W9-BCQ-519

ARCTIC OCEAN

80°N

60°N

EUROPE
LPS

Volga

URAL MTS.

Ob

40°N

ASIA

GOBI DESERT

HINDU KUSH

HIMALAYA MTS.

Indus

Ganges

Yangtze

SYRIAN
DESERT

HARA

Nile

AFRICA

DECCAN
PLATEAU

Tropic of Cancer

20°N

PACIFIC OCEAN

INDIAN OCEAN

Equator 0°

NAMIB DESERT

KALAHARI
DESERT

GREAT
SANDY
DESERT

20°S

Tropic of Capricorn

AUSTRALIA

Cape of
Good Hope

0   1000   2000   3000 Km.

0   1000   2000   3000 Mi.

60°S

Antarctic Circle

ANTARCTICA

80°S

180°

The Earth and Its Peoples:

A Global History

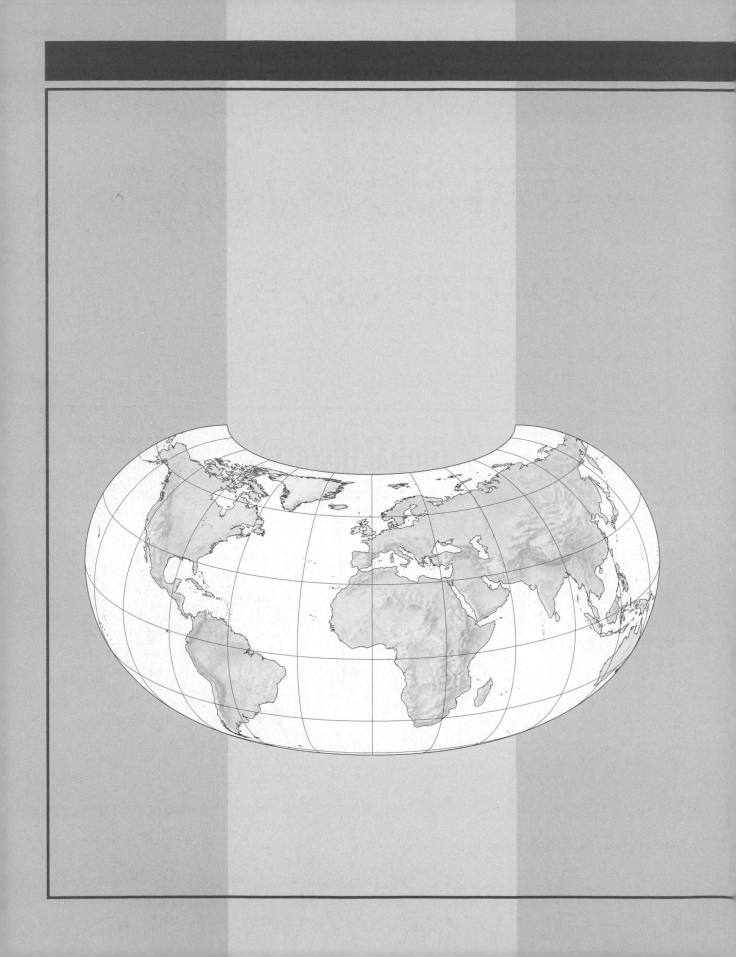

THE EARTH AND ITS PEOPLES:

A GLOBAL HISTORY

Richard W. Bulliet   COLUMBIA UNIVERSITY

Pamela Kyle Crossley   DARTMOUTH COLLEGE

Daniel R. Headrick   ROOSEVELT UNIVERSITY

Steven W. Hirsch   TUFTS UNIVERSITY

Lyman L. Johnson   UNIVERSITY OF NORTH CAROLINA—CHARLOTTE

David Northrup   BOSTON COLLEGE

Houghton Mifflin Company   BOSTON   NEW YORK

Senior Sponsoring Editor: *Patricia A. Coryell*
Senior Basic Book Editor: *Elizabeth M. Welch*
Senior Project Editor: *Susan Westendorf*
Senior Production/Design Coordinator: *Jill Haber*
Senior Manufacturing Coordinator: *Priscilla Bailey*

Cover designer: *Anthony Saizon*

Cover image research: *Rose Corbett Gordon*

Cover image: Kublai Khan Hunting *by Liu Kuan-tao, Yuan dynasty, National Palace Museum, Taipei, Taiwan, Republic of China.*

Printed in the U.S.A.

Library of Congress Catalog Card Number: 96-76875

ISBN: 0-395-52757-0

Examination Copy ISBN: 0-395-84295-6

23456789—VH—00 99 98 97

BRIEF CONTENTS

CONTENTS

P A R T   S I X

Revolutions Reshape the World, 1750–1870

C H A P T E R   2 2

Central and Eastern Asia, 1500–1800

C H A P T E R   2 3

The Industrial Revolution, 1760–1870

CHAPTER 27

The Ottoman Empire and East Asia, 1800–1870

PART SEVEN

Global Dominance and Diversity, 1850–1945

CHAPTER 28

The New Power Balance, 1850–1914

C H A P T E R   2 9

The New Imperialism, 1869–1914

C H A P T E R   3 0

The First World War and Its Aftermath, 1914–1929

MAPS

ENVIRONMENT & TECHNOLOGY

VOICES & VISIONS

PREFACE

History is not easy. We met in a conference room at Houghton Mifflin: six professional historians seated around a table hammering out our ideas on what a global history textbook at the start of a new millennium should be. Together we brought to the project a high level of knowledge about Africa, the Americas, Asia, Europe, the Middle East. We argued; we made up over dinner; we debated some more.

But there was no short cut. Though not by nature contentious people, we were determined to write the best global history we could. And that necessarily meant testing ideas aloud; considering alternatives put forward by smart, articulate colleagues; and bargaining over what to include and what, with regret, to pass over. We believe the result was worth the sweat.

Our goal was to write a textbook that would not only speak for the past but speak to today's student and today's teacher. By the time a class has completed it, students and instructor alike should have a strong sense that the history of the human species, throughout the globe, follows a particular trajectory: from sparse and disconnected communities reacting creatively to their individual circumstances; through ever more intensive stages of contact, interpenetration, and cultural expansion and amalgamation; to a twenty-first century world situation in which people increasingly visualize a single global community.

This trajectory of human development is not a fixed road map, however. Different parts of the world have moved or paused at different points in time and have followed their own paths. The chronology of the transition from the first domesticated plants and animals to broad territorial empires in the Western Hemisphere, for example, is unconnected with that of the Eastern Hemisphere, just as the industrialization of Western Europe and North America preceded by a century or two industrialization elsewhere. Yet the world all comes together in the late twentieth century, a paradoxical period of global political and economic forces confronting intensified reassertions of particular national and cultural identities. As in ages past, however large and encompassing social, cultural, and political systems become, human diversity persists. Those people who speak today of an emerging global community are answered by others who insist on their own distinctive identities.

The keynote of this book is not progress but process: a steady process of change over time, at first differently experienced in various regions of the world but eventually entangling peoples from all parts of the globe. Students should come away from this book with a sense that the problems and promises of their world are rooted in a past in which people of every sort, in every part of the world, confronted problems of a similar character and coped with them as best they could. We believe our efforts will help students see where their world has come from and learn thereby something useful for their own lives.

Central Theme

We have subtitled *The Earth and Its Peoples* "A Global History" because the book explores the common challenges and experiences that unite the human past. Although the dispersal of early humans to every livable environment resulted in myriad economic, social, political, and cultural systems, all societies displayed analogous patterns in meeting their needs and exploiting their environments. Our challenge was to select the particular data and episodes that would best illuminate these global patterns of human experience.

To meet this challenge, we adopted a central theme to serve as the spinal cord of our history. That theme is "technology and environment," the commonplace bases of all human societies at all times and a theme that grants no special favor to any cultural or social group even as it embraces subjects of the broadest topical, chronological, and geographical range.

It is vital for students to understand that technology, in the broad sense of experience-based knowledge of the physical world, underlies all human activity. Writing is a technology, but so is oral transmission from generation to generation of lore about medicinal or poisonous plants. The magnetic compass is a navigational technology, but so is the Polynesian mariners' hard-won knowledge of winds, currents, and tides that made possible the settlement of the Pacific islands.

All technological development, moreover, has come about in interaction with environments, both physical and human, and has, in turn, affected those environments. At the most basic level, concern with technology and the environment arises from the reality that all humans must eat. Yet less material cultural attainments are encompassed as well. Quite apart from such facilitating technologies as writing, papermaking, and printing, philosophies and religions have started from and sought to explain real world phenomena. Technological skills like stonecutting, paint mixing, and surveying have enabled creative artists to frame their works in response to specific environments: the indestructible rock paintings and engravings of the Sahara and Kalahari Desert, the Greek temple of Sounion on a high cliff by the sea, the grand mosques of Istanbul atop the city's seven hills, Daoist Chinese landscape painting capturing the mists of the Yangtze River gorges. Cultural achievements of these sorts reflect changing understandings of human relations to one another and to the world they live in. Thus they belong in this book, evidence of the technology and environment theme as a constant in human society and a solid basis for comparing different times, places, and communities.

Organization

The Earth and Its Peoples uses eight broad chronological divisions to define its conceptual scheme of global historical development. In **Part I: The Emergence of Human Communities, to 500** B.C.E., we examine important patterns of human communal organization. Early human communities were small, and most parts of the world were populated sparsely, if at all. As they spread worldwide, men and women encountered and responded to enormously diverse environmental conditions. Their responses gave rise to many technologies, from implements for meeting daily needs to the compilation of exhaustive lore about plants, animals, the climate, and the heavens. This lore, in turn, fueled speculations about the origin of the world and humanity, the nature of the gods or forces they felt controlled the world around them, the purpose of life, and the meaning of death. Though scarcity of written sources limits what we know about the world's first societies, the evolution of their technologies tells us much about gender relations, specialization of work activities, and patterns of everyday life—in short, about the growing complexity of human communities.

Part II: The Formation of New Cultural Communities, 1000 B.C.E.**–500** C.E., introduces the concept of a "cultural community," in the sense of a coherent pattern of activities and symbols pertaining to a specific human community. While all communities have distinctive cultures, the advances and conquests of some communities in this period magnified the geographical and historical imprint of their cultures.

In the geographically contiguous African-Eurasian landmass, the cultures that proved to have the most enduring influence traced their roots to the second and first millennia B.C.E. The long-term impact of these cultural communities involved competition with other cultures that did not prove so enduring. This frequently violent competition, culminating in the extensive empires of the Assyrians, Persians, Romans, and Han Chinese, was often marked by technological mixing across contested frontiers. Thus, non-Greek elements in Greek culture (such as the use of an alphabet invented by Phoenicians), the influence of non-Chinese steppe nomads on Chinese culture (as with the introduction of horse-related technologies), and other such examples are used to show how all cultural traditions become amalgams as they grow.

Part III: Growth and Interaction of Cultural Communities, 300 B.C.E.**–1200** C.E., deals with early episodes of technological, social, and cultural exchange and interaction on a continental scale outside the framework of imperial expansion. These are so different from earlier interactions arising from conquest or extension of political boundaries that they constitute a distinct era in world history, an era that set the world on the path of increasing global interaction and interdependence that it has been following ever since.

Exchange along long-distance trade routes and migrations by peoples equipped with advanced technologies played an especially important role in the coming together of the world's peoples. The Silk Road, for example, put China into contact with Mesopotamia and the Mediterranean lands, leading to a stimulating exchange of products and ideas and to the emergence of urban society in central Asia. In Africa, the Bantu migrations spread iron-working and cultivation of yams and other crops throughout most of the sub-Saharan region, while in the Americas a similar diffusion of corn, potatoes, and other domestic plants made possible the sophisticated states of the Mayas, Incas, and Aztecs. And throughout Europe, Asia, and much of Africa the universal religions of Buddhism, Christianity, and Islam gained so many adherents that they became defining elements of entire civilizations.

In **Part IV: Interregional Patterns of Culture and Contact, 1200–1500,** we take a look at the world during three centuries that saw both intensified cultural and commercial contact and increasingly confident self-definition of cultural communities in Europe, Asia, and Africa. The Mongol conquest of a vast empire extending from China to Iran and eastern Europe greatly stimulated trade and interaction while Chinese civilization itself extended its influence. Muslim religious expansion brought new cultural values and societal contacts to India, West Africa, and the Balkans and promoted trading networks around the Indian Ocean and across the Sahara. In the West, strengthened European kingdoms began maritime expansion in the Atlantic, forging direct ties with sub-Saharan Africa and laying the base for expanded global contacts after 1500.

Part V: The Globe Encompassed, 1500–1700, treats a period dominated by the global effects of European expansion and continued economic growth. European ships took over, expanded, and extended the maritime trade of the Indian Ocean, coastal Africa, and the Asian rim of the Pacific Ocean.

This maritime commercial enterprise had its counterpart in European colonial empires in the Americas and a new Atlantic trading system. In Asia, the Middle East, and Africa powerful new states emerged in this period that limited, challenged, or simply ignored the growing European dominance elsewhere. The contrasting capacities and fortunes of land empires and maritime empires, along with the exchange of domestic plants and animals between the hemispheres, underline the technological and environmental dimensions of this first era of complete global interaction.

In **Part VI: Revolutions Reshape the World, 1750–1870,** the word *revolution* is used in three senses: in the political sense of governmental overthrow, as in France and the Americas; in the metaphorical sense of radical transformative change, as in the Industrial Revolution; and in the broadest sense of a profound change in circumstances and world-view, as in the abolitionist movement, which in time completely destroyed an instrument of oppression that had been part of human life for thousands of years. These three senses of the word make it possible to integrate the experiences of a Western Europe intoxicated by the enormous power triggered by industrialization; a Western Hemisphere consumed with a passion for freedom from European domination; and Ottoman, Chinese, and Japanese states that saw their earlier conceptions of the world rapidly dissolve even as they struggled to adapt to the currents of change.

Technology and environment lie at the core of these developments. With the ascendancy of the Western belief that science and technology could overcome all challenges, environmental or otherwise, technology became not only an instrument of transformation but also an instrument of domination, threatening the integrity and autonomy of cultural traditions in nonindustrial lands. At the same time, other aspects of technology intensified social diversity by accentuating the difference between rich and poor, slave and free, and male and female.

Part VII: Global Dominance and Diversity, 1850–1945, examines the development of a world arena in which people conceived of events on a global scale. Imperialism, world war, international economic connections, and world-encompassing ideological forces, like nationalism and socialism, present the picture of an increasingly interconnected globe. European dominance took on a worldwide dimension, at times seeming to threaten permanent subordination to European values and philosophies while at other times triggering strong political or cultural resistance. The accelerating pace of technological change deepened other sorts of cleavages as well. Economic class divisions, for example, became part of the ideological struggle between socialism and capitalism; and a spreading desire for political participation led to demands by women for voting rights.

For **Part VIII: The Perils and Promises of a Global Community, 1945 to the Present**, we chose a thematic structure in keeping with how many people perceive the past half century. Countries throughout the world experienced more or less similar challenges in the era of Cold War and decolonization that culminated in 1991. In large measure, these challenges derived from global economic, technological, and political forces that limited the options for political and economic development open to the scores of new nations that emerged at the start of this period.

In a world contest for resources, the difference between growth and prosperity or overpopulation and poverty often hinged on technological and environmental factors, such as the development of high-yielding strains of rice and other crops. Yet even as the world faced the prospect of deepening gulfs between its rich and its poor regions, technological development simultaneously brought its peoples into closer contact than ever before. With the dimensions and the values of an increasingly globalized economy and society up for debate, issues such as gender equality, racial justice, human rights, and the demise or revitalization of human cultural diversity remained for the next century to resolve.

Distinctive Features

Learning and teaching aids are especially important in a book that extends its scope to all of human history. The pedagogical framework for *The Earth and Its Peoples* seeks to make the text accessible and memorable by reinforcing its theme and highlighting its subject matter.

To keep the technology and environment theme and the structural linkage between the parts clear, each part begins with an opening essay that sets the following chapters into the broad context of the book as a whole. A unique "geographic locator" map accompanies this opener to help the student visualize the world areas and developments that will be discussed in the part.

"Environment and Technology" boxes in each chapter further emphasize our central theme. Each feature expands on a particular topic in technological history—for example, ship design, camel saddles, coinage, military technology, writing systems, Indian mathematics, Copernican astronomy, the McCormick reaper, and compact disks. Accompanying illustrations enhance student understanding of the far-reaching impact of technological and environmental developments on human experience.

"Voices and Visions" features likewise accompany each chapter. These consist of excerpts from primary written, or occasionally visual, sources. While encouraging close study of historical evidence, they also enhance our narrative by giving clear voice to an array of individual viewpoints and cultural outlooks. Slavery in different periods and places receives attention, for example, as do witchcraft accusations and prosecutions, a Chinese official's views on the opium trade, a Nigerian woman's recollection of her childhood at the turn of the twentieth century, and Arthur Ashe's struggle against AIDS. Questions for analysis designed to stimulate critical interpretation of primary sources close each "Voices and Visions" feature.

Each chapter opens with a thematic introduction intended to engage the reader's interest while previewing what will follow. Extensive maps and illustrations serve to reinforce and complement, not merely ornament, surrounding discussion, while numerous charts and timelines help to organize and review major developments. Careful chapter conclusions draw together major topics and themes and link the present chapter to the one that follows. An annotated list of Suggested Reading at the end of each chapter contains a wide range of up-to-date references to help students pursue their interests.

For further assistance, *The Earth and Its Peoples* is issued in three formats to accommodate different academic calendars and approaches to the course. There is a one-volume hardcover version containing all 35 chapters, along with a two-volume paperback edition: Volume I, To 1500 (Chapters 1–16), and Volume II, Since 1500 (Chapters 17–35). For readers at institutions with the quarter system, we offer a three-volume paperback version: Volume A, To 1200 (Chapters 1–12); Volume B, From 1200 to 1870 (Chapters 13–27); and Volume C, Since 1750 (Chapters 23–35).

At the end of each volume, an extensive pronunciation guide shows the reader how to pronounce the many foreign terms and names necessary to a book of this scope.

Supplements

We have assembled with care an array of text supplements to aid students in learning and instructors in teaching. These supplements, including a *Study Guide*, a *Computerized Study Guide*, an *Instructor's Resource Manual*, *Test Items*, *Computerized Test Items*, *Map Transparencies*, and a *Power Presentation Manager*, are tied closely to the text, to provide a tightly integrated program of teaching and learning.

The *Study Guide*, authored by Michele G. Scott James of MiraCosta College, contains learning objectives, chapter outlines (with space for students' notes on particular sections), key-term identifications, multiple-choice questions, short-answer and essay questions, and map exercises. Included too are distinctive "comparison charts," to help students organize the range of information about different cultures and events discussed in each chapter. The *Study Guide* is published in two volumes, to correspond to Volumes I and II of the text: Volume I contains Chapters 1–16 and Volume II Chapters 17–35.

The *Study Guide* is also available in a computerized version for use with IBM PC and compatible computers. This *Computerized Study Guide* contains text references for all questions and rejoinders to each multiple-choice question that explain why the student's response is or is not correct.

The *Instructor's Resource Manual*, prepared by Rosanne J. Marek, Ball State University, provides useful teaching strategies for the global history course and tips for getting the most out of the text. Each chapter contains instructional objectives, a detailed chapter outline, discussion questions, individual learning activities, and audio-visual resources.

Each chapter of the *Test Items*, written by John Cashman of Boston College, offers 20 to 25 key-term identifications, 5 to 10 essay questions with answer guidelines, 35 to 40 multiple-choice questions, and 3 to 5 history and geography exercises. We also provide a computerized version of the *Test Items*, to enable instructors to alter, replace, or add questions. Each entry in the *Computerized Test Items* is numbered according to the printed test items to ease the creation of customized tests. The computerized test item file is available for use with both IBM PC and compatibles and Macintosh computers.

In addition, a set of *Transparencies* of all the maps in the text is available on adoption.

We are also pleased to offer the *Power Presentation Manager*, a software tool that enables teachers to prepare visual aids for lectures electronically, using both textual and visual material. Instructors can customize their lectures by incorporating their own material onto the PPM and combining it with the electronic resources provided, including adaptable chapter outlines as well as tables, illustrations, and maps from the text.

Acknowledgments

From our first to final draft, we have benefited from the critical readings of many colleagues. Our sincere thanks in particular to the following instructors: Kathleen Alaimo, St. Xavier University; Kenneth Andrian, Ohio State University; Norman Bennett, Boston University; Fritz Blackwell, Washington State University; Steven C. Davidson, Southwestern University; John E.

Davis, Radford University; Chandra de Silva, Indiana State University; Keven Doak, University of Illinois at Urbana-Champaign; Ellen Eslinger, DePaul University; Allen Greenberger, Pitzer College; Frances Harmon, College of Mount Saint Joseph; Janine Hartman, University of Cincinnati; Michele G. Scott James, MiraCosta College; Charles R. Lee, University of Wisconsin—La Crosse; Rosanne J. Marek, Ball State University; Peter Mellini, Sonoma State University; Shirley Mullen, Westmont College; Patricia O'Neill, Central Oregon College; William Parsons, Eckerd College; John P. Ryan, Kansas City Kansas Community College; Abraham Sherf, North Shore Community College; Steven R. Smith, Savannah State University; Sara W. Tucker, Washburn University; Sarah Watts, Wake Forest University; and Kenneth Wolf, Murray State University.

We would like to extend our collective thanks as well to Lynda Shaffer for her early conceptual contributions. Individually, Richard Bulliet thanks Jack Garraty and Isser Woloch for first involving him in world history; Pamela Crossley wishes to thank Gene Garthwaite, Charles Wood, and David Morgan; Steven Hirsch extends his gratitude to Dennis Trout; Lyman Johnson his to Kenneth J. Andrien, Richard Boyer, Grant D. Jones, William M. Ringle, Hendrik Kraay, Daniel Dupre, and Steven W. Usselman; and David Northrup thanks Mrinalini Sinha, Robin Fleming, Benjamin Braude, Alan Rogers, and John Tutino.

Over the years it took to bring this project to fruition, we worked with an excellent editorial and publishing team at Houghton Mifflin. Our hearts belong especially to Elizabeth M. Welch, Senior Basic Book Editor, who with unfailing good humor and sympathy (at least in our presence) guided us around every pitfall. At a somewhat earlier stage, Sean W. Wakely, our former Sponsoring Editor, and Jane Knetzger, Senior Associate Editor and our former Basic Book Editor, bore with remarkable aplomb the burden of listening to our lengthy debates while keeping us headed toward the final goal.

The rest of the Houghton Mifflin team, to each of whom we extend our deepest thanks, consisted of: Jean L. Woy, Editor-in-Chief for History and Political Science; Patricia A. Coryell, Senior Sponsoring Editor; Jeff Greene, Senior Associate Editor; Jeanne Herring, Assistant Editor; Susan Westendorf, Senior Project Editor; Charlotte Miller, map editor; Carole Frohlich, photo researcher; Jill Haber, Senior Production and Design Coordinator; Ron Kosciak, interior designer; Anthony L. Saizon, cover designer; and Rose Corbett-Gordon, cover image researcher.

We thank also the many students whose questions and concerns shaped much of this work, and we welcome all our readers' suggestions, queries, and criticisms. Please contact us at our respective institutions or at this e-mail address: history@hmco.com

Richard W. Bulliet   A professor of Middle Eastern history at Columbia University and director of its Middle East Institute, Richard W. Bulliet received his Ph.D. from Harvard University. He has written scholarly works on a number of topics: the social history of medieval Iran (*The Patricians of Nishapur*), the historical competition between pack camels and wheeled transport (*The Camel and the Wheel*), the process of conversion to Islam (*Conversion to Islam in the Medieval Period*), and the overall course of Islamic social history (*Islam: The View from the Edge*). He has also published four novels, co-edited *The Encyclopedia of the Modern Middle East*, and hosted an educational television series on the Middle East.

Pamela Kyle Crossley   Pamela Kyle Crossley received her Ph.D. in Modern Chinese History from Yale University and is Professor of History at Dartmouth College. Her research has been supported in recent years by the American Council of Learned Societies, the Marion and Jasper Whiting Foundation, the Woodrow Wilson International Center for Scholars, and the John Simon Guggenheim Memorial Foundation. She is author of the books *A Translucent Mirror: History and Identity in Qing Ideology*, *The Manchus*, and *Orphan Warriors: Three Manchu Generations and the End of the Qing World*, as well as articles in the *American Historical Review*, the *Journal of Asian Studies*, and the *Harvard Journal of Asiatic Studies*.

Daniel R. Headrick   Daniel R. Headrick received his Ph.D. in History from Princeton University. Professor of History and Social Science at Roosevelt University in Chicago, he is the author of several books on the history of technology, imperialism, and international relations, including *The Tools of Empire: Technology and European Imperialism in the Nineteenth Century*, *The Tentacles of Progress: Technology Transfer in the Age of Imperialism*, and *The Invisible Weapon: Telecommunications and International Politics*. His articles have appeared in the *Journal of World History* and the *Journal of Modern History* and he has been awarded fellowships by the National Endowment for the Humanities and the John Simon Guggenheim Memorial Foundation.

Steven W. Hirsch   Steven W. Hirsch holds a Ph.D. in Classics from Stanford University and is currently Associate Professor of Classics and History at Tufts University and Chair of the Department of Classics. He has received grants from the National Endowment for the Humanities and the Massachusetts Foundation for Humanities and Public Policy. His research and publications include *The Friendship of the Barbarians: Xenophon and the Persian Empire*, as well as articles and reviews in the *Classical Journal*, the *American Journal of Philology*, and the *Journal of Interdisciplinary History*.

Lyman L. Johnson   Professor of History at the University of North Carolina at Charlotte, Lyman L. Johnson earned his Ph.D. in Latin American history from the University of Connecticut. A two-time Senior Fulbright-Hays Lecturer, he has also received fellowships from the Tinker Foundation, the Social Science Research Council, the National Endowment for the Humanities, and the American Philosophical Society. His recent books include *The Problem of Order in Changing Societies*, *Essays on the Price History of Eighteenth-Century Latin America* (with Enrique Tandeter), and *Colonial Latin America* (with Mark A. Burkholder). The current President of the Conference on Latin American History (1997–1998), he has also published in journals, including the *Hispanic American Historical Review*, the *Journal of Latin American Studies*, the *International Review of Social History*, *Social History*, and *Desarrollo Económico*.

David Northrup   Professor of History at Boston College, David Northrup earned his Ph.D. from the University of California, Los Angeles. He has twice been awarded Fulbright-Hays Research Abroad Grants and National Endowment for the Humanities Summer Stipends, along with an African Studies Grant from the Social Science Research Council. He is the author of *Trade Without Rulers: Pre-Colonial Economic Development in South-Eastern Nigeria*, *Beyond the Bend in the River: A Labor History of Eastern Zaire, 1870–1940*, *Indentured Labor In the Age of Imperialism, 1834–1922*, and he compiled and edited *The Atlantic Slave Trade*. His research has appeared in the *Journal of African History*, the *Journal of Interdisciplinary History*, *History in Africa*, the *International Journal of African Historical Studies*, and the *Journal of Church and State*.

Where necessary for clarity, dates are followed by the letters C.E. or B.C.E. C.E. stands for "Common Era" and is equivalent to A.D. (*Anno Domini*, Latin for "in the year of the Lord"). B.C.E. stands for "Before the Common Era" and means the same as B.C. ("Before Christ"). In keeping with their goal of approaching world history without special concentration on one culture or another, the authors chose these neutral abbreviations as appropriate to their enterprise. Because many readers will be more familiar with English than with metric measurements, however, units of measure are generally given in the English system, with metric equivalents following in parentheses.

In general, Chinese has been romanized according to the *pinyin* method. Exceptions include proper names well established in English (e.g., Canton, Chiang Kai-shek) and a few English words borrowed from Chinese (e.g., kowtow). Spellings of Arabic, Ottoman Turkish, Persian, Mongolian, Manchu, Japanese, and Korean names and terms avoid special diacritical marks for letters that are pronounced only slightly differently in English. An apostrophe is used to indicate when two Chinese syllables are pronounced separately (e.g., Chang'an).

For words transliterated from languages that use the Arabic script—Arabic, Ottoman Turkish, Persian, Urdu—the apostrophe indicated separately pronounced syllables may represent either of two special consonants, the *hamza* or the *ain*. Because most English speakers do not hear distinction between these two, they have not been distinguished in transliteration, and they are not indicated when they occur at the beginning or end of a word. As with Chinese, some words and commonly used placenames from these languages are given familiar English spellings (e.g., Quran instead of Qur'an, Cairo instead of al-Qahira). Arabic romanization has normally been used for terms relating to Islam, even where the context justifies slightly different Turkish or Persian forms, again for ease of comprehension.

There is lively scholarly debate on how best to render Amerindian words in English letters. Nahuatl and Yacatec Maya words and placenames are given in familiar, conventional forms that some linguists now challenge. Thus terms like Tenochtitlán and Chichén Itzá contain accented vowels, contrary to some scholarly recommendations. Similarly, like most North American historians, we have not followed recent proposals for a new system of transliterating Aymara and Quechua words from the Andean region. Thus we retain Inca instead of Inka and *quipu* instead of *khipu*.

To help clarify placenames that have changed over time, the modern form of the name is often put in parentheses after the form appropriate to the period of history under discussion. Thus, Annam, an ancestor state of Vietnam, is referred to as such where appropriate historically, with its relationship to modern Vietnam noted in parentheses. In some cases, consideration of the reader has demanded careful anachronisms (e.g., "Inner China" and "Outer China" in discussion of the early history of territories that only much later became part of empires based in China, and eventually of China itself). Anachronisms of this sort are explained in the text.

PART ONE

The Emergence of Human Communities, TO 600 B.C.E.

Though remote from the present, the global events that we examine in the first part of *The Earth and Its Peoples* are fundamental for understanding the origins of human nature, culture, and society. These chapters examine two aspects of the earliest human interactions with the natural world: how environmental forces affected humans' physical evolution and how evolving humans gradually devised tools and acquired technical knowledge that enabled them to reshape environments to meet their needs. These chapters also detail how the movement of humans across the planet gave rise to cultural differences in language, customs, and beliefs and how the development of increasingly complex societies led to social distinctions based on occupation and status as well as on gender and age.

An unusually cool climate dominated the long era during which human beings first appeared on the earth. Great masses of ice slowly expanded and contracted over much of northern Eurasia and North America, soaking up so much water that sea levels and rainfall were affected even in tropical regions. During this "Great Ice Age," which lasted until about 10,000 years ago, the pace of change in human development was also glacially slow. Like other creatures, members of the human species *Homo* evolved physically in ways that improved their species' chances for survival.

During the later millennia of the Ice Age, a unique capacity for cultural change gave humans a survival strategy that unfolded more quickly and more easily than physical evolution. As physically modern people gradually evolved, their mental capacities enabled them to adapt to various environmental situations by devising new tools and strategies. Because many of the earliest tools that have been discovered are made of stone, researchers have named the expanse of time extended from 2 million years ago to 4,000 years ago the "Stone Age."

Those tools and learning ability enabled humans to fan out to the far reaches of the planet. Arriving in different environments, they learned how to hunt the local animals, gather native plants for food, make clothing, and build dwellings from materials at hand. They also used their mental powers to develop languages, create works of art, and speculate about the meaning of life.

The value of humans' ability to adapt their way of life to new environments became evident when the Ice Age ended and generally warmer temperatures returned. Humanity entered a new stage in its relationship with nature, and the pace of historical change quickened. No longer entirely dependent on wild plants and animals for food, people began to cultivate edible plants and to domesticate animals such as wild cattle, pigs, and water buffalo. In arid lands people depended on herds of domesticated animals for their livelihood. Their way of life is known as pastoralism. In places where water was more abundant, people established permanent communities where they cultivated food crops and improved their ability to manage and shape their environment. A series of "agricultural revolutions" occurring in Eurasia, Africa, and the Americas between 10,000 and 5,500 years ago supported a steady rise in populations. Some agricultural settlements grew into towns and cities.

The growth and concentration of population intensified humans' manipulation of the environment around 3500 B.C.E. (Before the Common Era)—that is, some fifty-five hundred years ago. In the floodplains of great river valleys in Egypt, Mesopotamia, India, and, later, China, communities constructed complex systems of irrigation to increase crop yields. Under the direction of powerful rulers, they built cities distinguished by monumental buildings, and they waged large-scale wars to defend and extend their territories.

One of the striking changes apparent in these river-valley civilizations was social stratification—the emergence of a class structure. At the top were powerful and wealthy kings who directed and controlled the lives of ordinary people, defending them from invaders, collecting taxes in goods and labor, and issuing and enforcing laws. Claiming to be far more than mere administrators, rulers enhanced their authority by taking on the attributes of gods. For example, a ruler might attribute a bountiful harvest to his mystical powers over nature rather than to his administrative skills.

Priests, who headed the state religion, were another exalted class. They performed religious rites, offered sacrifices to the gods, communicated the god's wishes, and conducted public festivals. At the bottom of the social ladder were the people conquered and enslaved in the course of frequent wars. In general, women seem to have lost standing to men in the social hierarchy of these civilizations.

Striking changes also appeared in the material culture of the river-valley civilizations, especially in architecture, writing, and recordkeeping. The cities and their outlying areas boasted splendid temples, palaces, and royal tombs, designed by master architects and built by armies of conscripted laborers. Stone became an important construction material. The development of tools made of bronze (an alloy of copper and tin) enabled builders to shape building stones with exquisite care. Bronze also was used in weapons and other implements. Just as the characteristic stone tools gave their name to the "Stone Age," so the "Bronze Age" that began about 3500 B.C.E., was named for its key technology.

Technology

2,000,000 B.C.E.—Stone tools (Africa)

1,000,000 B.C.E.—Controlled use of fire (Africa)

ca. 10,500 B.C.E.—First pottery in China

9000 B.C.E.—Domestication of animals and plants

7000 B.C.E.—Early metalworking (Middle East)

4000 B.C.E.—Bronze casting (Middle East)

3500 B.C.E.—Invention of wheel and plow (Mesopotamia)

3100 B.C.E.—First writing (Sumer)

3000 B.C.E.—Domestication of the camel (Arabia)

2500 B.C.E.—Domestication of the horse (Central Asia)

Environment

2,000,000–12,000 B.C.E.—Great Ice Age

32,000–12,000 B.C.E.—Last glacial period; animal extinctions

12,000 B.C.E.—Warming trend melts glaciers

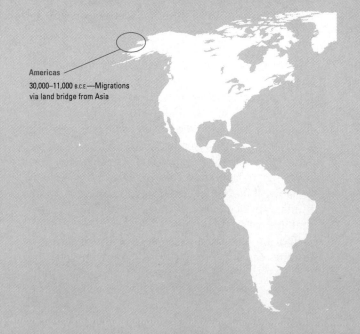

Americas
30,000–11,000 B.C.E.—Migrations via land bridge from Asia

The invention of writing was another achievement of enduring importance. Rulers employed a small number of specially trained writing specialists—scribes—to keep track of the collection of taxes, to record royal laws, and to memorialize military victories and other royal achievements. Temple scribes also began to record myths and other religious lore. At this time writing consisted of stylized pictures (pictographs) of the objects being represented; later, scribes developed simplified phonetic alphabets.

The influence of the river-valley civilizations extended beyond their borders, because members of the royal and priestly classes of these states traded with people living in distant parts of their realm. They used their wealth to trade for precious metals such as gold and silver; for the copper and other metals that went into bronze; for exotic jewels, animal skins, feathers, and other items of personal adornment; and for special woods, stones, and other materials for construction. Specialized artisans using various systems of counting kept accounts of these transactions.

In the Middle East merchants helped to spread aspects of their culture beyond the areas of conquest. Egyptian culture influenced Nubia to the south. The development of a sophisticated culture around the Aegean Sea in the eastern Mediterranean owed much to influence from Egypt and other parts of the middle East.

Yet on the whole, most of the world was little affected by the development of the river-valley civilizations. Most people continued to practice pastoralism, hunting, and gathering, and small-scale farming. Although their ways of life left no spectacular ruins, such societies did produce significant achievements. For example, in the third millennium B.C.E., pastoralists in Arabia domesticated the camel and other pastoralists in Central Asia domesticated the horse. Both animals became important for warfare, trade, and communication.

During the Late Bronze Age of the second and first millennia B.C.E., the reach, complexity, and sophistication of the civilizations in the eastern Mediterranean, Middle East, and East Asia grew. Building on earlier achievements, these civilizations also extended their influences by new conquests and trade. Despite disrupting invasions in the eastern Mediterranean and in Mesopotamia around 1200 B.C.E., these communities left enduring legacies.

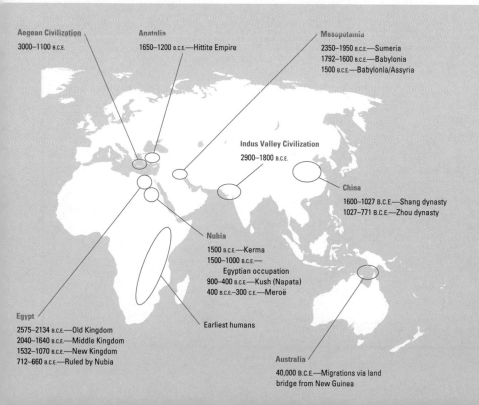

Aegean Civilization
3000–1100 B.C.E.

Anatolia
1650–1200 B.C.E.—Hittite Empire

Mesopotamia
2350–1950 B.C.E.—Sumeria
1792–1600 B.C.E.—Babylonia
1500 B.C.E.—Babylonia/Assyria

Indus Valley Civilization
2900–1800 B.C.E.

China
1600–1027 B.C.E.—Shang dynasty
1027–771 B.C.E.—Zhou dynasty

Nubia
1500 B.C.E.—Kerma
1500–1000 B.C.E.—
   Egyptian occupation
900–400 B.C.E.—Kush (Napata)
400 B.C.E.–300 C.E.—Meroë

Egypt
2575–2134 B.C.E.—Old Kingdom
2040–1640 B.C.E.—Middle Kingdom
1532–1070 B.C.E.—New Kingdom
712–660 B.C.E.—Ruled by Nubia

Earliest humans

Australia
40,000 B.C.E.—Migrations via land bridge from New Guinea

Society

1,000,000 B.C.E.—Gathering and hunting bands
9000 B.C.E.—Agricultural communities
ca. 8000 B.C.E.—First walled town (Jericho)
ca. 3500 B.C.E.—First religious elites
ca. 3100 B.C.E.—First kingdoms
ca. 3000 B.C.E.—First major cities (Mesopotamia)
237 B.C.E.—First empires (Middle East)

Culture

First languages
First music and dance
First religious practices
30,000 B.C.E.—Earliest known cave art
4000 B.C.E.—Megalithic tombs
2590 B.C.E.—Great Pyramid at Giza
1750 B.C.E.—Hammurabi's Law Code

CHAPTER ONE

Nature, Humanity, and History: The First Four Million Years

African Genesis · History and Culture in the Ice Age

The Agricultural Revolutions · Life in Neolithic Communities

According to a story handed down by the Yoruba people of West Africa, at one time there was only water below the sky. Then the divine Owner of the Sky let down a chain by which his son Oduduwa descended along with sixteen male companions. Oduduwa scattered a handful of soil across the water and set down a chicken that scratched the soil into the shape of the land. A palm nut that he planted in the soil grew to became the bountiful forest that is the home of the Yoruba people. Oduduwa was their first king.

At some point in their history most human societies began telling similar stories about their origins. In some the first humans came down from the sky; in others they emerged out of a hole in the ground. Historical accuracy was not the point of such creation myths. Like the story of Adam and Eve in the Hebrew Bible, their primary purpose was to define the moral principles that a society thought should govern humans' dealings with the supernatural world, with each other, and with the rest of nature. In addition, they provided an explanation of how a people's way of life, social divisions, and cultural system arose.

In the absence of any contradictory evidence, creation myths became embedded in the identities and beliefs of peoples throughout the world. However, in the nineteenth century evidence started to accumulate that human beings and ways of life based on farming and herding domesticated animals had quite different origins. Natural scientists were finding remains of early humans who resembled apes rather than gods. Other evidence suggested that the familiar ways of life based on farming and herding did not arise within a generation or two of creation, as the myths suggest, but after humans had been around for many hundreds of thousands of years.

Although such evidence has long stirred controversy, a careful consideration of it reveals insights into human identity that may be as meaningful as those propounded by the creation myths. First, humans began their existence not with the ability to control and manipulate nature but as part of the natural world, subject to its laws. Second, the physical and mental abilities humans gradually acquired in response to changes in the natural world gave them a unique capacity to adapt to new environments by altering their way of life rather than by evolving physically as other species did. Finally, after nearly 2 million years of physical and cultural development, human communities in different parts of the world opened up extraordinary possibilities for change when they learned how to manipulate the natural world, domesticating plants and animals for their food and use. In short, one of the fundamental themes of human history concerns how people have interacted with the environment.

AFRICAN GENESIS

The discovery in the mid-nineteenth century of the remains of ancient creatures that were at once humanlike and apelike generated both excitement and controversy. The evidence upset many because it challenged accepted beliefs about human origins. Others welcomed the new evidence as proof of what some researchers had long suspected: the physical characteristics of modern humans, like those of all other creatures, had evolved over incredibly long periods of time. But until recently the evidence was too fragmentary to be convincing.

Interpreting the Evidence

In 1856 in the Neander Valley of what is now Germany workmen discovered fossilized bones of a creature with a body much like that of modern humans but with a face that, like the faces of apes, had heavy brow ridges and a low forehead.

Although we now know these "Neanderthals" were a type of human common in Europe some 40,000 years ago, in the mid-nineteenth century the idea that earlier forms of humans could have existed was so novel that some scholars who first examined them argued they must have been deformed individuals from recent times.

Another perspective on human links to the distant past was already gaining ground. Three years after the Neanderthal finds, Charles Darwin, a young English naturalist (student of natural history), published *On the Origin of Species*. In this work he argued that the time frame for all biological life was far longer than most persons had supposed. Darwin based his conclusion on pioneering naturalists' research and on his own investigations of fossils and living plant and animal species in Latin America. He proposed that the great diversity of living species and the profound changes in them over time could be explained by *natural selection*, the process by which biological variations that enhanced a population's ability to survive became dominant in that species and over very long periods led to the formation of distinct new species.

Turning to the sensitive subject of human evolution in *The Descent of Man* (1871), Darwin summarized the growing consensus among naturalists that, by the same process of natural selection, humans were "descended from a hairy, tailed quadruped" (four-footed animal). Because humans shared so many physical similarities with African apes, he proposed that Africa must have been the home of the first humans, even though no evidence then existed to substantiate this hypothesis.

As it happened, the next major discoveries pointed to Asia, rather than Africa, as the original human home. On the Southeast Asian island of Java in 1891 Eugene Dubois uncovered an ancient skullcap of what was soon called "Java man," a find that has since been dated to between 1 million and 1.8 million years ago. In 1929 W. C. Pei discovered near Peking (Beijing), China, a similar skullcap that became known as "Peking man."

By then, even older fossils had been found in southern Africa. In 1924, while examining fossils from a lime quarry, Raymond Dart found the skull of an ancient creature that he named *Australopithecus africanus* (African southern ape), which he argued was transitional between apes and early humans. For many years most specialists disputed Dart's idea, because, while *Australopithecus africanus* walked upright like a human, its brain was ape-size. Such an idea went against their expectations that large brains would have evolved first and that Asia, not Africa, was the first home of humans. Biologists classify australophithecines as members of a family of primates known as *hominids*. Primates are members of a family of warm-blooded, four-limbed, social animals known as *mammals* that first appeared about 65 million years ago.

Since 1950, Louis and Mary Leakey, their son Richard, along with many others, have discovered a wealth of other hominid fossils in the exposed sediments of the Great Rift Valley of eastern Africa. These finds strongly support Dart's hypothesis and Darwin's guess that the tropical habitat of the African apes was the cradle of humanity. Although new discoveries could alter these conclusions, most researchers now believe that tropical Africa was the home of the earliest human ancestors.

The development of precise archaeological techniques has enhanced the quantity of evidence currently available. Rather than collect isolated bones, modern researchers literally sift the neighboring soils to extract the remains of other creatures existing at the time, locating fossilized seeds and even pollen by which to document the environment in which the humans lived. They can also determine the age of most finds by using dating the rate of molecular change in potassium, in minerals in lava flows, or in carbon from wood and bone.

As the result of this new work, is it now possible to trace the evolutionary changes that produced modern humans during a period of 4 million years. As Darwin suspected, the earliest transitional creatures have been found only in Africa; the later human species (including Java man and Peking man) had wider global distribution. By combining that evidence with the growing understanding of how other species adapt to their natural environments, scientists can describe with some precision when, where, and how early human beings evolved and how they lived.

"Rather Odd African Apes"?

The accumulating evidence that humans evolved gradually over millions of years has led to much debate about how our species should be defined. Some researchers focus on our similarities to other living creatures; others look at what makes us different. Each approach yields different and important insights. As close as humans are to other primates, small genetic oddities are responsible for immense differences in our capacities. Indeed, humans are unique in being able to contemplate the meaning of life and consider the question we are grappling with here: what is a human being?

Within the primate kingdom humans are most closely related to the African apes—chimpanzees and gorillas. Since Darwin's time it has been popular (and controversial) to say that we are descended from apes. Modern research has found that over 98 percent of human DNA, the basic genetic blueprint, is identical to that of the great apes. For this reason anthropologist David Philbeam has called human beings "rather odd African apes."[1]

From a biological perspective, three major traits distinguish humans from other primates. As Dart's australopithecines demonstrated, the earliest of these traits to appear was *bipedalism* (walking upright on two legs). This frees the forelimbs from any necessary role in locomotion and enhances an older primate trait: a hand that has a long thumb that can work with the fingers to manipulate objects skillfully. Modern humans' second trait, a very large brain, distinguishes us more profoundly from the australopithecines than does our somewhat more upright posture. Besides enabling humans to think abstractly, experience profound emotions, and construct complex social relations, this larger brain controls the fine motor movements of the hand and of the tongue, increasing humans' tool-using capacity and facilitating the development of speech. The physical possibility of language, however, depends on a third distinctive human trait: the

Fossilized footprints Archaeologist Mary Leakey (shown at top) found these remarkable footprints of a hominid adult and child at Laetoli, Tanzania. The pair had walked through fresh volcanic ash that solidified after being buried by a new volcanic eruption. Dated to 3.5 million years ago, the footprints are the oldest evidence of bipedalism yet found. (John Reader/Photo Researchers, Inc.)

human larynx (voice box) lies much lower in the neck than does the larynx of any other primate. This trait is associated with many other changes in the face and neck.

How and why did these immensely important biological changes take place? Scientists still employ Darwin's concept of natural selection, attributing the development of distinctive human

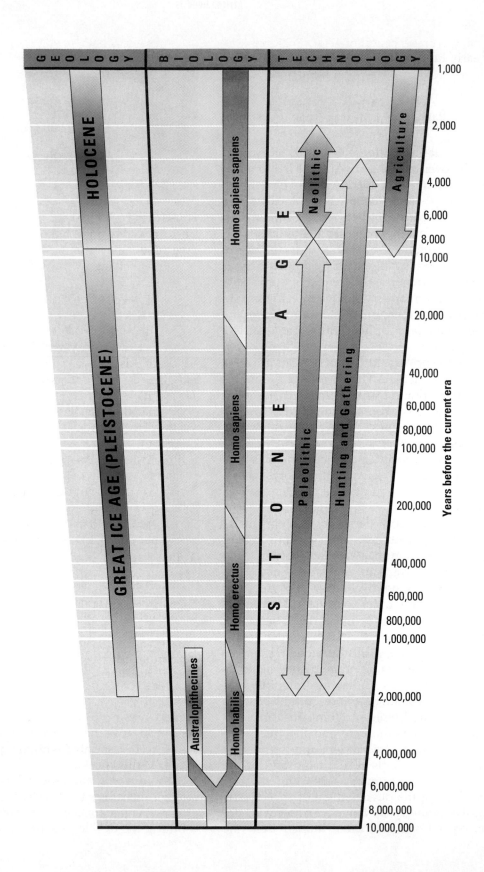

traits to the preservation of genetic changes that enhanced survivability. Although the details have not been fully worked out, it is widely accepted that major shifts in the world's climate led to evolutionary changes in human ancestors and other species. About 10 million years ago the earth entered a period of lower average temperatures that culminated in the Great Ice Age, or Pleistocene epoch, from about 2 million to about 11,000 years ago (see Figure 1.1). The Pleistocene epoch included more than a dozen very cold periods, each spanning several thousand years, separated by warmer periods. The changes that these climate shifts produced in rainfall, vegetation, and temperature imposed great strains on existing plant and animal species. As a result, large numbers of new species evolved during the Pleistocene.

In the temperate regions of the earth during the Pleistocene, massive glaciers of frozen water spread out from centers of snow accumulation. At their peak such glaciers covered a third of the earth's surface and contained so much frozen water that ocean levels were lowered by over 450 feet (140 meters), exposing land bridges between many places now isolated by water.

Unlike the frozen lands to the north and south, the equatorial regions of the world were not touched by the glaciers, but during the Pleistocene they probably experienced cooler and drier climates that led to the growth of open savanna grasslands in places once dominated by tropical forests. According to one popular theory, as the forests shrank, some tree-dwelling apes were forced to search for more of their food on the ground. Gradually the new family of primates—the hominids—evolved with a more upright way of walking.

Some recent evidence of ancient vegetation casts doubt on that scenario, but it is well established that between 3 million and 4 million years ago several new species of bipedal australopithecines inhabited eastern Africa. In a remarkable find in northern Ethiopia in 1974, Donald Johanson unearthed a remarkably well pre-

Figure 1.1   Human Biological Evolution and Technological Development in Geological and Historical Context

served skeleton of a twenty-five-year-old female, whom he nicknamed "Lucy." In northern Tanzania in 1977, Mary Leakey discovered fossilized footprints that provide spectacular visual evidence of how australopithecines walked.

Bipedalism evolved because it provided australopithecines with some advantage for survival. Some studies suggest that a decisive advantage of bipedalism may have come from its energy efficiency in walking and running. Another theory is that bipeds survived better because they could fill their arms with food to carry back to mates and children. Whatever its decisive advantage, bipedalism led to other changes.

Climate changes between 2 million and 3 million years ago led to the evolution of a new species, the first to be classified in the same genus (*Homo*) with modern humans. At Olduvai Gorge in northern Tanzania in the early 1960s Louis Leakey discovered the first fossilized remains of this creature, which he named *Homo habilis* (handy human). What most distinguished *Homo habilis* from the australopithecines was a brain that was nearly 50 percent larger. A larger brain would have added to the new species' intelligence. What was happening in this period that favored greater mental capacity? Some scientists believe that the answer had to do with food. Greater intelligence enabled *Homo habilis* to locate a vast number of different kinds of things to eat throughout the seasons of the year. They point to seeds and other fossilized remains in ancient *Homo habilis* camps that indicate the new species ate a greater variety of more nutritious seasonal foods than the australopithecines ate.

By about 1 million years ago *Homo habilis* and all the australopithecines had become extinct. In their habitat lived a new hominid, *Homo erectus* (upright human), which had first appeared in eastern Africa about 1.8 million years ago. These creatures possessed brains a third larger than those of *Homo habilis*, which presumably accounted for their better survivability. A nearly complete skeleton of a twelve-year-old male of the species discovered by Richard Leakey in 1984 on the shores of Lake Turkana in Kenya shows that *Homo erectus* closely resembled modern people from the neck down. *Homo erectus* was very successful in dealing with different environ-

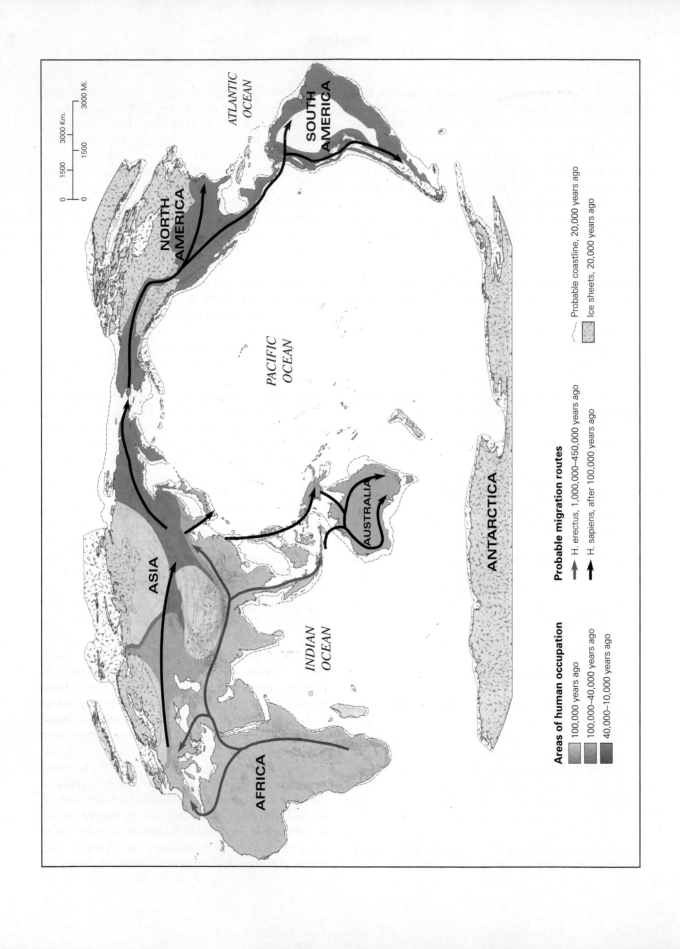

ATLANTIC OCEAN

SOUTH AMERICA

NORTH AMERICA

3000 Mi.
3000 Km.
1500
1500
0
0

PACIFIC OCEAN

ASIA

AUSTRALIA

ANTARCTICA

INDIAN OCEAN

AFRICA

Areas of human occupation

100,000 years ago

100,000–40,000 years ago

40,000–10,000 years ago

Probable coastline, 20,000 years ago

Ice sheets, 20,000 years ago

Probable migration routes

H. erectus, 1,000,000–450,000 years ago

H. sapiens, after 100,000 years ago

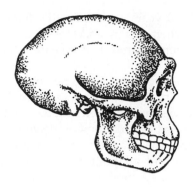 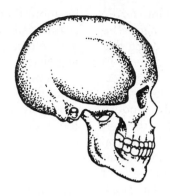 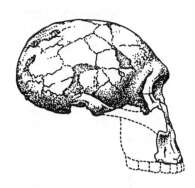

Evolution of the human brain   These drawings of skulls show the extensive cranial changes associated with the increase in brain size during the 3 million years from *Homo habilis* to *Homo sapiens sapiens*. (Left, middle: From *Origins Reconsidered* by Richard Leakey. Copyright © 1992 B. V. Sherma. Used by permission of Doubleday, a division of Bantam Doubleday Dell Publishing Group, Inc.; Right: Courtesy of A. Walker and Richard Leakey/*Scientific American*, 1978, all rights reserved.)

ments and underwent hardly any biological changes during a million years.

However, by a long, imperfectly understood evolutionary process between 400,000 and 100,000 years ago, a new human species emerged: *Homo sapiens* (wise human). The brains of *Homo sapiens* were a third larger than those of *Homo erectus*, whom they gradually superseded. *Homo sapiens* also had greater speech capacity.

This slow but remarkable process of physical evolution that distinguished humans by a small but significant degree from other primates was one part of what was happening. Equally remarkable was the way in which humans were extending their habitat.

Migrations from Africa

Early humans gradually expanded their range in eastern and southern Africa. Then they ventured out of Africa, perhaps following migrating herds of animals or searching for more abundant food

Map 1.1 Human dispersal to 10,000 years ago   Early migrations from Africa into southern Eurasia were followed by treks across land bridges during cold spells when giant ice sheets had lowered ocean levels.

supplies in time of drought. The details are unsettled, but the end result is vividly clear: humans learned to survive in every part of the globe from the arctic to the equator, from deserts to tropical rain forests. This dispersal demonstrates early humans' talent for adaptation (see Map 1.1).

Homo erectus was the first human species to inhabit all parts of Africa and the first to be found outside Africa. By migrating overland from Africa across southern Asia, *Homo erectus* reached Java as early as 1.8 million years ago. At that time sea levels caused by water being trapped in ice-age glaciers were so low that Java was not an island but was joined to the Southeast Asian mainland. Although Java's climate would have been no colder than East Africa's, Java's dense forests would have been very different from the open grasslands of eastern Africa. Even more challenging was adaptation to the harsh winters of northern Europe and northern China, where *Homo erectus* settled between 700,000 and 300,000 years ago.

Scientists disagree whether *Homo sapiens* also spread outward from Africa or evolved separately from *Homo erectus* populations in different parts of the world. If, as most scientists suppose, *Homo sapiens* first evolved in Africa, their migrations to the rest of the world would have been made easier by a wet period that transformed the normally arid Sahara and Middle East into fertile grasslands until about 40,000 years ago. The abundance of plant and animal food during this wet period would have promoted an increase in human populations.

By the end of that wet period further evolutionary changes had produced fully modern humans (*Homo sapiens sapiens*), which some evidence suggests may have originated in Africa. This new species displaced older human populations, such as the Neanderthals in Europe, and penetrated for the first time into the Americas, Australia, and the Arctic.

During the last glacial period, between 32,000 and 13,000 years ago, when the sea levels were low, hunters were able to cross a land bridge from northeastern Asia into North America. As these pioneers and later migrants moved southward (penetrating southern South America by 27,000 years ago), they passed through lands teeming with life, including easily hunted large animal species. Meanwhile, traveling by boat from Java, other *Homo sapiens sapiens* colonized New Guinea and Australia when both were part of a single landmass, and they crossed the land bridge then existing between the Asian mainland and Japan. Despite the generally cool climate of this period, human bands also followed reindeer even into northern arctic environments during the summer months.

As populations migrated, they may have undergone some minor evolutionary changes that helped them adapt to extreme environments. One such change was in skin color. The deeply pigmented skin of today's indigenous inhabitants of the tropics (and presumably of all early humans who evolved there) is an adaptation that reduces the harmful effects of the harsh tropical sun. At some point, possibly as recent as 5,000 years ago, especially pale skin became characteristic of Europeans living in northern latitudes with far less sunshine especially during winter months. The loss of pigment enabled their skins to produce more vitamin D from sunshine, though it exposed Europeans to a greater risk of sunburn and skin cancer when they migrated to sunnier climates. This was not the only possible way to adapt to the arctic. Eskimos who began moving into northern latitudes of North America

no more than 5,000 years ago retain the deeper pigmentation of their Asian ancestors but are able to gain sufficient vitamin D from eating fish and sea mammals.

As distinctive as skin color is in a person's appearance, it represents a very minor variation biologically. What was far more remarkable about the widely dispersed populations of *Homo sapiens sapiens* was that they varied so little. Despite a global dispersal and adaptation to many diverse environments, all modern human beings are members of the same species. Instead of needing to evolve physically like other species in order to adapt to new environments, modern humans were able to change their eating habits and devise new forms of clothing and shelter. As a result, human communities became culturally diverse while remaining physically homogeneous.

HISTORY AND CULTURE IN THE ICE AGE

Evidence of early humans' splendid creative abilities first came to light in 1940 near Lascaux in southern France. Examining a newly uprooted tree, youths discovered the entrance to a vast underground cavern. Once inside, they found that its walls were covered with paintings of animals, including many that had been extinct for thousands of years. Other collections of cave paintings have been found in Spain and elsewhere in southern France, including an enormous cavern near Vallon-Pont-d'Arc, discovered in 1994, containing hundreds of paintings from 20,000 years ago.

Observers of these cave paintings have been struck not only by the great age of this art but also by its high artistic quality. To even the most skeptical person, such rich finds are awesome demonstrations that thousands of years before the first "civilizations" (see Chapter 2), there existed individuals with richly developed imaginations and skill. Though less strikingly visible, great talent also can be perceived in the production of ever more specialized tools and in the development of complex social relations.

The fact that similar art and tools were produced over wide areas and long periods of time demonstrates that skills and ideas were not simply individual but were deliberately passed along within societies. These learned patterns of action and expression constitute *culture*. Culture includes material objects, such as dwellings, clothing, tools, and crafts, along with nonmaterial values, beliefs, and languages. Although it is true that some other species also learn new ways, all other species' activities are determined primarily by inherited instincts. Uniquely, among humans the proportions are reversed: instincts are less important than the cultural traditions that each new generation learns. The development, transmission, and transformation of cultural practices and events are the subject of *history*. All living creatures are part of natural history, which traces their biological development, but only human communities have a history that traces their varied cultural development over time.

Food Gathering and Stone Technology

Most early human activity centered on gathering food. Like the australopithecines, early humans depended heavily on vegetable foods such as leaves, seeds, and grasses, but one of the changes evident in the Ice Age is the growing consumption of highly nutritious animal flesh. Moreover, unlike australopithecines, humans regularly made tools. The first crude tools made their appearance with *Homo habilis*, later human species made much more sophisticated tools. These two changes—increased meat-eating and toolmaking—appear to be closely linked.

When archaeologists examine the remains of ancient human sites, the first thing that jumps out at them is the abundant evidence of human toolmaking—the first recognizable cultural activity. Because the tools that survive are made of stone, the extensive period of history from the appearance of the first fabricated stone tools around 2 million years ago until the appearance of metal tools around 4 thousand years ago has been called the Stone Age.

The name Stone Age can be quite misleading.

In the first place, not all tools were made of stone. Early humans would also have made useful objects and tools out of bone, skin, wood, and other natural materials less likely to survive the ravages of time. In the second place, as this period of nearly 2 million years has been better studied, it has become evident that there were so many distinct periods and cultures during the

Making stone tools About 35,000 years ago the manufacture of stone tools became highly specialized. Small blades, chipped from a rock core, were mounted in a bone or wooden handle. Not only were such composite tools more diverse than earlier all-purpose hand-axes, but the small blades required fewer rock cores—an important consideration in areas where suitable rocks were scarce. (From Jacques Bordaz, *Tools of the Old and New Stone Age.* Copyright 1970 by Jacques Bordaz. Redrawn by the permission of Addison-Wesley Educational Publishers, Inc.)

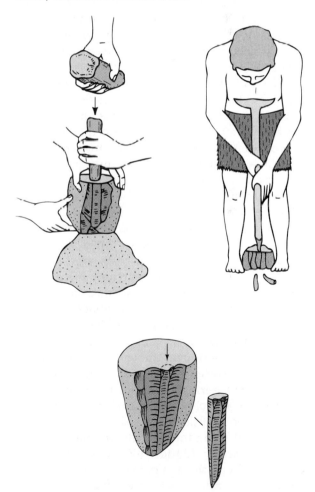

Stone Age that the old division into a Paleolithic (Old Stone) Age down to 10,000 years ago and a Neolithic (New Stone) Age is no longer adequate. Modern research scientists have largely abandoned the use of *Paleolithic* in favor of particular labels, but *Neolithic* remains in current usage.

Most stone tools made by *Homo habilis* have been found in the Great Rift Valley of eastern Africa, whose sides expose sediments laid down over millions of years. One branch of this valley, the Olduvai Gorge in Tanzania, explored by Louis and Mary Leakey, has been a particularly important source. The earliest tools were made by chipping flakes off the edges of volcanic stones. Modern experiments show that the razor-sharp edges of such flakes are highly effective in skinning and butchering wild animals.

The small-brained *Homo habilis*, however, probably lacked the skill to hunt large animals successfully and probably obtained animal protein by scavenging meat from kills made by animal predators or by accidents. There is evidence that they used large stone "choppers" for cracking open bones to get at the nutritious marrow. The fact that many such tools are found together far from the outcrops of volcanic rock suggests that people carried them long distances for use at killsites and camps.

Homo erectus were also scavengers, but their larger brains would have made them cleverer at it—capable, for example, of finding and stealing the kills of leopards and other large predators that drag their kills into trees. They also made more effective tools for butchering large animals, although the stone flakes and choppers of earlier eras continued to be made. The most characteristic stone tool used by *Homo erectus* was a hand ax formed by removing chips from both sides of a stone to produce a sharp outer edge.

Modern experiments show the hand ax to be an efficient multipurpose tool, suitable for skinning and butchering animals, for scraping skins clean for use as clothing and mats, for sharpening wooden tools, and for digging up edible roots. Since a hand ax can also be hurled accurately for nearly 100 feet (30 meters), it might also have been used as a projectile to fell animals. From sites in Spain there is evidence that *Homo erectus* even butchered elephants, which then ranged across southern Europe, by driving them into swamps where they became trapped and died.

Homo sapiens were far more skillful hunters. They tracked and killed large animals (including mastodons, mammoths, and bisons) throughout the world. Their success depended on their superior intelligence and on an array of finely made tools. Sharp stone flakes chipped from carefully prepared rock cores were often used in combination with other materials. A spear could be made by attaching a stone point to a wooden shaft. Embedding several sharp stone flakes in a bone handle produced a sawing tool.

Indeed, *Homo sapiens* were so skillful and successful as hunters that they may have caused or contributed to a series of ecological crises. Between 40,000 and 13,000 years ago the giant mastodons and mammoths gradually disappeared, first from Africa and Southeast Asia and then from northern Europe. In North America the sudden disappearance around 11,000 years ago of highly successful large-animal hunters known as the Clovis people was almost simultaneous with the extinction of three-fourths of the large mammals in the Americas, including giant bisons, camels, ground sloths, stag-moose, giant cats, mastodons, and mammoths. In Australia there was a similar event. Since these extinctions occurred during the last series of severe cold spells at the end of the Great Ice Age, it is difficult to measure which effects were the work of global and regional climate changes and which resulted from the excesses of human predators. Whichever the case, 10,000 years ago major changes in human food strategies were under way that would have far greater impact on the planet and its life forms (as the next section shows).

Finds of fossilized animal bones bearing the marks of butchering tools clearly attest to the scavenging and hunting activities of Stone Age peoples, but anthropologists do not believe that early humans depended primarily on meat for their food. Modern food-gathering peoples in the Kalahari Desert of Southern Africa and Ituri Forest of central Africa all derive the bulk of their day-to-day nourishment from wild vegetable foods; meat is the food of feasts. It is likely that Stone Age peoples would have done the same, even though the tools and equipment for gathering and processing vegetable foods have left few traces for they were made of materials too soft to survive for thousands of years.

Like modern hunter-gatherers, ancient humans would have used skins and mats woven from leaves for collecting fruits, berries, and wild seeds. They would have dug edible roots out of the ground with wooden sticks. Archaeologists believe that the donut-shaped stones often found at Stone Age sites may have been weights placed on wooden digging sticks to increase their effectiveness.

The evidence of early food preparation is also scarce and largely indirect. Modern societies pound and grind roots and seeds to make them more palatable, but this can be done with ordinary stones that would not appear distinctive in the archaeological remains. Both meat and vegetables become tastier and easier to digest when they are cooked. The first cooked foods were probably found by accident after wildfires, but there is new evidence from East and South Africa that humans were setting fires deliberately between 1 million and 1.5 million years ago. The wooden spits and hot rocks that would have been used for roasting, frying, or baking are not distinctive enough to stand out in an archaeological site. Only with the appearance of clay cooking pots some 12,500 years ago in East Asia is there hard evidence of cooking.

Gender Divisions and Social Life

To bring the mute material remains of Ice Age humans to life, anthropologists have studied the few surviving present-day hunter-gatherer societies. Although in many ways such societies must be quite different from hunting and gathering communities thousands of years earlier, in other ways they provide models of what such early societies could have been like.

For example, the gender division of labor in present-day hunting and gathering societies suggests that in the Ice Age women would have done most of the gathering and cooking (which can be performed while caring for small children). Men, with stronger arms and shoulders, would have been more suited than women to hunting, particularly for large animals. Some early cave art shows males in hunting activities.

Other aspects of social life in the Ice Age are suggested by studies of modern peoples. All modern hunter-gatherers live in small groups or bands. The community has to have enough members to defend itself from predators and to divide responsibility for the collection and preparation of animal and vegetable foods. However, if it has too many members, it risks exhausting the food available in its immediate vicinity. Even a band of optimal size has to move at regular intervals to follow migrating animals and take advantage of seasonally ripening plants in different places. Archaeological evidence from Ice Age campsites suggests early humans were organized in highly mobile bands.

Other researchers have studied the organization of nonhuman primates for clues about very early human society. Gorillas and chimpanzees live in groups consisting of several adult males and females and their offspring. Status varies with age and sex, and a dominant male usually heads the group. Sexual unions between males and females generally do not result in long-term pairing. Instead, the strongest ties are those between a female and her children and among siblings. Adult males are often recruited from neighboring bands.

Very early human groups likely shared some similar traits, but by the time of *Homo sapiens sapiens* the two-parent nuclear family would have been characteristic. How this change from a mother-centered family to a two-parent family developed over the intervening millennia can only be guessed at, but it is likely that physical and social evolution were linked. Larger brain size was a contributing factor. Big-headed humans have to be born in a less mature state than other mammals so they can pass through the narrow birth canal, and thus they take much longer to mature outside the womb. Other large mammals are mature at two or three years of age; humans at from twelve to fifteen. Human infants' and children's need for much longer nurturing makes care by mothers, fathers, and other relatives a biological imperative.

The human reproductive cycle also became unique at some point. In other species sexual contact is biologically restricted to a special mating season of the year or to the fertile part of the female's menstrual cycle. As well, among other primates the choice of mate is usually not a matter for long deliberation. To a female baboon in heat (estrus) any male will do, and to a male baboon any receptive female is a suitable sexual partner. In contrast, adult humans can mate at any time and are much choosier about their partners. Once they choose their mates, frequent sexual contacts promote deep emotional ties and long-term bonding.

An enduring bond between parents made it much easier for vulnerable offspring to receive the care they needed during the long period of their childhood. In addition, human couples could nurture dependent children of different ages at the same time, unlike other large mammals whose females must raise their offspring nearly to maturity before beginning another reproductive cycle. Spacing births close together also ensured offspring a high rate of survival and would have enabled humans to multiply more rapidly than other large mammals. The gender specialization in hunting and gathering food discussed earlier would also have maximized band members' chances for survival.

Hearths and Cultural Expressions

Because frequent moves were necessary to keep close to migrating herds and ripening plants, hunting and gathering peoples usually did not lavish much time on housing. Natural shelters under overhanging rocks or in caves in southern Africa and southern France are known to have been favorite camping places to which bands returned at regular intervals. Where the climate was severe or where natural shelters did not

Mammoth-bone architecture Composed of the different bones of giant mammoths, this reconstructed framework of a 15,000-year-old communal hut in the Ukraine would have been covered with hides to provide a durable shelter against the weather. (Novosti)

exist, people erected huts of branches, stones, bones, skins, and leaves as seasonal camps. More elaborate dwellings were common in areas where protection against harsh weather was necessary.

An interesting camp dating to 15,000 years ago has been excavated in the Ukraine southeast of Kiev. Its communal dwellings were framed with the bones of elephant-like mammoths, then covered with hides. Each oblong structure, measuring 15 to 20 feet (4.5 to 6 meters) by 40 to 50 feet (12 to 15 meters), was capable of holding fifty people and would have taken several days to construct. The camp had five such dwellings, making it a large settlement for a hunting-gathering community. Large, solid structures were common in fishing villages that grew up along rivers and lake shores where the abundance of fish permitted people to occupy the same site year-round.

Making clothing was another necessary technology in the Stone Age. Animal skins were an early form of clothing, and the oldest evidence of fibers woven into cloth dates from about 26,000 years ago. An "Iceman" from 5,300 years ago, whose frozen remains were found in the European Alps in 1991, was wearing many different garments made of animal skins sewn together with thread fashioned from vegetable fibers and rawhide.

Although accidents, erratic weather, and disease took a heavy toll on a hunting and gathering band, there is reason to believe that day-to-day existence was not particularly hard or unpleasant. Some studies suggest that under the conditions operating on the African savannas and other game-rich areas, securing the necessities of food, clothing, and shelter would have occupied only from three to five hours a day. This would have left a great deal of time for artistic endeavors as well as for toolmaking and social life.

Although the foundations of what later ages called science, art, and religion are harder to detect and interpret, they were established during the Stone Age. Basic to human survival was extensive and precise knowledge about the natural environment. Gatherers needed to know which local plants were best for food and the seasons when they were available. Successful hunting re-

The "Iceman" A 5,300-year-old body found frozen in the Alps preserved remarkable evidence of clothing and tools. Dressed for cold weather, he wore a fur hat, tailored deer-skin vest, and leather leggings. His tools included a copper-headed ax, a long bow and quiver of arrows, a flint knife in a string sheath, a flint scraper, a flint awl, and fire-starting tools. The Iceman also carried a birch bark cup. (New York Times Picture Sales)

quired intimate knowledge of the habits of game animals. People learned how to use plant and animal parts for clothing, twine, and building materials, as well as which natural substances were effective for medicine, consciousness altering, dyeing, and other purposes. Knowledge of the natural world included identifying minerals suitable for paints, stones for making the best tools, and so forth. Given humans' physical capacity for speech, it is likely that the transmission of such prescientific knowledge involved verbal communication, even though direct evidence for language appears only in later periods.

Early manifestations of music and dance have left no traces, but the evidence of painting and drawing is vivid and abundant. The use of pigment for painting or personal adornment is very old. Red-ochre sticks found at the site of Terra Amata on the French Riviera have been dated to between 200,000 and 300,000 years ago, for example. Cave paintings were being made in Europe and north Africa by 32,000 years ago and at later times in other parts of the world. Cave art that features wild animals such as oxen, reindeer, and horses, which were hunted for food, has led to speculation that the art was meant to record hunting scenes or that it formed part of some magical and religious rites to ensure success. However, the newly discovered cave at Vallon Pont-d'Arc features rhinoceroses, panthers, bears, owls, and a hyena, which probably were not the objects of hunting. Still other drawings include people dressed in animal skins and smeared with paint. In many caves there are large numbers of stencils of human hands. Are these the signatures of the artists or the world's oldest graffiti? Some scholars suspect that other marks in cave paintings and on bones from this period may represent efforts at counting or writing.

Theories about cave and rock art emphasize concerns with fertility, efforts to educate the young, and elaborate mechanisms for time reckoning. These different interpretations do not exclude each other, for there is no reason to think that a single purpose was in the minds of all the artists during several thousands of years and in distant parts of the world. Another way to view such art is from the perspective of living peoples. The San have been hunters, gatherers, and artists in southern Africa since time immemorial. Archaeologist David Lewis-Williams has argued that much, if not all, of the cave art of southern Africa can be interpreted in terms of potency and

trance—that is, it represents visions hallucinated by people in altered physical states brought on by meditation or psychoactive drinks and smokes (see Voices and Visions: Interpreting Rock Art).

Stone Age people possessed sufficiently well-developed brains to have wondered about the majesty of the heavens, the mystery of success in the hunt, and the fate of the dead. In other words, they could have devised the first religions. But without written religious texts it is very difficult to know exactly what early humans believed. Sites of deliberate human burials from about 100,000 years ago give some hints. The fact that an adult was often buried with stone implements, food, clothing, and red-ochre powder suggests that early people revered their leaders enough to honor them after death and may imply a belief in an afterlife.

It is likely that future discoveries will add substantially to the understanding of Stone Age life. Already this vast era, whose existence was scarcely dreamed of two centuries ago, can be recognized as a period of formative importance. Important in its own right, the period was also a necessary preparation for the major changes ahead as human communities passed from being food gatherers to being food producers.

THE AGRICULTURAL REVOLUTIONS

Like all other species, early humans depended on wild plants and animals for their food. But around 10,000 years ago some humans began to meet their food needs by raising domesticated plants and animals. Gradually over the next millennium most people became food producers, although hunting and gathering continued to exist in some places. This transition to food production was a major milestone in humans' manipulation of nature and had myriad implications for the human species and their planet (see Map 1.2).

The change from food gathering to food production at the end of the Stone Age has been called the "Neolithic revolution." The name can

Interpreting Rock Art

The drawings of animals and people found in caves or in rock shelters in many parts of the world are spectacular visually but hard to interpret. Some of the drawings seem to record common activities, such as hunting. Others are puzzling mixtures of realistic and fantastic shapes in odd configurations. Archaeologist David Lewis-Williams has extracted rich meaning from one school of cave art by connecting it with the beliefs and rituals of a southern African hunting and gathering people now known as the San.

The last San groups to create such paintings died out a century ago, but Lewis-Williams believes the records of their beliefs, customs, and symbols provide a way to interpret a tradition of rock art that extends back thousands of years. As he reconstructs it, the rock drawings were made by *shamans*, men and women in San society who acquired the power to cure sickness, control antelope herds, and make rain while in trances. He believes much of San art depicts trance scenes when the shamans shook, sweated, and fell into a deep sleep during which they had out-of-body experiences.

Lewis-Williams reads the scene reproduced here as representing a shaman's efforts to control the rain by leading a mystical animal across a parched landscape. The figure marked (1) is a shaman entering a trance,

holding his body characteristically bent over with his arms thrown back. Figure (2) is a shaman fully in a trance, lying down; the lines represent his spirit leaving his body. The partially obscured figure (3) above the rain animal has his hand to his nose in depiction of "snoring," which the San associated with curing illness. The line of small dots above the animal (4) are bees, whose swarming the San believed marked a particularly potent time for trance medicine.

Unfortunately, nowhere else in the world has rock art been connected to a recorded system of beliefs. However, Lewis-Williams's reconstructions do suggest how much symbolic belief and mystical lore may lie behind the cave art of these early periods.

If you had only the drawing to go by, could you make sense of it? Why is it important to understand the cultural context in which a work of art is made? What do you know about the San that helps explain why they attached such importance to animals? Why might they prize personal mystical experiences?

Source: Adapted from Martin Hall, *Farmers, Kings, and Traders: The People of Southern Africa, 200–1860* (Chicago: University of Chicago Press, 1990), 62. The illustration is reproduced by permission of David Lewis-Williams, "Introductory Essay. Science and Rock Art," *South African Archaeological Society, Goodwin Series* 4 (1983): 3–13.

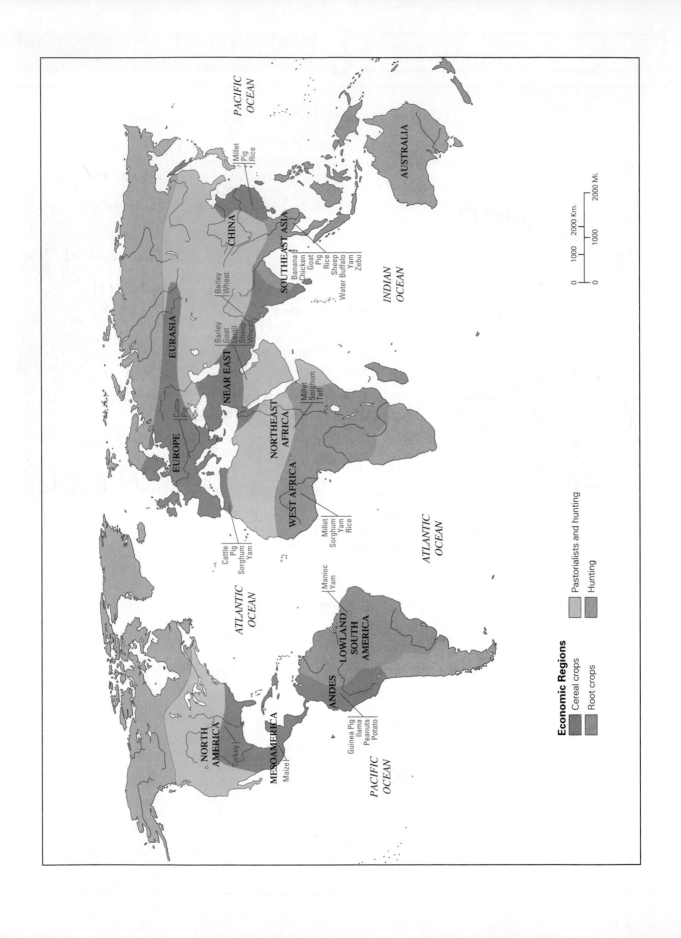

Economic Regions

Cereal crops

Root crops

Pastorialists and hunting

Hunting

PACIFIC OCEAN

AUSTRALIA

Millet
Pig
Rice

CHINA

SOUTHEAST ASIA

Banana
Chicken
Goat
Pig
Rice
Sheep
Water Buffalo
Yam
Zebu

INDIAN OCEAN

Barley
Wheat

EURASIA

Barley
Goat
Lentil
Sheep
Wheat

NEAR EAST

EUROPE

Cattle
Pig

NORTHEAST AFRICA

Millet
Sorghum
Teff

WEST AFRICA

Millet
Sorghum
Yam
Rice

Cattle
Pig
Sorghum
Yam

ATLANTIC OCEAN

ATLANTIC OCEAN

Manioc
Yam

LOWLAND SOUTH AMERICA

NORTH AMERICA

Turkey

MESOAMERICA

Maize

ANDES

Guinea Pig
Llama
Peanuts
Potato

PACIFIC OCEAN

0   1000   2000 Km.

0   1000   2000 Mi.

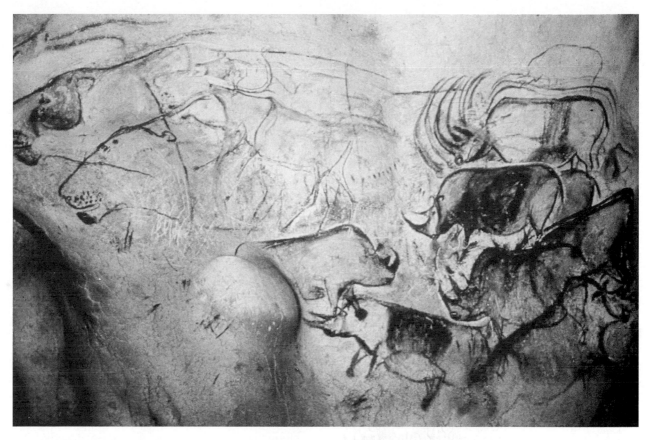

Cave art Remarkable paintings and engravings of 300 animals were discovered in cave at Vallon-Pont-d'Arc in southern France in 1994. Dated to about 20,000 years ago, the depictions in black and red include bison, rhinoceros, reindeer, lions, horses, oxen, and bears, as well as the only known portrayal of a panther. (Jean Clottes/Ministère de la Culture/Sygma)

be misleading because stone tools were not its essential component and because it was not a single event but a series of separate transformations in different parts of the world. "Agricultural revolutions" is a more precise label, stressing that the central change was in food production and that this momentous transformation occurred independently in many different parts of the world. In most cases agriculture included the domestication of animals for food as well as the cultivation of new food crops. Changes in global climate appear to have caused this transformation.

Map 1.2 Centers of plant and animal domestication Many different parts of the world made original contributions to domestication during the "agricultural revolutions" that began about 10,000 years ago. Later interactions helped spread these domesticated animals to new locations. In lands less suitable for crop cultivation, pastoralism and hunting predominated.

The Transition to Plant Cultivation

Food gathering gave way to food production in stages spread over hundreds of generations. The process may have begun when hunter-gatherer bands returning year after year to the same seasonal camps took measures to encourage the nearby growth of the foods they liked. They deliberately scattered the seeds of desirable plants in locations where they would thrive, and they discouraged the growth of competing plants by clearing them away. Such techniques of semicultivation could have supplemented food gathering for many generations. Families willing to devote their energies principally to food production, however, had to settle permanently in their formerly seasonal camp.

One component of settled agriculture was the production of new specialized tools and the development of techniques to enhance success. Indeed, the abundant evidence of new tools first alerted archaeologists to the significance of the food production revolutions. Many specialized stone tools were developed or improved for agricultural use, including sickle blades of small, sharp stone chips imbedded in bone or wooden handles, polished or ground stone heads used to work the soil, and stone mortars in which grain was pulverized.

However, stone axes were not very efficient in clearing shrubs and trees. For that a much older technology was used: fire. Farmers set fires to get rid of unwanted undergrowth, and from the ashes they received a bonus: natural fertilizer. After the burn-off they could use blades and axes to trim away the regrowth before it got too large.

More fundamental to the success of agriculture than new tools was the new technique of selecting the highest-yielding strains of wild plants, which over time led to the development of valuable new domesticated varieties. Because women were the principal gatherers of wild plant foods, they are likely to have played a major role in this transition to plant cultivation. The success of a farming community also would have required extensive male labor, especially to clear fields for planting.

The transition to agriculture has been traced in greatest detail in the Middle East. By 8000 B.C.E. (Before the Common Era) human selection had transformed certain wild grasses into higheryielding domesticated grains now known as emmer wheat and barley. Communities there also discovered that alternating the cultivation of grains and pulses (plants yielding edible seeds such as lentils and peas) helped to maintain soil fertility.

Crops that were first domesticated in the Middle East were later grown elsewhere, but the spread of agriculture was not essentially a process of diffusion. Agriculture arose independently in many parts of the world. Over time much borrowing occurred, but it was societies that already had begun to practice agriculture on their own that were most likely to borrow new plants, animals, and farming techniques from their neighbors.

The oldest traces of food production in northern Africa are in the eastern Sahara, which was able to support farming during a particularly wet period after 8000 B.C.E. As in the Middle East, emmer wheat and barley became the principal crops and sheep, goats, and cattle the main domesticated animals. The return of drier conditions about 5000 B.C.E. led many Saharan farmers to move to the Nile Valley, where the annual flooding of the Nile River provided moisture for cereal farming.

In Europe cultivation of wheat and barley began as early as 6000 B.C.E. in Greece, combining local experiments and Middle Eastern borrowings. Shortly after 4000 B.C.E. farming developed in the light-soiled plains of Central Europe and along the Danube River. As forests receded because of climate changes and human clearing efforts, agriculture spread to other parts of Europe over the next millennium.

Early farmers in Europe and elsewhere practiced shifting cultivation, also known as *swidden agriculture*. After a few growing seasons, the fields were left fallow (abandoned to natural vegetation), and new fields were cleared nearby. Between 4000 and 3000 B.C.E., for example, communities of from 40 to 60 people in the Danube Valley of Central Europe supported themselves on about 500 acres (200 hectares) of farmland, cultivating a third or less each year while leaving the rest fallow to restore its fertility. From around 2600 B.C.E. people in Central Europe began using ox-drawn wooden plows to till heavier and richer soils.

Although the lands around the Mediterranean seem to have shared a complex of crops and farming techniques, there were major geographical barriers to the spread of this complex. Wheat and barley were unsuited to the rainfall patterns

Agricultural Revolutions in Asia and the Americas

astern and southern Asia were major centers of plant domestication, although the details and dates are not so clearly documented as in the Middle East. Rice was one important food that was first domesticated in southern China, the northern half of Southeast Asia, or northeastern India, possibly as early as 10,000 B.C.E., but more likely closer to 5000 B.C.E. Rice cultivation thrived in the warm and wet conditions of southern China. The cooler, drier climate of northern China favored locally domesticated cereals, such as foxtail millet. In India several pulses (including hyacinth beans, green grams, and black grams) domesticated about 2000 B.C.E. were cultivated along with rice.

At the same time as food production was spreading in Eurasia and Africa, the inhabitants of the isolated American continents were creating another major center of crop domestication. As game animals declined in the Tehuacán Valley of Mexico after 8000 B.C.E., wild vegetable foods became increasingly important to the diet. New dating techniques indicate that agriculture based on maize (corn) developed there after 3500 B.C.E. and spread to what is now the southwestern United States about 500 B.C.E. About the same time as maize-based agriculture was emerging in Mexico, the inhabitants of Peru were developing a food production system based on squash and quinoa, a protein-rich seed grain. In the more tropical regions of Mesoamerica, tomatoes, peppers, and potatoes were cultivated.

It is significant for their own early history that Asia and the Americas were able to develop distinctive domesticated plants quite independent of outside influences. In later centuries many of their crops were carried to other lands, adding to the variety and abundance of the world's food supply.

---

south of the Sahara. Instead, farming in sub-Saharan Africa came to be based on a wide variety of locally domesticated grains, including sorghums, millets, and (in Ethiopia) teff. Grains could not be grown at all in the very humid regions of equatorial West Africa, where there is early evidence of indigenous domestication of root crops such as yams. Eastern Asia and the Americas were also major centers of food plant domestication (see Environment and Technology: Agricultural Revolutions in Asia and the Americas).

Animal Domestication and Pastoralism

The revolution in food production was not confined to plants; the domestication of animals also expanded rapidly during these same millennia. The first domesticated animal was probably the dog, tamed to assist early hunters in tracking game. Later animals were domesticated to provide meat, milk, and energy. Like the domestication of plants, this process is best known in the Middle East.

By studying the refuse dumped outside some Middle East villages during the centuries after 7000 B.C.E., archaeologists have been able to document a gradual decline in the quantity of wild gazelle bones. This finding probably reflects the depletion of such wild animals through over-hunting by the local farming communities. Meat eating, however, did not decline; the deposits show sheep and goat bones gradually replacing gazelle bones. It seems likely that wild sheep and goats had learned to scavenge for food scraps around agricultural villages and that people began to feed the tamer sheep and goats and protect them from wild predators in order to provide themselves with a ready supply of food. At first the biological differences between tame and wild species are too slight to date domestication precisely. Distinct domesticated species evolved as people controlled the breeding of their sheep and goats to produce desirable characteristics such as high milk production and long wool.

Elsewhere in the world other animal species were being domesticated during the centuries before 3000 B.C.E. Wild cattle were domesticated in northern Africa; pigs and water buffalo in

China; and humped-back Zebu cattle, buffalo, and pigs in India. As in the case of food plants, varieties of domesticated animals from abroad sometimes replaced the species initially domesticated. For example, the Zebu cattle originally domesticated in India first became important in sub-Saharan Africa about 2000 years ago.

In most parts of the world, farming populations depended on domesticated plants and animals for food and also used domesticated oxen, cattle, or (in China) water buffalo as draft animals. Animal droppings were important for fertilizing the soil and their wool and hides for clothing. However, there were two notable deviations from this pattern of mixed agriculture and animal husbandry.

One variation was in the Americas. There, comparatively few species of wild animals were suitable for domestication, other than llamas (for transport and wool) and guinea pigs and some fowls (for meat). No species could be borrowed from elsewhere because the Americas' land bridge to Asia had submerged as melting glaciers raised sea levels. Hunting remained an important source of meat for Amerindians, but perhaps their exceptional contributions to the world's domesticated plant crops were partly in compensation for the shortage of domesticated meat animals (see Chapter 12).

The other notable variation from mixed farming occurred in more arid parts of Africa and Central Asia. There, pastoralism, a way of life dependent on large herds of small and large stock, predominated. For example, pastoralists had replaced farmers in the Sahara as it became drier, up until about 2500 B.C.E., when desert conditions forced them to migrate southward. The necessity of moving their herds to new pastures and watering places throughout the year meant that pastoralists needed to be almost as mobile as hunter-gatherers and thus could accumulate little in the way of bulky possessions and substantial dwellings. Like modern pastoralists, early cattle-keeping people were probably not great meat eaters but relied heavily on the milk from their animals for their diet. During seasons when grasses for grazing and water were plentiful, they could also have done some hasty crop cultivation or bartered meat and skins for plant foods with nearby farming communities.

Agriculture and Ecological Crisis

Why in the Neolithic period did societies in so many parts of the world gradually abandon a way of life based on food gathering? Some theories assume that people were drawn to food production by its obvious advantages. For example, it has recently been suggested that people settled down in the Middle East so they could grow enough grains to ensure themselves a ready supply of beer. Beer drinking is frequently depicted in ancient Middle Eastern art and can be dated to as early as 3500 B.C.E.

However, most researchers today believe that some ecological crisis during the period of global warming after the ice age drove people to abandon hunting and gathering in favor of pastoralism and agriculture. Such a crisis would explain why so many places adopted food production during the same period. Although the precise nature of the crisis has not been identified, some scholars think food production may have been a response to shortages of wild food. In some places a warmer, wetter climate could have promoted rapid forest growth in former grasslands, reducing the supplies of game and wild grains. Or, because a warmer climate made it easier for more people to survive, rising population could have depleted supplies of wild food.

Additional support for an ecological explanation comes from the fact that in many drier parts of the world, where wild food remained abundant, agriculture was not adopted. The inhabitants of Australia continued to rely exclusively on hunting and gathering until recent centuries, as did some peoples in all the other continents. Many Amerindians in the arid grasslands from Alaska to the Gulf of Mexico hunted bison, while in the Pacific Northwest others took up salmon-fishing. Abundant supplies of fish, shellfish, and aquatic animals permitted food gatherers east of the Mississippi River in North America to become increasingly sedentary. In the equatorial rain forest and in the southern part of Africa conditions favored retention of the older ways. The reindeer-based societies of northern Eurasia were also unaffected by the spread of farming.

Whatever the causes, the effects of the gradual adoption of food production in most parts of the world between 12,000 and 2,000 years ago were momentous. A hundred thousand years ago there probably were fewer than 2 million humans, and their range was largely confined to the temperate and tropical regions of Africa and Eurasia. During the last glacial epoch, between 32,000 and 13,000 years ago, human population may have fallen even lower. As the glaciers retreated, humans expanded into new land and adopted agriculture, and their numbers gradually rose to 10 million by 5000 B.C.E. Then human population mushroomed, reaching from 50 million to 100 million by 1000 B.C.E. and 200 million or more a millennium later. This increase in numbers brought momentous changes to social and cultural life.

LIFE IN NEOLITHIC COMMUNITIES

The evidence that people were driven to food production by a crisis rather than drawn to it has led researchers to reexamine the disadvantages and advantages of agriculture compared to those of hunting and gathering. Modern studies suggest that food producers have to work much harder and for much longer periods than do food gatherers. In return for modest harvests, early farmers needed to put in long days of arduous labor clearing and cultivating the land. Pastoralists had to guard their herds from wild predators, guide them to fresh pastures, and tend to their many needs.

There is also evidence that even though the food supply of early farmers was more secure than that of food-gathering peoples and pastoralists, the farmers' diet was less varied and nutritious. Skeletal remains show that on average Neolithic farmers were shorter than earlier food-gathering peoples. Farmers were also likely to die at an earlier age because permanent villages

and towns were unhealthier than temporary camps. Contagious diseases could establish themselves more readily in densely settled communities because human waste contaminated drinking water, disease-bearing vermin and insects infested persons and buildings, and new diseases migrated to humans from their domesticated animals (especially pigs and cattle).

The most notable benefit of agriculture was a more dependable supply of food that could be stored between harvests to tide people over seasonal changes and short-term climate fluctuations such as droughts. Over several millennia, permanent settlements experienced slow but steady population growth. There were also profound changes in culture and the emergence of towns and craft specialization.

Rural Population and Settlement

Researchers have long wondered exactly how farmers displaced hunter-gatherers. Some have envisioned a violent struggle between practitioners of the two ways of life; others believe there was a more peaceful transition. Some violence was likely, especially as the amount of cleared land reduced the wild foods available to hunter-gatherers. Probable too were conflicts among farmers for control of the best land. A growing body of evidence, however, suggests that in most cases farmers displaced hunter-gatherers by a process of gradual infiltration rather than by rapid conquest.

The key to the food producers' expansion may have been the simple fact that their small surpluses gave them a long-term advantage in population growth, by ensuring slightly higher survival rates during times of drought or other crisis. The respected archaeologist Colin Renfrew argues, for example, that over a few centuries farming-population densities in Europe could have increased by from fifty to one hundred fold. According to his scenario, as population densities rose, those individuals who had to farm at a great distance from their native village eventually formed a new farming settlement.

Renfrew finds it consistent with the archaeological evidence for a steady nonviolent expansion of agricultural peoples—moving only 12 to 19 miles (20 or 30 kilometers) a generation—to have repopulated the whole of Europe from Greece to Britain between 6500 and 3500 B.C.E.[2] The process would have been so gradual that it need not have provoked any sharp conflicts with existing hunter-gatherers, who simply could have stayed clear of the agricultural frontier or gradually adopted agriculture themselves and been absorbed by the advancing farming communities. This hypothesis of a gradual spread of agricultural people across Europe from southeast to northwest is also supported by new studies that map similar genetic changes in the population.[3]

Like hunter-gatherer bands, the expanding farming communities were organized around kinship and marriage. Nuclear families (parents and their children) probably did not become larger, but people traced kinship relations back over more generations so that distant cousins were clearly aware of their membership in the same kin network. This was important because landholding was likely to be vested in large kinship units, known as *lineages* and *clans*.

Even if one assumes stable marriage patterns, tracing descent is a complex matter. Because each person has two parents, four grandparents, eight great-grandparents, and so on, each individual has a bewildering number of ancestors. Societies tend to trace descent primarily through a single parent. Some trace descent through mothers (*matrilineal societies*) and some through fathers (*patrilineal societies*).

Some scholars have argued that ancient peoples may have traced descent through women and may have been ruled by women. For example, the traditions of Kikuyu farmers on Mount Kenya in East Africa relate that women once ruled them, but the Kikiyu men conspired to get all the women pregnant at once and then overthrew them while the women were unable to fight back. No specific evidence can prove or disprove legends such as this, but it is important not to confuse tracing descent through women (*matrilineality*) with the rule of women (*matriarchy*). In both patrilineal and matrilineal societies today, men, particularly older men, are dominant.

Cultural Expressions

The importance of their kinship systems influenced early agricultural people's outlook on the world. Reverence for departed ancestors was an important part of group solidarity, and the deaths of old persons tended to be marked by elaborate burials. The existence of a plastered skull from Jericho in the Jordan Valley of modern Israel may be evidence of an early ancestor cult. (A cult is a system of religious rituals expressing reverence or worship.)

The religion of food producers also reflected their awareness of their relationship to nature. In contrast to food gatherers, whose religions tended to center on sacred groves, springs, and wild animals, many farming communities centered their religious activities on the Earth Mother, a female deity who was the source of all new life, along with other gods and goddesses representing fire, wind, and rain. Beliefs in an all-powerful (and usually) male Sky God were also common.

The story in an ancient Hindu text about the burning of a large forest near modern India's capital, New Delhi, may preserve a memory of the conflict between old and new beliefs. In the story the gods Krishna and Arjuna are picnicking in the forest when Agni, the fire-god, appears in disguise and asks them to satisfy his hunger by burning the forest along with every creature in it. As interpreted by some scholars, this story represents both the clearing of the land for cultivation and the destruction of the wildlife on which food gatherers depended.[4]

Religions placed different emphasis on the role of ancestors, the Sky God, and the Earth Mother, but most seem to have included all three in their religious practices, along with older rituals and deities. Large chambers called *megaliths* (meaning "big stones") dating from 4000 B.C.E. provide some evidence of an ancestor cult in western Europe. The early ones appear to have been communal burial chambers, which descent groups may have erected to mark their claims to farmlands. Megaliths were also built on eastern Mediterranean (Aegean) islands. In the Middle East, the Americas, and other parts of the world, giant earth burial mounds and ziggurats (mounds on which temples were later built) may have served similar functions.

Another fundamental cultural contribution of Neolithic period was the dissemination of the large language families that form the basis of most languages spoken today. Renfrew has suggested that the spread of the western half of the giant Indo-European language family (from which Germanic, Romance, and Celtic languages are derived) was the work of the pioneering agriculturalists who gradually moved across Europe. The age of the language family and its differentiation into many related but distinct languages are indeed more consistent with a pattern of gradual infiltration than with rapid conquest. Similarly, the Afro-Asiatic language family that spans the Middle East and northern Africa might have been the result of the food producers' expansion, as might the spread of the Sino-Tibetan family in East and Southeast Asia.

These interpretations of language diffusion must be considered speculative because there is no physical evidence of what languages were actually spoken during the Neolithic period. Indisputable instances of language and an agricultural population spreading together do exist from somewhat later times. One example is the great wave of Malayo-Polynesian colonization of the East Indies and the thousands of islands in the Pacific Ocean between 4000 B.C.E. and 1000 C.E. Everywhere they went, Pacific mariners introduced their principal crops—breadfruit, taro, coconut, yams, and bananas—along with the current version of their spoken language. Another example of agricultural and linguistic expansion, the spread of the Bantu-speaking people across central and southern Africa, occurred from about 500 B.C.E. to 1000 C.E. (see Chapter 8).

Early Towns and Specialists

Most early farmers lived in small villages, but in some parts of the world a few villages grew into towns, which were centers of trade and craft specialization. These larger communities were most notable in river valleys where rich soils and regular water supplies provided high agricultural

Neolithic goddess   Many versions of a well-nourished and pregnant female figure were found at Çatal Hüyük. Here she is supported by twin leopards whose tails curve over her shoulders. To those who inhabited the city some 8,000 years ago the figure likely represented fertility and power over nature. (C.M. Dixon)

yields that could support denser populations (see Chapters 2 and 3). Towns and cities had elaborate dwellings and ceremonial buildings made of mud brick, stone, and wood, as well as many large structures for storing the surplus production until the next harvest. Baskets and other woven containers held dry foods; pottery jugs, jars, and pots stored liquids.

Most of these structures and objects could be made by the agriculturalists in their spare time, but larger communities had craft specialists, who devoted their full energies to making products of unusual complexity or beauty. Such specialization was possible because the community produced a surplus of food and other necessities.

Two towns in the Middle East that have been extensively excavated are Jericho on the west bank of the Jordan River and Çatal Hüyük in central Anatolia (modern Turkey).

The excavations at Jericho revealed an unusually large and elaborate early agricultural settlement. Around 8000 B.C.E. dwellings at Jericho were round, mud-brick structures, perhaps imitating the shape of the tents of hunters who once had camped near Jericho's natural spring. A millennium later there were rectangular rooms with finely plastered walls and floors and wide doorways that opened on a central courtyard. Around the 10-acre (4-hectare) settlement extended a massive stone wall, to which tall towers were added about 7000 B.C.E. The walls were clearly for defense against invasion, presumably by local pastoralists.

Çatal Hüyük, an even larger Neolithic town, dates to between 7000 and 5000 B.C.E. and covered 32 acres (13 hectares) at its height. Its residents also occupied plastered mud-brick rooms that were elaborately decorated. Unlike Jericho, Çatal Hüyük had no defensive fortifications. But the outer walls of the houses formed a continuous barrier without doors or large windows, so invaders would have found it difficult to break in. Residents entered their house by climbing down a ladder through a hole in the roof.

Çatal Hüyük was a bustling town that prospered from long-distance trade in obsidian, a hard volcanic rock that craftspeople skillfully chipped, ground, and polished into tools, weapons, mirrors, and ornaments. Other residents made fine pottery and practiced many other crafts, including weaving baskets and woolen cloth, making stone and shell beads, and working leather and wood. House sizes varied, but there is no evidence that Çatal Hüyük had a dominant class or a centralized political structure.

Although the amount and the importance of craftwork in towns like Jericho and Çatal Hüyük were quite new in history, the two towns displayed many close links with older ways of living. The very extensive representational art at Çatal Hüyük makes it clear that hunting retained a powerful hold on people's minds. Elaborate wall paintings depict hunting scenes remarkably similar to those of earlier cave paintings, and

men were buried with weapons of war and hunting, not with the tools of farming. Moreover, many of the wall scenes depict persons, both males and females, adorned with the skins of wild leopards.

Discarded bones are proof that wild game featured prominently in the diet of Çatal Hüyük residents, but, however neglected in their art, agriculture was the basis of their existence. Fields around the town produced crops of barley and emmer wheat, as well as legumes and other vegetables. A species of pig was kept along with goats and sheep. Wild foods such as acorns and wild grains were also important in the diet.

Perhaps the most striking finds at Çatal Hüyük are concerned with religious practice. There is a religious shrine for every two houses. At least forty rooms contained shrines with depictions of horned wild bulls, female breasts, goddesses, leopards, and handprints. There are dishes where grains, legumes, and meat were burned as offerings, but there is no evidence of live animal sacrifice. The fact that statues of plump female deities far outnumber statues of male deities persuaded the principal excavator of Çatal Hüyük that a cult of the goddess was central to the town's religion. He further concluded that the large number of females who had received elaborate burials in the shrine rooms were priestesses of this cult. In his view, although male priests were also present, "It seems extremely likely that the cult of the goddess was administered mainly by women."[5]

Whether male or female, religious leaders were a specialized occupation in many Neolithic communities. Spectacular evidence is provided by the growing number of large stone structures constructed after 3000 B.C.E., including the stone circles of western Europe (of which Stonehenge is the most famous), the ziggurats of Mesopotamia and Mesoamerica, the pyramids of Egypt, and the citadels of the Indus Valley. There is no reason to think these widely scattered structures had any connection to each other. Like agriculture, each arose in its own cultural context as an expression of human communal ties, fears, and aspirations.

Metalworking was another important specialized occupation in the late Neolithic period. At Çatal Hüyük objects of copper and lead, metals that occur naturally in a fairly pure form, can be dated to about 6400 B.C.E. Silver and gold were also worked at an early date in many parts of the world. Because of their rarity and their softness these metals did not replace stone tools and weapons but instead were used primarily to make decorative or ceremonial objects. The discovery of many such objects in graves suggests they were symbols of status and power.

The growth of towns, specialized crafts, and elaborate religious shrines added to the workload of agriculturalists, who already had to work hard to till the soil. The towns' permanent houses needed much labor to build, as did Jericho's defensive walls and towers. Extra food had to be produced for the nonfarming full-time priests and craft specialists. Building religious monuments in stone must have occupied much time during the less busy season of the agricultural year. It is estimated, for example, that even a fairly small structure like Stonehenge took 30,000 person-hours to build. No evidence from this period indicates whether these tasks were performed freely or coerced. But after 3500 B.C.E. it is clear that political authorities coerced labor for large building projects (see Chapter 2).

CONCLUSION

The span of time that this chapter covers is immense, far longer than the combined time span of all the rest of the chapters in the book. Compressing so long a period into a single chapter highlights the fundamental and gradually evolving relationships between humans and their natural environment—relationships that underlie human history. In the first stage the struggle to survive in the changing environments of the early Ice Age gave rise to the physical evolution of human beings. Next, distinctive physical and mental abilities enabled humans to adapt culturally to many different natural environments. Since the Neolithic period, people

consciously and deliberately have modified parts of the natural world to suit their needs. These events suggest several themes that have been important throughout human history.

First, the fact that human nature and human cultures have been profoundly shaped by the struggle to survive the rigors of their environments strongly suggests that we humans must respect our place in nature. However much we use our unique abilities to reshape the land and develop new domesticated species by artificial selection, we must be careful not to upset the ecological balance on which our own existence depends.

Second, the use of tools, techniques, and specialized technical knowledge that societies passed down from one generation to the next enabled humans to exploit many natural environments. Technology enabled cultural change to become the alternative to biological change.

A third theme concerns diversity. Although many distinct species of humans once existed, by the late Neolithic period humans were the least varied biologically of any living organism. Yet they were also the earth's most widely dispersed mammals. A single species, *Homo sapiens sapiens*, had developed many diverse cultures and learned how to thrive in all the habitable continents.

The transition from food collection to food production brought the greatest modification of the natural environment and the greatest cultural changes since the first people walked our planet. Indeed, the agricultural revolution was one of the most momentous changes in all of human history. Agriculture brought many toils and hardships, but it enabled people to exercise over the natural environment a degree of control that no other species had ever attained. The transition to farming and settled life opened the way to still greater changes in technology and population size as well as in social and cultural diversity. The patterns of language and belief, of diet, dress, and dwelling, that emerged in the Neolithic period shaped the next several millennia. As Chapters 2 and 3 detail, specialization made possible by settled life gave rise to significant advances in architecture and metallurgy, to artistic achievements, and to the growth of complex religious and political systems.

SUGGESTED READING

Useful reference works for this period are Ian Tattersall, Eric Delson, and John Van Couvering, eds., *Encyclopedia of Human Evolution and Prehistory* (1988), and *The World Atlas of Archaeology* (1985). Reliable surveys for interested students are Brian Fagan's *People of the Earth: An Introduction to World Prehistory*, 8th ed. (1995), and Bernard G. Campbell, *Humankind Emerging*, 6th ed. (1992). Fagan has also written a popular survey, *The Journey from Eden: The Peopling of Our World* (1990).

Accounts of the discoveries of early human remains, written for the nonspecialist by eminent researchers, include Donald Johanson, Leorna Johanson, and Blake Edgar, *In Search of Human Origins* (1994), based on the *Nova* television series of the same name; Richard Leakey and Roger Lewin, *Origins Reconsidered: In Search of What Makes Us Human* (1992); and Donald C. Johanson and Maitland A. Edey, *Lucy: The Beginnings of Mankind* (1981). Other useful books that deal with this subject include George D. Brown, Jr., *Human Evolution* (1995), for a precise biological and geological perspective; Adam Kuper, *The Chosen Primate: Human Nature and Cultural Diversity* (1994), for an anthropological analysis; Glyn Daniel and Colin Renfrew, *The Idea of Prehistory*, 2d ed. (1988), detailing the development of the discipline and relying primarily on European examples; Robert Foley, *Another Unique Species: Patterns in Human Evolutionary Ecology* (1987), a thoughtful and readable attempt to bring together archaeological evidence and biological processes in the development of early humans.

More analytical overviews of the evolutionary evidence are Richard G. Klein, *The Human Career: Human Biological and Cultural Origins* (1989); and Paul Mellars, ed., *The Emergence of Modern Humans* (1991). Provocative and speculative explorations of key issues are Colin Renfrew, *Archaeology and Language: The Puzzle of Indo-European Origins* (1988); Ronald K. Siegel, *Intoxication: Life in Pursuit of Artificial Paradise* (1989); and Marija Gimbutas, *The Civilization of the Goddess: The World of Old Europe* (1991). Margaret Ehrenberg, *Women in Prehistory* (1989), and M. Kay Martin and Barbara Voorhies, *Female of the Species* (1975), provide interesting, though necessarily speculative, discussions of women's history.

Cave and rock art and their implications are the subject of many works. A broad, global introduction is Hans-Georg Bandi, *The Art of the Stone Age: Forty Thousand Years of Rock Art* (1961); Ann Sieveking, *The Cave Artists* (1979), provides a brief overview of the major European finds. Other specialized studies are Robert R. R. Brooks and Vishnu S. Wakankar, *Stone Age Painting in India* (1976); R. Townley Johnson, *Major Rock Paintings of Southern Africa* (1979); J. D. Lewis-Williams, *Believing and Seeing* (1981) and *Discovering Southern African Rock Art* (1990); Mario Ruspoli, *The Cave Art of Lascaux* (1986); and N. K. Sanders, *Prehistoric Art in Europe* (1968).

For the transition to food production see Allen W. Johnson and Timothy Earle, *The Evolution of Human Societies: From Foraging Group to Agrarian State* (1987), and J. D. Clark and Steven A. Brandt, eds., *From Hunters to Farmers: The Causes and Consequences of Food Production in Africa* (1984). James Mellaart, the principal excavator of Çatal Hüyük, has written an account of the town for the general reader: *Çatal Hüyük: A Neolithic Town in Anatolia* (1967). A pioneering work on human ecology, whose early sections are about this period, is Madhav Gadgil and Ramachandra Guha, *This Fissured Land: An Ecological History of India* (1992).

NOTES

1. Quoted in Richard Leakey and Roger Lewin, *Origins Reconsidered: In Search of What Makes Us Human* (New York: Doubleday, 1992), 81.

2. Colin Renfrew, *Archaeology and Language: The Puzzle of Indo-European Origins* (New York: Cambridge University Press, 1988), 125, 150.

3. Luigi Cavalli-Sforza, L. Luca, Paolo Menozzi, and Alberto Piazza, *The History and Geography of Human Genes* (Princeton, NJ: Princeton University Press, 1994).

4. Madhav Gadgil and Ramachandra Guha, *This Fissured Land: An Ecological History of India* (Berkeley: University of California Press, 1992), 79.

5. James Mellaart, *Çatal Hüyük: A Neolithic Town in Anatolia* (New York: McGraw-Hill, 1967), 202.

CHAPTER TWO

The First River-Valley Civilizations, 3500–1500 B.C.E.

Mesopotamia · Egypt · The Indus Valley Civilization

The Challenges and Opportunities of Great River Valleys

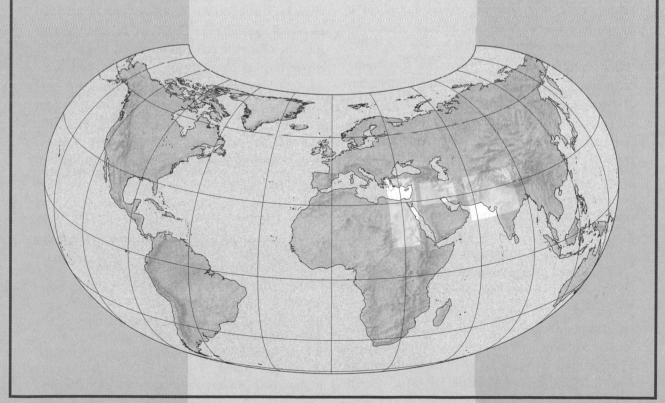

The *Epic of Gilgamesh*, whose roots date to some time before 2000 B.C.E., making it perhaps the oldest surviving work of literature in the world, provides a definition of *civilization* as the people of ancient Mesopotamia (present-day Iraq) understood it. Gilgamesh, an early king, sends a priestess to tame Enkidu, a wild man who lives like an animal in the grasslands. After using her sexual charms to win Enkidu's trust, she says to him:

> "Come with me to the city, to Uruk,
> to the temple of Anu and the goddess Ishtar . . .
> to Uruk, where the processions are and music,
> let us go together through the dancing
> to the palace hall where Gilgamesh presides."[1]

She then clothes Enkidu and teaches him to eat cooked food, drink brewed beer, and bathe and oil his body. By her actions she indicates some of the behavior and choices that ancient Mesopotamians associated with civilized life.

The tendency of the Mesopotamians, like other peoples throughout history, to equate civilization with their own way of life, should serve as a caution for us. What assumptions are hiding behind the frequently made claim that the "first" civilizations, or the first "advanced" or "high" civilizations, arose in western Asia and northeastern Africa sometime before 3000 B.C.E.? Given that *civilization* is a loaded and ambiguous concept, the idea that the "first" civilizations emerged in ancient Mesopotamia and Egypt needs to be explained carefully.

What we can say is that certain political, social, economic, and technological phenomena that scholars agree are indicators of civilization appeared in the Middle East before 3000 B.C.E.: (1) cities that served as administrative centers, (2) a political system based on territory rather than on kinship, (3) specialization of labor and a significant number of people engaged in non-food-producing activities, (4) class divisions and a substantial increase in the accumulation of wealth, (5) monumental building, (6) a system

for keeping permanent records, (7) long-distance trade, and (8) major advances in science and the arts.

We also know that the earliest societies in which those features are apparent developed in the floodplains of great rivers in Asia and Africa: the Tigris and Euphrates in Mesopotamia, the Indus in Pakistan, the Yellow (Huang He) in China, and the Nile in Egypt (see Map 2.1). The periodic flooding of the rivers brought benefits—deposits of fertile silt and irrigation for the fields—but also threatened lives and property. To protect themselves and channel these powerful forces of nature, people living near these rivers created new technologies and forms of political and social organization.

In this chapter, we trace the rise of civilization in Mesopotamia, Egypt, and the Indus River Valley from approximately 3500 to 1500 B.C.E. Our starting point roughly coincides with the origins of writing, so we can observe aspects of human experience that scholars cannot deduce from archaeological evidence alone. Events after 1500 B.C.E. are the subject of Chapter 3, which examines the new patterns that emerged as a result of expanding political and economic networks, new technologies, and the activities of new groups of people. Because the independent emergence of civilization based on river floods and irrigation occurred somewhat later in China than in Mesopotamia, Egypt, and the Indus Valley, early China is also taken up in the next chapter.

MESOPOTAMIA

Because of the unpredictable nature of the Tigris and Euphrates Rivers and the weather, the peoples of ancient Mesopotamia tended to see the world as a hazardous place where human beings were the playthings of fickle and uncompassionate gods who were personifications of natural forces. One of their explanations for the origins and nature of their world is what we know as the Babylonian Creation Myth (Babylon was the most powerful city in southern Mesopotamia in the second and first millennia B.C.E.). The high point of the myth is a cosmic battle between Marduk, the chief god of Babylon, and Tiamat, a female figure who personifies the salt sea. Marduk cuts up Tiamat and from her body fashions the earth and sky. He then creates the divisions of time, the celestial bodies, rivers, and weather phenomena, and from the blood of a defeated rebel god he creates human beings. Creation myths of this sort provided the ancient inhabitants of Mesopotamia with a satisfactory explanation for the environment in which they were living.

Settled Agriculture in an Unstable Landscape

Mesopotamia is a Greek word meaning "land between the rivers." It reflects the centrality of the Euphrates and Tigris Rivers to the way of life in this region. Mesopotamian civilization developed in the plain alongside and between the Tigris and Euphrates, which originate in the mountains of eastern Anatolia (modern Turkey) and empty into the Persian Gulf. This is an alluvial plain, built up over many millennia by silt that the rivers deposited.

Mesopotamia lies mostly within modern Iraq. Certain natural features establish its boundaries: to the north and east, the arc of mountains extending from northern Syria and southeastern Anatolia to the Zagros Mountains, which cut off the plain of the Tigris and Euphrates from the Iranian Plateau; to the west and southwest, the Syrian and Arabian deserts; and to the southeast, the Persian Gulf. This region is subject to unpredictable extremes of weather. Floods can be sudden and violent and tend to come at the wrong time for grain agriculture—in the spring when the crop is ripening in the field. There also is the ever-present danger of the rivers changing course, suddenly cutting off fields and population centers from water resources and avenues of communication.

Periods of Mesopotamian History	
3000–2350 B.C.E.	Early Dynastic (Sumerian)
2350–2200 B.C.E.	Akkadian (Semitic)
2112–2004 B.C.E.	Third Dynasty of Ur (Sumerian)
1900–1600 B.C.E.	Old Babylonian (Semitic)
1500–1150 B.C.E.	Kassite

The first domestication of plants and animals took place not far away, in the "Fertile Crescent" region of northern Syria and southeastern Anatolia, around 8000 B.C.E. Agriculture did not come to Mesopotamia until approximately 5000 B.C.E. Agriculture that depends on rain requires annual rainfall of at least 8 inches (20 centimeters). In hot, dry southern Mesopotamia, agriculture depended on irrigation. At first, people probably took advantage of the occasional flooding of the rivers over their banks and into the nearby fields, but shortly after 3000 B.C.E. they learned to construct canals to supply water as needed and to carry water to more distant parcels of land.

Barley was the main cereal crop in southern Mesopotamia. It was better able to withstand the effects of the salt drawn to the surface of the soil when the fields were flooded than the wheat grown in northern Mesopotamia. By 4000 B.C.E. farmers were using plows pulled by cattle to turn over the earth. A funnel attached to the plow dropped a carefully measured amount of seed. Fields were left fallow (unplanted) every other year, to replenish the nutrients in the soil. Date palms provided food, fibers, and some wood. Small garden plots produced vegetables. Reed plants, which grew on the river banks and in the marshy southern delta, could be woven into mats, baskets, huts, and boats. Fish from the rivers and marshes were an important part of people's diet. Herds of sheep and goats, which grazed on the fallow land and beyond the zone of cultivation, provided wool and milk. Cattle and donkeys carried or pulled burdens, joined in the third and second millennia B.C.E. by newly introduced camels and horses.

The earliest people living in Mesopotamia in the "historical period"—that is, the period for

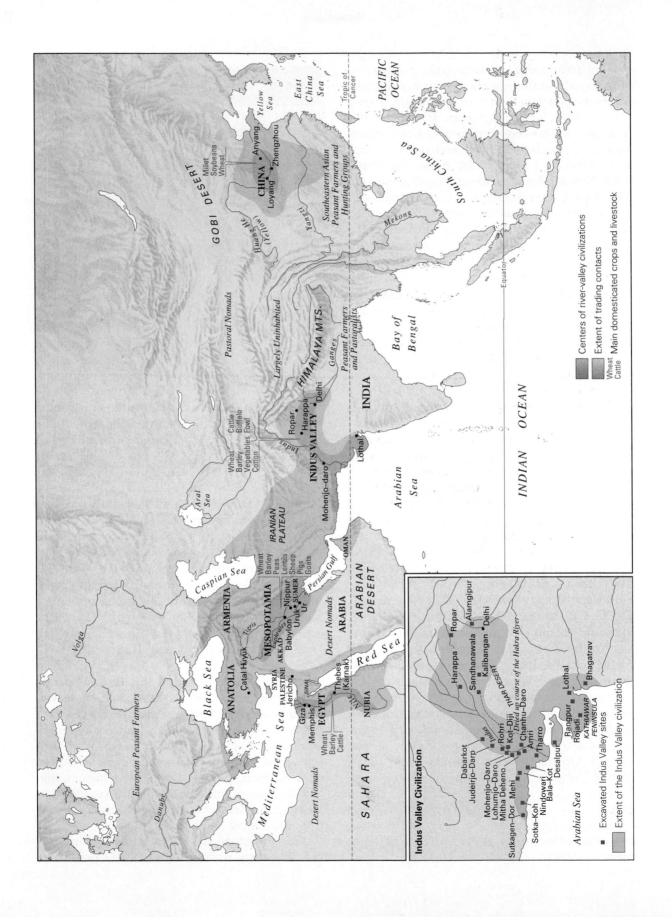

Centers of river-valley civilizations

Extent of trading contacts

Main domesticated crops and livestock

Wheat
Cattle

PACIFIC OCEAN

Tropic of Cancer

Yellow Sea

East China Sea

GOBI DESERT

Anyang
Zhengzhou
CHINA
Loyang

Millet
Soybeans
Wheat

Huang He (Yellow)

Yangzi

South China Sea

Mekong

Southeastern Asian Peasant Farmers and Hunting Groups

Pastoral Nomads

Largely Uninhabited

HIMALAYA MTS.

Ganges

Peasant Farmers and Pastoralists

Delhi

INDIA

Ropar
Harappa

INDUS VALLEY

Indus

Lothal

Mohenjo-daro

Bay of Bengal

Cattle
Buffalo
Fowl

Wheat
Barley
Vegetables
Cotton

Aral Sea

IRANIAN PLATEAU

Caspian Sea

Wheat
Barley
Peas
Lentils
Sheep
Pigs
Goats

ARMENIA

Tigris

MESOPOTAMIA

Euphrates

AKKAD

Nippur
SUMER
Uruk
Ur

Babylon

Persian Gulf

OMAN

Volga

Black Sea

ANATOLIA

Catal Huyuk

SYRIA

PALESTINE
Jericho

SINAI

Thebes (Karnak)

EGYPT

Giza
Memphis

Nile

NUBIA

Red Sea

Desert Nomads

ARABIA

ARABIAN DESERT

Desert Nomads

Wheat
Barley
Cattle

SAHARA

Mediterranean Sea

Desert Nomads

European Peasant Farmers

Danube

Equator

INDIAN OCEAN

Arabian Sea

Indus Valley Civilization

Ropar
Alamgipur
Sandhanawala
Kalibangan
Delhi
Harappa

Dried up course of the Hakra River

THAR DESERT

Dabarkot
Judeirjo-Darp
Mohenjo-Daro
Lohumjo-Daro
Mitha Deheno
Sutkagen-Dor Mehi
Sotka-Koh
Nindowari
Bala-Kot
Desalpur

Rohri
Kot-Diji
Chanhu-Daro
Amri
Tharro

Rangpur
Rojadi
Bhagatrav

Lothal

KATHIAWAR PENINSULA

Indus

Arabian Sea

■ Excavated Indus Valley sites

Extent of the Indus Valley civilization

which we have some written evidence—are the Sumerians. There is mounting archaeological evidence that they were in southern Mesopotamia at least by 5000 B.C.E. and perhaps even before then. The Sumerians created the main framework of civilization in Mesopotamia—a framework adopted and adapted by other ethnic groups that later rose to dominance in the region. The third millennium B.C.E. was primarily a Sumerian epoch. However, even in this period the Sumerians were not the only ethnic and linguistic group inhabiting the Tigris-Euphrates Valley. From as early as 2900 B.C.E. the names of individuals recorded in inscriptions from northerly cities in the southern plain suggest the presence of Semites—people who spoke a Semitic language. (The term *Semitic* refers to a family of related languages that have long been spoken across parts of western Asia and north Africa. In antiquity these languages included Hebrew, Aramaic, and Phoenician; the most widespread modern member of the Semitic family is Arabic.)

Historians believe that these Semites descended from nomadic peoples who had migrated into the Mesopotamian plain from the western desert. There is little indication of ethnic conflict between Sumerians and Semites. The Semites assimilated to Sumerian culture and sometimes gained positions of wealth and power.

By 2000 B.C.E. the Semitic peoples had become politically dominant, and from this time forward Akkadian, a Semitic language, was the primary language in Mesopotamia. Much of the Sumerian cultural legacy, however, was preserved. Sumerian-Akkadian dictionaries were compiled, Sumerian literature was translated, and from these stories we know that the Semitic gods borrowed characteristics and adventures of the Sumerian gods. This cultural synthesis parallels a biological merging of Sumerian and Semitic stocks through intermarriage. Other ethnic groups, including mountain peoples such as the

Map 2.1 River Valley Civilizations, 3500–1500 B.C.E. The earliest complex societies arose in the flood plains of large rivers: in the fourth millennium B.C.E. in the valley of the Tigris and Euphrates Rivers in Mesopotamia and the Nile River in Egypt, in the third millennium in the valley of the Indus River in Pakistan, and in the second millennium in the valley of the Yellow River in China.

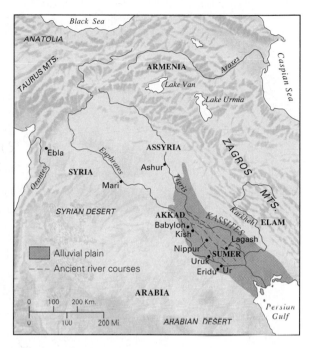

Map 2.2 Mesopotamia The Sumerians of southern Mesopotamia developed new technologies, complex political and social institutions, and distinctive cultural practices, responding to the need to organize labor resources to create and maintain an irrigation network in the Tigris-Euphrates Valley, a land of little rain.

Kassites as well as Elamites and Persians from Iran, played a part in Mesopotamian history. But not until the arrival of Greeks in the Middle East in the late fourth century B.C.E. would the Sumerian/Semitic cultural heritage of Mesopotamia be fundamentally altered.

Cities, Kings, and Trade

Mesopotamia was a land of villages and cities. Villages—groups of families that live close to one another—are common in agricultural societies. By banding together, families can protect each other, share farming implements and facilities such as barns and threshing floors, and help each other at key times in the agricultural cycle. Villages also serve human social needs, providing a pool of potential marriage partners and a variety of people to talk to.

Cities also depend on agriculture; indeed, the earliest known urban centers in the Middle East,

Lagash, Ur-Nanshe Stone wall plaque depicting the twenty-fifth century B.C.E. Sumerian ruler of Lagash, Ur-Nanshe. In the upper register the king carries on his head a basket with mud bricks, symbolizing his role as a builder. The figures to his right may be his wife and sons. In the lower register he is seated on a throne and approached by subjects or members of court. Note how the king's superior status is indicated by his greater size. (Louvre © R.M.N.)

such as Jericho and Çatal Hüyük, sprang up shortly after the first appearance of agriculture (see Chapter 1). In nonurban societies almost everyone engages in the basic tasks of subsistence, gathering or growing enough food to feed themselves and their families. Cities, however, depend on the ability of farmers to produce surplus food to feed people who are not engaged in food production but instead specialize in other kinds of activities, such as metallurgy (creating useful objects from metal), crafts, administration, and serving the gods. Even so, many people living in early Mesopotamian cities went out each day to labor in nearby fields.

Most cities evolved from villages. As a successful village grew, smaller satellite villages developed nearby, and eventually the main village and its satellites coalesced into an urban center.

Cities and villages continued to be linked in a relationship of mutual dependence. A city controlled the agricultural land and villages in its vicinity, requiring the surplus foodstuffs of the countryside to feed its population of specialists. At the same time the city provided the rural districts with military protection against bandits and raiders and a market where villagers could trade surplus products, often for manufactured goods produced by specialists in the city.

We use the term *city-state* to refer to independent ancient urban centers and the agricultural hinterlands they controlled. Early Mesopotamia was a land of many small city-states. Stretches of open and uncultivated land, whether desert or swamp, lay between the territories controlled by the various communities and served as buffers. However, disputes over land, water rights, and movable property often sparked hostilities between neighboring cities and prompted most to build protective walls of sun-dried mud bricks. But cities also cooperated in various ways, sharing water and allowing safe passage of trade goods through their territories.

The production of food surpluses in the Tigris-Euphrates Valley required new land to be opened up to agriculture by the construction and maintenance of an extensive irrigation network. Canals brought water to fields distant from the rivers. Drainage ditches carried water away from flooded fields before a damaging layer of salt and minerals was drawn to the surface of the soil. Dikes protected young plants emerging in fields near the riverbanks from being destroyed in flood season. Gravity moved the water through the network. Dams raised the water level of the river so that water could flow into the irrigation channels. A machine with counterweights was invented to lift water—for example, up from the river and over the dike to the land beyond. Because the rivers carried so much silt, channels got clogged and needed constant dredging.

The successful operation of such a sophisticated irrigation infrastructure depended on the emergence of individuals or groups wielding sufficient political power to compel and organize large numbers of people to work together. Other projects also relied on the cooperation of many people: the harvest, sheep shearing, the construction of fortification walls, the construction of monuments, and waging war. Little is known about the political institutions of early Mesopotamian city-states, although there are traces of some sort of citizens' assembly that may have evolved from the traditional village council. The two centers of power for which there are written records are the temple and the king.

Each Mesopotamian city contained one or more temples housing the cult of the deity or deities who watched over the community. The temples owned extensive tracts of agricultural land and stored the gifts that worshipers donated. The importance of the cults is confirmed by the central location of the temple buildings. The leading members of the priesthood, who controlled the shrine and managed the deity's considerable wealth, appear to have been the dominant political and economic force in early Mesopotamian communities.

In the third millennium B.C.E. another kind of leadership developed in the Sumerian cities. A figure who is referred to in Sumerian documents as *lugal*, or "big man"—what we would call a "king"—emerged. How this position evolved is not clear, but it may have been related to an increase in the frequency and scale of warfare as ever-larger communities quarreled over limited quantities of land, water, and raw materials. According to one plausible theory, certain men chosen by the community to lead the armies in time of war found ways to extend their authority into peacetime and to assume key judicial and ritual functions. The position of lugal was not automatically hereditary, but capable sons had a good chance of succeeding their fathers.

The later development of this secular authority is often reflected in the position of the palace, the seat of the king's power. The palace tends not to be as centrally located as the temple, having emerged after the heart of the city had been established. There must have been considerable jockeying for wealth and power between priests and kings, and the process of political evolution must have varied from community to community. The overall trend, however, favored the king, presumably because he had the army behind him. Though still influential because of their wealth and religious mystique, the priests and temples became dependent on the palace. By the late third millennium B.C.E. royal officials were supervising the temples. Some Mesopotamian kings claimed to be gods on earth, but this concept did not take root, and the normal pattern was for the king to portray himself as the earthly representative of the god.

Appointed and favored by the divinity, the king assumed responsibility for the upkeep and building of temples and the proper performance of ritual. Other key responsibilities of the king included maintenance of the city walls and defenses, upkeep and extension of the network of irrigation channels, preservation of property rights, and protection of the people from outside attackers and from perversions of justice at home. Some kings even took steps to correct economic inequalities, by setting prices and canceling debts.

We catch glimpses of the unchecked power, restless ambition and value to the community of this new breed of rulers in the epic of Gilgamesh. While the story, as we now have it, has gone through various changes over the centuries and relates many supernatural events in an otherworldly landscape, it is based on a historical figure who was king of Uruk. Gilgamesh is depicted as the strongest man in his community. His subjects resent his prerogative to demand sexual favors from new brides, but they depend upon his wisdom and courage to protect them. In his quest for everlasting glory, Gilgamesh built magnificent walls around the city and stamped his name on all the bricks. And his journey to the faraway Cedar Mountains reflects the king's role in bringing valuable resources to the community.

Over time certain political centers became powerful enough to extend their control over other city-states. Sargon, ruler of the city of Akkad around 2350 B.C.E., was the first to unite many cities under the control of one king and capital. His title, "King of Sumer and Akkad," became symbolic of this claim to universal dominion ("Sumer" and "Akkad" denoted, respectively, the southern and central portions of the Tigris-Euphrates Valley). Sargon and the four members of his family who succeeded him over a period of one hundred twenty years secured their power in a number of ways. They razed the walls of conquered cities, installing governors backed by garrisons of Akkadian troops. Soldiers received land to ensure their loyalty. Because Sargon and his people were of Semitic stock, the cuneiform system of writing used for Sumerian (discussed later in the chapter) was adapted to express their language. A uniform system of weights and measures and standardized formats for official documents facilitated tasks of administration such as the assessment and collection of taxes, recruitment of soldiers, and organization of large labor projects.

For reasons that are not completely clear to modern scholars, the Akkadian state fell around 2230 B.C.E. The so-called Sumerian King List, which claimed to catalog the rulers of Mesopotamia since the time of creation, wryly referred to the period after the fall of Akkad (a period in which the various cities regained their independence) by asking, "Who was King? Who was not King?" A last resurgence of Sumerian language and culture in the cities of the southern plain was seen under the Ur III Dynasty, (2112–2004 B.C.E.). Based on a combination of campaigns of conquest and alliances cemented by marriage, the dynasty encompassed five kings who ruled for a century. The Ur III state did not control territories as extensive as those of its Akkadian predecessor, but a rapidly expanding bureaucracy of government administrators led to tight government control of a wide range of activities and an obsessive degree of record keeping. A corps of messengers and well-maintained road stations facilitated rapid communication, and an official calendar, standardized weights and measures, and uniform scribal practices enhanced the effectiveness of the central administration. As the southern plain came under increasing pressure from Semitic Amorites in the northwest, the kings erected a great wall 125 miles (201 kilometers) in length to keep out the nomadic invaders. In the end, though, the Ur III state succumbed to the combined pressure of nomadic incursions and an attack of Elamites coming from the southeast.

The Amorites founded a new city at Babylon, not far from Akkad. During the reign of the aggressive Hammurabi (r. 1792–1750 B.C.E.), Babylon became the capital of what historians have named the "Old Babylonian" state, which extended its control not only over Sumer and Akkad but also far to the north and northwest from 1800 to 1600 B.C.E. Hammurabi is best known for his Law Code, inscribed on a polished black stone tablet. Though not a comprehensive list of all the laws of the time, Hammurabi's Code provided judges with a lengthy set of examples illustrating the principles they were to employ when deciding cases. Some of its formulations call for physical punishments to be inflicted on the body of an offender to compensate for a crime. Such laws are precursors of the Israelites' principle of "an eye for an eye, a tooth for a tooth" (see Chapter 4). When we compare them to the monetary penalties in the earlier Ur III codes, we see that the Amorites introduced their own principles of justice.

The far-reaching conquests of some Mesopotamian states were motivated, at least in part, by the need to obtain access to vital resources. The alternative was to trade for raw materials, and long-distance commerce did flourish in most periods. Evidence of boats used in sea trade goes back as far as the fifth millennium B.C.E. Wood, metals, and stone had to be imported from afar. In exchange, wool, cloth, barley, and oil were exported. Wood was acquired from cedar forests covering the slopes of mountain ranges in Lebanon and Syria. Silver came from Anatolia, gold from Egypt, copper from the eastern Mediterranean and Oman (on the Arabian peninsula), tin from Afghanistan (in south-central Asia). Chlorite, a greenish stone from which bowls were carved, came from the Iranian Plateau; black diorite, from the Persian Gulf; lapis lazuli, from eastern Iran and Afghanistan; and carnelian, from Pakistan (in south-central Asia) for jewelry and carved figurines.

In the third millennium B.C.E. merchants were in the employ of the palace or temple. Those were the only two institutions that had the financial resources and long-distance connections to organize the collection, transport, and protection of goods. Merchants exchanged the surplus from the agricultural estates of kings or priests for vital raw materials and luxury goods. In the second millennium B.C.E. commerce came more and more into the hands of independent merchants, and merchant guilds became powerful forces in the community and even assumed some official functions in periods of political crisis or decline.

Modern scholars do not know where in the Mesopotamian city the most important commercial activities took place. There does not appear to have been an open public area dedicated to this function. Two possible locations are the area just inside the city gates and in the vicinity of the docks. Wherever it occurred, all this commercial activity was accomplished without the benefit of money. Coins—that is, pieces of metal whose value the state guarantees—were not invented until the sixth century B.C.E. (see Chapter 5, Envi-

ronment and Technology: The Origins and Early Development of Coinage) and did not reach Mesopotamia until several centuries later. For most of Mesopotamian history, items could be bartered for one another or valued in relation to fixed weights of precious metal, primarily silver.

Mesopotamian Society

One of the persistent features of urbanized civilizations is the development of social divisions—that is, significant variation in the status and privileges of different groups of people due to differences in wealth, in social functions, and in legal and political rights. The rise of cities, specialization of function, centralization of power, and the use of written records enabled certain groups of people to accumulate wealth on an unprecedented scale. As we have seen, the temple leadership and the kings controlled large agricultural estates, and the palace administration also collected various kinds of taxes from its subjects. It is less apparent how certain other people, who made up what we might call an elite class, acquired large holdings of land, for the sale of land was rare. Debtors who could not pay back what they owed forfeited their land, and soldiers and religious officials received plots of land in return for their services.

Social divisions in Mesopotamian society must have varied considerably over time and place, but the situation that historians can infer from the Law Code of Hammurabi for Babylon in the eighteenth century B.C.E. may reveal fundamental distinctions valid for other places and times. There were three classes: (1) *awilum*, the free, landowning class, which included royalty, high-ranking officials, warriors, priests, merchants, and some artisans and shopkeepers; (2) *mushkenum*, the class of dependent farmers and artisans, who were legally attached to land that belonged to king, temple, or elite families and thus provided the bulk of the work force for the rural estates and temple complexes; and (3) *wardum*, the class of slaves, primarily employed in domestic service. In the Old Babylonian period, the awilum—the class of people who were not dependent on the great institutions of temple or palace—grew in numbers and importance, and the amount of land and other property in private hands increased. Penalties for crimes prescribed in the Law Code differed, depending on the class of the offender.

Slavery existed but was not as prevalent and fundamental to the economy as it would be in the later societies of Greece and Rome (see Chapters 5 and 6). Many of the slaves came from mountain tribes and either had been captured in war or sold by slave traders. There was a separate category of slavery for those who were unable to pay off a debt. Under normal circumstances slaves were not chained or otherwise constrained, but they had to wear a distinctive hairdo. If they were given their freedom, a barber shaved off the telltale mark. In the surviving documents it is often hard to distinguish slaves or dependent workers from free laborers, because both were paid in commodities such as food and oil and the quantities varied according to a person's age, gender, and task. There seems to be a trend toward the use of free labor in the second millennium B.C.E., when a larger percentage of the population was no longer dependent on the institutions of temple or palace.

It is difficult to reconstruct the life experiences of ordinary Mesopotamians, especially those who lived in villages or on large estates in the countryside, since they leave little trace in the archeological or literary record. Rural peasants built their houses out of materials such as mud-brick and reed, which quickly disintegrate, and they possessed little in the way of metals. Being illiterate, they were not able to write about their lives.

It is particularly difficult to discover very much about the experiences of women in ancient Mesopotamia. The written sources are the product of male scribes (trained professionals who applied their skills in reading and writing to tasks of administration) and, for the most part, reflect elite male activities. Archaeological remains provide only limited insight into attitudes, status, and gender roles.

Anthropologists theorize that women lost social standing and freedom as part of the transition from hunter-gatherer to agricultural

societies (see Chapter 1). Women previously had provided the bulk of the community's food from their gathering activities. But agricultural labor in a place like Mesopotamia depended on the hard physical work of dragging around a plow and digging irrigation channels and tended to be done by men. At the same time, the generation of a food surplus permitted families to have more children, and bearing and raising children became the primary occupation of many women. The amount of time given to the care of children made it hard for women to acquire the specialized skills of the scribe or artisan, though in rare instances women did fill these roles. Non-elite women who stayed at home must have been engaged in other tasks—helping with the harvest, planting vegetable gardens, milking cattle, cooking and baking, cleaning the house, fetching water, tending the household fire, and weaving baskets and textiles. Some women worked outside the household, in textile factories and breweries or as prostitutes, tavern keepers, bakers, or fortunetellers. Women had no apparent political role, but they had important economic rights and were able to own property, maintain control of their dowry, and even engage in trade.

There is evidence for a decline in the standing of women in the Semitic second millennium B.C.E. This development may be linked to the rise of an urbanized middle class and an increase in private wealth. Women could be used by their families to preserve and increase wealth through tactics such as (1) arranged marriages, which created alliances between families, and (2) the avoidance of marriage—and the resulting loss of a dowry—by dedicating certain girls to the service of a deity as "god's brides." The husband became more dominant in the household and had greater latitude in the laws relating to marriage and divorce. Although Mesopotamian society was generally monogamous, a man could obtain a second wife if the first gave him no children, and in the later stages of Mesopotamian history kings and others who could afford to do so had several wives. Some scholars believe that from the second millennium B.C.E. may originate the constraints on women that eventually became part of the Islamic tradition, such as the expectation that they confine themselves to

The impression made by a Mesopotamian cylinder seal Seals indicated the identity of an individual and were impressed into wet clay or wax to "sign" legal documents or to mark ownership of an object. Here the owner of the seal stands before the goddess Ishtar, recognizable by her characteristic star symbol and lion. Ishtar (Sumerian Inanna), whose domains encompassed both love and violence, is dressed as a warrior. (Courtesy, Trustees of the British Museum)

the household and go veiled in public (see Chapter 10).

Gods, Priests, and Temples

The ancient Mesopotamians believed in a multitude of gods who embodied the forces of nature. For the Sumerians the god Anu was the sky, Enlil the air, Enki the water, Utu the sun, Nanna the moon. The emotional impulses of sexual attraction and violence were the domain of the goddess Inanna. People believed these gods were *anthropomorphic*—that is, like humans in form and conduct. They thought their gods had bodies and senses, sought nourishment from sacrifice, enjoyed the worship and obedience of humanity, and were driven by lust, love, hate, anger, and all the other emotions that motivated human beings. Generally speaking, the Mesopotamians feared their gods, who they believed were responsible for the changes that occurred without warning in the unpredictable landscape in which they lived, and they sought to appease their deities by any means.

When the Semitic peoples became dominant, they equated their deities with those of the Sumerians. For example, the Sumerian gods Nanna and Utu became the Semitic Sin and Shamash, and the goddess Inanna became Ishtar. The myths of the Sumerian deities were transferred to their Semitic counterparts, and many of the same rituals continued to be practiced.

Particularly visible in the archaeological record is the public, state-organized religion. Each city contained temples to one or more patron divinities who protected the community and were given special devotion. Nippur, with its temple of the air-god Enlil, was especially venerated as a religious center for all the peoples of Sumer. The temple was regarded as the residence of the god, and the cult statue, which was located in a special interior shrine, was believed to be occupied by the life-force of the deity. Priests literally waited on this physical image of the divinity, anticipating and meeting its every need in a daily cycle of waking, bathing, dressing, feeding, moving around, entertaining, soothing, and revering. These efforts reflected the emphatic claim of the Babylonian Creation Myth that humankind had been created to be the servants of the gods. Several thousand priests may have staffed a large temple, such as the temple at Babylon of the chief god Marduk.

The office of priest was hereditary; fathers passed along sacred lore to their sons. Priests were paid in food taken from the crops raised on the deity's estates. The amount an individual received depended on his rank. Within the priesthood there was a complicated hierarchy of status and specialized function. The high priest performed the central acts in the great rituals. Certain priests made music to please the gods. Others knew the appropriate incantations for exorcising evil spirits. Still others were seers who interpreted dreams and divined the future by methods such as examining the organs of sacrificed animals, reading patterns in the rising incense smoke, or casting dice.

The temple precinct was surrounded by a high wall. The enclosed area contained the shrine of the chief deity, as well as open-air plazas, chapels for other gods, housing, dining facilities and offices for the priests and other members of the temple staff, and craft shops, storerooms, and service buildings to meet the needs of a large and busy organization. The most visible part of the temple precinct was the *ziqqurat*, a multistoried tower approached by ramps and stairs and built of mud brick. Modern scholars are not entirely certain of the ziqqurat's function and symbolic meaning.

Even harder to determine are the everyday beliefs and religious practices of the common people. Modern scholars do not know how accessible the temple buildings were to the general public. Individuals did place votive statues in the sanctuaries. They believed that these miniature replicas of themselves could continually beseech and seek the favor of the deity. The survival of many amulets (small charms meant to protect the bearer from evil) and representations of a host of demons suggest a widespread belief in the value of magic—the use of special words and rituals that allow people to manipulate and

control the forces of nature. A headache was believed to be caused by a demon that could be driven out of the ailing body. Lamashtu, who was held responsible for miscarriages, could be frightened off if a pregnant woman wore an amulet with the likeness of the hideous but beneficent demon Pazuzu. In return for an appropriate gift or sacrifice, a god or goddess might be prevailed on to reveal information about the future.

The religion of the elite and the religion of ordinary people came together in great festivals such as the twelve-day New Year's Festival held each spring in Babylon to mark the beginning of a new agricultural cycle. The Babylonians believed that the world went through a cycle from birth to death each year, but they did not assume that the cycle would automatically recur every year. The New Year's Festival was a virtual restaging of the act of creation, an effort by all members of society to ensure the victory of life over death and the restarting of time.

Technology and Science

The ancient Mesopotamians, like all complex societies, developed a set of technologies which allowed them to exert some degree of control over their environment. The term "technology" comes from the Greek word *techne,* meaning "skill" or "specialized knowledge." Technology in the broadest sense can encompass both tools and machinery to manipulate the physical world and ideas that can influence the intellectual, emotional, and spiritual spheres in which human beings also operate, as, for instance, the religious knowledge of the priests.

A particularly important example of the latter type of technology is writing, which first appeared in Mesopotamia before 3300 B.C.E. The earliest inscribed tablets were found in the chief temple at Uruk and date from a time when the temple was the most important economic institution in the community. According to a plausible recent theory, writing originated from a system of tokens used to keep track of property—sheep, cattle, wagon wheels, and the like—as increases in the amount of accumulated wealth and the volume and complexity of commercial transactions strained the capacity of people's memory to preserve an accurate record. These tokens were made in the shape of the commodity and were inserted and sealed in a clay envelope. Pictures of the tokens were incised on the outside of the envelope as a reminder of what was inside. Eventually people realized that the incised pictures were an adequate record of the transaction, rendering the tokens inside redundant. These pictures became the first written symbols.

The earliest symbols were thus pictures of the objects they represented, but they could also stand for the sound of that word if it was part of a longer word. For example, the symbols *shu* for "hand" and *mu* for "water" could be combined to form *shumu* for "name." The commonest method of writing was with a sharpened reed on a moist clay tablet. Because the reed made wedge-shaped impressions, the early pictures were increasingly stylized into a combination of strokes and wedges that evolved into the *cuneiform* (Latin for "wedge-shaped") system of writing. Mastering this system of writing required years of training and practice. Several hundred signs were in use at any one time, as compared to the twenty-five or so signs required for an alphabetic system. In the "tablet-house," which may have been attached to a temple or palace, students were taught writing and mathematics by a headmaster and were tutored by older students called "big brothers." Members of the scribal class had prestige and regular employment because of their skill and thus may have been reluctant to simplify the cuneiform system. In the Old Babylonian period, the growth of the private commercial sector was accompanied by an increase in the number of people who could read and write. Nevertheless, only a small percentage of the population was literate. Kings and commanders normally did not know how to read and write and paid scribes to exercise this skill on their behalf.

Cuneiform is not a language but a system of writing. Developed originally for the Sumerian language, it was later adapted to express the Akkadian language of the Mesopotamian Semites as well as other languages of western Asia such as Hittite, Eblaite (see Voices and Visions:

Baked clay model of a sheep's liver (about 1700 B.C.E.)   A diviner who examined the physical appearance of the liver of a sacrificed animal could deduce valuable information about the future or will of the gods. The cuneiform inscriptions on this model, which was probably used to teach divination, explain the significance of markings in different areas of the organ. (Courtesy, Trustees of the British Museum)

Ebla), Elamite, and Persian. The earliest documents are economic, but cuneiform is an outstanding example of a technology that had wide-ranging uses beyond the use for which it was originally conceived. In the early period, legal acts had been validated by the recitation of oral formulas and the performance of symbolic actions. After the development of cuneiform, written documents that were marked with the seal of the participants became the primary indicator of validation. In similar fashion the system of writing also came to be used for political, literary, religious, and scientific purposes.

Other technologies enabled the Mesopotamians to meet the challenges of their environment. As we have seen, irrigation was indispensable to agriculture and called for the construction and maintenance of canals, dams, and dikes. Appropriate means of transportation were developed for different terrains. Carts and sledges drawn

Ebla

One of the most exciting archaeological discoveries of the past half century was at Tell Mardih, near Aleppo in northern Syria, where, since the 1960's, Italian archaeologists have been unearthing the ancient city of Ebla (see Map 2.2). Excavation has focused both on the elevated citadel, where several palaces and temples have been found, and on the lower town. Besides the remains of buildings and artifacts, excavators stumbled upon the palace archives, several rooms filled with tablets. Approximately two thousand tablets were intact and many thousands more in fragmentary condition, the result of a fiery destruction of the palace. The tablets were inscribed with cuneiform symbols in two languages, Sumerian and the local Semitic dialect now called Eblaite. The tablets are mostly records of the palace economy, keeping track of the harvesting and distribution of food stocks, flocks of sheep, shearing of wool, manufacture of cloth, and collection of gold and silver tribute. There are also official letters and treaties between Ebla and other states, literary texts, and Sumerian-Eblaite dictionaries.

The pinnacle of its wealth and power occurred in the period from 2400 to 2250, when it controlled an extensive territory in northwest Syria and derived wealth from agriculture, sheepraising, and manufacturing cloth. Ebla played an important role in the trade routes between Mesopotamia and the Mediterranean, involving the exchange of timber, copper, and silver, available in the nearby mountains of Lebanon, Syria, and southwest Anatolia, and even blocks of lapis lazuli from distant Afghanistan.

This interstate commerce is illuminated by the following excerpts from a treaty between Ebla and the northern Mesopotamian city-state of Ashur:

Thus says Ebla's king to Ashur: Without my consent there will be no movement of emissaries in the country; you, Ja-dud, [will not authorize any movement of emissaries]; (only) I issue orders regarding commercial traffic. In case emissaries who have undertaken a journey of 20 days have exhausted all their supplies, you must, graciously, procure provisions for their stay at the trading post at market-price.

. . . In cases where emissaries go on a journey, their goods must not be touched; silver, oxen, sheep, son, daughter, wife, must not be taken, and you must not appropriate them.

The city-state of Kablul and (its) trade centers belong to Ebla's ruler; the city-state of Za-ar in Uziladu and (its) trade centers belong to Ebla's ruler; the city-state of Guttanum [and its trade centers] belong to Ebla's ruler. The subjects of Ebla's ruler in all the (aforesaid) trade centers are under the jurisdiction of Ebla's ruler, (whereas) the subjects of Ashur's ruler are under the jurisdiction of Ashur's ruler.

If an Eblaite fights with an Assyrian and the latter dies, then 50 rams will be given as penalty; [if an Assyrian fights with an Eblaite] and the latter dies, then 50 rams will be given as penalty.

(If) Ebla has received either a male or female citizen as a slave, and Ashur [requests] the house of Ebla for [their liberation], then Ebla will free the slaves, (but Ashur) must give 50 rams as compensation (to Ebla).

In case he (Ashur's ruler) does wrong, then the sun god, the storm god, and Venus, who are witnesses, will scatter his "word" on the steppe. Let there be no water for (his) emissaries who undertake a journey. You will have no permanent residence, but (on the contrary) you, Ja-dud, will begin a journey to perdition.

The discoveries at Ebla demonstrate the cultural vitality of third millennium Syria and the complexity of the relationships between various peoples in western Asia, as well as providing a wealth of detail about life in an early Middle Eastern city-state. What is the relationship between the kings of Ebla and Ashur? What common interests do they share? What kinds of problems and disputes are anticipated in this treaty, and how are they to be resolved? How are the terms of the treaty to be enforced?

Source: Giovanni Pettinato, *Ebla: A New Look at History* (1991), pp. 230–237.

by cattle were common in some locations. Boats and barges were more effective in the south, where numerous water channels cut up the landscape. In northern Mesopotamia, donkeys were the chief pack animals for overland caravans in the centuries before the advent of the camel (see Chapter 8).

Although the Mesopotamians had to import raw metal ore, they became quite skilled in metallurgy, mixing copper with arsenic or tin to make bronze. The stone implements of earlier eras continued to be produced in this period, for the poorest members of the population usually could not afford metal. Bronze, however, has the advantage of being more malleable than stone. Liquid bronze can be poured into molds, and hardened bronze takes a sharper edge than stone, is less likely to break, and is more easily repaired.

Resource-poor Mesopotamians possessed one commodity in abundance: clay. Mud bricks, whether dried in the sun or baked in an oven for greater durability, were their primary building material. Construction on a monumental scale—whether city walls, temples, or palaces—required considerable practical knowledge of architecture and engineering. For example, the reed mats that Mesopotamian builders laid between the mud-brick layers of ziggurats served the same stabilizing purpose as girders in modern high-rise construction. The abundance of good clay also meant that pottery was the most common form of dishware and storage vessel. The potter's wheel was in use by 4000 B.C.E.

In the military sphere as well there were innovative developments—in organization, tactics, and weapons and other machinery of warfare. Early military forces were rallied when needed by calls for the able-bodied members of the community. The powerful states of the later third and second millennia B.C.E. built up professional armies. In the early second millennium B.C.E. horses appeared in western Asia, and the horse-drawn chariot came into vogue, carrying close to enemy lines a driver and an archer who could unleash a volley of arrows. Using increasingly effective siege machinery, Mesopotamian soldiers could climb over, undermine, or knock down the walls protecting the cities of their enemies.

In many other ways the Mesopotamians sought to gain control of their physical environment. They used a base-60 number system (the origin of the seconds and minutes we use today) in which numbers were expressed as fractions or multiples of 60, in contrast to our base-10 system. Advances in mathematics and careful observation of celestial phenomena made the Mesopotamians sophisticated practitioners of astronomy. Mesopotamian priests compiled lists of omens or unusual sightings on earth and in the heavens together with a record of the events that coincided with them. They consulted these texts at critical times, for they believed that if, at some future time, a similar omen appeared, the event that originally occurred with the omen would occur again. The underlying premise here was that material phenomena, from the macrocosmic to the microscopic, were interconnected in mysterious but undeniable ways.

EGYPT

Nowhere is it more apparent how profoundly natural environment shapes the history and culture of a society than in ancient Egypt. Located at the intersection of Asia and Africa, Egypt is protected by surrounding barriers of desert and a harborless seacoast. Mesopotamia was open to migration or invasion and was dependent on imported resources. In contrast, natural isolation and essential self-sufficiency allowed Egypt to develop a unique culture that for long periods of time had relatively little to do with other civilizations.

The Land of Egypt: "Gift of the Nile"

The fundamental geographical feature of Egypt, ancient and modern, is the Nile River. The world's longest river, the Nile originates from Lake Victoria and from several large tributaries in the highlands of tropical Africa and flows northward, carving a narrow valley between the

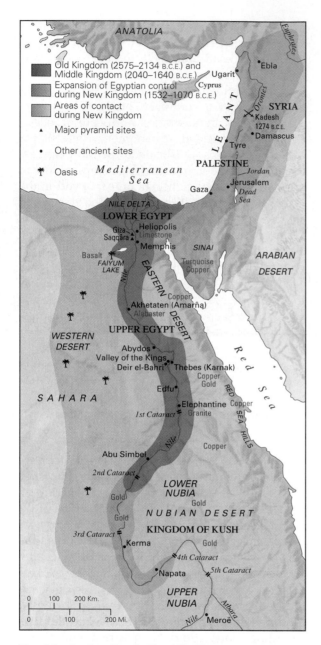

Map 2.3 Ancient Egypt The Nile River, flowing south to north, carved out of the surrounding desert a narrow green valley which became heavily settled in antiquity.

the Mediterranean the river breaks up into a number of channels to form a triangular delta. Virtually the entire population of the region lives in that twisting, green ribbon alongside the river or in the Nile Delta. The rest of the country, 90 percent or more, is a bleak and inhospitable desert of mountains, rocks, and dunes. The ancient Egyptians recognized this stark dichotomy between the low-lying, life-sustaining "Black Land" with its dark soil alongside the river and the elevated, deadly "Red Land" of the desert. With justification and insight did the fifth-century B.C.E. Greek traveler Herodotus call Egypt the "gift of the Nile."

The river was the main means of travel and communication. In antiquity, boats sailed southward, upriver, propelled by the perpetual following wind, and were rowed northward, downriver. The orientation of the country was along the axis of the river. The most important cities were located considerably upstream. Because the river flows from south to north, the Egyptians called the southern part of the country "Upper Egypt," the northern part "Lower Egypt." The southern boundary of Egypt in most periods was the First Cataract—the northernmost of a series of impassable rocks and rapids below Aswan (about 500 miles [800 kilometers] south of the Mediterranean)—though at times Egyptian control extended farther south into what they called "Kush" (later Nubia, the southern part of the modern state of Egypt and northern Sudan). The Egyptians also settled a number of large oases—green and habitable "islands" in the midst of the desert—which lay some distance west of the river.

The hot climate with plenty of sunshine was favorable for agriculture, but south of the delta there is virtually no rainfall. Thus agriculture was entirely dependent on river water. Throughout Egyptian history great efforts were made to increase the amount of land suitable for planting by digging irrigation channels to carry water out into the desert. And in the basin of Lake Faiyum, a large depression west of the Nile, successful drainage techniques rendered the lake smaller and allowed more land to be reclaimed for agriculture.

Each September, with considerable regularity, the river overflowed its banks, spreading water

chain of hills on either side, until it reaches the Mediterranean Sea (see Map 2.3). The land through which it flows is mostly desert, but the river makes green a narrow strip on either side of its banks. About 100 miles (160 kilometers) from

Limestone relief of an Egyptian cargo boat, from a tomb at Saqqara, ca. 2300 B.C.E. The large sail, used when going upstream, is rolled up at the moment as the vessel floats downstream with the current (northwards). The steersman uses the rudder at the rear (right), while men with long poles watch out for shallows. This vessel is carrying a large block of stone from one of the quarries upriver for use in a monumental construction project. (Egyptian Museum, Cairo)

out into the depressed basins. Unlike the Mesopotamians, the Egyptians did not need to construct dams and mechanical devices to lift river water to channels and fields. And unlike the Tigris and Euphrates, whose flood came at a disadvantageous time, the Nile flooded at just the right time for grain agriculture. When the waters receded, they left behind a fertile layer of mineral-rich silt, and farmers could easily plant their crops in the moist soil. The Egyptians had many versions of the Creation Myth, but it always involved the emergence of life from a primeval swamp.

The height of the river when it crested was crucial to the prosperity of the country. "Nilometers"—stone staircases with incised units of measure—were placed along the river's edge to gauge the flood surge. When the flood was too high, dikes were washed out and much damage resulted. When the flood was too low for a series of years, the country was plunged into famine and decline. Indeed, the ebb and flow of successful and failed regimes seems to be linked to the cycle of floods. Nevertheless, in most eras there was a remarkable stability to this landscape, and Egyptians viewed the universe as an orderly and beneficent place.

Egypt was well endowed with natural resources. Egyptians used reeds that grew in marshy areas and along the banks of the river to make sails, ropes, and a kind of paper. Hunters pursued the wild animals and birds that abounded in the marshes and on the edge of the desert, and fishermen lowered their nets into the river. Building stone could be quarried and floated downstream from a number of locations in southern Egypt. Clay for mud bricks and pottery could be found almost everywhere. Copper and turquoise deposits in the Sinai desert to the east and gold from Nubia to the south were within reach and the state organized armed expeditions and mustered forced labor to exploit these resources. Thus Egypt was self-sufficient to a much larger degree than Mesopotamia.

Farming villages appeared in Egypt as early as 5500 B.C.E. as inhabitants of the Nile Valley borrowed and adapted knowledge of how to do-mesticate various species of plants and animals that had emerged several millennia earlier in western Asia. However, the circumstances that led to Egypt becoming a focal point of civiliza-tion were due, at least in part, to a change in cli-mate that took place gradually from the fifth to the third millennium B.C.E. Until that time, the Sahara, the vast region that is now the world's largest desert, had a relatively mild and wet cli-mate and lakes and grasslands that supported a variety of plant and animal species as well as populations of hunter-gatherers (see Chapter 8). As the climate changed and the Sahara began to dry up and become a desert, some displaced groups migrated into the Nile Valley.

Divine Kingship

The increase in population produced new, more complex levels of political organization, includ-ing a form of local kingship. The pivotal event, in the view of later generations of Egyptians, was the conquest of these smaller units and the unifi-cation of all Egypt by Menes, a ruler from the south, around 3100 B.C.E. Although some schol-ars question whether Menes was a historical or mythical figure, many authorities equate him with Narmer, a historical ruler who is represent-ed on a decorated slate palette that shows a king exulting over defeated enemies. Later kings of Egypt were referred to as "Rulers of the Two Lands"—Upper and Lower Egypt—and were depicted with two crowns and implements sym-bolizing the unification of the country. In con-trast to Mesopotamia, Egypt was unified early in its history.

The system that historians use to organize Egyptian history is based on thirty dynasties (sequences of kings from the same family) identi-fied by Manetho, an Egyptian from the third cen-tury B.C.E. The rise and fall of dynasties often reflects the dominance of different parts of the country. At a broader level of generalization, scholars refer to the "Old," "Middle," and "New Kingdoms," each a period of centralized political power and brilliant cultural achievement, punc-tuated by "Intermediate Periods" of political fragmentation and cultural decline. Although experts disagree about specific dates for these periods, the chronology (see page 49) is represen-tative of current opinion.

The central institution in the Egyptian state was the *pharaoh*, or king. From the period of the Old Kingdom if not earlier, the principle was es-tablished that the king was the son of the sun-god, Re. Egyptians believed that their king was sent to earth by the gods and that his function on earth was to maintain *ma'at*, the divinely autho-rized order of the universe. He was the indis-pensable link between his people and the gods, and through his benevolent rule he ensured the welfare and prosperity of the country. The Egyp-tians' conception of a divine king who was the source of law and authority may explain the apparent lack of efforts to publish in Egypt an impersonal code of law comparable to Ham-murabi's Code in Mesopotamia.

In a very real sense, all of Egypt belonged to the king, and everyone served him. When the monarchy was strong, it controlled the country and virtually every facet of people's lives. An ex-tensive administrative apparatus began at the village level and progressed to the districts into which the country was divided and, finally, to the central government based in the capital city.

Various cities served as the royal capital at dif-ferent times, for the capital was usually the origi-nal power base of the dynasty that occupied the throne. Memphis, on the Lower Nile near the apex of the Delta (close to Cairo, the modern cap-ital), held this central position during the Old Kingdom. Thebes, far to the south, came to prominence during much of the Middle and New Kingdom periods.

The royal bureaucracy used writing to keep track of land, labor, products, and people. It en-abled the ruler to extract as taxes a substantial portion of the annual revenues of the country—at times as much as 50 percent. The income was used to subsidize the palace, bureaucracy, and army, to build and maintain temples, and to raise great monuments of the ruler's reign. Because the villages lined up along the river, it was easy for the government to monitor their activities and extract their surplus resources.

The royal administration maintained a monopoly over key sectors of the economy and controlled long-distance trade. Private enterprise was almost nonexistent. Everyone worked in some capacity for the state, though independent exchanges of goods surely took place on a small scale at the local level. This was quite different from Mesopotamia, where commerce increasingly fell into the hands of an acquisitive urban middle class.

This system of kingship and administration crystallized relatively quickly after the unification of the country. Early rulers may have been influenced by the emergent civilization of Mesopotamia, for in the late fourth millennium B.C.E. trading linked Egypt and western Asia. Nevertheless, they adapted what they borrowed and gave such institutions a uniquely Egyptian form. After this early rush of innovation, Egyptian civilization remained relatively static and resistant to change for nearly three millennia, in large part because of the natural isolation of the country.

The death of the king was a critical moment in the life of the country, because so much depended on him. Every effort was made to ensure the well-being of his soul on its perilous journey to rejoin the company of the gods. Massive resources were poured into the construction of royal tombs, the celebration of elaborate funerary rites, and the sustenance of kings' souls in the afterlife by perpetual offerings in funerary chapels attached to the royal tombs. Early rulers were buried in flat-topped, rectangular tombs made of mud brick. But around 2630 B.C.E., Djoser, a Third Dynasty king, ordered the construction for himself at Saqqara, about 20 miles south of the Delta, of a spectacular stepped pyramid consisting of a series of stone platforms laid one on top of the other. Rulers in the Fourth Dynasty filled in the steps to create the smooth-sided, limestone pyramids that have become the most memorable symbol of ancient Egypt. Between 2550 and 2490 B.C.E., the pharaohs Khufu and Khefren erected huge pyramids at Giza, several miles to the north of Saqqara, the largest stone structures ever built by human hands. Khufu's pyramid originally reached a height of 481 feet (147 meters).

Periods of Egyptian History

3100–2575 B.C.E.	Early Dynastic
2575–2134 B.C.E.	Old Kingdom
2134–2040 B.C.E.	First Intermediate Period
2040–1640 B.C.E.	Middle Kingdom
1640–1532 B.C.E.	Second Intermediate Period
1532–1070 B.C.E.	New Kingdom

Egyptians accomplished all this construction with bronze tools and no machinery other than simple levers, pulleys, and rollers. What really made it possible was almost unlimited human muscle power. Calculations of the human resources needed to build a pyramid within the lifetime of the ruler suggest that large numbers of people must have been pressed into service for part of each year, probably during the flood season, when no agricultural work could be done. Although this labor was compulsory, the Egyptian masses probably regarded it as a kind of religious service that helped to ensure the continuity of their beneficent environment. Virtually all the surplus resources of the country went into the construction of these artificial mountains of stone. In the end, the outlay was more than the country could sustain for long. The age of the great pyramids lasted only about a century, although pyramids continued to be built on a smaller scale for two millennia afterward.

Administration and Communication

The need for extensive records of the resources of the country led to the creation of a complex administrative bureaucracy. Officials received grants of land from the king and were supported by dependent peasants who worked the land.

The hallmark of this administrative class was literacy. A system of writing had been developed by the beginning of the Old Kingdom, perhaps under the influence of Mesopotamia but with distinctively Egyptian qualities. *Hieroglyphics,* the earliest form of this writing system, were picture symbols standing for words, syllables, or individual sounds. Our ability to read ancient Egyptian writing is due to the decipherment, in the early nineteenth century C.E., of the Rosetta Stone, a document from the second century B.C.E. that gave both hieroglyphic and Greek versions of the same text.

Hieroglyphic writing long continued in use on monuments and ornamental inscriptions. By 2500 B.C.E., however, a cursive script, in which the original pictorial nature of the symbol was less readily apparent, had been developed for the everyday needs of administrators and copyists working with ink on a writing material called *papyrus*, after the reed from which it was made. The stems of the papyrus reed were laid out in a vertical and horizontal grid pattern and then pounded with a soft mallet until the moist fibers merged to form a sheet of writing material. The plant grew only in Egypt but was in demand throughout the ancient world and was exported in large quantities. Indeed, the word *paper* is derived from Greek and Roman words for papyrus.

Writing came to be used for many purposes other than administrative recordkeeping. A large written literature developed—tales of adventure and magic, love poetry, religious hymns, and manuals of instruction on technical subjects. Workshops attached to the temples produced copies of traditional texts.

When the monarchy was strong, officials were appointed and promoted on the basis of merit and accomplishment. Lower-level officials were assigned to work in villages and district capitals; high-ranking officials served in the royal capital. When Old Kingdom officials died, they were buried in tombs laid out around the monumental tomb of the king so that they could serve him in death as they had done in life.

One sign of the breakdown of centralized power in the late Old Kingdom and First Intermediate Period was the presence of officials' tombs in their home districts, where they spent much of their time and exercised power more or less independently. Another sign was the tendency of administrative posts to become hereditary. Throughout Egyptian history there is an underlying tension between the centralizing power of the monarchy and the decentralizing forces created by the Egyptian bureaucracy. The early monarchs of the Middle Kingdom responded to the fragmentation of the preceding period by reducing the power and prerogatives of the old elite and creating a new middle class of administrators.

It has often been said that Egypt was a land of villages and did not have any real cities, because the political capitals were really extensions of the palace and central administration. In Mesopotamia, in contrast, cities were not only the basic political units but also centers of economic activity in which many people produced wealth through specialized, nonagricultural tasks. It is true that, in comparison with Mesopotamia, a far larger percentage of the Egyptian population lived in rural villages and engaged in agriculture, and that the essential wealth of Egypt resided to a higher degree in the land and its products. But there were towns and cities in ancient Egypt, although they were less crucial than Mesopotamian urban centers to the economic and cultural dynamism of the country. Unfortunately, archaeologists for the most part have been unable to excavate them, because many ancient urban sites in Egypt have been continuously inhabited and lie beneath modern communities.

During the Old and Middle Kingdoms, Egypt was isolationist in its foreign policy. The king maintained limited contact with the other advanced civilizations of the region but did not actively seek to expand beyond Egypt's natural boundaries. When necessary, local militia units backed up a small standing army of professional soldiers. The nomadic tribes living in the eastern and western deserts and the Libyans in the northwest were a nuisance rather than a real danger to the Nile Valley and were readily handled by the Egyptian military. Egypt's interests abroad focused primarily on maintaining access to valuable resources rather than on acquiring territory. Trade with the coastal towns of the Levant (modern Israel, Lebanon, and Syria) brought in cedar wood. In return, Egypt exported grain, papyrus, and gold.

In all periods the Egyptians had a particularly strong interest in goods that came from the

The pyramid of Khephren at Giza, ca. 2500 B.C.E.   With a width of 704 feet (214.5 meters) and a height of 471 feet (143.5 meters), it is only eight feet shorter than the nearby Great Pyramid of Khufu. The construction of these massive edifices depended on relatively simple techniques of stonecutting, transport (the stones were floated downriver on boats and rolled out to the site on sledges), and lifting (the stones were dragged up the face of the pyramid on mud brick ramps). However, the surveying and engineering skills required to level the platform, lay out the measurements, and securely position the blocks were very sophisticated and have withstood the test of time. (Werner Forman/Art Resource, NY)

south. Nubia contained rich sources of gold (in Chapter 3 we examine the rise of a civilization in Nubia that, though heavily influenced by Egypt, created a vital and original culture that lasted for more than two thousand years). The southern course of the Nile offered the only easily passable corridor to sub-Saharan Africa.

In the Old Kingdom, Egyptian noblemen living at Aswan on the southern border led donkey caravans south to trade for gold, incense, and products of tropical Africa such as ivory, ebony, and exotic animals. A line of forts along the southern border protected Egypt from attack. In the second millennium B.C.E., Egyptian forces struck south into Nubia, extending the Egyptian border as far as the Third Cataract and taking possession of the gold fields. Still farther to the south, perhaps in the northern coastal region of present-day Somalia, lay the fabled land of Punt, source of the fragrant myrrh resin that priests burned on the altars of the Egyptian gods. Normally this commodity passed through the hands of a series of intermediaries before reaching Egypt, but in the fifteenth century B.C.E. a naval expedition sailed down the Red Sea to initiate direct contacts between Punt and Egypt (see Chapter 3).

The People of Egypt

The population of ancient Egypt—perhaps between 1 million and 1½ million people—was physically heterogeneous, ranging from dark-skinned people related to the populations of sub-Saharan Africa to lighter-skinned people akin to the Berber and Arab populations of North Africa and western Asia. Although Egypt was not subject to the large-scale migrations and invasions that Mesopotamia experienced, throughout the historical period various groups of settlers trickled into the Nile Valley and assimilated with the people already living there.

Social stratification clearly existed in Egypt: some people possessed more status, wealth, and power than others. But it does not appear that a rigid class structure emerged. At the top of the social hierarchy were the king and high-level officials. In the middle were lower-level officials, local leaders, priests and other professionals, artisans, and well-to-do farmers. At the bottom were peasants, the vast majority of the population. Peasants lived in rural villages. Their lives were filled with the seasonally changing tasks of agriculture—plowing, sowing, tending emerging shoots, reaping, threshing, and storing grain or other products of the soil. Plowing was relatively easy in the soft, silt-laden soil left behind after the departure of the floodwaters. The irrigation network of channels, basins, and dikes had to be maintained, improved, and extended. Domesticated animals—cattle, sheep, goats, and fowl—and fish supplemented their diet. Inhabitants of the same village must have shared implements, work animals, and storage facilities, as well as helped one another at peak times in the agricultural cycle and in the construction of houses and other buildings. They also prayed and feasted together at festivals to the local gods and other public celebrations. Villagers periodically were required to contribute labor to state projects, such as construction of the pyramids. If the burden of taxation or compulsory service proved too great, few avenues of resistance were available to villagers other than running away into the inhospitable desert.

This account of the lives of ordinary Egyptians is largely conjectural because the numerous villages of ancient Egypt, like those of Mesopotamia, left few traces in the archaeological or literary record. Tomb paintings of the elite sometimes depict the lives of common folk. The artists employed pictorial conventions to indicate status, such as obesity for the possessors of wealth and comfort, baldness and deformity for members of the working classes. Poetry frequently uses metaphors of farming and hunting, and legal documents on papyruses preserved in the hot, dry sands tell of property transactions and the disputes of ordinary people.

Slavery existed on a limited scale but was of little significance for the economy. Prisoners of war, condemned criminals, and debtors could be found on the country estates or in the households of the king and the upper classes. Treatment of slaves was relatively humane, and they could be given their freedom.

Obstacles also deprive us of any vivid sense of the experiences of women in ancient Egypt. Some information is available about the lives of women of the upper classes, but it is filtered through the brushes and pens of male artists and scribes. Egyptian women had rights over their dowry in case of divorce, they could own property, and they could will their property to whomever they wished. Historical evidence suggests that at certain times queens and queen-mothers played a significant behind-the-scenes role in the politics of the royal court. Tomb paintings show women of the royal family and elite classes accompanying their husbands and engaging in typical activities of domestic life. They are depicted with dignity and affection, though clearly in a subordinate position to the men. The artistic convention of depicting men with a dark red and women with a yellow flesh tone implies that the elite woman's proper sphere was assumed to be indoors, away from the searing sun.

In the beautiful love poetry of the New Kingdom the lovers address each other in terms of apparent equality and express emotions akin to our own ideal of romantic love. We cannot be sure how accurately this poetry represents the prevalent attitude in other periods of Egyptian history or among groups other than the educated elite. The limited evidence, however, does suggest that women in ancient Egypt were treated more respectfully and had more social freedom than women in other ancient societies such as Mesopotamia.

Belief and Knowledge

The religion of the Egyptians was rooted in the physical landscape of the Nile Valley and in the vision of cosmic order that this environment evoked. The consistency of their environment—the sun rose every day into a clear and cloudless sky, and the river flooded on schedule every year, ensuring a bounteous harvest—persuaded the Egyptians that the natural world was a place of recurrent cycles and periodic renewal. The sun-god, Re, was said to journey in a boat through the Underworld at night, fighting off the attacks of demonic serpents so that he could be born anew each morning. The story of Osiris, a god who once ruled the land of Egypt, was especially popular. Osiris was slain by his adversary Seth, who then scattered the dismembered pieces. Isis, Osiris's devoted wife, found the remnants and Horus, his son, took revenge on Seth. Osiris was restored to life and installed as king of the Underworld, and his example gave people hope of a new life in a world beyond this one.

In normal times the king—himself the son of Re, the sun-god—was the chief priest of Egypt, intervening with the gods on behalf of his land and people. When a particular town attained special significance as the capital of a ruling dynasty, the chief god of that town became prominent across the land. Thus did Ptah of Memphis, Re of Heliopolis, and Amon of Thebes become gods of all Egypt, serving to unify the country and strengthen the monarchy.

Egyptian rulers took a special interest in building new temples, refurbishing old ones, and making lavish gifts to the gods, as well as overseeing the construction of their own monumental tombs. Thus a considerable portion of the wealth of Egypt was used for religious purposes as part of a ceaseless effort to win the gods' favor, maintain the continuity of divine kingship, and ensure the renewal of the life-giving forces that sustained the world.

The many gods of ancient Egypt were diverse in origin and nature. Some deities were normally depicted with animal heads; others were always given human form. Few myths about the origins and adventures of the gods have survived, but there must have been a rich oral tradition. Many towns had temples in which locally prominent deities were thought to reside. Cult activities were carried out in the privacy of the inner reaches of the temples, where priests daily served the needs of the deity by attending to his or her statue. As in Mesopotamia, some temples came to possess extensive landholdings worked by dependent peasants, and the priests who administered the deity's wealth played an influential role locally and sometimes even throughout the land.

During great festivals, a boat-shaped litter carrying the shrouded statue and cult items of the deity was paraded around the town. Such occasions allowed large numbers of people to have contact with the deity and to participate in a mass outpouring of devotion and celebration. Little is known about the day-to-day beliefs and practices of the common people, however. In the household family members revered and made small offerings to Bes, the grotesque god of marriage and domestic happiness, to local deities, and to the family's ancestors. Amulets and depictions of demonic figures reflect the prevalence of magical practices. In later times Greeks and Romans regarded Egypt as a place where the devotion to magic was especially strong.

Egyptians believed fervently in the reality of the afterlife and made extensive preparations for a safe and successful passage to the next world and a comfortable existence once they arrived there. One common belief was that death was a journey beset with hazards along the way. The Egyptian Book of the Dead, which has been found in many excavated tombs, provided guidance for those making the journey. It contained rituals and prayers to protect the soul of the deceased at each point of the trip. The final and most important challenge was the weighing of the deceased's heart in the presence of the judges of the Underworld to determine whether the traveler had led a good life and deserved to reach the ultimate blessed destination.

Along with Egyptians' obsession with the afterlife went great concern about the physical condition of the cadaver. The Egyptians perfected techniques of mummification to preserve the dead body. The idea probably derived from the early practice of burying the dead in the hot, dry sand on the edge of the desert, where bodies decomposed slowly. The elite classes utilized the most expensive kind of mummification. The brain and certain vital organs were removed, preserved, and stored in stone jars laid out around the corpse. Body cavities were filled with

A scene from the Egyptian Book of the Dead, ca. 1300 B.C.E. The mummy of the deceased, a royal scribe named Hunefar, is approached by members of his household before being placed in the tomb. Behind Hunefar is Anubis, the jackal-headed god, who will conduct the spirit of the deceased to the afterlife. The Book of the Dead provided Egyptians with the necessary instructions to complete this arduous journey and gain a blessed existence in the afterlife. (Courtesy, Trustees of the British Museum)

various packing materials. The cadaver was immersed for long periods in dehydrating and preserving chemicals and eventually was wrapped in linen cloth. The mummy was then placed in one or more decorated wooden caskets and was entombed.

Tombs usually were placed at the edge of the desert so as not to tie up valuable farmland. They were filled with pictures and samples of food and the objects of everyday life, so that the deceased would have whatever he or she might need in the next life. From this practice of stocking the tomb with utilitarian and luxury household objects we have gleaned much of what we know about ancient Egyptian life. Small figurines called *shawabtis* were included to play the part of servants and to take the place of the deceased in case the regimen of the afterlife included periodic calls for compulsory labor. The elite classes, at least, had chapels attached to their tombs and left endowments to subsidize the daily attendance of a priest and offerings of foodstuffs to sustain their souls for all eternity.

The form of the tomb also reflected the wealth and status of the deceased. Common people had to make do with simple pit graves or small mudbrick chambers. The privileged classes built larger tombs and covered the walls with pictures and inscriptions. Kings erected pyramids and other grand edifices, employing subterfuges to hide the sealed chamber containing the body and treasures, as well as curses and other magical precautions, to foil tomb robbers. Rarely did they succeed, however. Nearly all the tombs that archaeologists have discovered had been plundered.

The ancient Egyptians made remarkable advances in many areas of knowledge and developed an array of advantageous technologies. They learned much about chemistry through their experiments to find ever better methods for preserving the dead body. The process of mummification also provided ample opportunities to learn about human anatomy, and as a result Egyptian doctors were in high demand in the courts of western Asia because of their relatively advanced medical knowledge and techniques.

The centrality of the Nile flood to their way of life spurred the Egyptians to find ways to better control and profit from this critical event. They devoted much effort to constructing, maintaining, and expanding the network of irrigation channels and holding basins. They needed mathematics to survey and measure the dimensions of fields and calculate the quantity of agricultural produce owed to the state. Sophisticated astronomical knowledge resulted from their efforts to calculate the time when the Nile would rise.

The construction of pyramids, temple complexes, and other monumental building projects called for great skill in engineering and architecture. Vast quantities of earth had to be moved. Large stones had to be quarried, dragged on rollers, floated downstream on barges, lifted into place, then carved to the exact size needed and made smooth. Long underground passageways were excavated to connect the mortuary temple by the river with the tomb near the desert's edge, and on several occasions Egyptian kings dredged out a canal more than 50 miles (80 kilometers) long in order to join the Nile Valley to the Red Sea and expedite the transport of goods.

Archaeologists recently discovered an 8-mile-long road (13 kilometers), made of slabs of sandstone and limestone and connecting a rock quarry with Faiyum Lake. Dating to the second half of the third millennium B.C.E., it is the oldest known paved road in the world. Relatively simple technologies facilitated the transportation of goods and people: carts pulled by draft animals, river barges for floating huge stones from the quarries, and lightweight ships equipped with sails and oars—well suited for travel on the peaceful Nile and sometimes used for voyages on the Mediterranean and Red Seas.

THE INDUS VALLEY CIVILIZATION

C ivilization arose almost as early in India as it did in Mesopotamia and Egypt. Just as each of the Middle Eastern civilizations was centered on a great river valley, civilization in India originated on a fertile floodplain. In the valley of the Indus River, settled farming created the agricultural surplus essential to urbanized society.

Natural Environment

In the central portion of the Indus river valley, in the Sind region of modern Pakistan, a plain of more than 1 million acres (400,000 hectares) lies between the mountains to the west and the Thar Desert to the east (see Map 2.1). Because the Indus River carries a great load of silt, over the ages the riverbed and its containing banks have risen above the level of the plain. Twice a year the river overflows its banks and spreads for as much as 10 miles (16 kilometers). In the spring, in March and April, melting snow feeds the river's sources in the Pamir and Himalaya mountain ranges. Then in August, the great monsoon (seasonal wind) blowing off the ocean to the southwest brings rains that swell the streams flowing into the Indus. As a result, farmers in this region of little rainfall are able to plant and harvest two crops a year. In ancient times, the Hakra River, which has since dried up, ran parallel to the Indus about 25 miles (40 kilometers) to the east and provided a second area suitable for intensive cultivation.

Several adjacent regions were also part of this fertile zone. To the northeast is the Punjab, where five rivers converge to form the main course of the Indus. Lying beneath the shelter of the towering Himalaya range, the Punjab receives considerably more rainfall than the central plain but is less prone to flooding. From this region settlements spread as far as Delhi in northwest India. Another zone of settlement extended south into the great delta where the Indus empties into the Arabian Sea, and southeast into India's hook-shaped Kathiawar Peninsula, an area of alluvial plains and coastal marshes. The territory covered by the Indus Valley civilization is roughly equivalent in size to modern France—much larger than the zone of Mesopotamian civilization.

Material Culture

The Indus Valley civilization flourished from approximately 2900 to 1800 B.C.E. Although archaeologists have located several hundred sites, the culture is best known from the archaeological remains of two great cities first discovered nearly eighty years ago. The ancient names of these cities are unknown, so they are referred to by modern names: Harappa and Mohenjo-Daro. Unfortunately, a rise in the water table at these sites has made excavation of the lowest and earliest levels of settlement virtually impossible.

The identity, origins, and fate of the people who created and maintained this advanced civilization for more than a thousand years are in dispute. Until recently, scholars assumed that they were dark-skinned speakers of the Dravidian languages whose descendants were later pushed out of the north into central and southern India by invading Indo-European nomads around 1500 B.C.E. Studies of skeletal evidence, however, indicate that the population of these lands remained stable from ancient times to the present. Scholars now think that settled agriculture in this part of the world dates back to at least 5000 B.C.E. The precise relationship between the Indus Valley civilization and several earlier cultural complexes in the Indus Valley and in the hilly lands to the west is unclear. Also unclear are the forces giving rise to the urbanization, population increase, and technological advances that occurred in the early third millennium B.C.E. Nevertheless, the case for continuity seems stronger than the case for a sudden migration due to the movement of new peoples into the valley.

Like the Mesopotamians and Egyptians, the people of the Indus Valley had a system of writing. They used more than four hundred signs to represent syllables and words. Archaeologists have recovered thousands of inscribed seal stones and copper tablets. Unfortunately, these documents have not yet provided us with a picture of the society, because no one has been able to decipher them.

This society produced major urban centers. Harappa, the smaller of the major urban centers excavated so far, was 3½ miles (506 kilometers) in circumference and may have housed a population of 35,000. Mohenjo-Daro was several times larger. There are marked similarities in the planning and construction of these cities. High, thick brick walls surrounded each. The streets were laid out on a grid pattern. Covered drainpipes

carried away waste. The regular size of the streets and length of the city blocks, as well as the uniformity of the mud bricks used in construction, may be evidence of a strong central authority. The seat of this authority may have been located in the citadel—an elevated, enclosed compound containing large buildings. Nearby stood well-ventilated structures that scholars think were storehouses of grain for feeding the urban population and for export. The presence of barracks may point to some regimentation of the skilled artisans.

A common assumption has been that these urban centers dominated the rural hinterland around them, though there is no proof that they did. Various factors may account for the location of the chief centers, and different centers may have had different functions. Mohenjo-Daro seems to dominate the great floodplain of the Indus. Harappa, which is nearly 500 miles (805 kilometers) from Mohenjo-Daro, seems to be on a kind of frontier between farmland and herding land, for no other settlements have been found west of its location. Harappa may have served as a "gateway" to the natural resources of the northwest, such as copper, tin, and precious stones. Seaports to the south would also have had a commercial function, expediting seaborne trade with the Persian Gulf.

Mohenjo-Daro and Harappa have received the most attention from archaeologists, and published accounts of the Indus Valley civilization have tended to treat those urban centers as the norm. Most people, however, lived in smaller settlements. Two intriguing features of the Indus Valley civilization are the considerable standardization of styles and shapes for many kinds of artifacts and the fact that the full range of materials, as well as the types and styles of artifacts, is found not only in the large cities but also in the smaller settlements. Some scholars suggest that this standardization may be due not to a strong and authoritarian central government but rather to extensive exchange and trading of goods within the zone of this civilization.

There is a greater abundance of metal in the Indus Valley than in Mesopotamia or Egypt, and most of the metal objects that archaeologists have found in the Indus Valley are utilitarian—

tools and other useful objects. In contrast, metal objects unearthed in Mesopotamia and Egypt tend to be decorative—jewelry and the like. Moreover, these metal objects were available to a large cross-section of the Indus Valley population, but in the Middle East metals were primarily reserved for the elite classes.

The civilization of the Indus Valley possessed impressive technological capabilities. These people were adept in the technology of irrigation. They used the potter's wheel, and they laid the foundations of large public buildings with mud bricks baked in a kiln, because sun-dried bricks exposed to floodwaters would quickly dissolve. Smiths worked skillfully with various metals—gold, silver, copper, and tin. The varying ratios of tin to copper in their bronze objects suggest that they were acutely aware of the hardness of different mixtures and conserved the relatively rare tin by using the smallest amount necessary, since, for example, knives need not be as hard as axes.

Archaeological evidence proves the people of the Indus Valley had widespread trading contacts. Thanks to passes through the mountains in the northwest, they had ready access to the valuable resources found in eastern Iran and Afghanistan, as well as to ore deposits in western India. These resources included metals (such as copper and tin), precious stones (lapis lazuli, jade, and turquoise), building stone, and timber. Rivers served as major thoroughfares for the movement of goods within the zone of Indus Valley culture. It has been suggested that the undeciphered writing on the many seal stones that have been found may convey the names of merchants who stamped their wares.

The inhabitants of Mesopotamia and of the Indus Valley obtained raw materials from some of the same sources, and Indus Valley seal stones have been found in the Tigris-Euphrates Valley. Thus some scholars believe that Indus Valley merchants served as middlemen in the long-distance trade, obtaining raw materials from the lands of west-central Asia and shipping them to the Persian Gulf.

We know little about the political, social, economic, and religious structures of Indus Valley society. Attempts have been made to demon-

Bronze statuette from the Indus Valley Found in a house in Mohenjo-Daro, it represents a young woman whose only apparel is a necklace and an armful of bracelets. Appearing relaxed and confident, she has been identified by some scholars as a dancer. (National Museum, New Delhi)

strate the presence at this early date of many cultural features that are characteristic of later periods of Indian history (see Chapter 7), including sociopolitical institutions (a system of hereditary occupational groups, the predominant political role of priests), architectural forms (bathing tanks like those later found in Hindu temples, private interior courtyards in houses), and religious beliefs and practices (depictions of gods and sacred animals on the seal stones, a cult of the mother-goddess). Much of this work is highly speculative, however, and further knowledge about this society can only come from additional archaeological finds and decipherment of the Indus Valley script.

Transformation of the Indus Valley Civilization

The Indus Valley cities were abandoned sometime after 1800 B.C.E. Archaeologists once thought that invaders destroyed them, but now they believe that this civilization suffered "systems failure"—the breakdown of the fragile interrelationship of the political, social, and economic systems that sustain order and prosperity. The precipitating cause may have been one or more natural disasters, such as an earthquake or massive flooding. Gradual ecological changes may also have played a role.

The Hakra river system dried up, and salinization (an increase in the amount of salt in the soil, inhibiting plant growth) and erosion may have taken their toll (see Environment and Technology: Environmental Stress in the Indus Valley). Towns no longer on the river, ports no longer by the sea, and regions suffering a loss of fertile soil and water would have necessitated the relocation of large portions of the population and a change in the livelihood of those who remained. The causes, patterns, and pace of change probably varied in different areas; urbanization is likely to have persisted longer in some regions than in others. But in the end, the urban centers could not be sustained, and village-based farming and herding took their place. As the interaction between regions lessened, the standardization of technology and style of the previous era was replaced by distinct regional variations.

Historians can do little more than speculate about the causes behind the changes and the experiences of the people who lived in the Indus

Valley around 1800 B.C.E. But it is important to keep two tendencies in mind. In most cases like this, the majority of the population adjusts to the new circumstances. But members of the political and social elite, who depended on the urban centers and complex political and economic structures, lose the source of their authority and are merged with the population as a whole.

THE CHALLENGES AND OPPORTUNITIES OF GREAT RIVER VALLEYS

It is surely no accident that the first civilizations to develop high levels of political centralization, urbanization, and technology were situated in river valleys where rainfall was insufficient for dependable agriculture. Although the theories of earlier generations of scholars overstated the necessity of those three conditions for the emergence of powerful political centers, the combination of need and opportunity does seem to have spurred political and technological development in Mesopotamia, Egypt, and the Indus Valley as well as in other river valleys.

Dependent as they were on river water to irrigate the cultivated land that fed their populations, Mesopotamia, Egypt, and the Indus Valley civilization channeled significant human resources into the construction and maintenance of canals, dams, and dikes. This work required expertise in engineering, mathematics, and metallurgy, as well as the formation of political centers that could organize the necessary labor force. Failure to contain the forces of nature and to maintain a viable ecological balance led to immediate disaster or to gradual degradation of the environment, whether in the form of deadly floods, rivers changing course, meager harvests and attendant famines, or excess salinization of the soil.

Agriculture constituted the economic base of these societies, and agricultural labor was the chief activity of most of the people. Surpluses

Environmental Stress in the Indus Valley

All three river valley civilizations covered in this chapter were located in arid or semiarid regions with little rainfall. Such regions are particularly vulnerable to changes in the environment. The debates of scholars of the Indus Valley Civilization over the existence and impact of changes in the climate and landscape of that region illuminate some of the potential factors at work, as well as the difficulties of proving and interpreting such changes for the distant past.

One of the points at issue is climatic change. An earlier generation of scholars made a series of arguments to show that the climate of the Indus Valley must have been considerably wetter during the height of that civilization. They pointed to the amount of wood from extensive forests that would be needed to bake the millions of mud bricks used to construct the cities (see photo below), the distribution of human settlements on land that is now unfavorable for agriculture, and the representation of jungle and marsh animals on decorated seals. Other experts were skeptical about a dramatic climatic change, and countered with refined calculations of the amount of timber needed, instances of utilization of unbaked brick, the evidence of plant remains, and the growing of barley, a grain which is tolerant of dry conditions. Radiocarbon-dated samples of ancient pollen have been used to argue both for continuity and for change in the climate. Recent studies of the stabilization of sand dunes, which occurs in periods of greater rainfall, and analysis of the sediment deposited by rivers and winds, have been used to revive the claim that the Indus Valley zone used to be wetter, and entered a period of drier conditions in the early-to-mid second millennium that have persisted till the present day.

A much clearer case can be made for changes in the landscape caused by shifts in the courses of rivers. These shifts are due, in many cases, to tectonic forces such as earthquakes. Dry channels, whether detected in satellite photographs or on-the-ground inspection, reveal the location of old river beds. It appears that a second major river system once ran parallel to the Indus some distance to the east. Either the Sutlej, which now feeds into the Indus, or the Yamuna, which

Source: D. P. Agrawal and R. K. Sood in Gregory L. Possehl (ed.), *Harappan Civilization: A Contemporary Perspective*, p. 229. Photo from *The Cambridge History of India: The Indus Civilization*, Sir Mortimer Wheeler. With permission of the Syndics of the Cambridge University Press.

now pours into the Ganges basin, may have been the main source of water for this system. As for the Indus itself, the present-day course of the lower reaches of the river has shifted 100 miles to the west since the arrival of the Greek conqueror Alexander the Great in the late fourth century, and the deposit of massive volumes of silt has pushed the mouth of the river fifty miles further south.

As a recent study concludes: "It is obvious that ecological stresses, caused both climatically and technically, played an important role in the life and decay of the Harappan Civilization."

that the ruling class siphoned off made possible the emergence of towns and cities—crowded and lively urban environments inhabited by specialists of various sorts engaged in the work of administration, war, commerce, religion, arts, and crafts.

We have reached the limit of what we can say in our comparison of the three river-valley civilizations described in this chapter. Because of our limited information about the people of the Indus Valley, we must focus any further comparison on the better-documented civilizations of Mesopotamia and Egypt.

In both regions kingship emerged as the dominant political form. The monarch was assisted by a privileged administrative bureaucracy that used the technology of writing, known only to a relative few, to record, manage, and exploit the resources of the country.

The religious outlook of both cultures was polytheistic (believing in more than one god). There was a hierarchy of gods, ranging from protective demons and local deities that people worshiped in their homes to the gods of the state, whose importance rose or fell with the power of the political centers with which they were associated. The priests who administered major temples controlled vast sums of wealth and were politically influential, sometimes challenging the authority of the monarchy.

In both Egypt and Mesopotamia the population was ethnically heterogeneous, yet both regions experienced a remarkable tradition of cultural continuity over centuries and millennia, because the various groups of peoples who migrated into the central cultural zone were readily assimilated to the dominant language, belief system, and lifeways. Culture, not physical appearance, was the criterion by which people were identified.

So much for the similarities. There were also telling differences, beginning with the landscapes in which these civilizations were rooted. The unpredictable and violent floods of the Tigris-Euphrates Basin were a constant source of alarm for the people of Mesopotamia. In contrast, the predictable, opportune, and gradual Nile floods were eagerly anticipated events in Egypt. The relationship with nature stamped the world-view of both peoples. Mesopotamians nervously tried to appease their harsh deities so as to survive in a perverse world. Egyptians confidently trusted in, and nurtured, the supernatural powers, which they believed guaranteed orderliness and prosperity.

In Egypt, political unification and centralization of power were the norm. Both were weakened from time to time by economic crises and challenged by the autonomy of high-level administrators and priests, but they were restored as soon as conditions permitted. The central authority of the king and court may have inhibited the process of urbanization outside the capital. In Mesopotamia, urbanization reached a more advanced stage. The city was the central political, social, and economic unit. The proliferation of independent-minded cities made it hard for any one center of power to be dominant for long. The temporary nature of centralized power in Mesopotamia may help to explain why private enterprise was given relatively free reign there, whereas the economy of Egypt was largely controlled by the state.

Although both societies developed a form of kingship, the ideology of each was different. In Egypt, particularly during the Old Kingdom, the king's divine origins made him central to the welfare of the entire country and gave him a religious monopoly superseding the authority of the temples and priests. Egyptian monarchs lavished much of the wealth of the country on their tombs because proper burial helped to ensure the continuity of kingship and the attendant blessings that it brought to the land and people. Mesopotamian rulers, who were not normally regarded as divine, had to justify their position on other grounds. They built new cities, towering walls, splendid palaces, and religious edifices as advertisements of their power to contemporaries and reminders to posterity of their greatness.

The somewhat different position of women in these societies may be related to the higher degree of urbanization and class stratification in Mesopotamia. Constraints on women often are related to the emergence of a highly property-conscious urban and commercial middle class. And in general, women appear to have lost freedom and legal privilege in Mesopotamia in the second millennium B.C.E., whereas Egyptian pictorial documents, love poems, and legal records indicate an attitude of respect and a higher degree of equality for women in the valley of the Nile.

Cheered by the essential stability of their environment, the Egyptians tended to have a more positive conception of the gods' designs for humankind, both in this life and beyond the grave. The Egyptian imagination devised several different versions of paradise, and although the journey to the next world was beset with hazards, the righteous soul that overcame them could look forward to a blessed existence that included all the pleasures of life on earth. In contrast, Gilgamesh, the hero of the Mesopotamian epic, is tormented by terrifying visions of the afterlife: disembodied souls of the dead stumbling around in the darkness of the Underworld for all eternity, eating dust and clay, and slaving for the heartless gods of that realm.

CONCLUSION

I n sum, the demands of their respective environments sometimes evoked similar organizational and technological responses from the first advanced civilizations of the ancient world. However, each of these societies met the challenges of daily life with a particular spirit deriving from its own distinctive outlook on life and death, nature and the supernatural, and the individual and the state.

In the second millennium B.C.E., as the societies of Mesopotamia and Egypt consolidated their cultural achievements and entered new phases of political expansion, and as the Indus Valley centers went into irreversible decline, a new and distinctive civilization, based likewise on the exploitation of the agricultural potential of a floodplain, was emerging in the valley of the Yellow River in eastern China. It is to that area that we turn our attention in Chapter 3.

SUGGESTED READING

Jack M. Sasson (ed.), *Civilizations of the Ancient Near East*, 4 vols. (1993) contains up-to-date articles and bibliography on a wide range of topics. An excellent starting point for geography, chronology, and basic institutions and cultural concepts in ancient western Asia is Michael Roaf, *Cultural Atlas of Mesopotamia and the Ancient Near East* (1990). General historical introductions can be found in A. Bernard Knapp, *The History and Culture of Ancient Western Asia and Egypt* (1988); Hans J. Nissen, *The Early History of the Ancient Near East, 9000–2000 B.C.* (1988); H. W. F. Saggs, *Civilization Before Greece and Rome* (1989); and Georges Roux, *Ancient Iraq*, 3d ed. (1992). Joan Oates, *Babylon* (1979), focuses on the most important of all the Mesopotamian cities. J. N. Postgate, *Early Mesopotamia: Society and Economy at the Dawn of History* (1992), offers deep insights into the political, social, and economic dynamics of Mesopotamian society.

The most direct and exciting introduction to the world of early Mesopotamians is through the epic of Gilgamesh, in the attractive translation of David Ferry, *Gilgamesh* (Noonday Press, New York, 1992). Thorkild Jacobsen, *The Treasures of Darkness: A History of Mesopotamian Religion* (1976), is a classic study of the evolving mentality of Mesopotamian religion. Stephanie Dalley, *Myths from Mesopotamia* (1989), and Henrietta McCall, *Mesopotamian Myths* (1990), deal with the mythical literature. Jeremy Black and Anthony Green, *Gods, Demons and Symbols of Ancient Mesopotamia* (1992), is a handy illustrated encyclopedia of myth, religion, and religious symbolism.

C. B. F. Walker, *Cuneiform* (1987), is a concise guide to the Mesopotamian system of writing. James B. Pritchard, *Ancient Near Eastern Texts Relating to the Old Testament*, 2d ed. (1955), contains an extensive collection of translated documents and texts from western Asia and Egypt. Attitudes, roles, and the treatment of women are taken up by Barbara Lesko, "Women of Egypt and the Ancient Near East," in *Becoming Visible: Women in European History*, 2d ed., Renata Bridenthal, Claudia Koonz, and Susan Stuard (1994), and by Guity Nashat, "Women in the Ancient Middle East," in *Restoring Women to History* (1988). The significance of Ebla and ancient Syria is taken up in Harvey Weiss, ed., *Ebla to Damascus: Art and Archaeology of Ancient Syria* (1985), and Giovanni Pettinato, *Ebla: A New Look at History* (1991).

John Baines and Jaromir Malek, *Atlas of Ancient Egypt* (1980), and T. G. H. James, *Ancient Egypt: The Land and Its Legacy* (1988), are primarily organized around the sites of ancient Egypt and provide general introductions to Egyptian civilization. Historical treatments include B. G. Trigger, B. J. Kemp, D. O'Connor, and A. B. Lloyd, *Ancient Egypt: A Social History* (1983); Barry J. Kemp, *Ancient Egypt: Anatomy of a Civilization* (1989); and Nicholas-Cristophe Grimal, *A History of Ancient Egypt* (1992). John Romer, *People of the Nile: Everyday Life in Ancient Egypt* (1982); Miriam Stead, *Egyptian Life* (1986); and Eugen Strouhal, *Life of the Ancient Egyptians* (1992), emphasize social history. For women see the article by Lesko cited above; Barbara Watterson, *Women in Ancient Egypt* (1991); and Gay Robins, *Women in Ancient Egypt* (1993).

Stephen Quirke, *Ancient Egyptian Religion* (1990), is a highly regarded treatment of a complex subject. George Hart, *Egyptian Myths* (1990), gathers the limited written evidence for what must have been a thriving oral tradition. Pritchard's collection, cited above, and Miriam Lichtheim, *Ancient Egyptian Literature: A Book of Readings, Vol. 1, The Old and Middle Kingdoms* (1973), provide translated original texts and documents.

For the Indus Valley civilization, there is a brief treatment in Stanley Wolpert, *A New History of India*, 3d ed. (1989). More detailed are Mortimer Wheeler's *Civilizations of the Indus Valley and Beyond* (1966) and *The Indus Civilization*, 3d ed., (1968). Gregory L. Poschl has edited two collections of articles by Indus Valley scholars: *Ancient Cities of the Indus* (1979) and *Harappan Civilization* (1982).

NOTE

1. David Ferry, *Gilgamesh* (Noonday Press, New York, 1992).

CHAPTER THREE

The Late Bronze Age in the Eastern Hemisphere, 2200–500 B.C.E.

Early China · The Cosmopolitan Middle East · Nubia

The Aegean World · The Fall of Late Bronze Age Civilizations

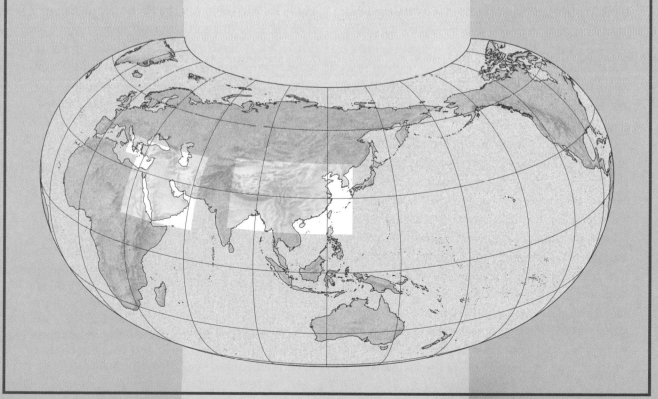

Around 1450 B.C.E. Queen Hatshepsut of Egypt sent a naval expedition down the Red Sea to the fabled land that the Egyptians called "Punt." Historians believe Punt was in the northern coastal region of modern Somalia. Myrrh exported from Punt usually passed through the hands of several intermediaries before reaching Egypt. Hatshepsut hoped to bypass the middlemen and establish direct trade between Punt and Egypt.

A fascinating written and pictorial record of this expedition and its aftermath is preserved in the mortuary temple of Hatshepsut at Deir el-Bahri, near Thebes. Besides bringing back myrrh resin and various sub-Saharan luxury goods— ebony and other rare woods, ivory, cosmetics, live monkeys, panther skins—the ships also carried young myrrh trees, probably to create a home-grown source of this precious substance which the Egyptians burned on the altars of their gods. These items are represented in the royal Egyptian tomb as tribute given by the people of Punt to their Egyptian overlord. Egyptian power, however, did not reach that far, so the Egyptian emissaries actually must have traded for them. Hatshepsut staged public displays of these treasures from southern lands and emphasized that she had accomplished what none of her predecessors had been able to do.

Hatshepsut's highly touted expedition to Punt reveals much that is important about the ancient world in the second millennium B.C.E. The major centers resolutely pursued access to important resources, by trade or conquest, because their power, wealth, and legitimacy depended on the acquisition of these commodities. A hallmark of this period in northeastern Africa, the eastern Mediterranean, western Asia, and East Asia was the interconnectedness of regions and states, large and small, in complex webs of political relationships and economic activities. Embassies, treaties, trade agreements, political marriages, and scribes utilizing widely recognized languages and writing systems were but some of the links connecting the heterogeneous peoples of these regions. Commerce over long distances, centering on the trade in metals, was vital to the power and prosperity of the ruling classes.

The movement of goods across long distances promoted the flow of ideas and technologies. These included concepts of kingship, methods of administration, systems of writing, religious beliefs and rituals, artistic tastes, metallurgical skills, and new forms of transportation. By the standards of the ancient world, the Late Bronze Age was a cosmopolitan and comfortable era, a time of stability and prosperity, of technological progress and cultural accomplishments.

The spread of ideas and technologies sparked important political changes across the Eastern Hemisphere (the vast landmass comprising the joined continents of Asia, Africa, and Europe). This period, which witnessed the last flourishing of the ancient centers of civilization in Egypt and southern Mesopotamia (introduced in Chapter 2), also saw the formation of new centers of power and the first stirrings of peoples who would take center stage in the first millennium B.C.E.:—Assyrians in northern Mesopotamia, Nubians in northeastern Africa, Greeks in the eastern Mediterranean, and the Shang and Zhou in northeastern China.

EARLY CHINA

On the eastern edge of the great Eurasian landmass, Chinese civilization evolved in the second millennium B.C.E. Under the political domination of the Shang and Zhou monarchs many of the characteristic institutions, patterns, and values of classical Chinese civilization emerged and spread south and west. As in

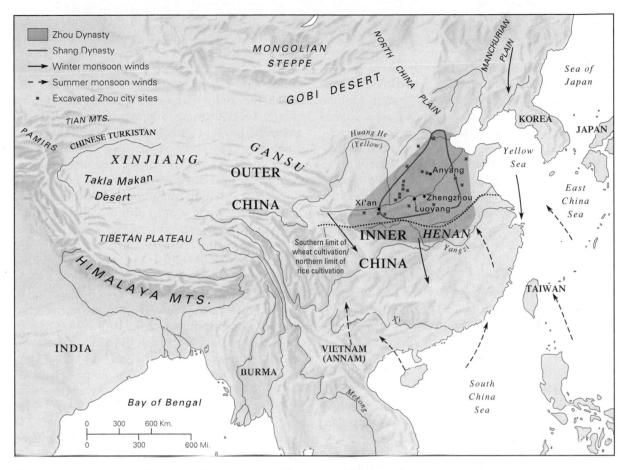

Map 3.1   China under the Shang and Zhou Dynasties, 1750–221 B.C.E.   A complex civilization arose in the second millennium B.C.E. in the floodplain of the Yellow River. While southern China benefits from the monsoon rains, northern China depends on irrigation. As population increased, the Han Chinese migrated to other parts of Inner China, carrying their technologies and cultural practices. Other ethnic groups predominated in Outer China, and the nomadic peoples of the northwest constantly challenged Chinese authority.

Mesopotamia, Egypt, and the Indus Valley, the rise of a complex society possessing cities, specialization of labor, bureaucratic government, writing, and other advanced technologies depended on the marshaling of human labor and exploitation of the waters of a great river system—the Yellow River (Huang He) and its tributaries—to support intensive agriculture in the plains. Although there is archaeological evidence of some movement of goods and ideas between western and eastern Asia, these developments were largely independent of the rise of complex societies in the Middle East and the Indus Valley.

Geography and Resources

China is isolated from the rest of the Eastern Hemisphere by formidable natural barriers: to the southwest the Himalayas, the highest mountains on the planet; to the west the Pamir and Tian Mountains and the Takla Makan Desert; to the northwest the Gobi Desert and the treeless and grassy hills and plains of the Mongolian steppe (see Map 3.1). To the east lies the vastness of the Pacific Ocean. Although China's separation was not total—trade goods, people, and ideas moved back and forth between China,

India, and Central Asia—its development in many instances was unique.

Most of the East Asian subcontinent is covered with mountains, making overland travel, transport, and communications difficult and slow. The great river systems of eastern China, however—the Yellow River, the Yangzi River, and their tributaries—facilitate internal movement along an east-west axis. It is useful to distinguish between Inner China and Outer China. Intensive agriculture was practiced and the population clustered in the eastern river valleys of Inner China. In Outer China—the steppe lands of Mongolia, the deserts and oases of Xinjiang, and the high plateau of Tibet—sparser populations practiced quite different forms of livelihood. The topographical diversity of East Asia is matched by climatic zones ranging from the dry, subarctic reaches of Manchuria in the north to the lush, subtropical forests of the south, and by rich variation in the plant and animal life adapted to these zones.

Even within Inner China there is a fundamental distinction between north and south. The same forces that create the great monsoon of India and Southeast Asia (see Chapter 2) also drench southern China with substantial amounts of rainfall in the summer months, the most beneficial time for agriculture. Northern China, in contrast, receives a much more erratic and restricted amount of moisture. As a result, in north and south there are different patterns for the use of land, the kinds of crops that can flourish, and the organization of agricultural labor. As in Mesopotamia, the Indus Valley, and southern Greece (see below), where technological and social developments also sprang up in a relatively adverse environment, the early history of China centered on the demanding environment of the northern plains. In that region arose important technologies, political traditions, and a set of philosophical and religious views that have been the hallmark of Chinese civilization. From the third century C.E. on, because of the gradual flow of population toward the warmer southern lands, the political and intellectual center of gravity also moved south.

The eastern river valleys and North China Plain contained timber, stone, and scattered deposits of metals. Above all, this region offered potentially productive land. Since prehistoric times, winds rising over the vast expanse of Central Asia have deposited a yellowish-brown silt called *loess* (silt in suspension in the water has given the Yellow River its distinctive hue and name). Over the ages this annual sprinkling has accumulated into a thick mantle of soil that is extremely fertile and soft enough to be worked with wooden digging sticks. The very lack of compactness of this soil is the reason why the region has been hit by catastrophic earthquakes.

In this landscape agriculture, which first appeared in the fourth millennium B.C.E., demanded immense human labor. In parts of northern China forests had to be cleared to open up land for planting. The Yellow River was prone to devastating floods, necessitating the construction of earthen dikes and channels to carry off the overflow. The region was equally vulnerable to prolonged droughts, for which the best defense was the digging of catch basins (reservoirs) to store river water and rainfall.

The staple crops in the northern region were millet, indigenous to China, and wheat, which spread to East Asia from the Middle East. The cultivation of rice in the Yangzi River Valley and the south required an even greater outlay of labor. The reward for this effort was a spectacular yield—rice can feed a larger number of people per cultivated acre than can any other grain. Rice prospered in the south because it requires a relatively high air temperature. Rice paddies must be absolutely flat and surrounded by water channels to bring and lead away water according to a precise schedule. Seedlings sprout in a nursery and then are transplanted one by one into the paddy and are flooded for a time. The flooding eliminates weeds and other rival plants and supports microscopic organisms that keep the soil fertile. When the crop is ripe, the paddy must be drained, the rice stalks harvested with a sickle, and the edible kernels separated out. As the population of ancient China expanded, people claimed more land for cultivation by building retaining walls to partition the hillsides into tiers of flat terraces. Thus, in both northern and southern China, agriculture required the coordinated efforts of large groups of people.

The Shang Period

Archaeologists have distinguished among several early cultural complexes in China, primarily on the basis of styles of pottery and forms of burial. These early populations grew millet and raised pigs and chickens. They made pottery on a wheel and fired it in high-temperature kilns. They mastered the techniques of silk-cloth production, fostering the growth of silkworms, which gorged on the leaves of mulberry trees and spun cocoons, which people carefully unraveled to produce silk thread. The early Chinese built walls of pounded earth by hammering the soil inside temporary wooden frames until it became hard as cement. By 2000 B.C.E. they had acquired bronze metallurgy.

Later generations of Chinese told stories about the dynasty of the Xia, who are said to have ruled the core region in the centuries before and after 2000 B.C.E. The validity of those stories, however, is difficult to gauge. For all practical purposes Chinese history begins with the rise to power of the Shang clans, coinciding with the earliest written records in the early second millennium B.C.E.

According to tradition, Tang, a subordinate of the last Xia monarch, overthrew his decadent master around 1750 B.C.E. The prominent class among the Shang was a warrior aristocracy whose greatest pleasures in life were warfare, hunting (both for recreation and to fine-tune the skills required for war), exchanging gifts, feasting, and wine-filled revelry. The Shang originated in the part of the Yellow River Valley that lies in the present-day province of Henan. Between approximately 1750 and 1027 B.C.E. they extended their control across a large swath of territory extending north into Mongolia, west as far as Gansu, and south into the Yangzi River Valley. Various cities served as the capital of the Shang Empire. The last and most important of them was near modern Anyang (see Map 3.1).

The core area of the empire was ruled directly by the king and his administrators, who were members of the aristocracy and served, as needed, as generals, ambassadors, and supervisors of public projects. Members of the royal family and

A bronze vessel with rams and dragons from the Shang Period   Such vessels were used in the rituals which allowed the Shang ruling class to make contact with its ancestors. As both the source and proof of the authority of this elite, these vessels were often buried in their tombs. The complex shape and elaborate decoration testify to the high level of artisans' skills. (Seth Joel/Laurie Platt Winfrey, Inc.)

high-ranking nobility managed provinces farther out. The most distant regions were governed by native rulers bound by ties of allegiance to the Shang king. The king was often on the road, traveling to the courts of his subordinates to reinforce their ties of loyalty.

Military campaigns were frequent. They provided the warrior aristocracy with a theater for brave achievements, and they yielded considerable plunder. The "barbarians," as the Chinese called the nomadic peoples who occupied the steppe and desert regions to the north and west, periodically were rolled back and given a reminder of Shang power. (The word *barbarian* reflects the language and view of Chinese sources.

Modern readers should be wary of the Chinese claim that these nomads were culturally backward and morally inferior to the Chinese.) The campaigns against peoples in the north and west produced large numbers of prisoners of war who were carried off to the Shang capital and used as slaves.

Far-reaching networks of trade sprang up across China, bringing to the core area of the Shang domain valued commodities such as jade, ivory, and mother of pearl (a hard, shiny substance from the interior of mollusk shells) used for jewelry, carved figurines, and decorative inlays. There are indications that Shang China was in contact with the civilization of Mesopotamia and that these centers exchanged goods and ideas with one another.

The Shang kings devised an ideology of kingship that reinforced their power. They presented themselves as indispensable intermediaries between their people and the gods. The Shang aristocracy worshiped the spirits of their male ancestors and believed that these ancestors were intensely interested in the fortunes of their descendants and had special influence with the gods. Before taking any action, the Shang used divination to ascertain the will of the gods (see Environment and Technology: Chinese and Mesopotamian Divination). Court ritual also called for sacrifices to gods and to ancestors in order to win divine favor. Burials of kings also entailed sacrifices, not only of animals but also of humans, including noble officials of the court, women, servants, soldiers, and prisoners of war.

Possession of bronze objects was a sign of authority and legitimacy and was mostly confined to members of the elite. Rural peasants were still using stone tools. Bronze was used in warfare and ritual, which, according to ancient sources, were the primary purposes of the state. Bronze weapons allowed the state to assert its authority, and the use of bronze ritual vessels was the best way to gain the support of ancestors and gods. The sheer quantity of bronze objects found in tombs of the Shang ruling class is very impressive, especially since copper and tin (the principal ingredients of bronze) were not plentiful in northern China. Clearly the Shang elite expended a huge effort on finding and mining deposits

of those elements, refining the mixed ores into pure metal, transporting the precious cargo to the capital, and commissioning the creation of skillfully made and beautifully decorated objects.

When the copper and tin had been mixed in the right proportions, artisans poured the molten bronze into clay molds. Separate hardened pieces were later joined together as necessary. The foundries were located outside the walls of the main cities. Artisans were sufficiently well rewarded to enjoy a comfortable lifestyle. They made weapons, chariot fittings, musical instruments, and, most important of all, the ritual vessels that held the liquids and solids used in religious ceremonies. Many of these elegant bronze vessels were vividly decorated with the stylized forms of real and imaginary animals. The decorations may indicate a belief that these creatures served as intermediaries between heaven and earth.

The Shang period was a time of other significant technological advances as well. The horse-drawn chariot, which the Shang may have adapted from the contemporary Middle East, was a formidable instrument of war. Domestication of the water buffalo provided additional muscle power. Growing knowledge of the principles of engineering and an effective administrative organization for mobilizing human labor led to the construction of cities, massive defensive walls of pounded earth, and monumental royal tombs.

A key to effective administration was the form of writing developed in this era. The original pictograms (pictures representing objects and concepts) were combined with phonetic symbols representing the sounds of syllables to form a complex system requiring scribes to memorize hundreds of signs. Because of the time needed to master this system, writing was the hallmark of the educated, elite class. The Chinese system has endured for thousands of years. Other ancient systems of writing that also were difficult to learn and brought special status and opportunities to those who did so—such as the cuneiform of Mesopotamia and the hieroglyphics of Egypt—were replaced by simpler alphabetic approaches.

Chinese and Mesopotamian Divination

The inhabitants of China and Mesopotamia and many other peoples of the ancient world believed that the gods controlled the forces of nature and foresaw events. Starting from this premise, they considered natural phenomena to be signs of the gods' will, and they tried to interpret these signs. Using various techniques of divination, the ancients sought to communicate with the gods and thereby anticipate, and even influence, the future.

The Shang ruling class in China frequently sought information from shamans, individuals who claimed to have the ability to make direct contact with ancestors and other higher powers (the king himself often functioned as a shaman). Chief among the tools of divination used by a shaman was oracle bones. The shaman touched a tortoise shell or the shoulder bone of an animal with the heated point of a stick. The shell or bone would crack, and the cracks could be "read" as a message from the spirit world.

Tens of thousands of oracle bones survive. They are a major source of information about Shang life, because usually the question that was being posed and the resulting answer were inscribed on the back side of the shell or bone. The rulers asked about the proper performance of ritual, the likely outcome of wars or hunting expeditions, the prospects for rainfall and the harvest, and the meaning of strange occurrences.

In Mesopotamia in the third and second millennium B.C.E. the most important divination involved the close inspection of the form, size, and markings of the organs of animals sacrificed. Archaeologists have found models of sheeps' livers accompanied by written explanations of the meaning of various features. Two other techniques of divination were following the trail of smoke from burning incense and examining the patterns that resulted when oil was thrown on water.

From about 2000 B.C.E. Mesopotamian diviners also foretold the future from their observation of the movements of the Sun, Moon, planets, stars, and constellations. In the centuries after 1000 B.C.E. celestial omens were the most important source of predictions about the future, and specialists maintained precise records of astronomical events. Mesopotamian mathematics, essential for calculations of the movements of celestial bodies, was the most sophisticated math in the ancient Middle East. A place-value system, in which a number stands for its value multiplied by the value of the particular column in which it appears (such as our ones, tens, and hundreds columns, moving from right to left), made possible complex operations with large numbers and small fractions.

Astrology, with its division of the sky into the twelve segments of the zodiac and its use of the position of the stars and planets to predict an individual's destiny, developed out of long-standing Mesopotamian attention to the movements of celestial objects. Horoscopes—charts with calculations and predictions based on an individual's date of birth—have been found from shortly before 400 B.C.E. In the Hellenistic period (323–30 B.C.E.), Greek settlers flooded into western Asia, built on this Mesopotamian foundation, and greatly advanced the study of astrology.

Chinese divination shell (Institute of History and Philology, Academia Sinica)

Women beating chimes   This scene, from a bronze vessel of the Zhou era, illustrates the important role of music in festivals, religious rituals, and court ceremonials. During the politically fragmented later (Eastern) Zhou era, many small states marked their independence by having their own musical scales and distinctive arrangement of orchestral instruments. (Courtesy, Imperial Palace Museum, Beijing)

The Zhou Period

Shang domination of central and northern China lasted more than six centuries. In the eleventh century B.C.E. the last Shang king was defeated by one of his dependents from the Wei River Valley, Duke Wu of Zhou. The Zhou line of kings (ca. 1027–221 B.C.E.) would prove to be the longest-lasting and most revered of all dynasties in Chinese history. As the Semitic peoples in Mesopotamia had adopted and adapted the Sumerian legacy (see Chapter 2), the Zhou preserved the foundations of culture created by their predecessors, adding important new elements of ideology and technology.

The positive image of Zhou rule, in many respects accurate, was skillfully constructed by propagandists for the new regime. The early Zhou monarchs had to formulate a new ideology of kingship to justify their seizure of power to the restive remnants of the Shang clans, as well as to their other subjects. The chief deity was now referred to as "Heaven," the monarch was called the "Son of Heaven," and his rule was called the "Mandate of Heaven." According to the new theory, the ruler would retain the backing of the gods as long as he served as a wise,

principled, and energetic guardian of his people. His mandate could be withdrawn if he misbehaved, as the last Shang ruler had done.

Although elements of Shang ritual were allowed to continue, there was a marked decline in the practice of divination and in the extravagant and bloody sacrifices and burials that had been hallmarks of Shang court ceremonial. The priestly power of the ruling class, which alone during the Shang period had been able to make contact with the powerful spirits of ancestors, was largely removed. The resulting separation of religion from political dealings allowed China to develop important secular philosophies in the Zhou period. The beautifully crafted bronze vessels that had been sacred implements in the Shang Period became family treasures.

The early period of Zhou rule—the eleventh through ninth centuries B.C.E.—is sometimes called the Western Zhou era. These centuries saw the development of a sophisticated administrative apparatus. The Zhou built a series of capital cities with pounded earth foundations and walls. The major buildings all faced south, beginning a long Chinese fascination with the orientation of structures. The king was supposed to be a model of morality, fairness, and concern for the welfare of the people—qualities that were expected of all imperial officials. The Zhou regime was highly decentralized. More than a hundred subject territories were ruled with considerable autonomy by members and allies of the royal family. The court was the scene of elaborate ceremonials, embellished by music and dance, which impressed on observers the glory of Zhou rule and reinforced the bonds of obligation between rulers and ruled. Standing armies were supplemented by local militias.

By around 800 B.C.E., Zhou power began to wane. Proud and ambitious local rulers operated ever more independently and waged war on one another, and nomadic peoples began to press on the borders from the northwest. Moreover, the center had lost its technological advantages over outlying regions. Knowledge of how to forge bronze tools and weapons and build sturdy city walls had spread to the subjects of the Zhou Empire and even to some of the "barbarian" groups.

The subsequent epoch of Chinese history is sometimes called the Eastern Zhou era. Members of the Zhou lineage who in 771 B.C.E. had relocated to a new, more secure, eastern capital near Luoyang continued to hold the imperial title and to receive at least nominal homage from the real power brokers of the age. This was a time of political fragmentation, rapidly shifting centers of power, and rampant competition and warfare among numerous small and independent states. The Eastern Zhou is also conventionally subdivided. The years between 771 and 481 B.C.E. are called the "Springs and Autumns Period," after a collection of chronicles that give annual entries for those two seasons. The period from 480 B.C.E. to the unification of China in 221 B.C.E. is called the "Warring States Period."

The many states of the Eastern Zhou era, when not paralyzed by internal power struggles, contended with one another for leadership. Cities, some of them quite large, spread across the Chinese landscape. Long walls of pounded earth, the ancestors of the Great Wall of China, protected the kingdoms from suspect neighbors and northern nomads. By 600 B.C.E. iron began to replace bronze as the primary metal for tools and weapons, and the Chinese had learned from the steppe nomads to put fighters on horseback.

In each of the states bureaucrats expanded in number and function. Codes of law were written

down. The government collected taxes from the peasants directly, and people's lives were regimented and regulated by the great rituals of court. The ruling class both justified its position and was steered toward right conduct by its claim that its actions were in accordance with a high standard of morality.

For those who lived through the political flux and social change, this was an anxious time. Their experiences led some to question old assumptions and begin to think in new ways. This was the historical setting for the life of Kong Fu Zi (Confucius 551–479 B.C.E.), an official and philosopher whose doctrine of duty and public service was to become one of the most influential strains in Chinese thought (see Chapter 6).

This era also saw the decline of the clan-based kinship structures that had characterized the Shang and early Zhou periods. Taking their place was the three-generation family—grandparents, parents, and children—which became the fundamental social unit. Related to this development was the emergence of the concept of private property. Land was considered to belong to the men of the family and was divided equally among the sons when the father died.

Very little is known about the conditions of life for women in early China. Some scholars believe that women may have had an important role as shamans, entering into trance states to communicate with supernatural forces, make requests on behalf of their communities, and receive predictions of the future. By the time written records begin to illuminate our knowledge of their experiences, however, women were in a subordinate position in the strongly patriarchal family.

The disparity in male and female roles was rationalized by the concept of *yin* and *yang*, which represented the complementary nature of male (yin) and female (yang) roles in the natural order. Male toughness was to be balanced by female gentleness, male action and initiation by female endurance and need for completion, male leadership by female willingness to follow. Only men were allowed to conduct the all-important rituals and make offerings to the ancestors; women helped to maintain the ancestral shrines in the household. Fathers held authority over the women and children, arranged marriages for

Periods of Early Chinese History

8000–2000 B.C.E.	Neolithic Cultures
1750–1027	Shang Dynasty
1027–772	Western Zhou
771–221	Eastern Zhou
771–481	Springs and Autumns Period
480–221	Warring States Period

their offspring, and were free to sell the labor of family members. A man was supposed to have only one wife but was permitted additional sexual partners, who had the lower status of concubines. Among the elite classes marriages were used to create political alliances, and it was common for the groom's family to offer a substantial "bride-gift" to the family of the prospective bride. A man whose wife died had a virtual duty to remarry in order to produce male heirs to keep alive the cult of the ancestors. Widows, however, were under considerable pressure not to remarry as proof of their devotion to their husbands.

In sum, during the long centuries of Zhou rule the classical Chinese patterns of family, property, and bureaucracy took shape. All that remained was for a strong central power to unify all the Chinese lands. This outcome would be achieved by the state of Qin, whose aggressive tendencies and disciplined way of life had made it the premier power among the warring states by the third century B.C.E. (see Chapter 6).

THE COSMOPOLITAN MIDDLE EAST

Both Mesopotamia and Egypt succumbed to outside invaders in the seventeenth century B.C.E. (see Chapter 2). Eventually the outsiders were either ejected or assimilated, and a new political equilibrium was achieved. In the period between 1500 and 1200 B.C.E. a number of large territorial states dominated the Middle East (see Map 3.2). Those centers of power controlled the smaller city-states, kingdoms, and kinship groups as they competed with, and sometimes fought against, one another for control of valuable commodities and trade routes.

Historians have called the Late Bronze Age in the Middle East a "cosmopolitan" era, meaning one in which elements of culture and lifestyle were widely shared among different groups. Extensive diplomatic relations and commercial contacts between states fostered the flow of ideas, and throughout the region one could find among the elite groups a relatively high standard of living and similar products and concepts. The majority of the population, peasants in the countryside, may have seen some improvement in their standard of living, but they reaped far fewer of the benefits deriving from increased contacts and trade among different societies.

Western Asia

By 1500 B.C.E. Mesopotamia was divided into two distinct political zones: Babylonia in the south and Assyria in the north (see Map 3.2). The city of Babylon had gained political and cultural ascendancy over the southern plain under the dynasty of Hammurabi in the eighteenth and seventeenth centuries B.C.E. Subsequently there was a persistent inflow of Kassites, peoples from the Zagros Mountains to the east who spoke a non-Semitic language, and by 1460 a Kassite dynasty had come to power in Babylon. The Kassites retained names in their native language but otherwise embraced Babylonian language and culture and intermarried with the native population. During their 250 years in power, the Kassite lords of Babylonia did not actively pursue territorial conquest and were content to defend their core area and trade for vital raw materials.

The Assyrians of the north had a more expansionist destiny. Back in the twentieth century B.C.E. the city of Ashur had become one pole of a busy trade route that crossed the northern Mesopotamian plain and ascended the Anatolian plateau, where representatives of Assyrian merchant families maintained trade settlements out-

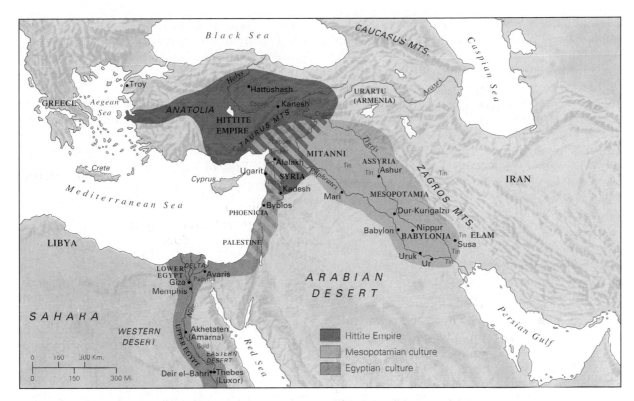

Map 3.2 The Middle East in the Second Millennium B.C.E.   While wars were not uncommon, treaties, diplomatic missions, and correspondence in Akkadian cuneiform helped relations between states. All were tied together by extensive networks of exchange centering on the trade in metals, and peripheral regions, such as Nubia and the Aegean Sea, were drawn into the web of commerce.

side the walls of important Anatolian cities. This commerce brought tin and textiles to Anatolia in exchange for silver. In the eighteenth century B.C.E. an Assyrian dynasty gained control of Mari, a key city-state on the upper Euphrates River near the present-day border of Syria and Iraq. Although this "Old Assyrian" kingdom, as it is now called, was short-lived, it illustrates the importance of the cities that lay astride the trade routes connecting Mesopotamia to Anatolia and the Syria-Palestine coast. After 1400 B.C.E. a resurgent "Middle Assyrian" kingdom was once again engaged in campaigns of conquest and economic imperialism.

Other ambitious states emerged on the periphery of the Mesopotamian heartland, including Elam in southwest Iran and Mitanni in the broad plain lying between the upper Euphrates

and Tigris Rivers. Most formidable of all were the Hittites, speakers of an Indo-European language who became the foremost power in Anatolia from around 1700 to 1200 B.C.E. From their capital at Hattushash, near present-day Ankara in central Turkey, they employed the fearsome new technology of horse-drawn war chariots. The hills of Anatolia contained rich deposits of some of the metals that were so prized in this age—copper, silver, and iron—and the Hittites came to play an indispensable role in international commerce. The Hittite king laid down a standardized code of law, demanded military service and labor in exchange for grants of land, and supported artists and craftsmen engaged in the construction and decoration of palaces and temples.

A distinctive feature of western Asia during the second millennium B.C.E. was the diffusion of

Mesopotamian political and cultural concepts from the original Sumerian core area in southern Mesopotamia across much of the region. The cuneiform system of writing was employed to communicate in Elamite, Hittite, and other languages. Mesopotamian myths and legends were taken over by other peoples, and Mesopotamian styles of art and architecture were imitated. In this new regional order the old center was often hard-pressed by newcomers who had learned well and improved on the lessons of Mesopotamian civilization. The small, fractious, Mesopotamian city-states of the third millennium B.C.E. had been concerned with their immediate neighbors in the southern plain. In contrast, the larger states of the second millennium B.C.E. interacted politically, militarily, and economically in a geopolitical sphere extending across western Asia.

New Kingdom Egypt

With the decline of the Middle Kingdom in the seventeenth century B.C.E., due to both the increased independence of high-level officials and the pressure of new groups migrating into the Nile Valley, Egypt entered a period of political fragmentation, economic regression, and cultural disruption. Around 1640 B.C.E. it came under foreign rule for the first time—at the hands of the Hyksos, or "Princes of Foreign Lands." Historians are uncertain about the precise identity of the Hyksos and how they came to power. Semitic peoples from the Syria-Palestine region to the northeast (today the countries of Israel, Palestine, Jordan, Lebanon, and Syria) had been migrating into the eastern Nile Delta for centuries, and it is likely that in the chaotic conditions of this time other peoples joined them and were able to establish control, first in the delta and then throughout lower Egypt (see Map 3.2). This process may not have been different from that by which the Amorites and Kassites first settled in and gained control in Babylonia.

The Hyksos intermarried with the Egyptian population and largely assimilated to native ways. They used the Egyptian language and maintained Egyptian institutions and culture. Nevertheless, in contrast to the relative ease with which outsiders were assimilated in Mesopotamia, the Egyptians, with their strong sense of ethnic identity and long tradition of political unity, continued to regard the Hyksos as "foreigners."

As with the formation of the Middle Kingdom approximately five hundred years earlier, the reunification of Egypt under a native dynasty again came from the princes of Thebes. Through three decades of unrelenting fighting, Kamose and Ahmose were able to expel the Hyksos from Egypt, thereby inaugurating the New Kingdom, which lasted from about 1532 to 1070 B.C.E.

A century of foreign domination had been a blow to Egyptian pride and shook the new leaders of Egypt out of the isolationist mindset of earlier eras. New Kingdom Egypt was an aggressive and expansionist state, engaging in frequent campaigns of conquest and extending its territorial control north into Syria-Palestine and south into Nubia. In this way Egypt won access to valuable commodities—including timber, copper, and gold—and to a constant infusion of wealth in the form of taxes and tribute, and a buffer zone of occupied territory protected Egypt against foreign attack. The mechanisms of Egyptian control in the Syria-Palestine region included strategically placed forts and garrisons of Egyptian soldiers and support for local rulers who were willing to collaborate. In Nubia, in contrast, Egypt imposed control directly and pressed the native population to adopt important elements of Egyptian language and culture.

At the same time, Egypt became a full-fledged participant in the network of diplomatic and commercial relations that linked the large and small states of western Asia. Egyptian soldiers, administrators, diplomats, and merchants spent much time outside Egypt. Their travels abroad exposed Egypt to new technologies, including improved potter's wheels and looms for weaving, new fruits and vegetables, new musical instruments, and the war chariot. In sum, the New Kingdom was a period of great innovation.

During this period at least one woman laid claim to the throne of Egypt. Hatshepsut was the queen of Pharaoh Tuthmosis II. When he died, she served at first as regent for her young stepson but soon claimed the royal title for herself

(r. 1473–1458 B.C.E.). In the inscriptions which she commissioned for her mortuary temple at Deir el-Bahri, she often used the male pronoun to refer to herself, and drawings show her wearing the long, conical beard symbolic of the king of Egypt. It was Hatshepsut who dispatched the naval expedition to Punt, described at the beginning of this chapter, to open up direct trade between Egypt and the source of the prized myrrh resin. She used the success of this expedition to bolster her claim to the throne. After her death, in a reaction that reflected simmering opposition in some official quarters to having a woman as ruler, her picture was defaced and her name blotted out wherever it appeared.

The reign of another ruler also saw sharp departures from the ways of the past. Originally called Amenhotep IV, this ruler began to refer to himself as Akhenaten (r. 1353–1335 B.C.E.) which means "beneficial to the *Aten* (the disk of the sun)." Changing his name was just one of the ways in which he emphasized the primacy of the Aten. He closed the temples of the other gods, directly challenging the long-standing supremacy of Amon among the gods and the temporal power and influence of the priests of Amon.

Scholars have drawn various conclusions about the spiritual impulses behind these changes, but it is likely that Akhenaten's motives were at least partly political and that he was attempting to reassert the superiority of the king over the priests and to renew belief in the divinity of the king. The worship of Aten was actually confined to the royal family in the palace. The population of Egypt was pressed to revere the divine ruler.

Akhenaten built a new capital at modern-day Amarna, halfway between Memphis and Thebes. He and his artists created a new style of realism: the king, his wife Nefertiti, and the family were depicted in fluid, natural poses. The discovery at Amarna of an archive containing correspondence between the Egyptian government and various local rulers in the Syria-Palestine dependencies illuminates the diplomatic currents of this so-called Amarna period (see Voices and Visions: The Amarna Letters).

Painting on a wooden casket from the tomb of Tutankhamun   The light, wooden chariot drawn by a pair of horses introduced into warfare a fearsome new level of speed and mobility. While Tutankhamun, here shown riding in a war chariot and slaughtering Nubian enemies, was pharaoh during the New Kingdom, a period in which Egypt abandoned its traditional isolation and extended its control over neighboring peoples in Nubia and Syria-Palestine, it is unlikely that this represents a real event in the brief reign of the boy-king (r. 1333-1323). (Griffiths Institute, Ashmokan Museum, Oxford)

The Amarna Letters

The Amarna Letters are nearly four hundred documents discovered in 1887 C.E. at modern Tell el-Amarna (ancient Akhetaten), the capital of the Egyptian pharaoh Akhenaten. The documents date from approximately 1355 to 1335 B.C.E.—from the last years of Akhenaten's father, Amenhotep III, through the reign of Akhenaten. Primarily they are correspondence between the Egyptian monarch and various subordinate local rulers within the territory of modern Israel, Palestine, Lebanon, and Syria.

Using Akkadian cuneiform, the vehicle for international communication at the time, the scribes sometimes betray their origins as Canaanites (the indigenous Semitic people of Syria-Palestine) by linguistic slips.

This archive reveals the complex and shifting political dynamics of the Egyptian empire, as can be seen in this letter from Lab'ayu, the Canaanite ruler of Shechem in central Israel, to Amenhotep III:

To the king, my lord and my Sun-god: Thus Lab'ayu, thy servant, and the dirt on which thou dost tread. At the feet of the king, my lord, and my Sun-god, seven times and seven times I fall. I have heard the words which the king wrote to me, and who am I that the king should lose his land because of me? Behold, I am a faithful servant of the king, and I have not rebelled and I have not sinned, and I do not withhold my tribute, and I do not refuse the requests of my commissioner. Now they wickedly slander me, but let the king, my lord, not impute rebellion to me!

The opening language of abject subordination to the divine king is a formula that appears in almost every document. Apparently Lab'ayu had been accused of disobedience by some of his neighbors and was writing to protest his innocence. In fact, Lab'ayu is frequently accused in the Amarna Letters of attacking the territory and robbing the caravans of other Egyptian subjects.

What can we deduce from this document about the relationship of the Egyptian government to the complex patchwork of subordinate local rulers in Syria-Palestine? What were the duties of Egyptian subjects? Why might the Egyptian government have tolerated quarreling and competition among the local chiefs?

Other documents in the archive provide glimpses of the goods (including human beings) traded through this region, a crossroads between Egypt, Syria, the Mediterranean, and Mesopotamia:

To Milkilu, prince of Gezer. Thus the king. Now I have sent thee this tablet to say to thee: Behold, I am sending to thee Hanya, the commissioner of the archers, together with goods, in order to procure fine concubines (i.e.) weaving women: silver, gold, linen garments, turquoise, all sorts of precious stones, chairs of ebony, as well as every good thing, totalling 160 deben. . . . So send very fine concubines in whom there is no blemish.

The appearance of Canaanite, Egyptian, and Indo-European names in the letters reveals the diverse mix of ethnic groups living in this region. There are also frequent references to the troubles caused by the Apiru, characterized as backward, nomadic peoples prone to prey on the farmlands and towns, as in this appeal to Akhenaten from Shuwardata, a local ruler from the Hebron region:

Let the king, my lord, learn that the chief of the Apiru has risen in arms against the lands which the god of the king, my lord, gave me; but I have smitten him. . . . So let it be agreeable to the king, my lord, and let him send Yanhamu, and let us make war in earnest, and let the lands of the king, my lord, be restored to their former limits!

What common interests bind together the Egyptian monarchy and the local rulers in Syria-Palestine? What forms might cooperation between these groups take?

The reforms of Akhenaten stirred resistance from the administration, the priesthood, and other groups whose privileges and wealth were linked to the traditional system. After his death the old ways were restored with a vengeance: the temples were reopened, Amon was returned to his position of primacy in the pantheon, and the institution of kingship was weakened to the advantage of the priests. The boy-king Tutankhamun (r. 1333–1323), one of the immediate successors of Akhenaten and famous solely because his is the only royal tomb found by archaeologists that had not been pillaged by tomb robbers, reveals both in his name (meaning "beautiful in life is *Amon*") and his insignificant reign the ultimate failure of Akhenaten's revolution.

Shortly thereafter the general Haremhab took possession of the throne for his family, the Ramessides, and this dynasty renewed the policy of conquest and expansion that had been neglected in the Amarna period. The greatest monarch of this line, Ramesses II—Ramesses the Great, as he is sometimes called—ruled for sixty-six years (r. 1290–1224) and dominated his age.

Early in his reign Ramesses II commanded Egyptian forces in a major battle against the Hittites at Kadesh in northern Syria (1285). Although Egyptian scribes presented this encounter as a great victory for their side, other evidence suggests that it was essentially a draw. In subsequent years Egyptian and Hittite diplomats negotiated a series of territorial agreements, which were strengthened by the marriage of Ramesses to a Hittite princess. Ramesses also looms large in the archaeological record because he undertook building projects all over Egypt, including the rock-cut temple at Abu Simbel, with its four colossal images of the seated king, and the two tall, needle-shaped obelisks at Luxor.

Commerce and Diplomacy

At issue in the great rivalry between Egypt and the Hittite kingdom was control of the region lying between them—Syria-Palestine—the pivot in the trade routes that bound together this part of the globe. Lying at a crossroads between the great powers of the Middle East and at the end of the east-west land route across Asia, the inland cities of Syria-Palestine—such as Mari on the upper Euphrates and Alalakh in western Syria—were meeting places where merchants from different lands could exchange goods. The coastal port towns—particularly Ugarit on the Syrian coast and the up-and-coming Phoenician towns of the Lebanese seaboard—served as transshipment points for products going to or coming from the lands ringing the Mediterranean Sea.

In the eastern Mediterranean, northeastern Africa, and western Asia in the Late Bronze Age, access to metal resources was vital for any state with pretensions to power. Indeed, commerce in metals energized the long-distance trade that bound together the economies of the various states of the time. We have seen the Assyrian traffic in silver from Anatolia, and later in this chapter we discuss the Egyptian passion for Nubian gold. The sources of the most important *utilitarian* metals—copper and tin to make bronze—lay in different directions. Copper came from Anatolia and Cyprus; tin came from Afghanistan and possibly the British Isles. Both ores had to be carried long distances and pass through a number of hands before arriving in the political centers where they were melded and shaped.

New modes of transportation expedited communications and commerce across great distances and inhospitable landscapes. Horses arrived in western Asia around 2000 B.C.E. Domesticated by nomadic peoples in Central Asia, they were brought into Mesopotamia from the northeastern mountains. They reached Egypt by about 1500 B.C.E. Horse-drawn chariots became the premier instrument of war, giving a terrifying advantage over soldiers on foot. The speed of travel and communication made possible by the horse opened up new opportunities for the creation of large territorial states and empires, because soldiers and government agents on horseback could cover great distances in a relatively short time.

Sometime after 1500 B.C.E., but not for another thousand years in Egypt, people began to make common use of camels, though the animal may have been domesticated a millennium earlier in southern Arabia. Thanks to their strength and ca-

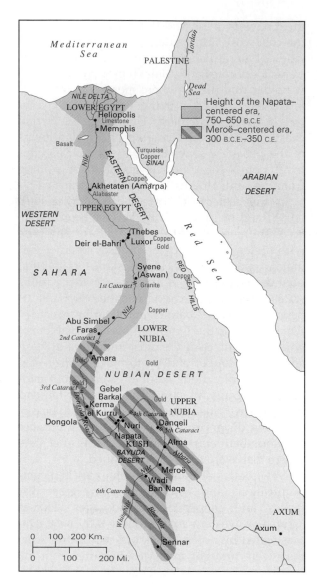

Map 3.3 Ancient Nubia The land route alongside the Nile River as it flows through Nubia (modern-day northern Sudan and southern Egypt) has long served as a corridor connecting sub-Saharan Africa with North Africa. The centuries of Egyptian occupation, as well as time spent in Egypt by Nubian hostages, mercenaries, and merchants, led to a marked Egyptian cultural influence in Nubia.

pacity to go long distances without water, camels were able to travel across barren terrain. Their fortitude led, eventually, to the emergence of a new desert nomad and to the creation of cross-desert trade routes (see Chapter 8).

NUBIA

The long-distance commerce in precious goods that flourished in the second millennium B.C.E. in western Asia and the eastern Mediterranean had repercussions to the south. Of even greater importance to Egypt than myrrh and other products from southern lands was the gold of Nubia.

Since the first century B.C.E. the name "Nubia" has been applied to a thousand-mile (1,600-kilometer) stretch of the Nile Valley lying between Aswan and Khartoum (see Map 3.3). The ancient Egyptians called it "Ta-sety," "Land of the Bow," after the favorite weapon of its warriors, and "Kush." This region straddles the southern part of the modern nation of Egypt and the northern part of Sudan. Nubia is the only continuously inhabited stretch of territory connecting the lands south of the vast Sahara with North Africa. For thousands of years it has served as a corridor for trade between tropical Africa and the Mediterranean. It also was richly endowed with coveted natural resources—gold, copper, and semiprecious stones like diorite—which it exported.

Nubia's vital intermediary position and natural wealth explain the early rise there of a civilization with a complex political organization, social stratification, metallurgy, monumental building, and writing. Egyptian efforts to secure control of Nubian gold sparked the emergence of this vital and long-lived civilization. Nubia traditionally has been considered a periphery of Egypt and its culture regarded as derivative. Now, however, most scholars emphasize the interactions between Egypt and Nubia and the mutually beneficial borrowings and syntheses that took place.

Early Cultures and Egyptian Domination

The central geographical feature of Nubia, as of Egypt, is the Nile River. In this part of its course the Nile flows through a landscape of rocky desert, grassland, and fertile plain. Water from

Wall painting of Nubians arriving in Egypt with rings and bags of gold   This scene was depicted in the fourteenth-century B.C.E. tomb of an Egyptian chief administrator in Nubia. Drawn by its rich gold deposits, during the New Kingdom Egyptian control extended deep into Nubia. Many Nubians also spent time in Egypt as emissaries, hostages, and soldiers. In this period Egypt exerted great influence on Nubian culture. (Courtesy of the Trustees of the British Museum)

the river was essential for agriculture in a climate that was severely hot and virtually without rainfall. Because of six cataracts—large boulders and threatening rapids—it was not possible for boats to follow the river continuously. Nevertheless, commerce and travel were made possible by boats operating over shorter distances between the cataracts and by tracks for walking and riding alongside the river or across the desert.

In the fourth millennium B.C.E. bands of people in northern Nubia—labeled the "A-Group" by archaeologists—made the transition from seminomadic hunting and gathering to a settled life based on grain agriculture and cattle herding. Peoples migrating into southern Nubia from the western desert around 2300 B.C.E. created the "C-Group" culture along similar lines. Egypt already must have been trading with Nubia before 3000 B.C.E., for Egyptian craftsmen of that period were working in ivory and in dark ebony wood—products of tropical Africa that had to come through Nubia.

Nubia first enters the historical record around 2300 B.C.E., in Old Kingdom Egyptian accounts of trade missions dispatched to southern lands. At that time Aswan, just north of the First Cataract, was the southern limit of Egyptian control. Egyptian noblemen stationed there led donkey caravans south in search of gold, incense, ebony, ivory, slaves, and exotic animals from tropical Africa. This was dangerous work, requiring delicate negotiations with local Nubian chiefs in order to secure protection, but it brought substantial rewards to those who succeeded. The following account was left by Harkhuf, who made several voyages south around 2250:

His majesty sent me a second time alone; I went forth upon the Elephantine road, and I descended . . . an affair of eight months. When I descended I brought gifts from this country in very great quantity. Never before was the like brought to this land. . . . Never had any companion or caravan-conductor who went forth to Yam before this, done (it). . . . His majesty now sent me a third time to Yam; I went forth. . . . and I found the chief of Yam going to the land of Temeh to smite Temeh. . . . I went forth after him . . . and I pacified him, until he praised all the gods for the king's sake. . . . I descended with 300 asses laden with incense, ebony, heknu, grain, panthers, ivory (throw sticks) and every good product. [Yam and Temeh were regions in Nubia.][1]

During the Middle Kingdom (ca. 2040–1640 B.C.E.) Egypt adopted a more aggressive stance toward Nubia. Egyptian rulers were eager to secure direct control of the gold mines located in the desert east of the Nile and to cut out the Nubian middlemen who drove up the cost of luxury goods from the tropics. The Egyptians erected a string of mud-brick forts on islands and riverbanks south of the Second Cataract. These forts and the garrisons residing within them protected the southern frontier of Egypt against Nubians and desert raiders and regulated the flow of commerce. There seem to have been peaceable relations but little interaction between the occupying Egyptian forces and the native population of northern Nubia, which continued to practice its age-old farming and herding ways.

Farther south, where the Nile makes a great U-shaped turn in the fertile plain of the Dongola Reach, a more complex political entity was evolving from the chiefdoms of the third millennium B.C.E. The Egyptians gave the name "Kush" to the kingdom whose capital was located at Kerma, one of the earliest urbanized centers in tropical Africa. The kings of Kush mustered and organized the labor to build monumental walls and structures of mud brick, and they were accompanied to the grave by dozens or even hundreds of servants and wives. These human sacrifices as well as the rich objects found in the tombs prove the wealth and power of the kings and suggest a belief in some sort of afterlife where attendants and possessions would be useful. Kushite craftsmen were skilled in metalworking, whether for weapons or jewelry, and their pottery surpassed in skill and beauty anything produced in Egypt.

During the expansionist New Kingdom (ca. 1532–1070 B.C.E.) the Egyptians penetrated even more deeply into Nubia. They destroyed the kingdom of Kush and its capital at Kerma, and they extended their frontier to the Fourth Cataract. The Egyptians built a new administrative center at Napata, near Gebel Barkal, "the Holy Mountain," believed to be the abode of a local god. A high-ranking Egyptian official called "Overseer of Southern Lands" or "King's Son of Kush" ruled Nubia. In an era of intense commerce among the states of the Middle East, when everyone was looking to Egypt as the prime source of gold, Egypt extensively exploited the mines of Nubia at considerable human cost. Fatalities were high among native workers in the brutal desert climate, and the army had to ward off attacks from the desert tribes.

Five hundred years of Egyptian domination in Nubia left many marks. The Egyptian government imposed Egyptian culture on the native population. The children of high-ranking natives were brought to the Egyptian royal court, simultaneously serving as hostages to ensure the good behavior of their families back in Nubia and absorbing Egyptian language, culture, and religion, which they later carried home with them. Many Nubians went north to serve as archers in the Egyptian armed forces. The manufactured goods that they brought back to Nubia have been found in their graves. The Nubians built towns on the Egyptian model and erected stone temples to Egyptian gods, particularly Amon. The frequent depiction of Amon with the head of a ram, however, may reflect a blending of the chief Egyptian god with a Nubian ram deity.

The Kingdom of Meroë

Egyptian weakness after 1200 B.C.E. led to the collapse of Egypt's authority in Nubia (see below). In the eighth century B.C.E. a powerful new native kingdom emerged in southern Nubia. The story of this civilization, which lasted for over a thousand years, can be divided into two parts. During the early period, between the eighth and fourth centuries B.C.E., Napata, the former Egyptian headquarters, was the primary center. During the later period, from the fourth century B.C.E. to the fourth century C.E., the center of gravity shifted farther south to the site of Meroë, near the Sixth Cataract.

For half a century, from around 712 to 660 B.C.E., the kings of Nubia ruled all of Egypt as the Twenty-fifth Dynasty. They conducted themselves in the age-old manner of Egyptian rulers. They were addressed by the royal titles, depicted in traditional costume, and buried according to Egyptian custom. However, they kept their Nubian names and were depicted with Nubian physical features. They inaugurated an artistic and cultural renaissance, building on a monumental scale for the first time in centuries and reinvigorating Egyptian art, architecture, and religion by drawing selectively on practices and motifs of various periods. In this period each Nubian king resided at Memphis, the Old Kingdom capital. Thebes, the capital of the New Kingdom, was the residence of a female member of the king's family who remained celibate and was titled "God's Wife of Amon."

The Nubian dynasty overextended itself beginning in 701 B.C.E. by assisting local rulers in Palestine in their resistance to the Assyrian Empire. The Assyrians retaliated by invading Egypt and driving the Nubian monarchs back to their southern domain by 660 B.C.E. Napata again became the chief royal residence and the religious center of the kingdom, and Egyptian cultural influences remained strong. Egyptian hieroglyphs were the medium of written communication. Pyramids of modest size made of sandstone blocks were erected over the subterranean burial chambers of royalty. Royal bodies were mummified and the tombs filled with *shawabtis*, human figurines intended to play the role of servants in the next life.

By the fourth century B.C.E. the center of gravity had shifted south to Meroë, perhaps because Meroë was better situated for both agriculture

Temple of the lion-headed god Apedemak at Naqa in Nubia, first century C.E. Queen Amanitore (right) and her husband, Natakamani, are shown here slaying their enemies. While the architectural forms are Egyptian, the deity is Nubian. The costumes of the monarchs and the important role of the queen also reflect the trend in the Meroitic era to draw upon sub-Saharan culture practices. (P. L. Shinnie)

and trade, the economic mainstays of the Nubian kingdom. One consequence was a movement in cultural patterns away from Egypt and toward sub-Saharan Africa. A clear sign is the abandonment of Egyptian hieroglyphs and the adoption of a new set of symbols to write the Meroitic language. This form of writing is still essentially undeciphered. People continued to worship Amon as well as Isis, an Egyptian goddess connected to fertility and sexuality. But those deities had to share the stage with Nubian deities like the lion-god Apedemak, and elephants had some religious significance. Meroitic art was an eclectic mixture of Egyptian, Greco-Roman, and indigenous traditions.

Women of the royal family played an important role in the Meroitic era, another reflection, perhaps, of the influence of cultural concepts from sub-Saharan Africa. The Nubians employed a matrilineal system in which the king was succeeded by the son of his sister. In a number of cases Nubia was ruled by queens, either by themselves or in partnership with their husbands. Greek, Roman, and biblical sources refer to a queen of Nubia named Candace. However, these sources relate to different times, so "Candace" was most likely a title borne by a succession of rulers rather than a proper name. At least seven of these queens can be dated to the period between 284 B.C.E. and 115 C.E. Few details of their reigns are known, but they played a part in warfare, diplomacy, and the building of great temples and pyramid tombs.

Meroë itself was a huge city for its time, more than a square mile in area, overlooking a fertile stretch of grasslands and dominating a converging set of trade routes. Great reservoirs were dug to catch precious rainfall. The city was a major center for iron smelting (after 1000 B.C.E. iron had replaced bronze as the primary metal for tools and weapons). The Temple of Amon was approached by an avenue of stone rams, and the enclosed "Royal City" was filled with palaces, temples, and administrative buildings. The ruler, who may have been regarded as divine, was assisted by a professional class of officials, priests, and army officers.

Weakened by shifts in the trade routes when profitable commerce with the Roman Empire

was diverted to the Red Sea and to the rising kingdom of Axum (in present-day Ethiopia), Meroë collapsed in the early fourth century C.E. Nomadic tribes from the western desert who had become more mobile because of the advent of the camel in North Africa may have overrun Meroë. In any case, the end of the Meroitic kingdom, and of this phase of civilization in Nubia, was as closely linked to Nubia's role in long-distance commerce as had been its beginning.

THE AEGEAN WORLD

Parallels between the rise of Nubian civilization in the second millennium B.C.E.— sparked by contact with the already ancient civilization of Egypt but striking out on its own path of cultural evolution—and concurrent developments in the lands of the Aegean Sea, a gulf of the eastern Mediterranean, are intriguing. The emergence of the Minoan civilization on the island of Crete and the Mycenaean civilization of Greece is another manifestation of the fertilizing influence of older centers on outlying lands and peoples.

The landscape of southern Greece and the Aegean islands is mostly rocky and arid, with small plains lying between the ranges of hills. The limited arable land is suitable for grains, grapevines, and olive trees. Flocks of sheep and goats graze the slopes. Sharply indented coastlines, natural harbors, and small islands lying virtually within sight of one another made sea travel the fastest and least costly mode of travel and transport. This region is resource-poor, having few deposits of metals and little timber. Those vital commodities, as well as surplus food for a large population, had to be imported from abroad. Thus the facts of geography and the lack of resources drew the inhabitants of the Aegean to the sea and brought them into contact with other peoples.

The Aegean peoples learned from the older, advanced civilizations of Mesopotamia, Syria, and Egypt and joined the diplomatic and economic networks of this "international" age. Indeed, because of their deficiency in important raw materials, the rise, success, and eventual fall of these societies was closely connected to their commercial and political relations with other peoples in the region.

The Minoan Civilization of Crete

Well before 2000 B.C.E. the island of Crete, which forms the southern boundary of the Aegean Sea (see Map 3.4), was the home of the first civilization in Europe to have complex political and social structures and advanced technologies such as were found in western Asia and northeastern Africa. These features include centralized government, monumental building, bronze metallurgy, writing, and recordkeeping. Archaeologists labeled this civilization "Minoan" after Greek legends about King Minos. The King ruled a vast naval empire and kept the monstrous Minotaur—half-man, half-bull—beneath his palace in a mazelike labyrinth built by the ingenious inventor Daedalus. Thus later Greeks recollected a time when Crete was home to many ships and sophisticated technologies.

Little is known about the ethnicity of the Cretans of this period, and their writings still cannot be translated. But archaeology has revealed sprawling palace complexes at the sites of Cnossus, Phaistos, and Mallia, and the distribution of Cretan pottery and other artifacts around the Mediterranean and Middle East testifies to widespread trading connections. The layout and architectural forms of the Minoan palaces, the methods of centralized government, and the system of writing all seem to owe much to the influence of the older civilizations of Egypt, Syria, and Mesopotamia. The absence of identifiable representations of the Cretan ruler, however, contrasts sharply with the grandiose depictions of the king in the Middle East and suggests a different conception of authority.

If small statues of women with elaborate headdresses and serpents trailing around their limbs have been correctly interpreted, we may say that the Cretans apparently worshiped female deities embodying the forces of fertility.

Gold cup with relief image of a young man capturing a wild bull Produced ca. 1500 B.C.E., by an artist from Crete but found in a tomb in southern Greece, this cup testifies both to the wealth of the ruling classes in the Bronze Age civilizations of the Aegean, who acquired precious and utilitarian metals from other parts of the Mediterranean and western Asia, and to the cultural influence of Minoan Crete on the Mycenaean Greeks. The elite seems to have enjoyed such idealized depictions of peasant life in romantic natural landscapes. (National Archaeological Museum Athens/Archaeological Receipts Fund)

Colorful fresco paintings applied to still-wet plaster on the walls of Cretan palaces portray groups of women in frilly, layered skirts enjoying themselves in conversation and observation of rituals or entertainments. We do not know whether pictures of young acrobats vaulting over the horns and back of an onrushing bull show a religious activity or mere sport. Scenes of servants briskly carrying jars and fishermen throwing nets and hooks from their boats suggest a joyful attitude toward work, though this portrayal may say more about the sentimental tastes of the elite classes than about the reality of daily toil for the masses. The stylized depictions of flora and fauna on painted vases—plants with swaying leaves and playful octopuses whose tendrils wind around the surface of the vase—reflect a delight in the beauty and order of the natural world.

Other than Cnossus, all the Cretan palaces, and even houses of the elite and peasant villages in the countryside, were deliberately destroyed

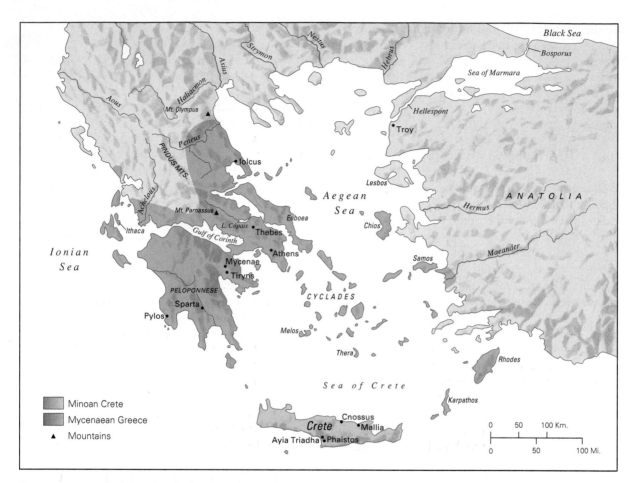

Map 3.4 Minoan and Mycenaean Civilizations of the Aegean   The earliest complex civilizations in Europe arose in the Aegean Sea. The Minoan civilization on the island of Crete evolved in the later third millennium B.C.E., and had a major cultural influence on the Mycenaean Greeks. Palaces decorated with fresco paintings, a centrally controlled economy, and the use of a system of writing for record-keeping are among the most conspicuous features of these societies.

around 1450 B.C.E. Because Mycenaean Greeks took over at Cnossus, most historians regard them as the likely culprits.

The Rise of Mycenaean Civilization

The standard view of Greek origins is that speakers of an Indo-European language ancestral to Greek migrated into the Greek peninsula around 2000 B.C.E., although some scholars argue for a much earlier date. A synthesis—through intermarriage, blending of languages, and melding of religious concepts—must have taken place be-

tween the indigenous population and the newcomers. Out of this mix emerged the first Greek culture. For centuries this society was simple and static. Farmers and shepherds lived in essentially Stone Age conditions, wringing a bare living from the land. Then, sometime around 1600 B.C.E. life on the Greek mainland changed relatively suddenly.

⇨ More than a century ago a German businessman, Heinrich Schliemann, set out to prove the historical veracity of the *Iliad* and the *Odyssey*, two great epics attributed to a poet named Homer, who probably lived shortly before 700 B.C.E. Homer's Greeks were led by Agamemnon, the king of Mycenae in southern Greece. In 1876 Schliemann stunned a skeptical scholarly world by his discovery at Mycenae of a circle of graves at the base of deep, rectangular shafts. These shaft graves, containing the bodies of men, women, and children, were filled with gold jewelry and ornaments, weapons, and utensils. Clearly, some people in this society had acquired a new level of wealth, authority, and the capacity to mobilize human labor. Subsequent excavation at Mycenae uncovered a large palace complex, massive fortification walls, another circle of shaft graves, and other components of a rich and technologically advanced civilization that lasted from around 1600 to 1150 B.C.E.

How is the sudden rise of Mycenae and other centers in mainland Greece to be explained? Greek legends later spoke of the arrival of immigrants from Phoenicia (modern Lebanon) and Egypt, but archaeology provides no confirmation. Another legend recalled the power of King Minos of Crete, who demanded from the Greek city of Athens an annual tribute of ten maidens and ten young men. The Athenian hero Theseus went to Crete, entered the labyrinth, and slew the Minotaur, thereby liberating his people.

Although there is no archaeological evidence for Cretan political control of the Greek mainland, there is much evidence of the powerful cultural influence exerted by Crete. From the Minoans the Mycenaeans borrowed the idea of the palace, the centralized economy, the administrative bureaucracy, and their writing system. Also from the Minoans they learned styles and techniques of architecture, pottery making, and fresco and vase painting. This explains where the Mycenaean Greeks got their technology. But how did they suddenly accumulate power and wealth? Most historians look to the profits from trade and piracy and perhaps also to the pay and booty brought back by mercenaries (soldiers who served for pay in foreign lands).

This first advanced civilization in Greece is called "Mycenaean" largely because Mycenae was the first site excavated. Other centers have been excavated since Schliemann's day—including Tiryns, about 10 miles (16 kilometers) from Mycenae; Pylos, in the southwest; Athens and Thebes in central Greece; and Iolcus in northern Greece.

Mycenae exemplifies the common pattern of these citadels: a commanding location on a hilltop surrounded by high, thick fortification walls made of stones so large that later Greeks believed the giant, one-eyed Cyclopes lifted them into place. Within the fortified perimeter were the palace and administrative complex. The large central hall with an open hearth and columned porch was surrounded by courtyards, by living quarters for the royal family, courtiers, and servants, and by offices, storerooms, and workshops. The palace walls were covered with brightly painted frescoes depicting scenes of war, the hunt, and daily life, as well as decorative motifs from nature. The fortified perimeter served as a place of refuge for the entire community in time of danger.

Nearby lay the tombs of the rulers and other leading families—shaft graves and later, much grander, beehive-shaped tombs made of rings of stone and covered with a mound of earth. Large houses, probably belonging to the aristocracy, lay just outside the walls. The peasants lived on the lower slopes and in the plain below, close to the land that they worked.

Additional information about Mycenaean life is provided by over four thousand baked clay tablets. The writing found on the tablets, today known as "Linear B," uses pictorial signs to represent syllables, like the earlier, still undeciphered system employed on Crete, but it is recognizably an early form of Greek. An unwieldy system of writing, it was probably known only to the palace administrators. These tablets are essentially lists: of chariot wheels piled up in palace storerooms, of rations paid to textile workers, of gifts dedicated to a particular deity, of ships stationed along the coasts. An extensive palace bureaucracy kept track of people, animals, and objects in exhaustive detail and exercised a high degree of control over the economy of the kingdom. Well-organized grain production supported large populations in certain regions, such as the territory controlled by Pylos in the southwest. (Archaeologists can make a rough estimate of population through surface surveys in which they tabulate the number of pieces of broken pottery from a given period that are visible on the ground.)

Certain industries seem to have been state monopolies. For instance, the state controlled the wool industry from raw material to finished product. Scribes kept track of the flocks in the field, the sheared wool, the distribution of raw wool to spinners and weavers, and the production, storage, and disbursal of cloth articles.

The view of this society that modern researchers can extract from the archaeological evidence and from the texts of the tablets is very limited. We know almost nothing about individual personalities—not even the name of a single Mycenaean king—very little about the political and legal systems, social structures, gender relations, and religious beliefs, and nothing about particular historical events and relations with other Mycenaean centers or peoples overseas.

The limited evidence for the overall political organization of Greece in this period is contradictory. In Homer's *Iliad* Agamemnon, the king of Mycenae, is in charge of a great expedition of Greeks from different regions against the city of Troy in northwest Anatolia. To this can be added the cultural uniformity to be found in all the Mycenaean centers: a remarkable similarity in the shapes, decorative styles, and production techniques of buildings, tombs, utensils, tools, clothing, and works of art. Some scholars argue that such cultural uniformity can be understood only within a context of political unity. The plot of the *Iliad*, however, revolves around the difficulties Agamemnon has in asserting control over other Greek leaders, such as the indomitable warrior Achilles. And the archaeological remains and contents of the Linear B tablets give strong indications of independent centers of power at Mycenae, Pylos, and elsewhere. Given this evidence, cultural uniformity might best be explained by extensive contacts and commerce between the various Greek kingdoms.

Overseas Commerce, Settlement, and Aggression

Long-distance contact and trade were made possible by the seafaring skill of Minoans and Mycenaeans. Two sources provide evidence of the appearance and functioning of Aegean vessels:

(1) wall paintings from Egypt and from Thera, an Aegean island, and (2) the excavation of vessels buried in sand at the bottom of the Mediterranean. Freighters depended entirely on wind and sail; the crews of warships could take down the mast and use oars when necessary. In general ancient sailors preferred to keep the land in sight and sail in daylight hours. Their sleek, light, wooden vessels had little decking, so the crew had to go ashore for food and sleep every night. With their low keels the ships could run right up onto the beach.

The wide dispersal of Cretan and Greek pottery and crafted goods indicates that Cretans and Greeks engaged in trade not only within the Aegean but with other parts of the Mediterranean and Middle East. At certain sites, where the quantity and range of artifacts suggest a settlement of Aegean peoples, an interesting pattern is evident. The oldest artifacts are Minoan, then Minoan and Mycenaean objects are found side by side, and eventually Greek wares replace Cretan goods altogether. The physical evidence seems to indicate that Cretan merchants opened up commercial routes and established trading posts in the Mediterranean, then admitted Mycenaean traders to these locations, and were supplanted by the Greeks in the fifteenth century B.C.E.

What commodities formed the basis of this widespread commercial activity? The numerous Aegean pots found throughout the Mediterranean and Middle East must once have contained products such as wine or oil. Other possible exports include weapons and other crafted goods, as well as slaves and mercenary soldiers, which leave no trace in the archaeological record. Minoan and Mycenaean sailors may also have served as middlemen along long-distance trading networks, making a tidy profit by carrying goods from and to other places.

As for imports, amber (a hard, translucent, yellowish-brown fossil resin used for jewelry) from northern Europe and ivory from Syria have been discovered at Aegean sites, and it seems likely that the large population of southwest Greece and other regions necessitated imports of grain. Above all, the Aegean lands needed metals, both the gold so highly prized by the rulers and the copper and tin needed to make bronze.

Fresco from the Aegean island of Thera, ca. 1600 B.C.E. This fresco depicts the arrival of a fleet in a harbor as people watch from the walls of the town. The Minoan civilization of Crete was famous in later legend for its naval power. This picture, originally painted on wet plaster, reveals the appearance and design of ships in the Bronze Age Aegean. The island of Thera was devastated by a massive volcanic explosion in the seventeenth century B.C.E., thought by many to be the origin of the myth of Atlantis sinking beneath the sea. (Archaeological Receipts Fund, Athens)

A number of sunken ships carrying copper ingots recently have been excavated on the floor of the Mediterranean. Scholars believe these ships probably carried metals from the island of Cyprus, in the northeast corner of the Mediterranean, to the Aegean. As in early China, members of the elite classes were virtually the only people who possessed things made of metal, and their near monopoly of metals may have had symbolic significance, working to legitimate their power. The bronze tripods piled up in the storerooms of Homer's heroes bring to mind the bronze vessels buried in Shang tombs.

In an unsettled world, the flip side of trade is piracy. Mycenaeans were tough, warlike, and acquisitive. They traded with those who were strong enough to hold their own and took from those who were too weak to resist. There is reason to believe that they became a thorn in the side of the Hittite kings of the fourteenth and thirteenth centuries B.C.E. A number of documents found in the archives at Hattusha, the Hittite capital, refer to the king and land of "Ahhijawa," most likely a Hittite rendering of *Achaeans*, the term used most frequently by Homer for the Greeks. The documents indicate that relations were sometimes friendly, sometimes strained, and they give the impression that the people of Ahhijawa were aggressive and taking advantage of Hittite preoccupation or weakness. Homer's tale of the ten-year Greek siege and eventual destruction of Troy, a city located on the fringes of Hittite territory and controlling an important commercial route connecting the Mediterranean and Black Seas, should be seen against this backdrop of Mycenaean belligerence and opportunism. Archaeology has confirmed a destruction at Troy around 1200 B.C.E.

THE FALL OF LATE BRONZE AGE CIVILIZATIONS

Hittite difficulties with Ahhijawa and the Greek attack on Troy foreshadow the troubles that culminated in the destruction of many of the old centers of the Middle East and Mediterranean around 1200 B.C.E. This was a momentous period in human history when, for reasons that historians do not completely understand, large numbers of people were on the move. As migrants or invaders swarmed into one region, they displaced other peoples, who then became part of the tide of refugees.

Around 1200 B.C.E. invaders from the north destroyed Hattusha, and the Hittite kingdom came crashing down (see Map 3.3). The tide of destruction moved south into Syria, and the great coastal city of Ugarit was swept away. Egypt managed to beat back two attacks. Around 1220 B.C.E., Pharaoh Merneptah, the son and successor of Ramesses II, repulsed an assault on the Nile Delta by "Libyans and Northerners coming from all lands," and about thirty years later Ramesses III checked a major invasion of "Peoples of the Sea" in Palestine. The Egyptian pharaoh claimed to have won a great victory, but the Philistines occupied the coast of Palestine. Egypt survived, barely, but gave up its territories in Syria-Palestine and lost contact with the rest of western Asia. The Egyptians also lost their foothold in Nubia, opening the way for the emergence of the native kingdom centered on Napata.

Among the invaders listed in the Egyptian inscriptions are the Ekwesh, a group that could be Achaeans—that is, Greeks. In this time of troubles it is easy to imagine opportunistic Mycenaeans taking a prominent role. Whether or not the Mycenaeans participated in the destructions elsewhere, in the first half of the twelfth century B.C.E. their own centers collapsed. The rulers apparently had seen trouble coming, for at some sites they began to build more extensive fortifications, and they took steps to guarantee the water supply of the citadels. But their efforts were in vain, and virtually all the palaces were destroyed. The Linear B tablets survived only because they were baked hard like pottery in the fires that consumed the palaces.

Scholars used to attribute the Mycenaean destruction to foreign invaders, but the archaeological record contains no trace of outsiders, and later Greek legends portrayed this as a time of internal dynastic struggles and wars between rival Greek kingdoms. A compelling explanation has been advanced that combines external and internal factors, since it is likely to be more than coincidence that the collapse of Mycenaean civilization occurred at roughly the same time as the fall of other great civilizations in the region. If the ruling class in the Mycenaean centers depended for their wealth and power on the import of vital commodities and the profits from trade, then the annihilation of major trading partners and disruption of trade routes would have weakened their position. Competition for limited resources may have led to the growth of internal unrest and, ultimately, political collapse.

The end of Mycenaean civilization illustrates the degree to which the major centers of the Late Bronze Age were interdependent. It also serves as a case study of the consequences of political and economic collapse. The destruction of the palaces meant the end of the political and economic domination of the ruling class. The massive administrative apparatus revealed in the Linear B tablets disappeared, and the technique of writing was forgotten, having no function outside the context of palace administration. People were displaced and on the move. Surface studies in various parts of Greece indicate depopulation in some regions and an inflow of people to other regions that had escaped the destruction. The Greek language, however, persisted, and a thousand years later people were still worshiping certain gods mentioned in the Linear B tablets. There was also continuity in material culture: people continued to make and use the vessels and implements that they were familiar with. But this society was much poorer, and there was a marked decline in artistic and technical skill. Different regions developed local shapes, styles, and techniques. This change from the uniformity of the Mycenaean Age was a consequence of the isolation of different parts of Greece from one another in this period of limited travel and communication.

Thus perished the cosmopolitan world of the Late Bronze Age in the Mediterranean and Middle East. The fragile infrastructure of civilization was shattered by a combination of external violence and internal weaknesses. Societies that had become interdependent through complex links of trade, diplomacy, and shared technologies, and had long prospered together, now fell together into a "Dark Age"—a period of poverty, isolation, and loss of knowledge—that lasted for four centuries. (The advent of the Iron Age and revival of complex and interdependent societies will be taken up for western Asia in Chapter 4, and for the eastern Mediterranean in Chapter 5.)

CONCLUSION

This chapter traces the development of a number of civilizations in Africa, Europe, and Asia in the second and first millennium B.C.E. Just as bronze metallurgy began at different times in different parts of the Eastern Hemisphere (in western Asia around 2500 B.C.E., in East Asia around 2000, in northeastern Africa around 1500), so too did the Bronze Age end at different times in different societies. The transition to iron as the primary metal came around 1000 B.C.E. in the eastern Mediterranean, northeastern Africa, and western Asia, and about five hundred years later in East Asia.

The acquisition of copper and tin to make bronze was a priority of Bronze Age elite classes. To a significant degree, political, military, and economic strategies reflected the demand for this commodity. Bronze was acquired in various ways in different parts of the hemisphere. In early China the state largely controlled the prospecting, mining, refining, alloying, and manufacturing processes. In western Asia long-distance networks of exchange were built up to

Important Events for the Late Bronze Age Civilizations of Western Asia, Northeastern Africa, and Southeastern Europe

1750 B.C.E.	Rise of Kingdom of Kush
1700	Hittites Become Dominant Power in Anatolia
1532	Hyksos Expelled from Egypt
1500	Egyptian Conquest of Nubia
1460	Kassites Assume Control of Southern Mesopotamia
1450	Queen Hatshepsut, Ruler of Egypt, Dispatches Expedition to Punt
1450	Destruction of Minoan Palaces in Crete
1353	Akhenaten Launches "Revolution" in Egypt
1285	Pharaoh Ramesses II Battles Hittites at Kadesh
1200–1150	Destruction of Late Bronze Age Centers in Anatolia and Greece

facilitate the trade in metals. Cities sprang up and achieved great prosperity as a result of their location on trade routes. Commercial crossroads became targets of military and diplomatic activity for the major powers of the time, as, for instance, the Syria-Palestine region was for the Egyptian and Hittite states.

The uses to which bronze was put also varied in different societies. Normally this costly metal was available only to the elite classes. Possession of bronze weapons with their hard, sharp edges enabled the warriors of the Mycenaean and Shang ruling classes, as well as the royal armies of Egypt and Mesopotamia, to dominate the peasant masses. In the poems of Homer, Greek aristocrats hoard bronze weapons and utensils in their heavy-gated storerooms and give them to one another in rituals of gift exchange that create bonds of friendship and obligation. In Shang China the most important use of bronze was to craft the bronze vessels that played a vital role in the rituals of contact with the spirits of ancestors.

The period from 2200 to 500 B.C.E. saw the rise of complex societies with social stratification, powerful governments, large bureaucracies, strong armies, systems of writing, and impressive technologies of manufacture and monumental building, in China, Iran, Syria-Palestine, Anatolia, Nubia, and the Aegean. Many of these new civilizations learned much from the already ancient centers in Mesopotamia and Egypt. At the same time, the old centers could hardly afford to remain static. In the competitive circumstances of this increasingly interconnected world, new means had to be found to expedite travel, transport, and communication. So, for instance, Akkadian cuneiform writing was used throughout western Asia, even in correspondence between the Egyptian throne and dependent rulers in Syria-Palestine. The use of horses speeded up communication between central governments and their outlying areas and facilitated the projection of power through fearsome squadrons of war chariots.

The interdependence of the societies of the eastern Mediterranean and western Asia promoted prosperity, development, and the spread of ideas and technologies in the Late Bronze Age. Ironically, that interdependence became a source of weakness at the end of the era, during the time of migrations and invasions around 1200 B.C.E. The disruption of trading networks weakened ruling classes accustomed to easy access to metals and other valuable commodities, and the attacks of invaders and the wanderings of displaced peoples brought down swollen bureaucracies.

In East Asia at roughly the same time there was no "fall," because China was far away and not tightly linked by trade relations to the eastern Mediterranean and western Asia. The Zhou replaced the Shang, but there was much continuity in political, religious, and cultural traditions. In contrast, in the eastern Mediterranean and western Asia the destruction was so great that the old centers did not survive or were severely weakened, and this part of the world entered a Dark Age. Within a few centuries new peoples

would come to the fore—in particular the Assyrians, Phoenicians, and Hebrews, whose story unfolds in the next chapter.

SUGGESTED READING

Caroline Blunden and Mark Elvin, *Cultural Atlas of China* (1983), contains general geographic, ethnographic, and historical information about China through the ages, as well as many maps and illustrations. Conrad Schirokauer, *A Brief History of Chinese Civilization* (1991), and John King Fairbank, *China: A New History* (1992), offer useful chapters on early China. John Hay, *Ancient China* (1973), and Kwang-chih Chang, *The Archaeology of Ancient China*, 4th ed. (1986), go into greater depth and emphasize archaeological evidence. W. Thomas Chase, *Ancient Chinese Bronze Art: Casting the Precious Sacral Vessel* (1991), contains a brief but useful discussion of the importance of bronzes in ancient China, as well as a detailed discussion of bronze-casting techniques. Robert Temple, *The Genius of China: 3,000 Years of Science, Discovery, and Invention* (1986), explores many aspects of Chinese technology, using a division into general topics such as agriculture, engineering, and medicine. Sharon L. Sievers, in *Restoring Women to History* (1988), and Patricia Ebrey, "Women, Marriage, and the Family in Chinese History," in *Heritage of China: Contemporary Perspectives on Chinese Civilization*, ed. Paul S. Ropp (1990), address the very limited evidence for women in early China.

Many of the books recommended in the Suggested Reading list for Chapter 2 are useful for Mesopotamia, Syria, and Egypt in the Late Bronze Age. In addition see Miriam Lichtheim, *Ancient Egyptian Literature: A Book of Readings, Vol. 2, The New Kingdom* (1973); Donald B. Redford, *Egypt, Canaan, and Israel in Ancient Times* (1992), which explores the relations of Egypt with the Syria-Palestine region in this period; and H. W. F. Saggs, *Babylonians* (1995), which devotes several chapters to this more thinly documented epoch in the history of southern Mesopotamia. On the Hittites see O. R. Gurney, *The Hittites*, 2d ed., rev. (1990), and J. G. Macqueen, *The Hittites and Their Contemporaries in Asia Minor* (1975). Tamsyn Barton, *Ancient Astrology* (1994), devotes her first chapter to early manifestations of astrology in Mesopotamia and Egypt.

After a long period of scholarly neglect—with an occasional exception such as Bruce G. Trigger, *Nubia Under the Pharaohs* (1976)—the study of ancient Nubia is beginning to receive considerable attention. David O'Connor, *Ancient Nubia: Egypt's Rival in Africa* (1993); Joyce L. Haynes, *Nubia: Ancient Kingdoms of Africa* (1992); Karl-Heinz Priese, *The Gold of Meroë* (1993)—all reflect the new interest of major museums in the art and artifacts of this society, as does John H. Taylor, *Egypt and Nubia* (1991), which also emphasizes the fruitful interaction of the Egyptian and Nubian cultures.

R. A. Higgins, *The Archaeology of Minoan Crete* (1973), O. Krzysz Kowska and L. Nixon, *Minoan Society* (1983), and N. Marinatos, *Minoan Religion* (1993), examine the archaeological evidence for the Minoan civilization. The brief discussion of M. I. Finley, *Early Greece: The Bronze and Archaic Ages* (1970), and the much fuller accounts of Emily Vermeule, *Greece in the Bronze Age* (1972), and J. T. Hooker, *Mycenaean Greece* (1976), are still useful treatments of Mycenaean Greece, based primarily on archaeological evidence.

For the evidence of the Linear B tablets see John Chadwick, *Linear B and Related Scripts* (1987) and *The Mycenaean World* (1976). J. V. Luce, *Homer and the Heroic Age* (1975), and Carol G. Thomas, *Myth Becomes History: Pre-Classical Greece* (1993), examine the usefulness of the Homeric poems for reconstructing the Greek past. For the disruptions and destructions of the Late Bronze Age in the eastern Mediterranean, see N. K. Sandars, *The Sea Peoples: Warriors of the Ancient Mediterranean* (1978), and Trude Dothan and Moshe Dothan, *People of the Sea: The Search for the Philistines* (1992).

NOTES

1. J. H. Breasted, *Ancient Records of Egypt*, vol. 1 (1906), pp. 153–154.

2. William L. Moran, *The Amarna Letters* (1992), pp. xxx.

PART TWO

The Formation of New Cultural Communities, 1000 B.C.E.–500 C.E.

For a number of reasons, the fifteen centuries from 1000 B.C.E. to 500 C.E. may be seen as a new chapter in the story of humanity, involving a vast expansion in the scale of human institutions and activities. First, new ethnic groups—Assyrians in northern Mesopotamia and Iranians in the high plateau to the east, Israelites at the crossroads between Asia and Africa, the Phoenicians of Lebanon and their Carthaginian offspring, Greeks and Romans in the Mediterranean, Aryans in India—arose to challenge the primacy of the old centers. These peoples occupied lands watered by rainfall rather than by river-water irrigation. Such environments sustained small farms worked by independent individuals and families, in contrast to the strong central authority and mass mobilization of dependent laborers required by the river-

Technology

Iron metallurgy in western Asia/eastern Mediterranean

Cavalry in Middle East and China

Shipbuilding and navigation (Phoenician, Greek, Indian Ocean, Polynesian)

Road networks, aqueducts, and watermills

Astronomy

Alphabetic system of Phoenicians and Greeks

700 B.C.E.—Hoplite infantry in Greece

700 B.C.E.—Coinage in Anatolia

500 C.E.—Mathematics (zero and place-value system) in India

300 B.C.E.—Horse-collar harness in China

Environment

Rainwater agriculture

Slash-and-burn agriculture in Southeast Asia

Polynesian settlement of Pacific islands

500 B.C.E.—Persian "paradise" (ancestor of Western garden)

valley civilizations. This difference led to new social structures, political traditions, religious institutions, and conceptions of humanity and of the gods.

The political and social traditions of these peoples discouraged exploitation of members of their own community, so elite groups devised new ways of gaining wealth and power. Thus, a second key phenomenon of the period was the formation of empires in which one ethnic group controlled the territory and taxed the surplus wealth of other groups. Technological innovations in metallurgy, military tactics, engineering, transportation, and communications made possible large political entities with diverse populations. Networks of cities connected by well-built roads permitted effective administration of far-flung territories. Greatly expanded trade over long distances brought essential raw materials and luxury goods to the ruling classes and facilitated the spread of new ideas—political ideologies explaining the relationship of individuals to the state and religious ideas promising knowledge and salvation.

Essential to empire formation was a third major development: significant enhancement of old technologies and the development of new ones. In many parts of the world iron replaced bronze as the preferred metal for tools and weapons. Political changes often reflected advances in military technology and tactics. In the Middle East and China soldiers on horseback replaced charioteers. The success of Greek armored infantrymen fighting in tight formations inspired Macedonian (northern Greek) and Roman foot soldiers, who forged empires of unprecedented size. Advances in siege and fortification techniques, ship design, and naval tactics accompanied these developments.

Utilizing new materials and techniques and mobilizing large pools of labor, governments undertook construction projects on unprecedented scales. To move troops, expedite communication, and protect frontier areas, the Roman and Chinese governments built thousands of miles of paved roads, long walls, and chains of forts. The technology of communication also underwent profound change. The development of an alphabetic system by Phoenicians and Greeks removed writing from the control of specialists. New, written literature emerged. Simplified writing systems also made possible the extensive

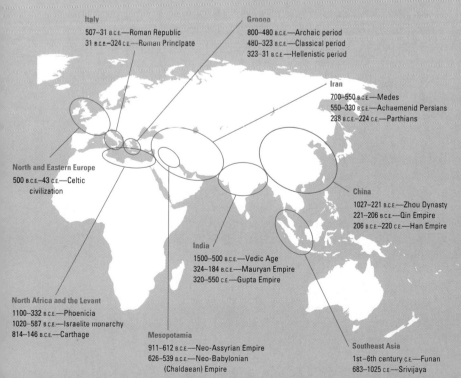

Italy
507–31 B.C.E.—Roman Republic
31 B.C.E.–324 C.E.—Roman Principate

Greece
800–480 B.C.E.—Archaic period
480–323 B.C.E.—Classical period
323–31 B.C.E.—Hellenistic period

Iran
700–550 B.C.E.—Medes
550–330 B.C.E.—Achaemenid Persians
238 B.C.E.–224 C.E.—Parthians

North and Eastern Europe
500 B.C.E.–43 C.E.—Celtic civilization

China
1027–221 B.C.E.—Zhou Dynasty
221–206 B.C.E.—Qin Empire
206 B.C.E.–220 C.E.—Han Empire

India
1500–500 B.C.E.—Vedic Age
324–184 B.C.E.—Mauryan Empire
320–550 C.E.—Gupta Empire

North Africa and the Levant
1100–332 B.C.E.—Phoenicia
1020–587 B.C.E.—Israelite monarchy
814–146 B.C.E.—Carthage

Mesopotamia
911–612 B.C.E.—Neo-Assyrian Empire
626–539 B.C.E.—Neo-Babylonian (Chaldaean) Empire

Southeast Asia
1st–6th century C.E.—Funan
683–1025 C.E.—Srivijaya

Society

Empire formation

Emergence of city-state

Urbanization and expanded trade

Slave-based economies

ca. 450 B.C.E.—Democracy and jury system in Greece

Culture

Astrology and geomancy

Wider literacy

New belief systems (Judaism, Christianity, Hinduism, Buddhism, Confucianism)

New literary forms (epic, drama, lyric poetry)

Libraries founded

Diffusion of imperial cultures (Greek, Roman, Chinese)

Scientific thought (from 600 B.C.E.) and historical writing (from 450 B.C.E.) in Greece

record keeping so important to the survival of large empires such as those of the Romans and Chinese, as well as new kinds of propaganda to bolster the position of the ruling classes.

Fourth, this period saw the emergence of cities with populations in the hundreds of thousands or more—Alexandria in Egypt, Rome in Italy, Chang'an in China, Pataliputra in India. Imperial capitals dotted with palaces, temples, monuments, storehouses, market centers, and places for public entertainment advertised the glory and power of the rulers, while stretching to the limit the capacities of ancient technology to carry water into crowded urban centers and carry sewage away. These giants were but the most extreme products of a process of urbanization that brought into being many smaller cities and towns. Most people, however, lived in the countryside and labored on the land. Without the agricultural surplus that the farming population was able to produce, city dwellers would not have been able to engage in specialized tasks of manufacture, trade, and services on such a large scale.

Fifth, trade took on a new character. The land and sea routes that expedited imperial control also became the highways by which long-distance trade expanded. Like writing, commerce was no longer the exclusive preserve of elite groups; emerging middle classes also sought imported goods. The advent of coinage in the first millennium B.C.E. further stimulated local and regional economies, making it easier for people to store wealth and facilitating exchanges.

The routes used for trade also carried ideas. Religious beliefs different from the largely localized cults of earlier times sprang up. Mystery religions that promised salvation after death and religions that taught belief in one universal god and demanded high ethical standards had broad appeal. The Zoroastrian religion of the Persians, one of the great ethical creeds of the ancient world, spread during the period of Persian rule and may have exerted considerable influence on Judaism. Jews dispersed far beyond their home-

land, paving the way for the spread of Christianity, itself an offshoot of Judaism. Hinduism evolved to become a cultural force unifying many political, social, and ethnic divisions in South Asia. Buddhism spread from its point of origin in northern India and began to make its way into central, southeast, and east Asia.

Sixth, this era saw dramatic movements of peoples. Members of *dominant* ethnic groups moved from the core area of empires, carrying with them their language, beliefs, technologies, and customs. The attractions of the Greek, Roman, and Chinese cultures, as well as the opportunities those cultures offered to ambitious members of *dominated* populations, led to the creation of large cultural zones in which elite groups participated in a luxurious way of life, while most members of the peasant population of the countryside retained their ancestral languages and cultures. Phoenicians, Greeks, and Italians moved to new homes all over the Mediterranean, attracted by the familiar climate, seasonal rhythms, and plants and animals of the region. Celts spread out from eastern Europe to occupy most of Europe north of the Alps. Aryans moved south and east from the Indus River Valley to occupy the Ganges basin and all but the southern portion of the Indian subcontinent.

In an inversion of this phenomenon, the Assyrians and, to a lesser extent, the Persians carried out forcible relocations of entire populations, usually rebellious groups. They were taken to strategic locations in the heart of the empire, where their labor was utilized to promote agriculture or construct imperial showplaces. The huge inflow of enslaved prisoners-of-war to Italy in the period of Roman expansion similarly altered the ethnic composition of Italy.

The end result of the interaction of these six forces was the creation of large cultural communities, some of them persisting to modern times. In the later second and first millennium B.C.E. in Israel, Greece, Iran, Rome, China, and India, cultural traditions sprang up that directly helped to shape the modern world.

CHAPTER FOUR

The Early Iron Age in Western Eurasia, 1000–300 B.C.E.

Celtic Europe · The First Empire: The Rise of Assyria

Israel · Phoenicia and the Mediterranean

The End of an Era: The Fall of Assyria

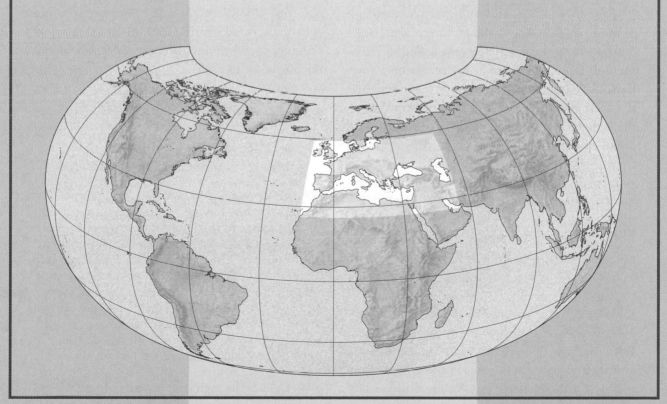

ncient peoples were very interested in the origins of their communities. One famous story concerned the great city of Carthage in present-day Tunisia, which for centuries dominated the waters and commerce of the western Mediterranean. Tradition held that Dido, a member of the royal family of the Phoenician city-state of Tyre in southern Lebanon, fled in 814 B.C.E. with her supporters to the western Mediterranean after her husband had been viciously murdered by her brother, the king of Tyre. Setting ashore on the North African coast, these refugees made friendly contact with the local population, who agreed to give them as much land as a cow's hide could cover. By cleverly cutting the hide into narrow strips, they were able to mark out a substantial piece of territory for their new foundation: Kart Chadasht, or "the New City" (*Carthago* on the tongues of their Roman enemies). At a later time, faithful to the memory of her dead husband, Dido committed suicide rather than marry a local chieftain.

This story evokes an important phenomenon of the Early Iron Age in the Mediterranean lands and western Asia: the migration and resettlement of peoples. For a variety of reasons, large numbers of people relocated during the first half of the first millennium B.C.E. Some populations fled when conquerors occupied their territories. Other conquered peoples were forcibly removed from their ancestral homes. Still others chose to settle in distant lands in response to political and military pressures or in the hope of improving their lot in life.

This chapter examines the history of Europe north of the Alps, western Asia, and North Africa in the Early Iron Age but carries the story farther forward when necessary. The focus is on four societies: the Celtic peoples of Europe; the Assyrians of northern Mesopotamia; the Israelites of Israel; and the Phoenicians of Lebanon and Syria and their colonies in the western Mediterranean, mainly Carthage. After the decline or demise of the ancient centers dominant throughout the third and second millennia B.C.E., these four societies evolved into new political, cultural, and commercial centers.

Of primary concern are the causes, means, and consequences of large-scale movements of people. But this chapter also focuses on how these societies developed different forms of political, social, and economic organization. In Celtic Western Europe an elite class of warriors and priests, operating out of hilltop fortresses, were the leaders of society. Under the direction of a powerful centralized monarchy, the Assyrians forged the first real empire in world history. The Israelites evolved from seminomadic herders belonging to a set of loosely federated tribes to settled agriculturalists in a small monarchic state in which the priests of their god Yahweh wielded considerable power and influence. The Phoenicians inhabited a string of autonomous city-states in which the leading merchant families, in concert with the monarch, played a dominant role. The Assyrian Empire eventually ruled nearly all of western Asia, thus bringing together the histories of Mesopotamia, Phoenicia, and Israel.

CELTIC EUROPE

To this point we have taken little note of Europe except for the emergence on its southeast fringe of the Late Bronze Age cultures of Crete and Greece (see Chapter 3). Humans had been living in Europe for a very long time (see Chapter 1), but the lack of any system of writing severely limits our knowledge of the earliest Europeans. Around 500 B.C.E. Celtic peoples spread across a substantial portion of Europe and, by coming into contact with the literate societies of the Mediterranean, entered the historical record.

Our main source of information about the early Celts is the archaeological record, which re-

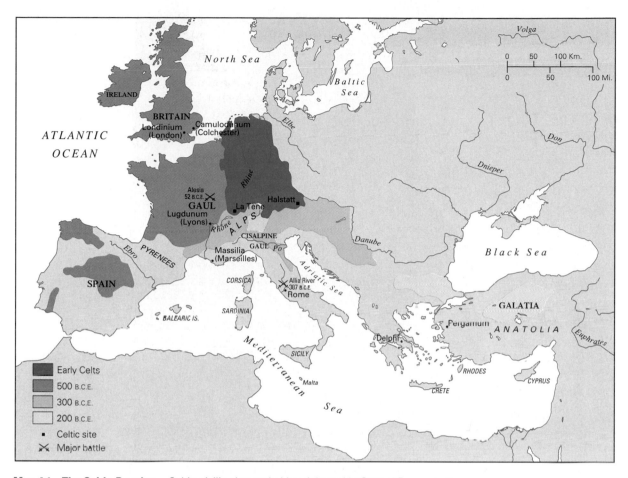

Map 4.1 The Celtic Peoples   Celtic civilization probably originated in Central Europe in the early part of the first millennium B.C.E. Around 500 B.C.E. Celtic peoples began to migrate, making Celtic civilization the dominant cultural style in Europe north of the Alps. The Celts' interactions with the peoples of the Mediterranean, including Greeks and Romans, encompassed both wars and trade.

veals a lot about the objects they made and used and the spaces in which they lived. The accounts of Greek and Roman travelers and conquerors also provide information about political and social organization, religion, and some historical personalities and events, although those outside observers sometimes may have been misinformed or biased. Another useful source is Celtic literature from Wales and Ireland that was written down centuries later during the European Middle Ages, and though colored by the Christianity of that era, probably descends from earlier oral traditions preserved by the bards, specialists who composed and transmitted stories of the legendary past.

The Spread of the Celts

The term *Celtic* is a linguistic designation referring to a branch of the Indo-European family of languages. Archaeologists link this language group to two cultural complexes, each named after an important site: (1) Hallstatt, in present-day Austria, which began in the eighth century B.C.E., and (2) La Tène, in Switzerland, dating from the fifth century B.C.E. Celtic civilization originated in Central Europe, in parts of present-day Germany, Austria, and the Czech Republic, in the early first millennium B.C.E. (see Map 4.1). The early Celts lived in or near hill forts—lofty

A Celtic hill fort in England   Such fortresses, of which hundreds have been found across Europe, served a variety of purposes: as centers of administration, gathering points for Celtic armies, manufacturing centers, storage depots for food and trade goods, and places of refuge. The natural defenses of a hill could be improved, as here, with elaborate sequences of ditches and earthwork walls. Particularly effective was the so-called "Gallic Wall," which combined earth, stone, and timber to create both strength and enough flexibility to absorb the pounding from siege engines. (Royal Commission for Historic Monuments)

natural locations made even more defensible by earthwork fortifications. Elite members of Celtic society were buried in wagons filled with extensive grave goods, suggesting belief in some sort of afterlife. By 500 B.C.E. these elites were trading with the Mediterranean lands, seeking crafted goods and wine. The contact may have stimulated the new styles of manufacture and art that launched the La Tène period.

The development of those new features coincides with a rapid expansion of Celtic groups in several directions. Moving to the west, Celtic groups occupied virtually all of France, much of Britain, and Ireland, and Celts and indigenous peoples merged to create the Celtiberian culture of northern Spain. Celts also migrated east and south. They overran northern Italy in the fifth century B.C.E. They made destructive raids into central Greece, and one group—Galatians—settled in central Anatolia (modern Turkey). By 300 B.C.E. Celtic peoples were spread across Europe north of the Alps, from present-day Hungary to Spain and Ireland. Their traces remain in the names of many places: rivers (Danube,

Rhine, Seine, Thames, and Shannon); countries (Belgium); regions (Bohemia, Aquitaine), and towns (Paris, Bologna, Leiden). They shared elements of language and culture, but there was no Celtic "state," for they were grouped into hundreds of small, loosely organized kinship groups.

Greeks and Romans were struck by the physical appearance of male Celts—their burly size, long red hair (which they often made stiff and upright by applying a cementlike solution of lime), shaggy mustaches, and loud, deep voices—as well as by their strange apparel—pants (usually an indication of horse-riding peoples) and twisted gold collars around their necks. Particularly terrifying were the warriors who fought naked and eagerly made trophies of the heads of defeated enemies. Their Mediterranean neighbors characterized the Celts as wildly fond of war, courageous, childishly impulsive and emotional, overly fond of boasting and exaggeration, yet quick-witted and eager to learn.

Celtic Society

Our greatest source of information about Celtic social and political organization is the Roman military commander Gaius Julius Caesar, who composed a detailed account of his eight-year conquest of Gaul (present-day France) between 58 and 51 B.C.E. Many of the Celtic groups in Gaul had been ruled by kings at an earlier time, but by about 60 B.C.E. they periodically chose public officials, perhaps under Greek and Roman influence.

Celtic society was divided into an elite class of warriors, professional groups of priests and bards, and the largest group of all: the common people. The warriors owned land and flocks of cattle and sheep and monopolized both wealth and power. The common people labored on their land. The warriors of Welsh and Irish legend reflect a stage of political and social development less complex than that of the Celts whom the Romans encountered in France. They bring to mind the heroes of Homer's *Iliad* and *Odyssey* (see Chapter 3), and the Indian *Mahabharata* (Chapter 7), raiding one another's flocks, reveling in

drunken feasts, and engaging in impromptu contests of strength and wit. At a banquet the bravest warrior could help himself to the choicest part of the animal, the "hero's portion," and men would fight to the death to win this privilege.

The priests, called Druids, belonged to a well-organized fraternity. Trainees received their knowledge of prayers, rituals, legal precedents, and traditions through a long program of memorization. The Druids were the teachers of Celtic society as well as the religious leaders. The priesthood was the one Celtic institution that crossed tribal lines. Sometimes the Druids were able to head off warfare between feuding groups, and they served as judges in cases that involved Celts from more than one group. In the first century C.E. the Roman government methodically set about stamping out the Druids, probably because of concern that they might serve as a rallying point for Celtic opposition to Roman rule, rather than because of their alleged involvement in bloody human sacrifices and forms of divination repugnant to Roman sensibilities.

Celtic women engaged primarily in child rearing, food production, and some crafts. Although they did not have true equality with men, their situation was superior to that of women in the Middle East or in the Greek and Roman Mediterranean. Marriage was a partnership to which both parties contributed property, and each party had the right to inherit the estate if the other died. Celtic women also had greater freedom in their sexual relations than did their southern counterparts.

Greek and Roman sources depict Celtic women as strong and proud. This portrayal corresponds to the representation of women in Welsh and Irish tales, where self-confident wives sit at banquet with their husbands, engage in witty conversation, and often provide ingenious solutions to vexing problems. Although women were not regular combatants, they might be present in the vicinity of the battlefield, and they would defend themselves fiercely if cornered.

Some of the Celtic burial chambers that archaeologists have excavated contain rich collections of clothing, jewelry, and furniture for use in the next world, identifying them as the tombs of elite women. Daughters of the elite were married to leading members of other tribes to create alliances. When the Romans invaded Celtic Britain in the first century C.E., they sometimes were opposed by Celtic tribes headed by queens (some experts see this as an abnormal circumstance created by the Roman invasion itself).

Belief and Knowledge

The condescending attitude of Greek and Roman sources gives a misleading impression of Celtic belief and knowledge. Historians know the names of more than four hundred Celtic gods and goddesses. Most of them are associated with particular localities and kinship groups, although certain deities have wider currency. Lug, for example, is the god of light, crafts, and inventions. Some are associated with animals or even depicted with animal features, such as the horse-goddess Epona or the horned god Cernunnos. "The Mothers," a set of three goddesses always depicted together and holding symbols of prosperity, must have played a part in some kind of fertility cult. The traditions of Halloween and May Day preserve the ancient Celtic holidays of Samhain and Beltaine, which took place at key moments in the growing cycle.

The early Celts did not build temples (later Celts learned to do so from the Mediterranean peoples). Instead, they worshiped at special places where they felt the presence of divinity, such as springs, groves, and hilltops. At the sources of the Seine and Marne Rivers, archaeologists have found huge caches of wooden statues thrown into the water by hopeful devotees.

In Irish and Welsh legends the barriers between the natural and supernatural worlds are far more permeable than they are in the mythology of other cultures. Celtic heroes and divinities pass back and forth from one to the other with relative ease, and magical occurrences are commonplace. Celtic priests set forth a doctrine of reincarnation—the rebirth of the soul in a new body.

The Celts were successful agriculturalists, able to support large populations by tilling the heavy but fertile soils of continental Europe. Their metallurgical skills probably surpassed those of the Mediterranean peoples. Celts living on the Atlantic shore of France built solid ships that could withstand ocean waves, winds, and currents. They used the large, navigable rivers as thoroughfares for extensive commerce, and by the first century B.C.E. some of the old hill-forts were evolving into urban centers.

The Roman conquest of many of the Celtic lands—Spain, southern Britain, France, and parts of Central Europe—from the second century B.C.E. to the first century C.E. curtailed the evolution of Celtic society, replacing it with an Italian model. The peoples in these lands were in large part assimilated to Roman ways (see Chapter 6). That is why the inhabitants of modern Spain and France speak languages that are descended from Latin. Germanic invaders from the third century C.E. on all but finished the job, and present-day inhabitants of Britain speak a language with a Germanic base. Only on the western fringes of the European continent—in Brittany (northwest France), Wales, Scotland, and Ireland—did Celtic peoples maintain their language, art, and culture into modern times.

THE FIRST EMPIRE: THE RISE OF ASSYRIA

Far to the south and east of the Celtic lands of continental Europe, the peoples of western Asia also were experiencing momentous changes in the first millennium B.C.E. The chief force for change was the rise of the powerful and aggressive Neo-Assyrian Empire. Although historians sometimes apply the term *empire* to earlier regional powers—such as the Akkadian state ruled by Sargon, the Babylonian kingdom of Hammurabi, and the expansionist New Kingdom in Egypt—the Assyrians of the early first millennium B.C.E. were the first to rule over far-flung lands and diverse peoples (see Map 4.2).

As we saw in Chapter 3, the Assyrian homeland in northern Mesopotamia differs in essential respects from the flat expanse of Sumer and Akkad to the south—hillier, more temperate in climate, with greater rainfall, and more exposed to raiders from the mountains to the east and north and from the arid steppe and desert to the west. Sturdy peasant farmers, accustomed to defending themselves against marauders, provided the military base for a revival of Assyrian power in the ninth century B.C.E. The rulers of the Neo-Assyrian Empire (911–612 B.C.E.) struck out in a ceaseless series of campaigns: westward across the steppe and desert as far as the Mediterranean, north into mountainous Urartu (modern Armenia), east across the Zagros range onto the Iranian plateau, and south along the Tigris River to Babylonia.

It is no accident that these tracks largely coincided with the most important long-distance trade routes in western Asia. These campaigns provided immediate booty and the prospect of tribute and taxes. They also guaranteed access to vital resources such as iron and silver and brought the Assyrians control of profitable international commerce.

What started out as an aggressive program of self-defense soon took on a far more ambitious agenda. Driven by pride, greed, and religious conviction, the Assyrians defeated all the rival great kingdoms of the day—Elam (southwest Iran), Urartu, Babylon, and Egypt. At its peak their empire stretched from Anatolia, Syria-Palestine, and Egypt in the west, across Armenia and Mesopotamia, as far as western Iran. In the end the Assyrians created a new kind of empire, larger in extent than anything seen before and dedicated to the enrichment of the imperial center at the expense of the subjugated periphery.

God and King

The king was both literally and symbolically the center of the Assyrian universe. Technically all the land belonged to him, and all the people—even the highest-ranking officials—were his "servants." Assyrians believed that the gods chose the king to rule as their earthly representative and instrument. Normally the sitting king chose one of his sons to be his successor, and the choice was confirmed both by divine oracles and by the Assyrian elite. The crown prince lived in the "House of Succession," where he was trained

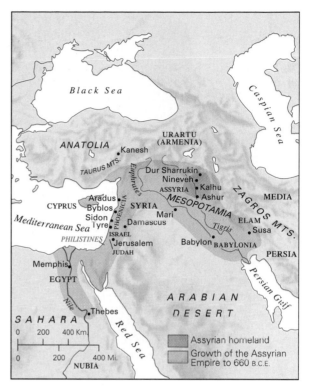

Map 4.2 The Assyrian Empire From the tenth to the seventh century B.C.E. the Assyrians of northern Mesopotamia created the largest empire the world had yet seen, extending from the Iranian plateau to the eastern shore of the Mediterranean and containing an array of peoples.

in the duties of the monarch and gradually given administrative and military responsibilities. In the ancient capital city of Ashur the high priest anointed the new king by sprinkling his head with oil and gave him insignia of kingship; a crown and scepter. The kings were buried in Ashur.

The duties of the king were enormous. Every day he received information carried by messengers and spies from all corners of the empire. He made decisions, appointed officials, heard complaints, corresponded with subordinates by dictating his wishes to an army of scribes, and received and entertained foreign envoys and high-ranking government figures. He was the military leader, responsible for the strategic planning of campaigns and often on tour inspecting the troops and commanding important operations. (Shalmaneser, who reigned from 858 to 824

Stone statue of Ashurnasirpal II, the ninth century B.C.E. **Assyrian king** This statue was found in a temple at Kalhu, the new royal capital which Ashurnasirpal built to advertise his greatness to contemporaries and posterity. Assyrian kings had themselves depicted in various guises. Here the scepter and flail in the king's hands are symbols of royal power, while the shawl indicates his role as a high priest. (Courtesy of the Trustees of the British Museum)

B.C.E., led his army in battle in thirty-one of the thirty-five years of his reign.) Hunting, the Assyrian kings' passion, whether shooting a bow from a chariot or stalking lions in a private preserve, was both recreation and preparation for the rigors of war.

Among the king's chief responsibilities was to fulfill his role as head of the state religion. He devoted much of his time to elaborate public and private rituals as well as to overseeing the upkeep of the temples. The king made no decisions of state without first consulting and gaining the approval of the gods through elaborate rituals of divination. All the decisions made by the king and central government were carried out under the banner of Ashur, the chief god, and were justified as being in accordance with Ashur's wishes. All victories were cited as proof of Ashur's superiority over the gods of the conquered peoples.

A relentless tide of government propaganda secured the acquiescence and participation of the Assyrian people in military campaigns that mostly benefited and enriched the king and nobility. Assyrian priests revised the Babylonian Creation Myth (see Chapter 2), replacing Marduk with Ashur as king of the gods, victor over the forces of evil and chaos, and creator of the world in its present form. Royal inscriptions cataloging the accomplishments of recent campaigns and harping on the power of Assyrian arms, the charisma and relentless will of the king, the backing of the all-powerful gods, and the ruthless punishments that would be given to those who resisted were put on public display (and presumably read aloud since most people were not literate) throughout the empire.

Art also served the Assyrian state. This use of art as political propaganda was an innovative departure in the ancient Middle East from the almost exclusive dedication of art to the worship of the gods. The walls of the royal palaces at Kalhu and Nineveh were covered with relief sculptures depicting hunts, battles, sieges, executions, and deportations. Looming over most scenes was the king, larger than anyone else, muscular and fierce, having the very visage of the gods. The purpose of these images was to overawe visitors to the court. The private, interior portions of the palace, probably off-limits to all but the royal family and high-ranking courtiers, contained a broader range of subjects, including many scenes of peaceful and pleasant pursuits.

Exploitation and Administration of the Empire

The Assyrians exploited to the maximum the wealth and resources of their subjects. The cost of military campaigns and administration had to be covered by the plunder the victors captured and the tribute they imposed. The wealth of the periphery was funneled to the center, where the king and nobility grew rich. As a result, proud kings seeking to display their magnificence to contemporaries and to leave a grand monument to posterity expanded the ancestral capital and religious center at Ashur and built magnificent new royal cities—Dur Sharrukin, Kalhu, and Nineveh—and adorned them with walls, palaces, and temples. Dur Sharrukin, "the Fortress of Sargon," was completed in a mere ten years, proof of the enormous human resources dedicated to the task. The labor force for these projects was drawn from prisoners of war transferred to the core zone, as well as from Assyrian citizens who owed periodic service to the state.

What made possible the Assyrians' conquest of their extensive and heterogeneous empire? A fundamental factor was their superior military organization and technology. Early Assyrian armies were put together one campaign at a time. They consisted not only of men who were obligated to give military service as part of the terms by which they held grants of land but also of peasants and slaves whose service was contributed by large landowners. Tiglathpileser (r. 744–727 B.C.E.) added a core army of professional soldiers drawn from both Assyrians and the most formidable subject peoples. At its peak the Assyrian state could mobilize a half-million troops, divided into contingents of light-armed bowmen and slingers who launched stone projectiles, spearmen with body armor, cavalry equipped with bow or spear, and four-man chariots.

Iron weapons gave Assyrian soldiers an advantage over opponents, and cavalry provided unprecedented speed and mobility. Assyrian engineers developed machinery and tactics for besieging fortified towns. They dug tunnels under the walls, built mobile towers to put their archers above the height of defenders, and brought up rams to batter weak points. The Assyrians destroyed some of the most ancient and best-fortified cities of the Middle East—Egyptian Thebes, Phoenician Tyre, Elamite Susa, and Babylon. Couriers and signal fires made communication across vast distances possible, and a network of spies gathered intelligence.

The Assyrian state also frequently used terror tactics—swift retribution, harsh punishments, brutal examples—to discourage resistance. The Assyrian state found in the practice of mass deportation—the forcible uprooting of entire communities from their homes in order to transport and resettle them—a means to accomplish a number of objectives simultaneously (see Voices and Visions: Mass Deportation in the Neo-Assyrian Empire). The deployment of deportees was also part of a grand economic strategy to shift human resources from the periphery to the center, where the deportees were employed as mass labor on the estates of king and nobility, to open up additional lands for agriculture, and to build the new palaces and cities. Skilled craftsmen and soldiers among the deportees could be assigned to units of the Assyrian army.

One particularly refined ploy involved exchanging two troublesome populations—that is, settling each people on the land of the other. Both groups were immediately rendered docile and even loyal to the interests of the very state that had removed them because submission was their only protection in an often hostile new environment. In addition to these concrete and immediate aims, the abrupt removal of a community also served as a conspicuous warning to others who might be contemplating resistance.

The need to control their empire posed enormous problems of organization and communication for the Assyrians. They had to contend with vast distances and diverse landscapes within which lived an array of peoples who differed in language, customs, religion, and political organization. Nomadic and sedentary kinship groups,

Wall relief from the Palace at Nineveh, depicting the Assyrian king Sennacherib's forces laying siege to the Israelite town of Lachish (701 B.C.E.) The Assyrians have built ramps, covered with wooden planks, to drag their equipment up close to the walls of the town. A long spear projecting from a tank-like siege machine is dislodging blocks from an enemy tower, while archers fire volleys of arrows to pin down the defenders. At right, we see the outcome of the battle. Prisoners from the captured town are marching into exile carrying but few possessions. (Courtesy of the Trustees of the British Museum)

temple-states, city-states, and, in a few instances, kingdoms composed the Assyrian domain.

Yet the Assyrians never found a single, enduring solution to the problem of how to govern such an empire. Control tended to be tight and effective at the center and in lands closest to the core area, less so as one moved outward. The Assyrian kings waged many campaigns to reimpose control on territories subdued in a previous campaign or reign. In the early days the Assyrians often backed a local ruler or faction willing to collaborate with them, but this arrangement made their position vulnerable whenever local authority changed hands. And some subject states chafing under Assyrian rule sought the protection of Egypt, Elam, or Urartu. As part of his plan to reshape the state apparatus, Tiglath-pileser extended direct Assyrian control over more outlying regions.

Towns and villages were headed by a council of elders who were responsible to a district commander and provincial governor. The primary duties of Assyrian provincial officials were to ensure payment of tribute and taxes, to maintain

Mass Deportation in the Neo-Assyrian Empire

We can gain some insight about the mentality of Assyrian rule by examining one of the most characteristic aspects of Assyrian imperial policy: mass deportation. This practice already had a long history in the ancient Middle East—in Sumer, Babylon, Urartu, Egypt, and the Hittite Empire. But the Neo-Assyrian monarchs employed it on an unprecedented scale. Surviving documents record the relocation of over 1 million people, and historians estimate the true figure exceeds 4 million.

The following entries from a set of inscriptions recording the year-by-year achievements of King Sargon II (r. 721–705 B.C.E.) reveal the fate of the people and territory of the northern Israelite kingdom and of several coastal cities:

[First Year] I besieged and conquered Samaria [the capital of the northern kingdom], led away as booty 27,290 inhabitants of it. I formed from among them a contingent of 50 chariots and made the remaining inhabitants resume their social positions. I installed over them an officer of mine and imposed upon them the tribute of the former king. . . . [Seventh Year] Upon a trust-inspiring oracle given by my lord Ashur, I crushed the tribes of Tamud, Ibadidi, Marsimanu, and Haiapa, the Arabs who live, far away, in the desert [and] who know neither overseers nor officials and who had not yet

brought their tribute to any I deported their survivors and settled them in Samaria. . . . [Eleventh Year] I besieged and conquered the cities Ashdod, Gath, Asdudimmu; I declared his [the ruler of Ashdod's] images, his wife, his children, all the possessions and treasures of his palace as well as the inhabitants of his country as booty. I reorganized the administration of these cities and settled therein people from the regions of the East which I had conquered personally. I installed an officer of mine over them and declared them Assyrian citizens and they pulled the straps of my yoke.

To what uses did the Assyrian government put deportees? What was the legal status of deportees? Looking at the deportations chronicled in Years 1 and 7, do you see any evidence of a master plan for where deportees were resettled? What might have been the emotional impact on deportees of being separated from the familiar environment in which they had grown up?

Source: Excerpt of translation of entries from transcriptions recording the year-by-year achievements of King Sargon II: James B. Pritchard, ed., *The Ancient Near East: An Anthology of Texts and Pictures*, 1958, pp. 195–197. Reprinted with permission of Princeton University Press.

law and order, to raise troops, and to undertake necessary public works. The central government intervened directly in provincial affairs, and local ruling classes and Assyrian provincial governors were subject to frequent inspections by royal overseers.

A large administrative bureaucracy was needed to carry out these multifaceted duties. At the top of the ladder was a group of dignitaries with titles like "commander-in-chief," "great chancellor," and "chief cup-bearer"; they served as advisers to the king and were dispatched on special missions. An army of courtiers, supervisors, scribes, and servants maintained the palace and the various offices of the central government. High-ranking officials had their own courts and estates worked by peasants tied to the land. This

elite class was bound to the monarchy by oaths of obedience, by fear of punishment for misbehavior, and by the expectation of rewards, such as grants of land and a share in booty and taxes, for loyalty and good performance. The support of the class of professionals—priests, diviners, scribes, doctors, and artisans—was also vital to the functioning of the state, and they too were bound to the monarchy by oaths and rewards.

When the ruling class grew too arrogant and abusive, an uprising of the rural nobility and free citizens of Assyria occurred in the late ninth and early eighth centuries B.C.E. This action led to Tiglathpileser's reforms, which strengthened the powers of the king and weakened the old aristocracy by breaking up provinces and administrative offices into numerous small jurisdictions.

Assyrian Society and Culture

The extant sources primarily shed light on the deeds of kings, victories of armies, and workings of government. Nevertheless, a certain amount is known about the lives and activities of the millions of subjects of the Assyrian Empire. In the core area people were assigned to the same three classes that had existed in Hammurabi's Babylon a millennium before (see Chapter 2): (1) free, landowning citizens, (2) farmers and artisans attached to the estates of the king or other rich landholders, and (3) slaves. Slaves—drawn from debtors who had failed to make good and from prisoners of war—had legal rights and, if sufficiently talented, could rise to positions of influence.

The government normally did not distinguish between native Assyrians and the increasingly large number of subjects and deportees residing in the Assyrian homeland. All were referred to as "human beings," entitled to the same legal protections and liable to the same obligations of labor and military service. Over time this inflow of outsiders led to changes in the ethnic makeup of the population of Assyria.

Agriculture constituted the economic foundation of the Assyrian Empire. The vast majority of subjects worked on the land, and the agricultural surpluses that they produced allowed a substantial number of people to engage in specialized activities—including the standing army, government officials, religious experts, merchants, artisans, and all manner of professionals in the towns and cities.

Individual artisans and small workshops in the towns manufactured goods. Most trade took place at the local level and involved foodstuffs and simple crafted goods like pottery, tools, and clothing. The state fostered long-distance trade, for imported luxury goods brought in substantial customs revenues and ultimately found their way into the possession of the royal family and elite classes. These included metals, fine textiles, dyes, gems, and ivory. Silver was the basic medium of exchange, weighed out for each transaction in a time before the invention of coins.

The Assyrian era saw both the preservation of old knowledge and the acquisition of new knowledge. When archaeologists excavated the palace of Ashurbanipal (r. 668–627 B.C.E.), one of the last Assyrian kings, at Nineveh, they discovered more than twenty-five thousand tablets or fragments of tablets. This "Library" contained official documents and an array of literary and scientific texts. Some were originals that had been brought to the capital; others were copies made at the king's request. Ashurbanipal was clearly an avid collector of the literary and scientific heritage of Mesopotamia, and the "House of Knowledge" referred to in some of the documents may have been an academy that attracted learned men to the imperial center. There is also evidence that libraries may have been attached to temples in various Assyrian cities.

Assyrians devoted much effort to the creation and preservation of lists covering all manner of subjects, such as plant and animal names, geographic terms, and astronomical occurrences. Building on the achievements of their Mesopotamian ancestors (see Environment and Technology: Chinese and Mesopotamian Divination, in Chapter 3), the Assyrians continued to make original contributions in mathematics and astronomy. Their assumption that gods or demons caused disease obstructed the investigation of natural causes, but in addition to the specialists whose job was to exorcise the demons thought to be possessing a sick person, another type of physician experimented with medicinal and surgical treatments to relieve symptoms.

The Assyrians preserved many of the achievements of Mesopotamian art, literature, and science, and much of what we know about earlier eras in Mesopotamian history comes to us through discoveries at Assyrian sites. Similarly, the Roman Empire later served as the conduit by which the achievements of Greek civilization were preserved in the West (see Chapter 6).

ISRAEL

On the western edge of the Assyrian Empire, in a land bordering on "the Upper Sea" as the Assyrians called the Mediterranean,

Ancient Textiles and Dyes

Throughout human history the production of textiles—cloth for clothing, blankets, carpets, and coverings of various sorts—may have required an expenditure of human labor second only to the amount of work necessary to provide food. Despite its importance, however, rather little is known about textile production in antiquity because it leaves so few traces in the archaeological record. The plant fibers and animal hair used for cloth are organic and quickly decompose except in rare and special circumstances. Some textile remains have been found in the hot, dry conditions of Egypt and adjacent desert locales, and others have been preserved in ice in the tombs of Siberian nomads and in the peat bogs of northern Europe. Most of our knowledge of ancient textiles, however, depends on the discovery of instruments used in textile production—such as spindles, loom weights, and dyeing vats—and on pictorial representations and descriptions in texts.

The production of cloth has usually been the work of women, for a simple but important reason. Women nearly always have the major responsibility for child rearing because only they can breast-feed the infant, often for several years. This responsibility limits their ability to participate in other activities but does not consume all their time, energy, and productive potential. In many societies textile production has been complementary to child-rearing activities, for it can be done in the home, is relatively safe, does not require great concentration, and can be interrupted and resumed without consequence. For many thousands of years cloth production has been one of the great common experiences of women around the globe.

The growing and harvesting of plants such as cotton or flax (from which linen is made) and the shearing of wool from sheep are outdoor activities, but the subsequent stages of production can be carried out indoors in the household environment. Various technological innovations improved the efficiency and quality of textile production. The basic methods, however, did not change much from early antiquity until the mid-eighteenth century C.E., when the fabrication of textiles was transferred to mills and mass production began.

When textile production has been considered "women's work," most of the output has been for domestic consumption. Men typically have become involved in commercial production, which increases the possibility of significant profit. One of these situations was in ancient Phoenicia, where fine textiles with bright, permanent colors became a major export product. These striking colors were produced by dyes derived from several species of snail: a blue-purple from the banded dye-murex and a red-purple from the spiny dye-murex. Most prized of all, the red-purple was known as Tyrian purple because Tyre was the major source. Robes dyed in this color were worn by Persian and Hellenistic kings, and a white toga with a purple border was the sign of a Roman senator.

The production of Tyrian purple was an exceedingly laborious process. The spiny dye-murex snail lives on the sandy Mediterranean bottom at depths ranging from 30 to 500 feet (10 to 150 meters). Nine thousand snails were needed to produce 1 gram (0.035 ounce) of dye. Particular techniques for the production of the best dyes were, no doubt, secrets carefully guarded by the Phoenician manufacturers. A Roman naturalist of the first century C.E., the elder Pliny, described the process of dye production as it existed in his day. The dye was made from a colorless liquid in the snail's hypobranchial gland. The gland sacs were removed, crushed, soaked with salt, and exposed to sunlight and air for some days; then they were subject to controlled boiling and heating.

Huge mounds of broken shells on the Phoenician coast are testimony to the ancient industry. It is likely that the snail was rendered virtually extinct at many locations, and some scholars have speculated that Phoenician colonization in the Mediterranean may have been motivated in part by the search for new sources of snails. The production of purple cloth in this region began before 1700 B.C.E. and continued until the seventh century C.E., when it fell victim to the destruction accompanying the Muslim conquest of Syria-Palestine.

Clothing of the Bog Body (The National Museum, Copenhagen)

lived a people who probably seemed of no great significance to the masters of western Asia but were destined to play an important role in world history. The history of ancient Israel is marked by two grand and interconnected dramas that played out over more than fifteen hundred years, from around 2000 to 500 B.C.E.: (1) a loose collection of tribes of nomadic herders and caravan drivers became a sedentary, agricultural people, developed complex political and social institutions, and became integrated into the commercial and diplomatic networks of the Middle East; and (2) the austere cult of a desert god evolved into a unique concept of deity and the exacting way of life of the Jewish people. Both the land and the people at the heart of this story have gone by various names: Canaan, Israel, Palestine; Hebrews, Israelites, Jews. For the sake of consistency, the people are referred to here as *Israelites*, the land they occupied in antiquity as *Israel*.

Israel is a crossroads, linking Anatolia, Egypt, Arabia, and Mesopotamia (see Map 4.3). This accident of geography has given the place an importance in history, both ancient and modern, out of all proportion to its size and economic or political potential. Its natural resources are few. The Negev Desert and the vaster wasteland of the Sinai lie to the south. The Mediterranean coastal plain was usually in the hands of others, particularly the Philistines throughout much of the biblical period. At the center are the rock-strewn hills of the Shephelah. Galilee to the north, with its sea of the same name, was a relatively fertile land of grassy hills and small plains. The narrow ribbon of the Jordan River runs down the eastern side of the region into the Dead Sea, so named because of its high salt content.

Israelite Origins

Information about the history of ancient Israel comes from several sources, including archaeological excavation and references in documents from other Middle Eastern societies, particularly Egyptian and Assyrian royal annals. However, the fundamental source is the extraordinarily rich yet problematic collection of writings preserved in the Hebrew Bible (called the Old Testament by Christians). The text of the Hebrew Bible is like a layer cake, having several collections of material superimposed on one another and choices made at each stage about what to include and exclude. Many traditions about the Israelites' early days were long transmitted orally. Not until the tenth century B.C.E. did they begin to be written down, by means of an alphabet borrowed from the nearby Phoenicians. The canonical text that we have today was compiled in the fifth century B.C.E. and reflects the point of view of the priests who controlled the Temple in Jerusalem. The Hebrew language of the Bible reflects the speech of the Israelites until about 500 B.C.E. It is a Semitic language, most closely related to Phoenician and to Aramaic (the language that later supplanted Hebrew in Israel), more distantly related to the Akkadian language of Mesopotamia and to Arabic. This linguistic affinity probably parallels the Israelites' ethnic relationship to the neighboring peoples.

In some respects the history of the ancient Israelites is unique, the primary source of the Judaeo-Christian tradition so central to Western civilization. But in another sense that history reflects a familiar pattern in the ancient Middle East. It is the story of nomadic pastoralists who occupied marginal land between the inhospitable desert and the settled agricultural areas. Early on, these nomads periodically raided the farms and villages of the settled peoples, but eventually they settled down to an agricultural way of life and at a somewhat later stage developed a state apparatus.

The Hebrew Bible preserves vivid traditions about the Patriarchs—the male leaders of the early Israelite groups—Abraham, Isaac, and Jacob. Abraham was born in the city of Ur in southern Mesopotamia, probably in the twentieth century B.C.E. He left the city of his birth, disgusted by the idol worship that predominated there, and moved with his herd animals (sheep, cattle, donkeys) and his extended family through the Syrian desert. Eventually he arrived in the land of Israel, which, according to the biblical account, had been promised to him and his descendants as part of a "covenant," or pact, with the Israelite god, Yahweh.

These "recollections" of the journey of Abraham may compress the experience of generations of pastoralists who moved through the grazing lands between the upper reaches of the Tigris and Euphrates Rivers and the Mediterranean coastal plain. Abraham, his family, and companions were following the usual pattern in this part of the world. They camped by a permanent water source in the dry season, then drove the herds of domesticated animals to a well-established sequence of grazing areas during the rest of the year. The animals provided for most needs—milk, cheese, meat, and cloth.

The early Israelites and the settled peoples of the region were suspicious of one another. This friction between nomadic herders and settled farmers, as well as the Israelites' view of their ancestors as being on the nomadic side of the equation, comes through in the story of the innocent shepherd Abel, who was killed by his farmer brother Cain, and in the story of Sodom and Gomorrah, two cities that Yaweh destroyed because of their wickedness.

Abraham's son and grandson, Isaac and Jacob, succeeded him as leaders of this wandering group of herders. In the next generation the story of Jacob's son Joseph, who was sold to passing merchants by his brothers, reveals the tensions that could arise within a leading family between children of different mothers. Through luck and ability Joseph became a high official at the court of the Egyptian king. Thus he was in a position to help his people when drought swept the land of Israel and the Israelites and their flocks migrated to Egypt. The sophisticated Egyptians, however, both feared and looked down on these rough herders and eventually reduced the Israelites to the status of slaves and put them to work on the grand building projects of the pharaoh.

That is the version of events given in the Hebrew Bible. Several points need to be made about it. First, the biblical account glosses over the very centuries (1700–1500 B.C.E.) during which Egypt was dominated by the Hyksos, who generally are identified as Semitic groups that infiltrated the Nile Delta from the northeast (see Chapter 3). The Israelites' migration to Egypt and their later enslavement may have been connected to the rise and fall of the Hyksos. Second, although extant Egyptian sources do not refer to Israelite slaves, they do complain about *Apiru*, a derogatory term applied to nomads, caravan drivers,

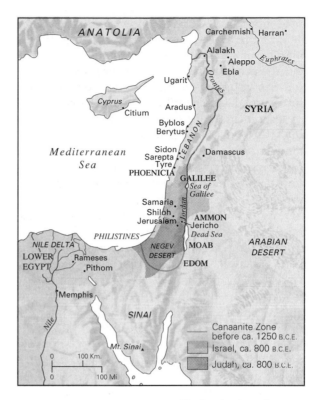

Map 4.3 Phoenicia and Israel The lands along the eastern shore of the Mediterranean Sea—sometimes called the Levant or Syria-Palestine—have always been a crossroads, traversed by migrants, nomads, merchants, and armies moving between Egypt, Arabia, Mesopotamia, and Anatolia.

bandits, and other marginal and stateless groups. The word seems to designate a class of people rather than a particular ethnic group, but some scholars have suggested an etymological connection between *Apiru* and *Hebrew* (see Voices and Visions: The Amarna Letters, in Chapter 3). Third, the period of Israelite slavery coincided with the Ramesside era of Egyptian history—1400 to 1200 B.C.E., during which pharaohs Sethos I and Ramesses II engaged in ambitious building programs (see Chapter 3).

Exodus from Egypt and Settlement in Canaan

According to the Hebrew Bible, the Israelite slaves were led out of captivity by Moses, an Israelite with connections to the Egyptian royal family. The narrative of the Exodus—the departure from Egypt—is overlaid with folktale motifs such as the ten plagues visited upon Egypt before the pharaoh allowed the Israelites to leave and the miraculous parting of the waters of the Red Sea, which enabled the refugees to escape the Egyptian army. Still, oral tradition may have preserved memories of an emigration from Egypt and years of wandering in the wilderness of Sinai.

During their forty-year sojourn in the desert the Israelites became devoted to a stern and warlike god. According to the Old Testament, Yahweh, who may have been localized at Mount Sinai, made a covenant with the Israelites: they promised to worship Yahweh exclusively, and he made them his "Chosen People." This pact was confirmed by tablets that Moses brought down from the top of Mount Sinai. Written on the tablets were the Ten Commandments, which laid down the basic tenets of Jewish belief and practice. This document prohibited murder, adultery, theft, lying, and envy, and demanded that the Israelites respect their parents and refrain from work on the Sabbath, the seventh day of the week.

In the later thirteenth century B.C.E. the Israelites came from the east into the land of Canaan (modern Israel and Palestine). Led by Joshua, Moses' successor, they attacked and destroyed Jericho and other Canaanite cities. The biblical account is confirmed by the evidence of archaeology. It shows the destruction of Canaanite towns at this time, followed shortly thereafter by the resettlement of lowland sites and the establishment of new sites in the hills—thanks in part to the development of cisterns for holding rainwater. The new settlers were a population with a cruder material culture than that of the Canaanites. This is yet another manifestation of the age-old pattern: nomadic pastoralists settle down and are assimilated into an agrarian economy.

It is unlikely that all members of the later Israelite population were descendants of the people who escaped from Egypt. The newcomers may have linked up with related peoples who had remained behind in Israel at the time of the migration into Egypt. And initial successes against the Canaanites probably attracted other nomad groups to join the Israelite rampage.

Throughout history, nomadic groups have formed new coalitions and then invented a common ancestry.

At this time there was no Israelite "state" as such. The "Children of Israel"—that is, descendants of the Patriarch Jacob—were members of twelve tribes that took their names from the sons of Jacob and Joseph. Each tribe installed itself in a different part of the conquered territory, and each tribe looked for guidance to one or more chiefs. Such leaders usually had limited coercive authority and were primarily responsible for mediating disputes and seeing to the welfare and protection of the group. Certain charismatic figures, famed for their daring in war or their genius in arbitration, were called "Judges" and (like the Celtic Druids) had a special standing that transcended tribal boundaries. The tribes were also bound together by their common access to a shrine in the hill country at Shiloh. The shrine housed the holy Ark of the Covenant, a chest containing the tablets of commandments that Yahweh had given to Moses.

Rise of the Israelite Monarchy

The Israelites were not the only triumphant newcomers in this region. The years around 1200 B.C.E. were a time of troubles throughout the eastern Mediterranean (see Chapter 3). In the early twelfth century B.C.E. the Philistines, who may be connected to the pre-Greek population of the island of Crete, occupied the coastal plain of Israel. Israelites and Philistines fought frequently in this period. Their wars were memorialized in the biblical traditions about the long-haired strongman Samson, who pulled down the walls of a Philistine temple, and the bravery of young David, whose slingshot felled the towering warrior Goliath.

An influential religious leader named Samuel, recognizing the need for a stronger central authority if the Israelites were to contend successfully against the Philistine city-states, anointed Saul as first king of Israel around 1020 B.C.E. Saul had mixed success, and when he perished in battle, the throne passed to David (r. ca. 1000–960 B.C.E.).

Gifted musician, brave warrior, and adroit politician, David completed the transition from tribal confederacy to unified monarchy. He strengthened royal authority by making the recently captured hill city of Jerusalem, which lay outside tribal boundaries, his new capital. Soon after, the Ark was brought to Jerusalem, making that city the religious as well as political center of the kingdom. To curtail the disorder caused by blood feuds, David designated "cities of refuge"—places to which those guilty of certain crimes could flee and escape retribution. A census was taken to facilitate the collection of taxes by the central government, and a standing army, with soldiers paid by and loyal to the king, was instituted. These innovations gave David the resources to win a string of military victories and substantially expand Israel's borders.

The reign of David's son Solomon (r. ca. 960–920 B.C.E.) marked the high point of the Israelite monarchy. Alliances and trade linked Israel with near and distant lands. Solomon and Hiram, the king of Phoenician Tyre, together commissioned a fleet that sailed south into the Red Sea and brought back gold, ivory, jewels, sandalwood, and exotic animals from distant Ophir. The story of the fabulous visit to Solomon by the queen of Sheba, who brought gold, precious stones, and spices, may be mythical, but it reflects the reality of trade with Saba (biblical

A model of the ancient city of Jerusalem, with the Temple at the center Strategically located in the middle of lands occupied by the Israelite tribes and on a high plateau overlooking the central hills and the Judaean desert, Jerusalem was captured c. 1000 B.C.E. by King David and made into his capital. The next king, Solomon, built the First Temple to serve as the center of the worship for the Israelite god, Yahweh. Solomon's Temple was destroyed during the Neo-Babylonian sack of the city in 587 B.C.E., but a modest structure was soon rebuilt and later replaced by the magnificent Second Temple was built by King Herod in the last decades of the first century B.C.E. This model represents the city in Second Temple times. (Private collection)

Sheba) in south Arabia (present-day Yemen) or the Horn of Africa (present-day Somalia). Considerable wealth flowed into the royal coffers, subsidizing the lavish lifestyle of Solomon's court, the expanding administrative bureaucracy, and a standing chariot army that made Israel into a regional power. Solomon undertook an ambitious building program employing slaves and the compulsory labor of citizens. To further link religious and secular authority, he built the First Temple in Jerusalem. Henceforth, the Israelites had a central shrine and an impressive set of rituals that could compete with the attractions of pagan cults.

The Temple priesthood, which carried out animal sacrifices to Yahweh on behalf of the community, received a percentage of the annual agricultural yield and evolved into a powerful and wealthy class. The expansion of Jerusalem, new commercial opportunities, and the increasing prestige of the Temple hierarchy began to change the social composition of Israelite society. A gap emerged between urban and rural, rich and poor, polarizing a people that previously had been relatively homogeneous.

The Israelites lived in extended families—the "house of the father" it was called; several generations lived together under the authority of the eldest male. Marriages, usually arranged between families, were an important economic as well as social institution. The groom gave a substantial gift to the father of the bride. Her entire family participated in the ceremonial weighing out of the silver or gold. Monogamy was the norm. The wife brought into the marriage a dowry that included a slave girl who attended her for life. Male heirs were of paramount importance. Firstborn sons received a double share of the inheritance. If no son was forthcoming from the marriage, the couple could adopt a son, or the husband could have a child by the wife's slave attendant. If a man died childless, his brother was expected to marry the widow and provide an heir.

Women suffered from certain legal disadvantages. They could not inherit, and they could not initiate divorce. Men could have extramarital relations, but equivalent behavior by wives was punishable by death. Women of the working classes labored with other family members in agriculture or herding, in addition to maintaining the household and raising the children. As the society became more urbanized, some women worked outside the home as cooks, bakers, perfumers, wet nurses (usually recent mothers, still producing milk, who were hired to provide nourishment to another person's child), prostitutes, and singers of laments at funerals. On occasion women reached positions of influence. For example, Deborah the Judge, a prophet and arbitrator of disputes, led troops in battle against the Canaanites. Women known collectively as "wise women" appear to have been educated and composed sacred texts in poetry and prose.

Fragmentation and Diaspora

After the death of Solomon around 920 B.C.E., resentment over the demands of the crown and royal neglect of tribal prerogatives led to the split of the monarchy into two kingdoms: Israel in the north, with its capital at Samaria; and Judah in the southern territory around Jerusalem. The two kingdoms were sometimes at war, sometimes in alliance with one another.

This period saw the crystallization of *monotheism*, the absolute belief in Yahweh as the one and only god. Nevertheless, religious leaders had to contend with the appeal of polytheistic (involving belief in multiple gods) cults. Many Israelites were attracted to the ecstatic rituals of the Canaanite storm-god, Baal, and the fertility goddess, Astarte. Fiery prophets claiming to convey messages from Yahweh, rose up to oppose the adoption of foreign ritual and to castigate the monarchs and aristocracy for their corruption, impiety, and neglect of the poor.

In response to the rise of the aggressive and brutal Neo-Assyrian Empire, the small states of Syria and Israel lay aside their rivalries and resisted together, but to no avail. In 721 B.C.E. the Assyrians destroyed the northern kingdom of Israel and deported a substantial portion of its population to the east (see Voices and Visions: Mass Deportation in the Neo-Assyrian Empire). New settlers were brought in, altering the ethnic composition, culture, and religious practices of this land and removing it from the mainstream of Jewish history. The southern kingdom of Judah hung on for over a century, at times paying tribute to the Neo-Assyrian Empire and then to the Neo-Babylonian kingdom that succeeded it, at other times breaking into rebellion. When the Neo-Babylonian monarch Nebuchadrezzar captured Jerusalem in 587 B.C.E., he destroyed the Temple and deported to Babylon the leading elements of the society—royal family, aristocracy, and workers with useful skills such as blacksmiths and scribes.

The deportees adapted quickly and prospered in their new home "by the waters of Babylon," and half a century later most of their descendants refused the offer of the Persian monarch Cyrus (see Chapter 5) to return to their homeland. This was the origin of the Jewish *Diaspora*—a Greek word meaning "dispersal" or "scattering"—which continues today. The communities of the Diaspora began to develop institutions that allowed them to maintain their religion and culture outside the homeland. One such institution was the *synagogue* (a Greek term meaning "bringing together"), a communal meeting place that came to serve religious, educational, and social functions.

Several groups of Babylonian Jews—as we may now begin to call these people, since an independent Israel no longer existed—did make the long trek back to Judah, where they met a cold reception from the local population. Nevertheless, the Temple was rebuilt in modest form and a new set of regulations, the Deuteronomic Code (*deuteronomic* is Greek for "second code of laws"), became the basis of law and conduct for the Jewish community. The fifth century B.C.E. also saw the compilation of the Hebrew Bible in roughly its present form.

The loss of political autonomy and the experience of exile had sharpened the Jewish identity and put an unyielding monotheism at the core of that identity. Jews lived by a rigid set of rules. Dietary restrictions forbade the eating of pork and shellfish and insisted that meat and dairy products not be consumed together. Rules of purity required women to take ritual baths to remove the taint of menstruation. The need to venerate the Sabbath (the seventh day of the week) meant

"Hezekiah's Tunnel" and the Pool of Siloam Anticipating an Assyrian siege in 701 B.C.E., the Israelite king Hezekiah constructed an underground tunnel through the rock of the hillside to bring water from a nearby spring to the city. Excavation began from both ends and a surviving inscription tells of the moment when the two crews met in the middle. (Garo Nalbandian)

refraining from work and from fighting, in imitation of their god, who rested on the seventh day according to the biblical story of the creation of the world (this is the origin of the concept of the weekend). There also was a ban on marrying non-Jews. These strictures tended to isolate the Jews from other peoples, but they also yielded a powerful sense of community and belief in the protection of a watchful and beneficent deity.

PHOENICIA AND THE MEDITERRANEAN

While the Assyrians were recovering from the disorders at the end of the Bronze Age and laying the foundation for future expansion, and the Israelite tribes were being forged into a united kingdom, important transformations also were taking place among another people who occupied the eastern shore of the Mediterranean. The ancient inhabitants of present-day Syria, Lebanon, and Israel (sometimes called the Levant or Syria-Palestine), are commonly designated Phoenicians, though they referred to themselves by the ethnic designation "Can'ani"—Canaanites. Their story is complicated by inconsistent terminology, sparse written evidence, and frequent migrations and invasions, which complicate the archaeological picture.

Yet, we can draw some insights into the history of this ethnic group. When western Asia and the eastern Mediterranean entered a period of violent upheavals and mass movements of population around 1200 B.C.E. (see Chapter 3), many settlements in Syria-Palestine were destroyed. Aramaeans migrated into the interior portions of Syria. Israelite tribes under the command of Joshua wandered into Canaan, destroyed

Wall relief of a Phoenician warship, ca. 700 B.C.E. This depiction in an Assyrian palace reflects the reliance of the Assyrians, and the Persians after them, on the Phoenicians for the core of their navy. The mast and broad square sail which these vessels used for cruising would be deposited on shore before battle. Manned by fifty rowers on two levels, the upper deck was protected by a screen of shields. The long, projecting "ram" at right was used to open a hole below the water line in an enemy vessel. (Courtesy, Trustees of the British Museum)

Canaanite cities, and settled down as herders and farmers. At the same time, the Philistines occupied the coast of much of present-day Israel and introduced iron-based metallurgy to this part of the world.

The Phoenician City-States

As a result of those invasions and migrations, by 1100 B.C.E. the zone that the Canaanites occupied was no more than a narrow strip of land lying between the mountains and the sea in present-day Lebanon (see Map 4.3). The inhabitants of this densely populated area adopted new political forms and sources of livelihood, particularly in manufacture and seaborne commerce. Rivers and rocky spurs of Mount Lebanon sliced the coastal plain into a series of small city-states. The most important were Aradus, Byblos, Berytus, Sidon, Sarepta, and Tyre. This region was the homeland of the Phoenicians, as the Canaanites came to be called by Greeks who encountered them in the early first millennium B.C.E. The Greek term *Phoinikes* may mean "red men" and have something to do with the color of the Canaanites' skin, or it may refer to the purple pigment that they produced from the murex snail and used to dye expensive garments (see Environment and Technology: Ancient Textiles and Dyes).

Thriving commerce brought in considerable wealth and gave the Phoenician city-states an important role in the international politics of the age. This commercial activity centered on raw materials, foodstuffs, and crafted luxury products: cedar and pine, metals, papyrus, wine, spices, salted fish, incense, textiles, carved ivory, and glass.

The Phoenicians developed earlier Canaanite models into the first alphabetic system of writing. In such a system each symbol stands for a sound, and only about two dozen symbols are needed. This technology was a considerable advance over cuneiform and hieroglyphics, which required hundreds of signs. Little indigenous written material survives from this period, however. Whatever "historical" records the Phoenicians may have had are lost, probably because they were written on perishable papyrus, though some information in Greek and Roman sources may be based on them. Equally regrettably, the archaeological remains from Phoenicia are very limited.

In the second millennium B.C.E. Byblos was the most important Phoenician city-state. It was a distribution center for cedar wood from the slopes of Mount Lebanon and for Egyptian papyrus, the precious writing medium of the age (the Greek word *biblion*, meaning "book written on papyrus," comes down as our word *bible*). In the early centuries of the first millennium B.C.E. Tyre, in southern Lebanon, came to play an ever more dominant role. King Hiram, who lived in the tenth century B.C.E., was responsible for Tyre's initial rise to prominence. According to the Hebrew Bible, he formed a close friendship and alliance with the Israelite king Solomon. When Solomon built the temple at Jerusalem, he used cedar from Lebanon and drew upon the skills of Phoenician craftsmen. In return, Tyre gained access to silver, surplus food, and trade routes to the east and south. In the ninth century B.C.E. Tyre extended its territorial control over nearby Sidon and monopolized the Mediterranean coastal trade.

The city itself was virtually impregnable because of its location on an island directly offshore. It had two harbors—one facing north, the other south—connected by a canal. It also had a large marketplace, a magnificent palace complex with treasury and archives, temples to the gods Melqart and Astarte, suburbs spilling onto the adjacent mainland, and a population of thirty thousand or more. Its one weakness was its dependence on the mainland for food and fresh water.

Little is known about the internal affairs of Tyre and the other Phoenician cities. The names of a series of kings are preserved, and the scant evidence suggests that leading merchant families dominated the political arena. Between the ninth and seventh centuries B.C.E. the Phoenician city-states had to contend with Assyrian aggression, followed in the sixth century B.C.E. by the expansion of the Neo-Babylonian kingdom and later the Persian Empire (see Chapter 5). Just as in the previous millennium, these small states of the

Levantine coast had to be adept at diplomacy, preserving their autonomy by playing the great powers off against one another when possible, accepting a subordinate relationship to a distant master when necessary.

Expansion into the Mediterranean

In the ninth century B.C.E. Tyre began to turn its attention westward into the Mediterranean. The colony of Citium was established on Cyprus, a large island 100 miles (161 kilometers) west of the Syrian coast (see Map 4.4). Phoenician merchants sailing into the Aegean Sea are mentioned in the *Iliad* and *Odyssey* of the Greek poet Homer (ca. 700 B.C.E.), and the Greeks imitated the Phoenicians by adapting the alphabet to their own language and sailing out into the Mediterranean in search of farmland and raw materials. In the ninth and eighth centuries B.C.E. a string of settlements in the western Mediterranean gradually formed a "Phoenician triangle" composed of the stretch of North African coast that today lies in western Libya, Tunisia, and Morocco, the south and southeast coast of Spain (including Gades—modern Cadiz—located astride the Strait of Gibraltar and controlling access into and out of the Mediterranean), and the major islands of Sardinia, Sicily, and Malta off the coast of Italy. Many of these new foundations were situated on promontories or offshore islands in imitation of Tyre. The result was a Phoenician trading network that spanned the entire Mediterranean.

Tyrian expansion westward in the Mediterranean was made possible by a combination of state enterprise and private initiative. It probably was a response both to the frequent and destructive invasions of the Syria-Palestine region by the Neo-Assyrian Empire and to the shortage of arable land to feed Tyre's swelling population. Overseas settlement provided an outlet for excess population, new sources of valuable trade commodities, and new trading partners. For a time Tyre maintained its autonomy by providing the considerable sums of money and goods that the Assyrian kings demanded as tribute. By the early seventh century B.C.E., however, the Assyrians conquered Tyre and stripped it of much of its territory and population, and the leading place in Phoenicia was taken over by Sidon in the sixth and fifth centuries B.C.E.

The Phoenicians' activities in the western Mediterranean often brought them into conflict with the Greeks, who at this time were also seeking out valuable resources in the western Mediterranean and colonizing southern Italy and Sicily. The focal point of this rivalry was Sicily. Phoenicians occupied the western end of the island, and Greeks colonized the eastern and central sectors. For centuries Greeks and Phoenicians fought for control of Sicily in some of the most savage wars in the history of the ancient Mediterranean. The sources contain many stories of atrocities, massacres, wholesale enslavements, and removals of populations. The unusual level of brutality must reflect the fact that each side felt its very existence to be at stake. In the end both communities survived, but the Carthaginians, who led the coalition of Phoenician communities in the western Mediterranean, had gained the upper hand and by the mid-third century B.C.E. controlled all of Sicily.

Carthage

Historians know far more about the new foundations in the western Mediterranean—particularly Carthage—than they know about the cities in the Phoenician homeland. Much of this knowledge comes from the Greeks' and Romans' reports of their wars with the western Phoenician communities.

This chapter opens with an account of the origins of Carthage—an account preserved by Roman sources but probably derived from a Carthaginian original. However much truth may lie behind the legend of Dido, archaeological excavation has roughly confirmed the traditional foundation date of 814 B.C.E. Carthage was established at a strategic location, very near the present-day city of Tunis in Tunisia, at that point in the middle portion of the Mediterranean where the sea crossing from Europe to Africa is narrowest. The new foundation prospered and grew rapidly, soon coming to dominate other Phoenician colonies in the west.

The city of Carthage was located on a narrow promontory jutting out into the Mediterranean

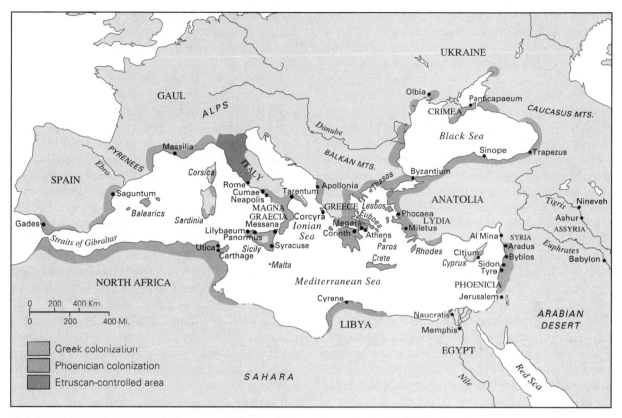

Map 4.4 Colonization of the Mediterranean In the ninth century B.C.E, the Phoenicians of Lebanon began to explore and colonize parts of the western Mediterranean, including the coast of North Africa, southern and eastern Spain, and the islands of Sicily and Sardinia. The Phoenicians were primarily interested in access to valuable raw materials and trading opportunities.

from the North African mainland. The crowded heart of the city stretched between Byrsa, the original fortified hilltop citadel of the community, and a double harbor. The inner harbor could accommodate up to 220 warships. Naval command headquarters were situated on an island in the middle of it. A watchtower allowed surveillance of the surrounding area, and high walls made it impossible to see in from the outside. The outer commercial harbor was filled with docks for merchant ships and with sheds and yards for shipbuilding and refitting. In a crisis the mouth of the harbor could be closed off by a huge chain.

Around the perimeter of a large central square lay government office buildings. Open space in the square itself was used by magistrates to hear legal cases outdoors. The inner city was a maze of narrow, winding streets, multistory apartment buildings, and sacred enclosures of the gods. Out from the center was Megara, a sprawling suburban district where fields and vegetable gardens separated the spacious houses of the well-to-do. This entire urban complex was enclosed by a wall 22 miles (35 kilometers) in length. At the most critical point—the 2½-mile-wide (4-kilometer-wide) isthmus connecting the promontory to the mainland—the wall was over 40 feet high (13 meters) and 30 feet thick (10 meters), and had high watchtowers at intervals.

With a population of roughly four hundred thousand, Carthage was one of the largest cities in the world in the mid-first millennium B.C.E. Given the limitations of ancient technology, the provision of food, water, and sanitation must have posed substantial challenges. The city housed an ethnically diverse population, including people of Phoenician stock, indigenous people likely to have been the ancestors of modern-day Berbers, and immigrants from all over the Mediterranean and sub-Saharan Africa who had come to Carthage to make their fortunes. Despite the reluctance of Dido in the foundation legend, the Phoenicians quite readily intermarried with other peoples.

Each year two *suffetes*, or "judges" (a word having the same Semitic root as the Israelites' word for their early leaders), were elected from the upper-class families. They served as heads of state and carried out administrative and judicial functions. The real seat of power was the Senate, made up of members of the leading merchant families, who sat for life, formulating policy and directing the affairs of the state. Within the Senate, an inner circle of heads of the thirty or so most influential families made the crucial decisions. Occasionally an Assembly of the people was called together to elect public officials and vote on important issues. Normally the Senate and officials made decisions, but if the leaders were divided or wanted to stir up popular enthusiasm for some venture, they would turn to the people as a whole.

There is little evidence at Carthage of the kind of social and political unrest that later plagued Greece and Rome (see Chapters 5 and 6). This perception may be due in part to the limited information in our sources about internal affairs at Carthage. However, a merchant aristocracy, unlike an aristocracy of birth, was not a closed circle, and in a climate of economic and social mobility ambitious and successful new families and individuals could push their way into the circle of politically influential citizens. The ruling class also saw to it that all benefited from the riches of empire, and the masses usually were ready to defer to those who made that prosperity possible.

A Commercial "Empire"

The most important arm of Carthaginian power was the navy. With citizens of Carthage playing an important role as rowers and navigators, the Carthaginian navy ruled the seas of the western Mediterranean for centuries. The many Phoenician towns along the shores of the western Mediterranean provided a chain of friendly ports.

Expert in the design and construction of ships and highly proficient as sailors, the Carthaginians had a large number of fast and maneuverable warships. These vessels were outfitted with a sturdy pointed ram in front that could be driven into an enemy vessel to open up a deadly hole at the water line. A deck allowed marines (soldiers onboard a ship) to take their positions and fire weapons at the enemy. Innovations in the placement of benches and oars made room for 30, 50, and eventually as many as 170 rowers to propel the ship at high speed. The Phoenicians of the eastern and western Mediterranean and their rivals the Greeks contributed to these technological advances and used similar vessels.

The foreign policy of the Carthaginian state reflected its economic interests. Protection of the sea lanes, access to raw materials, and fostering of trade opportunities mattered most to the dominant merchant class. Indeed, Carthage claimed the waters of the western Mediterranean as its own. Merchant vessels of other peoples were free to sail to Carthage to market their goods, but if they tried to operate on their own, they risked being sunk by the Carthaginian navy. Treaties between Carthage and other states included formal recognition of this maritime commercial monopoly.

Carthaginian merchants were active all around the Mediterranean, but the archaeological record provides little evidence of which commodities they traded. This commerce may have included perishable goods—for example, foodstuffs, textiles, and animal skins, as well as slaves, which would not survive in the archaeological record—and raw metals (silver, lead, iron, and tin) whose Carthaginian origin would not be evident. Goods manufactured elsewhere were carried by Carthaginian ships, and products brought to Carthage by foreign traders were re-exported for a profit.

There is also evidence for some form of trade with sub-Saharan Africans. Hanno, an eminent Carthaginian of the fifth century B.C.E., claimed to have sailed out of the Strait of Gibraltar, stopping at various points to found small settlements and explore the West African coast. A surviving Greek version of his adventure-filled official report includes descriptions of ferocious savages, drums in the night, and rivers of fire. Scholars have had difficulty matching up Hanno's topographic descriptions and distances with the actual geography of the Atlantic coast of Africa. Some regard the document as an outright fiction. Others surmise that Hanno purposely altered distances and exaggerated the dangers so that other explorers would not dare to follow in his tracks and compete in this new commercial sphere.

The Greek historian Herodotus describes a form of silent barter in which the Carthaginians deposited items on the beach and returned at a later time to pick up the gold that the local inhabitants left in exchange. Other Carthaginian commanders explored the Atlantic coast of Spain and France and secured control of an important source of tin (a component of bronze, still important in the Iron Age) in the "Tin Islands," as Greek sources call them, probably Cornwall in the British Isles.

It is important to be precise about the goals and methods of the Carthaginian "empire" in the western Mediterranean between the sixth and third centuries B.C.E. Unlike Assyria, Carthage did not seek direct rule of a large amount of territory. A belt of fertile land in northeastern Tunisia, owned by Carthaginians but worked by native peasants and imported slaves, provided a secure food supply. Indigenous groups in this territory were subject to taxation and military service.

Beyond this core area Carthaginian domination was usually indirect. Other Phoenician communities in the western Mediterranean were essentially independent. However, because of Carthage's superior economic and military resources and the shared interests of all the Phoenician communities of the west, they normally looked to Carthage for military protection, and they followed Carthage's lead in foreign policy. Sardinia and southern Spain were provinces under the direct control of a Carthaginian governor and garrison, probably because they contained vital agricultural, metal, and manpower resources.

Carthage's overarching emphasis on commerce may explain an unusual feature of the state: citizens were not required to serve in the military, because they were of more value in a civilian capacity. Carthage had little to fear from potential enemies close to home. The indigenous North African population was not well organized politically or militarily and thus was easily controlled. Carthage did need armies for military operations overseas, and it engaged in a series of fierce and destructive wars with Greeks and Romans from the fifth through third centuries B.C.E. For these conflicts it came to rely on mercenaries, soldiers hired from the most warlike peoples in their dominions or in neighboring areas—such as Numidians from North Africa, Iberians from Spain, Gauls from France, and various Italian peoples. These well-paid mercenaries were under the command of professional Carthaginian officers.

Another sign that the conduct of war was not seen as the primary business of the state was the separation of military command from civilian government. Generals were chosen intermittently by the Senate and kept in office for as long as they were needed. This practice led to the rise of a professional class of military experts, men who studied the art of war and gained experience and a high level of skill over the course of long commands. There is a telling contrast with Assyria and the other major states of the ancient Middle East, whose kings normally led the campaigns.

Gods and Cult

Carthaginian religion fascinated Greek and Roman writers. Like the deities of Mesopotamia (see Chapter 2), the gods of the Carthaginians—chief among them Baal Hammon, a male-storm god, and Tanit, a female fertility figure—were powerful and capricious entities whose worshipers sought to appease them at any price.

It was reported, for example, that members of the Carthaginian elite sacrificed their own male children at times of crisis. Excavations at Carthage and other Phoenician towns in the west have turned up *tophets*—walled enclosures in

The "Tophet" of Carthage   This is where the cremated bodies of sacrificed children were buried from the seventh to second centuries B.C.E. The claim in ancient sources that the Carthaginians sacrificed children to their gods at times of crisis has been confirmed by archaeological excavation. The stone markers, decorated with magical signs and symbols of divinities as well as the name of the family, were placed over ceramic urns containing the ashes and charred bones of one or more infants or, on occasion, older children. (Martha Cooper/Peter Arnold, Inc.)

which were buried thousands of small, sealed urns containing the burned bones of children. Some scholars see these compounds as the final resting place of infants born prematurely or taken by childhood illnesses. Most experts, however, maintain that the western Phoenicians practiced child sacrifice on a more or less regular basis.

The motivation behind this activity and the meanings that it held for its practitioners are not well understood. Presumably it was intended to win the favor of the gods at critical moments, such as the eve of decisive battles with Greek and Roman foes. Originally practiced by the upper classes, child sacrifice was later taken over by broader elements of the population and became increasingly common in the fourth and third centuries B.C.E.

Plutarch, a Greek who lived around 100 C.E., long after the demise of Carthage, but who had access to earlier sources, wrote the following about the Carthaginians:

> The Carthaginians are a hard and gloomy people, submissive to their rulers and harsh to their subjects, running to extremes of cowardice in times of fear and of cruelty in times of anger; they keep obstinately to their decisions, are austere, and care little for amusement or the graces of life.[1]

We should not take at face value what was said about the Carthaginians by their Greek and Roman enemies, but it is important to recognize that the Carthaginians were perceived as different and that cultural barriers, leading to misunderstanding and prejudice, played a significant role in the encounters of these peoples of the ancient Mediterranean. In Chapter 6 we follow the protracted and bloody struggle between Rome and Carthage for control of the western Mediterranean.

THE END OF AN ERA: THE FALL OF ASSYRIA

The extension of Assyrian power over the entire Middle East had enormous consequences for all the peoples of this region and caused the stories of Mesopotamia, Israel, and Phoenicia to converge. As we have seen, in 721 B.C.E. the

New Cultural Communities in Western Eurasia, ca. 1200–500 B.C.E.

	Israel	Phoenicia/Carthage	Mesopotamia
1250–1200 B.C.E.	Israelite conquest of Canaan		
1000	David establishes Jerusalem as capital		
969		Hiram of Tyre comes to power	
960	Solomon builds First Temple		
920	Division into two kingdoms		
911			Rise of Neo-Assyrian empire
814		Foundation of Carthage	
744–727			Reforms of Tiglath-Pileser
721	Assyrian conquest of northern kingdom		
701		Assyrian humiliation of Tyre	
668–627			Reign of Ashurbanipal
612			Fall of Assyria
626–539			Neo-Babylonian Kingdom
587	Neo-Babylonian capture of Jerusalem		
465		Voyage of Hanno the Carthaginian to West Africa	

Assyrians destroyed the northern kingdom of Israel and deported a substantial portion of the population, and for over a century the southern kingdom of Judah was exposed to relentless pressure (see Voices and Visions: Mass Deportation in the Neo-Assyrian Empire). Assyrian threats and demands for tribute spurred the Phoenicians to explore, colonize, and commercially exploit the western Mediterranean. The humiliation of Tyre, the leading Phoenician state, by the Assyrians in the seventh century B.C.E. accelerated the decline of the Phoenician homeland, but the western colonies, especially Carthage, lying far beyond Assyrian reach, flourished for centuries.

Even Egypt, for so long impregnable behind its desert barriers, was conquered and occupied for a time by Assyrian forces in the mid-seventh century B.C.E. Thebes, its ancient capital, was damaged beyond recovery. The southern plains of Sumer and Akkad, the birthplace of Mesopotamian civilization, were reduced to a protectorate. The venerable old metropolis at Babylon was alternately razed and rebuilt by Assyrian kings of differing dispositions. Urartu and Elam, Assyria's great power rivals close to home, were ultimately destroyed.

By the mid-seventh century B.C.E. Assyria stood seemingly unchallenged in western Asia. But the cost had been high. The arms race with Urartu, the frequent expensive campaigns, and protection of lengthy borders had overextended Assyrian resources. The brutality of Assyrian conduct and the exploitation of the conquered peoples had aroused the hatred of many subjects and neighbors. And changes in the ethnic composition of the army and in the population of the homeland had rendered both soldiers and civilians less committed to the interests of the Assyrian state.

Two dynamic new political entities spearheaded resistance to Assyria: a resurgent Babylonia under the Neo-Babylonian, or Chaldaean, dynasty, and the kingdom of the Medes, an Iranian people who by the seventh century B.C.E. were extending their control eastward across the Iranian plateau. These two powers launched a series of attacks on the Assyrian homeland, and by 612 B.C.E. the chief Assyrian cities had been destroyed. The rapidity of the Assyrian decline and fall is stunning. The destruction systematically carried out by the victorious attackers led to the depopulation of northern Mesopotamia. Two centuries later, when a corps of Greek mercenaries passed by mounds that concealed the ruins of the Assyrian capitals, the Athenian chronicler Xenophon had no inkling of the existence of the Assyrians and their once-mighty empire.

The Medes took over the Assyrian homeland and the northern steppe as far as eastern Anatolia, but most of the immediate benefits went to the Neo-Babylonian kingdom. Kings Nabopolassar (r. 625–605 B.C.E.) and Nebuchadrezzar (r. 604–562 B.C.E.), both energetic campaigners, took over much of the territory of the old empire. Babylonia underwent a cultural renaissance. The city of Babylon was enlarged and adorned, becoming the greatest urban complex in the world in the sixth century B.C.E. Old cults were reactivated, temples rebuilt, festivals resurrected. The related pursuits of mathematics, astronomy, and astrology reached new heights.

CONCLUSION

The history of Europe, North Africa, and western Asia shared two main themes in the first millennium B.C.E. First, this epoch witnessed the rise to prominence of peoples who had played a less significant role earlier—in particular the Assyrians of northern Mesopotamia and the Phoenicians (Canaanites) of the eastern Mediterranean coast—or whose way of life had undergone such significant changes as to constitute a new culture—as in Israel and among the Celts of Europe.

In each of those cases we can follow the evolution of new, more complex political, social, and economic structures. The Assyrians, using land-based military technologies, created an empire on a scale that never before had been seen in the world, extending over vast distances and encompassing many different ethnic groups. The distances involved and the slowness of communications made it difficult to maintain control. The Assyrian response was to employ and advertise brute force and terror in order to cow opponents into submission and keep reluctant subjects obedient. The Carthaginians, the most successful of the Phoenician colonists in the western Mediterranean, created an "empire" of a different sort, based on naval dominance of the waters of the western Mediterranean and commercial exploitation of the resources of adjacent lands. In both cases great wealth was funneled into the center. The Assyrian royal family and aristocracy were enriched by the booty, taxes, and labor exacted from conquered peoples. The Carthaginian merchant families grew prosperous from trade and manufacture.

The second main theme of this chapter is population movements and the relocation of large numbers of people to new homes. Other historical periods may be better known as eras of mass migration—the prehistoric diffusion of the human species across all the habitable regions of the planet (see Chapter 1), the eruption of the new religion of Islam across western Asia and North Africa in the seventh century C.E. (see Chapter 10), and our own highly mobile century, for example. But the population movements of the first millennium B.C.E., though less well documented, also sparked profound political, social, cultural, and economic changes in the lands of Europe, North Africa, and western Asia.

The Assyrians, with their military conquest of most of western Asia, exemplify a pattern of coerced population movements. Large numbers of prisoners of war were deported from outlying subject territories to the core area in northern Mesopotamia. The Phoenician colonization of the nearby island of Cyprus and the more distant shores of North Africa, Spain, and the islands off Italy was at least partially a response to Assyrian aggression but also exemplifies a different pattern: citizens voluntarily left their overpopulated homeland to make better lives for themselves in new settlements. And, as the next chapter discusses, while the Phoenicians were exploring and settling in the western Mediterranean, Greeks from the Aegean Sea region were colonizing and occupying coastal points in southern Italy, Sicily, southern France, western Libya, and the lands bordering the Black Sea.

The story of the Israelite settlement of Canaan and the radiation of Celtic peoples from a Central European point of origin across a wide swath of Europe north of the Alps describes yet another pattern of mass migration. Phoenician colonists largely duplicated in their new homes the forms they had been using in the old country. Celts and Israelites, in contrast, underwent a more profound political, social, and cultural transformation as they adapted to new zones of settlement.

It is no accident that several of the peoples featured in this chapter who settled in large numbers outside their places of origin had long and glorious destinies ahead of them. In the first millennium B.C.E., as in later historical eras, diasporas proved to be both fertile sources of innovation and safety valves for the preservation of culture. The Carthaginian enterprise was eventually cut short by the Romans, but Jews and Celts survive into our own time. Ironically the Assyrians, for a time the most powerful of all these societies, suffered the most complete termination of their way of life. Because Assyrians did not settle outside their homeland in significant numbers, when their state was toppled in the late seventh century B.C.E. their culture also fell victim.

The Neo-Babylonian kingdom that arose on the ashes of the Neo-Assyrian Empire would prove to be the last revival of the ancient Sumerian and Semitic cultural legacy in western Asia. The next chapter relates how the destiny of the peoples of the Middle East became enmeshed in the stories of Iran and Greece.

SUGGESTED READING

The best concise introduction to Celtic civilization is Simon James, *The World of the Celts* (1993). Also of use are T. G. E. Powell, *The Celts* (1980), and Barry Cunliffe, *The Celtic World* (1979). Miranda J. Green, *The Celtic World* (1995) is a large and comprehensive collection of articles on many aspects of Celtic civilization.

On Celtic religion and mythology see Proinsias Mac Cana, *Celtic Mythology* (1983); and two books by Miranda Green: *The Gods of the Celts* (1986) and *Dictionary of Celtic Myth and Legend* (1992). Celtic art is covered by Ruth and Vincent Megaw, *Celtic Art: From Its Beginnings to the Book of Kells* (1989), and I. M. Stead, *Celtic Art* (1985). For translations and brief discussion of Celtic legends see Patrick K. Ford, *The Mabinogi and Other Medieval Welsh Tales* (1977), and Jeffrey Gantz, *Early Irish Myths and Sagas* (1981).

Fundamental for all periods in the ancient Middle East is Jack M. Sasson, ed., *Civilizations of the Ancient Near East*, 4 vols. (1995). This collection, containing nearly two hundred articles with bibliography by contemporary experts, is divided into sections covering environment, population, social institutions, history and culture, economy and trade, technology and artistic production, religion and science, language, writing and literature, and visual and performing arts. Barbara Lesko, ed., *Women's Earliest Records: From Ancient Egypt and Western Asia* (1989), is a collection of papers on the experiences of women in the ancient Middle East. John Boardman, I. E. S. Edwards, N. G. L. Hammond, and E. Sollberger, *The Cambridge Ancient History*, 2d ed., vols. 3.1–3.3 (1982–1991), provides extremely detailed historical coverage of the entire Mediterranean and western Asia.

For general history and cultural information about the Neo-Assyrian Empire and Mesopotamia and western Asia in the first half of the first millennium B.C.E. see Michael Roaf, *Cultural Atlas of Mesopotamia and the Ancient Near East* (1990); H. W. F. Saggs, *Civilization Before Greece and Rome* (1989); and A. Bernard Knapp, *The History and Culture of Ancient Western Asia and Egypt* (1988). Jeremy Black and Anthony Green, *Gods, Demons and Symbols of Ancient Mesopotamia: An Illustrated Dictionary* (1992), is valuable for religious institutions and conceptions, mythology, and artistic representation.

H. W. F. Saggs, *Babylonians* (1995), has coverage of the fate of the old centers in southern Mesopotamia during this era in which the north attained dominance.

Julian Reade, *Assyrian Sculpture* (1983), provides a succinct introduction to the informative relief sculptures from the Assyrian palaces. Andre Parrot, *The Arts of Assyria* (1961), provides full coverage of all artistic media.

Primary texts in translation for Assyria and other parts of western Asia can be found in James B. Pritchard, ed., *Ancient Near Eastern Texts Relating to the Old Testament*, 3d ed. (1969).

For general historical introductions to ancient Israel see Michael Grant, *The History of Israel* (1984); J. Maxwell Miller and John H. Hayes, *A History of Ancient Israel and Judah* (1986); and J. Alberto Soggin, *A History of Israel: From the Beginnings to the Bar Kochba Revolt, A.D. 135* (1984). Amihai Mazar, *Archaeology of the Land of the Bible, 10,000–586* B.C.E. (1990), provides an overview of the discoveries of archaeological excavation in Israel. For the Philistines see Trude Dothan, *The Philistines and Their Material Culture* (1982).

Donald Harden, *The Phoenicians* (1962), and Gerhard Herm, *The Phoenicians: The Purple Empire of the Ancient World* (1975), are general introductions to the Phoenicians in their homeland. Maria Eugenia Aubet, *The Phoenicians and the West: Politics, Colonies and Trade* (1993), is a sophisticated investigation of the dynamics of Phoenician expansion into the western Mediterranean. Lionel Casson, *The Ancient Mariners: Seafarers and Sea Fighters of the Mediterranean in Ancient Times*, 2d ed. (1991), 75–79, discusses the design of warships and merchant vessels. For Carthage, David Soren, Aicha Ben Abed Ben Khader, and Hedi Slim, *Carthage: Uncovering the Mysteries and Splendors of Ancient Tunisia* (1990), fills a long-standing void. Aicha Ben Abed Ben Khader and David Soren, *Carthage: A Mosaic of Ancient Tunisia* (1987), includes articles by American and Tunisian scholars as well as the catalog of a museum exhibition. R. C. C. Law, "North Africa in the Period of Phoenician and Greek Colonization, c. 800 to 323 B.C.," Chapter 2 in *The Cambridge History of Africa*, vol. 2 (1978), places the history of Carthage in an African perspective.

Elizabeth Wayland Barber, *Women's Work: The First 20,000 Years: Women, Cloth, and Society in Early Times* (1994), is an intriguing account of textile manufacture in antiquity, with emphasis on the social implications and primary role of women. I. Irving Ziderman, "Seashells and Ancient Purple Dyeing," *Biblical Archaeologist* 53 (June 1990): 98–101, is a convenient summary of Phoenician purple-dyeing technology.

NOTE

1. Plutarch, *Moralia* 799 D, translated by B. H. Warmington, *Carthage* (Penguin, Harmondsworth, 1960), 163.

CHAPTER FIVE

Greece and Iran, 1000–30 B.C.E.

Ancient Iran · The Rise of the Greeks

The Struggle of Persia and Greece · The Hellenistic Synthesis

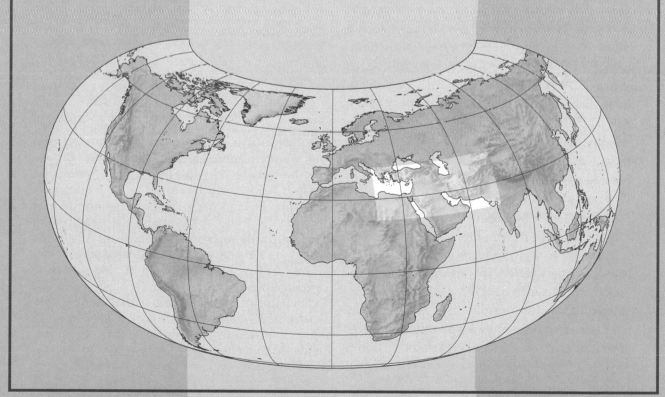

The Greek historian Herodotus (ca. 485–425 B.C.E.), chronicler of the struggles of Greece with the Persian Empire in the sixth and fifth centuries B.C.E., tells a revealing story about cultural differences. The Persian king Darius I, who ruled an empire stretching from eastern Europe to northwest India, summoned the Greek and Indian wise men who served him at court. He first asked the Greeks whether under any circumstances they would be willing to eat the bodies of their deceased fathers. The Greeks, who cremated their dead, recoiled at the impiety of such an act. Darius then asked the Indians whether they would be prepared to burn the bodies of their dead parents. The Indians were repulsed, because it was their practice to ritually partake of the bodies of the dead. The point, as Herodotus wryly points out, was that different peoples have very different practices but each regards its own way as "natural" and superior.

The effort of some thinkers to distinguish between what was natural and what was mere cultural convention was creating much discomfort among Greeks in Herodotus's lifetime, since it called into question their fundamental assumptions. Herodotus's story also reminds us that the Persian Empire (and the Hellenistic Greek kingdoms that succeeded it) brought together in Europe and in Asia lands, peoples, and cultural systems that previously had known little direct contact, and that this new cross-cultural interaction had the potential to be alarming and to stimulate new and exciting cultural syntheses.

In this chapter we look at the eastern Mediterranean and western Asia in the first millennium B.C.E., emphasizing the experiences of the Persians and the Greeks. The rivalry and wars of Greeks and Persians from the sixth to fourth centuries B.C.E. are traditionally seen as the first act of a drama that has continued intermittently ever since: the clash of the civilizations of East and West, of two peoples and two ways of life that

were fundamentally different and thus almost certain to come into conflict.

Ironically, Greeks and Persians had far more in common than they realized. They both spoke in tongues belonging to the same Indo-European family of languages found throughout Europe and western and southern Asia. Many scholars believe that all the ancient peoples who spoke languages belonging to this family inherited fundamental cultural traits, forms of social organization, and religious outlooks from their shared past.

By tracing the rise of Persian and Greek civilizations in very different physical landscapes and historical circumstances, and by looking at the characteristic institutions and values of each people, we can see how two centuries of rivalry and warfare affected the development of both peoples, and we can see what impact Persian and Greek domination made on the lands and other peoples of the eastern Mediterranean and western Asia from the sixth to second centuries B.C.E.

ANCIENT IRAN

The location of Iran, "the land of the Aryans," makes it a link between western Asia and southern and Central Asia, and its history has been marked by this mediating position (see Map 5.1). In the sixth century B.C.E. the vigorous Persians of southwest Iran created the largest empire the world had yet seen. Heirs to the long legacy of Mesopotamian history and culture, they fused it with distinctly Iranian elements and introduced new forms of political and economic organization in western Asia.

Relatively little written material from within that empire has survived, so we are forced to view it mostly through the eyes of Greeks—outsiders who were ignorant at best, usually hostile, and interested only in events that affected them-

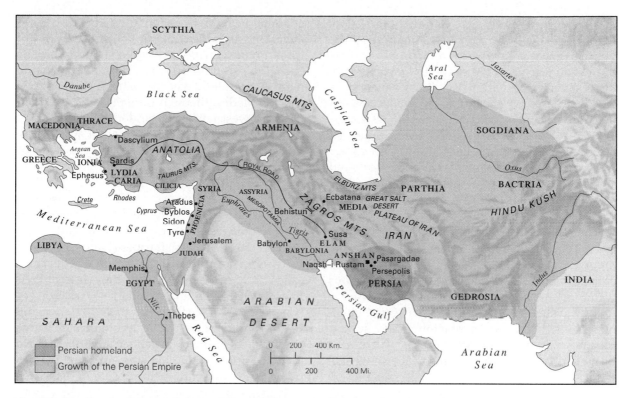

Map 5.1 The Persian Empire Between 550 and 522 B.C.E., the Persians of southwest Iran, under their kings Cyrus and Cambyses, conquered each of the major states of western Asia— Media, Babylonia, Lydia, and Egypt. The third king, Darius I, extended the boundaries as far as the Indus Valley in the east and the European shore of the Black Sea in the west. The first major setback came when the fourth king, Xerxes, failed in his invasion of Greece in 480 B.C.E. For their empire, which was considerably larger than its recent predecessor, the Assyrian Empire, the Persian rulers developed a system of provinces, governors, regular tribute, and communication via royal roads and couriers that allowed for efficient operations for almost two centuries.

selves. This Greek perspective leaves us unaware of developments in the central and eastern portions of the Persian Empire. Nevertheless, recent archaeological discoveries and close analysis of the limited written material from within the empire can be used to supplement and correct the perspective of the Greek sources.

Geography and Resources

Iran is bounded by the Zagros Mountains to the west, the Caucasus Mountains and Caspian Sea to the northwest and north, the mountains of Afghanistan and the desert of Baluchistan to the east and southeast, and the Persian Gulf to the southwest. The northeast is less protected by natural boundaries, and Iran has always been open to attacks from the nomads of Central Asia through that corridor.

The fundamental topographical facts about Iran are that there are high mountains at the edges, salt deserts in the interior depressions, and mountain streams traversing the sloping plateau and draining into seas or interior salt lakes and marshes. For humans to survive in these harsh lands, they must find ways to exploit limited water resources. Unlike the valleys of the Nile, Tigris-Euphrates, Ganges, and Yellow Rivers, ancient Iran never had a dense population. The most well-watered and populous parts of the country lie to the north and west; aridity increases and population decreases as one moves south and east. On the interior plateau, oasis settlements sprang up beside streams or springs. The Great Salt Desert, which covers most of eastern Iran, and Baluchistan in the southeast corner were extremely inhospitable, and the scattered settlements in the narrow plains beside the Persian Gulf were cut off by mountain barriers from the interior plateau.

The advent of irrigation in the first millennium B.C.E. enabled people to move down from the mountain valleys and open up the plains to agriculture. To prevent evaporation of precious water in the hot, dry climate, they devised a unique system of underground irrigation channels. Constructing and maintaining these subterranean channels and the vertical shafts that provided access at intervals was labor-intensive work. Normally, local leaders oversaw the expansion of the network in each district. Activity accelerated during periods when a strong central authority was able to organize large numbers of laborers. The connection between royal authority and prosperity is evident in the ideology of the first Persian Empire (see below). Even so, human survival depended on a delicate ecological balance, and increased levels of salt in the soil or a falling water table sometimes forced the abandonment of settlements.

Iran's mineral resources—copper, tin, iron, gold, and silver—were exploited on a limited scale in antiquity. Mountain slopes, more heavily wooded than they are now, provided fuel and materials for building and crafts. Since this austere land could not generate much of an agricultural surplus, minerals and crafted goods (such as textiles and carpets) tended to be the objects of trade.

Rise of the Persian Empire

In antiquity many groups of people, whom historians refer to collectively as Iranians because they spoke related languages and shared certain cultural features, spread out across a wide expanse of western and Central Asia, comprising not only the modern nation of Iran but also Turkmenistan, Afghanistan, and Pakistan. Several of these groups arrived in western Iran near the end of the second millennium B.C.E. The first to reach a complex level of political organization was the Medes (Mada in Iranian)* who settled in the northwest and came under the influence of the ancient centers in Mesopotamia and Urartu (modern Armenia). The Medes played a major role in the destruction of the Assyrian Empire in the late seventh century B.C.E. and extended their control westward across Assyria into Anatolia (modern Turkey). They also projected their power southeast toward the Persian Gulf, a region occupied by Persian tribes (Parsa).

The Persian rulers of the region of Anshan—called Achaemenids because they traced their lineage back to an ancestor named Achaemenes (Hachamanish)—cemented their relationship with the Median court through marriage. Cyrus (Kurush), the son of a Persian chieftain and a Median princess, united the various Persian tribes and overthrew the Median monarch Astyages sometime around 550 B.C.E. His victory should perhaps be seen less as a conquest than as an alteration of the relations between groups within the framework of the Median kingdom, for Cyrus placed both Medes and Persians in positions of responsibility. The differences between these two Iranian peoples were not great—principally dialectical differences in the way they spoke and variations in dress. The Greeks could not readily tell the two apart and used the term *Medoi* to refer to both Persians and Medes.

Like most Indo-European peoples, the early inhabitants of western Iran had a patriarchal organization: the male head of the household had virtually absolute authority over family members. Society was divided into three social and occupational castes: warriors, priests, and peasants. Warriors were the dominant element. A land owning aristocracy, they took pleasure in hunting, fighting, and gardening, and the king was the most illustrious member of this group. The Magi (*magush*) were ritual specialists who

---

*Iranian groups and individuals are known in the Western world by Greek approximations of their names; thus these familiar forms are used here. The original Iranian names are given in parentheses.

supervised the proper performance of sacrifices. The common people were primarily village-based farmers and shepherds.

The rise of the Persians was breathtakingly sudden. Cyrus, by his conquests, thrust his relatively backward society into the role of an imperial people. At first they retained the framework of Median rule. The Persians were always willing to adapt to local circumstances, to learn from those with more experience, and to employ non-Persians who had valuable skills.

Over the course of two decades the energetic Cyrus (r. 550–530 B.C.E.) redrew the map of western Asia. In 546 B.C.E. he prevailed in a cavalry battle outside the gates of Sardis, the capital of the kingdom of Lydia in western Anatolia, because the smell of his camels disconcerted his opponents' horses. All Anatolia, including the Greek city-states on the western coast, came under Persian control. In 539 he swept into Mesopotamia, where the Chaldaean, or Neo-Babylonian, dynasty had ruled since the collapse of Assyrian power (see Chapter 4). Cyrus made a deal with disaffected elements within Babylon, and when he and his army approached, the gates of the city were thrown open to him without a struggle. A skillful propagandist, Cyrus showed respect to the Babylonian priesthood and had his son crowned king in accordance with native traditions.

After Cyrus lost his life in 530 B.C.E. while campaigning against a coalition of nomadic Iranians in the northeast, his son Cambyses (Kambujiya r. 530–522 B.C.E.) set his sights on Egypt, the last of the great ancient kingdoms of the Middle East. The Persians prevailed over the Egyptians in a series of bloody battles, after which they sent exploratory expeditions south to Nubia and west to Libya. Greek sources depict Cambyses as a cruel and impious madman, but contemporary documents from Egypt show him operating in the same practical vein as his father, cultivating local priests and notables and respecting native traditions.

The manner in which Cambyses' eventual successor, Darius I (Darayavaush), came to the throne is shrouded in mystery. By birth he was from a junior branch of the ruling clan. Our primary account of the events that led to his accession is the great cuneiform inscription that he ordered to be carved into a cliff face at Behistun

Relief of two Persian magi A stone relief from Dascylium, the headquarters of the Persian governor in northwest Anatolia, showing two Iranian magi. The magi, who conducted religious rituals, are here seen wearing veils over their mouths and holding bundles of sticks used in the ceremony of sacrifice. The Persian kings and their subordinates were Zoroastrians, and it is likely that Zoroastrian religion spread to the provinces, where significant numbers of Persians lived, and influenced the beliefs of other peoples. (Courtesy, Archaeological Museums of Istanbul)

in Western Iran. According to Darius, Cambyses had secretly murdered his own brother and heir, Bardiya. When Cambyses died in 522 B.C.E., the throne was seized by a Median priest who claimed to be the surviving son of Cyrus. Darius and six other leading Persians discovered the masquerade and slew the impostor. Darius's account has struck commentators as improbable, and many believe that Darius and his fellow conspirators killed the real Bardiya. The choice of a Median scapegoat may have been an attempt to justify the dominance of Persians over Medes within the ruling class. Medes subsequently played a more junior role than they had enjoyed in the first two reigns, and all the major posts went to members of leading Persian families.

The elevation of Darius (r. 522–486 B.C.E.) was not well received everywhere. The rest of the Behistun inscription recounts how the new king and his deputies had to put down nine pretenders to the throne and fight nineteen battles across the length and breadth of the empire. The fact that Darius ultimately prevailed over all comers is testimony to his skill, energy, and ruthlessness. In the ensuing decade he extended Persian control eastward as far as the Indus Valley and westward into Europe, where he bridged the Danube River and chased the nomadic Scythian peoples north of the Black Sea. The Persians erected a string of forts in Thrace (modern-day northeast Greece and Bulgaria) and by 500 B.C.E. were on the doorstep of Greece. Darius also promoted the development of maritime routes, dispatching the Anatolian mariner Scylax to explore the waters from the Indus Delta to the Red Sea and completing a canal that linked the Red Sea with the Nile.

Imperial Organization and Ideology

The empire of Darius I was the largest the world had yet seen (see Map 5.1). Stretching from eastern Europe to Pakistan, from southern Russia to the Sudan, it encompassed a multitude of ethnic groups and every form of social and political organization, from nomadic tribe to subordinate kingdom to city-state. Darius can rightly be considered a second founder of the Persian Empire, after Cyrus, because he created a new organizational structure that was maintained throughout the remaining two centuries of the empire's existence.

Darius divided the empire into twenty provinces. Each one was under the supervision of a Persian *satrap*, or governor, who was often related or connected by marriage to the royal family. In his province the satrap was not just a representative but a replica of "the Great King"; the satrap's court was a miniature version of the royal court. The tendency for the position of satrap to become hereditary meant that satraps' families lived in the province governed by their

leader, acquired a fund of knowledge about local conditions, and formed connections with the local native elite. The farther a province was from the center of the empire, the more autonomy the satrap had, because slow communications made it impractical to refer most matters to the central administration.

One of the satrap's most important duties was to collect and then send tribute to the king. Darius had prescribed how much precious metal each province was to contribute annually (only in the western provinces were coins in circulation; see Environment and Technology: Origins and Early Development of Coinage). This amount was forwarded to the central treasury. Some of it was disbursed for necessary expenditures, but most of it was hoarded. As more and more precious metal was taken out of circulation, the price of gold and silver rose, and it became increasingly difficult for the provinces to meet their quotas. Evidence from Babylonia indicates a gradual economic decline setting in by the fourth century B.C.E. The increasing burden of taxation and official corruption worsened the economic downturn.

Royal roads connected the outlying provinces to the heart of the empire. Well maintained and patrolled, they had stations at intervals to receive important travelers and couriers carrying official correspondence. Garrisons were installed at strategic points, such as mountain passes, river crossings, and important urban centers. The administrative center was Susa, the ancient capital of Elam, in southwest Iran near the present-day border with Iraq. It was to Susa that Greeks and others went with requests and messages for the king. It took a party of Greek ambassadors at least three months to make the journey to Susa. Altogether, travel time, time spent waiting for an audience with the Persian king, delays due to weather, and the duration of the return trip probably kept the ambassadors away from home a year or more.

The king lived and traveled with his numerous wives and children. The little information that we have about the lives of Persian royal women comes from foreign sources and is thus suspect. The Book of Esther in the Hebrew Bible tells a romantic story of how King Ahasuerus

Origins and Early Development of Coinage

Numismatics, the study of coins, is a valuable source of information for historians. Coins from the ancient world survive in large numbers and can be used to trace commercial and political relations as well as the changing programs and slogans of the governments that issued them. Coins were invented in the early sixth century B.C.E., probably in Lydia. They soon spread throughout the Greek world and beyond. In the ancient world a coin was a piece of metal whose weight and purity, and thus value, were guaranteed by the state. Silver, gold, bronze, and other metals were an attractive choice for a medium of exchange: sufficiently rare to be perceived as valuable, relatively lightweight and portable (at least in the quantities available to most individuals), seemingly indestructible and therefore permanent, yet easily divided. Other items with similar qualities have been used as money in various historical societies, including beads, hard-shelled beans, and cowrie shells.

All such materials have no absolute value. They have only the value that a particular society attributes to them, based on rarity, desirability, and convention. In the modern world, paper money and even some coins lack any intrinsic value and only represent objects of value (such as the gold stored at Fort Knox) that underlie the collective wealth of the society.

Prior to the invention of coinage, people in the lands of the eastern Mediterranean and western Asia had to weigh out quantities of gold, silver, or bronze and exchange pieces of those metals for items they wanted to buy. Coinage allowed for more rapid exchanges of goods as well as for more efficient record keeping and storage of wealth. It stimulated trade and increased the total wealth of the society. However, international commerce could still be confusing because different states used different weight standards, which had to be reconciled.

At the height of their power, the Athenians required all the states in their maritime empire to use Athenian coins, weights, and measures. They probably argued that this standardization would promote commerce and be of benefit to all, and there would have been a degree of truth to this claim. However, besides being a blatant statement of Athenian domination, because the right to issue coins was a mark of sovereignty, the imposition of an Athenian monetary standard brought the lion's share of commerce to the ships and warehouses of Athens. The Athenian "owl" shown here—so called because of the portrait of Athena on one side of the coin and her symbol, the owl, on the other—became the standard for international exchange and was welcomed everywhere.

In the eastern parts of the Persian Empire coinage did not gain a foothold in the sixth to fourth centuries B.C.E. The Persian administration, however, did issue its own coin, the Daric, with a picture of Darius I, for use in the western regions that were, by then, accustomed to coinage. Several of the western satraps also issued coins with their own portraits, probably to pay Greek mercenary soldiers working for them. Later, in the Hellenistic period, Greek-style coins spread across the lands of western Asia.

Athenian coin   (Courtesy, Trustees of the British Museum)

(Xerxes) picked the Jewish woman Esther to be one of his wives because of her great beauty and how the courageous and clever queen later saved the Jewish people from a plot to massacre them. Greek sources make clear that women of the royal family could become pawns in the struggle for power. Darius strengthened his claim to the throne by marrying a daughter of Cyrus, and the Greek ruler Alexander the Great would later marry a daughter of the last Persian king. Greek sources portray Persian queens as vicious intriguers, poisoning rival wives in the

king's large harem and plotting to win the throne for their sons.

Besides the royal family, the king's large entourage included other groups: the sons of the Persian aristocracy, who were educated at court and also served as hostages for their parents' good behavior; many noblemen, who were expected to attend the king when they were not otherwise engaged; the central administration, including officials and employees of the treasury, secretariat, and archives; the royal bodyguard; and countless courtiers and slaves. Long gone was the simplicity of the days when the king hunted and caroused with his warrior companions. Inspired by Mesopotamian conceptions of monarchy, the king of Persia had become an aloof figure of majesty and splendor: "The Great King, King of Kings, King in Persia, King of countries." He referred to everyone, even the Persian nobility, as "my slaves," and those who approached were required to bow down before him. In sculptured reliefs he is larger than all the figures around him, and hovering overhead is a winged figure that represents *farna*, the charisma, glory, and fortune of kingship.

The king owned vast tracts of land throughout the empire. Some of this land he gave to his supporters. Donations called "bow land," "horse land," and "chariot land" in Babylonian documents obliged the recipient to provide military service. Scattered around the empire were gardens, orchards, and hunting preserves belonging to the king and the high nobility. The *paradayadam* (meaning "walled enclosure"—the term has come into English as *paradise*), a green oasis in an arid landscape, advertised the prosperity

Stone relief in Hall of 100 Columns   A stone relief from Persepolis, ca. 500 B.C.E., showing the Persian king on a throne supported by his subjects. Above the king hovers the *farna,* a winged figure representing the glory of kingship. Persian art, architecture, documentary language, and administrative methods often show the influence of the Assyrians, their imperial predecessors in this part of the world. Yet the Persians represented themselves as a new kind of master, concerned with the welfare of their subjects and tolerant of local practices. Persian artists have here transformed an Assyrian motif, depicting the subjects upright and happy to support the monarchy. (Courtesy, Trustees of the British Museum)

that the king and empire could bring to those who loyally served them.

Surviving administrative records from the Persian homeland give us a glimpse of how the complex tasks of administration were managed. The Persepolis Treasury and Fortification Texts, inscribed in Elamite Cuneiform on baked clay tablets show that government officials distributed food and other essential commodities to large numbers of workers of many different nationalities. Some of these workers may have been prisoners of war brought to the center of the empire to work on construction projects, maintain and expand the irrigation network, and farm on the royal estates. Workers are broken down into groups of men, women, and children. Women receive less than men of equivalent status, but pregnant women and women with babies receive more. Men and women performing skilled jobs receive more than their unskilled counterparts.

Tradition remembered Darius as a lawgiver who created a body of "laws of the King" and a system of royal judges operating throughout the empire and encouraged the codification and publication of the laws of the various subject peoples. In a manner that typifies the decentralized character of the Persian empire, he allowed each people to live in accordance with its own traditions and ordinances.

The central administration was based not in the Persian homeland (present-day Fars, directly north of the Persian Gulf) but farther west in Elam and Mesopotamia. This location was closer to the geographical center of the empire and allowed the kings to employ the trained administrators and scribes of these ancient civilizations. However, on certain occasions the king returned to one special place back in the homeland.

Darius began construction of a ceremonial capital at Persepolis (Parsa), an artificial platform on which were built a series of palaces, audience halls, treasury buildings, and barracks. Here, too, Darius (and his son Xerxes, who completed the project) was inspired by Mesopotamian traditions, for each of the great Assyrian kings had created a fortress-city as an advertisement of his wealth and power. Darius's approach can be seen in the luxuriant relief sculpture that covers the foundations, walls, and stairwells of the buildings at Persepolis.

Representatives of all the peoples of the empire—recognizable by their distinctive hair, beards, dress, hats, and footwear—are depicted in the act of of bringing gifts to the king. Historians used to think that the sculpture was a pictorial representation of a real event that transpired each year at Persepolis. In recent years this interpretation has lost support, and according to the new consensus the sculpture at Persepolis was an exercise in what today we would call public relations or propaganda: it is Darius's carefully crafted vision of an empire of vast extent and abundant resources in which all the subject peoples willingly cooperate. In one telling sculptural example, Darius subtly contrasted the character of his rule with that of the Assyrian Empire, the Persians' predecessors in these lands (see Chapter 4). The Assyrian kings had gloried in their raw power and depicted subjects staggering under the weight of a giant platform that supported the throne. Darius's artists altered the motif to show erect subjects shouldering the burden voluntarily and without strain.

What actually took place at Persepolis? This opulent retreat in the homeland probably was the scene of events of special significance for the king and his people: the New Year's Festival, coronation, marriage, death and burial. The kings, from Darius on, were buried in elaborate tombs cut into the cliffs at nearby Naqsh-i Rustam.

Another perspective on what the Persian monarchy claimed to stand for is provided by the several dozen inscriptions that have survived. At Naqsh-i Rustam Darius makes the following claim:

> Ahuramazda [god], when he saw this earth in commotion, thereafter bestowed it upon me, made me king. . . . By the favor of Ahuramazda I put it down in its place . . . I am of such a sort that I am a friend to right, I am not a friend to wrong. It is not my desire that the weak man should have wrong done to him by the mighty; nor is that my desire, that the mighty man should have wrong done to him by the weak.[1]

As this inscription makes clear, behind Darius and the empire lies the will of god. Ahuramazda made Darius king and gave him a mandate to

View of the east front of the Apadana (Audience Hall) at Persepolis, ca. 500 B.C.E.   To the right lies the Gateway of Xerxes. Persepolis, in the Persian homeland, was built by Darius I and his son Xerxes, and it was used for ceremonies of special importance for the Persian king and people—coronations, royal weddings, funerals, and the New Year's festival. The stone foundations, walls, and stairways of Persepolis are filled with sculpted images of members of the court and embassies bringing gifts, offering a vision of the grandeur and harmony of the Persian Empire. (Courtesy of the Oriental Institute, University of Chicago)

bring order to a world in turmoil, and, despite his sweet reasonableness, the king will brook no opposition. Ahuramazda is the great god of the Zoroastrian religion, and it is virtually certain that Darius and his successors were Zoroastrians.

The origins of this religion are shrouded in uncertainty. The Gathas, hymns in an archaic Iranian dialect, are said to be the work of Zoroaster (Zarathushtra). The dialect and the physical setting of the hymns indicate that Zoroaster lived in eastern Iran, but scholarly guesses about when he lived range from 1700 to 500 B.C.E. He revealed that the world had been created by Ahura Mazda, "the wise lord," but was threatened by the malevolent designs of Angra Mainyu, "the hostile spirit," backed by a host of demons. In this dualist universe the

struggle between good and evil plays out over a period of twelve thousand years. At the end of this period, good is destined to prevail, and the world will return to the pure state of creation. In the meantime, humanity is a participant in this cosmic struggle, and individuals are rewarded or punished in the afterlife for their actions.

The tenets of Zoroastrianism are best known from later periods, and it is difficult to determine how much the beliefs and practices of the Achaemenid period (550–331 B.C.E.) differed from later orthodoxy. Besides the teachings of Zoroaster, the Persians drew on moral and metaphysical conceptions with deep roots in the Iranian past. They were sensitive to the beauties of nature and venerated beneficent elements, such as water, which was not to be sullied, and fire, which was worshiped at fire altars. They were greatly concerned about the purity of the body. Corpses were exposed to wild beasts and the elements to prevent them from putrifying in the earth or tainting the sanctity of fire. The Persians still revered some of the major deities from the pagan past, such as Mithra, associated with the sun and defender of oaths and compacts. They were expected to keep promises and tell the truth. Darius castigated evildoers in his inscriptions as followers of "the Lie."

Zoroastrianism was one of the great religions of the ancient world. It believed in one supreme deity, held humans to a high ethical standard, and promised salvation. It traveled across western Asia with the advance of the Persian Empire, and it may have exerted a major influence on Judaism and thus, indirectly, on Christianity. God and the Devil, Heaven and Hell, reward and punishment, the Messiah and the End of Time, all appear to be legacies of this profound belief system, which, because of the accidents of history, has all but disappeared (except for a relatively small number of Parsees, as Zoroastrians are now called, in Iran and India).

THE RISE OF THE GREEKS

Because Greece was a relatively resource-poor region, the cultural features that emerged there in the first millennium B.C.E. came into being only because the Greeks had access to foreign sources of raw materials and to markets abroad. Greeks were in contact with other peoples, and Greek merchants and mercenaries brought home not only raw materials and crafted goods but also ideas. Under the pressure of population, poverty, war, or political crisis, Greeks moved to other parts of the Mediterranean and western Asia, carrying with them their language and culture and exerting a powerful influence on other societies. Awareness of the different practices and beliefs of other peoples stimulated the formation of a Greek identity and created an interest in geography, ethnography, and history. The two-century-long rivalry with the Persian Empire also played a large part in shaping the destinies of the Greek city-states.

Geography and Resources

Greece is part of a large ecological zone that encompasses the Mediterranean Sea and the lands surrounding it (see Map 4.4). This zone is bounded by the Atlantic Ocean to the west, the several ranges of the Alps to the north, the Syrian Desert to the east, and the Sahara to the south. The lands lying within this zone have a roughly uniform climate, experience a similar sequence of seasons, and are home to similar plants and animals. In the summer a weather front stalls near the entrance of the Mediterranean, impeding the passage of storms from the Atlantic and allowing hot, dry air from the Sahara to creep up over the region. In winter the front dissolves, and the ocean storms roll in, bringing waves, wind, and cold. Within this ecological zone, it was relatively easy for people to move around, whether driven by the pressures of war, the need for land, or the pursuit of trade.

Greek civilization arose in the lands bordering the Aegean Sea: the Greek mainland, the islands of the Aegean, and the western coast of Anatolia (see Map 5.2). As we saw in Chapter 3, southern Greece is a dry and rocky land with small plains carved up by low mountain ranges. There are no navigable rivers to ease travel or the transport of commodities across this difficult terrain. The small islands dotting the Aegean were inhabited from early times. People could cross the water from Greece to Anatolia almost without losing sight of land. From about 1000 B.C.E. Greeks began to settle on the western edge of Anatolia. Rivers that formed broad and fertile plains near the coast made Ionia, as the ancient Greeks called this region, a comfortable place. The interior of Anatolia is rugged plateau, and the Greeks of the coast were in much closer contact with their fellows across the Aegean than with the native peoples of the interior. The sea was always a connector, not a barrier.

Without large rivers, Greek farmers on the mainland depended entirely on rainfall to water

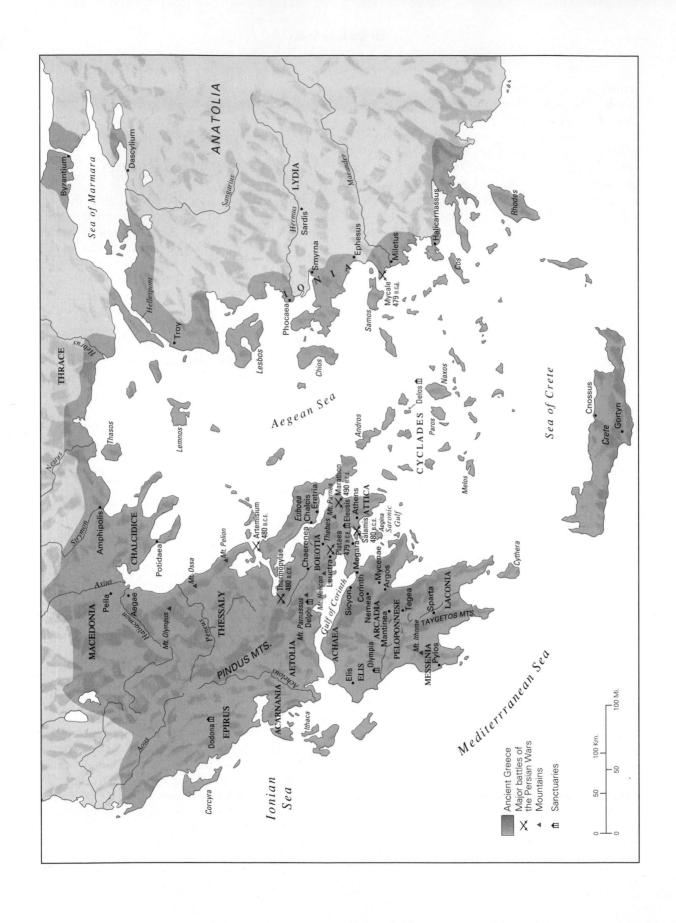

ANATOLIA

Sea of Marmara

Byzantium

Dascylium

THRACE

Hellespont

Sangarius

LYDIA

Hermus

Sardis

Smyrna

Maeander

Troy

Ephesus

Phocaea

I O N I A

Mycale
479 B.C.E.

Miletus

Halicarnassus

Rhodes

Lesbos

Chios

Samos

Cos

Aegean Sea

Sea of Crete

Thasos

Lemnos

Andros

CYCLADES

Delos

Naxos

Paros

Cnossus

Crete

Gortyn

Amphipolis

CHALCIDICE

Potidaea

Mt. Pelion

Euboea

Chalcis

Eretria

Mt. Parnes

Marathon
490 B.C.E.

ATTICA

Melos

Strymon

Axius

Mt. Ossa

Artemisium
480 B.C.E.

Chaeronea

BOEOTIA

Thebes

Eleusis

Athens

Aegina

Saronic
Gulf

MACEDONIA

Pella

Aegae

Mt. Olympus

Haliacmon

Peneus

THESSALY

Thermopylae
480 B.C.E.

Delphi

Mt. Parnassus

Mt. Helicon

Leuctra

Plataea
479 B.C.E.

Megara

Salamis
480 B.C.E.

Mycenae

Corinth

Sicyon

Argos

PINDUS MTS.

AETOLIA

Achelous

Gulf of Corinth

ACHAEA

Nemea

ARCADIA

Tegea

Sparta

LACONIA

TAYGETOS MTS.

Cythera

ACARNANIA

Ithaca

Elis

ELIS

Olympia

Mantinea

Mt. Ithome

MESSENIA

Pylos

EPIRUS

Dodona

Aous

Corcyra

Ionian
Sea

Mediterranean Sea

Nestus

Hebrus

PELOPONNESE

Ancient Greece

Major battles of
the Persian Wars

Mountains

Sanctuaries

X

100 Mi.

100 Km.

50

50

their crops. The limited arable land, thin topsoil, and sparse rainfall could not sustain large populations. In the historical period it was common practice to plant grain (mostly barley, which was hardier than wheat) in the flat plain, olive trees at the edge of the plain, and grapevines on the terraced lower slopes of the foothills. Sheep and goats were grazed in the hills during the growing season. In northern Greece, where the rainfall is greater and the land opens out into broad plains, cattle and horses were more abundant. These Greek lands had virtually no metal deposits and little timber, although both building stone, including some fine marble, and clay for the potter were abundant.

A glance at the map reveals a deeply pitted coastline with many natural harbors. A combination of circumstances—the difficulty of overland transport, the availability of good anchorages, and the need to import metals, timber, and grain—drew the Greeks to the sea. They would obtain timber from the northern Aegean, gold and iron from Anatolia, copper from Cyprus, tin from the western Mediterranean, and grain from the Black Sea, Egypt, and Sicily. Sea transport was much cheaper and faster than overland transport. To give a concrete example, a pair of oxen pulling a cart filled with grain will eat all the grain before traveling 50 miles (80 kilometers). Thus, though never comfortable with "the wine-dark sea," as Homer called it, the Greeks had no choice but to embark upon it in their small, frail ships, hugging the coastline or island-hopping where possible.

Map 5.2 Ancient Greece   By the early first millennium B.C.E., Greek-speaking peoples were dispersed throughout the Aegean region, occupying the Greek mainland, most of the islands, and the western coast of Anatolia. The rough landscape of central and southern Greece, with small plains separated by ranges of mountains, and the many islands in the Aegean favored the rise of hundreds of small, independent communities. The presence of adequate rainfall meant that agriculture was organized on the basis of self-sufficient family farms. As a result of the limited natural resources of this region, the Greeks had to resort to sea travel and trade with other lands in the Mediterranean to acquire metals and other vital raw materials.

The Emergence of the *Polis*

The first flowering of Greek culture in the Mycenaean civilization of the second millennium B.C.E. is described in Chapter 3. For several centuries after the destruction of the Mycenaean palace-states, c. 1150–800 B.C.E., Greece lapsed into a "Dark Age": dark for those who lived through it because of depopulation, poverty, and backwardness; dark for us because it left few traces in the archaeological record. One of the hallmarks of the Dark Age was isolation. Greece and the Aegean as a whole were isolated from the wider world. The importation of raw materials had been the chief source of Mycenaean prosperity. Lack of access to vital resources lay behind the poverty of the Dark Age. Within Greece, regions that had little contact with one another developed distinct regional styles in pottery and other crafts.

The isolation of Greece ended around 800 B.C.E. when Phoenician sailors arrived in the Aegean (see Chapter 4). The Phoenician city-states were dominated by a merchant class that was making ever more distant voyages west in search of valuable commodities and trading partners. By reestablishing contact between the Aegean and the Middle East, the Phoenicians gave Greek civilization an important push and inaugurated what scholars now term the "Archaic" period of Greek history (ca. 800-480 B.C.E.). Soon Greek ships were also plying the waters of the Mediterranean in search of raw materials, trade opportunities, and fertile farmland. The appearance of lifelike human and animal figures and imaginative mythical beasts on painted Greek pottery reveals the influx of new ideas from the east.

The most auspicious gift of the Phoenicians was a writing system. The Phoenicians used a set of twenty-two symbols to represent the consonants in their language, leaving the vowel sounds to be inferred by the reader. The Greeks utilized some of the symbols for which there was no equivalent sound in the Greek language to represent the vowel sounds, thus producing the first true alphabet. An alphabet has tremendous advantages over systems of writing employing ideographic and syllabic signs, such as cuneiform and hieroglyphics. Because they required years of training and the memorization of several hundred signs, cuneiform and hieroglyphics remained the preserve of a scribal class whose elevated social position stemmed from their mastery of this technology. An alphabet opens the door for more widespread literacy, because it requires only a few dozen signs to represent all the possible statements in a language and people can learn an alphabet in a relatively short period of time.

There is controversy over the first uses of the Greek alphabet. Some scholars maintain that it was first used for economic purposes, such as to keep inventories. Others propose that it originated as a vehicle for preserving the oral poetic tradition. Whatever its first use was, the new technology was soon being used to produce new forms of literature, law codes, religious dedications, and epitaphs on gravestones. This does not mean, however, that Greek society immediately became literate in the modern sense. For centuries to come, Greece remained a primarily oral culture in which people used oral means such as storytelling, rituals, and dramatic performances to preserve and transmit information.

One indicator of the powerful new forces at work was a veritable explosion of population. Studies of cemeteries in the vicinity of Athens show that there was a dramatic increase (perhaps as much as five- or sevenfold) during the eighth century B.C.E. The reasons for it are not fully understood, but it probably reflects a more intensive use of land as farming replaced herding, as well as increasing prosperity based on the importation of food and raw materials. Rising population density led to the merging of villages into urban centers. It also created the potential for specialization of labor: freed from agricultural tasks, some members of the society were able to develop skills in other areas, such as crafts, commerce, and religion.

Greece at this time consisted of hundreds of independent political entities, reflecting the facts of Greek geography—small plains separated from each other by mountain barriers. The Greek *polis* (usually translated "city-state") consisted of an urban center and the rural territory that it

controlled. City-states came in various sizes, having populations as small as several thousand or as large as several hundred thousand in the case of Athens.

Most urban centers had certain characteristic features. An *acropolis* ("top of the city") offered a place of refuge in an emergency. The town spread out around the base of this fortified high point. An *agora* ("gathering place") was an open area where the citizens came together to ratify the decisions of their leaders or to line up with their weapons before military ventures. Government buildings were located there, but the agora soon developed into a marketplace as well, since vendors everywhere are eager to set out their wares wherever crowds gather. Fortified walls surrounded the urban center; but as the population expanded, new buildings sprang up beyond the perimeter. City and country were not so sharply distinguished as in our society. The urban center depended on its agricultural hinterland to provide food, and many of the people living within the walls of the city went out to work nearby farms during the day.

Each polis was fiercely jealous of its independence and suspicious of its neighbors, and this state of mind led to frequent conflict. By the early seventh century B.C.E. the Greeks had developed a new kind of warfare, based on the *hoplite*, a heavily armored infantryman who fought in a close-packed formation called a *phalanx*. Protected by a helmet, a breastplate, and leg guards, each hoplite held a small round shield over his own left side and the right side of the man next to him and brandished a thrusting spear, with a sword in reserve. The key to victory in this style of combat was maintaining the cohesion of one's own formation while breaking open the enemy's line. Most of the casualties were suffered by the defeated army in flight.

Recent studies have emphasized the close relationship of hoplite warfare to the agricultural basis of Greek society. When a hoplite army marched into the fields of another community, the enraged farmers of that community, who had expended so much hard labor on their land and buildings, could not fail to meet the challenge. And, brutal and terrifying as the clash of two hoplite lines might be, it did offer a quick decision.

The Acropolis at Athens This steep, defensible plateau jutting up from the Attic plain served as a Mycenaean fortress in the second millennium B.C.E., and the site of Athens was continuously occupied from that time. In the mid-sixth century B.C.E. the tyrant Pisistratus built a temple to Athena, the patron goddess of the community, which was destroyed by the Persians when they invaded Greece in 480 B.C.E. The Acropolis was left in ruins for three decades as a reminder of what the Athenians had sacrificed in defense of Greek freedom, but in the 440s Pericules initiated a building program, using funds from the naval empire, which Athens now headed. These construction projects, including a new temple to Athena—the Parthenon—brought glory to the city and popularity to Pericles and the new democracy which he championed. (Robert Harding Picture Library)

Battles rarely lasted more than a few hours, and the survivors could promptly return home to tend their farms.

The expanding population soon surpassed what the small plains could support. Many communities were forced to send away their surplus population to establish independent "colonies" in distant lands. Not every colonist went willingly. Sources tell of people being chosen by lot and forbidden to return on pain of death. After obtaining the approval of the god Apollo, who spoke through a priestess at Delphi, the colonists set out, carrying with them fire from the communal hearth of the "mother-city," a symbol of the kinship and religious ties that would connect the two communities. They settled by the sea in the vicinity of a hill or other natural refuge. The "founder," a prominent member of the mother-city, allotted parcels of land and drafted laws for the new community. In some cases the indigenous population was driven away or reduced to a semiservile status; in other cases there was some intermarriage and mixing between colonists and natives.

A wave of colonization in the eighth through sixth centuries B.C.E. spread Greek culture far beyond the land of its origins. New settlements sprang up in the northern Aegean area, around the Black Sea, and on the Libyan coast of North Africa. In southern Italy and on the island of Sicily (see Map 4.4) a whole second Greek world was established. Not only did the colonies become trading partners for their mother-cities, but new developments first appearing in the colonial world traveled back to the Greek homeland—urban planning, new forms of political organization, and, as we shall see shortly, new intellectual currents. (See "Voices and Visions: Conceptions of Identity in Greece and Persia" for the impact of the frontier experience on Greek cultural identity.)

Conceptions of Identity in Greece and Persia

Most people in the ancient world were under the authority of a particular political entity, but their sense of relationship and obligation was far different from modern notions of citizenship. What were the components of Greek and Persian identity, and what was the significance of being inside or outside these groups?

During the early Archaic period Greeks began to use the term Hellenes (Graeci is what the Romans later called them) to distinguish themselves from barbaroi, the other peoples they were encountering on the frontiers created by exploration, colonization, and the expansion of long-distance commerce. Increasing interaction with new peoples and exposure to their different practices made the Greeks aware of the factors that bound them together: their language, religion, and life-style.

At first barbaroi was a descriptive, non-judgmental term meaning "non-Greeks." The struggle with Persia in the early fifth century B.C.E. strengthened the Greek sense of identity and caused a change in attitude, with the contrast between Hellenes and barbaroi beginning to take on a moral dimension that is still felt in our word "barbarian."

The Greek historian Herodotus, in his narrative of Xerxes' invasion, explicitly contrasts Greek and Persian characters. He reports a dialogue (whose historical accuracy is impossible to determine) between Xerxes and Demaratus, an exiled Spartan king, over whether the Spartans and other Greeks will stand their ground in the face of the Persians' overwhelming numerical advantage. Demaratus says:

Poverty has always been native in Greece, but the courage they have comes imported, and it is achieved by a compound of wisdom and the strength of their laws. By virtue of this Greece fights off poverty and despotism. . . . Fighting singly, they [the Spartans] are no worse than any other people; together, they are the most gallant men on earth. For they are free—but not altogether so. They have as despot over them Law, and they fear him much more than your men fear you.

The Athenians make similar claims when an envoy from the Persians offers them terms of peace if they will abandon the Greek alliance:

We know of ourselves that the power of the Mede is many times greater than our own. . . . Yet we have such a hunger for freedom that we will fight as long as we are able. . . . There is not enough gold in the world anywhere, nor territory beautiful and fertile enough, that

we should take it in return for turning to the Persian interest and enslaving Greece. . . . We are one in blood and one in language; those shrines of the gods belong to us all in common, and the sacrifices in common, and there are our habits, bred of a common upbringing.

What qualities do the Greeks particularly value? In what ways do they claim to be fundamentally different from barbarians? What might be the causes of these differences?

The lack of sources makes it more difficult to gauge the Persian sense of identity. Our best glimpse of the qualities that Persians valued comes from several inscriptions of Darius I:

I am Darius the Great King, King of Kings, King of countries containing all kinds of men, King in this great earth far and wide, son of Hystaspes, an Achaemenian, a Persian, son of a Persian, an Aryan, having Aryan lineage.

What is right, that is my desire. I am not a friend to the man who is a Lie-follower. I am not hot-tempered. What things develop in my anger, I hold firmly under control by my thinking power. I am firmly ruling over my own impulses. . . . Trained am I both with hands and with feet. As a horseman I am a good horseman. As a bowman I am a good bowman both afoot and on horseback. As a spearman I am a good spearman both afoot and on horseback.

What claims is Darius making here for a Persian character? Which qualities are especially valued?

Herodotus reports another story which, if true, might represent how the Persians viewed the Greeks. Cyrus allegedly said of the Greeks:

I never yet feared men who have a place set apart in the midst of their cities where they gather to cheat one another and exchange oaths, which they break.

Why might Zoroastrian Persians have looked down on the commercial and legal practices of the Greeks?

Sources: The first, second, and fourth quotations are from Herodotus, *The History*, trans. David Grene (Chicago: University of Chicago Press, 1988), 502–504, 610–611, 103 (=Herodotus 7.102–104, 8.143–144, 1.153). The third translation is from Roland G. Kent, *Old Persian: Grammar, Texts, Lexicon*, 2nd ed. (New Haven, CT: American Oriental Society, 1953), 138, 140.

By reducing surplus population, colonization helped to relieve pressures building within the Archaic Greek world. Nevertheless, it was an era of political instability. Kings ruled the Dark Age societies depicted in the great epic poems of Homer, the *Iliad* and the *Odyssey*, but at some point councils composed of the heads of noble families superseded the kings. This aristocracy derived its wealth and power from ownership of large tracts of land. The land was worked by peasant families who were allowed to occupy a plot and keep a portion of what they grew, or by debt-slaves, men who had borrowed money or seed from the lord and lost their freedom when unable to repay. A typical community also contained free peasants who owned small farms and urban-based craftsmen and merchants who began to constitute a growing "middle class."

In the seventh and sixth centuries B.C.E. in one city-state after another, an individual "tyrant"—by which the Greeks meant someone who held power contrary to the established traditions of the community—gained control. The individuals who seized power—often disgruntled members of the aristocracy—were backed by the emerging middle class. New opportunities for economic advancement and the declining cost of metals meant that a larger number of people could acquire arms. This group was playing an ever more important role as hoplite soldiers in the local militia and thus could put force at the disposal of their leader. Weary of the corruption and arrogance of the aristocrats who monopolized political power, this class must have demanded some political prerogatives as the price of their cooperation.

Ultimately, the tyrants of this age were unwitting catalysts in a process of political evolution. Although some were able to pass their position on to the next generation, sooner or later the tyrant-family was ejected, and authority in the community developed along one of two lines: toward *oligarchy*, in which only the wealthier members exercised political privilege; or toward *democracy*, in which all free, adult males could play a role.

Greek religion encompassed a wide range of cults and beliefs. The ancestors of the Greeks had brought a pantheon of sky-gods with them when they entered the Greek peninsula at the end of the third millennium B.C.E. Male gods predominated, but a number of female deities had important roles. These gods often represented forces in nature: Zeus sent storms and lightning, and Poseidon was master of the sea and earthquakes. The *Iliad* and the *Odyssey*, which Greek schoolboys memorized and professional performers recited, put a distinctive stamp on the personality and character of these deities. The gods that Homer portrayed were anthropomorphic, that is, conceived as humanlike in appearance and emotion. Indeed, the chief thing that separated them from humans was humans' mortality.

The worship of these gods at state-sponsored festivals was as much an expression of civic identity as of personal piety. Sacrifice was the central ritual of Greek religion. Carried out at altars in front of the temples that were the gods' places of residence in the town, it reveals how the Greeks thought about the relationship of humans and gods. The gods were given gifts, which could be as humble as a small cake deposited on the altar or a cup of wine poured out on the ground. In return the gods were expected to favor and protect the donor. Spectacular forms of ritual involved a group of people in the act of killing one or more animals, spraying the altar with the victim's blood, and burning parts of its body so that the aroma would ascend to the gods on high. The Greeks created a sense of community out of shared participation in the taking of life.

Greek individuals and poleis (the plural of polis) sought information, advice, or predictions of the future from oracles, sacred sites where the gods communicated with humans, especially from the prestigious oracle of Apollo at Delphi in central Greece. The god responded at Delphi through his priestess, the Pythia, whose obscure poetic utterances were interpreted by the male priests who administered the sanctuary. Because most Greeks were farmers, fertility cults, which worshiped and sought to enhance the productive forces in nature (for obvious reasons usually conceived of as female), were popular though often hidden from modern view because of our dependence on literary texts expressing the values of an educated, urban elite.

Vase painting depicting a sacrifice to the god Apollo, ca. 440 B.C.E.   For the Greeks, who believed in a multitude of gods who looked like humans and behaved in a similar fashion, the central act of worship was the sacrifice, the ritualized offering of a gift. This created a relationship between the human worshipper and the deity, with the expectation that the god would bestow favors in return. Here we see a number of male devotees, in their finest clothing with garlands in their hair, near the sacred outdoor altar and statue of Apollo holding his characteristic bow and laurel branch. The man on the right is offering to the god bones wrapped in fat, while the human celebrants will feast on the meat carried by the boy. (Museum für Vor-u. Frühgeschichte, Frankfurt)

New Intellectual Currents

The material changes taking place in Greece in the Archaic Period—new technologies, increased prosperity, and social and political development—led to distinctive innovations in the intellectual and artistic outlook of the Greeks. One distinctive feature of the age was a growing emphasis on the individual. In early Greek communities, the individual was enveloped by the family, and land belonged collectively to the family, including ancestors and descendants. Ripped out of this communal network and forced to establish a new life on a distant frontier, the colonist became a model of the rugged individualist, as was the tyrant who seized power for himself alone. These new patterns of activity led toward a concept of *humanism*, of the uniqueness, potentialities, and

prerogatives of the individual, which has remained a central tenet of western civilization.

We see signs of individualism clearly in the new *lyric poetry*, short compositions in which the subject matter is intensely personal, drawn from the immediate experience of the poet and highlighting his or her loves, hates, and views. Archilochus, a soldier and poet living in the first half of the seventh century B.C.E. made a surprising admission:

> Some barbarian is waving my shield, since I was obliged to
> leave that perfectly good piece of equipment behind
> under a bush. But I got away, so what does it matter?
> Let the shield go; I can buy another one equally good.[2]

Here Archilochus is making fun of the heroic ideal that scorned a soldier who ran away from the enemy.

Sappho, one of the few Greek women poets whose work has partially survived, composed exquisite poetry reflecting the lives and loves of the circle of young women whom she mentored on the Aegean island of Lesbos around 600 B.C.E. For example:

> She was like the sweetest apple
> That ripened highest on the tree,
> That the harvesters couldn't reach,
> And pretended they forgot.
> Like the mountain hyacinth trod underfoot
> By shepherd men, its flower purple on the ground.[3]

In challenging traditional values and exploiting the medium to disseminate personal feeling and opinion, lyric poets like Archilochus and Sappho paved the way for the modern Western conception of poetry.

There were also challenges to traditional religion, as when certain thinkers known as pre-Socratic philosophers called into question the kind of gods that Homer had popularized. Xenophanes, living in the sixth century B.C.E. protested:

> But if cattle and horses or lions had hands, or were able to draw with their hands and do the works that men can do, horses would draw the forms of the gods like horses, and cattle like cattle, and they would make their bodies such as they each had themselves.[4]

The pre-Socratic philosophers rejected traditional religious explanations for the origins and nature of the world and sought to explain things rationally. They were primarily concerned with questions of natural science: How was the world created? What is it made of? Why does change occur? (The term *pre-Socratic* reflects the the fact that Socrates, in the later fifth century B.C.E., turned the focus of philosophy to ethical questions.) Their science is theoretical rather than experimental, for the pre-Socratics developed conceptual models to account for the phenomenal world but did not test their validity.

Certain pre-Socratic thinkers postulated various combinations of earth, air, fire, and water as the primal elements that combine or dissolve to form the numerous substances found in nature. One advanced the theory that the world is composed of microscopic atoms (from a Greek word meaning "indivisible") moving through the void of space, colliding randomly, and combining in various ways to form the many substances of the natural world. In some respects startlingly similar to modern atomic theory, this model was merely a lucky intuition, but it is a testament to the sophistication of these thinkers. Espousing such views took courage, because more conventional Greeks regarded the pre-Socratics as impious. It is probably no coincidence that most of these theorists came from Ionia and southern Italy, two zones in which Greeks were in close contact with non-Greek peoples. The shock of encountering people with very different ideas may have stimulated new lines of inquiry.

Another important intellectual development also took place in Ionia in the sixth century B.C.E. A group of men later referred to as *logographers* ("writers of prose accounts") set about gathering information on a wide range of topics, including the geography and ethnography (description of the physical characteristics and cultural practices of a group of people) of Mediterranean lands and peoples, the foundation of important cities, and the origins of famous Greek families. They called the method they employed to collect, sort, and select information *historia*, "investigation/research." In the mid-fifth century B.C.E. Herodotus (ca. 485–425 B.C.E.), from Halicarnassus in southwest Anatolia, published his *Histories*. Early parts of the work are filled with the geographic and ethnographic reports, legends, folktales, and marvels dear to the logographers, but in later sections Herodotus focuses on the great event of the previous generation: the wars between the Greeks and the Persian Empire.

Herodotus declared his new conception of his mission in the first lines of the book:

> I, Herodotus of Halicarnassus, am here setting forth my history, that time may not draw the color from what man has brought into being, nor those great and wonderful deeds, manifested by both Greeks and barbarians, fail of their report, and, together with all this, the reason why they fought one another.[5]

When he states that he wants to find out *why* Greeks and Persians came to blows, he is a historian who is seeking the causes behind historical events. Herodotus directed the all-purpose techniques of *historia* to the service of *history* in the modern sense of the term, thereby narrowing the meaning of the word. For this achievement he is known as "the father of history."

Athens and Sparta

The two preeminent city-states of the later Archaic and Classical periods were Athens and Sparta. The remarkably different character of these two communities, both of which arose under the umbrella of Greek culture, underscores the immense potential for diversity in the evolution of human societies.

The ancestors of the Spartans had migrated into the Peloponnese, the southernmost part of the Greek mainland, around 1000 B.C.E. For a time Sparta followed a typical path of development, participating in trade and fostering the arts. Then in the seventh century B.C.E. something happened to alter the destiny of the Spartan state.

Like many other parts of Greece, the Spartan community was feeling the effects of rising population and a shortage of arable land. However, instead of sending out colonies, the Spartans crossed their mountainous western frontier and invaded the fertile plain of Messenia. Hoplite tactics may have given the Spartans the edge they needed to prevail over fierce Messenian resistance. The result was the takeover of Messenia and the virtual enslavement of the native population, who descended to the status of *helots*, the most abused and exploited population on the Greek mainland.

Fear of a future helot uprising led to the evolution of the unique Spartan way of life. The Spartan state became a military camp in a permanent state of preparedness. Territory in Messenia and Laconia (the Spartan homeland) was divided into several thousand lots and assigned to Spartan citizens. The helots worked the land and turned over a portion of what they grew to their Spartan masters, who were thereby freed from food production and able to spend their lives in military training and service.

The professional Spartan soldier was the best in Greece, and the Spartan army was superior to all others, since the other Greek states relied on citizen militias called out in time of crisis. The Spartans, however, paid a huge personal price for their military readiness. At age seven, boys were taken from their families and put into barracks, where they were toughened by a severe regimen of discipline, beatings, and deprivation. A Spartan male's whole life was subordinated to the demands of the state.

Sparta essentially stopped the clock, refusing to participate in the economic, political, and cultural revival taking place in the Archaic Greek world. There were no longer any poets or artists at Sparta. In an attempt to maintain equality among citizens, precious metals and coinage were banned, and Spartans were forbidden to engage in commerce. The fifth-century B.C.E. historian, Thucydides, a native of Athens, remarked that in his day Sparta appeared to be little more than a large village and that no future observer of the ruins of the site would be able to guess its power.

Other Greeks admired the Spartans for their courage and commitment but were put off by their arrogance, ignorance, and cruelty. The Spartans purposefully cultivated a mystique by rarely putting their reputation to the test. Under the leadership of a Council of Elders and two kings who commanded troops in the field, Sparta practiced a foreign policy that was cautious and isolationist. Reluctant to march far from home for fear of a helot uprising, the Spartans sought to maintain peace in the Peloponnese through the Peloponnesian League, a system of alliances between Sparta and its neighbors.

Athens followed a strikingly different path. By the standards of Greek city-states it possessed an unusually large and populous territory: the entire region of Attica. By the fifth century B.C.E. it had a population of approximately 300,000 people. Attica contained a number of moderately fertile plains and was ideally suited for cultivation of the olive tree. In addition to the urban center of Athens, located some 5 miles (8 kilometers) from the sea where the sheer-sided Acropolis towered above the Attic Plain, the peninsula was dotted with villages and a few larger towns.

The large land area of Attica provided a buffer against the initial stresses of the Archaic period, but by the early sixth century B.C.E. things had reached a critical point. In 594 B.C.E. Solon, a member of the aristocracy with ties to the merchant community, was appointed lawgiver with extraordinary powers to avert a looming crisis. He divided Athenian citizens into four classes based on the annual yield of their farms. Those in the top three classes could hold state offices. Members of the lowest class, who had little or no property, could not hold office but were allowed to participate in meetings of the Assembly. This arrangement, which made rights and privileges a function of wealth, was a far cry from democracy, but it broke the absolute monopoly on power of a small circle of aristocratic families, and it allowed for social and political mobility. And by abolishing the practice of enslaving individuals for failure to repay their debts, Solon guaranteed the freedom of Athenian citizens.

Despite Solon's efforts to defuse the crisis, political turmoil continued until 546 B.C.E., when an aristocrat named Pisistratus seized power. At this time most Athenians still lived in villages in the Attic countryside, identified primarily with their district, and were under the thumb of local lords, who lived in strongly constructed manor houses. To strengthen his position and weaken the aristocracy, Pisistratus tried to shift the allegiance of the rural population to the urban center of Athens, where he was the dominant figure. He undertook a number of monumental building projects, including a Temple of Athena on the Acropolis. He also instituted or expanded several major festivals: the City Dionysia, which was to become the setting for dramatic performances, and the Panathenaea, which drew people to Athens for a religious procession and athletic and poetic competitions.

Pisistratus passed the tyranny on to his sons, but with Spartan assistance the tyrant family was turned out in the last decade of the sixth century B.C.E. In the 460s and 450s B.C.E. Ephialtes and Pericles took the last steps in the evolution of democracy, transferring all power to popular organs of government: the Assembly, Council of 500, and People's Courts. Henceforth it was possible for men of moderate or little means to hold office and engage in the political process. In sensitive areas, such as managing public money and commanding military forces, offices were filled by means of election, to guarantee the ability of those chosen. But men were selected by lot to fill even the highest offices in the state, and they were paid for public service so they could afford to take time off from their work.

Henceforth, the focal point of political life was the Assembly of all citizens. Several times a month proposals were debated there, decisions were openly made, and anyone could speak to the issues of the day. There was no strong executive office; members of the Council took turns presiding and representing the Athenian state. Pericles (ca. 495–429 B.C.E.), who seems to have dominated Athenian politics for three decades, must have created an effective political organization that got out the vote on every important occasion.

In tandem with this century-and-a-half process of internal political evolution, Athens's economic clout and international reputation rose steadily. From the time of Pisistratus, Athenian pottery is increasingly prominent in the archaeological record at sites all around the Mediterranean, crowding out the products of former commercial powerhouses such as Corinth and Aegina. These pots often contained olive oil, Athens's chief export, but the elegant painted vases must have been desirable luxury commodities in their own right. Extensive trade increased the numbers and wealth of a burgeoning middle class and helps to account for why Athens took the path of increasing democratization.

THE STRUGGLE OF PERSIA AND GREECE

For the Greeks of the fifth and fourth centuries B.C.E., Persia was the great enemy of their civilization, and the wars with Persia were the decisive historical event of the era. No doubt Persians would have viewed these events differently, would have located the center of gravity farther to the east, and would not have seen the wars with the Greeks in the early fifth century B.C.E. as being so consequential. Nevertheless, the encounter with the Greeks over a period of two centuries was, in the end, of profound importance for the history of the eastern Mediterranean and western Asia.

Early Encounters

Cyrus's conquest of Lydia in 546 B.C.E. led to the subjugation of the Greek cities of the Anatolian seaboard. In the years that followed the Greek cities were ruled by local individuals or factions willing to collaborate with the Persian government so as to maintain themselves in power and allow their city to operate with minimal Persian interference. All this changed when the Ionian Revolt, a great uprising of Greeks and other subject peoples on the western frontier, broke out in 499 B.C.E. The Persians needed five years and a massive infusion of troops and resources to stamp out the insurrection.

This failed revolt led to the Persian Wars, two Persian attacks on Greece in the early fifth century B.C.E. In 490 B.C.E. Darius dispatched a naval fleet to punish Eretria and Athens, two states on the Greek mainland that had given assistance to the Ionian rebels, and to warn others about the foolhardiness of crossing the Persian king. After Eretria had been betrayed to the Persians by several of its own citizens, the survivors were marched off to permanent exile in southwest Iran. In this, as in many things, the Persians took over the practices of their Assyrian predecessors, although they resorted to mass deportation less often and were more reticent to advertise it. The Athenians were next on the list and no doubt would have had a similar fate, but their hoplites defeated the lighter-armed Persian troops in a short, sharp engagement at Marathon, 26 miles (42 kilometers) from Athens.

Xerxes (Khshayarsha r. 486–465 B.C.E.) succeeded his father on the Persian throne in 486 B.C.E. and soon turned his attention to the troublesome Greeks. He probably was moved by a desire to prove himself the equal of his predecessors, all of whom had made major acquisitions of territory for the empire. He and his advisers also must have recognized that the Aegean Sea did not provide a satisfactory boundary for the empire as long as Greeks under Persian control were in easy contact with independent Greeks across the waters.

In 480 B.C.E. Xerxes set out with a huge invasionary force. The Persian core army was supported by contingents summoned from all the peoples of the empire and by a large fleet of ships drawn from maritime subjects. Crossing the Hellespont (the narrow strait at the edge of the Aegean separating Europe and Asia) and journeying across Thrace, they descended into central and southern Greece (see Map 5.2). Xerxes sent messengers ahead to most of the Greek states, bidding them to offer up "earth and water," the tokens of submission.

Many Greek communities did indeed acknowledge Persian overlordship. But in southern Greece an alliance of states bent on resistance was formed under the leadership of the Spartans. This Hellenic League, as modern historians call it, failed to halt the Persian advance at the pass of Thermopylae in central Greece, where three hundred Spartans and their king gave their lives to buy time for their fellows to escape. However, after seizing and sacking the city of Athens in 480 B.C.E., the Persians allowed their navy to be lured into the narrow straits of nearby Salamis, where they gave up their advantage in numbers and maneuverability and suffered a devastating defeat. The following spring (479 B.C.E.), the Persian land army was routed at Plataea and the immediate threat to Greece receded.

For contemporary Greeks the victory over Xerxes' army and navy was a miracle. It was, to be sure, the first major setback for Persian arms after seventy years of expansion. A number of factors help to account for the outcome: the Persians' difficulty in provisioning a very large army in a distant land; the serious tactical error made by the Persian high command in being drawn into the narrow waters off Salamis; and the superiority of heavily armed and well-drilled Greek hoplite soldiers over lighter-armed Asiatic infantry.

The collapse of the threat to the Greek mainland did not mean the end of the war. The Greeks now went on the offensive. Athens's stubborn refusal to submit to the Persian king, even after the city had been sacked twice in two successive years, and the vital role played by the Athenian navy, which made up fully half of the allied Greek fleet, had earned the city a large measure of respect. The next phase of the war—the aim of which was to drive the Persians away from the Aegean and liberate Greek states still under Persian control—was naval. Thus Athens replaced isolationist and land-based Sparta as leader of the campaign against Persia.

In 477 B.C.E. the Delian League was formed. It was a voluntary alliance of Greek states eager to prosecute the war against Persia. Within less than twenty years, League forces, led by Athenian generals, had swept the Persians from the waters of the eastern Mediterranean and freed all Greek communities except those in distant Cyprus.

The Height of Athenian Power

By scholarly convention, the Classical period (480–323 B.C.E.) of Greek history begins with the successful defense of the Greek homeland against the forces of the Persian Empire. Ironically the Athenians, who had played such a crucial role, exploited these events to become an imperial power. Success and the passage of time led many of their Greek allies to assume an increasingly passive stance and, instead of contributing ships and men, to contribute money. The Athenians used this money to build and man an ever larger navy. Eventually they saw the other members of the Delian League as their empire. The Athenians demanded annual contributions and other signs of submission. States that tried to leave the League were brought back by force, stripped of their defenses, and rendered subordinate to Athens.

Athens's mastery of naval technology transformed Greek warfare and politics and brought power and wealth to Athens itself. Greek commercial ships were powered by wind and sail. They used a single square-rigged sheet, which was effective for sailing downwind but of little use in a headwind. Almost round in shape for stability and to allow maximum space for cargo,

these vessels could carry 100 tons or more. For the relatively small crews there was room on board to cook and sleep. Greek sailors were reluctant to go to sea in the winter months, both because of the increased danger of storms and because of the difficulty of navigating in cloudy weather, when they could see neither landmarks ashore nor the sun.

Unlike commercial ships, military vessels could not be left to drift if the wind failed. Thus they relied on large numbers of rowers. Having little deck room or storage space, these ships needed to hug the coastline and go ashore nightly to replenish food supplies and to give the crew a chance to sleep. For centuries the primary warship in Greek waters had been the *pentekonter*, a sturdy vessel powered by fifty oars in two tiers. Naval battles fought in pentekonters were crude engagements. Warriors from each side launched volleys of spears and arrows to clear the decks of the enemy ship before boarding and fighting hand to hand. By the late sixth century B.C.E. experimentation had begun with the *trireme*, a sleeker, faster vessel powered by 170 rowers.

The design of the trireme has long been a puzzle, but the unearthing at Athens of the slips where these vessels were moored, and recent experiments with full-scale replicas manned by international volunteers, have revealed much about the design of the trireme and the battle tactics that it made possible. The Greek trireme was sleek (approximately 115 by 15 feet or 35 by 6 meters) and fragile. Rowers using oars of differing lengths and carefully positioned on three levels so as not to run afoul of one another were able to achieve short bursts of speed of up to 7 knots. Athenian crews, by constant practice, became the best in the eastern Mediterranean. They could disable enemy vessels by sheering off their oars, smashing in their sides below the water line with an iron-tipped ram, or forcing them to collide with one another by running around them in ever-tighter circles.

The effectiveness of the new Athenian navy had significant consequences, both at home and abroad. The emergence at Athens of a democratic system in which each male citizen had, at least in principle, an equal voice is connected to the new primacy of the fleet. Hoplites were members of the middle and upper classes (they had to provide their own protective gear and weapons). Rowers, in contrast, came from the lower classes, and because they were providing the chief protection for the community and were the source of its power, they could insist on full rights.

Possession of a navy allowed Athens to project its power farther than it could have done with a citizen militia (which could be kept in arms for only short periods of time). In previous Greek wars, the victorious state had little capability to occupy a defeated neighbor permanently (with the exception, as we have seen, of Sparta's takeover of Messenia). Usually the victor satisfied itself with booty and, perhaps, minor adjustments to boundary lines. Athens was able to continually dominate and exploit other, weaker communities in an unprecedented way.

Athens did not hesitate to use political power to promote its commercial interests (see Environment and Technology: Origins and Early Development of Coinage). Athens's port, the Piraeus, grew into the most important commercial center in the eastern Mediterranean. The money collected each year from the subject states helped to subsidize the increasingly expensive Athenian democracy as well as underwrite the construction costs of the beautiful buildings on the Acropolis, including the majestic new temple of Athena, the Parthenon. Many Athenians worked on the construction and decoration of these monuments. Indeed, the building program was a means by which the Athenian leader, Pericles, redistributed the profits of empire to the Athenian people and gained extraordinary popularity. When his political enemies protested against the use of Delian League funds for the building program, Pericles replied: "They [Athens's subjects] do not give us a single horse, nor a soldier, nor a ship. All they supply is money. . . . It is no more than fair that after Athens has been equipped with all she needs to carry on the war, she should apply the surplus to public works, which, once completed, will bring her glory for all time."[6]

In other ways as well Athens's cultural achievements were dependent on the profits of empire. The economic advantages that empire brought to Athens subsidized indirectly the festivals at which the great dramatic tragedies of Aeschylus, Sophocles, and Euripides, and the comedies of Aristophanes, were performed. Money and power are a prerequisite for support of the arts and sciences, and the brightest and most creative artists and thinkers in the Greek world were drawn to Athens. Traveling teachers, called *Sophists,* or "wise men," provided advanced instruction in logic and public speaking to pupils who could afford their fees. The new discipline of *rhetoric*—the construction of attractive and persuasive arguments—gave those with training and quick wits a great advantage in politics and the courts. The Greek masses became connoisseurs of oratory, eagerly listening for each innovation yet so aware of the power of words that *sophist* came to mean one who uses cleverness to distort and manipulate reality.

These new intellectual currents came together in 399 B.C.E., when the philosopher Socrates (ca. 470–399 B.C.E.) was brought to trial on charges of corrupting the youth of Athens and not believing in the gods of the city. A sculptor by trade, Socrates spent most of his time in the company of young men who enjoyed conversing with him and observing him deflate the pretensions of those who thought themselves wise. He wryly commented that he knew one more thing than everyone else: that he knew nothing.

In an Athenian trial there was no guarantee that anyone involved had any legal expertise. Complainants and defendants spoke for themselves. The presiding magistrate was an ordinary citizen assigned to office by lot. Large juries of scores, or even hundreds, of citizens decided guilt and punishment, often motivated more by emotion than by legal principles.

At his trial, Socrates was easily able to dispose of the actual charges, because he was a deeply religious man and had the support of the families of the young men who had associated with him. He recognized that the real basis of the hostility he faced was twofold: (1) He was being held responsible for the actions of several of his aristocratic students who had badly harmed the state. (2) He was the target of popular prejudice against the Sophists and other intellectuals who raised questions about traditional religious beliefs and morality. The vote that found him guilty of the charges was fairly close. But his lack of

A segment of the marble frieze from the Parthenon, ca. 440 B.C.E. A continuous band of sculptured relief ran around the upper edge of the walls of the temple. Most scholars believe that it represents the great procession which was a central component of the most important civic festival in Athens, the Panathenaea, which celebrated the new year and the birthday of Athena. Here we see pairs of women carrying trays, as well as several cloaked men. Festivals were among the few occasions when Athenian women of the middle and upper classes would be out in public. Other scenes on the frieze depict young horsemen, priests with animals about to be sacrificed, and several gods looking on. Surviving records of the construction of the Parthenon indicate that the sculptors took two months to make each figure. (Giraudon/Art Resource, NY)

contrition in the penalty phase, in which he proposed that he be rewarded for his services to the state, led a larger majority of the jury to condemn him to death by drinking hemlock.

The trial of Socrates reveals a number of fault lines in Athens: between democrats and oligarchs, between members of the upper classes and commoners, and between the conservative majority and new-style intellectuals. Sophocles' disciples regarded his execution as a martyrdom. In response to it, smart young men such as Plato, who normally would have devoted their energies to political careers, withdrew from public life and dedicated themselves to the philosophical pursuit of knowledge and truth.

This period also encompasses the last stage in Greece of the transition from orality to literacy. Socrates himself wrote nothing, preferring to converse with people he met in the street. Plato (ca. 428–347 B.C.E.) may represent the first generation to be truly literate. He gained much of his knowledge from books and habitually wrote down his thoughts. Plato founded a school on the outskirts of Athens. In his Academy young men pursued a course of higher education. Yet even Plato retained vestiges of the orality of the world in which he had grown up. He wrote dialogues—an oral form—in which his protagonist, Socrates, uses the "Socratic method" of question and answer to reach a deeper understanding of the meaning of values such as justice, excellence, and wisdom. Plato refused to write down the most advanced stages of the philosophical and spiritual training that took place at his Academy. He believed that full apprehension of a higher reality, of which our own sensible world is but a pale reflection, was available only to "initiates" who had completed the earlier stages.

Inequality in Classical Greece

It is important to keep in mind that Athenian democracy, the inspiration for the concept of democracy in the Western tradition, was a democracy only for the relatively small percentage of the inhabitants of Attica who were truly citizens—free, adult males of pure Athenian ancestry. Excluding women, children, slaves, and foreigners, this came to only 10 or 15 percent—30,000 or 40,000 people out of a total population of approximately 300,000. Other democratic Greek poleis, less well known to us than Athens, were, no doubt, equally exclusive.

Slaves, mostly of foreign origin, constituted perhaps a third of the population of Attica in the fifth and fourth centuries B.C.E., and the average Athenian family owned one or more. Slaves were needed to run the shop or work on the farm while the master was attending meetings of the Assembly or serving on one of the countless boards that oversaw the day-to-day activities of the state. The slave was a "living piece of property," required to do any work, submit to any sexual acts, and receive any punishments that the owner ordained (some communities did prohibit arbitrarily killing a slave). For the most part, however, Greek slaves were not subjected to the extremes of cruelty and abuse that occurred in other places and times.

In the absence of huge estates there were no rural slave gangs, and the condition of Greek slaves was like that of the favored domestic servants in other slave-owning societies. Slaves were regarded as members of the household, and they often worked together with the master or mistress on the same tasks. The close daily contact between owners and slaves meant, in many cases, that a relationship developed, and this made it hard for Greek slave owners to deny the essential humanity of their slaves. Still, Greek thinkers rationalized the institution of slavery by arguing that *barbaroi* (non-Greeks; see Voices and Visions: Conceptions of Identity in Greece and Persia) lacked the capacity to reason and thus were better off under the direction of rational Greek owners. The social stigma attached to slavery was so great that most Athenians refused to work as wage laborers for another individual because following the orders of an employer was akin to being his slave.

Equally essential to providing Athenian men with the freedom to engage in political and social life were women. The position of women varied across Greek communities. The women of Sparta, because they were expected to bear and raise strong children, were encouraged to exercise and enjoyed a level of public visibility and outspokenness that shocked other Greeks. Athens—the case historians know best because of the abundance of written sources and vase paintings—may have been on the extreme end of Greek communities as regards the confinement and oppression of women. This situation, ironically, is linked to the high degree of freedom for men in a democratic state.

Athenian marriages were patently unequal affairs. The man might be thirty, reasonably well educated, a veteran of war, experienced in business and politics. Under law he had virtually absolute authority over the members of his household. He arranged a marriage with the parents of his prospective wife, who was likely to be a teenager who had been brought up in the women's quarters of her parents' house and had no formal education and only minimal training in weaving, cooking, and household management. Coming into the home of a husband she hardly knew, she had no political rights and limited legal protection. Given the differences in age, social experience, and authority, the relationship between husband and wife was in many ways similar to that of father and daughter.

The primary function of marriage was to produce children, preferably male. It is impossible to prove the extent of infanticide—the killing through exposure of unwanted children—because the ancients were sufficiently ashamed to say little about it. But it is likely that more girls than boys were abandoned.

Husbands and wives had limited contact in the daily round of activities. The man spent the day outdoors attending to work or political responsibilities; he dined with male friends at night; and usually he slept alone in the men's quarters. The closest relationship in the family was likely to be between the wife and her slave attendant—women of roughly the same age who spent enormous amounts of time together. The servant could be sent into town on errands while the wife stayed in the house, except to attend funerals and certain festivals and to make discreet visits to the houses of female relatives. Greek men justified the confinement of women by claiming that they were naturally promiscuous and likely to introduce other men's children into the household—an action that would threaten the family property and violate the strict regulation of citizenship rights. Athenian law allowed a husband to kill an adulterer caught in the act with his wife.

The wife's normal duties included the production of clothing, cooking, and cleaning, as well as raising the children and directing the household slaves. In wealthy families with many possessions and a large contingent of slaves, those duties might amount to extensive supervisory responsibilities.

Without any documents written by women in this period, we cannot tell the extent to which Athenian women resented their situation or accepted it because they knew little else. Women's festivals, such as the Thesmophoria, provided a rare opportunity to get out. During this three-day festival the women of Athens lived together and managed their own affairs in a great encampment, carrying out mysterious rituals meant to enhance the fertility of the land. The appearance of bold and self-assertive women on the Athenian stage is also suggestive: the defiant Antigone of Sophocles' play, who buried her brother despite the injunction of the king; and the wives of Aristophanes' comedy *Lysistrata*, who refused to have sex with their husbands until the men ended a war. Although these plays were written by men and probably reflect a male fear of strong women, the playwrights must have had models in their mothers, sisters, and wives.

The inequality of men and women also posed obstacles to creating a meaningful relationship between the sexes. To find his intellectual and emotional "equal," a man often looked to other men. Bisexuality was common in ancient Greece, as much a product of the social structure as of biological inclinations. A common pattern was that of an older man serving as admirer, pursuer, and men-

Vase painting depicting women at an Athenian fountain house, ca. 520 B.C.E. The paintings on Greek vases provide the most vivid pictorial record of ancient Greek life. The subject matter usually reflects the interests of the aristocratic males who purchased them—warfare, athletics, mythology, and drinking parties—but sometimes we are given glimpses into the lives of women and the working classes. These women are presumably domestic servants sent to fetch water for the household from a public fountain. On their heads they balance large water jars, like the one on which this scene is depicted. (William Francis Warden Fund. Courtesy, Museum of Fine Arts, Boston)

tor of a youth. Bisexuality became part of a system by which young men were educated and initiated into the community of adult males. At least this was true of the elite, intellectual groups that loom large in the written sources. It is hard to say how prevalent bisexuality and the confinement of women were among the Athenian masses.

Failure of the City-State and Triumph of the Macedonians

The emergence of Athens as an imperial power in the half-century after the Persian invasion aroused the suspicions of other Greek states and led to open hostilities between former allies. In the year 431 B.C.E. the Peloponnesian War broke out. This nightmarish struggle for survival between the Athenian and Spartan alliance systems encompassed most of the Greek world. It was a war unlike any previous Greek war because the Athenians had used their naval power to insulate themselves from the dangers of an attack by land. In mid century they had built three long walls connecting the city with the port of Piraeus and the adjacent shoreline. As long as Athens controlled the sea lanes and was able to provision itself, it could not be starved into submission by a land-based siege.

At the start of the war, Pericles formulated an unprecedented strategy, refusing to engage the Spartan-led armies that invaded Attica each year. Pericles knew that the enemy hoplites must soon return to their farms. Instead of being a short, sharp conflict typical of Greek hoplite warfare, the Peloponnesian War dragged on for nearly three decades with great loss of life and squandering of resources. It severely sapped the morale of all of Greece. The war ended only with the defeat of Athens in a naval battle in 404 B.C.E. The Persian Empire had bankrolled construction of ships by the Spartan alliance that were able to take the conflict into Athens's own element, the sea.

The Spartans, who had entered the war championing "the freedom of the Greeks," took over Athens's overseas empire until their own increasingly highhanded behavior aroused the opposition of other city-states. Indeed, the fourth century B.C.E. was a time of continuous skirmishing or warfare among Greek states. It is the tragedy of Greek history that this people, despite all its creativity and brilliance of intellect, failed to solve the problem of how to achieve peace. One can make the case that the independent *polis*, from one point of view the glory of Greek culture, was also the fundamental structural flaw.

Internal conflict in the Greek world had given the Persians their chance to recoup old losses. By the terms of the King's Peace of 387 B.C.E., to which most of the states of war-weary Greece subscribed, all of western Asia, including the Greek communities of the Anatolian seaboard, were conceded to Persia. The Persian king became the guarantor of a status quo that kept the Greeks divided and weak. Why, then, did the Persian kings of the fourth century B.C.E. not undertake another invasion of the Greek mainland? Luckily for the Greeks, rebellions in Egypt,

Cyprus, and Phoenicia as well as trouble with some of the satraps in the western provinces demanded the Persians' attention.

Meanwhile, in northern Greece developments were taking place that would irrevocably alter the balance of power in the eastern Mediterranean and western Asia. Philip II (r. 359–336 B.C.E. was transforming his previously backward kingdom of Macedonia into the premier military power in the Greek world. (Although southern Greeks had long doubted the "Greekness" of the rough and rowdy Macedonians, modern scholarship is inclined to regard their language and culture as Greek at base, though much influenced by contact with non-Greek neighbors.) Philip had made a number of improvements to the traditional hoplite format. He increased the striking power and mobility of his phalanx by equipping his soldiers with longer thrusting spears and less armor and experimenting with the coordinated use of infantry and cavalry (horses thrived in the broad, grassy plains of the north). He and his engineers had also developed new kinds of siege equipment, including the first catapults—machines using the power of twisted cords which, when relaxed, hurled arrows or stones great distances.

In 338 B.C.E. Philip defeated a coalition of southern states and established the Confederacy of Corinth as an instrument for controlling the Greek city-states. Philip was elected military commander for a planned all-Greek campaign against Persia, and his generals established a bridgehead on the Asiatic side of the Hellespont. It appears that Philip was following the advice of the Athenian educator Isocrates, who had pondered the lessons of the Persian Wars of the fifth century B.C.E. and urged a crusade against the national enemy as a means of unifying his quarrelsome countrymen.

We will never know how far Philip's ambitions extended, for an assassin killed him in 336 B.C.E. When Alexander (356–323 B.C.E.), his son and heir, crossed over into Asia in 334, his avowed purpose was to exact revenge for Xerxes' invasion a century and half before. Alexander defeated the Persian forces in three pitched battles—against the satraps of the western provinces at the Granicus River in northwest Anatolia and against King Darius III (r. 336–330

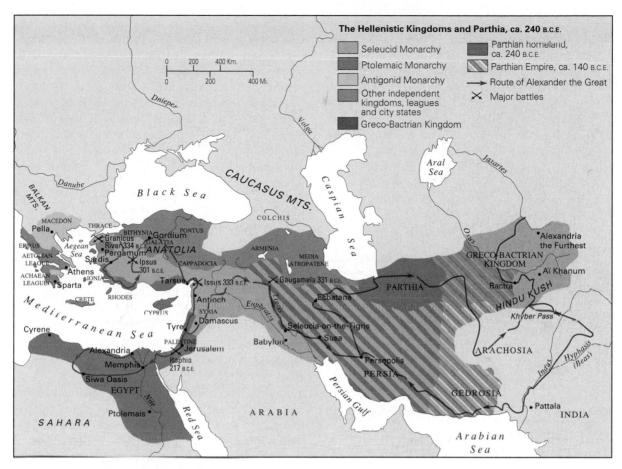

Map 5.3 Hellenistic Civilization After the death of Alexander the Great in 323 B.C.E., his vast empire soon split apart into a number of large and small political entities. A Macedonian dynasty was established on each continent: the Antigonids ruled the Macedonian homeland and endeavored, with varying success, to extend their control over southern Greece; the Ptolemies ruled Egypt; and the Seleucids inherited the majority of Alexander's conquests in Asia, though they lost control of the eastern portions due to the rise of the Parthians of Iran in the second century B.C.E. This period saw Greeks migrating in large numbers from their overcrowded homeland to serve as a privileged class of soldiers and administrators on the new frontiers, where they replicated the life style of the city-state.

B.C.E.) himself at Issus in southeast Anatolia and at Gaugamela, north of Babylon (see Map 5.3).

From the beginning Alexander the Great, as he came to be called, maintained the framework of Persian administration in the lands he conquered, recognizing that it was well adapted to local circumstances and reassuringly familiar to the subject peoples. But he replaced Persian officials with his own Macedonian and Greek comrades. As a way of controlling strategic points in

his expanding empire, Alexander also established a series of Greek-style cities, beginning with Alexandria in Egypt, and settled wounded and aged ex-soldiers in them. After his victory at Gaugamela (331 B.C.E.), he began to experiment with leaving cooperative Persian officials in place. He also admitted some Persians and other Iranians into the army and the circle of his courtiers, and he adopted elements of Persian dress and court ceremonial. Finally, he married several Iranian women who had useful royal or aristocratic connections, and he pressed his leading subordinates to do the same.

Scholars have reached widely varying conclusions about why Alexander adopted policies that were so unexpected and so fiercely resented by the Macedonian nobility. It is probably wisest to see Alexander as operating from a combination of motives, both pragmatic and idealistic. He set off on his Asian campaign with visions of glory, booty, and revenge. But the farther east he traveled, the more he began to see himself as the legitimate successor of the Persian king (a claim facilitated by the death of Darius III at the hands of subordinates). Alexander may have recognized that he had responsibilities to all the diverse peoples who fell under his control, and he may also have realized the difficulty of holding down so vast an empire by brute force and without the cooperation of important elements among the conquered peoples. In this, too, he was following the example of the Achaemenids.

THE HELLENISTIC SYNTHESIS

At the time of his sudden death in 323 B.C.E. at the age of thirty-two, Alexander apparently had made no plans for the succession. Thus his death ushered in a half-century of chaos, as the most ambitious and ruthless of his officers struggled for control of the vast empire. When the dust cleared, the empire had been broken up into three major kingdoms, each ruled by a Macedonian dynasty—the Seleucid, Ptolemaic, and Antigonid kingdoms (see Map 5.3). Each major kingdom faced a unique set of problems, and although they frequently were at odds with one another, a rough balance of power prevented anyone from gaining the upper hand and enabled smaller states to survive by playing off the great powers.

Historians call this new epoch ushered in by the conquests of Alexander the "Hellenistic Age" (323–30 B.C.E.), reflecting the tendency for the lands in northeastern Africa and western Asia that came under Greek rule to be *Hellenized*—

powerfully influenced by Greek culture. This was an age of large kingdoms with heterogeneous populations, great cities, powerful rulers, pervasive bureaucracies, and vast disparities in wealth between rich and poor—a far cry from the small, homogeneous, independent city-states of Archaic and Classical Greece. It was a cosmopolitan age of long-distance trade and communications, which saw the rise of new institutions like libraries and universities, new kinds of scholarship and science, and the cultivation of sophisticated tastes in art and literature. In many respects, it was a world much more like our own than like the preceding Classical era.

Of all the successor states, the Seleucids, who took over the bulk of Alexander's conquests, faced the greatest challenges. The Indus Valley and Afghanistan soon split off, and over the course of the third century B.C.E. Iran was lost to the Parthians. What remained for the Seleucids was a core in Mesopotamia, Syria, and parts of Anatolia, which the Seleucid monarchs ruled from their capital at Syrian Antioch. Their sprawling territories were open to attack from many directions, and, like the Persians before them, they had to administer lands inhabited by many different ethnic groups organized under various political and social forms. In the countryside, where the bulk of the native population resided, they maintained an administrative structure modeled on the Persian system. The Seleucids also continued Alexander's policy of founding Greek-style cities throughout their domains. These cities served as administrative centers and were also the lure that the Seleucids used to attract colonists from Greece, for many were willing to desert their economically depressed homeland for opportunities on the new frontier—as long as they could maintain a Greek way of life. The Seleucids desperately needed Greek soldiers, engineers, administrators, and other professionals.

The dynasty of the Ptolemies ruled Egypt and sometimes laid claim to adjacent Palestine. It faced a straightforward task. Natural boundaries of sea, mountains, and desert protected the Ptolemies' kingdom. The people of Egypt belonged to only one ethnic group and were fairly easily controlled because the vast majority of them were farmers living in villages alongside the

Nile. The Ptolemies were able to take over much of the administrative structure of the pharaohs, a system that had been perfected over the millennia to efficiently extract the surplus wealth of this populous and productive land. The Egyptian economy was centrally planned and highly controlled. Vast revenues poured into the royal treasury from rents (the king owned most of the land), taxes of all sorts, and royal monopolies on olive oil, salt, papyrus, and other key commodities.

The Ptolemies ruled from Alexandria, the first of the new cities laid out by Alexander himself. The orientation and status of this city says much about Ptolemaic policies and attitudes. The capitals of ancient Egypt, Memphis and Thebes, had been located upriver, reflecting the internal orientation of Egypt under the pharaohs. Alexandria was situated near to where the westernmost branch of the Nile runs into the Mediterranean Sea and clearly was meant to be a link between Egypt and the Mediterranean world. In the language of the Ptolemaic bureaucracy, Alexandria was technically "beside Egypt" rather than in it, as if to emphasize the gulf between rulers and subjects.

The Ptolemies, like the Seleucids, actively encouraged the immigration of Greeks from the homeland and, in return for their skills and collaboration in the military or civil administration, gave them land and a privileged position in the new society. But the Ptolemies did not seek to scatter Greek-style cities throughout the Egyptian countryside, and they made no effort to encourage the adoption of Greek language or ways by the native population. In fact, so separate was the Greek ruling class from the subject population that only the last Ptolemy, Queen Cleopatra (r. 51–30 B.C.E.), even bothered to learn the language of the Egyptians. For the Egyptian peasant population laboring on the land, life was little changed by the advent of new masters. Yet from the early second century B.C.E., periodic native insurrections in the countryside, which government forces in cooperation with Greek and Hellenized settlers quickly stamped out, were signs of Egyptians' growing resentment of the exploitation and arrogance of the Greeks.

Back in Europe the Antigonid dynasty ruled the Macedonian homeland and adjacent parts of northern Greece. This was a compact and ethnically homogeneous kingdom, so there was little of the hostility and occasional resistance that the Seleucid and Ptolemaic ruling classes faced. Macedonian garrisons at strongpoints gave the Antigonids a toehold in central and southern Greece, and the shadow of Macedonian intervention always hung over the south. The southern states met the threat by banding together into

A copy of a Hellenistic sculpture, ca. 300 B.C.E., depicting the head of the god Serapis. The cult of Serapis was created by Ptolemy I, the founder of the Macedonian dynasty in Egypt, to legitimize his rule. Meant to be accessible to both his Greek and Egyptian subjects, it was a syntheses of Greek religious conceptions with the mythology and ritual of the Egyptian god of the dead, Osiris. A great sanctuary was built to the new deity in Alexandria. In the art of the Hellenistic Period, the naturalism of the Classical Period was preserved but the style became more ornate, as seen here in the folds of the robe and the treatment of the hair. (Alinari/Art Resources, NY)

confederations, such as the Achaean League in the Peloponnese, in which the member-states maintained local autonomy but pooled resources and military power.

Athens and Sparta, the two leading cities of the Classical period, stood out from these confederations. The Spartans never quite abandoned the myth of their own invincibility and made a number of heroic but futile stands against Macedonian armies. Athens, which held a special place in the hearts of all Greeks because of the artistic and literary accomplishments of the fifth century B.C.E., pursued a foreign policy of neutrality. The city became a large museum, filled with the relics and memories of a glorious past, as well as a university town that attracted the children of the well-to-do from all over the Mediterranean and western Asia.

In an age of cities, the greatest city of all was Alexandria, with a population of nearly half a million. At the heart of this city was the royal compound. This precinct contained the palace and administrative buildings for the ruling dynasty and its massive bureaucracy. The centerpiece was the magnificent Mausoleum of Alexander. The first Ptolemy had stolen the body of Alexander while it was being brought back to Macedonia for burial. The theft was a move aimed at gaining legitimacy for Ptolemaic rule by claiming the blessing of the great conqueror, who was declared to be a god.

Alexandria gained further luster from its famous Library, which had several hundred thousand volumes, and from its Museum, or "House of the Muses" (the divinities presiding over the arts and sciences), a research institution that supported the work of the greatest poets, philosophers, doctors, and scientists of the day. Two harbors served the needs of the many trading ventures that linked the commerce of the Mediterranean with the Red Sea and Indian Ocean network. A great lighthouse—the first of its kind, a multistory tower with a fiery beacon visible at a distance of 30 miles (48 kilometers)—was one of the wonders of the ancient world.

Greek residents of Alexandria enjoyed citizenship in a Greek-style polis with Assembly, Council, and officials who dealt with purely local affairs, and they took advantage of public works and institutions that signified the Greek way of life. Public baths and shaded arcades were places to relax and socialize with friends. Ancient plays were revived in the theaters, and musical performances and demonstrations of oratory took place in the concert halls. The *gymnasium* offered facilities for exercise and fitness and also was the site where young men of the privileged classes were schooled in athletics, music, and literature. Jews had their own civic corporation, officials, and courts and predominated in two of the five main residential districts. Other quarters were filled with the sights, sounds, and smells of ethnic groups from Syria, Anatolia, and the Egyptian countryside.

In all the Hellenistic states, ambitious members of the indigenous populations learned the Greek language and adopted elements of the Greek way of life, because doing so put them in a position to become part of the privileged and wealthy ruling class. For the ancient Greeks, to be Greek was primarily a matter of language and lifestyle rather than physical traits. Now there was a spontaneous synthesis of Greek and indigenous ways. Egyptians migrated to Alexandria, and Greeks and Egyptians intermarried in the villages of the countryside, where their children were likely to grow up speaking and acting more Egyptian than Greek. Greeks living amid the monuments and descendants of the ancient civilizations of Egypt and western Asia were exposed to the mathematical and astronomical wisdom of Mesopotamia, the elaborate mortuary rituals of Egypt, and the many attractions of foreign religious cults. With little official planning or blessing, stemming for the most part from the day-to-day experiences and actions of ordinary people, this age saw a great multicultural experiment as Greek and Middle Eastern cultural traits clashed and merged in numerous ways.

CONCLUSION

Profound changes took place in the lands of the eastern Mediterranean and western Asia in the first millennium B.C.E., with pivotal roles played by Persians and Greeks. Let us compare the impacts of these two peoples and assess the broad significance of these centuries.

The empire of the Achaemenid Persians was the largest empire yet to appear in the world. It also was a new kind of empire because it encompassed such a wide variety of landscapes, peoples, and social, political, and economic systems. How did the Persians manage to hold together so diverse a collection of lands for more than two centuries?

The answer did not lie entirely in brute force. The Persians lacked the manpower to install garrisons everywhere, and communication between the central administration and provincial officials was sporadic and slow. They managed to co-opt leading elements of the subject peoples, who were willing to collaborate in return for being allowed to retain a dominant position among their own people. The Persian government demonstrated flexibility and tolerance in dealing with the laws, customs, and beliefs of subject peoples, and the Persian administration was superimposed on top of local structures, allowing a considerable role to local institutions.

The Persians also displayed a flair for public relations. The Zoroastrian religion underlined the authority of the king as the appointee of god and upholder of cosmic order. In their art and inscriptions, the Persian kings broadcast an image of a benevolent empire in which the dependent peoples contributed to the welfare of the realm.

Certain peoples with long and proud traditions, such as the Egyptians and Babylonians, revolted from time to time. But most subjects found the Persians to be decent enough masters and a great improvement over earlier Middle Eastern empires such as that of the Assyrians.

Western Asia underwent a number of significant changes in the period of Persian supremacy. First, the early Persian kings put an end to the ancient centers of power in Mesopotamia, Anatolia, and Egypt. Second, by imposing a uniform system of law and administration and by providing security and stability, the Persian government fostered commerce and prosperity, at least for some. Some historians have argued that this period was a turning point in the economic history of western Asia. The Achaemenid government possessed an unprecedented capacity to organize labor on a large scale, for the purposes of constructing an expanded water distribution network and working the extensive estates of the Persian royal family and nobility. The Persian "paradise" was not only the symbol but also the proof of the connection between political authority and the productivity of the earth.

Most difficult to assess is the cultural impact of Persian rule. The long dominant culture of Mesopotamia was fused with some Iranian elements to form a new synthesis, most visible in the art, architecture, and inscriptions of the Persian monarchs. The lands east of the Zagros Mountains as far as northwest India were brought within this cultural sphere. It has been suggested that the Zoroastrian religion spread across the empire and influenced other religious traditions, such as Judaism, but it does not appear that Zoroastrianism had a broad, popular appeal. Because the Persian administration relied heavily on the scribes and written languages of its Mesopotamian, Syrian, and Egyptian subjects, and because literacy remained the preserve of a small, professional class, the Persian language does not seem to have been widely adopted by the inhabitants of the empire. And even if there was a greater degree of Persianization in the provinces than is suggested by the extant evidence, it was so thoroughly swamped by Hellenism in the succeeding era that few traces are left.

Nearly two centuries of trouble with the Greeks on their western frontier were a vexation for the Persians but probably not their first priority. It appears that Persian kings were always more concerned about the security of their eastern and northeastern frontiers, where they were vulnerable to attack by the nomads of Central Asia. The technological differences between Greece and Persia were not great. The only difference that seems to have been of much significance was a set of arms and a military formation used by the Greeks that often allowed them to prevail over the Persians. The Persian king's response in the later fifth and fourth centuries B.C.E. was to hire Greek mercenaries to employ these hoplite tactics for his benefit. The claim is sometimes made that the Persian Empire was weak and crumbling by the time Alexander invaded, but no one could have anticipated the charismatic leadership and boundless ambition of Alexander of Macedonia.

The shadow of Persia loomed large over the affairs of the Greek city-states for more than two centuries, and even after the repulse of Xerxes' great expeditionary force there was a perpetual fear of another Persian invasion. The victories in 480 and 479 B.C.E. did allow the Greek city-states to continue to evolve politically and culturally at a critical time. Athens, in particular, vaulted into power, wealth, and intense cultural creativity as a result of its role in the Greek victory. It evolved into a new kind of Greek state, upsetting the rough equilibrium of the Archaic period by threatening the autonomy of other city-states and changing the rules of war. The result was the Peloponnesian War, which squandered lives and resources for a generation, raised serious doubts about the viability of the city-state, and diminished many people's allegiance to it.

Alexander's conquests brought to the Greek world changes virtually as radical as those suffered by the Persians. Greeks spilled out into the sprawling new frontiers in northeastern Africa and western Asia, and the independent city-state became inconsequential in a world of large kingdoms. The centuries of Greek domination had a far more pervasive cultural impact on the Middle East than did the Persian period. Alexander had been inclined to preserve the Persian administrative apparatus, leaving native institutions and personnel in place. His successors relied almost exclusively on a privileged class of Greek soldiers, officers, and administrators.

Equally significant were the foundation of Greek-style cities, which exerted a powerful cultural influence on important elements of the native populations, and a system of easily learned alphabetic Greek writing accompanied by frequent and diverse uses of the written medium, which led to more widespread literacy and far more effective dissemination of information. The end result of all this was that the Greeks had a profound impact on the peoples and lands of the Middle East, and Hellenism persisted as a cultural force for a thousand years. As we shall see in the next chapter, when the Romans arrived in the eastern Mediterranean in the second century B.C.E., they would be greatly influenced by the cultural and political practices of the Hellenistic kingdoms.

SUGGESTED READING

The most accessible treatment of the Persian Empire is J. M. Cook, *The Persian Empire* (1983). Richard N. Frye, *The History of Ancient Iran* (1984), and volume 2 of *The Cambridge History of Iran*, ed. Ilya Gershevitch (1985), are written by Iranian specialists and have abundant bibliography. John Curtis, *Ancient Persia* (1989), emphasizes the archaeological record. Roland G. Kent, *Old Persian: Grammar, Texts, Lexicon,* 2d ed. (1953), contains translations of the royal inscriptions.

William W. Malandra, *An Introduction to Ancient Iranian Religion: Readings from the Avesta and Achaemenid Inscriptions* (1983), contains documents in translation pertaining to religious subjects. Vesta Sarkhosh Curtis, *Persian Myths* (1993), is a concise, illustrated introduction to Iranian myths and legends.

The fullest treatment of Greek history and civilization in this period is in *The Cambridge Ancient History,* 3d ed., vol. 3–7 (1970–). Among the many standard one-volume histories of Greece are J. B. Bury and Russell Meiggs, *A History of Greece* (1975), and Nancy Demand, *A History of Ancient Greece* (1996). For the Archaic period see Oswyn Murray, *Early Greece,* 2d ed. (1993).

Social history is emphasized by Frank J. Frost, *Greek Society,* 3d ed. (1987). Peter Levi, *Atlas of the Greek World* (1980), is filled with maps and pictures. Michael Grant and Rachel Kitzinger, ed., *Civilization of the Ancient Mediterranean* (1987), is a three-volume collection of essays by contemporary experts on virtually every aspect of ancient Greco-Roman civilization and includes up-to-date bibliographies.

We are fortunate to have an abundant written literature from ancient Greece, and the testimony of the ancients themselves should be the starting point for any inquiry. Herodotus, Thucydides, and Xenophon chronicled the history of the Greeks and their Middle Eastern neighbors from the sixth through fourth centuries B.C.E. Arrian, who lived in the second century C.E., provides the most useful account of the career of Alexander the Great. Among the many collections of documents in translation, see Michael Crawford and David Whitehead, eds., *Archaic and Classical Greece: A Selection of Ancient Sources in Translation* (1983). David G. Rice and John E. Stambaugh, eds., *Sources for the Study of Greek Religion* (1979); Mary R. Lefkowitz and Maureen B. Fant, eds., *Women's Life in Greece and Rome: A Source Book in Translation* (1982); and Thomas

Wiedemann, ed., *Greek and Roman Slavery* (1981), are specialized collections.

Some of the most valuable treatments of particular topics include Elaine Fantham, Helene Peet Foley, Natalie Boymel Kampen, Sarah B. Pomeroy, and H. Alan Shapiro, *Women in the Classical World;* Yvon Garlan, *Slavery in Ancient Greece* (1988); Walter Burkert, *Greek Religion* (1985); Victor Davis Hanson, *The Western Way of War: Infantry Battle in Classical Greece* (1989); Lionel Casson, *The Ancient Mariners: Seafarers and Sea Fighters of the Mediterranean in Ancient Times,* 2d ed. (1991); Joint Association of Classical Teachers, *The World of Athens: An Introduction to Classical Athenian Culture* (1984); N. G. L. Hammond, *The Macedonian State: The Origins, Institutions and History* (1989); Joseph Roisman, ed., *Alexander the Great: Ancient and Modern Perspectives* (1995); and William R. Biers, *The Archaeology of Greece: an Introduction* (1990). Jack Martin Balcer, *Sparda by the Bitter Sea: Imperial Interaction in Western Anatolia* (1984), is a study of the interaction of Greeks and Persians.

For the Hellenistic world see F. W. Walbank, *The Hellenistic World,* rev. ed. (1993) and Michael Grant, *From Alexander to Cleopatra: The Hellenistic World* (1982). M. M. Austin, ed., *The Hellenistic World from Alexander to the Roman Conquest: A Selection of Ancient Sources in Translation* (1981) provides sources in translation.

NOTES

1. Quoted in Roland G. Kent, *Old Persian: Grammar, Texts, Lexicon,* 2d ed. (New Haven, CT: American Oriental Society, 1953), 138, 140.

2. Richmond Lattimore, *Greek Lyrics,* 2d ed. (Chicago, University of Chicago Press, 1960), 2.

3. Guy Davenport, *Sappho: Poems and Fragments* (Ann Arbor, University of Michigan Press, 1965), fragment 40.

4. G. S. Kirk and J. E. Raven, *The Presocratic Philosophers: A Critical History with a Selection of Texts* (Cambridge, Cambridge University Press, 1957), 169.

5. Herodotus, *The History,* trans. David Grene (Chicago: University of Chicago Press, 1988), 33. (Herodotus 1.1)

6. Plutarch, *Pericles* 12, translated by Ian Scott-Kilvert, *The Rise and Fall of Athens: Nine Greek Lives by Plutarch* (Harmondsworth, Penguin Books, 1960, 178.

CHAPTER SIX

An Age of Empires: Rome and Han China, 753 B.C.E. –330 C.E.

Imperial Parallels

Rome's Creation of a Mediterranean Empire, 753 B.C.E.–330 C.E.

The Origins of Imperial China, 221 B.C.E.–220 C.E.

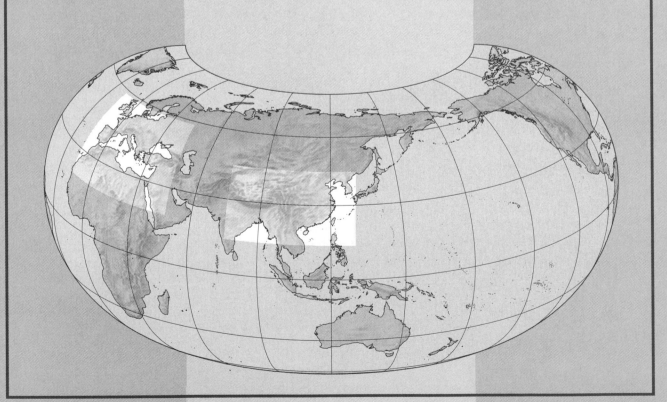

According to Chinese sources, in the year 166 C.E. a group of travelers identifying themselves as delegates from An-tun, the king of distant Da Qin, arrived at the court of the Chinese emperor Huan, who belonged to the Han dynasty. An-tun was Marcus Aurelius Antoninus, the emperor of Rome.

As far as we know, these men were the first "Romans" to reach China, although they probably were not natives of the Italian peninsula but residents of one of the eastern provinces, perhaps Egypt or Syria. They may have stretched the truth in claiming to be official representatives of the Roman emperor. More likely they were merchants hoping to set up a profitable trading arrangement at the source of the silk so highly prized in the West. Chinese officials, however, were in no position to disprove their claim, since there was no direct contact between the Roman and Chinese empires.

We do not know what became of these travelers, and their mission apparently did not lead to any more direct or regular contact between the emperors at opposite ends of the vast Eurasian landmass. Even so, the episode raises some interesting points. First, it is clear that in the early centuries C.E. Rome and China were linked by far-flung international trading networks encompassing the entire Eastern Hemisphere, and that they were dimly aware of each other's existence. Second, the period of the last centuries B.C.E. and the first centuries C.E. saw the emergence of two manifestations of a new kind of empire.

As we noted in Chapter 4, historians apply the term empire to political entities differing greatly in size, wealth, power, institutions, and longevity. The Roman and Han Chinese empires were both quantitatively and qualitatively different from earlier empires. The Roman Empire encompassed all the lands surrounding the Mediterranean Sea as well as substantial portions of continental Europe and the Middle East. The Han Empire stretched from the Pacific Ocean to the oases of Central Asia. They were the largest empires the world had yet seen, extending over a greater diversity of lands and peoples than the Assyrian and Persian Empires in the Middle East and the Mauryan Empire in India. Yet they were able to centralize control to a greater degree than the earlier empires, their cultural impact on the lands and peoples they dominated was more pervasive, and they were remarkably stable and lasted for many centuries.

Thousands of miles separated the empires of Rome and Han China; neither one influenced the other. Why, then, did two such unprecedented political entities flourish at the same time? Historians have put forth theories stressing supposedly common factors operating in both places—such as climatic change or the pressure of nomadic peoples from Central Asia on the Roman and Chinese frontiers—but none of them has won the support of most scholars. In this chapter, we examine why the Roman and Han Empires came into being, the sources of their stability or instability, and the benefits and liabilities that these empires brought to the dominant and the dominated parties.

We explore striking parallels between the Roman and Chinese Empires. These parallels suggest that rulers facing similar problems—problems that, perhaps, are bound to afflict empires of this magnitude—devise similar solutions. At the same time, we need to account for the equally important differences between the empires of East and West, to understand the unique cultural traditions that have evolved in these two parts of the world.

IMPERIAL PARALLELS

The similarities between ancient Rome and China begin at the level of the family. In both cultures the family comprised the living generations and was headed by an all-powerful patriarch. It was a tightly knit unit to which individual members were bound by strong loyalties and obligations. The family inculcated values—obedience, respect for superiors, piety, and a strong sense of duty and honor—that individuals carried with them into the wider social and political world, creating a pervasive social cohesion.

For each civilization, agriculture was the fundamental economic activity and source of wealth. The revenues of both imperial governments derived primarily from a percentage of the annual agricultural yield. Each empire depended on a free peasantry—sturdy farmers who could be pressed into military service or other forms of compulsory labor. Conflicts over who owned the land and how the land was to be used were at the heart of the political and social evolution that occurred in both places. The autocratic rulers of the Roman and Chinese states secured their positions by breaking the power of the old aristocratic families, seizing the excess land that they had amassed, and giving some land back to small farmers. The later reversal of this process, as wealthy noblemen once again gained control of vast tracts of land and reduced the peasants to dependent tenant farmers, signaled the erosion of the authority of the state.

Both empires spread out from an ethnically homogeneous core to encompass widespread territories having diverse ecosystems, populations, and ways of life. Both brought to those regions a cultural unity that has persisted, at least in part, to the present day. This development involved far more than military conquest and political domination. The skill of Roman and Chinese farmers and the high yields that they produced led to a dynamic expansion of population. As the population of the core areas outstripped the available resources, Italian and Han settlers moved into new regions, bringing their languages, beliefs, customs, and technologies with them. Many people in the conquered lands were attracted to the culture of the ruler nation and chose to adopt these practices and to attach themselves to a "winning cause."

Both empires found similar solutions to the problems of administering far-flung territories and large populations in an age in which travel and communications were slow. Technologies that facilitated imperial control also fostered cultural unification and improvements in the general standard of living. Roads built to expedite the movement of troops became the highways of commerce and the thoroughfares by which imperial culture spread. A network of cities and towns served as the nerve center of each empire, providing local administrative bases, further promoting commerce, and radiating imperial culture out into the surrounding countryside.

Cities and towns modeled themselves on the capital cities—Rome and Chang'an. Travelers throughout each empire could find in outlying regions the same types and styles of buildings and public spaces, as well as other attractive features of urban life, that they had seen in the capital, though on a smaller scale. The majority of the population still resided in the countryside, but most of the advantages of empire were enjoyed by people living in urban centers.

In an age when a message could not be transmitted faster than a man on horseback or on foot could carry it, the central government had to delegate considerable autonomy to officials at the local level. In both empires a kind of civil service developed. It was staffed by educated and capable members of a prosperous middle class.

The empires of Rome and Han China faced similar problems of defense: long borders located far from the administrative center and aggressive neighbors who coveted the prosperity of the empire. Both empires had to build walls and maintain a chain of forts and garrisons to protect against incursions. The cost of frontier defense was staggering and eventually eroded the economic prosperity of the two empires. Rough neighbors gradually learned the skills that had given the empires an initial advantage and were able to close the "technology gap." Eventually, both empires were so weakened that their borders were overrun and their central governments collapsed. Ironically, the new peoples who migrated in and took over political control had been so deeply influenced by imperial culture that they maintained it to the best of their abilities.

ROME'S CREATION OF A MEDITERRANEAN EMPIRE, 753 B.C.E.–330 C.E.

Rome's central location contributed to its success in unifying first Italy and then all the lands ringing the Mediterranean Sea (see Map 6.1). The second of three peninsulas that jut from the European landmass into the Mediterranean, the boot-shaped Italian peninsula and the large island of Sicily constitute a natural bridge almost linking Europe and North Africa. Italy was a crossroads in the Mediterranean, and the site of Rome was a crossroads within Italy. Rome lay at the midpoint of the peninsula, about 15 miles (24 kilometers) from the western coast, where a north-south road intersected an east-west river route. The Tiber River on one side and a double ring of seven hills on the other afforded natural protection to the site.

The burgeoning Roman state drew on the considerable natural resources of the peninsula. Italy is a land of hills and mountains. The Apennine range runs along its length like a spine, separating the eastern and western coastal plains. The arc of the Alps serves as a shield to the north. Many of the rivers of Italy are navigable, and passes through the central range and even through the snow-capped Alps allowed merchants and armies to travel overland. The mild Mediterranean climate affords a long growing season and conditions suitable for a wide variety of crops. The hillsides, largely denuded of cover today, were well forested in ancient times, providing timber for construction and fuel. The region of Etruria in the northwest was rich in iron and other metals.

Even though as much as 75 percent of the total area of the Italian peninsula is hilly, there is still ample arable land in the coastal plains and river valleys. Much of this land has extremely fertile volcanic soil and sustained a much larger population than was possible in Greece. While expanding within Italy, the Roman state created effective mechanisms for tapping the human resources of the countryside.

According to popular legend, the city of Rome was founded in 753 B.C.E. by Romulus, who, as a baby, had been cast adrift on the Tiber River and nursed by a she-wolf. Archaeological research, however, shows that the earliest occupation of the Palatine Hill—one of the seven hills on the site of Rome—took place as early as 1000 B.C.E. The merging of several hilltop communities to form an urban nucleus, made possible by the draining of a swamp on the site of the future Roman Forum (civic center), took place shortly before 600 B.C.E.

A Republic of Farmers

Agriculture was the essential economic activity and land was the basis of wealth in the early Roman state. As a consequence, social status, political privilege, and fundamental values were related to landownership. The vast majority of early Romans were self-sufficient independent farmers owning small plots of land. A relatively small number of families managed to acquire large tracts of land. The elders of these wealthy families were members of a council—the *senatus*, or Senate—that played a dominant role in the politics of the Roman state. These wealthy families constituted the senatorial class.

According to tradition, between 753 and 507 B.C.E. there were seven kings of Rome. The first was Romulus; the last was the tyrannical Tarquinius Superbus. In 507 B.C.E. members of the senatorial class, led by Brutus "the Liberator," deposed Tarquinius Superbus and instituted a *res publica*, a "public possession" or republic.

The Roman Republic, which lasted from 507 to 31 B.C.E., was hardly a democracy. In principle sovereign power resided in several assemblies that male citizens were eligible to attend, but the

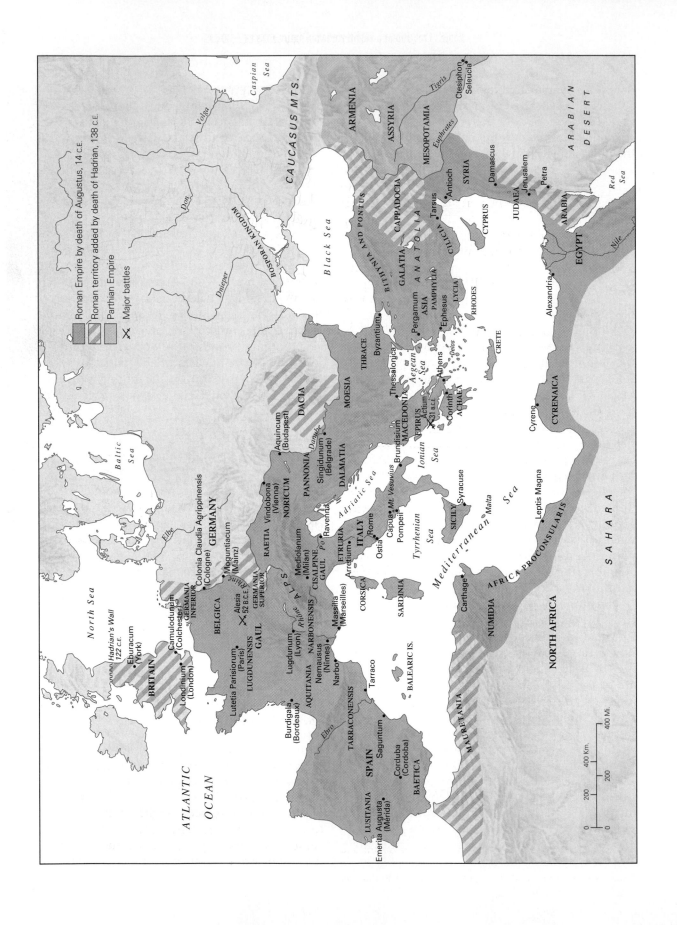

Roman Empire by death of Augustus, 14 C.E.

Roman territory added by death of Hadrian, 138 C.E.

Parthian Empire

✕ Major battles

Caspian Sea

Volga

CAUCASUS MTS.

ARMENIA

ASSYRIA

Tigris

MESOPOTAMIA

Ctesiphon
Seleucia

ARABIAN DESERT

Don

BOSPORAN KINGDOM

Dnieper

Black Sea

BITHYNIA AND PONTUS

CAPPADOCIA

GALATIA

ANATOLIA

Pergamum

ASIA

PAMPHYLIA

CILICIA

Tarsus

Antioch

SYRIA

CYPRUS

Damascus

Jerusalem

Petra

JUDAEA

ARABIA

EGYPT

Red Sea

Nile

Alexandria

Baltic Sea

Elbe

GERMANY

Colonia Claudia Agrippinensis (Cologne)

Moguntiacum (Mainz)

Rhine

GERMANIA INFERIOR

GERMANIA SUPERIOR

RAETIA

Vindobona (Vienna)

NORICUM

Aquincum (Budapest)

Danube

PANNONIA

Singidunum (Belgrade)

DALMATIA

DACIA

MOESIA

THRACE

Byzantium

MACEDONIA

Thessalonica

EPIRUS

Aegean Sea

Athens

ACHAEA

Corinth

Actium
31 B.C.E. ✕

Ephesus

Delos

RHODES

CRETE

North Sea

Hadrian's Wall
122 C.E.

Eburacum (York)

Camulodunum (Colchester)

Londinium (London)

BRITAIN

BELGICA

Lutetia Parisiorum (Paris)

LUGDUNENSIS

GAUL

Alesia
52 B.C.E. ✕

ALPS

Mediolanum (Milan)

CISALPINE GAUL

Po

Ravenna

Massilia (Marseilles)

NARBONENSIS

AQUITANIA

Lugdunum (Lyon)

Rhône

Nemausus (Nîmes)

Narbo

Burdigala (Bordeaux)

Tarraco

ETRURIA

Arretium

ITALY

Rome

Ostia

Capua

Mt. Vesuvius

Pompeii

Tyrrhenian Sea

CORSICA

SARDINIA

Adriatic Sea

Brundisium

Ionian Sea

Syracuse

SICILY

Malta

Mediterranean Sea

Leptis Magna

AFRICA PROCONSULARIS

Carthage

NUMIDIA

NORTH AFRICA

MAURETANIA

CYRENAICA

Cyrene

S A H A R A

ATLANTIC OCEAN

Tarraco

TARRACONENSIS

Ebro

BALEARIC IS.

Saguntum

SPAIN

Corduba (Cordoba)

BAETICA

LUSITANIA

Emerita Augusta (Mérida)

400 Mi.

400 Km.

200

200

0

0

system of voting was rigged so that the votes of the wealthiest classes counted for more than the votes of poorer citizens. A slate of civic officials was elected each year, and a hierarchy of state offices evolved. The culmination of a political career was to be selected as a *consul,* or chief magistrate. Each year two men were tapped to serve as consuls. When at home, the consuls presided over meetings of the Senate and assemblies. Often they were away from the city, commanding the army on military campaigns.

The real center of power was the Senate, the one permanent body in the Roman state (members sat for life). Technically an advisory council, first to the kings and later to the annually changing Republican officials, the Senate increasingly made policy and governed. The Senate nominated the sons of senators for lower-level public offices and filled vacancies in the Senate from the ranks of former officials. This self-selected body was the repository of wealth, influence, and political and military experience in the state and had both the competence and the will to rule.

The basic unit of Roman society was the family, consisting of several generations as well as the family slaves. Every member of the family was under the absolute authority of the oldest living male, the *paterfamilias.* The head of the family and the most important members of society as a whole—all men—were invested with *auctoritas,* the quality that enabled a man to inspire and demand obedience from his inferiors.

Roman society was unashamedly hierarchical. When a Roman man went for a walk, virtually everyone he met was of inferior or superior social status and expected to be treated accordingly. In this stratified society individuals and families were connected by complex ties of obligation. A fundamental social relationship existed

Statue of a Roman carrying busts of his ancestors, first century B.C.E. Roman society was extremely conscious of status, and an elite Roman family's status was determined, in large part, by the public achievements of ancestors and living members. A visitor to a Roman home would find portraits of distinguished ancestors in the entry hall, along with labels listing the offices they held, and portrait heads were carried in funeral processions. (Alinari/Art Resource, NY)

Map 6.1   The Roman Empire   The Roman Empire came to encompass all the lands surrounding the Mediterranean Sea, as well as parts of continental Europe. When Augustus died in 14 C.E., he left behind instructions to his successors not to expand beyond the limits he had set, but Claudius invaded southern Britain in the mid-first century and the soldier-emperor Trajan added Romania early in the second century. Deserts and seas provided solid natural boundaries, but the long and vulnerable river border in Central and Eastern Europe would eventually prove expensive to defend and vulnerable to invasion by Germanic and Central Asian peoples.

between a *patron,* a man of wealth and influence, and a *client,* a man who sought a patron's help and protection.

At Rome a senator might be the patron of dozens or even hundreds of men. He could provide his clients with legal advice and representation, physical protection, and loans of money in tough times. In turn, the client was expected to follow his patron out to battle, to support him in the political arena, to work on his land, and even to contribute toward the dowry of his daughter. A throng of clients awaited their patron in the morning and accompanied him from his house to the Forum for the day's business. A man with an especially large retinue enjoyed great prestige. Middle-class clients of the aristocracy might be patrons of poorer men. In sum, at Rome inequality was accepted, institutionalized, and turned into a system of mutual benefits and obligations.

Our sources do not often permit us to observe the activities of Roman women, largely because they played no public role. Virtually all our information about Roman women pertains to those in the upper classes. In a legal sense, a woman never ceased to be a child. She started out under the absolute authority of her paterfamilias. When she married, she came under the jurisdiction of the paterfamilias of her husband's family. Unable to own property or represent herself in legal proceedings, she had to depend on a male guardian to advocate her interests.

However, despite all the limitations put on them, Roman women seem to have been less constrained than their counterparts in the Greek world (see Chapter 5). New forms of marriage allowed them greater personal protection and economic independence. There are many stories of strong women who had great influence on their husbands or sons and thereby helped to shape Roman history. Roman poets confess their love for women who appear to be educated and outspoken, and the accounts of the careers of the early emperors are filled with tales of self-assured and assertive queen mothers and consorts.

How did the early Romans view the natural world and their place in it? Like other Italian peoples, they believed the world was filled with *numina*—invisible, shapeless forces. Vesta, the living, pulsating energy of fire, was in the hearth. Janus guarded the door. The Penates watched over food stored in the cupboard. Other deities resided in nearby hills, caves, grottoes, and springs. Small offerings of cakes and liquids were made to win the favor of these spirits. Certain gods had a larger sphere of operations—for example, Jupiter, the god of the sky, and Mars, initially a god of agriculture as well as war.

The Romans were especially concerned to maintain the *pax deorum* (peace of the gods), a covenant between the gods and the Roman state. Boards of priests drawn from the aristocracy performed sacrifices and other rituals to win the gods' favor. In return, the gods were expected to bring success to the undertakings of the Roman state. When the Romans came into contact with the Greeks of southern Italy (see Chapter 5), they equated their major deities with gods from the Greek pantheon, such as Zeus (Jupiter) and Ares (Mars), and took over the myths attached to the Greek gods.

Expansion in Italy and the Mediterranean

At the dawn of the Roman Republic, around 500 B.C.E., Rome was a relatively insignificant city-state among many in the region of central Italy called Latium. Three-and-a-half centuries later Rome was the center of a huge empire encompassing virtually all the lands surrounding the Mediterranean Sea. Expansion began slowly but picked up momentum, reaching a peak in the third and second centuries B.C.E.

Scholars have long debated the forces that propelled this expansion. Some credit the greed and aggressiveness of a people fond of war. Others observe that the very structure of the Roman state encouraged recourse to war, because consuls had only one year in office in which to gain glory through a military command. The Romans themselves, as part of the elaborate ceremonial accompanying their declarations of war, invariably claimed that they were only defending themselves. A strong case can be made that fear drove the Romans to expand the territory under their control in order to provide a buffer against attack: each new conquest became vulnerable, and a sense of insecurity led to further expansion. In any event, the Romans were quick to seize opportunities as they presented themselves.

Rome's conquest of Italy was sparked by ongoing friction between the hill tribes of central Italy—pastoral groups whose livelihood depended on driving their herds to seasonal grazing grounds—and the agriculturalists of the coastal plains. In the fifth century B.C.E. Rome rose to a position of leadership within a league of central Italian cities organized for defense against the nearby hill tribes. In the fourth century B.C.E. the Romans were called in to defend the wealthy and sophisticated cities of Campania, the region on the Bay of Naples possessing the richest farmland in the peninsula. By 290 B.C.E., in the course of three wars with the tribes of Samnium, in central Italy, the Romans had extended their "protection" over nearly the entire peninsula.

One key to the Romans' success in consolidating their hold over Italy was their willingness to extend Roman citizenship—with its attendant political, legal, and economic privileges—to conquered populations. In this they contrasted sharply with the Greeks, who were reluctant to share the privileges of citizenship with outsiders (see Chapter 5). In essence, the Romans co-opted the most influential elements within the conquered communities and made Rome's interests their interests. Rome demanded of its Italian subjects that they provide soldiers for the Roman military. A seemingly inexhaustible reservoir of manpower was another key to Rome's military success. In a number of crucial wars Rome was able to endure higher casualties than the enemy and to prevail by sheer numbers.

In the mid- and late third century B.C.E. Rome fought two protracted and bloody wars against the Carthaginians, those energetic descendants of Phoenicians from Lebanon who had settled in present-day Tunisia and dominated the waters and commerce of the western Mediterranean (see Chapter 4). In the end, the Roman state emerged as the unchallenged master of the western Mediterranean and acquired its first overseas colonies in Sicily, Sardinia, and Spain. Between 200 and 146 B.C.E. a series of wars pitted the Roman state against the major Greek kingdoms in the eastern Mediterranean. The Romans were at first reluctant to occupy such distant territories and withdrew their troops at the conclusion of several wars. But when the settlements that they imposed failed to hold up, a frustrated Roman government took over direct administration of these turbulent lands.

Initially the Romans did not find it feasible to extend to the overseas provinces the system of governance and the extension of citizenship rights that they had employed in Italy. Considerable autonomy, including responsibility for local administration and tax collection, was given to indigenous elite groups willing to collaborate with the Roman authorities. In addition, every year a member of the Senate, usually someone who recently had held a high public post, was dispatched to each province to serve as governor. The governor took with him a surprisingly small retinue of friends and relations to serve as advisers and deputies. The governor's primary responsibilities were to defend the province against outside attack and internal disruption, to oversee the collection of taxes and other revenues due Rome, and to decide legal cases.

Over time this system of provincial administration proved inadequate. Officials were chosen because of their political connections at Rome, not their competence or experience, and yearly changes of governor meant that the incumbent had little time to gain experience or make local contacts. Although many Roman governors were honest, some were notoriously unscrupulous and put all their ingenuity into discovering new ways to extort money from the provincial populace. While governing an ever-larger Mediterranean empire, the Romans maintained the institutions and attitudes which had developed when Rome was merely a city-state.

The Failure of the Republic

The spectacular achievement of Rome in creating an empire of unprecedented proportions unleashed powerful forces that eventually brought down the Republican system of government. As a result of the frequent wars and territorial expansion of the third and second centuries B.C.E., profound changes were taking place in the Italian landscape. Two factors were driving this complex process: Italian peasant farmers were away from home on military service for long periods of time, and most of the wealth acquired by conquest and control of new provinces ended up in the hands of members of the upper classes.

The upper classes naturally preferred to funnel the profits of empire into the purchase of Italian land. Because the soldier-farmers were away for long periods of time, it was relatively easy for investors to get possession of their farms by purchase, deception, or intimidation. As a result, the small, self-sufficient peasant farms of the Italian countryside, from which had come the soldiers who were the backbone of the Roman legions (units of 6,000 soldiers), were replaced by *latifundia,* literally "broad estates" or ranches.

The owners of these estates found it more lucrative to graze herds of cattle or to grow crops, such as grapes for wine, that brought in a big profit than to grow wheat, the staple food of ancient Italy. Thus large segments of the population of Italy, especially in the burgeoning cities, became dependent on expensive imported grain. Meanwhile, displaced peasants, who had lost their farms and could not find work in the countryside because of the cheapness of slave labor, moved to cities such as Rome (see Voices and Visions: Slavery in Rome and China). But there was no work for them in the cities, and they found themselves living in dire poverty. The growing urban masses, idle and prone to riot, would play a major role in the political struggles of the late Republic.

A critical factor contributing to the Senate's loss of authority was a change in the composition of the Roman army. One consequence of the decline of peasant farmers in Italy was a shortage of men who owned the minimum amount of property required for eligibility to serve in the legions. This shortage was felt acutely during a war that the Romans fought in North Africa at the end of the second century B.C.E.

Gaius Marius, a "new man" not from the traditional ruling class, reached a position of unprecedented political prominence by accepting into the legions poor, propertyless men and promising to give them farms when they retired from military service. These troops became devoted to the man who guaranteed their future. In the decades that followed, a series of ambitious

individuals—Sulla, Pompey, Julius Caesar, and Mark Antony—commanded armies whose primary loyalties were to their generals rather than to the state. These men did not hesitate to use the Roman legions to increase their personal power and influence. A number of bloody civil wars pitted Roman army against Roman army. The city of Rome itself was taken by force on several occasions, and victorious commanders executed their political opponents and exercised dictatorial control of the state.

Julius Caesar's grandnephew and heir, Octavian (63 B.C.E.–14 C.E.), eliminated all rivals by 31 B.C.E. and painstakingly set about refashioning the Roman system of government. He fundamentally altered the realities of power but was careful to maintain the forms of the Republic—the offices, the honors, and the social prerogatives of the senatorial class. A military dictator in fact, he never called himself king or emperor, claiming merely to be *princeps,* "first among equals" in a restored Republic. For this reason it is conventional to refer to the period following the Republic as the Principate.

Augustus, one of the many honorific titles that the Roman Senate gave Octavian, combines connotations of reverence, prosperity, and piety and became the name by which he is best known to posterity. Augustus succeeded thanks to a combination of ruthlessness, patience, and his intuitive grasp of the psychology of all elements of Roman society, which enabled him to manipulate each group in turn. He also had the good sense to live a long time. When he died in 14 C.E., after forty-five years of carefully veiled rule, almost no one was still alive who could remember the Republic. During his reign Egypt, parts of the Middle East, and Central Europe were added to the empire (the only significant later additions were the southern half of Britain and modern Romania).

So popular was Augustus when he died that four members of his family succeeded to the position of "emperor" (as we may call it) despite their serious personal and political shortcomings. The emperorship was never automatically regarded as a hereditary privilege, and after the mid-first century C.E. other families obtained the post. In theory, the early emperors were affirmed by the Senate. In reality they were chosen by the

Slavery in Rome and China

Although slaves were to be found in most ancient societies, Rome, was one of the few historical societies in which slave labor became the indispensable foundation of the economy. In the course of the frequent wars of the second century B.C.E., large numbers of prisoners were carried into slavery. Landowners and manufacturers found they could compel slaves to work longer and harder. Periodically, the harsh working and living conditions resulted in slave revolts.

The following excerpt comes from one of several surviving manuals on agriculture which give ample advice on the subject of controlling and efficiently exploiting slaves:

When the head of a household arrives at his estate, after he has prayed to the family god, he must go round his farm on a tour of inspection on the very same day, if that is possible. . . . On the next day after that he must call in his manager. . . . If the work doesn't seem to him to be sufficient, and the manager starts to say how hard he tried, but the slaves weren't any good, and the weather was awful, and the slaves ran away, and he was required to carry out some public works, then when he has finished mentioning these and all sorts of other excuses, you must draw his attention to your calculation of the labor employed and time taken. . . . There are all sorts of jobs that can be done in rainy weather—washing wine-jars, coating them with pitch, cleaning the house, storing grain, shifting muck, digging a manure pit, cleaning seed, mending ropes or making new ones. . . . The head of the household . . . should sell any old oxen, cattle or sheep that are not up to standard, wool and hides, an old cart or old tools, an old slave, a sick slave—anything else that is surplus to requirements. (Cato the Elder, *Agriculture* 2—second century B.C.E.)

What is the attitude of this Roman writer toward slaves, and how does he treat slaves? What forms of resistance do slaves put up? What precautions and punitive measures do slaveowners take to minimize the resistance and maximize the productivity of their slaves? What incentives exist for slaves to be productive?

Slavery was far less prominent in ancient China. During the Warring States Period, the large holdings of the landowning aristocracy were worked by slaves as well as by dependent peasants. The Qin government sought to abolish slavery, but the institution persisted into the Han period, although it involved only a small fraction of the population. The relatives of criminals could be seized and enslaved, and

poor families sometimes sold unwanted children into slavery. In China, whether they belonged to the state or to individuals, slaves generally performed domestic tasks.

Wang Ziyuan of Shu Commandery went to the Jian River on business, and went up to the home of the widow Yang Hui, who had a male slave named Bianliao. Wang Ziyuan requested him to go and buy some wine. Picking up a big stick, Bianliao climbed to the top of the grave mound and said: "When my master bought me, Bianliao, he only contracted for me to care for the grave and did not contract for me to buy wine for some other gentleman."

Wang Ziyuan was furious and said to the widow: "Wouldn't you prefer to sell this slave?". . . Wang Ziyuan immediately settled on the sale contract. . . .

The slave again said: "Enter in the contract everything you wish to order me to do. I, Bianliao, will not do anything not in the contract."

Wang Ziyuan said: "Agreed."

The text of the contract said: . . . The slave shall obey orders about all kinds of work and may not argue. He shall rise at dawn and do an early sweeping. After eating he shall wash up. Ordinarily he should pound the grain mortar, tie up broom straws, carve bowls and bore wells, scoop out ditches, tie up fallen fences, hoe the garden, trim up paths and dike up plats of land, cut big flails, bend bamboos to make rakes, and scrape and fix the well pulley . . . [the list of tasks continues for two-and-a-half pages]. . . .

The reading of the text of the contract came to an end. The slave was speechless and his lips were tied. Wildly he beat his head on the ground, and beat himself with his hands. He said: "If it is to be exactly as master Wang says, I would rather return soon along the yellow-soil road, with the grave worms boring through my head. Had I known before I would have bought the wine for master Wang." (Wang Bao—first century B.C.E.)

How does the situation of slaves in China seem to be somewhat different from that of Roman slaves? In what ways do the tasks of slaves and the relations between master and slave in China seem similar to those in Rome?

Sources: Thomas Wiedemann, *Greek and Roman Slavery* (1981), pp. 139–141, 183–184; C. Martin Wilbur, *Slavery in China During the Former Han Dynasty, 206 B.C.–A.D. 25* (1943), pp. 383, 388.

armies. By the second century C.E. a new mechanism of succession had been worked out by the so-called Good Emperors of that era: each designated as his successor a mature man of proven ability whom he adopted as his son and with whom he shared offices and privileges.

Augustus had allied himself with the *equites,* the class of well-to-do Italian merchants and landowners second in wealth and social status only to the senatorial class. This body of competent and self-assured individuals became the core of a new civil service that helped to run the Roman Empire. At last Rome had an administrative bureaucracy up to the task of managing a large empire with considerable honesty, consistency, and efficiency.

An Urban Empire

The Roman Empire of the first three centuries C.E. was an *urban empire.* This term does *not* mean that most people were living in cities and towns. Perhaps 80 percent of the 50 million or 60 million people living within the borders of the empire were engaged in agriculture and lived in villages or on isolated farms in the countryside. The empire, however, was administered through a network of towns and cities and brought the greatest benefits to the urban populace, and for that reason we characterize it as "urban."

The number of people living in urban centers varied widely. Numerous small towns had perhaps several thousand inhabitants. A handful of major cities—Alexandria in Egypt, Antioch in Syria, and Carthage—had populations of several hundred thousand. Rome itself had approximately a million residents. The largest cities put a huge strain on the limited technological capabilities of the ancients. Providing adequate supplies of food and water and removing sewage were always problems.

At Rome the upper classes lived in elegant townhouses on one or another of the seven hills. The house was centered around an *atrium,* a rectangular courtyard. In the ceiling of the atrium an open skylight let in light and rainwater, which fell into a basin for later use. Surrounding the atrium were a large dining room, for the dinner

and drinking parties that were an important part of the social life of the aristocracy, an interior garden, a kitchen, and, perhaps, a private bath. Bedrooms were on the upper level. The floors were decorated with pebble mosaics. The walls and ceilings were covered with frescoes (paintings done directly on wet plaster) representing mythological scenes or outdoor vistas, which gave a sense of openness in the absence of windows. The typical aristocrat also owned a number of villas in the Italian countryside, a retreat from the pressures of city life.

The poor of Rome lived in crowded slums in the low-lying parts of the city. Their wooden tenements were subject to frequent fires and must have been damp, dark, and smelly, with few furnishings. Fortunately, for much of the year they could spend the day outdoors.

The cities, towns, and even the ramshackle settlements that sprang up on the edge of frontier forts were miniature replicas of the capital city in political organization, physical layout, and appearance. A town council and two annually elected officials drawn from men of property were responsible for maintaining law and order and for collecting from both the urban center and the agricultural hinterland assigned to it the taxes due the state. In return for the privilege of running local affairs with considerable autonomy and in appreciation for how the Roman state protected their wealth and position, this municipal aristocracy loyally served the interests of Rome. In their drive to imitate the manners and values of Roman senators, they made lavish gifts to their communities. They endowed cities and towns, which had very little revenue of their own, with attractive elements of Roman urban life—a *forum* (an open plaza that served as a civic center), public office buildings, temples, gardens, baths, theaters, amphitheaters, and games and public entertainments of all sorts. Because of these amenities, the situation of the urban poor was superior to that of the rural poor. Poor people living in a city could pass time at the baths, seek refuge from the elements amid the colonnades, and attend the games.

Life in the countryside was much as it always had been. Hard work and drudgery were relieved by an occasional holiday or village festival and by the everyday pleasures of sex, family, and social exchange. Most of the time the rural population had to fend for itself in dealing with bandits, wild animals, and other hazards of country life. People living away from urban centers had little direct contact with the Roman government other than an occasional run-in with bullying soldiers and the dreaded arrival of the tax collector.

The process by which ownership of the land tended to become concentrated in ever fewer hands had been temporarily reversed during the civil wars that brought an end to the Roman Republic. In the era of the emperors it resumed. However, after the era of conquest ended in the early second century C.E., slaves were no longer plentiful or inexpensive, and landowners had to find a new source of labor. Over time the numbers of the independent farmers decreased, and they were replaced by *coloni*—tenant farmers—who had to give a portion of their crop to the landlord. In the early centuries C.E. the landowners still lived in the cities, operating their estates by means of foremen. Thus wealth was concen-

trated in the cities but was based on the productivity of rural agricultural laborers.

Another source of prosperity for some urban dwellers, was manufacture and trade. Commerce was greatly enhanced by the *pax romana* (Roman peace), the safety and stability guaranteed by Roman might. Grain, meat, vegetables, and other bulk foodstuffs usually could be exchanged only locally, because transporting them very far was not economical and many products spoiled quickly without refrigeration. The city of Rome depended on the import of massive quantities of grain from Sicily and Egypt to feed its huge population, and special naval squadrons were assigned this vital task.

Fine manufactured products, such as glass, metalwork and delicate pottery, were exported throughout the empire. Over time there was a tendency for the centers of production, which once had been located in Italy, to move outward into the provinces as knowledge of the necessary skills spread. The armies stationed on the frontiers were a large market of consumers, and their

Sign for a Roman shop　A woman behind the counter is selling fruit to one customer, while two other men are taking game hanging from a rack. The snail and two monkeys to the right of the shopkeeper may represent the name of the establishment. Towns served as markets where farmers brought their surplus products and exchanged them for crafted goods made by urban artisans. Local commerce in agricultural products must have been a major component of the economy of the Roman Empire but is hard to trace in the archaeological record. (Archivo Fotografico della Soprintendenza Archeologica di Ostia)

presence promoted the prosperity of border provinces. There also was a trade in luxury items coming from far beyond the boundaries of empire, especially silk from China and spices from India and Arabia.

Trade was of vital importance to the imperial system. Looking at the Roman Empire as a whole, we can see that the surplus revenues of rich interior provinces like Gaul (France) and Egypt were transferred in two directions: to Rome to support the emperor and the central government and to the frontier provinces to subsidize the armies. Two mechanisms made possible this transfer of wealth: the taxes demanded by the central government and the networks of trade that enabled armies on distant frontiers to buy much of what they needed on the spot.

One of the most enduring consequences of this empire, which encompassed such a wide diversity of ethnic and linguistic groups and forms of political and social organization, was *romanization*, the spread of the Latin language and the Roman way of life. This phenomenon was confined primarily to the western half of the empire, because the eastern Mediterranean already had Greek as a common idiom, a legacy of the Hellenistic kingdoms (see Chapter 5). Portuguese, Spanish, French, Italian, and Romanian all evolved from the Latin language, proving that the language of the conquerors eventually was taken over not just by elite groups in the provinces but also by the common people.

There is little evidence that the Roman government pursued a policy of forcibly Romanizing the provinces. The switch to Latin and adoption of the cultural habits that went with it were choices that the inhabitants of the provinces made for themselves. However, those who made this choice were responding to the very significant advantages available to individuals who spoke Latin and wore a toga (the traditional cloak of Roman citizens), just as today in developing nations there often are advantages to moving to the city, learning English, and putting on a suit and tie. The use of Latin facilitated dealings with the Roman administration, and a merchant who spoke Latin could get contracts to supply the military and be understood anywhere he went in the empire. Beyond these practical incen-

tives, many must have been drawn to the aura of success attached to the language and culture of a people who had conquered so vast an empire. The art, literature, and sophisticated lifestyle of the Romans had their own attractions.

As towns sprang up and acquired the characteristic features of Roman urban life, they served as magnets for ambitious members of the indigenous population. The Romans at first had been reluctant to grant Roman citizenship, with its attendant privileges, legal protections, and exemptions from certain types of taxation, to people living outside Italy. Nevertheless, a gradual extension of citizenship to individuals and communities did take place. Men who completed a twenty-six-year term of service in the native military units that backed up the Roman legions were granted citizenship and passed this coveted status on to their posterity. Emperors made grants of citizenship to individuals or entire communities as rewards for good service.

The culmination of this process occurred in 212 C.E., when the emperor Caracalla granted citizenship to all free, adult, male inhabitants of the empire. This gradual diffusion of citizenship epitomizes the process by which the empire was transformed from an Italian dominion over the Mediterranean lands into a commonwealth of peoples. Already in the first century C.E. some of the leading literary and intellectual figures came from the provinces, and by the second century even the emperors hailed from Spain, Gaul, and North Africa.

The Rise of Christianity

During this same period of general peace and prosperity, at the eastern end of the Mediterranean events were taking place that, though little noted at the moment, would prove to be of great historical significance. The Jewish homeland of Judaea (see Chapter 4), roughly equivalent to present-day Israel, was put under direct Roman rule in 6 C.E. Over the next half-century a series of Roman governors insensitive to the Jewish belief in one god managed to increase tensions. Among the Jews various kinds of opposition to Roman rule sprang up. Many waited for the arrival of the Messiah, the "Anointed One," who they thought would be a military leader who would liberate the Jewish people and drive the Romans out of the land.

It is in this context that we must see the career of Jesus, a young carpenter from the Galilee region in northern Israel. Offended by the materialism and lack of spirituality in the mainstream Jewish religion of his time, he prescribed a return to the fundamental spiritual tenets of an earlier age. Jesus eventually attracted the attention of the Jewish authorities in Jerusalem. They turned him over to the Roman governor, Pontius Pilate. Jesus was imprisoned, condemned, and executed by crucifixion, a punishment usually reserved for common criminals. His followers, the Apostles, carried on after his death and sought to spread the word of his mission and his resurrection (return from death to life) among their fellow Jews.

In the 40s C.E. Paul, a Jew from the Greek city of Tarsus in southeast Anatolia, became converted to the new creed and threw his enormous talent and energy into spreading the word. Traveling throughout Syria-Palestine, Anatolia, and Greece, he became increasingly frustrated with the refusal of most Jews to accept the revelation that he taught. Discovering a spiritual hunger among many non-Jews, he redirected his efforts toward this population (sometimes called "gentiles") and set up a string of Christian (from the Greek *Christ*, meaning "anointed one," given to Jesus by his followers) communities in the eastern Mediterranean.

The career of Paul exemplifies the cosmopolitan nature of the Roman Empire in this era. Speaking both Greek and Aramaic, he moved comfortably between the Greco-Roman and Jewish worlds. He used Roman roads, depended on the peace guaranteed by Roman arms, called on his Roman citizenship to protect him from the arbitrary action of local authorities, and moved from city to city in his quest for converts.

In 66 C.E. long-building tensions in Roman Judaea erupted into a full-scale revolt that lasted until 73. One of the casualties of the Roman reconquest of Judaea was the Jerusalem-based Christian community, which saw its primary

Important Events in Roman History	
1000 B.C.E.	First settlement on site of Rome
507 B.C.E.	Establishment of Republic
290 B.C.E.	Defeat of Samnites gives Rome control of Italy
201 B.C.E.	Defeat of Hannibal and Carthage guarantees Roman control of western Mediterranean
200–146 B.C.E.	Wars against Hellenistic kingdoms lead to control of eastern Mediterranean
88–31 B.C.E.	Civil Wars and failure of the Republic
31 B.C.E.–14 C.E.	Augustus establishes the Principate
45–58 C.E.	Paul spreads Christianity in the eastern Mediterranean
235–284 C.E.	Third Century Crisis
324 C.E.	Constantine moves capital to Constantinople

mission among the Jews. This left the field clear for Paul's non-Jewish converts, and Christianity began to diverge more and more from its Jewish roots.

For more than two centuries, the sect grew slowly but steadily. Many of the first converts were from disenfranchised groups—women, slaves, the urban poor. They could hope to receive respect and obtain positions of responsibility not accorded to them in the larger society when the members of early Christian communities assembled to democratically elect their leaders. However, as the religious movement grew and prospered, it developed a hierarchy of priests and bishops and became subject to bitter doctrinal disputes (see Chapter 9).

Early Christians were vulnerable to persecution because Roman officials regarded their refusal to worship the emperor (as monotheists they were forbidden to worship other gods) as a sign of disloyalty. Nevertheless, despite occasional attempts at suppression, or perhaps because of them, the young Christian movement continued to gain strength and attract converts.

By the late third century C.E. adherents to Christianity were a sizable minority within the population of the Roman Empire, and membership in the sect had spread up the social ranks to include many educated and prosperous people who held posts in local and imperial government.

Technology and Transformation

We have seen how the early Christians took advantage of the relative ease and safety of travel brought by Roman arms and engineering to spread their faith. Remnants of roads, walls, aqueducts, and buildings still visible today testify to the engineering expertise of the ancient Romans. Some of the best engineers served with the army, building bridges, siege works, and ballistic weapons that hurled stones and shafts. In peacetime the soldiers were often put to work on construction projects. Aqueducts—long, elevated or underground conduits—carried water from its source to urban centers, using only the force of gravity. The Romans were pioneers in the use of the arch, which distributes great weights evenly without thick supporting walls. The invention of concrete—a mixture of lime powder, sand, and water that could be poured into molds set on scaffolding—allowed the Romans to create vast vaulted and domed interior spaces and to move away from the strictly rectilinear forms of the pillar-and-post construction methods employed by the Greeks.

One of the greatest challenges for the Roman administration was the defense of borders that stretched for thousands of miles. Augustus's posthumous recommendation to his successors had been that they not expand the empire further, because any subsequent acquisition would cost more to administer and defend than the revenues it brought in. Thus after Augustus's death the Roman army was reorganized and redeployed to reflect the shift from an offensive to a defensive strategy. The empire was protected at most points by natural features—mountains, deserts, and seas. The long Rhine/Danube river frontier in Germany and Central Europe, however, was a vulnerable point. This lengthy frontier was guarded by a string of forts whose relatively small garrisons were adequate for dealing with raiders. On particularly desolate frontiers, such as in Britain and North Africa, long walls were built to keep out the peoples who lived beyond.

Fortunately for Rome, its neighbors, with one exception, were less technologically advanced and more loosely organized peoples who did not pose a serious threat to the security of the empire as a whole. That one exception was on the eastern frontier, where the Parthian kingdom, heir to earlier Mesopotamian and Persian empires, controlled the lands that are today Iran and Iraq. For centuries Rome and Parthia engaged in a rivalry that, in the end, sapped both sides without leading to any significant territorial gain for either party.

The Roman state prospered for two-and-a-half centuries after Augustus stabilized the internal political situation and addressed the needs of the empire with an ambitious program of reforms. In the third century C.E. cracks in the edifice became visible. Historians use the expression "third-century crisis" to refer to the period from 235 to 284 C.E., in which the Roman Empire was beset and nearly destroyed by political, military, and economic problems.

The most visible symptom of the crisis was the frequent change of rulers. It has been estimated that some twenty or more men claimed the office of emperor during this period. Most of them reigned for a very short time before being overthrown by a rival or killed by their own troops. Germanic tribesmen on the Rhine/Danube frontier took advantage of the frequent civil wars and periods of anarchy to raid deep into the empire. For the first time in centuries, cities began to erect walls to protect themselves. Several regions, feeling that the central government was not adequately protecting them, turned power over to a man on the spot who promised to put their interests first.

These political and military emergencies had a devastating impact on the economy of the empire. The cost of rewarding troops and defending the increasingly permeable frontiers drained the state treasury, and the incessant demands of the central government for more tax revenues, as well as the interruption of commerce by fighting, eroded the prosperity of the towns. Shortsighted emperors, desperate for cash, secretly cut back the amount of precious metal in the coins and pocketed the excess. But the public quickly caught on, and the devalued coinage became less and less acceptable as a medium for exchange. Indeed, the empire reverted to a barter economy, a far less efficient system that further curtailed large-scale and long-distance commerce.

The municipal aristocracy, once the most vital and public-spirited class in the empire, was slowly crushed out of existence. As town councilors its members were personally liable to make up any shortfall in the tax revenues owed to the state. But the decline in trade eroded, as did their wealth, which usually was based on manufacture and commerce. Many began to evade their civic duties and even go into hiding.

There was an overall shift of population away from the cities and into the countryside. Many people sought employment and protection—from raiders and from government officials—on the estates of wealthy and powerful country landowners. In the shrinking of cities and the movement of the population to the country estates, we can see the roots of the social and economic structures of the European Middle

The Roman aqueduct near Tarragona, Spain   Provisions of an adequate water supply was a problem associated with the growth of towns and cities during the Roman Empire. An aqueduct brought water from a source, sometimes many miles away, to an urban complex, using only the force of gravity. Roman engineers skillfully designed structures that maintained a steady downhill slope all the way from source to destination, and Roman troops were often used in such large-scale construction. Scholars can sometimes roughly estimate the population of an ancient city by calculating the amount of water available. (Rapho/Photo Researchers, Inc.)

Ages—a roughly seven-hundred-year period in which wealthy rural lords dominated a peasant population tied to the land (see Chapter 9).

Just when things looked bleakest, a man arose who pulled the empire back from the brink of self-destruction. Like many of the rulers of that age, Diocletian was from one of the eastern European provinces most vulnerable to invasion. A commoner by birth, he had risen through the ranks of the army and gained power in 284. The measure of his success is indicated by the fact that he ruled for more than twenty years and died in bed.

Diocletian implemented a series of radical solutions that saved the Roman state by transforming it. To halt inflation, he issued an edict that specified the maximum prices that could be charged for various commodities and services. To ensure an adequate supply of workers in vital services, many people were frozen into their professions and were required to train their sons to succeed them. This kind of government regulation of prices and vocations was completely new in Roman history and had some unforeseen consequences. One was the creation of a black market among buyers and sellers who chose to ignore the government's price controls and establish their own prices for goods and services. Another was a growing tendency among the inhabitants of the empire to consider the government an oppressive entity that no longer deserved their loyalty.

When Diocletian resigned in 305, the old divisiveness reemerged as various claimants battled for the throne. The eventual winner was Constantine. By 324 he was able to reunite the entire empire under his sole rule.

In 312 Constantine had won a key battle at the Milvian Bridge over the Tiber River near Rome. He later claimed that before this battle he saw in the sky a cross (the sign of the Christian God) superimposed on the sun. Believing that the Christian God had helped him achieve victory, the new emperor converted to Christianity. Throughout his reign he supported the Christian church, although he tolerated other beliefs as well.

Historians disagree about whether Constantine was motivated by purely spiritual motives or whether he was seeking to unify the peoples of the empire under a single religion. In either case his conversion was of tremendous historical significance. Large numbers of people began to convert, because they saw that Christians seeking political office or favors from the government had clear advantages over non-Christians.

The other decisive step taken by Constantine was the transfer of the capital from Rome to Byzantium, an ancient Greek city on the Bosporus strait leading into the Black Sea. The city was renamed Constantinople, "City of Constantine." This move both reflected and accelerated changes already taking place. Constantinople was closer than Rome to the most threatened borders of the empire, in eastern Europe. The urban centers and prosperous middle class of the eastern half of the empire had better withstood the third-century crisis than had those of the western half. In addition, more educated people and more Christians were living in the eastern provinces (see Chapter 9).

The conversion of Constantine and the transfer of the imperial capital away from Rome often have been considered events marking the end of Roman history. This conventional view, however, is open to question for at least two reasons: (1) Many of the important changes that culminated during Constantine's reign had their roots in events of the previous two centuries. (2) The Roman Empire as a whole survived for at least another century, and the eastern, or Byzantine, portion of it (discussed in Chapter 9), survived Constantine by more than a thousand years. It is true that the Roman Empire of the fourth century was fundamentally different from what had existed before, and for that reason it is convenient to see in Constantine's reign the beginning of a new epoch in the West.

THE ORIGINS OF IMPERIAL CHINA, 221 B.C.E.–220 C.E.

The early history of China (described in Chapter 3) was marked by the fragmentation that geography seemed to dictate. The authority of the first dynasties, Shang (ca. 1750–1027 B.C.E.)

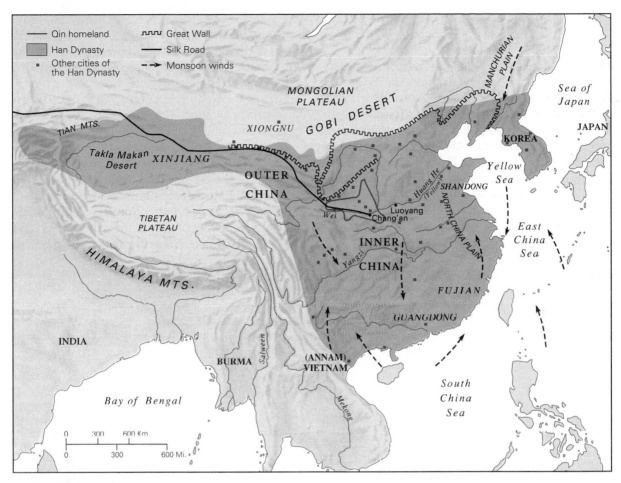

Map 6.2 Han China   The Qin and Han rulers of northeast China extended their control over all of Inner China and much of Outer China. A series of walls in the north and northwest, built to check the incursions of nomadic peoples from the steppes, were joined together to form the ancestor of the present-day Great Wall of China. An extensive network of roads connecting towns, cities, and frontier forts, promoted rapid communication and facilitated trade. The Silk Road carried China's most treasured product to Central, Southern, and Western Asia and the Mediterranean lands.

and Zhou (1027–221 B.C.E.), was confined to a relatively compact zone in northeastern China. The last few centuries of nominal Zhou rule—the Warring States Period—was an age of rivalry and belligerence among a group of small states. They differed to some extent in language and culture and in many ways bring to mind the contemporary Greek city-states (see Chapter 5). As in Greece, so also in China: an era of competition and conflict saw the formation of many of the distinctive elements of a national culture.

In the second half of the third century B.C.E. one of the warring states—the Qin state of the Wei Valley—rapidly conquered its rivals and created China's first empire (221–206 B.C.E.). But the Qin Empire, itself built at a great cost in human lives and labor, barely survived the death of its founder, Shi Huangdi. Power soon passed over to a new dynasty, the Han, which ruled over China for the next four centuries (206 B.C.E.–220 C.E.) (see Map 6.2). Thus began the long history of imperial China—a tradition of political and cultural unity and continuity that lasted into the early twentieth century C.E. and still resonates in the very different China of our own time.

Resources and Population

This achievement is especially remarkable for a region that was not only vast in extent but also marked by extreme diversity in its topography, climate, plant and animal life, and human population. An imperial state controlling these lands faced greater obstacles to long-distance communications and to a uniform way of life than did the Roman Empire. The Roman state encompassed lands whose climates and agricultural potentials were similar. The Roman Empire also had the benefit of an internal sea—the Mediterranean—which facilitated relatively rapid and inexpensive travel and transport of commodities. What were the resources, technologies, institutions and values that made possible the creation and maintenance of a Chinese empire?

Agricultural production was the primary source of the wealth and taxes that supported the institutions of state. The main tax, a percentage of the annual yield of the fields, was used to support the government in its many manifestations, from the luxurious life-style enjoyed by members of the royal court to the many levels of officials and the military units stationed throughout the country and on the frontiers. The capital cities, first Chang'an and later Luoyang, had large populations that had to be fed. As intensive

A thick deposit of loess soil in the Shanxi region   For thousands of years winds from Central Asia have deposited layers of fine sand in the plains of the Yellow River and its tributaries in northeast China, and the periodic flooding of the rivers has left behind water-borne silt. The thick mantle of fine, soft soil which accumulated was very fertile and easily worked with digging sticks, while networks of irrigation channels from the rivers provided the necessary moisture. The efficient systems of agriculture developed in this region by the indigenous Han people supported a large population and were later carried by them to other parts of China, along with other elements of Chinese civilization. (Courtesy, Caroline Blunden)

agriculture spread in the Yangzi River Valley, transporting southern crops to the north became important, and the first steps were taken toward construction of canals to connect the two great river systems, the Yangzi and the Yellow. The government also exercised foresight in collecting and storing in prosperous times surplus grain that could be distributed at reasonable prices in times of shortage.

The other fundamental commodity was human labor. The government periodically carried out a census of inhabitants. The results for the years 2 C.E. and 140 C.E. are preserved in extant historical writings. The earlier survey indicates totals of approximately 12 million households and 60 million people; the later, not quite 10 million households and 49 million people. Thus the average household contained 5 persons. Then, as now, the vast majority of the population lived in the eastern portion of the country, the river-valley regions where intensive agriculture could support a dense population. Initially the largest concentration was in the Yellow River Valley and North China Plain, but by the early Han Empire the demographic center had begun to shift to the Yangzi River Valley.

How did the Qin and Han governments take advantage of an expanding population? In the intervals between seasonal agricultural tasks, every able-bodied male was expected to donate one month of labor a year to public works projects—work on the construction of palaces, temples, fortifications, and roads; transporting goods; excavating and maintaining canal channels; labor on imperial estates; or service in the mines. Another obligation was two years of military service. Young Chinese men were marched to the frontiers, where they built walls and forts, kept an eye on barbarian neighbors, fought when necessary, and grew crops to support themselves. Annually updated registers of land and households enabled imperial officials to keep track of money and services due (see Environment and Technology: Writing as an Imperial Technology). We again see strong parallels between the Roman and Chinese governments in their dependence on a large population of free peasants who contributed both taxes and services to the state.

Throughout the Han period there was a persistent, gradual expansion of Han Chinese at the expense of other ethnic groups. The growth of population in the core regions and a shortage of good, arable land spurred pioneers to push into new areas. Sometimes the government organized the opening up of new areas, as when it resettled people in colonies at militarily strategic sites and on the frontiers. Neighboring kingdoms also invited in Chinese settlers in order to exploit their skills and learn their technologies.

The pattern of expansion is significant. Han people tended to move into regions suitable for the kind of agriculture with which they were familiar from living in the eastern river valleys. They took over land on the northern frontier, pushing back nomadic populations. They also expanded into the tropical forests of southern China and settled in the western oases. In places not suitable for their preferred kind of agriculture, particularly the steppe and the desert, Han Chinese were not able to displace other groups.

Hierarchy, Obedience, and Belief

As the Han Chinese expanded into new regions, they brought with them their social organization, values, and other elements of their culture. The basic unit of Chinese society was the family. The Chinese family included not only the living generations but also all the previous generations—the ancestors. The Chinese believed their ancestors maintained an ongoing interest in the fortunes of living members of the family. Thus people were careful to consult, appease, and venerate their ancestors in order to maintain their favor. The family was viewed as a living, self-renewing organism, and it was absolutely necessary for each generation to have sons to perpetuate the family and ensure the immortality offered by ancestor cult.

Within the family absolute authority rested with the father. He served as an intermediary between the living members and the ancestors, presiding over the rituals of ancestor worship. Every member of the family saw himself or herself as part of an interdependent unit rather than as an individual agent. Each person had a place

Writing as an Imperial Technology

One of the most important technologies in China and Rome was writing. The Chinese word for writing—*wen*—is also the term for "civilization." The origins of Chinese writing may go back as far as the fifth millennium B.C.E., even before the development of cuneiform writing in Mesopotamia. The earliest *surviving* Chinese writing, however, is from the late third or early second millennium B.C.E. Originally developed as a medium for communication with ancestors and gods, writing was essential for the maintenance of the official records on which the imperial system of government depended.

The Chinese use of characters, originally pictures, to represent a concept or word is different from the principles underlying the Roman alphabet. Each letter of the alphabet stands for a sound. The Chinese system requires a person to learn thousands of characters but permits people who speak different languages to read the same text. As part of its program of political and cultural unification, the Qin government imposed a standard system of writing and introduced new characters to represent novel concepts. Paper was invented in China in the first century C.E.

The Roman alphabet is still used for English and many other languages in the modern world. Its ultimate source is the system of writing developed in Phoenicia in the late second millennium B.C.E. and refined by the Greeks after 800 B.C.E. (see Chapters 4 and 5). As in China, the effective functioning of the Roman imperial administration depended on keeping detailed records. In recent years scholars have tried to discover how common literacy was among the peoples of the Roman Empire. Roman emperors put slogans on coins to communicate news and propaganda throughout the empire. Surviving coins indicate that they changed the slogans frequently and suggest the power of the written word even in those times.

A wooden slip with Chinese writing, first century B.C.E. or first century C.E. It gives instructions for soldiers using fire signals to send messages along a chain of forts on the northwest frontier. (Courtesy of the Trustees of the British Museum)

A coin of the emperor Vespasian, 71 C.E. On the obverse (shown here) the ruler's portrait, titles, and offices. The reverse shows a Roman soldier and a weeping female figure under a palm tree representing the province of Judea after suppression of a revolt. (Courtesy of the Trustees of the British Museum)

and responsibilities within the domestic hierarchy, based on his or her gender, age, and relationship to other family members. The family inculcated the basic values of Chinese society: loyalty, obedience to authority, respect for elders and ancestors, and concern for honor and appropriate conduct. Because the hierarchy in the state mirrored the hierarchy in the family, these same attitudes carried over into the relationship between the individual and the state.

Another fundamental source of values was the doctrine of the philosopher Kong Zi (551–479 B.C.E.)—known in the West by the Latin form of his name: Confucius. Confucius came from one of the small states in Shandong during the late Zhou period. He was not particularly successful in obtaining administrative posts, but he developed a system of precepts for people in positions of power.

Confucius started with two assumptions: (1) hierarchy was innate in the order of the universe, and (2) the patterns of human society should echo and harmonize with the cycles of the natural world. From these assumptions, Confucius said, it followed that each person had a particular role to play, with prescribed rules of conduct and proper ceremonial behavior, in order to maintain the social order. Fortunately, people can be guided to the right path through education, imitation of proper role models, and self-improvement. Government exists to serve the people, and the administrator or ruler gains respect and authority by displaying fairness and integrity.

Confucian teachings emphasized benevolence, avoidance of violence, justice, rationalism, loyalty, and decorum. They aimed to affirm and maintain the political and social order by improving it.

The experiences of women in ancient Chinese society are hard to pinpoint because, as elsewhere, contemporary written sources are largely silent on the subject. Confucian ethics, deeply ingrained in the consciousness of the intellectual and administrative classes, stressed the impropriety of women participating in public life. Within the family, males monopolized formal authority. They alone could communicate with the all-important ancestors. Traditional wisdom about the conduct appropriate for women is preserved in an account of the life of the mother of Mengzi (ca. 371–ca. 289 B.C.E.), a major Confucian philosopher known in the West as Mencius. According to this account:

> A woman's duties are to cook the five grains, heat the wine, look after her parents-in-law, make clothes, and that is all! . . . [She] has no ambition to manage affairs outside the house. . . . She must follow the "three submissions." When she is young, she must submit to her parents. After her marriage, she must submit to her husband. When she is widowed, she must submit to her son.[1]

That is an ideal perpetuated by males of the upper classes, the social stratum about which we are best informed because it is the source of most of the written texts. Female members of this group probably were under considerable pressure to conform to those expectations. In contrast, women of the lower classes, less affected by Confucian ways of thinking, may have been less constrained than their more "privileged" counterparts.

Marriages were arranged by parents. A young bride left home to reside with her husband's family. To them she was a stranger who had to prove herself. In such circumstances ability and force of personality (as well as the capacity to produce sons) could make a difference. Dissension between the wife and her mother-in-law and sisters-in-law was frequent as they competed for influence with husbands, sons, and brothers and a larger share of the economic resources held in common by the family.

Like the early Romans, the ancient Chinese believed that divinity resided within nature rather than being outside and above it, and they worshiped and tried to appease the forces of nature. The state erected and maintained shrines to the lords of rain and winds as well as to certain great rivers and high mountains. Gathering at mounds or altars where the local spirit of the soil was felt to reside, people sacrificed sheep and pigs and beat drums loudly to promote the fertility of the earth. Strange or disastrous natural phenomena, such as eclipses or heavy rains, called for symbolic restraint of the deity by tying a red cord around the sacred spot.

The natural world was seen as a balance of forces: *yin,* embodying the female principle, dark and cold, and *yang,* representing the male, light and heat. Within this overarching dichotomy lay a series of fives: five elements (fire, water, metal, wood, and earth), five directions (north, south, east, west, and center), five colors, five senses, and so forth. Because it was believed that supernatural forces, bringing good and evil fortune, flowed through the landscape, experts in geomancy ("earth divination") were consulted to determine the most favorable location and orientation for buildings and graves. The faithful learned to adapt their lives to the complex rhythms they perceived in nature.

There was widespread interest in ways of cheating death, whether by making the body immortal with life-enhancing drugs or providing

Terracotta (baked clay) soldiers from the tomb of the First Emperor of China, third century B.C.E.   First discovered in 1974 in the tomb of the Qin emperor Shi Huangdi, thousands of these life-size figures of soldiers and horses continue to be unearthed by archaeologists. The ground plan of the tomb represents an imperial city, and the figures were arranged in military formation. The individual figures differ from one another in hair and facial features, garments, and weaponry, and were originally brightly painted. This may represent an adaptation of the Shang practice of sacrificing members of the royal retinue and burying them with the deceased ruler. (China Pictorial Service)

for a blessed afterlife. The rich built ostentatious tombs, flanked by towers or covered by mounds of earth, and filled them with the equipment they believed they would need to maintain the quality of life they had enjoyed on earth. The objects in these tombs have provided archaeologists with a wealth of knowledge about Han society.

The First Chinese Empire

For centuries eastern China had been divided among the compact, rival states whose frequent hostilities gave rise to the label "Warring States Period." In the second half of the third century B.C.E. one of these states, that of the Qin, suddenly burst forth and took over the other states one by one. For the first time the northern plain and the Yangzi River Valley were unified under one rule, marking the creation of China and the inauguration of the imperial age. Many scholars maintain that the very name *China*, by which this land has been known in the Western world, is derived from *Qin*.

Several factors account for the meteoric rise of the Qin. The Qin ruler, who took the title *Shi Huangdi* ("First Emperor"), and his adviser and prime minister Li Si, were able and ruthless men who exploited the exhaustion resulting from the long centuries of interstate rivalry. The Qin homeland in the valley of the Wei, a tributary of the Yellow River, was less urbanized and commercialized than the kingdoms farther east, and the leadership could draw on a large pool of sturdy peasants to serve in the army. Moreover, long experience of mobilizing manpower for the construction of irrigation and flood-control works had strengthened the authority of the Qin king at the expense of the nobles and endowed his government with superior organizational skills.

Shi Huangdi and Li Si created a totalitarian structure in which the individual was subordinated to the needs of the state. They cracked down on Confucianism, regarding its demands for benevolent and non-violent conduct from rulers as a check on the absolute power that they claimed to hold. A new school of political thought—Legalism—emerged to justify the actions of the Qin government. According to this philosophy, whose major exponent was Li Si himself, the will of the ruler was supreme, and his subjects were to be trained in discipline and obedience through the rigid application of rewards and punishments.

The new regime was determined to eliminate any rival centers of authority. Its first target was the landowning aristocracy of the old kingdoms and the system on which aristocratic wealth and power had been based. The Qin government abolished *primogeniture*—the right of the eldest son to inherit all the landed property—because primogeniture allowed a small number of individuals to accumulate vast tracts of land. The Qin required estates to be broken up and passed on to several heirs.

The large estates of the aristocracy had been worked by slaves (see Voices and Visions: Slavery in Rome and China) and by a serf class of peasants who turned over to the landlord a substantial portion of what they grew. The Qin abolished slavery and took steps to bring into being a free peasantry. The members of this group were numerous small landholders who could not evade the government's demands for taxes and who would serve in the army and devote a portion of their labor each year to state projects.

The Qin government's commitment to standardization in many areas of life helped to create a unified Chinese civilization. During the Warring States Period (480 B.C.E.–221 B.C.E.), the small states had emphasized their independence through a wide array of symbolic practices. For example, each state had its own particular forms of music, with different scales, systems of notation, and instruments. The Qin imposed standard weights, measures, and coinage, a uniform law code, a common system of writing, and even regulations governing the axle length of carts so as to leave just one set of ruts on the roads.

Thousands of miles of roads were built—comparable in scale to the roads of the Roman Empire—to connect the parts of the empire and to facilitate the rapid movement of Qin armies. The various frontier walls of the old kingdoms began to be linked into a continuous barricade, the precursor of the Great Wall (see Chapter 11), to protect cultivated lands from incursions by nomadic invaders from the north. To build these walls and roads, large numbers of citizens were forced to donate their labor and often their lives. So op-

pressive were the financial exploitation and the demands for forced labor that when Shi Huangdi died, in 210 B.C.E., a series of rebellions broke out and brought down the Qin dynasty.

The Long Reign of the Han

When the dust cleared, Liu Bang, who may have been from a peasant background, had outlasted his rivals and established a new dynasty, the Han (206 B.C.E.–220 C.E.). The new emperor claimed to reject the excesses and mistakes of the Qin and to restore the institutions of a venerable past. In reality, the Han system of administration maintained much of the structure and Legalist ideology put in place by the Qin, though with less fanatical zeal. The Han system of administration became the standard for later ages, and the Chinese people refer to themselves ethnically as "Han."

The first eighty years of the new dynasty was a time of consolidation. Then, in the later second century B.C.E., Emperor Wu (r. 140–87 B.C.E.) launched a period of military expansion, south into Fujian, Guangdong, and present-day north Vietnam and north into Manchuria and present-day North Korea. Armies were also sent west, to inner Mongolia and Xinjiang, to secure the lucrative Silk Road (see Chapter 8). However, maintaining control of the newly acquired territories was expensive, and Wu's successors curtailed further expansion.

The Han Empire endured with a brief interruption between 9 and 23 C.E. for more than four hundred years. From 202 B.C.E. to 8 C.E.—the period of the Early, or Western, Han—the capital was at Chang'an, in the Wei Valley, an ancient seat of power from which the Zhou and Qin dynasties had emerged. From 23 to 220 C.E. the Later, or Eastern, Han established its base farther east, in the more centrally located Luoyang.

Chang'an, well protected by a ring of hills but having ready access to the fertile plain, was surrounded by a wall of pounded earth and brick 15 miles (24 kilometers) in circumference. We know from contemporary descriptions that it was a bustling place, filled with courtiers, officials, soldiers, merchants, craftsmen, and foreign visitors.

A population of 246,000 is recorded for 2 C.E. Part of the city was carefully planned. Broad thoroughfares running north and south intersected with those running east and west. High walls protected the palaces, administrative offices, barracks, and storehouses of the imperial compound, and access was restricted. Temples and marketplaces were scattered about the civic center. Chang'an became a model of urban planning, its main features imitated in the cities and towns that sprang up throughout the Han Empire.

The complaints of moralists provide glimpses of the private lives of well-to-do officials and merchants in the capital. Living in multistory houses, dressed in fine silks, traveling about the city in ornate horse-drawn carriages, they devoted their leisure time to art and literature, occult religious practices, elegant banquets, and diverse entertainments—music, dance, jugglers and acrobats, dog and horse races, cock and tiger fights. Far different were the lives of the common people of the capital. They inhabited a sprawling warren of alleys, living in dwellings packed "as closely as the teeth of a comb," as one poet put it.

As in the Zhou monarchy (see Chapter 3), the emperor was the "Son of Heaven," and he had the "Mandate of Heaven" to rule. The emperor stood at the center of government and society. As the father held authority in the family and was a link between the living generations and the ancestors, so the emperor was supreme in the state. He brought the support of powerful imperial ancestors and guaranteed the harmonious interaction of heaven and earth. To a much greater degree than his Roman counterpart, he was regarded as a virtual divinity on earth, and his word was law. If he failed to govern worthily, however, Heaven's mandate could be withdrawn. Since the Chinese believed there was a strong correspondence between events in heaven, in the natural world, and in human society, they viewed natural disasters such as floods, droughts, and earthquakes as both the consequence and the proof of the emperor's ethical failure and mismanagement. Successful revolutions were viewed as proof that Heaven's mandate had been withdrawn from an unworthy ruler.

The emperor lived in seclusion within the walled palace compound, surrounded by his many wives, eunuchs, courtiers, and officials. Life in the palace compound was an unceasing round of pomp and ritual emphasizing the worship of Heaven and imperial ancestors as well as the practical business of government. The royal compound was also a hive of intrigue, particularly when the emperor died. His chief widow had the prerogative of choosing the heir from among the male members of the ruling clan.

The central government was run by two top officials—a prime minister and a civil service director—by nine ministers with responsibility in areas such as recordkeeping, the treasury, court protocol, security, criminal punishment, and religious ceremonial, and by the army commanders. The empire was divided into commanderies and kingdoms under the direction of civil and military authorities and subordinate kings, usually members of the imperial family. These administrative regions were subdivided into prefectures, districts, and wards.

Like the imperial Roman government, the Han government depended on local officials to carry out the day-to-day business of administering the vast empire. Local people were responsible for collecting taxes and dispatching revenues to the central government, for regulating the system of conscription for the army and for labor projects, for protection of the area, and for settling disputes. The central government was a remote entity that rarely impinged on the lives of most citizens; their only experience of government was their contact with local officials. Who, then, made up the large bureaucracy of local officials in the Han Empire?

A significant development during the Han period was the rise of a class that scholars refer to as the "gentry." As part of their strategy to weaken the rural aristocrats and to exclude them from political posts, the Qin and Han emperors entered into an alliance with the class next in wealth below the aristocrats. The members of this class were moderately prosperous landowners and professionals. Like the Roman equites favored by Augustus and his successors, the gentry class was the source of the local officials that the central government required. These officials were a privileged and respected group within Chinese society, and they made the government more efficient and responsive than it had been in the past.

The Han period saw a revival of the code of ethics and conduct first advanced by Confucius in the fifth century B.C.E. The new gentry class of officials adopted a somewhat revised Confucianism. It provided them with a system of education for training generations of officials to be both intellectually capable and morally worthy of their role in administration, and it embodied a code of conduct against which to measure individual performance. An imperial university, located just outside of Chang'an and said to have as many as thirty thousand students, and provincial centers of learning were established. From these centers, students were chosen to enter various levels of government service.

As civil servants advanced in the bureaucracy, they received distinctive emblems and other privileges of rank, including preferential treatment at law and exemption from military service. In theory, young men from any class could rise in the state hierarchy. In practice, the sons of the gentry class had an advantage, because they were in the best position to receive the necessary training in the Confucian classics. Over time the gentry became a new aristocracy of sorts, banding together in cliques and family alliances that had considerable clout and worked to advance the careers of members of their group.

In the Han period Daoism took root. Based on the teachings of Lao Zi (whose date is unknown) and Zhuang Zi (369–286 B.C.E.), it soon attached to itself a mixture of popular beliefs, magic, and mysticism. Daoism was popular with the common people. Its religious and philosophical world-view in many respects was at odds with the Confucianism of the elite and provides a glimpse of the tensions within Chinese society.

Daoism emphasized the search for the *dao*, or "path," of nature and the value of harmonizing with the cycles and patterns of the natural world. But Daoists believed that the successful conclusion of the search was to be achieved not so much by education as by solitary contemplation, physical and mental discipline, and striving to reach that instant in which one suddenly, intu-

Important Events in Early Imperial China

221 B.C.E.	Qin emperor unites eastern China
206 B.C.E.	Han dynasty succeeds Qin
140–87 B.C.E.	Emperor Wu expands the Chinese empire
23 C.E.	Capital transfered from Chang'an to Luoyang
220 C.E.	Fall of Han empire

itively, grasps the nature of things. Daoism was skeptical, calling into question age-old beliefs and values and rejecting the hierarchy, rules, and rituals of Confucianism. In the end, it urged passive acceptance of the disorder of the world, denial of ambition, contentment with simple pleasures, and following one's instincts about what was right.

Technology and Trade

China was the home of many important inventions, and what the Chinese did not invent, they improved. Tradition seems to have recognized the importance of technology for the success and spread of Chinese civilization. The legendary first five emperors were all culture heroes whom the Chinese credited with the introduction of major new technologies.

The advent of bronze tools around 1500 B.C.E. had given a powerful impetus to the effort to clear the forests of the North China Plain in order to open up more land for agriculture. Almost a thousand years later, iron arrived. One possible explanation for the military superiority of the Qin is that they were among the first to take full advantage of the new iron technology. In later centuries, the crossbow and use of cavalry helped the Chinese military to beat off the attacks of nomads from the steppe regions. The watermill, which harnessed the power of running water to turn a grinding stone, was in use in China long before it appeared in Europe. The development of a horse collar that did not constrict the animal's breathing allowed horses in China to pull loads much heavier than the loads pulled by horses in Europe at the same time.

The Qin had undertaken an extensive program of road building, and the Han rulers continued this project. These roads connected an expanding network of urban centers. Growth in population and increasing trade resulted in the development of local market centers. The importance of these thriving towns grew as they became county seats from which imperial officials operated. Estimates of the proportion of the population living in towns and cities range from 10 to 30 percent.

Along with the growth of local and regional trade networks came the development of long-distance commerce. China's most important export commodity was silk. Silk cocoons are secreted onto the leaves of mulberry trees by silkworms. For a long time this simple fact was a closely guarded secret that gave the Chinese a monopoly on the manufacture of silk. Carried on a perilous journey westward through the Central Asian oases to the Middle East, India, and the Mediterranean, and passing through the hands of many middlemen, each of whom raised the price in order to make a profit, this beautiful textile may have increased in value a hundredfold by the time it reached its destination. The Chinese government sought to control the Silk Road and the profits that it carried by launching periodic campaigns into Central Asia. Garrisons were installed and colonies of Chinese settlers were sent out to occupy the oases.

Decline of the Han Empire

For the Han government, as for the Romans, maintaining the security of the frontiers—particularly the north and northwest frontiers—was a primary concern. Yet, in the end, the pressure of non-Chinese peoples raiding from across the frontier or moving into the prosperous lands of the Empire led to the decline of Han authority.

In general, the Han Empire had been able to consolidate its hold over lands occupied by sedentary farming peoples, but living in nearby regions were nomadic tribes whose livelihood depended on their horses and herds. The very different ways of life of farmers and herders gave rise to suspicions and insulting stereotypes on both sides. The settled Chinese tended to think of nomads as "barbarians"—rough, uncivilized peoples—much as the inhabitants of the Roman Empire looked down on the German tribes living beyond their frontier.

Along the boundary between settled agriculturalists and nomadic pastoralists there was frequent contact. Often the closeness of the two populations led to significant commercial activity. The nomads sought the food commodities and crafted goods produced by the farmers and townsfolk, and the settled peoples depended on the nomads for horses and other herd animals and products. Sometimes, however, contact took the form of raids on the settled lands by nomad bands, which seized what they needed or wanted. Tough and warlike because of the demands of their way of life, mounted nomads could strike swiftly and just as swiftly disappear.

Although nomadic groups tend to be relatively small and to fight often with each other, from time to time circumstances and a charismatic leader can create a large coalition of tribes. The major external threat to Chinese civilization in the Han period came from the Xiongnu, a great confederacy of Turkic peoples. For centuries Chinese policy had succeeded in containing the Xiongnu. The Chinese used a range of strategies: periodic campaigns onto the steppe, maintenance of military colonies and garrisons on the frontier, the settlement of compliant nomadic groups within the borders of the empire to serve as a buffer against warlike groups, bribes to promote dissension within the nomad leadership, and payment of protection money. One successful approach was the "tributary system," in which nomad rulers accepted Chinese supremacy and sent in payments of tribute in return for which they were rewarded with marriages to Chinese princesses, dazzling receptions at court, and gifts from the Han emperor which exceeded the value of the tribute.

In the first century C.E. the Xiongnu were defeated by the Chinese and pushed west. Several centuries later they arrived on the northern frontier of the Roman Empire and the Huns, as the Romans called them, plagued that other great empire and helped to bring about its downfall.

In the end, the cost of continuous military vigilance along the frontier imposed a crushing bur-

Han era (first century B.C.E.) stone rubbing of a horse-drawn carriage The "trace harness," a Chinese invention which attached a strap across the chest, allowed horses to pull far heavier loads than was possible with the constricting throat harness used in Europe at that time. In the Han period, towns and cities sprang up across the Chinese landscape. They were primarily inhabited by a growing class of officials, professionals, and soldiers who served the regime. This class used its social position and prosperity to create a conspicuous lifestyle that included fine clothing, comfortable transportation, servants, and delightful pastimes, at the same time that it was guided by a Confucian emphasis on duty, honesty, and appropriate behavior. (From Wu family shrine, Jiaxiang, Shantung. From *Chin-shih-so* [Jinshisuo]. Photographer: Eileen Tweedy)

den on Han finances and worsened the economic troubles of later Han times. And, despite the earnest efforts of Qin and Early Han emperors to reduce the power and wealth of the aristocracy and to turn land over to a free peasantry, by the end of the first century B.C.E. nobles and successful merchants again were beginning to acquire control of huge tracts of land, and many peasants were seeking their protection against the exactions of the government. This trend became widespread in the next two centuries. Strongmen largely independent of state control emerged, and the central government was deprived of tax revenues and manpower. The system of military conscription broke down, forcing the government to hire more and more foreign soldiers and officers. These men were willing to serve for pay, but their loyalty to the Han state was weak.

Several factors combined to weaken and eventually bring down the Han dynasty in 220 C.E.: factional intrigues within the ruling Han clan, official corruption and inefficiency, uprisings of desperate and hungry peasants, the spread of banditry, unsuccessful reform movements, attacks by nomadic groups on the northwest frontier, and the ambitions of rural warlords. After 220, China entered a period of political fragmentation and economic and cultural regression that lasted until the rise of the Sui and Tang dynasties in the late sixth and early seventh centuries C.E., a story that we take up in Chapter 11.

CONCLUSION

The parallels between the Roman Empire and the Han Empire are quite striking. Both employed similar means to control vast territories and large populations over a long period of time. In both, subject peoples adopted the language and culture of the rulers. A marked rise in prosperity and in the general standard of living, the growth of cities, increased long-distance trade, more widespread education and literacy, and significant technological developments occurred against a backdrop of peace and stability. Even in the manner of their demise there were strong similarities.

However, there also are significant differences between Rome and Han China. These differences become clear from an examination of the long-term effects of the failure of central authority. In China, the imperial tradition and the class structure and value system that maintained it were eventually revived (see Chapters 11 and 14), and they survived with remarkable continuity into the twentieth century C.E. In Europe, North Africa, and the Middle East, in contrast, there never has been a restoration of the Roman Empire, and the subsequent history of these lands has been marked by great political changes and cultural diversity. Several interrelated factors help to account for the different outcomes.

First, these cultures had different attitudes toward the importance of the individual and the obligations of individuals to the state. In China the individual was deeply embedded in the larger social group. The Chinese family, with its emphasis on a precisely defined hierarchy, unquestioning obedience, and solemn rituals of deference to elders and ancestors, served as the model for society and the state. Thus in China respect for authority always has been a deep-seated habit. The architects of Qin Legalism largely got their way, and the emperor's word was regarded as law. Although the Roman family had its own hierarchy and traditions of obedience, the cult of ancestors was not as strong among the Romans as it was among the Chinese, and the family did not serve as the model for the organization of Roman society and the Roman state.

It is probably also fair to say that economic and social mobility, which make it possible for some people to rise dramatically in wealth and status, tends to enhance a society's sense of the significance of the individual. In ancient China opportunities for individuals to improve their economic status were more limited than they were in the Roman Empire, and the merchant class in China was frequently disparaged and constrained by government control. The more important role played by commerce in the Roman Empire, and the resulting economic mobility, heightened Roman awareness of the uniqueness and prerogatives of individuals. To a much greater extent than the Chinese emperor, the Roman emperor had to resort to persuasion, threats, and promises in order to forge a consensus for his initiatives.

Another factor differentiating the empires of Han China and Rome is political and religious ideology. Although Roman emperors tried to create an ideology to bolster their position, they were hampered by the persistence of Republican traditions and the ambiguities about the position of emperor deliberately cultivated by Augustus. As a result, Roman rulers were likely to be chosen either by the army or by the Senate, the dynastic principle never took deep root, and the cult of the emperor had little spiritual content. This stands in sharp contrast to the iron-clad Chinese ideology of the Mandate of Heaven, the belief in the emperor as the divine Son of Heaven, and the imperial monopoly of access to the beneficent power of the royal ancestors. Thus, in the West, there was no compelling basis for reviving the position of emperor and the territorial claims of empire in later ages.

Finally, weight also must be given to differences in the new belief systems that took root in each empire. Christianity, with its insistence on monotheism and one doctrine of truth, negated the Roman emperor's pretensions to divinity and was essentially unwilling to come to terms with pagan beliefs. Thus the triumphant spread of Christianity through the provinces of the late Roman Empire, and the decline of the western half of the empire in the fifth century C.E. (see Chapter 9), constituted an irreversible break with the past. However, Buddhism, which came to China in the early centuries C.E. and flourished in the post-Han era (see Chapter 11), was easily reconciled with traditional Chinese values and beliefs. In the next chapter we turn to the homeland of Buddhism and Hinduism in South Asia and trace the development of Indian civilization.

SUGGESTED READING

Tim Cornell and John Matthews, *Atlas of the Roman World* (1982), offers a general introduction, pictures, and maps to illustrate many aspects of Roman civilization. Michael Grant and Rachel Kitzinger, eds., *Civilization of the Ancient Mediterranean*, 3 vols. (1988), is an invaluable collection of essays with bibliographies by specialists on every major facet of life in the Greek and Roman worlds. Among the many good surveys of Roman history is Michael Grant, *History of Rome* (1978). Naphtali Lewis and Meyer Reinhold, eds., *Roman Civilization*, 2 vols. (1951), contains extensive ancient sources in translation.

For Roman political and legal institutions, attitudes, and values see J. A. Crook, *Law and Life of Rome: 90 B.C.–A.D. 212* (1967). Michael Crawford, *The Roman Republic*, 2nd ed. (1993), and Chester G. Starr, *The Roman Empire, 27 B.C.–A.D. 476: A Study in Survival* (1982), assess the evolution of the Roman state during the Republic and Principate. Fergus Millar, *The Emperor in the Roman World (31 B.C.–A.D. 337)* (1977), is a comprehensive study of the position of the princeps.

For the Roman military expansion and defense of the frontiers, see W. V. Harris, *War and Imperialism in Republican Rome* (1979); and Stephen L. Dyson, *The Creation of the Roman Frontier* (1985). David Macaulay, *City: A Story of Roman Planning and Construction* (1974), uses copious illustrations to reveal the wonders of Roman engineering.

Kevin Greene, *The Archaeology of the Roman Economy* (1986), showcases new approaches to social and economic history. U. E. Paoli, *Rome: Its People, Life and Customs* (1983) looks at everyday life. Jo-Ann Shelton, ed., *As the Romans Did: A Sourcebook in Roman Social History* (1988), offers a selection of translated ancient sources. Elaine Fantham, Helene, Peet Foley, Natalie Boymel Kampen, Sarah B. Pomeroy, and H. Alan Shapiro, *Women in the Classical World: Image and Text* (1994), provide an up-to-date discussion of women in the Roman world. Many of the ancient sources on Roman women can be found in Mary R. Lefkowitz and Maureen B. Fant, eds., *Women's Life in Greece and Rome: A Source Book in Translation* (1982). Thomas Wiedemann, ed., *Greek and Roman Slavery* (1981), contains the ancient sources in translation.

A number of the chapters in John Boardman, Jasper Griffin, and Oswyn Murray, eds., *The Roman World* (1988) surveys the intellectual and literary achievements of the Romans. R. M. Ogilvie, *The Romans and Their Gods in the Age of Augustus* (1969) is an introduction to religion in both its public and its private manifestations. R. A. Markus, *Christianity in the Roman World* (1974), investigates the rise of Christianity.

For the geography and demography of China see the well-illustrated *Cultural Atlas of China* (1983) by Caroline Blunden and Mark Elvin. Basic surveys of Chinese history include Jacques Gernet, *A History of Chinese Civilization* (1982); and John K. Fairbank, *China: A New History* (1992). In greater depth for the ancient period is Denis Twitchett and Michael Loewe, eds., *The Cambridge History of China*, vol. 1, *The Ch'in and Han Empires, 221 B.C.–A.D. 220* (1986), and Michele Pirazzoli-t'Serstevens, *The Han Dynasty* (1982). Kwang-chih Chang, *The Archaeology of Ancient China*, 4th ed. (1986), emphasizes the archaeological record. W. de Bary, W. Chan, and B. Watson, eds., have assembled sources in translation in *Sources of Chinese Tradition* (1960).

For social history see Michael Loewe, *Everyday Life in Early Imperial China During the Han Period, 202 B.C.–A.D. 220* (1988); and the chapter by Sharon L. Sievers in *Restoring Women to History*, ed. (1988). For economic history and foreign relations see Ying-shih Yu, *Trade and Expansion in Han China* (1967). For scientific and technological achievements see Robert Temple, *The Genius of China: 3,000 Years of Science, Discovery, and Invention* (1986).

Benjamin I. Schwartz addresses intellectual history in *The World of Thought in Ancient China* (1985). Spiritual matters are taken up by Laurence G. Thompson, *Chinese Religion: An Introduction*, 3d ed. (1979). For art see Michael Sullivan, *A Short History of Chinese Art*, rev. ed. (1970).

NOTE

1. Patricia Buckley Ebrey, ed., *Chinese Civilization and Society: A Sourcebook* (The Free Press, New York, 1981) 33–34.

CHAPTER SEVEN

India and Southeast Asia,

1500 B.C.E. – 1100 C.E.

Foundations of Indian Civilization · Imperial Expansion and Collapse

Southeast Asia

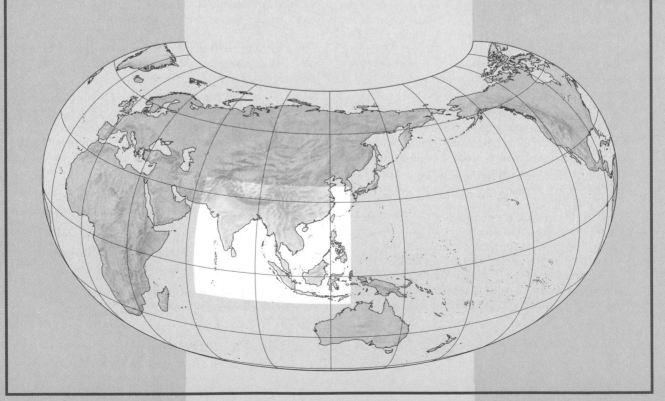

In the *Bhagavad-Gita*, the most renowned of all Indian sacred texts, Arjuna, the greatest warrior of Indian legend, rides out in his chariot between two armies preparing for battle. Torn between his social duty to fight for his family's claim to the throne and his conscience, which balks at the prospect of killing the relatives, friends, and former teachers who are in the enemy camp, Arjuna slumps down in his chariot and refuses to fight. But his chariot driver, the god Krishna in disguise, persuades him, in a carefully structured dialogue, both of the necessity to fulfill his duty as a warrior and of the proper frame of mind for performing these acts. In the climactic moment of the dialogue Krishna endows Arjuna with a "divine eye" and permits him to see the true appearance of god:

> It was a multiform, wondrous vision,
> with countless mouths and eyes
> and celestial ornaments,
> Everywhere was boundless divinity
> containing all astonishing things,
> wearing divine garlands and garments,
> anointed with divine perfume.
> If the light of a thousand suns
> were to rise in the sky at once,
> it would be like the light
> of that great spirit.
> Arjuna saw all the universe
> in its many ways and parts,
> standing as one in the body
> of the god of gods.[1]

In all of world literature, this is one of the most compelling attempts to depict the nature of deity. Graphic images emphasize the enormity, diversity, and multiplicity of the god, but in the end we learn that Krishna is the organizing principle behind all creation, that behind diversity and multiplicity lies a higher unity.

This is an apt metaphor for Indian civilization. If there is one word that might be used to characterize India in both ancient and modern times, it is *diversity*. The enormous variety of the Indian landscape is mirrored in the patchwork of ethnic and linguistic groups that occupy it, the political fragmentation that has marked most of Indian history, the elaborate hierarchy of social groups into which the Indian population is divided, and the thousands of deities who are worshiped at the innumerable holy places that dot the subcontinent. Yet, in the end, one can speak of an Indian civilization that is united by a set of shared views and values.

In this chapter we survey the history of South and Southeast Asia from approximately 1500 B.C.E. to 1100 C.E., focusing on the evolution of defining features of Indian civilization: economic activities, technologies, social divisions, and a religious tradition whose distinctive conceptions of space, time, gods, and the life cycle have shaped virtually every aspect of South Asian culture. Considerable attention is given to Indian religious conceptions. This is due, in part, to religion's profound role in shaping Indian society. It is also a consequence of the sources of information available to historians.

Lengthy epic poems, such as the *Mahabharata* and *Ramayana*, may preserve useful information about early Indian society, but most of the earliest texts are religious documents—such as the *Vedas, Upanishads*, and Buddhist stories—that were preserved and transmitted orally long before they were written down. In addition, Indian civilization held a conception of vast expanses of time during which creatures are repeatedly reincarnated and live many lives. This belief may account for why ancient Indians did not develop a historical consciousness like that of their Israelite and Greek contemporaries but instead took little interest in recording specific historical events: such events seemed relatively insignificant when set against the long cycles of time and lives.

Despite the limited evidence, the political history of early India is also our subject. In the face of powerful forces that tended to keep India politically fragmented, two great empires emerged:

the Mauryan Empire, which lasted from the fourth to the second century B.C.E., and the Gupta Empire, from the fourth to the sixth century C.E. The chapter concludes by looking at how a number of states in Southeast Asia became wealthy and powerful by exploiting their advantageous position on the international trade routes between India and China and by adapting Indian ideas and technologies to their needs.

FOUNDATIONS OF INDIAN CIVILIZATION

India is often called a *subcontinent* because it is a large—roughly 2,000 miles (3,200 kilometers) in both length and breadth—and physically isolated landmass within the continent of Asia. It is set off from the rest of Asia by the Himalayas, the highest mountains on the planet, to the north, and by the Indian Ocean on its eastern, southern, and western sides (see Map 7.1). The most permeable frontier, and the one used by a long series of invaders and migrating peoples, lies to the northwest. But people using even this corridor must cross over the mountain barrier of the Hindu Kush and the Thar Desert east of the Indus River.

The Indian Subcontinent

This region—which encompasses the modern nations of Pakistan, Nepal, Bhutan, Bangladesh, India, and the adjacent island of Sri Lanka—can be divided into three distinct topographical zones. The mountainous northern zone takes in the heavily forested foothills and high meadows on the edge of the Hindu Kush and Himalaya ranges. Next come the great basins of the Indus and Ganges Rivers. Originating in the ice of the Tibetan mountains to the north, through the millennia these rivers have repeatedly overflowed their banks and deposited layer on layer of silt,

creating large alluvial plains. Northern India is divided from the third zone, the peninsula proper, by the Vindhya range and the Deccan, an arid, rocky plateau that brings to mind parts of the American West. The tropical coastal strip of Kerala (Malabar) in the west, the Coromandel Coast in the east with its web of rivers descending from the central plateau, the flatlands of Tamil Nadu on the southern tip of the peninsula, and the island of Sri Lanka often have followed paths of political and cultural development separate from those of northern India.

The rim of mountains looming above India's northern frontier shelters the subcontinent from cold Arctic winds and gives it a subtropical climate. The most dramatic source of moisture is the monsoon (seasonal wind). The Indian Ocean is slow to warm or cool, and the vast landmass of Asia swings rapidly between seasonal extremes of heat and cold. The temperature difference between the water and the land acts like a bellows, producing a great wind in this and adjoining parts of the globe. The southwest monsoon begins in June. It carries huge amounts of moisture picked up from the Indian Ocean and deposits it over a swath of India that encompasses the rainforest belt on the western coast and the Ganges Basin. Three harvests a year are possible in some places. Rice is grown in the moist, flat Ganges Delta (the modern region of Bengal). Elsewhere the staples are wheat, barley, and millet.

The Indus Valley, by contrast, gets little precipitation (see Chapter 2). In this arid region the successful practice of agriculture depends on extensive irrigation. Moreover, the volume of water in the Indus is irregular, and the river has changed course from time to time.

Although invasions and migrations usually came by land through the northwest corridor, the ocean surrounding the peninsula has not been a barrier to travel and trade. Indian Ocean mariners learned to ride the monsoon winds across open waters from northeast to southwest in January and to reverse the process in July. Ships made their way west across the Arabian Sea to the Persian Gulf, the southern coast of Arabia, and East Africa, and east across the Bay of Bengal to Indochina and Indonesia (see Chapter 8).

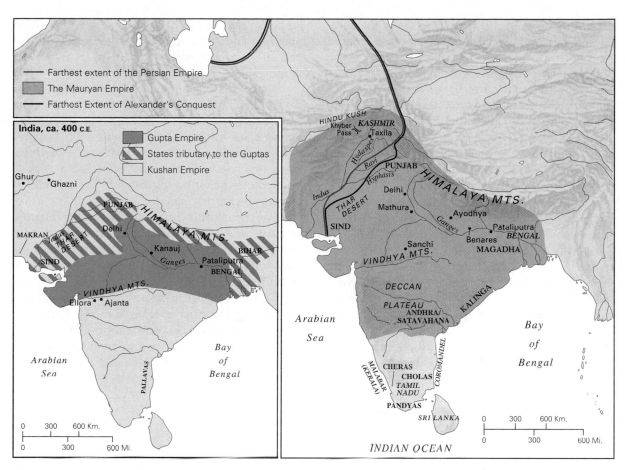

Map 7.1 Ancient India   The Indian subcontinent is largely cut off from the mass of Asia by mountains and sea. Migrations and invasions usually came through the northwest corridor (Hindu Kush). Sea-borne commerce with western Asia, Southeast Asia, and East Asia often flourished. While peoples speaking Indo-European languages migrated into the broad valleys of the Indus and Ganges Rivers in the north, Dravidian-speaking peoples remained the dominant population in the south. The diversity of the Indian landscape, the multiplicity of ethnic groups, and the primary identification of people with their class and caste, lie behind the division into many small states which characterizes much of Indian political history.

The Vedic Age, 1500–500 B.C.E.

It is tempting to trace many of the characteristic features of later Indian civilization back to the Indus Valley civilization of the third and early second millennia B.C.E., but proof is hard to come by because the writing from that period has not yet been deciphered. That society, which responded to the challenge of an arid terrain by developing high levels of social organization and technology, seems to have succumbed around 1800 B.C.E. to some kind of environmental crisis (see Chapter 2).

Historians call the period from 1500 to 500 B.C.E. the "Vedic Age," after the Vedas, religious texts that are our main source of information about the period. The foundations for Indian civilization were laid in the Vedic Age. Most historians believe that new groups of people—nomadic warriors speaking Indo-European languages—migrated into northwest India around 1500 B.C.E. Some argue for a much earlier Indo-European presence in this region in conjunction with the spread of agriculture. In any case, in the mid-second millennium B.C.E. northern India entered a new historical period associated with the dominance of Indo-European groups.

In the arid northwest, large-scale agriculture depends on irrigation. After the collapse of the Indus Valley civilization there was no central authority to direct these efforts, and the region became home to kinship groups that depended mostly on their herds of cattle for sustenance, and perhaps also on some gardening to supplement their diet. Like other Indo-European peoples—Celts, Greeks, Iranians, Romans—these societies were patriarchal. The father dominated the family as the king ruled the tribe. Members of the warrior class boasted of their martial skill and courage, relished combat, celebrated with lavish feasts of beef and rounds of heavy drinking, and filled their leisure time with chariot racing and gambling.

After 1000 B.C.E. some of these groups began to push east into the Ganges Plain. New technologies made this advance possible. Iron tools—harder than bronze, more durable, and able to hold a sharper edge—allowed settlers to fell trees and to work the newly cleared land with plows pulled by oxen. The soil of the Ganges Plain was fertile, well watered by the annual monsoon, and able to sustain two or three crops a year. As in Greece at roughly the same time (see Chapter 5), in India the use of iron tools to open up new land for agriculture must have led to a significant increase in population.

Stories about this era, not written down until much later but long preserved by memorization and oral recitation, speak of bitter rivalry and warfare between two groups of people: the Aryas, relatively light-skinned speakers of Indo-European languages, and the Dasas, dark-skinned speakers of Dravidian languages. Some scholars argue that the real process by which Arya groups became dominant in the north was more complicated, involving the absorption of some Dasas into Arya populations and a merging of elites from both groups. For the most part, however, Aryas pushed the Dasas south into central and southern India, where their descendants still live. A sign of the ultimate success of the

Aryas in the north is the languages spoken in northern India today: they are primarily members of the Indo-European language family. Dravidian speech prevails in the south.

Skin color has been a persistent concern of Indian society and is one of the bases for its historically sharp internal divisions. Over time there evolved a system of *varna*—literally "color," though the word came to indicate something akin to "class." There were four class designations into which individuals were born: *Brahmin*, the group comprising priests and scholars; *Kshatriya*, warriors and officials; *Vaishya*, merchants, artisans, and landowners; and *Shudra*, peasants and laborers. The designation *Shudra* originally may have been reserved for Dasas, who were given the menial jobs in society. Indeed, the very term *dasa* came to mean "slave." Eventually a fifth group was also marked off: the Untouchables. They were excluded from the class system, and members of the other groups literally avoided them because of the demeaning or polluting work to which they were relegated—such as leather tanning, which involved touching dead animals, or sweeping away ashes after cremations.

People at the top of the social pyramid in ancient India could explain why this hierarchy existed. According to one creation myth, a primordial creature named Purusha allowed himself to be sacrificed. From Purusha's mouth sprang the class of Brahmin priests, the embodiment of intellect and knowledge. From his arms came the Kshatriya warrior class, from his thighs the Vaishya landowners and merchants, and from his feet the Shudra workers.

The varna system was just one of the mechanisms that Indian society developed to regulate relations between different groups. Within the broad class divisions, the population was also further subdivided into numerous *jati*, or birth groups (sometimes called *castes* from a Portuguese term meaning "breed"). Each jati had its proper occupation, duties, and rituals. The individuals who belonged to a given jati lived with members of their group, married within the group, and ate only with members of the group. Elaborate rules governed their interactions with members of other groups. Members of higher-status groups feared pollution from contact with lower-caste individuals and had to undergo elaborate rituals of purification to remove the taint.

The class and caste systems came to be connected to a widespread belief in reincarnation. The Brahmin priests taught that every living creature had an immortal essence: the *atman*, or "breath." Separated from the body at death, at a later time the atman was reborn in another body. Whether the new body was that of an insect, an animal, or a human depended on the *karma*, or deeds, of the atman in its previous incarnations. People who lived exemplary lives would be reborn into the higher classes. Those who misbehaved would be punished in the next life by being relegated to a lower class or even a lower life form. The underlying message was: You are where you deserve to be, and the only way to improve your lot in the next cycle of existence is to accept your station and its attendant duties.

The dominant deities in Vedic religion were male and were associated with the heavens. To release the dawn, Indra, god of war and master of the thunderbolt, daily slew the demon encasing the universe. Varuna, lord of the sky, maintained universal order and dispensed justice. Agni, the force of fire, consumed the sacrifice and bridged the worlds of gods and humans.

Sacrifice was the essential ritual. People believed that the dedication to a god of a valued possession, often a living creature, created a relationship between themselves and the gods. These offerings were made to invigorate the gods and thereby sustain their creative powers and promote stability in the world. The person making the sacrifice also hoped that the deity would respond favorably to his or her request. An important ingredient of Vedic ritual was *soma*, the nectar of immortality, a hallucinogenic liquid of some kind. The chief religious event of the year was the soma sacrifice, held just before the arrival of the June monsoon and credited with the reappearance of the life-giving rains.

Brahmin priests controlled the technology of sacrifice, for only they knew the precise rituals and prayers. The *Rig Veda*, a collection of more than a thousand poetic hymns to various deities,

and the Brahmanas, detailed prose descriptions of procedures for ritual and sacrifice, were collections of priestly lore couched in the Sanskrit language of the Aryan upper classes. This information was handed down orally from one generation of priests to the next. Some scholars have hypothesized that the Brahmins opposed the introduction of writing. Their opposition would explain why this technology did not come into widespread use in India until the Gupta period (320–550 C.E.), long after it had begun to play a conspicuous role in other societies of equivalent complexity. The priests' "knowledge" (the term *veda* means just that) was the basis of their economic well-being. They were amply rewarded for officiating at sacrifices, and their knowledge provided them with social and political power because they were the indispensable intermediaries between gods and humans.

As in virtually all ancient societies, it is difficult to uncover the experiences of women in ancient India. Limited evidence indicates that in the Vedic period women studied sacred lore, composed religious hymns, and participated in the sacrificial ritual. They had the opportunity to own property and usually were not married until they reached their middle or late teens. A number of strong and resourceful women appear in the epic poem *Mahabharata*. One of them, the beautiful and educated Draupadi, married by her own choice the five royal Pandava brothers. This accomplishment probably should not be taken as evidence for the regular practice of polyandry (having more than one husband). In India, as in Greece, legendary figures could play by their own rules.

The rigid internal divisions of Indian society, the complex hierarchy of groups, and the claims of some to superior virtue and purity served important social functions in Indian culture. They provided each individual with a clear identity and role and offered the benefits of group solidarity and support. There is evidence that groups sometimes were able to upgrade their status. Thus the elaborate system of divisions was not static and provided a mechanism for working out social tensions. Many of these features persisted into modern times.

Challenges to the Old Order: Jainism and Buddhism

After 700 B.C.E. various forms of reaction against Brahmin power and privilege emerged. People who objected to the rigid hierarchy of classes and castes or the community's demands on the individual could always retreat to the forest. Despite the clearing of extensive tracts of land for agriculture, much of ancient India was covered with forest. These wild places which were never very far from the civilized areas, served as a refuge and symbolized freedom from societal constraints.

Certain individuals abandoned their town or village and moved to the forest. Sometimes these hermits attracted bands of followers. Calling into question the exclusive claims to wisdom of the priests and the necessity of Vedic chants and sacrifices, they offered, as an alternate path to salvation, the individual pursuit of insight into the nature of the self and the universe through physical and mental discipline (*yoga*), special dietary practices, and meditation. They taught that by distancing oneself from desire for the things of this world, one could achieve *moksha*, or "liberation," union with the divine force that animates the universe. This release from the cycle of reincarnations sometimes was likened to "a deep, dreamless sleep." The Upanishads—a collection of over one hundred mystical dialogues between teachers and disciples—reflect this questioning of the foundations of Vedic religion.

The most serious threat to Vedic religion and to the prerogatives of the Brahmin priestly class came from two new sects that emerged around this time: Jainism and Buddhism. Mahavira (540–468 B.C.E.) was known to his followers as *Jina*, "the Conqueror," from which is derived *Jainism*, the name of the belief system that he established. Emphasizing the holiness of the life force that animates all living creatures, Mahavira and his followers practiced strict nonviolence. They wore masks to prevent themselves from accidentally inhaling small insects, and before sitting down, they carefully brushed off the surface of the seat. Those who gave themselves over completely to Jainism practiced extreme asceticism and nudity, ate only what they were given by others, and eventually starved themselves to death. Less zealous Jainists, restricted from agricultural work by the injunction against killing, tended to be city dwellers engaged in commerce and banking.

Of far greater significance for Indian and world history was the rise of Buddhism. So many stories have been told about Siddhartha Gautama (563–483 B.C.E.), known as the *Buddha*, "the Enlightened One," that it is difficult to separate fact from legend. He came from a Kshatriya family of the Sakya tribe in the foothills of the Himalayas. As a young man he enjoyed the lifestyle to which he had been born, but at some point he experienced a change of heart and gave up family and privilege to become a wandering ascetic. After six years of self-deprivation, he came to regard asceticism as being no more likely to produce spiritual insights than the luxury of his previous life had been. He decided to adhere to a "Middle Path" of moderation. Sitting under a tree in a deer park near Benares on the Ganges River, he had a revelation of "Four Noble Truths": (1) life is suffering; (2) suffering arises from desire; (3) the solution to suffering lies in stemming desire; and (4) this can be achieved by following the "Eightfold Path" of right views, aspirations, speech, conduct, livelihood, effort, mindfulness, and meditation. Rising up, he preached his First Sermon, a central text of Buddhism, and set into motion the "Wheel of the Law." The Buddha soon attracted followers who took vows of celibacy, nonviolence, and poverty.

In its original form Buddhism centered on the individual. Although it did not quite reject the existence of gods, it denied their usefulness to a person seeking enlightenment. What mattered was living one's life in a manner that minimized desire and suffering and emphasized the search for spiritual truth. The ultimate reward was *nirvana*, literally "snuffing out the flame." With nirvana came release from the cycle of reincarnations and achievement of a state of eternal tranquillity. The Vedic tradition emphasized the survival beyond death of the atman, the "breath" or nonmaterial essence of the individ-

Stone relief of women adoring the Buddha, from the Great Stupa at Amaravati (central India), second century C.E. Many stories circulated concerning the life of the Buddha and his many previous lives. Such stories were represented in the rich carvings which decorated the gates and walls of *stupas*, mounds containing relics of the founder which became major pilgrimage sites. For centuries after his death, artists refrained from directly depicting the Buddha, instead using a repertoire of symbols: the tree under which he achieved enlightenment, his begging bowl, and, as here, his seat and footprints. The fact that he is not represented in human form emphasizes that he has achieved the state of *nirvana*, nonexistence. (Robert Fisher)

ual. In contrast, Buddhism regarded the individual as a composite without any soul-like component that survived death. Nirvana is an eternal state of nonexistence.

When the Buddha died, he left no rules or instructions, instead urging his disciples to "be their own lamp." As the Buddha's message spread throughout India and beyond into Central, Southeast, and East Asia, its very success began to subvert the individualistic and essentially atheistic tenets of the founder, however. Buddhist monasteries were established, and a hierarchy of Buddhist monks and nuns came into being. Worshipers erected *stupas* (large earthen mounds that symbolized the universe) over relics of the cremated founder and walked around them in a clockwise direction. Indeed, the Buddha himself began to be worshiped as a god. Buddhists also revered *bodhisattvas*, enlight-

ened men and women who had earned nirvana but chose to be reborn into mortal bodies to help others along the path to salvation.

The makers of early pictorial images had refused to show the Buddha as a living person and represented him only indirectly, through symbols such as his footprints, begging bowl, or the tree under which he achieved enlightenment, as if to emphasize his achievement of a state of nonexistence. From the second century C.E., however, statues of the Buddha and bodhisattvas began to proliferate, done in native sculptural styles and in a style that showed the influence of the Greek settlements established in Bactria (modern Afghanistan) by Alexander the Great (see Chapter 5). A deep schism emerged within Buddhism. Devotees of Mahayana, or "Great Vehicle," Buddhism embraced the popular new features. In contrast, practitioners of Theravada

Sculpture of the Buddha, second or third century C.E.   This depiction of the Buddha, showing the effects of a protracted fast, is from Gandhara in the northwest. It displays the influence of Greek artistic styles emanating from the settlements of Greeks which had been established in that region by Alexander the Great in the late fourth century B.C.E. This work illustrates how some of the Buddha's own precepts were superseded in the Mahayana form of Buddhism which gained popularity by the early centuries C.E. (Robert Fisher)

Buddhism, "The Way of the Elders" (also called Hinayana, or "Lesser Vehicle"), followed most of the original teachings of the founder.

The Rise of Hinduism

Challenged by new, spiritually satisfying, and egalitarian movements, Vedic religion made important adjustments, evolving into Hinduism,

the religion of hundreds of millions of people in South Asia today. (The term *Hinduism*, however, was imposed from outside. When Islamic invaders reached India in the eleventh century C.E., they labeled the diverse range of practices they saw there as Hinduism: "what the Indians do.")

The foundation of Hinduism is the Vedic religion of the Aryan tribes of northern India. But Hinduism also incorporated elements drawn from the Dravidian cultures of the south, such as an emphasis on intense devotion to the deity and the prominence of fertility rituals and symbolism, as well as elements of Buddhism. The process by which Vedic religion was transformed into Hinduism by the fourth century C.E. is largely hidden from us. The Brahmin priests emerged with their high social status and influence essentially intact. But sacrifice, though still part of traditional worship, was less central, and there was much more opportunity for direct contact between gods and individual worshipers.

The gods were altered, both in identity and in their relationships with humanity. Two formerly minor deities, Vishnu and Shiva, assumed a preeminent position in the Hindu pantheon. Hinduism emphasized the worshiper's personal devotion (*bhakti*) to a particular deity, usually Vishnu, Shiva, or Devi ("the Goddess"). These gods can appear in many guises. They are identified by various cult names and epithets and are represented by a complex symbolism of stories, companion animals, birds, and objects.

Vishnu, the preserver, is a benevolent deity who helps his devotees in time of need. Hindus believe that whenever demonic forces threaten the cosmic order, Vishu appears on earth in a series of *avataras*, or incarnations. Among his incarnations are the legendary hero Rama, the popular cowherd-god Krishna, and the Buddha (a blatant attempt to co-opt the rival religion's founder). Shiva, who lives in ascetic isolation on Mount Kailasa in the Himalayas, is a more ambivalent figure. He represents both creation and destruction, for both are part of a single, cyclical process. He often is represented performing dance steps that symbolize the acts of creation and destruction. Devi manifests herself in various ways—as a full-bodied mother-goddess who promotes fertility and procreation, as the docile and loving wife Parvati, and as the frightening deity who, under the name Kali or Durga, lets loose a torrent of violence and destruction.

Both Shiva and Devi appear to be derived from the Dravidian tradition, in which fertility cult and female deities played a prominent role. Their origin is a telling example of how Aryan and non-Aryan cultures fused to form classic Hindu civilization. It is interesting to note that Vishnu, who has a clear Aryan pedigree, remains more popular in northern India, while Shiva is dominant in the Dravidian south.

The multiplicity of gods (330 million according to one tradition), sects, and local practices within Hinduism is dazzling, reflecting the ethnic, linguistic, and cultural diversity of India. Yet within this variety there is unity. A worshiper's devotion to one god or goddess does not entail denial of the other main deities or the host of lesser divinities and spirits. Ultimately, all are seen as manifestations of a single divine force that pervades the universe. This sense of underlying unity is expressed in many ways: in texts such as the passage from the Bhagavad-Gita quoted at the beginning of this chapter; in the different potentials of women represented in the various manifestations of Devi, in composite statues that are split down the middle—half Shiva, half Vishnu—as if to say that they are complementary aspects of one cosmic principle.

Hinduism offers the worshiper a variety of ways to approach god and obtain divine favor, whether through special knowledge of sacred truths, mental and physical discipline, or extraordinary devotion to the deity. The activity of worship centers on the temples, which range from humble village shrines to magnificent, richly decorated stone edifices built under royal patronage. Beautifully proportioned statues beckon the deity to take up temporary residence within the image, where he or she can be reached and beseeched by eager worshipers. A common form of worship is *puja*, service to the deity, which can take the form of bathing, clothing, or feeding the statue. Potent blessings are conferred on the man or woman to whom *darsan*, a glimpse of the divine image, is given.

Pilgrimage to famous shrines and attendance at festivals offer additional opportunities to

Stone relief depicting Vishnu asleep and dreaming on the ocean floor, from a Vishnu temple at Deogarh (central India), fifth century c.e. Vishnu lies on the coiled body of a giant, multi-headed serpent which he had subdued. The beneficent god of preservation, Vishnu appears in a new *avatara* (incarnation) whenever the world is threatened by demonic forces. The Indian view of the vastness of time is embodied in this mythic image, which conceives of Vishnu as creating and destroying universes as he exhales and inhales. (John C. Huntington)

show devotion. The entire Indian subcontinent is dotted with sacred places where the worshiper can directly perceive and obtain benefit from the inherent power of divinity. Mountains, caves, and certain plants and rocks are enveloped in an aura of mystery and sanctity. The literal meaning of *tirthayatra*, the term for a pilgrimage site, is "journey to a river-crossing," pointing up the frequent association of Hindu sacred places with flowing water. Hindus consider the Ganges River to be especially sacred, and each year millions of devoted worshipers flock to its banks to bathe and receive the restorative and purifying power of its waters. The habit of pilgrimage to the major shrines promotes contact and the exchange of ideas among people from different parts of India and has helped to create a broad Hindu identity and the concept of India as a single civilization, despite enduring political fragmentation.

Religious duties may vary, depending not only on the worshiper's social standing and gender but also on his or her stage of life. A young man from one of the three highest classes (Brahmin, Kshatriya, or Vaishya) undergoes a ritual rebirth through the ceremony of the sacred thread, marking the attainment of manhood and access to religious knowledge. From this point, the ideal life cycle passes through four stages: (1) the young man becomes a student and studies the sacred texts; (2) he then becomes a householder, marries, has children, and acquires material wealth; (3) when his grandchildren are born, he gives up home and family and becomes a forest dweller, meditating on the nature and meaning of existence; (4) he abandons his personal identity altogether and becomes a wandering ascetic awaiting death. In the course of a virtuous life he has fulfilled first his duties to society and then his duties to himself, so that by the end of his life he is so disconnected from the world that he can achieve moksha (liberation).

The successful transformation of a religion based on Vedic antecedents and the ultimate victory of Hinduism over Buddhism—Buddhism was driven from the land of its birth, though it maintains deep roots in Central, East, and Southeast Asia (see Chapters 8 and 11)—is a remarkable phenomenon. Hinduism succeeded by responding to the needs of people for personal deities with whom they could establish direct connections. The austerity of Buddhism in its most authentic form, its denial of the importance of gods, and its expectation that individuals find their own path to enlightenment may have demanded too much of ordinary individuals. And the very features that made Mahayana Buddhism more accessible to the populace—gods, saints, and myths—also made it more easily absorbed into the vast social and cultural fabrics of Hinduism.

IMPERIAL EXPANSION AND COLLAPSE

Political unity, on those rare occasions when it has been achieved, has not lasted for long in India. A number of factors have contributed to India's habitual political fragmentation. The landscape of India—mountains, foothills, plains, forests, steppes, deserts—is extremely varied. Different terrains called forth different forms of organization and economic activity, and the peoples who occupied topographically diverse zones differed from one another in language and cultural practices. Perhaps the most significant barrier to political unity lay in the complex social hierarchy. Individuals identified themselves primarily in terms of their class and caste (birth group); allegiance to a higher political authority was of secondary concern.

Despite these divisive factors, two empires arose in the Ganges Plain: the Mauryan Empire of the fourth to second centuries B.C.E. and the Gupta Empire of the fourth to sixth centuries C.E. Each extended political control over a substantial portion of the subcontinent and expedited the formation of a common Indian civilization.

The Mauryan Empire, 324–184 B.C.E.

Around 600 B.C.E. the landscape of north India was dotted with many separate tribal groups and independent states. The kingdom of Magadha, in eastern India south of the Ganges (see Map 7.1), began to play an increasingly influential role, however, thanks to wealth based on agriculture, iron mines, and its strategic location astride the trade routes of the eastern Ganges Basin. In the late fourth century B.C.E. Chandragupta Maurya, a young man who may have belonged to the Vaishya or Shudra class, gained control of the kingdom of Magadha and expanded it into India's first centralized empire. He may have been inspired by the example of Alexander the Great, who had followed up his conquest of the Persian Empire with a foray into the Punjab (northern Pakistan) in 326 B.C.E. (see Chapter 5).

Indeed, Greek tradition claimed that Alexander met a young Indian native by the name of "Sandracottus," an apparent corruption of "Chandragupta."

The collapse of Greek rule in the Punjab after the death of Alexander created a power vacuum in the northwest. Chandragupta (r. 324–301 B.C.E.) and his successors Bindusara (r. 301–269 B.C.E.) and Ashoka (r. 269–232 B.C.E.) extended Mauryan control over the entire subcontinent except for the southern tip of the peninsula. Not until the height of the Mughal Empire of the seventeenth century C.E. or the advent of British rule in the nineteenth century would so much of India again be under the control of a single government.

Tradition holds that Kautilya, a crafty elderly Brahmin, guided Chandragupta in his conquests and consolidation of power. Kautilya is said to have written a surviving treatise on government, the *Arthashastra*. Although recent studies have shown that the *Arthashastra* in its present form is a product of the third century C.E., its core text may well go back to Kautilya. This coldly pragmatic guide to political success and survival advocates the so-called *mandala* (circle) theory of foreign policy: "My enemy's enemy is my friend." It also relates a long list of schemes for enforcing and increasing the collection of tax revenues, and it prescribes the use of spies to keep watch on everyone in the kingdom.

The Mauryan kings and government were supported by a tax equivalent to one-fourth of the value of the agricultural crop. Administrative districts, based on traditional tribal boundaries, were governed by close relatives and associates of the king. A large national army—with infantry, cavalry, chariot, and elephant divisions—and royal control of mines, shipbuilding, and the manufacture of armaments further secured the power of the central government. Standard coinage issued throughout the empire both fostered support for the government and military apparatus and promoted trade.

The Mauryan capital was at Pataliputra (modern Patna), where five tributaries join the Ganges. Several extant descriptions of the city composed by foreign visitors provide valuable information and testify to the international connections of the Indian monarchs. Surrounded by a timber wall and moat, the city extended along the river for 8 miles (13 kilometers). It was governed by six committees with responsibility for features of urban life such as manufacturing, trade, sales, taxes, the welfare of foreigners, and the registration of births and deaths.

Ashoka, Chandragupta's grandson, is a towering figure in Indian history. At the beginning of his reign he engaged in military campaigns that

A stone pillar inscribed with edicts of King Ashoka, ca. 240 B.C.E. Ashoka, the most powerful and charismatic of the Mauryan kings, became a convert to Buddhism early in his reign. He argued nonviolence, moderation, justice, and religious tolerance on his officials and subjects, and put up inscriptions on stone pillars and great rocks around his realm to broadcast his pronouncements. Many are preserved and constitute the first extant examples of writing in India. (Borromeo/Art Resource, NY)

extended the boundaries of the empire. During his conquest of Kalinga (modern Orissa, a coastal region southeast of Magadha), hundreds of thousands of people were killed, wounded, or deported. The brutality of this victory overwhelmed the young monarch. He became a convert to Buddhism and an exponent of nonviolence, morality, moderation, and religious tolerance both in government and in private life.

Ashoka publicized this program by inscribing edicts on great rocks and polished pillars of sandstone scattered throughout his enormous empire. Among the inscriptions that have survived and constitute the earliest decipherable Indian writing is the following:

> For a long time in the past, for many hundreds of years have increased the sacrificial slaughter of animals, violence toward creatures, unfilial conduct toward kinsmen, improper conduct toward Brahmans and ascetics. Now with the practice of morality by King Devanampiya Piyadasi [Ashoka], the sound of war drums has become the call to morality. . . . You [government officials] are appointed to rule over thousands of human beings in the expectation that you will win the affection of all men. All men are my children. Just as I desire that my children will fare well and be happy in this world and the next, I desire the same for all men. . . . King Devanampiya Piyadasi . . . desires that there should be the growth of the essential spirit of morality or holiness among all sects. . . . There should not be glorification of one's own sect and denunciation of the sect of others for little or no reason. For all the sects are worthy of reverence for one reason or another.[2]

Ashoka, however, was not naive. Despite his commitment to employ peaceful means where possible, he hastened to remind potential transgressors that "the king, remorseful as he is, has the strength to punish the wrongdoers who do not repent."

Commerce and Culture in an Era of Political Fragmentation

The Mauryan Empire prospered for a time after Ashoka's death in 232 B.C.E. Then, weakened by dynastic disputes, it collapsed from the pressure of attacks in the northwest in 184 B.C.E. Five hundred years would pass before another indigenous state was able to extend its control over northern India.

In the meantime, a series of foreign powers dominated the Indus Valley and extended their influence east and south. The first was the Greco-Bactrian kingdom (180–50 B.C.E.), descended from troops and settlers that Alexander the Great had left behind in Afghanistan. Domination by two nomadic peoples from Central Asia followed: the Shakas (known as Scythians in the Mediterranean world) from 50 B.C.E. to 50 C.E. and the Kushans from 50 to 240 C.E. Several foreign kings—most notably the Greco-Bactrian Milinda (Menander in Greek) and the Kushan Kanishka—were converts to Buddhism, a logical choice because Hinduism had no easy mechanism for working foreigners into its system of class and caste. The eastern Ganges region reverted to a patchwork of small principalities, as it had been before the Mauryan era.

This period of political fragmentation in the north also saw the rise of important states in central and southern India, particularly the Andhra, or Satavahana, dynasty in the Deccan (from the second century B.C.E. to the second century C.E.) and the three southern Tamil kingdoms of Cholas, Pandyas, and Cheras (see Map 7.1). Although there were frequent military conflicts among these societies, this was a period of great literary and artistic productivity that manifested itself in poetry, epic, and the performances of troupes of wandering actors and musicians (see Voices and Visions: Tamil Culture).

Indeed, despite the political fragmentation of India in the five centuries after the collapse of the Mauryan Empire, there were many signs of economic, cultural, and intellectual development. The network of roads and towns that had sprung up under the Mauryans fostered lively commerce within the subcontinent, and India was at the heart of international land and sea trade routes that linked China, Southeast Asia, Central Asia, the Middle East, East Africa, and the lands of the Mediterranean. In the absence of a strong central authority, guilds (shreni) of merchants and artisans in the Indian towns became politically powerful, regulating the lives of their members and

Tamil Culture

The majority of the population in southern India speak languages that belong to a non-Indo-European family of languages called Dravidian. The Tamil language of the inhabitants of the southern tip of the peninsula (as well as the northern part of the island of Sri Lanka) is one of these, and the Tamil people have an ancient conception of this region as Tamilakam, "the homeland of the Tamils." In their own traditions they have always lived in this region, but long ago it was much larger, before great floods and tidal waves swallowed up land that now lies beneath the ocean.

Historical evidence, while quite limited for southern India, does point to the existence of Tamil kingdoms from as early as the fifth century B.C.E. The three kingdoms of Pandyas, Cholas, and Cheras, which were in frequent conflict with one another, experienced periods of ascendancy and decline, but persisted in one form or another for two thousand years or more. The period from the third century B.C.E. to the third century C.E. is regarded as a "classical" period in which Tamil society, under the patronage of the Pandya kings and intellectual leadership of the sangham, an academy of 500 authors, produced works of literature on a wide range of topics, including grammatical treatises, collections of ethical proverbs, epics, and shorter poems about love, war, wealth, the beauty of nature, and the joys of music, dance, and drama.

The following passage, from an anthology called "The Ten Idylls," describes the port of Pukar at the mouth of Cauvery River:

At this great ancient and lovely port of Pukar, which has stood forever like a heaven of rare attainments, the fishermen bathe in the confluence to wash off their sin and bathe again in fresh water to wash off the salt. They dash into the waves, play with the crabs, make images in the sands and play throughout the day with never-abating enthusiasm.

In the well-lit storied mansions with high colonnades, young wives whose husbands have joined them, take off their silks and put on fine clothes of cotton. They enjoy the drinks poured out of the receptacles. . . . On the wide highways leading from the port lined with aloes of white blossoms and long leaves are the officials of the kings who collect the customs revenue of the land. They are famous for their honesty and untiring work. . . . The buildings in the bazaar streets rise up to the clouds with many floors and apartments, tall winding stairs of short steps, long corridors and wide and narrow doorways. . . . In the streets below, god-intoxicated girls sing and dance in honor of Muruga in tune to the call of the flute, the sound of the lute and the beat of the drums. . . . Flags fly over the decorated gates of temples, where gods of great repute are enshrined, before which many bow down. . . . Famous scholars, great authorities in knowledge and learning, have raised awe-inspiring flags as a sign of challenge for debates. Flags are seen on the top masts of ships lying at anchor in the beautiful open harbor of Pukar tossing in their moorings like restless elephants moving to and fro."

What physical features of an ancient Tamil city are evident in the passage above? What were the different elements of Tamil society? What kinds of work did they engage in, and what kinds of recreation were available to them?

In the religious sphere, in contrast to the primarily male orientation of Brahmin–dominated northern India, the Tamil south has had a pronounced female orientation. Worship of fertility goddesses in humble local temples has always been strong. The Tamils perceived a potent connection between female chastity and spiritual power, and in their stories they recollected how this power had protected the Tamil lands and culture from internal injustice and outside threats. The epic Silipathikaram *tells the story of Kannagi, a heroine who resolutely sets out to prove the innocence of her husband, who had been executed for a crime he did not commit:*

"She rose bewildered and fell down on earth
like the moon behind the pouring rain,
and with her eyes blood-shot, she cried and sighed,
'O husband mine, where have you sped'. . .
(She addresses the Sun)
'Thou knowest all in this wide sea-girt earth,
Say if my husband was a thief, O Sun!'
'No thief was he, O dame with jet-black eyes,
This town will be for fire a feast' said he. . .
(Kannagi speaks again)
'Where can I get this solved? This can't be truth.
Even so, unless my anger is appeased
I will not seek to join my husband dear.
The cruel king I will see and demand the right.'
So she said; she rose and stood and paused
Remembering her evil dream, and cried.
She stood and dried her blinding tears and went
And reached the gates of the palace of the king."

Kannagi's quest leads to the death of the unjust king who ordered the execution, the destruction by fire of his capital, and the transformation of Kannagi, who is transported to the skies in a chariot to become the goddess of chastity. What does this story tell us about the importance and influence of women in Tail society? What qualities are expected of them and admired in them? Why might Tamil society have valued these qualities?

Source: Translations from J. M. Somasundaram Pillai, *Two Thousand Years of Tamil Literature* (Madras, 1959), pp. 150–152, 205–211.

having an important say in local affairs. Their economic clout enabled them to serve as patrons of culture and to endow the religious sects to which they adhered—particularly Buddhism and Jainism—with richly decorated temples and monuments.

During the last centuries B.C.E. and first centuries C.E. the two greatest Indian epics, the *Ramayana* and the *Mahabharata*, based on oral predecessors dating back many centuries, achieved their final form. The events of both epics are said to have occurred several million years in the past, but the political forms, social organization, and other elements of cultural context—proud kings, beautiful queens, tribal wars, heroic conduct, and chivalric values—seem to reflect the conditions of the early Vedic period, when Aryan warrior societies were moving into the Ganges Plain.

The vast pageant of the *Mahabharata* (it is eight times the length of the Greek *Iliad* and *Odyssey* combined) tells the story of two sets of cousins, the Pandavas and Kauravas, whose quarrel over succession to the throne leads them to a cata-

Wall painting from the caves at Ajanta (central India), seventh century C.E.   Kings and other wealthy patrons donated lavishly for the construction and decoration of Buddhist, Hindu, and Jain religious shrines, including elaborate complexes of caves. At Ajanta, twenty-nine caves are filled with paintings and relief sculpture illustrating religious and secular scenes. This segment represents a visit of envoys from Persia or Central Asia to the court of an Indian monarch. The ruler, seen at left on his pillow-covered throne, is surrounded by male and female members of court. The envoys, at bottom right, who have non-Indian facial features and wear long coats, are presenting gifts to the king. (Harvard College Library)

clysmic battle at the field of Kurukshetra. The battle is so destructive on all sides that the eventual winner, Yudhishthira, is reluctant to accept the fruits of so tragic a victory.

The Bhagavad-Gita, quoted at the beginning of this chapter, is a self-contained (and perhaps originally separate) episode set in the midst of those events. The great hero Arjuna, at first reluctant to fight his own kinsmen, is tutored by the god Krishna and learns the necessity of fulfilling his duty as a warrior. Death means nothing in a universe in which souls will be reborn again and again. The climactic moment comes when Krishna reveals his true appearance—awesome and overwhelmingly powerful—and his identity as time itself, the force behind all creation and destruction. The Bhagavad Gita offers an attractive resolution to the tension in Indian civilization between duty to society and duty to one's own soul. Disciplined action—that is, action taken without regard for any personal benefits that might derive from it—is a form of service to the gods and will be rewarded by release from the cycle of rebirths.

This era also saw significant advances in science and technology. Indian doctors had a wide knowledge of herbal remedies and were in demand in the courts of western and southern Asia. Indian scholars made impressive strides in the field of linguistics. Panini (late fourth century B.C.E.) undertook a remarkably detailed analysis of the word forms and grammar of the Sanskrit language. He and the commentators who built on his work contributed to a standardization of Sanskrit usage which arrested its natural development and turned it into a formal, literary language. Prakrits—popular dialects—emerged to become the ancestors of the modern Indo-European languages of northern and central India.

The Gupta Empire, 320–550 C.E.

In the early fourth century C.E. a new imperial entity coalesced in northern India. Like its Mauryan predecessor, the Gupta Empire grew out of the kingdom of Magadha on the Ganges Plain and had its capital at Pataliputra. There can be no clearer proof that the founder of this empire consciously modeled himself on the Mauryans

than the fact that he called himself Chandra Gupta (r. 320–335), borrowing the very name of the Mauryan founder. A claim to wide dominion was embodied in the title that the monarchs of this dynasty assumed—"Great King of Kings"—although they never controlled territories as extensive as those of the Mauryans. Nevertheless, over the fifteen-year reign of Chandra Gupta and the forty-year reigns of his three successors—Samudra Gupta, Chandra Gupta II, and Kumara Gupta—Gupta power and influence reached across northern and central India, west to Punjab and east to Bengal, north to Kashmir and south into the Deccan (see Map 7.1).

This new empire enjoyed the same strategic advantages as its Mauryan predecessor, sitting astride important trade routes, exploiting the agricultural productivity of the Ganges Plain, and controlling nearby iron deposits. It adopted similar methods for raising revenue and administering broad territories. The chief source of revenue was a tax on agriculture, requiring that one-fourth of the annual produce be paid to the state. Those who used the irrigation network also had to pay for the service, and there were special taxes on particular commodities. The state maintained monopolies in key areas, such as the mining of metals and salt, owned extensive tracts of farmland, and demanded a specified number of days of labor annually from the citizens for the construction and upkeep of roads, wells, and the irrigation network.

Gupta control, however, was never as effectively centralized as Mauryan authority. The Gupta administrative bureaucracy and intelligence network were smaller and less pervasive. A powerful army maintained tight control and taxation in the core of the empire, but outlying areas were left to their governors to organize. The position of governor offered tempting opportunities to exploit the populace. It often was hereditary, passed on to high-ranking members of the civil and military administration. Distant subordinate vassal kingdoms and tribal areas were expected to make annual donations of tribute, and certain key frontier points were garrisoned to keep open the lines of trade and expedite the collection of customs duties.

Historians often point to the Gupta Empire as a good example of a "theater-state." Limited in its ability to enforce its will on outlying areas, it instead found ways to "persuade" others to follow its lead. One medium of persuasion was the splendor, beauty, and order of life at the capital and royal court. A constant round of rituals, ceremonies, and cultural events were a potent advertisement for the benefits that derived from association with the empire.

The relationship of ruler and subjects in a theater-state also has an economic base. The center is a focal point for the collection and redistribution of luxury goods and profits from trade through the exchange of gifts and other means of sharing accumulated resources with dependents. Subordinate princes sought to emulate the Gupta center on whatever scale they could manage, and to maintain close ties through visits, gifts, and intermarriage.

Because the moist climate of the Ganges Plain does not favor the preservation of buildings and artifacts, there is for the Gupta era, as for earlier eras in Indian history, relatively little archaeological data. An eyewitness account, however, provides valuable information about the Gupta kingdom and Pataliputra, its capital city. A Chinese Buddhist monk named Faxian made a pilgrimage to the homeland of his faith around 400 C.E. and left a record of his journey:

> The royal palace and halls in the midst of the city, which exist now as of old, were all made by spirits which [King Ashoka] employed, and which piled up the stones, reared the walls and gates, and executed the elegant carving and inlaid sculpture-work—in a way which no human hands of this world could accomplish. . . . By the side of the stupa of Ashoka, there has been made a Mahayana [Buddhist] monastery, very grand and beautiful; there is also a Hinayana one; the two together containing six hundred or seven hundred monks. The rules of demeanor and the scholastic arrangements in them are worthy of observation. . . . The cities and towns of this country are the greatest of all in the Middle Kingdom. The inhabitants are rich and prosperous, and vie with one another in the practice of benevolence and righteousness. . . . The heads of the Vaishya families in them establish in the cities houses for dispensing charity and medicines. All the poor and destitute in the country, orphans, widowers, and childless men, maimed people and cripples, and all who are diseased, go to those houses, and are provided with every kind of help.[3]

The endeavors of astronomers, mathematicians, and other scientists received royal support. Indian mathematicians invented the concept of zero and developed a revolutionary system of place-value notation that is in use in most parts of the world today (see Environment and Technology: Indian Mathematics).

The Gupta kings were also patrons of the arts. A number of the works of drama of this age were love stories, providing us glimpses of the lifestyle and manners of high society. The greatest of all ancient Indian dramatists, Kalidasa, was active in the reign of Chandra Gupta II (r. 375–415). Seven of his plays survive, written in the elite Sanskrit and everyday Prakrit of the time. As the Athenian dramatists of the fifth century B.C.E. had drawn their plots from the legendary tradition preserved in Homer but altered details and reworked the characters to comment on the values and issues of their own times, so Kalidasa refashioned elements drawn from the great Indian epics. In Indian legend a female heroine named Shakuntala resolutely pursued a prince who had forgotten his promise that the child who resulted from their brief love affair in the forest would inherit his throne. In *Shakuntala or the Ring of Recollection*, Kalidasa turned Shakuntala into a largely docile figure animated more by forlorn love than by confident self-assertion. In this way he validated the prevailing conception of women, emphasizing the importance of female passivity, chastity, and devotion to the husband. This and other evidence seem to indicate that women's situations worsened after the Vedic period.

In all likelihood, this development was similar to developments in Mesopotamia from the second millennium B.C.E., Archaic and Classical Greece, and China from the first millennium B.C.E. In these civilizations, several factors—urbanization, the formation of increasingly complex political and social structures, and the emergence of a nonagricultural middle class that placed high value on the acquisition and inheritance of property—led to a loss of women's rights and increased male control over women's

Indian Mathematics

The so-called Arabic numerals used in most parts of the world today were developed in India. The Indian system of place-value notation was far more efficient than the unwieldy numerical systems of Egyptians, Greeks, and Romans, and the invention of zero was a profound intellectual achievement. Indeed, it has to be ranked as one of the most important and influential discoveries in human history. This system is used even more widely than the alphabet derived from the Phoenicians (see Chapter 4) and is, in one sense, the only truly universal language.

In its fully developed form the Indian method of arithmetic notation employed a base-ten system. It had separate columns for ones, tens, hundreds, and so forth, as well as a zero sign to indicate the absence of units in a given column. This system makes possible the economical expression of even very large numbers. And it allows for the performance of calculations that were not possible in a system like the numerals of the Romans, where any real calculation had to be done mentally or on some sort of counting board.

A series of early Indian inscriptions using the numerals from 1 to 9 are deeds of property given to religious institutions by kings or other wealthy individuals. They were incised in the Sanskrit language on copper plates. The earliest known example has a date equivalent to 595 C.E. A sign for zero is attested by the eighth century. Other textual evidence leads to the inference that a place-value system and the zero concept were already known in the fifth century.

This Indian system spread to the Middle East, Southeast Asia, and East Asia by the seventh century. Other peoples quickly recognized its capabilities and adopted it, sometimes using indigenous symbols. Europe received the new technology somewhat later. Gerbert of Aurillac, a French Christian monk, spent time in Spain between 967 and 970, where he was exposed to the mathematics of the Arabs. A great scholar and teacher who eventually became Pope Sylvester II (r. 999–1003), he spread word of the "Arabic" system in the Christian West.

Knowledge of the Indian system of mathematical notation seems to have spread throughout Europe primarily through the use of a mechanical calculating device, an improved version of the Roman counting board, with counters inscribed with variants of the Indian numeral forms. Because the counters could be turned sideways or upside down, at first there was considerable variation in the forms. But by the twelfth century they had become standardized into forms close to those in use today. As the capabilities of the place-value system for written calculations became clear, the counting board fell into disuse. The abandonment of this device led to the adoption of the zero sign—not necessary on the counting board, where a column could be left empty—by the twelfth century.

Why was this marvelous system of mathematical notation invented in ancient India? The answer may lie in the way in which the range and versatility of this number system corresponds to elements of Indian cosmology. The Indians conceived of immense spans of time—trillions of years (far exceeding current scientific estimates of the age of the universe as between 15 billion and 20 billion years old)—during which innumerable universes like our own were created, existed for a finite time, then were destroyed. In one popular creation myth Vishnu is slumbering on the coils of a giant serpent at the bottom of the ocean and worlds are being created and destroyed as he exhales and inhales. In Indian thought our world, like others, has existed for a series of epochs lasting more than 4 million years, yet the period of its existence is but a brief and insignificant moment in the vast sweep of time. The Indians developed a number system that allowed them to express concepts of this magnitude.

From another perspective, the goal of both Hindu and Buddhist devotees was to escape from the toilsome cycle of lives and to achieve a state akin to nonexistence. The philosophical/religious concepts of moksha and nirvana correspond to the numerical concept of zero.

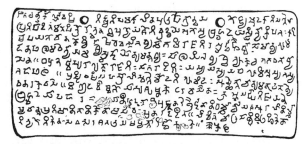

Copper plate from western India (Facsimile by Georges Ifrah. Reproduced by permission of Georges Ifrah)

behavior. Over time women in India lost the right to own or inherit property. They were barred from studying sacred texts and participating in the sacrificial ritual and in many respects were treated as equivalent to the lowest class, the Shudra. As in Confucian China, they were expected to obey first their father, then their husband, and finally their sons (see Chapter 6). Girls were married at an increasingly early age, sometimes as young as six or seven. This practice meant that the prospective husband could be sure of his wife's virginity and, by bringing her up in his own household, could train and shape her to suit his purposes.

Some women escaped these instruments of male control. One way to do so was by entering a Jainist or Buddhist religious community. Women who belonged to powerful families and courtesans trained in poetry and music as well as in ways of providing sexual pleasure had high social standing and sometimes gave money for the erection of Buddhist stupas and other shrines. In the emerging Hindu culture, however, a woman's primary *dharma*, or duty, was to be a mother and wife. The most extreme form of control of women's conduct took place in certain parts of India where a widow was expected to cremate herself on her husband's funeral pyre. This ritual, called *sati,* was seen as a way of keeping a woman "pure." Women who declined to make this ultimate gesture of devotion to a deceased husband were forbidden to remarry, shunned socially, and given little opportunity to earn a living.

The period of political fragmentation between the eclipse of the Mauryan Empire and the rise of the Guptas had seen the development of extensive networks of trade within India, as well as the creation of land and sea routes to foreign lands. This vibrant commerce continued into the Gupta period. Coined money served as the medium of exchange, and well-organized artisan guilds played an influential role in the economic, political, and religious life of the towns. The Guptas sought control of the ports on the Arabian Sea but saw a decline in trade with the weakened Roman Empire. In compensation, trade with Southeast and East Asia was on the rise. Adventurous merchants from the ports of eastern and southern India made the sea voyage to the Malay Peninsula and islands of Indonesia in order to exchange Indian cotton cloth, ivory, metalwork, and exotic animals for Chinese silk or Indonesian spices. The overland silk route from China also continued in operation but was vulnerable to disruption by Central Asian nomads.

The Mauryans had been Buddhists, but the Gupta monarchs were Hindus. They revived ancient Vedic practices to bring an aura of sanctity to their position, and this period also saw a reassertion of the importance of class and caste and the influence of Brahmin priests. Nevertheless, it was an era of religious tolerance. The Gupta kings were patrons for Hindu, Buddhist, and Jain endeavors. Buddhist monasteries with hundreds or even thousands of monks and nuns in residence flourished in the cities. Northern India was the destination of Buddhist pilgrims from Southeast and East Asia, traveling to visit the birthplace of their faith.

The classic form of the Hindu temple evolved during the Gupta era. Sitting atop a raised platform surmounted by high towers, the temple was patterned on the sacred mountain or palace in which the gods of mythology resided, and it represented the inherent order of the universe. From an exterior courtyard worshipers approached the central shrine, where the statue of the deity stood. In the best-endowed sanctuaries paintings or sculptured depictions of gods and mythical events covered the walls. Cave-temples carved out of rock were also richly adorned with frescoes or with sculpture.

By the later fifth century C.E. the Gupta Empire was coming under pressure from the Xiongnu. These nomadic invaders from the steppes of Central Asia poured into the northwest corridor. Defense of this distant frontier region eventually exhausted the imperial treasury, and the empire collapsed by 550.

The early seventh century saw a brief but glorious revival of imperial unity. Harsha Vardhana (r. 606–647), ruler of the region around Delhi, extended his power over the northern plain and moved his capital to Kanauj on the Ganges River. We have an account of the life and long reign of this fervent Buddhist, poet, patron of artists, and dynamic warrior, written by the courtier Bana. In addition, the Chinese Buddhist pilgrim Xuanzang (600–664) left an account of his travels in

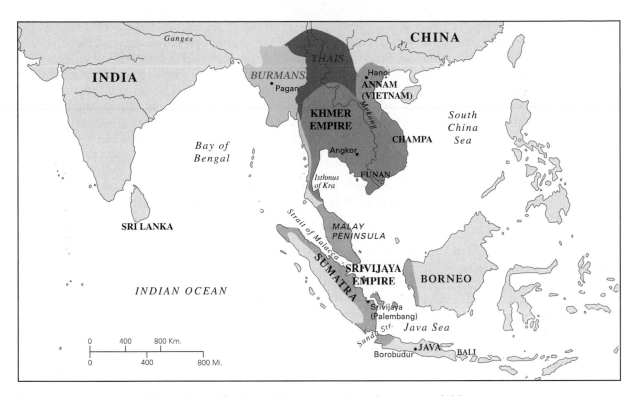

Map 7.2 Southeast Asia The position of Southeast Asia between the ancient centers of civilization in India and China had a major impact on its history. A series of powerful and wealthy states arose in the first millennium C.E. by gaining control of major trade routes: first Funan, based in southern Vietnam and the Malay peninsula, then Srivijaya on the island of Sumatra, followed by a number of states on the island of Java. Shifts in the trade route led to the demise of one and the rise of another.

India during Harsha's reign. After Harsha's death, northern India reverted to its customary state of political fragmentation and would remain divided until the Islamic invasions of the eleventh and twelfth centuries (see Chapter 15).

During the centuries of Gupta ascendancy and decline in the north, the Deccan Plateau in central India and the southern part of the peninsula had a separate existence. In this region the landscape was more segmented by mountains, rocky plateaus, tropical forests, and sharply cut river courses than in the broad northern plains, and there were multiple small centers of power. The village-based inhabitants of the lowland plains and river basins found themselves in conflict with tribal peoples from the uplands and forest.

From the seventh to twelfth centuries the Pallavas, Cholas, and other warrior dynasties collected tribute and plundered as far as their strength permitted, storing their wealth in urban

fortresses. These rulers sought legitimacy and fame as patrons of religion and culture, and much of the distinguished art and architecture of the period was produced in the kingdoms of the south (see Voices and Visions: Tamil Culture). These kingdoms also served as the conduit through which Indian religion and culture reached Southeast Asia.

SOUTHEAST ASIA

Southeast Asia consists of three geographical zones: the Indochina mainland, the Malay Peninsula, and thousands of islands extending on an east-west axis far out into the Pacific Ocean (see Map 7.2). Encompassing a vast area of land and water, today this region is occupied by the countries of Myanmar (Burma), Thailand, Laos, Cambodia, Vietnam, Malaysia, Singapore, Indonesia, Brunei, and the Philippines. Poised between the ancient centers of China and India, Southeast Asia has been influenced by the cultures of both civilizations. The region first rose to prominence and prosperity because of its intermediate role in the trade exchanges between southern and eastern Asia.

The strategic importance of Southeast Asia is enhanced by the region's natural resources. This is a geologically active zone; the islands are the tops of a chain of volcanoes. Lying along the equator, Southeast Asia has a tropical climate. The temperature hovers around 80 degrees Fahrenheit (30 degrees Celsius), and the monsoon winds provide dependable rainfall throughout the year. There are several growing cycles each year, so the region is capable of supporting a large human population. The most fertile agricultural lands lie along the floodplains of the largest silt-bearing rivers or contain rich volcanic soil deposited by ancient eruptions.

Early Civilization

Rain forest covers much of Southeast Asia. Rain forest ecosystems are particularly fragile because of the great local variation of plant forms within them and because of the vulnerability of their soil to loss of fertility if the protection of the forest canopy is removed. As early as 2000 B.C.E. this circumstance led to the development of *slash-and-burn agriculture*, a system in which a patch of land is cleared for farming by cutting and burning the vegetation growing on it. The land, known as *swidden*, is farmed for several years, then abandoned and reclaimed by the forest.

A number of plant and animal species that first developed in Southeast Asia spread to other regions. These included wet rice (rice cultivated in deliberately flooded fields), soybeans, sugar cane, yams, bananas, coconuts, cocoyams, chickens, and pigs. Rice was the staple food product, for even though rice cultivation is labor-intensive (see Chapter 3), it can support a large population.

The indigenous population of this region consisted primarily of Malay peoples. Historians believe that rising population and disputes within communities prompted streams of people to leave the Southeast Asian mainland in the longest-lasting movement of colonization in human history. By the first millennium B.C.E. the inhabitants of Southeast Asia had developed impressive navigational skills. They knew how to ride the monsoon winds and to interpret the patterns of swells, winds, clouds, and bird and sea life. Over a period of several thousand years groups of Malays in large double outrigger canoes spread out across the Pacific and Indian Oceans—half of the circumference of the earth—to settle thousands of islands.

The inhabitants of Southeast Asia tended to cluster along the banks of rivers or in the fertile volcanic plains. Fields and villages were never far from the rain forest, with its wild animals and numerous plant species. Forest trees provided fruit, wood, and spices. The shallow waters surrounding the islands teemed with fish. This region was also an early center of metallurgy, particularly bronze. Metalsmiths heated bronze to the requisite temperature for shaping by using hollow bamboo tubes to funnel a stream of oxygen to the furnace.

Political units at first were small. The size of the fundamental unit reflected the number of people who drew water from the same source. Water resource "boards," whose members were representatives from the leading families of the different villages involved, met periodically to allocate and schedule the use of this critical resource.

The early centuries C.E. saw the emergence of larger states. This development was a response to two powerful forces: commerce and Hindu/Buddhist culture. First, Southeast Asia was strategically sited along what turned out to be a new international trade route carrying Chinese silk to India and the Mediterranean. The movements of nomadic peoples had disrupted the old land route across Central Asia. But in India there was increasing demand for silk—for domestic use and for transshipment to the Arabian Gulf and Red Sea to satisfy the fast-growing luxury market in the Roman Empire. At first a sea-land-sea route developed between India, the Isthmus of Kra on the Malay peninsula, and the South China Sea. Over time merchants extended this exchange network to encompass goods from Southeast Asia, including aromatic woods, resins, and spices such as cinnamon, pepper, cloves, and nutmeg. Southeast Asian centers rose to prominence by serving this trade network and controlling key points.

The second force leading to the rise of larger political entities was the influence of Hindu/Buddhist culture imported from India. Commerce brought Indian merchants and sailors into the ports of Southeast Asia. As Buddhism spread, Southeast Asia became a way station for Indian missionaries and East Asian pilgrims on their way to and from the birthplace of their faith. Indian cosmology, rituals, art, and statecraft constituted a rich treasury of knowledge and a source of prestige and legitimacy for local rulers who adopted them. The use of Sanskrit terms such as *maharaja* (great king), the adaptation of Indian ceremonial practices and forms of artistic representation, and the employment of scribes skilled in writing all proved invaluable to the most ambitious and capable Southeast Asian rulers.

The first major Southeast Asian center, called "Funan" by Chinese visitors, flourished between the first and sixth centuries C.E. Its capital was at the modern site of Oc-Eo in southern Vietnam (see Map 7.2). Funan occupied the delta of the Mekong River, a "rice bowl" capable of supporting a large population.

By extending its control over most of southern Indochina and the Malay Peninsula, Funan was able to dominate a key point on the trade route from India to China—the Isthmus of Kra. Seaborne merchants from the ports of northeast India found that offloading their goods from ships and carrying them across the narrow strip of land was both safer and quicker than making the thousand-mile (sixteen-hundred-kilometer) voyage around the Malay Peninsula—a dangerous trip marked by treacherous currents, rocky shoals, and pirates. Once the portage across the isthmus was finished, the merchants needed food and lodging while they waited for the monsoon winds to shift so that they could make the

A stone image of Durga, a fierce manifestation of the Goddess, slaying the buffalo demon, from Java, thirteenth century C.E. The Goddess, one of the three major Hindu divinities, appeared in a number of complementary manifestations. The most dramatic is Durga, a murderous warrior equipped with multiple divine weapons. That the same divine figure could, in its other manifestations, represent life-bringing fertility and docile wifely duties in the household, shows how attuned was Indian thought to the interconnections among different aspects of life. (Eliot Elisofon Collection, Harry Ransom Humanities Center, University of Texas, Austin)

last leg of the voyage to China by sea. Funan stockpiled food and provided security for those engaged in this trade—in return, most probably, for customs duties and other fees.

According to one legend (a sure indicator of the influence of Indian culture in this region), the kingdom of Funan arose out of the marriage of an Indian Brahmin and a local princess. Chinese observers have left reports of the prosperity and sophistication of Funan, emphasizing the presence of walled cities, palaces, archives, systems of taxation, and state-organized agriculture. Nevertheless, for reasons not yet clear to modern historians, Funan declined in the sixth century. The most likely explanation is that international trade routes changed, bypassing Funan.

The Srivijayan Kingdom

By the sixth century, a new, all-sea route had developed. Merchants and travelers from south India and Sri Lanka sailed through the Strait of Malacca (lying between the west side of the Malay Peninsula and the northeast coast of the large island of Sumatra) and into the South China Sea. This route presented both human and navigational hazards, but it significantly shortened the journey.

Another factor promoting the use of this route was a decline in the demand of the Eastern Roman (Byzantine) Empire for imported Chinese silk. Christian monks had hidden silkworms in bamboo stalks, smuggled them out of China, and brought them to Constantinople, thereby exposing the secret of silk production and breaking the Chinese monopoly.

A new center of power, Srivijaya—Sanskrit for "Great Conquest"—was dominating the new southerly route by the late seventh century C.E. The capital of the Srivijayan kingdom was at modern-day Palembang, 50 miles (80 kilometers) up the Musi River from the southeastern coast of Sumatra. Srivijaya had a good natural harbor on a broad and navigable river and a productive agricultural hinterland. The kingdom was well situated to control the southern part of the Malay Peninsula, Sumatra, parts of Java and Borneo, and the Malacca and Sunda straits—vital passageways for shipping (see Map 7.2).

The Srivijayan capital, one of several thriving Sumatran river ports, gained ascendancy over its rivals and assumed control of the international trade route by fusing four distinct ecological zones into an interdependent network. The core area was the productive agricultural plain along the Musi River. The king and administrative specialists—clerks, scribes, judges, and tax collectors—whom he employed controlled this zone directly. Less direct was the king's control of the second zone, the upland regions of Sumatra's interior that were the source of commercially valuable forest products. The local rulers of this area were bound to the center in a dependent relationship held together by oaths of loyalty, elaborate court ceremonies, and the sharing of profits from trade. The third zone consisted of river ports that had been Srivijaya's main rivals. They were conquered and controlled thanks to an alliance between Srivijaya and neighboring sea nomads, pirates who served as a Srivijayan navy as long as the king guaranteed them a steady income.

The fourth zone was the fertile "rice bowl" on the central plain of the nearby island of Java—a region so productive, because of its volcanic soil, that it houses and feeds the majority of the population of present-day Indonesia. Srivijayan monarchs maintained alliances with several ruling dynasties that controlled this region. The alliances were cemented by intermarriage, and the Srivijayan kings even claimed descent from the main Javanese dynasty. These arrangements gave Srivijaya easy access to the large quantities of foodstuffs needed by the people living in the capital and by the merchants and sailors visiting the various ports.

The kings of Srivijaya who constructed and maintained this complex network of social, political, and economic relationships were men of extraordinary energy and skill. Although their authority depended in part on force, it owed much more to diplomatic and even theatrical talents. Like the Gupta monarchy, Srivijaya should be seen as a theater-state, securing its position of prominence and binding dependents to it by its sheer splendor and its ability to attract labor resources, talent, and luxury products. According to one tradition, the Srivijayan monarch was so wealthy that he deposited bricks of gold in the river estuary to appease the local gods, and a hillside near town was said to be covered with silver and gold images of the Buddha to which devotees brought lotus-shaped vessels of gold. The gold originated in West Africa and came to

Southeast Asia through trade with the Muslim world (see Chapter 8).

The Srivijayan king was believed to have great magical powers. He mediated between the spiritually potent realms of the mountains and the sea, and he embodied powerful forces of fertility associated with the rivers in flood. His capital and court were the scene of ceremonies designed to dazzle observers and reinforce the image of wealth, power, and sanctity surrounding the king. Subjects and visitors recognized the king as a "winner" and wanted to be associated with his success. Subordinate rulers took oaths of loyalty that carried dire threats of punishment for violations, and in their own home locales they imitated the splendid ceremonials of the capital.

The kings built and patronized Buddhist monasteries and schools. In central Java local dynasties allied with Srivijaya built magnificent temple complexes to advertise their glory. Borobodur, the most famous of these, was the largest human construction in the Southern Hemisphere. The winding ascent through the ten tiers of this virtual mountain of volcanic stone is a Buddhist allegory for the progressive enlightenment of the soul. Numerous sculptured reliefs depicting Buddhist legends provide modern viewers with glimpses of daily life in early Java.

In all of this, the cultural influence of India was paramount. Shrewd Malay rulers looked to Indian traditions to supply conceptual rationales for kingship and social order. They utilized Indian models of bureaucracy and the Sanskrit system of writing to expedite government business. Their special connection to powerful gods and higher knowledge raised them above their rivals. Southeast Asia's central position on long-distance trade routes and pilgrimage routes guaranteed the presence of foreigners with useful skills to serve as priests, scribes, and administrators. Hindu beliefs and social structures have survived to this day on the island of Bali, east of Java. Even more influential was Buddhism because of the flow of Buddhist pilgrims and missionaries between East Asia and India.

The Southeast Asian kingdoms, however, were not just passive recipients of Indian culture. They took what was useful to them and synthesized it with indigenous beliefs, values, and institutions—for example, local concepts of chiefship, ancestor worship, and forms of oaths. Moreover, they trained their own people in the new ways, so that the bureaucracy contained

View of the Buddhist monument at Borobodur, Java The powerful dynasties which emerged in Sumatra (Srivijaya) and Java were influenced by Indian religion and statecraft. The great monument at Borobodur in central Java was begun around 780 C.E. by the Sailendra dynasty. It is the largest human construction in the southern hemisphere, more than 300 feet (90 meters) in length and over 100 feet (30 meters) high. Pilgrims made a three-mile-long winding ascent through ten levels which represents the ideal Buddhist journey from ignorance to enlightenment. (From N. J. Krom and T. Van Erp, *Beschrijving van Barabudur* (The Hague: Martinus Nijhoff, 1916) Reproduced with permission)

Important Events in India and Southeast Asia

1500 B.C.E.	Migration of Indo-European peoples into northwest India
1000	Indo-European groups move into the Ganges Plain
500	Siddhartha Gautama (the Buddha) and Mahavira found Buddhism and Jainism
324	Chandragupta Maurya becomes king of Magadha and lays foundation for Mauryan Empire
184	Fall of Mauryan Empire
First Century C.E.	Establishment of Funan, first major center in Southeast Asia
320	Chandra Gupta establishes Gupta Empire
550	Collapse of Gupta Empire
606–647	Reign of Harsha Vardhana
683	Rise of Srivijaya in Sumatra
1025	Collapse of Srivijaya

both foreign experts and native disciples. The whole process was a cultural dialogue between India and Southeast Asia, one in which both partners were active participants.

The kings of Srivijaya carried out this marvelous balancing act for centuries. However, the system they erected was vulnerable to various external forces, including shifts in the pattern of international trade. Some such dynamic must have contributed to the collapse of Srivijaya in the eleventh century, even though the immediate cause was a destructive raid on the Srivijayan capital by forces of the Chola kingdom of southeast India.

Despite the decline of Srivijaya, the maritime realm of Southeast Asia remained prosperous and connected to the international network of trade. The impetus passed to new, vigorous kingdoms on the eastern end of the island of Java.

At one end of these long-distance trade routes lay the lands of western Europe. Goods and occasional reports from South and Southeast Asia long continued to filter west, and some Europeans were aware of this region as a source of spices and other luxury items. Some four centuries after the decline of Srivijaya, an Italian navigator serving under the flag of Spain—Christopher Columbus—would embark on a westward course across the Atlantic Ocean, seeking to establish a direct route to the fabled "Indies" from which the spices came.

CONCLUSION

This chapter traces the emergence of complex societies in South and Southeast Asia between the second millennium B.C.E. and the first millennium C.E. Because of the migrations of people, trade, and the spread of belief systems, an Indian style of civilization spread throughout the subcontinent and adjoining regions and eventually made its way to the mainland and island chains of Southeast Asia. In this period were laid cultural foundations that in large measure still characterize these regions.

The development and spread of belief systems—Vedism, Buddhism, Jainism, and Hinduism—has a central place in this chapter, because nearly all the sources from which scholars can reconstruct the story of antiquity in this part of the world come from the religious sphere. A visitor to a museum who examines the artifacts from ancient Mesopotamia, Egypt, the Greco-Roman Mediterranean, China, and India will find that objects originally located in a religious shrine or having a primarily cultic function compose a prominent part of the collection. Only in the Indian case, however, would the artifacts be almost exclusively drawn from the religious sphere.

The prolific use of writing came later to India than to other parts of the Eastern Hemisphere, for reasons particular to the Indian situation. As with artifacts, the vast majority of ancient Indian texts are of a religious nature. Ancient Indians did not generate historiographic texts of the kind written elsewhere in the ancient world, primarily because they held a strikingly different view of time. Mesopotamian scribes compiled lists of political and military events and the strange celestial and earthly phenomena that coincided with them. They were inspired by a cyclical conception of time and believed that the recurrence of an omen at some future date signaled a repetition of the historical event associated with it. Greek and Roman historians described and analyzed the progress of wars and the character of rulers. They believed that these accounts would prove useful because of the essential constancy of human nature and the value for future leaders and planners of understanding the past as a sequence of causally linked events. Chinese annalists set down the deeds and conduct of rulers as inspirational models of right conduct. In contrast, the distinctive Indian view of time—as vast epochs in which universes are created and destroyed again and again and the essential spirit of living creatures is reincarnated repeatedly—made the particulars of any brief moment appear to be relatively unilluminating.

The tension between divisive and unifying forces can be seen in many aspects of Indian life. Political and social division has been the norm throughout much of South Asian history. It is a consequence of the topographical and environmental diversity of the subcontinent and the complex mix of ethnic and linguistic groups inhabiting it. The elaborate structure of classes and castes was a response to this diversity—an attempt to organize the population and locate individuals within an accepted hierarchy, as well as to regulate group interactions. Strong central governments, like those of the Mauryan and Gupta kings, gained ascendancy for a time and promoted prosperity and development. However, as in Archaic Greece and Warring States China, the periods of fragmentation and multiple small centers of power seemed to be as economically and intellectually fertile and dynamic as the periods of unity.

India possessed many of the advanced technologies available elsewhere in the ancient world—agriculture, irrigation, metallurgy, textile manufacture, monumental construction, military technology, writing, and systems of administration. But of all the ancient societies, India made the most profound contribution to mathematics, devising the so-called Arabic numerals used al-most everywhere on the planet (see Environment and Technology: Indian Mathematics).

Many distinctive social and intellectual features of Indian civilization—the class and caste system, models of kingship and statecraft, and Vedic, Jainist, and Buddhist belief systems—originated in the great river valleys of the north, where descendants of Indo-European immigrants came to dominate. Hinduism, however, also contained elements drawn from the Dravidian cultures of the south and from Buddhism. Hindu beliefs and practices are less fixed and circumscribed than the beliefs and practices of Judaism, Christianity, and Islam, which rely on clearly defined textual and organizational sources of authority. The capacity of the Hindu tradition to absorb and assimilate a wide range of popular beliefs facilitated the gradual spread of a common Indian civilization across the subcontinent, although there was, and is, considerable variation from one region to another.

This same malleable quality also came into play as the pace of international commerce quickened in the first millennium C.E. and Indian merchants embarking by sea for East Asia passed through Funan, Srivijaya, and other commercial centers in Southeast Asia. Indigenous elites in Southeast Asia came into contact with Indian merchants, sailors, and pilgrims. They found elements of Indian civilization attractive and useful, and they fused it with their own traditions to create a culture unique to Southeast Asia. Chapter 8 describes how the networks of long-distance trade and communication established in the Eastern Hemisphere in antiquity continued to expand and foster technological and cultural development in the subsequent era.

SUGGESTED READING

A useful starting point for the Indian subcontinent is Karl J. Schmidt, *An Atlas and Survey of South Asian History* (1995), with maps and facing text illustrating geographic, environmental, cultural, and historical features of South Asian civilization. Concise discussions of the history of ancient India can be found in Stanley Wolpert, *A New History of India* (3rd edition, 1989), and Romila Thapar, *A History of India, volume I* (1966). D. D. Kosambi, *Ancient India: A History of Its Culture and Civilization* (1965) is a fuller presentation.

Ainslie T. Embree, *Sources of Indian Tradition, volume 1* (2nd edition, 1988), contains translations of primary texts, with the emphasis almost entirely on religion and few materials from southern India. Barbara Stoler Miller, *The Bhagavad-Gita: Krishna's Counsel in Time of War* (1986), is a readable translation of this ancient classic with a useful introduction and notes. An abbreviated version of the greatest Indian epic can be found in R. K. Narayan, *The Mahabharata: A Shortened Modern Prose Version of the Indian Epic* (1978). The filmed version of Peter Brook's stage production of *The Mahabharata* (3 videos—1989) generated much controversy because of its British director and multicultural cast, but is a painless introduction to the plot and main characters. For those who want to sample the fascinating document on state-building supposedly composed by the advisor to the founder of the Mauryan Empire, see T. N. Ramaswamy, *Essentials of Indian Statecraft: Kautilya's Arthasastra for Contemporary Readers* (1962). James Legge, *The Travels of Fa-hien: Fa-hien's Record of Buddhistic Kingdoms* (1971), and John W. McCrindle, *Ancient India as Described by Megasthenes and Arrian* (1877), provide translations of reports of foreign visitors to ancient India.

A number of works explore political institutions and ideas in ancient India: Charles Drekmeier, *Kingship and Community in Early India* (1962); John W. Spellman, *Political Theory of Ancient India: A Study of Kingship from the Earliest Times to Circa A.D. 300* (1964); and R. S. Sharma, *Aspects of Political Ideas and Institutions in Ancient India* (2nd edition, 1968). Romila Thapar, *Asoka and the Decline of the Mauryas* (1963), is a detailed study of the most interesting and important Maurya king.

For fundamental Indian social and religious conceptions, see David R. Kinsley, *Hinduism: A Cultural Perspective* (1982). See also David G. Mandelbaum, *Society in India, 2 volumes* (1970), who provides essential insights into the complex relationship of class and caste. Jacob Pandian, *The Making of India and Indian Tradition* (1995), contains much revealing historical material, with particular attention to often neglected regions such as southern India, in its effort to explain the diversity of contemporary India. Stella Kramrisch, *The Hindu Temple, 2 volumes* (1946), and Surinder M.

Bhardwaj, *Hindu Places of Pilgrimage in India: A Study in Cultural Geography* (1973), examine important elements of worship in the Hindu tradition.

Roy C. Craven, *Indian Art* (1976), is a clear, historically organized treatment of its subject. Mario Bussagli and Calembus Sivaramamurti, *5000 Years of the Art of India* (1971) is lavishly illustrated.

For the uniqueness and decisive historical impact of Indian mathematics, see Georges Ifrah, *From One to Zero: A Universal History of Numbers* (1985).

Jean W. Sedlar, *India and the Greek World: A Study in the Transmission of Culture* (1980), relates the interaction of Greek and Indian civilizations. Lionel Casson, *The Periplus Maris Erythraei: Text With Introduction, Translation and Commentary* (1989), explicates a fascinating mariner's guide to the ports, trade goods, and human and navigational hazards of Indian Ocean commerce in the Roman era.

Richard Ulack and Gyula Pauer, *Atlas of Southeast Asia* (1989), provides a very brief introduction and maps for the environment and early history of Southeast Asia. Nicholas Tarling (ed.), *The Cambridge History of Southeast Asia*, volume 1 (1992), and D. R. DeSai, *Southeast Asia: Past and Present* (3rd edition, 1994), provide general accounts of Southeast Asian history. Lynda Shaffer, *Maritime Southeast Asia to 1500* (1996), focuses on early Southeast Asian history in a world historical context. Also useful is Kenneth R. Hall, *Maritime Trade and State Development in Early Southeast Asia* (1985).

The art of Southeast Asia is taken up by M. C. S. Diskul, *The Art of Srivijaya* (1980), and B. P. Groslier, *The Art of Indochina, Including Thailand, Vietnam, Laos and Cambodia* (1962).

NOTES

1. Barbara Stoler Miller, *The Bhagavad-Gita: Krishna's Counsel in Time of War* (Bantam, N.Y., 1986) 98–99.

2. B. G. Gokhale, *Asoka Maurya* (Twayne, N.Y., 1966) 152–153, 156–157, 160.

3. James Legge, *The Travels of Fa-hien: Fa-hien's Record of Buddhistic Kingdoms* (Oriental Publishers, Delhi, 1971) 77–79.

PART THREE

Growth and Interaction of Cultural Communities, 300–1200

Technologies of food production and local religious and political systems long distinguished specific human societies from one another. The civilizations born in great river valleys differed markedly from one another in irrigation techniques, forms of worship, conceptions of government, and patterns of daily life despite similar environmental situations. The pastoral societies that came into existence in various regions similarly differed in types of animals herded, use of animal products, social organization, and relations with settled peoples. Around the world, even among peoples who were responding to parallel ecological challenges, or who had a linguistic kinship with neighboring peoples, diversity of all sorts was normal.

Over time, some groups prospered more than others, and a few expanded from localized states into extensive empires. As we have seen, the imperial armies of Assyria, Macedon, Rome, and Han China effectively united disparate societies under unified political rule for greater or lesser periods of time. But peaceful exchange along trade routes, folk migrations by people equipped with especially productive technologies, and missionary efforts to convert people to new religions regardless of their political allegiances had a more profound and long-lasting impact on the coming together of the world's peoples. The continent-spanning technological, social, and cultural exchange and interaction that marked the centuries from 300 to 1200 differed substantially from earlier instances of cultural expansion in

both mechanisms of exchange and eventual historical impact. Some of these interactions relate to trade, some to migration, some to religion, and some to political purpose. They do not add up to an easily summarized story, but they are so different from earlier interactions arising primarily from conquest or the extension of political boundaries that they constitute a distinct era in world history.

In the realm of trading connections, three types of long-distance routes rose and flourished: the Silk Road across Central Asia from Mesopotamia to China, trans-Saharan caravan routes linking northern with sub-Saharan Africa, and a variety of maritime routes connecting the coastal lands of the Indian Ocean. By means of such routes, Mesopotamian farmers started to plant rice, cotton, citrus trees, and other Eastern crops; African farmers acquired bananas and yams from Southeast Asia; and Chinese farmers learned about wine grapes, alfalfa, and other crops of the Mediterranean region. The techniques of silk production and papermaking spread westward from China, musical instruments and styles reached China from Iran, and gold dust reached the Mediterranean from West Africa in exchange for cloth and metal manufactures. Each of these exchanges, and many more, had a significant impact on the receiving societies and economies.

In the realm of change brought on by movements of human groups, the spread of the Bantu peoples eastward and southward from West

Africa brought iron implements and new techniques of food production to sub-Saharan Africa and helped foster a distinctive African cultural pattern. Quite differently, the Arabs of the Arabian peninsula, under the inspiration of the Prophet Muhammad, in the seventh century C.E. conquered an empire that stretched from Spain to India; and they implanted in it their language, their faith, and their cultural values.

In the realm of religion, while Arab military prowess set the stage for a centuries-long process of converting non-Arabs to Islam, the division of the Roman Empire into east and west and the decline of its western portion in the fifth century C.E. provided the background for the slow conversion of Europe to Christianity. As in the case of Islam, Christian beliefs became wedded to political structures: the Byzantine Empire in the eastern Mediterranean and the Carolingian and, later, the Holy Roman Empires in western Europe, as well as Christian kingdoms in Ethiopia, Armenia, and Russia. Simultaneously, Buddhism drew on the energies of missionaries and pilgrims as it made its way by land and sea from northern India and Afghanistan to Sri Lanka, Tibet, Southeast Asia, China, Korea, and Japan.

Finally, in the realm of political purpose, the era of the Crusades in the eleventh century saw European Christian armies attack Muslim territories in the eastern Mediterranean and Spain, thereby contributing to a reopening of contacts between lands long separated. While military arts such as siegecraft and castle building made significant advances on both sides, the impact of the Crusades had far-ranging consequences in fields such as philosophy and medicine.

Meanwhile, at the other end of Eurasia, the demise, at the close of the ninth century C.E., of the Tang Empire, which was strongly oriented toward contacts with the pastoral peoples of Central Asia, led the leaders of smaller successor states in the north to encourage a steady and ongoing migration toward the south. This contributed, under the Song Empire, to a clearer distinction between the civilization of the pastoral and trading peoples of Central Asia and the comparatively unified civilization that had come to cover most of China. The consequences of these developments included great strides forward in science, technology, and size of population under the Song.

This era also witnessed the culminating stages

Technology

ca. 800 B.C.E.—Iron smelting south of the Sahara

ca. 250 B.C.E.—Silk Road opens from China to Mesopotamia

ca. 100 C.E.—Stirrup spreads from northern Afghanistan

ca. 750—Trans-Saharan trade routes become active

ca. 800—Efficient horse harnessing in northern Europe

800s—Woodblock printing in East Asia, to a lesser extent in Islamic lands

1000s—Song Empire develops compasses, large ships; extensive coal and iron production

Environment

ca. 5000–1000 B.C.E.—Spread of maize, potatoes, and manioc in America

ca. 2500 B.C.E.—Sahara reaches maximum aridity

ca. 100 C.E.—Bananas and yams from Southeast Asia spread to Africa

ca. 200–400—Introduction of rice cultivation into Japan from Korea

ca. 300—Chinese crops in Mesopotamia: rice, sugar, and citrus

ca. 700–1000—Cotton becomes dominant fabric in Islamic lands

ca. 1100–1200—European population growth and agricultural expansion

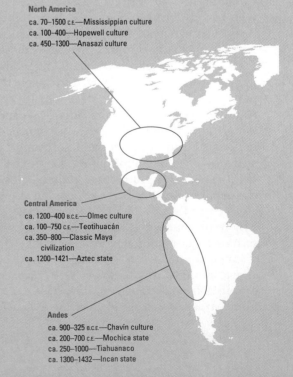

North America
ca. 70–1500 C.E.—Mississippian culture
ca. 100–400—Hopewell culture
ca. 450–1300—Anasazi culture

Central America
ca. 1200–400 B.C.E.—Olmec culture
ca. 100–750 C.E.—Teotihuacán
ca. 350–800—Classic Maya civilization
ca. 1200–1421—Aztec state

Andes
ca. 900–325 B.C.E.—Chavín culture
ca. 200–700 C.E.—Mochica state
ca. 250–1000—Tiahuanaco
ca. 1300–1432—Incan state

of technological, cultural, and civilizational development in the Western Hemisphere. The near absence of written records makes a detailed history impossible, but it is apparent that an early succession of urban, agricultural civilizations in the Andes, the Yucatán lowlands, and the central plateau of Mexico reached a climax in the Aztec and Incan Empires and the somewhat earlier flourishing of the Maya. All of the aspects of long-distance cultural exchange and interaction that mark this era in Eurasia and Africa have their counterparts in the Western Hemisphere. The spread of cultivated plants such as potatoes, manioc, and corn attests to long-distance exchanges of technology and to the impact of such exchanges on landscapes and lifestyles from the eastern woodlands of North America, through the Caribbean islands, to the far reaches of the Andes. Migrations of human groups were crucial to the peopling of the Caribbean islands and the formation of urban civilization in central Mexico. Similar religious ideas and ritual practices are found over broad areas. And the political policies of the Aztec and Incan rulers, in the only stage of this development that is well documented, testify abundantly to their interests in expansion and

their devising of economic and social means of advancing their aims.

In the long sweep of human history, civilizational expansion through increasing the size of political units could not remain the sole or dominant form of societal interaction. Empires lacked the technological means to communicate with or defend borders that were too distant from the imperial center. Thus, other mechanisms of interaction and exchange played stronger roles as distant peoples gradually became aware of one another. Trade, migration, travel for the purpose of telling people about new ideas or beliefs, and political determination to invade or make contact with peoples in distant lands did not begin in this era, but they characterize and dominated this era in an unprecedented fashion. And in so doing, they make the centuries from 300 to 1200 a critical link between an earlier world of societies living largely apart with only limited contact and, at the era's end, a world of pervasive interconnections among peoples and continent-spanning exchanges of technologies, products, and ideas.

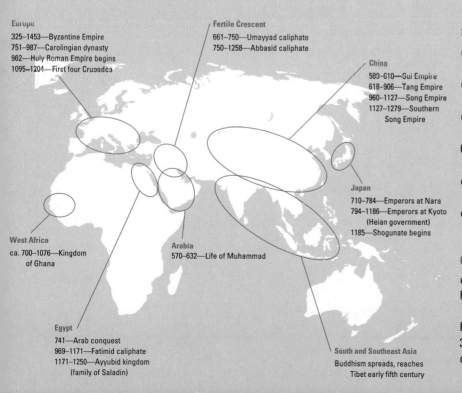

Europe
325–1453—Byzantine Empire
751–987—Carolingian dynasty
962—Holy Roman Empire begins
1095–1204—First four Crusades

Fertile Crescent
661–750—Umayyad caliphate
750–1258—Abbasid caliphate

China
589–610—Sui Empire
618–906—Tang Empire
960–1127—Song Empire
1127–1279—Southern Song Empire

Japan
710–784—Emperors at Nara
794–1186—Emperors at Kyoto (Heian government)
1185—Shogunate begins

West Africa
ca. 700–1076—Kingdom of Ghana

Arabia
570–632—Life of Muhammad

Egypt
741—Arab conquest
969–1171—Fatimid caliphate
1171–1250—Ayyubid kingdom (family of Saladin)

South and Southeast Asia
Buddhism spreads, reaches Tibet early fifth century

Society

ca. 2000 B.C.E.–1500 C.E.—Urban temple complexes in Central and South America

ca. 500 B.C.E.–1000 C.E.—Bantu migrations from West Africa

ca. 400–800 C.E.—Decline of urbanism and monetary economy in Europe

600s—Introduction of Chinese examination system

ca. 800–1000—Islamization leads to rapid urbanization in Iran

ca. 1000—Decline of Confucian elite in Japan, rise of warrior classes

Culture

ca. 4000–200 B.C.E.—Saharan rock art

From ca. 50 C.E.—Christianity spreads from Jerusalem

From ca. 100—Buddhism spreads eastward

325—Christianity becomes official Roman faith

ca. 600–840—Buddhist political and cultural influence in China

CHAPTER EIGHT

Expanding Networks of Communication and Exchange, 300 B.C.E.–1100 C.E.

The Silk Road · The Indian Ocean · Routes Across the Sahara
Sub-Saharan Africa · The Spread of Ideas

Around the year 800 C.E., a Chinese poet named Bo Zhuyi nostalgically wrote:

Iranian whirling girl, Iranian whirling
   girl—
Her heart answers to the strings,
Her hands answer to the drums.
At the sound of the strings and drums, she
   raises her arms,
Like whirling snowflakes tossed about, she
   turns in her twirling dance.

Iranian whirling girl,
You came from Sogdiana.
In vain did you labor to come east more
   than ten thousand tricents.
For in the central plains there were already
   some who could do the Iranian whirl,
And in a contest of wonderful abilities, you
   would not be their equal.[1]

An exotic foreign dancer would not seem particularly remarkable to us, accustomed as we are to a world closely interconnected through television and satellite communications. But the western part of Central Asia, the region around Samarkand and Bukhara known in the eighth century C.E. as Sogdiana, was 2,500 miles (4,000 kilometers) from the Chinese capital of Chang'an. The average caravan took more than four months to trek across the mostly unsettled deserts, mountains, and grasslands. How many Iranian dancing girls reached China by this route? Enough to make their style of dance legendary and the object of local imitation. Indeed, contemporary pottery figurines excavated from Chinese graves show troupes of Iranian performers.

The Silk Road connecting China and the Middle East across Central Asia was an important conduit for the exchange of agricultural goods, manufactured products, and ideas. But musicians and dancing girls traveled, too—as did camel pullers, merchants, monks, and pilgrims. The Silk Road, like any important trade route, was not just a means of bringing peoples and parts of the world into contact; it was a social system. However, it was a social system that nei-

ther lay within a state or empire nor gave rise to one. Consequently, this and other major trading networks that have had a deep impact on world history deserve special scrutiny.

As we have seen, political units in ancient times grew only slowly into kingdoms, and a few developed further into empires. With every expansion of territory, the accumulation of wealth by temple, leaders, kings, and emperors enticed traders to venture ever farther afield for cargoes of precious goods. For the most part, their customers were wealthy elites. But the knowledge of new products, agricultural and industrial processes, and foreign ideas and customs these long-distance traders brought with them sometimes affected an entire society.

Nevertheless, travelers and traders were not always admired or respected. They seldom owned much land, wielded political power, or achieved military glory. Moreover, they were often socially isolated (sometimes by law) and secretive since dissemination of knowledge about markets, products, routes, and travel conditions could give advantage to their competitors. On balance, however, their mostly anonymous efforts contributed more to drawing the world together than did the efforts of all but a few kings and emperors.

This chapter examines the social systems and historical impact of exchange networks that developed between 300 B.C.E. and 1100 C.E. in Europe, Asia, and Africa. The Silk Road, the Indian Ocean maritime system, and the trans-Saharan caravan routes in Africa illustrate the nature of long-distance trade in this era, when major parts of the globe began the slow process of getting to know one another.

Trading networks were not the only medium for the spread of new ideas, products, and customs over wide distances, however. Chapter 6 discussed the migration into the Roman Empire of peoples speaking Germanic languages and the

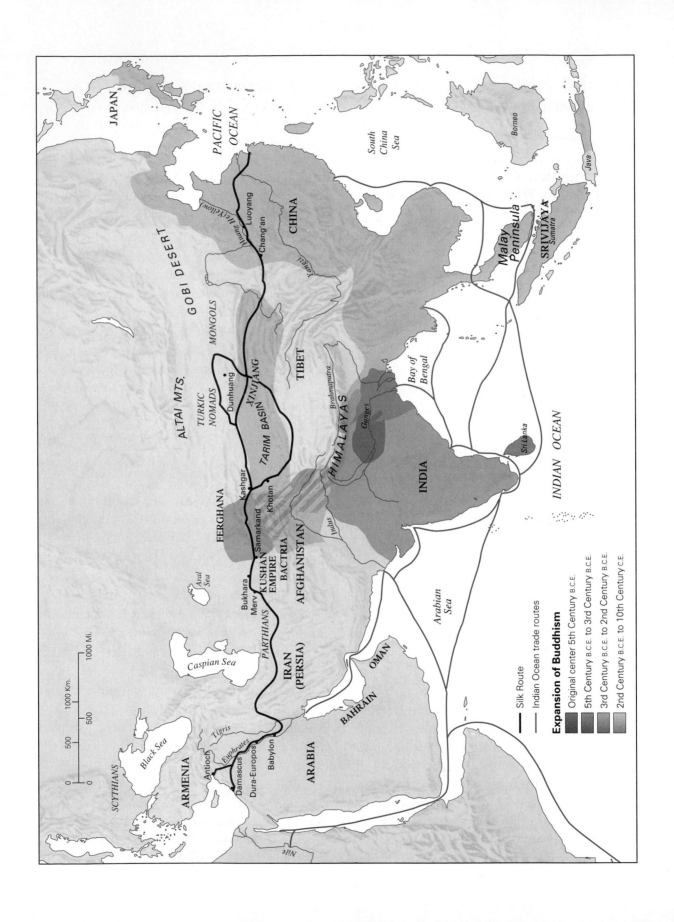

JAPAN

PACIFIC OCEAN

Huang He (Yellow)

Luoyang

Chang'an

CHINA

South China Sea

Borneo

Malay Peninsula

SRIVIJAYA

Sumatra

Java

GOBI DESERT

ALTAI MTS.

MONGOLS

TURKIC NOMADS

Dunhuang

XINJIANG

TARIM BASIN

TIBET

Yangzi

Brahmaputra

Bay of Bengal

INDIAN OCEAN

Sri Lanka

FERGHANA

Kashgar

Samarkand

Khotan

HIMALAYAS

Ganges

Aral Sea

Bukhara

Merv

KUSHAN EMPIRE

BACTRIA

AFGHANISTAN

Indus

INDIA

PARTHIANS

IRAN (PERSIA)

Caspian Sea

OMAN

BAHRAIN

Arabian Sea

1000 Mi.

1000 Km.

500

500

SCYTHIANS

Black Sea

Tigris

Euphrates

Antioch

Damascus

Dura-Europos

Babylon

ARABIA

ARMENIA

Nile

Expansion of Buddhism

Silk Route

Indian Ocean trade routes

Original center 5th Century B.C.E.

5th Century B.C.E. to 3rd Century B.C.E.

3rd Century B.C.E. to 2nd Century B.C.E.

2nd Century B.C.E. to 10th Century C.E.

beginning of Christian missionary activity in Europe. This chapter compares the development of the Saharan trading system of northern Africa with the simultaneous folk migrations of Bantu-speaking peoples within sub-Saharan Africa that laid the foundation for that region's special type of cultural unity. This chapter also discusses the spread of Buddhism in Asia and of Christianity in Africa that marked this period. The politically and militarily more consequential expansion of Islam is the subject of Chapter 10.

THE SILK ROAD

Archaeology and linguistic studies show that the peoples of Central Asia engaged in long-distance movement and exchange from at least the second millennium B.C.E. In Roman times the imagination of Europeans became captivated by the idea of the Silk Road. A trade route linking the lands of the Mediterranean with China by way of Mesopotamia, Iran, and Central Asia, the Silk Road experienced several periods of heavy use. The first extended from approximately 150 B.C.E. to 900 C.E., when the collapse of the Tang dynasty in China led to disruption at its eastern end (see Chapter 11). Another period of heavy use began in the thirteenth century C.E. and lasted until the 17th century. During that period, much of the Silk Road's traffic flowed north of Iran, skirted the northern shore of the Caspian Sea, and ended at ports on the Black Sea (see Map 8.1). The operation of that segment of the route is considered in Chapter 13. This chapter

Map 8.1 Asian Trade and Communication Routes The overland Silk Road was much shorter than the maritime route from the South China Sea to the Red Sea, and ships were more expensive than pack animals. Moreover, China's political centers were in the north. It was more vulnerable, however, to political disruption. Historians remain puzzled by the lack of Buddhist expansion westward from Afghanistan.

examines the origins of trade along the Silk Road and the importance of the Silk Road in drawing together different parts of the Eurasian landmass during its first centuries of use.

Origins and Operations

The Seleucid kings who succeeded to the eastern parts of Alexander the Great's empire in the third century B.C.E. focused their energies on Mesopotamia and Syria, allowing an Iranian nomadic leader to establish an independent kingdom in northeastern Iran. Historians disagree about the stages by which the Parthians, named after their homeland just east of the Caspian Sea, took over Iran and then Mesopotamia. The Parthians remained wedded to their nomadic origins. They left few written sources, and recurring wars between the Parthians and the Seleucids, and later between the Parthians and the Romans, prevented travelers from the Mediterranean region from gaining a firm knowledge of the Parthian kingdom. It seems most likely, however, that their place of origin on the threshold of Central Asia and the lifestyle they had in common with nomadic pastoral groups farther to the east were key to their encouragement of trade along what became known as the Silk Road.

In 128 B.C.E., a Chinese general named Chankien made his first exploratory journey westward across Central Asia on behalf of Emperor Wu of the Han dynasty. After crossing the broad and desolate Tarim Basin north of Tibet, he reached the fertile valley of Ferghana, nestled between the Pamir and Tian Mountains, and for the first time encountered westward-flowing rivers. There he found horse breeders whose animals far outclassed any other horses he had ever seen. In China these noble animals would be deemed descendants of a heavenly horse.

Later Chinese historians looked on General Zhang Qian as the originator of overland trade with the western lands, and they credited him with personally introducing into China a whole garden of new plants and trees. Zhang Qian's own account proves that the people of Ferghana were already receiving goods from China, though probably by way of India. Specifically, he saw them using canes

Felt funerary cloth from central Asia Fourth Century B.C.E. burial mounds at Pazaryk in the Peltai Mountains contain some of the earliest indications of life and art among central Asian nomads. Felt, made by wetting wool and matting it under pressure, was a common central Asian fabric. Here a horseman wearing characteristic nomad clothing approaches a figure in an ornamented robe. Metal horse harness parts also feature in archaeological finds from nomadic culture. (Hermitage, Leningrad)

made from a square type of bamboo that only grows in western China. But this does not diminish the fact that Chankien, as leader of some eighteen imperial expeditions, was an important pioneer on the more northerly route that became the Silk Road.

Long-distance travel was much more familiar to the Central Asians than to the Chinese. Kin to the trouser-wearing, horse-riding Parthians in language and customs, the populations of Ferghana and neighboring regions included many nomads. For more than a thousand years they had lived by following their herds of horses, cattle, and sheep across the Asian deserts, steppes, and mountains from the Black Sea to the Chinese frontier. But their migrations had had little to do with trade, despite the occasional piece of silk or Chinese manufactured item that found its way into their animals' packs.

We need to distinguish between, first, trips made by occasional travelers or the movements of migrating pastoralists and, second, the deliberate fostering of trading connections. The keys to the opening of the Silk Road were, on the eastern end, Chinese eagerness for western products, especially horses, and on the western end, the organized Parthian state controlling the flourishing markets of Mesopotamia and culturally linked to the pastoralists of Central Asia. In between were caravan cities to support the traders and camel- and horse-breeding nomads to supply them with livestock.

Historians put great emphasis on the long distances traveled: once the route was fully functioning, around 150 B.C.E., for example, Greeks could buy Chinese silk from Parthian traders in Mesopotamian border entrepôts. Yet caravans bought and sold goods along the way in prosperous Central Asian trading cities like Kashgar, Khotan, Samarkand, Bukhara, and Marv. These cities grew and flourished, often under the rule of local princes who cultivated good relations with the nomads who provided the camels, guides, and animal handlers for the caravans.

One industry that developed along with the caravan trade was the specialized breeding of hybrid camels. Figurines, graffiti, and other pictorial sources show that the two-humped Bactrian camel (named for Bactria in northern Afghanistan) was initially the mainstay of the Central Asian caravan trade. Closely related to the one-humped camel, or dromedary, of torrid Arabia, the Bactrian camel has a heavy coat of hair and is built to withstand the frigid winters of Central Asia.

Hybrid camels began to appear early in the Silk Road's operations. The historian Diodorus of Siculus wrote in the first century B.C.E. about an area that seems to be Parthian-controlled southern Mesopotamia where Arabs bred different types of camels, including "both the hairless and the shaggy, and those which have two humps, one behind the other, along their spines." Diodorus's "shaggy" camel is the first evidence of the hybrid camel, which combined the merits of both Bactrian camel and dromedary: it was larger and stronger than either parent and had a

Caravan Cities

Archaeology reveals a lot about daily life in caravan cities, but travelers' descriptions give a better indication of the impact that such cities made at the time. Two geographer-historians from the first century B.C.E., Diodorus of Siculus and Strabo, provide valuable descriptions of the terminal cities of the Arabian caravan route that linked the incense-producing region of southern Arabia with Jordan and Syria. At the southern end was Sabae, in Yemen. At the northern end of the route was Petra, in Jordan.

SABAE

And a natural sweet odor pervades the entire land because practically all the things which excel in fragrance grow there unceasingly. Along the coast, for instance, grow balsam . . . and cassia. . . . And throughout the interior of the land there are thick forests, in which are great trees which yield frankincense and myrrh, as well as palms and reeds, cinnamon trees and every other kind which possesses a sweet odor such as these have. . . .

This people surpassed not only the neighboring Arabs but also all other men in wealth and in their several extravagancies besides. For in the exchange and sale of their wares they, of all men who carry on trade for the sake of the silver they receive in exchange, obtain the highest price in return for things of the smallest weight. Consequently, since they have never for ages suffered the ravages of war because of their secluded position, and since an abundance of both gold and silver abounds in the country, especially in Sabae, where the royal palace is situated, they have embossed goblets of every description, made of silver and gold, couches and tripods with silver feet, and every other furnishing of incredible costliness, and halls encircled by large columns, some of them gilded, and others having silver figures on the capitals. . . . For the fact is that these people have enjoyed their felicity unshaken since ages past because they have been entire strangers to those whose own covetousness leads them to feel that another man's wealth is their own godsend. . . . And there are prosperous islands nearby, containing unwalled cities. . . . These islands are visited by sailors from every part and especially from Potana, the city which Alexander founded on the Indus River.

Source: Diodorus Siculus, Book III, 46–47.

PETRA

The Nabataeans are a sensible people, and are so much inclined to acquire possessions that they publicly fine anyone who has diminished his possessions and also confer honors on anyone who has increased them. Since they have but few slaves, they are served by their kinsfolk for the most part, or by one another, or by themselves; so that the custom extends even to their kings. They prepare common meals together in groups of thirteen persons; and they have two girl-singers for each banquet. The king holds many drinking bouts in magnificent style, but no one drinks more than eleven cupfuls, each time using a different golden cup. The king is so democratic that, in addition to serving himself, he sometimes even serves the rest himself in his turn. He often renders an account of his kingship in the popular assembly; and sometimes his mode of life is examined. Their homes, through the use of stone, are costly; but, on account of peace, the cities are not walled. . . . The sheep are white-fleeced and the oxen are large, but the country produces no horses. Camels afford the service they require instead of horses. Some things are imported wholly from other countries, but others not altogether so, especially in the case of those that are native products, as, for example, gold and silver and most of the aromatics, whereas brass and iron, as also purple garb [for the kings], styrax, crocus, costaria, embossed works, paintings, and molded works are not produced in their country.

What role do imported goods play in the economy of these cities? To what degree is monarchy associated with trade?

Source: Strabo, Book 16, 4.26.

Caravan animals from either end of the Silk Road   Though the elongated two-humped camel from the sixth century C.E. Sui dynasty in China is more elegant than the broken two-humped Parthian camel, they carry what appear to be identical rounded loads, possibly silk cloth or thread. The similarity in loads proves that some commodities traveled the entire distance from China to Mesopotamia. Caravan camels carried approximately 500 pounds of cargo carefully balanced on either side of the animal. Most two-humped camels disappeared in Mesopotamia by the first century C.E., being replaced by the one-humped camels of Arabia as Arab nomads became increasingly involved in caravan trade. (Private collection)

heavy coat that suited it to the Central Asian climate. The hybrid was so perfectly adapted for work on the Silk Road that the eventual decline of the route after 1600 C.E. led to its almost total disappearance.

The breeding of hybrid camels called for careful herd management and is an example of how the caravan trade itself generated new economic activities. Of greater importance, however, was the exchange of products between East and West. Chinese sources abound in references to products imported across the Silk Road, sometimes specifically mentioning the Anxi (the Parthians) or Bose (the Persians).

General Zhang Qian seems to have brought back two plants during one of his many trips west: alfalfa and domestic grapes. The former provided the best fodder for the growing Chinese herds of Ferghana horses. The latter were integral to the famous trio of "wine, women, and song" that Chinese explorers noted as central to Central Asian life. Later images of Iranian musicians and whirling dancing girls confirm the allure of these western ways.

In addition, Chinese farmers adopted pistachios, walnuts, pomegranates, sesame, corian-

der, spinach, and many other new crops. Chinese artisans and physicians used other trade products, such as jasmine oil, oak galls (used in tanning animal hides, dyeing, and ink making), sal ammoniac (for medicines), copper oxides, zinc, and precious stones.

Caravan traders going from east to west brought back from China new fruits such as the peach and the apricot, which the Romans attributed to Persia and Armenia, respectively, demonstrating the route of dissemination farther westward. They also brought cinnamon, ginger, and other spices that could not be grown in the West. Above all, however, China was known for its manufactured goods—particularly silk, pottery, and paper—all of which were eventually adopted or imitated in western lands, starting with Iran.

Chinese pottery figurines of pack camels usually show them with almost hemispherical loads hanging on either side of the animal, as do figurines of the Parthian period found in Mesopotamia. If we assume that the potters depicted items of special distinction, these loads most likely contained silk. Thus, despite the great diversity of goods exchanged by caravan across Central Asia, the traditional name of the Silk Road seems well justified.

The Impact of Silk Road Trade

As trade became a more important part of Central Asian life, the Iranian-speaking peoples settled increasingly in trading cities and surrounding farm villages. This allowed nomads originally from the Altai Mountains farther east to spread west across the steppes and become the dominant pastoral group. These peoples spoke Turkic languages unrelated to the Iranian tongues and are well in evidence by the sixth century C.E. The prosperity that trade created affected not only the ethnic mix of the region but also cultural values. The nomads continued to live in the round, portable felt huts called yurts that can still be seen occasionally in Central Asia, but prosperous merchants and landholders built stately homes decorated with brightly colored wall paintings. The paintings show these merchants and landholders wearing Chinese silks and Iranian brocades and riding on richly outfitted horses and camels. They also give evidence of an avid interest in Buddhism, which competed with Christianity, Zoroastrianism, and—eventually—Islam in a lively and inquiring intellectual milieu.

Religion (discussed later in this chapter) exemplifies the impact of foreign customs and beliefs on the Central Asian peoples, but their culture also affected surrounding areas. For example, Central Asian military practices had a profound impact on both East and West. Chariot warfare, horse-harnessing techniques, and the use of mounted bowmen all originated in Central Asia and spread eastward and westward through military campaigns and folk migrations that began in the second millennium B.C.E. and recurred throughout the period of the Silk Road.

Evidence of the use of stirrups, one of the most important inventions, comes first from the Kushan people in northern Afghanistan in approximately the first century C.E. Ideas and styles from farther east and west along the Silk Road strongly influenced the culture of these people, and we may presume that their use of the stirrup spread by means of the same route. At first a solid bar, then a loop of leather to support the rider's big toe, and finally a device of leather and metal or wood supporting the instep, the stirrup gave riders far greater stability in the saddle—which in all likelihood was an earlier central Asian invention.

Using stirrups, a mounted warrior could supplement his bow and arrow with a long lance, and, leaning forward, he could charge his enemy

Iranian musicians from Silk Road This three-color glazed pottery figurine, 23 inches (58.4 centimeters) high, is one of hundreds of Silk Road camels and horses found in northern Chinese tombs from the sixth to ninth centuries C.E. The musicians playing Iranian instruments testify to the migration of Iranian culture across the Silk Road. At the same time dishes decorated by the Chinese three-color glaze technique were in vogue in northern Iran. (The National Museum of Chinese History)

Linkages between World Regions

ca. 1200 B.C.E.	Horse herders supplant cattle herders in central Sahara
500 B.C.E.–1000 C.E.	Bantu migrations from west Africa
ca. 250 B.C.E.–900 C.E.	Silk Road flourishes from China to Mesopotamia
From ca. 50 C.E.	Christianity spreads in all directions from Jerusalem
From ca. 100	Buddhism spreads eastward by land and sea
ca. 750–1076	Islam spreads in Ghana south of Sahara
ca. 900	Hindu and Arab merchants in Canton

at a gallop without fear that the impact of his attack would push him backward off his mount. Nevertheless, the bow and arrow remained the weapon of choice in Central Asia. The Parthians were famous for what the Romans called "the Parthian shot"—an arrow shot backward while the warrior was riding away from his enemy. Far to the west, however, the stirrup made possible the armored knights who dominated the battlefields of Europe (see Chapter 9), and it contributed to the superiority of the Tang cavalry in China (see Chapter 11).

The success of the Silk Road sowed the seeds of eventual change. From Parthian times until well after the Arab invasions of the 7th century C.E. (see Chapter 10), each Central Asian caravan city and mountain valley seems to have had its own ruling family. These many small states enjoyed various sorts of relations, presumably centered on their common interest in trade. Fear of disrupting the trade may be why none seems to have tried to conquer the others and establish an empire. Yet the Turkic-speaking pastoral nomads who initially provided traders with animals and animal handlers gradually came to grasp the potential for political activity on a larger scale. Although traffic along the Silk Road tapered off for awhile after 900 C.E., in large part because of the collapse of the Tang state in China, the following

two centuries saw the emergence of larger territorial states based on the military force of the Turkic nomads (see Chapter 14).

THE INDIAN OCEAN

Some Chinese and western products were exchanged by sea rather than by land. Just as nomads and city traders in Central Asia played the major role in trade along the Silk Road, so a multilingual, multiethnic society of seafarers carried on most of the trade across the Indian Ocean and the South China Sea. These people left few records and seldom played a visible part in the rise and fall of kingdoms and empires, but they forged increasingly strong economic and social ties between the coastal lands of East Africa, southern Arabia, the Persian Gulf, India, Southeast Asia, and southern China.

This trade took place in three distinct regions: (1) In the South China Sea, Chinese and Malays (including Indonesians) dominated trade. (2) From the east coast of India to the islands of Southeast Asia, Indians and Malays were the main traders. (3) From the west coast of India to the Persian Gulf and the east coast of Africa, merchants and sailors were predominantly Persians and Arabs. These ethnic divisions were customary rather than politically formalized, however. Chinese and Malay sailors could and did voyage to East Africa, and Arab and Persian traders reached southern China.

In coastal areas, small groups of seafarers sometimes had a significant social impact despite their usual lack of political power. Women seldom accompanied their menfolk on long sea voyages, so sailors and merchants often married local women in port cities. The families thus established were bilingual and bicultural. As in many other situations in world history, women played a crucial, if not well-documented, role as mediators between cultures. Not only did they raise their children to be more cosmopolitan than children from inland regions, but they introduced their menfolk to customs and attitudes that they carried off when they returned to sea. As a consequence, the designation of specific seafarers as Persian, Arab, Indian, or Malay often conceals mixed heritages and a rich cultural diversity.

The Indian Ocean Maritime System

With their frequent reliance on written records, historians sometimes exaggerate the importance of chance literary references and overlook other types of historical evidence. From the time of Herodotus in the fifth century B.C.E., Greek writers regaled their readers with stories of marvelous voyages down the Red Sea into the Indian Ocean and around Africa from the east, or out of the Mediterranean Sea through the Pillars of Hercules and around Africa from the west. Most often, they attributed such trips to the Phoenicians, the most fearless of Mediterranean seafarers. But occasionally a Greek appears. One such was Hippalus, a Greek ship's pilot who was said to have discovered the seasonal monsoon winds that facilitate sailing across the Indian Ocean. Though this story is questionable, it highlights the importance of the monsoon.

In early spring, the warming of the East African landmass gives rise to a northward wind along the coast. Laden with ocean moisture, this wind brings rain to the highlands of Ethiopia (causing the Nile flood) and Yemen and then veers due east until it encounters the southern part of the Indian subcontinent, which it drenches with rains during the summer months before proceeding to the islands and mainland of Southeast Asia. Six months later, again impelled by temperature differentials between water and land, a reverse monsoon blows westward from Southeast Asia to the East African coast.

This regular rotation of steady winds could not have remained unnoticed for thousands of years, waiting for an alert Greek to happen along. Looked at more realistically, the great voyages and discoveries made before written records became common should surely be attributed to the peoples who lived around the Indian Ocean—Africans, Arabs, Persians, Indians, Malays—rather than to interlopers from the Mediterranean Sea. The story of Hippalus resembles the Chinese story of General Chankien, whose role in opening up trade with Central Asia so strongly overshadows the anonymous contributions made by the indigenous peoples.

The sailing traditions and techniques of the Indian Ocean differed markedly from those of the Mediterranean. Mediterranean sailors of the time of Alexander used square sails and long banks of oars to maneuver among the sea's many islands and small harbors. Indian Ocean vessels relied on triangular lateen sails and normally did without oars in running before the wind on long ocean stretches. The triangular sail made for greater stability, since the pressure of the wind was strongest on its lower portion; and it was somewhat more maneuverable than a square rig. Mediterranean shipbuilders nailed their vessels together. The planks of Indian Ocean ships were pierced, tied together with palm fiber, and caulked with bitumen. Mediterranean sailors rarely ventured out of sight of land. Indian Ocean sailors, thanks to the monsoon winds, could cover the long reaches between southern Arabia and India entirely at sea.

The world of the Indian Ocean developed differently from the world of the Mediterranean Sea. The Phoenicians and the Greeks fostered trade around the Mediterranean by establishing colonies that maintained contact with their home city, thus giving rise to the maritime empires of Carthage and Athens (see Chapters 4 and 5). The traders of the Indian Ocean, where distances were greater and contacts less frequent, seldom retained political affiliations with their homelands. The colonies they established were sometimes socially distinctive but rarely independent of the local political powers. The Mediterranean region was smaller than the Indian Ocean basin and more competitive with respect to a small number of exchangeable goods—copper, tin, wine, olive oil, pottery. These political and environmental factors contributed to the recurrent war and intense rivalry that marked the Mediterranean world, a political situation favoring rowed warships that retained great maneuverability even in windless conditions. By contrast, war seldom beset the Indian Ocean maritime system prior to the arrival of the European explorers at the end of the fifteenth century C.E. Its early history is primarily concerned with population movements and the exchange of goods and ideas.

These two examples illustrate the difficulty historians encounter in writing the history of the Indian Ocean trading system. Written sources are extremely rare, and archaeological finds are often hard to interpret. Yet the historical importance of communication across the Indian Ocean is unquestionable.

Origins of Contact and Trade

As early as the third millennium B.C.E., Sumerian records spoke of regular trading contacts between Mesopotamia, the islands of the Persian Gulf, Oman, and the Indus Valley. However, this early trading contact eastward broke off, and later Mesopotamian trade references refer more often to East Africa than to India.

A similarly early chapter in Indian Ocean history concerns migrations from Southeast Asia to Madagascar, the world's fourth largest island, situated off the southeastern coast of Africa. Some two thousand years ago, people from one of the many islands of Southeast Asia established themselves in that forested, mountainous land some 6,000 miles (9,500 kilometers) from home. Since they could not possibly have carried enough supplies for a direct voyage across the Indian Ocean, their route must have touched the coasts of India and southern Arabia. No remains of their journeys have been discovered, however.

Apparently, their sailing canoes plied the seas along the increasingly familiar route for several hundred years. The settlers farmed the new land and entered into relations with Africans, who found their way across the 250-mile-wide (400 kilometers) Mozambique Channel around the 5th century C.E. The descendants of the seafarers preserved the language of their homeland and some of its culture, such as xylophone music and the cultivation of bananas, yams, and other native Southeast Asian plants. Both musical instruments and food crops spread to mainland Africa. But gradually the memory of their distant origins faded away, not to be recovered until modern times, when scholars established the linguistic link between the two lands.

The Impact of Indian Ocean Trade

The only extensive written account of trade in the Indian Ocean before the rise of Islam in the seventh century C.E. is an anonymous work by a Greco-Egyptian of the first century C.E. *The Periplus of the Erythraean Sea* (that is the Red Sea) describes ports of call along the Red Sea and down the East African coast to somewhere south of the island of Zanzibar. Then it describes the ports of southern Arabia and the Persian Gulf before continuing eastward to India, mentioning ports all the way around the subcontinent to the mouth of the Ganges River. Though the geographer Ptolemy, who lived slightly later, had heard of ports as far away as Southeast Asia, the author of the *Periplus* had obviously voyaged to the places he mentions and was not merely an armchair traveler. What he describes is unquestionably a trading *system* and is clear evidence of a steady growth of interconnections in the region during the preceding centuries.

What inspired mariners to persist in their long ocean voyages was the demand for products from the coastal lands. Africa produced exotic animals, wood, and ivory. However, since ivory also came from India, Mesopotamia, and North Africa, the extent of African ivory export cannot be determined. The highlands of northern Somalia and southern Arabia grew the scrubby trees whose aromatic resins were valued as frankincense and myrrh. Trees on the island of Socotra near the entrance of the Red Sea produced "dragon's blood," a scarlet resin that Roman artists highly valued as a pigment. Pearls abounded in the Persian Gulf, and evidence of ancient copper mines has been found in Oman in Southeast Arabia. India shipped spices and manufactured goods, and more spices came from Southeast Asia, along with manufactured goods, particularly pottery, obtained in trade with China. In sum, the Indian Ocean trading region was one of enormous potential richness. Given the long distances and the comparative lack of islands, however, the volume of trade there was undoubtedly much lower than in the Mediterranean Sea.

The culture of the ports was often isolated from the hinterlands, particularly in the west. The coasts of the Arabian peninsula, the African side of the Red Sea, southern Iran, and northern India (today Pakistan) were mostly barren desert. Ports in all these areas tended to be small, and many suffered from meager supplies of fresh water. Farther south in India, the monsoon provided ample water, but steep mountains—the Western Ghats—cut the coastal plain off from the interior of the country. Thus few ports between Zanzibar and Sri Lanka had substantial inland populations within easy reach. The head of the Persian Gulf was one exception: shipborne trade was possible as far north as Babylon and, from the eighth century C.E., nearby Baghdad.

By contrast, eastern India, the Malay Peninsula, and Indonesia afforded more hospitable and densely populated shores with easier access to inland populations. Though the fishers, sailors, and traders of the western Indian Ocean system supplied a long series of kingdoms and empires with precious goods, none of these consumer societies became primarily maritime in orientation, as did the Greeks and Phoenicians in the Mediterranean. In the east, on the other hand, seaborne trade and influence seem to have been important even to the earliest states, such as that of Srivijaya (see Chapter 7). The inland forest dwellers of Malaysia were far less potent politically than the citizens of the port cities.

The pace of communication across the Indian Ocean increased over time. By the early Islamic era of the eighth century C.E., eastern products were well known in the Middle East, Javanese and Indian communities had been established in Mesopotamia, a partially seaborne Arab expedition had conquered the lower Indus Valley, and a large colony of Arab and Persian traders was growing up in southern China. Evidence of the worship of Hindu gods by Indian traders can be found in caves in southwestern Iran, and close relations exist to this day between Arab families long settled in Singapore and Jakarta and the land of their ancestors in southern Yemen.

ROUTES ACROSS THE SAHARA

The windswept Sahara, stretching from the Red Sea to the Atlantic Ocean and broken only by the Nile River, isolates sub-Saharan Africa from the Mediterranean world. The current dryness of the Sahara dates only to about 2500 B.C.E., however. The period of drying out that preceded that date was twenty-five centuries long and encompassed several cultural changes. During that time, travel between an only slowly shrinking number of grassy areas was comparatively easy. However, by 300 B.C.E., scarcity of water was restricting travel to a few difficult routes initially known only to desert nomads. Trans-Saharan trade over these routes was at first only a trickle, but it eventually expanded into a significant stream. By 1100 C.E., the riches in gold, slaves, and tropical goods flowing northward had begun to excite the envy of the Europeans, whose desire to find the source of the Saharan trading wealth helped trigger their farflung explorations after the year 1400 C.E.

Early Saharan Cultures

Sprawling sand dunes, flat sand plains, and vast expanses of exposed rock make up most of the great desert. Stark and rugged mountain and highland areas—Air, Ahaggar, Tassili, Tibesti, and others—separate its northern and southern portions. The cliffs and caves of these highlands, which were the last spots where water and grassland could be found as the climate changed, preserve a vast treasury of rock paintings and

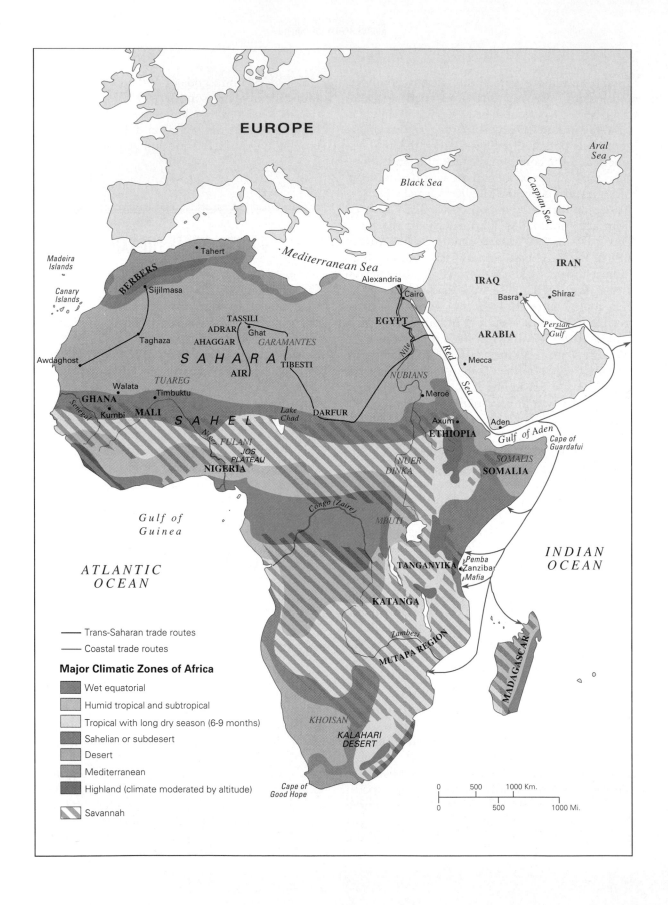

EUROPE

Madeira Islands

Canary Islands

Black Sea

Caspian Sea

Aral Sea

Mediterranean Sea

IRAN

IRAQ

Alexandria

Cairo

Basra

Shiraz

BERBERS

Tahert

Sijilmasa

TASSILI

ADRAR

AHAGGAR

Ghat

GARAMANTES

EGYPT

ARABIA

Persian Gulf

Taghaza

S A H A R A

TIBESTI

Mecca

Awdaghost

A I R

Nile

Red Sea

Walata

TUAREG

Timbuktu

GHANA

Kumbi

MALI

S A H E L

Lake Chad

DARFUR

NUBIANS

Meroë

Axum

Aden

Gulf of Aden

Cape of Guardafui

Senegal

Niger

FULANI

JOS PLATEAU

NIGERIA

ETHIOPIA

NUER
DINKA

SOMALIS

SOMALIA

Gulf of Guinea

Congo (Zaire)

MBUTI

ATLANTIC OCEAN

TANGANYIKA

Pemba
Zanzibar
Mafia

INDIAN OCEAN

KATANGA

Zambezi

MUTAPA REGION

MADAGASCAR

KHOISAN

KALAHARI DESERT

Cape of Good Hope

—— Trans-Saharan trade routes

—— Coastal trade routes

Major Climatic Zones of Africa

Wet equatorial

Humid tropical and subtropical

Tropical with long dry season (6-9 months)

Sahelian or subdesert

Desert

Mediterranean

Highland (climate moderated by altitude)

Savannah

0   500   1000 Km.

0   500   1000 Mi.

Cattle herders in Saharan rock art   These paintings, the most artistically accomplished type of Saharan art, succeeded the depictions of hunters characteristic of the earliest art. Herding societies of modern times living in the Sahel region just south of the Sahara strongly resemble the society depicted here. This suggests that as the Sahara became completely arid, the cattle herders moved south and played a role in the formation of sub-Saharan African culture. (Henri Lhote)

engravings that constitute the primary evidence for early Saharan history.

Scholars have never discovered a method of dating these pictures. Some are darker than others because of longer exposure to the sun, which draws minerals to the surface of the rock to form

Map 8.2 Africa and the Saharan Trade Routes   The Sahara desert and the surrounding oceans isolated most of Africa from foreign contact before 1000 C.E. The Nile valley, a few trading points on the east coast, and limited transdesert trade provided exceptions to this rule; but the dominant forms of sub-Saharan African culture originated fare to the west, north of the Gulf of Guinea.

a hard film. This difference in brightness, however, indicates only that one picture is older than another; it does not yield a fixed date. Since artists sometimes used the same flat surfaces again and again, relative dating can also be accomplished by seeing which paintings or engravings overlap others. Regrettably, no archaeological remains such as charcoal, which might be dated by means of carbon 14, or stone projectiles, which might be compared with datable materials from elsewhere, have ever been found in clear association with any of this rock art. Ashes from a prehistoric campfire at the foot of a rock painting, after all, could date from centuries earlier or later than the painting itself.

In what appear to be the earliest images, left by hunters in obviously much wetter times, elephants, giraffes, rhinoceroses, crocodiles, and other animals that have long been extinct in the region come vividly alive. Presumably these early hunting peoples followed their game animals southward or northward as the rivers and luxuriant grasslands disappeared because of climatic change. But whether they were more closely related to the later peoples of sub-Saharan Africa or to the Berber-speaking peoples who inhabited the mountains and plains of North Africa in Greco-Roman times cannot be determined.

Overlaps in the artwork indicate that the hunters were gradually replaced by new cultures based on cattle breeding and well adapted to the sparse grazing that remained. Cattle domestication probably originated in western Asia and reached Africa before the Sahara became completely dry. However, the beautiful paintings of cattle and detailed scenes of daily life found in the Sahara depict pastoral societies that bear little similarity to any in Asia. Rather, the people seem physically akin to today's West Africans, and the customs depicted, such as dancing and wearing masks, as well as the long-horned breeds of cattle, strongly suggest later sub-Saharan societies. These factors support the hypothesis that some sub-Saharan cultural patterns originated in the Sahara and migrated southward. In the Sahara itself, however, the cattle herders seem little related to the peoples who followed them.

Overlaps in artwork also clearly indicate that horse herders succeeded the cattle herders. The rock art changes dramatically in style. The superb realism of the cattle pictures is replaced by sketchier images that are often strongly geometric. Moreover, the horses are frequently shown drawing light chariots. This phase of Saharan rock art has provoked numerous theories. According to the most common theory, the charioteers were intrepid travelers from the Mediterranean shore who drove their flimsy vehicles across the desert and established societies in the few remaining green areas of the central Saharan highlands. The characteristic "flying gallop" posture of the horses—all four legs are extended in a dramatic though unrealistic fashion—has been compared with similar representations in early Greek art. Some scholars have suggested possible chariot routes that refugees from the collapse of the Mycenaean and Minoan civilizations of Greece and Crete might have followed deep into the desert around the twelfth century B.C.E.

However, no archaeological evidence of actual chariot use in the Sahara has ever been discovered, much less any convincing indication of extensive migration along chariot routes. Moreover, though rock art in the mountainous areas of North Africa is rare compared with the abundant images from the central Saharan highlands, images of chariots are strikingly absent. Given the extreme aridity of the Sahara by the twelfth century B.C.E. and the absence of indications that charioteers penetrated the more inviting lands north of the desert, it is difficult to imagine large numbers of refugees from the politically chaotic Mediterranean region trekking and driving their chariots into the trackless desert in search of a new homeland somewhere to the south.

As in the case of the cattle herders, therefore, the identity of the Saharan horse breeders, and the source of their passion for drawing chariots, remain a mystery. Only with the coming of the camel is it possible to make firm connections with the Saharan nomads of today through the depiction of objects and geometric patterns still used by the veiled, blue-robed Tuareg people of the highlands in Algeria, Niger, and Mali.

The Coming of the Camel

Taking note of two Roman military expeditions into central Libya in the first century B.C.E., some historians maintain that the Romans inaugurated an important trans-Saharan trade, but only scanty archaeological evidence supports this theory. More plausible is the idea that the Saharan trade and the spread of camel domestication developed together. Supporting evidence is visible in the highland rock art, where overlaps of paintings and engravings imply that camel riders in desert costume constitute the latest Saharan population. As in the transition from cattle to horses,

Chariot in Saharan rock art   Horse herding followed cattle herding as the Sahara became a desert in the second millennium B.C.E. Art became less naturalistic. The motif of spoked chariot wheels seen in profile with almost no place to stand appears in Indo-European cultures as far away as Sweden and central Asia. The "flying gallop" motif with the horses' legs unrealistically extended forward and backward resembles early Greek imagery. (Gerard Franceschi)

artistic styles again change. The camel-oriented images are decidedly the crudest and most elementary to be found in the region.

Latin texts from the first century B.C.E. first mention camels in North Africa. The camel is not native to Africa, so it must have reached the Sahara from Arabia. Scholars do not know exactly when, but scattered sources hint that camels probably came into use in Egypt in the first millennium B.C.E. and from there became known to the people who lived in the deserts bordering the Nile Valley. From the upper Nile region in the Sudan they could have been adopted by peoples farther and farther to the west, from one central Saharan highland to the next, only much later becoming disseminated northward and coming to the attention of the Romans.

Evidence for this south-to-north diffusion of camels comes not from written sources but from the design of camel saddles and patterns of camel use (see Environment and Technology: Camel Saddles). In North Africa, including the northern Sahara, pack saddles of obvious Middle Eastern design predominate, and Greco-Roman sources stress the fact that the camel-using Berber groups native to the region did not fight on camelback but dismounted and used their animals as shields. By contrast, the peoples in the central and southern Sahara used riding saddles of an entirely different design and are regularly depicted, both in art and in later historical texts, as fighting with sword and spear while on camelback.

The southern riding saddles undoubtedly developed in a warrior society rather than a commercial society. Indeed, the forms of camel use in the south fit much more closely the military image conveyed by the preceding chariot-riding

Camel Saddles

As seemingly simple a technology as saddle design can be an indicator of a society's economic structure. The South Arabian saddle was good for riding, and baggage could easily be tied to the wooden arches that attached it to the animal in the front. It was comparatively inefficient militarily, however, because the rider knelt on the cushion behind the camel's hump and was thus poorly positioned both to control his mount and to use his weapons.

The North Arabian saddle was a significant improvement that came into use in the first centuries B.C.E. Its wooden framework made tying on cargo easy, and its prominent front and back arches and placement over the camel's hump gave warriors a decent perch from which to wield their swords and spears. Arabs in northern Arabia took control of the caravan trade in that region by using these saddles.

The best riding saddles were developed by the peoples south of the Sahara. The saddles of the Tuareg seated the rider on the camel's shoulders, giving him complete freedom to use his sword and allowing him to control his mount by pressure from his toes on the animal's neck. These excellent war saddles could not be used for baggage, however, because they did not offer a convenient place to tie bundles.

Two styles of camel saddles The South Arabian saddle, featuring two closely spaced arches in front holding a pad that extends behind the camel's hump, is used for baggage purposes from Morocco to India, and for riding in southern and eastern Arabia. The saddle of the Tuaregs, with a pommel shaped like a cross, is a superior riding saddle but cannot be used for carrying baggage. (Private collection)

society than they fit the later image of long-distance caravan trade. Once camel herding was established in the south, it became easier for people to move away from the highlands and roam the deep desert. Through contacts made by the new society of far-ranging camel herders, the people north of the Sahara finally gained access to camels. Because they were within the economic sphere of the Roman Empire, however, they adopted the saddling technology of Rome's Middle Eastern provinces because it was better suited than the riding saddles of the south to carrying baggage. Ignoring the camel's military potential, they exploited it primarily as a work animal, even developing harnesses for attaching camels to plows and carts. These practices, entirely unknown in the southern Sahara, are still in evidence in Tunisia today.

Trade Across the Sahara

The coming of the camel did not automatically stimulate the beginning of trade across the Sahara. People on both sides of the desert used camels, but in different ways, and they seem to have had little influence on each other even though most of them spoke Berber languages. Trade between two different trading systems, one in the south, the other in the north, developed slowly.

The southern traders concentrated on supplying salt from large deposits in the southern desert to the peoples of sub-Saharan Africa. Salt is a physiological necessity in torrid climates, and natural deposits are rare outside the desert. Traders from the equatorial forest zone brought forest products, such as kola nuts or palm oil, to trading centers near the desert's southern fringe. Each received from the other, or from the farming peoples of the Sahel—literally "the coast" in Arabic, the southern borderlands of the Sahara—the products they needed in their homelands. Middlemen who were native to the Sahel played an important role in this trade, but precise historical details are lacking.

In the north, the main trade of Roman North Africa consisted of supplying Italy with agricultural products, primarily wheat and olives, and with wild animals from the Atlas Mountains for the arena. Cities near the coast, such as Carthage (rebuilt as a Roman city after its destruction in the Punic Wars), Hippo in Tunisia, and Leptis Magna in Libya, were centers of exchange. People living on the farms and in the towns of the interior consumed Roman manufactured goods and shared Roman styles, as is evident from abundant ruins with mosaic pavements depicting scenes from daily life.

This northern pattern began to change with the decline of the Roman Empire, which saw the abandonment of many Roman farms, the growth of nomadism, and a lessening of trade across the Mediterranean. After the Arabs invaded North Africa in the middle of the seventh century C.E., the direction of trade shifted to the Middle East, the center of Arab rule. Since the Arab conquests were inspired by the new religion of Islam (see Chapter 10), and the Christian lands of Europe constituted enemy territory, trans-Mediterranean trade diminished still further. Meanwhile, an east-west overland trade grew to compete with the coastal sea route, which was limited in effectiveness in Algeria and Morocco because high mountains separated most seaports from the interior. Since many of the Arabs belonged to camel-breeding tribes back in their Arabian homeland, they felt a cultural kinship with those Berbers who had taken up camel pastoralism during the preceding few centuries and thus related better to the peoples of the interior than any previous conquerors had done.

A series of Berber revolts against Arab rule from 740 onward led to the appearance of several small principalities in what are today Morocco and Algeria. The rulers of these city-states on the northern fringe of the Sahara held Islamic beliefs somewhat different from those of the Arab rulers in the east. Their religious differences may have interfered with their east-west overland trade and led them to look for new possibilities elsewhere. From the fragmentary records that survive, it appears that traders from these city-states, Sijilmasa and Tahert, were the first places to develop significant and regular trading contact with the south in the 9th century. Most of their populations were Berbers, so it is reasonable to assume that they already knew that nomads speaking closely related languages were roaming the central and southern reaches of the great desert. But prior to 740, they had little reason to explore the possibilities of trade with the south.

Once they did look south, however, they discovered that gold dust was one of the products the southern nomads received in exchange for salt. The gold came from deposits along the Niger and other West African rivers. The people who panned for the gold seem not to have used it extensively, and they did not value it nearly as highly as did the traders from Sijilmasa. For the latter, trading salt for gold was a dream come true. They were able to provide the nomads of the southern desert, who controlled the salt sources but had little use for gold, with products not available from the south, such as copper and certain manufactured goods. Thus everyone benefited from the creation of the new trade link. Sijilmasa and Tahert became wealthy cities, the former minting gold coins that circulated as far away as Egypt and Syria. The high value placed on gold in the Mediterranean lands greatly increased the profitability of the trade at every stage.

The Kingdom of Ghana

The earliest known sub-Saharan beneficiary of the new exchange system was the kingdom of Ghana. First mentioned in an Arabic text of the late eighth century as "the land of gold," Ghana inaugurates the documentable political history of West Africa. Yet until the mid-eleventh century, few details are available about this realm, established by the Soninke people and covering parts of Mali, Mauritania, and Senegal. Then the Arab geographer al-Bakri (d. 1094) described it as follows:

> The city of Ghana consists of two towns situated on a plain. One of these towns is inhabited by Muslims. It is large and possesses a dozen mosques, one being for the Friday prayer, and each having imams [prayer leaders], muezzins [people to make the call to prayer], and salaried reciters of the Quran. There are jurisconsults [legal specialists] and scholars. Around the town are sweet wells, which they use for drinking and for cultivating vegetables. The royal city, called al-Ghaba ["the grove"], is six miles away, and the area between the two towns is covered with habitations. Their houses are constructed of stone and acacia wood. The king has a palace with conical huts, surrounded by a fence like a wall. In the king's town, not far from the royal court, is a mosque for the use of Muslims who visit the king on missions. . . . The interpreters of the king are Muslims, as are his treasurer and the majority of his ministers.
>
> Their religion is paganism, and the worship of idols. . . . Around the royal town are domed dwellings, woods and copses where live their sorcerers, those in charge of their religious cults. There are also their idols and their kings' tombs.[2]

Typical of monarchs with imperial powers, the king of Ghana required the sons of vassal kings to attend his court. He meted out justice and controlled trade, collecting taxes on the salt

and copper coming from the north. His large army of bowmen and cavalry made Ghana the dominant power in the entire region. By the end of the tenth century, the king's sway extended even to Awdaghost, the trade entrepôt that had grown up in the desert at the southern end of the track to Sijilmasa. Awdaghost was populated by Arabs and Berbers.

After 1076, Ghana fell prey to a new state formed by desert nomads who had been drawn into the trade in the region of Awdaghost. These conquerors, the Muslim Almoravids, ruled both sides of the desert from their newly built capital city of Marrakesh in Morocco. After little more than a decade, during which later Muslim historians assert many people in Ghana converted to Islam, Almoravid strength in the south dwindled because of demands for military manpower in the north. Although Ghana thereby regained its independence, many of its former provinces had been permanently lost, and it never recovered its former greatness. Ghana's strength had clearly derived from its dominance of the new trading system. But with the Almoravids still powerful in Morocco, the old system could not easily be recreated.

Prior to the arrival of the religiously zealous Almoravids, the traders who had reached Ghana from the north had not been overly insistent on propagating Islam. Over the three centuries separating al-Bakri's account in the eleventh century from the earliest mention of Ghana, Muslims had come to hold high economic positions in Ghana, and the kings tolerated their religious practices. But, in general, the people of Ghana had not been stirred to convert to Islam. General adoption of the Islamic religion, with consequent impact on the way of life of the Sahel peoples, would only come under later kingdoms.

SUB-SAHARAN AFRICA

The Indian Ocean network and, somewhat later, trade across the Sahara provided the vast region of sub-Saharan Africa with a few external contacts. The most important African network of cultural exchange from 300 B.C.E. to 1100 C.E., however, was within sub-Saharan Africa, and it led to the formation of enduring characteristics of African culture.

That a significant degree of cultural unity developed in sub-Saharan Africa is especially remarkable because of the many geographic obstacles to movement. The Sahara, the Atlantic and Indian Oceans, and the Red Sea form the boundaries of the region. With the exception of the Nile, a ribbon of green traversing the Sahara from south to north, the major river systems empty either into the South Atlantic, in the case of the Senegal, Niger, and Zaire, or into the Mozambique Channel of the Indian Ocean, in the case of the Zambezi. Moreover, rapids limit the use of these rivers for navigation.

Stretching over 80 degrees of latitude, Africa encompasses a large number of dramatically different environments. A 4,000-mile (6,500 kilometers) trek from the southern edge of the Sahara to the Cape of Good Hope would take a traveler from the semiarid steppes of the Sahel region to tropical savanna covered by long grasses and scattered forest, next to tropical rain forest on the lower Niger and in the Zaire Basin. The rain forest then gives way to another broad expanse of savanna, followed by more steppe and desert, and finally a region of temperate highlands at the southern extremity, located as far south of the equator as Greece and Sicily are to its north. East-west travel is comparatively easy in the steppe and savanna regions but difficult in the equatorial rain-forest belt and across the mountains and deep rift valleys that abut the rain forest to the east and separate East from West Africa.

The Development of Cultural Unity

As we learned in Part II, by the first millennium C.E., distinctive cultural regions had come into existence from China to the Mediterranean as the result of political expansion and conquest. More enduring than the political units, however, were cultural heritages shared by the educated elites within each region—heritages that some anthropologists call "great traditions." They typically included a written language, common legal and belief systems, ethical codes, and other intellectual traditions. They loom large in surviving written records as traditions that rise above the diversity of local customs and beliefs commonly distinguished as "small traditions."

By the first millennium C.E., sub-Saharan Africa, too, had become a distinct cultural region, but one that was not shaped by imperial conquest and not characterized by a shared elite culture, a "great tradition." The cultural unity of sub-Saharan Africa was especially complex because it rested on similar characteristics shared to varying degrees by myriad popular cultures, or "small traditions." These popular cultures had developed during sub-Saharan Africa's long period of isolation from the rest of the world and had been refined, renewed, and interwoven by repeated episodes of migration and social interaction. Unfortunately, historians know very little about this complex prehistory. Thus, to a greater degree than in other regions, they call on anthropological descriptions, oral history, and comparatively late records of various "small traditions" to reconstruct the broad outlines of prehistoric cultural formation.

Sub-Saharan Africa's cultural unity is less immediately apparent than its diversity. Indeed, both students and scholars find the number and variety of the continent's social and cultural forms bewildering. By one estimate, for example, two thousand distinct languages are spoken on the continent, many of them corresponding to social and belief systems endowed with distinctive rituals and cosmologies. There are likewise numerous food production systems, ranging from hunting and gathering—very differently carried out by the Mbuti Pygmies of the equatorial rain forest and the Khoisan peoples of the southwestern deserts—to the cultivation of bananas, yams, and other root crops in forest clearings and of sorghum and other grains in the savanna lands. Pastoral societies display a similar diversity. Among cattle herders, the Dinka and Nuer of the upper Nile have customs quite unlike those of the Fulani in West Africa. Among camel herders, the practices of the Somalis living in the Horn of East Africa bear little resemblance to those of the Tuareg far to the west in the southern Sahara.

Such diversity is not surprising. Sub-Saharan Africa covers an area much larger than any of the other cultural regions of the first millennium C.E., and the diversity of its climate, terrain, and vegetation is more pronounced. Africans adapted to these many environments in distinctive ways. Moreover, the overall density of population was in most areas lower than in the temperate lands to the north. Thus societies and polities had abundant room to form and reform, and a substantial amount of space separated different groups. The contacts that did occur were neither so frequent nor so long lasting as to produce rigid cultural uniformity.

Another factor accounts for the persisting diversity of sub-Saharan Africa—the inability for centuries of external conquerors to penetrate the region's natural barriers and impose any sort of uniform culture. The Egyptians occupied Nubia for long periods but were blocked from going farther south by the Nile cataracts and the vast swampland in the Nile's upper reaches. The Romans sent expeditions against people living in the Libyan Sahara but could not incorporate them into the Roman world. Arabic sources tell of military expeditions reaching the southern parts of the Sahara in the seventh century C.E., but these accounts are tinged with legend and had little, if any, effect. Indeed, not until the nineteenth century would outsiders gain control of the continent and begin the process of establishing an elite culture, that of western Europe.

African Cultural Characteristics

Despite these great cultural variations, outside visitors who got to know the sub-Saharan region well in the nineteenth and twentieth centuries were always struck by the broad commonalities that underlay African life and culture. Though there were many varieties of African kingdoms, kingship displayed common features, most notably the ritual isolation of the King (see Voices & Visions: Personal Styles of Rule in India and Mali in Chapter 15). Even in societies too small to organize themselves into kingdoms, there was a strong concern for distinct and parallel social categories—age groupings, fixed kinship divisions, distinct gender roles and relations, and occupational groupings. Though not hierarchial, these filled a role similar to the prevalent divisions between noble, commoner, and slave where kings ruled.

Commonalities are also evident in music. Africans played many musical instruments, yet there were underlying traditions, particularly in rhythm, that made African music as a whole distinctive. Music played an important role in social rituals, as did dancing and wearing masks. In agriculture, the common technique was cultivation by hoe and digging stick instead of plowing with a team of animals.

These and other indications of underlying cultural unity have led modern observers to identify a common African quality throughout most of the region, even though most sub-Saharan Africans themselves did not perceive it—just as Greeks and Persians, though both part of a broad Indo-European linguistic and cultural grouping, did not recognize the shared features of their pantheons, social structures, and languages. An eminent Belgian anthropologist, Jacques Maquet, has called this quality "Africanity."

Some historians hypothesize that this cultural unity emanated originally from the peoples who once occupied the southern Sahara. In Paleolithic times, periods of dryness alternated with periods of wetness as the ice ages that locked up much of the world's fresh water in glaciers and icecaps came and went. As European glaciers receded with the waning of the last ice age, a storm belt brought increased wetness to the Saharan region. Deep canyons were scoured by rushing rivers. Now filled with fine sand, those canyons are easily visible on flights over the southern parts of the desert, which long ago were among the most habitable parts of the continent and perhaps the most densely populated. As the glaciers receded still farther, the storm belt moved northward to Europe, and a dry belt that had been farther south moved northward between 5000 and 2500 B.C.E. As a consequence, runs the hypothesis, the region's population migrated south, where it became increasingly concentrated in what is now the Sahel. That region may have been the initial incubation center for what were to become Pan-African cultural patterns.

Eventually, however, the dryness of the land and the pressures of population concentration drove some people out of this cultural core into more sparsely settled lands to the east, west, and south. A parallel process may have occurred in the northern Sahara, but the evidence there is much more limited. As for the Nile Valley, migration away from the desert was surely one of the triggers for the emergence of the Old Kingdom of Egypt at the start of the third millennium B.C.E.

The Advent of Iron and the Bantu Migrations

Although some aspects of this reconstruction are speculative, archaeological investigation has shown that sub-Saharan agriculture first became common north of the equator by the early second millennium B.C.E., and then spread southward, displacing hunting and gathering as a way of life. Moreover, there is botanical evidence that banana trees, probably introduced to southeastern Africa from Southeast Asia, made their way north and west, retracing the presumed migrations of the first agriculturalists.

A second dispersal involved metallurgy. Copper mining is in evidence in the Sahara from the early first millennium B.C.E., in the Niger Valley somewhat later, and in the Central African copper belt between 400 and 900 C.E. Gold mining is evident in Zimbabwe by the eighth and ninth centuries C.E. Most important of all, iron smelting is documented in northern sub-Saharan Africa in the early first millennium C.E., and from there it spread southward to the rest of the continent, becoming firmly established in southern Africa by the year 800.

Iron does not naturally occur in metallic form, except in meteorites, and a very high temperature is necessary to extract it from ores. Thus many historians believe that the secret of smelting iron was discovered only once, by the Hittites of Anatolia (modern Turkey) around 1500 B.C.E. (see Chapter 3). But while its spread from this presumed point of origin can generally be traced in Europe and Asia, how iron smelting reached sub-Saharan Africa is not clear. By way of the Nile Valley is one possibility, but the earliest evidence of ironworking from the kingdom of Meroë, on the upper Nile, is no earlier than the evidence from West Africa (northern Nigeria). Even less plausible is the idea of a spread southward from Phoenician settlements in North Africa, since archaeological evidence has not substantiated vague Greek and Latin accounts of Phoenician contacts with the south by land.

Some historians, therefore, suggest that Africans may have discovered for themselves how to smelt iron. They might have done so while firing pottery in kilns. No firm evidence exists to prove or disprove this theory.

Linguistic analysis provides the strongest evidence of extensive contacts among sub-Saharan Africans in the first millennium C.E.—and offers suggestions about the spread of iron. Linguists recognize that most of the people of sub-Saharan Africa speak languages belonging to one giant family, often called the Niger-Kongo, that stretches from the Senegal River in West Africa to the southern tip of the continent. Virtually all of the more than three hundred languages spoken south of the equator are closely related, belonging to the branch of the Niger-Kongo family known as Bantu after the word meaning "people" in most of the languages.

The distribution of the Bantu languages both north and south of the equator is consistent with a divergence beginning in the first millennium B.C.E. By comparing core words common to most of the languages, linguists have drawn some conclusions about the original Bantu-speakers, whom they call "proto-Bantu." The proto-Bantu engaged in fishing, using canoes, nets, lines, and hooks. They lived in sedentary villages on the edge of the rain forest, where they grew yams and grains and harvested wild oil palms. They possessed domesticated goats, dogs, and perhaps other animals. They made pottery and cloth. From this and other evidence, linguists surmise that the proto-Bantu homeland was near the modern boundary of Nigeria and Cameroon, from which they trace western and eastern routes of linguistic dispersal into the equatorial rain forests to the south. Although dates for this long process are scarce, Bantu-speaking people are evident in East Africa by the eighth century C.E.

Because the presumed home of the proto-Bantu lies near the known sites of early iron smelting, migration by Bantu-speakers seems a likely mechanism for the southward spread of iron. Supplied with iron axes and iron hoes, the migrating Bantus are presumed to have hacked out forest clearings and planted crops. According to this scenario, they established an economic basis for new societies that were able to sustain much denser populations than could earlier societies dependent on hunting and gathering. Thus the period from 500 B.C.E. to 1000 C.E. saw a massive transfer of Bantu traditions and practices southward, eastward, and westward and their transformation into Pan-African traditions and practices.

THE SPREAD OF IDEAS

Ideas, like social customs, religious attitudes, and artistic styles, can spread along trade routes and through folk migrations. In either event, documenting the dissemination of ideas, particularly in preliterate societies, poses a difficult historical problem. Customs surrounding the eating of pork are a case in point. Scholars disagree about whether the idea to domesticate pigs occurred only once and spread or whether several different peoples hit on the same idea.

Southeast Asia was an important and possibly the earliest center of pig domestication. There the eating of pork became highly ritualized, sometimes being prohibited except on ceremonial occasions. On the other side of the Indian Ocean, in ancient Egypt, wild swine were common in the Nile swamps, pigs were considered sacred to the underworld god Set, and eating them was prohibited. The biblical prohibition on the Israelites' eating pork, echoed later by the Muslims, probably came from Egypt in the second millennium B.C.E.

In eastern Iran, an archaeological site dating from the third millennium B.C.E. provides strong evidence of another religious taboo on eating pig. Although the area around the site was swampy and home to many wild pigs, not a single pig bone has been found there. Yet small pig figurines seem to have been used as symbolic religious offerings.

What accounts for the apparent connection between the domestication of pigs and religion in these widespread areas? There is no way of knowing. It has been hypothesized that pigs were first domesticated in Southeast Asia by people who had no herd animals—sheep, goat, cattle, horses—and who relied on fish for most of their animal protein. The pig was thus a special animal to them. From Southeast Asia, pig domestication and the religious beliefs and rituals associated with the consumption of pork could have spread along the maritime routes of the Indian Ocean, eventually reaching Iran and Egypt.

A more certain example of the spread of an idea is the practice of hammering a carved die onto a piece of precious metal and using the resulting coin as a medium of exchange. From its origin in Anatolia in the first millennium B.C.E., the idea of trading by means of struck coinage spread rapidly to Europe, North Africa, and India. Was the low-value copper coinage of China, made by pouring molten metal into a mold, also inspired by this practice from far away? It may have been, but it might also derive from indigenous Chinese metalworking. There is no way to be sure. Theoretically, all that is needed for an idea to spread is a single returning traveler telling about some wonder that he or she saw abroad.

The Spread of Buddhism

The spread of ideas in an organized way emerges as a new phenomenon in the first millennium B.C.E. From its original home in northern India in the fifth century B.C.E., Buddhism grew to become, with Christianity and Islam, one of the three most popular and widespread religions in the world (see Chapter 7). In all three cases, the religious ideas being spread were distinctive because of *not* being associated with specific ethnic or kinship groups.

King Ashoka, the Maurya ruler of India, and Kanishka, the greatest king of the Kushans of northern Afghanistan, were powerful royal advocates of Buddhism between the third century B.C.E. and the second century C.E. However, monks, missionaries, and pilgrims were the people who crisscrossed India, followed the Silk Road, or took ship in the Indian Ocean to bring the Buddha's teachings to Southeast Asia, China, Korea, and ultimately Japan.

The Chinese pilgrims Faxian (died between 418 and 423 C.E.) and Xuanzang (600–664 C.E.) left written accounts of their travels (see Chapter 7). Both followed the Silk Road, from which Buddhism had arrived in China, encountering along the way Buddhist communities and monasteries that previous generations of missionaries and pilgrims had established. Faxian began his trip in the company of a Chinese envoy to an unspecified ruler or people in Central Asia. After working his way from one Buddhist site to another across Afghanistan and India, he reached Sri Lanka, a Buddhist land where he lived for two years. Then he embarked for China on a merchant ship with two hundred men aboard. A storm drove the ship to Java, which he did not describe because its religion was Hindu rather than Buddhist (the presence of Hinduism is an indication of earlier seaborne influences from India on island Southeast Asia). After five months ashore, Faxian finally reached China on another ship. The narrative of Xuanzang's journey two centuries later is quite similar, though he returned to China the way he had come, along the Silk Road.

Less reliable accounts make reference to missionaries traveling to Syria, Egypt, and Macedonia, as well as to Southeast Asia. One of Ashoka's sons allegedly led a band of missionaries to Sri Lanka. Later his sister brought a company of nuns along with a branch of the sacred Bo tree under which the Buddha received enlightenment. According to Buddhist tradition, she accomplished her journey by air. At the same time, there are reports of other monks traveling to Burma, Thailand, and Sumatra. Ashoka's missionaries may also have reached Tibet by way of trade routes across the Himalayas. A firmer tradition maintains that in 622 C.E. a minister of the

Textile with Buddha image from northwest China Images of the Buddha, with or without various attendants, are central in the art of all Buddhist countries. The image of the Buddha first emerged in Gandhara in northwest Pakistan around the third century B.C.E. Originally influenced by Greek artistic styles introduced by Alexander the Great, it developed many variations as Buddhism spread across the Silk Road and Indian Ocean. (Courtesy of the Trustees of the British Museum)

Tibetan king traveled to India to study Buddhism and on his return introduced writing to his homeland.

The different lands that received the story and teachings of the Buddha preserved or adapted them in different ways. Theravada Buddhism, "Teachings of the Elders," centered in Sri Lanka. Holding closely to the Buddha's earliest teachings, it maintained that the goal of religion, available only to monks, is *nirvana*, the total absence of suffering and the end of the cycle of rebirth (see Chapter 7). This teaching contrasted with

Mahayana, or "The Greater Vehicle," Buddhism, which stressed becoming a *bodhisattva,* a "being striving for enlightenment," a status all Buddhists could aspire to. Compassion for others and helping to relieve their suffering were more important in this system than achieving nirvana.

An offshoot of Mahayana Buddhism stressing ritual prayer and personal guidance by "perfected ones" became dominant in Tibet after the 8th century C.E. In China, another offshoot, Chan (called Zen in its Japanese form), focused on meditation and sudden enlightenment. It and Pure Land Buddhism, also derived from Mahayana scriptures and devoted to repetition of the name of the Buddha Amitabha, became the dominant sects in China, Korea, and Japan (see Chapter 11).

The Spread of Christianity

The post-Roman development of Christianity in Europe is discussed in Chapter 9. The Christian faith spread earlier in northern Africa and Asia, however. Aksum, the first Christian kingdom of Ethiopia, provides an illuminating example of the role of trade routes. In the fourth century C.E., a Syrian philosopher, traveling with two youths, took ship for India to acquaint himself with distant lands. Returning, they put into a port on the Red Sea occupied by Ethiopians who had had a falling out with the Romans. The Ethiopians killed everyone aboard the ship except for the two boys, Aedesius—who later narrated this story—and Frumentius. They were taken before the king. He was strongly impressed with their learning and made the former his cupbearer and the latter his treasurer and secretary.

When the king died, his wife pleaded with Frumentius to take over the reins of government on behalf of her and her infant son, Ezana. Vested with such power, Frumentius sought out Roman Christians among the merchants who visited the country and urged them to establish Christian communities. It is not stated whether he converted Ezana before he reached his majority and became king. Once Ezana was in power, however, Aedesius and Frumentius were free to

return to Syria. From there, Frumentius traveled to Egypt to report to the patriarch of Alexandria on the progress of Christianity in Aksum. Though Frumentius had not previously been a clergyman, the patriarch elevated him to the rank of bishop and in approximately 330 sent him back to inaugurate that post at Aksum, thus beginning the still-continuing tradition of the patriarch of Alexandria appointing the head of the Ethiopian church.

As in Europe, where Christmas trees, Easter eggs, and many other customs preserve pre-Christian traditions, Ethiopian Christianity developed its own unique features. One popular belief, perhaps deriving from the Ethiopian Jewish community was that the Ark of the Covenant, the most sacred object of worship of the ancient Hebrews (see Chapter 4), had been transferred from Jerusalem to the Ethiopian church of Our Lady Mary of Zion. Another tradition maintains that Christ miraculously dried up a lake to serve as the site for this church, which became the place of coronation for Ethiopia's rulers.

Christianity, Buddhism, and Islam (as will be discussed in Chapter 10) all developed local customs and understandings as they spread, despite the overall doctrinal unity of each. As "great traditions," these religions linked priests, monks, nuns, and religious scholars across vast distances. The masses of believers, however, seldom considered their faith in such broad contexts. Missionary religions imported through long-distance trading networks merged with myriad "small traditions" to provide for the social and spiritual needs of peoples living in many lands under widely varying circumstances.

CONCLUSION

Exchange within early long-distance trading systems differed in many ways from the ebb and flow of culture, language, and custom that folk migrations brought about. New technologies and agricultural products worked great changes on the landscape and in people's lives, but nothing akin to the Africanity observed south of the Sahara can be attributed to the societies involved in the Silk Road, Indian Ocean, or trans-Saharan exchanges. The peoples directly involved in travel and trade were not very numerous in comparison with the agricultural populations their routes brought into contact, and their specialized lifestyles as pastoral nomads or seafarers isolated them still further. The Bantu, however, if current theories are correct, brought with them metallurgical skills and agricultural practices that permitted much denser habitation in the lands they spread to. Moreover, they themselves settled among and merged with the previous inhabitants, becoming not just the bearers of new technologies but their primary beneficiaries as well.

The most obvious exception to this generalization lies in the intangible area of ideas. Circumstantial evidence, reinforced by legendary accounts of missionary exploits, offer the persuasive argument that trade routes and networks of exchange played vital roles in the spread of religion. How people received, adapted, and utilized each religion as it spread from one country to the next is difficult to determine. But, as the next two chapters will show, the spread of religion plays as important a role as agricultural and technological innovation in shaping the patterns of cultural change and diversity in this first era of long-distance interchange among the peoples of the earth.

SUGGESTED READING

Broad and suggestive overviews on issues of cross-cultural exchange in this era may be found in Philip D. Curtin, *Cross-Cultural Trade in World History* (1985), and C. G. F. Simkin, *The Traditional Trade of Asia* (1968).

For readable overviews of the Silk Road see Luce Boulnois, *The Silk Road* (1966), and Irene M. Franck and David M. Brownstone, *The Silk Road: A History*

(1986). A more detailed examination of products traded across Central Asia in the eighth century based on a famous Japanese collection is provided by Ryoichi Hayashi, *The Silk Road and the Shoso-in* (1975). Owen Lattimore gives a superb first-person account of traveling by camel caravan in the region in *The Desert Road to Turkestan* (1928). More generally on peoples and historical developments in Central Asia see Denis Sinor, *Inner Asia, History-Civilization-Languages: A Syllabus* (1987), and Karl Jettmar, *Art of the Steppes*, rev. ed. (1967). The Middle Eastern trading entrepôts are treated by M. Rostovzeff, *Caravan Cities* (1975).

For a readable but rather sketchy historical overview of the history of connections across the Indian Ocean see August Toussaint, *History of the Indian Ocean* (1966). Alan Villiers provides a stimulating account of what it was like to sail dhows between East Africa and the Persian Gulf in *Sons of Sinbad* (1940).

On a more scholarly plane, K. N. Chaudhuri's *Trade and Civilization in the Indian Ocean: An Economic History from the Rise of Islam to 1750* (1985), stresses the economic aspect of trading relations. Pierre Vérin gives an archaeologist's perspective on the special problem of Madagascar in *The History of Civilisation in North Madagascar* (1986). The question of Roman contact with India is the topic of E. H. Warmington's *The Commerce Between the Roman Empire and India* (1974); J. Innes Miller's *The Spice Trade of the Roman Empire, 29 B.C. to A.D. 641* (1969); and Vimala Begley and Richard Daniel De Puma's edited collection of articles, *Rome and India: The Ancient Sea Trade* (1991). The indispensable primary source for early Indian Ocean history is Lionel Casson, ed. and trans., *The Periplus Maris Arythraei: Text with Introduction, Translation, and Commentary* (1989). Seafaring as revealed in Arabic texts is the topic of George F. Hourani's brief book *Arab Seafaring in the Indian Ocean in Ancient and Early Medieval Times* (1975).

Richard W. Bulliet's *The Camel and the Wheel* (1975) deals with the development of camel use in the Middle East, along the Silk Road, and in North Africa and the Sahara. For an entertaining and well-illustrated account of the discovery of Saharan rock art, see Henri Lhote, *The Search for the Tassili Frescoes: The Story of the Prehistoric Rock-Paintings of the Sahara* (1959). Additional views on the history and impact of Saharan trade may be found in E. Ann McDougall, "The Sahara Reconsidered: Pastoralism, Politics and Salt from the Ninth Through the Twelfth Centuries," *History in Africa* 12 (1983): 263–286, and Nehemia Levtzion, *Ancient Ghana and Mali*, 2d ed. (1980). The latter work is also essential to the broader topic of early West

African history. For translated texts relating to both the Sahara and West Africa see J. F. P. Hopkins and Nehemia Levtzion, eds., *Corpus of Early Arabic Sources for West African History* (1981).

Two general works on the early history of sub-Saharan Africa containing many articles by numerous authors are J. F. A. Ajayi and Michael Crowder, *A History of West Africa*, vol. 1 (1976), and G. Mokhtar, ed., *General History of Africa II: Ancient Civilizations of Africa* (1981). The latter work contains extensive treatments of the issues of ironworking and the Bantu migrations.

The spread of Christianity and the spread of Buddhism are enormous topics. To follow up the particular aspects treated in this chapter see Stuart Munro-Hay, *Aksum: An African Civilisation of Late Antiquity* (1991); Xinru Liu, *Ancient India and Ancient China: Trade and Religious Exchanges, A.D. 1–600* (1988); Rolf A. Stein, *Tibetan Civilization* (1972); Tilak Hettiarachchy, *History of Kingship in Ceylon up to the Fourth Century A.D.* (1972); and Yoneo Ishii, *Sangha, State, and Society: Thai Buddhism in History* (1986). The Chinese travelers, accounts cited are Fa-hsien [Faxian], *The Travels of Fa-hsien (399–414 A.D.), or, Record of the Buddhistic Kingdoms*, trans. H. A. Giles (1923; reprint, 1981), and Hiuen Tsiang [Xuanzang], *Si-Yu-Ki: Buddhist Records of the Western World*, trans. Samuel Beal (1884; reprint, 1981).

NOTES

1. Victor H. Mair, ed. *The Columbia Anthology of Traditional Chinese Literature* (New York, 1994) p. 485. Translated by Victor H. Mair.

2. J. F. A. Ajayi and Michael Crowder, eds. *History of West Africa* (New York, 1976) vol. 1, pp. 120–121.

CHAPTER NINE

Christian Europe Emerges, 300–1200

The Post-Roman Transformation · The Western Church

The Byzantine Empire · Western Europe Revives

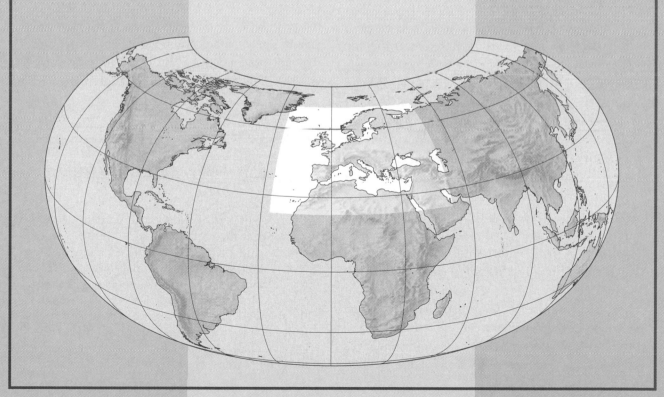

Christmas Day of the year 800 found Charles, the king of the Franks, in Rome instead of his palace in Aachen, in northeastern France. At six-foot-three, Charles was a foot taller than the average man of his time, and his royal career had been equally gargantuan. Crowned king in his mid-twenties in 768, he had spent three decades crisscrossing western Europe, waging war on Muslim invaders from Spain, Avar invaders from Hungary, and a myriad of German princes.

Charles subdued many enemies and established himself as the protector of the papacy. So it is hard to believe the eyewitness report of his secretary and biographer, the Saxon Einhard, that Charles was surprised when Pope Leo III stepped forward as the king rose from his prayers in the church of Saint Peter and placed a new crown on his head. "Life and victory to Charles the August, crowned by God the great and pacific Emperor of the Romans," proclaimed the pope.[1] Then, amid the cheers of the crowd, he humbly knelt before the new emperor.

Charlemagne (from the Latin *Carolus magnus*, "Charles the Great") was the first to bear the title *emperor* in western Europe since 476, when a Germanic commander had deposed the Roman emperor in the West. Rome's decline and Charlemagne's rise marked a shift of focus for Europe—away from the Mediterranean and toward the north and west. The world of Charlemagne, dominated by the Germanic peoples of the north, opened a new era in European history, in which German custom and Christian piety transformed a Roman heritage to create a new civilization. This civilization is commonly called medieval, literally "middle age," because it comes between the era of Greco-Roman civilization and the intellectual, artistic, and economic changes of the Renaissance in the fourteenth century. Irish monks replaced Greek philosophers as the leading intellectuals. Crimes were defined

the German way, as offenses against family, not against society, as in Rome. The sumptuous villas of the Roman emperors gave way to cold, stone castles. One of Charlemagne's consisted of a simple stone building with three large rooms and eleven small ones, surrounded by a wooden stockade enclosing stables, kitchen, and bakery, and stocked with 355 pigs, 22 peacocks, one set of bedding, and one tablecloth.

The imperial title did not survive Charlemagne. The unity of his realm fell apart under less able successors; and even he had to acknowledge a rival emperor in the East, where the political and legal heritage of Rome continued in the Eastern Roman, or Byzantine Empire. Western Europeans lived amid the ruins of an empire that haunted their dreams but was never rebuilt. The Byzantines, in contrast, continued and reinterpreted Roman traditions for centuries. In the East, the authority of the Byzantine emperors blended with the influence of the Christian church to form a new and creative synthesis. The western area of the old Roman Empire, despite the respite of Charlemagne's reign, experienced generations of chaos among scores of competing regional powers; there the only unifying force was the growing authority of the church.

THE POST-ROMAN TRANSFORMATION

The migrations of the Germanic peoples, the disappearance of the legal framework of unity and order that persisted even in the final days of the Western Roman Empire, and the fragmentation of political allegiance among scores of kings, nobles, and chieftains dramatically changed the landscape in western Europe during the period 500–800 leading up to the reign of Charlemagne. In region after region, the traditional, family-based law of the Germanic peoples supplanted the imperial edicts of the emperors.

The Roman order broke down in other ways, as well. Fear and physical insecurity, particularly in areas subject to Viking raids, was one of several factors that induced many communities to adopt defensive attitudes and seek the protection of local strongmen. When looters and pillagers from the sea were likely to appear at any moment, a distant king was not nearly so important as a local lord with a fortified castle where peasants could take refuge. This sort of personal dependency became a hallmark of the post-Roman period in the Latin West.

From Roman Empire to Germanic Kingdoms

Rome's decline, beginning in the third century, marked not just the end of an empire but the end of a long era during which the eastern Mediterranean Sea was the geographic center of a group of interrelated societies and economies. Although Rome's political institutions and military prowess had united the Mediterranean Basin, (see Chapter 6), Rome always had been on its western fringe, far from the great Eastern cities such as Athens, Antioch, Damascus, Jerusalem, and Alexandria. Thus it is not surprising that when the empire weakened, the emperors Diocletian and Constantine concerned themselves most with preserving power in the East in what became known as the Byzantine Empire.

Left on its own, the Western Roman Empire fragmented in the fifth century into a handful of kingdoms under Germanic rulers: Frankish kings of the Merovingian family, who preceded the Carolingians (family of Charlemagne) in much of Gaul, Visigothic kings in Spain, Burgundians in eastern Gaul, Saxons on the eastern side of the Rhine, among others (see Map 9.1). Italy itself saw the establishment in the sixth century of a strong Lombard kingdom in its north and a Byzantine foothold around Ravenna along the northeast coast. Rome proper lost virtually all political importance even though it retained prominence as the seat of the papacy, which local noble families competed to control.

Visigothic crown of King Recceswinth from 7th century Spain Jewelry was one of the best developed Germanic arts. Set with 30 pearls and 30 sapphires, this gold crown featured pendant letters spelling "Reccesvinthus Rex Offerata"—"KING RECCESWINTH OFFERS IT." (Museo Archeologico, Madrid)

Local versions of Latin were understood only by speakers for whom they were a native language. The educated few, more and more to be found among Christian priests and monks, retained a somewhat simplified form of Latin. The speech of the uneducated masses rapidly evolved into Romance dialects—Portuguese, Spanish, Catalan, Provençal, French, Italian, Romanian—except in northern and northeastern Europe, where Latin was too poorly established to stand in the way of the Germanic and Scandinavian di-

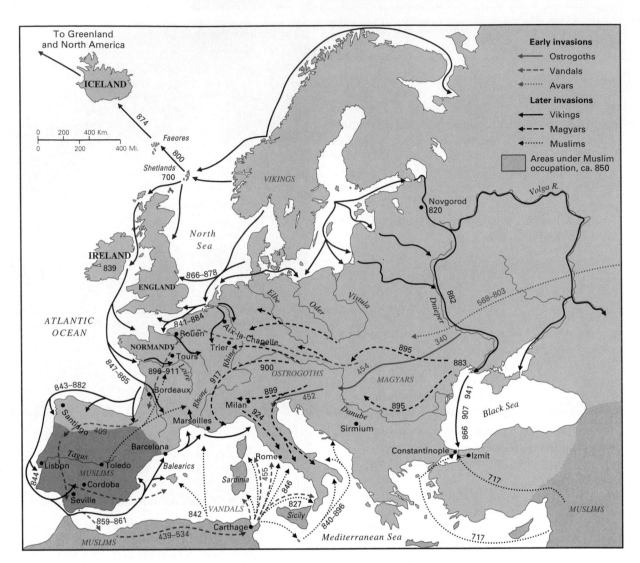

Map 9.1 Raids and Invasions in the Era of Political Disruption   Early invasions focused on the primary care centers of Roman imperial authority: Rome, Milan, Carthage, and Constantinople. Later invasions reflect the shift of power to northern Europe. In contrast to raids in the northwest, extensive Viking activity along the rivers of eastern Europe consisted partly of establishing authority over Slavic peoples and partly of opening up trade routes to Byzantium and Iran.

alects. Thus Europe came to be divided roughly into three linguistic zones: countries in the west and south speaking Romance tongues, countries in the north and center speaking Germanic and Scandinavian tongues, and countries in the east speaking the Slavic languages of peoples who moved westward on the heels of the Germanic folk migrations (see Voices and Visions: The Evolution of the Germanic Languages).

Despite the warlike behavior of the new rulers in the West, lack of unity impaired their military strength. In 711 a frontier raiding party of Arabs and Berbers, acting under the authority of the Muslim ruler in Damascus, in Syria, crossed the Strait of Gibraltar and overturned the kingdom of the Visigoths in Spain. The Europeans were too disunited to stop them from consolidating their hold on the Iberian Peninsula. After push-

The Evolution of the Germanic Languages

People in almost every country in Europe speak a distinctive language because of the consolidation of kingdoms between 1200 and 1500 and the rise of modern nation-states. In post-Roman Europe, however, language was in flux. Literacy was mostly confined to Latin, which changed only slowly because it was a written tongue. A great variety of spoken dialects that were seldom written evolved more rapidly from intermixtures of Italic, Celtic, Germanic, and Slavic tongues—all belonging to the Indo-European language family that extended as far as India and Central Asia.

The following quotations from the Gospel of Saint Luke indicate the variety and change over time in the Germanic dialects that eventually developed into modern English and German.

And shepherds were in that same land abiding and keeping watch by night over their flocks. But the angel of the lord approached them and the glory of the lord shone about them, and they feared greatly.

Gothic (fourth century)
Jah hairdjos wesun in thamma samin landa thairhwakandans jah witandans wahtwom nahts ufaro hairdai seinai. Ith aggilus fraujins anaqam ins jah wulthus fraujins biskain ins, jah ohtedun agisa mikilamma.

Old English (tenth/eleventh century)
& hydras waeron on tham ylcan rice waciende. & nihtwaeccan healdende ofer heora heorda. Tha stod drihtnes engel with hig & godes beorhtnes him ymbescean. & hi him mycelum ege adredon.

Middle English
And schepherdis weren in the same cuntre, wakinge and hepinge the watchis of the nyzt on her fick. And loo! The aungel of the Lord stood by sydis hem, and the clerenesse of God schynedet aboute hem; and thei dredden with greet drede.

Low German (fifteenth century)
Unde de herden weren in der suluen iegenode wakende. Unde helden de wake auer ere schape. Unde seet de engel des heren stunt by en unde de clarheit godes ummevench se unde se vruchteden sick myt groten vruchten.

High German (sixteenth century)
Und es woren Hirten in derselbigen Gegend auf dem Felde bei den Hurden, die huteten des Nachts ihrer Herde. Und siehe, des Herrn Engel trat zu ihnen, und die Klarheit des Herrn leuchtete um sie; und sie furchteten sich.

What do these quotations indicate about the similarities of English and German? How important is language as a social bond?

Source: J. P. Mallory, *The Search for the Indo-Europeans* (London: Thames and Hudson, 1989), p. 86.

ing the remaining Christian chieftains into the Pyrenees Mountains, the Muslims moved on to France. There they conquered much of the southern coast and penetrated as far north as Tours, less than 150 miles (240 kilometers) from the English Channel, before Charlemagne's grandfather, Charles Martel, stopped their most advanced raiding party in 732.

The Arabs never returned to northern Europe, but Viking sea raiders from Scandinavia perpetuated feelings of insecurity in coastal regions in the succeeding centuries. Local sources from France, the British Isles, and Muslim Spain attest to widespread dread of Viking warriors descending from multi-oared dragon-prowed boats to pillage monasteries, villages, and towns. In the ninth century, raiders from Denmark and Norway harried the British and French coasts while the Swedes pursued raiding and trading interests along the rivers of eastern Europe. Although many Viking attacks were private pirate raids for booty and slaves, the eleventh century saw concerted efforts at colonization and political expansion with the settlement of Iceland, Greenland, and, for a brief time, Vinland on the eastern coast of Canada.

The most important and ambitious expeditions in terms of numbers of men and horses and long-lasting impact were by Vikings long settled in Normandy (in northeastern France). These Norman (from "North men") conquests of England in 1066 by the Duke of Normandy, William the Conqueror, and of Muslim Sicily from the 1060s to the 1090s resulted in permanent changes of government.

A Basic Economy

Archaeological investigations and analyses of records kept by Christian monasteries and nunneries reveal that a profound economic transformation was under way beneath the political jumble of the newly arising Germanic kingdoms. With the ascent of the Germanic peoples, the urban-based civilization of the Romans withered and shrank. Cities built according to Roman architectural and institutional models lost population, in some cases becoming villages. Roads the Romans had built to facilitate the march of their legions, and secondarily to foster commerce, fell into disuse and disrepair. Small thatched houses sprang up beside abandoned villas, and public buildings made of marble became dilapidated in the absence of the laborers, money, and civic leadership needed to maintain them. Purchases paid for in coin largely gave way to the bartering of goods and services.

Trade languished. The wheat that had once been shipped from Egypt to feed the multitudes of Rome now went to Constantinople. The wheat-growing lands of Tunisia, another of Rome's breadbaskets, were cut off in 439 by an invasion of Germanic Vandals from Spain, never to be effectively reintegrated with Europe. Although occasional shipments of goods from Egypt and Syria continued to reach Western ports, for the most part western Europe had to rely on its own resources. These meager resources, however, underwent a redistribution.

Roman centralization had long diverted the wealth and production of the empire toward the capital, from which Roman culture radiated outward to the provinces. As Germanic and other territorial lords replaced Roman governors, local self-sufficiency became ever more important, and the general disappearance of literacy and other aspects of Roman civilized life made room for new trends to flourish. These trends were based on local folk cultures, the "small traditions" of the various Germanic and Celtic peoples.

The diet in the northern countries was based on beer, lard or butter, and bread made of barley, rye, or wheat, all amply supplemented by pork from herds of swine fed with forest acorns and beechnuts, and by game from the same forests. The Roman diet based on wheat, wine, and olive oil persisted in the south. Nutritionally, the average western European of the ninth century probably did better than his or her descendants three hundred years later, when population was increasing and the forests were more and more reserved for the nobility.

In both north and south, self-sufficient farming estates, known as *manors* or *villas*, became the primary centers of agricultural production. Wealthy Romans had commonly owned country houses situated on their lands. From the fourth century onward, political insecurity prompted common farmers to give their lands to large landowners in return for political and physical protection. The warfare and instability of the post-Roman centuries made unprotected country houses even more vulnerable to pillaging and encouraged the fortification of manors. Isolated by poor communications and lack of organized government, landowners depended on their own resources for survival. Many became warriors or maintained a force of armed men. Others swore allegiance to landowners who had the armed force to protect them.

A well-appointed manor possessed fields, gardens, grazing lands, fish ponds, a mill, a church, workshops for making whatever implements or goods were needed, and a village for the farmers dependent on its lord. The degree of protection that a manor required, ranging from a ditch and wooden stockade to a stone wall surrounding a fortified keep (a stone building), varied with local conditions. The trend was toward ever greater fortification down to the twelfth century (see Environment and Technology: Castles and Fortifications).

Castles and Fortifications

The word *castle* most often brings to mind great stone fortresses like Krak des Chevalliers. These came as the climax of a long evolution, however. The Romans had built square army camps surrounded by stockades to protect their frontiers. Once those frontiers were breached, the new rulers of Europe, each with far fewer men than a Roman legion, turned to smaller fortifications: either a ringwork (a circular wooden stockade surrounding a group of wooden buildings) or, more often, a motte-and-bailey. The motte was an artificial mound with a trench around it and a wooden tower of some sort on top. The bailey was a courtyard or enclosed area with a wooden stockade at the foot of the mound. Archaeologists have identified the remains of over 200 ringworks and 1,050 mottes in Britain, Wales, and Scotland alone, but wood construction has caused most of their buildings to perish.

As security needs increased, some lords and rulers built a keep within the bailey or atop the motte. A keep was a fortified stone building. Castle Acre in England began as a country house surrounded by a fairly weak ringwork. In the mid-twelfth century the mound was raised and the house redesigned as a keep within a smaller, more imposing ringwork. The builders doubled the thickness of the house walls and buried much of the first floor to strengthen the house's foundation. The final twelfth-century version of the keep, looking more like today's image of a castle, was taller, smaller, and surrounded by a still more formidable wall.

Stone walls steadily replaced wooden stockades. Most interior buildings, except for the keep, were of wood, as were drawbridges, stairways, and other essential parts of the fortification. Further advances in castle design featured towers along the walls from which archers shooting through arrow slits could flank enemies attacking the walls; heavily fortified gateways; and a barbican, or fortified gateway, on the far side of the bridge over a moat.

Source: All illustrations are from John R. Kenyon, *Medieval Fortifications* (Leicester, England: Leicester University Press, 1990). Used with permission of Girando/Art Resource, NY.

Life on the manor depended on one's personal status. The lord and his family exercised almost unlimited power over their serfs—agricultural workers who belonged to the manor. Serfs were obligated to till their lord's fields and were subject to other dues and obligations. Moreover, they were prohibited from leaving the manor where they were born and attaching themselves to another lord. Particular conditions varied from region to region. The majority of peasants in England, France, and western Germany were unfree serfs in the tenth and eleventh centuries. In Bordeaux, Saxony, and a few other regions a tradition of free peasantry stemming from the egalitarian social structure of the Germanic peoples during their period of migration still survived. Outright slavery, the mainstay of the Roman economy (see Chapter 6), diminished as more and more peasants became serfs in return for a lord's protection.

Feudal Society

Although Europe's reversion to a basic economy limited the freedom and potential for personal achievement of most of the population, an emerging class of nobles reaped great personal benefits. During the period of Germanic migrations, and continuing much later among the Vikings of Scandinavia, men regularly answered the call to arms of the war chiefs to whom they swore allegiance. All warriors shared in the booty gained from raiding. But as settlement enhanced the importance of agricultural tasks as compared with swineherding and hunting, trading the plow for the sword at the chieftain's call became harder.

Those who, out of loyalty or desire for adventure, continued to join the war parties included a growing number of horsemen. The mounted warrior was the mainstay of the Carolingian army, but fighting from horseback did not make a person either a noble or a landowner. Women could be landowners and perform important administrative duties on their domains. By the tenth century, however, nearly constant warfare to protect rights to land or to support the claims

of a superior lord brought about the gradual transformation of the mounted warrior into the noble knight—a transformation that eventually led to landholding becoming inseparable from military service.

This process, culminated in what later historians labeled "feudal" society, was a specifically European response to conditions of weak central government, a lack of effective law, the need to defend one's land militarily, and respect for personal oaths of loyalty. It brought together the Roman practice of granting land in return for military service and the German custom of swearing allegiance to a war chief. Other parts of the world developed similar social and political structures to which some historians apply the term *feudalism*, but each instance has its own particular features as, indeed, does feudal society in different regions of Europe itself.

The German foes of the Roman legions had equipped themselves with a helmet, a shield, and a sword, spear, or throwing ax. They did not wear body armor. Some rode horses, but most fought on foot. The rise of the mounted warrior as the paramount force on the battlefield is associated with the use of stirrups. For hundreds of years horsemen had gripped their mounts with their legs and fought with bow and arrow, throwing javelin, stabbing spear, and sword. Stirrups allowed the rider to stand in the saddle, lean forward with a sturdy lance held under his arm, and thus absorb the impact of striking his enemy at full gallop.

This type of warfare required heavy, grain-fed horses rather than the small, grass-fed animals of the Central Asian pastoralists who seem to have invented the stirrup around the first century C.E. Thus it was in predominantly agricultural Europe rather than among the nomads of the steppe that charges of mounted knights came to dominate the battlefield.

By the eleventh century, the knight had emerged as the central figure in medieval warfare. He wore an open-faced helmet and a long linen shirt, or hauberk, studded with small metal disks. A century later, knightly equipment commonly included a visored helmet that covered the head and neck and a hauberk of chain mail.

Armor was made for the knight's horse, too. From these evolved, in the thirteenth century, metal plate protection for the knight's chest, thighs, and other vulnerable areas, and in the fifteenth century, completely enclosed iron plating.

Each increase in armor for knight and horse entailed a greater financial outlay. Since land was the basis of all wealth, it rapidly became impossible for anyone to serve as a knight who did not have financial support from land revenues. Accordingly, kings took to rewarding meritorious armed service with grants of land from their own property. Nobles with extensive properties did the same to build up their own military retinues.

A grant of land in return for a sworn oath to provide specified military service was called a *feudum*, or *fief*. At first, kings granted fiefs only on a temporary basis, but by the tenth century, most fiefs could be inherited—by sons from their fathers, for example—as long as the specified military service continued to be provided. Although feudalism varied greatly from one part of Europe to another, and generally was more developed in the north and west than in the Mediterranean region, it lent a distinctive cast to medieval European history.

In feudal societies kings tended to be weak and dependent on their *vassals*, noble followers whose services a king or some other noble might be able to command for only part of the year depending on the agreement between them. A lord granted land and owed protection to a vassal; the vassal swore an oath of loyalty and service to the lord. Vassals who held land from several different lords were likely to swear loyalty to each one. Moreover, the allegiance that a vassal owed to one lord was likely to entail military service to that lord's master in time of need.

A "typical" feudal realm—actual practices varied between and within realms—consisted of some lands directly owned by a king or a count and administered by his royal officers. Other lands, often the greater portion, were held and administered by the king's or count's major vassals in return for military service. These vassals, in turn, granted land to their own vassals. Instead of taxes, therefore, the lands of kings and other nobles yielded primarily military service.

The Rise of Christendom in Europe

313	Edict of Milan; Christianity tolerated in Roman Empire
325	Constantine convenes Council of Nicaea
476	End of Roman Empire in the west
ca. 547	Death of St. Benedict
800	Coronation of Charlemagne
910	Monastery of Cluny founded
936	Beginning of Holy Roman Empire
989	Ruler of Russia adopts Orthodox Christianity
1054	Final schism between Catholic and Orthodox churches
1007	Pope Gregory VII and Emperor Henry IV at Canossa
1095	Pope Urban II preaches First Crusade

A lord's manor was the effective source of governance and justice in most areas. Direct royal government was quite limited. The king had few financial resources at his disposal and seldom exercised legal jurisdiction at a local level. The fact that all members of the clergy, as well as the extensive agricultural lands owned by monasteries and nunneries, fell under the supervision and legal jurisdiction of the church further limited the reach and authority of the feudal monarch.

Noblewomen became enmeshed in the tangle of feudal obligations as heiresses and as candidates for marriage. A man who married the widow or daughter of a lord with no sons could gain for himself control of that lord's property. Entire kingdoms were put together or taken apart through marriage alliances. Noble daughters and sons had little say in marriage matters, for the important issues were land, power, and military service, not the feelings or preferences of individuals. Noblemen guarded the women in their families as closely as they guarded their other valuables.

Noblewoman directing construction of a church   This picture of Berthe, wife of Girat de Rouissillion, acting as mistress of the works is from a tenth-century manuscript but shows a scene from the ninth-century. Wheel-barrows rarely appear in medieval building scenes. (Copyright Bibliothèque royale Albert Ier, Bruxelles, Ms. 6, fol. 554 verso.)

This does not mean that all women lived powerless, sheltered lives. Some noblewomen exercised real power, administering their husband's lands when they were away at war. Women of the manor who were not of the noble class usually worked alongside their menfolk, performing agricultural tasks such as raking and stacking hay, shearing sheep, and picking vegetables. As artisans, women spun, wove, and sewed clothing. Indeed, one of the greatest works of craft and art surviving from medieval Europe is the Bayeux Tapestry, a piece of embroidery 230 feet (70 meters) long and 20 inches (51 centimeters) wide designed and executed entirely by women.

It depicts in cartoon form the story of the invasion of England in 1066 by William the Conqueror, duke of Normandy.

Dhuoda, a ninth-century Frankish noblewoman, reflected the social distinctions of an emerging feudal society in the counsel she gave her son on how to direct his prayers. She urged young William to pray for "kings and all those of the highest ranks" at the pinnacle of society, then, in descending order, for his lord, his father, his enemies, and a final group consisting of the wayfarer, the infirm, the poor and suffering, and "all sorts of others whom I have omitted here." Among the omitted are the serfs of the manor.

Notably, Dhouda placed one category above even the king. "Pray first," she writes, "for the bishops and all the priests, that they may pour forth to God pure and worthy prayers for you and for all the people."[2] Already by her time the Christian church was showing promise of being the one institution capable of combating the political fragmentation, social stratification, and warfare of post-Roman Europe.

THE WESTERN CHURCH

The Christian church was the sole institution claiming jurisdiction over, and the loyalty of, large segments of Europe's population. The growing Christian populations in eastern Europe recognized the authority of the patriarch of Constantinople even in Slavic lands beyond the control of the Byzantine emperor (see Map 9.2). The pope commanded similar authority over church affairs in the Latin west. There, missionaries added territory to Christendom with forays into the British Isles and the lands of the Germans. Yet travels by Christian preachers did not necessarily mean significant conversions among those who heard their words, which must have been tiny minorities of the population. Lists of bishops and wonder-filled lives of missionaries are often historians' only sources for assessing the penetration of Christianity into new lands, and these say little about the actual pattern of adoption of the new religion or about the effectiveness of the pope's control of bishops far from Italy.

Regional disagreements over church regulations, shortages of educated and trained clergy, difficult communications, political disorder, and the general insecurity of the period were formidable obstacles to unifying church standards and practices. By the eleventh century, clerics in some parts of western Europe were still issuing prohibitions against the worship of rivers, trees, and mountains and other superstitions. In the face of residual paganism and lax enforcement of prohibitions against practices such as clergy marrying, nepotism (giving preferment to one's close kin), simony (selling ecclesiastical appointments, often to people who were not members of the clergy), and even the wearing of beards, the persistence of the papacy in asserting its legal jurisdiction over clergy, combating heretical beliefs, and calling on secular rulers to recognize its authority constituted a rare force for unity and order in a time of disunity and chaos.

Faith and Rule

From the fourth century onward, divisions on matters of doctrine endangered the Christian church. Jesus' disciples had established Christian communities in Jerusalem, Antioch, Alexandria, and Rome, and most Christians recognized the successors of these early authorities, called patriarchs or, in the Roman case, popes, as the paramount leaders of the church. The emperor Constantine made his capital city, Constantinople, a fifth patriarchate in the fourth century. The patriarchs and popes appointed bishops throughout the regions that recognized their authority, and the bishops consecrated priests in smaller localities. Church rules could be set by the patriarch or by councils of bishops.

Priests were expected to follow these rules in servicing the needs of the ordinary believers. These needs focused on major life events: baptism after birth; admission to participation in and personal performance of the ritual of communion, which consisted of consuming the body and blood of Jesus in the form of sacred wine and bread; performance of marriage ceremonies; and anointing the dead. These ceremonies and rituals, along with the ordination of priests, were considered sacred mysteries, or sacraments, that only priests—bishops and patriarchs were also priests—could perform.

The hierarchy of church ranks theoretically ensured a consistency in Christian ritual and belief throughout the Christian community. In fact, patriarchs, popes, and bishops sometimes disagreed on important religious issues. One area of

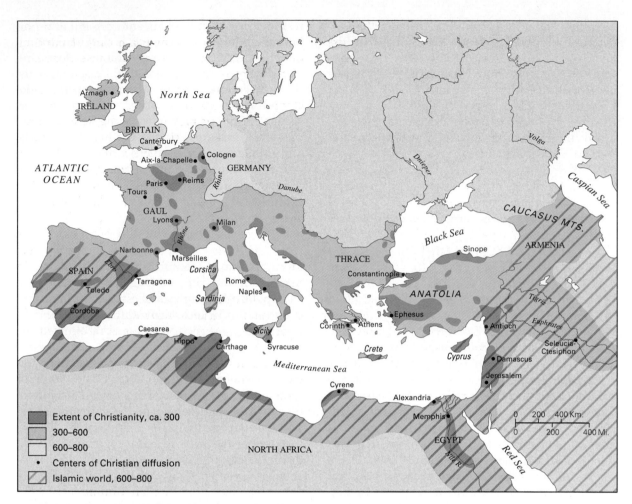

Map 9.2   The Spread of Christianity   By the early eighth century, Christian areas around the southern Mediterranean from northern Syria to northern Spain, accounting for most of the Christian population, had fallen under Muslim rule; and the slow process of conversion to Islam had begun. This accentuated the importance of the patriarchs of Constantinople, the popes in Rome, and the later converting regions of northern and eastern Europe.

confusion and disagreement centered on Jesus' relationship to God the Father and to the Holy Spirit. Christians generally agreed that these together formed a divine Trinity in which three aspects or manifestations of God were somehow united, but they did not all understand the Trinity in the same way. They also disagreed on such matters as whether Mary was the mother of God, or the mother of a man named Jesus; and on whether images of God or Jesus or Mary, called icons, were proper objects to pray toward because they stimulated pious thoughts, or whether praying toward them was too much like praying to pagan statues.

Disagreements like these could lead to charges and countercharges of heresy, defined as beliefs or practices that were so unacceptable as to be un-Christian. Charges of heresy were important to ordinary people, even when they involved hard-to-understand theological issues, because they brought into question the sacraments performed by the priests or bishops charged as heretics. They also threatened the unity of the Christian church at a time when political fragmentation was rapidly increasing.

The most severe challenges to ecclesiastical authority arose in North Africa and the lands of the eastern Mediterranean and resulted in schism—a formal division over differences in doctrine. Some doctrinal disagreements, such as Monophysite doctrine, which puts primacy on the divine character of Jesus Christ and minimizes his human characteristics, persist to this day. The Coptic Church of Egypt, the Ethiopian Church, and the Armenian Apostolic Church all accept Monophysitism. Other potential sources of schism were stamped out. One of these was the Donatist Church of North Africa, which denied the authority of the Roman pope because of disagreements over whether a sacrament like baptism was still valid if a person temporarily gave in to persecution and abandoned Christianity.

The common way of dealing with such challenges to Christian unity was for a council of bishops to deliberate and declare a particular doctrine true or false. In the East, the Byzantine emperor claimed the prerogative of calling such conferences. In the West, the pope took the lead. Schismatics could call conferences of their own. The bishops of particular regions often met in council to set rules, called *canons*, to regulate the priests and lay people (men and women who were not members of the clergy) under their jurisdiction. The doctrine that most endangered papal authority was Arianism, which was widespread among the Germanic peoples. Although the teaching of the Alexandrian bishop Arius that Jesus was a creation of God the father and a lesser sort of divinity was declared heretical in 325 at the Council of Nicaea called by the emperor Constantine (see Chapter 6), it did not quickly disappear.

Charges of heresy focused on matters of dogma but often reflected underlying social or political issues, such as the desire of Monophysite Egyptians to resist the authority of Con-

stantinople or the desire of North African Berbers to use Donatism as a means of standing up to Roman colonizers. In some cases, practices as ordinary as the wearing of beards—permitted in the Byzantine East but forbidden in the Latin West—or the way of shaving the priest's head stirred local desires for ecclesiastical independence. The overriding issue in such cases was *orthopraxy*, "correct practices," rather than *orthodoxy*, "correct beliefs." Ireland, in particular, challenged Rome in the eighth and ninth centuries by extolling its own church practices and exporting them to Scotland, Britain, France, and Switzerland by means of missionaries who established important monasteries like Iona, off the Scottish coast, and Saint Gall in Switzerland.

In politically fragmented western Europe, the pope needed allies. He found them in rulers like Charlemagne, who upheld papal rights in return for religious legitimation of his rule. Charlemagne's descendants did not maintain his empire intact, however, and it was not until 962, with the papal coronation of a Holy Roman Emperor (Charlemagne never held this title), that a secular political authority came into being that claimed to represent general Christian interests. Essentially a loose confederation of German princes who named one of their own to the highest office, the Holy Roman Empire held little sway west of the Rhine River.

Although the pope crowned the Holy Roman Emperors, the law of the church (known as *canon law*) and the various secular laws in effect in different regions were on a collision course. According to canon law, the pope had exclusive legal jurisdiction over all clergy and all church property wherever located. Kings and princes saw this claim as an intrusion on their territory, but one that they generally were fearful of objecting to because the pope could excommunicate them, that is, bar them from all church activities and sacraments. Complicating things, many bishops controlled lands that owed military support or other feudal services and dues to the kings and princes. The secular rulers argued that they should have the power to appoint those bishops because that was the only way to ensure that they would fulfill their duties as feudal vassals. The popes disagreed.

In the eleventh century, this conflict came to a head. Hildebrand, an Italian monk, capped a career of reforming and reorganizing church finances by being named Pope Gregory VII in 1073. His personal notion of the papacy (preserved among his letters) represents an extreme position, stating among other claims, that

§ The pope can be judged by no one;
§ The Roman church has never erred and never will err till the end of time;
§ The pope alone can depose and restore bishops;
§ He alone can call general councils and authorize canon law;
§ He can depose emperors;
§ He can absolve subjects from their allegiance;
§ All princes should kiss his feet.[3]

Such claims antagonized lords and monarchs, who had become accustomed to controlling the nomination, or *investiture*, of bishops and abbots in their domains. Historians use the term *investiture controversy* to refer specifically to the struggle to control ecclesiastical appointments; the term also refers to the broader conflict of popes versus emperors and kings. When Holy Roman Emperor Henry IV opposed Gregory's reforms, Gregory excommunicated him in 1076. Stung by the resulting decline in his influence, Henry stood barefoot in the snow for three days outside a castle in northern Italy waiting for Gregory, a guest there, to receive him. Henry's formal act of penance forced Gregory to forgive him and return him to the church, but the reconciliation, amounting to a defeat for the pope, did not last. In 1078, Gregory declared Henry deposed. The emperor forced the pope to flee from Rome to Salerno, where two years later, Gregory died, supported only by Sicily's Norman rulers.

However, the reforming legacy of Gregory VII survived. The struggle between the popes and emperors continued until 1122, when a compromise was reached at Worms, a town in Germany. In the Concordat of Worms, Emperor Henry V renounced his rights to choose bishops and abbots or confer them with spiritual symbols such as a staff and a ring. In return, Pope Calixtus II permitted the emperor to invest papal nominees for the position of bishop or abbot with any lay rights or obligations before their spiritual consecration. This was essentially a victory for the church, though not a complete one.

Conflicts between secular and ecclesiastical authority erupted in other areas as well. Though barely twenty when he became king of England in 1154 (see below), Henry II instituted reforms designed to strengthen the power of the Crown and weaken the feudal lords. He appointed traveling justices to enforce his laws. He made juries, a holdover from traditional Germanic law, into powerful legal instruments. He established the principle that criminal acts violated the "king's peace" and should be tried and punished in accordance with charges brought by the crown instead of in response to charges brought by victims.

Henry had a harder time controlling the church. His closest friend, the chancellor, or chief administrator, of England, was Thomas Becket (ca. 1118–1170). A supporter of the king, Becket was a typical courtier who lived in a grand and luxurious manner. In 1162 Henry persuaded Becket to become a priest in order to assume the position of archbishop of Canterbury, the highest church office in England. Becket agreed but warned Henry that if he became an official of the church, he would act solely in the interest of the church when it came into conflict with the Crown. Accordingly, when Henry sought to try clerics accused of crimes in royal instead of ecclesiastical courts, Archbishop Becket, now leading an austere and pious life away from court luxuries, resisted.

In 1170 four of Henry's knights, knowing that the king desired Becket's death, murdered the archbishop in Canterbury Cathedral. Their crime backfired, however. An outpouring of sympathy caused Canterbury to become a major pilgrimage center, and in 1173 the pope declared the martyred Becket to be a saint. Henry allowed himself twice to be publicly whipped in penance for the crime, but his authority had been badly damaged.

Although the Latin Church repeatedly and effectively defended its claim as the sole arbiter of doctrinal religious truth, the investiture controversy and Henry II's conflict with Thomas Becket yielded no clear victor. Western Europe was heir to three legal traditions: (1) feudal law, based in large part on Germanic custom; (2) canon law, based in large part on Roman law in its visualization of a single hierarchical legal institution covering all of Western Christendom; and (3) Roman law, which, after centuries of disregard, began to be studied anew at the fledgling University of Bologna, in Italy, around 1088. This pattern of church-state division became a noteworthy feature of western European civilization and one that set the region apart from both the Byzantine Empire and the Muslim states that succeeded the Byzantines in Syria, Egypt, and Tunisia (see Chapter 10).

Monasticism

Another distinctive feature of Western Christendom rooted in the period from 300 to 1200 was monasticism. The origins of monasticism lay in the eastern lands of the Roman Empire. Practices such as celibacy, continual devotion to prayer, and living apart from society (alone or in small groups) were not new, but they came together in

Cloister of Benedictine Monastery Interior courtyards with fountains and gardens, also a common feature of Muslim palaces in Spain, recall the architecture of Roman villas. The semicircular arches identify this architectural style as Romanesque. (Rheinisches Archiv)

Christian guise in Egypt. Athanasius (d. 373), the patriarch of Alexandria, portrays Anthony, perhaps the most important early hermit monk, as a pious desert dweller continually tempted by Satan. On one occasion, "when he was weaving palm leaves . . . that he might make baskets to give as gifts to people who were continually coming to visit him . . . he saw an animal which had the following form: from its head to its side it was like a man, and its legs and feet were those of an ass."[4] As was his custom, Anthony prayed to God upon seeing this sight, and Satan left him alone.

In western Europe holy hermits given to mystic visions were comparatively few. The most important form of monasticism involved groups of monks or nuns living together in a single community. Benedict of Nursia (ca. 480–547), in Italy, began his pious career as a hermit in a cave but eventually organized several monasteries, each headed by an abbot. The Rule he promulgated to govern the monks' behavior emphasizes celibacy, poverty, and obedience to the abbot; but it is moderate compared with some Eastern practices. The Rule of Benedict was the starting point for most forms of western European monastic life and remains in force today in Benedictine monasteries. It discusses both ritual activities and everyday life in passages like the following:

> § Since the spirit of silence is so important, permission to speak should rarely be granted even to perfect disciples, even though it be for good, holy, edifying conversation. . . . If anything has to be asked of the Superior, it should be asked with all the humility and submission inspired by reverence. But as for coarse jests and idle words or words that move to laughter, these we condemn everywhere with a perpetual ban. . . .
> § Let clothing be given to the brethren according to the nature of the place in which they dwell and its climate. . . . In ordinary places the following dress is sufficient for each monk: a tunic, a cowl (thick and woolly for winter, thin or worn for summer), a scapular [sleeveless cloak] for work, stockings and shoes to cover the feet. The monks should not complain about the color or the coarseness of any of these things, but be content with what can be found in the district where they live and can be purchased cheaply.[5]

Monastic life removed thousands of pious men and women from towns and villages and thus reinforced a tendency toward separation between religious affairs and secular politics and economics. Jesus' axiom that one should "render unto Caesar what is Caesar's and unto God what is God's" was taken seriously in the monastery despite the fact that many bishops who were based in towns came to control vast properties and numerous retainers and behave like secular lords. Monasteries were also the primary centers of literacy and learning in the centuries following the decline of the Western Empire. Many lay nobles were illiterate and interested in little other than warfare and hunting. Monks (but seldom nuns) saw copying manuscripts and even writing books as part of their religious calling. Were it not for monks of the ninth century, most ancient works in Latin would have disappeared.

Monasteries and nunneries served other functions as well. Although a few planted Christianity in new lands, as the Irish monks did in parts of Germany, most of them serviced the needs of travelers, organized agricultural production on their lands, and took in foundlings. Nunneries provided refuges for widows and other women who lacked male protection in a harsh world or who desired a spiritual life. All such religious houses, however, presented problems of oversight to the church. A bishop might have authority over an abbot or abbess (head of a nunnery), but there was no way to exercise constant vigilance over what transpired behind monastery walls.

An influential movement of reform and centralization of monastic authority is named for the Benedictine abbey of Cluny in eastern France. Cluny was founded in 910 by William the Pious, the first duke of Aquitaine, who freed it completely of lay authority. A century later Cluny gained similar freedom from the local bishop. Its abbots then embarked on a vigorous campaign, in alliance with reforming popes like Gregory VII, to improve the discipline and administration of European monasteries. A magnificent new abbey church, designed in the Romanesque style with small arched windows and heavy stone walls, symbolized Cluny's claims to eminence.

With later additions, it became the largest church in the world.

At the peak of Cluny's influence, nearly a thousand Benedictine abbeys and priories (lower-level monastic houses) in various countries accepted the authority of the abbot of Cluny. Where the original Benedictine Rule presumed that each monastery would be independent, the Cluniac reformers stipulated that every abbot and every prior (head of a priory) be appointed by the abbot of Cluny and have had personal experience of the religious life of Cluny. The Cluniac movement set the pattern for the organizations of monasteries, cathedral clergy, and preaching friars that would dominate ecclesiastical life in the thirteenth century.

Shaping European Society

The magnitude of the changes in the society of Western Europe that took place under the influence of Christianity is difficult to overestimate. Roman society in Jesus' time had felt comfortable with slavery, religious pluralism, and overt sexuality. Christian society demanded a celibate clergy and discouraged sexual activities outside marriage, advocated monogamy while deploring divorce and concubinage, frowned on slavery, and looked on non-Christians with suspicion and sometimes hatred.

The fragile legal status of the Jews led them into money-changing, goldsmithing, and other trades that they could practice anywhere. Rulers and popes protected or expelled Jews to suit their own political and economic ends and whims. When crusading enthusiasm overtook Europe in the early eleventh century (see below), some Christian zealots decided to murder and loot local Jewish communities rather than trek to the Holy Land. Muslims were even more unwelcome than Jews because Islam was seen as a political threat (see Chapter 10).

Where Roman society had been based on extended kinship lineages (see Chapter 6), Christian Europe conceived the family in a somewhat narrower sense. The lines of social division separating nobles from clergy or landowners from

serfs were quite different from those of the Roman era. Festivals and rituals, monumental building programs, artistic endeavor of all kinds—everything that conveyed a sense of civilization—manifested itself in Christian form rather than in the trappings of the secular empire of Rome. In the fourth and fifth centuries, Germanic customs and tastes were seen as overriding and destroying the more sophisticated traditions of Rome. However, by the year 1200, Christianity had forged in Western Europe a new civilization that preserved selected features of the Roman and German past while evolving its own distinctive features.

THE BYZANTINE EMPIRE

In the eastern region of the old Roman Empire, European Christian civilization was very different from its counterpart in the West. The Byzantine emperors represented the continuation of Roman imperial rule and tradition and brought to political, social, and religious life a continuity that was almost entirely absent in the West. Roman law, which the Eastern emperors inherited intact, lessened the impact of church proscriptions, and the Byzantine emperors, exercising an authority known as *caesaropapism*, combining both the imperial ("Caesar") and the papal, made a comfortable transition into the role of all-powerful Christian monarchs.

The Byzantine drama, however, played on a smaller and steadily shrinking stage. The loss of Syria, Egypt, and Tunisia to Muslim invaders in the seventh century, Slavic pressure on Byzantium's Balkan frontiers, and the eventual Byzantine failure to prevent the Muslims from overwhelming Anatolia (modern Turkey) in the late eleventh century deprived the empire of long-lasting periods of peace. Christianity progressively withered in lands that fell to the Muslims, despite occasional bursts of imperial military power, such as occurred in the tenth century, when Christian forces temporarily recaptured the city of Antioch. By the end of the twelfth century, at least two-thirds of the Christians in the former Byzantine territories had adopted the Muslim faith.

The peoples to the north, however, provided room for Christian missionary expansion. As the Slavs gradually adopted Christianity—except for the Poles, who were brought into Latin Christianity by German missionaries and knights—they also adopted a reverence for the customs, rituals, and imperial tradition of Byzantium. These factors were to have a profound impact on the later history of Russia.

The Fortunes of Empire

The Roman emperors who ruled in the East retained many imperial traditions and outlooks that disappeared in the West. In 324, in the nineteenth year of his reign, Constantine led a procession marking out the expanded limits of the city he had selected as his new capital: the millennium-old Greek city of Byzantium, located on a long, narrow inlet at the entrance to the Bosporus strait. In the forum of the new Constantinople, he erected a 120-foot-tall (36-meter) column topped with a statue of Apollo, and he retained the old Roman title *pontifex maximus* (chief priest). Nevertheless, he was a Christian, and he studded the city with churches.

The pope in Rome was chosen by ecclesiastical election and eventually claimed complete independence and authority over Western Christendom. In contrast, the Byzantine emperor appointed the patriarch of Constantinople and became closely involved in doctrinal disputes over which beliefs constituted heresy. In 325 Constantine called hundreds of bishops to a council at the city of Nicaea (modern Iznik in northwestern Turkey) and persuaded them to reject the Arian doctrine that Jesus was of lesser importance than God the Father. In doing this, he was applying the characteristically Eastern principle of caesaropapism. Nevertheless, the Byzantine Empire was torn for centuries by disputes over theology and by quarrels among the

patriarchs of Constantinople, Alexandria, and Antioch. Much of the surviving literature of the Byzantine period is devoted to religious affairs, and it is apparent that religious differences permeated society. As the fourth-century bishop Gregory of Nyssa reports: "Everything is full of those who are speaking of unintelligible things. . . . I wish to know the price of bread; one answers, 'The Father is greater than the Son.' I inquire whether my bath is ready; one says, 'The Son has been made out of nothing.'"[6]

In contrast with the West, polytheism died fairly quickly in the Byzantine world, surviving longest among the country folk. (Latin *pagani*, whence the word "pagan" for people who believe in strange gods). The emperor Julian (r. 361–363) tried in vain to restore the old polytheistic faith. When a blind Christian called Julian an apostate (a renegade from Christianity) he said, "You are blind, and your God will not cure you," to which the Christian replied, "I thank God for my blindness, since it prevents me from beholding your impiety." In 392 the emperor Theodosius banned all pagan ceremonies. The following year he terminated the Olympic games. He also removed the pagan altar of victory from the Senate in Rome.

Having a single ruler endowed with supreme legal and religious authority prevented the breakup of the Eastern Empire into a mosaic of petty feudal principalities, but it did not guarantee either peace or prosperity. In the fourth century the empire was threatened from the east, along its Euphrates River frontier, by a new Iranian empire ruled by the Sasanid family (see Chapter 10), and from the north by Germanic Goths and the nomadic Huns from Central Asia. Bribes, diplomacy, and occasional military victories persuaded the Goths and Huns either to settle peacefully or move on toward targets in western Europe. War with the Sasanids recurred for almost three hundred years, however, until a new enemy appeared from the Arabian peninsula in the form of marauding tribes led by followers of the Arab prophet Muhammad. During the first half of the seventh century, these Muslim invaders destroyed the Sasanid Empire and captured Egypt, Syria, and Tunisia.

The loss of some of its most populous and prosperous provinces permanently reduced the power of the Byzantine Empire, and its political trajectory was generally downward. Although it survived until 1453, its later emperors were continually threatened by the Muslims to their south and by newly arriving Slavic and Turkic peoples to their north. At the same time, relations with the popes and princes of western Europe steadily worsened. As early as the mid-ninth century the patriarchs of Constantinople had challenged the territorial jurisdiction of the popes of Rome and some of the established practices of the Latin Church. Rather than going away, these arguments worsened over time and in 1054 culminated in a formal schism between the Latin Church and the Orthodox Church—a break that has never been mended. This ill will did not prevent Eastern and Western Christians from cooperating in some measure during the crusading era of the twelfth century. But it contributed to the decision by the leaders of the Fourth Crusade (see below) to sack Constantinople in 1204, send the Byzantine emperor fleeing to an outlying province, and establish Latin principalities on Byzantine territory.

Society and Urban Life

The maintenance of imperial authority, and the accompanying urban prosperity, in the eastern provinces of the old Roman Empire buffered Byzantium against the population decline and severe economic regression suffered in the West from the third century on. Nevertheless, a similar though less pronounced transformation set in around the seventh century, possibly sparked by the loss of Egypt and Syria to the Muslims. Narrative histories give scant coverage to this period, but saints' lives show a transition from stories about educated saints hailing from cities to stories about saints originating as peasants. In many areas, barter replaced money transactions, and cities declined in population and prosperity, causing the virtual disappearance of the traditional class of local urban notables.

The disappearance of that class left a social gap between the high aristocracy centered on the imperial court and the rural landowners and peasants. By the end of the eleventh century, a family-based military aristocracy somewhat similar to the feudal nobility of western Europe had emerged, though without being institutionalized in feudal law codes. Of Byzantine emperor Alexius Comnenus (r. 1081–1118) it was said: "He considered himself not a ruler, but a lord, conceiving and calling the empire his own house."

The situation of women changed, too. Earlier Roman family structure had been loose, and women had been comparatively active in public life. Now the family became a more rigid unit, and women increasingly found themselves confined to the home by their husbands and by social custom. When they went out in public, they concealed their faces behind veils. The only males they socialized with were family members. Paradoxically, however, from 1028 to 1056 women ruled the Byzantine Empire with their husbands.

To what extent these changes are related to the social conditions that brought about a parallel seclusion of women in the neighboring Islamic countries has not yet been established. It is likely, however, that the two developments are linked despite the differences in religion. By comparison with Christianity in western Europe, Byzantine Christianity manifested less interest in, or felt less need for, the provision of refuge for women in nunneries. This, too, finds its parallel in the development of Islam.

Economically, the Byzantine emperors continued a late Roman inclination to set prices, control the provision of grain to the capital city, and monopolize trade in certain goods, like purple cloth. Whether government intervention contributed to the comparative lack of technological development and economic innovation in Byzantium is difficult to determine. As long as merchants and pilgrims hastened to the metropolis of Constantinople from all corners of the compass, rare and costly goods were readily available for aristocratic consumption. The decline of other Eastern cities, however, emphasized the basis of the economy in agriculture and animal husbandry.

There Byzantine farmers continued to use light scratch plows and creaky oxcarts long after farmers in western Europe had adopted heavy plows and efficiently harnessed horses. Despite this stagnation, the Byzantines continued for a time to outclass western Europe in the variety and quality of manufactured goods.

Because Byzantium's inheritance from the earlier Roman Empire was so much richer than western Europe's, there was little recognition that the slow deterioration that set in during the seventh century constituted a problem. Gradually, however, pilgrims and visitors from the West began to see the reality beyond the awe-inspiring, incense-filled domes of cathedrals like Constantinople's Hagia Sophia and beneath the glitter and silken garments of the royal court. An eleventh-century French visitor wrote:

> The city itself [Constantinople] is squalid and fetid and in many places harmed by permanent darkness, for the wealthy overshadow the streets with buildings and leave these dirty, dark places to the poor and to travelers; there murders and robberies and other crimes which love the darkness are committed. Moreover, since people live lawlessly in this city, which has as many lords as rich men and almost as many thieves as poor men, a criminal knows neither fear nor shame, because crime is not punished by law and never entirely comes to light. In every respect she exceeds moderation; for, just as she surpasses other cities in wealth, so too, does she surpass them in vice.[7]

The view from the other side was expressed by Anna Comnena, the brilliant daughter of Emperor Alexius Comnenus. She described the Western knights of the First Crusade (1096–1099) as uncouth barbarians, albeit sometimes gifted with an impressive manliness. She even turned her scorn on a prominent churchman and philosopher who happened to be from Italy: "Italos . . . was unable with his barbaric, stupid temperament to grasp the profound truths of philosophy; even in the act of learning he utterly rejected the teacher's guiding hand, and full of temerity and barbaric folly, [believed] even before study that he excelled all others."[8]

By the time of the Crusades, the Byzantines were being surpassed by the western Europeans. Their most valuable provinces had been lost. Their army played only a supporting role in the conquest of the Holy Land. And their maritime commerce was mostly carried in ships from Genoa, Venice, and Pisa. From the sack of Constantinople during the Fourth Crusade in 1204 to its fall to the Ottoman sultan Mehmed the Conqueror in 1453, vestiges of the legendary Byzantine imperial pomp and political intrigue remained, but this heir to the Roman Empire amounted to little more than a small, weak principality centered on a shrunken, looted, and dilapidated Constantinople and a few outlying cities.

Byzantine church as shown in twelfth century manuscript Upper portion shows church facade and domes—one over each arm of a Greek cross and one over the central crossing. Lower portion shows interior with picture or mosaic of Christ enthroned at the altar end. (Bibliothèque nationale de France)

Cathedral of St. Dmitry in Vladimir Built between 1193 and 1197, this Russian Orthodox cathedral shows Byzantine influence. Three-arch facade, small dome, and symmetrical Greek-cross floor plan strongly resemble the painting on page 266. (Sovfoto)

Cultural Achievements

Just as the maintenance of imperial authority facilitated the emergence of the Byzantine emperor as the ultimate arbiter of religious disputes, so his power persisted in secular legal affairs. Sev-

eral emperors had collections of laws and edicts made. The most famous and complete collection was the *Corpus Juris Civilis* (*Body of Civil Law*) compiled in Latin by seventeen legal scholars at the behest of the emperor Justinian (r. 527–565). In the late eleventh century, it began to be studied at the University of Bologna and became the basis for *civil* law (as opposed to *canon* and *feudal* law) in western Europe as well. Many modern principles of law were thereby handed on from Roman models, a fact that accounts for the use of Latin expressions in the legal profession today.

Also of lasting importance from the time of Justinian is the architectural tradition represented by Hagia Sophia, the great domed cathedral of Constantinople. Domed buildings, which required a careful calculation of the stress of the stone dome's weight, were comparatively rare in the western lands of the Roman Empire, but they evolved splendidly in Byzantium, creating enormous spaces with an aesthetic appeal completely different from that of the long, lofty naves of Western cathedrals. After capturing Constantinople in 1453, the Ottoman Turks patterned a series of majestic mosques on Hagia Sophia, which they also turned from a cathedral into a mosque. Byzantine models were also in mind much later when the great architects of the Italian Renaissance (fifteenth and sixteenth centuries) turned their hand to designing domes.

Other important Byzantine achievements date to the empire's long period of political decline. In the ninth century, two brothers named Cyril and Methodius embarked on a highly successful missionary enterprise among the Slavs of Moravia (part of the modern Czech Republic). They preached in the local language, and their followers perfected a writing system, called Cyrillic, that came to be used by Slavic Christians adhering to the Orthodox—that is, Byzantine—rite.

In the following century the Russians, who were then enjoying an upsurge of power in the form of a new state centered on the city of Kiev (see Chapter 13), turned more and more toward Christianity. Russian preferences for domed churches and the display of religious icons are direct inheritances from Byzantium, as is the use of the title *tsar*, a contraction of the Latin title *caesar*. Thus slowly declining Byzantium witnessed the triumph of Orthodox Christianity and Byzantine ecclesiastical culture in the lands of the Slavs.

WESTERN EUROPE REVIVES

Between 1000 and 1300, western Europe slowly emerged from almost seven centuries of subsistence economy—an economy in which most people who worked on the land and could meet only their basic needs for food, clothing, and shelter. Population and agricultural production climbed, and a growing food surplus found its way to town markets, enhancing the return of a money-based exchange economy, as opposed to one where people ate most of what they grew, and providing support for larger numbers of craftspeople, construction workers, traders, and artisans engaged in cloth making: spinners, bleachers, dyers, weavers, and so forth.

One sign of the upturn in economic activity was more abundant circulation of coinage. In the ninth and tenth centuries, most gold coins had come from Muslim lands and Byzantium. They were rarely seen in Germany, France, and Britain because they were worth too much for most trading purposes. In western Europe the standard coin for centuries was the widely imitated Carolingian silver penny. With the economic revival of the twelfth century, silver coins began to be minted locally in Scandinavia, Poland, and other outlying regions. In the following century the reinvigoration of Mediterranean trade made possible a new and abundant gold coinage, the Florentine florin and the Venetian ducat, the former first minted in 1252 and the latter in 1284. The ducat, in particular, became the new standard of trade.

Historians have attributed western Europe's revival to population growth spurred by new technologies and to the appearance in Italy and Flanders (modern Belgium and Holland) of self-governing cities devoted primarily to trade and seafaring. Among the beneficiaries of these changes were kings, who began the long process of improving central administration, gaining greater control over their vassals, and consolidating realms that eventually would become strong national kingdoms.

The Role of Technology

A lack of concrete evidence indicating how widespread various technological innovations were and exactly when they appeared frustrates efforts to relate the exact course of Europe's revival to technological change. Nevertheless, most historians agree that technology played a significant role in the approximate tripling of the population of western Europe between 1000 and 1300. The population of England, for example, seems to have risen from 1.1 million in 1086 to 3.3 million in 1300, and the population of the territory of modern France seems to have risen from 5.2 million to 15.7 million over the same period.

A group of innovations that seem to have become increasingly widespread after the year 1000 is credited with launching the economy of western Europe into a robust and productive stage. Notable among them were efficient draft harnesses for pulling wagons and a new type of plow. The Roman plow, which farmers in southern Europe continued to use, merely scratched the soil. The new plow had a curved plate (a moldboard) that turned the sod over as the plowshare (blade) bit through the heavy, wet soil of the northern river valleys. Over time, the new harness and new plow contributed to the emergence of the horse as western Europe's primary work animal, replacing the ox in many areas. In no other part of the world did the draft horse become so important.

A mystery surrounds the adoption of harnesses that did not strangle a horse pulling a heavy load, as the old-style harnesses derived from the yoke tended to do. The horse collar, which lowers the point of traction from the animal's neck to its shoulders, first appears around 800 in a miniature painting, and it is shown clearly as a harness for plow horses in the Bayeux Tapestry, embroidered after 1066. The breast-strap harness, which is less well adapted for the heaviest work but was preferred in southern Europe, seems to have appeared around the year 500. In both cases, linguists have tried to trace key technical terms to Chinese or Turko-Mongol words and have argued for technological diffusion across the breadth of Eurasia. Yet third-century Roman farmers in Tunisia and Libya used both types of efficient harness to hitch horses and camels to plows and carts. This technology, which is still employed in Tunisia, is clearly depicted on bas-reliefs and lamps, but there is no more evidence of its movement northward into Europe than there is of efficient harnessing moving across Asia. Thus the question of whether efficient harnessing began in 500 or in 800, or was known even earlier but not extensively used, cannot easily be resolved.

Hinging on this problem is the question of when and why landowners in northern Europe

Farming scene on border of Bayeux Tapestry By the late eleventh century, new harnessing techniques permitted the use of heavier plows. Here a mule harnessed with a horse collar pulls a wheeled plow with a mould board and coulter, the knife-like piece behind the wheels that cuts the turf that is then turned over by the share (blade). (Tapisserie de Bayeux et avec autorisation spéciale de la Ville de Bayeux)

began to use teams of horses to pull plows through the moist, fertile river-valley soils that were too heavy for teams of oxen. Stronger and faster than oxen, horses increased the productivity of these and other lands by reducing the number of hours needed for plowing. This development undoubtedly contributed to a greater agricultural surplus, but the breeding of larger horses for knightly warfare may have been as important a factor as the new technology in starting the move away from oxen.

Accompanying improvements in tilling the soil was improved understanding of how to maximize its productivity. A three-field system of cultivation emerged. Two-thirds of the land of a manor or village was planted in grain or other foodstuffs each year; this land was plowed once and then sown with seed. The other third was left fallow but was plowed twice a year to turn under the weeds and thus return nitrogen to the soil. Some fallow (unplanted) land was also used for grazing. We will take a village with 300 acres (120 hectares) of farmland as an example. Under the earlier half-and-half system, 150 acres (60 hectares) would be plowed once and the other 150 acres twice for a total of 450 acres (180 hectares) of plowing. Under the three-field system, 200 acres (80 hectares) would be plowed once, and the remaining 100 acres (40 hectares) twice for a total of 400 acres (160 hectares) of plowing. The time and energy that farmers saved could go into other productive activities, including increasing the total area under cultivation.

Cities and the Rebirth of Trade

Associated with the growth of population was the appearance, first in Italy and Flanders and then elsewhere, of independent cities governed and defended by communes of leading citizens. Lacking the extensive farmlands that had been virtually the sole basis of wealth in western Europe since the decline of Rome, these cities turned to manufacturing and trade. Equally important, they won for themselves a legally independent position between the jurisdiction of the church and that of the feudal lord and therefore could frame their laws specifically to favor manufacturing and trade. These laws made serfs free, so these cities attracted many migrants from the countryside.

Cities in Italy that had shrunk within walls built by the Romans now filled those walls to overflowing, forcing the construction of new ones. Pisa built a new wall in 1000 and expanded it in 1156. Other twelfth-century cities that built new walls include Florence, Brescia, Piacenza, Pavia, Pistoia, and Siena. Bologna, Lucca, Mantua, and Parma followed in the thirteenth century.

Venice was a new city situated on a group of islands at the northern end of the Adriatic Sea that had been largely uninhabited in Roman times. In the eleventh century it rose to be the dominant seapower in the Adriatic. With its rivals Pisa and Genoa from the western side of Italy, Venice competed for leadership in the trade of goods from Muslim ports in North Africa and the eastern Mediterranean. A merchant's list from 1310 mentions some 300 "spices" (including dyestuffs, textile fibers, and raw materials) then traded, among them alum (for dyeing), 11 types; wax, 11 types; cotton, 8 types; indigo, 4 types; ginger, 5 types; paper, 4 types; and sugar, 15 types; along with cloves, caraway, tamarind, dragon's blood (a scarlet pigment), and fresh oranges.

Ghent, Bruges, and Ypres in Flanders were the only cities in western Europe—except Cordoba and Seville in Muslim Spain—that could rival the Italian cities in prosperity, trade, and industry. Enjoying comparable independence based on privileges gained by their communes from the counts of Flanders, these cities centralized the wool trade of the North Sea, transforming raw wool from Britain into woolen cloth that enjoyed a very wide market.

The Crusades

The Crusades dominated the politics of Europe from 1000 to 1200. Though touted as a series of religiously inspired military campaigns designed to recapture the Holy Land, on the Eastern shore

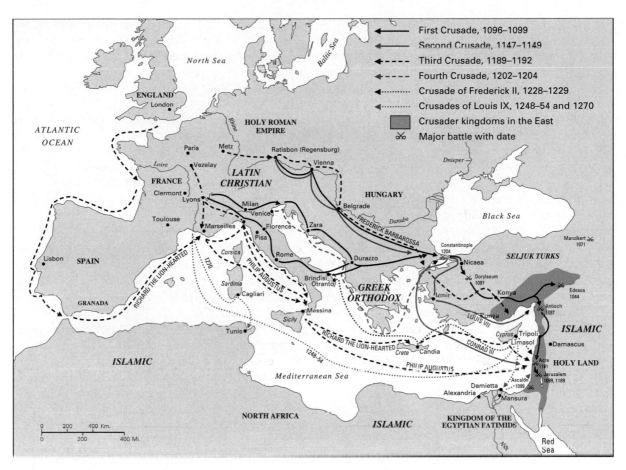

Map 9.3 The Crusades The first two crusades proceeded overland through Byzantine territory. The third crusade included contingents under the French and English kings, Philip Augustus and Richard the Lion-Hearted, that traveled by sea, and a contingent under the Holy Roman Emperor Frederick Barbarossa that took the overland route. Frederick died in southern Anatolia. Later crusades were mostly seaborne, with Sicily, Crete, and Cyprus playing important roles.

of the Mediterranean, from the Muslims, they actually were a manifestation of many of the social and economic currents of the eleventh century. Reforming leaders of the Latin Church interested in softening the warlike tone of society worked to popularize the Peace of God. This was a movement to limit fighting between feudal lords by specifying times of truce, such as during Lent (the 40 days before Easter) and on the Sunday sabbath. Ambitious rulers were looking for new lands to conquer, an objective best represented by the Norman invasions of England and Sicily. Feudal knights, particularly younger sons in

areas where the oldest son inherited everything, were becoming increasingly anxious about lacking the land they needed to maintain their noble status. Italian merchants were eager to increase trade in the eastern Mediterranean and to acquire trading posts in Muslim territory.

Several influences focused attention on the Holy Land, which had been under Muslim rule for four centuries. Pilgrimages were particularly important. Pilgrimage was an important aspect of religious life in western Europe. Pilgrims traveled in special costume under royal protection. Some were actually tramps, thieves,

Battle of knights   Though the stirrups are not shown, the triumphant knight's posture indicates that the force of his blow has forced him back in his saddle and he is bracing himself in place by pushing his feet against stirrups and his body against the cantle (back) of his saddle. Without stirrups he would fall off over his horse's rump. (British Library)

beggars, peddlers, and merchants using pilgrimage as a safe way of traveling. Others were deeply affected by the old churches and sacred relics preserved in ecclesiastical centers like Rome, Constantinople, and Jerusalem. Genuinely pious pilgrims often journeyed to fulfill a vow or as a penance for sin.

Knights who followed the popular pilgrimage route across northern Spain to pray at the shrine of Santiago de Compostela at its northwest corner learned of the expanding campaigns of the Christian kings to dislodge the Muslims. Others heard of the war conducted by seafaring Normans against the Muslims in Sicily, whom they

finally defeated in the 1090s after thirty years of fighting.

The tales of pilgrims returning from the East further induced both churchmen and nobles to think of the Muslims as a proper target of Christian militancy. Muslim rulers, who had controlled Jerusalem, Antioch, and Alexandria ever since the seventh century, generally tolerated and protected Christian pilgrims. But after 1071 that changed when a Turkish army defeated the Byzantine emperor at the Battle of Manzikert and opened the way for Turkish tribal bands, generally associated with the rise of the Seljuk Empire in Iran and Iraq (see Chapter 10), to spread throughout Anatolia. Ancient centers of Christianity previously under Byzantine control were now threatened with absorption into a growing Muslim political realm, and this peril was duly reported back to western Europe.

From time to time the Byzantine emperor Alexius Comnenus suggested to the pope and western European rulers that they help him confront the Muslim threat. In 1095, at the Council of Clermont, Pope Urban II responded. He addressed a huge crowd of people gathered in a field and called on them, as Christians, to stop fighting one another and go to the Holy Land to fight Muslims.

"God wills it!" exclaimed voices in the crowd. People cut cloth into crosses and sewed them on their shirts to symbolize their willingness to march on Jerusalem. And thus began the holy war now known as the "First Crusade," a word taken from Latin *crux* for "cross." People at the time, however, spoke not of a "crusade" but of *peregrinatio*, a "pilgrimage." Indeed, the Crusades were basically armed pilgrimages. Urban promised that crusaders who had committed sins would be freed from the normal penance, the usual reward for peaceful pilgrims to Jerusalem.

The three crusades of the eleventh and twelfth centuries signaled the end of western Europe's centuries of isolation, not just political but also intellectual. Sicily, seized from the Muslims, yielded treasures in the form of Arabic translations of Greek philosophical and scientific works and equally important original works by Arabs and Iranians. Spain yielded an even greater bounty to translators who worked in both the Christian and the Muslim kingdoms. Later, Greece was ransacked for ancient Greek manuscripts after the Venetians persuaded the leaders of the Fourth Crusade in 1204 to satisfy their financial debts by capturing Constantinople and taking over, for a century, most of the shrunken Byzantine Empire. Generations passed before all these works were translated into Latin and studied, but they eventually transformed the thought of the western Europeans, who hitherto had had little familiarity with Greek writings except through Latin intermediaries.

The impact of the Crusades on the Islamic world was not nearly so great as on Europe, even though the invaders did establish four small principalities along the eastern Mediterranean at Jerusalem, Edessa, Antioch, and Tripoli, the last surviving until 1289. Knights of the higher nobility who became the rulers of these new principalities instituted feudal laws and granted Latin clergy ecclesiastical jurisdiction despite the fact that most local Christians owed allegiance to Constantinople. Later Crusades saw western Europe's most powerful kings embarking on lengthy campaigns to show their might and prove their piety, but they seldom stayed long in the Holy Land.

The Decline of Feudal Society

The interplay of manufacturing and commercial revival in the Italian and Flemish city-states, aggressive papal and monastic reform of the Latin Church, and mass military (and thus financial) mobilization to launch the Crusades tolled the death knell of feudal society though its actual demise extended over several centuries. Feudal society had emerged unevenly and haphazardly from the fifth century onward as a response to the collapse of a unified political order, widespread violence, and severe economic regression accompanied by a decline in interregional communication. Based on Germanic custom and on remnants and recollections of Roman practices, feudal society had protected populations and productive capacities in western Europe and had generated a distinctive culture centered on the court life of the nobility. Moreover, it had provided the political and social framework within which western Europe became a truly Christian land.

Born of disunity, chaos, and poverty, feudal society was ill suited to the economic, political, and ecclesiastical revival that began to stir Europe to new life in the twelfth century and ultimately gave birth to a robust and expansive Europe in the following centuries (see Chapter 16). Nobles and serfs subsisting on the agricultural and craft production of isolated manors and minimally connected to any broader monetary or market network gradually became obsolete in a time of urban-based manufacturing, large-scale imports from the East, and the need for cash to support a noble's long trip to the Holy Land. Steady improvements in fortifications and armaments added to the financial burden of nobility, enabling a few kings and great nobles to achieve an unprecedented degree of dominance and desire to enlarge, consolidate, and economically exploit their domains.

All of these tendencies had counterparts in the area of religion. Monasteries that had lived from the yield of their lands and from the work of their serfs had been little different from feudal manors. Their abbots had played the role of ecclesiastical lords. With monastic reform, whether under Cluny or later reforming movements, the independence of abbots dwindled along with the power of many petty nobles. In the growing cities, belatedly including royal capitals like Paris and London, cathedrals took on growing importance, both as symbols of civic pride and as ecclesiastical centers of a new, reviving Europe. Cathedral building brought together the political authority, financial resources, and technical skills of urban communities. The impact of a new cathedral was therefore much greater than that of a rural monastery.

The decline of feudal society, like its initial growth, was quite diverse in different parts of Europe. In Germany and eastern Europe monarchs actually became weaker in the twelfth century and great nobles stronger. In Spain, the objective of expelling the Muslims seemed achievable after the Muslim defeat at the Battle of Las Navas de Tolosa in 1212, and this objective provided in Spain a unifying focus for political action, and eventually for national unity, that was lacking elsewhere. In Italy and Flanders, the cities protected their new-found autonomy, thwarting the efforts of monarchs and popes to draw them into their own domains.

The struggle waged by King Henry II (r. 1154–1189) to gain control of the church in England (see above) was an extension of measures to centralize the realm that had begun under Henry I (r. 1100–1135). Under the first

Henry's predecessors, the king's *curia*, or court, had been made up of his noble companions of the moment. Henry I turned it into a more formal body possessed of specialized skills. More and better records were kept. Financial and judicial functions became more professional and developed into separate government departments (financial functions were called the "Exchequer" because of the practice of calculating accounts on a table marked off like a checkerboard).

These factors did not in themselves bring feudalism to an end. Noble society seemed to be flourishing, and most of the nobility of the twelfth century never imagined that their great-grandchildren would lose many of their privileges to increasingly powerful kings. Even as the seeds of feudal decline were germinating, long-lasting expressions of feudal culture such as ideas of chivalry and courtly love were receiving their highest expression in poetry and story.

The life of western Europe's leading female noble illustrates many of the changes taking place in the turbulent twelfth century. It is also representative of the degree to which people of that era saw the political order revolving around the lives and passions of the high nobility.

In 1137, a fifteen-year-old woman named Eleanor came into a vast inheritance upon the death of her father William, duke of Aquitaine and count of Poitou. Her lands in southwestern France were richer and more extensive than those of the French king, Louis the Fat. William had nevertheless been a vassal of Louis, and Louis feared that Eleanor of Aquitaine (as she is known to history) would marry one of his enemies. So he decided to marry her to his son, the future Louis VII. Five hundred of the king's most important vassals escorted the seventeen-year-old prince to Bordeaux, the capital of Aquitaine, for the wedding. During their return to Paris, the newlyweds learned that Louis the Fat was dead. Eleanor thus left Bordeaux a duchess and arrived in Paris a queen.

Louis and Eleanor ruled with little regard for the interests of the church until 1141, when a dispute broke out between Louis and Bernard, abbot of the monastery of Clairvaux, over the appointment of a bishop. As shrewd politically as he was influential as a theologian and mystic, Bernard easily won his contest with the young king and forced him to undertake a crusade to the Holy Land. Eleanor, who had given birth to a daughter in 1145, accompanied Louis along with her own band of women equipped as knights.

Once in Antioch, Eleanor became enamored of her attractive uncle, the poet Raymond of Toulouse, and decided to renounce her royal throne and remain in Antioch as duchess of Aquitaine and countess of Poitou. One of the many ballads later written about her imagines her saying to King Louis: "Why do I renounce you? Because of your weakness. You are not worth a rotten pear." Louis, however, seized her and carried her back to France because he did not want to lose control of her valuable properties.

After a second daughter was born in 1150, Louis began to worry about the lack of a son to succeed him as king. For her part, Eleanor became interested in Count Geoffrey of Anjou, called "Plantagenet" because he always wore on his helmet a sprig of yellow broom, the plant called *genista* in Latin. In 1152 Louis had their marriage annulled. Geoffrey had died in the meantime, so Eleanor married his son Henry, soon to become King Henry II of England.

While her new husband was reforming his monarchy, Queen Eleanor gave birth to three more daughters and five sons between 1153 and 1167. At about the time the last was born, Henry fell in love with Rosamond Clifford, the daughter of a Norman knight. Although Eleanor had overlooked earlier infidelities, she became enraged by the public nature of his dalliance with Rosamond and returned to Poitiers, the capital of Poitou. A majestic, commanding personality, she attracted knights, troubadours, and storytellers from all over France to her court. The idea of chivalry as an elaborate type of courtesy paid by knights to noble ladies reached a peak in Eleanor's court.

When a revolt against King Henry by his sons misfired, he captured Poitiers and took Eleanor back to England as a prisoner. Refusing to retire from the world as abbess of a nunnery, Eleanor remained under loose detention for fifteen years.

When Henry II died in 1189, their son Richard, known as "the Lion Hearted," became king and set his mother free.

While King Richard was on crusade in the Holy Land, Eleanor ruled England, using the title *queen*. On his way back, Richard was shipwrecked and captured by enemies in Europe. Queen Eleanor raised a ransom of 100,000 silver pieces to free him and then accompanied him back to England, where he easily suppressed the revolt of his usurping brother John Lackland. When Richard died in 1199 of a chance arrow shot while fighting against King Philip Augustus of France, he left no sons. So John succeeded legitimately to the throne. Eleanor died in 1204 at the age of eighty-two.

In 1215, King John was forced by a rebellion of his greatest vassals to put his seal to Magna Carta ("Great Charter"), a document that confirmed the rights of England's great barons with respect to the Crown (see Chapter 16). This was ostensibly a victory for the idea of feudalism, though it set a precedent for negotiating limitations on the king's power that later worked in favor of the common people and against the nobility. Its objective was not to dismantle the centralized administration that John's predecessors had established but to prevent future rulers from using it tyrannically.

In France, which witnessed parallel efforts at royal centralization under Philip Augustus (r. 1180–1223), the inevitable wave of feudal resistance to growing royal power came exactly a century later (1314–1315) and resulted in a series of provincial agreements that subsequent kings were able to whittle down one by one, ultimately giving rise to unlimited power for the French kings.

CONCLUSION

T he collapse of imperial Rome was not a unique phenomenon in world history. China's Han dynasty (see Chapter 6) and the

Abbassid caliphate (discussed in Chapter 10) both dissolved into a myriad of successor states, as had Alexander the Great's short-lived empire in the fourth century B.C.E. (see Chapter 5). Although the chaos, disunity, and economic regression experienced in post-Roman western Europe were particularly severe, the cultural vitality that eventually emerged from the centuries of disorder bears comparison with other instances. The Hellenistic Age, which followed the death of Alexander in 323 B.C.E., was a remarkable period of intellectual, religious, and scientific ferment and creativity. The Tang Empire, which emerged in China in the seventh century C.E. (see Chapter 11), was a powerful new state with a distinctive and lively culture, based only in part on survivals from the Han era. And in the Middle East the emergence of a mass society based on the Islamic religion was largely a phenomenon of the period following the collapse of the central Islamic state in the tenth century (see Chapter 10). The dynamic development of Islam after this political collapse is remarkably parallel to the overwhelming influence gained by Christianity in western Europe by the end of the twelfth century.

In contrast, the Byzantine Empire continued and built on Roman practices in an economic and political environment that was both more prosperous and more peaceful than that of western Europe. Furthermore, Byzantine society became deeply Christian well before a comparable degree of Christianization had been reached in western Europe. Yet despite their success in transmitting their own version both of Christianity and of the imperial tradition to Russia and to the peoples of the Balkans, the Byzantines largely failed to demonstrate the dynamism and ferment that characterized both the Europeans to their west and the Muslims to their south.

Although historians often have been limited by their sources to the investigation of imperial greatness and expansion, the intermediate periods between empires seem to be unusually creative and culturally dynamic times, as these examples show. Perhaps one reason for this is the opportunity that imperial dissolution affords different localities and peoples to follow their own particular lines of social, economic, and cultural

development. The history of the rise and development of Islam told in the next chapter will offer an opportunity to test this hypothesis.

SUGGESTED READING

Of the many general histories of Europe during this period, Roger Collins's *Early Medieval Europe, 300–1000* (1991) is the best survey stressing institutional and political developments. Georges Duby, *The Early Growth of the European Economy* (1974), provides an outstanding overview of economic and social history reflecting up-to-date historical methods. Jacques Le Goff, *Medieval Civilization, 400–1500* (1989), puts more stress on questions of social structure. Richard W. Southern, *Western Society and the Church in the Middle Ages* (1970), offers a survey concentrating on the all-important history of the church. The same author's *The Making of the Middle Ages* (1953) is a classic that gives a memorable impression of the period based on specific lives and events. Archibald R. Lewis, *Naval Power and Trade in the Mediterranean, A.D. 500–1100* (1951), offers an unusual focus on war and trade in the Mediterranean Sea and the ebb and flow of power between Christians and Muslims.

More specialized studies of economic and technological issues include Lynn White, Jr., *Medieval Technology and Social Change* (1962), a pathbreaking work on technological history; C. M. Cipolla, *Money, Prices and Civilization in the Mediterranean World, Fifth to Seventeenth Century* (1956), an insightful and easily understood explanation of important economic matters, and Cipolla's more general history, *Before the Industrial Revolution: European Society and Economy, 1000–1700* (1980); J. C. Russell, *The Control of Late Ancient and Medieval Population* (1985), a thorough analysis of demographic history and the problems of interpreting medieval European data; and Georges Duby, *Rural Economy and Country Life in the Medieval West* (1990), a detailed portrayal of rural life accompanied by translated documents.

Good works focusing on specific countries include, on France, Pierre Riché, *Daily Life in the World of Charlemagne* (1978), and Georges Duby, *The Chivalrous Society* (1977); on England, Dorothy Whitelock, *The Beginnings of English Society* (1952), and Doris Mary Stenton,

English Society in the Early Middle Ages (1066–1307) (1951); on Italy, Edward Burman, Emperor to Emperor: Italy Before the Renaissance (1991); on Germany and the Holy Roman Empire, Timothy Reuter, Germany in the Early Middle Ages, c. 800–1056 (1991); and on Viking Scandinavia, Gwyn Jones, A History of the Vikings (1984).

Amy Kelly, Eleanor of Aquitaine and the Four Kings (1950), is an extraordinary biography of an extraordinary woman. Dhuoda, Handbook for William: A Carolingian Woman's Counsel for Her Son, trans. Carol Neel (1991), offers a firsthand look at the life of a noblewoman of the Carolingian era. More general works on women include Margaret Wade's classic popular history, A Small Sound of the Trumpet: Women in Medieval Life (1986), and Bonnie S. Anderson and Judith P. Zinsser's A History of Their Own: Women in Europe from Prehistory to the Present (1989). In the area of religion, Caroline Bynum's Jesus as Mother: Studies in the Spirituality of the High Middle Ages (1982) illustrates new trends in the study of women in this period.

Hans Eberhard Mayer's The Crusades (1988) is an excellent brief history of the crusading era. For a longer masterful account, stressing particularly the Byzantine standpoint, see Steven Runciman, A History of the Crusades, 3 vols. (1987). Benjamin Z. Kedar, Crusade and Mission: European Approaches Toward the Muslims (1988), explains the religious issues underlying the conflict.

The classic account of the revival of trade and urban life is Henri Pirenne's Medieval Cities: Their Origins and the Revival of Trade (1952). A similarly influential work is Robert S. Lopez, The Commercial Revolution of the Middle Ages, 950–1350 (1971). Lopez and Irving W. Raymond have compiled and translated an excellent collection of primary documents dealing with trade and urban life: Medieval Trade in the Mediterranean World: Illustrative Documents with Introductions and Notes (1990).

The standard histories of the Byzantine Empire are Georgij A. Ostrogorsky, History of the Byzantine State (1969), and Alexander Aleksandrovich Vasiliev, History of the Byzantine Empire, 2 vols. (1952). Volume 1 of Vasiliev's work takes the history down to 1081. Cyril Mango's Byzantium: The Empire of New Rome (1980) provides a synthesis with a strong emphasis on cultural matters. Later Byzantine history, for which conventional narratives are scarce, is unusually well covered by A. P. Kazhdan and Ann Wharton Epstein in Change in Byzantine Culture in the Eleventh and Twelfth Centuries (1985). This book stresses social and economic issues instead of religion and politics and covers broader topics than its title indicates.

NOTES

1. Lewis G. M. Thorpe, *Two Lives of Charlemagne* (Harmondsworth: Penguin, 1969).

2. Dhuoda, *Handbook for William: A Carolingian Woman's Counsel for her Son* (Lincoln: University of Nebraska Press, 1991), pp. 83–89.

3. R. W. Southern, *Western Society and the Church in the Middle Ages* (Harmondsworth: Penguin, 1970), p. 102.

4. Anne Fremantle, *A Treasury of Early Christianity* (New York: New American Library of World Literature, 1960), pp. 400–401.

5. *St. Benedict's Rule for Monasteries*, tr. Leonard J. Doyle (Collegeville, Minn.: The Liturgical Press, 1948), pp. 20–21, 75–76.

6. A. A. Vasiliev, *History of the Byzantine Empire 324–1453* (Madison: University of Wisconsin Press, 1978), Vol. I, pp. 79–80.

7. A. P. Kazhdan and Ann Wharton Epstein, *Change in Byzantine Culture in the Eleventh and Twelfth Centuries* (Berkeley: University of California Press, 1985), p. 255.

8. *Ibid.* p. 248.

CHAPTER TEN

The Sasanid Empire and the Rise of Islam, 600 B.C.E.–1200

The Sasanid Empire · The Origins of Islam

The Caliphate in Power · Islamic Civilization

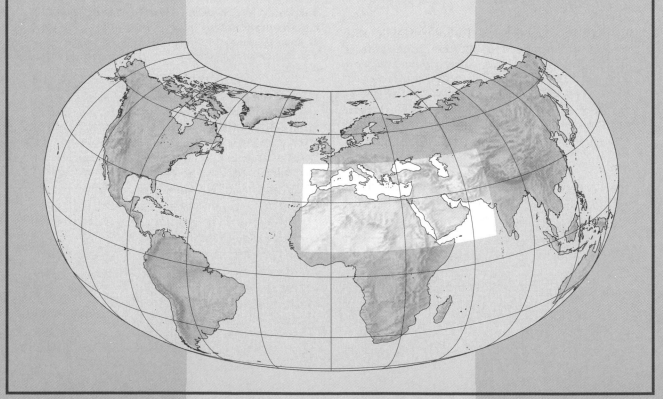

In 803 Harun al-Rashid, the ruler of the empire of Islam, abruptly dismissed and executed his long-time favorite, Ja'far, a member of the illustrious Barmakid family. He also threw Ja'far's father and brother into a dungeon, where they died. Arabic chronicles give conflicting reasons for the disgrace of the Barmakids, who had controlled the financial and administrative affairs of the empire for over twenty-five years. One report has Harun arranging a marriage of convenience between his beloved sister Abbasa and Ja'far and then becoming enraged when the pair actually engaged in marital relations. Harun's only purpose in arranging the marriage had been to facilitate social contact without violating the prohibition on Abbasa being with a man she was not related to.

The story is probably a fiction embodying a favorite theme in Islamic historical writing: the negative influence of women on government affairs. It had the zest of court gossip, however, and contributed significantly to the legendary stature of the Barmakids.

The most extraordinary part of the story was not the Barmakids' fall but their rise. Ja'far's great-grandfather had been the chief monk of a Buddhist monastery in northern Afghanistan. How did an Afghan Buddhist family acquire such power in an empire established by Arab armies, embodying Persian traditions of rule, and devoted to the religion of Islam? Although the story of Islam begins in Arabia with the Prophet Muhammad, the dramatic growth of Islam as a political, social, and cultural community involved many peoples and had roots in developments that long preceded him.

Arab conquerors in the seventh century established an empire that maintained its political cohesion for less than three centuries. But this was long enough to sustain a massive religious conversion that turned Islam from a religion of desert Arabs into a multiethnic universal faith. Islam fostered a vibrant and productive urban culture that contrasted dramatically with the urban decline of the Latin Christian West. Islamic society developed approaches to law, piety, and social relations that differed from those of the Christians, despite the Judaic roots that both religions shared.

THE SASANID EMPIRE

The rise in the third century of a new Iranian empire—the Sasanid Empire—as the foe of the Byzantine Empire seems superficially to continue the old rivalry between Rome's legions and the Parthians along the Euphrates frontier. However, behind this façade of continuity, a social and economic transformation was in the making in the Middle East. The outcome of this transformation was not a return to a simpler, more fragmented, and less urbanized pattern of life, as in western Europe. Rather, together the Sasanid Empire and the Byzantine Empire made possible a new and powerful religio-political movement: Islam.

Ardashir, a descendant of one Sasan, defeated the Parthians around 224 and established a new Iranian kingdom: the Sasanid. Unlike the Parthians, their nomadic predecessors from the northeast, the Sasanids hailed from Fars province (Persis in Greek) in southwestern Iran, the homeland of the Achaemenid dynasty, which had fallen to Alexander the Great (see Chapter 5). The Sasanids were urbane and sophisticated and established their capital on the Tigris River at Ctesiphon, near the later site of Baghdad. Thus Mesopotamia, a land populated mostly by speakers of Semitic rather than Iranian languages, was the capital province of the new Iranian dynasty.

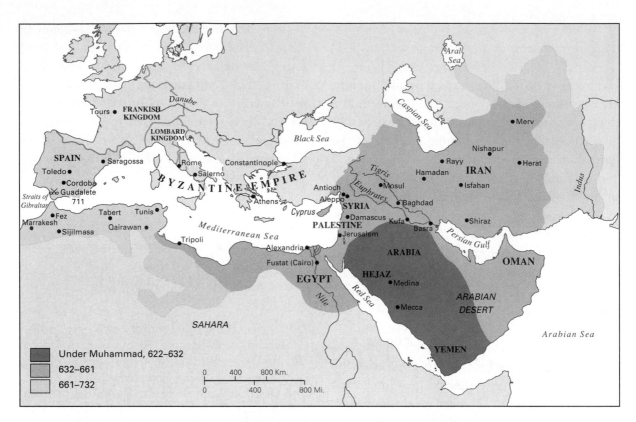

Map 10.1 Early Expansion of Muslim Rule The territory brought under Muslim rule during the Arab conquests of the first Islamic century was vast. However, the expansion of Islam as the religion of the majority of the population was much slower. In most areas outside the Arabian peninsula, the only region where Arabic was then spoken, conversion was uncommon during the first century but accelerated during the second.

Politics and Society

To their west, the new rulers confronted first the Romans and then, after 330, the Byzantines. Along their desert frontier west of the Euphrates, the Sasanids subsidized the chieftains of nomadic Arab groups to protect their empire from invasion, just as the Byzantines did with Arabs on their Jordanian frontier. This practice served to bring some Arab pastoralists into the orbit of imperial politics and culture, though others farther to the south remained isolated and independent. Farther north, the international frontier ran down the upper Euphrates River in Mesopotamia, and the rival Sasanid and Byzan-tine Empires launched numerous attacks on each other across that frontier between the 340s and 628.

Nevertheless, in times of peace, exchange between the empires flourished, allowing goods transported over the Silk Road to enter the zone of Mediterranean trade. Cities like Antioch, Damascus, and Aleppo—all in Syria—were thriving cultural, commercial, and manufacturing centers and benefited greatly from contacts with the Sasanids to the east. Just as the Arabs who traversed the desert between Syria and Mesopotamia were drawn into imperial political affairs, so these pastoralists benefited from the trade between the empires. They not only supplied camels and guides but played a significant role as merchants and organizers of caravans, especially during the mid third century flourishing of the Arab kingdom of Palmyra in the middle of the Syrian desert (see Map 10.1). Roman conquerors destroyed Palmyra's temples and colonnaded avenues in 273, but depictions of the Palmyrene caravan-god leading his camel are still visible in the ruins.

The mountains and plateaus of Iran proper formed the Sasanids' political hinterland, often ruled by the Shah's (King's) cousins or by powerful nobles. Cities there were small walled communities that served more as military strongpoints than as major centers of population and production. Society revolved around a minor, local aristocracy who lived on rural estates and cultivated the arts of hunting and war just like the noble warriors described in the sagas of ancient kings and heroes sung at their banquets. The small principalities of Central Asia that mostly lay beyond Sasanid control were home to a more developed urban culture imbued

Sasanid Shah Shapur II (309–379) The ruler hunting or banqueting is a common symbol of royalty in pre-Islamic Iran, seen here on a silver plate. Wild boar were dangerous prey. Later Muslim society considered them unclean and prohibited eating them. Aristocratic Sasanid society favored silver plates like these. After the Muslim Arabs conquered Iran in the seventh century, landed aristocracy gradually disappeared. Prosperous city dwellers made do with elegant, but cheaper, glazed pottery plates. (Smithsonian Institution, Courtesy of the Freer Gallery of Art, Washington, D.C. Neg. #34.23)

with Buddhism and buoyed by the prosperity of the Silk Road (see Chapter 8).

Sasanid political structure was unlike the feudal relationships of western Europe. Despite the dominance of powerful baronial families on the Iranian Plateau, long-lasting political fragmentation along feudal lines did not develop. Also, although Arabs and other nomadic or seminomadic peoples were numerous in mountain and desert regions, no folk migration arose comparable to that of the Germanic peoples of the late Roman empire. The Sasanid and Byzantine Empires successfully maintained central control of imperial finances and military power and found effective ways of integrating frontier peoples as mercenaries or caravaneers.

Nor did urban life and the money-based economy erode as it did in the West. The silver coins of the Sasanid rulers and the gold coins of the Byzantine emperors were plentiful, and trade with the East remained robust. The Silk Road brought new products to Mesopotamia, some of which became part of the agricultural landscape. Sasanid farmers pioneered in planting cotton, sugar cane, rice, citrus trees, eggplants, and other crops adopted from India and China. Although the acreage devoted to new crops spread slowly, these products were to become important consumption and trade items during the Islamic period following the fall of the Sasanid Empire.

Religion and Empire

The Sasanids were Zoroastrians (see Chapter 5) and established their faith, which the Parthians before them had never particularly stressed, as a state religion just as Constantine made Christianity the official religion of the Byzantine Empire in the 320s (see Chapter 6). The Zoroastrian equivalent of the patriarch of Constantinople was the *Mobadan-mobad*, "Priest of Priests," appointed by the Sasanid *Shahan-shah*, "King of Kings."

The Hellenistic kingdoms that arose from Alexander's empire and, after them, the early Roman Empire, had sponsored official cults focusing on the deified ruler, but they also had recognized the great variety of religious beliefs among their diverse populations. Moreover, the rulers and the urban upper class were often more interested in varieties of Greek philosophy than in a specific religious sect. But the proclamation of Christianity and Zoroastrianism as official faiths marked the emergence of religion as an instrument of politics both within and between the empires, thus setting a precedent for the subsequent rise of Islam as the focus of a political empire.

Both Zoroastrianism and Christianity embraced intolerance. A late-third-century inscription in Iran boasts of the persecutions of Christians, Jews, and Buddhists carried out by the Zoroastrian high priest Kartir, and the councils of Christian bishops declared many theological beliefs heretical from the fourth century onward. Yet sizable Christian and Jewish communities remained, especially in Mesopotamia, and the Christians became pawns in the political rivalry with the Byzantines, sometimes persecuted and sometimes patronized by the Sasanid kings.

Sasanid policy took advantage of the bitter schisms among the Christian sects of Byzantium. In 431 a council of bishops called by the Byzantine emperor declared the Nestorian Christians heretics for overemphasizing the human side of Christ's nature. The Nestorians believed that human and divine natures existed side by side in Jesus and that Mary was not the mother of God, as many other Christians maintained, but the mother of the human Jesus. After the ruling the Nestorians sought refuge under the Sasanid shah and eventually spread their missionary activities across Central Asia. Ten years earlier, in 421, war had broken out with Byzantium because of Sasanid persecution of Christians. Moreover, Armenia, whose Christian population had cultural links with Iran, was a bone of contention between the empires. The Armenian Apostolic Church used the Armenian language in its services and hewed to Monophysite doctrine, which was considered heretical by the Byzantine state (see Chapter 9).

In the third century a preacher named Mani founded a new religion in Mesopotamia known as Manichaeism. He preached a dualist faith—a struggle between good and evil—theologically derived from Zoroastrianism. Although he first enjoyed the favor of the shah, Mani was martyred in 276 with many of his followers. Yet his religion survived and spread widely. The Nestorian missionaries in Central Asia competed with Manichaean missionaries for converts.

The Arabs who guarded the desert frontiers of the two empires became enmeshed in this web of religious conflict. Those subsidized by the Byzantines adopted the Monophysite faith; the allies of the Sasanids, the Nestorian. Thus both Arab groups retained a measure of religious independence from their patrons; and through them, knowledge of Christianity penetrated deeper into the Arabian peninsula during the fifth and sixth centuries.

The politicizing of religion contrasts sharply with earlier periods of East-West rivalry along the Euphrates frontier during the time of the Greek city states (see Chapter 5) and the Roman-Parthian rivalry (see Chapter 8) when language, ethnic identity, or citizenship in a particular city-state defined political allegiances. Now, religion penetrated into all aspects of community life. Most subjects of the Byzantine emperors and Sasanid shahs identified themselves first and foremost as members of a religious community. Their schools and law courts were religious. They looked on priests, monks, rabbis, and mobads as moral guides in daily life. Most books were on religious subjects. And in some areas, religious leaders represented their flocks even in secular matters such as tax collection.

As we saw in Chapter 9, western Europe was experiencing a thoroughgoing reorientation toward Christianity during the centuries following the fall of the Western Roman empire. The Sasanid and Byzantine territories, however, were marked by much more religious diversity. They included many different Christian, Jewish, and Zoroastrian communities along with smaller groups adhering to other faiths. Relations between religious groups, fluctuating between tolerance and intolerance, were a major determinant of social order or conflict.

THE ORIGINS OF ISLAM

The activities of the Arabs who lived beyond the frontiers of the empire were seldom of interest to the Sasanid rulers. The Sasanids displayed some interest in the Arab side of the Persian Gulf and to Yemen, which were along their maritime trade routes. But as for the interior of the Arabian peninsula, the Sasanid view, evident in a phrase attributed in later centuries to Muhammad, was that the Arabs were "monkeys on the backs of camels."

Yet it was precisely in the interior of Arabia, far from the gaze and political reach of the Sasanid and Byzantine Empires, that the religion of Islam was to take form and inspire a movement that would humble the proud emperors. Both the socioreligious complexity of the Sasanid and Byzantine Empires and their inattention to events far from their borders are key to understanding the phenomenal rise and success of Islam.

The Arabian Peninsula Before Muhammad

Throughout history most of the people living on the Arabian peninsula have lived in settled communities rather than as pastoral nomads. The highlands of Yemen are fertile and abundantly watered by the spring monsoon blowing northward along the East African coast. The interior mountains farther east in southern Arabia are much more arid but in some places receive enough water to support farming and village life. And small inlets along the coast favored the rise of an occasional fishing and trading community. These regions are largely cut off from the Arabian interior by the enormous sea of sand known as the "Empty Quarter." In the seventh century, most people in southern Arabia knew more about Africa, India, and the Persian Gulf than about the forbidding interior of the great peninsula and the scattered camel- and sheep-herding nomads who lived there.

Exceptions to this pattern were mostly associated with caravan trading. Several kingdoms—Qataban, Himyar, Sabae (biblical Sheba)—rose and fell in Yemen, leaving stone ruins and enigmatic inscriptions to testify to their bygone prosperity. From these commercial entrepôts came frankincense and myrrh (crystallized resins harvested from low trees that grew in eastern Yemen). Nomads derived income from providing camels, guides, and safe passage to merchants wanting to transport incense northward, where the fragrant substances had long been burned in religious rituals. Return caravans brought manufactured products from Mesopotamia and the Mediterranean.

Just as the Silk Road enabled small towns in Central Asia to become major trading centers, so the trans-Arabian trade gave rise to desert caravan cities (see Voices and Visions: Caravan Cities, in Chapter 8). The earliest and most prosperous, Petra in southern Jordan and Palmyra in northern Syria, were swallowed up by Rome. This, coupled with early Christians' distaste for incense, which seemed too much a feature of pagan worship, contributed to a slackening of trade in high-value goods in Sasanid times and a period of political turbulence among the nomadic groups. Nevertheless, trade across the Arabian desert did not lapse altogether. Camels, leather, and gold and other minerals mined in the mountains of western Arabia, took the place of frankincense and myrrh as exports, and grain and manufactured goods were imported. This reduced trade kept alive the relations between the Arabs and the settled farming regions to the north forged in earlier centuries, and it familiarized the Arabs who accompanied the caravans with the cultures and lifestyles of the Sasanid and Byzantine empires.

In the desert, Semitic polytheism, with its worship of natural forces and celestial bodies, still thrived but was affected by other religions. Christianity, as practiced by the Arab tribes guarding the imperial frontiers in Jordan and southern Mesopotamia, and Judaism, possibly carried by refugees from the Roman expulsion of the Jews from their homeland in the first century C.E., made inroads on polytheism.

Mecca, a late-blooming caravan city, lies in a barren mountain valley halfway between Yemen and Syria along the Red Sea coast of Arabia (see Map 10.2). The torrid coastal plain was ill suited to caravan travel, giving Mecca a good position in the trade from Yemen to the north and east. A nomadic kin group known as the Quraysh settled in Mecca in the fifth century and assumed control of this trade. Mecca rapidly achieved a measure of prosperity, partly because it was too far from Byzantine Syria, Sasanid Iraq, and Ethiopian-controlled Yemen for them to attack. It came nowhere near to rivaling the earlier luxuries of Palmyra and Petra, but some subgroups of the Quraysh became wealthy.

Mecca was also a cult center. A cubical shrine called the Ka'ba, a holy well called Zamzam, and a sacred precinct surrounding the two wherein killing was prohibited contributed to the emergence of Mecca as a pilgrimage site. Some Meccans associated the shrine with stories known to Jews and Christians. They regarded Abraham (Ibrahim in Arabic) as the builder of the Ka'ba, and they identified a site outside Mecca as the location where God asked Abraham to sacrifice his son. The son was not Isaac (Ishaq in Arabic), the son of Sarah, but Ishmael (Isma'il in Arabic), the son of Hagar, cited in the Hebrew Old Testament as the forefather of the Arabs.

Muhammad in Mecca

Muhammad was born in Mecca in 570 and grew up an orphan in the house of his uncle, Abu Talib. He engaged in trade and married a widow named Khadija, also a member of the Quraysh, whose caravan interests he superintended. They had several children, but their one son died in childhood. Around the year 610, Muhammad adopted the practice of meditating at night in the mountainous terrain around Mecca. During one night vigil, known to later religious tradition as "The Night of Power and Excellence," a being whom Muhammad later understood to be the angel Gabriel (Jibra'il in Arabic) spoke to him:

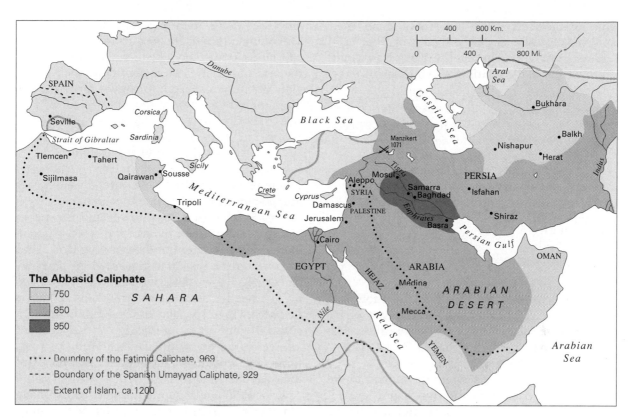

Map 10.2 Rise and Fall of the Abbasid Caliphate Though Abbasid rulers occupied the caliphal seat in Iraq from 750 to 1250, when Mongol armies destroyed Baghdad, real political power waned sharply and steadily after 850. Nevertheless, the idea of the caliphate remained central to Sunni Muslim political theory. The rival caliphates of the Fatimids (909–1171) and Spanish Umayyads (929–976) were comparatively short-lived.

Proclaim! In the name of your Lord who created.
Created man from a clot of congealed blood.
Proclaim! And your Lord is the Most Bountiful.
He who has taught by the pen.
Taught man that which he knew not.[1]

Over the next three years he shared this and subsequent revelations only with his closest friends and family members. This period culminated in Muhammad's conviction that the words he was hearing were from God (Allah in Arabic). Khadija, his uncle Abu Talib's son Ali, his friend Abu Bakr, and others close to him shared this conviction. The revelations continued until Muhammad's death in 632.

Like most people in the ancient world, includ-

ing Christians and Jews, the Arabs believed in unseen spirits: gods, desert spirits called *jinns*, demons known as *shaitans*, and so forth. They further believed, just as most other ancient peoples did, that certain individuals had contact with the spirit world. Some were oracles or seers; others poets, who were thought to be possessed by a jinn. Therefore, when Muhammad began to recite his sonorous rhymed revelations in public, many people believed that he was inspired by an unseen spirit even as they questioned whether that spirit was, as Muhammad asserted, the one true god.

The content of Muhammad's earliest revelations called on people to witness that one god had created the universe and everything in it, including themselves. At the end of time, their souls would be judged, their sins balanced against their good deeds. The blameless would go to paradise; the sinful would taste hellfire:

> By the night as it conceals the light;
> By the day as it appears in glory;
> By the mystery of the creation of male and female;
> Verily, the ends ye strive for are diverse.
> So he who gives in charity and fears God,
> And in all sincerity testifies to the best,
> We will indeed make smooth for him the path to Bliss.
> But he who is a greedy miser and thinks himself self-sufficient,
> And gives the lie to the best,
> We will indeed make smooth for him the path to misery.[2]

All people were called to submit themselves to God and accept Muhammad as the last of his messengers. Those who did so were called *muslim*, meaning one who makes "submission," *islam*, to the will of God.

Because earlier messengers mentioned in the revelations included Noah, Moses, and Jesus, it was clear to Muhammad's hearers that what he was saying was in agreement with the Judaism and Christianity they were already somewhat familiar with. Yet his revelations were distinctly different. They charged the Jews and Christians with being negligent in preserving God's revealed word, just as other peoples, such as those of Sodom and Gomorrah, to whom God had sent the prophet Lot, had rejected it outright. Thus, even though the Ka'ba, which superseded Jerusalem as the focus of Muslim prayer in 624, was founded by Abraham/Ibrahim, whom Muslims consider the first Muslim, and even though many revelations narrated stories also found in the Bible, Muhammad's followers considered his revelation more perfect than that of the Bible.

Some non-Muslim scholars have maintained that Muhammad's revelations appealed especially to Meccans who were distressed that wealth was replacing kinship as the most important aspect of social relations. Verses criticizing taking pride in wealth and neglecting obligations to orphans and other powerless people are seen as conveying a message of social reform. Other scholars, along with most Muslims, consider Muhammad's revelations an oral document of enormous power and beauty. The force of its rhetoric and poetic vision, coming in the Muslim view directly from God, thus goes far to explain Muhammad's early success.

The Formation of the Umma

Though conceding that Muhammad's eloquence might stem from possession by a jinn, most Meccan leaders felt that their power and prosperity would be threatened by acceptance of Muhammad as the sole agent of the one true God. They put pressure on his kin to disavow him, and they persecuted the weakest of his followers. Stymied by this hostility, Muhammad and his followers fled Mecca in 622 to take up residence in the agricultural community of Medina 215 miles (346 kilometers) to the north. This carefully planned flight, the *hijra*, marks the beginning of the Muslim calendar.

Prior to the hijra, representatives of the major kin groups of Medina had met with Muhammad and agreed to accept and protect him and his community of Muslims because they saw him as an inspired leader who could calm their perpetual feuding. Together, the Meccan migrants and major groups in Medina bound themselves into a single *umma*, a community defined solely by acceptance of Islam and of Muhammad as the "Messenger of God," his most common title. Three Jewish kin groups chose to retain their own faith. Their decision is one reason why Muslims changed the direction of their prayer away from Jerusalem and toward the Ka'ba in 624.

During the last decade of his life, Muhammad took active responsibility for his umma. The Meccan immigrants in the community were terribly vulnerable without the support of their Meccan kinsmen. Fresh revelations provided a framework for regulating social and legal affairs and stirred the Muslims to fight against the still-unbelieving city of Mecca. Sporadic war, much of it conducted by raiding and negotiation with desert nomads, sapped Mecca's strength and convinced many Meccans that God was on

Muhammad's side. In 630 Mecca surrendered, and Muhammad and his followers made the pilgrimage to the Ka'ba unhindered.

Muhammad did not return to Mecca again. Medina had grown into a bustling Muslim city-state. The Jews, whom he accused of disloyalty during the war, had been expelled or eliminated. Delegations from tribes all over Arabia came to meet the new leader, and Muhammad sent emissaries back with them to teach them about Islam and collect their alms. Whether he planned or desired it or not, Muhammad's mission to bring God's message to humanity had resulted in his unchallenged control of a state that was coming to dominate the Arabian peninsula. Yet unlike preceding short-lived nomadic kingdoms, the supremacy of the Medinan state was based not on kinship but on a common faith in a single god.

In 632, after a brief illness, Muhammad died. Within twenty-four hours a group of Medinan leaders, along with three of Muhammad's close friends, determined that Abu Bakr, one of the earliest believers and the father of Muhammad's favorite wife A'isha, should succeed him. They called him the *khalifa*, or "successor," the English version of which is *caliph*. But calling Abu Bakr a successor did not clarify the capacity in which he was succeeding the Prophet. Everyone knew that neither Abu Bakr nor anyone else could receive revelations, and they likewise knew that Muhammad's revelations had made no provision for succession, or for any government purpose beyond maintaining the Muslim community, the *umma*. Indeed, some people thought the world would soon end because God's last messenger was dead.

Abu Bakr's immediate task was to reestablish and expand Muslim authority over Arabia's many nomadic and settled communities. After Muhammad's death, some had abandoned their allegiance to Medina or even switched allegiance to would-be prophets of their own. Muslim armies fought hard to confirm the authority of the newborn caliphate. In the process, some fighting spilled over into non-Arab areas in Iraq.

Abu Bakr summoned those who had acted as secretaries for Muhammad and ordered them to organize the revelations into a book. Hitherto

Rise and Fall of the Caliphate

611	Muhammad's first revelations
632–634	Abu Bakr first caliph
661	Civil war ends; Umayyads rule from Damascus
750	Abbasids overthrow Umayyads, caliphate moves to Iraq
836–892	Capital at Samarra: Turkish troops dominate caliphate
909	Shi'ite Fatimid caliphate in Tunisia
945	Buyids occupy Baghdad, strip caliph of temporal power
976	Spanish Umayyad caliphate dissolves, successor states quarrel
1171	End of Fatimid caliphate; Saladin restores Sunni rule in Egypt
1258	Mongols sack Baghdad, kill Abbasid caliph
1517	Last Abbasid caliph dies; Ottomans take Cairo

written haphazardly on pieces of leather or bone, the verses of revelation were now written as a single document on parchment and gathered into chapters. The resulting book, which acquired its final form when Uthman, the third caliph, ordered a definitive fixing of its short vowels, which are not normally indicated in Arabic script, was called the Quran, or the Recitation. Muslims regard it not as the words of Muhammad but as the unalterable word of God. As such, it is comparable not so much to the Bible, a book written by many hands over a long period of time, as to the person of Jesus Christ, who, according to Christian belief, is a direct manifestation of God.

Though theoretically united in its acceptance of God's will, the umma soon fell prey to human disagreement over the succession to the caliphate. The first civil war in Islam followed the assassination of the third caliph, Uthman, in 656. His assassins, rebels from the army, nominated to succeed him Ali, Muhammad's first cousin and husband of his daughter Fatima. Ali had been passed over three times previously even though many people considered him to be the natural heir to the Prophet's mantle. Indeed, he and his supporters felt that Muhammad had indicated as much in public remarks, though other Muslims interpreted his words differently.

When Ali accepted the nomination to be caliph, two of Muhammad's close companions and his favorite wife A'isha challenged him. Ali defeated them in the Battle of the Camel (656), so called because the fighting raged around the camel on which A'isha was seated in an enclosed woman's saddle. But blood had been spilled within the umma. After the battle, the governor of Syria, Mu'awiya, a kinsman of Uthman from the Umayya subgroup of the Quraysh, renewed the challenge. Inconclusive battle gave way to arbitration. The arbitrators decided that Uthman had been killed unjustly and that Ali had been at fault in accepting the nomination. Ali rejected the arbitrators' findings, but before he could resume fighting, he was killed by one of his own supporters, who faulted him for agreeing to arbitration in the first place. Mu'awiya offered Ali's son Hasan a dignified retirement in the holy cities and thus emerged as caliph in 661.

Mu'awiya chose his own son, Yazid, to succeed him and thus instituted the Umayyad dynasty. Yazid aroused opposition in 680 when he ordered the interception and killing of Hasan's brother Husain, and his family, when Husain tried to reestablish the right of Ali's family to rule. Sympathy for Husain's martyrdom was pivotal in the transformation of a political movement, the Party of Ali—in Arabic, Shi'at Ali, or Shi'ites for short—into a religious sect.

Several variations in Shi'ite belief developed, but Shi'ites have always agreed that Ali was the rightful successor to Muhammad and that God's choice as *Imam*, or leader of the Muslim community, at any given time is one or another of Ali's descendants. Because the Shi'ites were seldom strong enough to establish their Imams in power, their religious feelings came to focus on outpourings of sympathy for Husain and other martyrs and on messianic dreams of one of their Imam's someday triumphing.

Those Muslims who thought the first three caliphs had been properly selected gradually came to be called the People of Tradition and Community—in Arabic, Ahl al-Sunna wa'l-Jama'a, or Sunnis for short. As for Ali's militant followers who had abhorred his acceptance of arbitration in a matter they regarded as already determined by God, they evolved into small and rebellious Kharijite sects (from *kharaja* meaning "to secede or rebel"). These three main divisions of Islam, the last one now quite minor, still survive. Today the umma has grown to over 800 million people.

THE CALIPHATE IN POWER

The Islamic caliphate was transformed into a mighty empire by the conquests carried out by the Arabs after Muhammad's death. It lasted until 1923, when the secular government of the newly established Republic of Turkey voted to abolish it. During the last thousand years or so of its existence, however, it only occasionally exerted real power. By the late 800s the caliphs already were losing control as one piece after another of their huge realm broke away. Yet they always retained the respect of the Sunni community, and the idea of a caliphate, however unrealistic it became, remained a touchstone of Sunni belief in the unity of the umma.

The residual religious authority of the declining caliphate cannot be compared with the authority of the popes in Rome or the patriarchs in Constantinople. Islam never recognized a single person as the absolute arbiter of true belief with the power to expel heretics and discipline clergy. Thus the caliphs had little theoretical basis for reestablishing their originally universal authority over the umma once they began to lose political and military power.

The Islamic Conquests

Arab conquests outside Arabia began under the second caliph, Umar (r. 634–644), possibly prompted by the first forays into Iraq. Within

Tomb of the Samanids in Bukhara   This early tenth century structure has the basic layout of a Zoroastrian fire temple: a dome on top of a cube. However, geometric ornamentation in baked brick marks it as an early masterpiece of Islamic architecture. The Samanid family achieved independence as rulers of northeastern Iran and western central Asia in the tenth century. (Private collection)

fifteen years Arab armies, organized according to kin groups, had wrenched Syria and Egypt— twenty years later Tunisia—away from the Byzantine Empire and defeated the Sasanid shah, Yazdigird III (r. 632–651) (see Map 10.1). After a decade-long lull, expansion began again. In 711, Spain fell to an Arab-led army mostly composed of Algerian and Moroccan Berbers, who, as nomads, had fallen in rather easily with Arab plans. In the same year, Sind, the southern Indus River valley and westernmost region of India, succumbed to partially seaborne invaders from Iraq.

Although a few pieces of territory were added later, such as Sicily in the ninth century, the extent of Muslim dominion remained roughly stable for the next three centuries. After that, conquest began anew in India, Anatolia, and Africa even as Islam was expanding peacefully by trade in these and other areas (see Chapter 15).

Muslim chroniclers portray the Arab conquests as manifestations of God's will. Non-Muslim historians have had a more difficult time explaining them. The speed and political cohesiveness of the campaigns of these warriors from Arabia set them apart from the piecemeal incursions of the Germanic peoples or the Vikings. Lust for booty, a frequently offered explanation, exaggerates the idea that pastoral Arab society was naturally war-like. A majority of the Arabs lived in settled communities, and many of the nomadic groups had long experience in servicing the caravan trade. Greed also fails to explain the persistence of the campaigns in regions where difficult terrain slowed the conquest and booty was scarce. Yet the alternative theory—fanatic religious fervor—ignores the fact that most of the warriors had no firsthand experience of life in Medina and knew comparatively little about Islam. Moreover, non-Arab converts to Islam were limited to a marginal role in the fighting, and certain Christian Arab kin groups were allowed to participate in the conquests without converting, as if Arab ethnicity rather than religion defined the movement.

Nor were the Arabs' adversaries powerless or fatally divided by religious quarrels as some historians have suggested. Although the Byzantine and Sasanid Empires had pummeled each other in a war that shortly preceded the Arab conquests, they still resisted the initial Muslim onslaught. Indeed, the Byzantines successfully defended their Anatolian heartland, despite recurrent Muslim attacks, for four centuries after their loss of Syria, Egypt, and Tunisia. Moreover, even though the Muslim rulers tolerated their non-Muslim subjects, most Christians, Zoroastrians, and Jews knew absolutely nothing about Muhammad or Islam while the conquests were under way and thus could not have acquiesced in Arab rule in anticipation of its leniency.

Historians have further been puzzled by the absence of a single great war leader like Alexander the Great. Three possible explanations present themselves. First, Muhammad himself died before the conquests began. Second, the caliphs rarely led an army. And third, the kin-group organization of the armies and the geographical sweep of the campaigns called for many commanders, whose abilities ranged from outstanding to mediocre.

The best explanation for this watershed in world history, the establishment of the caliphate through conquest as a great empire, is that the close Meccan companions of the Prophet were men of political and economic sophistication who were truly inspired by their experience of his charisma. They guided the conquests. The social structure and hardy nature of Arab society lent itself to flexible military operations, and the authority of Medina, reconfirmed during the caliphate of Abu Bakr, assured obedience.

More important than any specific military quality, however, was the decision taken during Umar's caliphate to prohibit the Arab pastoral groups from taking over conquered territory for their own use. Umar tied army service, with its regular pay and occasional windfalls of booty, to residence in large military camps—two in Iraq, one in Egypt, and one in Tunisia. The desert fringe areas of Syria seem to have been more open to dispersed Arab occupation. East of Iraq, Arabs were assigned to much smaller garrison towns at strategically crucial locations, though one large garrison was established at Marv in present-day Turkmenistan.

Down to the early eighth century, this policy not only kept the armies together and ready for action but preserved life in the countryside, where at least three-fourths of the population lived, virtually unchanged. Most people who became subjects of the caliphate by conquest probably never saw an Arab during their lifetimes, and only a tiny proportion, in Syria and Iraq, understood the Arabic language.

Spread over the largest territorial empire ever achieved, the million or so Arabs who participated in the conquests constituted a small, self-isolated ruling minority living on the taxes paid by a vastly larger non-Arab, non-Muslim subject population. Far from requiring their conquered subjects to convert, the Arabs had little material incentive to encourage conversion; and there is no evidence of a coherent missionary effort to spread Islam during the conquest period. All of these factors contradict the common assumption that the Arabs sought to force their faith on the peoples they conquered.

The Umayyad and Abbasid Caliphates

The Umayyad caliphs who came to power in 661 presided more over an ethnically defined Arab realm than over an Islamic empire. Ruling from Damascus, they stemmed from a wealthy Meccan family that initially had opposed Muhammad. Their military forces were composed almost entirely of Muslim Arab warriors. They adopted and adapted the administrative practices of their Sasanid and Byzantine predecessors, as had the four caliphs who preceded them. Only gradually did they replace non-Muslim secretaries and tax officials with Muslims and introduce Arabic as the language of government. A major symbolic step was the introduction of distinctively Muslim silver and gold coins early in the eighth century. From that time on, silver dirhams and gold dinars bearing Arabic religious phrases but devoid of images held pride of place in monetary exchanges from Morocco to the borders of China. Islamic coins were even imitated occasionally in England and France.

The Umayyad dynasty fell in 750 after a decade of growing unrest from many quarters. Converts to Islam by that date were no more than 10 percent of the indigenous population, but they were numerically significant because of the comparatively small number of Arab warriors, and they resented not achieving equal status with the Arabs. The Arabs of Iraq and elsewhere felt the Syrian Arabs were too powerful in caliphal affairs. Pious Muslims looked askance at the secular and even irreligious behavior of the caliphs. And Shi'ites and Kharijites attacked the Umayyad family's religious legiti-

Frescoes from the caliphal palace in the Syrian desert Painted early in the eighth century, these scenes show a stage of Islamic art before calligraphy and geometric ornament became standard. The bottom scene is strikingly similar to the royal hunt depicted on page 281, but the rider has been stripped of royal crown and fancy dress. The top scene reflects Sasanian banqueting and entertainment motifs. The lute and flute became popular instruments in Muslim society, but some religious authorities frown on music. (Syria Museum, Damascus)

macy as rulers, giving rise to a number of rebellions.

One rebellion, in the region of Khurasan in northeastern Iran, Afghanistan, and Central Asia, overthrew the last Umayyad caliph. Even with triumph at hand, however, it was uncertain on whose behalf the fight had been fought. Many supporters of the rebellion were Shi'ites who thought they were fighting for the family of Ali.

Dome of the Rock of Jerusalem   Begun in 687 with a Byzantine architectural layout, this shrine is a monument to the Muslim belief that Muhammad, riding a miraculous steed called al-Buraq, ascended to heaven on a night journey from this point. It is located on the great artificial mound where the Jewish temple was situated before its destruction by the Romans in 70 C.E. (Laurie Platt Winfrey, Inc.)

As it turned out, the secret organization that coordinated the revolt was loyal to the family of Abbas, one of Muhammad's uncles. Some of the Abbasid caliphs who ruled after 750 were lenient toward their relatives in Ali's family, and one even flirted with transferring the caliphate to them. The Abbasid family, however, held on to the caliphate until 1258, when Mongol invaders killed the last of them in Baghdad (see Chapter 13). A branch of the family resumed the title in Cairo a few years later, establishing a new caliphate that lasted until 1517, but the Cairo Abbasids were mere puppets of local warlords.

At the outset the Abbasid dynasty made a fine show of leadership and concern for Islam. Theology and religious law became preoccupations at court and among a growing community of scholars, along with interpretation of the Quran, collection of the sayings of the Prophet, and Arabic grammar. Some caliphs fought on the Byzantine frontier to expand Islam. Others sponsored ambitious projects to translate the great works of Greek, Persian, and Indian thought into Arabic such as the writings of Aristotle and the Sanskrit book of instructive animal fables, the *Panchatantra.*

At the same time, the new dynasty, with its roots among the semi-Persianized Arabs of Khurasan, gradually adopted many of the ceremonials and customs of the Sasanid shahs. Government grew increasingly complex in Baghdad, the newly built capital city. As more and more non-Arabs converted to Islam, the ruling elite became more cosmopolitan. Greek, Iranian, Central Asian, and African cultural currents met in the capital and gave rise to an abundance of literary products, a process greatly facilitated by the timely introduction of papermaking from China. Arab poets neglected the traditional odes extolling life in the desert and wrote instead to praise their patrons, the drinking of wine (despite its prohibition in Islam), or other features of the vibrant urban scene.

The translations of Aristotle into Arabic, the founding of the main currents of theology and law, and the splendor of the Abbasid court—reflected in stories of *The Arabian Nights* set in the time of Harun al-Rashid (r. 776–809)—in some respects warrant the designation of the early Abbasid period as a "golden age." Yet the refinement of Baghdad culture only slowly made its way into the provinces. Egypt was still predominantly Christian and Coptic-speaking in the early Abbasid period. Iran never did adopt the Arabic language as a spoken tongue. Spain (in Arabic al-Andalus), where an Umayyad fleeing the overthrow of his family in 750 had created an independent state, was affected by Berber, Visigothic, Jewish, and Roman traditions quite different from those in the East. And North Africa freed itself almost entirely of caliphal rule: Morocco and Algeria through Kharijite revolts in 740, Tunisia after 800 by agreeing to pay a regular tribute to Baghdad.

Moreover, the gradual conversion to Islam of the conquered population did not accelerate until the second quarter of the ninth century. But by that time most social discrimination against non-Arab converts had faded away, and the Arabs themselves—at least those living in cosmopolitan urban settings—had abandoned their previously strong attachment to kinship and ethnic identity. If the expression "golden age of Islam" implies a mass, multilingual, multiethnic society of Muslims with only minority non-Muslim elements, it existed around the end of the tenth century. By then, however, the Abbasid caliphate had lost most of its power.

Political Fragmentation

The decline of Abbasid power became evident in the second half of the ninth century when the pace of conversion to Islam was at its peak (see Map 10.2). The idea of a single government ruling an empire stretching almost a quarter of the way around the world would be hard to entertain even under modern conditions. But the Abbasids had to reckon with the fact that caravans traveled only 20 miles (32 kilometers) a day, and dispatches through the official post system usually did not exceed a hundred miles (160 kilometers) a day. News of revolts on the frontier took weeks to reach Baghdad. Military responses might take months. Economically, it was hard to centralize tax payments, which were often made in grain or other produce rather than in cash, and to ensure that provincial governors forwarded the proper amounts to Baghdad. Moreover, coins were minted in many locations, providing yet another opportunity for local strongmen to profit from seizing power.

When the first Arab garrisons with their surrounding communities of Muslims had been strung like beads along communication routes that crossed territory populated mostly by non-Muslims, revolts against Arab rule had always been feared. Hence, the Muslim community, the umma, had had every reason to cling together, despite the long distances. Nobody knew whether Islam would become a permanent feature of society or whether someday, somehow, foreign foes or a resurgence of non-Muslim strength within the caliphate would reverse the apparent tide of history.

With the massive conversion of the population to Islam, this perception fundamentally changed. The idea that Islam might pass away or be destroyed faded as Muslims became the overwhelming majority. At the same time, it became increasingly apparent that a highly centralized empire meant wealth and splendor for the capital but did not necessarily serve the interests of people in the provinces. Many eighth-century revolts had been directed against Arab or Muslim domination. By the middle of the ninth century, this type of rebellion gave way to movements within the Islamic community that concentrated on seizure of territory and formation of a principality. None of the states carved out of the Abbasid caliphate after 850 repudiated or even threatened Islam. What they did was prevent tax revenues from flowing to Baghdad, thereby increasing the prosperity of the locality. It is hardly surprising that the local Muslim communities either supported such rebels or remained neutral.

Increasingly starved for funds by breakaway provinces and by a fall in revenues from Iraq itself, the caliphate entered a period of crisis in the late ninth century. Distrusting the generals and troops from outlying areas, the caliphs purchased Turkic slaves (*Mamluks*) from Central Asia and established them as a standing army. Well trained and hardy, the Turks proved an effective military force. But they were also expensive. When the government could not pay them, the Mamluks took it on themselves to seat and unseat caliphs, a process made easier by the construction of a new capital at Samarra, north of Baghdad on the Tigris River. There the Turks dominated the court without interference from an unruly Baghdad population that regarded them as rude and highhanded. Samarra weakened the caliphate in another way as well. The money and effort that went into building the huge city, which was occupied only from 835 to 892, sapped the caliphs' financial strength and deflected labor from more productive pursuits.

In 945, after several attempts at finding a strongman who would reform government administration and restore military power, the Abbasid caliphate itself fell under the control of new rulers from the mountains of northern Iran, the remote and unsophisticated province of Daylam. Led by the Buyid family, they conquered western Iran as well as Iraq and divided their territory among leading family members, each of whom ruled his own principality. After almost two centuries of glory, the sun began to set on Baghdad. The Abbasid caliph remained, but he was subject to the control of a Buyid prince or his lieutenant. Being Shi'ites, the Buyids had no special reverence for the Sunni caliph. But, according to their particular Shi'ite sect, the twelfth and

last divinely appointed Imam had disappeared around 873 and would return as a messiah only at the end of the world. Thus they retained the caliph to help control their predominantly Sunni subjects, who regarded him as a rightful ruler, while the Bayids themselves disregarded his views.

Dynamic growth in outlying provinces paralleled the caliphate's gradual loss of temporal power. In the east, the dynasty of the Samanids, one of several Iranian families to achieve independent rule, presided over a glittering court in Bukhara, a major city on the Silk Road (see Map 10.1). The Samanid princes patronized literature and learning much as the early Abbasids had, but the language they favored was Persian written in Arabic letters. For the first time, a non-Arabic literature rose to challenge the eminence of Arabic within the Islamic world. The new Persian poetry and belles lettres foreshadowed the world of today, in which Iran sharply distinguishes itself from the Arab world.

In Egypt a Shi'ite ruler established himself as a rival caliph in 969 after the sixty-year struggle of his family, the Fatimids, to extend their power beyond an initial base in Tunisia. His governing complex outside Fustat was named Cairo, and for the first time Egypt became a major cultural, intellectual, and political center of Islam (see Map 10.2). The al-Azhar Mosque built at this time remains a paramount religious and educational center to this day. Although the Fatimid family was Shi'ite, their religious influence on Egypt was rather slight during their two centuries of rule. Most of the population remained Sunni. Nevertheless, the abundance of their gold coinage, derived from West African sources, made them an economic power in the Mediterranean.

Cut off from the rest of the Islamic world by the Strait of Gibraltar and, from 740 onward, by independent city-states in Morocco and Algeria, Spain developed a distinctive Islamic culture (see Map 10.1). Historians disagree on how rapidly and completely the Spanish population converted to Islam. If we assume that the process was similar to what took place in the eastern re-

The Fraternity of Beggars

Beggars, tricksters, and street performers were considered members of a single loose fraternity: Banu Sasan, or Tribe of Sasan. Tales of their tricks and exploits amused staid, pious Muslims, who often encountered them in cities and on their scholarly travels. Beggars and scholars were among the most mobile elements of the population. These descriptive verses come from a tenth-century poet who studied beggars' jargon and way of life.

For we are the lads, the only lads who really matter, on land or on sea.
We exact a tax from all mankind, from China to Egypt,
And to Tangier; indeed, our steeds range over every land of the world.
When one region gets too hot for us, we simply leave it for another one.
The whole world is ours, and whatever is in it, the lands of Islam and the lands of unbelief alike.
Hence we spend the summers in snowy lands, whilst in winter we migrate to the lands where the dates grow.
We are the beggars' brotherhood, and no one can deny us our lofty pride . . .
And of our number if the feigned madman and mad woman, with metal charms strung from their [sic] necks.
And the ones with ornaments drooping from their ears, and with collars of leather or brass round their necks . . .
And the one who simulates a festering internal wound, and the people with false bandages round their heads and sickly, jaundiced faces.

And the one who slashes himself, alleging that he has been mutilated by assailants, or the one who darkens his skin artificially pretending that he has been beaten up and wounded . . .
And the one who practices as a manipulator and quack dentist, or who escapes from chains wound round his body, or the one who uses almost invisible silk thread mysteriously to draw off rings . . .
And of our number are those who claim to be refugees from the Byzantine frontier regions, those who go round begging on pretext of having left behind captive families . . .
And the one who feigns an internal discharge, or who showers the passers-by with his urine, or who farts in the mosque and makes a nuisance of himself, thus wheedling money out of people . . .
And of our number are the ones who purvey objects of veneration made from clay, and those who have their beards smeared with red dye.
And the one who brings up secret writing by immersing it in what looks like water, and the one who similarly brings up the writing by exposing it to burning embers.

Source: Clifford Edmund Bosworth, *The Mediaeval Islamic Underworld: The Banu Sasan in Arabic Society and Literature* (Leiden: E. I. Brill, 1976), 191–199.

gions, it seems likely that the most rapid surge in Islamization occurred in the mid-tenth century.

Just as in the east, governing cities were at the core of the Islamic presence in al-Andalus, as the Muslims called the regions they ruled in Spain. Cordoba, Seville, Toledo, and other cities grew substantially, becoming much larger than comparable cities in neighboring France. Converts to Islam and their descendants, unconverted Arabic-speaking Christians, and Jews joined with the comparatively few descendants of the Arab invaders to create new architectural and literary styles. In the countryside, where the Berbers preferred to settle, a fusion of preexisting agricultural technologies with new crops, notably citrus fruits, and irrigation techniques from the east gave Spain the most diverse and sophisticated agricultural economy in Europe.

The rulers of al-Andalus did not take the title *caliph* until 929, when Abd al-Rahman III

(r. 912–961) did so in response to a similar step taken by the newly established Fatimid ruler in Tunisia. Toward the end of the tenth century, this caliphate encountered challenges from breakaway movements that eventually splintered al-Andalus into a number of small states. But political decay did not stand in the way of cultural growth. Some of the greatest writers and thinkers in Jewish history—Judah Halevi, Solomon ibn Gabirol, Abraham ibn Ezra—worked in Muslim Spain in the eleventh and twelfth centuries, sometimes writing in Arabic. At the same time, Islamic thought in Spain was attaining its loftiest peaks in Ibn Hazm's treatises on love and other subjects, the philosophical writings of Ibn Rushd (known in Latin as Averroës) and Ibn Tufayl, and the mystic speculations of Ibn al-Arabi.

Several dozen principalities came and went between the tenth and the twelfth centuries while these states were flourishing. The Samanids, Fatimids, and Spanish Umayyads are representative of the political diversity and awakening of local awareness that characterized the period of Abbasid decline. Yet drawing and redrawing political boundaries did not result in a rigid division of the Islamic world into kingdoms as was then occurring in Europe. Religious and cultural developments, particularly the rise in cities throughout the Islamic world of a social group of religious scholars known as the *ulama*—Arabic for "people with (religious) knowledge"—worked against the permanent division of the Islamic umma.

Assault from Within and Without

Outside the urban milieu, political fragmentation enabled nomadic groups to assert themselves. In the west, trade across the Sahara had brought prosperity to northern city-states—Sijilmasa in Morocco and Tahert in Algeria—and to the kingdom of Ghana in Senegal and Mali (see Chapter 8). In the mid-eleventh century, however, recently converted Berber nomads from the western Sahara overpowered these trading centers and established a kingdom that stretched from Morocco to Mali (see Chapter 15) and even penetrated into Spain. These Almoravid rulers, established in their new capital of Marrakesh, wore blue veils over their faces and retained other traits from their Saharan past. A century later, such practices offended Ibn Tumart, a zealous Muslim preacher. He recruited a Berber army in the Atlas Mountains and launched a movement that, after his death in 1130, supplanted the Almoravids and established an Almohad empire that ruled from Tunisia to Spain from Fez, its capital, located in Morocco. In both instances, the rulers were sometimes sophisticated and urbane, but they depended on unruly rural warrior peoples and often resorted to harsh and intolerant measures.

More gradually, Arabs from southern Egypt slowly made their way across North Africa. Contemporary historians portray these invaders of the Bani Hilal and Bani Sulaim as locusts bent on destroying the agrarian-based prosperity of the region. Modern historians are still debating the actual impact of the so-called Hilali invasions. The question is the role they may have played in a significant economic change that took place in North Africa during this period. Prior to the eleventh century, Muslim rule in North Africa had been based on cities surrounded by agricultural hinterlands. Tahert, Sijilmasa, and, in Tunisia, Qairawan, were interior cities in contact with the desert. Coastal cities were less important, at least until the rise of the Fatimids. The farmers and the pastoralists of the mountains and deserts were largely Berber-speaking and little affected by Islam.

The Hilali tribal incursions coincided with a shift of the North African economy toward the Mediterranean Sea. Ports and cities situated between the mountains and the coast—Tunis and Sousse in Tunisia, Tlemcen in Algeria, Marrakesh and Fez in Morocco—flourished while cities connected with the desert dwindled. Trading contact across the Mediterranean grew, and Andalusian culture influenced urban styles throughout the region. Meanwhile, agriculture languished. The interior plains and habitable parts of the northern Sahara became mostly Arabic-speaking. Berber became the language of the mountains and of the Tuareg tribes in the southern Sahara. Trans-Saharan trade continued, but the new Muslim societies south of the desert developed in substantial isolation from the urban culture of the Mediterranean.

Syria and Iraq experienced nomadic upsurges as well. Political life along the eastern Mediterranean became increasingly fragmented. Nomad-based Arab kingdoms came and went, subjecting cities like Damascus, Aleppo, and Jerusalem to an ever-shifting array of political forces. Here, too, coastal cities like Acre and Tripoli began to grow as Mediterranean trade revived. In the Tigris and Euphrates valley Shi'ite Arabs from the desert and Sunni Kurds from the mountains competed in building small principalities.

But a powerful new Turkish presence overshadowed both Arabs and Kurds. Nomadic groups speaking one or another Turkic language had been known as allies or enemies ever since the Arab conquests. After 1000, these horse-breeding pastoralists from the steppes and deserts north and east of the Black, Caspian, and Aral Seas filtered into more central Islamic lands.

The role played by Turkish Mamluks in the decline of Abbasid power had established an enduring stereotype of the Turk as a trained and ferocious warrior little interested in religion or the sophistication of urban life. This image was reinforced in the 1030s when the Seljuk family established the first Turkish Muslim state based on nomadic power. Taking the Arabic title *Sultan*, meaning "power," and the revived Persian title *Shahan-shah*, the Seljuk ruler Tughril Beg created a kingdom that stretched from northern Afghanistan to Baghdad, which he occupied in 1055. After a century under the thumb of the Shi'ite Buyids, the Abbasid caliph breathed a bit easier under the slightly lighter thumb of the Sunni Turks. The Seljuks pressed on into Syria and Anatolia, administering a lethal blow to Byzantine power at the Battle of Manzikert in 1071. The Byzantine army fell back on Constantinople, leaving Anatolia open to the entry of the Turks.

Under Turkish rule, cities shrank as their agricultural hinterlands, already short on labor because of migration to the cities, were overrun by pastoralists. Irrigation works suffered from lack of maintenance in the unsettled countryside. Tax revenues fell. Cities were fought over as Seljuk princes contested for power in the twelfth century. But few Turks participated in urban cultural and religious life. Thus a gulf that had arisen between the religiously based urban society and the culture and personnel of the government deepened. When factional riots broke out between Sunnis and Shi'ites, or between rival schools of Sunni law, the government remained aloof, even when destruction and loss of life were extensive. Similarly, when princes fought for the title *sultan*, religious leaders advised citizens to remain neutral.

By the early twelfth century, unrepaired damage from floods, fires, and civil disorder had reduced old Baghdad on the west side of the Tigris to ruins. The caliphs took advantage of fighting among the Seljuks to regain some power locally and built a wall around the palace precinct on the east side of the river. Nevertheless, the heart of the city died, not to be restored to prosperity until the twentieth century. The withering of Baghdad, moreover, betrayed an even broader change in the environment: the collapse of the canal system that irrigated the Tigris and Euphrates valley. For millennia a world center of civilization, Mesopotamia suffered population losses that today still make Iraq an underpopulated country.

The Turks alone cannot be blamed for the demographic and economic misfortunes of Iran and Iraq. Their rise to power is as much symptom as cause. Too-robust urbanization that strained food resources, political fragmentation that resulted in reduced revenues, and the growing practice of using land grants (*iqta'*) to pay soldiers and courtiers also played a role. When absentee grant holders used agents to collect taxes, the inevitable result was a tendency to gouge the villagers and to take little interest in improving production, all of which weakened the agricultural base of the regime.

Just as the Seljuk Empire was beset by internal quarreling, the first crusading armies reached the Holy Land. Chapter 9 recounts the expeditions of Christian soldiers who trekked across the Balkans or sailed across the Mediterranean to fight for the cross. Though charged with the stuff of romance, the Crusades had little lasting impact on the Islamic lands. The four principalities of Edessa, Antioch, Tripoli, and Jerusalem simply became parts of the shifting pattern of politics already in place. Newly arrived knights were eager to attack the Muslim enemy, whom they called "Saracens." But those who had lived in the region longer, including the religious orders of the Knights of the Temple (Templars) and the Knights of the Hospital of St. John (Hospitallers), recognized that diplomacy and seeking partners of convenience among the rival Muslim princes was a sounder strategy.

The challenge to the Muslims, with their impotent caliph and endemic political fragmentation, was unification to face the European enemy. That unification finally came in the late twelfth century under Nur al-Din ibn Zangi and his military commander Salah al-Din, known in the West as Saladin (ca. 1137–1193). The former established a strong state based on Damascus and sent an army to terminate the Fatimid caliphate in Egypt. The latter, a nephew of the Kurdish commander of the expedition to Egypt, profited by Nur al-Din's timely death to unify Egypt and Syria and, in 1187, recapture Jerusalem from the Europeans.

Although the Christians of Spain would eventually succeed in destroying Islamic rule there, Saladin's descendants fought off all subsequent Crusades to the Holy Land. However, after one such battle, in 1250, their Turkish Mamluk troops seized control of the government, thus ending Saladin's dynasty. In 1260 these Mamluks rode east to confront a new invading force. At the Battle of Ain Jalut (Spring of Goliath), in Syria, they met and defeated an army of Mongols from Central Asia, thus stemming an invasion that had begun several decades before and legitimizing their claim to dominion over Egypt and Syria.

The Mongol invasions administered a great shock to the world of Islam. The full story of their conquests is told in Chapters 13 and 14, but the impact of their destruction of the Abbasid caliphate in Baghdad in 1258 and their imposi-tion of non-Muslim rule from Iraq eastward for most of the thirteenth century bears mention here. Although the Mongols left few ethnic or linguistic traces in these lands, their initial destruction of cities, their subsequent promotion of trans-Asian trade along northerly routes instead of by way of the traditional Silk Road, and their casual disregard for urban and religious life, even after they themselves converted to Islam, hastened currents of change already under way.

ISLAMIC CIVILIZATION

Though complex and unsettled in its political dimension, life in the ever-expanding Islamic world underwent a creative, supportive, and fruitful evolution in the areas of law, social structure, and religious expression. From the interlocking phenomena of religious conversion and urbanization emerged a distinct Islamic civilization. Because of the immense geographical and human diversity of the Muslim lands, many "little traditions" coexisted with the developing "big tradition" of Islam—a "big tradition" that was more an urban than a rural phenomenon. Nevertheless, the adaptability of Islamic civilization to new situations was one of its most salient features.

Law and Dogma

The hallmark of Islamic civilization is the Shari'a, the law of Islam. Yet aside from certain parts of the Quran that conveyed specific divine ordinances—most pertaining to personal and family matters—no legal system was in place in the time of Muhammad. Only Arab custom and the Prophet's own authority offered guidance. After Muhammad died, the umma tried to conduct itself according to his *sunna*, or tradition. This became harder and harder to do, however, as those who knew Muhammad best passed away and many Arabs found themselves living in far-off parts of the conquered territories. Living in accordance with the sunna was even harder for non-Arab converts to Islam, who at first were expected to follow Arab customs they had little familiarity with.

Islam slowly developed laws to shape social and religious life. Certain basic matters are likely to have been a part of Islam from the beginning—namely, the so-called Five Pillars, all referred to in the Quran: (1) avowal that there is only one god and Muhammad is his messenger, (2) prayer five times a day, (3) fasting during the lunar month of Ramadan, (4) paying alms, and (5) making the pilgrimage to Mecca at least once during one's lifetime. The full sense of Islamic civilization, however, goes well beyond these basics.

Some Muslim thinkers felt that the reasoned consideration of a mature and intelligent man—women were only rarely heard in religious matters—provided the best way of resolving issues not covered by Quranic revelation. Others argued that the best guide was the sunna of the Prophet and that the best way to understand that sunna was to collect and study the many reports in circulation purporting to describe the precise words or deeds of Muhammad. These reports were called *hadith*, and it gradually became customary to precede each hadith with a statement indicating whom the speaker had heard it from, whom that person had heard it from, and so on, back to the Prophet personally.

Some hadith dealt with ritual matters, such as how to perform ablutions before prayer; others were simply anecdotes. A significant number provided answers to legal questions not covered by Quranic revelation, or they suggested principles for resolving such matters. By the eleventh century, most specialists on Islamic legal thought had accepted the idea that Muhammad's personal behavior was the best model for society in general, and that the hadith were therefore the most authoritative basis for Islamic law after the Quran itself.

Yet the hadith themselves posed a problem. This body of lore, numbering tens of thousands of anecdotes, included not only genuine reports

Spanish Muslim textile of the twelfth century This fragment of woven silk, featuring confronted peacocks and Arabic writing, is one of the finest examples of Islamic weaving. While the cotton industry flourished in the early Islamic centuries, silk remained a highly valued product. Some fabrics were treasured in Christian Europe. (Victoria & Albert Museum)

about the Prophet but also invented ones, politically motivated ones, and stories derived from non-Muslim religious traditions. Only a specialist could separate a sound from a weak tradition. As the importance of hadith grew, so did the branch of learning devoted to their analysis. Thousands of hadith were deemed weak and were discarded. The most reliable ones were collected into books that gradually were accorded a canonical, or irrefutable, status. Sunnis placed six books in this category; Shi'ites, four.

The Shari'a was built up over centuries. It incorporated the ideas of many legal scholars as well as the implications of thousands of hadith, a body of material whose origin in the very mouth of the Prophet is sometimes disputed by modern scholars.

Nevertheless, the Shari'a embodies a vision of an umma in which all Muslims are brothers and sisters and subscribe to the same moral values. From this perspective, political or ethnic divisions are not important, for the Shari'a assumes that a Muslim ruler will abide by and enforce the religious law. In practice, this vision was often lost in the hurly-burly of political life. Even so, it was an important basis for an urban lifestyle that varied surprisingly little from Morocco to India.

Converts and Cities

The caliphs' determination that Arab warriors should live in garrisons at governing centers led to a significant change in the social and economic landscape of the conquered lands by encouraging urbanization. The early political history of Islam concentrates on Mecca and Medina; Damascus and Baghdad, which became capitals in 661 and 762 respectively; and a few military encampments that grew into major cities: Kufa and Basra in Iraq, Fustat in Egypt, and Qairawan in Tunisia.

A major cause of urbanization was conversion to Islam. Conversion was more an outcome of the gradual communication of knowledge about the new rulers' religion than it was a step that people took to escape the tax on non-Muslims, as some scholars have suggested. Conversion was fairly simple. No extensive knowledge of the faith was required. To become a Muslim, a person recited, in the presence of a Muslim, the profession of faith in Arabic: "There is no God but God, and Muhammad is the Messenger of God."

Few converts knew Arabic, and most people were illiterate and hence unable to read the Quran. Indeed, many converts knew no more of the Quran than the few verses necessary for their daily prayers. Moreover, Muhammad had established no priesthood to define and propagate the faith. Thus new converts, whether Arab or non-

Arab, faced the problem of finding out for themselves what Islam was about and how they should act as Muslims.

The best way to solve this problem was to congregate with other Muslims, learn their language, imitate their behavior, and gradually acquire a Muslim social identity. In many areas, the only way to do this was to migrate to an Arab governing center. The alternative, to convert to Islam but remain in one's home community, posed an additional problem. Even before the emergence of Islam, religion had become the main component of individuals' social identity in the Middle East. Converts to Islam thus encountered discrimination if they went on living within their Christian, Jewish, or Zoroastrian communities. Again, one solution was migration, an option made attractive by the fact that tax revenues from the conquered lands flowed into the Arab governing centers, providing many economic opportunities for converts.

Kufa and Basra in Iraq were the first new Arab settlements to blossom as cities. Both became important centers for Muslim cultural activities. But as conversion rapidly spread in the mid-ninth century, urbanization increased in other regions as well. It was particularly noticeable in Iran, where most cities previously had been quite small. Nishapur in the northeast grew from less than 10,000 at the time of conquest to between 100,000 and 200,000 by the year 1000. Other Iranian cities—Marv, Isfahan, Ray, Balkh, Herat, Shiraz, and Hamadan—experienced similar growth. In Iraq, Baghdad and Mosul joined Kufa and Basra as major cities. In Syria, Aleppo and Damascus flourished under Muslim rule. New districts were added to Fustat—the final one in 969 was named Cairo—to form one of the largest and greatest of the Islamic cities. The primarily Christian patriarchal cities of Jerusalem, Antioch, and Alexandria were not Muslim governing centers, did not benefit from this wave of migration, and consequently shrank and stagnated.

In Europe, the spread of Christianity by missionaries roaming the countryside coincided with a sharp decline of urban life. The spread of Islam was just the opposite. Cities were the centers of Islam; the countryside was slower to con-

Teacher and students This is a typical scene from urban Muslim society of the eleventh century. Teachers or storytellers usually sat on a mat or stool, or rested against a pillar while their listeners sat before them. Hadith were either recited from memory or read from the teachers' notes while the students copied them down for their own use. Note the variety of headdress and robes. (Topkapi Saray Museum)

vert. Muhammad and his first followers had lived in a commercial city, and Islam acquired a peculiarly urban character very different from that of medieval European Christianity. Mosques in large cities were not just ritual centers but places for learning and all sorts of social activities.

Urban social life was colored by Islam. Without religious officials to instruct them, the new Muslims imitated Arab dress and customs and sought out for guidance individual Muslims whom they regarded as particularly pious. Inevitably, in the absence of a central religious authority comparable to a pope or patriarch, there was great local variation in the way people practiced Islam and in the collection of hadith attributed to the Prophet. That same absence of a centralized organization gave to the rapidly growing religion a flexibility that accommodated many different social situations. The fundamental profession of Islamic faith called only for the acknowledgment of God's unity and Muhammad's prophethood and did not involve intrinsically difficult concepts such as the Trinity or divine incarnation in human form. So Islam escaped most of the severe conflicts over heresy that beset the Christians at a comparable stage of development.

By the tenth century, the growth of cities was also affecting the countryside by producing an expanding market of consumers. Citrus fruits, rice, and sugar cane increased in acreage and were introduced to new areas. Cotton became a major crop in Iran and elsewhere and gave rise to a diverse and profitable textile industry. Irrigation works, too, expanded in certain areas. Diet diversified. Abundant Islamic coinage made for a largely monetized economy. Intercity and long-distance trade flourished, providing regular links between isolated districts and integrating into the region's economy the pastoral nomads who provided the necessary animals. Manufacturing expanded as well, particularly the production of cloth, metal goods, and pottery. The market economy grew under the strong influence of Islamic ethics and law. Indeed, one of the few officials specified by the Shari'a was the market inspector.

Islam, Women, and Slaves

Women rarely traveled. Those living in rural areas worked in the fields and tended animals. Urban women, particularly members of the elite, lived in seclusion and did not leave their homes without covering themselves completely. The practice of secluding women in their houses and veiling them in public already existed in Byzantine and Sasanid urban society. With textual support from the Quran, these practices now became fixtures of Muslim social life. Although women sometimes studied and became literate, they did so in seclusion from the gaze of men who were not related to them. Although women played an influential role within the family, any public role had to be indirect, through their husbands. Slave women were an exception. They alone were permitted to perform before men as musicians and dancers, and a man could have sexual relations with as many slave concubines as he pleased, in addition to as many as four wives.

In some ways, however, Muslim women fared better legally under the developing practices of Islamic law than did Christian and Jewish women under the practices of Christianity and Judaism. Muslim women could own property and retain it in marriage. They could remarry if their husbands divorced them, and they were entitled to a cash payment upon divorce. Although a man could divorce his wife without stating a cause, a woman was able to initiate divorce

under specified conditions. Women could practice birth control. They could testify in court, although their testimony was weighed as half that of a man. And they could go on pilgrimage. Nevertheless, a mysogynistic tone is sometimes evident in Islamic writings. One saying attributed to the Prophet observed: "I was raised up to heaven and saw that most of its denizens were poor people; I was raised into the hellfire and saw that most of its denizens were women."[3]

Because writings by women about women are almost unknown from this period, the status of women must be deduced from the writings of men. The Prophet's wife A'isha, the daughter of Abu Bakr, provides an example of how Muslim men appraised the role of women in society. A'isha was only eighteen when Muhammad died. She lived for another fifty years. The earliest reports stress her status as Muhammad's favorite and the only virgin he married. She was the only wife to see the angel Gabriel. These reports emanate from A'isha herself, who was an abundant source of hadith.

A'isha was especially known, however, for two episodes. As a fourteen-year-old she became separated from a caravan and rejoined it only after traveling through the night with a man who found her alone in the desert. Gossips accused her of being untrue to the Prophet, and it took a revelation from God to prove her innocence. The other event was her participation in the Battle of the Camel, fought to prevent Ali from becoming the fourth caliph. These two episodes came to epitomize what Muslim men feared most about women: sexual infidelity and meddling in politics. As a result, even though the earliest literature dealing with A'isha stresses her position as Muhammad's favorite, his first wife, Khadija, and his daughter, Fatima, who was married to Ali, eventually surpass A'isha as ideal women. Both were portrayed as model wives and mothers, and neither aroused suspicions of sexual irregularity or political manipulation.

As the seclusion of women became commonplace in urban Muslim society, some writers recommended that men cultivate homosexual relations, partly because a male lover was presentable in public or on a journey. Although Islam frowned on homosexuality, one ruler

Slave girls from Samarra This early ninth century wall painting is from the harem quarters of the Abbasid palace in Samarra. Women were expected to be veiled outside the house and in the presence of unrelated men, but unveiled slave girls commonly sang, danced, and played instruments at parties. Islamic law prohibited wine but wine songs feature prominently in Arabic poetry in this period. (Bildarchiv Preussischer Kulturbesitz)

wrote a book in which he advised his son to follow moderation in all things and thus to share his affections equally between men and women. Another ruler and his slaveboy became models of perfect love extolled in the verses of mystic poets.

Islam sanctioned slavery, with the provision that Muslims could not enslave other Muslims or so-called People of the Book—Jews, Christians, and Zoroastrians, who revered holy books re-spected by the Muslims—living under their protection, except when slavery resulted from being made a prisoner of war. In later centuries there was a constant flow of slaves into Islamic territory from lands conquered by the Arabs in Africa and Central Asia. A hereditary slave society, however, did not develop. Usually slaves converted to Islam, which caused many masters to free them as a pious deed; and the offspring of slave women and Muslim men were born free.

The Recentering of Islam

The caliphate had originally been the center of Islam, the concrete political expression of the unity of the umma. The process of conversion, however, was not directed by any formal organization or hierarchy. Thus there emerged a multitude of local Islamic communities that were so disconnected from each other that numerous competing interpretations of the developing religion arose. Inevitably, the centrality of the caliphate diminished (see Map 10.2). The appearance of rival caliphates in Tunisia and Cordoba accentuated the problem of decentralization just when the Abbasids were losing the last of their temporal power.

The rise of the ulama as the leaders of Muslim communities did not at first ameliorate the growing fragmentation because the leaders themselves were often divided into contentious factions. During the twelfth century, however, this factionalism began to abate, and a new set of socioreligious institutions emerged to provide the umma with a different sort of religious center.

These new developments stemmed in part from an exodus of religious scholars from Iran in response to the economic and political disintegration of the late eleventh and twelfth centuries. This flow of Iranians to the Arab countries and to newly conquered territories in India and Anatolia became a flood after the Mongol invasion. As scholars fully versed in Arabic as well as their native Persian, they were well received wherever they went, and they brought with them a view of religion developed in the urban centers of Iran. A new sort of higher religious college, a *madrasa*, thus gained sudden popularity outside Iran, where madrasas had been known since the tenth century. Scores of madrasas, many under the patronage of local rulers, were established throughout the Islamic world.

Also in the twelfth and thirteenth centuries, and with a strong input from Iranians, mystic fraternities known as *Sufi brotherhoods* developed. The spread of the doctrines and rituals of certain Sufis from city to city gave rise to the first geographically extensive Islamic religious organizations. The doctrines of various Sufis varied enormously, but the common denominator was the quest for a sense of union with God through rituals and training. This type of spiritual endeavor had begun in early Islamic times and had doubtless benefited from the ideas and beliefs of converts to Islam from other religions with mystic traditions.

The early Sufis had been saintly individuals given to ecstatic and poetic utterances and wonderworking. They attracted disciples but did not try to organize them. The growth of brotherhoods, an altogether less ecstatic form of Sufism, set a tone for society in general. It soon became common for most Muslim males to belong to at least one Sufi brotherhood, particularly in the cities.

A sense of the social climate that the Sufi brotherhoods fostered can be gained from a twelfth-century manual:

> Every limb has its own special ethics. . . . The ethics of the tongue. The tongue should always be busy in reciting God's names (*dhikr*) and in saying good things of the brethren, praying for them, and giving them counsel. . . . The ethics of hearing. One should not listen to indecencies and slander. . . . The ethics of sight. One should lower one's eyes in order not to see forbidden things. . . . The ethics of the hands: to give charity and serve the brethren and not use them in acts of disobedience.[4]

For people who merely wanted to emulate the Sufis and enjoy their company there were special dispensations that allowed them to follow less demanding rules:

> It is allowed by way of dispensation to possess an estate or to rely on a regular income. The Sufis' rule in this matter is that one should not use all of it for himself, but should dedicate this to public charities and should take from it only enough for one year for himself and his family. . . .
>
> There is a dispensation allowing one to be occupied in business; this dispensation is granted to him who has to support a family. But this should not keep him away from the regular performance of prayers. . . .
>
> There is a dispensation allowing one to watch all kinds of amusement. This is, however, limited by the rule: What you are forbidden from doing, you are also forbidden from watching.[5]

Some Sufi brotherhoods spread to the countryside, where there was a simultaneous proliferation of local shrines and pilgrimages to the

Automata

Muslim scientists made discoveries and advances in almost every field, from mathematics and astronomy to chemistry and optics. Many worked under the patronage of rulers who paid for translations from Greek and other languages into Arabic and built libraries and observatories to facilitate their work. In return, some engineers designed elaborate mechanical devices for the entertainment of the rulers.

In this example, a conventional-looking *saqiya* of a type in use from Morocco to Afghanistan to raise water appears to be powered by a wooden cow. A saqiya is a chain of buckets descending to a water source from a spoked drum attached to interlocking gears. An animal walks in a circle turning the first gear and setting the rest in motion. In this device the real power comes from a water wheel and gears hidden underground. These turn the platform the cow is mounted on, causing the gears above it to operate the chain of buckets lifting water to the outlet trough on the upper left.

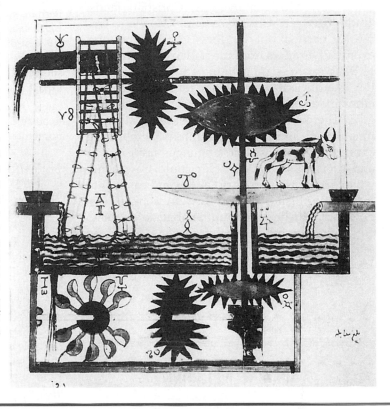

Saqiya   (Widener Library Photographic Services)

tombs of Muhammad's descendants and saintly Sufis. The pilgrimage to Mecca, too, received new prominence as a religious duty. The end of the Abbasid caliphate enhanced the religious centrality of Mecca, which eventually became an important center of madrasa education.

Altogether, the twelfth and thirteenth centuries saw a transition from the politically volatile and socially and religiously effervescent earliest centuries of Islamic history to the later centuries, in which the weight of the fully developed Shari'a, of madrasa education, and of the Sufi brotherhoods would create a more regimented, though more organized and supportive, society. The Islamic civilization that spread into

Asia, Africa, and Europe after the period of the Mongols was of this later form.

CONCLUSION

The centuries surveyed in this chapter witnessed profound changes in the political, religious, social, and economic environment of the Middle East, North Africa, and Central Asia. Despite the renewal of trade with Europe in the twelfth century, the rise of Islam permanently severed long-standing links among the various Mediterranean lands. Islam was tolerant of Jews, Christians, and Zoroastrians but demanded that they remain subordinate and do nothing to threaten Muslim dominance. Christianity was even more intolerant of Muslims than it was of Jews. Few Muslims lived in Christian lands. Trade between Christians and Muslims was mostly carried out by Jews, Armenians, and eventually traders from the Italian city-states.

Religiously, Islam culminated the transition in the late ancient world from identity based on ethnicity and localism to identity based on religion. The concept of the umma united all Muslims in a universal community, embracing enormous diversity of language, appearance, and social custom. A scholar could travel anywhere in the Islamic world and blend easily into the local Muslim community. In some areas, however, Muslim communities had to adapt to equally powerful cultural traditions. This was particularly true in China and the lands influenced by Chinese civilization as will be discussed in the next chapter.

SUGGESTED READING

Two comprehensive surveys of Islamic history devote substantial space to the period covered in this chapter and set it in broader contexts. Ira M. Lapidus, *A History of Islamic Societies* (1990), focuses on social developments and includes the histories of Islam in India, Southeast Asia, sub-Saharan Africa, and other parts of the world. Marshall G. S. Hodgson, *The Venture of Islam*, 3 vols. (1974), presents a critique of traditional ways of studying the Islamic Middle East while offering an interpretation based on the contributions of major intellectual and religious figures.

For a much shorter but eminently readable survey see J. J. Saunders, *History of Medieval Islam* (1965; reprint, 1990). Richard W. Bulliet, *Islam: The View from the Edge* (1993), provides, in a fairly brief book, a different approach by minimizing discussion of major political events and concentrating on the lives of converts to Islam and of the local religious notables who guided their lives.

R. Stephen Humphreys, *Islamic History: A Framework for Inquiry*, rev. ed. (1991), provides the best introduction to issues of historiography and some of the major issues in current scholarship. Gerhard Endress, *An Introduction to Islam* (1988), is less insightful but contains an excellent bibliography and chronology and deals with many more subjects than Humphreys does. Bernard Lewis, ed. and trans., *Islam: From the Prophet Muhammad to the Capture of Constantinople*, 2 vols. (1974; reprint, 1987), is an excellent selection of brief, well-introduced translations from primary historical sources.

Muslims believe that the Quran is untranslatable because they consider the Arabic in which it is couched to be an inseparable part of God's message. There are numerous "interpretations" in English, however. Most of these adhere reasonably closely to the Arabic text, and there is no agreement on which is the best. Arthur J. Arberry, *The Koran Interpreted*, 2 vols. in 1 (1955; reprint, 1986), represents more than most an effort to capture the poetic quality of Quranic language.

Muslims and non-Muslims disagree strongly on the best way to narrate the life of the Prophet Muhammad. Muslims prefer biographies that accept the basic lines of the story as contained in the earliest Muslim sources. Non-Muslims display greater skepticism about those sources and often lean toward social and economic interpretations. Martin Lings, *Muhammad: His Life Based on the Earliest Sources*, rev. ed. (1991), is a readable biography incorporating the Muslim point of view. The standard Western treatments have long been W. Montgomery Watt's *Muhammad at Mecca* (1953) and *Muhammad at Medina* (1956; reprint, 1981); there is a one-volume abbreviated version of those two works: *Muhammad, Prophet and Statesman* (1974). Michael A. Cook, *Muhammad* (1983), is a brief, intelligent discussion of the historiographical problems and source difficulties inherent in the subject.

G. R. Hawting, *The First Dynasty of Islam: The Umayyad Caliphate, A.D. 661–750* (1987), offers a sophisticated but easily readable history of a crucial century.

Western historians have much debated the beginning of the Abbasid caliphate. Moshe Sharon, *Black Banners from the East: The Establishment of the 'Abbasid State— Incubation of a Revolt* (1983), gives a lively account based on recently discovered sources. For a broader history that puts the first three centuries of Abbasid rule into the context of the earlier periods see Hugh N. Kennedy, *The Prophet and the Age of the Caliphates: The Islamic Near East from the Sixth to the Eleventh Century* (1986). Harold Bowen, *The Life and Times of Ali ibn Isa "The Good Vizier"* (1928; reprint, 1975), supplements Kennedy's narrative superbly with a detailed study of corrupt caliphal politics in the tumultuous early tenth century.

With the fragmentation of the Abbasid caliphate beginning in the ninth century, studies of separate areas become more useful than general histories. Richard N. Frye, *The Golden Age of Persia: The Arabs in the East* (1975), skillfully evokes the complicated world of early Islamic Iran and the survival and revival of Iranian national identity. Thomas F. Glick, *Islamic and Christian Spain in the Early Middle Ages* (1979), gives a geographically and technologically oriented interpretation that provocatively questions standard ideas about Christians and Muslims in Spain. For North Africa, Charles-André Julien, *History of North Africa: Tunisia, Algeria, Morocco, From the Arab Conquest to 1830* (1970) summarizes the dominant ideas of a literature primarily written in French. This same French historiographical tradition is challenged and revised by Abdallah Laroui, *The History of the Maghrib: An Interpretive Essay* (1977).

Few medieval historical narratives are available in good, readable translations. An excellent one is Usamah ibn Munqidh, *An Arab-Syrian Gentleman and Warrior in the Period of the Crusades*, trans. Philip Hitti (1929; reprint, 1987).

Studies of particular aspects of Islamic history are useful for comparison with other regions. Roy P. Mottahedeh, *Loyalty and Leadership in an Early Islamic Society* (1980), deals with the ethos and organization of tenth-century Iranian politics and society. Ira Marvin Lapidus, *Muslim Cities in the Later Middle Ages* (1984), deals with similar questions in fourteenth-century Syria, particularly in cities. These books make for an interesting comparison with each other and with similar books on medieval Europe and China.

Ahmad Y. al-Hassan and Donald R. Hill, *Islamic Technology: An Illustrated History* (1986), is a well-illustrated introduction to this little-studied field. For a less theoretical and more crafts-oriented look at the same subject see Hans E. Wulff, *The Traditional Crafts of Persia: Their Development, Technology, and Influence on Eastern and Western Civilizations* (1966).

The study of women is difficult in Islamic contexts because of the lack of sources. Denise Spellberg, *Politics, Gender, and the Islamic Past: The Legacy of 'A'isha bint Abi Bakr* (1994), provides pathbreaking guidance. Basim Musallam, *Sex and Society in Islamic Civilization* (1983), is an excellent treatment of the social, medical, and legal history of birth control in medieval Islam.

Islamic prohibitions on the taking of interest have raised many questions about the economic ideology of the medieval Islamic world and its capacity for capitalistic expansion. Maxime Rodinson, *Islam and Capitalism* (1978), is a good introduction to this problem.

Among the numerous introductory books on Islam as a religion, a reliable starting point is Hamilton A. R. Gibb, *Mohammedanism: An Historical Survey*, 2d ed. (1969). For more advanced work, Fazlur Rahman, *Islam*, 2d ed. (1979), skillfully discusses some of the subject's difficulties.

Islamic law, one of the most important specialized fields of Islamic studies, is well covered in Noel J. Coulson, *A History of Islamic Law* (1979). For Sufism, the mystic tradition in Islam, see Annemarie Schimmel, *Mystical Dimensions of Islam* (1975).

Two particularly valuable religious texts available in translation are Abu Hamid al-Ghazali, *The Faith and Practice of al-Ghazali*, trans. W. Montgomery Watt (1967; reprint, 1982), and Abu al-Najib al-Suhrawardi, *A Sufi Rule for Novices*, trans. Menahem Milson (1975). Both date from the twelfth- and thirteenth-century transition period of Islamic history and show the variety of religious perspectives then common. Al-Ghazali's view is that of a scholar and teacher, al-Suhrawardi's that of a Sufi who is concerned about everyday behavior.

Jere L. Bacharach, *A Middle East Studies Handbook*, 2d rev. ed. (1984), contains many useful reference features designed for students: outline maps, dynasty charts, a chronology, a glossary of common terms, and a table giving equivalents between dates A.H. (*anno Hegirae*, "in the year of the hijra") and dates A.D. (*anno Domini*, "in the year of the Lord"). For more detailed maps see William C. Brice, ed., *An Historical Atlas of Islam* (1981) The most complete reference work for people working in Islamic studies is *The Encyclopedia of Islam*, new ed. (1960–).

NOTES

1. Quran. Sura 96, verses 1–5.

2. Quran. Sura 92, verses 1–10.

3. Richard W. Bulliet. *Islam: The View from the Edge* (1994), p. 87.

4. Abu Najib al-Suhrawardi. *A Sufi Rule for Novices*, tr. Menahem Milson (1975), pp. 45–58.

5. Ibid., pp. 73–82.

CHAPTER ELEVEN

Central and Eastern Asia, 400–1200

The Tang Empire and the Power of Transmission

Localism and Specialization After the Tang

In the fourth century C.E., the multiply talented scholar Ge Hong (281–361 C.E.) provided a vivid description of epidemics that had afflicted populations in north China. In detail the diseases strongly resembled measles or smallpox. Ge described several partial remedies and then commented sharply on the circumstances under which the diseases had been introduced in his time: "Because the epidemic was introduced . . . when Chinese armies attacked the barbarians . . . it was given the name of `Barbarian pox.'"[1] This was a profound comment on the times. After the fall of the Han Empire in 220 C.E., the Chinese territories were divided among smaller states which frequently were at war with one another. Certain diseases could be transmitted between warring armies and spread rapidly from the soldiers to noncombatant populations. Refugees from war were continually driven from north of the Yellow River toward the south. They carried with them waves of infectious disease, earlier arriving in northern China from Central Asia.

But Ge Hong was more than a medical commentator, and the diversity of his achievements is a reminder that the turmoil of these times produced not only social dislocation and disease but remarkable discovery and innovation. Ge himself was a Daoist with strong interests in both medicine and alchemy. He combined these interests in his search for the elixir of life, the formula for immortality. He passed to later ages his knowledge on such diverse topics as hallucinogenic drugs, the prevention of rabies, and magnetism. His contemporaries knew how to refine and use the stimulant ephedrine, and they understood the basic functioning of the digestive and circulatory systems. Drawing on the ideas of Daoism, these groups of scholars also made and recorded significant advances in metallurgy and pharmacology (thanks to their interest in alchemy) and in mathematics.

When China was reunified in the late sixth century, skills and theoretical knowledge gained in the period of disunity could be collected and disseminated. The knowledge discovered in China during the third to sixth centuries would later produce advances in such dissimilar fields as iron and steel smelting, the production of more durable and more reliable compasses, and the development of variolation (an early form of vaccination). The Sui Empire, which reunited China in 589, and the Tang Empire, which followed it (618–906 C.E.), were the greatest disseminators of knowledge and cultural influence in medieval Asia.

After the Tang Empire ended in the early tenth century, East Asia comprised a number of local kingdoms, including the Liao and Jin in northern China and Mongolia, the Song in southern China, the Tangguts to the west of China, and the countries of Tibet, Japan, Korea, Annam (the ancestor of modern Vietnam), Champa (in what is now southern Vietnam), and the Turkic khanates of Central Asia. In many of these societies, the cultural and political heritage of the Tang Empire persisted. These small, often highly centralized regimes were able to take the cultural traditions and technological methods introduced under the Tang and develop them in local, specialized, and often advanced ways. Song China, in particular, became famous for its achievements in science, mathematics, and engineering. This specialization and diversification of knowledge in turn created rich new sciences and technologies that could be disseminated again once East Asia was reunified—which happened when the Mongols invaded after the year 1200 (see Chapters 13 and 14).

THE TANG EMPIRE AND THE POWER OF TRANSMISSION

Some of the kingdoms that sprang up from the ruins of the Han Empire were run in the Chinese style, with an emperor, a bureaucracy using the Chinese language exclusively, and a Confucian state philosophy. Others were affected by the Xiongnu, Tibetan, Turkic, and other regional cultures that predominated in some parts of the former Han domain. These kingdoms often used the emperorship to support unorthodox cultural influences, primarily Buddhism. When China was later reunified under the Sui Empire at the end of the sixth century, Buddhism became a profoundly important political and cultural influence.

Reunification Under the Sui and Tang

In less than forty years the Sui Empire (among other achievements) reunified China, Korea, and parts of Southeast Asia under its rule; designed a new imperial capital near Chang'an, the old capital of the Han Empire; and built the Grand Canal, a waterway linking the Yellow and Yangzi Rivers. Although traditional histories have explained the brevity of the Sui Empire (it lasted less than forty years) in terms of its "good first emperor" Wendi and its "bad last emperor" Yangdi, the empire probably was exhausted by its extraordinary pace of expansion and its overcentralization.

In 618 the militarily powerful Li family ended the Sui and created a new empire of their own, the Tang (Map 11.1). They maintained the eastern borders established by the Sui and expanded primarily westward into Central Asia, under the brilliant emperor Li Shimin (r. 627–649). The Tang avoided the problem of overcentralization by allowing significant power to local nobles, gentry, officials, and religious establishments. And they relied on a variety of political ideologies—not only Confucianism but also Buddhism and the central Asian respect for the title *khan*

(leader)—to legitimate their power and increase their appeal.

The Tang emperors were descendants of the Turkic elites of small kingdoms existing in northern China after the Han, and of Chinese officials and settlers who had intermarried with them. Consequently the Tang nobility were heavily influenced by central Asian culture but were also knowledgeable about Chinese political traditions. In warfare, for instance, the Tang were ready to combine Chinese weapons—the crossbow and armored infantrymen—with central Asian expertise in horsemanship and the use of iron stirrups. As a result, from about 650 to 750, the Tang armies were the most formidable on earth. Among Li Shimin's political allies were powerful Turkic and Sogdian (a people of eastern Iran) generals, and the first king of Tibet married into Li's family. The Tang drive westward across Central Asia was stopped only in the middle 700s by a combined force from Central and western Asia. Thereafter the Tang Empire was stable until it began to decline in the ninth century.

Chang'an at the Eastern Terminus of the Silk Road

The hub of Tang communications was at its primary capital, Chang'an (modern-day Xi'an in Shaanxi province, China). This was near the site of old Chang'an, the Han capital, in the Wei Valley (see Chapter 6), but it was a newly designed city. Tang Chang'an was a terminus of the overland trade with Central Asia, the Middle East, Tibet, and India. It was connected by well-maintained road and water transport to the rudimentary coastal towns of south China, of which Canton (Guangzhou) was most important. Chang'an was also the center for the ambassadors and students sent to the Tang capital as part of the *tributary system*. This was a practice, begun in Han times, in which countries not conquered by the empire acknowledged the empire's supremacy by sending regular embassies to the capital to pay tribute. Thus Chang'an was regarded as the cultural and economic capital of eastern Asia.

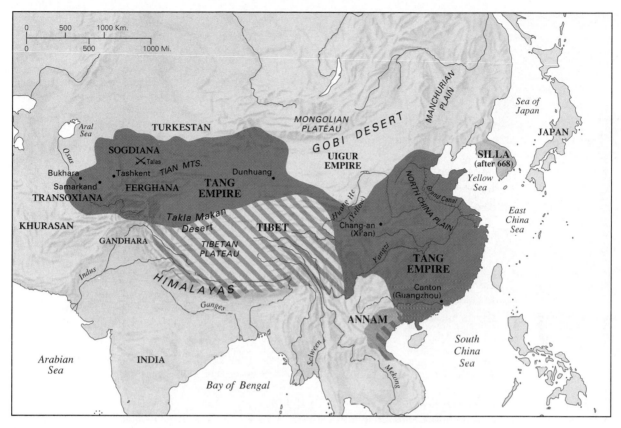

Map 11.1 Eastern Asia in the Tang Era The Tang Empire controlled not only China but also a very large part of Central Asia. Tibet was closely associated with the Tang by political and marital ties, while Japan, the Korean kingdom of Silla, and Annam were leading tributary states.

The Wei Valley had been heavily populated since the time of the Han Empire. During the Tang period, Chang'an was the most populous city in the world, with possibly as many as 2 million inhabitants. Its original ground plan, completed under the Sui, called for construction on 30 square miles (78 kilometers²); under the Tang, the city grew to occupy a much larger area. Only a minority of the population lived in the central city. Most people lived in the suburbs that extended out from each of the main gates. Many dwelt in specialized towns in the countryside— such as those responsible for maintaining the imperial tombs in the Wei Valley or those operating the imperial resort at Huaqing Pool at the foot of Mount Li, where the aristocracy relaxed in sunken tile tubs while the steamy waters of the springs swirled around them.

The market networks of Chang'an, both within the city and in its suburbs, kept the city's economy vibrating. A system of roads connected the central city and the suburbs to the smaller cities, towns, and villages that extended south and east along the Yellow River. Special compounds, including living accommodations and general stores, were established for foreign merchants, students, and ambassadors drawn from all over Asia by the tributary system and by trade. Along the main streets were restaurants, inns, temples, mosques, and street stalls that kept the population entertained every evening. At curfew, generally between eight and ten o'clock, commoners

Iron stirrups   This bas-relief from the tomb of Li Shimin depicts in detail the type of horse on which the Tang emperor's armies conquered China and Central Asia. The horses were equipped with saddles having high supports in front and back, breastplate and crupper, all indicating the importance of high speeds and quick maneuvering on the field of battle. Most significant, perhaps, were the iron stirrups, which were generally used in Central Asia from the time of the Huns (fifth century). The stirrups could support the weight of fully shielded and well-armed soldiers who rose in the saddle to shoot arrows, use lances, or simply urge the horse to greater speeds. (University of Pennsylvania Museum, neg. #S8-62844)

had to return to their neighborhoods, which were surrounded by brick walls and wooden gates that guards locked until dawn to control crime.

Market roads, major long-distance roads, caravan routes (the Silk Road), sea routes, and canals all brought people and commerce toward Chang'an. Under the Sui and Tang, for the first time the 1,100-mile (1,771 kilometers) distance between the Yellow and the Yangzi Rivers was spanned by construction of the Grand Canal (see Map 11.1). Special armies patrolled the canal, special boats were designed for travel on it, spe-

cial towns appeared along its route, and a special budget for its maintenance was established. The Grand Canal allowed the integration of the Yangzi Valley with north China and contributed to the development of an economic and cultural center in the eastern part of China. After the fall of the Tang Empire, rulers of China made their capitals in the eastern part of the country, largely because of the economic and political effects of the Grand Canal.

The Grand Canal was the eastward extension and enhancement of overland routes reaching Chang'an from Central Asia and other westerly points over the Silk Road (see Chapter 8). Into the markets of Chang'an came caravans of camels originating in Iran or north India, led by bearded Arab and Iranian camel drivers and bringing a variety of passengers—including Indian monks, Turkic soldiers, Arab merchants, and enslaved female musicians and dancers. They brought tea from India, and horses, cotton, grape wine in soft leather sacks, fruits and vegetables, musical instruments, beaten gold and silver jewelry, and glassware. From Chang'an, ceramics, paper, ink, and silk went westward with the caravans toward the Middle East.

Chang'an was also the terminus of the Persian Gulf trade route that began by sea in the Strait of Hormuz, landed at Canton in the south, then continued north overland. By this circuit, Chang'an was linked with the Mediterranean, East Africa, India, and Southeast Asia. These regions benefited from Chinese skills in compass design and shipbuilding in the late Tang period, and China drew much from them as well. The overland route to India by way of Central Asia and Tibet was not the only access that East Asia had to Indian culture. During the Tang, Chinese control of what is now coastal southern China was consolidated, and this, together with geographical information of the sort provided in earlier times by Faxian (see Chapter 8) and other religious travelers, increased Chinese access to the Indian Ocean. These sea routes also were a factor in the spread of Islam to East Asia. Indeed an uncle of Muhammad is credited with having erected the small, pagoda-like "red mosque" at Canton in the middle seventh century.

The sea route between the Middle East and Canton was also the means of transmission of bubonic plague to East Asia. In the fifth century, bubonic plague had moved from North Africa into the Middle East. From there, the sea trade brought it to East Asia. Evidence of plague is found in references to Canton and south China in the early 600s. The plague found a hospitable environment in parts of southwestern China and lingered there after the virtual eradication of the disease in the Middle East and Europe. The trade and embassy routes of the Tang Empire quickly became channels for transmission of plague to Korea, Japan, and Tibet, all of which experienced their first outbreaks after the establishment of diplomatic ties with Chang'an in the seventh century. Plague was soon controlled in urban East Asia but remained active in some isolated rural pockets until the Mongol invasions in the thirteenth century, when a new outbreak occurred.

Buddhism and Society

Along the trade routes of East Asia came Buddhism, which had been influential in Central Asia and northern China for centuries before the Tang Empire (see Map 8.1). Buddhism set forth a religious function for kings and emperors: to bring humankind into the Buddhist realm. Buddhists believed that protective spirits would aid the king in the governing of the state and prevent harm from coming to the people living under him. State cults based on this idea were important in the kingdoms of Central Asia and north China during the period of disunity after the fall of the Han Empire. China's next unifying empires, the Sui and the Tang, inherited the cults from those kingdoms. From there, they spread quickly to Korea, Japan, and Tibet.

The most important Buddhist school of teaching in Central and eastern Asia was Mahayana, or "Great Vehicle," Buddhism. Like all Buddhist sects, Mahayana Buddhism considered belief in the reality of the material world to be the root of suffering. But Mahayana specifically fostered a faith in enlightened beings—*bodhisattvas*—who have postponed achieving *nirvana* (eternal bliss) in order to help others achieve enlightenment. Faith in bodhisattvas led to the acceptance of many local gods and goddesses into Buddhist sainthood. In contrast to some other schools of Buddhism, Mahayana encouraged the translation of Buddhist scripture into local languages, and it accepted forms of religious practice that had little or no connection with written texts. These qualities allowed Mahayana Buddhism to assert its influence over many diverse societies and over many classes of people within those societies. The tremendous reach of Mahayana invigorated travel, language learning, and cultural exchange throughout northern India, Central Asia, and East Asia.

Precisely because of its social, cultural, and political influence, Buddhism was first an important ally of the Tang emperors and later their enemy. In 840 the state moved to crush the economic power and the influence of the Buddhist monasteries, and the Tang elites strongly reasserted Confucian ideology. The repression reflected the wish of the state to decrease Buddhist interference in court politics and to increase tax revenues by repealing exemptions granted to the monasteries. The repression also reflected the elites' anxiety that Buddhism was encouraging both the dissolution of the family (as idealized by Confucians) and the empowerment of women.

The family estates of the Tang period were a fundamental component of the economic and political structure of the empire. Thus the government and the elites regarded with suspicion anything that endangered the stability of these estates or endangered the values of family cohesiveness on which they rested.

Because of Buddhism's disapproval of earthly ties, a man or woman had to sever relations with the secular world in order to begin the journey to salvation. Monasteries, where monks continually prayed for the preservation of the state and the salvation of souls, were exempt from taxes. This economic edge allowed them to employ large numbers of serfs and to purchase large tracts of land as well as precious objects. Many poor people flocked to the monasteries and nunneries as artisans, fieldworkers, cooks, housekeepers, and guards. Some eventually converted to Buddhism and took up the monastic life. Others came as beggars and then began to study the religion. Among the gentry and nobility were some who turned away from their families for the peace and spirituality of the religious life. Wealthy believers often gave large tracts of land to the monasteries.

By the ninth century, hundreds of thousands of people had entered monasteries and nunneries. Those people were exempt from taxes and military service. They deprived their families of the advantages that might have resulted from their marriages. And they denied descendants to their ancestors, which was strictly contrary to Confucian teaching, an element of the religion that eventually aroused the suspicion of the gentry.

Equally obvious to the Tang court was the subversive influence of Buddhism on politics: Buddhism could be used as a legitimating philosophy opposed to the Confucian idea of the family as the model for the state. A woman who had married into the imperial family, Wu Zhao, seized control of the government in 690, declared herself a female emperor, and reigned until 705. She legitimated herself by claiming she was a bodhisattva, and she favored Buddhists and Daoists over Confucianists. In the later Tang era, Emperor Wu and other powerful women such as the concubine Yang Guifei were despised by Confucian critics such as the poet Bo Zhuyi. In his poem "Everlasting Remorse" Bo lamented women's influence at the Tang court—influence that had caused "the hearts of fathers and mothers everywhere not to value the birth of boys, but the birth of girls."[2]

When the Tang forced dissolution of the monasteries, the loss in cultural artifacts was incalculable, and many of the great sculptures and grottoes that survived were permanently defaced. Most of the temples and the façades built to shelter the great stone carvings from the weather were made of wood and disappeared in the fires that accompanied the suppression of Buddhism. The suppression also created the population of wandering, impoverished monks who became a common theme in Tang and Song art, and were also transmitters of information they picked up on their travels (see Voices & Visions: Ennin in China). In later times monasteries would be legalized again, but Buddhism in China was never afterward the profound social, political, and cultural force it had been in early Tang times.

Central Asia as the Crossroads of Trade

Since prehistoric times, exchanges of technology between Central Asia and the peripheries of Eurasia had resulted in major advances in methods of transport, modes of warfare, differentiation of languages and development of written literatures, and the spread of religious ideas. The religious influences in Central Asia might be

Ennin in China

Since the spread of Buddhism to eastern Asia in Han times, monks making pilgrimages to China and India had been a major source of new knowledge about geography, travel routes, languages, and economic conditions. The notes of these monks remain from as early as the third century C.E., *when pilgrims from the Korean kingdoms recorded part of their travels through China. In the 400s Faxian and in the 600s Xuanzang brought to China new knowledge of India, Southeast Asia, and Tibet. Perhaps the most famous traveler of the period 400–1200, however, was the Japanese monk Ennin (794–864).*

By the 800s Japan was recognized throughout East Asia as a center of Buddhist worship and study. Ennin intended in 838 to follow in the steps of many other Japanese monks who had made pilgrimages to sacred sites in China and to return promptly to Japan. His plans were disrupted when he was shipwrecked on the coast of Shandong, the peninsula stretching into the Sea of Bohai, through which the increasing traffic of Japanese and Korean monks regularly passed. He spent the next nine years wandering eastern China during the height of the suppression of Buddhism, and he learned the esoteric folk doctrines that were the predecessors of Zen Buddhism.

Ennin's diary provides many details of the everyday life of the people he encountered and often had to depend on. His petition to a local monastery reveals something of the life in this poor and isolated region:

There have been plagues of locusts for the past three or four years which have eaten up the five grains so that the officials and commoners alike have gone hungry. In the [Shandong] region they have been using only acorns for food. It is difficult for travelling monks passing through this rugged area to obtain provisions. Millet costs eighty cash per dou and non-glutinous rice one hundred cash per dou. We are without provisions to eat . . . .

The said Ennin and others left their homeland far away in order to search for Buddhist teachings, but, because he is asking for official credentials, he has not yet moved on. He makes his home anywhere and finds his hunger beyond endurance, but, because he speaks a different tongue, he is unable to beg for food himself. He humbly hopes that in your compassion you will give the surplus of your food to the poor monk from abroad. You have already given him a certain amount, and he is extremely embarrassed to be troubling you again. He humbly sends his disciple Isho to inform you. Respectfully stated . . . .

What does Ennin's presence in China and the pattern of his travels tell you about the international Buddhist world of his time? What was the status of Buddhism and Buddhist priests in China at the time? How did this compare to the situation in Japan and Korea?

Source: "Ennin's Diary of His Pilgrimage to China," in David John Lu, *Sources of Japanese History*, Volume 1 (New York: McGraw-Hill, 1974), .58–59.

seen as streams flowing from the Mediterranean toward eastern Asia. Earliest was Iranian culture and religion, which left a lasting impression on the royal traditions, city architecture, and the religious character of Central Asia.

Another early influence, and one well remembered in the Tang Empire, was the campaigns of Alexander the Great (see Chapter 5). In the third century B.C.E. he had conquered the lands between Iran, India, and Central Asia. In the "Alexandrias"—cities established by Alexander, including Samarkand and Gandhara—a partial Greek heritage persisted. The stone bas-reliefs and full-figure statuary that would become characteristic of Indian Buddhist art and later be transmitted to East Asia, for instance, were Greek in inspiration. Hellenic knowledge of mathematics, astronomy, and physiology had been transmitted from these centers to northern India, and had also gone eastward into Central Asia and Tibet. These regions were also familiar with the *Romance of Alexander*, which was first

Tang Developments

581	Reunification of China under the Sui empire
618	Founding of the Tang empire
627–649	Reign of Li Shimin
645–710	Taika era of state formation in Japan
668	Silla state unifies Korea
690–705	Reign of Empress Wu
751	End of Tang expansion in Central Asia at Battle of Talas
752	"Eye opening" ceremony makes Nara Japan prominent in Buddhist world
755–757	An Lushan rebellion
880	Outbreak of Huang Chao rebellion
906	Last Tang emperor deposed

written in Egypt, in Greek, to celebrate Alexander's adventures. Literate men of Central Asia who read Greek in the third and fourth centuries C.E. translated, illustrated, and elaborated on the Alexander stories. By the time of the Mongols, all the peoples of Central Asia and Tibet were acquainted with the *Romance*, and a Mongolian version of the epic later reached China and Korea by the 1300s.

The fortunes of the Tang Empire were related to the development of Turkic power in the region extending from Siberia to the eastern borders of Iran. The original homeland of the Turks was north and east of China, in the vicinity of modern Mongolia. After the fall of the Han Empire in 220 C.E., Turkic populations began moving westward, through Mongolia, then on to Central Asia. This long migration eventually would take them to Anatolia and the region we now call Turkey. During the period of disunion in East Asia between the Han and the Tang Empires, Central Asia was united under the rule of the Turks. But as East Asia was reunited around 600 C.E., internal warfare weakened the Turks' control of Central Asia. In the mid-seventh century the Turkic Empire was split in two. It was partly this fracturing of the Turks' power that allowed the Tang Empire to establish control over Central Asia. Within about fifty years, however, a new Turkic order arose, and by the early 700s much of Central Asia was under the control of a new Turkic group, the Uigurs (see Map 11.1).

As part of the Uigur Empire, Central Asia's great cities of Bukhara, Samarkand, and Tashkent—all critical to the caravan trade—had a literate culture with strong ties to both the Middle East and to China. The Uigurs were famous as merchants and as professional scribes who were specially skilled to deal with the many languages of the region. In the time of the earlier Turkic empires a simple script had been used, and on occasion it was employed in Central Asia by the Tang Empire as well. But from the borders of Iran, the Sogdians introduced a running syllabic script, related to the Semitic Syriac script of the Middle East. The spread of Nestorian Christianity in Central Asia made the running syllabic script widely familiar. The Uigurs adopted it and refined it for the writing of their language (see Environment & Technology: Writing in East Asia). The new script made possible several innovations in Uigur government, including the change from a tax paid in kind (with products or services) to a money tax and, subsequently, the minting of coins.

An urban culture embracing the Buddhist classics, religious art based on the styles of northern India, and clothing, tools, and architecture revealing the mixture of East Asian and Middle Eastern styles flourished. By the mid-ninth century Uigur power in Central Asia was in eclipse, but Uigur culture continued to influence urban life in the region for centuries.

In the 1000s many of the intellectual and artistic treasures of Central Asia were sealed in the caves at Dunhuang, a settlement in modern-day Gansu province, China, that lay on the caravan route to Tibet and India. These paintings and manuscripts lay undisturbed until the nineteenth century, when intense competition among European explorers and collectors brought them to light. The treasures give us a vivid picture of the religious and material life of Central Asia before

Writing in East Asia, 600–1200

Chinese ideographic writing—script based on the depiction of ideas rather than the representation of sounds (syllabic or phonetic script)—was widespread throughout East Asia by the reunification of China in the late sixth century under the Sui Empire. Many of the peoples of East Asia attempted to adapt the characters to the writing of their own languages, which were not related to Chinese in grammar or in sound.

In Korea and in Japan, Chinese characters were often simplified and associated with the sounds of the Korean or Japanese languages. For instance, the Chinese character *an,* meaning peace (figure 1), was pronounced *an* in Japanese and was familiar as a Chinese character to Confucian scholars in the Heian period. But others besides scholars simplified the character and began to use it to write the Japanese sound *a* (figure 2). With a set of more than thirty of these syllabic symbols adapted from Chinese characters, any Japanese word could be written, complete with all its grammatical inflections. It was with a syllabic system of this sort that Murasaki Shikibu wrote the *Tale of Genji* around 1000 C.E.

A more complex change occurred in northern Asia. The Kitans, who spoke a language related to early Mongolian, developed an ideographic system of their own, inspired by Chinese characters. For instance, the Chinese character *wang* (figure 3), meaning "king, prince, ruler," was changed slightly to represent the Kitan word for an emperor (figure 4) by adding an upward stroke, representing a "superior" ruler. Because the system was ideographic, we do not now know exactly how this Kitan word was pronounced. But following the same ideographic logic, a further innovation was the Kitan character for "God" or "Heaven" (figure 5)—the symbol for ruler, but with a top stroke added, meaning the "ultimate" ruler or power. Though inspired by Chinese characters, the Kitan characters could not be read by any who were not specially educated in them.

Like the Koreans and Japanese, the Kitans developed a second method of writing, that was intended to represent the sounds and the grammar of the language. They used small, simplified elements arranged together within a frame, to indicate the several sounds in any word. This practice might have been inspired by Kitan knowledge of the phonetic script used by the Uigur Turks. In this example (figure 6), we see three words from a Kitan inscription. Only the second one

("horse") has been deciphered. This method of fitting sound elements within a frame also occurred later in *han'gul,* the Korean phonetic system introduced in the 1400s. Here (figure 7), we see the two words of the city name "Pyong-yang."

Though the Chinese ideographic writing system was powerful and has served well the needs of the Chinese elite to nearly the present day, peoples speaking unrelated languages were continually experimenting with the Chinese invention to produce new ways of expressing their own cultures. The result was the emergence of several sound-based writing systems in East Asia, some of them still being deciphered today.

Figure 1

Figure 2

Figure 3

Figure 4

Figure 5

Figure 6

Figure 7

the dominance of Islam. The culture they recall was predominantly Buddhist, but strong Greek and Iranian influences are apparent in textile designs, sculpture, painting, and architecture.

After the Tang empire reunited Central Asia with China in the early seventh century, the material culture of China was vividly affected by influences from Central Asia and the Middle East of the sort depicted by the Dunhuang artifacts. Lively new animal motifs and colors from Iran and Central Asia brightened the ceramics, painting, and silk designs of the Tang period, and life-size sculpture became common. In north China, the mode of dress changed. Working people no longer wore robes but adopted pants, which horse-riding Turks from Central Asia had introduced. Cotton, which the Central Asian trade imported in large and affordable quantities, gradually replaced hemp in the clothes worn by commoners. Pastimes now included polo, also

Tang women playing polo   The Tang empire, like the Sui, was strongly influenced by Central Asian as well as Chinese traditions. As in many Central Asian cultures, women were likely to exercise greater influence in the management of property, in the arts, and in politics than women in Chinese society of later times. They were not excluded from public view, and noblewomen could even compete at polo. The game, which was widely known in various forms in Central Asia from a very early date, combined the Tang love of riding, military arts, and festive spectacles. (The Nelson-Atkins Museum of Art)

introduced from Central Asia and strongly promoted by the Tang court (which, in accord with Central Asian tradition, allowed noblewomen to compete). Music changed as a host of stringed instruments were imported by means of the Silk Road, along with the folk melodies of the Central Asian peoples. Food changed, too, particularly with the introduction of grape wine and tea.

China also influenced the Middle East across the central Asian connection—not only through trade but also through warfare. Chinese technicians captured by the Muslim armies in the middle 700s, for instance, took to the Middle East their knowledge of papermaking, woodblock printing, ironworking, and ceramics. In ensuing centuries, knowledge of the crossbow and of gunpowder also filtered from East Asia westward. These technologies profoundly changed the societies of the Middle East and Europe.

Renewed Migrations and Fragmentation of the Tang

The Tang order was destroyed by the very forces that were essential to its creation and maintenance. The campaigns of expansion in the seventh century had left the empire large and powerful but dependent on local military commanders and on a complex system of tax collection. A series of ruinous westward campaigns ended in 751 at the Battle of the Talas River, near Samarkand. There, a combined army of Arabs, Turks, and Tibetans defeated the Tang forces. The reverses contributed to the demoralization and underfunding of the Tang armies. In 755 the rebellion of An Lushan, a Sogdian general close to the Tang imperial family and supported by the influential concubine Yang Guifei, broke out. In a few years it was suppressed, but at the price of the establishment of independent military governors whose power grew steadily to the end of the Tang period. These governors virtually assumed control of the empire when it was engulfed by the great Huang Chao peasant rebellion of 880. Residents of north China were uprooted and

driven toward the frontier regions of southern China as renewed migrations of Central Asians moved into northern China.

In the later eighth and ninth centuries, Turkic populations moving in from the east buffeted both the Uigur and the Tang Empires—as well as their western contemporary, the Abbasid caliphate (see Map 10.2). After the final decline of the Uigur and Tang Empires, control of Central Asia passed from Turks to Arabs in the west and to the Kitans and Tangguts in the east. The politically weakened Turkic populations continued the westward migrations that would eventually transform portions of the Middle East.

When the Tang empire ended in 906, a set of smaller states succeeded it. Each of them controlled considerable territory, and some of them had lasting historical influence. But none could match the capacity of the Tang for integrating the economic and cultural interests of vastly disparate territories or for transmitting knowledge across huge distances. In the ensuing three centuries East Asia was fragmented, and its communication with Europe and the Middle East was crippled. Important artistic styles, technical advances, and philosophical developments emerged in East Asia, but the particular brilliance that had resulted from the cosmopolitanism of the Tang was not seen again for centuries. Instead, regional states refined and implemented much of the cultural influence and technological knowledge introduced during the Tang.

LOCALISM AND SPECIALIZATION AFTER THE TANG

Just as in the aftermath of the Han, so in the aftermath of the Tang new states emerged and competed to inherit the legacy of the dissolved empire. Earliest and in some ways most distinctive was the Liao Empire of the Kitan people (related to the Mongols), who est-

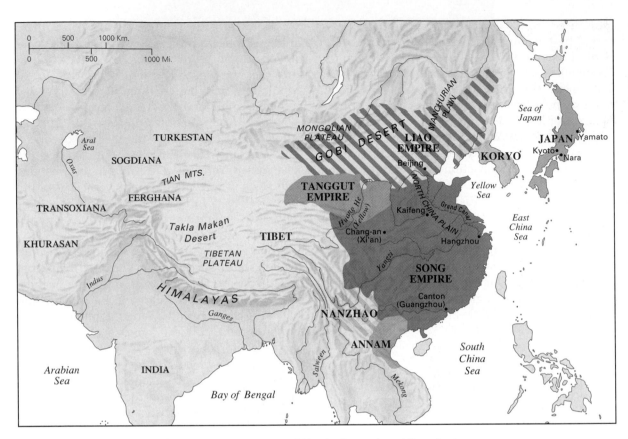

Map 11.2 Liao and Song Empires The hostile states of Liao in the north and Song in the south generally ceased open hostilities after a treaty in 1005 stabilized the border and imposed an annual tribute upon Song.

ablished their rule in 906 at what is now Beijing immediately following the overthrow of the last Tang emperor. Not long after, the Minyak people (closely related to the Tibetans) established a large empire in what is now western China and called themselves "Tangguts" to show their own connection with the former empire (see Map 11.2).

By the end of the tenth century, an empire adopting the name Song was established in central China. In the early 1100s the Jurchens (distantly related to the Koreans and closely related to the hunting peoples of northeastern Asia) destroyed the Liao Empire and eventually took northern China from the Song (see Map 11.3). There ensued years of continuous warfare among the Jin, Song, and Tangguts, until in the

1200s the Mongols subjugated or destroyed them all.

The period in which East Asia was dominated by the smaller empires that emerged after disintegration of the Tang was a complex time. The continuous relations between Eastern and Central Asia that had existed in earlier times ended. Sea connections among East Asia, the Middle East, and Southeast Asia continued, and the Song in particular distinguished themselves in seafaring technologies. But the intensity of the demands on Song resources fundamentally changed the relationships of the east Asian perimeter with the rest of Asia.

The Song state struggled under enormous military demands, and Song elite society rejected what it considered "barbaric" or "foreign" influ-

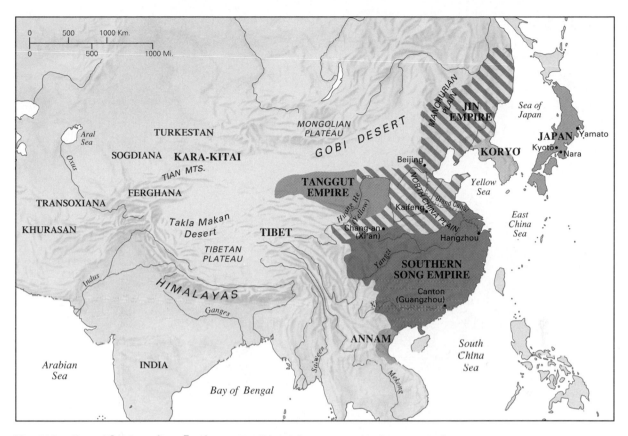

Map 11.3 Jin and Southern Song Empires The Jin and Song engaged in frequent warfare, which resulted in the loss of Song control over the region between the Yellow and the Yangzi Rivers. The diminished Song domain is generally referred to as the "Southern Song."

ences from Central and southern Asia. Korea and Japan forged strong political and cultural ties with Song China, and some states of Southeast Asia, relieved that they were no longer threatened by the military power of the Tang, entered into new, friendly relations with the Song court. The allied societies of East and Southeast Asia formed a Confucian milieu in which goods, resources, and knowledge were vigorously traded.

The Northern and Central Asian Empires: Nomadism and Buddhism

In the Liao, Jin, and Tanggut Empires, the state ideology differed dramatically from that used in Song China, in Korea, Japan, and Annam. In each of these northern empires, a significant portion of the population was nomadic or relocated seasonally. The rulers of these empires had to accommodate economies and the social structures of these parts of the population within the empire as a whole. This meant that the languages, religions, and political ideologies of the nomadic peoples were recognized and preserved alongside those of the agriculturalist.

In these multinational empires, no attempt was made to consolidate a single elite culture. Chinese elites within these empires were encouraged by the emperors to use their own language, study their own classics, and see the emperor through Confucian eyes. Other peoples were instructed to use their own languages and see the

Hunters with falcons   The Liao period was distinguished for its achievements in the arts, particularly porcelain, architecture, and water colors. In this painting, a small group of Kitan hunters have paused to rest their horses and hounds. The artist details the distinctive soft riding boots, leggings, and robes of the Kitans, much like those later used by the Mongols. Their hairstyle, with part of the scalp shaved and part of the hair worn long, was a shared tradition in central and northern Asia (including Japan) by which men used patterned hairstyles to show their political allegiance. The custom was documented in the 400s (and is certainly much older) and continued up to the famous queue (pigtail) worn by the Manchus, who conquered China in 1644 and governed it till the twentieth century. (National Palace Museum, Taiwan, Republic of China)

emperor as a champion of Buddhism or as a nomadic leader. As a consequence, Buddhism was far more powerful than Confucianism in these states, where emperors depended on their roles as bodhisattvas or as Buddhist kings to legitimate their power.

The earliest of the states to emerge from the ruins of the Tang was the Liao Empire of the Kitan people, who ruled a tremendous expanse from Siberia to Central Asia (see Map 11.2). They were the intermediaries between the Chinese territories and all other regions to the north and west. As a result, variations on the name of the Kitans became the name for China in these regions of the world: "Kitai" for the Mongols, "Khitai" for the Russians, and "Cathay" for those, like the contemporaries of Marco Polo, reaching China from the medieval West. In all, the Liao Empire of the Kitans was one of the largest and most long-lived in medieval history, lasting from 906 to 1121. It was also the first empire to make the city we now know as Beijing one of its capitals; relics of the Liao period can still be seen there. In ceramics, painting, horsemanship, religion, and some forms of architecture, Liao made a lasting contribution to Asian civilization and constructed much of the foundation on which the Mongols would build their great empire.

The Liao had a fascinating postscript. After losing their primary capital in Mongolia to the Jurchens in 1121, the imperial family went westward into Central Asia. There they established a new empire, the "black Kitans," or Kara-Kitai, which mixed Confucian bureaucratic philosophy with a culture that was part Buddhist and part Islamic with traces of Christianity and other religious influences. Among its distinctive features was the fact that several of the Kara-Kitai rulers were women. This multinational and multicultural empire survived for almost a century, until the Mongols destroyed it, as they destroyed the other states in its region. But the Kara-Kitai made a unique impression on Europe: their ruling family was probably the inspiration for the legends of Prester John, a mysterious Asiatic Christian king whom Europeans hoped would help them conquer religious sites in Palestine, Lebanon, and Syria.

The Minyaks, like the Liao, also believed themselves to be the rightful heirs of the Tang Empire, although they were not Chinese. Their culture was Tibetan, and their Tanggut Empire was in a sense the last empire sustained by a Tibetan people (see Map 11.3).

In earlier centuries, Tibet itself had been a large empire. At roughly the same time that Tang power was consolidated under Li Shimin in the early 600s, Tibet's first king centralized political power in Tibet. The Tang and Tibetan Empires declared their friendship when a Tang princess,

Tang Successor States

907	Liao Empire establishes "southern" capital at Beijing
935	Koryo state succeeds Silla in Korea
939	Annam wins independence from Tang Empire
960	Song Empire establishes its capital at Kaifeng
990	Tanggut Empire created
1000	Murasaki depicts life of Fujiwara Japan in *Tale of Genji*
1005	Peace treaty between Liao and Song
1125	Jin Empire destroys Liao
1185	Creation of Kamakura shogunate in Japan

whom the Tibetans called Kongjo, was sent to Tibet as the king's wife in 634. The arrival of Kongjo was also the arrival in Tibet of Mahayana Buddhism, which combined there with the native shamanic religion, Bon, to create a distinctive local religious style. Kongjo's entourage introduced to Tibet the technologies for which China was famous at the time: the manufacture of millstones, paper, ink, and rice wine. Tibetans thereafter joined Koreans, Japanese, and other nationalities as students in the imperial capital at Chang'an.

Because of Tibet's location between Central, East, South, and Southeast Asia, the variety of cultural influences in Tibet was extraordinary. In the seventh century, Chinese Buddhists began to route their pilgrimages to India through Tibet, so contacts between India and Tibet flourished. It was from India that Tibetans took their alphabet, and from India also came various artistic and architectural influences. From both India and China the Tibetans learned of mathematics, astronomy, and divination. From Central Asia and the Middle East came knowledge of Islam and of the monarchical traditions of Iran and Rome. From Iran came knowledge of the medical science of the Greeks, which in medieval Tibet the royal family favored over all other forms of healing.

The Tibetan Empire also excelled in military arts. Horses and armor, both of which were introduced through contacts with the Turks, were used and improved by the Tibetans, to a level that startled even the Tang. In the later 600s and the 700s Tibet and the Tang fought each other frequently. Tibet was extending its influence over what are now Qinghai, Sichuan, and Xinjiang provinces in China.

By the end of the 700s relations between Tang and Tibet had improved, probably because of the influence of Buddhism in Tibet. Like the early emperors of the Tang, the Tibetan kings encouraged the growth of Buddhist religious establishments and prided themselves on their role as intermediaries between India and China. At about the time of the persecutions of Buddhism in China in the 800s, a new king in Tibet decided to follow the Tang lead and eradicate the political and social influence of the monasteries.

The result in Tibet was very different from the outcome in China. Monks assassinated the king, and control of the Tibetan royal family passed into the hands of religious leaders. In later years the system of monastic domination, which continued into modern times, isolated Tibet from neighboring territories and drew around Tibet the veil of timeless mysticism for which modern Tibet is still known.

While the Tibetans secluded themselves, their cultural relatives, the Tangguts, continued an expansive, militaristic (though intensely Buddhist) government. The Tangguts successfully fended off both the Jurchens of the Jin Empire and the Chinese of the Song, falling only to the Mongols (see Chapter 14).

The Emergence of East Asia: Rice and Confucianism

With these alien and often hostile regions to the north and west, it is not surprising that the Song looked east and south for their closest allies, and during the tenth and eleventh centuries the eastern perimeter of Asia—East Asia—became a distinctive region. In Korea, Japan, and Annam, Song China found societies that, like itself, were overwhelmingly agricultural. Throughout East Asia, many crops were important, but rice was being widely disseminated. Rice fit well with Confucianism as a social ideology, because tending the young rice plants, irrigating the rice paddies, and managing the harvest required the coordination of considerable numbers of village and kin groups.

In East Asian societies, the Confucian emphasis on hierarchy, obedience, and self-sacrifice was increasingly important, and these values were instilled into the minds of ordinary people through popular education and indoctrination by members of the elite. Since Han times, the spread of Confucianism through East Asia had been strongly associated with the spread of the Chinese system of writing. In all these countries, the elite learned to read Chinese and the Confucian classics. Literate Koreans used Chinese characters to write the Korean language even before China was reunited under the Tang Empire. This method was later adopted in Japan, and a similar technique was developed independently in Annam (see Environment & Technology: Writing in East Asia).

Political ideologies in Korea, Japan, and Annam varied somewhat from the ideology of the Song, which asserted the predominance of Confucianism over all other philosophies, particularly Buddhism. These three East Asian neighbors of the Song had first centralized power under a ruling house in the early Tang period, and their state ideologies continued to resemble the ideology of the early Tang period, when Buddhism and Confucianism were compatible political philosophies. The states of East Asia nevertheless had far more in common with the Song than did their rivals—the Liao, Jin, and Tangguts—to the north and west and were able to agree that the Song Empire was the rightful successor of the Tang.

Chinese bureaucrats of the third century B.C.E. first documented Korean history when the Qin Empire established its first colony in Korea. During the Han Empire, the small kingdoms of Korea were distinguished for their knowledge of the horse, their strong hereditary elites, and their shamanism. But they quickly absorbed Confucianism and Buddhism, both of which they transmitted to Japan. Examinations in Korea (unlike those in China) never were able to influence the social structure. The hereditary elites remained strong and in the early 500s made the system of inherited status—the "bone ranks"—permanent in the leading state of Shilla. Professional training was limited to the ranks of scribes, translators, bookkeepers, and some artisans.

The same hereditary specialization applied to woodblock printing in Korea, which was introduced during the Tang period. The oldest surviving example of Chinese characters printed from wood blocks comes from Korea and is dated to the middle 700s. Korean printers rapidly made their own advances in printing techniques, and by Song times China was benefiting from Korean experiments with movable type.

Immediately after the fall of the Tang in the early 900s, a coup in the leading Korean kingdom led to establishment of a new dynasty, the Koryo, from which the modern name "Korea" is taken (see Map 11.2). The Koryo governed the peninsula, as a state friendly to China, until the fourteenth century (see Chapter 14). The Koryo kings were great patrons of Buddhism, and among their outstanding achievements are superb printed editions of Buddhist texts.

Japan's earliest history, like Korea's, is first known from Chinese records. The first description, dating from the fourth century C.E., tells of an island at the eastern edge of the world, divided into hundreds of small countries and ruled over by a shamaness named Himiko or Pimiko. Japan is mountainous and has small pockets and stretches of land suitable for agriculture (see Map 11.2). So this early account hints at the ways in which Japan's terrain influenced the social and political structures of the period.

The unification of central Japan appears to have occurred in the fourth or fifth century C.E. There is evidence that unification may have involved a significant immigration from Korea—possibly warriors on horseback who brought the small countries of Japan under the control of a new central government at Yamato, on the central plain of Honshu Island. It is also possible that Korean immigrants made a fundamental contribution to early Japanese agriculture (particularly the importation and cultivation of rice), writing, and knowledge of ceramics and metallurgy, and it is certain that in the early period of recorded Japanese history Korea was a fundamental conduit to Japan of major elements of continental Asian civilization.

By the middle of the seventh century the Taika Reforms were implemented by the rulers based at Yamato, allowing the Yamato regime in Japan to assume many of the features of the Chinese government, with which it was now in direct contact through embassies to Chang'an. There was a legal code, an official variety of Confucianism, a strong state interest in Buddhism, and within a century a complex system of state documentation, including the production of a massive history in the Confucian style. The Japanese mastered Chinese architectural science and styles so well that Japan's ancient cities of Nara and Kyoto have been invaluable for the study of Chinese wooden buildings that have vanished. During the eighth century Japan in some ways surpassed China as a center of Buddhist study. In 752 the enormous statue of the Buddha Vairocana (Roshana) was unveiled in its "eye-opening" ceremony (at which priests painted in the great statue's eyes), and dignitaries from all over Buddhist Asia gathered at the great Todaiji temple, near the capital at Nara, to celebrate the event.

There were also significant departures from Chinese practice. Chinese buildings and some street plans were reproduced in Japan, but Chinese city walls were not. Unlike central China, central Japan of the seventh and eighth centuries was not a site of constant warfare, so Japanese cities were built without fortifications. Chinese Confucianism emphasized the importance of the Mandate of Heaven for legitimating the government; but there was no need for the Mandate of Heaven in Japan. The *tenno*, or hereditary head of state—often called "emperor" in English—was a member of the line that had ruled Japan continuously since the beginning of its known history. And by the seventh century the Japanese regarded him as a direct descendant of the sun-goddess Amaterasu, who they believed created Japan and the Japanese people. Because there

The Great Buddha Hall The central hall in the enormous Todaiji temple complex is the largest wooden building in the world. It housed the gigantic statue of the Buddha of light, the object of the "eye-opening" ceremony in 752, when a priest from India painted the eyes onto the statue and completed it. The Todaiji complex was ruined in the civil war that led to establishment of the Kamakura shogunate in the late 1100s, but reconstruction began soon afterward. Today, the Todaiji is a monument to Nara civilization, and to the Chinese influence which shaped its architecture. (Werner Forman/Art Resource, NY)

had been no dynastic changes in Japan, there was no need of the Mandate of Heaven to justify such a change.

The primary reason for the continuation of the royal line in Japan was that only in exceptional cases did the emperors wield any real political power. Control was in the hands of a prime minister and of the leaders of the native religion, which in later times would be called *Shinto*, the "way of the gods." This distinct outlook was also preserved in historical writing that, unlike the Confucian style, emphasized the authority of myths and religious ideas. The *Kojiki*, completed in 712, exemplified this approach and existed alongside the more Confucian histories also produced under court sponsorship.

At the time of the Tang Empire, members of an ancient family, the Fujiwara, were the leading priests, bureaucrats, and warriors in Japan. They controlled power in the country and assumed responsibility for protecting the emperor from harm. The Fujiwara elevated men of Confucian learning over the warriors, who generally were illiterate. Japanese noblemen spent their time reading the Chinese classics, appreciating painting and poetry, and refining their sense of wardrobe and interior decoration. But to sustain their highly aesthetic life, the nobles of the Fujiwara period had to entrust responsibility for local government, policing, and tax collection to the warriors in their employ. Although many of these warrior clans had humble beginnings, by the late 1000s a small number of them had become wealthy, cultivated, and very powerful. The nobility's control over these ambitious and violent men began to weaken. By the middle 1100s the capital was engulfed in a civil war.

A literary epic, the *Tale of the Heike,* later commemorated the heroic losers in this first clash of warrior clans and celebrated the rise of a new elite culture based on military values. The standing of the Fujiwara family at court was destroyed, as nobles hurried to accommodate the new warlords. The emperor, too, had to acknowledge them as his protectors. Though the new warrior class (in later times called *samurai*) would in coming years absorb some of the values of the Fujiwara aristocracy, the age of the civil elite in Japan was ending.

In 1185 the Kamakura shogunate, the first of three decentralized military regimes, was established in eastern Honshu, far from the old religious and political center at Kyoto. Until the nineteenth century, Japan would remain under the control of hereditary warrior elites.

Annam, like Korea, had been under Chinese influence since the Qin Empires (see Map 11.2). The rice-based agriculture of this area made it well suited to integration with southern China. Wet climate and hilly terrain called for expertise in irrigation. The early Annamese were perhaps ahead of the Chinese in their use of draft animals in farming, in their metalworking, and in their mastery of certain forms of ceramics. With the collapse of Han military control in Southeast Asia in the third century C.E., Annam became vulnerable to aggression from the south. Not until the eighth century did the Tang Empire restabilize Annam as an outpost of Chinese elite culture. Confucian bureaucratic training revived, and Mahayana Buddhism was given pride of place among the varied religious influences of the region. When the Tang Empire was destroyed at the beginning of the tenth century, Annamese elites decided to continue a government resembling the early Tang. Annam maintained good relations with Song China but as an independent country.

Champa was the greatest challenger to Annam for influence in continental Southeast Asia (see Map 13.1). Cultural affinity and commercial activities made Champa part of the networks of trade and cultural influence that linked the Indian Ocean, the Malay Peninsula, Sumatra, Java, Indonesia, the Philippines, and the Pacific Ocean. The impact on Champa of the cultures of India and Malaya was particularly strong. During the period of Tang domination of Annam, the posture of Champa toward its northern neighbor was hostile. But during the Song period, when Annam was independent, Champa voluntarily became a tributary state of Song China. Indeed "Champa rice," a fast-maturing rice of the region, was sent to the Song by Champa as a tribute gift and became critical in the advancement and specialization of Song agriculture.

Elite Life in East Asia Under the Song

Perhaps because of the incessant military troubles of the Song period, Song elite culture idealized civil pursuits. In the social hierarchy the civilian man outranked the military man, and a classical revival marked the Song period. Private academies, designed to train men for the official examinations and to develop their intellectual interests, became influential in culture and politics. In the aftermath of the rejection of Buddhism in China, speculative philosophy flourished, and the rationalist school of neo-Confucianism predominated. In its theorizing about the sources of material experience, energy, and morality, this type of philosophy would have a later impact on Korea and Japan also.

But popular sects of Buddhism remained vigorous in the Song period, and elites adopted some folk practices. Most remarkable of these was Chan Buddhism (in Japan known as *Zen* and in Korea as *Sŏn*). It was inspired by varieties of Buddhist belief introduced under the Tang dynasty, and it asserted that salvation was possible through mental discipline alone.

Under the Song, the examination system for officials assumed the form it would retain for nearly a thousand years. Introduced during the Tang period, it was a dramatic departure from the tradition of the Han Empire, when officials were hired and promoted on the basis of recommendations. In theory the written examinations were intended to recruit the most talented men for government service, whether their backgrounds were prestigious or humble. In practice, however, it was generally men from wealthy families who did well in the examinations. They excelled because the tests were based on the Confucian classics, which, along with commentaries written over the centuries, had to have been memorized by anyone who hoped to pass the examinations. Preparation for the examinations was so time-consuming that peasant boys, who had to spend their days working the fields with their families, could rarely compete.

The examination system is another case of a Tang institution taking on complexity and refinement under the Song, who made it more specialized and practical. A large bureaucracy oversaw the design and administration of the examinations, in which candidates competed for degrees at the county, provincial, and national levels. Test questions often related to fiscal management or foreign policy.

In the new context, the social implications of the examinations were stronger, for Song society was less bound by hereditary class distinctions than Tang society had been. Many men from the gentry and merchant classes who hoped to enter government service spent much of their adult lives studying for and taking the examinations. Through study and testing, men established lifelong bonds that they could use to advantage. Success in the examinations brought good marriage prospects, hope of a high salary, and enormous prestige. Failure, however, could bankrupt a family and ruin a man both socially and psychologically. These were not comforting thoughts for degree candidates who had to endure days at a time in tiny, airless, almost lightless examination cells, attempting to produce in beautiful calligraphy their answers to that year's examination questions.

The gentry—powerful landholding classes below the aristocracy—had emerged in Han times and remained prominent in the ensuing centuries. In the Song period many men from gentry families chose not to compete in the examinations even if they were well educated. They saw that agriculture and commerce could be extremely rewarding. Patterns of landholding in central and south China promoted the concentration of ownership in the hands of comparatively few, very wealthy, people. This was partly a consequence of the fact that in Tang times what is now south China was still a frontier for Chinese settlers, who claimed extensive tracts of land for themselves before later colonists arrived on the scene. During the period of settlement, the indigenous inhabitants of the region, who were related to modern-day populations of Malaysia, Thailand, and Laos, were driven into the mountains and southward toward Annam.

The concentration of landownership in southern China reflected the type of agriculture practiced in the region. Northern China is dry, and the soil is sandy. Millet, beans, and wheat grew well there and could be cultivated by individual families. In the south of China, there are more rivers and the land is more adaptable to the cultivation of rice. Productive rice growing demands large concentrations of land and labor and generally involves village or family cooperatives working together. In the south, small landowners lost out and had to sell their land to larger ones.

Under these conditions, well-off farmers tended not to divide their property among multiple sons, a practice also widespread in Korea, Japan, and Annam. Brothers lived together and worked the fields, and the family remained cohesive as long as its lands and yields grew. Family members could pool their resources to avoid debts to outsiders and could command high interest rates when lending money. A family with large holdings could afford to set aside some land for specialized crops such as mulberry trees for feeding silkworms. One or two brothers could take charge of managing the land. Other brothers could become merchants, selling the family's rice or raw silk in nearby towns. In China, still other brothers might prepare for the official examinations and increase the family's influence through government service.

Women, Commerce, and Private Wealth

Song China is renowned for its brilliant achievements in speculative philosophy, in technology, in the arts, and in the creation of a highly urbanized commercial economy. But not everyone's lot in life improved during the period, and for women the Song era marked the beginning of a long period of cultural subordination, legal disenfranchisement, and social restriction. This outcome was consistent with the backlash against Buddhism and elevation of Confucianism that began under the Tang and intensified under the Song. It also was closely tied to the economic and status concerns of the gentry and rising merchant classes.

Merchants needed to be away from their homes for long periods of time, and many maintained more than one household. Frequently these men depended on their wives (a wealthy man would have more than one wife and perhaps numerous concubines) to manage their homes and even their businesses. As women were obliged to assume some responsibility for the management of their husbands' property, they were systematically deprived of the right to have and control property of their own. Laws relating to dowries were changed in the Song period, so that a woman's property automatically passed to her husband, and women were forbidden to remarry if their husbands divorced them or died.

Confucianism could be interpreted to require the absolute subordination of women to men, so it became fashionable to educate girls in gentry or noble families just enough to read simple versions of Confucian philosophy, edited to emphasize the lowly role of women. Modest education increased the value of these young women in the eyes of gentry or noble families and made them more desirable as wives and mothers. The poet Li Qingzhao (1083–1141) was one of the very few women of extremely high station and unusual personal determination who were permitted extensive education and freedom to pursue literary arts.

The most dramatic change in the status of Chinese women resulted from footbinding. When the foot is bound, the toes are forced under and toward the heel, the bones eventually break, and the woman cannot walk on her own. This practice first appeared among dancing slave women of the Tang court and was not widespread in China before the Song period.

In families of the gentry and nobles, footbinding typically began when a girl was between five and seven years old. In many less wealthy families girls had to work until they were older, so footbinding began later, perhaps even as late as their teen years. Protests, most strongly voiced by many literate men, condemned this maiming of innocent girls and the general uselessness of the practice. Nevertheless, bound feet became a powerful status symbol in rapidly changing Song society, and by the year 1200 footbinding was firmly entrenched among elites. Almost without exception, families that were members of the elite or that aspired to elite status bound the feet of their girls. Mothers generally oversaw the binding of their daughters' feet. They knew that girls without bound feet would be rejected by society, by prospective husbands, and ultimately by their own families.

Among working women in general and among the native peoples of what is now southern China, footbinding was unknown. Women in these classes and cultures enjoyed considerably more independence than did elite women.

Despite the importance of Confucian influence in East Asian societies, footbinding did not spread beyond China. In medieval Korea, strong lineage alliances that functioned like political and economic organizations allowed women to retain a role in the negotiation and disposition of property. In Annam, before the arrival of Confucianism from China, it appears that women enjoyed higher status than women in China, perhaps because of the need for the whole community—both women and men—to participate in wet-rice cultivation. This suggests that the women of south and southeastern China may also have enjoyed relatively high status prior to the growth of influence from northern China. The Trung sisters of Annam, who lived in the second century C.E. and led local farmers in resistance against the invading forces of the Han Empire, have been revered for almost two thousand years as national symbols in Vietnam and as

The players Women—often enslaved—were used as entertainers at the courts of China from very early times. These Song singers, however, show some significant differences from their predecessors of Tang times. While Tang art often depicts women with slender figures, there was clearly also great tolerance for, even admiration of, more robust physiques. By Song times, pale women with willowy figures were favored. In a more dramatic change, these women clearly have bound feet. Though foot-binding appears to have first been practiced in Tang times, it was not a widespread custom until the Song. Then, foot-binding was nearly universal among the gentry, and became increasingly common in merchant families and those who hoped to move upward on the social ladder. The image of weak, housebound women who were unable to work became a powerful status symbol, and pushed aside the earlier enthusiasm for healthy women who participated in the business of their families. (The Palace Museum, Beijing)

Going up the river   Song cities hummed with commercial and industrial activity, much of it concentrated on the rivers and canals linking the capital of Kaifeng to the provinces. This detail from the famous painting *Going Upriver at the Qingming [Spring] Festival*, shows only a tiny portion of the panorama that the great scroll represents. Zhang Zeduan, who completed the painting sometime before 1125, was a master at the depiction of daily life, and this scroll is one of the most important sources of information on the activities of working people. Here, the open shop fronts and tea houses are clearly displayed, a camel caravan departs, goods are offloaded from donkey carts, a scholar rides loftily (if gingerly) on horseback above the crowd, and sedan chair carriers transport shaded women of wealth. (The Palace Museum, Beijing)

local heroes in southern China. They represented a memory of when women were visible and active in community and political life.

Japan, like China, valued a limited amount of education for elite women. The hero of the novel *The Tale of Genji*, written around the year 1000, remarks, "Women should have a general knowledge of several subjects, but it gives a bad impression if they show themselves to be attached to a particular branch of learning."[3] The author of the novels, the noblewoman Murasaki Shikibu, was both accurate and ironic in her observation.

Fujiwara noblewomen were expected to live in virtual isolation. Generally they spent their leisure time studying Buddhism. To communicate with their families or among themselves, they depended on writing. The simplified syllabic script that they used permitted them to write the Japanese language in its fully inflected form (Fujiwara men using the Chinese classical script that they had been taught could not do so). The combination of loneliness, free time, and a ready instrument for expression produced an outpouring of poetry, diaries, and storytelling by women of the Fujiwara era. Their best-known achievement, however, remains Murasaki's stunning portrait of Fujiwara court culture.

During the twelfth century the total population of the Chinese territories rose above 100 million for the first time. Increasing numbers of people were living in large towns and cities. The Northern Song capital at Kaifeng and the Southern Song capital at Hangzhou probably did not exceed a million people by very much, but they were the largest cities in the world at the time, as Chang'an had been earlier, and they dwarfed all other cities in East Asia (see Map 11.3).

In the Song cities, multistory wooden apartment houses were common, and the narrow streets—sometimes little more than 4 or 5 feet wide (1.2 or 1.5 m)—were often impassable. The crush of people made expertise in the management of waste and the water supply and expertise in firefighting necessities. Song cities were also adept at controlling rodent and insect infestations and thus kept the bubonic plague isolated in certain rural pockets for most of the period.

Hangzhou, in particular, was engineered in such a way that the currents of the nearby Qiantang River generated a steady movement of water and air through the city, flushing away waste and disease. Turkic, Arab, and European travelers of the 1200s—sensitive to the urban crowding that troubled their own societies—recorded their amazement at Hangzhou's effective management of the dangers stemming from tremendous population density and the presence in the Southern Song capital of restaurants, parks, bookstores, wine shops, tea houses, and theaters that gave beauty and pleasure to the inhabitants.

To handle the growth of regional and national trade, Song merchants and traders developed institutions of credit. "Flying money"—paper money that could be redeemed for silver or gold in another city—made possible the transportation of goods without cumbersome guarantees and allowed the rise of a new industry based on banking and usury. The idea of credit had been introduced during the Tang but, like many other innovations, was not widely applied until the Song.

Economic growth under the Song was so rapid that the government could not maintain the huge monopolies and strict regulation that had been traditional in China before the Song period. As a consequence the government was hard pressed to gain the revenue it needed to maintain the army, the canals, the roads, the waterworks, and other state functions. Some government processes, including tax collection, were sold off to privateers. The result was exorbitant rates for services and much heavier tax burdens on the common people.

But the privatization of the economy created new opportunities for those with capital to enter businesses which had previously been monopolized by the state. Now merchants and artisans as well as gentry and officials could make fortunes, and urban life, in particular, was transformed by the elite's growing taste for fine cloth, porcelain, exotic foods, larger houses, and exquisite paintings and books.

Printing and Society

In Song China, the influence of Korean printing with movable type was felt, and improvements in printing technology profoundly changed the social impact of the official examinations. Woodblock printing, in common use during the Tang period, required time-consuming work by skilled artisans who had to carve hundreds of characters on a single piece of wood before a single printed page could be produced. In Song China, page molds and individual Chinese characters were cast in metal or porcelain. Movable pieces of type set in reusable page molds made possible the accurate printing of texts. Thanks to these new techniques, printers could quickly publish study materials for young men hoping to sit for the examinations.

The government recognized the potential of the new printing technology and by the year 1000 was mass-producing official preparation books for the examinations. In this way, the government was able to influence the ideological development of students, and more students gained a hope of competing in the examinations. Though the examination system did not become egalitarian in this way (a man had to be literate to buy even the cheap preparation books, and basic education was still not common), the opportunities for men of humbler background to take the examinations increased, and a moderate number of men without a noble, gentry, or elite background entered government service. The new printing technology also brought changes to the practical arts and sciences. Increasing numbers of illustrated books transmitted knowledge of ceramics, loom building, carpentry, iron and steel smelting, and medicine.

Landlords frequently gathered their tenants and workers together to show them the illustrated texts and explain what they meant. Printed materials provided information about planting and irrigation, harvesting, tree cultivation, threshing, and weaving. In combination with other technological advances, the dissemination of knowledge by means of texts printed from movable type contributed to the colonization of what is now southern China. Plows, rakes, and other iron agricultural implements, that had been introduced during the Tang dynasty were modified during the Song for use in wet-rice cultivation as the population moved south. Landowners and village leaders gained information about the control of malaria, which bedeviled the southern regions. With malaria under control, more and more northerners moved south, and there was a sharp increase in the local population.

The Song Technological Explosion

Technological innovations in farming introduced in Tang times were widely applied in the Song period. Iron plows facilitated the planting of seeds, prevented the loss of seeds to birds and deer, and improved the efficiency of land use. Such implements were not common in Europe until the beginning of the nineteenth century. New crops, such as cotton (brought to northern China from Central Asia) and quick-ripening rice (brought into southern China from Champa), were planted soon after they were introduced. Information about these and other agricultural advances—in seed selection, double cropping, soil preparation, and mechanization—was widely accessible because of the new printing technology. In some instances, the in-

formation had been available in China since Han times but never had been distributed.

Like Indian, Uigur, and Middle Eastern scholars of the time, Song scholars were absorbed in the arts of measurement and observation. Song specialization in these areas was a consequence of the migration of Indian and West Asian mathematicians and astronomers to China during the Tang period. Song mathematicians are the first known to have used fractions, which they originally employed to describe the phases of the moon. On the basis of their lunar observations, Song astronomers constructed a very precise calendar. They were extremely persistent and methodical. As an outgrowth of their work in astronomy and mathematics, Chinese scholars made significant contributions to timekeeping and development of the compass.

The most spectacular Song achievement in timekeeping was a gigantic mechanical celestial clock constructed by Su Song in 1088. Escapement mechanisms for the control of the revolving wheels in water-powered clocks had been developed under the Tang, as had the application of water wheels to weaving and threshing machines. But this knowledge had not been generalized and widely applied. Su Song adapted the escapement and water wheel to his chain-driven clock, the earliest known chain-drive mechanism in history. The clock told not only the time of day but the day of the month, and it indicated the movement of the moon and certain stars and planets across the night sky. The 80-foot (24-meter) structure was topped by an observation deck and a mechanically rotated armillary sphere (a globe with moving markers indicating the positions of stars and planets). The celestial clock was a monument to the Song ability to integrate observational astronomy, applied mathematics, and engineering.

Familiarity with celestial coordinates, particularly the Pole Star, refined the production of compasses in the Song era. Long known in China, in Song times the magnetic compass was reduced in size and attached to a fixed stem and in some instances was put into a small protective case that had a glass covering for the needle. These changes made the compass suitable for seafaring; the first attested naval application was in

Su Song's astronomical clock   Song expertise in observational astronomy later made great contributions to integrated Eurasian knowledge of mathematics, astronomy, and calendar-making. The gigantic clock built at Kaifeng 1088–1092, however, joined these skills with an equally dramatic aspect of Song achievement: engineering. The team overseen by Su Song combined an observation platform with an armillary sphere. The sphere was automatic, powered by chains attached to the water-driven central mechanism shown here. Also motored from the central wheel were rotating Buddhas in a small pagoda, and devices to display the daily, monthly, and annual time. All the technologies of Su Song's clocktower had been known in China for some time, but had not before been combined into a public display. The clocktower was the inspiration for the large mechanical clocks in churches and towers that appeared in medieval Europe a few centuries later. (Courtesy, Joseph Needham, *Science and Civilization in China*)

1090. The Chinese compass and the Greek astrolabe, introduced later, would improve navigation throughout Southeast Asia and the Indian Ocean in ensuing centuries.

Development of a seaworthy compass coincided with the improvement of techniques in the building of junks. A stern-mounted rudder improved the steering of these large ships in rough seas, and watertight bulkheads helped keep them afloat in emergencies. Mariners on the Persian Gulf quickly adopted these features. Chinese traders in gigantic junks were able to reach the Middle East, the Philippines, and possibly more-distant points by sea. China's Grand Canal was fitted with a series of locks, which allowed large vessels to travel far inland.

The Song technological explosion that gave rise to these and other advances was stimulated not only by a vibrant and expanding economy but also by military pressure. East Asia in general, and Song China in particular, were under constant military pressure from the northern empires. Liao, Tanggut, and Jin societies were fundamentally nomadic and excelled in the use of cavalry in warfare. The Song defended the empire with an infantry-based army, which made up for its strategic disadvantages with its enormous size. Although the Song Empire was less than half the size of the Tang Empire, it maintained an army four times as large, about 1.25 million men. For military leadership, the Song employed men educated specially for the task, examined on military subjects, and paid regular salaries.

In addition to meeting the cost of the military, Song rulers made annual, large tribute payments to the Liao to prevent warfare. In some years, military expenditures consumed as much as 80 percent of the Song government budget—a burden that threatened to crush the state. Thanks to the advances in printing, the government attempted to alleviate some of its financial troubles by distributing paper money, the first of its kind. But the result was inflation so severe that by the beginning of the 1100s Song paper money traded for 1 percent of its face value. Eventually it was withdrawn, and the government attempted to meet its expenses with new taxes, monopolies, and financial incentives to merchants. The only real solution to Song financial problems would have been peace, which was not achieved until after the Mongol conquest in the thirteenth century.

Because of the importance of iron and steel to warfare, the ore- and coal-producing regions of north China were constantly a site of military confrontation between the Song and their northern rivals. The volume of Song mining and iron production (which once again became a government monopoly in the eleventh century) was huge. By the end of the eleventh century, Song production of cast iron was 125,000 tons (113,700 metric tons), which in absolute terms would have rivaled the output of eighteenth-century Britain. Song engineers became skilled at high-temperature metallurgy. They produced steel weapons of unprecedented strength through the use of enormous bellows, often driven by water wheels, to superheat the molten ore. Casting and assembly were made more efficient by the refinement of mass-production techniques that had been used in China with bronze and ceramics for nearly two thousand years.

Song defensive works also incorporated iron, which was impervious to fire or concussion. Bridges and small buildings were made of iron, and so was mass-produced body armor for soldiers in small, medium, and large sizes. To counter the devastating cavalry assaults made by the Liao and Jin, the Song experimented with projectiles that could destroy groups of men and horses. The explosive properties of gunpowder were well known in China, but a formula that could produce an intense charge had not yet been developed (see Chapter 14). At this time, gunpowder was used to propel flaming arrows into oncoming cavalry. Not until the wars against the Jin in the 1100s did the Song introduce a new and terrifying weapon. Shells launched from Song fortifications exploded in the midst of the enemy, sending out shards of iron. The Jin were horrified by the resulting carnage—wholesale dismemberment of men and animals. But the small range of the shells limited them to defensive uses, and they made no major impact on the overall conduct of war.

CONCLUSION

The fragmentation of Asia that followed the end of the Tang Empire in 906 allowed the emergence of regional cultures that experimented with and in many cases improved the cultural, military, architectural, and scientific technologies whose transmission had been facilitated by Tang rule. In northern and Central Asia, these refinements included state ideologies based on Buddhism, bureaucratic practices based on Chinese traditions, and military techniques combining nomadic horsemanship and strategies with Chinese armaments and weapons. In Song China, the application of technological knowledge introduced during the Tang years transformed society. The results were privatization of commerce; production of larger ships and exploitation of long-distance sea trade; rapid advancement in the iron, steel, and porcelain industries; increased productivity in agriculture; the colonization of new regions; and deeper exploration of ideas about time, cosmology, and mathematics. China, however, was not self-reliant. Like its East Asian neighbors—Korea, Japan, and Annam—China was enriched by the mutual sharing of improvements in agriculture, ceramics, and printing.

At the same time, the relatively small scale of political organization and attendant inability to amass military resources left most of East Asia vulnerable to attack from a large and well-organized force. The test of the local systems arising in Asia from the tenth century on would arrive in the early thirteenth century. Some of the states would survive, most would be swept away in the persisting, systematic conquests of the Mongols. As they united the Eurasian world that had been so strongly linked in the time of the Tang and Abbasid empires, the Mongols and their subordinates would decide whether to nurture, exploit, suppress, or ignore the technological and cultural legacies of the independent Asian kingdoms that had thrived in the tenth to twelfth centuries.

These large patterns of contact and change would appear to their participants to literally affect the whole world. In fact, they omitted vast lands and peoples in the Americas, which a few Eurasian societies knew only as legend, and most could not have imagined in any form.

SUGGESTED READING

Moss Roberts's *Three Kingdoms* (1991) is an excellent abridged translation of Luo Guanzhong's *Romance of the Three Kingdoms.* There are many good books on the history and cultures of Central Asia. Rene Grousset's *The Empire of the Steppes: A History of Central Asia* (1988) is a classic text. It can be very profitably supplemented by selected chapters from Denis Sinor, ed., *The Cambridge History of Early Inner Asia* (1990). On the transport technologies of early Central Asia see Richard Bulliet, *The Camel and the Wheel* (1975). On the Uigur Empire, see Colin MacKerras, *The Uighur Empire* (1968).

Arthur Wright's *The Sui Dynasty* (1978) is a readable narrative about the reunification of China in the sixth century. The Tang Empire is the topic of a huge literature, but for a variety of enduring essays see Arthur F. Wright and David Twitchett, eds., *Perspectives on the T'ang* (1973). On the contacts of the Tang Empire with the cultures of Central, South, and Southeast Asia see Edward Schafer, *The Golden Peaches of Samarkand* (1963), *The Vermilion Bird* (1967), and *Pacing the Void* (1977). For an introduction to medieval Tibet see Christopher I. Beckwith, *The Tibetan Empire in Central Asia* (1987), and Rolf Stein, *Tibetan Civilization* (1972).

There is comparatively little literature on the Central and northern Asian empires that succeeded the Tang. But for a classic text see Karl Wittfogel and Chia-sheng Feng, *History of Chinese Society: Liao* (1949). On the Jurchen Jin see Jin-sheng Tao, *The Jurchens in Twelfth Century China* (1976); and on the Tangguts see Ruth Dunnell, *Buddhism and the State in Eleventh-Century Xia* (1996).

On the Song, there is a large volume of material, particularly relating to technological achievements. For an introduction to the monumental work of Joseph Needham see his *Science in Traditional China* (1981). For a large and now classic thesis on Song advancement (and Ming backwardness) see Mark Elvin, *The Pattern of the Chinese Past* (1973), particularly Part II. Joel

Mokyr, *The Lever of Riches* (1990), is a more recent, comparative treatment. On Li Qingzhao, see Hu Pinch'ing, *Li Ch'ing-chao* (1966). See also W. T. de Bary, W-T Chan, and B. Watson, compilers, *Sources of Chinese Tradition, Volume I* (1964); Miyazaki Ichisada, *China's Examination Hell* (1976); Richard von Glahn, *The Country of Streams and Grottoes* (1987); and Patricia Ebrey, *The Inner Quarters: Marriage and the Lives of Chinese Women in the Sung Period* (1993).

On the history of Korea see Andrew C. Nahm, *Introduction to Korean History and Culture* (1993), and Ki-Baik Kim, *A New History of Korea* (1984). An excellent introduction to Japanese history is Paul H. Varley, *Japanese Culture*, 3d ed. (1984). Relevant documents are reprinted in David John Lu, *Sources of Japanese History, Volume One* (1974), and R. Tsunoda, W. T. de Bary, and D. Keene, compilers, *Sources of Japanese Tradition, Volume I* (1964). Ivan Morris's *The World of the Shining Prince: Court Life in Ancient Japan* (1979), is a classic introduction to the literature and culture of Fujiwara Japan at the time of the writing of Murasaki Shikibu's novel *The Tale of Genji*. For Annam see Keith Weller Taylor, *The Birth of Vietnam* (1983).

NOTES

1. Edited quotation from William H. McNeill, *Plagues and Peoples* (Garden City: Anchor Press, 1976), 118. McNeill, following his translator, has mistaken Ge Hong as "Ho Kung" (pinyin romanization "He Gong").

2. Quoted in David Lattimore, "Allusion in T'ang Poetry," in A. Wright and D. Twitchett, eds., *Perspectives on the T'ang* (New Haven: Yale University Press, 1973), 436.

3. Quoted in Ivan Morris, *The World of the Shining Prince: Court Life in Ancient Japan* (New York: Penguin Books, 1979), 221–222.

CHAPTER TWELVE

Peoples and Civilizations of the Americas, to 1500

First Peoples • Mesoamerica, 2000 B.C.E.–800 C.E.

The Postclassic Period in Mesoamerica, 800–1500 • Northern Peoples

Andean Civilizations

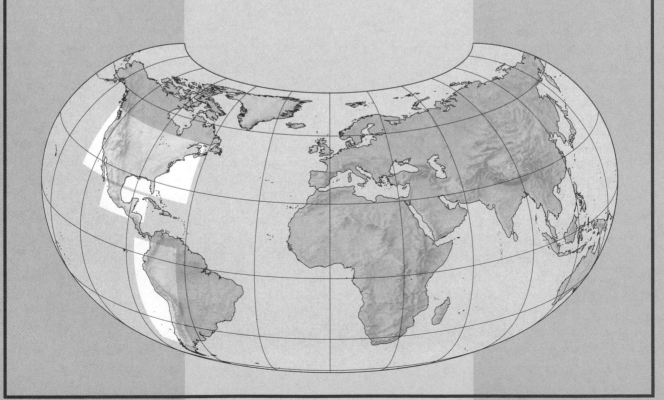

The Maya kingdoms of Tikal and Uaxactún were located less than 12 miles (19 kilometers) apart. Led by their kings and great nobles, the armies of the two kingdoms had met often in battle to secure captives for the gods. War and sacrifice held a central place in the Maya social order, but war seldom threatened the survival of dynasties or territorial boundaries. These limits were overturned on January 16, 378 C.E., when the forces of Uaxactún were decisively defeated by Great-Jaguar-Paw, king of Tikal.

The battle began in the traditional way: the opposing armies shouted challenges and insults at each other across the grassy plain that separated them. Filled with anger by these taunts, individual warriors broke ranks and rushed to engage their tormentors. As individuals and small groups struggled with clubs and stabbing spears, subdued warriors were dragged away from the battle for later sacrifice.

After hours of hand-to-hand combat, many warriors on both sides had been wounded, but only a few had been killed or taken captive. It was then that Smoking-Frog, war leader of Tikal's forces and kinsman of the king, ordered a reserve force hidden in the nearby forest to attack. These warriors were armed with atlatls, a device for throwing obsidian-tipped spears long distances (obsidian is a hard, glassy volcanic rock). Used before by the Maya only for hunting large game, the atlatl was an efficient killing weapon that transformed the battlefield. Uaxactún's forces had no response. When a massed counterattack collapsed under repeated volleys of spears, the king of Uaxactún and the remnants of his army fled the battlefield.

Customary preparations for war had failed the royal house of Uaxactún. Days of fasting, prayers, and rituals had not won for Uaxactún the support of the gods. Elaborate war regalia and carefully painted faces had not protected the king and his nobles. Their courage and skill were no match for the weapons and tactics of Tikal. In the aftermath of defeat, the ancient lineage of Uaxactún was extinguished by ritual sacrifice. Tikal's war leader, Smoking-Frog, and his heirs would reign in their place. New technology had altered warfare and geopolitics in the Maya world. War for the first time in the Americas was associated with the conquest and subordination of a rival dynasty.[1]

For more than ten thousand years peoples in the Western Hemisphere lived in virtual isolation from the rest of the world. Although some scholars suggest that limited contacts with the Old World may have occurred, most experts believe that the Americas developed without significant cultural influence from elsewhere. The duration and comprehensiveness of this isolation distinguishes the history of the Americas from the world's other major cultural regions. While technological innovations passed back and forth among the civilizations of Asia, Africa, and Europe, the peoples of the Americas faced the challenges of the natural environment on their own.

As suggested by the story of Smoking-Frog's victory over Uaxactún, the indigenous peoples of the Americas were in constant competition for resources. Although political and technological innovations helped to determine events, no single set of political institutions or technologies worked in every environment, and enormous cultural diversity existed in the ancient Americas. In Mesoamerica (Mexico and northern Central America) and in the Andes, indigenous peoples developed some of the world's most productive and diversified agriculture. They also built great cities that rivaled in size and beauty the capitals of the Chinese and Roman Empires. In the rest of the hemisphere, indigenous peoples adapted combinations of hunting and agriculture to maintain a wide variety of settlement patterns, political forms, and cultural traditions. These cultural traditions, as well as the civilizations of Mesoamerica and the Andes, experienced cycles of expansion and vitality followed by contraction and reorganization as they were challenged by environmental changes, population growth, class conflict, and warfare.

FIRST PEOPLES

The Western Hemisphere became inhabited as the result of migrations from the Asian mainland (see Chapter 1). The lower sea levels of the late Ice Age linked Siberia and Alaska and made it possible for groups of hunters to cross to the Americas on foot. Given that Australia had been peopled by seaborne migrants as early as 50,000 B.C.E., it is possible that some migrants arrived in small boats as well. Some scholars believe the first migrations occurred as early as the period 35,000–25,000 B.C.E. Others, relying on physical evidence from archaeological excavations, insist on a later date, between 20,000 and 13,000 B.C.E.

Great variation in the Western Hemisphere's environments and climates contributed to the development of enduring cultural differences among these first peoples.[2] Unique strategies were needed to adapt to environments as different as the frozen regions of the polar extremes, the tropical rain forest of the Amazon and Orinoco Basins, the deserts of coastal Peru and the southwest of the present-day United States, the high altitudes of the Andes and Rocky mountain ranges, and the woodlands and prairies of both North and South America. Within each of these regions human communities produced new technologies and uncovered useful natural resources.

Early Cultures

The early residents of the Americas first lived in small hunting bands made up of related adults and children. Because these bands moved often to follow game and collect edible plants, they had no fixed settlements. These early peoples depended on hunting, but seeds, nuts, and berries gained a larger place in their diet with the passage of centuries. Men were the primary hunters of large game. Women supplemented the unreliable results of their hunts with small game and edible plants. Because women found and harvested edible plants, they probably played a central role in the development of plant domestication.

Like the peoples of the Stone Age cultures of the Old World, these peoples had a rich religious life that gave meaning to their collective experience and provided motifs for the decoration of both utilitarian and ritual objects. They also had a sophisticated knowledge of the natural environment, allowing them to identify a remarkable number of medicinal and hallucinogenic plants. Technological innovations, like improved projectile points, the spear thrower (atlatl) and, later, the bow and arrow, increased their efficiency as hunters. The success of hunters was also increased by tactics such as stampeding herds of bison over cliffs. This maneuver resulted in the deaths of many more animals than could be killed by individual hunters. These advances in hunting technology were accompanied by the development of grinding devices, baskets, and pottery that eased the processing and storage of seeds and nuts.

The Beginnings of Agriculture

Between 5000 and 3000 B.C.E. advances in plant domestication and agricultural technology permitted growth in the number and size of settlements in the Americas. Although domesticated plant varieties and related technologies were commonly disseminated over vast distances, four distinct regional agricultural complexes based on different staple crops eventually appeared. Between approximately 4000 and 3000 B.C.E. inhabitants of the central Mexican plateau domesticated maize. Maize eventually became the most important staple in the Americas. As climatically suitable varieties were developed, maize cultivation soon spread south to South America and then north and east through North America, reaching Canada and the northeast of what is now the United States after 1000 C.E.

The great civilizations of the Andean region relied in similar ways on the potato. Varieties of potato became the most important staple crop at higher elevations of the Andean region after 1000 B.C.E. It was supplemented where possible by maize cultivation after 2500 B.C.E. and, at high elevations, by quinoa, an indigenous grain.

The third region was also in South America. In the Amazonian and Orinocan regions of South America, manioc (a tuber) became the staple after 1500 B.C.E. It then spread to the Caribbean. Though little known in temperate regions even today, manioc is a hearty plant that produces more calories per acre than any other staple crop. Located between the maize and manioc regions, societies of the Caribbean cultivated both crops.

Between 2000 and 1000 B.C.E. eastern North America became the fourth center of independent plant domestication. By 100 C.E. a complex agriculture based on varieties of squash and locally domesticated seed crops sustained the first permanent North American agricultural societies along the Ohio and Mississippi river valleys. Unlike the maize, potato, and manioc agricultures, this seed-based agricultural economy did not survive into the modern era. It was abandoned soon after 100 C.E. in favor of growing a frost-resistant maize.

In addition to the development of improved plant varieties, the progress of agriculture depended on increasingly sophisticated and costly technological solutions to environmental challenges. Long before the appearance of Europeans, the first peoples of the Americas had dramatically altered the landscape as they met these challenges. In sparsely populated regions with limited agriculture, like the northeast of North America and the Amazon region, periodic burning and the introduction of new plant species altered the natural landscape. In Mesoamerica and in the southern Andes, expanding agricultural productivity and growing population had an even more profound environmental impact beginning about 1000 B.C.E. In both regions powerful states with populous and prosperous cities appeared at about the time that the Hittite kingdom of the Middle East was destroyed and the Shang period ended in China. The cultural legacies of the two most important of these early civilizations, the Olmec of Mesoamerica and Chavín of the Andean region, persisted for more than a thousand years.

MESOAMERICA, 2000 B.C.E.–800 C.E.

Mesoamerica is a region of great geographic and climatic diversity located between the large landmasses of North and South America. It includes central and southern Mexico and most of Central America north of the isthmus of Panama. In the centuries before 1000 C.E., it sustained a coherent and dynamic regional culture that produced the most highly urbanized civilizations of the Americas. Mesoamerica has three distinct ecological zones, each hosting a great variety of plant and animal life. The hot and humid plains of the Gulf coast are bordered to the west by the temperate areas of the coastal foothills and fertile basin of the central mesa (tableland). These regions are surrounded by semi-arid high mountains. Differences in rainfall, temperature, and soil create micro environments where early agriculturalists produced both staples and specialized products for trade with neighbors. Within these ecological niches, Mesoamerican societies developed specialized agricultural technologies and exploited useful minerals like obsidian and chert (flintlike quartz) to make sharp tools and weapons.

The Development of Cultural Unity

Although large areas of Mesoamerica were sometimes controlled by powerful imperial states, the region was never united politically. Instead, Mesoamerica was unified by cultural traditions. Important regional differences were always present, but in agriculture, religion, political organization, art, architecture, and sport shared characteristics were found throughout the region. Scholars have created broad historical categories to represent changes in levels of urbanization, increased class distinctions, the growing power of state authority, and an escalation in levels of military conflict.

The economic basis for Mesoamerican culture was a highly diverse and productive agriculture. Maize, squash, and beans became dietary staples by 2500 B.C.E. Supplementing them were such foods as avocado, tomato, cacao (chocolate beans), chilies, and amaranth (an edible flowering plant). As populations grew and political institutions gained the power to mobilize labor for collective tasks, the environment was transformed. In the lowlands of the Gulf coast and along lake shores of the central mesa labor was organized to construct raised fields and drainage canals to reduce the threat of flooding during the rainy season. Similar efforts terraced the coastal foothills and mountains of the interior to slow erosion and increase available land for planting. In semiarid regions massive irrigation works, reservoirs, and aqueducts allowed farmers to grow food on marginal lands. Even in heavily forested regions the use of fire and seed selection altered the distribution of plant varieties to favor those most useful to nearby populations.

There was great variation in the names and personas of the gods that inhabited the pantheons of Mesoamerica's peoples, but nearly all the region's cultures accepted that the gods had dual (male/female) natures. A form of kingship that melded religious and secular powers and roles was also common. Kings, priests, and shamans were assumed to have the power to transform themselves into powerful supernatural actors through bloodletting rituals and the use of hallucinogens. Images of men transformed into jaguars were common decorative motifs. Warfare and the sacrifice of prisoners were tied to ritual needs and a general belief that bloodletting was central to the survival and well-being of human society.

Other shared characteristics included monumental sculpture, a number system based on 20, the development of both ritual and solar calendars, and writing. There were also similarities in urban planning. Cities were architecturally dominated by high temple pyramids, the residences of elite families, and ball courts. The ball game was played with a solid rubber ball on steep-sided courts. In some cases elite captives were forced to play this game before being sacrificed.

These cultural attributes were shared by linguistically distinct local cultures organized in most cases as independent political states. In Mesoamerica cultural exchange depended more on long distance trade and well-developed markets than on political integration or military expansion. Technologies, beliefs, and ritual practices were exchanged along with subsistence goods and the valuable products of skilled artisans who worked with jade, shell, and feathers.

The Preclassic Olmecs

The preclassic period witnessed increased levels of urbanization, growth in the power of hereditary aristocracies and kings, and expanded long-distance trade. The Olmecs were the most influential Mesoamerican preclassic civilization (see Figure 12.1, p. 354). They flourished between 1200 and 400 B.C.E., roughly the period of the golden age of Athens. The major Olmec centers were located along the tropical coast of Vera Cruz and Tabasco in Mexico. San Lorenzo (1200–900 B.C.E.) was the largest early Olmec center. La Venta inherited cultural primacy when San Lorenzo was abandoned or destroyed. Tres Zapotes became the principal center when La Venta underwent a similar collapse around 600 B.C.E. (see Map 12.1). In each case monuments were defaced and buried before the abandonment of a center. Archaeologists have recently excavated other important

Olmec head Giant heads sculpted from basalt are one of the most widely recognized legacies of the Olmec culture of Mesoamerica (1200 to 400 B.C.E.). Sixteen heads have been found, the largest approximately 11 feet tall. Each head has a unique personality and highly individualized appearance. Experts in Olmec archaeology believe the heads are portraits of individual rulers, warriors, or ballplayers. (Georg Gerster/Comstock)

Olmec sites along the Pacific coast of southern Mexico and in Central America.

The Olmecs made extensive use of raised fields. They dug drainage canals and used the excavated mud to build up planting areas. This technology enabled them to farm more intensively and produce the surpluses needed to sustain large-scale construction and craft specialization of their urban centers. Little is known about the political structure of Olmec civilization, but it is clear that there was no Olmec empire. Olmec influence depended more on the control of rare and desirable commodities, like jade and colored clays, and on the apparent appeal of their religious practices than on political control. The Olmecs' jaguar-god, some have suggested, was the precursor to the important rain deity found in all the later cultures of Mesoamerica. Jaguars and men being transformed into jaguars were common decorative motifs throughout the Olmec region.

The architectural and artistic accomplishments of the Olmecs were extraordinary given the absence of the wheel and draft animals (oxen, horses, burros). Their greatest artistic achievements were in jade carving. Figurines, necklaces, and ceremonial knives of jade were common in elite burials. All the major centers included large artificial platforms and mounds of packed earth and smaller temples with stone veneers. The best-known monuments of Olmec culture, however, were colossal carved stone heads as big as 11 feet (3.4 meters) high. Since each head is

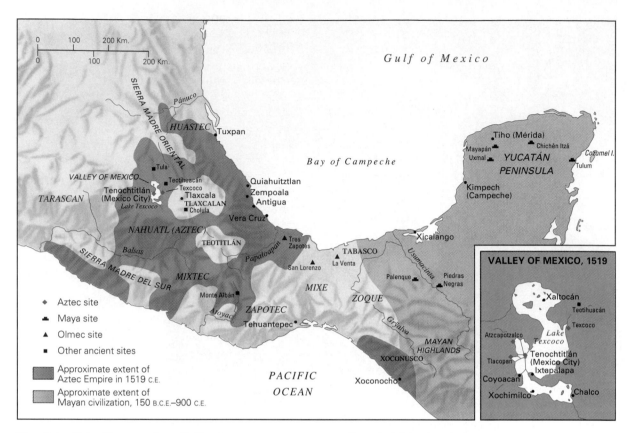

Map 12.1   Major Mesoamerican Civilizations, 1000 B.C.E.–1519 C.E.   From their island capital of Tenochtitlán, the Aztecs militarily and commercially dominated a large region. Aztec achievements were built on the legacy of earlier civilizations such as the Olmecs and Maya.

unique, most archaeologists believe that they represent individual rulers.

Both skilled artisans and large amounts of less skilled labor were needed to construct the urban centers. Only a powerful political class that commanded thousands of laborers could manage the quarrying and transportation of heavy stones. Other skilled craftsmen worked in stone, clay, and jade. Olmec society also had an important class of priests or shamans. Long-distance trade in luxury and ritual goods was probably carried on by a merchant class.

The Olmec played a crucial role in the early development of writing and astronomy, and they devised a calendar. It is likely that the ritual ball game eventually played widely throughout

Mesoamerica also originated with the Olmecs. The legacy of the Olmecs is most visible in the Maya lands to the south.

Two Classic Civilizations: Teotihuacán and the Maya

Located about 30 miles (48 kilometers) northeast of modern Mexico City, Teotihuacán (100 B.C.E.–750 C.E.) was one of Mesoamerica's most important classic-period civilizations (see Map 12.1). At the height of its power, from 450 to 600 C.E., Teotihuacán was the largest city in the Americas. With between 125,000 and 200,000 inhabitants, it was larger than all but a small number of contemporary European and Asian cities.

Religious architecture dominated the city center. Enormous pyramids dedicated to the Sun and Moon and more than twenty smaller temples devoted to other gods were arranged along a central avenue. The people recognized and worshiped many gods and lesser spirits. Among the gods were the Sun, the Moon, a storm-god, and Quetzalcóatl, the feathered serpent. Quetzalcóatl was a culture-god believed to be the originator of agriculture and the arts. Like the earlier Olmecs, people living at Teotihuacán practiced human sacrifice. More than sixty sacrificial victims were found during the excavation of the temple of Quetzalcóatl at Teotihuacán. Sacrifice was viewed as a sacred duty toward the gods and as essential to the well being of human society.

The rapid growth in urban population was the result of the forced relocation of farm families from smaller villages in the region. More than two-thirds of the city's residents continued to work in agriculture, walking out from urban residences to their fields. The elite of Teotihuacán used the city's growing labor resources to bring marginal lands into production. Swamps were drained, irrigation works were constructed, terraces were built into hillsides, and the use of chinampas was expanded. *Chinampas*, sometimes called "floating gardens," were narrow artificial islands anchored by trees and created by heaping lake muck and waste material on beds of reeds. Chinampas permitted year-round agriculture—because of subsurface irrigation and resistance to frost—and thus played a crucial role in sustaining the region's growing population. The productivity of the city's agriculture made possible its accomplishments in art, architecture, and trade.

As population grew, the housing of commoners underwent dramatic change. Apartment-like stone buildings were constructed for the first time. Among the residents of these early apartment blocks were the craftsmen who produced the pottery and obsidian tools that were the most important articles of long-distance trade. Teotihuacán pottery has been found throughout central Mexico and even in the Maya region of Guatemala. More than 2 percent of the urban population was engaged in making obsidian tools and weapons.

The city's role as a religious center and commercial power provided both divine sanction and a material basis for the elite's increased wealth and status. This elite controlled the state bureaucracy, tax collection, and commerce. The prestige and wealth of the elite were reflected in growing class distinctions in dress and diet and in the construction of separate residence compounds for the families of the aristocracy. The central position and great prestige of the priestly class are made clear in temple and palace murals. Teotihuacán's religious influence drew pilgrims from as far away as Oaxaca and Vera Cruz. Some of them became permanent residents.

Historians debate the role of the military in the development of Teotihuacán. The city's location in a valley and the absence of defensive structures before 500 C.E. suggest that Teotihuacán enjoyed relative peace during its early development. Archaeological evidence, however, reveals that the city's powerful military protected long-distance trade and enforced the elite's effort to compel peasant agriculturalists to transfer their surplus production to the city. The discovery of representations of soldiers in typical Teotihuacán dress in the Maya region of Guatemala suggests to some that Teotihuacán used its military to expand trade relations. But unlike later postclassic civilizations, Teotihuacán was not an imperial state controlled by a military elite.

It is unclear what forces brought about the collapse of Teotihuacán about 650 C.E. Weakness was evident as early as 500 C.E., when the urban population declined to about 40,000 and the city built defensive walls. These fortifications and pictorial evidence from murals suggest that the city's final decades were violent. Early scholars suggested that the city was overwhelmed militarily by Cholula, a rival city-state located in the Valley of Puebla, or by nomadic warrior peoples from the northern frontier. More recently, investigators have uncovered evidence of conflict within the ruling elite and the mismanagement of resources. This, they argue, led to class conflict and the breakdown of public order. As a result, most important temples in the city center were pulled down and religious images defaced. Elite palaces were also systematically burned and many of the residents killed. Regardless of the causes, the eclipse of Teotihuacán was felt throughout Mexico and into Central America.

During Teotihuacán's ascendancy in the north, the Maya developed an impressive civilization in the region that today includes Guatemala, Honduras, Belize, and southern Mexico (see Map 12.1). Given the difficulties imposed by a tropical climate and fragile soils, the cultural and architectural achievements of the Maya were remarkable. Although they shared a single culture, they were never unified politically. Instead, rival kingdoms led by hereditary rulers struggled with each other for regional dominance, much like the Mycenaean-era Greeks (see Chapter 3).

Modern Maya farmers prepare their fields by cutting down small trees and brush and then burning the dead vegetation. This *swidden agriculture* can produce high yields for a few years, but it uses up the soil's nutrients, eventually forcing people to move to more fertile land. The high population levels of the classic period (250–800 C.E.) required more intensive forms of agriculture. Maya living near the major urban centers achieved high agricultural yields by draining swamps and building elevated fields. They used irrigation in areas with long dry seasons, and they terraced hillsides in the cooler highlands. Nearly every household planted a garden to provide condiments and fruits to supplement dietary staples. Maya agriculturalists also managed nearby forests, favoring the growth of the trees and shrubs that were most useful to them, as well as promoting the conservation of deer and other semitame animals.

During the classic period, Maya city-states proliferated. Each city concentrated religious and political functions and controlled groups of smaller dependent cities and a broad agricultural zone. Classic-era cities, unlike earlier sites, had dense central precincts visually dominated by monumental architecture. These political and ceremonial centers were commonly positioned to reflect the movement of the Sun and Venus.

Open plazas were surrounded by high pyramids and by elaborately decorated palaces often built on high ground or on constructed mounds. The effect was to awe the masses drawn to these centers for religious and political rituals.

The Maya loved decoration. Nearly all of their public buildings were covered with bas-relief and painted in bright colors. Religious allegories, the genealogies of rulers, and important historical events were the most common motifs. Beautifully carved altars and stone monoliths were erected near major temples. This rich legacy of monumental architecture was constructed without the aid wheels—no pulleys, wheelbarrows, or carts—or metal tools. Masses of men and women aided only by levers and stone tools cut, carried, and put construction materials in place.

The Maya cosmos was divided into three layers connected along a vertical axis that traced the course of the Sun. The earthly arena of human existence held an intermediate position between the heavens, conceptualized by the Maya as a sky-monster, and a dark underworld. A sacred tree rose through the three layers; its roots were in the underworld, and its branches reached into the heavens. The temple precincts of Maya cities physically represented essential elements of this religious cosmology. The pyramids were sacred mountains reaching to the heavens. The doorways of the pyramids were portals to the underworld.

Rulers and other members of the elite served both priestly and political functions. They decorated their bodies with paint and tattoos and wore elaborate costumes of textiles, animal skins, and feathers to project both secular power and divine sanction. Kings communicated directly with the supernatural residents of the other worlds and with deified royal ancestors through bloodletting rituals and hallucinogenic trances. Scenes of rulers drawing blood from lips, ears, and penises are common in surviving frescoes and on painted pottery.

Even warfare, like the battle between Tikal and Uaxactún described at the beginning of the chapter, was infused with religious meaning and elaborate ritual. Battle scenes and the depiction of the torture and sacrifice of captives were fre-

The Great Plaza at Tikal   The ruins of Tikal, in modern Guatemala, demonstrate the impressive architectural and artistic achievements of the Classic Era Maya. The arrangement and construction of Maya centers provided a dramatic setting for the numerous rituals that dominated public life. This is one of a number of complexes dominated by one or more temples at Tikal. Early construction of this complex began before 150 B.C.E. The site was abandoned about 900 C.E. Temple I is on the right and Temple II on the left. In the background is an elevated platform with additional temples. The plaza also included elite residences and a ballcourt. (William Ferguson)

quent decorative themes. Typically, Maya military forces fought to secure captives rather than territory. Days of fasting, sacred ritual, and rites of purification preceded battle. The king, his kinsmen, and other ranking nobles actively participated in war. Elite captives were nearly always sacrificed; captured commoners were more likely to be enslaved.

Only two women are known to have ruled Maya kingdoms. At Palenque, Kan'anal-Ik'al ruled from 583 to 604 C.E., and Sak-K'uk ruled from 612 to 615 C.E. Maya women of the ruling

lineages did play important political and religious roles, however. The consorts of male rulers participated in bloodletting rituals and in other important public ceremonies, and their noble blood helped legitimate the rule of their husbands. Although Maya society was patrilineal (tracing descent in the male line), there is evidence that some male rulers traced their lineages bilaterally (in both the male and the female lines) and emphasized the female line if it held higher status. Much less is known about the lives of the women of the lower classes, but scholars believe that they played a central role in the household economy, maintaining essential garden plots and weaving, and in the management of family life.

Building on what the Olmecs had done, the Maya made important contributions to the development of the Mesoamerican calendar and to mathematics and writing. Their interest in time and in the cosmos was reflected in the complexity of their calendric system. Each day was identified by three separate dating systems. Like other peoples throughout Mesoamerica, the Maya had a calendar that tracked the ritual cycle (260 days divided into 13 months of 20 days) and a solar calendar (365 days divided into 18 months of 20 days, plus 5 unfavorable days at the end of the year). The concurrence of these two calendars every 52 years was believed to be especially ominous. The Maya, alone among Mesoamerican peoples, also maintained a continuous "long count" calendar, which began at a fixed date in the past that modern scholars identify as 3114 B.C.E., a date that was likely associated with creation.

These accurate calendric systems and the astronomical observations on which they were based depended on Maya contributions to mathematics and writing. Their system of mathematics incorporated the concept of the zero and place value but had limited notational signs. Maya writing was a form of hieroglyphic inscription that signified whole words or concepts as well as phonetic cues or syllables (see Environment & Technology: The Maya Writing System). Aspects of public life, religious belief, and the biographies of rulers and their ancestors were recorded in deerskin and bark-paper books, on pottery, and on the stone columns and monumental buildings of the urban centers. In this sense every Maya city was a sacred text.

Between 800 and 900 C.E. many of the major urban centers of the Maya were abandoned or

The Mesoamerican ball game   Archaeologists have found evidence from Guatemala to Arizona of an ancient ball game played with a solid rubber ball on slope-sided courts shaped like the capital letter T. Among the Maya the game was mythologically associated with creation, and thus had deep religious meaning. There is evidence that some players were sacrificed. In this scene found on a ceramic jar, players in elaborate ritual clothing which includes heavy, protective pads around the chest and waist play with a ball much larger than that actually used in games. In some representations, balls were drawn so as to suggest a human head. (Dallas Art Museum/Justin Kerr)

The Maya Writing System

Of all the cultures of precolombian America, only the Maya produced a written literature that has survived to the modern era. The literary legacy of the Maya is inscribed on stone monuments, ceramics, jade, shell, and bone. Books of bark paper were the original and most common medium of Maya scribes, but only four of these books exist today.

The historical and literary importance of the written record of the Maya has been recognized only recently. In the early nineteenth century, visitors to southern Mexico and Guatemala began to record and decipher the symbols they found on stone monuments. By the end of the nineteenth century, the Maya system of numbers and the Maya calendar were decoded.

Not until the 1960s did scholars recognize that Maya writing reflects spoken language by having a set word order. We now know that Maya writing was capable of capturing the rich meaning of spoken language.

Maya scribes could use signs that represented sounds or signs that represented whole words. *Jaguar* (*balam* in Maya) could be written by using the head of this big cat in symbolic form. Because there were other large cats in the Maya region, scribes commonly added a pronunciation cue like a prefix or suffix to the front or back of the symbol to clarify meaning. In this case they might affix the syllable sign *ba* to the front of the jaguar head or the syllable sign *ma* to the end. Because the Maya word for no other feline began with *ba* or ended with *ma*, the reader knew to pronounce the word as *balam* for "jaguar." Alternatively, because the last vowel was not sounded, *balam* could be written with three syllable signs: *ba la ma*.

These signs were expressed in a rich and varied array of stylized forms, much like illustrated European medieval texts, that make translation difficult. But these stylistic devices helped convey meaning. Readers detected meaning not only in what the text "said" but also in how and where the text was written.

The work of Maya scribes was not intended as mass communication, since few Maya could read these texts. Instead, as two of the most respected experts in this field explain, "Writing was a sacred proposition that had the capacity to capture the order of the cosmos, to inform history, to give form to ritual, and to transform the profane material of everyday life into the supernatural."

Source: Adapted from Linda Schele and David Freidel, *A Forest of Kings: The Untold Story of the Ancient Maya*, 1990 with figure of *balaam*. Copyright © 1990 by Linda Schele and David Freidel. Reprinted by permission of William Morrow & Co., Inc.

balam   *ba - balam*   *balam - ma*   *ba - balam - ma*   *ba - la - m(a)*

destroyed, although a small number of classic-period centers survived for centuries. This collapse was preceded in some areas by decades of urban population decline and increased warfare. Some experts have argued that the destruction of Teotihuacán about 750 C.E. disrupted trade, thus undermining the legitimacy of Maya rulers. Other scholars suggest that growing population pressure led to environmental degradation and falling agricultural productivity. This environmental crisis, in turn, might have led to class conflict and increased levels of warfare as desperate elites sought to acquire additional agricultural land through conquest. Although little evidence has been found, some scholars have proposed that epidemic disease and pestilence were the prime causes of the catastrophe. Most probably, a combination of factors caused the end of the classic period.

THE POSTCLASSIC PERIOD IN MESOAMERICA, 800–1500

The division between classic and postclassic periods is somewhat arbitrary. Not only is there no single explanation for the collapse of Teotihuacán and many of the major Maya centers, but these events occurred over more than a century and a half. In fact, some important classic-period civilizations, like Cholula in the Valley of Puebla, survived unscathed. Moreover, the essential cultural characteristics of the classic period were carried over to the postclassic. Similarities in religious belief and practice, in architecture and urban planning, and in social organization all link the two periods.

There were, however, some important differences between these periods. There is evidence that the population of Mesoamerica expanded during the postclassic period. Resulting pressures led to an intensification of agricultural practices and to increased warfare. The governing elites of the major postclassic states—the Toltecs and the Aztecs—responded to these harsh realities by increasing the size of their armies and by developing political institutions that facilitated their control of large and culturally diverse territories acquired through conquest.

The Toltecs

Little is known about the Toltecs prior to their arrival in central Mexico. Some scholars speculate that they were originally a satellite population that Teotihuacán placed on the northern frontier to protect against the incursions of nomads. After their migration south, the Toltecs borrowed from the cultural legacy of Teotihuacán and created an important postclassic civilization. Memories of their military achievements and the violent imagery of their political and religious rituals dominated the Mesoamerican imagination in the late postclassic period. In the fourteenth century, the Aztecs and their contemporaries erroneously believed that the Toltecs were the authors of nearly all the great cultural achievements of the Mesoamerican world. The actual accomplishments of the Toltecs, however, were primarily political and military.

The Toltecs created a powerful conquest state and extended their influence from the area north of modern Mexico City to Central America. Established about 968 C.E., Tula, the Toltec capital, was constructed in a grand style (see Map 12.1). Its public architecture featured colonnaded patios and numerous temples. Although the population of Tula never reached the levels of classic-period Teotihuacán, the Toltec capital dominated central Mexico. Toltec decoration had a more warlike and violent character than the decoration of earlier Mesoamerican cultures. Nearly all Toltec public buildings and temples were decorated with representations of warriors or with scenes suggesting human sacrifice.

The Toltec state apparently was ruled by two chieftains or kings at the same time. Evidence suggests that this division of responsibility eventually weakened Toltec power and led to the destruction of Tula. Sometime after 1000 C.E., a struggle between elite groups identified with rival religious cults undermined the Toltec state. According to legends that survived among the Aztecs, Topiltzin—one of the rulers and a priest of the cult of Quetzalcóatl—and his followers bitterly accepted exile in the east, "the land of the rising sun." These legendary events coincided with a growing Toltec influence among the Maya of the Yucatán Peninsula. One of the ancient texts relates these events in the following manner:

> Thereupon he [Topiltzin] looked toward Tula, and then wept. . . . And when he had done these things . . . he went to reach the seacoast. Then he fashioned a raft of serpents. When he had arranged the

raft, he placed himself as if it were his boat. Then he set off across the sea.[3]

The Toltec state began to decline after the exile of Topiltzin, and around 1168 C.E. Tula was overcome by northern invaders. After its destruction, a centuries-long process of cultural and political assimilation produced a new Mesoamerican political order based on the urbanized culture and statecraft of the Toltecs. Like Semitic peoples of the third millennium B.C.E. interacting with Sumerian culture, the new Mesoamerican elites were drawn in part from the invading cultures. The Aztecs of the Valley of Mexico would become the most important of these late postclassic peoples.

The Aztecs

The Mexica, more commonly known as Aztecs, were among the northern peoples who pushed into central Mexico in the wake of the collapse of

Costumes of Aztec warriors In Mesoamerican warfare individual warriors sought to gain prestige and improve their status by taking captives. This illustration from the sixteenth-century Codex Mendoza was drawn by a Amerindian artist. It shows how the Aztecs used distinctive costumes to acknowledge the prowess of warriors. These costumes indicate the taking of two (top left) to six captives (bottom center). The individual on the bottom right shown without a weapon was a military leader. As was common in Mesoamerican illustrations of military conflict, the captives, held by their hair, are shown kneeling before the victors. (The Bodleian Library, Oxford, Ma. Arch. Selder. A.I. fol. 64r.)

Tula. Once settled, they grafted onto their clan-based social organization elements of the political and social practices that they found among the urbanized agriculturalists of the valley. At first, the Aztecs served their more powerful neighbors as serfs and mercenaries. As their strength grew, they relocated to small uninhabited islands near the shore of Lake Texcoco and began the construction of their twin capitals, Tenochtitlán and Tlateloco, around 1325 C.E.

From this strong point, they became valued mercenaries of the region's dominant political power, Azcapotzalco. Military successes allowed the Aztecs to seize control of additional agricultural land along the lake shore. With the increased economic independence and greater political security that resulted from this expansion, the Aztecs transformed their political organization by introducing a monarchical system similar to that found in more powerful neighboring states. Clans survived to the era of Spanish conquest but increasingly lost influence to monarchs and hereditary aristocrats.

As the power of the nobility grew and the authority of kinship-based clans declined, class distinctions became more important. These alterations in social structure and political life were made possible by Aztec military expansion. Territorial conquest allowed the warrior elite of Aztec society to seize land and peasant labor as spoils of war (see Map 12.1). In time, the royal family and high aristocracy possessed extensive estates that were cultivated by slaves and landless peasants. Although commoners received some material rewards from imperial expansion, their ability to influence or control decisions was largely lost. Some commoners were able to achieve some social mobility through success on the battlefield or by entering the priesthood, but the highest social ranks were always reserved for hereditary nobles.

Nevertheless, the urban plan of Tenochtitlán and Tlateloco continued to be organized around the clans, whose members maintained a common ritual life and accepted civic responsibilities such as caring for the sick and elderly. Clan members also fought together as military units. However, the clans' historical control over common agricultural land and other scarce resources, such as fishing and hunting rights, was diminished. By 1500 C.E., Aztec society was characterized by great inequalities in wealth and privilege.

The kings and aristocracy legitimated their new ascendancy by creating elaborate rituals and ceremonies that separated them from the commoners. One of the Spaniards who participated in the conquest of the Aztec Empire remembered his first meeting with the Aztec ruler Moctezuma II (r. 1502–1520): "many great lords walked before the great Montezuma [Moctezuma II], sweeping the ground on which he was to tread and laying down cloaks so that his feet should not touch the earth. Not one of these chieftains dared look him in the face."[4] Commoners lived in small dwellings and ate a limited diet of staples, but members of the nobility lived in large, well-constructed two-story houses and consumed a diet rich in animal protein and flavored by condiments and expensive imports like chocolate. The elite were also set apart by their rich dress and jewelry. Even marriage customs in the two groups were different. Commoners were monogamous; nobles, polygamous.

The Aztec state met the challenge of feeding an urban population of approximately 150,000 by efficiently organizing the labor of the clans and additional laborers sent as tribute by defeated peoples to expand agricultural land. The construction of a dike more than 5½ miles (9 kilometers) long by 23 feet (7 meters) wide to separate the fresh and saltwater parts of Lake Texcoco was the Aztecs' most impressive land reclamation project. Once constructed, the dike allowed a significant extension of irrigated fields and the construction of additional chinampas. One expert has estimated that the project consumed 4 million person-days to complete. Aztec chinampas contributed maize, fruits, and vegetables to the markets of Tenochtitlán. The imposition of tribute obligations on conquered peoples also helped relieve some of the pressure of Tenochtitlán's growing population. Approximately one quarter of the Aztec capital's food requirements were satisfied by tribute payments of maize, beans, and other foods from nearby dependencies. The Aztecs also demanded cotton cloth, military equipment, luxury goods like jade and feathers, and sacrificial victims as tribute. They acquired other goods by trade.

A specialized class of merchants controlled long-distance trade. Given the absence of draft animals and wheeled vehicles, this commerce was dominated by lightweight and valuable products like gold, jewels, feathered garments, cacao, and animal skins. Merchants also provided essential political and military intelligence for the Aztec elite. Operating outside the protection of Aztec military power, merchant expeditions were armed and often had to defend themselves. Although merchants became wealthy and powerful as the Aztecs expanded their empire, they were denied the privileges of the high nobility and feared to publicly display their affluence.

As was true throughout the Mesoamerican world, Aztec commerce was carried on without money and credit. Barter was facilitated by the use of cacao, quills filled with gold, and cotton cloth as standard units of value to compensate for differences in the value of bartered goods. Aztec expansion facilitated the integration of producers and consumers in the central Mexican economy. As a result, the markets of Tenochtitlán and Tlateloco offered a rich array of goods produced from as far away as Central America and what is now the southwestern border of the United States. Hernán Cortés (1485–1547), the Spanish explorer who eventually conquered the Aztecs, expressed his admiration for the abundance of the Aztec marketplace:

> One square in particular is twice as big as that of Salamanca and completely surrounded by arcades where there are daily more than sixty thousand folk buying and selling. Every kind of merchandise such as may be met with in every land is for sale. . . . There is nothing to be found in all the land which is not sold in these markets, for over and above what I have mentioned there are so many and such various things that on account of their very number . . . I cannot detail them.[5]

The Aztecs succeeded in developing a remarkable urban landscape. The combined population of Tenochtitlán and Tlateloco and the nearby cities and hamlets of the surrounding lake shore was approximately 500,000 by 1500 C.E. The is-land capital was designed so that canals and streets intersected at right angles. Three causeways connected the city to the lake shore. Startled by the size and orderliness of Tenochtitlán, the Spaniards compared it favorably to the largest cities in Spain.

Religious rituals dominated public life in Tenochtitlán. Like the other cultures of the Mesoamerican world, the Aztecs believed in and worshiped a large number of gods. Most of these gods had a dual nature—both male and female personas. The major contribution of the Aztecs to the religious life of Mesoamerica was the cult of Huitzilopochtli, the southern hummingbird. As the Aztec state grew in power and wealth, the importance of this cult grew as well. Eventually, Huitzilopochtli became associated with the Sun. It was believed that he required a diet of human hearts to sustain him in his daily struggle to bring the Sun's warmth to the world. Tenochtitlán was architecturally dominated by a great twin temple devoted to Huitzilopochtli and Tlaloc, the rain god, symbolizing the two bases of the Aztec economy: war and agriculture.

War captives were preferred as sacrificial victims, but criminals, slaves, and people provided as tribute by dependent regions were also sacrificed in large numbers. Although human sacrifice had been practiced since early times in Mesoamerica, the Aztecs and other societies of the late postclassic period transformed this religious ritual by dramatically increasing its scale. There are no reliable estimates for the total number of sacrifices, but the numbers clearly reached into the thousands each year, some say as high as 20,000 per year. In 1487, the rededication of the temple of Huitzilopochtli alone was celebrated by the sacrifice of more than 10,000 victims. Clearly this form of violent public ritual had political consequences and was not simply the celebration of religious belief. Some scholars have emphasized the political nature of this rising tide of sacrifice. Since sacrifices were carried out in front of large crowds that included leaders from enemy and subject states as well as the masses of Aztec society, a political subtext must have been clear: rebellion, deviancy, and opposition were extremely dangerous.

NORTHERN PEOPLES

By the end of the classic period in Mesoamerica, around 800 C.E., important cultural centers had appeared in the southwestern desert region and along the Ohio and Mississippi river valleys of what is now the United States (see Figure 12.1). In both regions improved agricultural productivity and population growth led to increased urbanization and more complex social and political structures. The introduction of maize, beans, and squash played an important role in these developments, but in the Ohio Valley large villages with monumental earthworks were sustained at first by locally domesticated seed crops combined with traditional hunting and gathering practices.

In both the southwestern desert cultures and the eastern river-valley cultures, large-scale irrigation projects were associated with growing dependence on maize. This development, in turn, indicates more centralized political power and greater social stratification. The two regions, however, evolved different political traditions. The Anasazi and their neighbors in the southwest maintained a more egalitarian social structure and retained collective forms of political organization based on kinship and age. The mound builders of the eastern river valleys evolved more hierarchical political institutions. Groups of smaller towns were subordinate to a political center ruled by a

Figure 12.1   Mesoamerican, North American, and Andean Civilizations, to 1500

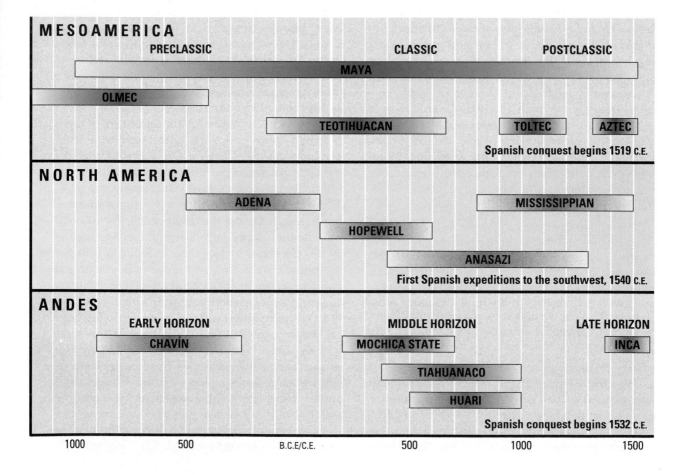

Pueblo Bonito Located in Chaco Canyon in modern New Mexico, Pueblo Bonito was the largest Anasazi settlement. At the height of its power around 1100 C.E., Pueblo Bonito was the center of an extensive religious and commercial network. This multistory structure included small apartments for individual families, storage chambers, and many subterranean rooms called kivas. The Anasazi believed that humans had emerged from within the earth. By locating much of their religious life in the kiva, they reconnected themselves to this mystical origin. (CGI/Pathway Productions)

hereditary chief who wielded both secular and religious authority.

The Southwestern Desert Cultures

Immigrants from Mexico introduced agriculture based on irrigation to present-day Arizona around 300 B.C.E. Because irrigation allowed the planting of two crops per year, the population grew, and settled village life soon appeared. Of all the southwestern cultures, the Hohokam of the Salt and Gila river valleys show the strongest Mexican influence. Hohokam sites have platform mounds and ball courts similar to those of Mesoamerica. Their pottery, clay figurines, cast copper bells, and turquoise mosaics also show southern influence. By 1000 C.E., the Hohokam

had constructed an elaborate irrigation system that included one canal more than 18 miles (30 kilometers) in length. Hohokam agriculture and ceramic technology spread over the centuries to neighboring peoples, but it was the Anasazi of the north who left the most vivid legacy of these desert cultures.

Archaeologists used *Anasazi*, a Navajo word meaning "ancient ones," to identify a number of dispersed, though similar, desert cultures located in what is now called the Four Corners region of Arizona, New Mexico, Colorado, and Utah. Between 450 and 750 C.E. the Anasazi embraced maize, beans, and squash. Their successful adaptation of these crops permitted the formation of larger villages and led to an enriched cultural life centered on underground ritual buildings called *kivas*. Evidence suggests that the Anasazi may also have used kivas for weaving and pottery making. They produced pottery decorated in geometric patterns, learned to weave cotton cloth, and, after 900 C.E., began to construct large multistory residential and ritual centers.

One of the largest Anasazi communities was located in Chaco Canyon in what is now northwestern New Mexico. Eight large communities were built in the canyon and four more on surrounding mesas, suggesting a regional population of approximately 15,000. Smaller villages were also located in the region. Each town contained hundreds of contiguous rooms arranged in tiers around a central plaza. At Pueblo Bonito, the largest town, more than 650 rooms were arranged in a four-story block of residences and storage rooms. Pueblo Bonito had 38 kivas, including a great kiva more than 65 feet (19 meters) in diameter. Social life and craft activities were concentrated in small open plazas or common rooms. Men were often drawn away from the village by hunting, by trade, and by the need to maintain irrigation works. Women shared in agricultural tasks and were specialists in many crafts. They were also responsible for food preparation and child care. If the practice of modern Pueblos, cultural descendants of the Anasazi, is a guide, houses and furnishings may have belonged to the women who formed extended families with their mothers and sisters.

The high quality construction at Chaco Canyon, the size and number of kivas, and the discovery of a system of roads linking the canyon to outlying towns suggest that Pueblo Bonito and its nearest neighbors exerted some kind of political or religious preeminence over a large region. Some archaeologists have suggested that the Chaco Canyon culture originated as a colonial appendage of Mesoamerica, but there is little evidence for this theory in the archaeological record. Merchants from Chaco provided Toltec-period peoples of northern Mexico with turquoise in exchange for shell jewelry, copper bells, macaws, and trumpets. But these exchanges occurred late in Chaco's development, and more important signs of Mesoamerican influence like pyramid-shaped mounds and ball courts are not found at Chaco. Nor is there evidence from the excavation of burials and residences of clear class distinctions, which were so prominent in Mesoamerica. Instead, it appears that the Chaco Canyon culture developed from earlier societies in the region.

The abandonment of the major sites in Chaco Canyon in the twelfth century most likely resulted from a long drought that undermined the culture's fragile agricultural economy. Nevertheless, Anasazi continued in the Four Corners region for more than a century after the abandonment of Chaco Canyon. There were major centers at Mesa Verde in present-day Colorado and Canyon de Chelly and Kiet Siel in Arizona (see Map 12.2). The Anasazi settlements on the Colorado Plateau and in Arizona were constructed in large natural caves located above valley floors. This hard-to-reach location suggests increased levels of warfare, probably provoked by population pressure on limited arable land. Although the Anasazi disappeared before the arrival of Europeans, the Pueblo peoples of the Rio Grande Valley and Arizona live in multistory villages and worship in kivas today.

The Mound Builders: Hopewell and Mississippian Cultures

The Adena culture of the Ohio Valley constructed large villages with monumental earthworks from about 500 B.C.E. This early mound-building culture was based on traditional hunting and gathering supplemented by limited agriculture of locally domesticated seed crops. Most, but not all, of the Adena mounds contained burials. Items found in these graves indicate a hierarchical society with an elite distinguished by its access to rare and valuable goods like mica from North Carolina and copper from the Great Lakes region.

Map 12.2 Culture Areas of North America   In each of the large ecological regions of North America, native peoples evolved distinctive cultures and technologies. Here the Anasazi of the arid southwest and the mound-building cultures of the Ohio and Mississippi River valleys are highlighted.

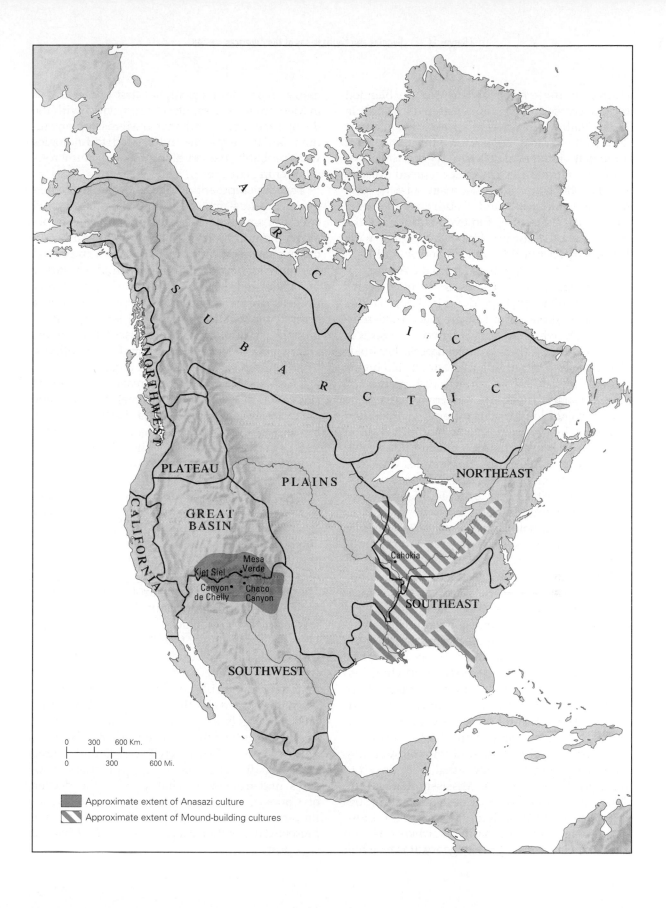

A R C T I C

S U B A R C T I C

NORTHWEST

PLATEAU

CALIFORNIA

GREAT
BASIN

PLAINS

NORTHEAST

Mesa
Verde
Kiet Siel
Canyon
de Chelly
Chaco
Canyon

Cahokia

SOUTHEAST

SOUTHWEST

0   300   600 Km.

0   300   600 Mi.

Approximate extent of Anasazi culture

Approximate extent of Mound-building cultures

Around 100 C.E. the Adena culture blended into a successor culture, also centered in the Ohio River Valley, called Hopewell. The largest Hopewell centers appeared in Ohio, but Hopewell influence, either in the form of colonies or trade dependencies, spread west to Illinois, Michigan, and Wisconsin, east to New York and Ontario, and south to Alabama, Louisiana, Mississippi, and even Florida. For the necessities of daily life Hopewell people were dependent on hunting and gathering and on a limited agriculture inherited from the Adena.

Hopewell is an early example of a North American chiefdom. Chiefdoms had populations of up to ten thousand and were ruled by hereditary leaders who had both religious and secular responsibilities. Chiefs organized periodic rituals of feasting and gift giving that established bonds among diverse kinship groups and guaranteed access to specialized crops and craft goods. They also managed long-distance trade relations that provided luxury goods and additional food supplies. The large mounds built to house elite burials and as platforms for temples and elite residences dominated Hopewell centers.

Hopewell sites were ordered hierarchically. The largest towns in the Ohio Valley served as ceremonial and political centers and had populations that reached several thousand inhabitants. Smaller villages had populations of a few hundred. Modern excavations of Hopewell mounds have found strong evidence of social stratification as well. Chiefs and other elite members were buried in vaults surrounded by valuable goods such as river pearls, copper jewelry, and, in some cases, women and retainers who apparently were sacrificed to accompany a dead chief into the afterlife. As was true with the earlier Olmec culture of Mexico, the abandonment of major Hopewell sites around 400 C.E. has no clear environmental or political explanation.

Hopewell technology and mound building continued in smaller centers that were linked to the development of the Mississippian culture (700–1500 C.E.). Although some experts have suggested that contacts with Mesoamerica influenced Mississippian culture, there is no convincing evidence for this theory. It is true that maize, beans, and squash, all first domesticated in Mesoamerica, were closely associated with the development of the urbanized Mississippian culture. But these plants and related technologies were probably passed along through numerous intervening cultures.

The development of these urbanized chiefdoms resulted instead from the accumulated effects of small increases in agricultural productivity, the adoption of the bow and arrow, and the expansion of trade networks. An improved economy led to population growth, the building of cities, and social stratification. The larger towns shared a common urban plan based on a central plaza surrounded by large platform mounds. Major towns were also trade centers where people bartered essential commodities, like flint used for weapons and tools.

The Mississippian culture reached its highest stage of evolution with the development of the great urban center of Cahokia, located near the modern city of East St. Louis, Illinois (see Map 12.2). At the center of this site was the largest mound constructed in North America, a terraced structure 100 feet (30 meters) high and 1,037 by 790 feet (316 by 241 meters) at the base. The center area of elite housing and temples was ringed by areas where commoners lived. At its height in about 1200 C.E., Cahokia had a population of about 30,000—about the same population as the great Maya city Tikal.

Like Tikal, Cahokia controlled surrounding agricultural lands and a number of secondary towns ruled by subchiefs. Burial evidence suggests that the rulers of Cahokia enjoyed an exalted position. In one burial more than fifty young women and retainers were apparently sacrificed to accompany a ruler on his travels after death. As with Hopewell, there is no evidence that links the decline and eventual abandonment of Cahokia (which occurred after 1250 C.E.) with military defeat or civil war. Experts argue that climatic changes and population pressures undermined its vitality. After the decline of Cahokia, smaller Mississippian centers continued to flourish in the southeast of the present-day United States until the arrival of Europeans.

ANDEAN CIVILIZATIONS

Geography played a greater role in directing the development of human society in the Andes than in any other area of the Americas. Much of the region's mountainous core is at altitudes that at first glance might seem too high for agriculture and human habitation. The arid coastal plain also posed difficult challenges to human populations. Yet Amerindian peoples in this area produced some of the most socially complex and politically advanced societies of the Americas. Perhaps the very harshness of the environment compelled the development of the administrative structures and supporting social and economic relationships that were central features of Andean civilization.

Cultural Response to Environmental Challenge

People living in the high mountain valleys and on the dry coastal plain were able to overcome the challenges posed by their environment through the effective organization of human labor. The remarkable collective achievements of Andean peoples were organized without writing, although a system of knotted colored cords, *quipus*, were used to aid administration. Large-scale drainage and irrigation works and the terracing of hillsides to control erosion and provide additional farmland led to an increase in agricultural production. Andean people also undertook road building, urban construction, and even textile production collectively.

The sharing of responsibilities began at the household level. But it was the clan, or *ayllu*, that provided the foundation for Andean achievement. Members of an ayllu held land communally. All members claimed descent from a common ancestor, but all members were not necessarily related. Ayllu members thought of each other as brothers and sisters and were obligated to aid each other in tasks that required more labor than a single household could provide. These reciprocal obligations provided the model for the organization of labor and the distribution of goods at every level of Andean society. Just as individuals and families were expected to provide labor to kinsmen, members of an ayllu were expected to provide labor and goods to their hereditary chief.

With the development of territorial states ruled by hereditary aristocracies and kings after 1000 B.C.E., these obligations were organized on a larger scale. The *mit'a*, or rotational labor obligation, required members of ayllus to work the fields and care for the herds of llamas and alpacas owned by religious establishments, the royal court, and the aristocracy. Mit'a laborers also built and maintained roads, bridges, temples, palaces, and large irrigation and drainage projects. Mit'a workers produced textiles and goods essential to ritual life such as beer made from maize and coca (dried leaves chewed as a stimulant and now also a source of cocaine). Once developed, the mit'a system remained an essential part of the Andean world for more than a thousand years.

Work was divided along gender lines, but the work of men and women was interdependent. Hunting, military tasks, and government were reserved largely for men. Women had numerous responsibilities in agriculture and the home. One early Spanish commentator described the responsibilities of Andean women in terms that sound very modern:

> [T]hey did not just perform domestic tasks, but also [labored] in the fields, in the cultivation of their lands, in building houses, and carrying burdens. . . . [A]nd more than once I heard that while women were carrying these burdens, they would feel labor pains, and giving birth, they would go to a place where there was water and wash the baby and themselves. Putting the baby on top of the load they were carrying, they would then continue walking as before they gave birth. In sum, there was nothing their husbands did where their wives did not help.[6]

The ayllu was intimately tied to a uniquely Andean system of production and exchange.

Because the region's mountain ranges created a multitude of small ecological areas with specialized resources, each community sought to control a mix of environments so as to guarantee access to essential goods. Coastal regions produced maize, fish, and cotton. Mountain valleys contributed quinoa (the local grain), plus potatoes and other tubers. Higher elevations contributed the wool and meat of llamas and alpacas, and the Amazonian region provided coca and fruits. Ayllus sent out colonies to exploit the resources of these ecological niches. Colonists remained linked to their original region and kin group by marriage custom and ritual. Historians commonly refer to this system of controlled exchange across ecological boundaries as *vertical integration,* or *verticality.*

The historical periodization of Andean history is similar to that of Mesoamerica (see Figure 12.1). Both regions developed highly integrated political and economic systems long before 1500. The pace of agricultural development, urbanization, and state formation in the Andes also approximated that in Mesoamerica. However, in the Andean region unique environmental challenges led to distinctive highland and coastal cultures with separate periodizations. Here, more than in Mesoamerica, geography influenced the process of regional cultural integration and state formation.

Chavín and Moche

Chavín was the first major urban civilization in South America. Its capital, Chavín de Huántar, was located at 10,300 feet (3,139 meters) in the eastern range of the Andes north of the modern city of Lima (see Map 12.3). Between 900 and 250 B.C.E., a period that roughly coincides with the Olmec culture of Mesoamerica, Chavín became politically and economically dominant in a densely populated region that included large areas of the coastal plain. Chavín de Huántar's location at the intersection of trade routes connecting the coast with populous mountain valleys provided an initial advantage. Military force may have spread its influence. The enormous scale of the capital and the dispersal of Chavín pottery styles, religious motifs, and architectural forms over a wide area suggest that Chavín imposed some form of political integration and trade dependency on its neighbors.

Chavín's development as a commercial center was probably associated with the spread of llamas to the coastal lowlands. Domesticated earlier in the mountainous region, their diffusion was crucial to regional development. The importance of llamas to Andean developments was similar to that of camels in the development of trans-Saharan trade (see Chapter 8). Llamas provided meat as well as wool. More important, they multiplied the scale of commercial exchange by decreasing the labor needed to transport goods, since a single driver could control from 10 to 30 animals, each carrying up to 70 pounds (32 kilograms).

At Chavín the essential characteristics found in later Andean civilizations were all present. The architectural signature for these civilizations was a large complex of multilevel platforms, usually packed earth or rubble faced with cut stone or adobe (sun-dried brick made of clay and straw). Although the construction was superior to that of the Ohio Valley mound builders, these platforms (like those in the Ohio Valley) held small buildings used for ritual purposes and residences for the elite. There is strong evidence of class differences and the growing authority of a chief or king. Platforms were decorated with relief carvings of serpents, condors, jaguars, and human forms. The largest of these constructions at Chavín de Huántar, the Castillo, measured 250 feet (76 meters) on each side and rose to a height of 50 feet (15 meters). About one third of its interior is hollow, containing narrow galleries and small rooms that may have housed the remains of important royal ancestors.

Archaeological investigations of Chavín de Huántar have revealed gold ornaments produced by means of revolutionary techniques that permitted artisans to forge three-dimensional objects. Chavín's artisans also introduced improvements in textile production. The most common decorative motif in sculpture and pottery was a jaguar-man similar in conception to the Olmec symbol of supernatural transformation.

Recent investigations suggest that increased warfare disrupted trade and eventually caused the collapse of Chavín around 200 B.C.E. Nevertheless, the material culture, statecraft, architecture, and urban planning associated with Chavín continued to influence the Andean region for centuries.

Some four centuries later, around 200 C.E., the next major Andean civilization appeared. The Mochica dominated the north coastal region of Peru between 200 and 700 C.E. from a capital, Moche, located near the modern Peruvian city of Trujillo (see Map 12.3). Archaeological evidence indicates that the Mochica cultivated maize, quinoa, beans, and potatoes with the aid of massive irrigation works. Since Moche itself was seriously damaged by a massive flood, the most important excavations have been carried out at secondary cities. A network of canals and aqueducts connected Moche's fields with water sources as far away as 75 miles (121 kilometers). These hydraulic works were maintained by mit'a labor imposed on commoners and subject peoples. Textile production, long-distance trade, and subsistence were all supported by large herds of llamas used for transporting goods as well as for wool and food.

Evidence from murals and decorated ceramics suggests that Moche was a highly stratified theocratic society controlled by priests and war leaders. The organizational requirements of the Mochica irrigation system promoted class division and ultimately gave political control to a small group. Hierarchy was then reinforced by military conquests of neighboring regions. The social elevation of the elite was architecturally represented by the placing of their residences on the top of platforms erected at ceremonial centers. Social distinctions were also evident in burial practices. A recent excavation in the Lambeyeque Valley discovered the tomb of a warrior-priest who was buried with a rich treasure that included gold, silver, and copper jewelry, textiles, feather ornaments, and shells. Also buried with this powerful man were two women and three men who accompanied him in his journey to the afterlife. The retainers had each had a foot amputated

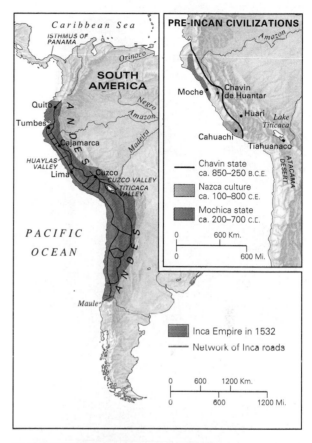

Map 12.3 Andean Civilizations, 900 B.C.E.–1432 C.E. In response to the environmental challenges posed by an arid coastal plain and high interior mountain ranges, Andean peoples made complex social and technological adaptations. Irrigation systems, the domestication of the llama, metallurgy, and shared labor obligations helped provide an abundant economic foundation for powerful, centralized states. In 1532, the Inca empire's vast territory stretched from modern Chile in the south to Colombia in the north.

to ensure their continued subservience and dependence.

Commoners devoted most of their time to subsistence farming and to the payment of labor dues owed to their ayllu and to the elite. They lived in one-room buildings clustered in the outlying areas of cities and in the surrounding agricultural zone. The high quality of Mochica metallurgy, textiles, and ceramics indicates the presence of a skilled artisan class involved full-time in their crafts. Both men and women were

A Moche portrait vase The Mochica of ancient Peru (100–800 C.E.) were among the most accomplished ceramic artists of the Americas. Mochica potters produced representations of gods and spirits, scenes of daily life, and portrait vases of important people. Both men and women were captured in stirrup jars such as the one shown here. This man wears a headdress adorned by two birds and sea shells. The stains next to the eyes of the birds represent tears. (Museo de Arqueologica y Antropologia, Lima/Lee Bolton Picture Library)

involved in agriculture and the household economy. Women had a special role in the production of textiles.

Mochica culture developed a brilliant representational art. Portrait vases produced by

Mochica craftsmen adorn museum collections in nearly every city of the world. Among the most original products of these ceramic artisans were pottery vessels decorated with explicit sexual acts. In addition, the Mochica were accomplished weavers and metalsmiths. Their metallurgy was largely devoted to religious and decorative functions, but they also produced heavy copper and copper alloy tools for agricultural and military purposes. There is some evidence that the Mochica originated the quipu, a coded form of numeric recordkeeping that later became common throughout the Andes.

A detailed history of the Mochica will never be written, but it is clear that the culture was conquered by the Huari in the ninth or tenth century. The Mochica had been weakened some centuries earlier when the course of the Moche River was altered by earthquakes around 450 C.E. and the river flooded the capital of Moche. Although a new capital was constructed at Pampa Grande in the north after Moche was abandoned, the Mochica never fully recovered from this flood.

Tiahuanaco and Huari

After 500 C.E. two powerful civilizations developed in the Andean highlands. At nearly 13,000 feet (3,962 meters) on the high treeless plain near Lake Titicaca in modern Bolivia stand the ruins of Tiahuanaco (see Map 12.3). Initial occupation may have occurred as early as 400 B.C.E., but significant urbanization began only after 200 C.E. Tiahuanaco's expansion depended on the adoption of technologies that increased agricultural productivity. Modern excavations provide the outline of vast drainage projects that reclaimed nearly 200,000 acres (8,000 hectares) of rich lakeside marshes for agriculture. This system of raised fields and ditches permitted intensive cultivation similar to that achieved by use of chinampas in Mesoamerica. Fish from the nearby lake and llamas added protein to a diet largely dependent on potatoes and grains. Llamas were also crucial for the maintenance of long-distance trade relationships that brought in corn, coca, tropical fruits, and medicinal plants.

The urban center of Tiahuanaco was distinguished by the scale of its construction and by the high quality of its stone masonry. Large stones and quarried blocks were moved many miles to construct a large terraced pyramid, walled enclosures, and a reservoir—projects that probably required the mobilization of thousands of laborers over a period of years. Despite a limited metallurgy that only produced tools of copper alloy, Tiahuanaco's artisans built large structures of finely cut stone that required little mortar to fit the blocks. They also produced gigantic human statuary. The largest example, a stern figure with a military bearing, is cut from a single block of stone 24 feet (7 meters) high.

Little is known of the social structure or daily life of this civilization. Neither surviving murals nor other decorative arts offer the suggestive guidance found in the burial goods of the Mochica. Nevertheless, it is clear that Tiahuanaco was a highly stratified society ruled by a hereditary elite. Most women and men devoted their time to agriculture and the care of llama herds. However, the presence of specialized artisans is demonstrated by the high quality construction in public buildings and in locally produced ceramics. The distribution of these ceramics to distant places suggests the presence of a specialized merchant class as well.

Many scholars portray Tiahuanaco as the capital of a vast empire, a clear precursor to the later Inca state. It is clear that the elite controlled a large disciplined labor force in the surrounding region. Military conquests and the establishment of colonial populations linked the highland capital to dependable supplies of products produced in ecologically distinct zones. Despite this cultural influence eastward to the jungles and southward to the coastal regions and oases of the Atacama Desert in Chile, archaeological evidence suggests that Tiahuanaco had, in comparison with contemporary Teotihuacán in central Mexico, a relatively small full-time population of around 30,000. It was a ceremonial and political center for a large regional population, but not a metropolis like the largest Mesoamerican cities.

The contemporary site of Huari was located about 450 miles (751 kilometers) to the northwest of Tiahuanaco near the modern Peruvian city of Ayacucho. The site was larger than Tiahuanaco, measuring nearly 4 square miles (10 square kilometers). The city center was surrounded by a massive wall and included a large temple. The center had numerous multifamily housing blocks. Less-concentrated housing for commoners was located in a sprawling suburban zone. Unlike most other major urban centers in the Andes, Huari's development appears to have occurred without central planning.

The culture and technology of Huari were clearly tied to Tiahuanaco, but the exact nature of this relationship remains unclear. Some scholars argue that Huari began as a dependency of Tiahuanaco. Others suggest that they were joint capitals of a single empire. However, there is little evidence for either position. Clearly there were sustained cultural contacts between the two societies, but each had a unique cultural signature.

Huari was distinguished by the small scale of its monumental architecture and the near absence of cut stone masonry in the construction of both public and private buildings. It is not clear that these characteristics resulted from the relative weakness of the elite or the absence of specialized construction crafts. Huari ceramic style was also different from that of Tiahuanaco. This difference has allowed experts to trace Huari's expanding power to the coastal area earlier controlled by the Mochica and to the northern highlands. Huari's military expansion occurred at a time of increasing warfare throughout the Andes. As a result, roads were built to maintain communication with remote fortified dependencies. Perhaps as a consequence of military conflict, both Tiahuanaco and Huari declined to insignificance by about 1000 C.E. Their political legacy was inherited by the Inca.

The Incas

In little more than one hundred years, the Inca developed a vast imperial state, which they called Tawantinsuyu, "the Land of Four Corners." By 1525 the empire had a population of more than 6 million inhabitants and stretched from the Maule River in Chile to northern

Ecuador and from the Pacific coast across the Andes to the hot country of the upper Amazon and, in the south, into Argentina (see Map 12.3). In the early fifteenth century the Inca were one of many competing military powers in the southern highlands, an area of limited political significance since the collapse of Huari. Centered in the valley of Cuzco, the Inca were initially organized as a chiefdom based on reciprocal gift giving and the redistribution of food and textiles. Strong and resourceful leaders consolidated political authority in the early fifteenth century and undertook an ambitious campaign of military expansion.

The Inca state, like earlier highland powers, was built on traditional Andean social customs and economic practices. Tiahuanaco had extended the traditional use of colonists to incorporate distant resources. The Inca built on this legacy by adding more distant territories through military conquest and by increasing the scale of forced exchanges. Crucial to this process was the development of a larger and more professional military. Unlike the peoples of Mesoamerica, who distributed specialized goods by developing markets and tribute relationships, Andean peoples used state power to broaden and expand the vertical exchange system that had permitted ayllus to exploit a range of ecological niches.

Like earlier highland civilizations, the Inca were pastoralists. Inca prosperity and military strength depended on vast herds of llamas and alpacas, which provided food and clothing as well as transport for goods. Both men and women were involved in the care of these herds. Women were primarily responsible for weaving; men were drivers in long-distance trade. This pastoral tradition provided the Inca with powerful metaphors that helped to shape their political and religious beliefs. They believed that both the gods and their ruler shared the obligations of the shepherd to his flock—an idea akin to the Old Testament references to "The Lord is my Shepherd."

The collective efforts of mit'a laborers made the empire possible. Cuzco, the imperial capital, and the provincial cities, the royal court, the imperial armies, and the state's religious cults all rested on this foundation. This system also created the material surplus that provided the bare necessities for the old, weak, and ill of Inca society. Each ayllu contributed approximately one-seventh of its adult male population to meet these collective obligations. These draft laborers served as soldiers, construction workers, runners to carry messages along post roads, and craftsmen. They also drained swamps, terraced mountainsides, filled in valley floors, built and maintained irrigation works, and built storage facilities and roads. The scale of their achievements is illustrated by the construction of nearly 13,000 miles (20,930 kilometers) of road that facilitated military troop movements, administration, and trade.

Imperial administration was similarly superimposed on existing political structures and established elite groups. Hereditary chiefs at the level of the ayllu carried out administrative and judicial functions. As the Inca expanded, they generally left local rulers in place. By leaving in place the rulers of defeated societies, the Inca risked rebellion, but they controlled these risks by means of a thinly veiled system of hostage taking and the use of military garrisons. The rulers of defeated regions were required to send their heirs to live at the Inca royal court in Cuzco. Even representations of important local gods were brought to Cuzco and made a part of the imperial pantheon. These measures promoted imperial integration while at the same time providing hostages to ensure the good behavior of subject peoples.

Conquests magnified the authority of the Inca ruler and led to the creation of an imperial bureaucracy drawn from among his kinsmen. The royal family claimed descent from the Sun, the primary god in the Inca pantheon. Members of the royal family lived in palaces maintained by armies of servants. The lives of the ruler and members of the royal family were dominated by political and religious rituals that helped to legitimate their authority. Among the many obligations associated with kingship was the requirement to extend imperial boundaries by warfare. Thus each new ruler began his reign with conquest.

The Aztec capital of Tenochtitlán had a population of about 150,000 in 1520, but Cuzco at the height of Inca power in 1530 had a population of under 30,000. Nevertheless, Cuzco was a remarkable place. The Inca were highly skilled stone craftsmen: their most impressive buildings were constructed of carefully cut stones fitted together without mortar. The city was laid out in the shape of a giant puma (a mountain lion). At the center were palaces that each ruler built when he ascended to the throne, as well as the major temples. The richest was the Temple of the Sun. Its interior was lined with sheets of gold, and its patio was decorated with golden representations of llamas and corn. The ruler made every effort to awe and intimidate visitors and residents alike with a nearly continuous series of rituals, feasts, and sacrifices. Sacrifices of textiles, animals, and other goods sent as tribute dominated the city's calendar. The destruction of these valuable commodities, and a small number of human sacrifices, helped give the impression of splendor and sumptuous abundance that legitimated the ruler's claimed descent from the Sun.

Inca cultural achievement was built on the strong foundation of earlier Andean civilizations. We know that astronomical observation was a central concern of the priestly class, as in Mesoamerica; the Inca calendar, however, is lost to us. All communication other than oral was transmitted by the quipus borrowed from earlier Andean civilizations. In weaving and metallurgy, Inca technology, building on earlier regional developments, was more advanced than Mesoamerican. Inca craftsmen produced utilitarian tools and weapons of copper and bronze as well as decorative objects of gold and silver. Inca women produced textiles of extraordinary beauty from cotton and the wool of llamas and alpacas.

Although the Inca did not introduce new technologies, they did increase economic output and added to the region's prosperity. The conquest of large populations in environmentally distinct regions permitted the Inca to multiply the productive potential of traditional forms of production and exchange. But the growth of imperial economic and political power was purchased at the cost of reduced equality and local autonomy. The imperial elite was almost cut off from the masses of society, living in richly decorated palaces in

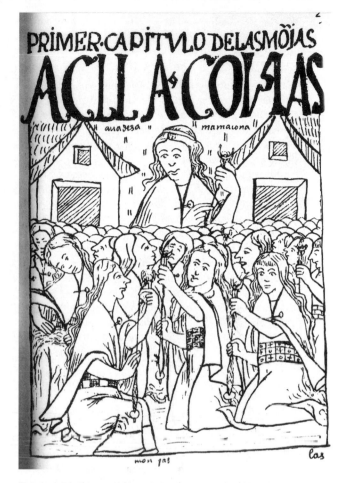

Acllas Representatives of the Inca ruler selected young virgins to serve the official religious cult devoted to Sun worship. Selection was generally seen as a sign of favor by the women's parents. Some of the women were given as wives or concubines to the Inca ruler and other favored nobles, but most lived celibate lives devoted to religious rituals and the production of beautiful textiles. This illustration drawn in the sixteenth century by Guaman Poma de Ayala, a member of the native aristocracy, shows acllas spinning thread. (Courtesy, Institut d'Ethnologie, Musee de l'Hommel)

Cuzco or other urban centers. Even members of the provincial nobility were held at arm's length by the royal court, subject to execution if they dared to look directly at the ruler's face.

The Inca Empire was in crisis on the eve of the Spanish conquest. In 1525 Huayna Capac, the Inca ruler, died, and two of his sons began a

Acllas

Acllas were young virgins selected by representatives of the Inca ruler to serve the cult of the Sun or be given as marriage partners and concubines to the Inca himself or to Inca nobles and favored nobles from dependencies. These young women were commonly chosen for their beauty from among the daughters of local rulers.

Eventually, selection came to be seen as a special sign of favor that strengthened the legitimacy and political authority of the woman's family. Yet close association with imperial power, while enhancing a family's social prestige, also weakened its traditional cultural position in the defeated community. With the passage of time, the interests of imperial and conquered elites melded. Assigning women from conquered regions as wives and concubines was essential to this process.

Our understanding of the acllas' lives and their place in Inca society is based primarily on Spanish-era sources. We know these women lived within the closely guarded walls of convent-like buildings located in the large towns of the empire and that their days were dedicated to religious observances and the production of fine textiles.

The following account was written in the early seventeenth century by Felipe Guaman Poma de Ayala. Although not a descendent of the Inca royal line, the author was proud of his high-ranking noble family. After long neglect, Guaman Poma's illustrated history of Inca and early Spanish colonial society study has become a fundamental source for Andean history. In this text, the word Inca is used to refer to both the people and to their ruler. Although obviously proud of the indigenous past, Guaman Poma's description of ancient images of gods as "idols" suggests the depth of cultural change among Amerindian people following the conquest.

During the time of the Incas certain women, who were called *acllas* or "the Chosen," were destined for lifelong virginity. Mostly they were confined in houses and they belonged to one of two main categories, namely sacred virgins and common virgins.

The so-called "virgins with red cheeks" entered upon their duties at the age of twenty and were dedicated to the service of the Sun, the Moon, and the Day-Star. In their whole life they were never allowed to speak to a man.

The virgins of the Inca's own shrine of Huanacauri were known for their beauty as well as their chastity. The other principal shrines had similar girls in attendance. At the less important shrines there were older virgins who occupied themselves with spinning and weaving the silk-like clothes worn by their idols. There was a still lower class of virgins, over 40 years of age and no longer very beautiful, who performed unimportant religious duties and worked in the fields or as ordinary seamstresses.

There was yet another class of aclla or "chosen," only some of whom kept their virginity and others not. These were the Inca's (the ruler of the Inca people) beautiful attendants and concubines, who were drawn from noble families and lived in his palaces. They made clothing for him out of material finer than taffeta or silk. They also prepared a maize spirit of extraordinary richness, which was matured for an entire month, and they cooked delicious dishes for the Inca. They also lay with him, but never with any other man.

Thus chastity was greatly prized in our country. It was the Inca who received our girls from the Sun and who allotted them, always as virgins, to his subjects. Until that time the man did not know the woman nor the woman the man. The man might be in Quito or Chile and might be assigned a woman from quite a different region but a contract of marriage was made with the help of the woman's brother.

What special qualities were most valued in the selection of acllas? What categories of acllas are described? What were their lives like? What do we know about how the Inca ruler was viewed from this description of his relationship with the acllas?

Source: From Felipe Guaman Poma de Ayala, *Letter to a King, A Peruvian Chief's Account of Life Under the Incas and Under Spanish Rule.* edited and translated by Christopher Dilke. New York: E.P. Dutton (1978), pp. 84–86.

bloody struggle for the throne. The ambitions and rivalries that divided professional military leaders from the elite of Cuzco, the resentments of conquered peoples, and the problems associated with governing a vast territorial state spread over more than 3,000 miles (4,830 kilometers) of mountainous terrain magnified the destructive consequences of the succession struggle. The scale and violence of this conflict suggest that its resolution would have imposed political and social changes as great as those associated with the collapse of earlier civilizations.

were challenged by powerful neighbors or by internal revolts. Similar challenges had contributed to the decline of earlier powers in both Mesoamerica and the Andean region. Previously, the collapse of a civilization was followed by a long period of adjustment and the creation of new indigenous institutions. With the arrival of Europeans, this cycle of crisis and adjustment would be transformed, and the future of Amerindian peoples would become linked to the cultures of the Old World.

CONCLUSION

The indigenous societies of the Western Hemisphere developed unique technologies and cultural forms in mountainous regions, tropical rain forests, deserts, woodlands, and arctic regions. In Mesoamerica, North America, and the Andean region, societies of hunters and gatherers as well as urbanized agricultural societies produced rich religious and aesthetic traditions as well as useful technologies and effective social institutions. Once established, these cultural traditions proved very durable.

The Aztec and Inca Empires represented the culmination of a long developmental process that had begun before the Olmec and Chavín civilizations. Each imperial state controlled extensive and diverse territories with populations that numbered in the millions. The capital cities of Tenochtitlán and Cuzco were great cultural and political centers that displayed some of the finest achievements of Amerindian technology, art, and architecture. Both states were based on conquests and were ruled by powerful hereditary elites who depended on the tribute of subject peoples.

The Aztec and Inca Empires were created militarily, their survival depending as much on the power of their armies as on the productivity of their economies or the wisdom of their rulers. As the Western Hemisphere's long isolation drew to a close in the late fifteenth century, these empires

SUGGESTED READING

In *Prehistory of the Americas* (1987) Stuart Fiedel provides an excellent summary of the early history of the Western Hemisphere. Alvin M. Josephy, Jr., in *The Indian Heritage of America* (1968), also provides a thorough introduction to the topic. *Canada's First Nations* (1992) by Olive Patricia Dickason is a well-written survey that traces the history of Canada's Amerindian peoples to the modern era.

Early Man in the New World, ed. Richard Shutler, Jr. (1983), provides a helpful addition to these works. *Atlas of Ancient America* (1986) by Michael Coe, Elizabeth P. Benson, and Dean R. Snow is a useful compendium of maps and information. George Kubler, *The Art and Architecture of Ancient America* (1962), is a valuable resource, though now dated.

Eric Wolf provides an enduring synthesis of Mesoamerican history in *Sons of the Shaking Earth* (1959). Linda Schele and David Freidel summarize the most recent research on the classic-period Maya in their excellent *A Forest of Kings* (1990). The best summary of Aztec history is Nigel Davies, *The Aztec Empire: The Toltec Resurgence* (1987). Jacques Soustelle, *Daily Life of the Aztecs*, trans. Patrick O'Brian (1961), is a good introduction. Though controversial in some of its analysis, Inga Clendinnen's *Aztecs* (1991) is also an important contribution.

Chaco and Hohokam (1991), ed. Patricia L. Crown and W. James Judge, is a good summary of research issues. Robert Silverberg, *Mound Builders of Ancient America* (1968), supplies a good introduction to this topic.

A helpful introduction to the scholarship on early Andean societies is provided by Richard W. Keatinge, ed., *Peruvian Prehistory* (1988). *The History of the Incas* (1970) by Alfred Metraux is dated but offers a useful summary. John Murra, *The Economic Organization of the Inca State* (1980), and Irene Silverblatt, *Moon, Sun, and Witches: Gender Ideologies and Class in Inca and Colonial Peru* (1987), are challenging, important works on Peru before the arrival of Columbus in the Western Hemisphere. Frederich Katz, *The Ancient Civilizations of the Americas* (1972), offers a useful comparative perspective on ancient American developments.

NOTES

1. This summary follows closely the narrative offered by Linda Schele and David Freidel in *A Forest of Kings: The Untold Story of the Ancient Maya* (New York: Morrow, 1990), 145–153.

2. Before 1492 the inhabitants of the Western Hemisphere had no single name for themselves. They had neither a racial con-sciousness nor a racial identity. Identity was derived from kin groups, language, cultural practices, and political structures. There was no sense that physical similarities created a shared identity. Racial consciousness and racial identity were imposed on America's original inhabitants by conquest and by the occupation of their lands by Europeans after 1492. All of the collective terms for these first American peoples are tainted by this history. *Indians, Native Americans, Amerindians, First Peoples,* and *Indigenous Peoples* are among the words in common usage. In this book the names of individual cultures and states are used wherever possible. *Amerindian* and other terms that suggest transcultural identity and experience are used most commonly for the period after 1492.

3. Quoted in Nigel Davies, *The Toltec Heritage: From the Fall of Tula to the Rise of Tenochtitlán* (Norman: University of Oklahoma Press (1980), 3.

4. Bernal Díazl del Castillo, *The Conquest of New Spain*, translated with an introduction by J. M. Cohen (London: Penguin Books, 1963), 217.

5. Hernando Cortés, *Five Letters, 1519–1526,* translated with an introduction by J. Bayard Morris (New York: W. W. Norton & Company, 1991), 87.

6. Quoted in Irene Silverblatt, *Moon, Sun, and Witches: Gender Ideologies and Class in Inca and Colonial Peru* (Princeton, NJ: Princeton University Press, 1987), 10.

Interregional Patterns of Culture and Contact, 1200–1500

Between 1200 and 1500, dynamic events intensified cultural and commercial contacts across wide expanses of Eurasia, Africa, and the Indian Ocean. The Mongols established vast empires in Eurasia, greatly stimulating trade and cultural interaction. Muslim influence grew as well—through religious conversion, through the founding of new empires in West Africa, India, and the Balkans, and through the extension of trading networks among the Indian Ocean states and across the Sahara. In the Latin West, strong European kingdoms began maritime expansion in the Atlantic, creating direct ties with sub-Saharan Africa.

Interregional contact depended on the massive networks of trade—on both land and sea—that by the 1200s had come into existence in several parts of Eurasia and Africa. Trade on the Silk Road became even more vigorous under the Mongol empires, and men and women of many classes and occupations traveled it. From 1200 to 1500, the Mediterranean continuously served as a focus of commercial exchange for the peoples of Europe, Africa, and the Middle East. At the other end of Eurasia, both China and Japan sent regular trade missions to Southeast Asia, Indonesia, and the Philippines. Underlying the greatest maritime network, however, was the Indian Ocean, where Hindu, Muslim, Jewish, Malay, Chinese, and other merchants engaged in a vigorous and profitable trade. Indeed, Chinese fleets occasionally ranged as far as the Middle East and eastern Africa.

Between 1200 and 1500, new and more complex links developed between the cultural regions. The earliest of these were achieved by the empires of the Mongols, who arose in central Asia in the very late 1100s. Using their extraordinary command of the horse and refinements in traditional forms of military and social organization, Mongols and allied groups united under Genghis Khan in the early thirteenth century. By the later part of the century, a Mongol empire spread over Eurasia from Poland to Korea. It was segmented into four separate regimes: one based in Russia, one in Iran, one in central Asia, and one in China. Along with intensified commercial and cultural exchanges, the Mongols brought changes to the peoples and the environments of many parts of Eurasia.

Some of those changes affected local cultures, creating an early nationalist effect. Mongol rulers, who were not usually familiar with the agricultural systems or governments of the peoples they conquered, tended to seek native helpers. At the same time, the Mongols often became interested in local customs and pastimes. Consequently, they sponsored the vernacular languages and often the folk customs of the local peoples, laying a foundation for the later literatures of these countries. The political influence of the capitals the Mongols established in China, Iran, and Russia lingered after them, creating bases for the formation of new national regimes. Also long lasting was hatred of the Mongols, which unified the peoples of these regions both during and after the period of Mongol rule. Perhaps the most distinctive Mongol legacy to later centuries was the memory of a Eurasian commercial prosperity that had tied together the cities of Mediterranean Europe, the Middle East, and East Asia.

Population change stimulated use of new land and sea contacts arising in the Mongol period. After a long period of stagnation, or very slow growth, the population of the world shot up from about 200 million in 600 C.E. to over 350 million between 1200 and 1500. Scholars do not fully understand the reasons for this phenomenon but believe it may reflect climatic changes as well as improved political stability before about 1250 in China and Europe, where the greatest increases took place. The factors that halted this population growth are better known. At the end of the 1200s, the Chinese population, for instance, stood at about 100 million. In the following century that population declined by a third or more as a result of warfare, disease, and the disruption of agriculture during Mongol conquest and rule. In Europe, rapid population growth peaked at about 80 million around 1300. This produced a heavy strain on the environment before the bubonic plague—also a result of the contacts created by the Mongol campaigns—swept away millions of malnourished people. By 1500, however, the populations of both China and Europe were back to their former peaks. Chinese seeking to escape the crowding of the coastal regions migrated along the trade routes to Southeast Asia. Europeans in crowded Mediterranean cities looked outward for new sources of occupation and wealth.

The rise and fall of the Mongol empires interacted with the rise of political powers elsewhere in Eurasia. Especially worth noting are rising powers dominated by Turkic Muslims. First, Turkic war leaders from what is now Afghanistan created an imperial capital at Delhi, overwhelming the many small states that had dotted north and central India before the 1200s. Second, during the 1300s the Ottoman Turks took advantage of the weakness of the Christian Byzantine Empire to establish their rule over western Anatolia and the southern Balkans. In the late 1300s, the invasions of India and Iran by the central Asian conqueror Timur (Tamerlane) shattered the Delhi

Technology

Wind and water mills and iron and copper mining spread in China, Middle East, Europe

Sailors use dhows to ply monsoon winds of Indian Ocean

1100s–1200s—Mathematics and astronomy spread from Islamic world to Europe

1300–1450—Invention of cannon spreads from East Asia to Middle East and Europe

1300–1500—Use of movable type spreads in East Asia and Europe

1400s—Improved firearms and rise of infantry in Europe

1403–1433—Chinese imperial voyages through Southeast Asia and Indian Ocean

1454—Gutenberg Bible printed in Europe

1498—Portuguese complete sea route to India

Environment

West Africans clear fields in rain forest

1200–1500—Between 1200 and 1350, Chinese population falls from above 100 million to 60 million or 70 million; rises above 100 million by 1500

1340–1450—Bubonic plague spreads from southwest China westward across Eurasia; urban populations in Europe fall as much as 30 percent

Sultanate and stopped the growth of Ottoman power. Only after the decline of Timur's empire in the 1400s could the Ottomans reconstitute their dominion. Exploiting their knowledge of both cavalry and artillery, the Ottomans extended their sway deeper into Europe (taking the last of the Byzantine Empire in 1453) and southward into the Middle East, establishing an empire that endured into the twentieth century.

At the very end of the fifteenth century a new commercial and political force entered the Indian Ocean from politically decentralized western Europe. The stories recounted by many travelers—including Marco Polo—about the Mongol courts of Asia inspired merchants to seek greater riches in the lands bordering the Indian Ocean and in China. When European merchants found their access to the usual routes through the Mediterranean or the Persian Gulf disrupted by the expansion of Ottoman power, they sought new routes. Building on decades of explorations down the Atlantic coast of Africa, a Portuguese fleet rounded the southern tip of the continent and continued on to India in 1498. This sea route between western Europe and Asia proved more durable and adaptable than the ancient overland routes of central Asia.

Mongol, Muslim, and European expansions all amplified the transmission of technologies. Printing, compasses, crossbows, gunpowder, and firearms had all originated in Asia, and the Mongol conquests had hastened their spread westward. The recipients of these technologies significantly improved them and explored new applications. Both the Ottomans and the regional powers of Europe based their expansions on gunpowder. The Portuguese, for instance, mounted cannon on ships designed to bear the weight and withstand the recoil shock of such weapons. In circumnavigating Africa, they also employed navigational and sailing devices that put them at the forefront of maritime technology. By 1500, the Eurasian overland links that had been central to the Mongol empires were in eclipse. The armed, trade-oriented, resource-hungry empires emerging in Europe would use the seas to forge new global patterns, presenting unprecedented technological and economic challenges to the peoples of Africa, Asia, and America.

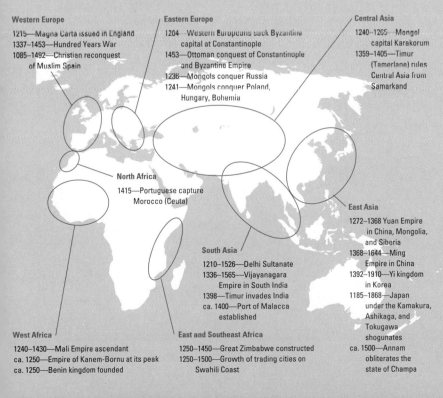

Western Europe
1215—Magna Carta issued in England
1337–1453—Hundred Years War
1085–1492—Christian reconquest of Muslim Spain

Eastern Europe
1204—Western Europeans sack Byzantine capital at Constantinople
1453—Ottoman conquest of Constantinople and Byzantine Empire
1236—Mongols conquer Russia
1241—Mongols conquer Poland, Hungary, Bohemia

Central Asia
1240–1265—Mongol capital Karakorum
1359–1405—Timur (Tamerlane) rules Central Asia from Samarkand

North Africa
1415—Portuguese capture Morocco (Ceuta)

South Asia
1210–1526—Delhi Sultanate
1336–1565—Vijayanagara Empire in South India
1398—Timur invades India
ca. 1400—Port of Malacca established

East Asia
1272–1368 Yuan Empire in China, Mongolia, and Siberia
1368–1644—Ming Empire in China
1392–1910—Yi kingdom in Korea
1185–1868—Japan under the Kamakura, Ashikaga, and Tokugawa shogunates
ca. 1500—Annam obliterates the state of Champa

West Africa
1240–1430—Mali Empire ascendant
ca. 1250—Empire of Kanem-Bornu at its peak
ca. 1250—Benin kingdom founded

East and Southeast Africa
1250–1450—Great Zimbabwe constructed
1250–1500—Growth of trading cities on Swahili Coast

Society
1220s–1260—Mongol conquests of northern China, Russia, and Iran
1295—Beginning of Il-khan conversion to Islam
1450–1500—Peasant rebellions and decline of serfdom in western Europe
1470s—Civil war in Japan results in rise of new class of warrior-commanders

Culture
1100–1300—Universities founded in Europe
After 1140—Gothic architecture in Europe
Bronze art at Ife and Benin in Nigeria
Islam spreads in Anatolia, sub-Saharan Africa, China, India, and Southeast Asia
1298—Publication of Marco Polo's Travels
1325–1354—Travels of Ibn Battuta
1368—Ming Empire reestablishes the examination system and state Confucianism in China
1378–1415—Great Schism in Western Christianity
1450–1500—Reunification of Mongolia with dominance of Tibetan Buddhism

Western Eurasia, 1200–1500

Central Asia in the Thirteenth Century · The Fall and Rise of Islam

National Definition in Response to the Mongols

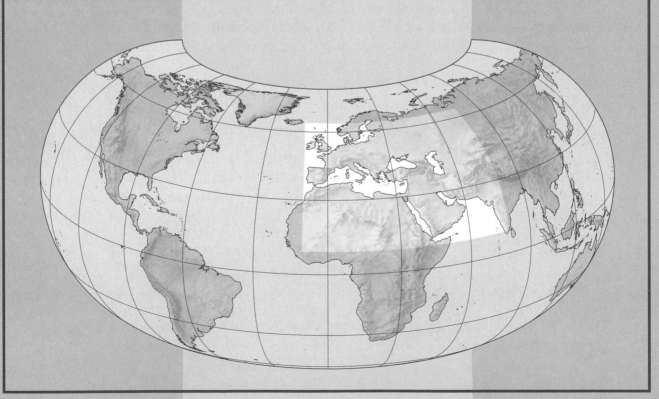

When Temüjin was a boy, his father was murdered by a rival group. Though Temüjin's mother tried hard to feed and shelter him (and to protect him from dogs, which he feared), she could not find a safe haven for him. At the age of fifteen Temüjin sought a place for himself in the care of Toghoril, leader of the Keraits. Among the many warring confederations of Mongolia, the Keraits were Turkic-speakers who used the Uigur writing system and had a strong interest in both the Christian and the Buddhist religions. During his years with the Keraits, Temüjin learned much that would be fundamental to the power and the scope of the empire he would someday build: the charisma of personal strength, courage and intelligence, the importance of religious breadth and tolerance, the necessity to show no mercy to determined enemies, and the versatility of the cultural and economic institutions of Central Asia.

When, in 1206, Temüjin was acknowledged as Genghis Khan (r. 1206–1227), or supreme leader (later "Great Khan") of the Mongols and their allies, he counted among his followers adherents of all the major religions of the Middle East and East Asia, as well as speakers of many of its languages. All were able to guide him in finding ways to make his rule more effective among and more appealing to the diverse civilizations of Eurasia. The historian Ala al-Din Ata Malik Juvaini recorded the following as Genghis's deathbed speech. It can hardly be literally true, but it captures the essential strategy behind Mongol success: "If you want to retain your possessions and conquer your enemies, you must make your subjects submit willingly and unite your diverse energies to a single end."[1]

By 1250 the segmented empire created under the successors of Genghis Khan stretched from Poland to Korea and from Siberia to Burma. The empire was partially reconstituted more than half a century after its demise by the self-proclaimed heir of Genghis, Timur (Timur-i lang, Tamerlane), who on his deathbed in 1405 was dreaming of a second Mongol subjugation of China. Both the Mongol wars of conquest and the subsequent peace enforced by the Mongol governments promoted the rapid movement of people and ideas from one end of Eurasia to the other. But they also brought distress, disease, and the germ of nationalism—the sense that distinct peoples should have their own rulers—to the various regions under Mongol control. In the aftermath of this last unification of Eurasia, the outlines of the nations of the early modern period—Iran, Russia, China, among others—emerged. Through their conscious policies and as a result of local reactions to those policies, the Mongols profoundly affected the cultural, political, and economic character of early modern Eurasia.

The unity of Eurasia achieved under the Mongol Empire speeded transmission of the specialized skills that had developed in many parts of the world in the preceding centuries. Trade routes were improved, markets expanded, and a demand for products grew both in the Middle East and in East Asia. As a result, goods, ideas, skills, and people steadily moved from one side of the Eurasian landmass to the other, often by means of the Silk Road that ran from northern Iran, around the Caspian Sea, across Central Asia and Turkestan to northern China.

Despite modern appreciation for the importance of the Mongol period in the development of the later medieval world, however, the association of the Mongols with death, gore, suffering, and conflagration is nearly overwhelming. Bloody encounters, involving levels of slaughter that were previously unknown in some parts, accompanied most of the Mongol conquests. The rapid movement of Mongol soldiers, their equipment, and their captives opened the way to the spread of virulent diseases. In the Middle East and China, Mongol rulers reduced the status of the traditional political and cultural elites or excluded them from state service, thereby forcing a change in the values and practices of government. In the Middle East, Russia, and East Asia generally, resentment of the Mongol occupation gave rise to aggressive nationalist feelings, which in subsequent centuries would bring grief to cultural minorities and to many neighboring states.

CENTRAL ASIA IN THE THIRTEENTH CENTURY

Large federations of nomads had dominated the steppes and deserts of Central Asia many times since the beginnings of recorded history. The Scythians, the Xiongnu (the nomadic rivals of the Han Empire), Turks, and Kitans all preceded the Mongols. The environment, economic life, cultural institutions, and political traditions of the steppes and deserts all contributed to the rise and contraction of empires. Similarly, the rise of the Mongols can be attributed at least as much to the long-term trends and particular pressures of Central Asia as to any special abilities of Genghis Khan and his followers.

Nomadism's Effects on Political and Social Organization

Nomadism is a way of life forced by a scarcity of resources. Nomadic groups have by far the lowest rates of population density. To find pastures and water for their livestock, they are continually on the move. In the course of their migrations they frequently come into contact with other nomadic groups seeking the same resources, and the outcomes of these encounters are commonly warfare, alliance, or both. In times of ecological stress such as drought, conflicts increase. The result is the extermination of small groups, the growth of alliances, and frequent outmigration from groups that have grown too large. It is believed that such a period of environmental stress afflicted northern Eurasia around 1000 C.E. and

contributed to the dislocations and conflicts out of which the Mongols eventually emerged.

Because nomads are constantly moving but also always under pressure to make their movements efficient and accurate, centralized decision making is a necessary part of their life. Nomadic groups in Central Asia frequently engaged in violence, and so every man was a full-time herdsman, full-time hunter, and full-time warrior. From childhood Mongols developed skills that were useful in wartime, such as riding and shooting arrows (see Environment & Technology: Horses). But mobility had a political effect as well, since the independence of Mongol individuals and their families forced decision making to be public, with many people voicing their views. Even at the height of a military campaign nomad warriors moved with their families and their possessions and sometimes struck off on their own if they disagreed with a decision. The political structures of the Central Asian empires all were designed to accommodate the conflicting centralizing and decentralizing forces of traditional nomadic life. Mongol groups had strong hierarchies, but the leader—the *khan*—was always required to have his decisions ratified by a council of the leaders of powerful families.

Competition for resources reinforced slavery and tribute in Central Asia. Many of the men and women captured during warfare or raids became slaves and were forced to do menial work in nomadic camps. Some individuals evidently entered into slavery willingly, to avoid starvation. Slaves were valuable not only for their labor but also as currency. Weak groups secured land rights and protection from strong groups by providing them with slaves, livestock, weapons, silk, or cash. Many powerful groups (such as the one to which Genghis Khan's father belonged) found that they could live almost entirely off tribute, so they spent less time and resources on herding and more on the warlike activities that would secure greater tribute. As each group grew in numbers and in wealth, its political institutions became more complex. Federations arose based on an increasing number of alliances among groups, almost always expressed in arranged marriages between the leading families. Children readily became pawns of diplomacy: their marriages were arranged for them in

Horses

Prior to the rise of the Mongols, the many breeds of horses in Eurasia had been improved and specialized by interbreeding with the large, quick, graceful horses of the Caucasus and the Middle East. In Mongolia, however, the early form of domesticated horse was preserved. The mounts on which the Mongols assaulted Europe looked not very different from the prehistoric horses that very early Europeans had painted on cave walls.

These ponies were an excellent example of the adaptation of traditional technologies (in this case horsebreeding) to environment. They were uniquely able to survive the very cold, very dry climate of Mongolia. Mongols never fed or sheltered their horses, so by natural selection the breed was able to survive on a minimal diet, to forage in the snow that covers some parts of Mongolia for most of the year, and to brave the plunging night temperatures of the region. The breeding technique required that the ponies be kept in a semiwild state. During the Tang Empire, the Central Asian ponies had been crossbred with specialized strains from the Middle East to produce larger, stronger, more beautiful horses. On occasion such horses were brought to Mongolia by the Turks and bred with the local horses. But only after the time of Genghis did the numbers of the Mongolian pony decline dramatically. The breed, or a near version of it, now survives only in game preserves.

Central Asian riding radically altered the conduct of war in Eurasia. The charioteers who had dominated warfare in ancient Middle East and East Asia were no match for well-coordinated and well-armed light horsemen, and chariot driving disappeared as a war art wherever extensive campaigns against Central Asian riders occurred. The Parthians of eastern Iran, whose riding skills astonished the empires of the Middle East, were legendary for their ability to shoot arrows at the enemy while retreating from them. In China, the Xiongnu drove out the chariot and forced Chinese soldiers to fight on horseback. The Huns were, for similar reasons, a revelation to Europe, which adopted the use of the iron stirrup from them.

Not only as a technology but also as a social institution, Central Asian horsemanship fundamentally altered the meaning of the horse. In the ancient Middle East, the use of horse teams and chariots in warfare was extremely expensive and demanded a select group of warriors wealthy enough to maintain their equipment and powerful enough to control grazing land for their animals. Horses had to be carefully bred to be large enough to pull the chariots and carefully trained to manage their loads with rather inefficient harnessing. In Central Asia, riding was an ability that all men and women in good health possessed. It required only a rudimentary saddle and experience. The deployment of riders in warfare blurred the distinction between a riding herdsman (or hunter) and a riding soldier, and there was no specialization of function along class lines. Because Central Asians did not enclose their herds but left them to forage, no question of individual landownership arose.

Like all their predecessors on the steppe, the Mongols were superb riders, both in agility and in endurance. They continued a tradition that Herodotus had noted among the Scythians—putting infants on goats in order to accustom them to riding. And like all Central Asian warriors the Mongols were adept at the special skill (for which there is a specialized word in all Central Asian languages) of shooting arrows from a moving horse. In Russia, the Middle East, and East Asia, the skills necessary for the use of the horse, including breeding, tacking, and military riding, were all adapted from the nomads. Under the Abbasids in western Asia and the Tang in eastern Asia, trousers became part of male dress through the influence of riding, and the sport of polo became popular, all, again, through nomadic influence.

Mongol ponies The stocky body and coarse mane of the Mongol pony are reminders of its descent from the northern ponies familiar to Paleolithic peoples of Europe. By the laws of Genghis Khan, the Mongols could not lead their ponies on the bit, but had to change to a gentle head-collar, as shown here. (National Palace Museum, Taipei, Taiwan)

childhood—in Temüjin's own case, at the age of eight. Because of the relationship between marriage and politics, women from prestigious families were often tremendously powerful in negotiation and management. And, when things became violent, they were just as likely as men to suffer assassination or execution.

Nomadic groups achieved a high degree of independence by attempting to restrict their diet to the products—primarily meat and milk—that they could provide for themselves and by wearing clothes produced from pastoral animals—felt (from wool), leather, and furs. Women generally oversaw the breeding and birthing of livestock and the preparation of furs, both of which were fundamental to the nomadic economy. But it was impossible for a large nomadic group to be completely independent forever. Trade with sedentary cultures—the agricultural societies such as

Animal husbandry In nomadic societies, it was common for men and boys to tend to the herds in the pastures. But the more technical tasks associated with animal husbandry—breeding, birthing, shearing, milking, and the processing of pelts—were usually performed by women who worked together in teams and passed the knowledge from older to younger members of the community. Their various activities are depicted in this contemporary painting. (Ulan Bator Fine Arts Museum)

Iran and China—was necessary for the acquisition of iron, wood, cotton and cotton seed, silk (the favored dress of the Central Asian elites), vegetables, and grains. Many nomads learned the value of having permanent settlements for the farming of grains and cotton, as well as for the working of iron, and they established their own villages—often with the help of migrants from the agricultural regions—at strategic points.

The result was extensive frontier regions, particularly east of the Caspian Sea and in northern China, where nomadic peoples and agricultural peoples created pluralistic civilizations in which farming, animal husbandry, ironworking, and long-distance trade were all important activities. Nevertheless, contact with the central agricultural zones, particularly in the Middle East and China, could not cease. When policy changes or economic difficulties within the sedentary societies obstructed trade, nomads frequently resorted to raiding or even to large-scale invasion to obtain what they needed.

Trade and Technology

The trade with sedentary societies that Central Asian nomads came to depend on normally benefited both groups. Because of their specialized way of life, nomads were important contributors to the industries of the cultural cores. Cotton, wool, leather, and many breeds of horses are among the products that nomadic peoples introduced to eastern Eurasia.

Iron was also important in nomadic Central Asia. It was used in bridles and stirrups, in wagons, and in weapons. Nomads did not develop large mining enterprises, but they eagerly acquired iron implements in trade and then reworked them to suit their own purposes. The Turks, for instance, had been famous for their large ironworking stations south of Mount Altai even before the rise of the Abbasid and Tang empires in the 600s. Agricultural empires in East Asia and the Middle East attempted to restrict the export of iron in any form to Central Asia. These attempts were never successful.

Central Asians not only continued to work in iron but improved many of the sedentary technologies and then exported them back to the sedentary regions. The effects of this exchange were strikingly illustrated in the seventh century, when the nearly invincible Tang imperial cavalry spread use of the Turkic iron stirrup throughout Eurasia (see Chapter 11). The Mongols retained the traditional Central Asian reverence for the qualities of iron and the secrets of ironworking. Temüjin, Genghis Khan's personal name, meant "blacksmith," and several of his prominent followers were sons of blacksmiths. The name of a later conqueror, Timur, meant "iron" in Turkish.

Movement and Cultural Diversity

The nomads of Central Asia were transmitters of cultural influences across Eurasia. Many of these influences were religious. As we have seen, Central Asian nomads aided in the spread of Manichaeism, Judaism, Christianity, and Buddhism across the continent. By the end of the Abbasid and Tang eras, Turkic nomads of Central Asia were increasingly active in the transmission of Islam, which quickly eroded the dominance of Buddhism, particularly in the cities of Central Asia. On the steppe, however, a mix of religious affiliations remained. There it was not unique to find within a single family individual believers in Buddhism, Manichaenism, Islam, Christianity, and Judaism, in combination with traditional shamanism (the ancient practices by which special individuals visited and influenced the supernatural world).

This plurality of religious practice reflected the fact that Central Asian nomads did not always associate ideas about rulership with ideas about religion. Since very early times, Central Asian societies had been permeated by the idea of world rulership by a khan, who, with the aid of his shamans, would speak to and for an ultimate god, represented in Central Asia as Sky, or Heaven. It was believed that this universal ruler, by virtue of his role as the speaker for Heaven, would transcend particular cultures and dominate them all. This idea may have derived from Iranian influences. It was evident in the government of the Xiongnu and was explicitly stated on numerous occasions in the Turkic empires. This idea was extremely important in the rise of the Mongols. It permitted them to appeal to any and all religions to legitimate their rule. And it authorized the Great Khan to claim superiority over all religious leaders.

Genghis Khan at first patronized only the Mongol shamans. Soon, however, he seemed to listen to the arguments of Buddhists, Daoists, Christians, and Muslims, all of whom believed they were about to convert the Great Khan and his family to their beliefs.

Unification of Eurasia and Overland Exchange

Religious zeal, hopes for power and wealth, and curiosity drew learned men, religious leaders, and merchants over long distances to the Mongol courts. These journeys produced travel literature that gives us vivid insights into the Eurasian world of the thirteenth century. The accounts were intriguing to their contemporary readers. Chinese and Westerners alike regarded the diet and hygiene of the Mongols as shocking and their powers of endurance as nearly superhuman. Some narratives, such as that of the Venetian traveler, Marco Polo (1254–1324), freely mixed the fantastic with the factual, to the delight of the audience. Most important, these books left an image of the inexhaustible wealth of the Mongols, and of Asia generally, that created in Europe a persisting ambition to find easier routes to Asia for trade and conquest.

Though the accounts of these travelers mesmerized readers for centuries, their unembellished experiences were not rare for their time. In the towns they visited in Central Asia or China, they regularly encountered other Europeans, sometimes from their own home regions. Some were travelers and some were captives, but all were part of the steady flow of people across Eurasia in these times. The economic, political, and cultural benefits of this traffic were great. Technical knowledge, whether of pharmacology, engineering, mathematics, or financial management, flowed between China and Iran.

At the same time, the steady stream of knowledge between Europe and the Middle East was widened by Mongol policy and occasionally by Mongol competition. For instance, the wish of the Mongols in the Middle East to drive the

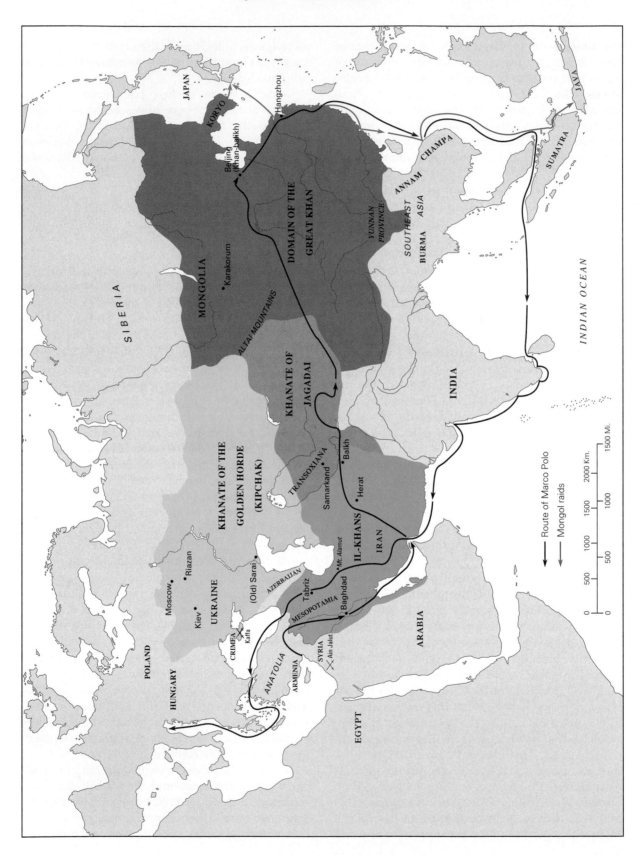

SIBERIA

JAPAN

KORYO

Hangzhou

Beijing (Khan-balikh)

MONGOLIA

Karakorum

DOMAIN OF THE GREAT KHAN

ALTAI MOUNTAINS

KHANATE OF JAGADAI

YUNNAN PROVINCE

CHAMPA

ANNAM

SOUTHEAST ASIA

BURMA

JAVA

SUMATRA

INDIAN OCEAN

KHANATE OF THE GOLDEN HORDE (KIPCHAK)

TRANSOXIANA

Balkh

Samarkand

Herat

INDIA

Moscow

Riazan

(Old) Sarai

AZERBAIJAN

IL-KHANS

IRAN

Mt. Alamut

POLAND

Kiev

UKRAINE

Tabriz

CRIMEA   Kaffa

MESOPOTAMIA

Baghdad

SYRIA   Ain Jalut

ARABIA

HUNGARY

ANATOLIA

ARMENIA

EGYPT

→ Route of Marco Polo

→ Mongol raids

1500 Mi.

2000 Km.

1500

1000

1500

1000

500

500

0

0

Mongols of Russia out of the Caucasus in the 1260s helped create a half-century of complex diplomacy in which Muslims often allied themselves with the European sponsors of the Crusader states—sometimes against Christians, sometimes against the Mongols. When the Mongols in Russia granted a special trade charter to merchants from Genoa, the Mongols in the Middle East granted a similar privilege to traders from Venice. It was this policy that brought Marco Polo, his uncles, and many others across Eurasia (Map 13.1). And it was probably also by this route that the cosmological ideas and technical knowledge of scholars working under Mongol patrons were communicated to Europe and helped to profoundly change its intellectual life.

There were also great dangers to the exchange. Europe had been free of bubonic plague—the Black Death (see Chapter 16)—since about 700. The Middle East had seen no plague since about the year 1200. In southwestern China, however, the plague had festered continuously in Yunnan province since the early Tang period. In the mid-thirteenth century, Mongol troops arrived in Yunnan and established a garrison. From that point, the military and supply traffic into and out of Yunnan provided the means for flea-infested rats carrying bubonic plague to be ferried from Yunnan to central China, to northwestern China, and across Central Asia. Along the routes, marmots and other desert rodents were massively infected and passed the disease on to dogs and to people. The caravan traffic across Central Asia infected the oasis towns, where the rats and fleas could disembark from overloaded camels, covered wagons, and the wagon-mounted felt tents (*yurts*) of the nomads. Finally, the Mongols themselves were incapacitated by the plague during their assault on Kaffa in Crimea in 1346. They withdrew, but Crimea was infiltrated by plague. From there, both Europe and Egypt would be repeatedly in-

Map 13.1 The Mongol Domains in Eurasia about 1300 Following the death of Genghis Khan in 1227, the empire was broken up into four large parts for his descendants: The Il-khans (founded by Hulegu) in the Middle East, the Golden Horde (founded by Batu) in southern Russia, the Jagadai khanate (founded by Genghis' son) in Central Asia, and the Yuan empire (founded by Khubilai) in eastern Asia.

Paisa The Mongol empire that united Eurasia in the middle 1200s provided good roads and protection for the movement of products, merchants, and diplomats. Under this system, individuals often traveled from one culture area to another via many intermediate zones, constantly encountering new languages, laws, and customs. The *paisa* (from a Chinese word for "card" or "sign"), with its inscription in Mongolian, proclaimed to all that the traveler had received the permission of the Khan to travel through the region. Europeans learned the practice and later applied it to travel through their small and diverse countries. The *paisa* was thus the ancestor of our modern passports. (The Metropolitan Museum of Art, neg. #257002)

fected by fleas from rats seeking the comfort of ships bound across the Mediterranean.

Bubonic plague was only one of the diseases at work, weakening the resistance of urban populations in particular and unleashing new waves of latent illness. Typhus, influenza, and smallpox traveled with the plague. The combination of these and other diseases created what is often called the "great pandemic" of 1347–1352. The human and cultural damage that resulted was far greater than any of the direct consequences of the Mongol military conquests. It is tempting to associate the social disorder of conquest and the plague as twin illnesses, but it was not the Mongol invaders who brought the disease westward. Rather, trade made possible by the Mongols assured the safety and order of the Eurasian trade routes. Peace and profit, in this case, were the channels by which pandemic illness terrorized Eurasia in the mid-fourteenth century.

THE FALL AND RISE OF ISLAM

Shortly after being acclaimed the Great Khan in 1206, Genghis began to carry out his plan to convince the kingdoms of Eurasia to surrender tribute to him. The ensuing two decades saw the bursting forth of Mongol aggression in nearly all directions. The earliest sustained action was westward, against Central Asia, the Middle East, and Russia. Genghis Khan died in 1227, possibly of the effects of alcoholism, but the campaigns continued. The Tanggut and then the Jin empires were destroyed, and their territories were put under Mongol governors (see Chapter 14). In 1236 a major offensive in the Russian territories gained the Mongols control of all the towns along the Volga River (see Map 13.1). Under siege by the Mongols in the 1230s, Europe would have suffered grave damage in 1241 had the Mongol forces not lifted their attack because of the death of the Great Khan Ogodei, and the necessity to head east for the election of a new Great Khan. After the installation of the new Great Khan Guyuk in 1246, Mongol pressure on the Middle East intensified and climaxed in 1258 in the capture and sacking of Baghdad and the murder of the last Abbasid caliph (see Chapter 10).

Mongols and Muslims

By 1260 the Mongols under Genghis' son Hulegu (ca. 1217–1265) controlled parts of Armenia and all of Azerbaijan, Anatolia, Mesopotamia, and Iran. The rulers of this regime became known as Il-khans, or "secondary" khans, subordinate only to the Great Khans in Mongolia. The role of Muslims in the Mongol conquest of the region known as Transoxiana was critical. There is evidence that some members of the Mongol imperial family were believers in Islam before the Mongol assault on the Middle East, and Mongols frequently relied upon Muslims as advance men and intermediaries. In addition, certain of the Il-khans showed favoritism toward some Muslim groups. Hulegu, for instance, was a Buddhist but was inclined to give privileges to the Shi'ite sect to which his most trusted adviser belonged. As a whole, however, the Mongols under the command of Hulegu were slow to become exposed to the Muslim religion.

In the same way that the Mongols had utilized Muslim resentment against nonbelievers in their conquest of cities in Central Asia, they utilized Christian resentment of Muslim rule in their seizure of some cities in Syria (where Christians were a large group), forcing the conversion of mosques to churches. When Baghdad, which had been the capital both of the Abbasid caliphs and of the Seljuk sultans, was captured by the Mongols in 1258, Hulegu agreed to the requests of his Christian wife that Christians be sought out and put in prominent posts. More shocking to the Muslim world was the murder of the last Abbasid caliph. In accordance with Mongol customs for the execution of high-born persons, he was rolled in a rug and trampled to death by horses, to prevent his blood from spilling on the ground.

Until the end of the thirteenth century, the Il-khans were officially adherents of Buddhism, and they championed that religion in Iran and Iraq. One reason was conflicts between the doctrines of Islam and the Mongol way of life. A most stubborn problem was the contradiction between the traditional shamanic method of animal slaughter among the Mongols, which required that no blood be spilled, and the Islamic code of cleanliness, *halal*, which required the draining of blood from the carcass. Litigation on this and closely related matters flooded the law courts of the Il-khans. For their part, Muslims were repelled by the Mongol worship of idols that is fundamental to shamanism, and were unwilling to forgive the apparently wanton murder of the caliph in 1258.

Islam posed other dangers to the Mongol mission in the Middle East. At the time that Hulegu was leading the Mongol armies into Iran and Iraq, Mongols were also conquering southern Russia, north of the Caspian Sea. By the 1260s the Mongol leader in Russia had declared himself a Muslim, announced his intention to avenge the last caliph, and claimed the Caucasus, between the Black and Caspian Seas. By this route, the Mongols of Russia could gain direct access to the Il-khan territories, and particularly to the capital at Tabriz in Azerbaijan. The conflict was the first between the Mongol domains, and the fact that one of the parties was avowedly Muslim led the leaders of Europe to believe that they could enlist the other party, the Il-khans, to drive Muslims out of the contested religious sites in Syria, Lebanon, and Palestine. The result was a brief diplomatic correspondence between the Il-khan court and Pope Nicholas IV (r. 1288–1292) and an exchange of ambassadors that sent two Christian Turks—Markuz and Rabban Sauma—on a remarkable tour of western Europe as Il-khan ambassadors in the late 1200s.

The Il-khans, who were still Buddhists, attempted to enlist the aid of European countries to eject the Golden Horde—the Mongols based in southern Russia—from the Caucasus. Many Crusaders individually enlisted in the Il-khan effort, and some were later excommunicated by the pope for doing so. For their part, the Mongols in Russia attempted to forge a Muslim alliance with the Mamluks in Egypt, to oppose the Crusaders and the Il-khans. The net result was prolongation of the life of the Crusader kingdoms in Palestine and Syria and of European influence there; the Mamluks did not succeed in completely ejecting them until the fifteenth century.

Before the Europeans could realize their plan of allying with the Mongols, the new Il-khan, Ghazan (1271–1304), declared himself a Muslim in 1295. Ghazan had been convinced to convert by his prime minister and confidant, Rashid al-Din Fadl Allah, who was a convert from Judaism to Islam.

It was years before the Il-khans made the crucial decision to support Sunna and not Shi'a Islam, but they were not completely consistent. Some of the Il-khans were baptized Christians as children, and at least one Il-khan reversed dynastic policy and supported Shi'ism instead of Sunnism. Nevertheless, the public stance of the Il-khans as Muslims radically changed the relationship of state and religion in the Middle East. The Il-khans, like all the large Middle Eastern states before them since the time of Muhammad, were the declared protectors and advocates of Islam, and all Mongols under the Il-khans were ordered to convert to Islam. The Il-khan legal code was ordered brought into agreement with the principles of Islam.

Technologies of Conquest

The Mongols were particularly creative in the use of cavalry, and they exploited the special properties of the Mongol bow. These bows could shoot one-third farther (and were significantly more difficult to pull) than Middle Eastern or European bows of the same period. Their accuracy was improved not only by the composite structure of the bows but also by the use of a jade thumbring to allow the archer's hands to withstand the tremendous tension of the drawn bowstring.

Mounted Mongol archers rarely exhausted the five-dozen or more arrows they carried in their quivers. At the opening of battle, they used these arrows from a distance to destroy the ranks of enemy marksmen, then rode their swift horses virtually without challenge into sword, lance, javelin, and mace combat against enemy infantry. The Mongol cavalry met its match only at the Battle of Ain Jalut (Spring of Goliath) near Jerusalem in 1260, where it confronted the forces of the Mamluks, who had also based their war techniques on the riding traditions of Central Asia. Thus it was Central Asian knowledge that prevented the westward advance of the Mongols toward the Mediterranean seaboard.

The Mongols besieged walled cities with flaming arrows, then with enormous projectiles—frequently also on fire—hurled from catapults. The first Mongol catapults were taken from the Chinese and, though easy to transport, had short ranges and poor accuracy. From the defeated Khwarazmshahs in Central Asia the Mongols adapted a catapult design that was half again as powerful as the Chinese catapult, and with this improved weapon they set upon the cities of Iran and Iraq.

Mongol warfare   The Mongols were in a long line of Central Asian conquerors who had mastered the art of shooting arrows from a galloping horse. They were renowned not only for their mobility, but the unusual distance and accuracy their archers could attain. This was largely due to the distinctive compound bow of the Mongols, which was more difficult to pull but much deadlier than the bows of Chinese or European archers. In combination with the advantage of using this deadly weapon from a speeding horse, the bow allowed the Mongols to overcome conventional infantry. (Courtesy, Edinburgh University Library)

Populations within the cities faced the prospect of immediate slaughter by the Mongols if they opened their gates to fight, or slow starvation followed by slaughter if they did not. On the other hand, the invaders offered their prospective victims food, shelter, and protection if they surrendered without a fight. The terrible bloodletting that the Mongols inflicted on cities such as Balkh in their early conquests gave staggering force to these appeals, and throughout the Middle East the Mongols found populations willing to acknowledge their overlordship in return for life. With each captured city the "Mongol" armies swelled in number, so that by its middle stage the conquest was accomplished by a small Mongol elite overseeing armies of recently recruited Turks, Iranians, and Arabs.

Muslims and the State

The original strategy of the Il-khans was to extract wealth from the country by peaceful means whenever possible but in any case to extract the maximum. This goal was most efficiently achieved through taxation, and the Mongols in many of their domains became masters of extraction. The method they used is generally called *tax farming*, a practice well developed in the Middle East before the coming of the Mongols. The government sold contracts for the collection of taxes to small corporations, most of which were owned by merchants who might work together to finance the caravan trade, small industries, or military expeditions. Those who bid to produce the highest revenues won the contracts and then proceeded by their own methods to collect the tax. The corporation kept anything over the contracted amount.

The short-term results for the government were good, for with a minimum of bureaucratic overhead the state collected large amounts of grain, cash, and silk. But the long-term results were different. The exorbitant rates to which the countryside was subjected drove many landowners into debt and servitude and prevented the reinvestment necessary to maintain productivity. Because many taxes were collected in kind, the price of grain rose so much that the government had difficulty in procuring supplies for the soldiers' granaries. As a consequence the state was forced to appropriate land to grow its own grain. These estates joined religious land grants, *auqaf*, in being tax exempt, and the tax base shrank further even though the demands of the army and the Mongol nobility for revenue continued to grow.

Economic troubles had become acute by the time Ghazan became Il-khan in 1295 and converted to Islam. To address the economic crisis, Ghazan appealed to the humane values of Islam and announced his intention to lessen the government's tax demands. At the same time, he used the international contacts of the Mongol empire to seek new methods of economic management. He believed he found one in the Chinese practice of using paper money, and at the time of his accession to the throne he ordered that paper money be used. But because the peoples of the Middle East had no previous exposure to paper money and no confidence in its value, the economy quickly sank into a depression from which it did not recover until after the end of the Il-khan period in the middle 1300s.

After Ghazan, the Il-khans experienced a slow decline that was like the decline of Mongol regimes elsewhere. The extraction of revenues from the population for the support of the Mongol military elite caused widespread popular unrest and elite resentment. The Mongol nobles themselves competed fiercely for the decreasing revenues, and fighting among Mongol factions destabilized the government. As the power of the Il-khans fragmented, the expansive ambitions of Mongols north of the Caspian were aroused again. In the mid-fourteenth century, the

Mongols of the Golden Horde came down through the Caucasus into the western regions of the Il-khan empire and soon into the Il-khan's central territory, Azerbaijan. The Golden Horde aided in the dismemberment of the Il-khan empire and briefly occupied its major cities.

As the power of the Il-khans in the Middle East and of the Mongols in Russia weakened in the fourteenth century, a new power emerged in

Islamic conversion The Il-khan ruler Ghazan (r. 1295–1304) was the first Mongol lord of Iran to convert to Islam. When a majority of Mongols in Iran followed his example, the Middle East became once again an overwhelmingly Muslim region, which altered balances of power in Europe, Russia, and Egypt. Il-khan law was altered to accommodate Islamic principles, and economic reforms were begun to alleviate the distress of farmers. But in many ways Ghazan remained Mongol. In this painting he is shown side by side with his primary wife, a standard practice in depicting Mongol leaders. She retains her distinctive Mongol hairstyle, while Ghazan is dressed in traditional Mongol robes and boots. (Bibliotheque Nationale de France)

Central Asia, where the Mongol rulers were descendants of Genghis's son Jagadai (d. 1242). Under the leader Timur (1336–1405), the Jagadai khanate drew on the political traditions of the Mongols and on Islam. The campaigns of Timur in western Eurasia were even more brutal than earlier Mongol campaigns had been, and by the late fourteenth century much of the Middle East was once again united under a single ruler. The Timurids (descendants of Timur) held the Middle East together long enough to deepen and consolidate Islamic influence, and they laid the groundwork for the later establishment in India of a Muslim Mongol regime, the Moguls, in the sixteenth century. But Timur was the last great Central Asian conqueror. After his time Central Asia was no longer the crossroads of Eurasia, as it had been since the earliest times.

Art and Science in Islamic Eurasia

Thanks partly to the wide-ranging cultural exchange fostered by the Mongols, the Il-khans and Timurids presided over a brilliant period in Islamic civilization. Many of the intellectual developments of the era had a strong direct effect on Europe. Others had an indirect but equally important influence. The sharing of artistic influences and political ideas between Iran and China created the illusion in European eyes that east of the Mediterranean there existed an "Orient" that was uniform in its tastes and its political cultures. In fact, the intimacy of Iran and China was a product of the millennia of Silk Road trade and only more recently of the Mongol Empire. It was not evidence of any fundamental "Oriental" character. Timur was not successful in his wish to reunite Iran and China under Mongol rule, but he made possible the advancement of some specific arts because of his practice, followed by his descendants, of forcibly concentrating scholars, artists, and craftsmen in his capital.

The historian Juvaini, who noted Genghis Khan's deathbed speech, was a central figure in literary development. His family came from the city of Balkh, which the Mongols devastated in 1221. At that time the family switched allegiance to the Mongols, and both Juvaini and his older brother assumed high government posts. Juvaini had among his interests the composition of historical works. Il-khan Hulegu, seeing an opportunity to both immortalize and justify the Mongol conquest of the Middle East, enthusiastically supported Juvaini's projects. The result was the first comprehensive narrative describing the rise of the Mongols under Genghis Khan.

Juvaini's work and his methods—he often was critical of his subjects—were the inspiration for even more profound work by Rashid al-Din, the prime minister of the later Il-khan, Ghazan. Rashid al-Din completed the first attempt at a history of the world. It contains the earliest known general history of Europe, based on information from European monks. Editions of Rashid al-Din's world history were often richly illustrated with pictures adapted from European paintings to depict European persons or events and from Chinese paintings to depict Chinese people or events. In this way, the principles of watercolor composition and portraiture in China—where watercolor painting was extremely well developed—were introduced into Iran, where they exercised a lasting influence. Reproduction and distribution of Rashid al-Din's work spread throughout Eurasia knowledge of the arts and histories of the lands under Mongol rule.

The cosmopolitan influence of Rashid al-Din's world history was personified by Rashid himself. As a Jew converted to Islam, serving the Mongols and traveling very widely in their service, he was aware of many cultures and many points of view. He was in constant touch with the officials of Central Asia and China. When he could not see them in person, he often wrote letters to them explaining his ideas on economic management. It was partly as a result of these lines of communication that similar financial and monetary reforms occurred at roughly the same time in Iran, Russia, and China. Rashid was above all practical. It was he who advocated conducting government in accord with the moral principles of a majority of the population, and it was he who convinced Ghazan to convert to Islam.

Under the Timurids, the magnificent achievement of the Il-khan historians was augmented. Timur himself was acquainted with the greatest historian and geographer of the age, Ibn Khaldun (1332–1406), a Moroccan. Like his Mongol predecessors, Timur was an enthusiastic supporter of historical narratives in which he himself acted as the primary informant. In a scene reminiscent of the times when Ghazan had sat patiently answering Rashid al-Din's questions on the history of the Mongols, Timur and Ibn Khaldun sat in Damascus, exchanging historical, philosophical, and geographical viewpoints. Like Genghis, Timur saw himself as a world conqueror, so the story of his conquests was necessarily the story of the world. At their capitals of Samarkand and Herat (in modern-day Afghanistan), later Timurid rulers sponsored historical writing both in Iranian and in Turkish. Under them, the art of illustrating historical and fictional works, employed so strikingly in Rashid al-Din's history, reached a very high point of development.

Juvaini had accompanied Hulegu in 1256 in the campaigns against the Assassins, a radical religious sect, at Mount Alamut, and he worked to preserve the enormous historical archives that

Jonah and the whale Rashid al-Din was Ghazan's closest advisor. Rashid was a Jew who converted to Islam, and was influential in Ghazan's decision to become a Muslim. In addition to his roles as bureaucrat and political advisor, Rashid was one of the most important historians who ever lived. With the encouragement of Ghazan and of Ghazan's successor as Il-khan, Rashid completed the first comprehensive world history, drawing upon sources from Latin, Greek, Arabic, Persian, Mongolian, and Chinese. The work was illustrated with distinctive art from the regions he discussed, relating their folklore and artistic styles. In this panel, the story of Jonah and the whale is depicted. (Courtesy, Edinburgh University Library)

the Assassins maintained there. It was possibly the archives and libraries of the Assassins that had drawn the multi-talented Shi'ite believer Nasir al-Din Tusi to Mount Alamut, where Mongol forces took him into custody. Hülegü was quickly charmed by Nasir al-Din and used him in ensuing years as one of his most trusted advisers.

Nasir al-Din was interested in history, poetry, ethics, and religion, but his outstanding contributions were in mathematics and cosmology. He drew on the work of the great poet and mathematician of the Seljuk period, Omar Khayyam (1038?–1131), to lay the foundations for complex algebra and trigonometry. The impact of Nasir al-Din's work on later thinkers was considerable. A group of his followers, working at their Maraga observatory and academy near the Il-khan capital of Tabriz in Azerbaijan, were able to solve a fundamental problem in classical cosmology.

In astronomy and in mathematics, Islamic scholars had preserved and elaborated on the insights of the Greeks. They adopted the cosmological model of Ptolemy, which assumed a universe with the Earth at its center and the Sun and planets rotating around it in circular orbits. Astronomers knew Ptolemy's model was flawed, because the motions of the five visible planets were not in agreement with its predictions. Since Ptolemy's time, astronomers and mathematicians of the Middle East had been searching for mathematically consistent explanations that would account for the movement of the planets and reconcile them with Ptolemy's model.

Nasir al-Din proposed such a model. His approach was based on a concept of small circles rotating within a large circle, changing vectors in such a way as to account for their movement when viewed from the Earth. A student of Nasir al-Din reconciled the model with the ancient Greek idea of epicycles (small circles rotating around a larger circle) to explain the movement of the moon around the earth, and here occurred the breakthrough that changed cosmological thought. The mathematical tables and geometric models of this student were later transferred in their entirety to Europe and became known to the Polish astronomer Nicholas Copernicus (1473–1543). The means of transmission is still one of the tantalizing unknowns in world his-

tory. Copernicus adopted the lunar model as his own, virtually without revision. He then proposed that the model of lunar movement developed under the Il-khans was the proper model for planetary movement also—with the planets moving around the Sun.

Europe was indebted to the Il-khans not just for cosmological insights. Perhaps because of the Central Asian nomads' traditional dependence on the stars to guide their movement, or because of the suitability of high, dry, Central Asia for astronomical observation, Central Asian empires —particularly the Uigurs and the Seljuks—had excelled in their sponsorship of observational astronomy and the making of calendars. Under the Il-khans, Maraga became a sort of world center for the prediction of lunar and solar eclipses. Astrolabes, armillary spheres, three-dimensional quadrants, and other instruments in use there were much more precise than those used earlier.

The Il-khans made a deliberate attempt to amass at their observatory astronomical data from all parts of the Islamic world, as well as from China. In this way they achieved unprecedented accuracy in the prediction of eclipses. The predictions of the Il-khan astronomers were translated into Arabic for use in the hostile Mamluk territories. Byzantine monks took them to Constantinople and translated them into Greek. They were taken to Muslim Spain and translated into Latin. They were taken to India, where the Sultan of Delhi ordered them translated into Sanskrit. The Great Khan Khubilai was so impressed that he demanded a team of Iranians to come to Beijing to build an observatory for him. The Timurids continued to sponsor large observatories. Indeed, the Timurid ruler Ulugh Beg (1394–1449) was an astronomer and actively participated in the construction of the great observatory at Samarkand.

Such work required a system for writing numbers that would give mathematical calculations a precision that was not possible with the numerical systems inherited—both in the Middle East and in Europe—from the Greeks. By the 700s, Middle Eastern scholars had adapted the Indian numerical system, including the symbol for zero, to their own script. This advance made possible work on the level of the Nasir al-Din group. Until Leonardo of Pisa (also called Fibonacci, the discoverer of Fibonacci's Numbers) studied Iranian texts and used them to introduce Europeans to the abacus in the 1200s, Europeans were still using the clumsy Roman numerals to do their calculations. In his text, Leonardo adapted the "Arabic" numerals of the Middle East and in this way introduced columnar calculation and the zero. With this technology, Europeans were finally able to participate again in the study of complex mathematics, astronomy and astrology, music theory, and logic—scholarship that had begun in the ancient Greek world and had been advanced in Islamic and Indian civilizations.

The Timurids continued the Seljuk and Ilkhan policies of sponsoring advanced work in astronomy and mathematics that integrated the traditions of Eurasia, and they underwrote another major advance in mathematics. Ghiyas al-Din Jamshid al-Kashi, in his studies of Chinese calendars, noted that Chinese astronomers had long used a unit for the measurement of new moons that was calculated as 1/10,000th of a day. It appears that this was the inspiration for al-Kashi's use of the decimal fraction, by which quantities less than 1 may be represented by the manipulation of a marker to show place value (a technology to which the zero was also crucial). With this means for representing decimal fractions, al-Kashi went on to propose a far more precise calculation for pi (π) than had been achieved since the value was established in classical times. This innovation, too, was transmitted to Europe by way of Constantinople, where al-Kashi's famous work on mathematics was translated into Greek in the fifteenth century.

NATIONAL DEFINITION IN RESPONSE TO THE MONGOLS

Major features of Iran and Iraq under the Ilkhans were characteristic of many regions that the Mongols occupied. One was a marked disparity between the fortunes of the cities and the countryside. After the conquest, the volume of safe, reliable overland trade

Ulugh Beg's observatory The Timurid ruler Ulugh Beg (1394–1449) continued the reunification of Central Asia and the Middle East under Islamic rule that had begun under his grandfather Timur (Tamerlane). Even before the rise of the Mongols, empires of Central Asia had been distinguished for their achievements in observational astronomy and in calendar making. The foundations of Ulugh Beg's observatory near Samarkand are still standing, though the instruments have all been removed and the most distinctive feature is the gigantic groove in the floor that once guided the canopy around the enclosure. (Novosti)

throughout Eurasia economically stimulated many of the commercial cities of Iran and Iraq. But the countryside, subjected to extensive damage in the conquest, sporadically continuing violence, and crushing taxes, suffered terribly. Although from the time of Ghazan the Il-khan policy changed from maximum extraction from the rural sector to a policy that was more constructive and protective, the change came too late to stop the decline in population and further deterioration of agriculture.

There were also distinctive cultural changes under the Il-khans and Timurids. Both empires were inclined to promote the use of the written Iranian language, often in connection with popular or secular forms of writing such as poetry, epic writing, and songs. Similarly, both showed a strong interest in popular religious practices, especially the mystical form of Islam known as *Sufism*. This was somewhat in tension with the official stance of the later Il-khan and the Timurid courts as adherents of Sunna orthodoxy.

After 1500 a new regime was established in Iran, the Safavids. They were not Iranian—they were part of the ongoing westward migration of Turkic peoples that began before the Mongols and continued after them. Nevertheless, they were able to position themselves against the Mongols and Timurids, using nationalist sentiments to unite the population. In contrast to the Il-khans and Timurids, for instance, the Safavids were not Sunnites but Shi'ites. Yet the tools they used to create a nationalist consciousness—the Iranian language, popular religion, the geographical unity of Iran itself—were products of the Il-khan and Timurid periods. Thus, both by direct and indirect influence, the Mongol period shaped Iran as an early modern "nation."

Similar dynamics can be observed in Russia. In the Middle East the Mongols ended the long period of the political and cultural dominance of Baghdad and encouraged the emergence of new centers of power and commerce. In Russia the Mongols ended the dominance of Kiev and encouraged the rise of Moscow. As when they first occupied Iran, the Mongols in Russia had little interest in the dominant religious system. But in Russia, as we shall see, the distance between the Mongols and the local people never moved the Mongols to become patrons of the local religion.

The result was not only survival of the religious hierarchy but also the strong association of the Russian Orthodox Church with native identity and aspirations to independence. In connection with these religious influences, the Russian language for the first time became the dominant written language of Russia. Finally, in Russia as elsewhere, the Mongols were an impetus to centralization. In the aftermath of the Mongol period, Russia's strongest leaders and its most centralized political system emerged.

Russia and Rule from Afar

The first conflict between the Kievan state and the Mongols occurred in 1223, when the Mongols defeated a combined Russian and Kipchak (a Turkic people) army in southeastern Russia. The great onslaught did not come until the late 1230s, when a series of defeats for the Russians climaxed in the capture and spectacular pillage of the town of Riazan. Unlike others who invaded Russia before and after, the Mongols were capable of successful winter campaigning and found that only the springtime mud of Russia hindered their cavalry. The Russian princes failed to unite to oppose the invaders, and in 1240 the central town of Kiev fell. The princes of Hungary acknowledged the superiority of Genghis's grandson Batu (d. 1255) shortly afterward, and the entire region came under Mongol domination. Batu and his descendants established their own regime and were known as the "Golden Horde" (see Map 13.1). This was really a collection of small khanates, many of which survived when others died out at the end of the 1300s. The White Horde, for instance, ruled much of southeastern Russia until the 1480s, and the khan of Crimea was not overthrown until 1783.

The Mongols placed their capitals at the ends of the overland caravan routes, which were the infrastructure of their empires. But in Russia only the region at the mouth of the Volga could be connected to the steppe networks. Therefore the Mongols of the Golden Horde settled well to the south and west of their Russian domains, at Sarai just north of the Caspian Sea. As part of their rule-from-afar, the Mongols allowed great privileges to the Orthodox Church, which aided in reconciling the Russian population to their distant masters. Old Church Slavonic was revived, Russian chronicle-writing remained vigorous, and Greek was shunned by Russian scholars even though the khans of the Golden Horde gave their blessing to renewed contacts with Constantinople. The Golden Horde also enlisted Russian princes to act as their agents (primarily their tax collectors and census takers) and frequently as their ambassadors to the court of the Great Khans in Mongolia.

As in their other domains, the Mongols' primary concern in Russia was the extraction of wealth. The flow of silver and gold into the hands of the Mongols starved the local economy for currency. Like the Il-khans, the Khans of the Golden Horde attempted to introduce paper money. So vivid was the impression left by this Mongol innovation that the word in Russian for money (*denga*) comes from the Mongolian word for stamp (*tamga*).

Mongol domination strongly affected urban development and population movement in Russia, in part because of the role played by Alexander Nevskii (ca. 1220–1263), the prince of Novgorod. Alexander aided in the Mongol conquest by persuading many of the Russian princes that it would be better to submit to the Mongols than to resist them. In recognition of Alexander's service, the Mongols favored both Novgorod (under the rule of Alexander) and the emerging town of Moscow (under the rule of Alexander's brother Daniel). These towns eclipsed devastated Kiev as political, cultural, and economic centers during the period of Mongol domination. This, in turn, encouraged people to move northward, away from the Mongol pasture lands in the southwest, and it led to the opening of new agricultural land far north of the Caspian Sea. During the 1300s, Moscow emerged as the new center of Russia, and control of Moscow was equivalent to control of the entire country (see Map 13.2).

Russia preserved reminders of the Mongol presence for many years. Some regions of southern Russia, particularly Crimea, remained breeding grounds for the bubonic plague long after the caravans that were encouraged and protected by the Mongols had introduced the disease. In the late Kievan period, the Ukraine had been a fertile and well-populated region. But under the Mongols, the Ukraine underwent a severe loss of population. The Mongols crossed the region repeatedly in their campaigns against eastern Europe and raided it continually to discipline villages that were slow to hand over their tax payments.

Historians debate the effect of the Mongol period of domination on the shaping of Russia. The destructiveness of the Mongol capture of Riazan, like the capture of Balkh in the Middle East,

Transformation of the Kremlin Like many peoples of northern medieval Europe, the Russians of the Kievan period had preferred to build in wood, which was easy to handle and comfortable to live in. But the fortification of the important political centers, which were vulnerable to assault, had to be constructed of stone. In the 1300s, the city of Moscow emerged as a leading political center, and its old palace, the Kremlin, was gradually transformed from a wooden to a stone structure. (Novosti)

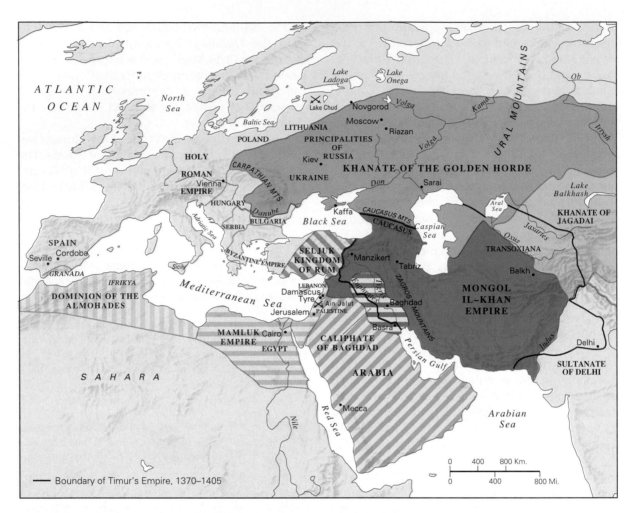

Map 13.2 Western Eurasia, 1258–1405 This map of the Mongol domains in the Middle East demonstrates the delicate balance of power that was upset by Ghazan's conversion to Islam in 1295. The Golden Horde became Muslim first, and began the first war between the Mongol domains in the 1260s when they combatted the Il-khans for control of the Caucasus, between the Black Sea and the Caspian Sea. Europeans hoped to exploit the conflict by enlisting the Il-khans against the Mamluks, but realized the cause was lost after Ghazan became Muslim. The Mamluks and the Golden Horde remained allies against the Il-khans, which aided Europeans in retaining their lands in Palestine and Syria.

seems to many to be typical of the Mongol conquests. In the opinion of many historians—as well as the eighteenth-century Russian poet Alexander Pushkin—the Mongol conquest of Russia and parts of eastern Europe isolated Russia from the great currents of development in early modern Europe, including the secularizing, neoclassical movements often called the *Renaissance* (see Chapter 16). These historians refer to

"the Mongol yoke" and hypothesize a sluggish economy and a dormant culture under the Mongols.

Other historians offer a different interpretation. They point out that the Kievan economy was in decline well before the coming of the Mongols and that the Kievan princes had already ceased to mint money. In addition, even though the Mongols' demands were high and their internationally oriented monetary measures sometimes inappropriate, the Russian territories regularly managed to pay their taxes in silver. These tax payments in silver suggest regular surpluses in income and an economy sufficiently well developed to make the conversion of goods to cash convenient. It is also clear that the tax burden was significantly increased not by the Mongols directly but by their tax collectors, Russian princes who often exempted their own lands from the tax and shifted the additional burden to the peasants. When the princes requested and received a lowering of the tax rate from the Mongols, the outcome was not necessarily more money in the hands of the common people.

More problematic is the cultural argument. Before the Mongol invasion, Russia was under the domination of the Byzantine Empire, which was not greatly affected by the Renaissance in western Europe. Prior to the time of the Russian ruler Peter the Great (r. 1682–1725), who did in fact establish strong relations with western Europe in the late 1600s, it is hard to see how Russian elites would have circumvented the influence of the Orthodox Church, with or without the influence of the Mongols.

The Mongols in Russia, as elsewhere, tended to undermine the local elites or to alter the status of individuals within the elite in order to enhance their ability to control the country. In the specific case of Russia, the question is whether the Mongols destroyed the traditional forms of elite participation in government. It does not appear that they did. There is good evidence that the structure of local government in Russia did not change significantly in this period. On the regional level, the princely families continued to battle among themselves for dominance as they had in the past. The Mongols were merely an additional factor in those struggles. It was Ivan III, the prince of Moscow (r. 1462–1505), who established himself as an autocratic ruler in the late 1400s. Before Ivan, the title *tsar* (from "caesar"), by which the rulers of Russia after the Mongols were known, had previously been used only for foreign rulers (whether the emperors of Byzantium or the Turkic khans of the steppe) who had dominated the disunited principalities of Russia. After being free of Mongol dominion, Russian leaders adopted the title *tsar* to show that Russia should be ruled by Russians and not from afar. This nationalistic response was not unlike others that occurred in the regions that for a time came under Mongol rule.

At the peripheries of Eurasia were countries that encountered the Mongols but remained independent. In many cases, these regions experienced the same upwellings of nationalist sentiment that arose in countries under Mongol domination. Yet those societies that were challenged but not conquered also tended to experience a centralization and strengthening of their institutions of command. It is probable that the long life of many of these regimes is partly due to the challenge of the Mongols, and the same is true for those regions where new, centralized, well-defined nations arose.

Social Change and Centralization in Europe and Anatolia

Communications between the Il-khans and Constantinople gave Europe a second doorway (Spain provided the first) to the scientific and philosophical achievements of Islamic culture. However, there were more direct consequences of the Mongol Empire for Europe. One was a shift in the power balances in the Middle East. Another was the invasion of Europe by Mongol forces in the very late 1230s and the 1240s.

The division of the western part of the Mongol Empire between the Golden Horde and the Il-khans had a parallel in the division of Europe at the same time between the political forces of the papacy and those of the Holy Roman Emperor and hereditary ruler of the German territories, Frederick II (r. 1212–1250) of the Hohenstaufen family (see Chapter 16). Frederick had been raised in Sicily and was sympathetic to Muslim culture. When the pope threatened Frederick with excommunication unless he participated in the Crusades waged by Europeans to capture religious sites in Palestine and Syria, Frederick conspired with the Mamluks to present the illusion of having captured Jerusalem.

Attempts by European leaders—including the popes—and the Il-khans to forge a diplomatic alliance against the Golden Horde alarmed the

Mamluks. They suspected that the Roman Catholic Church would use the alliance to destroy Frederick's power and then would turn its full force on the Mamluk territories in Syria and Egypt. In defense, the Mamluks created their long-lasting alliance with the Golden Horde. Frederick and his son Manfred became magnets for the hopes of some Islamic groups. The Assassins, who had been banished by the Seljuks to their stronghold on Mount Alamut and lived in fear of the Mongol onslaught, sent their ambassadors to Frederick in Sicily. The pieces for a medieval world war were in place.

With Europe divided between the pope and the Holy Roman Emperor, the kingdoms of eastern Europe—particularly Hungary, Poland, and Transylvania—were left on their own to deal with the onslaught of the Golden Horde. Many of the eastern princes decided to capitulate and went to Sarai to declare themselves slaves of Batu. One of the minority of the eastern groups unwilling to capitulate was the Teutonic Knights.

Like the Knights Templar in the Middle East, the Teutonic Knights had been sent on a crusade to Christianize the Slavic and Kipchak populations of northern Europe. Also like the Knights Templar, the Teutonic Knights were licensed to colonize their conquered territories, and they imported many thousands of German farmers, artisans, and clerics to populate their kingdoms. Alexander Nevskii, the prince of Novgorod, led the Mongol campaigns against the Knights and their Finnish allies, who lost so many of their number through the ice at Lake Chud that their power was broken and the northern crusades virtually ceased.

The role of Alexander Nevskii in the defeat of the Teutonic Knights is a reminder that the "Mongol" armies whom the Europeans encountered were barely Mongol at all. Commanders, of course, were Mongols. Sübüdei, who oversaw the campaigns in western Eurasia, has been ranked by historians as one of the world's great military geniuses. The Mongol policies of recruitment and conscription had created an international force in which combatants and support forces were composed of Mongols, Turks, Chinese, Iranians, and many Europeans, including at least one Englishman who went to the Middle East as a crusading knight and through capture or capitulation joined the Mongol forces, turning up in the Hungarian campaigns.

Eastern Europe came under direct assault from these forces in the winter of 1241, when the Danube River froze. Sübüdei's troops rode over it and inflicted a series of dazzling defeats on the eastern European kingdoms. Mongol forces appeared at the foot of the Alps, apparently menacing northern Italy and possibly Venice. They were also on the outskirts of Vienna. While Poles, Hungarians, Austrians, and Bohemians struggled frantically to safeguard themselves and mount some resistance, the rest of Europe was panicked by the sudden, terrifying onslaught by the unknown invaders.

Rumors and some written accounts described the Mongols as having bodies that were part dog. They were theorized to have come from Hell or from the caves where the monsters of ancient times had been banished by Alexander the Great. They were asserted to be cannibals. In Germany it was claimed that the Mongols were the lost tribes of Israel, returned, and in the eastern German territories there were instances of the lynching of Jews who were believed to be in secret alliance with the invaders. In Hungary, the recently Christianized Kipchaks were accused of aiding the Mongols; some were imprisoned, and some were killed. The king of France resigned himself to the destruction of his country, welcoming it as the will of God. The pope, despite his wish to keep pressure on Frederick II, authorized a crusade against the Mongols, and the liturgies for daily worship were altered to include a line begging God for deliverance from them.

It seemed that the prayers were answered. Before the Europeans could mount a united force to repel the Mongols, Sübüdei's forces turned and left in December 1241. The Great Khan Ögödei had died, and the Mongol princes wished to return to Mongolia to participate in the intense struggle that would elect the new Great Khan.

After the sudden retreat of Sübüdei's troops from Europe in 1241, several European leaders attempted to open peaceful channels of communication with the Il-khans, hoping through them to reach the Great Khans in Mongolia. Some

VOICES & VISIONS

Dueling Pieties

Much of the written communication between Europe and the Mongols survives, but only as a result of an extraordinarily complex process. Europeans wrote to the Mongols in Latin, which was normally translated into Persian when the parties reached the Il-khan territories. On the route to the Mongol capital, a means had to be found to translate the Persian into Mongolian, although this translating could be done orally if the ambassadors received an audience with the Great Khan or his representatives. For messages going from east to west, the opposite process was applied.

Fortunately, the messages were not complicated, though each side found the other's ideas so bizarre that mistakes in translation were very often suspected. This passage in a letter from Pope Innocent IV to the Great Khan in 1245 is typical (Innocent did not know that there was no one to receive the letter, for Ögödei had died in 1241, and Güyük had not yet been installed as the next Great Khan):

It is not without cause that we are driven to express in strong terms our amazement that you, according to what we have heard, have invaded many countries belonging both to Christians and to others and are laying them waste in a horrible desolation, and with a fury still unabated you do not cease from breaking the bond of natural ties, sparing neither sex nor age, you rage against all indiscriminately with the sword of chastisement.

Like other popes before and after him, Innocent proceeded to explain that he was sending monks to convert the Great Khan to Christianity, to baptize him, and to make him not a waster of the Christian lands but their protector (an echo of the Prester John dream). Group after group of missionaries came from the church to convert the Mongols, and all were disappointed.

When Güyük was proclaimed Great Khan in 1246, he answered Innocent's letter. He expressed befuddlement at the idea that he should be chastised for invading Christian lands and at the suggestion that he himself should be baptized. Güyük satirized Innocent's arrogance in presuming to know God's intentions:

Though you also say that I should become a trembling Christian, worship God, and be an ascetic, how do you know whom God absolves, or in truth to whom He shows mercy? How do you know that such words as you speak are with God's approval? From the rising of the sun to its setting, all the lands have been made subject to me. Who could do this contrary to the command of God?

The Mongol Great Khans were consistent with traditional Central Asian religion in their belief that Heaven shows its will in the unfolding of history, that victors are necessarily the messengers of Heaven's will, and that the supreme victor is the supreme messenger. As often as the Popes warned the Great Khans to be baptized and submit to the guidance of the Vatican, the Great Khans responded with the simple message that they were not about to submit to the church and that all Europe had best submit to the Great Khans—or suffer the consequences.

Güyük sternly closed his letter to Innocent:

If you do not observe God's command, and if you ignore my command, I shall know you as my enemy. Likewise I shall make you understand. If you do otherwise, God knows what I know.

In 1254, the Great Khan Mongke—the last to rule the united Mongol Empire in Eurasia—used similarly ringing rhetoric on Louis IX of France:

If, when you hear and understand the decree of the eternal God, you are still unwilling to pay attention and believe it, saying "Our country is far away, our mountains are mighty, our sea is vast," and in this confidence you bring an army against us—we know what we can do: He who made what was difficult easy and what was far away near, the eternal God, He knows.

What did the Popes regard as the primary evidence that the Mongols were evil? What did the Mongols see as the basic test of their supreme righteousness?

Source: Adapted from Christopher Dawson, ed., *Mission to Asia*, Medieval Academy Reprints for Teaching Series (Toronto: University of Toronto Press, 1981), 75, 85–86, 204. Archaic language has been amended to make the quotations more readable.

kings of Europe, trade federations, and the popes sent repeated embassies to Iran, and many passed eastward toward the Mongol capital. The Mongol rulers often received merchants and craftsmen favorably, but they welcomed ambassadors from kings or from the Vatican only if they brought messages of submission from their lords (see Voices & Visions: Dueling Pieties).

European embassies to the Golden Horde and to the Great Khans in Mongolia increased in number through the thirteenth century. As Europeans learned to utilize the Mongol trade routes, and to exploit Mongol divisions in the Middle East, their terror of the Mongols was replaced by their awe of, and eventual idealization of, the wealth and power of the Mongol empires. From their contacts with the Mongols the Europeans gained their first systematic knowledge of Eurasian geography, cultural configuration, natural resources, and commerce. They learned about the use of diplomatic passports, the mining and uses of coal, movable type, high-temperature metallurgy, efficient enumeration and higher mathematics, gunpowder, and, in the fourteenth century, the casting and use of bronze cannon.

Nevertheless, Europe suffered greatly from the effects of Mongol domination of eastern Europe and Russia. The terror created by the Mongol invasion combined with other factors to ignite a storm of religious questioning and anxiety, most intense in regions of eastern and central Europe that had been virtually under the hooves of the Mongol horses. More devastating than the religious anxiety was an outbreak of bubonic plague in the 1340s (see Chapter 16). Europeans thought it was not a product of the trade encouraged by the Mongols but a disaster independently visited upon them by God.

Because in its later stages the plague can be passed from person to person by airborne particles, the crowded cities of Europe were mercilessly gutted. Overall Europe lost perhaps a third of its population in a decade, and many cities lost the vast majority of their residents. Eventually, changes in building practices, and new methods of controlling the rat population, eradicated the plague again from western Europe. How-

ever, whole strata of society, particularly those classes and occupations based in the cities, were undermined by disease.

One of the effects was the lessening of the influence of the professions and of those educated in Latin, resulting in the rise of popular culture and vernacular literatures. Thus the indirect effects on Europe of the Mongol invasion parallel the direct effects of Mongol policy throughout Eurasia: traditional elites and their languages were displaced in favor of new professional elites and literatures in local languages.

When, in the fourteenth century, the Mongol grip on eastern Europe was weakened, several regions emerged considerably centralized from the century of Mongol pressure. Lithuania was one of the European regions energized by the Mongol threat (see Map 13.2). Just as Russia fell to the Mongols and eastern Europe was first invaded, Lithuania was undergoing an unprecedented degree of centralization and military strengthening. Like Alexander Nevskii, the Lithuanian leaders struck a deal with the Mongols and maintained much independence for the country. In the late 1300s, when Mongol power in Russia was waning, Lithuania capitalized on its privileged position to dominate its neighbors, particularly Poland. Lithuania ended all hopes of a revival of the power of the Teutonic Knights in eastern Europe. In the Balkans, too, independent and well-organized kingdoms separated themselves from the chaos of the Byzantine Empire and thrived until the Turkic Ottomans conquered them in the 1500s and 1600s.

The Ottomans arose from the region of Anatolia formerly dominated by the Seljuks of Rum. In the time of the Il-khan Ghazan, the Ottomans began to struggle for autonomy on this western perimeter. As the Il-khans weakened, the emerging Ottomans gained local dominance, but Timur and his successors checked their power. Not until the disintegration of the Timurid Empire did the Ottomans gain free rein in Anatolia and parts of the Middle East. By the end of the 1400s they had delivered a fatal blow to the Byzantine navy and taken the Byzantine capital at Constantinople for their own, renaming it Istanbul. Like other empires arising in the wake of the Mongols, the Ottomans defined themselves by their opposition to the Il-khans and later to the Timurids. But in their institutions the Ottomans evinced both the Central Asian origins they shared with the Mongols and the direct adaptation of many Mongol techniques of government.

Stabilization of Mamluk Rule in Egypt

In the Middle East, the Mamluks were the outstanding example of a government that was strengthened, was centralized, and even gained some international support for its resistance to the Mongol advance. (In Abbasid times, mamluk was a term used for military slaves; later, the mamluks who established an empire in Egypt and Syria used the name Mamluk for their regime and its ruling class.) They retained control of their base in Egypt and their separated lands in Syria. During the campaigns against the Il-khans in the 1250s and 1260s, the Crusaders allowed the Mamluks to cross Palestine to maintain lines of supply and command. The Mamluks were brilliantly successful in their campaigns against the Il-khans, and this same strength was evident in the later defeat and destruction of the Crusader kingdoms. It was also demonstrated in the Mamluks' ruthless suppression of the well-organized and violent Assassins, which made the Mamluks one of the pillars (far more reliable than the Il-khans) of Sunni orthodoxy in the Middle East.

Mamluk society, particularly in Egypt, became very diverse. In the Abbasid and Seljuk eras the Mamluks had been Turkic immigrants from Central Asia, but by the thirteenth century the military servants who gave their name to the regime were drawn from sub-Saharan Africa, from parts of Europe, and from throughout the Middle East. Under the Mamluks, Egypt remained a military dictatorship until the forces of the Ottoman Empire conquered it in the 1500s. Even then, the Mamluks persisted as the dominant elites in Egypt until Napoleonic times at the end of the eighteenth century.

The Mamluks were cosmopolitan and practical in outlook. They continued their friendship

Western Eurasia, 1200–1500	
1206	Temujin chosen as Genghis Khan of the Mongols
1221–1223	Mongol attacks on Iran, Russia
1227	Death of Genghis Khan
1241	Death of Ogodei, withdrawal of Mongol forces from Eastern Europe
1242	Alexander Nevskii defeats the Teutonic Knights
1258	Mongols take Baghdad, kill last Abbasid caliph
1260	First war between Il-khans and Golden Horde
1295–1304	Reign of Ghazan Khan in Iran
1346	Plague outbreak at Kaffa
1370–1405	Rule of Timur in Central Asia
1462–1505	Ivan III unites Russia under rule of Moscow

with the Hohenstaufen family and sent the Syrian diarist and judge Jamal al-Din Muhammad ibn Salim as ambassador to Frederick's son Manfred in Italy. Mamluk links with the Golden Horde, established during the conflict with the Il-khans, kept a steady stream of people and goods moving by ship between Cairo and Russia, particularly the port of Kaffa in Crimea. Historians now know that Kaffa was the primary point of embarkation for carriers of the plague to points on the Mediterranean, and it was by this route that Egypt suffered a continuing tragedy.

From the late 1300s to the very end of the 1700s, the Mamluks and their successors continued to import soldiers from Crimea. At the height of the fourteenth-century pandemic, Egypt may have lost as much as a third of its population. Lebanon, Palestine, and Syria all had many towns receiving caravan traffic from the east and ship traffic from the Mediterranean, and although plague spread swiftly through the urban populations, the epidemic was brief. Egypt, however, was continually reinfected by the traffic from Crimea, where plague lingered into the modern period.

CONCLUSION

Despite the official enmity and disdain that later national governments expressed against the Mongols, the effects of the Mongol occupation in the Middle East were profound. In Iran under the late Abbasid and Seljuk orders, the decentralization of control had effectively divided the country into northern and southern halves. The Il-khans destroyed those regimes and united Iran under their control. They also fostered the elevation, wider application, and standardization of the written Iranian language. The Timurids, by their patronage of Sunni doctrine, inspired their opponents to identify with Shi'ism and often with ecstatic sects such as Sufism. Thus, both positively and negatively, the period of Il-khan and Timurid domination established the terms of nationalism that became very important under the succeeding Safavid state.

Similarly, it was both by positive and negative influences that the Mongols helped to establish the terms of national identity in Russia. To efficiently control the Russian territories, the Mongols stabilized the rule of the Russian princes and solidified the control of powerful families over certain towns and cities. In this way, native control was unbroken during Mongol domination of Russia and parts of eastern Europe. In Russia, the Mongols showed the same favoritism toward the native language that they had shown in Iran. And as in Iran, the Mongols not only tolerated but strengthened the identification of the established religion with regional identity. Under the Russian leaders who succeeded the Mongols, the Orthodox Church would become a symbol of Russian nationhood.

Finally, in the same way that the Mongols ended the domination of the city of Baghdad in the Middle East, they ended the domination of Kiev in Russia. By establishing new centers, the Mongols redefined the elites, reshuffled the hierarchy of elite families, and shifted patterns of population. Moscow was largely a creation of the Mongols, and its continuing centrality in Russian life is a mark of the cultural and structural impact of the period of Mongol domination. Indeed, centralized government in Russia was an inspiration of the Mongols. Iran, which had a long history of unity and centralization, had been disunited during the late Abbasid centuries and was reunited under the Mongols.

It is important to compare the experiences of the Mongol domains to the Mongol peripheries. The domains frequently gained national definition and cultural coherence under the Mongols, and many sectors of the economy benefited economically from their participation in the Eurasian trade system. But in general their century or so of subjugation left them drained of wealth, sometimes demographically depressed, and—ironically—deprived of the technological stimulation they might have gained had the Mongols not imposed on them nearly a century of peace.

The peripheries, in contrast, frequently integrated themselves with the Mongol trade networks and enjoyed a flow of information, experience, and often wealth (as in the cases of Genoa and Venice) that aided in their growth. Under military pressure from the Mongols they tightened and strengthened their leadership (as in the cases of Lithuania and the Mamluks), or they explored new working alliances (as between the Mamluks and the Holy Roman Emperor). It was at the peripheries of the Mongol realm that Mongol influence over Eurasia was completed, and, as we shall see, the effects in eastern Eurasia were as marked as they were farther west.

SUGGESTED READING

An enormous amount has been written on the history of the Mongol Empire. An accessible recent introduction, now available in paperback, is David Morgan's *The Mongols* (1986). A more specialized study is Thomas T. Allsen, *Mongol Imperialism: The Policies of the Grand Qan Möngke in China, Russia, and the Islamic Lands, 1251–1259* (1987). Also in paperback is Rene

Grousset's classic *The Empire of the Steppes: A History of Central Asia* (1970; reprint, 1988). Two accessible but scholarly texts link early and modern Mongol history and culture: Sechin Jagchid and Paul Hyer, *Mongolia's Culture and Society* (1979), and Larry Moses and Stephen A. Halkovic, Jr., *Introduction to Mongolian History and Culture* (1985). Tim Severin's *In Search of Chinggis Khan* (1992) is a fascinating revisit by a modern writer to the paths of Genghis's conquest. The demographic effects of the Mongol conquests are outlined by William H. McNeill in *Plagues and Peoples* (1976), and Joel Mokyr discusses the technological effects in *The Lever of Riches: Technological Creativity and Economic Progress* (1990). For a thesis of global development that discusses the thirteenth century in depth, see Janet L. Abu-Lughod, *Before European Hegemony: The World System A.D. 1250–1350* (1989).

The history of Central Asia during the Mongol period, when it first came under the rule of the Jagadai khanate, is important but difficult. The best overview is S. A. M. Adshead, *Central Asia in World History* (1993). The most recent scholarly study of Timur is Beatrice Manz, *The Rise and Rule of Tamerlane* (1989).

The only "primary" document relating to Genghis Khan, *Secret History of the Mongols,* has been reconstructed in Mongolian from Chinese script and has been variously produced in scholarly editions by Igor de Rachewilz and Francis Woodman Cleaves, among others. Paul Kahn produced a readable prose English paraphrase of the work in 1984. Also of interest is the only version of the *Secret History* by a modern Mongol author: *The History and the Life of Chinggis Khan: The Secret History of the Mongols, Translated and Annotated by Urgunge Onon* (1990). Outstanding among recent biographies of Genghis Khan are Leo de Hartog, *Genghis Khan, Conqueror of the World* (1989); Michel Hoang, *Genghis Khan,* trans. Ingrid Canfield (1991); and Paul Ratchnevsky, *Genghis Khan: His Life and Legacy,* trans. and ed. Thomas Nivison Haining (1992), which is most detailed on Genghis's childhood and youth.

The best single volume in English on the Mongols in Russia is Charles Halperin, *Russia and the Golden Horde: The Mongol Impact on Medieval Russian History* (1987). A more detailed study is John Lister Illingworth Fennell, *The Crisis of Medieval Russia, 1200–1304* (1983) and those with a special interest might consult Devin DeWeese, *Islamization and Native Religion in the Golden Horde* (1994).

No single volume in English has yet been devoted to a history of the Il-khans. David Morgan, cited above, is a Persianist, and his chapters on the Il-khans in *The Mongols* (1986) are presently the best general introduction to the history of the Il-khans in Azerbaijan and Iran. Interestingly, the great historians of the Il-khan period have been translated into several European languages. Available in English are Juvaini's history of the Mongols, Joveyni, 'Ala al-Din 'Ata Malek, *The History of the World-Conqueror, translated from the text of Mirza Muhammad Qazvini* by John Andrew Boyle (1958); a small portion of Rashid al-Din's work translated by: David Talbot Rice, *The Illustrations to the World History of Rashid al-Din*, ed. Basil Gray (1976); and *The Successors of Genghis Khan,* trans. John Andrew Boyle (1971). Equally important as illustrative reading are works related to Ibn Battuta. See C. Defremery and B. R. Sanguinetti, eds., *The Travels of Ibn Battuta, A.D. 1325–1354,* translated with revisions and notes from the Arabic text by H. A. R. Gibb (1994), and Ross E. Dunn, *The Adventures of Ibn Battuta, a Muslim Traveler of the 14th Century* (1986).

For Europe, a lively and well-known narrative is James Chambers, *The Devil's Horsemen: The Mongol Invasion of Europe* (1979). Many of the individuals who traveled from Europe to the Mongol courts—not only Marco Polo but also the Franciscan friars John of Plano Carpini and William of Rubruck—have had their accounts translated and annotated in modern editions. Christopher Dawson, ed., *Mission to Asia* (1955; reprint, 1981), is a compilation of some of the best known. But see also Frances Wood, *Did Marco Polo Really Go to China?* (1995). There is also some published material on the travels of Rabban Sauma, a Christian Turk, to Europe; the most recent and most comprehensive is Morris Rossabi, *Visitor from Xanadu* (1992). Some of the possible effects of the exposure of medieval Europe to Central Asian influence is suggested in Jacques Le Goff, *The Birth of Purgatory,* trans. Arthur Goldhammer (1984), and Carlo Ginzburg, *Ecstasies: Deciphering the Witch's Sabbath* (1991).

NOTES

1. Quotation adapted from Desmond Martin, *Chingis Khan and His Conquest of North China*:303.

Eastern Eurasia, 1200–1500

The Shaping of Eastern Eurasia

Social Change and National Definition in East Asia

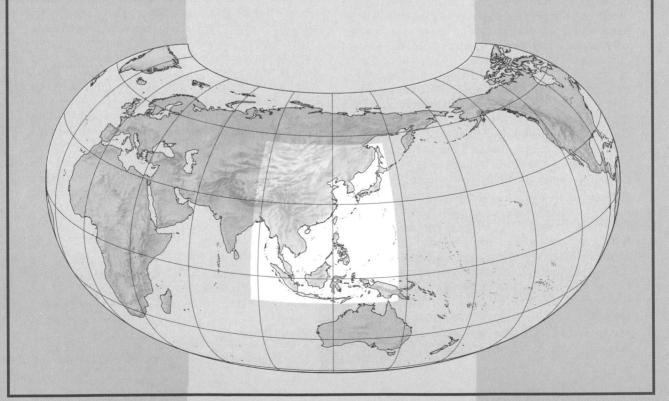

When Ogodei, Genghis's third son and successor as Great Khan, achieved stable Mongol control of northern China in the 1230s, he told his newly recruited Confucian adviser, Yelu Chucai, that he planned to turn the heavily populated North China Plain into a grazing pasture for the Mongols' livestock. Yelu was able to convince Ogodei that he could extract more wealth through taxation than by razing the cities to the ground. Ogodei quickly grasped the advantages of taxation as a means of redistributing wealth from Chinese to Mongol hands. What this oft-told story does not emphasize, however, is that the tax system Ogodei instituted was not the fixed-rate method traditional to China but the oppressive tax farming already in use in the Mongol empires of western Eurasia.

The Chinese in the early years of the Mongol occupation suffered under this system, but they also learned new sciences and technologies, thanks to the Mongols, and eventually turned them to their own ends. In eastern Eurasia as in western Eurasia, the enormous expanse of the Mongol empires and the Mongol emphasis on trade led to the spread of knowledge and skills. In western Eurasia, European countries and many Muslim cultures were able to exploit for their own military advancement or economic enrichment knowledge gained under the Mongols. Likewise in eastern Eurasia, knowledge first introduced under the Yuan Empire of the Mongols (1272–1368) enabled the societies of China, Korea, Southeast Asia, and Japan to experience unprecedented power and wealth. The economic and political practices of the Mongols, however, often created conditions that made the application and further development of these skills difficult.

Song China and Korea were able to resist the Mongols for decades, and Japan was invaded by the Mongols twice in the late 1200s but not conquered. This resistance prolonged the warfare in eastern Asia through virtually the entire thirteenth century. Technological developments of this century, particularly in warfare, were rapidly appropriated by the Mongols and disseminated westward. As a consequence, the Mongol period of Eurasian unity was a watershed in the refinement and dissemination of the technologies—both martial and peaceful—associated with gunpowder, metal casting, and the building of wagons and bridges. It also initiated the period in which large-scale trade in iron ore, sulfur, coal, and copper created new economies in eastern Eurasia. The Ming empire (1368–1644) in China and Yi kingdom (1392–1910) in Korea were beneficiaries of the technological developments that arose during the century of warfare in the 1200s.

THE SHAPING OF EASTERN EURASIA

The substitution of taxation for warfare is also a reminder of the changing effects of conflict in eastern Asia over the three centuries of the Yuan and early Ming empires. The Mongol conquest of southern China in the late 1200s marked the end of the prolonged struggle of the Song against northern invaders that had produced a centralization of government and many technological advances (see Chapter 11). After the fall of the Song, the Yuan empire absorbed much of the technology and disseminated it westward toward the Middle East and Europe. But in eastern Asia after the fall of the Yuan to the Ming in 1368 the intense need for technological advances in warfare waned, while an increase in population decreased the need to mechanize in agriculture and some manufacturing. Though, as will be discussed below, eastern Asia was a wealthy and culturally brilliant region after the fall of the Mongols, the long-term consequences for China of having no technologically innovative, ambitious rivals on the northern frontier led to a marked slowdown in technological change.

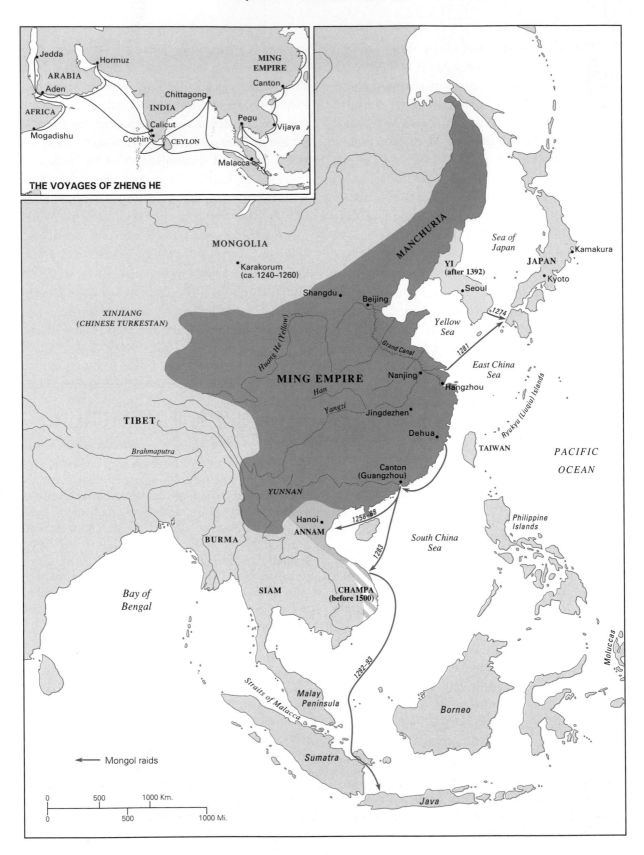

THE VOYAGES OF ZHENG HE

Jedda
Hormuz
ARABIA
Aden
AFRICA
Mogadishu

MING
EMPIRE
Canton

Chittagong

INDIA

Pegu
Calicut
Vijaya
Cochin
CEYLON

Malacca

MONGOLIA

MANCHURIA

Sea of
Japan

Kamakura

Karakorum
(ca. 1240–1260)

YI
(after 1392)

JAPAN

Shangdu

Beijing

Seoul

Kyoto

XINJIANG
(CHINESE TURKESTAN)

Huang He (Yellow)

Grand Canal

Yellow
Sea

1274

1281

MING EMPIRE

Nanjing

East China
Sea

Han

Hangzhou

Ryukyu (Liuqiu) Islands

TIBET

Yangzi

Jingdezhen

Brahmaputra

Dehua

TAIWAN

PACIFIC
OCEAN

YUNNAN

Canton
(Guangzhou)

Philippine
Islands

Hanoi

1258–88

BURMA

ANNAM

1283

South China
Sea

Bay of
Bengal

SIAM

CHAMPA
(before 1500)

Moluccas

1292–93

Straits of Malacca

Malay
Peninsula

Borneo

Mongol raids

Sumatra

Java

0   500   1000 Km.

0   500   1000 Mi.

The Impact of Trade and War

The Mongol assaults of the 1220s on the Jin Empire in northern Asia and on the Tangguts in northwestern China happened about the same time as the first Mongol invasions of Russia and the Middle East (see Chapter 13). Although the purpose of these campaigns was to convince the Jin and the Tanggut rulers to render tribute, Genghis Khan was also interested in establishing communications with the ruling elites and institutions. Buddhists, Daoists, and Confucianists from China visited the Great Khan and, like the Muslims and Christians from western Eurasia, believed that they had all but convinced him to convert to their religions or accept their philosophies. But only the religious leaders of Tibet seem to have exercised real influence over the Mongol rulers. The Tibetan idea of a militant universal ruler, bringing the whole world under control of the Buddha and thus bringing it nearer to salvation, was in agreement with the ancient idea of universal rulership in Central Asia.

Thus the Tibetan religious elite established a special place for itself in the Mongol order. In addition, Mongol leaders considered Tibet strategically important to their power in western Mongolia and Central Asia. When necessary, they supported their interests with military invasions. The Mongol Great Khans personally oversaw the governance of Tibet during the imperial period, and reinforced the dominance of the Tibetan variant of Buddhism, often called "Lamaism." A *lama* in Tibet was a teacher of special techniques for contacting the spirits, and Tibetan Buddhism was increasingly popular among Mongols after the time of Genghis Khan. After the fall of the Mongol Empire, Mongol leaders still tried to use

Lamaism to legitimate themselves and to keep some portion of the Mongols united. This attempt ultimately led to invention of the title *Dalai* (a Mongolian word for "universal") *Lama* by Mongol khans in the 1500s.

Central Asia remained under the control of the descendants of Genghis's second son, Jagadai (d. 1242). In their attempts to hold on to their pastoral life, the Jagadai Mongols often came into conflict with the Yuan Empire in China, founded in 1272 by Genghis's grandson Khubilai (1215–1294) (see Map 14.1). The political prestige of the Jagadai domains and the ability of the Jagadai Mongols to defend themselves prevented the absorption of Central Asia by the Yuan. Moreover, the independence of the Jagadai Mongols contributed to the tendency of Central Asian Mongols to continue to strengthen their ties to Islam and to Turkic language and culture. Both the Islamic and the Turkic links were important to the rise of Timur in the later fourteenth century (Timur's empire is described in Chapter 13). The long-standing enmity between the Jagadai ruling family and the Yuan Empire may also have inspired Timur's wish to conquer China.

Mongolia itself had been subdued by Genghis Khan. While the Mongol Empire was united, the Mongol khans of the Golden Horde, the Jagadai domains in Central Asia, and the Il-khans in the Middle East were subordinate to the Great Khans in Mongolia. These Great Khans were chosen in the *khuriltai* gatherings of Mongol aristocrats, which took years to come to a conclusion. In the interim, the widow of the deceased Khan sometimes acted as head of the government. Genghis's son and successor as Great Khan, Ögödei (1185–1241), created the Mongol capital at Karakorum. Between 1240 and 1260 it functioned as the supreme center of the Eurasian empire. When the European missionary Giovanni di Piano Carpini (John of Plano Carpini) visited it in 1246, he found it isolated but very well populated and extremely cosmopolitan, with residents and visitors from all over Eurasia.

Karakorum disappeared virtually without a trace. The city was destroyed between 1260 and 1265 in a civil war between Khubilai and his younger brother, contesting the Great Khanship. Khubilai won, transferred his capital to China, and later declared himself the founder of a new

Map 14.1 Eastern Eurasia The Ming empire controlled China, but otherwise had a hostile relationship to peoples in Mongolia and Central Asia who had been under the rule of the Mongol emperors of the Yuan. The Mongol attempts at conquest by sea, which are marked on this map, were continued by the Ming mariner Zheng He, who between 1405 and 1433 sailed to Southeast Asia and then beyond, to India, the Persian Gulf, and East Africa.

empire, called by the Chinese name *Yuan*, meaning "origin." Some of the Mongols refused to accept Khubilai as Great Khan and withdrew further into Mongolia, where, like the Jagadai Mongols, they remained enemies of the Yuan.

To the north and east of Mongolia lived various peoples who depended on hunting, gathering, and fishing for their living. These peoples, some of whom were reindeer-riding nomads, were frequently seen in the trading villages of the region and were loosely under the control of the Great Khans. They paid the demanded tax on their trade and sometimes joined the Mongol armies. Their languages and their dress were slightly affected by the Mongols, but in general these peoples were too scattered and mobile to be effectively subjugated. In extreme northeastern Asia, these groups continued their ancient way of life and, by means of the Aleutian islands, maintained contact with the peoples of Alaska, who were their cultural and linguistic relatives.

Manchuria (see Map. 14.1) was more thickly populated and in addition to the traditional trades had a good number of farmers. Since the 600s there had been a steady influx of Chinese and Korean settlers, all of whom helped develop the agriculture and the towns of the region. Manchuria was more directly controlled by the Mongols and became their steppingstone to Korea. Using Mongolian terms and Mongol organizational institutions, the dominant indigenous people—the Jurchens, who had once ruled the area under the Jin empire—gained greater economic and military power. By the late 1400s they were a challenge to the Ming empire in China, which uneasily suppressed Jurchen power until the late 1500s.

War among these groups was frequent after decline of the Yuan empire in the middle 1300s. Overland Eurasian trade was hindered by the growing disorder but remained an important economic resource for the western and Jagadai Mongols in particular. There was also new trouble for Ming China, which hoped to bring all the Mongols under its domination and to convince them to participate in the tributary system (see Chapter 11). The Mongols did participate, but only to the extent that doing so made it easy for them to trade with the Chinese. They were other-

wise hostile, and Ming attempts to suppress a resurgence of Mongol power led to the disastrous war of the middle 1400s in which the Mongols captured the Ming emperor and briefly attacked the Chinese capital at Beijing.

The Yuan Empire

Khubilai Khan, a grandson of Genghis Khan, was the ruler among the Mongols who best understood the advantages of the Chinese traditions of imperial rule. He transferred the capital to Beijing in northern China in 1265 and reunified the Chinese territories for the first time since the Tang (see Map 14.1). The capital of Khubilai's empire, like the capitals of the regional Mongol empires, was placed at a critical spot on the overland trade routes that were the infrastructure of the Mongol world. Beijing was the easternmost terminus of the caravan routes of the Silk Road that began near Tabriz and Sarai.

Khubilai created the spirit, if not all the features that remain today, of Beijing, naming it his Great Capital (Dadu) or, as it was also called, City of the Khan (*khan-balikh*, Marco Polo's "Cambaluc"). Khubilai ordered massive mud walls built around Beijing (a tiny portion of them can still be seen) and designed the main streets to be broad and wide (Mongols needed good clear stretches for their horse runs). He also developed the linked lakes and artificial islands at the city's northwest edge as a closed imperial complex. As a summer retreat, Khubilai maintained the palace and parks at Shangdu, now in Inner Mongolia. This was the "Xanadu" celebrated by the English romantic poet Samuel Taylor Coleridge, and its "stately pleasure dome" was the hunting preserve where Khubilai and his courtiers practiced the traditional skills of riding and shooting.

When the Mongols came to Chinese territory in the 1220s, there was no "China" as we think of it today. Northern China was under the control of the Jin empire of the Jurchens, who a hundred years before had wrested it from the Liao empire of the Kitans (see Chapter 11). China south of the Yellow River was ruled by the Song. Western China was controlled by the Tangguts. Yunnan and its surrounding mountainous terrain were governed by the small Nanzhao kingdom of a people related to the Thais. These states had separate languages, separate writing systems, and variant forms of imperial government, and each had a distinctive elite culture. The Mongols had the power to subjugate or obliterate such states, co-opt or decimate their aristocracies, and impose Mongol control on them, reconstituting "China" as a base on which the Ming and later governments would stand.

In their creation of civil government in China, the Mongols did not merely copy and perpetuate the style of government that had developed under the Song. On the contrary, they introduced a radical restructuring of government. As they had in the Middle East, they put primary emphasis on counting the population and collecting taxes. In the early period, direct taxation was replaced by taxfarming in the Middle Eastern style. For this purpose the Yuan government brought to China a large number of Persian, Arab, Uigur, and Turkic administrators, who virtually controlled the offices of taxation and finance. Muslim scholars were also relied on to lead the offices of calendar making and astronomy.

By law, the status of individuals within the regime was dictated by where they or their ancestors had originated. Mongols were highest on the ladder, then came Central Asians and Middle Easterners, then came northern Chinese, and finally southern Chinese. This apparent racial ranking, it should be noted, was also a hierarchy of professions. The Mongols were the conquering caste, the warriors of the empire. The Central Asians and the Middle Easterners contributed the highly valued political functions of census taking, tax collection, and managing the calendar. The northern Chinese had come under Mongol control almost two generations before the southern Chinese and thus outranked them. The southern Chinese, the last to be conquered, were strongest in their attachment to the principles of Confucian thought.

Many Confucians were permanently alienated from the Yuan government because of their comparatively low status and their philosophical disagreements with the Yuan. The Confucians, for instance, were opposed to any elevation in status of merchants. But in the Yuan Empire, merchants were a privileged group, and most were of central Asian or Middle Eastern origin or were northern Chinese. Similarly, the Confucians regarded doctors as at best technicians and at worst heretical practitioners of Daoist mysticism. The Yuan, however, encouraged the theory and practice of medicine, and under the Yuan began the very long process of integrating the medical and herbal knowledge of China and the rest of Eurasia.

In China as in the Middle East, the Mongols found it convenient to redistrict the country for purposes of census taking and administration. China had previously been organized along the lines of the commandaries established in Qin and Han times (see Chapter 6). But the Mongols reorganized China's political administration into provinces, each one much larger than the previous units had been. Governors, tax collectors, and garrison commanders were also organized along provincial lines. The creation of the provinces was a strong assertion of Mongol ownership of the country. It marked a radical change in the regional configuration of China while increasing central control over selected matters.

Our understanding of the economy in the Yuan Empire, as in the other Mongol domains, is obscured by the vast difference between the experiences of the cities and of the countryside. The Yuan economic situation is also difficult to assess because of the scarcity of contemporary records and the influence of the later Chinese view of this period. In general, however, many cities in China seem to have prospered under the Mongols—not only the cities of north China that were on the caravan routes but also the cities of the interior that were on the Grand Canal and the well-developed cities along the coast. One outcome of the reunification of the country was the revitalization of trade between north and south China, the original purpose of the Grand Canal. Early in the Yuan period, Khubilai discovered that it was more economical to move grain from south China to Beijing by sea than by land, so the ports of eastern China also were invigorated. The urban economies were further stimulated by the reintegration of East Asia (though not Japan) with the overland Eurasian trade.

Mongol and wife (tomb painting)   Mongols who settled in China adopted many of the country's practices, including the use of tombs and of portraits on tomb walls, of the sort depicted here. But the couple are portrayed side by side according to the Mongol custom, which for a time became influential among northern Chinese. (From *Wenwu*, 1986 #4, pp. 40–46)

The isolation of Japan during the Mongol period actually helped to keep the Chinese economy stable. During the Song period, China and Japan had enjoyed a strong trade relationship (see Chapter 11). One of the Chinese exports to Japan had been copper coinage. The result of this trade had been a shortage of copper coins in China, which elevated the value of copper coins and destructively distorted the price ratio of copper to silver. There is evidence that Song trade and taxation were affected by the copper drain. But after the Mongol conquest of China, trade with Japan—which continued to resist the Mongol conquest—ceased. The stabilization in copper coinage helped encourage trade and credit in China and other regions of the Yuan Empire.

In addition to fostering long-distance transport and monetary stabilization, the privileges given merchants and the prestige they enjoyed under the Mongols changed urban life and the economy of China. The official examinations prevalent in Tang and Song times to select government personnel were suspended, and Chinese elites were eligible for only a limited number of posts in the government, many of which were hereditary. The great families who in the Song period had spent their fortunes on the education of their sons for competition in the examinations and entry into government service had to find other uses for their money. Many gentry families used their money to enter the mercantile professions, even though according to traditional Chinese values, merchants were a despised class.

Most commercial activities, from the financing of caravans to tax farming to lending money to the Mongol aristocracy, were managed through corporations. These corporations had evolved from the caravan-financing groups in the cities of Central Asia and the Middle East and were based on mutual risk sharing. In the early Yuan Empire, these corporations were mostly made up of Central Asians and Middle Easterners, but the Chinese quickly began to purchase an interest in them. Soon most of the corporations were mixed in membership, and many were entirely Chinese.

The financial and commercial life of Yuan China encouraged the gentry to live in the cities rather than in the countryside, a change from earlier times. The cities themselves began to cater to the tastes of merchants rather than to the tastes of the traditional scholars. Special shops dedicated to the sale of clothing, grape wine, furniture, and properly butchered meats (reflecting customers' religious convictions) were common. Teahouses—particularly those featuring sing-song girls, drum singers, operas, and other arts previously considered coarse—thrived. One result was a lasting cultural change: the rise of literature written in a popular style and the increasing influence of the northern, Mongolian-influenced Chinese language that in the West is often called *Mandarin*.

The countryside, where more than 90 percent of the population lived, presents a much darker picture. Cottage industries linked to the urban economies and agricultural engineering continued to advance. The cultivation of mulberry trees and cotton fields and the construction of new irrigation systems (encouraged by the Mongols, who favored the irrigation systems of the Middle East), dams, and water wheels were all common features of village technology. The production and dissemination of literature describing techniques for farming, harvesting, threshing, and butchering continued under the Mongols, and some of the most famous treatises were first published in this period. Villagers also continued to worship technological innovators as local gods. One of the most interesting of these cults began in the Yuan period: the worship of Huang

Dao Po, who brought her special knowledge of cotton growing, spinning, and weaving from her native Hainan Island to the fertile Yangzi Delta.

But the vast majority of farmers were less involved in producing cotton and other cash crops and more involved in producing rice and other staples. For them the Yuan period appears to have been one of persistent, often intense, hardship. Their troubles began with the conquests. After the fighting subsided, the Mongol princes summarily evicted many farmers from their land. Those who retained land rights were subjected to the exactions and the brutality of the tax farmers, their agents, and their enforcers. There is evidence that by the end of the 1200s the Mongol government in China had, as in Iran, begun to change its policies toward the farmers from exploitation to protection and encouragement. But, as in Iran, by this time serious damage had already been done. Many farmers had been driven into servitude or homelessness, and dams and dikes had been neglected to the point where flooding, particularly of the Yellow River, was recurring and disastrous.

In the 1340s, power contests among the Mongol princes shredded the political fabric of the Yuan Empire, and the countryside was in increasing turmoil. During this crisis, Zhu Yuanzhang, who previously had been a monk, a soldier, and a bandit, vanquished his own rivals in rebellion and established the Ming Empire in 1368.

Ming China on a Mongol Foundation

In many ways the change from Yuan to Ming was more ideological than structural. The Ming were strong in their nationalist passions, and partly to symbolize their rejection of the Mongols, they established their imperial capital at Nanjing ("southern capital") on the Yangzi River, rather than at Beijing ("northern capital") (see Map 14.1). The Ming were also aggressive in their attempts to intimidate the remaining Mongols and the other peoples of Central Asia and Southeast Asia. In these wars, Confucianism was used to depict the Ming emperor as the champion of civilization and virtue, justified in making war on uncivilized "barbarians."

But in its basic outlines the Ming government resembled that of the Yuan. In their new capital at Nanjing, the Ming built a replica of the observatory at Beijing and attached to it their own Muslim academy of astronomy and mathematics. They kept the academy that had been established for Mongol princes, and they employed Mongols who could handle the translation of communications between the Ming court and the Mongol powers of Central Asia and Mongolia. They retained the provincial style of administration, including the military garrison system introduced under the Yuan. In a continuation of Mongol social legislation, the Ming maintained hereditary professional categories. And though the reinstitution of the examinations allowed a return of the Confucian majority to the bureaucracy, the Ming also retained Muslims in the special tasks for which they had been imported by the Yuan. These tasks included the making of calendars, and the Ming continued to use the calendar promulgated by the Mongols.

In the early 1400s, the Yongle emperor (r. 1403–1421) of the Ming returned the capital to Beijing and set about improving on and enlarging the imperial complex that the Yuan had built there. Though the central part of this complex—the "Forbidden City" now visited by millions of people from all over the world each year—was elaborated in the centuries afterward, it was primarily during the 1400s that the enormous structure took on its present character, with moats, outer vermilion walls, enormous gates arranged in accordance with Chinese geomantic beliefs (see Chapter 6), golden roofs, paved interior courtyards, artificial streams, alabaster bridges, and dozens of palaces. This combination fortress, religious site, bureaucratic center, and imperial residential park was intended by the Yongle emperor to overshadow the imperial architecture at Nanjing, and in fact it is the most imposing traditional architectural complex still extant in any country. A significant portion of it is still reserved for China's rulers, closed to either foreign or native observers.

It appears that in their first half century the Ming also intended to pursue the Mongol program of aggression against Southeast Asia. This goal was partly inspired by the wish of the early Ming emperors—and the Yongle emperor in particular—to act out the role of universal ruler, which the Mongol Great Khans had embodied. Economic revitalization was also a consideration, and the Ming attempted, after an initial policy of isolation was reversed under the Yongle emperor, to restore commercial links with the Middle East. Because the hostile western Mongols controlled much of the territory through which the Eurasian land routes passed, the Ming attempted to establish their own imperial connection by sea. This was one reason for the expeditions of Zheng He from 1405 to 1433.

Historians have long been intrigued by the extraordinary adventure in Chinese seafaring that took place under the command of Zheng He in 1403 and continued sporadically until the 1430s, after Zheng He's death. The feat itself was remarkable, but to many it has appeared even more remarkable that the voyages were not continued and led to no sea-based colonialism by the Ming Empire. On the contrary, Chinese interest in the sea seemed to evaporate, and the country was set upon in the following centuries by nations that had acquired and exploited the skills that the Chinese had had earlier and then abandoned. The more closely the Zheng He episode is examined, however, the less mysterious it appears (see Voices & Visions: Pursuit and Renunciation of Universal Rule).

The Chinese and many of the peoples of Southeast Asia had been exchanging seafaring knowledge for many centuries. By the time Zheng He's fleet was outfitted, many thousands of ancestral Chinese had settled throughout Southeast Asia, in the regions ringing the Indian Ocean, almost certainly in some parts of coastal Australia, and quite possibly in some sites in eastern Africa. The hypothesis that Chinese also reached the Americas in this early period is technologically possible but unproven. From one point of view, Zheng He was merely attempting to trace the routes that the Chinese had been exploring for centuries but was doing so in a public, organized, and very dramatic way. In any event, he was a superb sea captain who believed that his exploits were measurably increasing the glory of the Yongle emperor, whom he served unflinchingly.

Pursuit and Renunciation of Universal Rule

Zheng He and his fellow eunuchs were not dispatched by the Yongle emperor to explore or to colonize. Their intention was to, in the words of the emperor, ". . . announce our Mandate to foreign nations." They had detailed maps of the regions they expected to visit and ample technical manuals for navigation. They were to attempt to open trade contacts that had been shunned in the beginning of the Ming, to seek out exotic products and medicines that would have a market in China (and be exempt from the taxes normally levied on trade), and to carry out such tasks as might seem necessary to demonstrate the universal jurisdiction of the Yongle emperor. Some of these tasks were pressing. The densely populated regions of southern China were experiencing repeated epidemics in the first years of the fifteenth century, and the herbs believed to be effective in controlling them had become impossible to attain because of the earlier ban on foreign trade. And revenue expected from the taxation of overseas Chinese populations who had lost contact with the court would be helpful in the Yongle emperor's plans for building his new capital at Beijing, sponsoring his grandiose cultural projects, and conquering the unruly Mongol groups to China's north and west.

Not all the business conducted by Zheng He and his crews focused on the pleasantries of making new friends and transporting exotic creatures. On many occasions, the troops accompanying the "Treasure Ships" got rough. In 1407 a Chinese community refused to acknowledge or pay tribute to the emperor, and it was devastated by the armada. In 1409, Zheng He decided to abduct the residents of a hostile village in Sri Lanka: "Straight away, their dens and hideouts we ravaged, and made captive that entire country, bringing back to our august capital their women, children, families, and retainers, leaving not one . . ." The next year, Zheng He gained the good will of a petty ruler in Sumatra (and demonstrated the omnipotence of the Yongle emperor) by capturing a rebel leader and bringing him to Beijing, where his execution was summarily ordered by the Yongle emperor.

The empire had enormous possibilities of expansion over land by the 1430s, and pressing responsibilities on its Mongol frontiers. Contacts had indeed been reopened with Southeast Asia, India, and the Middle East, and private traders followed in Zheng He's wake—their trade, unlike his, all to be taxed by the Ming state. When the Yongle emperor died in 1424, the greatest force behind the expeditions was gone. Government moneys were desperately needed to maintain public works and strengthen defenses in many areas. The new Xuande emperor waited long enough to show respect for the grand designs of his late father, and then ordered that

voyages should cease. He sent one of the last expeditions out with this message, a graceful fairwell to the universal ambitions that his dynasty had previously claimed:

The new reign has commenced, and everything has begun anew. But distant lands beyond the seas have not yet been informed. I send eunuchs Zheng He and Wang Jinghong with this imperial order to instruct these countries to follow the way of Heaven with reverence and to watch over their people so that all might enjoy the good fortune of lasting peace.

Moreover, after the death of the Yongle emperor, many high-ranking bureaucrats felt increasingly free to condemn Zheng He and anything he might have achieved: As a Muslim and a eunuch he was doubly repugnant to them, and there may well have been jealousy over the glamorous reputation he had procured. Not only were the voyages to cease, but all record of them—including the private accounts of at least three of the crew members— was to be suppressed.

The expeditions wasted uncountable money and grain, and moreover the people who met their deaths on these expeditions may be counted by the tens of thousands. Although he returned with wonderful precious things, what benefit was it to the state? This was merely an action of bad government of which ministers should severely disapprove. Even if the old archives were still preserved they should be destroyed in order to suppress a repetition of these things at the root.

The expeditions may indeed have been a less than efficient way to secure the goals of the Yongle emperor, but the fact is that they did succeed—which is the most important explanation for their cessation. China remained securely linked by sea as well as by land to a large number of markets, and for the remainder of the Ming period it was never again closed to foreign trade.

How did Zheng He see his mission in relation to the emperor? Why were later officials so anxious to bury the record of the Zheng He expeditions?

Source: The first three quotations are adapted from Louise Levathes, *When China Ruled the Seas* (New York: Simon & Schuster, 1993), 113, 115, 169. The fourth quotation is adapted from Joseph Levenson, *European Expansion* (Englewood, N.J.: Prentice-Hall, 1967), 88.

Because Zheng He had been castrated and entered the service of the imperial family, he was trusted to carry out a special mission from the ambitious Yongle emperor. He was also a eunuch. Thanks to Islam, he had knowledge of the Middle East. His paternal ancestors had come from the Strait of Hormuz, and both his father and his grandfather had made the pilgrimage to Mecca. Zheng He's religion also made him a good ambassador to the states of the Indian subcontinent, which was the destination of his first three voyages. On subsequent voyages similar ships reached Hormuz, sailed along the entire southern coast of the Arabian peninsula and the northeast coast of Africa, and reached as far south, perhaps, as the Strait of Madagascar (see Map 14.1).

An important objective of Zheng He's early voyages was to visit Chinese merchant communities in Southeast Asia, affirm their allegiance to the Ming empire, and demand taxes from them. If they resisted, as did a community on Sumatra, they were subject to severe military punishment from Zheng He's marines (who in Sumatra slaughtered the men of the community in question). The Ming court also hoped to establish lucrative trade relationships with the Middle East and possibly with Africa but was not successful in this. The primary achievement was to introduce the Ming empire to new countries and to sign them on as tributary states.

Zheng He's expeditions added as many as fifty new tributaries. The result was sporadic embassies to Beijing from rulers in India, the Middle East, Africa, and Southeast Asia. An early ruler of Brunei died in Beijing during such a visit and was buried at the Chinese capital with great fanfare and praise from the emperor.

The cessation of the voyages has raised many questions. Having accomplished long-distance navigation far in advance of the Europeans, why did the Chinese not develop seafaring for commercial and military gain? It might first be pointed out that the voyages of the Zheng He group were not based on developing technology. The design of the enormous junks and of the compasses that Zheng He used were not new, and neither were his navigation techniques. Most dated from the Song period (see Chapter 11). Any empire based in China since the eleventh

century that might have wanted to spread its reputation through the sponsorship of such voyages could have done so, but neither the Song nor the Yuan had considered it worth the trouble.

The expectation that the voyages would create new commercial opportunities, or awe overseas Chinese and foreign nations into immediate submission to the Ming, also was not realized. In the meantime, Japanese piracy along the coast had intensified, and the Mongol threat in the north and west had grown. The human and financial demands of fortifying the north, remodeling and strengthening Beijing, and outfitting new military expeditions against the Mongols were more than enough for a government that had outgrown its initial enthusiasm for world dominion.

Perhaps the Zheng He voyages are best seen as what people at the time understood them to be: the personal project of the Yongle emperor. This ruler had wrested control from a branch of the imperial family in 1403 and felt he was constantly being forced to prove his worthiness. In Beijing he accomplished most of the intense building that now represents the Forbidden City. He sponsored gigantic encyclopedia projects designed to collect and organize all known knowledge and literature. And he prosecuted effective campaigns against the nomadic and seminomadic peoples of Mongolia and northeastern Asia. His nearest model for what he wished to achieve in the voyages west may well have been Khubilai Khan, who also hoped to use enormous fleets of ships to demand the submission of Japan and Southeast Asia. Indeed, the self-image of the Yongle emperor was so like that of the Great Khans that he was rumored to be a Mongol.

It is important to remember that the cessation of the voyages did not represent a Chinese turning away from the sea. Zheng He's phenomenal fleet was only one episode in the saga of Chinese seafaring, which continued to be wide-ranging and vigorous after Zheng He's voyages had ceased. The question to be answered is not about Chinese involvement with the sea but about the Ming emperors' lack of interest in centralizing the organization of such voyages and turning them to military and mercantilist uses. The Ming empire was a large, complex, and constantly challenged land-based empire, and the Ming em-

Aerial of the Forbidden City   The general shape of the imperial complex at Beijing and the set of artificial lakes at its northwest corner were planned under the Mongol ruler Khubilai Khan in the late 1200s. It was during the Ming period (1368–1644), however, that the now-famous architecture was built. In addition to the gold-tiled roofs and the vermilion walls, the Forbidden City is noted for its marble-paved courtyards and three large central palaces, all set on a north-south axis that was part of a spatial pattern that the Forbidden City's planners believed would give it supernatural protection. (Reproduced by permission of the Commercial Press [Hong Kong] Limited, from *The Forbidden City*)

perors saw little reason to attempt to impose and sustain rule over distant and far-flung sea-based colonies. It was more than a century after the death of the Yongle emperor before the small, resource-starved kingdoms of Europe were forced to devise such strategies (see Chapter 16).

Technology and Population

It is tempting to link the cessation of Zheng He's long-distance voyages to the general slowdown in technological growth in Ming China, but they are two separate problems. The slowing of technological development took many forms and perhaps occurred first in mining and metallurgy. Following prodigious accomplishments during the Song period, the slowdown may have begun under the Yuan. One reason for it was the peace brought to the region by the Mongol conquest: peace removed the pressure to constantly manufacture weapons.

More surprising than the fall in the amount of mining and metal manufacture is the evaporation from China of the technical knowledge that had made possible the production of extremely high-quality bronze and steel. When instruments were cast for Khubilai's observatory at Beijing, for instance, the work was done not by Chinese technicians but by Central Asian and Middle Eastern technicians. The failure in China to preserve Song knowledge of high-temperature metallurgy has not been fully explained.

During the Ming period, Japan quickly surpassed China in the production of swords demanding extremely high-quality steel. It appears that at this time copper (which was once again draining away to Japan in the form of coins), iron, and steel had become very expensive commodities in China, so expensive that farm implements and well-caps made of these materials became prohibitive to manufacture. Shipbuilding

declined sharply, particularly after the death of the Yongle emperor in 1424. There were few advances in printing, timekeeping, or agricultural technology. Through the fifteenth century, it appears that some innovations in the mechanization of weaving occurred, but after the year 1500 such advances also became rare. Agricultural productivity peaked and remained stagnant for centuries.

The slowing of technological development might be at least partly due to the significant shift in the career patterns of educated men at this time. During the Yuan periods the examinations had been suspended, and comparatively few Chinese entered state service. Some went into the arts. But most men were not artistically inclined, and it must have been the case that commerce and agriculture in China were also

Observatory at Beijing   The Jurchens of the Jin empire were the first to build an observatory at Beijing in the 1200s. Later, the Mongols built a new observatory, expanded to include instruments designed and built by Islamic astronomers from the Middle East. In 1442 the Ming built a third observatory, at this site on Beijing's main street, with sighting tubes and armillary spheres, depicted here, built and maintained by Chinese Muslims. It was restored and enlarged by the Qing, and now is a major tourist and museum site in the capital. (Museum of History of Science, Oxford)

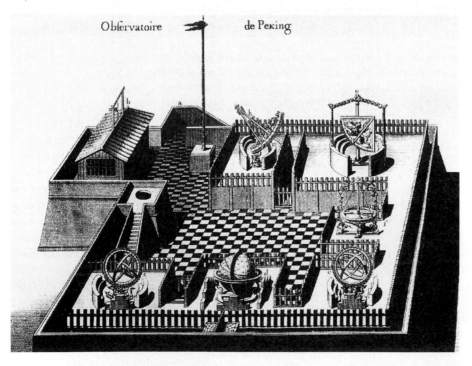

Observatoire de Peking

stimulated in this period by China's educated, entrepreneurial elite. After the overthrow of the Mongols, the new Ming government reinstituted the examinations and began to employ large numbers of educated men in government again. The economy may have been deprived of the participation of some of its best educated, most ambitious leadership.

Another factor behind the economic and technological decline was the very rapid population growth of the early Ming period, following a steep drop in population under the Yuan. If the Song records of population levels before the Mongol conquest and the Ming census taken after the overthrow of the Mongols are reliable (each may be exaggerated in one direction or another), it appears that China may have lost as much as 40 percent of its population in the eighty years of Mongol rule. Many localities in northern China lost as much as five-sixths of their populations during the 1200s and early 1300s.

The reasons were complex. One was the continuous warfare of the 1220s due to effective resistance by the Southern Song to the Mongol invasion. Another was the massive, continuous, southward movements of population attempting to flee the Mongols. This might explain why population losses in northern China were greater than in southern China, though it is clear that the fall of the Southern Song also sparked large and panicked migrations to Southeast Asia. Among those who left was the last Song emperor, who drowned in 1279 with his entourage while trying to escape southward from Hangzhou. Those who stayed behind, particularly in the countryside, were subjected not only to crushing taxes and floods but also to the sporadic violence of the Mongol princes, Tibetan monks, and bandits.

Perhaps more important was the effect of bubonic plague and its attendant diseases, the spread of which was increased by the constant population movements of the period. The Mongol opening of Yunnan reexposed inland China to plague. The cities may have been better equipped to lessen or avoid outbreaks than the countryside. Rural portions of northern China were extensively affected by plague in the 1300s, and it is probable that the south was exposed before then. Privations in the countryside may

have been extreme enough to depress the rate of population growth, particularly if the traditional practice of female infanticide was employed.

From perhaps as low as 60 million at the end of the Yuan period in 1368, the population seems to have neared 100 million again by the year 1400. This growth is dwarfed by the population explosion of later centuries, but at the time it constituted a boom to which the economy may have adjusted very awkwardly.

The rapid growth shifted relative economic importance away from the commercial sectors, where innovation had been rewarded in the Song period, to the production of agricultural staples—primarily grain in the north and rice in the south. Staple crops, though necessary to sustain farming families and feed the rest of the population, did not have the profit margins of more specialized commercial crops and did not provide farmers with money to pay for capital improvements. Moreover, planting and harvesting were not easy to mechanize, and cheap labor caused by the growth of population may have lessened the incentives for mechanization.

Finally, remember that the materials necessary for the building of machines had become scarce. Iron was difficult to obtain, and wood was becoming expensive because of the progressive deforestation of southern and central China during the Ming period as trees were cut to provide houses and coffins for the expanding population.

The Mongols with whom the Ming were often at war were not, as the earlier imperial Mongols had been, avid students of the technological advances of the sedentary societies. They fought as their early Mongol ancestors had fought, and the Ming fought back with technology that was roughly as ancient: arrows, scattershot mortars, and explosive canisters. The Ming used a small number of cannon, but used them selectively. Thus they were not under pressure to innovate and advance in the technologies of warfare, as the Song had been (see Environment and Technology: Explosive Power).

Fear of technology transfer—whether from the state to the people or from China to foreign nations—seems evident in much of the behavior of the Ming government. Encyclopedias of practical knowledge, for instance, were produced in

Explosive Power

China is often credited with the invention of gunpowder. But anecdotal evidence in Chinese records gives credit for its introduction to a Sogdian Buddhist monk of the 500s and thus suggests that gunpowder was a Central Asian invention. The monk described the wondrous alchemical transformation of elements produced by a combination of charcoal and saltpeter. In this connection he also mentioned sulfur. Naphtha distillation, too, seems to have been a skill first developed in Central Asia, for some of the earliest devices for distilling naphtha have been found in the Gandhara region (in modern Pakistan).

By the eleventh century, the Chinese had made and used flamethrowers based on the slow igniting of naphtha, sulfur, or gunpowder in a long tube. They used these weapons not only to intimidate and injure foot soldiers and horses but also to set fire to thatched roofs in hostile villages and, occasionally, the rigging of enemy ships.

During their war against the Mongols, the Song learned to enrich saltpeter to increase the amount of nitrate in gunpowder and thereby produce forceful explosions that could cause destruction. Launched from catapults, canisters filled with the explosive material could rupture fortifications and inflict mass casualties. Ships could be set afire or sunk by an explosive hurled from a distance.

The Song also seem to have been the first to experiment with the construction of metal gun barrels from which to fire projectiles propelled by the explosion of gunpowder. The earliest of these gun barrels were broad and squat and were carried on special wagons to their emplacements. From the mouths of the barrels projected saltpeter mixed with scatter-shot minerals that were ignited by the firing of the gun. The Chinese and then the Koreans also learned to use gunpowder to shoot masses of arrows, as well as flaming arrows, at enemy fortifications. But it was the Mongols who used Song expertise to devise cannon.

In 1280, in the aftermath of the conquest of the Southern Song, the Yuan Empire produced a device featuring a projectile that completely filled the mouth of the cannon and thus concentrated the explosive force. They used cast bronze for the barrel and iron for the cannonball. The new weapon could be aimed better and shot farther than the earlier devices of the Song. Its ability to smash through brick, wood, and flesh without suffering destruction itself was unprecedented.

Knowledge of the cannon and cannonball moved westward across Eurasia. By the end of the thirteenth century, more accurate, more mobile cannon were being produced in the Middle East. By 1327, small, squat cannon called "bombards" were being produced and used in Europe (see Chapter 16, Environment and Technology: Cannon).

The development and improvement of guns and cannon by the Mongols is only one example of the application of knowledge about gunpowder. Gunpowder was used in China and Korea to do the excavation necessary for mining, canal building, and irrigation. Alchemists in China used formulas related to gunpowder to construct noxious gas pellets that they believed would not only paralyze enemies but also expel evil spirits and reduce the populations of disease-carrying insects—an aid to the colonization of malarial regions in China and Southeast Asia. And gunpowder was used in the Mongol Empire for fireworks displays on ceremonial occasions, delighting European visitors to Karakorum who saw them for the first time.

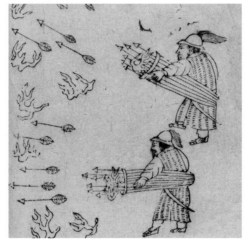

Gunpowder Though the formula for explosive gunpowder was known in China since the sixth century, it was only in the Southern Song period, as the last of China was being conquered by the Mongols in the late 1200s, that the Song devised cannon to allow gunpowder to propel large projectiles. The Mongols immediately adopted the technology, and it quickly spread to the Middle East and Europe. (British Library)

the early Ming as much as in the Song. But in the Ming case, the chapters on gunpowder and guns were censored. Ming shipyards and ports were closed to avoid contact with Japanese pirates and to prevent more Chinese from migrating to Southeast Asia. The Ming state, unlike the Song before it, did not encourage the rapid dissemination and application of technology. New crops, such as sweet potatoes, that were available were not adopted. Guns and cannon, known from contacts with the Middle East and later with Europeans, were not manufactured or used on any significant scale. Advanced printing techniques were not developed. When rapidly printed editions of rare books of the Tang or Song periods were desired, they were purchased from Korea. When superior steel was needed, it was purchased from Japan.

The Ming Achievement in Fine Arts

Despite those problems in the Ming period, the late 1300s and the 1400s were a time of cultural brilliance, particularly in literature. The interest in vernacular style that had been encouraged under the Yuan came to fruition in the early Ming in some of the world's earliest novels. One of the most famous, *Water Margin*, is based on the raucous drum-song performances famous during the Yuan (and loosely related to another famous entertainment, the Chinese opera). Its subject is the adventures of a group of dashing Chinese bandits opposed to Mongol rule (as Robin Hood and his merry men had been opposed to Norman rule). The fictional work distorts many of the original stories on which it is based, and it is clear that many authors were involved in its final commission to paper and print.

Luo Guanzhong (1330–1400), one of the authors of *Water Margin*, is the reputed author of *Romance of the Three Kingdoms*. Based on a much older series of story cycles, the saga resembles in some ways the Arthurian stories. It deals with the attempts of an upright but doomed war leader and his variously talented followers to restore the Han Empire (see Chapter 6) and resist the growing power of the cynical but brilliant villain, Cao Cao. *Romance of the Three Kingdoms* and *Water Margin* expressed much of the militant

but joyous nationalistic sentiment of the early Ming and have remained among the best appreciated fictional works in China.

The early Ming also elevated the arts and technology of porcelain, which had already been very accomplished in the Song and Yuan periods. The great imperial ceramic works at Jingdezhen, for instance, was a constant site not only of technological improvement but also of the organization and rationalization of labor (see Map 14.1). Ming patterns—most famous is the blue on white that is widely recognized as Ming "ware"—were stimulated in the 1400s by motifs from India, Central Asia, and the Middle East. In the later Ming, the foundations of a vigorous global trade in Chinese porcelain would be built on these achievements of the fifteenth century.

Nevertheless, the technological disparity between China and Europe that would have dramatic consequences in later centuries had its roots in the Ming period. It was unprecedented, for instance, for Korea to move ahead of China in the design and production of firearms and ships and in the sciences of weather prediction and calendar making. It was also unprecedented for Japan to surpass China in mining and metallurgy and in the manufacture of novel household goods. During the Ming period, China began to be afflicted with an underdevelopment complex—relative to its own past, relative to its immediate neighbors, and ultimately relative to its more distant rivals.

Continued Dissemination of Eurasian Knowledge

Despite the lack of relative material advance in China in the Ming, there was considerable growth in theoretical knowledge. During the Mongol period, technological, medical, mathematical, and astronomical knowledge was freely shared from one end of Asia to the other. Khubilai in China and Hülegü in Iran were brothers, and their primary advisers were constantly in touch. The economic and financial policies of the Yuan Empire and the Il-khans were similar, and so was their devotion to the sponsorship of engineering, astronomical study, and mathematics.

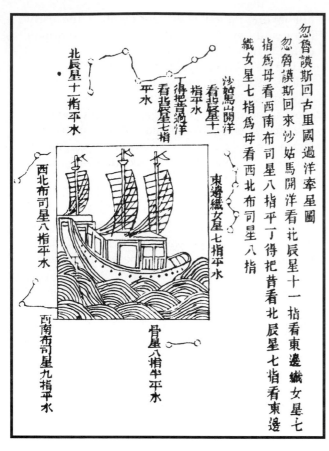

Zheng He's navigational manual The navigational techniques used by Zheng He and his crew were well established and precise, as his manual shows. Ships were guided by reference to the Pole Star, and the routes to India, the Middle East, and East Africa were well known. The manual underscores that Zheng He's mission was not to explore, but to carry out political and, if possible, economic mandates. (From the *Wubei zhi* [records of military preparations], 1621.)

During the Ming period in China, knowledge continued to be developed in both the government and the private spheres.

Muslims from the Middle East had overseen most of the weapons manufacture and engineering projects for Khubilai's armies. From China, the Il-khans imported the scholars and the texts that made possible their understanding of the use of many technological advances, including sighting tubes on equatorial mounts, mechanically driven armillary spheres, and techniques for measuring the movement of the moon. Just as Chinese knowledge was integrated with other Eurasian knowledge at the Il-khan observatory and academy, so Il-khan science was reimported to China and Korea under Khubilai. He commissioned the Iranian philosopher Jamal al-Din to come to Beijing to construct an observatory and an institute for astronomical studies based on the Il-khans' facility at Maraga. For the remainder of the imperial period in China, maintaining and staffing the observatory continued to be regarded as an imperial responsibility. It was rebuilt in the Ming period and recently was rebuilt again, now standing on its original grounds on the main street in Beijing.

In mathematics as in astronomy, the Yuan Empire promoted an integration of Chinese skills with new ideas from the Middle East. The Chinese had contributed the concept of fractions to Middle Eastern mathematics, and Middle Easterners coming to China brought along their developments—algebra and trigonometry. In the Yuan period, brilliant Chinese mathematicians were encouraged to develop and publish their treatises. Two in particular, Guo Shoujing and Zhu Shijie, wrote and published advanced theses on mathematics, astronomy, calendrical science, and agronomy. Into the late Ming period, mathematics continued to be an obsession with some groups of scholars. Li Zhi, a descendant of Muslims who was himself a Confucian who converted to Buddhism, believed that moral realities were clearly revealed only in mathematics and dimly suggested by all other phenomena.

Islamic scholars from the Middle East were also important in the development of medicine and pharmacology in China. Before the Mongols, medicine had been a lowly profession in China, but the Yuan emperors—particularly Khubilai, who had alcoholism, gout, and many other health complaints—gave doctors an influential position. Chinese scholarship on herbs, drugs, and potions had been well developed before the Mongol period, but the introduction during the Yuan of new seeds, plants, and formulas from the Middle East stimulated an explosion of experimentation and publication. Again, it was a Ming scholar, Li Shizhen (living about the same time as Li Zhi), who brought the knowledge of previous centuries together into a encyclopedia of pharmacology.

When the Ming Empire succeeded the Yuan, the new emperors continued to employ Muslims as astronomers and calendar makers, and a few Muslim officials remained in charge of international relations with the Muslim countries. After 1368 the Ming continued the overland Eurasian trade, so Muslim livelihoods, apart from government work, were little affected by the transition from Yuan to Ming. For their overseas explorations, too, the Ming turned to Muslims and Chinese descended from Muslims (such as Zheng He), hoping to exploit the community's knowledge of outfitting, sustaining, and navigating fleets across the Indian Ocean to the Middle East and Africa.

SOCIAL CHANGE AND NATIONAL DEFINITION IN EAST ASIA

During the 1200s, the forty-five-year battle against the Southern Song led the Mongols to seek greater control of the coasts of East Asia. They hoped to find new launching sites for naval expeditions against the south and for strategic points to choke off Song sea trade. Once Korea was conquered in the mid-thirteenth century, Japan was the likely next stop. Japan was easily accessible by sea from Korea's southern tip, and from Japan's islands the coast of southern China might be controlled. But, as the Mongols were stopped in the west by the Mamluks (see Chapter 13), so they were stopped in the east by the Japanese. In both instances, there was an element of luck: the Mamluks benefited from the fact that the Mongol forces were diminished and their leaders were distracted by the need to elect a new Great Khan, and the Japanese benefited from unruly summer weather in the Strait of Tsushima and along the coast of Japan. But in both cases overextended Mongol forces were confronting strong regimes that, under pressure from the Mongols, had successfully pursued centralization and militarization.

Map 14.2 Korea and Japan before 1500 The proximity of Korea and of northern China to Japan gave the Mongols the opportunity for launching their enormous fleets. They were defeated by the warriors of the Kamakura shogunate which controlled most of the three islands (Honshu, Shikoku, and Kyushu) of central Japan. The northernmost island, Hokkaido, was not yet under colonization by Japanese settlers. It was the home of the Ainu and other Northeast Asian peoples who lived by fishing, hunting, and gathering.

Transmission and Specialization: The Case of Korea

In contrast to Ming China, other parts of East Asia after the fall of the Mongols managed to develop and use on a large scale the knowledge they had gained. A dramatic example is Korea (see Map 14.2). Formally, Korea was not a part of the Mongol Empire or the Yuan Empire, because the royal house of Koryŏ continued to govern. But in experience Korea resembles a Mongol domain. The Korean royal house became an extension of the Mongol imperial family, and Korea was subjected to the heavy tax burdens and military obligations of a Mongol domain. After the fall of the Mongols, however, a new royal family used its military knowledge to make Korea independent of China and to generate new wealth.

When the Mongols attacked in 1231, the leader of a prominent Korean family assumed the role of military commander and protector of the king (not unlike the shoguns of Japan or the hegemons of ancient China). Under this leader, Korean forces waged defensive warfare against the Mongol invaders for over twenty years, until the countryside and the Korean armies were exhausted. The cultural as well as the material losses that Korea experienced in the war were heavy. One of the most important wooden buildings in East Asia, the nine-story pagoda at Hwangnyong-sa, was destroyed, and the wooden printing blocks of the *Tripitaka*—the ninth-century masterpiece of printing art under the Koryŏ dynasty—were burned. In 1258 (the year the Abbasid caliph was executed in Baghdad) the Korean military commander was killed by his own underlings. Soon afterward, the Koryŏ king surrendered to the Mongols, and his family was joined by marriage to the family of the Great Khans.

By the middle 1300s the Koryŏ kings were mostly Mongol by descent and were comfortable with the Mongolian language, dress, and customs. Many resided at Khubilai's capital, Beijing, and the travel of the kings, princes, their families, and their entourages between China and Korea was steady. In this way, the Mongols opened Korea to direct influence from the most recent philosophical and artistic styles of China, including neo-Confucianism, Chan Buddhism (in Korea, called *Sŏn*), and celadon ceramics (see Chapter 11). Koryŏ attachment to the Mongol imperial family was so strong that when the Yuan Empire fell, Koryŏ decided to remain loyal to the Mongols and had to be forced to recognize the new Ming Empire in China. But soon afterward Koryŏ collapsed and was succeeded by the Yi kingdom in 1392.

The capacity of the Mongol Empire to facilitate the sharing of information among distant cultures strongly influenced medieval Korea.

Since the tenth century Korea had been somewhat isolated. Under the Mongols, the growing of cotton (introduced to northern China from Central Asia in Song times) was begun in southern Korea. Gunpowder, created in China but not used in artillery and firearms until the time of the Mongols, arrived in Korea for the first time. The arts of astronomical observation, at which the Chinese excelled, were combined with cosmological theories and mathematical skills from Central Asia and the Middle East, and all were introduced at once to Korea as a unified science of calendar making, eclipse prediction, and vector calculation. The direct influence of Central Asia is evident in the Korean celestial clocks built for the royal observatory at Seoul. A superficial resemblance to the Chinese celestial clock built by Su Song (see Chapter 11) is apparent in a machine that in its mechanics and its astronomical orientation is Islamic in inspiration.

The Mongols' conquest of Korea opened new avenues of advancement to Korean scholars who were willing to learn and translate Mongolian, to Korean landowners who were willing to open their lands to falconry and to grazing, to Korean merchants who capitalized on the new royal traffic to Beijing. In this and other ways, the Mongols encouraged the rise of a new, landed, educated class in Korea.

After the fall of the Mongol empires and of the Koryŏ kingdom, Korea's rulers were anxious to reestablish a national identity. Like Safavid Iran, Muscovite Russia, and Ming China, the Yi regime in Korea publicly rejected the period of Mongol domination but also adopted Mongol government practices and institutions. Mongol-style land surveys, techniques in the administration of military garrisons, and taxation in kind were all continued.

Like the Ming Empire, the Yi kingdom revived study of the Confucian classics. This scholarly activity required the Korean elites to retain their literacy in Chinese, and it also showed the dedication of the state to the promotion of reading and study. The revival of interest in the Confucian classics may have been the primary factor leading to a technological breakthrough.

Since the 700s, Koreans had been using Chinese woodblock printing, and Koryŏ later adopt-

Korean printing   Movable type was being experimented with by several peoples of eastern Asia before the Mongol period, but the Koreans were the first to create a reliable and efficient method using cast metal elements in a stable frame. Historical records first refer to the use of this method in 1234 in Korea. In combination with the phonetic system later used to write Korean in the 1400s, the country gained an unprecedented level of literacy and access to printed documents in this period. (Courtesy, Yushin Yoo)

ed the Song practice of printing from cast metal plates. These technologies were well suited to China, where a comparatively large number of literate men demanded many copies of a comparatively small number of texts. In Korea, however, the readership was comparatively small, and the range of reading demanded was comparatively great. Movable type had been used in Korea since the early thirteenth century and may have been invented there. But texts printed from movable type were frequently inaccurate and mostly difficult to read. Yi printers, working

directly with the king in the 1400s, developed a reliable device to anchor the pieces of type to the printing plate. They replaced the old beeswax adhesive with solid copper frames. As a result, the legibility of the printed page improved, and high-volume, accurate reproduction of many pages in rapid succession became possible. In combination with the creation in Korea of the phonetic *han'gul* writing system (see the Environment & Technology feature in Chapter 11), this printing technology laid the foundation for a very high rate of literacy in early modern Korea.

Displaying their willingness to adapt and shape Eurasian knowledge imported by the Mongols, the Yi Koreans used the astronomical arts of the Koryŏ period to develop a meteorological science of their own. The astronomical clock and armillary spheres of the royal observatory at Seoul were augmented by redesigned and newly invented instruments to measure wind speed and rainfall, the first of their kind. Keen interest in agricultural specialization inspired the development of a local calendar based on minute comparisons with the calendrical systems of China and of the Islamic world. Interest in agriculture also sparked improvements in the production and use of fertilizer, the transplanting of seedlings in rice paddies, and the engineering of reservoirs (of which there were thousands in Yi times), all disseminated through the powerful new publishing abilities of the Yi government.

Yi agriculture was so well developed that the growing of cash crops became common. Cotton, introduced under the Mongols, was the primary cash crop. It was so highly valued by the state that it was accepted as payment for taxes. Demand was stimulated by the need of the large and frequently mobilized Yi army for cotton uniforms. Cotton also displaced traditional fabrics in the clothing worn by the Korean civil elite. Artisans built cotton gins and spinning wheels, often powered by water, to produce this profitable cloth. In mechanizing the processing of cotton, Korea advanced more rapidly than China. Soon, Korea was exporting considerable amounts of cotton both to China and to Japan.

The Yi also succeeded in reclaiming their coastlines from Japanese pirates who had previously operated at will and driven harassed farmers inland. In the 1400s, Koreans were innovators in military technology. Although both the Yuan and the Ming withheld the formula for destructive gunpowder from the Korean government, Korean officials acquired the information by subterfuge. By the later 1300s the Koreans had mounted cannon on their patrol ships and used gunpowder-driven arrow launchers against enemy personnel and to propel flaming arrows into the rigging of enemy ships. In combination with Koreans' skill in armoring ships, these techniques made the Yi navy, though small, a formidable defense force.

Power Imbalances and Political Transformation in Japan

The Mongols launched their first naval invasion against Japan in 1274. The invading force was diverse and formidable. It included not only the horses and riders of the Mongols, but also light catapults and incendiary and explosive projectiles manufactured by the Chinese. Some captains of the fleet were Koreans. Additional warriors were drawn from the Jurchens and other peoples from northeastern Asia, many of whom were both excellent archers and experienced sailors. They were joined by Korean foot soldiers and archers. In numbers—perhaps thirty thousand combatants—and in technical outfitting, the expedition presented a clear threat to the independence of Japan. But it was not equal to the weather of Hakata Bay on the north side of Kyushu Island (see Map 14.2). The Mongol forces were able to land and inflict stunning damage on mounted Japanese warriors, but a storm prevented them from establishing a base on the beach. The Mongol invaders returned to their ships and sailed back to the mainland for refitting.

The appearance of the Mongols, their large invasion force, and their superior military technology made a deep impression on the leaders of Japan and hastened social and political changes already under way. At the time Japan was organized under the Kamakura shogunate (see Chapter 11), although another powerful family had actually assumed control. The shogun distributed land and privileges to his followers, who paid him tribute and supplied him with soldiers. Based on the balancing of power among warlords, this system was comparatively stable, but it was also decentralized. Lords in the north and east of Japan were remote from those in the south and west, and beyond their declared devotion to the emperor and to the shogun, little united them. The Mongol threat served to pull them together, because it was alien, terrifying, and prolonged.

After the initial shocking foray in 1274, Khubilai sent envoys to Japan insisting on Japanese submission. Japanese leaders executed the ambassadors, but they knew the Mongols would return eventually.

Mongol sea invasion of Japan   The two unsuccessful Mongol attempts to invade Japan were the largest sea mobilizations of the medieval period. The ships, built and outfitted in northern China and in Korea, were designed to transport the war machines, horses, and armor of the invading force—as well as the tens of thousands of Turkic, Mongol, Korean, and Chinese warriors. The Japanese resisted the invaders both on the water and on land, but may well have owed thanks for failure of the Mongol campaigns to heavy seas and erratic weather—the *kamikaze,* or "wind of the gods," that destroyed the second and last Mongol fleet in 1281. (© Museum of Imperial Collections [Kunaityo Sannomal Shozokan])

The preparations to defend against a new attack included strengthening the position of middle-level military officials throughout Japan. Local military commanders hoping to increase their own power frequently had ignored the civil code that had been created under the Kamakura shoguns. In response to the Mongol attack, the shogun took steps to centralize his military government and his methods of communication. Warlords from the south and west of Honshu (Japan's main island) and from the island of Kyushu, which was closest to the expected point of attack, rose in influence.

Preparations also included an attempt by the Japanese military planners to imitate what they had observed of Mongol war tactics. Efforts were made to retrain Japanese warriors and to outfit the Japanese for defense against the advanced weaponry of the attackers. The entire realm was involved in attempts to construct fortifications for defense at Hakata and other points along the Honshu and Kyushu shores. This effort demanded, for the first time, a national system to move resources from elsewhere in Japan to western points.

The Mongols attacked again in 1281. They came in a sea force greater than any ever before amassed anywhere. They brought 140,000 warriors, including Mongols, Chinese, Koreans, and Jurchens, in hundreds of ships. Since the first Mongol attack, however, the Japanese had built a wall cutting off Hakata Bay from the mainland and depriving the Mongol forces of a reliable landing point. After a standoff lasting months, a typhoon struck and sent perhaps half of the Mongol ships to the bottom of the sea. The remainder of the fleet returned to the mainland, never again to harass Japan. The Japanese gave thanks to the "wind of the Gods"—*kamikaze*—for driving away the Mongols.

The belief that the Mongols still posed a threat continued to influence Japanese development. On his deathbed in 1294 Khubilai was planning a third expedition to Japan. His successors did not carry through with it, but the shoguns did not know that the Mongols had given up the idea of conquering Japan. They continued to make plans for coastal defense well into the fourteenth century. This planning helped to consolidate the social position of Japan's warrior elite. It also

Painting by Sesshu Sesshu Toyo (1420–1506) is renowned as the creator of a distinctive style in ink painting that contrasted with the Chinese styles that predominated earlier in Japan. He owed much of his training to the development of Japanese commerce in the period of the Ashikaga shogunate, because as a youth he was patronized by a great commercial family of southern Japan who financed his travel to China, where he first learned his techniques. As he developed a new style, a market for his art and those following in his footsteps developed among the merchant communities of the great castle towns of the Ashikaga periods, and spread to other urban elites. (Collection of the Tokyo National Museum)

stimulated the development of a national infrastructure for trade and communication. On the downside, it hastened the bankruptcy of the failing Kamakura regime.

In the 1330s a civil war ignited by the wish of the emperor Go-Daigo to reclaim power for himself from the shoguns and from rivals within his own family destroyed the shogunate, the power of its military overseers, and the political ambitions of the imperial family itself. In 1338 a new shogunate, the Ashikaga, was established.

The Ashikaga shogunate, not threatened by Mongols, was based at the imperial center of Kyoto. Government authority was more decentralized in the Ashikaga shogunate than in the Kamakura. The provincial warlords enjoyed greater independence. Around their imposing castles, these men sponsored the development of thriving market towns, religious institutions, and occasionally schools. The application of technologies imported in earlier periods, including the water wheel, improved plows, and Champa rice, increased the productivity of the land. The growing wealth and relative peace of the period stimulated artistic creativity, most of which reflected the Zen Buddhist beliefs of the warrior elite. In the simple elegance of the architecture and gardens, in the contemplative landscapes of such artists as Sesshu, and in the eerie, ritualized performances of the No theater, the unified aesthetic code of Zen became established in the Ashikaga era.

Despite the technological advancement, artistic productivity, and rapid urbanization of this period, the progressive aggrandizement of the warlords and their followers led to regional military conflicts. By the later 1400s these conflicts were so severe that they resulted in the virtual destruction of the warlords. In the aftermath of the great Onin War in 1477 Kyoto was devastated, and the Ashikaga shogunate remained a central government only in name. Ambitious but low-ranking warriors began to scramble for control of the provinces, eager to exploit political and economic resources in order to increase their power. They were aided by the revival of trade with continental Asia.

After the fall of the Yuan Empire, the sea trade among China, Korea, and the islands of Japan and Okinawa resumed. Although Japan, unlike

Korea, did not take the lead in the adaptation and application of gun and gunpowder technology, it benefited from the development of firearms on the Asian continent and exported to Korea and China copper, sulfur, and other raw resources. The folding fan, invented in Japan during the period of isolation, quickly became a desired item in Korea and China. The same was true of swords, for which Japan quickly became famous. From China, Japan imported books, porcelain, and copper coins, which it had absorbed in great quantity before the Mongol invasion. In the late Ashikaga period, this trade combined with the volatile political environment in Japan to produce energetic partnerships between warlords and their local merchants. All of them worked to strengthen their own towns and treasuries through exploitation of the overseas trade and, sometimes, through piracy.

Eastern Eurasia, 1200–1500

1206	Temujin chosen as Genghis Khan of the Mongols
1223	Deaths of last ruling emperors of the Tangguts and of the Jin Jurchens
1227	Death of Genghis Khan
1234	Mongol conquest of north China
1279	Mongol conquest of south China; end of southern Song
1333–1336	End of Kamakara shogunate in Japan; beginning of Ashikaga Shogunate
1368	Founding of Ming empire in China
1392	Founding of Yi kingdom in Korea
1403–1424	Yongle emperor's reign in China
1471–1500	Conquest of Champa by Annam

The Rise of Annam as a Conquest State

With the Southern Song destroyed in 1279, Khubilai was determined to subdue the independent state of Annam next. His troops crossed south of the Red River and attacked Hanoi three times. On each occasion the Mongol troops occupied the city, attained an agreement for the paying of tribute, and then withdrew. Later, the Mongols moved farther south, invading Champa in 1283 and making it a tribute nation as well. In 1293 a combined Mongol, Uigur, and Chinese force, numbering perhaps 40,000, set out from the southeast China coast for Java (see Map 14.1). The campaign was ruined by internal dissension among the commanders. There they became embroiled in an internal dispute and wasted their resources without conquering the island. In the case of Southeast Asia, as in the case of Eastern Europe, the ultimate extension of Mongol effort and the limits of Mongol war techniques were reached.

The Ming Empire adopted the Mongol program in Southeast Asia, but with greater success. In 1400, when Annam was distracted by a war with Champa (see Chapter 11), Ming troops occupied Hanoi and installed a puppet government. The new regime lasted until 1428, when it was destroyed in a war for Annamese independence. Ming troops withdrew, and Annam returned to the tributary status it had assumed with Song China. But like Lithuania, the Ottomans, and Korea, Annam was forged into a conquest state by its struggle against a greater empire. In a series of ruthless campaigns, Annamese armies moved southward and systematically annexed the territories of Champa. By 1500 the process was complete. Champa disappeared, and the ancestor of the modern state of Vietnam was born.

The new state reinforced its centralization with Confucian bureaucratic government and an examination system. But it differed from the Ming state in two important ways. The Vietnamese legal code preserved the tradition of group land-owning and decision making within the villages. It also preserved women's property rights. Both developments were probably related to the rural culture based on the growing of rice in wet paddies, but by this time they also were regarded by Annamese as distinctive features of a national culture.

CONCLUSION

The period of Mongol domination of Eurasia had different consequences for peoples of different regions and different classes. Partly because of the decentralized hierarchy that held Mongol regimes together, state expenditures, especially on the military, were always high. Mongol governments were primarily machines of extraction, and the collection of taxes kept intense pressure on farmers and on their rapidly exhausted farmlands. Later Mongol rulers in China and in Iran tried to lessen this burden, but the farming and laboring populations remained in distress. In the 1300s, when the Mongols' political control was weakened throughout their domains, the combination of rebellions and civil wars among the Mongol leaders brought to an end most of the Mongol khanates.

Peasants everywhere suffered under Mongol domination, but new vistas of experience and opportunities for advancement opened to merchants, artists, scholars, high-ranking soldiers, and many religious leaders. The Mongols were actively interested in developing the overland trade among Europe, the Middle East, and East Asia. A great variety of goods and knowledge crisscrossed Eurasia under their rule. Middle Eastern financial administrators immigrated to China to serve the Mongols. As a consequence, thousands of large Muslim communities and several long-lived Jewish communities were established in the Asian interior. They brought with them advanced knowledge of astronomy and mathematics, and Chinese scholars rapidly assimilated their expertise. In exchange, Chinese financial innovations, including paper money and a rudimentary form of banking, were brought to Iran.

Religious influences too were very mobile in the Mongol domains. The Mongol Great Khans patronized Buddhist, Confucianist, and Daoist leaders. The Il-khans reconciled themselves to Islam, and after them the Timurids elevated Sunni Islam to the dominant religious system of Central Asia as well as the Middle East. In Russia, the Mongols tolerated and in a few instances encouraged the continued domination of the Orthodox Church over local affairs.

Although the Mongol invasion of Europe in the mid-thirteenth century had excited terror (partly because the Mongols brought with them the bubonic plague, which had first afflicted them during their conquest of China), the Mongol Empire attracted European merchants and adventurers. Some Christian leaders hoped that the Mongols would play a role in the capture of religious sites in the Middle East from Muslim control. These hopes proved to be ill founded, for a large and growing portion of the Mongols who settled in the Middle East became Muslim. Nevertheless, the expectations of some European rulers led to diplomatic exchanges with the Mongols and to the appearance at European courts of emissaries from Asia. The European dream of harnessing Asian power and wealth that helped to inspire Marco Polo and others who, eager to discover the riches of the "East," would be followed centuries later by Christopher Columbus.

The legacy of the Mongols did not cease when their control over major cultural and political centers ended. Throughout Eurasia, succeeding regimes showed the marks of Mongol influence. Some were direct—for example, changes in modes of dress in the Middle East and the institutionalization of some aspects of Mongol rule in China and in Russia. More profound were the direct and indirect effects of the Mongol empires on the formation of nations in the post-Mongol period.

The Mongols brought unity to China, Iran, and Russia by destroying the small states within each region and gathering each region under the control of a single khanate. The Mongols established new capitals, and each of them remained a center of regional unity for centuries after the end of Mongol rule. The Mongol khans encouraged the use of vernacular languages, and in later times those languages became the vehicles for the creation of the literature of China, Iran, and Russia. Perhaps most important, Ming China, Safavid Iran, and Muscovite Russia all benefited from a state ideology that clearly defined each of them in contrast to the late, hated Mongol overlords.

Areas not actually invaded or dominated by

the Mongols nevertheless felt their impact. Lands as widely separated as Armenia and Thailand were regularly harassed by Mongol forces and received waves of refugees from the areas of warfare. Lithuania, Egypt, Japan, and Annam underwent surges of military centralization in anticipation of Mongol attacks.

The period of Mongol rule was a dynamic period for Eurasia and in many ways an unhappy one for the majority populations. It nevertheless changed the world. Heightened regional definition and centralization were critical to the major nations that emerged from the decaying Mongol empires. After the period of Mongol dominance, the land connections that the Mongols had established between Europe and Asia declined, permanently eclipsed by new sea routes. The age of exploration was the primary heir of the age of Mongol rule, and the early modern empires were its stepchildren. The quest for trade, new resources, exploration, conquest, and colonization that China had undertaken in the 1400s continued to draw Europeans toward Asia and, on the way, to East Africa. By the early sixteenth century, Portuguese and Spanish traders were familiar with the shorelines of the whole African continent and Southeast Asia, and they would be followed by the Dutch, the British, and ultimately traders from most of the major nations of Europe.

SUGGESTED READING

See Chapter 13 for works on the general history of the Mongols. For China under the Mongols see Morris Rossabi's *Khubilai Khan: His Life and Times* (1988). On the effects of the Mongol period on economy and technology in Yuan and Ming China see Mark Elvin, *The Pattern of the Chinese Past* (1973); Joel Mokyr, *The Lever of Riches: Technological Creativity and Economic Progress* (1990); and Joseph Needham, *Science in Traditional China* (1981).

Scholarly studies in English on the early Ming period are not so well developed as studies on some other periods of Chinese history. But see Albert Chan, *The Glory and Fall of the Ming Dynasty* (1982), and Edward L. Farmer, *Early Ming Government: The Evolution of Dual Capitals* (1976).

On early Ming literature see Lo Kuan-chung, *Three Kingdoms: A Historical Novel Attributed to Luo Guanzhong,* translated and annotated by Moss Roberts (1991); Pearl Buck's translation of *Water Margin,* entitled *All Men Are Brothers,* 2 vols. (1933), and a later translation by J. H. Jackson, *Water Margin, Written by Shih Nai-an* (1937); Richard Gregg Irwin, *The Evolution of a Chinese Novel: Shui-hu-chuan* (1953); Ellen Widmer, *The Margins of Utopia: Shui-hu hou-chuan and the Literature of Ming Loyalism* (1987); and Shelley Hsüeh-lun Chang, *History and Legend: Ideas and Images in the Ming Historical Novels* (1990).

On Ming painting see James Cahill, *Parting at the Shore: Chinese Painting of the Early and Middle Ming Dynasty* (1978). See also selected essays in Paul S. Ropp, ed. *Heritage of China* (1990).

The Zheng He expeditions are extensively discussed in secondary works. A classic interpretation is Joseph R. Levenson, ed., *European Expansion and the Counter-Example of Asia, 1300–1600* (1967). More recent scholarship is available in Philip Snow, *The Star Raft* (1988), and a full and lively account is Louise Levathes, *When China Ruled the Seas* (1993).

For a general history of Korea in this period see Andrew C. Nahm, *Introduction to Korean History and Culture* (1993); Ki-Baik Lee, *A New History of Korea* (1984); and William E. Henthorn, *Korea: the Mongol Invasions* (1963). On a more specialized topic, see Joseph Needham et al., *The Hall of Heavenly Records: Korean Astronomical Instruments and Clocks, 1380–1780* (1986).

Narrative histories of Japan are cited in Chapter 11, but see also John W. Hall and Toyoda Takeshi, eds., *Japan in the Muromachi Age* (1977), and H. Paul Varley, trans., *The Onin War: History of Its Origins and Background with a Selective Translation of the Chronicle of Onin* (1967). On the Mongol invasion see Yamada Nakaba, *Ghenko, the Mongol Invasion of Japan, with an Introduction by Lord Armstrong* (1916), and the novel *Fûtô* by Inoue Yasushi, translated by James T. Araki as *Wind and Waves* (1989). On the Nō theater and Zen aesthetics there is a great deal of writing. Perhaps most direct and charming are Donald Keene, *No: The Classical Theatre of Japan* (1966), and Ueda Makoto, trans., *The Old Pine Tree and Other Noh Plays* (1962).

Tropical Africa and Asia, 1200–1500

Tropical Lands and Peoples • New Islamic Empires • Indian Ocean Trade

Social and Cultural Change

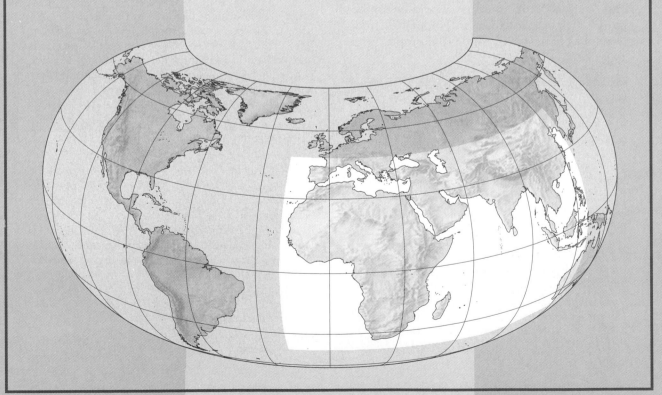

Sultan Abu Bakr customarily offered his personal hospitality to all distinguished visitors arriving at his city of Mogadishu, an Indian Ocean port on the northeast coast of Africa. In 1331 he provided food and lodging for Muhammad ibn Abdullah ibn Battuta (1304–1369), a young Muslim scholar from Morocco, who had set out to explore the Islamic world. Having already completed a pilgrimage to Mecca and traveled throughout the Middle East, Ibn Battuta was touring the trading cities of the Red Sea and East Africa. Subsequent travels took him to Central Asia and India, China and Southeast Asia, Muslim Spain, and sub-Saharan West Africa. Logging some 75,000 miles (120,000 kilometers) in the course of his twenty-nine years of travel, Ibn Battuta became the most widely traveled man of his times. For this reason his journal, which describes where he went and what he saw, is a valuable historical source for these lands.

Other Muslim princes and merchants welcomed Ibn Battuta as graciously as did the ruler of Mogadishu. Hospitality was a highly respected Muslim virtue, which ignored individuals' physical and cultural differences. Although the Moroccan traveler noted that Sultan Abu Bakr had skin darker than his own and spoke a different native language (Somali), that made little difference. They were brothers in faith when they prayed together at Friday services in the Mogadishu mosque, where the sultan greeted his foreign guest in Arabic, the common language of the Islamic world: "You are heartily welcome, and you have honored our land and given us pleasure." When Sultan Abu Bakr and his jurists heard and decided cases after the mosque service, they used the law code familiar in all the lands of Islam.

Islam was not the only tie that bound the peoples of Africa and southern Asia together. A network of land and sea trade routes joined their lands. These routes were older than Islam and an important means for the spread of beliefs and technologies as well as goods. Ibn Battuta made his way down the coast of East Africa in merchants' ships and joined their camel caravans to cross the Sahara to West Africa. He reached India by overland trade routes and sailed for China on another merchant ship.

An even more fundamental link among the diverse peoples of Africa and southern Asia was the tropical environment itself. Environmental differences had helped shape the region's cultural differences. Cultural and ecological differences, in turn, helped generate the trade in specialized products from one place to another. And the twice-a-year shift in the Indian Ocean winds made the ocean voyages possible.

During the period 1200 to 1500, commercial and cultural exchange among tropical peoples reached a much greater level of intensity than ever before. Human interaction was catching up with its geographical potential.

TROPICAL LANDS AND PEOPLES

The people who inhabited the tropical regions of Africa and Asia were profoundly affected by their natural setting. Members of each community obtained food by using methods that generations of experimentation had proved most successful in dealing with their particular environment, whether desert edge, grasslands, or tropical rain forest. Much of their success lay in learning how to blend human activities with the natural order, but their ability to modify the environment to suit their needs was also evident in their irrigation works and mining.

The Tropical Environment

Because of the angle of earth's axis, the tropics are warmed by the sun's rays year-round, instead of having alternating hot and cold seasons as in the temperate zones. The equator marks the

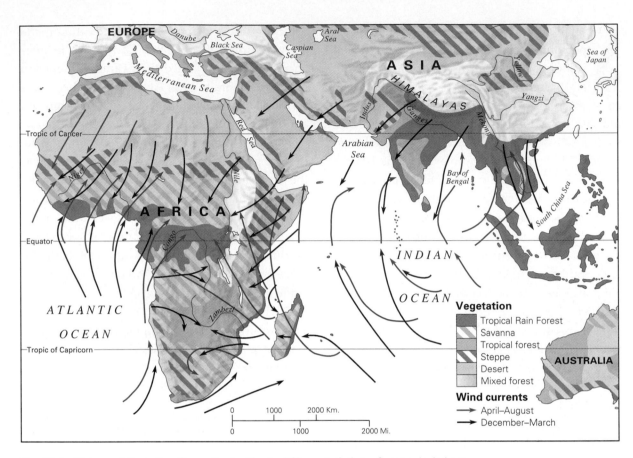

Map 15.1 Africa and the Indian Ocean Basin: Physical Characteristics   Seasonal wind patterns controlled the rainfall in the tropics and produced the different tropical vegetation zones to which human societies adapted over thousands of years. The wind patterns also dominated sea travel in the Indian Ocean.

center of the tropical zone, and the Tropic of Cancer and Tropic of Capricorn mark its outer limits. As Map 15.1 shows, Africa lies almost entirely within the tropics, and southern Arabia, most of India, and all of mainland Southeast Asia and the East Indies also fall within the tropics.

Lacking the hot and cold seasons of temperate lands, the Afro-Asian tropics have their own cycle of rainy and dry seasons caused by changes in wind patterns across the surrounding oceans. Winds from a permanent high-pressure air mass over the South Atlantic deliver heavy rainfall to the western coast of Africa during much of the year. However, in December and January large high-pressure zones over northern Africa and Arabia produce a southward movement of dry

air that limits the inland penetration of the moist ocean winds.

In the lands around the Indian Ocean the rainy and dry seasons reflect the influence of similar alternating wind patterns. A gigantic high-pressure zone over the Himalayas that is at its peak from December to March produces a strong southward air movement (the northeast monsoon) in the western Indian Ocean. This is southern Asia's dry season. Between April and August a low-pressure zone over India creates a northward movement of air from across the ocean (the southwest monsoon) that brings southern Asia its heaviest rains. This is the wet season.

Along with geographical features, these wind and rain patterns are responsible for the variations in tropical lands, from desert to rain forest. Where rainfall is exceptionally abundant, as in the broad belt along the equator in coastal West Africa and west-central Africa, the natural vegetation is dense tropical rain forest. Rain forests also characterize Southeast Asia and parts of coastal India. Somewhat lighter rains produce other tropical forests. The English word *jungle* comes from a Hindi word for the tangled undergrowth in the tropical forests that once covered most of India.

Although heavy rainfall is common in some of the tropics, other parts rarely see rain at all. Stretching clear across the width of northern Africa is the world's largest desert, the Sahara. This arid zone continues eastward, to include the Arabian Desert and the Thar Desert of northwest India. Another desert zone in southwestern Africa includes the Namib and Kalahari Deserts. In between the deserts and the rain forests are lands that receive moderate amounts of moisture during the rainy seasons. These are the majority of lands in tropical India and Africa and range from fairly wet woodlands to the much drier grasslands characteristic of much of East Africa and the desert edges.

Other variations in tropical climate result from the topography of the landmasses. Thin atmospheres at high altitudes can hold less of the tropical heat than can atmospheres at lower elevations. The volcanic mountains of eastern Africa rise to such heights that some are covered with snow all or part of the year. The Himalayas that form the northern frontier of India are also snow capped and so high that they block the movement of cold air into the northern India plains, giving this region a milder climate than its latitude would suggest. The many plateaus of inland Africa and the Deccan Plateau of central India also make these regions somewhat cooler than the coastal plains.

The mighty rivers that descend to the oceans from these mountains and plateaus carry water far from where it falls. The heavy rains falling in the highlands of Central Africa and Ethiopia supply the Nile's annual floods that make Egypt bloom in the desert. On its long route to the Atlantic, the Niger River of West Africa flows northward to the Sahara's edge, creating a rich floodplain (the inland Niger Delta) and providing waters to the trading cities that clustered along its great bend. In like fashion, the Indus River provides nourishing waters from the Himalayas to arid northwest India. The Ganges and its tributaries provide valuable moisture to northeastern India during the dry season. Mainland Southeast Asia's great rivers, such as the Mekong, are similarly valuable.

Human Ecosystems

Thinkers in temperate lands once imagined that, because of the absence of a harsh winter season, surviving in the tropics was as easy as picking wild fruit off a tree. In fact, mastering the tropics' many different environments had been a long and difficult struggle. A careful observer touring the tropics in 1200 would have noticed how much the differences in societies could be attributed to their particular ecosystems—that is, to how they made use of the plants, animals, and other resources of their physical environments. Tropical peoples' success in adapting to their natural worlds was fundamental to all their other achievements.

Centuries before 1200, most tropical Africans and Asians had taken up raising domesticated plants and animals as the best way to feed themselves. But in some environments people found it preferable to rely primarily on wild food that they obtained by hunting, fishing, and gathering. This was true of the dense forests of Central Africa where the small size of the Pygmy hunters was itself a physical adaptation that permitted them to pursue their prey through the dense undergrowth. Hunting was also a way of life in the upper altitudes of the Himalayas and in some desert environments. A Portuguese expedition led by Vasco da Gama visited the arid coast of southwestern Africa in 1497 and recorded the presence there of a healthy group of people who lived off both land and sea creatures, feeding themselves on "the flesh of seals, whales, and gazelles, and the roots of wild plants." Fishing was a highly skilled and successful form of food gathering everywhere in the region along all the major lakes and rivers as well as in the oceans, though it might be combined with farming. The ocean fishermen of the East African coast and the East Indies were particularly distinguished, as were those of coastal India. The boating skills of fishermen often led to their playing an important role in ocean trade.

In areas too arid for agriculture, tending herds of domesticated animals was common. Unencumbered by bulky personal possessions and elaborate dwellings, pastoralists' knowledge of the local waterholes and observation of the scattered rains enabled them to find adequate grazing for their animals in all but the severest droughts. They fed themselves with milk from their herds and with grain and vegetables obtained from farmers in exchange for hides and meat. The world's largest concentration of pastoralists was in the arid and semiarid lands of northeastern Africa and Arabia. Like Ibn Battuta's host at Mogadishu, some Somali were urban dwellers, but most grazed their herds of goats and camels in the desert hinterland of the Horn of Africa. The western Sahara sustained herds of sheep and camels belonging to the Tuareg, whose intimate knowledge of the desert also made them invaluable as guides to caravans, such as the one Ibn Battuta joined on the two-month-long journey across the desert. Along the Sahara's southern edge the cattle-herding Fulani people gradually extended their range during this period, so that by 1500 they were found throughout the western and central Sudan. A few weeks after its encounter with the hunter-gatherers of southern Africa, Vasco da Gama's expedition bartered for meat with a pastoral people possessing fat cattle and sheep.

Although food gathering and animal husbandry continued, farming was the dominant way of life for most tropical peoples between 1200 and 1500. The density of agricultural populations was closely tied to the adequacy of rainfall and soils. South and Southeast Asia were generally much better watered than tropical Africa and so could support much greater populations. In 1200 there were probably over 100 million people living in South and Southeast Asia, more than four-fifths of them on the fertile Indian mainland. This was three times the number of people living in all of Africa at that time and nearly twice as many as

in Europe, though still a little less than the population of China.

Because of India's lush vegetation, one Middle Eastern writer of the time identified it as "the most agreeable abode on earth . . . its delightful plains resemble the garden of Paradise."[1] Rice cultivation was particularly important in places such as the fertile Gangeatic plain of northeast India, mainland Southeast Asia, and southern China. In drier areas tropical farmers grew grains (such as wheat, sorghum, millet, and ensete) and legumes (such as peas and beans), whose ripening cycle matched the pattern of the rainy and dry seasons. A variety of tubers and tree crops were characteristic of farming in rain forest clearings.

By the year 1200 human migrations had spread many useful domesticated plants and animals around the tropics. Bantu-speaking farmers (see Chapter 8) had introduced grains and tubers from West Africa throughout the southern half of the continent. Bananas, brought to southern Africa centuries earlier by mariners from Southeast Asia, had become the stable food for people farming the rich soils around the Great Lakes of East Africa. Yams and cocoyams of Asian origin had spread clear across equatorial Africa. Asian cattle breeds grazed contentedly in pastures throughout Africa, while coffee of Ethiopian origin would shortly become common drink in the Middle East.

The spread of farming did not always create permanent changes in the natural environment. In most parts of sub-Saharan Africa and many parts of the East Indies until quite recent times, the basic form of cultivation was extensive rather than intensive. Instead of enriching fields with manure and vegetable compost so they could be cultivated year after year, farmers abandoned fields every few years when the natural fertility of the soil was exhausted and cleared new fields. Ashes from the brush, grasses, and tree limbs that were cut down and burned gave the new fields a significant boost in fertility. Even though a great deal of work was needed to clear the fields initially, modern research suggests that such shifting cultivation was an efficient use of labor in areas where soils were not naturally rich in nutrients.

Water Systems and Irrigation

In other parts of the tropics environmental necessity and population pressure led to the adoption of more intensive forms of agriculture. A rare area of intensive cultivation in sub-Saharan Africa was the inland delta of the Niger River, where large crops of rice were grown using the river's naturally fertilizing annual floods. The rice was probably sold to the trading cities along the Niger bend.

One of the great challenges of the tropical environment in parts of Asia was the uneven distribution of rainfall during the year. Unlike pastoralists who could move their herds to the water, farmers had to find ways of moving the water to their crops. Farmers met the challenge by conserving some of the monsoon rainfall for use during the drier parts of the year. Farming communities in Vietnam, Java, Malaya, and Burma constructed terraced hillsides with special water-control systems for growing rice. Water-storage dams and irrigation canals were also becoming common in both north and south India. For example, during these centuries Tamil villagers in southeast India built a series of stone and earthen dams across rivers to store water for gradual release through elaborate irrigation canals. Over many generations these canals were extended to irrigate more and more land. Although these dams and channels covered large areas, they were relatively simple structures that local people could keep working by routine maintenance.

As had been true since the days of the first river-valley civilizations (see Chapter 2), the largest irrigation systems in the tropics were government public works projects. Under the government of the Delhi Sultanate (1206–1526) northern India acquired extensive new water-control systems. Ibn Battuta commented appreciatively on a large reservoir, constructed under one ruler in the first quarter of the thirteenth century, that supplied the city of Delhi with water. Enterprising farmers planted sugar cane, cucumbers, and melons along the reservoir's shore as the water level fell during the dry season. In the fourteenth century the Delhi Sultanate built in the Gangeatic plain a large network of irrigation canals that would not be surpassed in size until the nineteenth century. These irrigation systems made it possible to grow crops throughout the year.

Since the tenth century the Indian Ocean island of Ceylon (modern Sri Lanka) had been home to the greatest concentration of irrigation reservoirs and canals in the world. These facilities enabled the powerful Sinhalese kingdom in arid northern Ceylon to support a large population. There was another impressive waterworks in Southeast Asia, where a system of reservoirs and canals served Cambodia's capital city Angkor.

Yet such complex systems were vulnerable to disruption. Between 1250 and 1400 the irrigation complex in Ceylon fell into ruin when invading Tamils from South India disrupted the Sinhalese government. The population of Ceylon then suffered from the effects of malaria, a tropical disease spread by mosquitoes breeding in the irrigation canals. The great Cambodian system fell into ruin in the fifteenth century when the government that maintained it collapsed. Neither system was ever rebuilt.

The vulnerability of complex irrigation systems built by powerful governments suggests an instructive contrast. Although village-based irrigation systems could be damaged by invasion and natural calamity, except in the most extreme cases they usually bounded back because they were the product of local initiatives, not centralized direction, and they depended on simpler technologies.

Mineral Resources

Metalworking was another way in which people made use of their environment's resources. Skilled metalworkers furnished their customers with tools, weapons, and decorative objects. The mining and processing of metals was also important for long-distance trade.

Iron was the most abundant of the metals worked in the tropics. People in most parts of the tropical world produced sufficient quantities of iron tools and implements to satisfy their own needs. The iron hoes, axes, and knives that enabled farmers to clear and cultivate their fields

Ife bronze head, thirteenth century   This sensuously beautiful head and some companion pieces unearthed at Ife in southwestern Nigeria in 1912 changed the world's image of African art and artistry. Such discoveries showed that sub-Saharan African artists were casting naturalistic images in copper with great skill in the thirteenth century. The crowned head represents a woman or a young man associated with the ancient rulers of the kingdom of Ife. (Werner Forman/Art Resource NY)

seem to have been used between 1200 and 1500 to open up the rain forests of coastal West Africa and Southeast Asia for farming. Iron-tipped spears and arrows improved hunting success. Needles were used in sewing clothes, nails in building. The skill of Indian metalsmiths was renowned, especially in making strong and beautiful swords. So great was the skill of

African iron smelters and blacksmiths that they were believed to possess magical powers.

Copper was of special importance in Africa, where copper and its alloys were used for jewelry and artistic casting. In the Copperbelt of south-eastern Africa, copper mining was in full production in the fourteenth and fifteenth centuries. The refined metal was cast into large X-shaped ingots (metal castings). Local coppersmiths made these ingots into wire and decorative objects. Copper mining was also important in the western Sudan, where Ibn Battuta described a mining town that produced two sizes of copper bars that were used as a currency of exchange in place of coins. The skill of coppersmiths in West Africa reached a high level during these centuries, enabling them to cast copper and brass (an alloy of copper and zinc) statues and heads that are considered among the masterpieces of world art. These works were made by the lost-wax method, in which a thin layer of wax sandwiched between clay forms is replaced by molten metal that hardens and assumes the shape of the wax.

During this period, Africans also acquired an international reputation for their production of gold, which was exported in quantity across the Sahara and into the Indian Ocean and Red Sea trades. Gold was mined and collected from stream beds along the upper Niger River and further south in modern Ghana. In the hills south of the Zambezi River (in modern Zimbabwe) archaeologists have discovered thousands of mine shafts, dating from this period, that were sunk up to a 100 feet (30 meters) into the ground to get at gold ores. The gold and silver mines in India seem to have been exhausted by this period, although panning for gold remained important in the streams descending from the mountains of northern India. For that reason, Indians imported from Southeast Asia and Africa considerable quantities of gold for jewelry and temple decoration.

Metalworking and food-producing systems were important to tropical peoples for two reasons. First, most people made a successful livelihood through such skilled exploitation of their environment. Second, the labors and skills of such ordinary people made possible the rise of powerful states and profitable commercial systems. When considering the better documented lives of rulers and merchants described elsewhere in this chapter, ask yourself: Could the caravans have crossed the Sahara without the skilled guidance of desert pastoralists? Could the trade of the Indian Ocean have reached its full importance were it not for the seafaring skills of the coastal fishermen? Could the city-based empires of Delhi and Mali have endured without the food taxed from rural farmers? Could the long-distance trade routes have prospered without the precious metals, the spices, and the grains produced by such ordinary folks?

NEW ISLAMIC EMPIRES

The empires of Mali in West Africa and Delhi in northern India were the two largest and richest tropical states of the period between 1200 and 1500. Both utilized Islamic administrative and military systems introduced from the Islamic heartland, but in other ways these two Muslim sultanates were very different. Mali was founded by an indigenous African dynasty, which had earlier adopted Islam through the peaceful influence of Muslim merchants and scholars. In contrast, the Delhi Sultanate of northern India was founded and ruled by invading Turkish and Afghan Muslims. Mali depended heavily for its wealth on its participation in the trans-Saharan trade, but long-distance trade played only a minor role in Delhi's wealth.

Mali in the Western Sudan

The consolidation of the Middle East and North Africa under Muslim rule during the seventh and eighth centuries (see Chapter 10) greatly increased the volume of trade along the routes that crossed the Sahara. In the centuries that followed, the faith of Muhammad gradually spread to the lands south of the desert, which the Arabs called the *bilad al-sudan*, the "land of the blacks." The rulers of Ghana, the empire that preceded Mali in the western Sudan (see Chapter 8), had

employed foreign Muslims in government posts but were not Muslims themselves.

The role of force in spreading Islam south of the Sahara was limited. Muslim Berbers invading out of the desert in 1076 captured Ghana's capital and caused the collapse of that empire, but their conquest did little to spread Islam. To the east, the Muslim attacks that destroyed the Christian Nubian kingdoms on the upper Nile in the late thirteenth century opened that area to Muslim influences, but Christian Ethiopia successfully withstood Muslim advances. Instead, the usual pattern for the spread of Islam south of the Sahara was through gradual and peaceful conversion. The expansion of commercial contacts in the western Sudan and on the East African coast greatly promoted the process of conversion.

Africans adopted Islam because they believed in its teachings and found it suited their interests. The first sub-Saharan African state to adopt the new faith was Takrur in the far western Sudan, whose rulers accepted Islam about 1030. Shortly after the year 1200 Takrur expanded in importance under King Sumanguru. Then in about 1240 Sundiata, the upstart leader of the Malinke people, handed Sumanguru a major defeat. Even though both leaders were Muslims, Malinke legends recall their battles as the clash of two powerful magicians. Sumanguru is said to have been able to appear and disappear at will, assume dozens of shapes, and catch arrows in midflight. Sundiata defeated Sumanguru's much larger forces through superior military maneuvers and by successfully wounding his adversary with a special arrow that robbed him of his magical powers. This victory was followed by others that created Sundiata's Empire of Mali (see Map 15.2).

Mali's strength, like that of Ghana before it, rested on a well-developed agricultural base combined with control over lucrative regional and trans-Saharan trade routes. But Mali differed from Ghana in two ways. First, it was much larger in size. Mali controlled not only the core trading area of the upper Niger but the gold fields of the Niger headwaters to the southwest as well. Second, its rulers were Muslims, who fostered the spread of Islam among the political and trading elites of the empire. Control of the

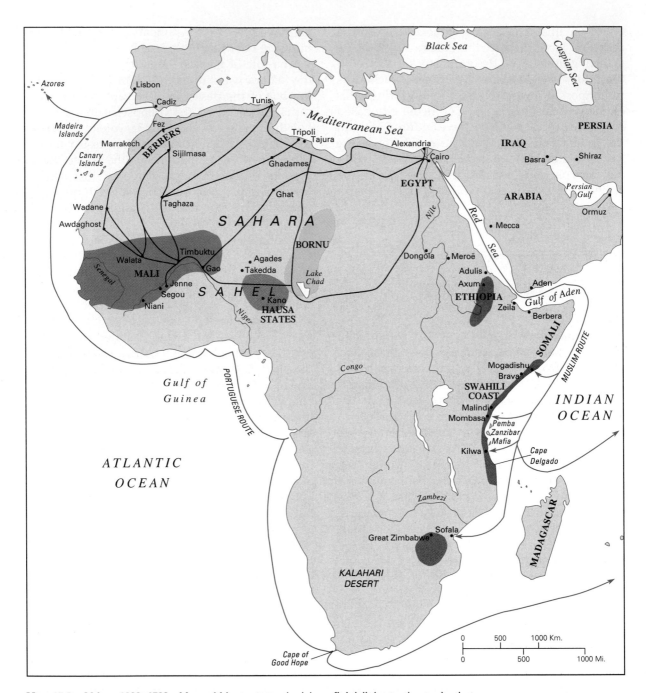

Map 15.2 Africa, 1200–1500 Many African states had beneficial links to the trade that crossed the Sahara and the Indian Ocean. Before 1500, sub-Saharan Africa's external ties were primarily with the Islamic world.

The Western Sudan (1375) A Jewish geographer on the Mediterranean island of Majorca drew this lavish map in 1375, incorporating all that was known in Europe of the rest of the world. This portion of the Catalan Atlas shows a North African trader approaching the king of Mali, who holds a gold nugget in one hand and a golden scepter in the other. A caption identifies the black ruler as Mansa Musa, "the richest and noblest king in all the land." (Bibliotheque nationale de France)

important gold and copper trades and contacts with North African Muslim traders gave Mali and its rulers unprecedented prosperity.

Under the Mali ruler Mansa Kankan Musa (r. 1312–1337), the empire's reputation for wealth spread far and wide. Mansa Musa's pilgrimage to Mecca in 1324–1325, in fulfillment of his personal duty as a Muslim, also became an occasion for him to display the exceptional wealth of his empire. As befitted a powerful ruler, he traveled with a large entourage. Besides his senior wife and 500 of her ladies in waiting and their slaves, one account says there were also 60,000 porters and a vast caravan of camels carrying supplies and provisions. Even more lavish was the gold that Mansa Musa is reported to have taken along. For purchases and gifts he took 80 packages of gold each weighing 122 ounces (3.8 kilo-

grams). In addition, 500 slaves each carried a golden staff. When the entourage passed through Cairo, Mansa Musa gave away and spent so much gold that its value was depressed for years.

Mansa Musa returned from his pilgrimage eager to promote the religious and cultural influence of Islam in his empire. He built new mosques and opened Quranic schools in the cities along the Niger bend. When Ibn Battuta visited Mali from 1352 to 1354, during the reign of Mansa Musa's successor Mansa Suleiman (r. 1341–1360), the practice of Islam in the empire met with his approval. He lauded Malians for their faithful recitation of prayers and for their zeal in teaching children the Quran.

Ibn Battuta also had high praise for Mali's government. He reported that "complete and general safety" prevailed in the vast territories ruled by Suleiman and that foreign travelers had no reason to fear being robbed by thieves or having their goods confiscated if they died. (For Ibn Battuta's account of the sultan's court and his subjects' respect see Voices & Visions: Personal Styles of Rule in India and Mali.)

Two centuries after Sundiata founded the empire, Mali began to disintegrate. When Mansa Suleiman's successors proved to be less able rulers, rebellions broke out among the diverse peoples who had been subjected to Malinke rule. Avid for Mali's wealth, other groups attacked from without. The desert Tuareg retook their city of Timbuktu in 1433. By 1500 the rulers of Mali had dominion over little more than the Malinke heartland.

The cities of the upper Niger survived Mali's collapse, but some of the western Sudan's former trade and intellectual life moved east to other African states in the central Sudan. Shortly after 1450 the rulers of several of the Hausa city-states adopted Islam as their official religion. The Hausa states were also able to increase their importance as manufacturing and trading centers, becoming famous for their cotton textiles and leatherworking. Also expanding in the late fifteenth century was the central Sudanic state of Kanen-Bornu. It was descended from the ancient kingdom of Kanem, whose rulers had accepted

Sankore Mosque, Timbuktu   The wall and tower at the left and center represent traditional styles of construction in clay in a region where building stone is rare. At its peak in the fourteenth through the sixteenth centuries, Timbuktu was a major emporium for trade at the southern edge of the Sahara and a center of Islamic religion and education. (Aldona Sabalis/Photo Researchers, Inc.)

Personal Styles of Rule in India and Mali

Ibn Battuta wrote vividly of the powerful men who ruled the Muslim states he visited. His account of Sultan Muhammad ibn Tughluq of Delhi reflects a familiarity he acquired during a long stay in India in the 1340s.

Muhammad is a man who, above all others, is fond of making presents and shedding blood. There may always be seen at his gate some poor person becoming rich, or some living one condemned to death. His generous and brave actions, and his cruel and violent deeds, have obtained notoriety among the people. In spite of this, he is the most humble of men, and the one who exhibits the greatest equity. The ceremonies of religion are dear to his ears, and he is very severe in respect of prayer and the punishment which follows its neglect . . . . When drought prevailed . . . the Sultan gave orders that provisions for six months should be supplied to all the inhabitants of Delhi from the royal granaries . . . .

One of the most serious charges against this Sultan is that he forced all the inhabitants of Delhi to leave their homes. [After] the people of Delhi wrote letters full of insults and invectives against [him,] the Sultan . . . decided to ruin Delhi, so he purchased all the houses and inns from the inhabitants, paid them the price, and then ordered them to remove to Daulatabad . . . .

The greater part of the inhabitants departed, but [h]is slaves found two men in the streets: one was paralyzed, the other blind. They were brought before the sovereign, who ordered the paralytic to be shot away from a *manjanik* [catapult], and the blind man to be dragged from Delhi to Daulatabad, a journey of forty days' distance. The poor wretch fell to pieces during the journey, and only one of his legs reached Daulatabad.

In contrast, Ibn Battuta's description of 1353 Mansa Suleiman of Mali is remote and impersonal, which accords with African political traditions.

On certain days the sultan holds audiences in the palace yard, where there is a platform under a tree . . . . carpeted with silk, [over which] is raised the umbrella, . . . surmounted by a bird in gold, about the size of a falcon. The sultan comes out of a door in a corner of the palace, carrying a bow in his hand and a quiver on his back. On his head he has a golden skullcap, bound with a gold band which has narrow ends shaped like knives, more than a span in length. His usual dress is a velvety red tunic, made of the European fabrics called *mutanfas*. The sultan is preceded by his musicians, who carry gold and silver [two stringed guitars], and behind him come three hundred armed slaves. He walks in a leisurely fashion, affecting a very slow movement, and even stops and looks round the assembly, then ascends [the platform] in the sedate manner of a preacher ascending a mosque-pulpit. As he takes his seat, the drums, trumpets, and bugles are sounded. Three slaves go at a run to summon the sovereign's deputy and the military commanders, who enter and sit down . . . .

The blacks are of all people the most submissive to their king and the most abject in their behavior before him. They swear by his name, saying *Mansa Suleiman ki* [by Mansa Suleiman's law]. If he summons any of them while he is holding an audience in his pavilion, the person summoned takes off his clothes and puts on worn garments, removes his turban and dons a dirty skullcap and enters with his garments and trousers raised knee-high. He goes forward in an attitude of humility and dejection, and knocks the ground hard with his elbows, then stands with bowed head and bent back listening to what he says. If anyone addresses the king and receives a reply from him, he uncovers his back and throws dust over his head and back, for all the world like a bather splashing himself with water. I used to wonder how it was that they did not blind themselves.

How can the kind and cruel sides of Sultan Muhammad be reconciled? What role would Islam have played in his generosity? Could cruelty have brought any benefits to the ruler of a conquest state?

How did Mansa Suleiman's ritual appearances serve to enhance his majesty? What attitudes toward the ruler do his subjects' actions suggest? How different were the ruling styles of Muhammad and Suleiman?

Source: The first excerpt is from Henry M. Elliot, *The History of India as Told by Its Own Historians* (London: Trübner and Co., 1869-1871) 3: 609–614. The second excerpt is adapted from H. A. R. Gibb, ed., *Selections from the Travels of Ibn Battuta in Asia and Africa* (London: Cambridge University Press, 1929), pp. 326–327.

Islam in about 1085. At its peak about 1250, Kanem had absorbed the state of Bornu south and west of Lake Chad and gained control of important trade routes crossing the Sahara. As Kanem-Bornu's armies conquered new territories in the late fifteenth century, they also spread the rule of Islam.

The Delhi Sultanate in India

The arrival of Islam in India was in violent contrast to its peaceful penetration of West Africa. Having long ago lost the defensive unity of the Gupta Empire (see Chapter 7), the divided states of northwest India were subject to raids by Afghan warlords from the early eleventh century. Motivated jointly by a wish to spread their Islamic faith and by a desire for plunder, the raiders looted Hindu temples of their gold and jewels, kidnapped women for their harems, and slew Hindu defenders by the thousands. In the last decades of the twelfth century a new Turkish dynasty armed with powerful crossbows, which warriors could fire from the backs of their galloping horses thanks to the use of iron stirrups, mounted a furious assault that succeeded in capturing the important northern Indian cities of Lahore and Delhi. One partisan Muslim chronicler recorded, "The city [Delhi] and its vicinity was freed from idols and idol-worship, and in the sanctuaries of the images of the [Hindu] Gods, mosques were raised by the worshippers of one God."[2] The invaders' strength was bolstered by a ready supply of Turkish adventurers from Central Asia eager to follow individual leaders and by the unifying force of their common religious faith. Although the Indians fought back bravely, centuries of security from outside invasion and a lack of interest in the rising military aggressiveness of the peoples around them had left them unprepared to present an effective united front.

Between 1206 and 1236 the Muslim invaders extended their rule over the Hindu princes and chiefs in much of northern India. Sultan Iltutmish (r. 1211–1236) consolidated the conquest of northern India in a series of military expeditions that made his empire the largest state in India (see Map 15.3). He also secured official recognition of the Delhi Sultanate as a Muslim state by the caliph of Baghdad. Although the looting and destruction of temples, enslavement, and massacres continued, especially on the frontiers of the empire, the incorporation of north India into the Islamic world marked the beginning of the Muslim invaders' transformation from brutal conquerors to somewhat more benign rulers. Hindus, whose land came under the control of foreign Muslim military officials, were accorded special measures of protection, which freed them from persecution in return for the payment of a special tax. Yet Hindus never forgot the intolerance and destruction of their first contacts with the invaders.

To the astonishment of his ministers, Iltutmish passed over his weak and pleasure-seeking sons and designated as his heir his beloved and talented daughter Raziya. When they questioned the unprecedented idea of a woman ruling a Muslim state, he said, "My sons are devoted to the pleasures of youth: no one of them is qualified to be king. . . . there is no one more competent to guide the State than my daughter." In fact, his wish was not immediately carried out after his death, but after seven months of rule by the generous but inept Firoz—whose great delight was riding his elephant through the bazaar, showering the crowds with coins—the ministers relented and put Raziya on the throne. A chronicler of the time, who knew her, explained why the reign of this able ruler lasted less than four years (r. 1236–1240):

> Sultan Raziya was a great monarch. She was wise, just, and generous, a benefactor to her kingdom, a dispenser of justice, the protector of her subjects, and the leader of her armies. She was endowed with all the qualities befitting a king, but that she was not born of the right sex, and so in the estimation of men all these virtues were worthless. May God have mercy upon her![3]

Doing her best to prove herself a proper king, Raziya dressed like a man and rode at the head of her troops atop an elephant. Nothing, however, could overcome the prejudices of the Turkish chiefs against a woman ruler. In the end, she was imprisoned and later killed by a robber while trying to escape.

After a half-century of stagnation and rebel-

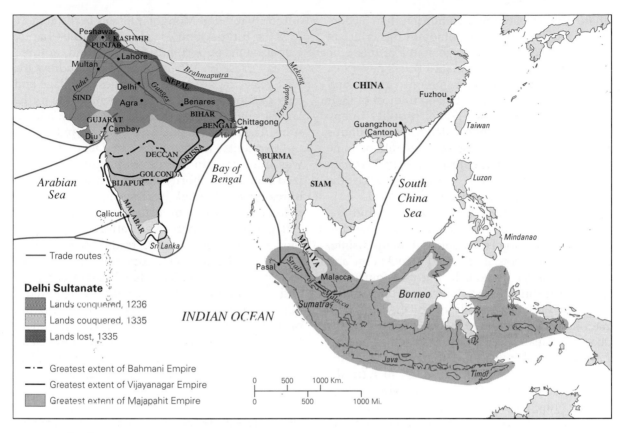

Map 15.3 South and Southeast Asia, 1200–1500 The rise of new empires and the expansion of maritime trade reshaped the lives of many tropical Asians.

lion, the ruthless but efficient policies of Sultan Ala-ud-din Khalji (r. 1296–1316) increased his control over the empire's outlying provinces. Successful frontier raids and high taxes kept his treasury full, wage and price controls in Delhi kept down the cost of maintaining a large army, and a network of spies stifled intrigue. When a Mongol threat from the northeast eased, Ala-ud-din's forces extended the sultanate's southern flank, seizing the rich trading state of Gujarat in 1298. Then troops drove into South India and briefly held the southern tip of the Indian peninsula.

At the time of Ibn Battuta's visit, Delhi's ruler was Sultan Muhammad ibn Tughluq (1325–1351), who received his visitor at his palace's celebrated Hall of a Thousand Pillars. The world traveler praised the sultan's piety and generosity—traditional Muslim virtues—but also recounted his cruelties (see Voices & Visions: Personal Styles of

Rule in India and Mali). In keeping with these complexities, the sultan resumed a policy of aggressive expansion against independent Indian states that enlarged the sultanate to its greatest extent. He balanced that policy with one of religious toleration intended to win the loyalty of Hindus and other non-Muslims. He even attended Hindu religious festivals. However, his successor Firuz Shah (r. 1351–1388) alienated powerful Hindus by taxing the Brahmins, preferring to cultivate good relations with the Muslim elite. Muslim chroniclers praised him for constructing forty mosques, thirty colleges, and a hundred hospitals.

A small minority in a giant land, the Turkish rulers relied on terror to keep their subjects submissive, on harsh military reprisals to put down rebellion, and on pillage and high taxes to sustain the ruling elite in luxury and power. Even under its most enlightened rulers, the Delhi Sultanate was probably more a burden than a benefit to most of its subjects. Although this criticism could be made of most large states of this time (including Mali), the sultanate's rulers never lost the disadvantage of their foreign origins and their membership in a faith alien to most of their subjects. Over time their initial hostility to any Hindu participation moderated as some Hindus were incorporated into the administration. Some members of the ruling elite also married women from prominent Hindu families, though the brides had to become Muslims.

Personal and religious rivalries within the Muslim elite, as well as the discontent of the Hindus, threatened the Delhi Sultanate with disintegration whenever it showed weakness and finally hastened its end. In the mid-fourteenth century Muslim nobles challenged the sultan's dominion and successfully established the Bahmani kingdom (1347–1482), which controlled the Deccan Plateau. To defend themselves against the southward push of Bahmani armies, the Hindu states of South India united to form the Vijayanagar Empire (1336–1565), which at its height controlled the rich trading ports on both coasts of south India and held Ceylon as a tributary state.

The conflict between Vijayanagar and the Bahmani was as much a struggle among different elites as it was a conflict between Muslims and Hindus, since both states pursued policies that turned a blind eye to religious differences when doing so favored their interests. Bahmani rulers sought to balance devotion to Muslim domination and the practical importance of incorporating the leaders of the majority Hindu population into the government, marrying Hindu wives and appointing Brahmins to high offices. Vijayanagar rulers hired Muslim cavalry specialists and archers to strengthen their military forces and formed an alliance with the Muslim-ruled state of Gujarat.

By 1351, when all of South India was independent, much of north India was also in rebellion. In the northeast, Bengal successfully broke away from Delhi's rule in 1338, becoming a center of the mystical Sufi tradition of Islam (see Chapter 10). In the west Gujarat regained its independence by 1390. The weakening of Delhi's central authority revived Mongol interests in the area. In 1398 the Turko-Mongol leader Timur (see Chapter 13) seized the opportunity to invade and captured the city of Delhi. When his armies withdrew the next year, dragging vast quantities of pillage and tens of thousands of captives behind them, the largest city in southern Asia lay empty and in ruins. The Delhi Sultanate never recovered.

Despite its shortcomings, the Delhi Sultanate was important in the development of centralized political authority in India. It established a bureaucracy headed by the sultan, who was aided by the prime minister (*wazir*) and provincial governors. There were efforts to improve food production, promote trade and economic growth, and establish a common currency. Despite the many conflicts that Muslim conquest and rule provoked, Islam gradually acquired a permanent place in South Asia. Yet the mixture of indigenous political traditions with these Islamic practices served to distinguish the Delhi Sultanate, like Mali, from the states in the Middle East, where Islam had first flourished.

INDIAN OCEAN TRADE

Food producers sustained the region's life; sultans and kings directed its political affairs. Merchants were a third force uniting the tropics. Their maritime network stretched across the Indian Ocean from the Islamic heartlands of Iran and Arabia to Southeast Asia and the East Indies. Connecting routes extended to Europe, Africa, and China. The world's richest maritime trading network at this time, the Indian Ocean routes also facilitated the spread of Islam.

Monsoon Mariners

Between 1200 and 1500 the volume of trade in the Indian Ocean increased, stimulated by the prosperity of Islamic and Mongol empires in Asia, of Latin Europe, as well as of Africa and the East Indies. There was greater demand for luxuries for the wealthy: precious metals and jewels, rare spices, fine textiles, and other manufactures. The construction of much larger ships in these centuries also made it profitable to ship bulk cargoes of ordinary cotton textiles, pepper, food grains (rice, wheat, barley), timber, horses, and other goods. When the collapse of the Mongol Empire in the fourteenth century disrupted the overland trade routes across Central Asia, the Indian Ocean routes assumed greater strategic importance in tying the peoples of Eurasia and Africa together.

Although some goods were transported from one end of this trading network to the other, few ships or crews made a complete circuit. Instead the trade was divided between the two sections of the Indian Ocean (the Arabian Sea in the west and the Bay of Bengal in the east) and among the three mainlands that bordered them (the Middle East, India, and the East Indies). This division was also true of the sailing vessels used in these two seas.

The characteristic cargo and passenger ship of the Arabian Sea was the *dhow* (see Environment & Technology: The Indian Ocean Dhow). Large numbers of these ships, which grew from an average capacity of 100 tons in 1200 to 400 tons in 1500, were constructed in Malabar coastal ports of southwestern India in this period. On a typical expedition a dhow might sail west from India to Arabia and Africa on the northeast monsoon winds (December to March) and return on the southwest monsoons (April to August). Small dhows kept the coast in sight. Relying on the stars to guide them, skilled pilots steered large vessels by the quicker route straight across the water. A large dhow could sail from the Red Sea to mainland Southeast Asia in from two to four months with stopovers in south India, Ceylon, and Sumatra. From 1200 onward, however, cargoes and passengers from dhows arriving on the Malabar Coast were more likely to be transferred to *junks*, which dominated the eastern half of the Indian Ocean and the South China Sea.

The largest, most technologically advanced, and most seaworthy vessels of this time, junks had been developed in China and spread with Chinese influence. They were built from heavy spruce or fir planks held together with enormous nails. The space below the deck was divided into watertight compartments to minimize flooding in case of damage to the hull of the ship. According to Ibn Battuta, the largest junks had twelve sails made of bamboo and carried a crew of a thousand men, of whom 400 were soldiers. A large junk might have up to a hundred passenger cabins and could carry a cargo of over 1,000 tons. Chinese junks dominated China's foreign shipping to the East Indies and India, but not all of the junks that plied these waters were under Chinese control. During the fifteenth century, vessels of this type were built in Bengal and Malacca and were sailed by crews from South and Southeast Asia.

The trade of the Indian Ocean was decentralized and cooperative. Commercial interests, not political authorities, united the several distinct regions that participated in it (see Map 15.4). The Swahili Coast supplied gold from inland areas of eastern Africa. Ports around the Arabian Peninsula supplied horses and goods from the northern parts of the Middle East, the Mediterranean, and eastern Europe. In the center of the Indian Ocean trade, merchants in the cities of coastal India received goods from east and west, sold some locally, passed others along, and added vast quantities of Indian goods to the trade. The Strait of Malacca, between the eastern end of the Indian Ocean and the South China Sea, was the meeting point of trade from the East Indies, mainland Southeast Asia, China, and the Indian Ocean. In each region certain ports functioned as giant emporia for the trade, consolidating goods from smaller ports and inland areas for transport across the seas. The operation of this complex trading system can best be understood by looking at some of these regions and their emporia in greater detail.

Africa: The Swahili Coast and Zimbabwe

Trade expanded steadily along the East African coast from about 1250, giving rise to between thirty and forty separate city-states by 1500. Archaeological excavations reveal that after 1200 many mud and thatch African fishing villages were rebuilt with new masonry buildings, some-

The Indian Ocean Dhow

The sailing vessels that crossed the Indian Ocean shared the diversity of that trading area. The name by which we know them, *dhow*, comes from the Swahili language of the East African coast. The planks of teak from which their hulls were constructed were hewn from the tropical forests of south India and Southeast Asia. Their pilots, who navigated by stars at night, used an ancient technique that Arabs had used to find their way across the desert. Some pilots used a magnetic compass, which had originated in China.

Dhows came in various sizes and designs, but they all had two distinctive features in common. The first was the construction of their hulls. They consisted of planks that were sewn together, not nailed. Cord made of fiber from the husk of coconuts or other materials was passed through rows of holes drilled in the planks. Because cord is weaker than nails, outsiders considered this shipbuilding technique strange. Marco Polo fancifully suggested that it indicated sailors' fear that large ocean magnets would pull any nails out of their ships. The most likely explanations are that pliant sewn hulls were less likely than rigid nailed hulls to be damaged by groundings on coral reefs and were cheaper to build.

The second distinctive feature of dhows was their triangular (lateen) sails made of palm leaves or cotton. The sails were suspended from tall masts and could be turned to catch the wind.

The sewn hull and lateen sails were technologies developed centuries earlier, but there were two innovations in this period. First, a rudder positioned at the stern (rear end) of the ship replaced the large side oar that had formerly controlled steering. Second, shipbuilders increased the size of dhows to accommodate bulkier cargoes.

Modern reconstruction of a dhow (National Maritime Museum, London)

times three or four stories high. Archaeology also reveals the growing presence of imported glass beads, Chinese porcelain, and other exotic goods. This narrow strip of coast and islands, some 1,500 miles (2,400 kilometers) long, shared a common culture and language, African in grammar and vocabulary but enriched with many Arabic terms. In time it became known as *Swahili*, from the Arabic name *sawahil al-sudan*, meaning "the shores of the blacks."

Until shortly before Ibn Battuta's visit in 1331 the northern city of Mogadishu had been the Swahili Coast's most important commercial center, but in the fourteenth century the southern city of Kilwa surpassed it in importance. After visiting Kilwa, Ibn Battuta declared it "one of the most beautiful and well-constructed towns in the world." He noted that its dark-skinned inhabi-

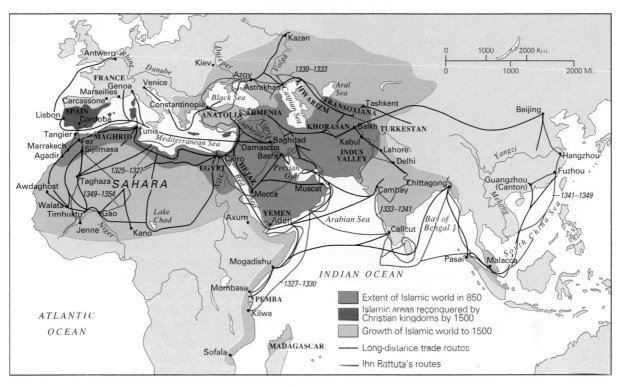

Map 15.4   Arteries of Trade and Travel in the Islamic World to 1500   Ibn Battuta's journeys across the vast expanse of Africa and Asia made use of land and sea routes, along which Muslim traders and the Islamic faith had long traveled.

tants were devout and pious Muslims, and he took special pains to praise their ruler as a man rich in the traditional Muslim virtues of humility and generosity.

Oral traditions associate the Swahili Coast's commercial expansion with the arrival of Arab and Iranian merchants, but what had attracted them? In Kilwa's case the answer is gold. By the late fifteenth century the city was exporting a ton of gold a year. It is also clear that the gold came from mines worked by Africans much farther south and inland from the coast. Much of it came from or passed through a powerful state on the plateau south of the Zambezi River, whose capital city is known as Great Zimbabwe. At its peak in about 1400, the city, which occupied 193 acres (78 hectares) may have had 18,000 inhabitants, the wealthiest of whom lived in dwellings made

of stone.

The stone ruins of Great Zimbabwe are one of the most famous historical sites in sub-Saharan Africa. The largest structure is a walled enclosure the size and shape of a large football stadium, carefully constructed of drystone masonry up to 17 feet (5 meters) thick and 32 feet (10 meters) high. Inside it were many buildings, including a large conical stone tower. Local African craftsmen built these stone structures between about 1250 and 1450 to serve as their king's court.

Like Mali, the Great Zimbabwe state rested on a mixed farming and cattle-herding economy, but its wealth depended on its role in long-distance trade. It first prospered in a regional trade based on copper ingots from the upper Zambezi Valley, salt, and local manufactures. The great expansion in the export of gold into the

Conical tower, Great Zimbabwe This graceful stone structure, situated inside the high-walled royal enclosure at Great Zimbabwe, was not used as a look out tower. Archaeologists believe the tower was a symbol of the African ruler's power, perhaps representing on a grand scale the clay granaries in which local chiefs stored the grain they received in tribute from their people. (Robert Aberman/Barbara Heller/Art Resource NY)

Indian Ocean in the fourteenth and fifteenth centuries brought Zimbabwe to the peak of its political and economic power. However, historians suspect that the city's residents depleted nearby forests for firewood while their cattle overgrazed surrounding grasslands. The result was an ecological crisis that hastened the empire's decline in the fifteenth century.

Arabia: Aden and the Red Sea

The city of Aden brought a double benefit to the Indian Ocean trade. Most of Arabia is desert, but monsoon winds brought Aden enough rainfall to supply drinking water to a large population and to grow grain for export. In addition, Aden's location (see Map 15.2) made it a convenient stopover for trade with India, the Persian Gulf, East Africa, and Egypt. Aden's merchants sorted out the goods from one place and sent them on to another: cotton cloths and beads from India, spices from the East Indies, horses from Arabia and Ethiopia, pearls from the Red Sea, luxurious manufactures from Cairo, slaves, gold, and ivory from Ethiopia. There were also grain, opium, and dyes from Aden's own hinterland.

After leaving Mecca, Ibn Battuta sailed to Aden in 1331 on his journey through the Red Sea, probably wedged in among bales of trade goods. He commented at length on the great wealth of Aden's leading merchants, telling a story about the slave of one merchant who paid the fabulous sum of 400 dinars for a ram in order to keep the slave of another merchant from buying it. Instead of punishing him for this extravagance, the master freed his slave as a reward for outdoing his rival. Ninety years later a Chinese Muslim visitor, Ma Huan, found "the country . . . rich, and the people numerous," with stone residences several stories high.

Common commercial interests generally promoted good relations among the different religions and cultures of this region. For example, in the mid-thirteenth century a wealthy Jew from Aden named Yosef settled in Christian Ethiopia, where he acted as an adviser. South Arabia had been trading with neighboring parts of Africa since before the times of King Solomon of Israel. The dynasty that ruled Ethiopia after 1270 claimed descent from Solomon and from the South Arabian princess Sheba. Solomonic Ethiopia's consolidation was associated with a great increase in trade through the Red Sea port of Zeila, including slaves, amber, and animal pelts, which went to Aden and on to other destinations.

Nevertheless, some religious and political conflict occurred. In the fourteenth century the

Sunni Muslim king of Yemen sent materials for the building of a large mosque in Zeila, but the local Somalis (who were Shiite Muslims) threw the stones into the sea. The result was a year-long embargo of Zeila ships in Aden. In the late fifteenth century Ethiopia's territorial expansion and efforts to increase control over the trade provoked conflicts with Muslims who ruled the coastal states of the Red Sea.

India: Gujarat and the Malabar Coast

The state of Gujarat in western India prospered as its ports shared in the expanding trade of the Arabian Sea and the rise of the Delhi Sultanate. Blessed with a rich agricultural hinterland and a long coastline, Gujarat attracted new trade after the Mongol capture of Baghdad in 1258 disrupted the northern land routes. Gujarat's forcible incorporation into the Delhi Sultanate in 1298 had mixed results. The state suffered from the violence of the initial conquest and from subsequent military crackdowns, but it also prospered from increased trade with Delhi's wealthy ruling class. Independent again after 1390, the Muslim rulers of Gujarat extended their control over neighboring Hindu states and regained their preeminent position in the Indian Ocean trade.

Much of the wealth of the state derived from its export of cotton textiles and indigo to the Middle East and Europe, largely in return for gold and silver. Gujaratis also dominated the trade from India to the Swahili Coast, selling cottons, carnelian beads, and foodstuffs in exchange for ebony, slaves, ivory, and gold. During the fifteenth century traders expanded their trade from Gujarat eastward to the Strait of Malacca. These Gujarati merchants helped spread the Islamic faith among East Indian traders, some of whom even imported specially carved gravestones from Gujarat.

Unlike Kilwa and Aden, Gujarat was important for its manufactures as well as its commerce. According to the thirteenth-century Venetian traveler Marco Polo, Gujarat's leatherworkers dressed enough skins in a year to fill several ships to Arabia and other places and also made beautiful sleeping mats for export to the Middle East "in red and blue leather, exquisitely inlaid with figures of birds and beasts, and skilfully embroidered with gold and silver wire," as well as leather cushions embroidered in gold. Later observers considered the Gujarati city of Cambay the equal of cities in Flanders and northern Italy (see Chapter 16) in the size, skill, and diversity of its textile industries. Gujarat's cotton, linen, and silk cloths, as well as its carpets and quilts, found a large market in Europe, Africa, the Middle East, and the East Indies. Cambay was also famous for its polished gemstones, gold jewelry, carved ivory, stone beads, and both natural and artificial pearls. At the height of its prosperity in the fifteenth century, this substantial city's well-laid-out streets and open places were lined with fine stone houses with tiled roofs. Although most of Gujarat's overseas trade was in the hands of its Muslim residents, its Hindu merchant caste profited so much from related commercial activities that their wealth and luxurious lives were the envy of other Indians.

Gujarat's importance in trade and manufacturing was duplicated farther south in the cities of the Malabar Coast. Calicut and other coastal cities prospered from their commerce in locally made cotton textiles and locally grown grains and spices, and as clearing-houses for the long-distance trade of the Indian Ocean. The Malabar Coast was united under a loose federation of its Hindu rulers, presided over by the Zamorin (ruler) of Calicut. As in eastern Africa and Arabia, rulers were generally tolerant of other religious and ethnic groups who were important to commercial profits. Most trading activity lay in the hands of Muslims, many originally from Iran and Arabia, who intermarried with local Indian Muslims. Jewish merchants also operated from Malabar's trading cities.

Southeast Asia: The Rise of Malacca

At the eastern end of the Indian Ocean, the principal passage into the South China Sea was through the Strait of Malacca between the Malay Peninsula and the island of Sumatra. As trade increased in the fourteenth and fifteenth centuries, this commercial choke point became the object of considerable political activity. The mainland kingdom of Siam gained control of most of the upper Malay Peninsula, while the Java-based kingdom of Majapahit extended its dominion over the lower Malay Peninsula and much of Sumatra. Majapahit, however, was not strong enough to suppress a nest of Chinese pirates who had gained control of the Sumatran city of Palembang and preyed on ships sailing through the strait. In 1407 a fleet sent by the Chinese government smashed the pirates' power and took their chief back to China for trial.

Weakened by internal struggles, Majapahit was unable to take advantage of China's intervention. The chief beneficiary of the safer commerce was the newer port of Malacca (or Melaka), which dominated the narrowest part of the strait. Under the leadership of a prince from Palembang, Malacca had quickly grown from an obscure fishing village into an important port by means of a series of astute alliances. Nominally subject to the king of Siam, Malacca also secured a tributary relationship with China that was officially conferred by the visit of the imperial fleet in 1407. The conversion of an early ruler from Hinduism to Islam helped promote trade with the Gujarati and other Muslim merchants who dominated so much of the Indian Ocean commerce. Merchants also appreciated Malacca's ability to offer them security and its absence of port duties except for presents to the ruler.

Besides serving as the meeting point for traders from India and China, Malacca also served as an emporium for Southeast Asian trade: rubies and musk from Burma, tin from Malaya, gold from Sumatra, as well as cloves and nutmeg from the Moluccas (or Spice Islands) to the east. Shortly after 1500, when Malacca was at its height, one resident counted eighty-four languages spoken among the merchants gathered there, who came from as far away as Turkey, Ethiopia, and the Swahili Coast. Four officials administered the large foreign merchant communities: one official for the very numerous Gujaratis, one for other Indians and Burmese, one for Southeast Asians, and one for the Chinese and Japanese. Malacca's wealth and its cosmopolitan residents set the standard for luxury in Malaya for centuries to come.

SOCIAL AND CULTURAL CHANGE

State growth, commercial expansion, and the spread of Islam between 1200 and 1500 led to many changes in the social and cultural life of tropical peoples. The political and commercial elites at the top of society grew in size and power. To serve their needs, the number of slaves increased considerably. There were also changes in lives of women in different social classes. The spread of Islamic practices and beliefs in many parts of the African and Asian tropics was a major aspect of social and cultural change, evident from the fact that the words *Sahara, Sudan, Swahili,* and *monsoon* are all Arabic in origin. Even so, traditional religious and social customs remained important.

Architecture, Learning, and Religion

As in other periods of history, social and cultural changes were more obvious in the cities than in rural areas. Some urban change was physical. As Ibn Battuta and other travelers observed, the merchants and ruling elites spent some of their wealth building new mansions, palaces, and places of worship. In architecture, as well as in education and religious practice, the spread of Islam was a major force for change in many tropical societies.

Most of the buildings that survive from this period are places of worship that exhibit fascinating blends of older traditions and new influences. Muslims in the western Sudan produced striking renditions of Middle Eastern mosque designs in local building materials of sun-baked clay and wood; Swahili cities built mosques of local coral stone. In India mosques were often influenced by the styles of existing temple architecture and even incorporated elements of older structures. Gujarati architecture of this period exhibited the finest blend of Hindu and Muslim styles. The congregational mosque at Cambay, built in 1325 with courtyard, cloisters, and porches typical of Islamic mosques, was assembled primarily out of pillars, porches, and arches taken from sacked Hindu and Jain temples of earlier generations. The congregational mosque erected at the Gujarati capital of Ahmadabad in 1423 was the culmination of a mature Hindu-Muslim architecture. It had an open courtyard typical of mosques everywhere, but the surrounding verandahs incorporated many typical Gujarati details and architectural conventions.

In some ways even more striking than these Islamic architectural amalgams were the Christian churches of King Lalibela of Ethiopia, constructed during the first third of the thirteenth century. As part of his new capital, Lalibela directed Ethiopian sculptors to carve eleven churches out of solid rock, each commemorating a sacred Christian site in Jerusalem. These unique structures carried on an old Ethiopian tradition of rock sculpture, though on a far grander scale.

Mosques were centers of education as well as of prayer. Muslims promoted literacy among their sons (and sometimes their daughters) so that they could read the religion's classic texts. Ibn Battuta reported seeing several boys in Mali who had been placed in chains until they completed memorizing passages of the Quran. In sub-Saharan Africa the spread of Islam was associated with the spread of literacy, which had previously been confined largely to Christian

Church of Saint George, Ethiopia   King Lalibela, who ruled the Christian kingdom of Ethiopia between about 1180 and 1220, had a series of churches carved out of solid volcanic rock to adorn his kingdom's new capital (also named Lalibela). The church of Saint George, excavated to a depth of 40 feet (13 meters) and hollowed out inside, has the shape of a Greek cross. (Robert Harding Picture Library)

Qutb Minar, India   A ruler of the Delhi Sultanate built this unusually tall minaret and mosque near Delhi in the early thirteenth century to display the power of Islam. Five times a day the muezzin climbed the 240-foot (73-meter) tower of red sandstone and white marble to call Muslims to prayer. (Jean Nou)

tion of written texts in India, even though they still had to be copied by hand.

Although most of the education was concerned with basic literacy and the recitation of the Quran, advanced Muslim scholars studied Islamic law, theology, and administration, as well as classical Greek works of mathematics, medicine, and science. By the sixteenth century the West African city of Timbuktu had over 150 Quranic schools, and advanced classes were held in the mosques and homes of the leading clerics. So great was the demand that books were the most profitable item to bring from North Africa to Timbuktu. At his death in 1536 one West African scholar, al-Hajj Ahmed of Timbuktu, possessed some 700 volumes, an unusually large library for that time. In the East Indies, Malacca became a center of Islamic learning from where scholars spread Islam throughout the region. Other important centers of learning developed in Muslim India, particularly in Delhi, the capital.

As the changes in architecture and education suggest, the spread of Islam as a religion was a major theme of the period. Even where Islam entered as the result of conquest, as in India, conversions were rarely forced. Example and persuasion seem to have been far more important to the spread of Islam. The communities of Muslim merchants throughout the region, along with the large number of Muslim warriors and administrators who moved into India during these centuries, attracted interest in their religion. Many Muslims were active missionaries for their faith and worked hard to persuade others of its superiority.

Muslim domination of long-distance trade and markets was particularly important in fostering the adoption of Islam. Many commercial transactions took place between people of different religions, but trust was easier among individuals who shared the common code of morality and law that Islam provided. For this reason many local merchants were attracted to Islam. From the major trading centers along the Swahili Coast, in the Sudan, in coastal India, and in the East Indies, Islam's influence spread along regional trade routes.

Another important way in which Islam spread was through marriage. Most of the foreign Muslims who settled in tropical Africa and Asia were

Ethiopia. Initially literacy was in Arabic, but in time Arabic characters were used to write local languages.

India already had a long literate heritage, so the impact of Islam on literacy there was less dramatic. Arabic spread among Indian scholars along with Persian (the language of Iran), which was considered more refined. Many new works of prose and poetry were written in Urdu, a Persian-influenced literary form of Hindi written in Arabic characters. Muslims also introduced papermaking in India, a second-century Chinese invention that had spread through the Indian Ocean trade routes. Paper facilitated the distribu-

single men. They often married local women, whom they required to be (or become) Muslims and to raise their children in the Islamic faith. Since Islam permitted a man to have up to four legal wives, as well as concubines, some wealthy men had dozens of children. In such large Muslim households the many servants, both free and enslaved, were also required by large elite Muslim households to be Muslims. Although such conversions were not fully voluntary, individuals could still find personal fulfillment in the Islamic faith.

In parts of southern Asia the upheavals of this period also promoted the spread of Islam. In India, Islamic invasions virtually destroyed the last strongholds of a long declining Buddhism. In 1196 the great Buddhist center of study at Nalanda in Bihar was overrun, its manuscripts were burned, and thousands of its monks were killed or driven into exile in Nepal and Tibet. Buddhism became a minor faith in the land of its birth (see Chapter 8), while Islam, swelled by substantial immigration, emerged as India's second most important religion. Hinduism remained India's dominant faith in 1500, but in most of maritime Southeast Asia the combined impact of Mongol invasion and the peaceful expansion of Muslim merchants led to the displacement of Hinduism by Islam.

Outside the cities, some peoples were attracted to Islam in this period. The seed of Islamic belief was planted among the pastoral Fulani of West Africa and Somali of northeastern Africa, as well as among pastoralists in northwest India. Low-caste rural Bengalis also began to adopt Islam, perhaps because they saw more hope in the universalism of Islam than in the fixed inequalities of the Hindu hierarchy. Yet the spread of Islam was not a simple process by which one set of beliefs was replaced by new ones. Islam too was changed by the cultures of the regions it penetrated, developing African, Indian, and Indonesian varieties.

Social and Gender Distinctions

The political, commercial, and religious changes of these centuries significantly affected the class structure and the status of at least some women. The gap widened between the elites and the masses. It is not clear that the poor became poorer—the 50 percent of the harvest that peasants in India paid in tax to the Delhi Sultanate may have been no more than what they formerly had paid to local lords—but the rich surely became richer and more numerous as a result of conquests and commerce.

The rising prosperity of the elites was accompanied by a growth in slavery. Many slaves were the product of wars of expansion by the powerful new states. The campaigns of conquest and pillage in India, according to Islamic sources, reduced Hindu "infidels" to slavery by the hundreds of thousands. The courts of the ruling elites of Delhi overflowed with slaves. Sultan Ala ud-Din owned 50,000; Sultan Firuz Shah had 180,000, including 12,000 skilled artisans. Sultan Tughluq sent 100 male slaves and 100 female slaves as a gift to the emperor of China in return for a similar gift. His successor prohibited any more exports of slaves, perhaps because of reduced supplies in the smaller empire.

In Africa, the growth of powerful states had also led to an increase in domestic slavery, as well as to a rising export trade in slaves. As Ibn Battuta reported, Mali and Bornu sent slaves across the Sahara to North Africa, including beautiful maidens and eunuchs (castrated males). The expanding Ethiopian Empire regularly sent captives for sale to Aden traders at Zeila. According to modern estimates, about 2.5 million enslaved Africans were sent across the Sahara and the Red Sea between 1200 and 1500. Some slaves were also shipped from the Swahili Coast to India, where Africans played conspicuous roles in the navies, armies, and administrations of some Indian states, especially in the fifteenth century. A few African slaves even found their way to China, where a Chinese source dating from about 1225 says rich families preferred gatekeepers whose bodies were "black as lacquer."

The status of slaves varied enormously, depending on their skill and sex. Relatively few in this period were used as field hands since "free" labor was so abundant and cheap. Most slaves were trained for special purposes. In some places, skilled trades and military service were dominated by hereditary castes of slaves, some of whom were rich and powerful. Indeed, the earliest rulers of the Delhi Sultanate were military slaves, though their status had long ceased to be a disadvantage. A slave general in the western Sudan named Askia Muhammad seized control of the Songhai Empire (Mali's successor) in 1493. Less fortunate were slaves who did hard menial work, such as those men and women who mined copper in Mali.

In all wealthy households there was a tremendous demand for slaves to be employed as servants. Ibn Battuta observed large numbers at the sultan of Mali's palace. Some servants were males, including the eunuchs who guarded the harems of wealthy Muslims, but most household slaves were female. Female slaves were also in great demand as entertainers and concubines. Having a concubine from every part of the world was a rich man's ambition in some Muslim circles. One of Firuz's nobles was said to have two thousand harem slaves, including women from Turkey and China.

Sultan Ala ud-Din's campaigns against Gujarat at the end of the thirteenth century yielded a booty of twenty thousand maidens in addition to innumerable younger children of both sexes. The supply of captives became so great that the lowest grade of horse sold for five times as much as an ordinary female destined for service, although beautiful young virgins destined for the harems of powerful nobles commanded far higher prices. Some decades later when Ibn Battuta was given ten girls captured from among the "infidels," he commented: "Female captives [in Delhi] are very cheap because they are dirty and do not know civilized ways. Even the educated ones are cheap." It would seem fairer to say that such slaves were cheap because the large numbers offered for sale had made them so.

How much the status of tropical women—whether slave or free—changed during this period is a subject needing more study. No one has yet offered a general opinion about Africa. Based on a reading of contemporary Hindu legal digests and commentaries (*Smiriti*), some authors speculate that the position of Hindu women may have improved somewhat compared to earlier periods, but in the absence of detailed information it is impossible to be sure. Hindu women continued to suffer from social and religious disabilities, but some restrictions on their lives may

have been relaxed—or, at the very least, not expanded—during these centuries. For example, the ancient practice of *sati*—that is, of an upper-caste widow throwing herself on her husband's funeral pyre—remained a meritorious act strongly approved by social custom. But Ibn Battuta leaves no doubt that, in his observation at least, sati was strictly optional. Since the *Smiriti* devote considerable attention to the rights of widows without sons to inherit their husbands' estates, one may conclude that sati was exceptional.

It remained the custom for Indian girls to be given in marriage before the age of puberty, although the consummation of the marriage was not to take place until the young woman was ready. Wives were expected to observe far stricter rules of fidelity and chastity than were their husbands and could be abandoned for many serious breaches. But women often were punished by lighter penalties than men for offenses against law and custom.

A female's status was largely determined by the status of her male master—father, husband, or owner. Women usually were not permitted to play the kind of active roles in commerce, administration, or religion that would have given them scope for personal achievements. Even so, women possessed considerable skills within those areas of activity that social norms allotted to them.

Besides child rearing, one of the most widespread female skills was food preparation. So far historians have paid little attention to the development of culinary skills, but preparing meals that were healthful and tasty required much training and practice, especially given the limited range of foods available in most places. One kitchen skill that has received greater attention is brewing, perhaps because it was the men who were the principal consumers. In many parts of Africa women commonly made beer from grains or bananas. These mildly alcoholic beverages, taken in moderation, were a nutritious source of vitamins and minerals. Socially they were an important part of male rituals of hospitality and relaxation that promoted social harmony.

Women's activities were not confined to the hearth, however. Throughout tropical Africa and Asia women did much of the farm work. They

Indian woman spinning, ca. 1500 This drawing of a Muslim woman by an Indian artist shows the influence of Persian styles. The female task of spinning cotton fiber into thread was made much easier by the spinning wheel, which the Muslim invaders introduced. The threads were woven into the cotton textiles for which India was celebrated. (British Library)

also toted home heavy loads of food, firewood, and water for cooking balanced on their heads. Other common female activities included making clay pots for cooking and storage and making clothing. In India the spinning wheel, introduced by the Muslim invaders, greatly reduced the cost of making yarn for weaving. Spinning was a woman's activity done in the home; the weavers were generally men. Marketing was a common activity among women, especially in West Africa, where they sold their agricultural surplus, pottery, and other craftwork.

It is difficult to judge how the spread of Islam affected the status of women. Women of some social classes found their status improved by becoming part of a Muslim household. The rare exception, such as Sultan Raziya, might even command supreme authority. Of course, many other women were incorporated into Muslim households as servants, concubines, and slaves.

Yet not all places that adopted Islam accepted all the social customs of the Arab world. In Mali's capital Ibn Battuta was appalled that Muslim women both free and slave did not completely cover their bodies and veil their faces when appearing in public. He considered their nakedness an offense to women's (and men's) modesty. In another part of Mali he berated a Muslim merchant from Morocco for permitting his wife to sit on a couch and chat with a male friend of hers. The husband replied, "The association of women with men is agreeable to us and part of good manners, to which no suspicion attaches." Ibn Battuta's shock at this "laxity" and his refusal to

ever visit the merchant again reveal the patriarchal precepts that were dear to most elite Muslims. So does the fate of Sultan Raziya of Delhi.

many ways more profound and disruptive. The
changes there would have great implications for
tropical peoples after 1500.

CONCLUSION

With nearly 40 percent of the world's population and over a quarter of its habitable
land, tropical Africa and Asia was a large
and diverse place. In the centuries between 1200
and 1500 commercial, political, and cultural expansion drew the region's peoples closer together. The Indian Ocean became the world's most
important and richest trading area. The Delhi
Sultanate brought the greatest political unity to
India since the decline of the Guptas. Mali extended the political and trading role pioneered
by Ghana in the western Sudan. The growth of
trade and empires was closely connected with
the enlargement of Islam's presence in the tropical world along with the introduction of greater
diversity into Islamic practice.

But if change was an important theme of this
period, so too was social and cultural stability.
Most tropical Africans and Asians never ventured far outside the rural communities where
their families had lived for generations. Their
lives followed the familiar pattern of the seasons,
the cycle of religious rituals and festivals, and the
stages from childhood to elder status. Occupations were defined by custom and necessity.
Most people engaged in food production by
farming, herding, and fishing; some specialized
in crafts or religious leadership. Based on the accumulated wisdom of how best to deal with their
environment, such village communities were remarkably hardy. They might be ravaged by natural disaster or pillaged by advancing armies,
but over time most recovered. Empires and kingdoms rose and fell in these centuries, but the villages endured.

In comparison, the social, political, and environmental changes taking place in the Latin
West, described in the next chapter, were in

SUGGESTED READING

The trading links among the lands around the Indian
Ocean have attracted the attention of recent scholars,
who include many details of the ecological underpin-
nings of that trade. Most ambitious, broadest (touching on all the regions), and perhaps most inclined to
overreach the evidence is Janet Abu-Lughod, *Before
European Hegemony: The World System A.D. 1250–1350*
(1989), which may usefully be read with K. N. Chaudhuri, *Asia Before Europe: Economy and Civilization of the
Indian Ocean from the Rise of Islam to 1750* (1991). Students will find clear summaries of Islam's influences
in tropical Asia and Africa in Ira Lapidus, *A History of
Islamic Societies* (1988), part II, and of commercial relations in Philip D. Curtin, *Cross-Cultural Trade in World
History* (1984).

Greater detail about tropical lands is found in regional
studies. For Southeast Asia see Nicholas Tarling, ed.,
The Cambridge History of Southeast Asia, vol. 1 (1992);
John F. Cady, *Southeast Asia: Its Historical Development*
(1964); and G. Coedes, *The Indianized States of Southeast
Asia,* ed. Walter F. Vella (1968). India is covered com-
prehensively by R. C. Majumdar, ed., *The History and
Culture of the Indian People,* vol. 4, *The Delhi Sultanate,*
2d ed. (1967); with brevity by Stanley Wolpert, *A New
History of India,* 4th ed. (1993); and from an intriguing
perspective by David Ludden, *A Peasant History of
South India* (1985). For advanced topics see Tapan Ray-
chaudhuri and Irfan Habib, eds., *The Cambridge Economic History of India,* vol. 1, *c. 1200–c. 1750* (1982).

Africa in this period is well served by the later parts of
Graham Connah's *African Civilizations: Precolonial
Cities and States in Tropical Africa: An Archaeological Perspective* (1987) and in greater depth by the relevant
chapters in D. T. Niane, ed., *UNESCO General History
of Africa,* vol. 4, *Africa from the Twelfth to the Sixteenth
Century* (1984), and in Roland Oliver, ed., *The Cambridge History of Africa,* vol. 3, *c. 1050 to c. 1600* (1977).

For accounts of slavery and the slave trade see Salim
Kidwai, "Sultans, Eunuchs and Domestics: New
Forms of Bondage in Medieval India," in *Chains of*

Servitude: Bondage and Slavery in India, eds. Utsa Pat-naik and Manjari Dingwaney (1985), and the first two chapters of Paul E. Lovejoy, *Transformations in Slavery: A History of Slavery in Africa* (1983).

Three volumes of Ibn Battuta's writings have been translated by H. A. R. Gibb, *The Travels of Ibn Battuta A.D. 1325–1354* (1958–1971); the fourth volume is in preparation. Ross E. Dunn, *The Adventures of Ibn Battuta: A Muslim of the 14th Century* (1986), provides a modern retelling of his travels with commentary. For annotated selections see Said Hamdun and Noël King, *Ibn Battuta in Black Africa* (1995).

The most accessible survey of Indian Ocean sea travel is George F. Hourani, *Arab Seafaring,* expanded ed. (1995). For a Muslim Chinese traveler's observations see Ma Huan, *Ying-yai Sheng-lan, "The Overall Survey of the Ocean's Shore" [1433],* trans. and ed. J. V. G. Mills (1970). Another valuable contemporary account of trade and navigation in the Indian Ocean is G. R. Tibbetts, *Arab Navigation in the Indian Ocean before the Coming of the Portuguese, Being a Translation of the Kitab al-Fawa'id . . . of Ahmad b. Majidal-Najdi* (1981).

NOTES

1. *Tarikh-i-Wassaf,* in Henry M. Elliot, *The History of India as Told by Its Own Historians,* ed. John Dowson (London: Trübner and Co., 1869–1871), 2:28.

2. Hasan Nizami, *Taju-l Ma-asir,* ibid., 2:219.

3. Minhaju-s Siraj, *Tabakat-i Nasiri,* ibid., 2:332–333.

CHAPTER SIXTEEN

The Latin West, 1200–1500

Rural Growth and Crisis • Urban Revival • Cultural Advances and the Renaissance

The Rise of the New Monarchies

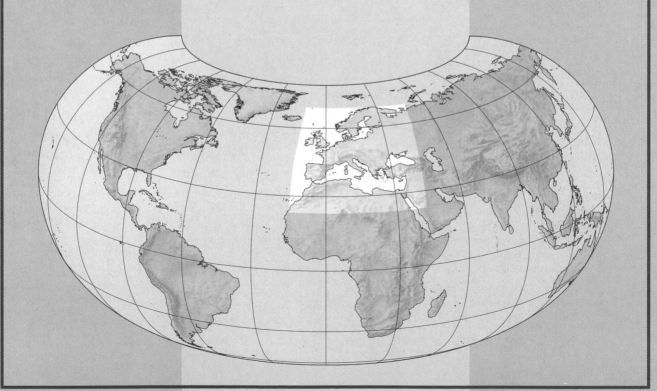

In the summer of 1454, Aeneas Sylvius Piccolomini was pessimistic about western Europe's future. A year earlier the Ottoman Turks, already in control of much of the Middle East and the Balkans, had captured the historic city of Constantinople, the last Christian stronghold in the eastern Mediterranean. As the pope's chief delegate in Germany, Aeneas Sylvius was charged with generating support for a crusade to halt further Muslim advances, but he doubted he would succeed. "How can you persuade the many rulers of the Christian world to take up arms under a single standard?" asked the man who in four years would be pope himself; "Christendom has no head whom all will obey—neither the pope nor the emperor receives his due."

Aeneas Sylvius reflected that, although French forces had recently won a decisive victory over the English in a series of conflicts that had begun in 1337 (now known as the Hundred Years War), the peace might easily be broken. The German emperor presided over dozens of states that were virtually independent of his control. The Spanish and Italians were divided into numerous kingdoms and principalities that often turned to war. With only slight exaggeration he lamented, "Every city has its own king, and there are as many princes as there are households," most more willing to fight with each other than to join a common front against the Turks.

This lack of unity, he believed, was due to Europeans' growing preoccupation with personal welfare and material gain:

> behold the huge and yawning maw of avarice, see how much inertia and how much greed there are. No one is devoted to letters or to the studies of the good arts. And do you think that an army of Turks could be destroyed by men of such morals?[1]

Such pessimism and materialism had increased during the previous century, partly in reaction to a devastating plague known in Europe as the Black Death. By 1351 it had carried off a third of western Europe's population.

Yet despite all these divisions, disasters, and wars, historians now see the period from 1200 to 1500 (Europe's later Middle Ages) as a time of unusual progress. The avarice and greed Aeneas Sylvius lamented were the dark side of the material prosperity that was most evident in the cities with their splendid architecture, institutions of higher learning, and cultural achievements. Frequent wars caused havoc and destruction, but in the long run they promoted the development of more powerful weapons and more unified monarchies.

Clearly the period looks rosier when one knows that the Turks did not overrun Europe, that the Hundred Years War had really ended, and that by 1500 explorers sent by Portugal and a newly united Spain would extend Europe's reach to other continents. Aeneas Sylvius knew only what had been, and the conflicts and calamities of the past made him shudder.

Although their contemporary Muslim and Byzantine neighbors commonly called western Europeans "Franks," they ordinarily referred to themselves as "Latins." That term underscored their allegiance to the Latin rite of Christianity (and to its patriarch, the pope) as well as the use by their literate members of the Latin language. The Latin West deserves special attention because its achievements during this period had profound implications for the future of the world. It was emerging from the economic and cultural shadow of its Islamic neighbors and, despite grave disruptions caused by plague and warfare, boldly setting out to extend its dominance into new regions. Some common elements promoted the Latin West's remarkable resurgence: competition, the pursuit of success, and the effective use of borrowed technology and learning.

Competition may be too mild a term to describe the often violent political, economic, and social conflicts of these centuries. Yet in the course of battles among themselves the people of the Latin West acquired the skills, tools, and determination that enabled them to challenge other parts of the world. Prolonged competition naturally promoted excellence, since besting one's rivals—whether in war, business, learning, or architecture—meant coming up with superior methods or tools. Technological and cultural borrowings in fields as different as milling and manufacturing, universities and printing, and weapons and navigation were vital to the pace of change. Although the Latin West's achievements ultimately depended on the activities of its own people, the ability to borrow from Muslim and Byzantine neighbors sped the region's rise, just as the Latin West's expansion overseas would accelerate new global exchanges.

RURAL GROWTH AND CRISIS

Between 1200 and 1500 the Latin West brought more land under cultivation, introduced new farming techniques, and made greater use of machinery and mechanical forms of energy. Yet for most rural Europeans—and more than nine out of ten people were rural—the period from 1200 to 1500 was a time of calamity and struggle. Most rural men and women worked hard for their meager returns and suffered mightily from the effects of famine, epidemics, warfare, and social exploitation. From the low point caused by the Black Death in 1347–1351, peasant revolts sped social changes that released many persons from the bondage of serfdom and made some improvements in rural welfare.

Peasants, Population, and Plague

In 1200 most western Europeans were serfs, obliged to till the soil on large estates owned by the feudal nobility and the church (see Chapter 9). In return for using a portion of their lord's land, serfs had to provide their Lord with a share of their harvests, perform numerous labor services, and meet other obligations. Such rigid social relations slowed improvements in agricultural production.

As a consequence of the inefficiency of farming practices and of the obligations they owed to landowners, peasants worked hard for very meager returns. Despite the existence of numerous religious holidays, peasant cultivators probably devoted an average of 54 hours of hard labor a week in their fields. More than half of that labor went to support the local nobility. Each noble household typically rested on the labors of from fifteen to thirty peasant families. The standard of life in the lord's stone castle or manor house stood in sharp contrast to the peasant's one-room thatched cottage with little furniture and no luxuries.

Scenes of rural life show both men and women at work in the fields, although there is no reason to believe that equality of labor meant equality of decision making at home. In the peasant's hut as elsewhere in medieval Europe, women were subordinate to men. The influential theologian Thomas Aquinas (1225–1274) spoke for his age when he argued that, although men and women were both created in God's image, there was a sense in which "the image of God is found in man, and not in woman: for man is the beginning and end of woman; as God is the beginning and end of every creature."[2]

Rural poverty was not simply the product of inefficient farming methods and an unequal social system. It also resulted from the rapid growth of Europe's population. In 1200 Chinese may have outnumbered Europeans by two to one; by 1300 each population was about 80 million. China's population fell because of the Mongol conquest (see Chapter 14), but why Europe's population rose is not so clear. Some historians believe that the reviving economy may have stimulated population increase. Others argue that warmer-than-usual temperatures reduced the number of deaths from starvation and exposure while the absence of severe epidemics lessened deaths from disease.

Whatever the cause, more people required more productive ways of farming new agricultural settlements. One change gaining widespread acceptance in the region around Paris in the thirteenth century was to reduce the amount of farmland left fallow (uncultivated). Instead of following the custom of leaving half of the land fallow for a year to regain its fertility, more and more farmers tried a new three-field system in which they grew crops on two-thirds of the land each year. Many farmers using this system grew one field in oats to feed horses, which they could use to pull plows. In most of western Europe, however, farmers still let half of their land lie fallow and used oxen (less efficient but cheaper than horses) to pull their plows.

Population growth also led to the foundation of new agricultural settlements. In the twelfth and thirteenth centuries large numbers of German immigrants migrated into the fertile lands east of the Elbe River and in the eastern Baltic. Knights belonging to Latin Christian religious orders slaughtered or drove away the native inhabitants, who had not yet adopted Christianity. For example, during the century after its founding in 1231, the Order of Teutonic Knights conquered and resettled a vast area along the eastern Baltic that became Prussia (see Map 16.3). Latin Christians also founded new settlements on lands conquered from the Muslims and Byzantines in southern Europe and on Celtic lands in the British Isles.

By draining swamps and clearing forests, people also brought new land under cultivation within the existing boundaries of the Latin West. But as population continued to rise, people had to farm marginal lands that had poor soils or were vulnerable to flooding, frost, or drought. Because of the growing dependence on such marginal lands, average crop yields began to decline after 1250. More and more people lived at the edge of starvation, vulnerable to even slight changes in the food supply resulting from bad

weather or the disruptions of war. According to one knowledgeable historian, "By 1300, almost every child born in western Europe faced the probability of extreme hunger at least once or twice during his expected 30 to 35 years of life."[3] One unusually cold spell led to the Great Famine of 1315–1317, during which there was widespread starvation in Europe. Other famines were more localized.

In time the cumulative effect of such crises might have reduced the population to a size that existing agricultural methods could more readily support. However, what actually eased population pressure was not famine but the *Black Death*. This terrible plague seems to have originated in India and then struck Mongol armies attacking the city of Caffa on the Black Sea in 1346 (see Chapter 13). A year later Genoese traders in Caffa carried the disease back to Italy and southern France. During the next two years the Black Death spread throughout western Europe, in some places carrying off two-thirds of the population. Overall the epidemic may have killed one of every three western Europeans by the time it subsided in 1351.

The plague's symptoms were ghastly to behold. Victims developed boils the size of eggs in their groins and armpits, black blotches on their skin, foul body odors, and severe pain. In most cases, death came within a few days. To prevent the plague from spreading, town officials closed their gates to people from infected areas and burned the victims' possessions. Such measures helped to spare some communities, but they could not halt the advance of the disease across Europe (see Map 16.1). It is now known that the Black Death was the bubonic plague, a disease that was spread not just from person to person but also by the bites of fleas that infested the fur of a certain black rat. But even if medieval Europeans had been aware of that route of infection, they could have done little to eliminate the rats, which thrived on urban refuse.

The plague left its mark not only physically but psychologically, bringing home to people how sudden and unexpected death could be. In response to the plague some people became more religious, giving money to the church or

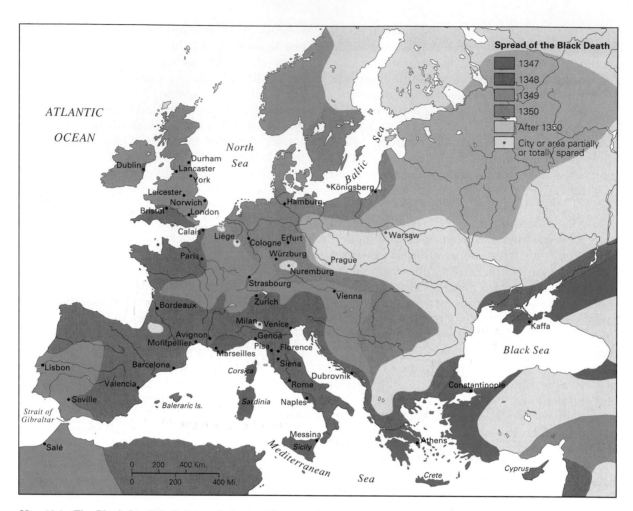

Map 16.1   The Black Death in Fourteenth-Century Europe   Spreading out of southwestern China along the routes opened by Mongol expansion, the bubonic plague reached the Black Sea port of Caffa in 1346. This map documents its deadly progress year by year from there into the Mediterranean and north and east across the face of Europe.

hitting themselves with iron-tipped whips to atone for their sins. Others chose to enjoy life while they still had it, spending their money on fancy clothes, feasts, and drinking. Whatever their mood, most people soon resumed their daily routines. Life went on.

Although population gradually rebounded from the low point of 1351, recovery was slow and uneven because of periodic returns of plague. By 1400 Europe's population had re-

gained only the levels of 1200; not until after 1500 did it rise above its preplague levels. Meanwhile, China was recovering from its thirteenth-century losses (see Chapter 14).

Social Rebellion

Besides its demographic and psychological effects, the Black Death also set off social changes in western Europe. Skilled and manual laborers who survived demanded higher pay for their services. At first authorities tried to freeze wages at the old levels. Seeing such repressive measures as a plot by the rich, peasants rose up against wealthy nobles and churchmen. During a widespread revolt in France in 1358, known as the *Jacquerie*, peasants looted dozens of castles, killing dozens of persons. In another large revolt led by Wat Tyler in 1381, English peasants invaded London, calling for an end to all forms of serfdom and to most kinds of manorial dues. Some angry demonstrators murdered the archbishop of Canterbury and many royal officials. Authorities put down these rebellions with even greater bloodshed and cruelty, but they could not stave off the higher wages and other social changes the rebels demanded.

Serfdom practically disappeared in western Europe as peasants bought their freedom or just ran away. Many free persons who got higher wages from the landowners saved their money and bought their own land in depopulated areas. Unable to afford hiring enough fieldworkers to farm their lands, many large English landowners turned to pasturing sheep for their wool or to less labor-intensive crops and made greater use of draft animals and labor-saving tools. Because the plague had not killed wild and domesticated animals, more meat was available for each survivor and more leather for shoes. Thus the welfare of the rural masses generally improved after the Black Death, though the gap between rich and poor remained wide.

In urban areas employers had to raise wages to attract enough workers to replace those killed by the plague. Merchant guilds (see below) found it necessary to reduce the period of apprenticeship. Competition within crafts also became more common. Although the overall economy shrank with the decline in population, per capita production actually rose.

Mills and Mines

Despite calamities and conflicts, the use of mechanical energy, mining, and metallurgy grew so much in the centuries before 1500 that some historians have spoken of an "industrial revolution" in medieval Europe. That may be too strong a term, but the landscape fairly bristled with mechanical devices. England's many rivers had some 5,600 functioning watermills in 1086. After 1200 such mills spread rapidly across the western European mainland. By the early fourteenth century, for example, entrepreneurs had crammed 68 watermills into a one-mile section of the Seine River in Paris.

The lower part of a water wheel could be turned by a river, or water could be directed to flow over the top of the wheel. Some medieval designs made use of varying water flows, but for maximum efficiency dams were built to ensure the water wheels had a steady flow of water throughout the year. Ingenious machinery even enabled some watermills in France and England to harness the power of ocean tides.

Windmills were also common, especially in dry lands like Spain, where the flow of rivers was too irregular for efficient watermills, and in northern Europe, where the power of the wind could be tapped even in winter when ice made water wheels useless. Neither type of mill was a new invention nor unique to Europe. Water wheels and windmills had long been common in the Islamic world, but the medieval Latin West used such devices to harness the power of nature on a much larger scale than in any other part of the world.[4]

Mills were expensive to build, but they cost little to operate because free natural energy powered them. Thus, over time, they returned great profits to their owners. It was these profits that led to the proliferation of mills in medieval Europe. This also was the cause of conflicts among investors to secure prime sites and local monopolies. Some mills were built by individuals or by monasteries. Many more mills were built by groups of investors. The ability of mill owners to grow rich by grinding grain with wind or water power often aroused the jealousy of their neighbors. The English poet Geoffrey Chaucer (c. 1340–1400) captured many a miller's unsavory reputation (not always deserved) in this portrait in his *Canterbury Tales*:

Water mill, Paris Sacks of grain were brought to these mills under the Grand Pont to be ground into flour. These "undershot" water wheels were turned by the River Seine flowing under them. Gears translated the vertical motion of the wheel into the horizontal motion of the millstone. (Bibliotheque nationale de France)

He was a master-hand at stealing grain.
He felt it with his thumb and thus he knew
Its quality and took three times his due—
A thumb of gold, by God, to gauge an oat![5]

Water power also made possible such a great expansion of iron making that some historians say Europe's true Iron Age was in the later Middle Ages. Water powered the stamping mills that broke up the iron, the trip hammers that pounded it, and the bellows (first documented in 1323) that raised temperatures to the point where the iron was liquid enough to be poured into molds. Blast furnaces capable of producing high-quality iron are documented from 1380. The finished products included everything from armor to nails, from horseshoes to agricultural tools.

The demand for iron stimulated iron mining in many parts of Europe. There were also important new silver, lead, and copper mines in Austria and Hungary that supplied metals for coins and church bells, cannon and statues. Techniques of deep mining developed in central Europe were introduced farther west in the latter part of the fifteenth century. A building boom also led to more stone quarrying in France during the eleventh, twelfth, and thirteenth centuries than during all of the millennia of ancient Egypt.

The rapid growth of industry produced significant changes in the Latin West's landscape. Forests were cleared for farming, towns grew outward and new ones were founded, dams and canals changed the flow of rivers, and the countryside was marked by quarry pits and mines tunneled into hillsides. Pollution sometimes became a serious problem. Urban tanneries (factories that cured and processed leather) dumped large quantities of acidified waste water back into streams, where it mixed with human waste and the runoff of slaughterhouses. The first recorded antipollution law was passed by the British Parliament in 1388, although enforcement was difficult.

One of the most dramatic environmental changes during these centuries was deforestation. Trees were cut to provide timbers for buildings and for ships. Tanneries stripped bark to make acid for tanning leather. Many forests were cleared to make room for farming. The use of wood for fuel, especially by the glass and iron industries, was also a great consumer of forests. Charcoal was made by controlled burning of oak or other hardwood; then the charcoal was used to produce the high temperatures these industries required. It is estimated that a single iron furnace could consume all the trees within five-eighths of a mile (1 kilometer) in just 40 days. As a consequence of all these demands, many once dense forests in western Europe were greatly depleted in the later Middle Ages, except for those that powerful landowners protected as hunting preserves.

URBAN REVIVAL

In the tenth century not a single town in the Latin West could compare in wealth and comfort—still less in size—with the cities in the Byzantine Empire and the Islamic caliphates. Yet by the later Middle Ages wealthy commercial centers stood all along the Mediterranean, the Baltic, and the Atlantic, as well as on major rivers draining into these bodies of water (see Map 16.2). The greatest cities in the East were still larger, but those in the West were undergoing greater commercial, cultural, and administrative changes. Their prosperity was visible in impressive new churches, guild halls, and residences. This urban revival is a measure of the Latin West's recovery from the economic decline that had followed the collapse of the Roman Empire

(see Chapter 9) as well as an illustration of how the West's rise was aided by its ties to other parts of the world.

Trading Cities

Most urban growth in the Latin West after 1200 stemmed from the revival of trade and manufacturing. The greatest part of the trade was between cities and their hinterlands, but long-distance trade also stimulated urban revival. Cities in northern Italy in particular benefited from maritime trade with the bustling port cities of the eastern Mediterranean and, through them, with the great markets of the Indian Ocean and East Asia. In northern Europe commercial cities in the County of Flanders (roughly today's Belgium) and around the Baltic Sea profited from growing regional networks and from overland and sea routes to the Mediterranean.

Two events in the thirteenth century strengthened Italian trade with the eastern Mediterranean. One was the Venetian-inspired assault in 1204 against the city of Constantinople, which dominated the passage between the Mediterranean and Black Seas. Misleadingly named the "Fourth Crusade," this assault by Latin Christians on Greek Christians had little to do with the religious differences between them and much to do with Venice's desire to gain better access to the rich trade of the East. By crippling Byzantine power, Venetians were able to seize the strategic island of Crete in the eastern Mediterranean and expand their trading colonies around the Black Sea. The other boon to Italian trade was the westward expansion of the Mongol Empire, which opened up trade routes from the Mediterranean to China (see Chapter 13).

To take advantage of that trade the young Marco Polo set out from Venice in 1271 on the long trek across inner Asia. After reaching the Mongol court, the talented Marco spent many years serving the emperor Khubilai Khan as an ambassador and as the governor of a Chinese province. Marco later authored an immensely popular account of these adventures and of the

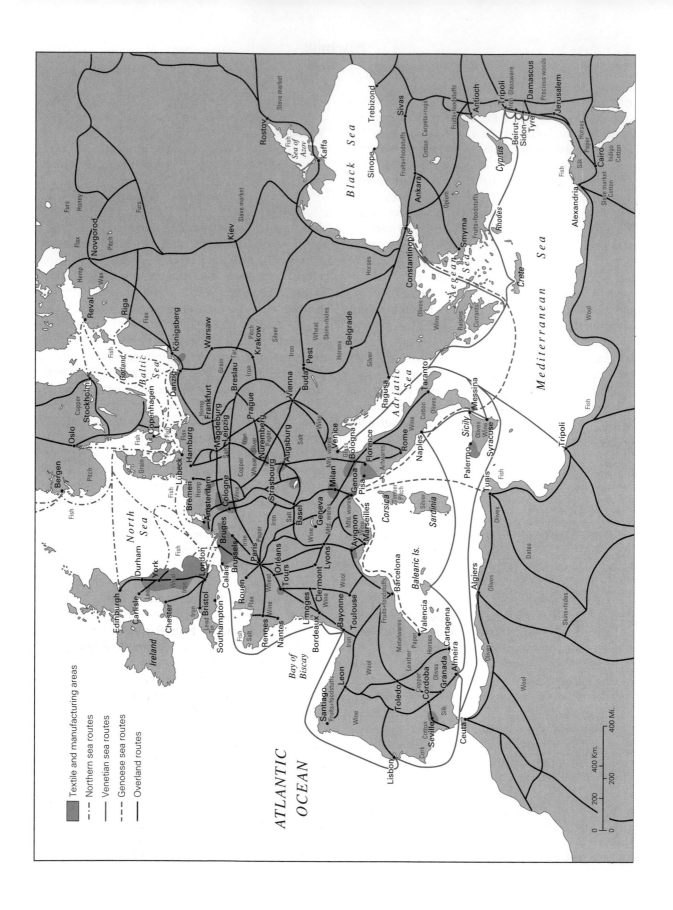

treacherous return voyage through the Indian Ocean that finally brought him back to Venice in 1295 after an absence of twenty-four years. Yet even in relatively prosperous Venice, few who had not seen for themselves could believe the stories of fabulous wealth of eastern lands.

While the disintegration of the Mongol Empire in the fourteenth century halted direct European contact with distant Asian cities, Venetian merchants continued to purchase eastern silks and spices brought by other middlemen to Constantinople, Beirut, and Alexandria. Three times a year galleys (ships powered by some sixty oarsmen each) sailed in convoys of two or three from Venice, bringing back some 2,000 tons of goods. Other merchants began to explore new overland or sea routes.

Venice was not the only Latin city whose trade expanded in the thirteenth century. The sea trade of Genoa on the west coast of northern Italy probably equaled that of Venice. Genoese merchants built up colonies on the shores of the eastern Mediterranean and around the Black Sea as well as in the western Mediterranean. In northern Europe an association of trading cities known as the *Hanseatic League* conducted extensive trade in the Baltic, including the newly conquered coasts of Prussia, and as far east as Novgorod in Russia and westward across the North Sea to London.

By the late thirteenth century, Genoese galleys from the Mediterranean and Hanseatic ships from the Baltic were converging on a third area, the trading and manufacturing cities in Flanders. In the Flemish towns of Bruges, Ghent, and Ypres skilled artisans turned raw wool from English sheep into a fine cloth that was softer and smoother than the coarse "homespuns" from simple village looms. Dyed in vivid hues, these

Map 16.2 Trade and Manufacturing in Later Medieval Europe The economic revival of European cities was associated with great expansion of commerce. Notice the concentrations of wool and linen textile manufacturing in northern Italy, the Netherlands, and England; the importance of trade in various kinds of foodstuffs; and the slave-exporting markets in Cairo, Kiev, and Rostov.

Flemish textiles appealed to wealthy Europeans who formerly had imported their fine textiles from Asia.

Along the overland route connecting Flanders and northern Italy important trading fairs developed in the Champagne region of Burgundy. These trading fairs began as regional markets, meeting once or twice a year, where manufactured goods, livestock, and farm produce were exchanged. When Champagne came under the control of the king of France at the end of the twelfth century, royal guarantees of safe conduct to all merchants turned the regional markets into international fairs. A century later fifteen Italian cities had permanent consulates in Champagne to represent the interests of their citizens who brought goods from Italy and eastern ports across the Alpine passes to exchange for Flemish cloths. The fairs were also important for exchanging currencies and conducting other financial transactions. During the fourteenth century the volume of trade grew so large that it became cheaper to send Flemish woolens to Italy by sea rather than overland on pack animals. As a consequence the fairs of Champagne lost some of their international trade but remained important regional markets.

Textile manufacturing also spread beyond Flanders. To increase revenue, in the late thirteenth century the English monarchy raised taxes on the export of raw wool, and it became more profitable to turn wool into cloth in England rather than in Flanders. Flemish textile specialists crossed the English Channel and introduced the spinning wheel and other devices to England. As a consequence the number of sacks of raw wool exported annually from England fell from 35,000 at the beginning of the fourteenth century to 8,000 in the mid-fifteenth, while exports of English wool cloth rose from 4,000 pieces in about 1350 to 54,000 a century later.

Florence was also developing as a wool-making center. Local banking families financed the profitable production of much of the high-quality cloth that in the past Florence had bought from the Flemish cities. In 1338, for example, Florence manufactured 80,000 lengths of cloth, while importing only 10,000. These changes in the textile industry

Flemish weavers, Ypres The spread of textile weaving gave employment to many people in the Netherlands. The city of Ypres in Flanders (now northern Belgium) was an important textile center in the thirteenth century. This drawing from a fourteenth-century manuscript shows a man and a woman weaving cloth on a horizontal loom, while a child makes thread on a spinning wheel. The cloth diaper takes it name from Ypres. (Stedelijke Openbare Bibliotheek, Ieper (Ypres))

show how competition promoted the spread of manufacturing and encouraged new specialties.

These growing industries made extensive use of windmills and water wheels. The power of wind and water was channeled through gears, pulleys, and belts to drive all sorts of machinery. The thriving textile industry in Flanders, for example, used mills to clean and thicken woven cloth by beating it in water, a process known as *fulling*. Another application of mill power was in papermaking. Although papermaking had been common in China and the Muslim world for centuries before it spread to southern Europe in the thirteenth century, Westerners were the first to use machines to do the heavy work in its manufacturing.

Fifteenth-century Venice surpassed all of its European rivals in the volume of its trade in the Mediterranean as well as across the Alps into Central Europe. Its skilled craftspeople also manufactured luxury goods once obtainable only from eastern sources. Notable in this regard were its silk and cotton weaving, its glass and mirror industries, its jewelry, and its papermaking. At the same time exports of Italian and northern European woolens to the eastern Mediterranean were also on the rise. In the space of a few centuries western European cities used the eastern trade to increase their prosperity and then reduced their dependence on eastern goods.

Civic Life

As in the Indian Ocean basin (see Chapter 15), trading cities in Europe generally had more social mobility and religious diversity than rural places. Most northern Italian and German cities were independent states, sometimes controlling considerable land outside their gates. Cities in the larger European kingdoms commonly held special royal charters that exempted them from the authority of local nobles. Because of their autonomy, they were able to adapt to changing market conditions more quickly than cities in China and the Islamic world, which were controlled by imperial authorities. Social mobility was also easier in the Latin West because anyone who lived in a chartered city for over a year became free of all claims on his or her person. This made these cities a refuge for all sorts of ambitious individuals, whose labor and talent added to their wealth.

Cities were also home to most of Europe's Jews. The largest Jewish population was in Spain, where earlier Arab rulers had made them welcome. Before their expulsion in 1492, Jews numbered 3 percent of Spain's population. Other commercial cities had small Jewish communities, but nowhere else in the West were Jews more than 1 percent of the population. City officials welcomed Jews for their manufacturing and business skills, especially as moneylenders, because Latin Christians generally considered charging interest (usury) sinful. Despite their official protection, Jews were periodically subject to violent religious persecutions or expulsions (see Voices & Visions: Blaming the Black Death on the Jews). In all of the medieval West only the papal city of Rome left its Jews undisturbed throughout the centuries before 1500.

Along with opportunities, there were many restrictions on individual enterprise in European cities. Within most towns and cities powerful associations known as *guilds* dominated civic life. A guild was an association of persons, such as silversmiths or merchants, who worked in a particular trade. Each guild regulated the business practices of its members and the prices that they charged, trained apprentices, and promoted the interests of its members with the city government. By denying membership to newcomers and all Jews, guilds perpetuated the interests of the families that already belonged.

Guilds also perpetuated male dominance of most skilled jobs. Despite serious restrictions, some women were able to join guilds either on their own or as the wives, widows, or daughters of male guild members. Large numbers of poor women also toiled in non-guild jobs in urban textile industries and in the food and beverage trades, generally receiving lower wages than their male counterparts.

For many women marriage was an important means of social advancement. In *The Canterbury Tales* Chaucer includes a woman from the city of Bath in southern England, who had become wealthy by marrying a succession of old men for their money (and then two other husbands for love), "aside from other company in youth." She was also a skilled weaver, Chaucer says: "In making cloth she showed so great a bent,/She bettered those of Ypres and of Ghent."[6]

By the fifteenth century, growing commerce gave rise to a new class of merchant-bankers who had the wealth to operate on a vast scale and who often specialized in money changing, loans, and investments on behalf of other parties. Merchants great and small used their services, but the merchant-bankers also handled the financial transactions of ecclesiastical and secular officials. For example, they arranged for the transmission to the pope of the funds known as *Peter's pence*, a collection taken up annually in every church in the Latin West. Merchant-bankers also advanced large sums of money to the princes and kings of Europe to support their wars and lavish courts. Some merchant-bankers even developed their own news services, amassing information on every topic that could affect their businesses.

Florence had special importance in banking services. Its financiers invented checking accounts, organized private shareholding companies (the

Blaming the Black Death on the Jews, Strasbourg, 1349

Prejudice against Jews was common in the Latin West, as one can see in this selection from the official Chronicles of the Upper-Rhineland Towns.

In the year 1349 there occurred the greatest epidemic that ever happened. Death went from one end of the earth to the other, on that side and this side of the [Mediterranean] sea . . . . This epidemic also came to Strasbourg in the summer of [that] year, and . . . about sixteen thousand people died.

In the matter of this plague the Jews throughout the world were reviled and accused in all lands of having caused it through the poison which they are said to have put into the water and the wells—that is what they were accused of—and for this reason the Jews were burnt all the way from the Mediterranean into Germany, but not in Avignon, for the pope protected them there.

. . . The deputies of the city of Strasbourg were asked what they were going to do with their Jews. They answered and said that they knew no evil of them. [The town-council was deposed. A new council gave in to the mob and arrested the Jews.]

On Saturday—that was St. Valentine's Day—they burnt the Jews on a wooden platform in their cemetery. There were about two thousand people of them. Those who wanted to baptize themselves were spared. Many small children were taken out of the fire and baptized against the will of their fathers and mothers. And everything that was owed to the Jews was cancelled, and the Jews had to surrender all pledges and notes that they had taken for debts. The council, however, took the cash that the Jews possessed and divided it among the working-men proportionately. The money was indeed the thing that killed the Jews. If they had been poor and if the feudal lords had not been in debt to them, they would not have been burnt.

To what extent was the massacre of the Strasbourg Jews due to fear of the plague, to prejudice, and to greed? Why did some officials try to protect them?

Source: Jacob R. Marcus, ed., *The Jew in the Medieval World: A Source Book*, 315–1791, 1938, pp. 45–47. Reprinted with permission of the Hebrew Union College Press, Cincinnati.

Massacre of the Strasbourg Jews (From the Chronicarum Mundi, Nurnberg, 1493)

forerunners of modern corporations), and improved bookkeeping techniques. In the fifteenth century, the Medici family of Florence operated banks in Italy, Flanders, and London. They also controlled the government of Florence and were important patrons of the arts. By 1500 the greatest banking family in western Europe was the Fuggers of Augsburg, who had ten times the Medici bank's lending capital. Starting out as cloth merchants under Jacob "the Rich" (1459–1525), the family branched into many other activities, including the trade in Hungarian copper that was essential for casting cannon.

Bankers had to devise ways to profit from loans indirectly in order to get around the Latin Church's condemnation of usury. Some borrowers agreed to repay a loan in another currency at a rate of exchange favorable to the lender. Others added to the borrowed sum a "gift" in thanks to the lender. For example, in 1501 church officials agreed to repay a loan of 6,000 gold ducats in five months to the Fuggers along with a "gift" of 400 ducats, amounting to an effective interest rate of 16 percent a year. In fact, the return was much smaller since the church failed to repay the loan on time.

Gothic Cathedrals

Among the skilled people in greatest demand in the thriving cities of later medieval Europe were master builders and associated craftsmen. These craftsmen designed and erected buildings in a new style, later called *Gothic*, that were the wonders of the later Middle Ages. Cities competed with one another in the magnificence of their guild halls, town halls, and episcopal palaces, but especially in the size and beauty of their cathedrals, which symbolized their religious faith.

One distinctive feature of the new cathedrals that made their appearance about 1140 in France was the pointed, or Gothic, arch, which replaced the older round, or Roman, arch. Another was their incredible height. The arches stood atop high, thin stone columns stabilized by external

Portrait of a bourgeois marriage, 1434 In this picture, the Flemish artist Jan van Eyck, one of the masters of the new Renaissance oil paints, recorded the marriage of Giovanni Arnolfini and Giovanna Cenami, members of Italian merchant families that were resident in the cities of what is now Belgium. Fifteenth-century Europeans would have understood that the dog symbolized fidelity and the mirror reflected purity. (Reproduced by courtesy of the Trustees, The National Gallery, London)

buttresses. This method of construction permitted the outside walls to be filled with giant windows depicting religious scenes in brilliantly colored stained glass. During the next four centuries, interior heights soared heavenward, towers went ever higher, and walls became dazzling curtains of stained glass. The cathedral spire in Strasbourg reached 466 feet (142 meters) into the air—the height of a 40-story building. The record heights achieved by such thirteenth-century

Strasbourg cathedral   Only one of the two spires that were originally planned for this Gothic cathedral was completed when work ceased in 1439. But the Strasbourg Cathedral was still the tallest masonry structure of medieval Europe. This engraving is from 1630. (Courtesy of the Trustees of the British Museum)

teacher, and as they constantly invented novel solutions to the problems they encountered, success rose from the rubble of their mistakes.

For most residents of western European cities, however, the wonders of new cathedrals provided only temporary distractions from the poverty and squalor of their lives. Even for the wealthy, European cities generally lacked the civic amenities, such as public baths and water supply systems, that had existed in the cities of Western antiquity and still survived in cities of the Islamic Middle East. Though thriving, the cities of the Latin West were still smaller than those of the eastern Mediterranean. On the eve of the Black Death, the largest, Venice, had nearly 200,000 inhabitants and Florence about half as many. To the north, Paris had some 80,000 inhabitants, but London (between 35,000 and 40,000) was no larger than the Flemish cities of Ghent (56,000) and Bruges (35,000). In comparison, Constantinople may have had a million inhabitants and Cairo even more.

CULTURAL ADVANCES AND THE RENAISSANCE

Urban revival involved more than markets and buildings. These cities were also centers of intellectual and artistic life. In part they rediscovered the cultural achievements of antiquity, and in some ways they surpassed them.

Throughout the Middle Ages people in the Latin West lived amid reminders of the achievements of the Roman Empire. They wrote and worshiped in its language, traveled its roads, and obeyed its laws. Even the vestments and robes of medieval popes, kings, and emperors were modeled on the regalia of Roman officials. Yet early medieval Europeans lost touch with much of the learning of classical antiquity. More vivid was the biblical world they heard about in the Hebrew and Christian scriptures.

structures would not be surpassed until the twentieth century.

These cathedrals were designed and built by men with little or no formal education and limited understanding of the mathematical principles of modern civil engineering. Master masons sometimes miscalculated, and parts of some overly ambitious cathedrals collapsed. The record-high choir vault of Beauvais Cathedral—154 feet (47 meters) high—for instance, came tumbling down in 1284. But practical experience was their greatest

Some fifteenth-century Italian authors proclaimed that their era had rediscovered the intellectual and artistic values of classical antiquity, ending a millennium of medieval superstition and ignorance. The Italian Renaissance ("rebirth") and its northern European extension were indeed a time of great intellectual and artistic achievement, but modern historians see the "Renaissance" less as a sudden break with the medieval past than as the culmination of a process of cultural enrichment that had been under way for several centuries. They also stress the importance of the Byzantine and Muslim worlds, where classical culture had never died out, in transmitting the learning of antiquity to their neighbors in the Latin West.

Though indebted to borrowings from its neighbors, Europe's cultural revival rested solidly on the prodigious talents of its own scholars and artists. The Latin West's cultural achievements were also fostered by new institutions of higher learning and by the perfection of mechanical printing as a means of disseminating knowledge. Moreover, it was not a coincidence that cultural revival was concentrated in Europe's thriving commercial centers. By itself the patronage of merchants and church prelates could not create great art, but it did give individuals the means to express their talents.

Universities

Before 1100 Byzantine and Islamic scholarship generally surpassed scholarship in Latin Europe. When southern Italy was wrested from the Byzantines and Sicily and Toledo from the Muslims in the eleventh century, many manuscripts of Greek and Arabic works came into Western hands and were translated into Latin for readers eager for new ideas. The manuscripts included previously unknown works of ancient philosophy by Plato and Aristotle and Greek treatises on medicine, mathematics, and geography. In addition there were scientific and philosophical writings by medieval Muslims. The works of the Iranian philosopher Ibn Sina (980–1037), known to the West as "Avicenna," were particularly influential. The Jewish scholarly community contributed significantly to the translation and explication of Arabic and other manuscripts.

The spread of these new classical manuscripts was intimately associated with new institutions of higher learning in the Latin West. Joining the older monastic schools were new independent colleges, endowed by contributions to provide subsidized housing for poor students and to pay the salaries of their teachers. The colleges first established in Paris and Oxford in the late twelfth and thirteenth centuries may have been modeled after similar places of study (*madrasa*) long known in the Islamic world.

However, the Latin West was the first part of the world to establish modern "universities," degree-granting corporations specializing in multidisciplinary research and advanced teaching. Some of the first universities were started by students; others were founded as guilds to which all the professors of a city belonged. These teaching guilds, like the guilds overseeing manufacturing and commerce, set the standards for membership in their profession, trained apprentices and masters, and defended their professional interests. The new universities set the curriculum of study for each discipline and instituted comprehensive final examinations for degrees. After passing exams at the end of their apprenticeship, students received a first diploma known as a "license" to teach. More advanced students, who completed longer training and defended a masterwork of scholarship, became "masters" and "doctors." In Paris the colleges were gradually absorbed into the city's university, but at Oxford and Cambridge the colleges remained independent, self-governing organizations.

Universally recognized degrees, well-trained professors, and exciting new texts promoted the rapid spread of universities in late medieval Europe. Between 1300 and 1500 the twenty oldest universities in Italy, France, England, and Iberia were joined by some sixty others throughout the Latin West. Because university courses were taught in Latin, students and masters could move freely across political and linguistic lines, seeking out the university that offered the courses they wanted and had the most interesting professors.

Universities offered a variety of programs of study but generally were identified with a particular specialty. Bologna was famous for the study of law; Montpellier and Salerno specialized in medicine; Paris and Oxford were best known for theology.

The importance of theology partly reflected the fact that many students were destined for ecclesiastical careers, but theology was also seen as the "queen of the sciences," the central discipline that encompassed all knowledge. For this reason thirteenth-century theologians sought to synthesize the newly rediscovered philosophical works of Aristotle, as well as the commentaries by Avicenna, with the revealed truth of the Bible. Their daring efforts were often controversial. The most notable case was the *Summa Theologica* issued between 1267 and 1273 by Thomas Aquinas, a doctor of theology at the University of Paris. Although his exposition of Christian belief organized on Aristotelian principles was eventually accepted as a brilliant demonstration of the reasonableness of Christianity, it upset many traditional thinkers. Some church authorities even tried to ban Aristotle from the curriculum. However, the considerable freedom of medieval universities from both secular and religious authorities enabled the new ideas of accredited scholars to prevail over the fears of church administrators.

Not all who studied theology followed careers in church administration. Chaucer's threadbare Oxford cleric, who "found no preferment [salaried post] in the church and . . . was too unworldly to make search for secular employment," became an independent scholar, repaying his benefactors with his prayers and spending their gifts on more books. "The thought of moral virtue filled his speech/And he would gladly learn, and gladly teach."[7] Many masters of theology preferred the freedom of the university over the cares of parish work or the discipline of monastic life.

In their quest for deeper understanding some fifteenth-century scholars studied classical texts in their original languages instead of in Latin translations. By comparing many different manuscripts, they produced critical editions of important works, correcting the errors intro-duced by generations of copyists. To aid in this task, Pope Nicholas V (r. 1447–1455) created the Vatican Library, buying scrolls of classical writings and paying to have expert copies and translations made. Working independently, the respected Dutch scholar Erasmus of Rotterdam (ca. 1466–1536) produced a critical edition of the Greek text of the New Testament. Erasmus was able to correct many errors in the Latin text that had been in general use throughout the Middle Ages, and he was able to issue hundreds of identical copies by means of the new technology of printing.

Printing

The Chinese were the first to use carved wood blocks for printing. During the tenth and eleventh centuries Chinese government presses had printed comprehensive editions of Confucian, Buddhist, and Taoist scriptures, but it seems that the direct inspiration for printing in Europe may have come from Chinese playing cards, which first appeared in Germany and Spain in 1377. Whatever the model, the high-quality books and pamphlets printed in the Latin West from the middle of the fifteenth century onward were a significant advance on Chinese printing techniques.

The man who did most to perfect the process was Johann Gutenberg (ca. 1394–1468) of Mainz, a goldsmith by training, who used his metal-working skills to cast individual letters of uniform style and size. He also developed a mechanical printing press and devised an ink suitable for printing. The Gutenberg Bible of 1454 was not only the first book in the West printed from moveable type but also an extremely beautiful and finely crafted work that bore witness to the printer's years of diligent experimentation. In addition to Gutenberg's Latin Bible, printers published critical editions of classical Latin writers. As interest in the past was stirred, the great Italian scholar-printer Aldo Manuzio (1449–1515) published classical Greek texts as well.

Printing spread with extraordinary speed. Paris alone had 75 printing presses in 1500; Venice had twice that number. By that date at least 10 million books had issued forth from presses in 238 towns in western Europe. Many of these presses were privately owned and printed whatever would sell, not just literary and religious texts.

Books were a boon to universities because students could buy a text rather than rent one or laboriously copy it by hand. Printing encouraged the spread of literacy and fostered the standardization of European languages. It also increased the circulation of works voicing unorthodox political and religious views. Not surprisingly, both church and state officials responded with efforts at censorship. The Catholic Church issued its first Index of Prohibited Books in 1564, but stopping the flow of works printed secretly in cellars and smuggled across political boundaries was difficult.

Renaissance Artists

The fourteenth and fifteenth centuries were as distinguished for their masterpieces of painting, sculpture, architecture, and literature as they were for their scholarship. Although artists continued to depict biblical subjects, the dissemination of classical knowledge led many artists especially in Italy to portray the deities and mythical tales of antiquity. Italy, where the Gothic style had never put down very deep roots, also pioneered the revival of Roman architectural motifs, including rounded arches, domes, and columned entrances.

This era abounded with artists of extraordinary talent. In Italy it was the age of Leonardo da Vinci (1452–1519), whose diverse works included the fresco (painting in wet plaster) *The Last Supper*, the oil painting *Mona Lisa,* and bronze sculptures, as well as imaginative designs for airplanes, submarines, and tanks. His younger contemporary Michelangelo (1472–1564) executed celebrated biblical frescoes on the ceiling of the Sistine Chapel in the Vatican, sculpted stat-

A French printshop, 1537   A workman operates the "press," quite literally a screw device that presses the paper to the inked type. Other employees examine the printed sheets, each of which holds four pages. When folded the sheets make a book. (Giraudon/Art Resource NY)

ues of David and Moses, and designed the dome for Saint Peter's Basilica. North of the Alps, the Flemish painter Jan van Eyck (ca. 1390–1441) created masterful realistic paintings on religious and domestic themes, and Hieronymus Bosch (ca. 1450–1516) produced complex allegorical fantasies.

The patronage of wealthy and educated merchants and prelates did much to foster this artistic blossoming in the cities of northern Italy and Flanders. The Florentine banker Cosimo de' Medici (1389–1464), for example, spent immense sums on paintings, sculpture, and public

buildings. His grandson Lorenzo (1449–1492), known as "the Magnificent," was even more lavish. The church also remained an important source of artistic commissions. In particular, the papacy launched an immense building program to restore Rome as the capital of the Latin church, culminating in the construction of the giant new Saint Peter's Basilica and a residence for the pope.

The achievements of Renaissance artists included several new techniques. Better understanding of perspective enabled painters to depict scenes of greater reality and depth on flat surfaces. The Flemish invention of oil paints in the fifteenth century provided artists with a medium that was easier to work in than the fast-drying frescoes, and the linseed-oil base of oil paints gave scenes an enduring luster. Da Vinci's ability to cast large statues in bronze owed much to techniques perfected in the casting of cannon.

Renaissance art, like Renaissance scholarship, owed a major debt not only to the contributions of individual artists but also to earlier generations. In Florentine painting, for example, the key precursor of the Renaissance was Giotto (ca. 1267–1337), of whom an influential modern art historian has said, "There are few men in the entire history of art to equal the stature of Giotto as a radical reformer."[8] In his religious scenes Giotto replaced the staring, otherworldly figures of the Byzantine style, which were intended to overawe viewers, with more natural and human portraits with whose emotions viewers could easily identify. Rather than floating on backgrounds of gold leaf, the saints of his Gothic style inhabit earthly landscapes. Renaissance artists

Africans in Renaissance Europe   Fifteenth-century Renaissance artists regularly portrayed black Africans, often as regal princes as in this nativity scene of about 1500 by the Dutch artist Hieronymus Bosch. Portuguese explorers brought several delegations of African rulers and ambassadors to Europe in the fifteenth century. African servants are also shown in many artworks, reflecting the growing population of African slaves in Iberia and Italy. (Museo del Prado)

credited Giotto with singlehandedly reviving "the lost art of painting." In Leonardo da Vinci's view, Giotto set standards of artistic perfection so high that it was only in his own century that Italian painting regained Giotto's level.

Italian Renaissance literature similarly depended greatly on earlier achievements. Giotto's Florentine contemporary Dante Alighieri (1265–1321) completed his long, elegant poem, the *Divine Comedy*, just before his death. Written in the Italian dialect of Tuscany, this supreme expression of medieval preoccupations tells the allegorical story of Dante's journey through the nine circles of hell and the seven terraces of purgatory, guided by the Roman poet Virgil, and then his entry into Paradise guided by Beatrice, a woman whom he had loved from afar since childhood. In the view of some scholars the *Divine Comedy* may have been influenced by Islamic literary conventions from India and Persia. Dante's lead in writing in the spoken vernacular was followed by the Italian writers Francesco Petrarch (1304–1374) and Giovanni Boccaccio (1313–1375).

These scholarly and artistic achievements exemplify the innovation and striving for excellence of the later medieval centuries. The new literary themes and artistic styles of this period had lasting influence on Western culture, but the innovations in the organization of universities, in printing, and in oil painting had wider implications, for they were later adopted by cultures all over the world.

THE RISE OF THE NEW MONARCHIES

A consolidation and expansion of royal power paralleled the economic and cultural revivals under way in western Europe. The emergence of these "new monarchies" was due to three closely related transformations: monarchs' success in struggles with their vassals, the development of new weapons of war, and a closer relationship of rulers with commercial elites and with the church. The process unfolded somewhat differently in each state (see Map 16.3). In France and England, the events of the Hundred Years War played a critical role. In the Iberian kingdoms that became Spain and Portugal, the process depended heavily on territorial expansion against Muslim states.

Dynastic Conflict

In some of the Italian and Flemish city-states merchant elites displaced older ruling classes after 1200, but in most of the Latin West feudal aristocrats retained their political and economic power. Noble families controlled vast estates—even entire provinces—because of royal grants to their ancestors as rewards for loyal service and battlefield bravery. In theory the nobles were vassals of the reigning monarchs, obliged to furnish knights for their service whenever the monarch called them to do so. In practice vassals sought to protect their entrenched rights and increase their independence. Monarchs, in turn, fought hard to increase their political power at the expense of the feudal nobility. By 1500 the rulers of England, France, Spain, and Portugal had gained the upper hand in this struggle.

By conquering England in 1066 and subduing or replacing its nobility with his own men, the duke of Normandy greatly strengthened the power of the dynasty he founded. The Anglo-Norman kings also extended their realm by assaults on their Celtic neighbors. Between 1200 and 1400 they effectively incorporated Wales and reasserted control over most of Ireland. Persistent rebellion, however, frustrated their efforts to subdue Scotland.

Nevertheless, English royal power was not absolute. For example, in the span of just three years the ambitions of King John (r. 1199–1216) were severely set back. First he was compelled to acknowledge the pope as his overlord (1213). Then he lost his bid to reassert claims to Aquitaine in southern France (1214). Finally he was forced to sign the Magna Carta ("Great

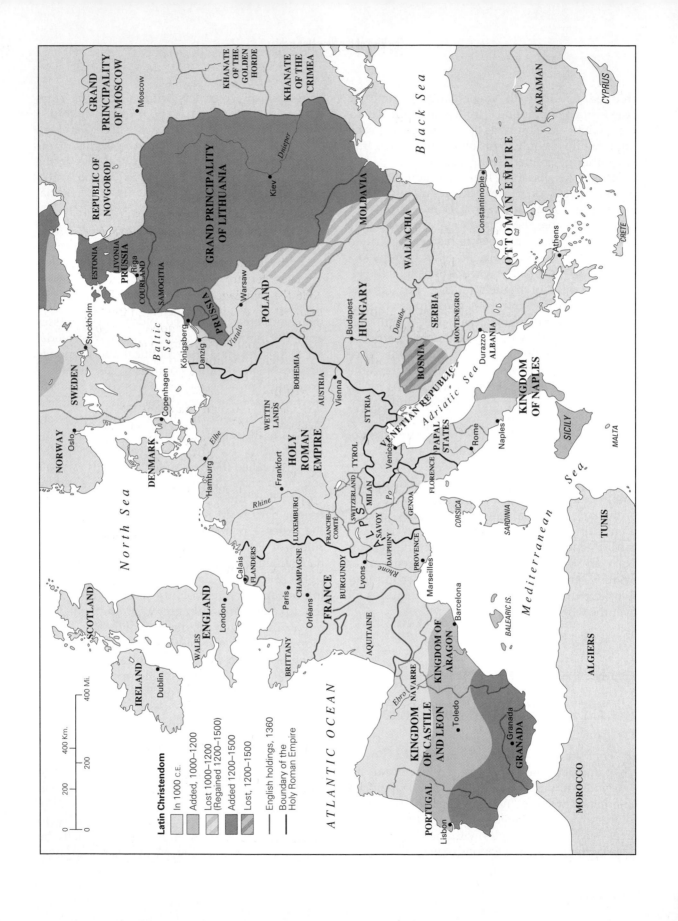

Latin Christendom

In 1000 C.E.

Added, 1000–1200

Lost 1000–1200
(Regained 1200–1500)

Added 1200–1500

Lost, 1200–1500

— — English holdings, 1360

—— Boundary of the
Holy Roman Empire

400 Mi.

0   200   400 Km.

0   200   400

GRAND
PRINCIPALITY
OF MOSCOW

• Moscow

KHANATE
OF THE
GOLDEN
HORDE

KHANATE
OF THE
CRIMEA

Black Sea

KARAMAN

CYPRUS

REPUBLIC OF
NOVGOROD

GRAND PRINCIPALITY
OF LITHUANIA

Kiev •

Dnieper

MOLDAVIA

WALLACHIA

OTTOMAN EMPIRE

Constantinople •

Athens •

CRETE

ESTONIA
LIVONIA
Riga •
PRUSSIA
COURLAND
SAMOGITIA

Stockholm •

*Baltic
Sea*

Königsberg •
Danzig •

PRUSSIA

Warsaw •

POLAND

Vistula

Budapest •

HUNGARY

Danube

SERBIA

BOSNIA

MONTENEGRO

Durazzo •

ALBANIA

KINGDOM
OF NAPLES

SICILY

MALTA

SWEDEN

NORWAY

Oslo •

DENMARK

Copenhagen •

Hamburg •

North Sea

BOHEMIA

WETTIN
LANDS

HOLY
ROMAN
EMPIRE

Frankfort •

Elbe

Rhine

LUXEMBURG

FRANCHE-
COMTÉ

AUSTRIA

Vienna •

STYRIA

TYROL

SWITZERLAND

MILAN

A L P S

Po

FLORENCE

GENOA

VENETIAN REPUBLIC

Venice •

PAPAL
STATES

Rome •

Naples •

Adriatic Sea

CORSICA

SARDINIA

*Mediterranean
Sea*

TUNIS

SCOTLAND

IRELAND

Dublin •

WALES

ENGLAND

London •

BRITTANY

Paris •

Orléans •

FRANCE

CHAMPAGNE

BURGUNDY

Lyons •

Rhône

SAVOY

DAUPHINY

PROVENCE

Marseilles •

Calais •
FLANDERS

AQUITAINE

NAVARRE

KINGDOM OF
ARAGON

Barcelona •

BALEARIC IS.

Ebro

KINGDOM
OF CASTILE
AND LEON

Toledo •

GRANADA

Granada •

PORTUGAL

Lisbon •

MOROCCO

ALGIERS

ATLANTIC OCEAN

Charter," 1215), which affirmed that monarchs were subject to established law, confirmed the independence of the church and the city of London, and guaranteed nobles' hereditary rights.

The kings of France began this period ruling a much larger and more populous kingdom than did the English monarchs but having less control of their noble vassals. By adroitly using the support of the towns, the saintly King Louis IX (r. 1226–1270) was able to issue ordinances that applied throughout his kingdom without first obtaining the nobles' consent. But there was prolonged resistance by the most powerful vassals to later kings' efforts to extend royal authority. These vassals included the kings of England (for lands that belonged to their Norman ancestors), the counts of prosperous and independent-minded Flanders in the north, the dukes of Brittany, and, later in the struggle, the dukes of Burgundy. For more than a century royal power in France rose and fell on the outcome of the battles that made up the Hundred Years War (1337–1453).

One of the factors central to these struggles was the hereditary nature of political authority. Both monarchs and vassals entered into strategic marriages with a view to strengthening their power and increasing their lands. Dynastic marriages sometimes produced unexpected results. For example, the marriage of Princess Isabella of France to King Edward II (r. 1307–1327) of England was meant to ensure that this powerful vassal remained loyal to the French monarchy. However, when Isabella's three brothers served in turn as kings of France without leaving a male heir, this gave her son, King Edward III (r. 1327–1377) of England, a possible claim to the French throne. When French courts instead awarded the throne to a more distant (and more

French) cousin, Edward decided to fight for his rights, beginning the Hundred Years War.

As this case shows, French rules of succession excluded women like Isabella both from inheriting the throne themselves and from passing on royal claims to their children. Elsewhere in the Latin West rules permitting royal women to rule in their own right when no male heir was available made marriage alliances even more important. An unmarried woman ruler was a most attractive bride, since such a union might join the spouses' territories as well as their persons. In 1386 the marriage of the queen of Poland to the grand duke of Lithuania created the largest state in Europe and also expanded the boundaries of Latin Christianity, for the duke agreed to accept that religion for himself and all his subjects as a condition of the marriage. (The Lithuanians were one of the last European peoples to adopt Christianity.) In 1469 the marriage of Ferdinand of Aragon (r. 1479–1516) and Isabella of Castile (r. 1474–1504) completed the amalgamation of several medieval Iberian kingdoms into Spain, sixteenth-century Europe's most powerful state.

Not all dynastic marriages benefited the female spouse. Despite her strategic marriage to an Austrian prince, Mary of Burgundy (1457–1482) was forced to surrender most of Burgundy to the king of France. In 1491 Anne of Brittany was compelled to marry the king of France, a step that led to the eventual incorporation of her duchy into France.

As these examples show, dynastic politics was in part a struggle among powerful families to retain control over ancestral lands and enlarge them by conquest, marriage, and inheritance. In this process both royal and noble families showed scant regard for "national" interests, regularly marrying across ethnic and linguistic lines and fighting to defend their claims to the diverse territories that resulted from such dynastic alliances. The resulting conflicts and boundary shifts make the political history of these centuries appear chaotic and unstable. Yet other parts of the tug of war between monarchs and vassals favored the strengthening of central authority and the creation of more stable (but not entirely fixed) state boundaries within which

Map 16.3 Europe in 1453 This year marked the end of the Hundred Years War between France and England and the fall of the Byzantine capital city of Constantinople to the Ottoman Turks. Muslim advances into southeastern Europe were offset by the Latin Christian reconquests of Islamic holdings in southern Italy and the Iberian Peninsula and by the conversion of Lithuania.

the nations of western Europe would in time develop. New technologies of war and the growing economy helped turn family dynasties into national monarchies.

New Weapons of War

Royal power rose as its dependence on feudal cavalry declined. The privileged economic and social position of the feudal nobility rested on the large estates that had been granted to their ancestors as fiefs so that they could support and train knights in armor to serve in a royal army. In the year 1200 the feudal knights were still the backbone of western European fighting forces, but by 1500 knights in armor were relics of the past. Two changes in weaponry did them in.

The first involved the humble arrow. Improved crossbows could shoot metal-tipped arrows with such force that they could pierce helmets and light body armor. Professional crossbowmen became more common and much feared. Indeed, a church council in 1139 outlawed the weapon as being too deadly for use against other Christians. The ban was largely ignored.

Early in the Hundred Years War French cavalry was reinforced by hired Italian crossbowmen, but arrows from another late medieval innovation, the English longbow, nearly annihilated the French force. Adopted from the Welsh, the six-foot longbow could shoot farther and more rapidly than the crossbow. Although arrows from longbows could not pierce armor, in concentrated showers they often found gaps in the knights' defenses or struck their less-well-protected horses. To defend against these weapons, armor became heavier and more encompassing, making it harder for a knight to move. If pulled off his steed by a foot soldier armed with a pike (hooked pole), a knight was usually unable to get up to defend himself.

The second innovation in military technology that weakened the feudal system was the firearm. This Chinese invention, using gunpowder to shoot stone or metal projectiles (see Environment

& Technology: Explosive Power in Chapter 14), completed the transformation of the medieval army. In the mid-fourteenth century, as Petrarch noted, "instruments which discharge balls of metal with most tremendous noise and flashes of fire [had] become as common and familiar as any other kind of arms"[9] (see Environment & Technology: Cannon).

On the battlefield the smoke and fire pouring forth from cannon may have been more useful in frightening the horses of advancing cavalry than the modest number of cannonballs were in causing damage. Large cannon, however, were quite effective in blasting holes through the heavy walls of medieval castles, ending the ability of their noble owners to withstand a royal siege. The first use of such siege artillery against the French, in the Battle of Agincourt (1415), gave the English an important victory. In the final battles of the Hundred Years War, French forces used heavy artillery to demolish the walls of once-secure castles held by the English and their allies.

With the English defeated, the French monarchs turned their armies on the duke of Burgundy, the most powerful remaining vassal, eventually seizing direct control of Flanders and Burgundy in 1477. During that struggle much smaller and more mobile cannon that could be fired more rapidly were developed. Made with greater precision and loaded with an improved gunpowder, these smaller cannon were nearly as powerful as the earlier behemoths. With only slight changes these weapons formed the basis of field artillery until the 1840s.

The final rout of the cavalry was due to improvements in hand-held firearms. By the late fifteenth century, projectiles shot from muskets could pierce even the heaviest armor, and the noise and smoke that muskets produced spooked the horses.

As a consequence of these changes in military hardware, armies depended less and less on knights and more on bowmen, pikemen, and musketeers, along with specialized artillery units. These new armed forces had to be financed from the royal treasury, not from feudal fiefs. Thus a third requirement of the new

Cannon

With some modifications the techniques and materials long used in the casting of bronze church bells were transferred to the casting of cannon. Europeans quickly surpassed all others in the qualities and quantities of cannon they produced. Until the mid-fifteenth century the tendency was for cannon to grow larger and larger. The largest, such as those used by the Turks to destroy the walls of Constantinople, were up to 15 feet (4.5 meters) long and so heavy that the German and Hungarian craftsmen who made them had to cast them on the spot. After firing stone projectiles 30 inches (76 centimeters) or more in diameter, such giants had to cool for hours before they could be fired again.

This illustration from the late fifteenth century depicts a large cannon being readied for use in blasting through a wooden rampart. As the scene shows, the cannon is not the center of the siege strategy. It is being used to supplement older forms of assault. Some of the attackers are attempting to scale the wall on a ladder. Note that none of the soldiers has a firearm. Most are armed with bows and arrows; a couple have crossbows.

Cannon, late fifteenth century   (British Library)

monarchies was a system for financing a standing army.

Controlling the Purse and the Church

Rulers had not been slow to recognize the new revenue they could extract from the expansion of trade. Many of them taxed goods entering or leaving their realms. Some Christian princes and kings who gave Jewish merchants their protection taxed them heavily for the privilege. In addition, merchant towns were willing to make generous contributions to monarchs who freed them from the demands made by local nobles. Individual merchants curried royal favor with loans, even though such debts could be difficult or dangerous to collect. For example, the wealthy fifteenth-century French merchant Jacques Coeur gained many social and financial benefits for himself and his family by lending money to important members of the French court, but he was ruined when his jealous debtors accused him of murder and had his fortune confiscated.

Nobles were also willing to convert their feudal obligations to monarchs into money payments and to cough up taxes for wars they supported. For example, in 1439 and 1445 Charles VII of France (r. 1422–1461) won from his vassals the right to levy a new tax on land. The tax not only enabled him to pay the costs of the current war with England but provided the financial base of the French monarchy for the next 350 years.

Royal efforts to gain access to the wealth of the church met with greater resistance. When English and French kings tried to impose taxes on their clergy during the Hundred Years War, they set off major conflicts over the independence of the church from state control. In 1302 the outraged Pope Boniface VIII (r. 1294–1303) went so far as to assert that divine law made the papacy superior not just to monarchs but to "every human creature."

Issuing his own claims to superiority, King Philip "the Fair" of France (r. 1285–1314) sent an army to arrest the pope. After this treatment hastened Pope Boniface's death, Philip engineered the election of a French pope who established a new papal residence at Avignon in southern France in 1309. With the support of the French monarchy, a succession of popes residing in Avignon improved church discipline—but at the price of compromising the papacy's neutrality in the eyes of other rulers. Papal authority was further eroded by the Great Western Schism (1378–1415), a period when rival papal claimants at Avignon and Rome vied for the loyalties of Latin Christians. The conflict was eventually resolved by returning the papal residence to its traditional location, the city of Rome, but the long crisis broke the pope's ability to resist the rising power of the new monarchies.

By then, French and English rulers controlled all high ecclesiastical appointments within their realms and thus could use the wealth attached to such offices to reward their supporters. Other states secured similar control over the church appointments and finances in their territories. In so doing, the monarchs were not abandoning the church. Indeed, they often used state power to enforce religious orthodoxy in their realms more vigorously than the popes had even been able to do. But, as reformers complained, the church's spiritual mission could be subordinated to political and economic concerns.

One of the tragic ironies of the closer association of church and state was the fate of a young French peasant woman, Joan of Arc. Believing she was instructed by God to save France, she donned a knight's armor and rallied the French troops that defeated the English in 1429 just as they seemed close to conquering France. When she had the misfortune to fall into English hands shortly after this victory, she was tried by English churchmen for being a witch and was burned at the stake in 1431.

As a result of these complex dynastic and military struggles, by the end of the fifteenth century England and France stood unified under strong kings, and the nobility and the church had lost much of their independence. In future centuries nobles rebelled many times when kings were weak or unpopular, or when, as English dynastic rules permitted, a woman occupied the throne. But never again would the trend toward centralized rule be seriously deflected.

Iberian Unification and Exploration

The growth of Spain and Portugal into strong, centralized states was also marked by struggles between kings and vassals, dynastic marriages and mergers, and wars (though firearms were less important). But their story was also related to another form of territorial expansion in the Middle Ages: the crusade to expand the boundaries of Latin Christianity. Religious motives featured prominently in the wars to reclaim the lands of southern Iberia from the Muslims.

Such religious zeal did not exclude personal gain. The Iberian knights who gradually pushed the frontiers of their kingdoms southward knew that to the victors went the spoils. The spoils included irrigated fields capable of producing an abundance of food, rich cities of glittering Moorish architecture, and ports offering access to the Mediterranean and the South Atlantic. Victorious Christian knights were often rewarded with a grant (an *encomienda*) over the land and people in a newly conquered territory. The pattern of serving God, growing rich, and living off the labor of others became ingrained in the Iberian nobility.

The reconquest advanced in waves over several centuries; there were long pauses to consolidate the conquered territory and unify the Christian kingdoms. Toledo was taken in 1085 and made into a Christian outpost. The Atlantic port of Lisbon fell to a multinational assault in 1147. The beautiful cities of Cordoba and Seville succumbed respectively in 1236 and 1248, leaving only the Muslim kingdom of Grenada hugging the Mediterranean coast. Aragon and Castile's joint conquest of Grenada in 1492 secured the final piece of Muslim territory in Iberia for the new kingdom. The crusading mentality of this conquest showed in the order issued less than three months after Grenada's fall expelling all Jews from the Spanish kingdoms. That year was also memorable because of Ferdinand and Isabella's sponsorship of a voyage of exploration from Seville led by Christopher Columbus. The objective was to reach the riches of the Indian Ocean, but the eventual outcome was the extension of Spain's crusading system across the Atlantic.

The Atlantic kingdom of Portugal had driven Muslim rulers from its southern limits in 1249. After a long pause to colonize, Christianize, and consolidate this land, Portugal also set out on new conquests. In 1415 Portuguese knights seized the port city of Ceuta in Morocco. During the next few decades Portuguese mariners sailing out into the Atlantic discovered and colonized the island chains of the Madeiras and the Azores.

As in the case of their conquest of the mainland, Iberian maritime explorers were motivated by a mixture of religious and economic motives. When the leader of the assault on Ceuta and its first Portuguese governor, the young Prince Henry (1394–1460), returned to Lisbon to plan a far greater expansion south along the Atlantic coast of Africa, his goals were to spread the Christian faith, find allies against Muslim power, and secure wealth for his kingdom. The Azores became centers of fishing, sugar cane plantations were introduced into the Madeiras and other Atlantic islands, and a flourishing trade in gold and slaves was established with coastal Africans.

Portuguese overseas expansion depended on more than royal backing and a crusading tradition. New knowledge of world geography and improvements in sailing technology were equally important to success. From 1409 a Latin translation of a world geography attributed to Ptolemy, a second-century Greek, circulated widely in Europe. The geography was in fact substantially the work of medieval Byzantine and Arab scholars trading on Ptolemy's reputation as a geographer. One of the important contributions of this work was to teach European mariners how to compute their location on the open sea. In other respects maps attributed to Ptolemy were highly inaccurate. They represented the Indian Ocean as being enclosed by land at the bottom, they had no knowledge of the Americas, and they underestimated the earth's circumference and thus the distance westward from Europe to China. The last two mistakes were the reason why Columbus thought he could reach Asia by a relatively short voyage westward across the Atlantic instead of by sailing around Africa.

Not all Europeans were so in awe of the authority of "Ptolemy." Under the direction of Prince Henry of Portugal (later called "the Navigator"), detailed geographical information was collected from sailors and other travelers as part of a determined effort to overcome Europe's ignorance of the South Atlantic. Four years before Columbus first sailed west across the Atlantic, Portuguese mariners had completed nearly seven decades of careful exploration of the Atlantic coast of Africa and proven that, contrary to Ptolemy's *Geography*, there was a water passage around the southern tip of Africa into the Indian Ocean.

In 1498 Portuguese mariners reached India, and that same year Columbus, on his second voyage in the service of Castile and Aragon, touched the mainland of the previously unknown continents of the Americas. Immense new worlds to conquer to the east and the west had been opened up to the most expansive western Europeans. Already in 1494 an agreement brokered by the pope had divided the world between the Spanish and the Portuguese. Just behind them were merchants, mariners, and missionaries from other parts of Europe eager to continue the overseas expansion of the Latin West.

CONCLUSION

From an ecological perspective the later medieval history of the Latin West is a story of triumphs and disasters. Westerners excelled in harnessing the inanimate forces of nature with their windmills, water wheels, and sails. They excelled at finding, mining, and refining the mineral wealth of the earth as well, although localized pollution and deforestation were among the results. Their inability to improve food production and distribution as rapidly as their population grew created a demographic crisis that became a demographic calamity when the bubonic plague swept through Europe in the mid-fourteenth century.

From a regional perspective the centuries from 1200 to 1500 witnessed the coming together of the basic features of the modern West. States were of moderate size but had exceptional military capacity honed by frequent wars with one another. The ruling class, convinced that economic strength and political strength were inseparable, promoted the welfare of the urban populations that specialized in trade, manufacturing, and finance—and taxed their profits. Autonomous universities fostered intellectual excellence, and printing diffused the latest advances in knowledge. Art and architecture reached peaks of design and execution that set the standard for subsequent centuries. Perhaps most fundamentally, later medieval western Europe was a society fascinated by tools and techniques. In commerce, warfare, industry, and navigation, new inventions and improved versions of old ones underpinned the region's continuing dynamism.

From a global perspective, in these centuries the Latin West changed from a region dependent on cultural and commercial flows from the East to a region poised to export its culture and impose its power on the rest of the world. It is one of history's great ironies that many of the tools that the Latin West used to challenge Eastern supremacy had originally been borrowed from the East. Medieval Europe's mills, printing, firearms, and navigational devices owed much to Eastern designs, just as its agriculture, alphabet, and numerals had in earlier times.

Western European success depended as much on strong motives for expansion as on adequate means. Long before the first voyages overseas, population pressure, religious zeal, economic motives, and intellectual curiosity had expanded the territory and resources of the Latin West. From the late eleventh century onward such expansion of frontiers was notable in the English conquest of Celtic lands, in the establishment of Crusader and commercial outposts in the eastern Mediterranean and Black Seas, in the massive German settlement east of the Elbe River, and in the reconquest of southern Iberia from the Muslims. The early voyages into the Atlantic were an extension of similar motives in a new direction.

SUGGESTED READING

A fine guide to the Latin West (including its ties to eastern Europe, Africa, and the Middle East) is Robert Fossier, ed., *The Cambridge Illustrated History of the Middle Ages*, vol. 3, *1250–1520* (1986). Daniel Waley, *Later Medieval Europe* (1975), is briefer and emphasizes Italy. For the West's economic revival and growth see Robert S. Lopez, *The Commercial Revolution of the Middle Ages, 950–1350* (1976), and Harry A. Miskimin, *The Economy of Early Renaissance Europe, 1300–1460* (1975). Fernand Braudel provides wide-ranging global perspectives from 1400 onward in his *Civilization and Capitalism, 15th–18th Century*, 3 vols. (1982).

Students will find fascinating primary sources in James Bruce Ross and Mary Martin McLaughlin, eds., *The Portable Medieval Reader* (1977) and *The Portable Renaissance Reader* (1977). *The Notebooks of Leonardo da Vinci*, ed. Pamela Taylor (1960), show this versatile genius at work.

Technological change is surveyed by Carlo M. Cipolla, *Guns, Sails, and Empires: Technological Innovation and the Early Phases of European Expansion, 1400–1700* (1965); Jean Gimpel, *The Medieval Machine: The Industrial Revolution of the Middle Ages* (1977); and William H. McNeill, *The Pursuit of Power: Technology, Armed Force, and Society Since A.D. 1000* (1982). For a key aspect of the environment see Roland Bechmann, *Trees and Man: The Forest in the Middle Ages* (1990).

Charles Homer Haskins, *The Rise of the Universities* (1923; reprint, 1957), is a brief, lighthearted introduction; more detailed and up-to-date is Alan Cobban, *The Medieval Universities: Their Development and Organization* (1975). Johan Huizinga, *The Waning of the Middle Ages* (1924), is the classic account of the "mind" of the fifteenth century.

For social history see Georges Duby, *Rural Economy and Country Life in the Medieval West* (1990), for the earlier centuries; George Huppert, *After the Black Death: A Social History of Early Modern Europe* (1986), takes the analysis past 1500. Brief lives of individuals are found in Eileen Power, *Medieval People* (1924), and Frances Gies and Joseph Gies, *Women in the Middle Ages* (1978). More systematic are the essays in Mary Erler and Maryanne Kowaleski, eds., *Women and Power in the Middle Ages* (1988). Vita Sackville-West, *Saint Joan of Arc* (1926; reprint, 1991), is a readable introduction to this extraordinary person.

Key events in Anglo-French dynastic conflict are examined by Christopher Alland, *The Hundred Years War: England and France at War, ca. 1300–ca. 1450* (1988). Joseph F. O'Callaghan, *A History of Medieval Spain* (1975), provides the best one-volume coverage; for more detail see Jocelyn N. Hillgarth, *The Spanish Kingdoms*, 2 vols. (1976, 1978). Barbara W. Tuchman, *A Distant Mirror: The Calamitous 14th Century* (1978), gives a popular account of the crises of that era. P. Ziegler, *The Black Death* (1969), supplies a thorough introduction.

The Latin West's territorial expansion is well treated by Robert Bartlett, *The Making of Europe: Conquest, Colonization, and Cultural Change* (1993); Pierre Chaunu, *European Expansion from the Thirteenth to the Fifteenth Centuries* (1978); and, more narrowly, Bailey W. Diffie, *Prelude to Empire: Portugal Overseas before Henry the Navigator* (1960).

Francis C. Oakley, *The Western Church in the Later Middle Ages* (1985), is a reliable summary of modern scholarship. Kenneth R. Stow, *Alienated Minority: The Jews of Medieval Latin Europe* (1992), provides a fine survey up through the fourteenth century. For pioneering essays on the Latin West's external ties see Khalil I. Semaan, ed., *Islam and the Medieval West: Aspects of Intercultural Relations* (1980).

NOTES

1. Quoted in *The Portable Renaissance Reader*, ed. James Bruce Ross and Mary Martin McLaughlin (New York: Penguin Books, 1968), 75, 78.

2. Quoted in Marina Warner, *Alone of All Her Sex: The Myth and Cult of the Virgin Mary* (New York: Random House, 1983), 179.

3. Harry Miskimin, *The Economy of the Early Renaissance, 1300–1460* (Englewood Cliffs, NJ: Prentice-Hall, 1969), 26–27.

4. George Basalla, *The Evolution of Technology* (New York: Cambridge University Press, 1988), 144.

5. Geoffrey Chaucer, *The Canterbury Tales*, trans. Nevill Coghill (New York: Penguin Books, 1952), 32.

6. Ibid., 29.

7. Ibid., 25.

8. H. W. Janson, *History of Art* (Englewood Cliffs, NJ: Prentice-Hall, 1962), 272.

9. Quoted in Carlo M. Cipolla, *Guns, Sails, & Empires: Technological Innovation and the Early Phases of European Expansion, 1400–1700* (New York: Minerva Press, 1965), 22.

PART FIVE

The Globe Encompassed, 1500–1700

New sea routes pioneered by the Iberian kingdoms of Portugal and Spain brought the cultural regions of the world into more frequent and more intense contact between 1500 and 1750. Although the early effects of this dramatic expansion of commercial, cultural, and biological exchanges varied widely from place to place, in the long term the global consequences of these encounters were significant.

Europeans were the greatest beneficiaries of new and expanded trade. Powerful western European governments promoted far-flung trading ventures and overseas colonization. Profits from these ventures helped enrich a growing middle class and stimulated the expansion of European manufacturing. New crops from the Americas and improved farming efficiency also increased Europe's food supply.

The indigenous peoples of the Americas suffered devastating consequences from Iberian expansion. Violent conquest, forced conversion to Christianity, and severe population losses weakened traditional cultures and toppled or undermined native elites. Long isolation from the Old World made New World peoples vulnerable to new diseases arriving from Europe. Abusive labor demands and epidemic disease eliminated virtually the entire indigenous population of the West Indies within thirty years of these new contacts. As the original populations and states in the Americas collapsed during the course of the sixteenth century, Spain and Portugal erected vast colonial empires that stretched from California to the southern tip of South America. Other European nations soon established American colonies of their own.

For the rest of the world the European voyages produced no such abrupt or devastating results. Indeed, in Asia and Africa the most important political changes sprang from internal sources. The Ottoman Empire continued its drive through the Balkans to the gates of Vienna before being stopped in 1529 by a coalition of European states. Ottoman fleets dominated the eastern Mediterranean until defeated at Lepanto in 1571 by a Spanish-led coalition in the largest sea battle of the sixteenth century. The disunity of India was ended about 1530 by the formation of the Mughal Empire, whose policies of toleration reduced conflicts between Muslims and Hindus. New Muslim empires also emerged in Iran and in West Africa during this time. By the early eighteenth century, however, various regional and internal factors had led to the disappearance or decline of all of these states.

In East Asia, political reorganization and centralization brought more enduring stability to China and Japan. The formation of the Qing Empire laid the basis for Chinese military expansion, population growth, and security from external penetration. Japan's feudal decentralization was ended by the establishment of a strong national government known as the Tokugawa shogunate. This government promoted economic development and reduced foreign influence through a policy of nearly total isolation.

Far more important globally than these political events were the economic changes occurring during this era. The capture of the Indian Ocean trade routes in the early sixteenth century gave tiny Portugal control of the world's most important maritime trading network. Profits from Asian spices, textiles, and other goods helped finance commercial growth and military expansion. In the Americas, new mechanisms of production and exchange introduced by Spain and Portugal created an Atlantic trade based on exports of precious metals, sugar, and dyewood. From its colonial base in Mexico, Spain pioneered new trade routes across the Pacific to the Philippines and China.

In the seventeenth century the Dutch pushed the Portuguese aside in the Indian Ocean, established a new commercial and colonial base in the East Indies, and challenged Iberian dominance in the Americas. Although the ascendancy of the Dutch was short-lived, their actions and investments greatly stimulated the Atlantic economy. Particularly important was their transplanting from Brazil to the West Indies of a sugar plantation system based on slave labor.

The English and French joined the Dutch in establishing new colonies in the Caribbean and North America and bringing large numbers of enslaved Africans across the Atlantic to provide the labor for the plantation colonies. By 1750 African slaves were the dominant population of the West Indies. The slave trade's destructive effects in Africa grew with its volume, yet the continent escaped European conquest. In fact, important new African states continued to make their appearance during this period.

The new trading and territorial empires promoted growing cultural exchanges among the regions of the world. Efforts by Europeans to spread Christianity in the wake of their commercial and military expansions met with mixed results. In Asia, both China and Japan took measures to suppress the disruptive influence of Christian converts, and early Portuguese missionary efforts in Africa were not sustained. Evangelical efforts had more lasting effects in the

Technology

European ships expand global maritime trade

Gunpowder empires in Europe and Middle East

Increased metal production in Europe, the Americas, Africa, and East Asia

Printed works spread in Europe

Early agricultural revolution in Europe

Environment

Cold weather in seventeenth century causes food shortages in northern Europe and northeast Asia

Rising human population deforests China, India, Europe, and West Indies

Food crops spread from Americas to Eurasia and Africa

Old World diseases, livestock, and plants introduced to Americas

Drastic fall in Amerindian population due to new diseases

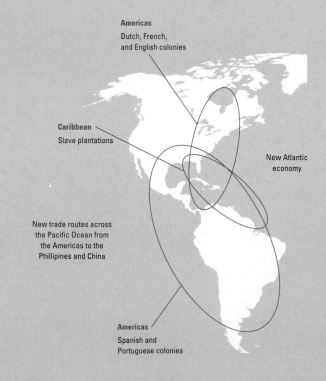

Americas
Dutch, French, and English colonies

Caribbean
Slave plantations

New Atlantic economy

New trade routes across the Pacific Ocean from the Americas to the Phillipines and China

Americas
Spanish and Portuguese colonies

Americas, where military conquest and demographic decline made the surviving native peoples more susceptible to conversion. Other elements of European culture, including food, clothing, housing, and language, gained a central place in evolving American colonial cultures. Religious practices, languages, and other cultural traits introduced by African slaves also had lasting influence.

Similar kinds of cultural change were occurring along the expanding frontiers of the Islamic world in sub-Saharan Africa, southeastern Europe, and southern Asia. In addition, important cultural changes were occurring within long-established regions. In China the expansion of educational institutions reinforced traditional values among the upper classes. In Japan the development of an indigenous merchant class widened the gap between popular and elite cultures. Europe experienced some of the farthest-reaching cultural changes in this period. Religious, social, and political conflicts threatened established institutions of church and state,

while new scientific discoveries and humanist concerns challenged traditional values and beliefs.

In areas where population and economic activity were rising, there were also important ecological changes. Japan and China suffered from deforestation, as did lands in the Americas that were cleared for agriculture and timber. The growth of shipbuilding and metallurgy in Europe also led to rapid deforestation. As new plants and animals spread from one continent to another, labor forms and land-use practices were altered, such as in the Americas, where horses and other newly introduced grazing animals often damaged fragile environments. But the most significant environmental change of this period was the growing human mastery over the power of the wind that propelled ships in growing numbers across the oceans and even around the world. Though far from tamed, by 1750 the oceans were being transformed from barriers into highways.

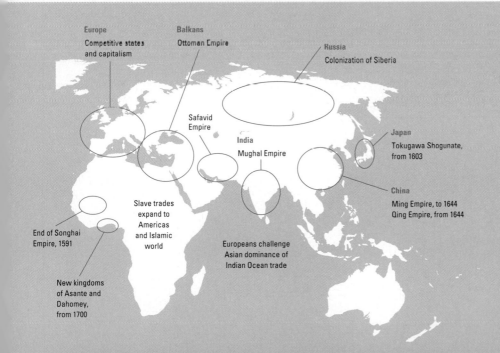

Europe
Competitive states and capitalism

Balkans
Ottoman Empire

Russia
Colonization of Siberia

Safavid Empire

India
Mughal Empire

Japan
Tokugawa Shogunate, from 1603

China
Ming Empire, to 1644
Qing Empire, from 1644

Slave trades expand to Americas and Islamic world

End of Songhai Empire, 1591

New kingdoms of Asante and Dahomey, from 1700

Europeans challenge Asian dominance of Indian Ocean trade

Society and Culture

Increased cultural interaction around the world

Missionaries spread Christianity in Americas, Africa, and Asia

Islam expands in Africa and South and Southeast Asia

First Dalai Lama of Tibetan Buddhism named in late 1500s

Sikh religion founded in Punjab

Muslims and Jews persecuted in Iberia

Protestant Reformation in Europe

Forced labor and slavery expand in the Americas

Scientific revolution in Europe

Literary flowering in late Ming China

CHAPTER SEVENTEEN

Global Expansion and Encounters, to 1550

Global Patterns of Expansion Before 1450 • European Expansion, 1450–1550

Encounters with Europe, 1450–1550

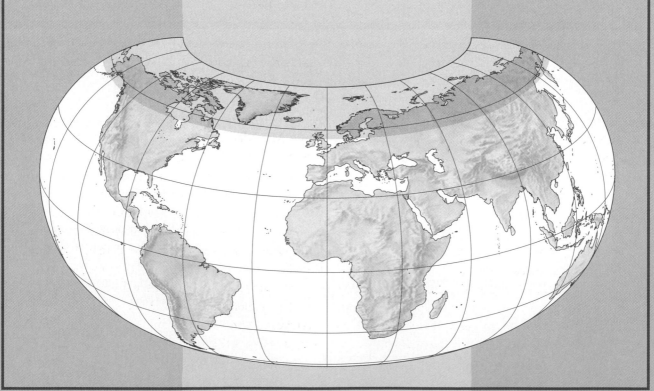

In 1511 the young Ferdinand Magellan sailed from Europe around the southern tip of Africa and eastward across the Indian Ocean as a member of the first Portuguese expedition to explore the East Indies (maritime Southeast Asia). Eight years later, this time in the service of Spain, he headed an expedition that sought to demonstrate the feasibility of reaching the East Indies by sailing westward from Europe. By the middle of 1521 Magellan's expedition had achieved its goal by sailing across the Atlantic, rounding the southern tip of South America, and traversing the Pacific Ocean, but at a high price. Of the five ships that set out from Spain in 1519, one had been wrecked on a reef, and the captain of another had deserted back to Spain. The passage across the vast Pacific had taken much longer than anticipated, resulting in the deaths of dozens of sailors due to starvation and disease. In the Philippines, Magellan had been killed on April 27, 1521, while aiding a local king who had promised to become a Christian. Magellan's successor met the same fate a few days later.

To consolidate their dwindling resources, the expedition's survivors burned the least seaworthy of their remaining three ships and transferred its men and supplies to the smaller *Victoria*, which continued westward across the Indian Ocean, around Africa, and back to Europe. Magellan's old flagship, the *Trinidad*, in no condition to continue, turned back across the Pacific, intending to reach the new Spanish colony in Panama in Central America. But after many weeks, with the health of the crew deteriorating, its officers gave up their search for westerly winds to power them back to South America and returned to the East Indies.

The *Victoria*'s successful return to Spain on September 8, 1522, was a crowning example of Europeans' new ability and determination to make themselves masters of the oceans. A century of daring and dangerous voyages backed by the Portuguese crown had opened new routes through the South Atlantic to coastal Africa and to the rich trade of the Indian Ocean. Rival voyages sponsored by Spain beginning in 1492 had revealed the existence of the American continents across the Atlantic. Now the unexpectedly gigantic Pacific Ocean had been crossed as well.

The *Trinidad*'s unsuccessful effort to reach Panama also teaches an important historical lesson. Not until 1565 did Europeans discover a route whose winds would carry a ship across the Pacific from west to east. For many centuries before 1450, historical influences in Eurasia, like the Pacific winds, tended to move from east to west. Most overland and maritime expansion had come from Asia, as had the most useful technologies and the most influential systems of belief. Asia was also home to the most powerful states and the richest trading networks. It was to reach such Eastern markets that Europeans set out on their voyages of exploration. Yet the Europeans' voyages began a new era in which the West gradually became the world's center of power, wealth, and innovation.

A third theme can also be teased out of Magellan's death fighting in alliance with one Philippine chief against another. The conquest of the oceans led to many new contacts, alliances, and conflicts. Some ended tragically for individuals like Magellan; some were disastrous for entire populations, as in the case of the Amerindians who endured conquest and suffered a rapid decline in numbers. Other contacts led to beneficial exchanges of goods, plants, animals, and ideas (see Chapter 19). In the long run Europeans' dominance gradually became global, but their initial contacts with other parts of the world between 1450 and 1550 had very diverse outcomes. In the Americas Spaniards established a new territorial empire. Elsewhere, despite the Portuguese establishment of a new trading empire in the Indian Ocean, Asians and Africans formed mutually beneficial relations with the visitors from Europe.

GLOBAL PATTERNS OF EXPANSION BEFORE 1450

The impulse to explore, settle, and conquer new lands did not originate with the peoples of western Europe. During the centuries before 1450 many other peoples had extended their areas of contact, commerce, and colonization—often on a grand scale (see Map 17.1). Some of these movements followed older patterns of overland conquest and empire building; others, like the later European voyages of exploration, involved crossing vast stretches of ocean. The motives for these earlier expansions included curiosity about the rest of the world, the quest for riches, and the search for new lands to settle. All sea voyages required daring, exceptional navigating skills, and ships specially equipped for long times at sea. These earlier global movements were important in themselves and help to provide a context for understanding the significance of European expansion.

Mongol and Chinese Expansion

East Asian peoples made two powerful thrusts westward between 1200 and 1450. In the thirteenth century the Mongols of northeastern Asia conquered a vast land empire that stretched from China to eastern Europe and the Middle East. In the first half of the fifteenth century there was a second dramatic westward thrust when the Ming dynasty of China launched a series of large fleets that enlarged China's contacts all across the Indian Ocean. Both expansions were important in their times but produced few effects that lasted beyond 1500.

The man the Mongols chose to be their leader (*khan*) in 1206, Genghis Khan (ca.1162–1227), would be little remembered by the rest of the world if he had confined himself to directing the affairs of those pastoral people. Instead he became the greatest conqueror in history. During a period of Chinese weakness and disunity lasting from 1205 to 1215, Mongol armies overran northern China and then set out across Central Asia. Over the next several decades Genghis's successors conquered Russia and parts of Eastern Europe, Iran, and Iraq, and by 1279 they had gained control of the rest of China.

The Venetian traveler Marco Polo (1254–1324) attributed the Mongols' military success to their discipline, endurance, and horsemanship. He reported they could launch "vast volleys of arrows" from the saddle and ride for as long as ten days "without lighting a fire or taking a meal." Without bothering to dismount, a Mongol horseman fed himself during such marches on a mixture of dried milk and water prepared in a leather bottle, and he punctured a vein in his horse's neck so he could drink the blood.

By ensuring traders protection from robbers and excessive tolls, the Mongol Empire revitalized the Silk Road across Eurasia, the ancient caravan route by which Chinese silks and other goods had moved westward for two thousand years. In Polo's day there were so many foreign merchants in Beijing buying silk and other goods that twenty thousand prostitutes made their living off them. Easier travel also helped Islam and Buddhism to spread to new parts of Central Asia.

In time the strains of holding such vast territories together caused the Mongol Empire to disintegrate. It first broke into a series of autonomous provinces known as *khanates,* each still of considerable size. Then over the course of the fourteenth and early fifteenth centuries the Mongol khanates collapsed one by one. The Ming dynasty of China overthrew Mongol rule in 1368 and launched expansionist foreign policies to reestablish China's predominance and prestige. Ming armies repeatedly invaded Mongolia, reestablished dominion over Korea, and occupied Annam (central Vietnam).

Having reestablished their dominance in East Asia, the Ming next enlarged their contacts with Southeast Asia, India, and other lands around the Indian Ocean. In choosing to sponsor the

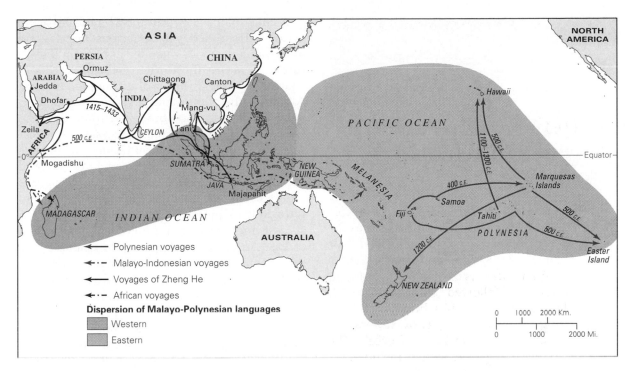

Map 17.1 Exploration and Settlement in the Indian and Pacific Oceans Before 1500 Over many centuries mariners originating in Southeast Asia gradually colonized the islands of the Pacific and Indian Oceans. The official Chinese voyages led by Zheng He in the fifteenth century were lavish official expeditions.

seven imperial fleets sent out between 1405 and 1433, the Ming may have been motivated partly by curiosity. The fact that most of the ports the fleets visited were important in the Indian Ocean trade suggests that enhancing China's commerce was also a motive. Yet because the expeditions were far larger than needed for exploration or to promote trade, it is likely that their main purpose was to enhance other peoples' awe of Ming power and achievements.

The Ming expeditions into the Indian Ocean basin were launched on a scale that reflected imperial China's resources and importance. The first consisted of sixty-two specially built "treasure ships," large Chinese *junks* each about 300 feet long by 150 feet wide (90 by 45 meters). There were also at least a hundred smaller vessels, most of which were larger than the flagship in which Columbus later sailed across the Atlantic. Each treasure ship had nine masts, twelve

sails, many decks, and a carrying capacity of 3,000 tons (six times the capacity of Columbus's entire fleet). One expedition carried 27,000 individuals, including infantry and cavalry troops. The ships would have been armed with small cannon, but in most Chinese sea battles arrows from highly accurate crossbows dominated the fighting.

At the command of the expeditions was Admiral Zheng He (1371–1435). A Chinese Muslim with ancestral connections to the Persian Gulf, Zheng was a fitting emissary to the increasingly Muslim-dominated Indian Ocean basin. The expeditions carried other Arabic-speaking Chinese as interpreters.

One of these interpreters, Ma Huan, kept a journal recording the customs, dress, and beliefs of the people visited, along with the trade, towns, and animals of their countries. Among his observations were these: exotic animals such as

Chinese junk A three-masted model of a junk shows the sails of pleated bamboo matting and a stern rudder for steering. Watertight interior bulkheads made junks the most seaworthy large ships of the fifteenth century. (National Maritime Museum, London)

As their name suggests, the Chinese "treasure ships" carried rich silks, precious metals, and other valuable goods intended as gifts for distant rulers. In return those rulers sent back gifts of equal or greater value to the Chinese emperor. Although their main purpose was diplomatic, these exchanges also stimulated trade between China and their southern neighbors. For that reason they were welcomed by Chinese merchants and manufacturers. Yet commercial profits could not have offset the huge cost of the fleets.

Interest in new contacts was by no means confined to the Chinese. For example, in 1415–1416 at least three trading cities on the Swahili Coast of East Africa sent delegations to China. When the delegates from one of them, Malindi, presented the emperor of China with a giraffe, this exotic animal created quite a stir among the normally reserved imperial officials. Such African delegations may have encouraged more contacts, for the next three of Zheng's voyages were extended to the African coast. Unfortunately no documents record how Africans and Chinese reacted to each other during these historic meetings between 1417 and 1433. It appears that China's lavish gifts stimulated the Swahili market for silk and porcelain. An increase in Chinese imports of pepper from southern Asian lands also resulted from these expeditions.

Had the Ming court concluded that commercial profits were an important end in themselves, the Chinese fleets might have continued to play a dominant role in Indian Ocean trade. But some high Chinese officials opposed increased contact with peoples whom they regarded as barbarians with no real contribution to make to China. Such opposition caused a suspension in the voyages from 1424 to 1431, and after the final expedition of 1432 to 1433, no new fleets were sent out. Later Ming emperors focused their attention on internal matters in their vast empire.

the black panther of Malaya and the tapir of Sumatra; beliefs in legendary "corpse headed barbarians" whose heads left their bodies at night and caused infants to die; the division of coastal Indians into five classes, which correspond to the four Hindu *varna* and a separate Muslim class; the fact that traders in the rich Indian trading port of Calicut could perform error-free calculations by counting on their fingers and toes rather than using the Chinese abacus. After his return, Ma Huan went on tour in China, telling of these exotic places and "how far the majestic virtue of [China's] imperial dynasty extended."[1]

Muslim Expansion

Muslim peoples were also expanding in southern Asia and Africa during the centuries after 1200. Some conquered new land empires in India and the Middle East, and others expanded their participation in the maritime trades of the Indian Ocean and Mediterranean Sea. The Mongol conquests set in motion across Eurasia some of this political and commercial expansion.

After conquering part of the Middle East, the Mongols recruited Turkish-speaking Muslims from Central Asia as their agents. As a consequence of this policy, there came to be a large Turkish community in Anatolia (now Turkey). In the second half of the thirteenth century Turks known as Ottomans (after Osman, their original leader) extended their base in Anatolia and then crossed into the Balkan Peninsula of southeastern Europe. Despite suffering a serious defeat by the Mongol warlord Timur (1336–1405) at the beginning of the fourteenth century, the Ottomans soon resumed their expansion. With the aid of large cannon in 1453, Ottoman armies were able to overrun the city of Constantinople, founded in 330, the last surviving remnant of the eastern Roman (or Byzantine) Empire.

During the sixteenth century the Ottomans brought Syria, Palestine, Iraq, and the shores of Arabia under their control, along with the North African states of Egypt, Libya, and Algeria. Their vast empire was defended by a powerful navy. By 1538 Ottoman fleets controlled the Ionian and Aegean Seas in the Mediterranean, as well as the Red Sea and the Persian Gulf.

Another example of Islamic territorial expansion occurred in northern India, where Turkish and Afghan Muslim conquests in the early thirteenth century established the Delhi Sultanate, a large empire ruled from the northern city of Delhi. The subsequent migration of large numbers of Muslims into India and the prestige and power of the Muslim ruling class brought India into the Islamic world.

Conquest and pillage at the hands of Timur's armies in 1398 left the Delhi Sultanate a shadow of its former self. Not until 1526 would Babur, a Muslim descendant of Timur, reestablish a larger and more illustrious Indian empire, known as the Mughal Empire. Under Babur's grandson, Akbar (r. 1556–1605), the Mughal Empire would reach its peak (see Chapter 21).

Besides the formation of these land empires, a different form of Islamic expansion was under way in the centuries before 1500. Muslim merchants of many nationalities formed trading alliances that gave them the predominant role in the trade of the Indian Ocean, the world's richest trading area. Merchant ships called *dhows* passed among the trading ports, carrying cotton textiles, leather goods, grains, pepper, jewelry, carpets, horses, ivory, and many other goods. Chinese silk and porcelain and Indonesian spices entered from the east, meeting Middle Eastern and European goods from the west. Gold and slaves of Muslim-ruled African states below the Sahara were also joined to this system by means of Muslim-controlled camel caravan routes across the desert.

As a consequence of the Islamic world's political and commercial expansion, the number of adherents to the Muslim faith also grew. By 1500 Islam had replaced Buddhism as the second most important faith in India and was on its way to displacing Hinduism and Buddhism in Southeast Asia. The faith was spreading in the Balkans. Raids by Arab pastoralists undermined ancient Christian states along Africa's upper Nile, leaving Ethiopia the only Christian state below the Sahara. In the trading cities below the Sahara and along the Indian Ocean coast where Islam had established itself well before 1200, the strength and sophistication of Islamic religious practice was growing.

Malayo-Polynesian, African, and Amerindian Voyages

The Chinese treasure fleets and the Muslim dhows in the Indian Ocean were not the only examples of maritime expansion in the centuries before 1450. Using smaller craft, Malayo-Polynesians, Africans, and Amerindians also engaged in significant voyages of exploration and settlement.

Considering the distances covered out of sight of land, the Pacific Ocean voyages of the Polynesians are among the most impressive in human history before 1450. Though there are no written records of them, linguistic evidence indicates that over several thousand years intrepid mariners from the Malay Peninsula of Southeast

Asia explored and settled the island chains of the East Indies and moved onto New Guinea and the smaller islands of Melanesia. Beginning some time before the Common Era (C.E.), a new wave of expansion from the area of Fiji brought the first humans to the islands of the central Pacific known as Polynesia. The easternmost of the Marquesa Islands were reached about 400 C.E.; Easter Island, 2,200 miles (3,540 kilometers) off the coast of South America, was settled a century later. From the Marquesas Polynesian sailors sailed to the Hawaiian Islands as early as 500 C.E. They settled New Zealand about 1200. Then between 1100 and 1300, new voyages northward from Tahiti to Hawaii brought more Polynesian settlers across the more than 2,000 nautical miles (4,000 kilometers) to Hawaii.

Until recent decades some historians argued that Polynesians could have reached the eastern Pacific islands only by accident since they lacked navigational devices to plot their way. Others wondered how Polynesians could have overcome the difficulties, illustrated by Magellan's flagship, *Trinidad*, of sailing eastward across the Pacific. In 1947 one energetic amateur historian of the sea, Thor Heyerdahl, even argued that Easter Island and Hawaii were actually settled from the Americas—a theory that he sought to prove by sailing his balsawood raft *Kon Tiki* westward from Peru.

Although some Amerindian voyagers did use ocean currents to travel northward from Peru to Mexico between 300 and 900 C.E., there is now considerable evidence that the settlement of the islands of the eastern Pacific was the result of planned expansion by Polynesian mariners. The first piece of evidence is the fact that the languages of these islanders are all closely related to the languages of the western Pacific and ultimately to those of Malaya. The second is the finding that accidental voyages could not have brought sufficient numbers of men and women for founding a new colony along with all the plants and domesticated animals that were basic to other Polynesian islands.

In 1976 a Polynesian crew led by Ben Finney used traditional navigational methods to sail an ocean canoe from Hawaii south to Tahiti. Their *Hokulea* was a 62-foot (19-meter) long double canoe patterned after old oceangoing canoes that sometimes were as long as 120 feet (37 meters). Not only did the *Hokulea* prove seaworthy, but, powered by an inverted triangular sail and steered by paddles (not by a rudder), it was able to sail across the winds at a sharp enough angle to make the difficult voyage, just as ancient mariners must have done. Perhaps even more remarkable, the *Hokulea*'s crew was able to navigate to its destination using only their observation of the currents, stars, and evidence of land.

While Polynesian mariners were settling Pacific islands, other Malayo-Indonesians were sailing westward across the Indian Ocean and colonizing the large island of Madagascar off the southeastern coast of Africa. These voyages continued up through the fifteenth century. To this day the inhabitants of Madagascar speak Malayo-Polynesian languages. However, part of the island's population is descended from Africans who had crossed the 600 miles (1,000 kilometers) from the mainland to Madagascar, most likely in the centuries just before 1500.

In West Africa, fishermen using large oceangoing canoes regularly ventured into coastal waters before 1450, but they did not establish permanent settlements on the many islands along Africa's Atlantic coast. There is also written evidence of African voyages of exploration in the Atlantic in this period. The celebrated Syrian geographer al-Umari (1301–1349) relates that when Mansa Kankan Musa, the ruler of the West African empire of Mali, passed through Egypt on his lavish pilgrimage to Mecca in 1324, he told of voyages to cross the Atlantic undertaken by his predecessor, Mansa Muhammad. Muhammad sent out four hundred vessels with men and supplies, telling them, "do not return until you have reached the other side of the ocean or if you have exhausted your food or water." After a long time one canoe returned, reporting the others had been swept away by a "violent current in the middle of the sea." Muhammad himself then set out at the head of a second, even larger, expedition, from which no one returned. Some writers have argued that these early-fourteenth-century Mali mariners may have reached the Americas; one even claims that the inhabitants of some

Polynesian canoes such as these, shown in an eighteenth century painting, carried Pacific Ocean mariners on epic voyages of exploration and settlement. The large vessel at the left has a platform connecting the two canoes and a sail to supplement the paddlers. ("Tereoboo, King of Owyhee, bringing presents to Captain Cook," (D. L. Ref. pxx 2f. 35). Courtesy, State Library of New South Wales)

parts of Mesoamerica in 1500 were of African descent.[2] Convincing proof is lacking, but as al-Umari's account makes clear, Mansa Musa had no reason to believe that any of his ancestor's canoes had reached the Americas, because no Mali explorer ever returned from there.

In addition to sailing up the Pacific coast, early voyagers from South America also colonized the West Indies. By the year 1000 Arawaks from northeast South America had gradually moved up the smaller islands of Lesser Antilles and into the Greater Antilles (Cuba, Hispaniola, Jamaica, and Puerto Rico) as well as into the Bahamas (see Map 17.2). Their route was followed in later centuries by the Caribs, who by the late fifteenth century had overrun most Arawak settlements in the Lesser Antilles and were raiding parts of the Greater Antilles. From the West Indies Arawaks and Caribs also undertook voyages to the North American mainland.

EUROPEAN EXPANSION, 1450-1550

The preceding survey shows that expansion by land and sea was under way in many parts of the world before 1450. Yet the epic sea voyages by Europeans from 1450 to 1550 merit special attention because, by creating new and closer ties among different regions of the world, they profoundly altered the course of world history. Expeditions like Magellan's marked the end of isolation and the acceleration of interaction. By dominating the maritime routes of interaction, Europeans' influence in world affairs rose steadily in the centuries after 1500.

European overseas expansion up to 1550 was the product of two related phenomena. First,

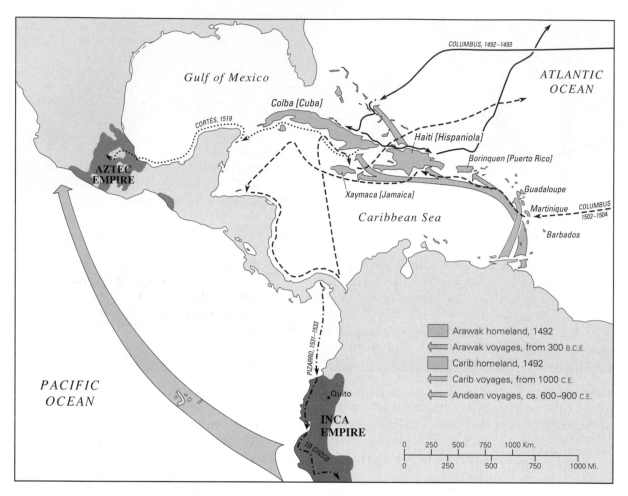

Map 17.2 Middle America to 1533 Early Amerindian voyages from South America brought new settlers to the West Indies and western Mexico. The arrival of Europeans in 1492 soon led to the conquest and depopulation of Amerindians.

Europeans had strong economic, religious, and political motives to expand their contacts and increase their dominance. Second, improvements in their maritime and military technologies gave them the means to master treacherous and unfamiliar ocean environments, seize control of existing maritime trade routes, and conquer new lands.

European Motives and Methods

In many ways overseas expansion continued the commercial, religious, and political expansion that had been under way in the Latin West for several centuries. Since the year 1000 manufacturing and trading cities had been gaining size and wealth along Europe's Mediterranean, Atlantic, and Baltic coasts, and along overland trade routes from northern Italy to the Netherlands. At first, this commercial revival was largely due to western Europe's strengthening domestic economy, but by 1300 imports of Asian silks, spices, and cottons from the Indian Ocean were becoming increasingly important.

Commercial goals sometimes worked together with religious motives; sometimes they were in conflict. The first of a series of Crusades (holy wars) between 1096 and 1270 against the Muslim-controlled eastern Mediterranean had succeeded in putting parts of the biblical Holy Land under Latin Christian control and making Europeans more aware of the luxuries of the East. Later Crusades often combined religious motives with actions to improve Latin Christians' competitive advantage in the trades from the East.

After the decline of the Mongol Empire disrupted the Silk Road across central Eurasia in the fourteenth century, European connections across the Muslim Middle East to the sea routes of the Indian Ocean assumed greater prominence. When the expansion of the Ottoman Empire disrupted these, Latin Christians launched new anti-Muslim Crusades in 1396 and 1444, but failed to halt Turkish advances. When the Turks captured Constantinople in 1453, the pope urged Europeans to stop fighting among themselves and form a united front. As he feared, Christian rulers would neither set aside their political rivalries nor reconcile their conflicting commercial and religious interests. The trading states of Venice and Genoa even made alliances with the Ottomans to protect their merchants' privileged access to the lucrative trade from the East. The king of France later sided with the Turks to prevent his Austrian Hapsburg rivals from achieving too much success in uniting Europe.

The Crusades to the Holy Land had a counterpart in the reconquest of parts of the Iberian Peninsula in southwestern Europe, which had been under Muslim rule since the seventh century. By about 1250 the Iberian kingdoms of Portugal, Castile, and Aragon had conquered all the Muslim lands in Iberia except the southern kingdom of Granada. United by a dynastic marriage in 1469, Castile and Aragon conquered Granada in 1492. These territories were gradually amalgamated into Spain, sixteenth-century Europe's most powerful state.

The Europeans' near constant fighting among themselves and with Muslim neighbors promoted the development of new military technology. In the course of the Hundred Years War (1337–1453) in France, medieval knights in armor were displaced by foot soldiers equipped with powerful crossbows and longbows and later by men using new gunpowder weapons: field cannon and hand-held muskets.

To pay for large and expensive standing armies, European monarchs promoted trade at home as well as overseas. The commercial and ruling classes had worked in close harmony in small trading states in many parts of the world, but the alliances that developed between the larger western European states and their merchants were something new. Such mutually beneficial arrangements stood in sharp contrast to the practice common in China, the Mughal Empire, and the Ottoman Empire of taxing merchants heavily without regard to their long-term interests.

Although these commercial, religious, and military dynamics affected most parts of western Europe, the first phase of western expansion was dominated by the nations of Spain and Portugal on the Iberian Peninsula between the Mediterranean Sea and the Atlantic Ocean. With only a modest share of the Mediterranean trade, Portugal and Spain had much to gain by finding new routes through the Atlantic to the rich trade of the East since these routes would bypass those dominated by the merchant states of northern Italy (see Map 17.3). Moreover, the long Crusades to reclaim lands from earlier Muslim conquests left the Iberian kingdoms with strong religious and economic motives for challenging Muslim control of the Indian Ocean trade. As it happened, both states were also blessed with exceptional leaders.

The Portuguese Voyages

Iberian voyagers were building on earlier efforts to explore the Atlantic. In the eleventh century, Vikings from Scandinavia had made successful voyages in their "long ships" across the North Atlantic and established several settlements in Greenland and parts of North America. In 1291 two Vivaldo brothers from Genoa had even set out to sail through the South Atlantic and around Africa to India—like the Mali canoemen, never to be heard of again. Small Portuguese and Genoese expeditions had discovered the Atlantic islands of Madeira, the Azores, and the Canaries farther south in the course of the fourteenth century.

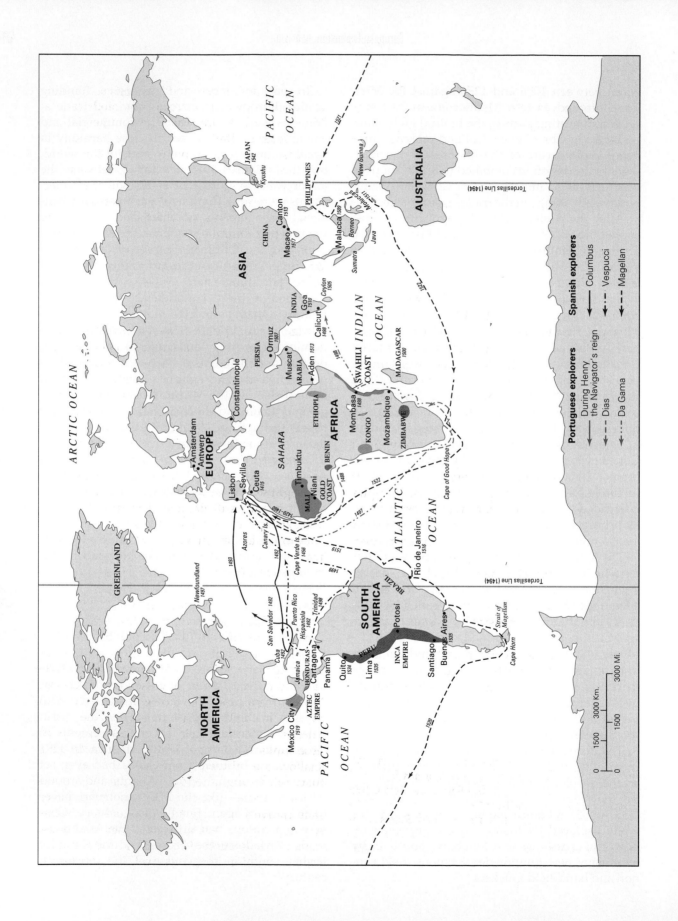

PACIFIC OCEAN

JAPAN
1542
Kyushu

CHINA

Canton
1513

Macao
1517

ASIA

Malacca

Borneo

Java

Sumatra

Moluccas
1511

New Guinea

PHILIPPINES

1521

1542

AUSTRALIA

Tordesillas Line (1494)

INDIA

Goa
1510

Ceylon
1505

Calicut
1498

Ormuz
1507

PERSIA

Muscat

ARABIA

Aden 1513

1488

SWAHILI
COAST

INDIAN
OCEAN

MADAGASCAR
1500

Constantinople

EUROPE

Amsterdam
Antwerp

ETHIOPIA

AFRICA

Mombasa
1498

Mozambique

ZIMBABWE

KONGO

ARCTIC OCEAN

Lisbon
Seville
Ceuta
1415

SAHARA

Timbuktu

Niani

MALI

BENIN

GOLD
COAST

1488

1420–1460

1522

Cape of Good Hope

ATLANTIC

OCEAN

1497

Azores

Canary Is.

Cape Verde Is.
1456

1492

GREENLAND

Newfoundland
1497

1493

1519

1499

1497

BRAZIL

Rio de Janeiro
1516

Tordesillas Line (1494)

San Salvador 1492

Puerto Rico
1492

Trinidad
1498

Hispaniola

Cuba
1492

Jamaica

HONDURAS

Cartagena

Panama

SOUTH
AMERICA

Quito
1534

Lima
1535

PERU

INCA
EMPIRE

Potosi

Santiago

Buenos Aires
1535

Strait of
Magellan

Cape Horn

1520

AZTEC
EMPIRE

Mexico City
1519

NORTH
AMERICA

PACIFIC
OCEAN

Portuguese explorers

During Henry
the Navigator's reign

Dias

Da Gama

Spanish explorers

Columbus

Vespucci

Magellan

3000 Mi.

3000 Km.

1500

1500

0

0

Portugal's decision to invest significant resources in new exploration built on well-established Atlantic fishing and a history of anti-Muslim warfare. When the Muslim government of Morocco in northwestern Africa showed weakness in the fifteenth century, the Portuguese went on the attack, beginning with the city of Ceuta in 1415. This assault combined aspects of a religious crusade, a plundering expedition, and a military tournament in which young Portuguese knights might display their bravery. The capture of this rich city, whose splendid homes, they reported, made those of Portugal look like pigsties, also made the Portuguese better informed about the caravans that brought gold to Ceuta from the African states to the south of the Sahara. Despite the capture of several more ports along Morocco's Atlantic coast, the Portuguese were unable to push inland and gain access to the gold trade. So they sought more direct contact with the gold producers by sailing down the African coast.

The attack on Ceuta had been led by the young Prince Henry (1394–1460), third son of the king of Portugal. Prince Henry devoted the rest of his life to promoting exploration of the South Atlantic. His official biographer Azurara emphasized Henry's religious motives for exploration, which included converting Africans to Christianity, making contact with existing Christian rulers in Africa, and launching joint crusades with them against the Ottomans. According to Azurara, Prince Henry also wished to discover new places and hoped that such new contacts would be profitable. Not surprisingly, most early profits came from gold.

Prince Henry is celebrated as "the Navigator" (though he never ventured much farther from home than Ceuta), because of his sponsorship of new explorations in the Atlantic. His staff collected existing knowledge about the lands beyond Muslim North Africa. They drew on the pioneering efforts of Italian merchants, especially the Genoese, who had learned some of the secrets of the trans-Saharan trade, and of fourteenth-century Jewish cartographers who used information from Arab and European sources to produce remarkably accurate sea charts and maps of distant places. Henry also oversaw the collection of new geographical information from sailors and travelers and sent out ships to explore the Atlantic. His ships established permanent contact with the islands of Madeira in 1418 and the Azores in 1439.

Henry also devoted his resources to solving problems of sailing in unknown waters and open seas. His staff studied and improved navigational instruments that had earlier come into Europe from China and the Islamic world. These instruments included the magnetic compass, first developed in China, and the astrolabe, an instrument of Arab or Greek invention that enabled mariners to determine their location at sea by measuring the position of the sun or the stars in the night sky. Even with such instruments, however, voyages still depended most on the skill and experience of the navigators.

Another achievement of Portuguese mariners was the design of vessels appropriate for the voyages of exploration. Galleys in the Mediterranean were powered by large numbers of oarsmen and were impractical for long ocean voyages. The square sails of the three-masted European ships of the Atlantic were propelled by friendly winds but could not sail at much of an angle against the wind. The voyages of exploration made use of a new vessel, the *caravel* (see Environment and Technology: Caravel). Caravels were small, only a fifth as big as the largest European ships of their day and the large Chinese junks. Their size permitted them to enter shallow coastal waters and explore upriver, but they were strong enough to weather ocean storms. When equipped with triangular lateen sails caravels had great maneuverability; when sporting square Atlantic sails, they had great speed. The addition of small cannon made them superb fighting ships as well. The caravels'

Map 17.3 European Exploration, 1420–1542 The Portuguese and Spanish explorers show the possibility and practicality of intercontinental maritime trade. Before 1450 European trade with Africa and Asia was much more important than that with the Americas, but with the Spanish conquest of the Aztec and Inca Empires the transatlantic trade began to rise. Note the Tordesillas line that in theory separated the Spanish and Portuguese spheres of activity.

combination of economy, speed, agility, and power justified a contemporary's claim that they were "the best ships that sailed the seas."[3]

Besides conquering the seas, pioneering captains also had to overcome their crew's fears that the South Atlantic's waters were boiling hot or contained ocean currents that would prevent any ship entering them from ever returning to Europe. It took Prince Henry fourteen years—from 1420 to 1434—to coax an expedition to venture beyond Cape Bojador in southern Morocco (see Map 17.3). Their fears proved unfounded, but the next stretch of coast, 800 miles (1,300 kilometers) of desert, offered little of interest to the explorers. Finally in 1444 the mariners reached the well-watered and populated lands below the Sahara beginning at what they named "Cape Verde" (the Green Cape) because of its vegetation. By the time of Henry's death in 1460, his explorers had established a secure base of operations in the uninhabited Cape Verde Islands, explored 600 miles (950 kilometers) of coast beyond Cape Verde, as far as what they named "Sierra Leone" (Lion Mountain). From there they knew the coast curved sharply toward the east.

To pay for the research, the ships, and the expeditions during the many decades before the voyages became profitable, Prince Henry drew on the income of the Order of Christ, a Catholic religious society of which he was the governor. In return the Order received the exclusive right to promote Christianity in all the lands that were discovered. The first income from the voyages came from selling into slavery Africans who had been captured in raids on the northwest coast of Africa and the Canary Islands during the 1440s. Raiding for slaves was soon surpassed by trading for gold as the Portuguese made contact with the trading networks that flourished in West Africa and reached across the Sahara. By 1457 enough African gold was coming back to Portugal for the kingdom to issue a new gold coin called the *cruzado* (crusade), a reminder of another Portuguese motive.

It had taken the Portuguese four decades to cover the 1,500 miles (2,400 kilometers) from Lisbon to Sierra Leone; it took only three decades to explore the remaining 4,000 miles (6,400 kilometers) to the southern tip of the African continent. The Portuguese crown continued to sponsor the voyages of exploration, but speedier progress resulted from the growing participation of private commercial interests. In 1469 a prominent Lisbon merchant named Fernão Gomes purchased from the Crown the privilege of exploring 400 miles (650 kilometers) of new coast a year for five years

Portuguese map of Western Africa, 1502   This map shows in great detail the African coastline that Portuguese explorers had charted and named in the fifteenth century. The cartographer has filled in the interior of the continent, which was almost completely unknown to Europeans, with drawings of birds and views of coastal sights: Sierra Leone (*Serra lioa*), named for a mountain shaped like a lion, and the Portuguese Castle of the Mine (*Castello damina*) on the Gold Coast. (From the American Geographical Society Collection, University of Wisconsin—Milwaukee Library)

Caravel: Ship of Exploration

Voyagers who braved the open oceans before 1500 sailed many types of ships from the double canoes of the Polynesians to the giant junks of the Ming expeditions. In their pioneering ocean voyages Europeans used several different vessels, but the newly designed caravel was of special importance in the early decades of Portuguese and Spanish exploration.

Caravels were of modest size, typically 65 to 100 feet (20 to 30 meters) long, about the same length as an oceangoing Polynesian canoe. A large junk might be three times that size. Initially rigged with triangular lateen sails on two masts, most caravels by the end of the fifteenth century flew square sails on the main mast and on a new foremast for greater speed. The lateen sail on the aftermast gave the caravel added maneuverability, as did the rudder, which was attached by iron hinges to the sternpost. Like the junk the caravel had internal compartments and above decks at the rear a structure of rooms known to Europeans as the "castle."

The caravels' sails and sleek lines gave them great speed, while they were still small and maneuverable enough to sail up rivers along the African coast. An important additional feature of the caravel was its armory of small cannon. Fifteen or so mounted on the top deck and in the castle could be fired through openings in the superstructure. After 1500, additional rows of cannon were mounted on lower decks. The desire to increase the firepower of their ships was a major factor in the evolution of the larger European vessels that were used in the conquest of the Indian Ocean.

in return for a monopoly on the trade he developed there. During the period of his contract, Gomes discovered the uninhabited island of São Tomé along the equator; in the next century it became a major source of sugar produced with African slave labor (see Chapter 20). He also explored what later Europeans called the Gold Coast, which became the headquarters of Portugal's West African trade.

The final thrust down the African coast was spurred along by the expectation of finding a passage around Africa to the rich trade of the Indian Ocean. Bartolomeu Dias was the first Portuguese explorer to reach the southern tip of Africa (in 1488) and sight the Indian Ocean beyond. In 1497–1498 a Portuguese expedition led by Vasco da Gama sailed around Africa and reached India. In 1500 an expedition under Pedro Alvares Cabral, while swinging wide to the west in the South Atlantic to catch the winds that would sweep them around southern Africa and on to India, came on the eastern coast of South America, laying the basis for Portugal's claim to Brazil. The gamble that Prince Henry had begun eight decades earlier was about to pay off handsomely.

The Spanish Voyages

Portugal's century-long efforts to explore the South Atlantic are a testimony to persistence, but the new contacts exploited by the Iberians in the sixteenth century were also due to unexpected developments. Two months after Vasco da Gama reached India in 1498, Christopher Columbus (1451–1506), a Genoese mariner in the service of the Spanish kingdom of Castile, sighted the mainland of South America. On two previous voyages of exploration in the West Indies, Columbus had founded settlements and brought enslaved Amerindians and gold back to Spain.

As a younger man Columbus had gained considerable experience of the South Atlantic while participating in Portuguese explorations along the African coast, but he had become convinced there was a shorter way to reach the riches of the East than the route around Africa. By his reckoning (based on a serious misreading of a ninth-century Arab authority), the Canaries were a mere 2,400 nautical miles (4,450 kilometers) from Japan, only one-fifth of the actual distance.

Though absolutely convinced of the feasibility of reaching Asia by sailing west, Columbus struggled for many years to persuade a sponsor to underwrite the costs of the voyage necessary to validate his theory. Portuguese authorities had twice rejected his plan, first in 1485 following a careful study and again in 1488 after Bartholomeu Dias had established the feasibility of a route around Africa. Columbus had received a sympathetic hearing in 1486 from Castile's able ruler, Queen Isabella, but no commitment of support. After a four-year study a Castilian commission appointed by Isabella had found the geographical foundations of Columbus's plan weak, but his persistence finally won over the queen and her husband, King Ferdinand of Aragon. In 1492 they agreed to fund a modest expedition. Their elation at expelling the Muslims from Granada may have put them in a favorable mood.

Columbus and his largely Spanish crew of ninety men "departed Friday the third day of August of the year 1492," he recorded in his log book toward "the regions of India." Their mis-

sion, the royal contract stated, was "to discover and acquire certain islands and mainland in the Ocean Sea." He carried letters of introduction from the Spanish sovereigns to Eastern rulers, including one to the "Grand Khan" (meaning the Chinese emperor). Also on board was a Jewish convert to Christianity whose knowledge of Arabic was expected to facilitate communication with the peoples of eastern Asia. The expedition traveled in three small ships, the *Santa María*, and two caravels, the *Santa Clara* (nicknamed the *Niña*), and a third vessel now known only by its nickname, the *Pinta*.

The expedition began well. Other attempts to explore the Atlantic west of the Azores had been impeded by unfavorable headwinds. But on his earlier voyages along the African coast, Columbus had learned that he could find west-blowing winds in the latitudes of the Canaries, which is why he chose that southern route. After reaching the Canaries, he even had the *Niña*'s lateen sails replaced with square sails, for he knew that from then on speed would be more important than maneuverability.

In October 1492 the expedition reached the islands of the Caribbean, whose inhabitants Columbus insisted on calling "Indians," since he believed that the islands were part of the East Indies. His three subsequent voyages of exploration did nothing to change his mind, but other Europeans were convinced he had reached not the East Indies but came upon islands and continents previously unknown to them. Amerigo Vespucci's explorations, first on behalf of Spain and then for Portugal, led mapmakers to name the new continents "America" after him, rather than "Columbia" after Columbus.

To prevent disputes, Spain and Portugal agreed by the Treaty of Tordesillas in 1494 to divide the world into two hemispheres along an imaginary line down the middle of the North Atlantic Ocean. Lands east of the line in Africa and southern Asia could be claimed by Portugal; lands to the west in the Americas were Spain's. Cabral's discovery of Brazil, however, gave Portugal a valid claim to a part of South America bulging east of the line.

But when the line was extended around the earth, where would Spain's and Portugal's spheres of influence divide in the East? Given Europeans' still limited geographical knowledge in 1494, it was not clear whether the valuable Spice Islands (the Moluccas) that had been the goal of Columbus's voyages were on Portugal's or Spain's side of the line. By chance, in 1513 a Spanish adventurer named Vasco Núñez de Balboa crossed the isthmus (a narrow neck of land) of Panama from the east and sighted the Pacific Ocean on the other side. The 1519 expedition of Ferdinand Magellan (ca. 1480–1521) was designed to complete Columbus's interrupted westward voyage by sailing around the Americas and across the Pacific, whose vast size no European then guessed.

Although the Spice Islands turned out to lie well within Portugal's sphere, as Spain formally acknowledged in 1529, Magellan's voyage laid the basis for Spanish colonization of the Philippine Islands after 1564. Nor did Magellan's death prevent him from being considered the first person to encircle the globe, for a decade earlier he had sailed from Europe to the East Indies as part of an expedition by his native Portugal. His separate voyages thus mirrored the separate spheres claimed by Portugal and Spain—at least until other Europeans began demanding a share. Of course, in the year 1500 European claims were largely theoretical; Portugal and Spain had only modest settlements overseas.

The fact that Columbus failed to find a new route to the East does not detract from the momentous consequences of his voyages for European expansion. Although Spain received little immediate recompense from Columbus's four expeditions, those who followed in his wake laid the basis for Spain's large colonial empires in the Americas and the empires of other European nations (see Chapter 19). In turn, these empires promoted the growth of a major new trading network among the four Atlantic continents that rivaled and eventually surpassed that of the Indian Ocean in importance (see Chapter 20). But the more immediately important consequence was Portugal's entry into the Indian Ocean, which quickly led to a major European presence and profit. Both the eastward and the westward voyages of exploration marked a tremendous expansion of Europe's role in world history.

ENCOUNTERS WITH EUROPE, 1450–1550

What resulted from these new contacts was not determined just by European actions. The ways in which Africans, Asians, and Amerindians perceived their new visitors and reacted to them also influenced their future relations. Some welcomed the Europeans as potential allies; others viewed them as rivals or enemies. In general, Africans and Asians had little difficulty in recognizing the benefits and dangers occasioned by the arrival of European visitors. However, the Amerindians' long isolation from the rest of the world added to the strangeness of their encounter with the Spanish and made them more vulnerable to the unfamiliar diseases that these explorers inadvertently introduced.

Western Africa

Along the West African coast, many Africans were eager for trade with the Portuguese since it would give them new markets for their exports and access to imports cheaper than those that reached them through the middlemen of the overland routes to the Mediterranean. This reaction was evident along the Gold Coast of West Africa first visited by the Portuguese in 1471. Miners in the hinterland had long sold their gold to African traders who took it to the trading cities along the southern edge of the Sahara, where in turn it was sold to traders who had crossed the desert from North Africa. Recognizing that they might get more favorable terms from the new sea visitors, coastal Africans were ready to negotiate with the representative of King John II of Portugal who arrived in 1482 seeking permission to erect a trading fort.

The Portuguese noble in charge, Diogo da Azambuja, and his officers (likely including the young Christopher Columbus, who had entered Portuguese service in 1476) were eager to make a proper impression. They dressed in their best

Portuguese soldier at Benin This detail from a bronze plaque by an African artist at Benin shows an armored European carrying a sword and an early firearm known as a matchlock. The many depictions of European visitors on other plaques that once decorated the palace of the Oba of Benin suggest the interest that West Africans had in making contact with the Portuguese. (Courtesy of the Trustees of the British Museum)

clothes, erected and decorated a reception platform, celebrated a Catholic Mass, and signaled the start of negotiations with trumpets, tambourines, and drums. The African king, Caramansa, staged his entrance with equal ceremony, arriving with a large retinue of attendants and musicians. Through an African interpreter, the two leaders exchanged flowery speeches pledging goodwill and mutual benefit. Caramansa then gave his permission for a small trading fort to be built, assured, he said, by their appearance that these royal delegates were honorable persons, unlike the "few, foul, and vile" Portuguese visitors of the previous decade.

Neither side made a show of force, but the Africans' upper hand was evident in Caramansa's warning that, should the Portuguese fail to be peaceful and honest traders, he and his people would simply move away, depriving their post of food and trade. Trade at the post of Saint George of the Mina (later called Elmina) enriched both sides. From there the Portuguese crown was soon purchasing gold equal to a tenth of the world's production at the time, in return for which Africans received large quantities of goods that Portuguese ships brought from Asia, Europe, and other parts of Africa.

Elsewhere, early contacts involved a mixture of commercial, military, and religious interests. Some African rulers were quick to appreciate that the Europeans' firearms could be a useful addition to their spears and arrows in conflicts with their enemies. Because African religions did not presume to have a monopoly on religious knowledge, coastal rulers were also willing to test the value of Christian practices that the Portuguese eagerly promoted. The rulers of Benin and Kongo, the two largest coastal kingdoms, both invited Portuguese missionaries and soldiers to accompany them into battle to test the power of the Christians' religion along with the power of their muskets.

After a century of aggressive expansion, the kingdom of Benin in the Niger Delta was near the peak of its power when it first encountered the Portuguese. Its *oba* (king) presided over an elaborate bureaucracy from a spacious palace in his large capital city, also known as Benin. In response to a Portuguese visit in 1486, the oba sent an ambassador to Portugal to learn more about the homeland of these strangers. Then he established a royal monopoly on trade with the Portuguese, selling pepper and ivory tusks (to be taken back to Portugal) as well as stone beads, textiles, and prisoners of war (to be resold at Elmina). In return, the Portuguese royal merchants provided Benin with copper and brass, fine textiles, glass beads, and a horse for the king's royal procession. In the early sixteenth century, as the demand for slaves for the Portuguese sugar plantations on the nearby island of São Tomé grew, the oba first raised the price of slaves and then imposed restrictions that limited their sale.

Portuguese efforts to persuade the king and nobles of Benin to accept the Catholic faith ultimately failed. Early kings showed some interest, but after 1538 the obas declined to receive further missionaries. They also closed down the market in male slaves for the rest of the sixteenth century. Exactly why Benin chose to limit its contacts with the Portuguese is uncertain, but the obas clearly had the power to control how much interaction they wanted.

Farther south on the lower Congo River, relations between the Kingdom of Kongo and the Portuguese began similarly in 1482 but had a quite different outcome. Like the oba of Benin, the *manikongo* (king of Kongo) sent delegates to Portugal, established a royal monopoly on trade with the Portuguese, and expressed interest in missionary teachings. Deeply impressed with the new religion, the royal family even made Catholicism the kingdom's official faith. But Kongo, lacking ivory and pepper, had less to trade than Benin. So to acquire the goods brought by Portugal and to pay the costs of the missionaries, it had to sell more and more slaves. Soon the manikongo began to lose his royal monopoly over the slave trade. In 1526 the Christian manikongo, Afonso I (r. 1506–ca. 1540), wrote to his royal "brother," the king of Portugal, begging for his help in stopping the trade because unauthorized Kongolese were kidnapping and selling people, even members of good families. Afonso's appeal that contacts be limited to "some priests and a few people to teach in the schools, and no other goods except wine and flour for the holy sacrament" received no reply. Other subjects took advantage of the manikongo's weakness to rebel against his authority. Indeed, after 1540 the major part of the slave trade from this part of Africa moved farther south (see Chapter 20).

Eastern Africa

Different still were the reactions of the Muslim rulers of the trading coastal states of eastern Africa. As Da Gama's fleet sailed up the coast in 1498, most rulers gave him a cool reception, suspicious of the intentions of these visitors who painted crusaders' crosses on their sails. But one of the cities, Malindi, saw in the Portuguese an ally who could help them expand their trading position, and they provided Da Gama with a pilot to guide him to India. The suspicions of most rulers were justified seven years later when a Portuguese war fleet bombarded and looted most of the coastal cities of eastern Africa in the name of Christ and commerce, though they spared Malindi.

Another eastern African state that saw potential benefit in an alliance with the Portuguese was Christian Ethiopia. In the fourteenth and early fifteenth centuries, Ethiopia faced increasing conflicts with Muslim states along the Red Sea. Emboldened by the rise of the Ottoman Turks, who conquered Egypt in 1517 and launched a major fleet in the Indian Ocean to counter the Portuguese, the talented warlord of the Muslim state of Adal launched a furious assault on Ethiopia. Adal's decisive victory in 1529 reduced the Christian kingdom to a precarious state. At that point Ethiopia's contacts with the Portuguese became crucial.

Since 1452, delegations from Portugal and Ethiopia had been exploring a possible alliance between their states based on their mutual adherence to Christianity. A key figure was the Queen Helena of Ethiopia. A convert from Islam after her marriage to the Ethiopian king, she acted as regent for her young sons after her husband's death in 1478. In 1509 Helena sent a letter to "our very dear and well-beloved brother," the king of Portugal, along with a gift of two tiny crucifixes said to be made of wood from the cross on which Christ had died in Jerusalem. In her letter she proposed an alliance of her land army and Portugal's fleet against the Turks. No such alliance was completed by the time Helena died in 1522. But as Ethiopia's situation grew increasingly desperate, renewed appeals for help were made.

Finally a small Portuguese force commanded by Vasco da Gama's son Christopher reached Ethiopia in 1539, at a time when what was left of the empire was being held together by another woman ruler, Queen Sabla Wangel. With Portuguese help the queen rallied the Ethiopians to renew their struggle. Christopher da Gama was captured and tortured to death, but the Muslim forces lost heart when their leader, Ahmed Gran, was mortally wounded in a later battle. Portuguese aid helped the Ethiopian kingdom save itself from extinction, but a permanent alliance faltered because Ethiopian rulers refused to transfer their Christian affiliation from the patriarch of Alexandria to the Latin patriarch of Rome (the pope) as the Portuguese wanted.

As these examples illustrate, African encounters with the Portuguese before 1550 varied considerably, as much because of the strategies and leadership of particular African states as because of Portuguese policies. Africans and Portuguese might become royal brothers, bitter opponents, or partners in a mutually profitable trade, but Europeans remained a minor presence in most of Africa in 1550. By then the Portuguese had become far more interested in the Indian Ocean trade.

Indian Ocean States

Vasco da Gama's arrival on the Malabar Coast of India in May 1498 did not make a great impression on the citizens of Calicut. After more than ten months at sea, many members of the crew were in ill health. And Da Gama's four small ships were far less imposing than the Chinese fleets of gigantic junks that had called at Calicut sixty-five years earlier and no larger than many of the dhows that filled the harbor of this rich and important trading city. The *samorin* (ruler) of Calicut and his Muslim officials showed mild interest in the Portuguese as new trading partners, but the gifts Da Gama had brought for the samorin evoked derisive laughter. Twelve pieces of fairly ordinary striped cloth, four scarlet hoods, six hats, and six wash basins seemed inferior goods to those accustomed to the luxuries of the Indian Ocean trade. When Da Gama tried to defend his gifts as those of an explorer, not a rich merchant, the samorin cut him short, asking whether he had come to discover men or stones: "If he had come to discover men, as he said, why had he brought nothing?"

Coastal rulers soon discovered that the Portuguese had no intention of remaining poor competitors in the rich trade of the Indian Ocean. Upon Da Gama's return to Portugal in 1499 the jubilant King Manuel styled himself "Lord of the Conquest, Navigation, and Commerce of Ethiopia, Arabia, Persia, and India," setting forth the ambitious scope of his plans. Previously the Indian Ocean had been *mare librum*, an "open sea," used by merchants (and pirates) of all the surrounding states. Now the Portuguese crown intended to make it *mare nostrum*, "our sea," the private property of Portugal alone, which others might use only on its terms.

The ability of little Portugal to assert control over the Indian Ocean stemmed from the superiority of its ships and weapons over the smaller and lightly armed merchant dhows. Indian ports were next on the list of the Portuguese fleet of 81 ships and some 7,000 men, which devastated the Swahili coast cities. Goa, on the west coast of India, fell to a well-armed fleet under the Duke of Albuquerque in 1510, becoming the base from which the Portuguese could menace the trading cities of Gujarat to the north and the Malabar Coast to the south. The port of Hormuz, controlling the entry to the Persian Gulf, was taken in 1515. Aden, at the entrance to the Red Sea, with its intricate natural defenses was able to preserve its independence. The addition of the Gujarati port Diu in 1535 consolidated Portuguese dominance of the western Indian Ocean.

Meanwhile, Portuguese explorers had been reconnoitering the Bay of Bengal and the waters farther east. The independent city of Malacca on the strait between the Malay Peninsula and Sumatra became the focus of their attention. During the fifteenth century Malacca had become the main entrepôt for the trade from China and Japan, from India, and from the Southeast Asian mainland and the Spice Islands. Among the city's more than 100,000 residents an early Portuguese counted eighty-four different languages, including those of merchants from as far west as Cairo, Ethiopia, and the Swahili Coast of East Africa. Many non-Muslim residents supported letting the Portuguese join this cosmopolitan trading community, perhaps to offset the growing solidarity of Muslim traders. In 1511, however, the Portuguese seized this strategic trading center with a force of a thousand fighting men, including three hundred recruited in southern India.

Force was not always necessary. In Macao on the China coast local officials and merchants interested in profitable new trade with the Portuguese persuaded the Chinese government to sanction Portuguese occupation of the port in 1557. From Macao the Portuguese established a virtual monopoly over the trade between China and Japan.

The Portuguese used their control of the major port cities to enforce an even larger trading mo-

nopoly over the main routes in the Indian Ocean. All spices were to be carried in Portuguese ships, as were goods carried between distant ports such as Goa and Macao. Beyond this the Portuguese also tried to control and tax other trade of the Indian Ocean. They required all ships entering and leaving one of their ports to carry a Portuguese passport and to pay customs duties both on their way out and on their return with goods from elsewhere. Portuguese patrols seized vessels attempting to avoid these monopolies, confiscated their cargoes, and either killed the captain and crew or sentenced them to forced labor.

Reactions to this power grab varied. Like the emperors of China, the Mughal emperors of India largely ignored Portugal's maritime intrusions, seeing their interests as maintaining control over their vast land possessions. The Ottomans responded more aggressively. They supported Egypt's fleet of fifteen thousand men against the Christian intruders in the years 1507–1509. Then, having absorbed Egypt into their empire, in 1538 they sent another large expedition against the Portuguese. Both expeditions failed because the Ottoman galleys were no

Portuguese in India Portuguese administrators and traders moved to the Indian Ocean basin following the Portuguese conquests in the early fifteenth century. This Indo-Portuguese drawing of ca. 1540 shows turbaned Indian men carrying a Portuguese noblewoman, trailed by two Portuguese men. The small female figures are probably servants, one of whom may be an African slave. (Ms. 1889, c. 97, Biblioteca Casanateuse Rome. Courtesy, Ministero per I Beui Culturali e Ambientali)

match for the faster, better-armed Portuguese vessels in the open ocean. However, the Ottomans had the advantage in the Red Sea and Persian Gulf, where they had many ports of supply.

The smaller trading states of the region were even less capable of challenging Portuguese domination head on, since their mutual rivalry impeded the formation of any common front. Some chose to cooperate with the Portuguese as the best way to maintain their prosperity and security. Others engaged in evasion and resistance. Two examples illustrate the range of responses among Indian Ocean peoples.

The merchants of Calicut, who were even less welcoming to later Portuguese than they had been to Vasco da Gama, put up some of the most sustained local resistance. In retaliation the Portuguese embargoed all trade with Aden, Calicut's principal trading partner, and centered their trade on the port of Cochin, which had once been a dependency of Calicut. Some Calicut merchants became adept at evading the patrol, but the price of Calicut's resistance was that it shrank in importance as Cochin gradually became the major pepper-exporting port on the Malabar Coast.

The traders and rulers of the state of Gujarat farther north had less success in keeping the Portuguese at bay. At first they resisted Portuguese attempts at monopoly and in 1509 joined Egypt's effort to sweep the Portuguese from the Arabian Sea. But in 1535, finding his state at a military disadvantage due to Mughal attacks, the ruler of Gujarat made the fateful decision to allow the Portuguese to build a fort at Diu in return for their support. Once established, the Portuguese gradually extended their control, so that by midcentury they were licensing and taxing all Gujarati ships. Even after the Mughals took control of Gujarat in 1572, the Mughal emperor Akbar permitted the Portuguese to continue their maritime monopoly in return for giving him one free passport a year for pilgrims to Mecca.

The Portuguese never gained complete control of the Indian Ocean trade, but their domination of key ports and the main trade routes during the sixteenth century brought them considerable profit, which they sent back to Europe in the form of spices and other luxury goods. Asian and East African traders were at the mercy of Portuguese warships, but their individual responses also affected their fates. Some were devastated, but others prospered by meeting the Portuguese demands or evading their patrols. The Portuguese strength was ocean based, however, and had little impact on the Asian and African mainland, in sharp contrast to what was occurring in the Americas.

The Americas

In the Americas the Spanish quickly established a vast territorial empire, in contrast to the trading empires the Portuguese created in Africa and Asia. Their varying approaches had little to do with differences between the two states. In fact, Spain and Portugal had similar motives for expansion and used identical ships and weapons, though the Spanish kingdoms did have somewhat greater resources to draw on. Rather, the isolation of the Amerindian peoples from significant outside contacts produced responses to outside contacts that differed from the responses of peoples in Africa and the Indian Ocean cities. In dealing with the small communities in the Caribbean, the first European settlers resorted to conquest and plunder (rather than trade), a pattern that was later extended to the more powerful Amerindian kingdoms on the American mainland. Moreover, the spread of deadly new diseases among the Amerindians after 1518 weakened their ability to sustain resistance.

The first Amerindians to encounter Columbus were the Arawak of the Greater Antilles (the large Caribbean islands) and the Bahamas to the north (see Map 17.3). They cultivated maize (corn), cassava (a tuber), sweet potatoes, and hot peppers, as well as cotton and tobacco, and they met their other material needs from the sea and wild plants. Although they were skilled at mining and working gold, the Arawak did not trade gold over long distances as Africans did. In 1493 Columbus returned to Hispaniola with several hundred settlers from southern Iberia who hoped to make their fortune. The Arawak extended a cautious welcome. Unprepared to sell large quantities of gold to the Spanish, they told Columbus exaggerated stories about gold in other places to persuade him to move on.

However, the Hispaniola Arawak were provoked to war in 1495 after the settlers stole gold ornaments, confiscated food, and raped women (see Voices and Visions: European Male Sexual Dominance Overseas). In this and later conflicts, the Spaniards' horses and body armor gave them a great advantage, and Arawak were slaughtered by the tens of thousands. The remaining Arawak were forced to pay a heavy tax in gold, spun cotton, and food. Those who failed to meet the quotas were condemned to forced labor. Meanwhile, the cattle, pigs, and goats introduced by the settlers were eating the Arawaks' food crops, causing deaths from famine and disease. Under a new governor appointed by the government of Spain in 1502, the remaining Arawak on Hispaniola were all assigned as forced laborers to Spanish settlers.

The actions of the Spanish in the Antilles reflected patterns and ambitions developed during the wars against the Muslims in Spain in the previous centuries: seeking to serve God by defeating the nonbelievers and placing them under Christian control—and becoming rich in the process. Individual *conquistadores* (conquerors) extended that pattern around the Caribbean. Some attacked the Bahamas to get gold and labor as these became scarce on Hispaniola. Many Arawak were taken to Hispaniola as slaves. In 1508, Juan Ponce de León (1460–1521), who had participated in the conquest of Muslim Spain and the seizure of Hispaniola, conquered the island of Boriquén (Puerto Rico), and in 1513 from there he explored southeast Florida. On a subsequent expedition to the west coast of Florida in 1521, he was fatally wounded in a battle with the Amerindians.

The most audacious expedition to the mainland was led by an ambitious and ruthless nobleman, Hernándo Cortés (1485–1547). He left Cuba in 1519 with six hundred fighting men and most of the island's stock of weapons to assault the rich Aztec Empire in central Mexico, bringing the exploitation and conquest that had begun in the Greater Antilles to the American mainland on a massive scale.

Arawak women making tortillas This sixteenth-century woodcut depicts techniques of food preparation in the West Indies. The woman at the left grinds cornmeal on a *metate;* the woman in the center pats cornmeal dough flat and fries the tortillas; the third woman serves tortillas with a bowl of stew. (Courtesy of the John Carter Brown Library at Brown University)

Like the Caribbean Indians, the people of Mexico had no precedent by which to judge these strange visitors. Later accounts suggest that some Indians believed Cortés to be the legendary ruler Quetzalcóatl, whose return to earth had been prophesied, and treated him with great deference. Other Indians saw the Spaniards as powerful human allies against the Aztecs, who had imposed their rule during the previous century.

From his glorious capital city Tenochtitlán, the Aztec emperor Moctezuma II (r. 1502–1520) sent messengers to greet Cortés and to try to figure out whether he was god or man, friend or foe. Cortés advanced steadily toward the capital, overcoming Aztec opposition with cavalry charges and steel swords and gaining the support of thousands of Amerindian allies from among the Aztecs' unhappy subjects. When they were near, the emperor went out in a great procession, dressed in all his finery, to welcome Cortés with gifts and flower garlands.

Tenochtitlan.

Moctezuma and Cortés, November 1519   In the palace at Tenochtitlan the Emperor Moctezu-ma and his advisers receive the Spaniard Cortés and his Indian translator Dona Marina or La Malinche. Offerings to the Spaniards of a deer, various birds, and maize are shown at the bot-tom. Curiously, the Tlaxcalan artist has shown the Aztec ruler and his companions in Tlaxcalan dress. (Neg. #330880, Courtesy, Department of Library Services, American Museum of Natural History)

Despite Cortés's initial promise that he came in friendship, Moctezuma quickly found himself a prisoner in his own palace, his treasury looted, and its gold melted down. Soon a major battle was raging in and about the capital between the Spaniards with their allies and the supporters of the Aztecs. At one point the Aztecs gained the upper hand, destroying half the Spanish force and four thousand of their Amerindian allies and offering their gods a sacrifice of fifty-three Span-ish prisoners and four horses, their severed heads displayed in rows on pikes. Reinforced by new troops from Cuba, Cortés was able to regain the advantage by means of Spanish cannon and clever battle strategies. The capture of Tenochti-tlán was also greatly facilitated by the spread of smallpox from the Antilles, which weakened and

killed many of the city's defenders. When the capital fell, the conquistadores overcame other parts of Mexico.

As Mexico capitulated, other Spaniards were eyeing the vast empire of the Inca, stretching nearly 3,000 miles (5,000 kilometers) south from the equator and containing half of the population in South America. The Inca had conquered the inhabitants of the Andes Mountains and the Pa-cific coast of South America during the previous century, and their rule was not fully accepted by all of the peoples whom they had defeated. With the vast Pacific Ocean on one side of their realm and the sparsely inhabited Amazon forests on the other, it is not surprising that the Incan rulers believed they controlled most of the world worth having. Theirs was indeed a great empire with

European Male Sexual Dominance Overseas: A Metaphor?

European expansion and colonization were overwhelmingly the work of men. Missionaries chose to remain celibate by choice; other men did not, as these two letters make clear. Some historians consider the exploitation of local women to be a metaphor for European dominance in other respects. The first letter, dated 1495, is from Michele de Cuneo, an officer on Columbus's second voyage across the Atlantic.

While I was in the boat I captured a very beautiful Carib woman, whom the said Lord Admiral [Columbus] gave to me, and with whom, having taken her into my cabin, she being naked according to their custom, I conceived desire to take pleasure. I wanted to put my desire into execution but she did not want it and treated me with her finger nails in such a manner that I wished I had never begun. But seeing that, (to tell you the end of it all), I took a rope and thrashed her well, for which she raised such unheard of screams that you would not have believed your ears. Finally we came to an agreement in such manner that I can tell you that she seemed to have been brought up in a school of harlots.

The second letter, dated 1550, is from an Italian Jesuit missionary in India to Ignatius Loyola, the founder of the Jesuits, in Rome.

Your reverence must know that the sin of licentiousness is so widespread in these regions [India] that no check is placed upon it, which leads to great inconveniences, and to great disrespect of the sacraments. I say this of the Portuguese, who have adopted the vices and customs of the land without reserve, including the evil custom of buying droves of slaves, male and female, just as if they were sheep, large and small. There are countless men who buy droves of girls and sleep with all of them, and subsequently sell them. There are innumerable married settlers who have four, eight, or ten female slaves and sleep with them, as is common knowledge. This is carried to such excess that there was one man in Malacca who had twenty-four women of various races, all of whom were his slaves, and all of whom he enjoyed. I quote this city because it is a thing that everybody knows. Most men, as soon as they can afford to buy a female slave, almost invariably use her as a girl-friend (*amiga*), besides many other dishonesties, in my poor understanding.

What circumstances made it virtually impossible for the women in question to resist the European men's advances? What phrases in the letters suggest that the writers attribute some responsibility for these encounters to the sexual license of the women involved? Are such inferences credible? Are such situations an appropriate metaphor for the growing global dominance of Europeans?

Sources: The first letter is reprinted from Samuel Eliot Morison, trans. and ed., *Journals and Other Documents in the Life and Voyages of Christopher Columbus* (New York: Heritage Press, 1963), 212; the second is from *The Portuguese Seaborne Empire: 1415–1825* by C. R. Boxer. Copyright © 1969 by C. R. Boxer. Reprinted by permission of Alfred A. Knopf, Inc.

highly productive agriculture, exquisite stone cities (such as the capital, Cuzco), and rich gold and silver mines. The power of the Incan emperor was sustained by beliefs that he was descended from the Sun God and by an efficient system of roads and messengers that kept him informed about major events in his empire.

Yet all was not well. At the end of the 1520s, before even a whisper of news about the Spanish reached them, an epidemic of smallpox unwittingly introduced from the Old World claimed countless lives, perhaps including the Incan emperor in 1530. Even more devastating was the threat awaiting the empire from Francisco

Pizarro (ca. 1478–1541) and his motley band of 180 men, 37 horses, and two cannon. With limited education and some military experience, Pizarro had come to the Americas in 1502 at the age of 25 to seek his fortune. He had participated in the conquest of Hispaniola and in Balboa's expedition across the isthmus of Panama. By 1520 Pizarro had grown wealthy as a landowner and official in Panama, yet he gambled his wealth on more adventures, exploring the Pacific coast to a point south of the equator, where he learned of the wealth of the Inca. With a license from the king of Spain, he set out from Panama in 1531 to conquer them.

In November 1532 Pizarro arranged to meet the new Incan emperor, Atahualpa (r. 1531–1533), in the valley of Cajamarca. With supreme boldness and brutality, Pizarro's men seized Emperor Atahualpa off a rich litter borne by eighty nobles as it passed through an enclosed courtyard. Though surrounded by an Incan army of at least forty thousand, the Spaniards were able to use their cannon to create confusion while their swords sliced the emperor's lightly armed retainers and servants to pieces by the thousands.

Noting the glee with which the Spaniards seized gold, silver, and emeralds, the captive Atahualpa offered them what he thought would satisfy even the greediest among them in exchange for his freedom: a roomful of gold and silver. But when the ransom of 13,400 pounds (6,000 kilograms) of gold and 26,000 pounds (12,000 kilograms) of silver was paid, the Spaniards gave Atahualpa a choice: he could be burned at the stake as a heathen or baptized as a Christian and then strangled. He chose the latter, and with him went the central unity of the complex Incan Empire.

In 1533 the Spaniards took Cuzco and from there set out to conquer and loot the rest of the empire. The defeat of a final rebellion in 1536 spelled the end of Incan rule. Five years later Governor Pizarro himself met a violent death at the hands of Spanish rivals, but the conquest of the mainland continued. Incited by the fabulous wealth of the Aztecs and Incas, conquistadores extended Spanish conquest and exploration in South and North America, dreaming of new treasuries to loot.

Patterns of Dominance

Within fifty years of Columbus's first landing in 1492, the Spanish had located and occupied all of the major population centers of the Americas and the penetration of the more thinly populated areas was well underway. In no other part of the world was the pattern of European dominance so complete. Why did the peoples of the Americas suffer such a different fate from that of peoples in Africa and Asia? Why were the Spanish able to erect a vast land empire in the Americas so quickly? Three factors seem crucial.

First, long isolation from the rest of humanity made the inhabitants of the Americas vulnerable to new diseases. The unfamiliar illnesses first devastated the native inhabitants of the Caribbean islands and then were unknowingly spread to the mainland by the conquistadores. Contemporaries estimated that between 25 and 50 percent of those infected with smallpox soon died. Repeated epidemics inhibited Amerindians' ability to regain control. Because evidence is very limited, estimates of the size of the population before Columbus's arrival vary widely, but there is no disputing the fact that the Amerindian population fell sharply during the sixteenth century. The Americas became a "widowed land," open to resettlement from across the Atlantic.

A second major factor was military. In many battles steel swords, protective armor, and horses gave the Spaniards an advantage over their Amerindian opponents. Though few in number, muskets and cannon gave the Spaniards a significant psychological as well as military edge. However, it should not be forgotten that the Spanish conquests depended heavily on large numbers of Amerindian allies armed with weapons the same as those of the people they defeated. But perhaps the Spaniards' most decisive military advantage came from the no-holds-barred fighting techniques they had developed during a long history of violent war at home.

The third factor in the Spanish conquest of the New World were patterns already established in Spain's reconquest of Granada in 1492. The reconquest provided precedents for imposing forced labor and forced conversion on conquered peoples and incorporating their conquered lands into a new empire.

The same three factors help explain the quite different outcomes elsewhere. Because of centuries of contact before 1500 peoples in Europe, Africans, and Asians shared the same Old World diseases. Only small numbers of very isolated peoples in Africa and Asia suffered the demographic calamity that undercut the ability of Amerindians to retain control of their lands. The Europeans' greatest military advantage was at sea, as the conquest of the Indian Ocean trade routes showed. On land, however, they had no decisive advantage against more numerous indigenous populations that were not weakened by disease. The religious zeal of the reconquest showed itself in the attacks on Muslims and other non-Christians, but existing trading networks in Africa and Asia helped ensure that commerce, not conquest, was the paramount objective in Africa and Asia in the first century of European expansion.

Ocean, and conquered a vast land empire in the Americas.

As dramatic and momentous as these events were, they were not completely unprecedented. The riches of the Indian Ocean trade that brought a gleam to the eye of many Europeans had been developed over many centuries by the trading peoples who inhabited the surrounding lands. Europeans' ships were less impressive than the treasure fleets of Zheng He. Their conquests of the Americas were no more rapid or brutal than the earlier Mongol conquests of Eurasia. Even the crossing of the Pacific had been done before, though in stages.

What made the European expansion unprecedented had less to do with what happened between 1450 and 1550 than with what happened later. Europeans' overseas empires endured longer than the Mongols' and continued to expand for three-and-a-half centuries after 1550. Unlike the Chinese, the Europeans did not turn their backs on the world after an impressive burst of exploration. Not content with dominance in the Indian Ocean trade, Europeans opened a second maritime network in the Atlantic that grew to rival the Indian Ocean network in the wealth of its trade. It was this growing dominance that made the period from 1450 to 1550 seem to mark the beginning of a new age—one that in time would affect areas of the world untouched by the first century of European expansion.

CONCLUSION

Historians are in wide agreement that the century between 1450 and 1550 was a major turning point in world history, the beginning of an age that they have called the "Vasco da Gama epoch," the "Columbian era," the "age of Magellan," or simply the "modern period." During those years European explorers opened new long-distance trade routes across the world's three major oceans, establishing regular contact among all the continents for the first time. By 1550 those who followed them had broadened trading contacts with sub-Saharan Africa, gained mastery of the rich trade routes of the Indian

SUGGESTED READING

There is no single survey of the different expansions covered by this chapter, but the selections edited by Joseph R. Levenson, *European Expansion and the Counter Example of Asia, 1300–1600* (1967), remain a good introduction to Chinese expansion and Western impressions of China. Janet Abu-Lughod, *Before European Hegemony: The World System A.D. 1250–1350* (1989), is a stimulating speculative reassessment of the importance of the Mongols and the Indian Ocean trade in the creation of the modern world system; she summarizes her thesis in the American Historical Association (AHA) booklet *The World System in the Thirteenth Century: Dead-End or Precursor?* (1993).

The Chinese account of Zheng He's voyages is Ma Huan, *Ying-yai Sheng-lan: "The Overall Survey of the Ocean's Shores"* [1433], ed. and trans. J. V. G. Mills (1970). Halil Inalcik, *The Ottoman Empire: The Classical Age, 1300–1600,* trans. N. Itzkowitz and C. Imber (1989), is a readable introduction to that empire's rise. William H. McNeill's AHA booklet *The Age of Gunpowder Empires 1450–1800* (1989) provides a brief overview of European, Muslim, and East Asian arms and politics. See also Michael Adas, ed., *Islamic and European Expansion: The Forging of a Global Order* (1993), and Bernard Lewis, *Cultures in Conflict: Christians, Muslims, and Jews in the Age of Discovery* (1995). A reliable guide to Polynesian expansion is Jesse D. Jennings, ed., *The Prehistory of Polynesia* (1979), especially the excellent chapter "Voyaging," by Ben R. Finney, which summarizes his *Voyage of Rediscovery: A Cultural Odyssey Through Polynesia* (1994). Ivan Van Sertima, *They Came Before Columbus: The African Presence in Ancient America* (1976), speculates on the basis of limited evidence that voyagers from West Africa not only reached the Americas but established a significant presence there.

A simple introduction to the technologies of European expansion is Carlo M. Cipolla, *Guns, Sails, and Empires: Technological Innovation and the Early Phases of European Expansion, 1400–1700* (1965; reprint, 1985). More advanced is Roger C. Smith, *Vanguard of Empire: Ships of Exploration in the Age of Columbus* (1993).

The European exploration is well documented and the subject of intense historical investigation. Clear general accounts based on the contemporary records are Boies Penrose, *Travel and Discovery in the Age of the Renaissance, 1420–1620* (1952); J. H. Parry, *The Age of Reconnaissance: Discovery, Exploration, and Settlement, 1450–1650* (1963); and G. V. Scammell, *The World Encompassed: The First European Maritime Empires, c. 800–1650* (1981). A clear and scholarly examination of the naval technology underlying European expansion is Roger C. Smith, *Vanguard of Empire: Ships of Exploration in the Age of Columbus* (1993).

An excellent general introduction to Portuguese exploration is C. R. Boxer, *The Portuguese Seaborne Empire, 1415–1825* (1969). More detail can be found in Bailey W. Diffie and George D. Winius, *Foundations of the Portuguese Empire, 1415–1580* (1977). The medieval background to European intercontinental voyages is summarized by Felipe Fernandez-Armesto, *Before Columbus: Exploration and Colonization from the Mediter-*

ranean to the Atlantic, 1229–1492 (1987). John William Blake, ed., *Europeans in West Africa, 1450–1560* (1942), is an excellent two-volume collection of contemporary Portuguese, Castilian, and English sources. Elaine Sanceau, *The Life of Prester John: A Chronicle of Portuguese Exploration* (1941), is a very readable account of Portuguese relations with Ethiopia. *The Summa Oriental of Tomé Pires: An Account of the East, from the Red Sea to Japan, Written in Malacca and India in 1512–1515,* trans. Armando Cortesão (1944), provides a detailed firsthand account of the Indian Ocean during the Portuguese's first two decades there.

The other Iberian kingdoms' expansion is well summarized by J. H. Parry, *The Spanish Seaborne Empire* (1967). Samuel Eliot Morison's *Admiral of the Ocean Sea: A Life of Christopher Columbus* (1942) is a fine scholarly celebration of the epic mariner, also available in an abridged version as *Christopher Columbus, Mariner* (1955). More focused on the shortcomings of Columbus and his Spanish peers is Tzvetan Todorov, *The Conquest of America,* trans. Richard Howard (1985). William D. Phillips and Carla Rhan Phillips, *The Worlds of Christopher Columbus* (1992), examines the mariner and his times in terms of modern concerns. Peggy K. Liss, *Isabel the Queen: Life and Times* (1992), is a sympathetic examination of Queen Isabella of Castile. Detailed individual biographies of each of the individuals in Pizarro's band are the subject of James Lockhart's *Men of Cajamarca: A Social and Biographical Study of the First Conquerors of Peru* (1972). A firsthand account of Magellan's expedition is Antonio Pigafetta, *Magellan's Voyage: A Narrative Account of the First Circumnavigation,* available in a two-volume edition (1969) that includes a facsimile reprint of the manuscript.

The trans-Atlantic encounters of Europe and the Americas are described by J. H. Elliott, *The Old World and the New, 1492–1650* (1970). Alfred W. Crosby, *The Columbian Voyages, the Columbian Exchange, and Their Historians* (1987), available as an AHA booklet, provides a brief overview of the first encounters in the Americas and their long-term consequences. The early chapters of Mark A. Burkholder and Lyman L. Johnson, *Colonial Latin America,* 2d ed. (1994), give a clear and balanced account of the Spanish conquest. For the Caribbean see Irvina Rouse, *The Tainos: Rise and Decline of the People Who Greeted Columbus* (1992).

The perceptions of the peoples European explorers encountered are not usually so well documented. John Thornton, *Africa and Africans in the Making of the Atlantic World, 1400–1680* (1992), examines Africans' encounters with Europeans, importance in the Atlantic economy, and impact in the New World. *The Broken Spears: The Aztec Account of the Conquest of Mexico*, ed. Miguel Leon-Portilla (1962), presents Amerindian chronicles in a readable package, as does Nathan Wachtel, *The Vision of the Vanquished: The Spanish Conquest of Peru Through Indian Eyes* (1977). Anthony Reid, *Southeast Asia in the Age of Commerce, 1450–1680* (1988), deals with events in that region.

NOTES

1. Ma Huan, *Ying-yai Sheng-lan: "The Overall Survey of the Ocean's Shores,"* ed. Feng Ch'eng-Chün, trans. J. V. G. Mills (Cambridge, England: Cambridge University Press, 1970), 180.

2. Ivan Van Sertima, *They Came Before Columbus: The African Presence in Ancient America* (New York: Random House, 1976). Most historians are unconvinced by Van Sertima's thesis, which suffers from problems similar to those of Heyerdahl's thesis about the settlement of the Pacific.

3. Alvise da Cadamosto in *The Voyages of Cadamosto and Other Documents*, ed. and trans. G. R. Crone (London: Hakluyt Society, 1937), 2.

CHAPTER EIGHTEEN

The Transformation of Europe,

1500–1750

Religious and Political Innovations · Building State Power

Urban Society and Commercial Technology

Rural Society and Environmental Change · The Realm of Ideas

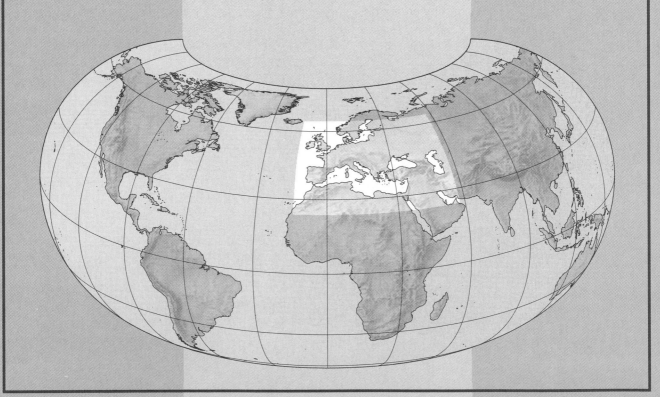

In the winter of 1697–1698 Tsar Peter I, the young ruler of Russia, traveled in disguise through the Netherlands and England, eager to discover how western European societies were becoming so powerful and wealthy. A practical man, Peter paid special attention to ships and weapons, even working for a time as a ship's carpenter in the Netherlands. With great insight, he perceived that western European success owed as much to trade and toleration as to technology. Trade generated the money to spend on weapons, while toleration attracted talented persons fleeing persecution.

Upon his return to Russia, Peter resolved to "open a window onto Europe," to reform features of his vast empire that he believed were backward. He ended the servile status of women and personally trimmed his noblemen's long beards to conform to Western styles. Peter also put the skilled technical advisers he had brought back with him to work modernizing Russia's industry and military forces. His reformed armies soon gained success against Sweden for possession of a port on the Baltic Sea and against the Ottoman Turks for access to the warm waters of the Black Sea. Then Peter turned to redesigning Russia's government on a French model, imitating King Louis XIV's new palace and his rituals of absolute royal power.

As Peter's actions illustrate, by the end of the seventeenth century, western European achievements in state administration, warfare, business, and ideas were setting a standard that others wished to imitate. Added to the maritime expansion that was examined in Chapter 17, these internal transformations promoted Western global ascendancy. Yet as this chapter shows, such achievements did not come smoothly. Warfare, poverty, persecution, and environmental degradation were also widespread in Europe between 1500 and 1750. Men like Tsar Peter, concerned with increasing state power, were little troubled by the misery that rapid change produced, but for ordinary men and women these early modern times were difficult and dangerous.

RELIGIOUS AND POLITICAL INNOVATIONS

Two bitter struggles in the early sixteenth century marked the end of Europe's medieval era and the beginning of the early modern period. One was the Reformation, a movement that succeeded in implementing many religious reforms but at the cost of shattering Latin Christian unity. The other was the unsuccessful attempt to unite Christian Europe to block the inroads of the Muslim armies of the Ottoman Empire. In place of unity, early modern Europe was plagued by divisions and warfare among its national monarchies.

Yet such disunity helped foster Europe's growing strength in the world. Competition and conflict promoted technological, administrative, social, and economic changes that propelled western Europe ahead of the more unified and peaceful empires of China and India and even ahead of the militarily aggressive Ottoman Empire.

Religious Reformation

In 1500 the papacy, the central administration of Latin Christianity, was simultaneously gaining stature and suffering from corruption and dissent. Economic prosperity was increasing revenues from taxes and donations, allowing successive popes to fund ambitious reconstruction projects in Rome, their capital city. During the sixteenth century they built fifty-four new churches and other buildings that were showcases of the artistic Renaissance then under way. The church's wealth and power also attracted into ecclesiastical careers some ambitious individuals whose personal lives became the source of scandal.

St. Peter's Basilica   Constructed between 1506 and 1626, the new St. Peter's displayed the prestige of the papacy and the artistry of Renaissance Italy. This 1774 engraving shows the splendid quadruple colonnade added by Gianlorenzo Bernini between 1629 and 1662 enclosing St. Peter's piazza. (Courtesy of the Trustees of the British Museum, BM Dept. Prints and Drawings)

The jewel of the new building projects was the magnificent new Saint Peter's basilica in Rome. The unprecedented size and splendor of this church were intended to glorify the Christian faith, display the skill of Renaissance artists and builders, and enhance the standing of the papacy. Such a project required refined tastes and vast sums of money. The skillful overseer of the design and financing of the new Saint Peter's was Pope Leo X (r. 1513–1521), a member of the wealthy Medici family of Florence, which was famous for its patronage of the arts.

Pope Leo's artistic taste was superb and his personal life free from scandal, but he was more a man of action than a spiritual leader. One technique that he used to raise funds for the basilica was to authorize an *indulgence*—forgiveness of the punishment due for past sins, granted as a reward for a pious act such as making a pilgrimage, saying a particular prayer, or making a donation to a religious cause. Pope Leo's agents preached the indulgence in ways that many felt emphasized fundraising more than religious piety.

In one German state where the new indulgence was being preached lived a young professor of sacred scripture named Martin Luther (1483–1546), whose personal religious quest had led him to forsake money and marriage for a monastery. While seeking salvation through prayer and self-denial, Luther formed a view of sin and salvation different from Pope Leo's. In Saint Paul's Epistle to the Romans he read that salvation came not by "doing certain things" but from religious faith. Thus Luther was very upset by preachers who emphasized the act of giving money, not the faith behind it. He wrote to Pope Leo, asking him to end the abuses and challenged the preachers to a debate on the theology of indulgences.

The conflict between these two churchmen quickly moved beyond the preaching of indulgences. Largely ignoring Luther's theological objections, Pope Leo regarded his letter as a challenge to papal power and acted to silence him. During a debate in 1519 a papal representative led Luther into open disagreement with some church doctrines, for which the papacy condemned him.

Blocked in his effort to reform the church from within, Luther burned the papal bull (document) of condemnation, rejecting the pope's authority and beginning the movement known as the *Protestant Reformation.* Accusing what he called "Romanists" (Roman Catholics) of relying on "good works," Luther insisted that the only way to salvation was through faith in Jesus Christ. He further declared that Christian belief must be based on the word of God in the Bible and on Christian tradition, not on the authority of the pope, as Catholics held. His conclusions led him to abandon his monastery, and he later married a former nun. Today Roman Catholics and most Lutherans have resolved their differences on many of these theological issues. But in the sixteenth century, stubbornness on both sides made reconciliation impossible.

Inspired by Luther, others raised their voices to denounce the ostentation and corruption of church leaders and to call for a return to authentic Christian practices and beliefs. John Calvin (1509–1564), a well-educated Frenchman who turned from the study of law to theology after experiencing a religious conversion, became a highly influential Protestant leader. As a young man in 1535, Calvin published *The Institutes of the Christian Religion,* a masterful synthesis of Chris-

tian teachings. Much of the *Institutes* was traditional medieval theology, but in two respects Calvin's teaching differed from that of Roman Catholics and Lutherans.

First, while agreeing with Luther's emphasis on faith over works, Calvin denied that even human faith could merit salvation. Salvation, said Calvin, was God's free gift to those "predestined" for it. Second, Calvin went further than Luther in curtailing the power of ordained clergymen and in simplifying religious rituals. Calvinist congregations elected their governing committees and in time created regional and national synods (councils) to regulate doctrinal issues. Calvinists were also distinguished by their simplicity in dress, life, and worship. In an age of ornate garments, they wore simple black clothes, avoided ostentatious living, and worshiped in churches devoid of statues, most musical instruments, stained-glass windows, incense, and vestments.

The Reformers appealed to sincere religious sentiments. But many who joined them brought along other political and economic agendas. Rising national consciousness often became identified with religious affiliation, as in the spread of Lutheranism in the German-speaking states. Peasants and urban laborers sometimes adopted a different faith in defiance of their masters. Since Protestants and Roman Catholics believed in male dominance in both the church and the family, neither tradition had a special attraction for women. Most Protestants, however, rejected the medieval tradition of celibate priests and nuns and advocated Christian marriage for all adults.

Shaken by the intensity of the Protestant Reformers' appeal, the Catholic Church undertook its own reforms. A council that met at the city of Trent, in northern Italy, in three sessions between 1545 and 1563 issued decrees reforming the education, discipline, and practices of the Roman Catholic clergy. The council also reaffirmed the supremacy of the pope and clarified Catholic beliefs (including those concerning indulgences) in light of Protestant challenges. Also important to this "Catholic Reformation" were the activities of a new religious order—the Society of Jesus, or "Jesuits," that had been founded by the Spanish nobleman Ignatius of Loyola (1491–1556) in 1534. Well-educated Jesuits helped stem the Protestant tide and win back some adherents by their teaching and preaching (see Map 18.1). Other Jesuits became important missionaries overseas (see Chapter 22).

Given the complexity of the issues and the intensity of the emotions that the Protestant Reformation raised, it is not surprising that violence often flared up. Both sides persecuted and sometimes executed those of differing views. Bitter "wars of religion," fought over a mixture of religious and secular issues, continued until 1648.

The Failure of Empire

Meanwhile, another great medieval institution, the Holy Roman Empire, was also in trouble. The threat to Europe that the Ottoman Turks posed after their capture of the important Greek Christian city of Constantinople in 1453 stirred interest in a pan-European coalition to stop the Muslim advances. Hope centered on a young man named Charles (1500–1557), descended from the powerful Hapsburg family of Vienna and the rulers of Burgundy on his father's side and from the rulers of Spain on his mother's. After the deaths of his maternal grandfather, Ferdinand of Spain, and his father, Philip of Burgundy, in rapid succession in 1516, Charles inherited the Spanish thrones of Castile and Aragon along with their extensive European and American possessions. In 1519 the young king also secured election as Emperor Charles V, ruler of the Holy Roman Empire, a loose federation of Germanic states and principalities that the Hapsburgs had headed for three generations (see Map 18.2).

A Christian coalition led by Charles eventually halted the Ottomans at the very gates of Vienna in 1529, but Charles's efforts to amalgamate his several possessions into Europe's strongest state met strong resistance. King Francis I of France, who had lost to Charles in the election for Holy Roman Emperor, openly supported the Muslim Turks to weaken his rival. Nor were the heads of the many states that made up the Holy Roman Empire eager to share their powers and revenues with the emperor. Luther's Reforma-

tion played into their hands. In the imperial Diet (assembly) many German princes, swayed by Luther's appeals to German nationalism against an Italian pope, also opposed Charles, a French-speaking emperor who defended the pope. Some Lutheran princes enriched themselves by seizing the church's lands within their states in the name of reform. The origins of the new kingdom of Prussia (created in 1701) were in lands that a Lutheran prince seized from a Catholic religious order in 1525.

After decades of bitter fighting, Charles V gave up his efforts at unification. He brought peace to the empire in 1555 by giving the princes the right to choose whether Catholicism or Lutheranism would prevail in their particular states, and he allowed them to keep any church lands they had seized before 1552. Then the prematurely aged Charles retired to a monastery, passing the throne of Spain to his son, Philip II, and securing the election of his brother Maximilian as Holy Roman Emperor, the titular head of a decentralized collection of German states.

Thus the two institutions that had symbolized Western unity during the Middle Ages—the papacy and the Holy Roman Empire—had been seriously weakened by the mid-sixteenth century. Luther emerged from a monastery to break the papacy; Charles retired to a monastery, broken by opposition to an effective pan-European empire. Neither the papacy nor the Holy Roman Empire disappeared, but after the year 1500 national kingdoms took over religious and political leadership in western Europe. Indeed, the collapse of religious and imperial unity was partly the work of their ambitious rulers, who were eager to enhance their own states by bringing all other institutions under their control and preventing the emergence of any imperial superpower.

Royal Centralization

Talented rulers and their able ministers guided the rise of these European kingdoms. When the system of monarchical succession worked best, it brought to the throne a creative, energetic young person who gained experience and loyalty over

Map 18.1 The Reformation in Europe   The Reformation brought greater religious freedom and devotion but also led to religious conflict and persecution. In many places the Reformation accelerated the trend toward state control of religion and added religious differences to the motives for wars among Europeans.

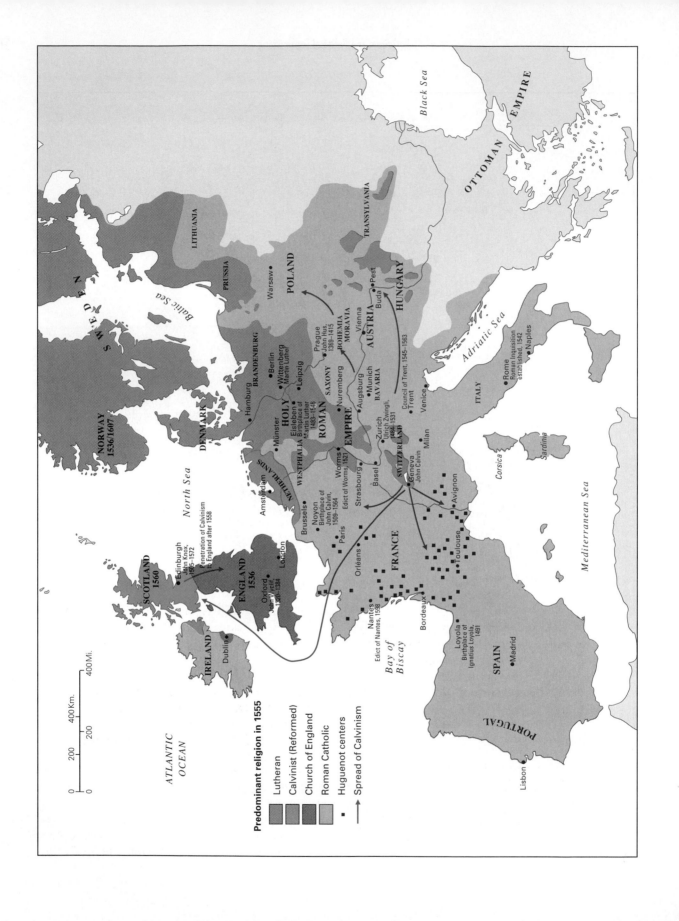

Predominant religion in 1555

Lutheran

Calvinist (Reformed)

Church of England

Roman Catholic

■ Huguenot centers

→ Spread of Calvinism

ATLANTIC
OCEAN

0   200   400 Km.
0   200   400 Mi.

IRELAND
Dublin

SCOTLAND
1560
Edinburgh
John Knox,
1505–1572

North Sea

ENGLAND 1536
Oxford
John Wyclif,
1320–1384
London

Penetration of Calvinism
to England after 1558

NETHERLANDS
Amsterdam

NORWAY
1536/1607

SWEDEN

DENMARK

Baltic Sea

Hamburg

Münster

WESTPHALIA

Brussels

Noyon
Birthplace of
John Calvin,
1509–1564

Paris

FRANCE

Orléans

Nantes
Edict of Nantes, 1598

Bay of
Biscay

Bordeaux

Toulouse

Avignon

Eisleben
Birthplace of
Martin Luther
1483–1546

HOLY
ROMAN
EMPIRE

Worms
Edict of Worms, 1521

Strasbourg

Basel

SWITZERLAND

Geneva
John Calvin

Zurich
Ulrich Zwingli,
1484–1531

BRANDENBURG
Berlin

Wittenberg
Martin Luther

Leipzig

SAXONY

Nuremberg

Augsburg

Munich

BAVARIA

PRUSSIA

LITHUANIA

Warsaw

POLAND

Prague
John Hus,
1369–1415

BOHEMIA

MORAVIA

AUSTRIA
Vienna

Trent
Council of Trent, 1545–1563

Venice

Milan

Pest
Buda

HUNGARY

TRANSYLVANIA

Black Sea

OTTOMAN EMPIRE

Adriatic Sea

ITALY

Rome
Roman Inquisition
established, 1542

Naples

Corsica

Sardinia

Mediterranean Sea

SPAIN
Madrid

Loyola
Birthplace of
Ignatius Loyola,
1491

PORTUGAL

Lisbon

Spain	France	England/Great Britain
Hapsburg Dynasty	**Valois Dynasty**	**Tudor Dynasty**
Charles I (1516–1556)	Francis I (1515–1547)	Henry VIII (1509–1547)
	Henry II (1547–1559)	Edward VI (1547–1553)
Philip II (1556–1598)	Francis II (1559–1560)	Mary I (1553–1558)
	Charles IX (1560–1574)	Elizabeth I (1558–1603)
	Henry III (1574–1589)	**Stuart Dynasty**
	Bourbon Dynasty	James I (1603–1625)
Philip III (1598–1621)	Henry IV (1589–1610)[a]	Charles I (1625–1649)[a, b]
Philip IV (1621–1665)	Louis XIII (1610–1643)	(Puritan Republic, 1649–1660)
Charles II (1665–1700)	Louis XIV (1643–1715)	Charles II (1660–1685)
		James II (1685–1688)[b]
		William III (1689–1702)
		and Mary II (1689–1694)
Bourbon Dynasty		Anne (1702–1714)
Philip V (1700–1746)		**Hanoverian Dynasty**
	Louis XV (1715–1774)	George I (1714–1727)
Ferdinand VI (1746–1759)		George II (1727–1760)

[a]Died a violent death.
[b]Was overthrown.

Table 18.1 Rulers and Dynasties in Early Modern Western Europe

many decades. By good fortune the leading states produced many such talented, hard-working, and long-lived rulers. Spain had only six rulers in the two centuries from 1556 to 1759, and France had but five between 1574 and 1774 (see Table 18.1). The long reigns of Henry VIII and his

Map 18.2 The European Empire of Charles V Charles was Europe's most powerful ruler from 1519 to 1556, but his efforts failed to unify the Christian West. In addition to being the elected head of the Holy Roman Empire, he was the hereditary ruler of the Spanish realms of Castile and Aragon and the central European possessions of the Austrian Habsburgs. The map does not show his extensive American and Asian empire.

Protestant daughter Elizabeth I helped stabilize sixteenth-century England, but their Stuart successors were twice overthrown by revolution during the next century .

Successful monarchs depended heavily on their chief advisers, who also eased the transition between rulers. Cardinal Jiménez guided the nineteen-year-old Charles V's entry to the throne of Spain. Cardinal Richelieu oversaw the policies of the young Louis XIII in France, and Richelieu's successor Cardinal Mazarin guided the youthful Louis XIV, who came to the throne at the age of five. By the seventeenth century, kings were beginning to draw on the talents of successful businessmen, such as Jean Baptiste Colbert (1619–1683), Louis XIV's able minister of finance.

In England, Robert Walpole, the powerful prime minister from 1721 to 1742, dominated the early Hanoverian kings.

Able monarchs and their advisers worked to enhance royal authority by limiting the autonomy of the church. Well before the Reformation, rulers in Spain, Portugal, and France had gained control over church appointments and had used church revenues to enhance royal power. This absorption of the church into the state helps explain why religious uniformity was such a hot political issue. Following a pattern used by his predecessors to suppress Jewish and Muslim practices, King Philip II of Spain used an ecclesiastical court, the Spanish Inquisition, to bring into line those who resisted his authority. It was the one institution common to his three Spanish kingdoms. Suspected Protestants, as well as critics of the king, found themselves accused of heresy, an offense punishable by death. Even those who were acquitted of the charge learned not to oppose the king again.

In France, Prince Henry of Navarre switched his faith from Calvinist to Catholic after gaining the military advantage in the French Wars of Religion (1566–1598), so that, as King Henry IV, he would share the faith of the majority of his subjects. His son and grandson, kings Louis XIII and Louis XIV, were as devoted to French Catholic religious uniformity as their counterparts in Spain. In 1685 Louis XIV even revoked the Edict of Nantes, by which his grandfather had granted religious freedom to his Protestant supporters in 1598.

Elsewhere, the Protestant Reformation made it easier for monarchs to increase their control of the church. The church in England lost its remaining autonomy after the pope turned down King Henry VIII's petition for an annulment of his marriage to Katharine of Aragon. Distressed that Katharine had not furnished him with a male heir, Henry had the English archbishop of Canterbury annul the marriage in 1533. The breach with Rome was sealed the next year when Parliament made the English monarch head of the Church of England.

Henry subsequently used his authority to disband the monasteries and convents. He gave some of their landholdings to his powerful allies and sold others to pay for his new navy. In other respects religion changed little under Henry and his successors, despite growing pressures from English Calvinists known as *Puritans,* to "purify" the Anglican Church of Catholic practices and beliefs. In 1603, the first Stuart king, James I, dismissed a Puritan petition to eliminate bishops with the statement, "No bishops, no king"—a reminder of the essential role that bishops played in royal administration.

Besides gaining control of the church, western European kings and queens enhanced their powers by promoting national institutions. In 1500 many of the separate provinces of Spain and France had their own laws and institutions, reflecting their piecemeal acquisition by inheritance and conquest. By 1750 rulers had been able to achieve greater uniformity in law and administration. Seventeenth-century French kings increased royal power by appointing new royal officials (known as *intendants*) over the provincial noble courts, effectively diluting their power, and by using the army to tear down the fortifications behind which powerful nobles and towns often asserted their independence.

The growth of a common language, especially among the elites, further strengthened national unity. In Spain the Castilian dialect was increasingly spoken, while in France people increasingly imitated the speech of Paris. The Protestant emphasis on reading the Bible in the vernacular (instead of in Latin) sped the replacement of many dialects with a standardized national language. Luther's magnificent translation of the Bible into the High German of Saxony laid the basis for modern German. The biblical translation prepared under the direction of King James I did the same for English, as did Calvin's translation for French. Important new secular literatures also helped to standardize national languages. These included the English plays of William Shakespeare (1564–1616), the French satires of François Rabelais (1483–1553), the Spanish novel *Don Quixote* by Miguel de Cervantes (1547–1616), and *The Lusiads,* an epic poem celebrating overseas exploration, by the Portuguese poet Luís de Camões (1524?–1580).

Absolutism and Constitutionalism

As monarchs sought to concentrate power in their own hands, they had to confront another central institution, the representative assemblies that traditionally had to approve important royal actions, such as making war and levying new taxes. As we have seen, the princes in the imperial Diet of the Holy Roman Empire effectively resisted Charles V. In contrast, French kings succeeded in circumventing the Estates General. The absence of any constitutional check on royal power is called *absolutism*, a theory that many seventeenth- and eighteenth-century European rulers admired and imitated. In England, Parliament checked royal absolutism and established *constitutionalism*, a theory of government in which royal power is subject to specified limits.

The French Estates General represented three estates, of the clergy, the nobility, and the towns (that is, townspeople with wealth and high status). The Estates General had asserted its prominence during the French Wars of Religion (1566–1598) when the monarchy was weak. But, except in 1614 when Queen Marie de Medici was ruling in the name of her young son, the new Bourbon kings refused to summon it into session. Unable to impose new taxes without summoning the Estates General, Louis XIV's astute finance minister, Colbert, instead devised efficient tax collection methods that tripled the funds reaching the royal treasury. Colbert also promoted economic development both in France and overseas to increase the tax base. When the wars waged by Louis XIV strained the treasury to the breaking point, the king raised additional sums by selling high offices.

Louis XIV's gigantic new palace at Versailles symbolized the French monarch's triumph over the traditional rights of the nobility. Capable of

Versailles, 1688 King Louis XIV inspects plans for a reservoir to provide water for his new suburban palace and its many fountains. The main palace buildings are in the background and the old village of Versailles is on the right. (Giraudon/Art Resource NY)

housing ten thousand people and surrounded by elaborately landscaped grounds and parks, the palace can be seen as a sort of theme park of royal absolutism. Occupied with elaborate ceremonies and banquets centered on the king, the nobles who lived at Versailles were kept away from the real politics of the kingdom. According to one of them, the duke of Saint-Simon, "no one was so clever in devising petty distractions" as the king. So successful was Versailles in taming the nobles that not only Tsar Peter in Russia but other kings, princes, and even a powerful German archbishop built imitations of it.

As eager as his French counterparts to promote royal absolutism, King Charles I of England ruled for eleven years without summoning Parliament, his kingdom's representative body. To raise money, he coerced "loans" from wealthy subjects and twisted tax laws to new uses. Then in 1640, a rebellion in Scotland forced him to summon the members of Parliament to approve new taxes to pay for an army. Nobles and churchmen sat in the House of Lords; representatives from the towns and counties sat in the House of Commons. Before authorizing new taxes, Parliament insisted on strict guarantees that the king would never again ignore its traditional rights. These King Charles refused to grant. When he ordered the arrest of his leading critics in the House of Commons in 1642, he plunged the kingdom into civil war.

Defending Parliament's traditional rights were the rich commoners and the well-organized religious Puritans, who had not given up on their plans to cleanse the English church of Catholic traits. Supporting the king were most of the established nobility and the more conservative northern parts of the kingdom. When Charles refused to compromise even after being defeated on the battlefield, a "Rump" Parliament purged of its opponents ordered him executed in 1649 and replaced the monarchy with a Puritan Republic under the Puritan general Oliver Cromwell.

Cromwell expanded England's power overseas and imposed firm control over Ireland and Scotland, but he was as unwilling as the Stuart kings to share power with Parliament. After his death the Stuart line was restored in 1660, and for a time it was unclear which side had won the civil war.

However, when King James II refused to respect Parliament's rights and had his heir baptized a Roman Catholic, Parliament offered the throne to his Protestant daughter Mary and her husband, the Dutch Prince William of Orange. Their triumphal arrival in England forced James into exile in the bloodless Glorious Revolution of 1688. This time, there was no doubt about the outcome. The Bill of Rights of 1689 specified that Parliament had to be called "frequently" and had to consent to changes in laws and to the raising of an army in peacetime. Another law reaffirmed the official status of the Church of England but gave religious toleration to Puritans.

BUILDING STATE POWER

The remarkable successes of early modern European states in unifying under powerful rulers, whether absolutist or constitutional, would have been of modest global significance if they had not achieved notable success in two other areas of greater importance. One was developing some of the world's most powerful armed forces. The second was ensuring sufficient economic growth to support the heavy costs of royal administration and warfare.

War and Diplomacy

Warfare was almost constant in early modern Europe (see Table 18.2). These struggles for dominance first produced a dramatic change in the size, skill, and armaments of armed forces and then an advance in diplomacy. The military revolution began in the late Middle Ages when firearms became the preferred weapons of war: cannon replaced catapults as siege weapons, muskets displaced lances and crossbows, and gun-toting commoners on foot supplanted aristocratic knights on horseback.

The numbers of men in arms increased steadily throughout the early modern period. Spanish armies doubled from about 150,000 in the 1550s to 300,000 in the 1630s. French forces, about half the size of the Spanish in the 1630s, grew to an estimated 300,000 to 400,000 by the early eighteenth century. Even smaller European states built up impressive armies. Sweden, with under a million people, had one of the finest and best-armed military forces in seventeenth-century Europe. Prussia, with fewer than 2 million inhabitants in 1700, devoted so many resources to building a splendid army that it was recognized as one of Europe's major powers. Indeed, Prussia was sometimes described as an army with a state attached. Of course, armies were largest in wartime, but only England, the island nation, was safe from attack by overland armies and, with Parliament guarding the purse strings, did not maintain a standing army in peacetime.

Larger armies required better command structures. Long before the development of modern field communications systems, European armies, in the words of a modern historian, "evolved . . . the equivalent of a central nervous system, capable of activating technologically differentiated claws and teeth."[1] New signaling techniques improved control of battlefield maneuvers, while better discipline was achieved by frequent marching drills, which trained troops to obey orders instantly and gave them a close sense of comradeship. First developed in the Netherlands during a long struggle for independence from Spain, the drilling techniques were quickly imitated by the best armies in Europe.

Military victories by these giant land armies were not assured, however. New fortifications able to withstand cannon bombardments made cities harder to capture, and battles between evenly matched armies often ended in stalemates, as in the prolonged Thirty Years War (1618–1648). As a result, victory in war increasingly depended on naval superiority. Warships were redesigned to accommodate several tiers of cannon that had the power to blow holes in the thick sides of enemy ships. Improved four-wheel

German Wars of Religion	1546–1555
Ottoman wars	1526–1571
French Wars of Religion	1562–1598
Revolt of the Netherlands	1566–1609, 1621–1648
Thirty Years War	1618–1648
English Civil War	1642–1648
Anglo-Dutch Wars	1652–1678
Wars of Louis XIV	1667–1697
Ottoman wars	1683–1697
War of Spanish Succession	1702–1714
Great Northern War	1702–1721
Ottoman wars	1714–1718
War of Austrian Succession	1740–1748

Table 18.2 Major Wars in Early Modern Europe

carriages made cannon easier to pull back and reload.

The rapid changes in naval warfare are evident in two fleets used by Philip II of Spain. In the greatest naval battle of the sixteenth century, a combined Spanish and Italian fleet of 200 ships met an even larger Ottoman force off Lepanto on the Greek coast in 1571. Both fleets consisted principally of oar-powered galleys, which had only light armaments. To attack, one galley rammed another so that armed men could climb aboard for hand-to-hand combat. Superior Venetian ships, loaded with Spanish troops and having a decisive edge in firepower, gave the Christian coalition victory, while the Ottomans lost 25,000 men and 200 ships. Only 40 Ottoman galleys escaped.

A very different Spanish fleet, the Catholic Armada, sailed from Lisbon in 1588 hoping to repeat the Lepanto success over the Protestant enemies of the north. The complex mission of these 130 heavily armed ships was to replace the Protestant ruler of England, Queen Elizabeth, with a Roman Catholic, then put down the rebellion in the Netherlands, and finally intervene in the French Wars of Religion on the Catholic side. But history did not repeat itself. The English could fire more rapidly because of their new cannon carriages, and their smaller, quicker ships successfully evaded the ram-and-board technique, which the Spanish retained from their Mediterranean victory. Moreover, a chance storm, celebrated by the English as a providential "Protestant wind," scattered and sank many Spanish ships that had survived the sea battles, thus dooming Philip's other plans for the armada.

The armada's defeat signaled the end of Spain's military dominance in Europe. By the time of the Thirty Years War, France had recovered from its Wars of Religion to become Europe's most powerful state. With twice the population of Spain at their command, France's forceful kings of the new Bourbon dynasty could field Europe's largest armies, whether to squelch domestic unrest, extend France's boundaries, or intervene in the affairs of neighboring states.

After emerging from its own civil wars in 1689, England became France's major rival. By then England had acquired Ireland and a North American empire, and in 1707 England merged with Scotland to become Great Britain. England's rise as a sea power had begun in the time of King Henry VIII, who spent heavily on ships and promoted a domestic iron-smelting industry to supply cannon. Queen Elizabeth's victorious fleet of 1588 was considerably improved by the copying of innovative ship designs from the Dutch in the second half of the seventeenth century. The Royal Navy grew in numbers, surpassing the French fleet by the early eighteenth century.

Britain's naval strength combined with the land armies of its Austrian and Prussian allies defeated the French expansionist efforts in a series of eighteenth-century wars, beginning with the War of Spanish Succession (1702–1714), which blocked France from uniting the thrones of France and Spain. This defeat of the French monarchy's empire-building efforts illustrated a major development in international relations—the principle of *balance of power*, by which the major European states combined to prevent any one of them from becoming too powerful.

Meanwhile, Russia emerged as a major power in Europe when Peter the Great's modernized armies succeeded in defeating Sweden in the Great Northern War (1702–1721). Though adhering to four different branches of Christianity, Catholic France, Anglican Britain, Catholic Austria, Lutheran Prussia, and Orthodox Russia (see Map 18.3) maintained an effective balance of power in Europe during the next two centuries by shifting their alliances for geopolitical rather than religious reasons.

Politics and the Economy

To pay the extremely heavy military costs of their wars, European rulers had to increase their revenues. The most successful of them in the seventeenth and eighteenth centuries promoted mutually beneficial alliances with the rising commercial elites. Both parties understood that trade thrived where government taxation and regulation were not excessive, where courts enforced contracts and collected debts, and where military power stood ready to protect overseas expansion by force when necessary.

Spain, sixteenth-century Europe's mightiest state, illustrates how the financial drains of an aggressive military policy and the failure to promote economic development could lead to decline. Expensive wars against the Ottomans, northern European Protestants, and rebellious Dutch subjects caused the treasury of King Philip II to default on its debts four times. In hindsight it is clear that Spanish rulers' concerns for religious uniformity, traditional aristocratic privilege, and expensive foreign wars undermined the country's economy. In the name of religious uniformity they expelled Jewish merchants, persecuted Protestant dissenters, and forced tens of thousands of skilled farmers and artisans into exile because of their Muslim ancestry. While exempting the landed aristocracy from taxation, Spanish rulers imposed high sales taxes that discouraged manufacturing.

For a time the government treasury was filled by vast imports of silver and gold bullion from

Austrian siege of Belgrade, 1688 The Ottoman Turks, in control of the Balkan Peninsula since the early sixteenth century, again assaulted the city of Vienna in 1683. Revitalized Austrian Hapsburg armies successfully defended their capital and then took the offensive against the Muslim invaders, retaking Hungary and capturing the city of Belgrade, south of the Danube River. Although the Turks soon regained Belgrade, the annexation of Hungary doubled the size of the Austrian empire and altered the balance of power in southeastern Europe. (Giraudon/Art Resource NY)

Spanish American colonies, but these bullion shipments also caused severe inflation (rising prices), worst in Spain but bad throughout the rest of western Europe as well. A Spanish saying captured the problem: American silver was like rain on the roof—it poured down and washed away. Huge debts for foreign wars drained bullion from Spain to its creditors. More wealth flowed out to purchase manufactured goods and even food in the seventeenth century.

The rise of the Netherlands to prosperity stemmed from opposite policies. The Spanish crown had acquired these resource-poor but commercially successful provinces as part of Charles V's inheritance. But King Philip II's deci-

sion to impose Spain's ruinously heavy sales tax and enforce Catholic orthodoxy drove the Dutch to revolt in the 1580s. Those measures would have discouraged business and driven away the Calvinists, Jews, and others who were essential to Dutch prosperity. The small colony fought with skill and ingenuity, raising and training an army and a navy that were among the most effective in Europe. By 1609 Spain was forced to agree to a truce that recognized the autonomy of the northern part of the Netherlands. In 1648, after eight decades of warfare, the independence of these seven United Provinces of the Free Netherlands (to give their full name) became final.

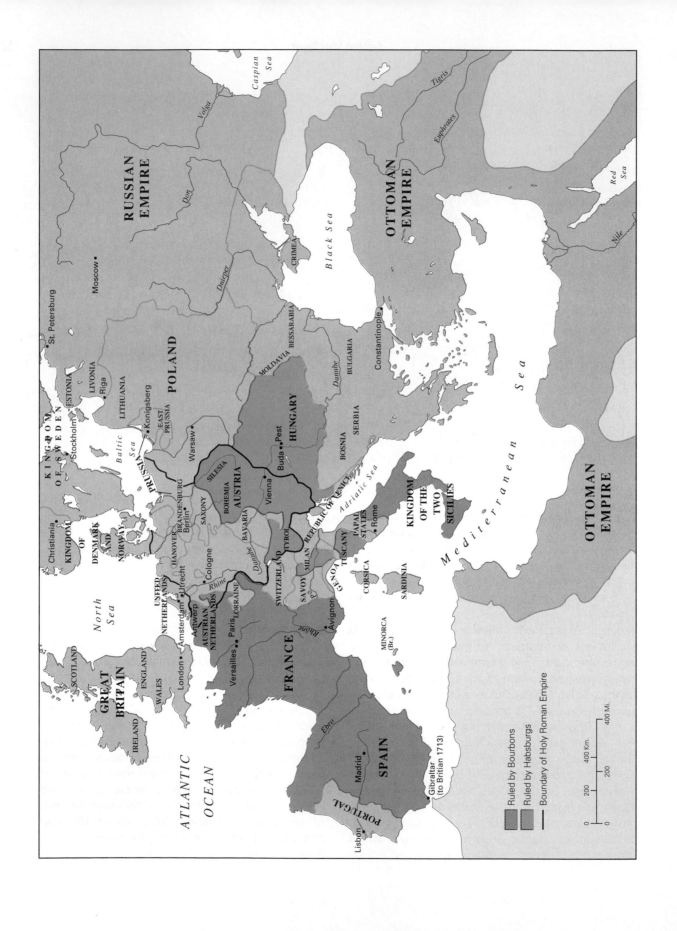

RUSSIAN EMPIRE

OTTOMAN EMPIRE

Caspian Sea

Volga

Don

Moscow •

St. Petersburg •

Baltic Sea

KINGDOM OF SWEDEN

Stockholm •

Christiania •

KINGDOM OF DENMARK AND NORWAY

ESTONIA

LIVONIA

Riga •

LITHUANIA

Königsberg •

EAST PRUSSIA

POLAND

Warsaw •

Dnieper

BESSARABIA

MOLDAVIA

HUNGARY

Buda • Pest

SILESIA

Vienna •

BOHEMIA

AUSTRIA

BRANDENBURG

Berlin •

SAXONY

HANOVER

PRUSSIA

BULGARIA

SERBIA

BOSNIA

Danube

Black Sea

Constantinople •

CRIMEA

Tigris

Euphrates

Red Sea

Nile

OTTOMAN EMPIRE

Mediterranean Sea

KINGDOM OF THE TWO SICILIES

REPUBLIC OF VENICE

Adriatic Sea

PAPAL STATES

Rome •

TUSCANY

TYROL

SWITZERLAND

MILAN

SAVOY

GENOA

Genoa

BAVARIA

Cologne •

UNITED NETHERLANDS

Amsterdam •

Utrecht •

Rhine

AUSTRIAN NETHERLANDS

Antwerp •

LORRAINE

Paris •

Versailles •

FRANCE

Rhône

Danube

CORSICA

SARDINIA

MINORCA (Br.)

North Sea

GREAT BRITAIN

SCOTLAND

ENGLAND

WALES

IRELAND

London •

ATLANTIC OCEAN

SPAIN

Madrid •

Ebro

PORTUGAL

Lisbon •

Gibraltar (to Britian 1713) •

Ruled by Bourbons

Ruled by Habsburgs

Boundary of Holy Roman Empire

400 Mi.

400 Km.

200

200

0

0

Port of Amsterdam Ships, barges, and boats of all types are visible in this busy seventeenth-century scene. The large building in the center is the Admiralty House, which housed the headquarters of the Dutch East India Company. (The Mansell Collection Limited)

Rather than being ruined by the long war, the United Netherlands emerged in the seventeenth century as the dominant commercial power in Europe and the world's greatest trading nation. During this golden century the wealth of the United Netherlands multiplied instead of flowing away. Their economic success owed much to an unusually decentralized government that let each of the seven provinces pursue its own interests. During the long struggle against Spain, the provinces united around the Prince of Orange, their sovereign, who served as commander-in-chief of the armed forces. But in economic matters each province was free to pursue its own

interests. The maritime province of Holland grew rich by favoring commercial interests.

Holland's many towns and cities were filled with skilled craftsmen. Factories and workshops turned out goods of exceptional quality at a moderate price and on a vast scale. Their textile industry concentrated on the highly profitable finishing and printing of cloth, transforming the cloths spun and woven by low-paid workers into fine textiles. Other factories refined West Indian sugar, brewed beer from Baltic grain, cut Virginia tobacco, and made imitations of Chinese ceramics. Holland's printers published books in many languages, free from the censorship imposed by political and religious authorities in neighboring countries. For a small province, barely above sea level, lacking timber and other natural resources, this was a remarkable achievement.

Amsterdam, Holland's major city, became seventeenth-century Europe's financial center and major port. From there Dutch ships dominated the sea trade of Europe, carrying over 80

Map 18.3 Europe in 1740 By the middle of the eighteenth century the great powers of Europe were France, Austria-Hungary, Great Britain, Prussia, and Russia. Spain, the Holy Roman Empire, and the Ottoman Empire were far weaker in 1740 than they had been two centuries earlier.

percent of the trade to Spain from northern Europe, even while Spain and the Netherlands were at war. The Dutch dominance of Atlantic and the Indian Ocean trade was such that, by one estimate, they conducted more than half of all the oceangoing commercial shipping in the world (for details see Chapters 20 and 21).

After 1650, the Dutch faced growing competition from the English, who were developing their own close association of business and government. In a series of wars (1652–1678) England used its naval might to break Dutch dominance in overseas trade and to extend England's colonial empire. With government support, the English merchant fleet doubled between 1660 and 1700, foreign trade rose by 50 percent, and, as a result, state revenue from customs duties tripled. During the eighteenth century Britain's trading position strengthened still more.

The debts run up by the Anglo-Dutch Wars helped persuade the English monarchy to enlarge the government's role in managing the economy to such a degree that it has been called a "financial revolution." The government increased revenues by taxing the formerly exempt landed estates of the aristocrats and by collecting taxes directly. Previously known as tax farmers private individuals had advanced the government a fixed sum of money; in return they could keep whatever money they were able to collect from taxpayers. To secure cash quickly for war and other emergencies and to reduce the burden of debts from earlier wars, England also followed the Dutch lead in creating a central bank, from which the government was able to obtain long-term loans at low rates.

The French government was also developing its national economy, especially under Colbert. He streamlined tax collection, promoted French manufacturing and shipping by imposing taxes on foreign goods, and improved transportation within France itself. Yet the power of the wealthy aristocrats kept the French government from following England's lead in taxing wealthy landowners, collecting taxes directly, and securing low-cost loans. Nor did France succeed in managing its debt as efficiently as England.

URBAN SOCIETY AND COMMERCIAL TECHNOLOGY

Just as palaces were early modern Europe's centers of political power, cities were its economic power centers. The urban growth underway since the eleventh century was accelerating and spreading. In 1500, Paris was the only northern European city with over 100,000 inhabitants. By 1700, both Paris and London had populations over 500,000, Amsterdam had burgeoned from a fishing village to a metropolis of some 200,000, and twenty other European cities contained over 60,000 people.

Most city dwellers had to struggle for a living and many were very poor. The cities' growth depended primarily on the prosperous merchants who managed the great expansion of regional and overseas commerce. Improved business techniques and manufacturing technologies also sped the growth of commerce.

Urban Social Classes

When asked by the mayor of the French city of Bordeaux what impressed them most about European cities in about 1580, a group of visiting Amerindian chiefs is said to have expressed their astonishment at the disparity between the fat, well-fed people and the poor, half-starved men and women in rags. Why, the visitors wondered, did the poor not grab the rich by the throat or set fire to their homes? The contrasts of wealth in European cities were indeed startling, and social tension often ran high.[2]

The well-off who dominated the cities were what the French called the *bourgeoisie* (town dwellers). Their wealth came from manufacturing, finance, and especially trade, both regional and overseas.

Grain for bread was brought by carts and barges from the surrounding countryside or, in the largest cities of western Europe, transported by special fleets from the eastern Baltic lands. Other fleets brought wine from southern to northern Europe. Parisians downed 100,000 barrels of wine a year at the end of the seventeenth century. The poor also consumed large amounts of beer. In 1750 Parisian breweries made 23 million quarts (22 million liters) for local consumption, another stimulus to the grain trade. In the seventeenth and eighteenth centuries wealthier urban classes could buy exotic luxuries imported from the far corners of the earth—Caribbean and Brazilian sugar and rum, Mexican chocolate, Virginian tobacco, North American furs, East Indian cotton textiles and spices, and Chinese tea.

As related above, the rise of the bourgeoisie was aided by mutually beneficial alliances with monarchs who saw economic growth as the best means of increasing state revenues. Unlike the old nobility, who shunned productive labor, the bourgeoisie devoted long hours to their businesses and poured their profits into new business ventures or other investments rather than spending them. Even so, they still had enough money to live comfortably in large houses with many servants.

Like merchants in the Islamic world, Europe's merchants relied on family and ethnic networks. In addition to families of local origin, many northern European cities contained merchant colonies from Venice, Florence, Genoa, and other Italian cities. In Amsterdam and Hamburg lived many Jewish merchants who had fled from religious persecution in Iberia. Other Jewish communities expanded out of eastern Europe into

The Fishwife, 1572 Women were essential partners in most Dutch family businesses. This scene by the Dutch artist Adriaen van Ostade shows a woman preparing seafood for retail sale. (Rijksmuseum-Stichting)

the German states, especially after the Thirty Years War. Armenian merchants from Iran were moving into the Mediterranean and became important in Russia in the seventeenth century.

Besides the bourgeoisie, Europe's cities included a middle category of craftworkers and many poor people. From 10 to 20 percent of the city dwellers were so poor that they were exempt from taxation, but this number included only those "deserving poor," whom officials considered permanent residents. In addition, cities contained large numbers of "unworthy poor," including recent migrants from impoverished rural areas, peddlers traveling from place to place, and beggars (many with horrible deformities and sores) who tried to survive on charity. There were also criminals, usually organized in gangs, ranging from youthful pickpockets to highway robbers.

Some people managed to improve their lot in life and others slipped lower, but most followed the careers of their parents. In contrast to the arranged marriages common to most of the rest of the world, young men and women in early modern Europe generally sought out their own spouses and set up their own households after marriage rather than living with their parents. For that reason, they had to delay marriage until they could afford to live on their own. Young men had to serve a long apprenticeship to learn a trade. Young women had to work—helping their parents, as domestic servants, or in some other capacity—to save money for the dowry they were expected to bring into the marriage. A dowry was the money and household goods—the amount varied by social class—that enabled a young couple to begin marriage independent of their parents. The typical groom in early modern Europe could not hope to marry before his late twenties, and his bride would be a few years younger—in contrast the rest of the world, where people usually married in their teens.

Besides enabling young people to be independent of their parents, the late age of marriage in early modern Europe also held down the birthrate and thus limited family size. Even so, about a tenth of the births in a city were to unmarried women, often servants, who generally abandoned their infants on the doorsteps of churches, convents, or rich families. Despite efforts to raise such abandoned children, many perished. Delayed marriage was also connected to the existence of public brothels, where young men satisfied their lusts in cheap and impersonal encounters with unfortunate young women, often newly arrived from impoverished rural villages. Nevertheless, rape was a common occurrence, usually perpetrated by gangs of young men who attacked young women rumored to be free with their favors. Some historians believe that such gang rapes reflect poor, young men's jealousy at older men's easier access to women.

Marriage also came late in bourgeois families. One reason for the delay was to allow men to finish their education. Although bourgeois parents did not formally arrange their children's marriages, the fact that nearly all found spouses within their social class strongly suggests that parents promoted marriages that forged business alliances with other families. Bourgeois parents were also very concerned that their children have the education and training necessary for success. They promoted the establishment of municipal schools to provide a solid education, including Latin and perhaps Greek, for their sons, who were then sent abroad to learn modern languages or to a university to earn a law degree. Legal training was useful for conducting business and was a prerequisite for obtaining government judgeships and treasury positions. Daughters were less likely to be groomed for a business career, but wives often helped their husbands as bookkeepers and sometimes inherited businesses.

Commercial Techniques and Technology

The expansion of trade in early modern Europe prompted the development of new techniques to manage far-flung business enterprises and invest the profits they produced. As elsewhere in the world, most European businesses operated on family-owned funds or used private moneylenders, but a key change in Europe was the rise of large financial institutions to serve the interests of big business and big government. In the seventeenth century, even though private Dutch banks paid modest rates of interest on deposits, they developed such a reputation for security that wealthy individuals and governments from all over western Europe entrusted them with their money. To make a profit, the banks then invested these funds in real estate, local industries, loans to governments, and overseas trade.

Another innovation was the *joint-stock company*, which sold shares to individuals. Often backed by a government charter, such companies were a way of raising large sums for overseas trading enterprises while spreading the risks (and profits) among many investors (how chartered joint-stock companies operated overseas trade is examined in Chapter 20). After the initial offerings, shares could be bought and sold in specialized financial markets called *stock exchanges*, another Italian innovation transferred to the cities of northwestern Europe in the sixteenth century. The greatest stock market in the seventeenth and eighteenth centuries was the Amsterdam Exchange, founded in 1530. Large insurance companies also emerged in this period, and insuring long voyages against loss became a standard practice after 1700.

Changes in technology also facilitated economic growth. As in the case of military developments, this was more an age of technological refinement and multiplication than innovation. For example, water wheels—a traditional source of mechanical energy for mills and factories—gradually increased in size. In the Dutch province of Holland, improved systems of gears made it possible to adapt windmills for new uses, such as driving a saw. Information about new devices was spread by means of printed manuals about machines, metallurgy, agriculture, and other technical subjects.

Improvements in water transport expanded Europe's superb natural network of seas and navigable rivers for moving bulk items such as grain, wine, and timber. The Dutch built numerous canals to drain the lowlands for agriculture and for transport. Other canals, with elaborate systems of locks to cross hills, were built in France, Germany, Italy, and England. One of the most important was the 150-mile (240-kilometer) Canal du Midi in France, built by the French gov-

ernment between 1661 and 1682 to link the Atlantic and the Mediterranean.

The expansion of maritime trade also led to new designs for merchant ships. In this too the Dutch played a dominant role. Using timber imported from northern Europe, shipyards in Dutch ports built ships for their own vast fleets and for export. Especially successful was the *fluit*, or "flyboat," a capacious cargo ship developed in the 1590s. It was cheap to build and required only a small crew to sail. Another successful type of merchant ship, the heavily armed "East Indiaman," helped the Dutch establish their supremacy in the Indian Ocean.

RURAL SOCIETY AND THE ENVIRONMENT

For all its new political, military, and commercial strengths, early modern Europe rested on a fragile agrarian base. The techniques and efficiency of European agriculture had improved little since 1300. The result of this slow progress was famine in bad years and only limited surpluses in good ones. Overall the circumstances of the majority of rural Europeans worsened between 1500 and 1750 as adverse economic conditions, warfare, environmental deterioration, and social change added to their misery.

Rural Lives

The bright side of western European rural life was the remarkable personal freedom of the peasantry compared to people of similar status in many other parts of the world. Serfdom, which bound peasant men and women to land owned by a local lord, had declined sharply after the great plague of the mid-fourteenth century. Most remaining serfs in western Europe gained their freedom by 1600. By that date slavery in southern Iberia, which had been fed by large numbers of captives from Africa, had also come to an end. Ironically this appearance of a free peasantry in early modern western Europe parallels the rapid increase of serfdom in much of eastern Europe.

The peasants' legal freedom in western Europe did little to make their lives less precarious. Peasant producers with surplus crops to sell benefited from higher prices brought about by the sixteenth-century inflation, but the broader trend was for peasants to fall deeper and deeper into debt until they lost their land through indebtedness. This transformation of rural ownership was accelerated by the desire of many successful members of the bourgeoisie to turn their wealth into social status by retiring from their professions and purchasing country estates. Landowning permitted them to become *gentry*, adopting the rural lifestyle—and the exemption from taxation—of the old feudal aristocracy.

Such rural gentry invested their money in loans both to impoverished peasants and to members of the feudal nobility, and in time they increased their lands. Some sought aristocratic husbands for their daughters, an alliance attractive to the old nobility because of the exceptional dowries that rich merchants provided. In France a family could gain the exemption from taxation by living in gentility for three generations but could gain noble status more quickly by purchasing a title. French kings sold so many new patents of nobility there arose a new social category, the *noblesse de robe* (dress nobility), in contrast to the medieval *noblesse d'épée* (sword nobility).

In Spain the old nobility were responsible for the consolidation of landownership and the impoverishment of the peasantry. By 1600 only 3 percent of the population controlled 97 percent of the land. When Spanish landowners decided that they could increase their incomes by turning cropland into pastures for their sheep, food production and population declined.

Environmental Crises

Rural Europeans also felt the adverse effects of a century-long period of cooler climate that began in the 1590s. Average temperatures fell only a few degrees during this "Little Ice Age," but the effects were startling. Glaciers in the Alps grew much larger. Rivers and canals important to commerce froze solid from bank to bank. In some places during the coldest years the growing season shrank by two months. As a result, food crops ripened more slowly during cooler summers and were often damaged by early fall frosts. In spring late frosts withered the tender shoots of newly planted crops.

People could survive a smaller-than-average harvest in one year with reserves left from the year before. But when there were successive cold years, the consequences were devastating. Records show that when average summer temperatures in northern Europe were 2.7°F (1.5°C) lower in 1674 and 1675 and again in 1694 and 1695, deaths due to malnutrition and cold increased sharply. The cold spell of 1694–1695 caused a famine in Finland that carried off from one-quarter to one-third of the population. It is difficult to isolate the harm done by the Little Ice Age, however, since European wars, changing patterns of landownership, and other social and economic circumstances also had adverse effects.

Another threat to the rural life was deforestation. Early modern Europeans consumed their great hardwood forests rapidly to provide timbers for ships and lumber for buildings, wagons, and barrels. Trees were also converted into fuel for heating, for cooking, and, in the form of charcoal, for smelting ores and other industrial processes. The three hundred ironworks in England in the late seventeenth century each consumed a thousand loads of oak a year. Wood shortages resulting from such high consumption led to increased imports of timber and charcoal from more heavily forested Scandinavian countries and Russia. Sweden used its vast forest resources to become a major iron producer in the seventeenth century, using fuel-efficient blast furnaces introduced from Liège, in present-day Belgium. After 1716 Russia was Europe's largest producer of iron.

Given this consumption of wood for Europe's rising population and expanding economy, it is not surprising that forest depletion emerged as a serious issue in the seventeenth and eighteenth centuries. The shortages were particularly acute in England, where one early-seventeenth-

Winter in Flanders, 1565 This January scene by the Flemish artist Pieter Bruegel shows many activities of everyday life besides the one featured in the painting's usual title, *Hunters in the Snow*. The women under the sign are singeing the bristles off a slaughtered pig. On the frozen ponds people skate and play hockey and curling. An old woman trudges home under a load of faggots. A February scene Bruegel painted as part of this series shows the snow all melted, but a century later winters became longer and colder. (Rijksmuseum-Stichting)

century observer lamented: "within man's memory, it was held impossible to have any want of wood in England. But . . . at present, through the great consuming of wood . . . and the neglect of planting of woods, there is a great scarcity of wood throughout the whole kingdom."[3] Shortages in England drove the price of ordinary firewood up five times faster than other prices between the late fifteenth and the mid-seventeenth centuries.

High wood prices encouraged the use of coal as an alternative fuel. England's coal mining in-

creased twelvefold from 210,000 tons in 1550 to 2.5 million tons in 1700. From 1709, when it was discovered how to remove impurities, coal (in the form of coke) began to replace charcoal in the smelting of iron. By 1750 English coal production was approaching 5 million tons a year.

France was much more forested than England, but increasing consumption there caused Colbert to predict that "France will perish for lack of wood." By the late eighteenth century, deforestation was becoming an issue even in Sweden and Russia. New laws in France and England designed to protect the forests were largely inspired by fears of shortages for naval vessels, whose keels required high-quality timbers of exceptional size and particular curvature. Although wood consumption remained high, rising prices encouraged some individuals to plant trees for future harvest.

Everywhere in Europe the depletion of the forests was felt most by the rural poor, who traditionally had depended on them for abundant supplies of wild nuts and berries, free firewood and building materials, and wild game. Many poor men and women flocked to the cities in hopes of finding better jobs, but most were disappointed. As we have seen, begging, theft, and prostitution were the result. Even in the prosperous Dutch towns half of the population lived in acute poverty. Other rural poor in the eighteenth century worked at home spinning yarn and weaving cloth from materials supplied by entrepreneurs. So many single women supported themselves by spinning yarn that *spinster* became the normal English word for an unmarried woman. Despite some changes, most Europeans continued to live at a precarious level of existence.

Land Enclosure and the "Agricultural Revolution"

In parts of the Netherlands and southeastern England consolidation of land led to the adoption of more productive agricultural practices. The Dutch had pioneered these practices, reclaiming 350,000 acres (150,000 hectares) of land from the sea between 1540 and 1715. In the late seventeenth century, Dutch engineers introduced their drainage techniques into England, transforming large marshes into fertile fields. Such reclaiming of wasteland was connected with the *enclosure movement*. Large landowners built fences or other barriers to enclose land formerly in common use. Such large enclosed fields made farming and pasturing sheep more efficient. New laws accelerated the enclosures after 1750.

Another technique for increasing production was to abandon the traditional practice of allowing a field to lie idle every second or third year so as to regain its fertility. Instead, progressive English farmers adopted the Dutch technique of alternating nitrogen-using crops (such as grain) with nitrogen-restoring crops (such as peas and beans) or using idled fields as pastures so that the animal droppings would fertilize the soil. This rotation of fields put more land under cultivation and increased crop yields per unit of land.

Large English landowners also tried to improve their animal stocks. Instead of letting farm animals reproduce randomly, they mated animals selectively to enhance desirable characteristics. Though not yet scientific, such selective breeding resulted in larger hogs, cows that gave more milk, and faster horses.

In 1750 this "agricultural revolution" was confined to a small area of northwestern Europe and so did little to relieve the general wretchedness. Indeed, under the pressure of social and environmental change and inflation, the condition of the average person in western Europe seems to have fallen sharply during the century after 1530. English peasants were reduced to a diet of black bread and little else. In other parts of Europe, new crops from the Americas helped the rural poor avert starvation. Initially eaten only in desperate times, these crops became staples for the rural poor in the eighteenth century because they yielded more abundant food from small garden plots. In northeastern and Central Europe and in Ireland the potato sustained life. Peasants along the Mediterranean, who could not afford to eat the wheat they raised for urban markets, grew maize (corn) for their own consumption.

Social Rebellion and Witch-Hunts

Rising discontent in early modern Europe led to many rebellions. For example, in 1525 peasant rebels in the Tyrolian Alps attacked both nobles and clergy as representatives of the privileged and landowning class. They had no more love of the merchants, whose lending at interest and high prices they also denounced. Rebellions multiplied as rural conditions worsened. In southwestern France alone some 450 uprisings were recorded between 1590 and 1715, often set off by food shortages and tax increases. The injustice of the wealthy being exempt from taxation was a frequent complaint. A rebellion in Languedoc in 1670 began when a mob of townswomen attacked the tax collector. It quickly spread to the country, where peasant leaders cried, "Death to the people's oppressors!" Authorities dealt severely with such revolts and executed or maimed their leaders.

Not all discontent expressed itself in open rebellion. Many distressed individuals turned their anger and jealousy inward or against their neighbors. The most extraordinary expression of social tension was the rash of witchcraft trials that were conducted across northern Europe in the late sixteenth and seventeenth centuries. It is estimated that nearly one hundred thousand people—some three-fourths of whom were women—were tried for practicing witchcraft. Some were acquitted, some recanted, but as many as a third were executed. The records of these trials make it clear that neither the accusers nor the accused doubted that Satanic magic could make people and domesticated animals sicken or die, or make crops wither in the fields. Indeed, many accused witches confessed to casting such spells and described in vivid detail their encounters with the Devil and their attendance at nighttime assemblies of witches (see Voices and Visions: Witchcraft).

Unable to accept that such confessions could be true, modern historians have sought to explain why witch-hunting increased and why so many of those accused were women. Reformation differences seem not to have been a factor since both Catholic and Protestant churches held such trials. The fact that many of the accused were older women, especially widows, may reflect the widespread belief that women not directly under the control of fathers or husbands were likely to turn to evil. Their confessions may have been coerced by torture or shaped by leading questions from the prosecutors. Such explanations do not seem entirely adequate, however, for the records show that large numbers of men were also tried for witchcraft and that some accused persons seem to have been eager to admit to witchcraft.

Another perspective comes from modern researchers who have studied witchcraft in parts of the world where the belief in witches still exists and actual witch-hunts still take place. They find that witch-hunts tend to arise at times of social stress and that people marginalized by poverty and social suspicion often relish the celebrity that public confession brings. Self-confessed "witches" may even find release from the guilt they feel for wishing evil on their neighbors. From this perspective there is a plausible linkage between the rise in witchcraft accusations and fears in early modern Europe and the rising social tension, rural poverty, and environmental strains.

No single explanation can account for all the possibilities raised by the surge of witch-hunts, but the different perspectives suggest that, far from being a bizarre aberration, this phenomenon was directly linked to the larger social structures of early modern Europe.

THE REALM OF IDEAS

As the widespread witch-hunts suggest, a blend of biblical and folk beliefs dominated the thinking of most early modern Europeans. The educated were also influenced by writings from Greco-Roman antiquity as well as from the Renaissance and Reformation. A few thinkers broke new scientific ground in deciphering the motion of the planets. Such scientific advances encouraged a reevaluation of traditional social and political systems. Although these new ideas had only limited effects before 1750, they illustrate the dynamic changes under way in Europe.

Traditional Thinking

Prevailing European ideas about the natural world drew on three distinct traditions. The oldest tradition was the stories and images of European folk cultures and pre-Christian religions,

Witchcraft

A widowed old woman, Walpurga Hausmännin was fairly typical of the kind of person accused of witchcraft in the Holy Roman Empire. In her confession, given in 1587, she mentioned activities commonly associated with witches: fornicating with demons, murdering children, desecrating the Blessed Sacrament, causing destructive storms, and night flying—though on a pitchfork, not a broomstick.

The herein mentioned, malefic and miserable woman, Walpurga Hausmännin, now imprisoned and in chains, has, upon kindly questioning and also torture, . . . confessed her witchcraft and admitted the following. When one-and-thirty years ago, she became a widow, she cut corn for Hans Schlumperger, of this place, together with his former servant, Bis im Pfarrhof, by name. Him she enticed with lewd speeches and gestures and they convened that they should, on an appointed night, meet in her, Walpurga's, dwelling, there to indulge in lustful intercourse. So when Walpurga in expectation of this, sat awaiting him at night in her chamber, meditating upon evil and fleshy thoughts, it was not the said bondsman who appeared unto her, but the Evil One in the latter's guise and raiment and indulged in fornication with her. . . . After the act of fornication she saw and felt the cloven foot of her whoremonger, and that his hand was not natural, but as if made of wood. She was greatly affrighted thereat and called upon the name of Jesus, whereupon the Devil left her and vanished.

On the ensuing night the Evil Spirit visited her again in the same shape and whored with her. . . . Further, the above-mentioned Walpurga confesses that she oft and much rode on a pitchfork by night with her paramour, but not far on account of her duties [as a midwife]. At such devilish trysts she met a big man with a grey beard, who sat in a chair, like a great prince and was richly attired. That was the Great Devil to whom she had once more dedicated and promised herself body and soul. . . .

At those devilish meetings, she ate, drank, and fornicated with her paramour. Because she would not allow him to drag her along everywhere he had beaten her harshly and cruelly. For food she often had a good roast or an innocent child, which was also roasted, or a suckling pig, and red and white wine, but no salt.

Since she surrendered to the Devil, she had seemingly oft received the Blessed Sacrament of the true Body and Blood of Jesus Christ, apparently by the mouth, but had not partaken of it, but (which once more is terrible to relate) had always taken it out of her mouth again and delivered it up to Federlin, her paramour. At their nightly gatherings she had oft with her other playfellows trodden under foot the Holy and Blessed Sacrament and the image of the Holy Cross. . . .

He also compelled her to do away with and to kill young infants at birth, even before they had been taken to Holy Baptism. This she did whenever possible. . . . She had used the said little bones to manufacture hail; this she was wont to do once or twice a year. . . .

After all this, the Judges and Jury of the Court of this Town of Dillingen . . . at last unanimously gave the verdict that the aforesaid Walpurga Hausmännin be punished and dispatched from life to death by burning at the stake as being a maleficent and well-known witch and sorceress, convicted according to the context of Common Law and the Criminal Code of the Emperor Charles V and the Holy Roman Empire. All her goods and chattels and estate left after her to go to the Treasury of our Most High Prince and Lord. The aforesaid Walpurga to be led, seated on a cart, to which she is tied, to the place of her execution, and her body first to be torn five times with red-hot irons. The first time outside the town hall in the left breast and the right arm, the second time at the lower gate in the right breast, the third time at the mill brook outside the hospital gate in the left arm, the fourth time in the place of execution in the left hand. But since for nineteen years she was a licensed and pledged midwife of the city of Dillingen, yet has acted so vilely, her right hand with which she did such knavish tricks is to be cut off at the place of execution. Neither are her ashes after burning to remain lying on the ground, but are thereafter to be carried to the nearest flowing water and thrown thereinto.

Under what circumstances did the widow confess to these deeds? Why was she so brutally executed?

Source: *The Fugger News-Letters*, ed. Victor von Klarwill, trans. Pauline de Chary (London: John Lane, The Bodley Head Ltd., 1924); reissued as *News and Rumor in Renaissance Europe: The Fugger Newsletters*, trans. Pauline de Chary (New York: Putnam, 1924), 137–39, 142–43.

which had a strong hold on the minds of the uneducated. On to this had been grafted the biblical tradition of the Christian and Jewish scriptures, heard by all in church and read by growing numbers in vernacular translations. Third was the classical tradition of ancient Greece and Rome, which had been rediscovered and blended with the biblical by the philosophers and artists of the Middle Ages.

Like people in other parts of the world, most early modern Europeans believed that natural events could have supernatural causes. When crops failed and people or domestic animals died unexpectedly, they held the unseen world of spirits responsible. Also common was the belief in supernatural causes of human triumph and tragedy. When much of Lisbon, Portugal's capital city, was destroyed by an earthquake in November 1755, for example, both educated and uneducated saw the event as a punishment sent by God. A Jesuit charged it "scandalous to pretend that the earthquake was just a natural event." An English Protestant, John Wesley, agreed, comparing Lisbon's fate with that of Sodom, a city that, according to the Hebrew Bible, God destroyed because of the sinfulness of its citizens.

The small number of systematic investigators of the natural world also believed in mystical or magical explanations. For example, alchemists (those who studied the properties of different metals and chemicals) searched for a secret formula that would magically transform ordinary metals into gold. Similarly, European astrologers who studied the heavens and carefully recorded the movements of the planets and stars, like their counterparts elsewhere in the world, believed these heavenly bodies governed the lives of people on earth.

Even university professors followed the ancient Greek founders of natural philosophy (the study of natural phenomena) in blending observation with mystical interpretation. The prevailing orthodoxy was the physics of Aristotle, which held that everything on Earth was reducible to four elements: two heavy elements, earth and water, that composed the surface of the planet and two lighter elements, air and fire, that floated above the surface. High above were the sun, moon, planets, and stars, which, according to Aristotelian physics, were so light and pure that they floated in crystalline spheres. This division between the ponderous, heavy earth and the airy, celestial bodies accorded perfectly with the common-sense perception that all heavenly bodies revolved around earth.

The prevailing conception of the universe was also influenced by the mathematical tradition derived from the ancient Greek mathematician Pythagoras. Pythagoreans attributed the ability of simple mathematical equations to describe physical objects to mystical properties (as in Pythagoras's famous theorem that the sum of the squares of the sides of a right triangle equals the square of its hypotenuse: $a^2 + b^2 = c^2$). Thus they attached special significance to the simplest (to them perfect) geometrical shapes: the circle (a point rotated around another point) and the sphere (a circle rotated on its axis). From their point of view celestial objects ought to be perfect spheres orbiting the earth in perfectly circular orbits.

Scientific Thinking

Combining careful observation and mathematical calculation, some daring and imaginative European investigators began to challenge the prevailing conceptions of the physical world. Without questioning the existence of a spiritual world, they demonstrated that the workings of the universe could be explained by natural causes, thereby founding modern science. However, the efforts of these scientific pioneers to separate the natural from the supernatural aroused tremendous opposition from those who were unwilling to accept this new approach or fearful that it undercut the privileged teaching role of organized religion.

This "scientific revolution" began with a Polish monk and mathematician named Nicholas Kopernik (1473–1543), best known by the Latin form of his name, Copernicus. Over the centuries, observers of the nighttime skies had plotted the movements of the different heavenly bodies, and mathematicians had worked to fit these observations into the prevailing theories of circular orbits. To make all the evidence fit, they had come up with eighty different spheres and some ingenious theories to explain the many seemingly irregular movements. Pondering these complications, Copernicus came up with a mathematically simpler solution: switching the center of the different orbits from the earth to the sun could reduce the number of spheres that were needed. Copernicus did not challenge the idea that the sun, moon, and planets were light, perfect spheres, or that they moved in circular orbits. But his placement of the sun, not the earth, at the center of things began a revolution in understanding about the structure of the heavens and about the central place of humans in the universe (see Environment and Technology: New Cosmologies).

To escape the anticipated controversies, Copernicus delayed the publication of his heliocentric (sun-centered) theory until after his death in 1543. Other astronomers, including the Danish Tycho Brahe (1546–1601) and his German assistant Johannes Kepler (1571–1630), strengthened and improved on Copernicus's model, showing that planets moved in elliptical, not circular orbits. The most brilliant of the Copernicans was the Italian Galileo Galilei (1564–1642), who built a telescope through which he took a closer look at the heavens. Able to magnify distant objects thirty times beyond the powers of the naked eye, Galileo saw that heavenly bodies were not the perfectly smooth spheres of the Aristotelians. The moon, he reported in *The Starry Messenger* (1610), had mountains and valleys; the sun had spots; other planets had their own moons. In other words, the earth was not unique in being heavy and changeable; instead all celestial bodies shared these qualities.

The Copernican universe at first found more critics than supporters because it so directly challenged not just popular ideas but the intellectual synthesis of classical and biblical authorities. How, demanded Aristotle's defenders, could the heavy earth move without producing vibrations that would shake the planet apart? Is the Bible wrong, asked the theologians, when the Book of Joshua says that, by God's command, "the sun [not the earth] stood still . . . for

about a whole day" to give the ancient Israelites victory in their conquest of Palestine? If Aristotle's physics was wrong, wondered other traditionalists, would not the theological synthesis built on other parts of his philosophy be open to question?

Intellectual and religious leaders encouraged political authorities to suppress the new formulation. Most Protestant leaders, following the lead of Martin Luther, condemned the heliocentric universe as contrary to the Bible. Catholic authorities waited longer to act. After all, both Copernicus and Galileo were Roman Catholics. Copernicus had dedicated his book to one pope, and another pope, Gregory XIII, had in 1582 issued a new and more accurate calendar (still used today) based on the latest astronomical findings. Galileo ingeniously argued that the conflict between scripture and science was only apparent. The word of God revealed in the Bible was expressed of necessity in the imperfect language of ordinary people, but in nature God's truth was revealed more perfectly in a language that could be learned by careful observation and scientific reasoning.

Unfortunately, Galileo also ridiculed those who were slow to accept his findings, charging that Copernican ideas were "mocked and hooted at by an infinite multitude . . . of fools." Jesuits and other critics, smarting under his stinging sarcasm, got Galileo's ideas condemned by the Roman Inquisition in 1616, which put *The Starry Messenger* on the Index of Forbidden Books and prohibited Galileo from publishing further on the subject. When in 1630 he published a new book, *Dialogue on the Two Chief Systems of the World*, the Inquisition forced him to recant his views and put him under house arrest in 1633. (In 1992 the Catholic Church officially retracted its condemnation of Galileo.)

Despite official opposition, printed books spread the new scientific ideas among scholars across Europe. The work begun by Copernicus, Brahe, Kepler, and Galileo was carried to completion by the English scientist Isaac Newton (1642–1727), living in a freer country and time. Newton devised a new branch of mathematics, calculus, which he used to show that the force of gravity—not angels—produced the elliptical or-

New Cosmologies

The classical Ptolemaic plan (below left), widely accepted in sixteenth- and seventeenth-century Europe, placed the earth at the center of the universe. The earth was surrounded by spheres of air and fire. Around them circled the moon and the seven known planets in individual orbits; farther out lay the stars, divided into the astrological sectors devised in antiquity.

In contrast, the Copernican system (below right) placed the sun at the center with the planets in orbit around it. The moon's orbit around the earth was shown. The circular spheres and the outer parts of the plan were unchanged.

Why did Copernicus's simple adjustment in the structure of the universe arouse so much opposition from theologians? Why might some delight in the human mind's ability to figure out the structure of the solar system while others saw humans as diminished by the Copernican plan?

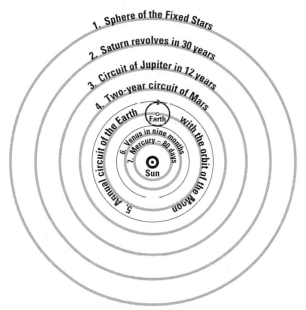

bits of heavenly bodies. His famous laws of motion applied equally to the orbit of planet Mercury and to the trajectory of a cannonball on the earth.

Scholars have often speculated about why the scientific revolution began in Europe, rather than in China, which also had a strong tradition of intellectual inquiry, mathematics, and innovative technology. Many explanations have been suggested. Some contrast China's orderly society with the competition prevailing in Europe. Others stress that the Chinese sought to live in harmony with nature rather than control it. Weaknesses in Chinese geometry have been pointed out. Explaining why something did *not* happen is virtually impossible, but Albert Einstein, one of the leading scientists of the twentieth century, proposed a different way of approaching the debate. In his opinion, "one has not to be astonished that the Chinese sages have not made these steps. The astonishing thing is that these discoveries were made at all."

Enlightened Thinking

Though scientific advances had little practical application until long after 1750, they inspired reconsiderations of other traditional beliefs and customs in early modern Europe. Official and unofficial groups in many countries examined everything from agricultural methods to law, religion, and social hierarchies. The belief that one could discover scientific laws that governed social behavior like the laws that governed physical objects characterized a movement known as the *Enlightenment*. Like the Scientific Revolution, this was the work of a few educated and "enlightened" individuals, who often faced bitter opposition from the political, intellectual, and religious establishment. The leading thinkers of the Enlightenment became accustomed to having their books burned or banned and, to escape similar fates themselves, often spent long periods in exile.

Influences besides the Scientific Revolution affected the Enlightenment. The Reformation had aroused many to champion one creed or another, but partisan bigotry and bloodshed led others to doubt the truth of any of the theological positions and to recommend religious toleration. The killing of suspected witches also shocked many thoughtful people. In the words of Voltaire (the pen name of François Marie Arouet, 1694–1778), a leading French thinker, "No opinion is worth burning your neighbor for."

The accounts of cultures in other parts of the world had also led some European thinkers to wonder about the supposed superiority of European political institutions, moral standards, and religious beliefs. Reports of Amerindian life, though romanticized, led some to conclude that those whom they had called savages were in many ways nobler than European Christians. Matteo Ricci, a Jesuit missionary to China whose journals made a strong impression in Europe, contrasted the lack of territorial ambition of the Chinese with the constant warfare in the West and attributed the difference to the fact that China was ruled by educated men called "Philosophers."

Another influence on the Enlightened thinkers of the eighteenth century was the English Revolution. In the wake of the Glorious Revolution of 1688 and the English Bill of Rights, the English political philosopher John Locke, who had sat out Oliver Cromwell's reign in the Netherlands, published his influential *Second Treatise of Civil Government* (1690). Disputing the prevailing idea that government was sacred, that kings ruled by divine right, Locke argued that rulers derived their power from the consent of the governed, who surrendered some of their rights to the state in order that they might better preserve their life, liberty, and property. This led Locke to dispute the common claim of continental monarchs—that they held absolute authority over their subjects. For Locke, absolute monarchy contradicted the basis of civil society. He believed that the monarch, like everyone else, was subject to the law that lay at the basis of the compact that had brought civil society into existence. If monarchs overstepped the law, Locke argued, citizens had not only the right but the duty to rebel. The consequences of this idea are considered in Chapter 24.

Though many circumstances thus shaped the new enlightened thinkers, the new scientific methods and discoveries provided their clearest model for changing European society. Voltaire posed the issues in these terms: "it would be very peculiar that all nature, all the planets, should obey eternal laws" but a human being, "in contempt of these laws, could act as he pleased solely according to his caprice." The English poet Alexander Pope (1688–1774) made the same point in verse: "Nature and Nature's laws lay hidden in night;/God said, 'Let Newton be' and all was light."

Despite all the enthusiasm it aroused in some circles, the Enlightenment was decidedly unpopular with many absolutist rulers and with clergymen of all faiths. Eighteenth-century Europe was neither enlightened nor scientific, but it was a place where political and religious division, growing literacy, and the printing press made possible the survival of a community of new ideas that profoundly changed life in the centuries that followed.

CONCLUSION

The word *revolution* has been applied to many different changes in Europe between 1500 and 1750. The inflation of the sixteenth century has been called a price revolution, the expansion of trade a commercial revolution, the reform of state spending a financial revolution, the changes in weapons and warfare a military revolution. We have also encountered the scientific revolution, the agricultural revolution, not to mention the religious revolution of the Reformation.

These important changes in early modern European government, economy, society, and thought were parts of a dynamic process that began in the later Middle Ages and led to even bigger industrial and political revolutions before the eighteenth century was over. Yet the years from 1500 to 1750 were not simply—perhaps not even primarily—an age of progress for Europe. For many, the ferocious competition of European armies, merchants, and ideas was a wrenching experience. The growth of powerful states extracted a terrible price in death, destruction, and misery. The Reformation brought greater individual choice in religion but widespread religious persecution as well. Individual women rose or fell with their social class, but few gained equality with men. The expanding economy benefited the emerging merchant elite and their political allies, but most Europeans became worse off as prices rose faster than wages. New scientific and enlightened ideas produced new controversies that did not immediately yield tangible benefits.

The historical significance of this period of European history is clearer when viewed in a global context. What stands out are the powerful and efficient armies, economies, and governments that emerged in Europe during this period and that were envied, and sometimes imitated, by other people such as Tsar Peter the Great. From a global perspective, the balance of political and economic power had shifted slowly but inexorably in the Europeans' favor. In 1500 Europe had been threatened by the Ottomans; but in 1750, as the remaining chapters of Part Five detail, Europeans had brought much of the world's seas and a growing part of its land and people under their control. To be sure, no single group of Europeans accomplished this. The early lead of the Portuguese and Spanish was eclipsed by the Dutch and then by the English and French, but that succession was also part of the European success.

Other changes in Europe during this period had no great overseas significance during this period. The more representative and financially stable government begun in Britain, the new ideas of the scientific revolution and the Enlightenment, and the innovations in agriculture and manufacturing were still of minor significance. Their full effects in furthering Europeans' global dominion would be felt after 1750, as Parts Six and Seven will explore.

SUGGESTED READING

Overviews of this period include H. G. Koenigsberger, *Early Modern Europe: Fifteen Hundred to Seventeen Eighty-Nine* (1987); Eugene F. Rice, Jr., *The Foundations of Early Modern Europe, 1460–1559* (1970); and Richard S. Dunn, *The Age of Religious Wars, 1559–1715*, 2d ed. (1979). More global perspectives are offered by Fernand Braudel, *Civilization and Capitalism, 15th-18th Century*, trans. Siân Reynolds, 3 vols. (1979), and Immanuel Wallerstein, *The Modern World-System*, vol. 2, *Mercantilism and the Consolidation of the European World-Economy, 1600–1750* (1980).

Excellent and accessible overviews of social and economic life are George Huppert, *After the Black Death: A Social History of Early Modern Europe* (1986), and Carlo M. Cipolla, *Before the Industrial Revolution: European Society and Economy, 1000–1700*, 2d ed. (1980). Peter Burke, *Popular Culture in Early Modern Europe* (1978), offers a broad treatment of nonelite perspectives, as does Robert Jütte, *Poverty and Deviance in Early Modern Europe* (1994). For more economic detail see Myron P. Gutmann, *Toward the Modern Economy: Early Industry in Europe, 1500–1800* (1988); Jan De Vries, *The Economy of Europe in an Age of Crisis, 1600–1750* (1976); and Carlo M. Cipolla, ed., *The Fontana Economic History of Europe*, vol. 2, *The Sixteenth and Seventeenth Centuries*

(1974). Merry E. Wiesner summarizes a body of new research in *Women and Gender in Early Modern Europe* (1994).

Technological and environmental changes are the focus of Geoffrey Parker, *Military Revolution: Military Innovation and the Rise of the West, 1500–1800*, 2nd ed. (1996); (1988); William H. McNeill, *The Pursuit of Power: Technology, Armed Force, and Society since A.D. 1000* (1982); Robert Greenhalgh Albion, *Forests and Sea Power: The Timber Problem of the Royal Navy, 1652–1862* (1965); Emmanuel Le Roy Ladurie, *Times of Feast, Times of Famine: A History of Climate since the Year 1000*, trans. Barbara Bray (1971); and Jean M. Grove, *The Little Ice Age* (1988). Robert C. Allen, *Enclosure and the Yeoman: The Agricultural Development of the South Midlands, 1450–1850* (1992), focuses on England.

A. R. Hall, *The Scientific Revolution, 1500–1800: The Formation of the Modern Scientific Attitude*, 2d ed. (1962), is the classic study of the scientific revolution; but Hugh Kearney, *Science and Change, 1500–1700* (1971), is a more accessible introduction. Carolyn Merchant, *The Death of Nature: Women, Ecology and the Scientific Revolution* (1980), tries to combine several broad perspectives. Dorinda Outram, *The Enlightenment* (1995), provides a recent summary of research on that subject.

Witchcraft is a complex subject that has been approached from many angles: H. R. Trevor-Roper, *The European Witch-Craze of the Sixteenth and Seventeenth Centuries and Other Essays* (1967), remains a useful introduction. Carlo Ginzburg, *The Night Battles: Witchcraft & Agrarian Cults in the Sixteenth & Seventeenth Centuries*, trans. Hohn and Anne Tedechi (1983), and Bengt Ankarloo and Gustav Hennisen, eds., *Early Modern Witchcraft: Centres and Peripheries* (1990), are more recent additions. A cross-cultural perspective is presented by Lucy Mair, *Witchcraft* (1969), and Geoffrey Parrinder, *Witchcraft: European and African* (1963).

Good single-country surveys are John Greg and John Morrill, *The Tudors and Stuarts*, vol. 3 of *The Oxford History of Britain*, ed. Kenneth Morgan (1992); Christopher Hill, *Reformation to Industrial Revolution, 1530–1780* (1969); Jonathan Israel, *The Dutch Republic: Its Rise, Greatness and Fall, 1477–1806* (1995); and J. H. Elliott, *Imperial Spain, 1469–1716*, rev. ed. (1977).

NOTES

1. William H. McNeill, *The Pursuit of Power: Technology, Armed Force, and Society Since A.D. 1000* (Chicago: University of Chicago Press, 1982), 124.

2. Michel de Montaigne, *Essais*, ch. 31, "Des Cannibales."

3. Quoted by Carlo M. Cipolla, "Introduction," *The Fontana Economic History of Europe*, vol. 2, *The Sixteenth and Seventeenth Centuries* (Glasgow: Collins/Fontana Books, 1974), 11–12.

CHAPTER NINETEEN

The Diversity of American Colonial Societies, 1530–1770

The Columbian Exchange • Spanish America and Brazil

The English and French Colonies of North America • Colonial Expansion and Conflict

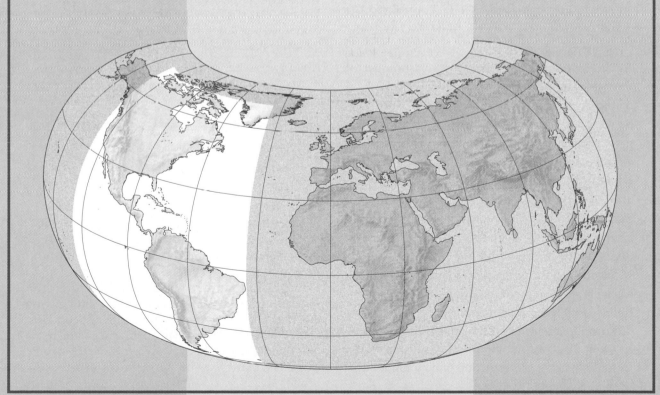

Shulush Homa—the eighteenth-century Choctaw leader called "Red Shoes" by the English—faced a dilemma common to many Amerindian leaders. For years he had befriended the French who had moved into the lower Mississippi Valley, protecting outlying settlements from other native groups and producing a steady flow of deerskins for trade. In return, he received guns and gifts as well as honors previously given only to chiefs. Though born a commoner, he had parlayed his skillful politicking with the French—and the shrewd distribution of the gifts he received—to enhance his position in Choctaw society. Then his fortunes turned. In the course of yet another war between England and France, the English cut off French shipping. Faced with followers unhappy over his sudden inability to supply French guns, Red Shoes decided to make a deal with the English. Unfortunately, the new tactic backfired. His former allies, the French, put a price on his head, which was soon collected. His murder in 1747 launched a Choctaw civil war, a conflict that left the French settlements unprotected and the Choctaw people weakened.

The story of Red Shoes reveals a number of themes from the period of European colonization of the Americas. First, although the wars, epidemics, and territorial loss associated with European settlement threatened Amerindians, many adapted the new technologies and new political possibilities to their own purposes and thrived—at least for a time. In the end, though, the best that they could achieve was a holding action. The people of the New World were becoming dominated by people from the Old.

Second, after centuries of isolation, the Americas were now being drawn into global events, influenced by the political and economic demands of Europe. The influx of Europeans and Africans resulted in a vast biological and cultural transformation, as the introduction of new plants, animals, diseases, peoples, and technologies fundamentally altered the natural environment of the Western Hemisphere. This transfer was not a one-way street, however. The technologies and resources of the New World contributed to profound changes in the Old. Staple crops introduced from the Americas provided highly nutritious foods that helped fuel a population spurt in Europe, Asia, and Africa. As we saw in Chapter 18, riches and products funneled from the Americas changed economic, social, and political relations in Europe.

Finally, the fluidity of the Choctaw's political situation reflects the complexity of colonial society, where Amerindians, Europeans, and Africans all contributed to the creation of new cultures. Although similar processes took place throughout the Americas, the particulars varied from place to place, creating a diverse range of cultures. The society that arose in each colony depended on its mix of native peoples, its connections to the slave trade, and the characteristics of the European society establishing the colony. As the colonies matured, new concepts of identity developed, and those living in the Americas began to see themselves as unique.

THE COLUMBIAN EXCHANGE

The term Columbian Exchange refers to the transfer of peoples, animals, plants and diseases between the New and Old Worlds. The European invasion and settlement of the Western Hemisphere opened a long era of biological and technological transfers that altered American environments. Within a century of first settlement, the domesticated livestock and major agricultural crops of the Old World had spread over much of the Americas, and the New World's useful staple crops had enriched the agricultures of Europe,

Asia, and Africa. Old World diseases that entered the Americas with European immigrants and African slaves devastated indigenous populations. These dramatic population changes weakened native peoples' capacity for resistance and facilitated the transfer of plants, animals, and related technologies. As a result, the colonies of Spain, Portugal, England, and France became vast arenas of cultural and social experimentation.

Demographic Changes

Because of their long isolation from other continents (see Chapter 17), the peoples of the New World lacked immunity to diseases introduced from the Old World. As a result, the death rates among Amerindian peoples during the epidemics of the early colonial period were very high.

The lack of reliable data has frustrated efforts to measure the deadly impact of these diseases in the Americas. Scholars disagree about the size of the precontact population but generally agree that native populations were overwhelmed by Old World diseases following contact. According to one estimate, in the century that followed the triumph of Hernán Cortés in 1521, the population of central Mexico fell from between 13 million and 25 million to approximately 700,000, and nearly 75 percent of the Maya population disappeared. In the region of the Inca Empire, population fell from about 9 million to approximately 600,000. Brazil's native population was similarly ravaged, falling from 2.5 million to under a million within a century of the arrival of the Portuguese. Other estimates begin with smaller precontact populations but agree that the epidemics had a catastrophic effect on indigenous peoples.

Smallpox was the most deadly of the early epidemics. It appeared for the first time on the island of Hispaniola in 1519 and was then transmitted to Mexico by an infected member of the Cortés expedition in 1520. It spread with deadly efficiency. During the siege of the Aztec capital Tenochtitlán, many more Amerindians died of smallpox than from fighting. One source remembered:

> It was [the month of] Tepeilhuitl when it began, and it spread over the people as great destruction.

Some it quite covered [with pustules] on all parts— their faces, their heads, [and] their breasts. . . . There was great havoc. Very many died of it.

In Mexico and Central America, 50 percent or more of the Amerindian population died during the first wave of smallpox epidemics. And even before Francisco Pizarro's arrival farther south (see Chapter 17), smallpox had reduced the Inca population, perhaps even causing the death of the Inca ruler.

Measles arrived in the New World in the 1530s and was followed by diphtheria, typhus, influenza, and the bubonic plague. Mortality was often greatest when two or more deadly diseases struck at the same time. Between 1520 and 1521 influenza in combination with other ailments attacked the Cakchiquel of Guatemala. Their chronicle recalls:

> Great was the stench of the dead. After our fathers and grandfathers succumbed, half the people fled to the fields. The dogs and vultures devoured the bodies. . . . So it was that we became orphans, oh my sons! . . . We were born to die![1]

By the mid-seventeenth century, malaria and yellow fever were also present in tropical regions. Malaria arrived with the African slave trade, ravaging the already reduced native populations and afflicting European immigrants as well. Although most scholars believe that yellow fever was also brought from Africa, new research suggests that the disease was present before the conquest in the tropical low country near present-day Veracruz on the Gulf of Mexico. Whatever its origins, yellow fever killed Europeans in the Caribbean Basin and in other tropical regions nearly as efficiently as smallpox had earlier extinguished Amerindians. Syphilis is the only significant disease believed to have been transferred from the Americas to Europe.

The development of English and French colonies in North America in the seventeenth century led to similar patterns of contagion and mortality. In 1616 and 1617 epidemics spread through New England, nearly exterminating some tribes. French fur traders transmitted measles, smallpox, and other diseases as far as Hudson Bay and the Great Lakes. Although there is very little evidence that Europeans consciously used disease as a tool of empire, the deadly results of contact clearly undermined the ability of native peoples to resist settlement.

Transfer of Plants and Animals

Even as epidemics swept through the indigenous population, the New and the Old Worlds were participating in a vast exchange of plants and ani-

The Columbian exchange Following the conquest, the American environment was dramatically altered by the introduction of plants and animals from the Old World. Here a group of Amerindian women are seen milking cows. Even though livestock sometimes destroyed the fields of native peoples, cows, sheep, pigs, and goats also provided food, leather, and wool that were valued. (Harvard College Library)

mals that radically altered diet and lifestyles in both regions. All the staples of southern European agriculture—including wheat, olives, grapes, and garden vegetables—were being grown in the Americas in a remarkably short time. African and Asian crops—such as bananas, coconuts, breadfruit, and sugar cane—were soon introduced as well. Native peoples remained loyal to traditional staples but added many Old World plants to their diet. Citrus fruits, melons, figs, and sugar as well as onions, radishes, and salad greens all found a place in Amerindian cuisines.

In return the Americas offered the Old World an abundance of useful plants. The New World staples—maize, potatoes, and manioc—revolutionized agriculture and diet in parts of Europe, Africa, and Asia (see Chapter 20, Environment and Technology: Amerindian Foods in Africa). Many experts assert that the rapid growth of world population after 1700 resulted in large measure from the dissemination of these useful crops, which provided more calories per acre than any of the Old World staples except rice. Beans, squash, tomatoes, sweet potatoes, peanuts, chilies, and chocolate also gained widespread acceptance in the Old World. The New World provided the Old with many other useful plants including plants that provided dyes, medicinal plants, varieties of cotton, and tobacco.

The introduction of European livestock had a dramatic impact on the environments and cultures of the New World. Faced with few natural predators, cattle, pigs, horses, and sheep, as well as pests like rats and rabbits, multiplied rapidly in the open spaces of the Americas. On the vast plains of present-day southern Brazil, Uruguay, and Argentina, herds of wild cattle and horses exceeded 50 million by 1700. Large herds of both animals also appeared in northern Mexico and what became the southwest of the United States.

Where Old World livestock spread most rapidly, environmental changes were most dramatic. Many priests and officials noted the destructive impact that marauding livestock had on Amerindian agriculturalists. The first viceroy of Mexico, Antonio de Mendoza, wrote to the Spanish king, "May your Lordship realize that if cattle are allowed, the Indians will be destroyed." However, Mendoza's stark choice misrepresented the complex response of indigenous peoples to these new animals. On the plains of South America, northern Mexico, and Texas, wild cattle provided indigenous peoples with abundant supplies of meat and hides. In the present-day southwestern United States, the Navaho became sheepherders and weavers. Even in the centers of European settlement, individual Amerindians turned European animals to their own advantage by becoming muleteers, cowboys, and sheepherders.

No animal had a more striking effect on the cultures of native peoples than the horse, which increased the efficiency of hunters and the military capacity of warriors on the plains. The horse permitted the Apache, Sioux, Blackfoot, Comanche, Assiniboine, and others to hunt more efficiently the vast herds of buffalo in North America. The horse revolutionized the cultures of the Araucanian and Pampas peoples in South America as well.

SPANISH AMERICA AND BRAZIL

The frontiers of conquest and settlement expanded rapidly. Within one hundred years of Columbus's first voyage to the Western Hemisphere, the Spanish Empire in America included most of the islands of the Caribbean, Mexico, the American southwest, Central America, the Caribbean and Pacific coast of South America, the Andean highlands, and the vast plains of the Rio de la Plata region (the region that includes the modern nations of Argentina, Uruguay, and Paraguay). Although Portuguese settlement in the New World developed more slowly, most of the Brazilian coast was occupied before the end of the sixteenth century.

Settlers from Spain and Portugal sought to create colonial societies based on the institutions and customs of their still-feudal homelands. They viewed society as a vertical arrangement of estates (classes of society), as uniformly Catholic, and as an arrangement of patriarchal extended-family networks. Early settlers moved quickly to recreate the religious, social, and administrative institutions of their homelands.

Despite the massive loss of life caused by epidemics in the sixteenth century, indigenous peoples exercised a powerful influence on the development of colonial societies. Once defeated, Aztec and Inca elite families actively sought to protect traditional privileges and rights through marriage or less formal alliances with *conquistadores* (conquerors). They also quickly learned to use Spanish courts to defend their lands. Nearly everywhere, Amerindian religious beliefs and practices survived beneath the surface of the Christianity imposed on them. Amerindian languages, cuisines, medical practices, and agricultural techniques also survived the conquest and influenced the development of Latin American culture.

The African slave trade added a third cultural stream to colonial Latin American society. At first, African slaves were concentrated in plantation regions of Brazil and the Caribbean (see Chapter 20), but by the end of the colonial era, Africans and their descendants were found throughout Latin America, providing a rich legacy of agricultural practices, music, religious beliefs, cuisine, and social customs to these colonial societies.

State and Church

The Spanish crown moved quickly to curb the independent power of the conquistadores and to establish royal authority over both the defeated native populations and the rising tide of European settlers. Created in 1524, the Council of the Indies in Spain supervised all government, ecclesiastical, and commercial activity in the Spanish colonies. Actual control was limited by technology, however. A ship needed more than two hundred days to make a roundtrip from Spain to Veracruz, Mexico, and additional months of travel to reach Pacific coast cities.

Distance from Europe increased the authority of the viceroys of New Spain and Peru, who were the highest-ranking Spanish officials in the colonies. In 1535, the Viceroyalty of New Spain, with its capital in Mexico City, included Mexico, Central America, and the islands of the Caribbean. The Viceroyalty of Peru, with its capital in Lima, was formed in the 1540s to govern

NEW FRANCE

Mississippi

Colorado

Effective frontier
of Spanish settlement

ENGLISH COLONIES
(Independence declared, 1776)

ATLANTIC
OCEAN

Silver
Silver

Rio Grande

COAHUILA

FLORIDA
(Ceded to England, 1763–1783)

Gulf of Mexico

VICEROYALTY OF NEW SPAIN
(1535)

Silver

Sugar cane
Beef
Tobacco

Havana

HAITI [SAINT DOMINGUE]
(Ceded to France, 1697)

BAJIO LEÓN

Silver

Guadalajara •

Mexico City •

• Veracruz

Sugar cane
Indigo

Sugar cane

Beef

Sugar cane

PUERTO RICO

Silver

Cacao

BRITISH
HONDURAS

SANTO DOMINGO

Sugar
cane
Cochineal

Cochineal
Cacao
Indigo

• Guatemala

Silver

JAMAICA
(Conquered by England, 1655)

Sugar cane

*Caribbean
Sea*

Pearls

Sugar cane

Caracas •

Cacao

PACIFIC
OCEAN

Magdalena

Gold
Suarez

• Bogotá

VICEROYALTY OF
NEW GRANADA
(Separated from
Viceroyalty of Peru,
1717, 1739)

GUIANA

Quito •

ANDES

Amazon

Forest
products

VICEROYALTY
OF PERU
(1590s)

Sugar cane

VICEROYALTY
OF BRAZIL
(1720)

Pernambuco •

Sugar
cane

Lima •

• Cuzco

Sugar
cane

Sugar
cane

• Bahia

Sugar
cane

• La Paz

Cacao

Chuquisaca
• (La Plata; Sucre)

Silver

• Potosí

Paraná

Diamonds
Gold

Yerba
Tobacco

São Paulo •

Rio de Janeiro
(Capital, 1763)

Spanish colonies

	Viceroyalty of New Spain
	Viceroyalty of New Granada
	Viceroyalty of Peru and Audiencia of Chile
	Viceroyalty of La Plata

Portuguese colonies

| | Viceroyalty of Brazil |

ANDES

VICEROYALTY OF
LA PLATA
(Separated from
Viceroyalty of Peru,
1776)

Wheat

Beef and
hides

Santiago •

Buenos Aires •

AUDIENCIA
OF CHILE
(Retained by
Viceroyalty of Peru,
1776)

• Montevideo

Beef and
hides

Claimed but
not settled by Spain

| 0 | 500 | 1000 Km. |
| 0 | 500 | 1000 Mi. |

*Islas Malvinas
(Falkland Islands)*

Cape Horn

Spanish South America (see Map 19.1). Each viceroyalty was subdivided into a number of judicial and administrative districts. Until the seventeenth century, almost all of the officials appointed to high positions in the colonial bureaucracy were born in Spain. Eventually, an economic crisis in Spain forced the Crown to begin selling appointments to these offices and, as a result, local-born members of the colonial elite gained many offices.

In the sixteenth century Portugal's resources and energies were concentrated on Asia. Portugal hesitated to establish expensive mechanisms of colonial government in Brazil, since its explorers had found neither mineral wealth nor native empires there. An effort in the 1530s to colonize and defend Brazil by granting twelve hereditary captaincies to court favorites failed. Finally, in 1549, the king of Portugal appointed a governor-general and established a colonial capital in Salvador, in the northern province of Bahia. The position was upgraded to viceroy in 1720.

The government institutions of the Spanish and Portuguese empires had a more uniform character and were much more extensive and costly than those later established in North America by France and Great Britain. Taxes paid by the silver and gold mines of Spanish America and by the sugar plantations of Portuguese Brazil funded these large colonial bureaucracies. Although these institutions made the colonies more responsive to the initiatives of Spain and Portugal, they also thwarted local economic and political experimentation.

The Catholic Church became the primary agent for the introduction and transmission of both Christian belief and European secular culture in Spanish America and Brazil. It undertook the conversion of Amerindians, ministered to the spiritual needs of European settlers and their children, and provided the institutional setting

Saint Martín de Porres (1579–1639) Martín de Porres was the illegitimate son of a Spanish nobleman and his black servant. Eventually recognized by his father, he entered the Dominican order in Lima, Peru. Known for his generosity, he experienced visions and gained the ability to heal the sick. As was common in colonial religious art, the painter both celebrates Martín de Porres' spirituality and represents him doing the type of work assumed most suitable for castes. (Mint Museum of Art, Charlotte, NC)

Map 19.1 Colonial Latin America in the Eighteenth Century Spain and Portugal controlled most of the Western hemisphere in the eighteenth century. New administrative jurisdictions were created to defend the colonies against European rivals. Taxes assessed on colonial products helped pay for this extension of governmental authority.

for intellectual life and formal education throughout the colonies.

Spain and Portugal justified their American conquests by accepting an obligation to convert native populations to Christianity. Although this religious objective was sometimes forgotten and some members of the clergy were themselves exploiters of native populations, the evangelical effort among America's native peoples imitated in

Dominican church, Cuzco, Peru The Dominican Church was built on the ruins of the Temple of the Sun, the holiest place in the Inca Empire. The construction of the church visually symbolized the overturning of the old order and the victory of Christianity. You can see the rounded outer wall of the Temple of the Sun below the arched portals of the church. (Courtesy, Dr. Valerie Fraser, University of Essex, England)

that many converts were secretly observing old beliefs and rituals. In the 1530s, two converted Aztec nobles were tried and punished for heresy. Then, three decades later, Bishop Diego de Landa used torture, executions, and the destruction of native manuscripts to eradicate idolatry among the Maya. Repelled by these events, the church hierarchy ended both the violent repression of native religious practice and efforts to recruit a native clergy.

Indeed, the church often protected native peoples from abuse and exploitation by the Spanish. Bartolomé de las Casas was the most influential defender of the Amerindians in the early colonial period. Arriving in Hispaniola in 1502, he was given a grant of Amerindian laborers—an *encomienda*—which allowed him to extract both labor and tribute from a group of Amerindians. Deeply moved by the deaths of so many Amerindians and by the misdeeds of the Spanish, Las Casas entered the Dominican Order. He eventually became the first bishop of Chiapas, in southern Mexico, where he took up the cause of the native peoples, writing a number of books that detailed their mistreatment by the Spanish. Among his many achievements was the enactment of The New Laws of 1542—reforms that outlawed the enslavement of Amerindians and limited other forms of forced labor.

Evangelization had led to the appearance of an Amerindian Christianity that, while superficially Catholic, included essential elements of traditional native cosmology and ritual. Indigenous beliefs and rituals were commonly blended with the celebration of saints' days or rituals associated with the Virgin Mary. The Catholic clergy and most settlers saw this mixture as either the work of the Devil or evidence of Amerindian inferiority. Instead it was one component of the process of cultural borrowing and innovation that contributed to a distinct and original Latin American culture.

Evangelical enthusiasm waned after 1600, and the church redirected most of its resources from the largely Amerindian countryside to the European cities and towns of colonial society. The founding of universities and secondary schools and the stimulation of intellectual life were the greatest achievements of this mature period.

scale and reach Christianity's expansion in the era of Constantine, some three or four hundred years after the death of Christ. In Mexico alone hundreds of thousands of conversions and baptisms were achieved within a few years of the conquest.

The Catholic clergy sought to convert the Amerindians by first converting native elites. Some early church leaders like the first bishop of Mexico, Juan de Zumárraga, sponsored the creation of schools devoted to the education of a native clergy. But these idealistic efforts were abandoned when church authorities discovered

Over time, the church would become the richest institution in the Spanish colonies, controlling ranches, plantations, and vineyards as well as serving as the society's banker.

Colonial Economies

The silver mines of Peru and Mexico and the sugar plantations of Brazil dominated regional economic development. The mineral wealth of the New World fueled the early development of European capitalism and funded a greatly expanded trade with Asia. Profits produced in these centers of production promoted the growth of colonial cities, concentrated scarce investment capital and labor resources, and stimulated the development of livestock raising and agriculture in neighboring rural areas (see Map 19.1). Once established, this dependence on mineral and agricultural exports endured to the end of the colonial period.

Although millions of pesos of gold were produced in the mines of Latin America, the silver mines of the Spanish colonies generated more wealth and exercised greater economic influence. The first important silver strikes occurred in Mexico in the 1530s and 1540s. In 1545 the single richest silver deposit in the Americas was discovered at Potosí in Bolivia. After 1680, however, Mexican silver production was nearly always twice that of the Andean region.

At first silver was extracted from ore by smelting. The ore was crushed in giant stamping mills, packed with charcoal in a furnace, and fired. Within a short time the need for fuel had stripped many mining regions of their forests. Mexican miners then developed an efficient method of chemical extraction using mercury to refine silver from ore (see Environment and Technology: The Silver Refinery at Potosí, Bolivia, 1700). Mercury amalgamation led to greater yields, but use of the poison mercury contaminated the environment and sickened the work force.

In the early years Spanish mines in both Mexico and Peru depended on the forced labor of Amerindians. Because the mines of Mexico were located away from the major Amerindian populations, mineowners there soon relied on wage laborers. In Peru, by contrast, a rotational labor draft called the *mita*, was imposed on Amerindian communities, and was retained to the end of the colonial period despite the slow development of a supplemental wage labor system.* The colonial mita required Amerindian communities to send one-seventh of all adult males to silver mines or other Spanish enterprises. It had a destructive impact on indigenous villages already struggling against epidemics and other dislocations. Deaths, injuries, and the decisions of some mita workers to stay at the mines as wage laborers imposed ever heavier labor and tax burdens on those who remained in the villages. As time went on, thousands of Amerindians fled from these obligations by becoming wage laborers in cities or on Spanish ranches and farms.

The Portuguese first developed sugar plantations that relied on slave labor on the Atlantic islands of Madeira, the Azores, the Cape Verdes, and São Tomé. Because of those experiences, they brought this profitable form of agriculture to Brazil in the first decades of settlement. After 1550, sugar production expanded rapidly in the northern provinces of Pernambuco and Bahia. By the seventeenth century, sugar dominated the Brazilian economy.

Brazil's sugar plantations depended on slave labor. At first the Portuguese enslaved Amerindians captured in war or seized from their villages, sending them to work on the plantations. Planters ignored Amerindian culture, which gave primary responsibility for agriculture to women. Efforts to resist or flee led to harsh punishments. Many committed suicide. Thousands of others died during the epidemics that raged across Brazil in the sixteenth and seventeenth centuries. The high death rate and rapid development of the sugar plantations created an insatiable demand for Amerindian slaves. In response, settlers from the southern region of São Paulo organized slave raids deep into the interior to supply the plantations of northeastern Brazil.

---

*This was based on the ancient Andean mit'a (see Chapter 12) which was a reciprocal system of labor obligations that provided protections for the elderly and incapacitated as well as support for the elite.

The Silver Refinery at Potosí, Bolivia, 1700

The silver refineries of Spanish America were among the largest and most heavily capitalized industrial enterprises in the Western Hemisphere during the colonial period. By the middle of the seventeenth century the mines of Potosí, Bolivia, had attracted a population of more than 120,000.

A typical refinery (*ingenio*) is presented in the accompanying illustration. Aqueducts carried water from large reservoirs on nearby mountainsides to the refineries. In this particular refinery the water wheel shown on the right drove two sets of vertical stamps that crushed ore. Each iron-shod stamp was about the size and weight of a telephone pole. Crushed ore was sorted, dried, and mixed with mercury and other catalysts to extract the silver. The amalgam was then separated by a combination of washing and heating. The end result was a nearly pure ingot of silver that would later be assayed and taxed at the mint.

Silver production carried a high environmental cost. Forests were cut down to provide fuel and the timbers needed to shore up mine shafts and construct stamping mills and other machinery. Unwanted base metals produced in the refining process poisoned the soil. In addition, the need for tens of thousands of horses, mules, and oxen to drive machinery and transport material led to overgrazing and widespread erosion.

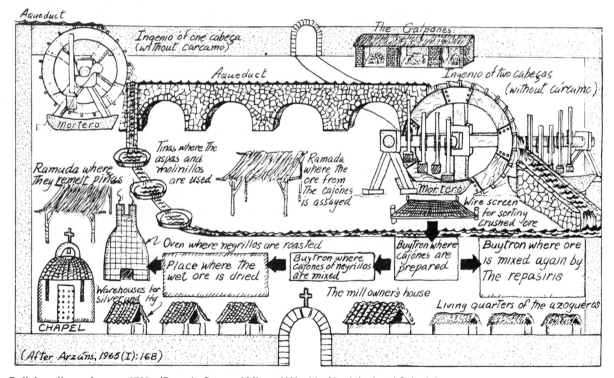

Bolivian silver mine, ca. 1700   (From *In Quest of Mineral Wealth: Aboriginal and Colonial Mining and Metallurgy in Spanish America*, edited by Alan K. Craig and Robert C. West, 1994. Vol. 33 of *Geoscience and Man.* Courtesy, Geoscience Publications)

Sugar planters eventually came to rely more on African slaves, although Amerindians continued to be enslaved as late as the eighteenth century. Africans cost much more than Amerindian slaves, but planters found them to be more productive and more resistant to disease. With rising profits from the plantations, imports of African slaves rose from an average of 2,000 per year in the late sixteenth century to approximately 7,000 per year a century later. Between 1650 and 1750, more than three African slaves arrived in Brazil for every free European immigrant.

Within Spanish America, the mining centers of Mexico and Peru exercised a broad economic influence. American silver increased the European money supply. The outcome was commercial expansion and, later, industrialization. American silver also flowed across the Pacific to the Spanish colony of the Philippines, where it was exchanged for spices, silks, and pottery. In the Americas, the rich mines of Peru, Bolivia, and Mexico stimulated the production of agriculturalists, livestock producers, and textile manufacturers in distant regions. By the end of the sixteenth century, the mining center at Potosí contained at least 120,000 inhabitants—a population larger than that of most contemporary European cities. Residents of Potosí were at the center of a vast regional market that consumed Chile's wheat, the livestock of Argentina, and the textiles of Ecuador.

The sugar plantations of Brazil played a similar role in integrating the economy of the south Atlantic region, connecting Brazil to the Spanish settlements in Argentina, Uruguay, and Paraguay. The ports of Bahia and Rio de Janeiro managed the exchange of sugar, tobacco, and reexported slaves from Brazil for the yerba (Paraguayan tea), hides, livestock, and silver produced in the Spanish colonies. Portugal's increasing openness to British trade also allowed Brazil to become a conduit for illegal trade with the Spanish colonies. At the end of the seventeenth century the discovery of gold in Brazil helped overcome this large region's currency shortage and promoted further economic integration.

In 1503 the government of Spain had designated Seville as the only Spanish port permitted to trade with Spain's American colonies, and it authorized a single institution, the House of Trade, to supervise colonial commerce. Merchant guilds were granted monopoly control of trade both in Spain and in the colonies. Because the fleets of foreign rivals and pirates attacked ships returning to Spain with silver and gold, the Spanish government came to rely on escorted convoys to supply the colonies. By 1650, Portugal had instituted a similar system of monopoly trade and fleets.

The combination of monopoly commerce and convoy systems that Spain and Portugal imposed proved to be remarkably effective in protecting shipping and facilitating the collection of taxes. It also slowed the flow of European goods to the New World and kept prices high. Colonial populations, however, became frustrated in their efforts to promote a greater volume of trade with Europe. As a result, colonial merchants eventually established illegal commercial relations with the English, French, and Dutch. By the middle of the seventeenth century a majority of European imports were arriving in Latin America illegally.

Society in Colonial Latin America

With the exception of a few early viceroys, few members of Spain's great noble families came to the New World. Lesser nobles (called *hidalgos*) were well represented as were Spanish merchants, artisans, miners, priests, and lawyers. Small numbers of criminals, beggars, and prostitutes also found their way to the colonies. This flow of immigrants from Spain was never large, and Spanish settlers were a tiny minority in a colonial society numerically dominated by Amerindians and rapidly growing populations of Africans, American-born whites (called *creoles*), and people of mixed ancestry (see Voices & Visions: Society in Colonial Mexico).

Encomenderos, conquistadores who received grants of labor and tribute (encomiendas) from Amerindian communities as rewards for service to the Crown, dominated society in early Spanish America. Encomiendas were initially based on obligations that Amerindian communities owed to native rulers before the conquest. Although laws attempted to prevent the mistreatment of Amerindians, abuse was common. Encomenderos sought to create a hereditary social and political power similar to European feudalism, but their position was undermined by the catastrophic loss of Amerindian life during the epidemics of the sixteenth century and by the growing power of viceroys, judges, and bishops appointed by the king.

By the end of the sixteenth century, the elite of Spanish America included both European immigrants and American-born creoles. Europeans dominated the highest levels of the church and government as well as trade with Europe. Creoles controlled colonial agriculture and mining. Wealthy creole families with extensive holdings in land and mines commonly sought to arrange for their daughters' marriage with successful Spanish merchants or officials. Often richer in reputation than in wealth, Spanish officials and merchants welcomed the opportunity to forge such connections. Although tensions between Spaniards and creoles were inevitable, most elite families had members from both groups.

When Europeans arrived in the Americas, native peoples were divided among a large number of distinct cultural and linguistic groups. Remarkable cultural diversity and class distinctions were found even in the highly centralized Aztec and Inca empires. The loss of life provoked by the European conquest undermined this complex and diverse mix of cultures and classes. The imposition of Catholic Christianity further eroded ethnic boundaries among native peoples. In place of the ethnic diversity that characterized the precontact Americas, colonial administrators and settlers evolved a racial label, "Indian," which facilitated the imposition of special taxes and labor obligations by ignoring the indigenous class and ethnic differences.

The indigenous Amerindian elites survived only briefly in the Spanish colonies and Brazil. Some of the conquistadores and early settlers married or established less formal relations with Amerindian women of this class, but fewer of these alliances occurred when European women arrived on the scene. By 1600 the descendants of the once-powerful Amerindian families were indistinguishable from the village rulers who had been subordinate to them. Both groups of heredi-

tary leaders, however, proved indispensable in the Spanish colonies, where they helped organize draft labor and collect taxes. Some members of this class prospered in the colonial period as ranchers, muleteers, and merchants; many others lived in the same materially deprived conditions as Amerindian commoners.

Thousands of blacks participated in the conquest and settlement of Spanish America. The majority were Spanish-speaking, Catholic slaves who had been born in Spain or Portugal, although some black freemen were also present. More than four hundred blacks, most of them slaves, participated in the conquest of Peru and Chile. In the fluid social environment of the conquest era, many slaves gained their freedom. Many simply fled from their masters. Juan Valiente escaped his master in Mexico, participated in Francisco Pizarro's conquest of the Inca Empire, and later became one of the most prominent early settlers of Chile, where he received an encomienda.

The status of the black population of colonial Latin America declined with the opening of a direct slave trade with Africa (for details, see Chapter 20). Africans were culturally different from blacks who had been brought to the New World from Spain and Portugal. Their differences in language, religious belief, and cultural practice were viewed as signs of their inferiority and ultimately served as a justification for enslaving them. Soon anyone with black ancestry was barred from positions in church and government as well as from many skilled crafts.

The rich mosaic of African identities was retained in colonial Latin America. Many cultural groups struggled in slavery to retain their languages, religious beliefs, and marriage customs. But, in regions with large slave majorities, these cultural and linguistic barriers often divided slaves and made resistance more difficult. Over time elements from many African traditions blended and mixed with European (and in some cases Amerindian) language and beliefs to forge distinct local cultures. The rapid growth of an American-born slave population accelerated this process of cultural change.

Slave resistance took many forms, including sabotage, malingering, running away, and rebellion. Although many slave rebellions occurred,

Society in Colonial Mexico

Great inequalities in wealth and power developed in the wake of conquest and European settlement in colonial Spanish America. The vast majority of the Amerindians lived in poverty and were excluded from full participation in the institutions of church and state. In 1799 Antonio de San Miguel, bishop of Michoacán in Mexico, wrote to the king of Spain to warn that these injustices would lead to violence. As preface to a suggested program of necessary reforms, the bishop provided the following summary of social conditions.

The population of New Spain is composed of three classes of men: whites or Spaniards, Indians, and castes. I suppose the Spaniards to compose the tenth part of the whole mass. In their hands almost all the property and all the wealth of the kingdom are centered. The Indians and the castes cultivate the soil; they are in the service of the better sort of people; and they live by the work of their hands. Hence there results between Indians and whites that opposition of interests and that mutual hatred which universally takes place between those who possess all and those who possess nothing, between masters and those who live in servitude. Thus we see, on the one hand, the effects of envy and discord, deception, theft, and the inclination to prejudice the interests of the rich, and on the other, arrogance, severity and the desire to take every advantage of the helplessness of the Indian. I am not ignorant that these evils everywhere spring from a great inequality of condition. But in America they are rendered still more terrific because there exists no intermediate state; we are rich or miserable, noble or degraded. . . .

Now, Sire, what attachment can the Indian have to the government, despised and degraded as he is, and almost without property and without hope of ameliorating his existence? He is merely attached to social life by a tie which affords him no advantage. Let not your majesty believe that the dread of punishment alone is sufficient to preserve tranquillity in this country; there must be other motives, there must be more powerful motives. If new legislation . . . do[es] not occupy itself with the situation of the Indians and people of color, the influence which the clergy possess over the hearts of these unfortunate people, however great it may be, will not be sufficient to contain them in the submission and respect due to their sovereign.

What are the conditions imposed on Amerindians and castes? What are the obstacles to progress discussed by the bishop? Does the bishop believe that these problems threaten Spanish rule in New Spain (Mexico)?

Source: Alexander von Humboldt, *Political Essay on the Kingdom of New Spain,* edited with an introduction by Mary Maples Dunn (Alfred A. Knopf, New York: 1972), 67.

---

colonial authorities were always able to reestablish control. Groups of runaway slaves, on the other hand, were sometimes able to defend themselves for years. In both Spanish America and Brazil communities of runaways (called *quilombos* in Brazil and *palenques* in Spanish colonies) were common. The largest quilombo was Palmares, where thousands of slaves defended themselves against Brazilian authorities for sixty years until they were overrun in 1694.

Slaves were skilled artisans, musicians, servants, artists, cowboys, and even soldiers. However, the vast majority worked in agriculture. Conditions for slaves were worst on the sugar plantations of Brazil and the Caribbean, where harsh discipline, brutal punishments, and backbreaking labor were common. Because planters preferred to buy male slaves, there was always a gender imbalance on plantations. As a result, neither the traditional marriage and family patterns of Africa nor those of Europe developed. The disease environment of the tropics, as well as the poor housing, diet, hygiene, and medical care offered to slaves, also weakened slave families.

The colonial development of Brazil was distinguished from that of Spanish America by the absence of rich and powerful indigenous civilizations such as the Aztecs and Incas and by lower levels of European immigration. Nevertheless, Portuguese immigrants came to exercise the same domination in Brazil as the Spanish exercised in their colonies. Eventually the growth of cities and the creation of imperial institutions duplicated in outline the social structures found in Spanish America—but with a difference: by the early seventeenth century, Africans and their American-born descendants were the largest racial group in Brazil, and, as a result, Brazilian colonial society was influenced more by African culture than by Amerindian culture.

Both Spanish and Portuguese law provided for *manumission*, the granting of freedom to individual slaves. Among those gaining their liberty, the majority had saved money and purchased their freedom. This was easiest in cities where slave artisans and market women had the opportunity to earn and save money. Some slaves were freed by owners without compensation. Household servants were the most likely beneficiaries of this form of manumission. Only about 1 percent of the slave population gained freedom each year, but the large percentage of women among this group led to the rapid growth of a large free colored population, for the children of free women were free.

Within a century of settlement, groups of mixed descent had become the majority in many regions. Although there were few marriages between Amerindian women and European men, less formal relationships were common. Few European or creole fathers recognized their mixed offspring, called *mestizos*. Nevertheless, this rapidly expanding class came to have a middle position in colonial society, dominating urban artisan trades and small-scale agriculture and ranching. In frontier regions many members of the elite came from this group, some proudly asserting their descent from Amerindian nobility. Colonial ethnic diversity is discussed in the Voices and Visions feature.

The African slave trade led to the appearance of additional mixed groups. Mulattos, individuals of European and African descent, came to hold an intermediate position in the tropics similar to that held by mestizos in Mesoamerica and the Andean region. In Spanish Mexico and Peru and in Brazil, mixtures of Amerindians and Africans were also common. All these mixed-descent groups were commonly called *castas*. Castas dominated small-scale retailing and construction trades in cities. In the countryside, many small ranchers and farmers as well as wage laborers were castas. Members of these mixed groups who gained high status or significant wealth generally spoke Spanish or Portuguese, observed the requirements of Catholicism, and, whenever possible, lived the life of Europeans in their residence, dress, and diet.

THE ENGLISH AND FRENCH COLONIES OF NORTH AMERICA

The North American colonial empires of England and France shared many characteristics with the colonies of Spain and Portugal (see Map 19.1). The governments of England and France hoped to find easily extracted forms of wealth or great indigenous empires like those of the Aztecs or Incas. English and French settlers responded to native peoples with a mixture of diplomacy and violence, as had the Spanish and Portuguese. African slaves also proved crucial to the development of these colonial economies.

Some important differences, however, distinguished North American colonial development from the Latin American model. The English and French colonies were developed nearly a century after Cortés's conquest of Mexico, a hundred-year period of significant economic and demographic growth in Europe. Distracted by ventures elsewhere, neither England nor France had the fiscal resources or political will necessary to imitate the bureaucracy established in the Spanish and Portuguese colonies. As a result, private companies and individual proprietors were granted the right to develop the English and French colonies. This practice led to greater regional variety among these colonies in economic activity, political culture, and social structure than was evident in Latin America.

Early English Experiments

England's first efforts to gain a foothold in the Americas produced more failures than successes. The first attempt was made by a group of west country gentry and merchants led by Sir Humphrey Gilbert. In the 1580s their effort to establish a colony in Newfoundland, Canada failed. Following Gilbert's death in 1584, leadership passed to his half-brother Sir Walter Raleigh, who organized private financing for a new colonization scheme. A year later, 108 men attempted a settlement on Roanoke Island off the coast of present-day North Carolina. Afflicted with poor leadership, undersupplied, and threatened by neighboring Amerindian groups, the colony was abandoned within a year. A final effort to settle Roanoke was made in 1587 when 117 men, women, and children were disembarked. Because of England's need to mobilize against the Spanish Armada, a relief expedition did not arrive until 1590. Raleigh's colonial experiment was given up when no sign of the settlers could be found.

When England's efforts to establish colonies in North America were renewed, essential elements of these failed experiments were retained. Primary among them were reliance on private capital to finance settlement and an unrealistic belief that these colonies would produce the high-value products of the Mediterranean economy—silk, citrus, and wine. English success in colonizing Ireland following the conquest in 1566 also encouraged new experiments in America. Property confiscated in Ulster was cleared of its native population and offered for sale to English investors. The city of London, merchant guilds, and wealthy private investors all purchased Irish "plantations." By 1650 nearly 150,000 English and Scottish settlers were established in Ireland. Ireland, therefore, was England's first successful colony. Indeed, it attracted six times as many colonists in the early seventeenth century as New England.

Painting of Castas   This is an example of a common genre of colonial Spanish American painting. In the eighteenth century there was increased interest in ethnic mixing and wealthy colonials as well as some Europeans commissioned sets of paintings that showed mixed families. Commonly the paintings also indicated what the artist believed was an appropriate class setting for each of these castes. In this painting a richly dressed Spaniard is depicted with his Amerindian wife dressed in European clothing. Notice that the painter has the mestiza daughter appear to look to her European father for guidance. (Private Collection. Photographer: Camilo Garza/Fotocam, Monterrey, Mexico)

The South

A privately funded colonial venture first appeared in the New World when London investors, organized as the Virginia Company, took up the challenge of colonizing Virginia in 1606. A year later 144 settlers disembarked at Jamestown, an island 30 miles (48 kilometers) up the James River in the region of Chesapeake Bay. Additional settlers arrived in 1609. Although the location was easily defended, it was a swampy and unhealthy place; indeed, nearly 80 percent of all settlers in the first fifteen years died from disease or Amerindian attacks. All hopes for immediate profits were dashed. There was no mineral wealth, no passage to Asia, and no docile and exploitable native population. By concentrating energies on these false hopes, settlers failed to grow enough food and were saved on more than one occasion by the generosity of natives.

The English crown dissolved the Virginia Company in 1624 because of its mismanagement of the colony. Freed from the company's commitment to Jamestown's unhealthy environment, colonists pushed deeper into the interior, developing a sustainable economy based on furs, timber, and, increasingly, tobacco. The profits from tobacco soon attracted new immigrants and new capital. Along the shoreline of the Chesapeake and the rivers that fed it, settlers spread out, developing plantations and farms. From this early date Virginia's population would remain dispersed. Unlike Latin America, where large and powerful capital cities dominated networks of secondary towns, no city of any significant size would develop in colonial Virginia.

Early settlement in the Chesapeake Bay saw one group absent from the colonies of Latin America: white indentured servants, who accounted for approximately 80 percent of the English immigrants to Virginia and neighboring Maryland. Young men and women unable to pay their transportation to the New World accepted indentures (contracts) that bound them to a term of from four to seven years of labor in return for passage, a small parcel of land, and some tools and clothes. During the seventeenth century, approximately 1,500 indentured servants, mostly male, arrived each year (see Chapter 20 for details on the indentured labor system). As mortality rates declined, however, the pattern changed. White planters relied less on indentured servants and more on slaves. Virginia's slave population grew from 300 in 1650 to 10,000 by 1700.

By the 1660s many of the elements of the mature colony were in place in Virginia. In politics, the governor and his council were joined by the representatives of "burghs," called *burgesses*. These representatives began meeting alone as a deliberative body, thus originating a system of representation that would distinguish the English colonies of North America from those of other European powers. Ironically, this expansion in colonial liberties and political rights occurred along with the development of slavery. The intertwined evolution of American freedom and American slavery gave England's southern colonies a unique and conflicted political character that remained after independence.

At the same time, the English were expanding their settlements in the South. The northern part of Carolina was settled from Virginia and followed that colony's mixed economy of tobacco and forest products. Charleston, South Carolina, was settled by planters from the Caribbean island of Barbados in 1670 and, within decades, developed many of the economic and social characteristics of the Caribbean islands and Brazil.

Despite an unhealthy climate, Charleston attracted a diverse array of immigrants that included French Protestants (Huguenots), colonists from Barbados, and English dissenters. The colony prospered at first from the profits of the fur trade. Fur traders pushed into the interior, eventually threatening the French trading networks organized from New Orleans and Mobile. By this trade, native peoples eventually contributed over 100,000 deerskins annually to the economy.

At the same time, native population was weakened by epidemics, alcoholism, and growing intertribal conflict. Amerindians captured in these wars were sold as slaves to the colonists, who used them as agricultural workers or exported them to the Caribbean islands. Dissatisfied with the terms of trade imposed by fur traders and angered by the abuses of the slave trade, various Amerindian groups attacked English settlements in the early 1700s. Defeat forced these Amerindian peoples from their traditional lands.

African slaves were present from the founding of Charleston and were instrumental in introducing irrigated rice agriculture along the coastal lowlands and in developing indigo (a plant that produced a blue dye) plantations at higher elevations away from the coast. Slaves were often given significant responsibilities. As one planter sending two slaves and their families to a frontier region put it: "[They] are likely young people, well acquainted with Rice & every kind of plantation business, and in short [are] capable of the management of a plantation themselves."[2]

As profits from rice and indigo rose, the importation of African slaves created a black majority. African languages and Gullah, a dialect derived from African and English roots, as well as African religious beliefs and diet, strongly influenced this unique colonial culture. These cultural divisions also contributed, in 1739, to the revolt known as the Stono Rebellion. After a group of about twenty slaves, many of them Africans, seized firearms, they were joined by about a hundred slaves from nearby plantations. The rebels were soon defeated by the militia, and many were executed. Nevertheless, the rebellion shocked slave owners throughout the South and led to greater repression.

Colonial South Carolina was the most hierarchical society in British North America. Planters controlled both the economy and political life. The richest maintained households both in the countryside and in Charleston, the largest city in the southern colonies. Small farmers, cattlemen, artisans, merchants, and fur traders held an intermediate but clearly subordinate social position. Although native peoples remained influential participants in colonial society through commercial contacts and alliances, they were increasingly marginalized. As had occurred in colonial Latin America, the growth of a large mixed population blurred racial and cultural boundaries. On the frontier, the children of white men and Indian women held an important place in the fur trade. In the plantation regions and Charleston, mulattos often held preferred positions within the slave workforce or, if they were freedmen, in skilled trades such as carpentry, and blacksmithing.

New England

The next area of English settlement was New England, where colonization sprang from different origins and took a different course. Two separate groups of Protestant dissenters, the Pilgrims and the Puritans, undertook the settlement of this region.

The Pilgrims, who came first, wished to break completely with what they saw as a still-Catholic Church of England. Unwilling to confront the power of the established church and monarch, they sought an opportunity to pursue their spiritual ends without persecution. As a result, approximately one hundred settlers—men, women, and children—established the colony of Plymouth on the coast. Although nearly half of the settlers died during the first winter, the colony survived. Plymouth benefited from strong leadership and from the discipline and cooperative nature of the settlers. Nevertheless, this experiment failed. The religious enthusiasm and purpose that first sustained the pilgrims was dissipated by new immigrants who did not share the founders' religious beliefs, and geographic dispersal to new towns. In 1691, Plymouth was absorbed into the larger Massachusetts Bay Colony of the Puritans.

The Puritan leaders of the Massachusetts Bay Company carried the charter that set out rights and obligations as well as the direction of company government with them from England to Massachusetts, thereby limiting Crown efforts to control them. Subjected to increased discrimination in England for their efforts to transform what they saw as a corrupted church, large numbers of Puritans began emigrating in 1630. By 1643, more than 20,000 had settled in the Bay Colony.

Immigration to Massachusetts differed from contemporary immigration to the Chesapeake and to South Carolina. Most immigrants to Massachusetts arrived with their families. Whereas 84 percent of Virginia's population in 1625 was male, Massachusetts had a normal gender balance in its population almost from the beginning. Massachusetts was also more racially and culturally homogeneous and, at the same time, less hierarchical than the southern colonies, in large measure because of the small number of indentured servants or African slaves drawn to this region of small farms.

Political institutions evolved out of the original colonial charter. A governor was elected, along with a council of magistrates drawn from the board of directors of the Massachusetts Bay Company. Disagreements between this council and elected representatives of the towns led, by

1650, to the creation of a lower legislative house that selected its own speaker and began to develop procedures and rules similar to those of the House of Commons.

Economically, Massachusetts Bay differed dramatically from the southern colonies. Agriculture met basic needs, but poor soils and harsh climate offered no opportunity to develop cash crops like tobacco or rice. To pay for imported tools, textiles, and other essentials, the colonists needed to discover some profit-making niche in the growing Atlantic market. Fur, timber and other ship stores, and fish provided the initial economic foundation, but New England's economic well-being soon depended on providing commercial and shipping services in a dynamic and far-flung commercial arena that included the southern colonies, the smaller Caribbean islands, Africa, and Europe.

In Spanish and Portuguese America, heavily capitalized monopolies dominated international trade. In New England, by contrast, merchants survived by discovering smaller but more sustainable profits in diversified trade across the Atlantic. The colony's commercial success required superior market intelligence, flexibility, and streamlined organization. The success of this development strategy is demonstrated by urban population growth. With 16,000 inhabitants in 1740, Boston was the largest city in British North America.

Social stratification was less extreme in New England than in the southern plantation colonies. Slaves were present in very small numbers as were indentured servants. Epidemics and military defeats at the hands of the settlers had dramatically reduced the Amerindian population by 1700. As a result, there were fewer differences in wealth and status, and the social structure was more uniformly British and Protestant than in the South.

The Middle Atlantic

The future success of English-speaking America was rooted in the rapid economic development and remarkable cultural diversity that appeared in the Middle Atlantic colonies—diversity that grew in part from non-English origin. In 1624 the Dutch West India Company established a colony called "New Netherland" and located its capital on Manhattan Island. The colony was poorly managed and underfinanced from the start, but its location commanded the potentially profitable and strategically important Hudson River. Dutch merchants established with the Iroquois Confederacy and other native peoples alliances and trading relationships that gave them access to the rich fur trade of Canada.

When confronted by substantial British military power in 1664, the Dutch surrendered without a fight. James, duke of York and later king of England, became proprietor of the colony. Renamed "New York," the colony was characterized by tumultuous politics and corrupt administration.

New York's success was guaranteed in large measure by the development of New York City as a commercial entrepôt. Inexpensive transportation by boat gave the region's grain farmers access to the booming markets of the Caribbean and southern Europe. By the early eighteenth century, New York had a diverse population that included (in addition to English colonists) Dutch, German, and Swedish settlers as well as a large slave community.

Pennsylvania began as a proprietary colony and as a refuge for a persecuted religious minority, the Quakers. The proprietor, William Penn, secured in 1682 an enormous grant of territory (nearly the size of England) because the English King Charles II was indebted to Penn's father. As owner of the land, Penn had sole right to establish a government, subject only to the requirement that he provide for an assembly of freemen.

Penn quickly lost control of the political process, but his colony was an immediate success. By 1700 Pennsylvania had a population of more than 21,000, and Philadelphia, its capital, soon passed Boston to become the largest city in the British colonies. Healthy climate, excellent land, relatively peaceful relations with native peoples (prompted by Penn's emphasis on negotiation rather than warfare), and access through Philadelphia to good markets led to rapid economic and demographic growth in the colony.

Pennsylvania and South Carolina were both grain-exporting colonies, but they were very dif-

The home of Sir William Johnson, British superintendent for Indian affairs, Northern District
As the colonial era drew to a close, the British attempted to limit colonial defense costs by negotiating land settlements between native peoples and settlers. These agreements were doomed to failure by the growing tide of western migration. William Johnson maintained a fragile peace along the northern frontier by building strong personal relations with influential native leaders. His home shows the mixed nature of the frontier—the relative opulence of the main house offset by the two defensive blockhouses built for protection. (Detail, "Johnson Hall," by E.L. Henry. Courtesy, Albany Institute of History and Art)

ferent societies. Whereas South Carolina's rice plantations required large numbers of slaves, Pennsylvania's grains were overwhelmingly produced on family farms by free workers, including a large number of German families. As a result, Pennsylvania's economic expansion in the late seventeenth century occurred without reproducing South Carolina's hierarchical and repressive social order. The prosperous city of Philadelphia, however, did have a large population of black slaves and freedmen by the early eighteenth century. Many were servants in the homes of wealthy merchants, but the fast-growing economy offered many opportunities in skilled trades as well.

French America

French settlement patterns more closely resembled those of Spain and Portugal than of England. There was a strong commitment to missionary activity and emphasis on extracting resources—in this case, furs. France's interest in North America was first stirred by the navigator and promoter Jacques Cartier. In three voyages between 1524 and 1542, he explored the region of

Newfoundland and the Gulf of St. Lawrence. A contemporary of Cortés and Pizarro, Cartier also hoped to find mineral wealth, but the stones he brought back to France turned out to be quartz and iron pyrite, "fool's gold."

The French waited more than fifty years before establishing settlements in North America. Coming to Canada after spending years in the West Indies, Samuel de Champlain founded Quebec on the banks of the St. Lawrence River in 1608. This location provided ready access to existing Amerindian trade routes, but it also compelled French settlers to take sides in the region's ongoing warfare. Champlain allied France with the Huron and Algonquin peoples, the traditional enemies of the powerful Iroquois Confederacy of five (later six) tribes. Although French firearms and armor at first tipped the balance of power to their native allies, the Iroquois proved to be resourceful and persistent enemies.

The European market for fur, especially beaver, fueled French settlement. Young Frenchmen were sent to live among native peoples to master languages and customs. These *coureurs de bois*, or runners of the woods, dominated the fur trade and led French expansion into the West and South. Amerindians actively participated in this trade because they quickly came to depend on the goods that they received in exchange—firearms, metal tools and utensils, textiles, and alcohol. These changes in the material culture of native peoples led to overhunting and increased competition for hunting grounds.

The Iroquois Confederation responded to the increased military strength of their Algonquin enemies by forging commercial and military links with Dutch and later English settlements in the Hudson river valley. At the high point of their power in the early 1680s, Iroquois hunters and war parties ranged to the Great Lakes region and the Ohio river valley. Increased attacks by French forces on Iroquois villages, burning fields and destroying stored crops, led to peace in 1701.

Although Spain had effectively limited the spread of firearms in its colonies, the fur trade, together with the growing military rivalry between Algonquin and Iroquois peoples and their respective European allies, led to the rapid spread of firearms in North America. Use of firearms in hunting and warfare moved west and south, reaching indigenous plains cultures that previously had adopted the horse introduced by the Spanish. This intersection of horse and gun frontiers dramatically increased the military power and hunting efficiency of the Sioux, Comanche, Cheyenne, and other indigenous peoples, slowing the pace of European settlement.

In French Canada, the Jesuits led the effort to convert native peoples to Christianity. Building on earlier evangelical efforts in Latin America, Catholic missionaries mastered native languages, created boarding schools for young boys and girls, and set up model agricultural communities for converted Amerindians. The Jesuits' greatest successes coincided with a destructive wave of epidemics and renewed warfare among native peoples in the 1630s. Eventually, churches were established throughout Huron and Algonquin territories. Nevertheless, local culture persisted. A French nun who had devoted her life to instructing Amerindian girls expressed the frustration of many missionaries in 1688:

> We have observed that of a hundred that have passed through our hands we have scarcely civilized one. . . . When we are least expecting it, they clamber over our wall and go off to run with their kinsmen in the woods, finding more to please them there than in all the amenities of our French house.[3]

Responsibility for finding settlers and supervising the colonial economy was first granted to a monopoly company chartered in France. Even though the fur trade flourished, population growth was slow. Founded at about the same time as French Canada, Virginia had twenty times as many European residents as Canada in 1627. Following the establishment of royal authority in the 1660s, the colonial population grew to nearly 7,000 by 1673. Improved fiscal management and more effective government led to agricultural expansion and a reduced reliance on the fur trade. The church redirected some of its resources from Amerindian conversion and became more active in larger French settlements, founding schools, hospitals, and churches.

Despite Canada's small population, limited resources, and increasing vulnerability to attack by the English and their indigenous allies, the

French aggressively expanded to the west and south. Louisiana was founded in 1699, but by 1708 there were fewer than 300 soldiers, settlers, and slaves in the territory. Like Canada, Louisiana depended on the fur trade, exporting more than 50,000 deerskins in 1726. As in Canada, Amerindians, driven by a desire for European goods, eagerly embraced this trade. In 1753 a French official reported a Choctaw leader as saying, "[The French] were the first . . . who made [us] subject to the different needs that [we] can no longer now do without."[4]

France's North American colonies were threatened by a series of wars fought by France and England and by the population growth and increasing prosperity of neighboring English colonies. The "French and Indian War" (also known as the Seven Years War, 1756–1763), however, proved to be the final contest for North American empire (see Map 19.2). England committed a larger military force to the struggle and, despite early defeats, took the French capital of Quebec in 1759. Although resistance continued briefly, French forces in Canada surrendered in 1760. The peace agreement forced France to yield Canada to the English and cede Louisiana to Spain. The French then concentrated their efforts on protecting their sugar-producing colonies in the Caribbean (see Chapter 20).

Canadian fur trader The fur trade provided the economic foundation of early Canadian settlement. The trade depended on a mix of native and European skills and resources. The fur trader's canoe was developed from native technology to carry larger loads over greater distances. (Hudson's Bay Company Archives, Provincial Archives of Manitoba)

COLONIAL EXPANSION AND CONFLICT

Starting in the last decades of the seventeenth century, all of the European colonies in America experienced a long period of economic and demographic expansion. The imperial powers responded by strengthening their own administrative and economic controls in the colonies. They also sought to force colonial populations to pay a larger share of the costs of administration and defense. These efforts at reform and restructuring coincided with a series of wars fought along Atlantic trade routes and in the Americas. France's loss of its North American colonies was one of the most important results of these struggles. Equally significant, colonial populations throughout the Americas became more aware of separate national identities and more aggressive in asserting local interests against the will of distant monarchs.

Imperial Reform in Spanish America and Brazil

Spain's Hapsburg dynasty ended when Charles II died without an heir in 1700 (see Chapter 18). After thirteen years of conflict involving the major European powers and factions within

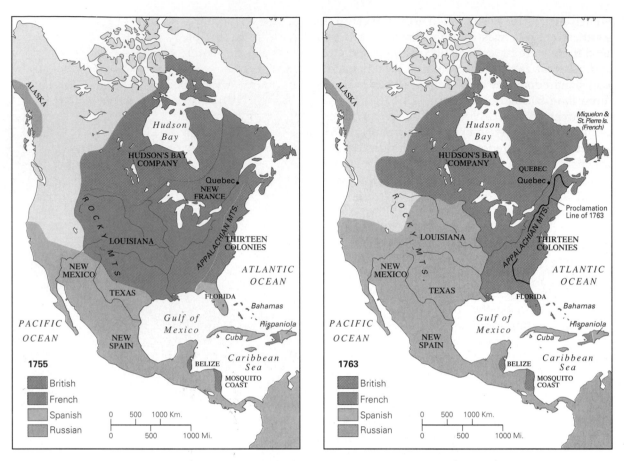

Map 19.2 European Claims in North America, 1755–1763 The results of the French and Indian War dramatically altered the map of North America. France's losses precipitated conflicts between Amerindian peoples and the rapidly expanding population of the British colonies.

Spain, the grandson of Louis XIV of France, Philip of Bourbon, gained the Spanish throne. Under Philip V and his heirs, colonial administration and tax collection were reorganized. The fleet system was gradually abolished, more colonial ports were permitted to trade with Spain, and inter-colonial trade was expanded. Spain created new commercial monopolies to produce tobacco, some alcoholic beverages, and chocolate. The Spanish navy was strengthened, and contraband trade was more effectively policed.

For most of the Spanish Empire, the eighteenth century was a period of remarkable economic expansion. Colonial population recovered from the early epidemics, as natural growth was supplemented by a slightly increased flow of Spanish immigrants and expansion of the slave trade to the plantation colonies. Silver production in Mexico and Peru rose steadily into the 1780s. The expanded production of tobacco, dyes, hides, chocolate, cotton, and sugar opened once-marginal regions to rapid growth.

But these reforms carried unforeseen consequences that threatened the survival of the Spanish Empire. Despite expanded silver production, the economic growth of the eighteenth century was led by the previously minor agricultural and grazing economies of the Rio de la Plata region,

Venezuela, Chile, and Central America. Unlike the bullion economies of Mexico and Peru, these export economies were less able to weather breaks in trade caused by imperial wars. With each such disruption, landowning elites were forced to turn to alternative, often illegal, trade with English, French, or Dutch merchants. By the 1790s, important sectors of the colonial elite viewed the Spanish Empire as an impediment to prosperity and growth.

Bourbon political reforms contributed to a growing sense of colonial distinctiveness by further limiting creole access to colonial offices. Local elites, unable to place their sons and relations in office, were frustrated by their inability to bend imperial policy to local interests. Only in the expanded colonial militias did creoles find opportunity for improved status and greater responsibility.

Because the reforms produced a more intrusive and expensive colonial government that interfered with established business practices, many colonists saw these changes as an abuse of the informal constitution that had long governed

Brazilian diamond mine   From the late seventeenth century into the early eighteenth century, Brazil experienced gold, emerald, and diamond booms. Slave labor was essential to the exploitation of these new resources. Here you can see the close supervision used to prevent slaves from hiding diamonds in order to purchase their freedom. (Courtesy, Fundacao Biblioteca Nacional, Rio de Janeiro)

the empire. One important result was a proliferation of tax rebellions, urban riots, and Amerindian uprisings after 1760.

The most spectacular of these was the rebellion initiated in 1780 by the Peruvian Amerindian leader José Gabriel Condorcanqui. Once in rebellion, he took the name of his Inca ancestor Tupac Amaru, who had been executed as a rebel in 1572. Tupac Amaru II was well connected in Peruvian society. He had been educated by the Jesuits and was actively involved in the trade to Potosí.

Historians still debate the objectives of this rebellion. Tupac Amaru's own pronouncements did not clearly state whether he sought to end local abuses or overthrow Spanish rule. It appears that the violence began as a quarrel between Tupac Amaru and a local Spanish judge. As thousands joined him, Tupac Amaru dared to contemplate the overthrow of Spanish rule. Although Amerindian communities suffering under labor and tribute obligations provided the majority of Tupac Amaru's army, he was also supported by some creoles, mestizos, and slaves.* After his capture, he was brutally executed, as were his wife, other family members, and closest allies. Even after his execution allies and kinsmen continued the struggle for two more years. By the time Spanish authority was firmly reestablished, more than 100,000 lives had been lost and enormous amounts of property destroyed.

Brazil experienced a similar period of expansion and reform, especially during the tenure of the royal minister the marquis of Pombal (1750–1777). New administrative positions were created and monopoly companies given exclusive rights to little-developed regions. The reforms were made possible by an economic expansion fueled by the discovery of gold and diamonds and by the development of export markets for coffee and cotton. This expansion led to the importation of nearly 2 million African slaves. However, unlike Spanish America, where a reinvigorated Crown sought to reimpose commercial controls, Portugal had fallen into the economic orbit of England. As a result, English imports to Brazil increased.

Reform and Reorganization in British North America

England's efforts to reform and reorganize its North American colonies began earlier than the Bourbon initiative in Spanish America. Following the period of Cromwell's Puritan Republic, the restored Stuart king, Charles II, and his brother and heir, James II, undertook an ambitious campaign to establish greater control over the colonies. Between 1651 and 1673 a series of navigation acts sought to severely limit both colonial trading and colonial production that competed directly with English manufacturers.

James II also attempted to increase his control over colonial political life. The proprietorships of New Hampshire, Massachusetts, and the Carolinas were replaced by royal governments. Because the New England colonies were viewed as centers of smuggling, the king temporarily suspended their elected assemblies. At the same time, he appointed governors who were granted new fiscal and legislative powers.

James II's overthrow in the Glorious Revolution of 1688 ended this confrontation, but not before colonists were provoked to resist and, in some cases, rebel. They overthrew the governors of New York and Massachusetts and removed the Catholic proprietor of Maryland. Relative peace was restored by William and Mary, but these conflicts alerted the colonists to the potential for aggression by the English government. Colonial politics would remain confrontational until the American Revolution (see Chapter 24).

During the eighteenth century the English colonies experienced renewed economic growth and attracted a new wave of European immigration, but social divisions were increasingly evident. The colonial population in 1770 was more urban, more clearly divided by class and race, and more vulnerable to economic downturns. Crises were provoked when imperial wars with France and Spain disrupted trade in the Atlantic,

---

*As was true in Spanish colonies, economic expansion and administrative reforms coincided with tax protests and rebellions.

increased tax burdens, forced military mobilizations, and provoked frontier conflicts with the Amerindians. On the eve of the American Revolution, England had defeated France and weakened Spain. The cost, however, had been great. Administrative, military, and tax policies imposed to gain empire-wide victory had alienated much of the American colonial population.

CONCLUSION

The colonial empires of Spain, Portugal, France, and England shared many characteristics. All subjugated Amerindian peoples and introduced large numbers of African slaves. Within all four empires, forests were cut down, virgin soils were turned with the plow, and Old World animals and plants were introduced. Colonists applied the technologies of the Old World to the resources of the New, producing wealth and engaging the commercial possibilities of the emerging Atlantic market. Yet each of these American empires reflected the distinct cultural and institutional heritages of the colonizing power.

Mineral wealth allowed Spain to develop the most centralized empire. Political and economic power was concentrated in the great capital cities of Mexico City and Lima. The Portuguese and French pursued similar objectives in their colonies. However, neither Brazil's agricultural economy nor French Canada's fur trade produced the fiscal resources necessary to imitate Spanish controls. As a result, political and commercial controls were weaker. Nevertheless, all three of these Catholic powers were able to impose and enforce significant levels of religious and cultural uniformity relative to the British.

British North America was characterized by much greater cultural and religious diversity. Settlers were drawn from throughout the British Isles and included all of Britain's numerous religious traditions. They were joined by Germans, Swedes, French Huguenots, and Dutch immigrants. Colonial government was also less uniform and more controlled by local interests. The British colonists, therefore, were better able to respond to changing economic and political circumstances. Most important, the British colonies attracted many more European immigrants than did the other American empires. While New France received only 11,000 immigrants between 1608 and 1763, the British settlements welcomed nearly a half-million European immigrants between 1630 and 1780. Combined with a growing slave trade, population in British North America reached 2.5 million by 1775.

By the eighteenth century, colonial societies across the Americas had matured as wealth increased, populations grew, and contacts with the rest of the world became more common as discussed in Chapter 20. Colonial elites were more confident of their ability to define and defend local interests. Colonists were in general increasingly aware of their unique and distinctive cultural identities and willing to defend American experience and practice in the face of European presumptions of superiority. Moreover, influential groups in all the colonies were drawn toward the liberating ideas of Europe's Enlightenment. In the open and less inhibited spaces of the Western Hemisphere, these ideas, as Chapter 24 examines, would soon provide a potent intellectual basis for opposing the continuation of empire.

SUGGESTED READING

Alfred W. Crosby, Jr., is justifiably the best-known student of the Columbian exchange. See his *The Columbian Exchange: Biological and Cultural Consequences of 1492* (1972) and *Ecological Imperialism* (1986). William H. McNeill, *Plagues and People* (1976), puts the discussion of the American exchange in a world history context. Elinor G. K. Melville, *A Plague of Sheep: Environmental Consequences of the Spanish Conquest of Mexico* (1994), is the most important recent contribution to this field.

Colonial Latin America, 2d ed. (1994), by Mark A. Burkholder and Lyman L. Johnson, provides a good introduction to colonial Latin American history. *Early Latin*

America (1983) by James Lockhart and Stuart B. Schwartz and *Spain and Portugal in the New World, 1492–1700* (1984) by Lyle N. McAlister are both useful introductions as well.

The specialized historical literature on the American colonial empires is extensive and deep. A sampling of useful works follows. For the early colonial period see Inga Clendinnen, *Ambivalent Conquests* (1987); James Lockhart, *The Nahuas After the Conquest* (1992); and John Hemming, *Red Gold: The Conquest of the Brazilian Indians* (1978). Nancy M. Farriss, *Maya Society Under Spanish Rule: The Collective Enterprise of Survival* (1984), is also one of the most important books on colonial Spanish America. On political culture see Colin M. MacLachlan, *Spain's Empire in the New World: The Role of Ideas in Institutional and Social Change* (1988). For the place of women see Asunción Lavrin, ed., *Sexuality and Marriage in Colonial Latin America* (1989).

On the slave trade, Herbert S. Klein, *The Middle Passage* (1978); and Philip D. Curtin, *The Atlantic Slave Trade: A Census* (1969), are indispensable. Frederick P. Bowser, *The African Slave in Colonial Peru, 1524–1650* (1973); Mary C. Karasch, *Slave Life and Culture in Rio de Janeiro, 1808–1850* (1986); and Stuart B. Schwartz, *Sugar Plantations in the Formation of Brazilian Society: Bahia, 1550–1835* (1985), are excellent introductions to the African experience in two very different Latin American societies.

Among the useful general studies of the British colonies are Charles M. Andrews, *The Colonial Period of American History: The Settlements*, 3 vols. (1934–1937); David Hackett Fischer, *Albion's Seed: Four British Folkways in America* (1989); and Gary B. Nash, *Red, White, and Black: The Peoples of Early America*, 2d ed. (1982). On the economy see John J. McCusker and Russell R. Menard, *The Economy of British America, 1607–1789* (1979). For slavery see David Brion Davis, *The Problem of Slavery in Western Culture* (1966); Allan Kulikoff, *Tobacco and Slaves: The Development of Southern Cultures in the Chesapeake, 1680–1800* (1986); and Peter H. Wood, *Black Majority: Negroes in Colonial South Carolina from 1670 Through the Stono Rebellion* (1974). Two very useful works on the relations between Europeans and Indians are James Merrill, *The Indians' New World: Catawbas and Their Neighbors from European Contact*

Through the Era of Removal (1989); and Daniel H. Usner, Jr., *Indians, Settlers, and Slaves in a Frontier Exchange Economy: The Lower Mississippi Valley Before 1783* (1992).

For late colonial politics see Gary B. Nash, *Urban Crucible: Social Change, Political Consciousness, and the Origins of the American Revolution* (1979); Bernard Bailyn, *The Origins of American Politics* (1986); Jack P. Greene, *The Quest for Power: The Lower Houses of Assembly in the Southern Royal Colonies* (1963); and Richard Bushman, *King and People in Provincial Massachusetts* (1985). On immigration see Bernard Bailyn, *The Peopling of British North America* (1986).

On French North America, William J. Eccles, *France in America*, rev. ed. (1990), is an excellent overview; see also his *The Canadian Frontier, 1534–1760* (1969). R. Cole Harris, *The Seigneurial System in Canada: A Geographical Study* (1966), provides an excellent analysis of the topic. Harold Innis, *The Fur Trade in Canada: An Introduction to Canadian Economic History* (1927), remains indispensable. Also of value are Cornelius Jaenen, *The Role of the Church in New France* (1976) and Alison L. Prentice, *Canadian Women: A History* (1988).

NOTES

1. Quoted in Alfred W. Crosby, Jr., *The Columbian Exchange: Biological and Cultural Consequences of 1492* (Greenwood Press, Westport, CT: 1972), 58.

2. Quoted in Alfred W. Crosby, Jr. *The Columbian Exchange*, 58.

3. Quoted in R. Douglas Francis, Richard Jones, and Donald B. Smith, Origins. *Canadian History to Confederation* (Holt, Rinehart, and Winston of Canada Limited, Toronto: 1992), 52.

4. Quoted in Daniel H. Usner, Jr., Indians, Settlers and Slaves in a Frontier Exchange Economy. *The Lower Mississippi Valley Before 1783* (Institute of Early American History and Culture, Williamsburg, VA, University of North Carolina Press, Chapel Hill, NC: 1992), 96.

CHAPTER TWENTY

The Atlantic System and Africa,

1550–1800

Plantations in the West Indies • Plantation Life in the Eighteenth Century

Creating the Atlantic Economy • Africa, the Atlantic, and Islam

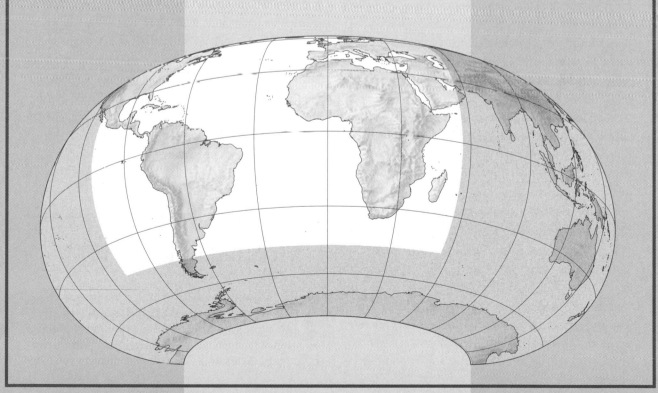

As the ship bearing a cargo of slaves from West Africa neared the West Indian island of Barbados in 1757, the English crew gave a joyful shout, glad that this leg of their trading tour around the Atlantic was over. Since leaving England, some of their number had died of African tropical diseases, and one had been flogged to death for insubordination. The survivors, thankful to put the risk of disease and slave insurrection behind them, looked forward to returning to England.

According to the autobiography of Olaudah Equiano, one of the slaves on board, the sight of Barbados filled his shackled African shipmates with apprehension. Although fortunate to have survived long weeks of suffocating heat and loathsome smells packed side by side in the cargo hold, the captive African men, women, and children feared they were going to be eaten by the white people who rushed to inspect them after the ship anchored in the harbor of Bridgetown. To ease the new arrivals' panic, local sugar planters sent veteran slaves on board to assure them in several African languages that they would not be eaten. Instead, most were destined to work on the island's sugar plantations. After landing, Equiano relates, he and his companions were relieved to discover that most of the island's inhabitants were Africans. The eleven-year-old Equiano found many of his own Igbo people there.

After examining the slaves for physical defects, the local merchants divided them into "parcels" of several slaves each and penned them up in a yard, in Equiano's words, "like so many sheep in a fold without regard to sex or age." A few days later they were sold to the planters, not by auction, but in a terrifying "scramble." At the beat of a drum, buyers rushed into the yard and seized the parcel of slaves they wanted. "In this manner," Equiano commented, "without scruple, are relations and friends separated, most of them never to see each other again."

By the time this ship arrived in Barbados, the island was past its prime as a sugar colony, so Equiano and some companions were shipped off to the colony of Virginia. There for a time he was put to work weeding; he later worked on a ship. In 1766 at the age of twenty-one, Equiano was able to buy his freedom with money he earned in private trading. During the rest of his life he worked as a seaman and then resided in England, where he joined the campaign against the slave trade.

The slave trade from Africa and the sugar plantations in the West Indies were pieces of a major business enterprise in the Atlantic Ocean. European investors, with the help of their governments, created a vast trading circuit that linked Europe, Africa, and the Americas. This Atlantic trade and the plantations the investors established in the Americas brought them profit, but the lasting effects were far broader. The forced migration of so many slaves across the Atlantic transformed the West Indies and other parts of the Americas into centers of African population and culture. In Africa the many cultural and economic impacts of growing European trade were added to the older influences from the Islamic world. The Atlantic system is a prime example of the growing global impact of European commercial expansion.

PLANTATIONS IN THE WEST INDIES

Spanish settlers had introduced sugar-cane cultivation into the West Indies shortly after 1500, but soon these colonies fell into neglect as attention shifted to colonizing the American mainland. After 1600 the West Indies revived as a focus of colonization, this time by northern Europeans interested in growing tobacco and other crops. The colonies' value mushroomed after the Dutch reintroduced the cultivation of sugar from Brazil in the 1640s and organized the supply of African slaves and European capital sufficient to sustain rapid growth.

Colonization Before 1650

In the 1620s and 1630s English colonization societies founded small European settlements on Montserrat, Barbados, Trinidad, and other Caribbean islands, while the French colonized Martinique, Guadeloupe, and some other islands. Because of greater support from their government, the English colonies prospered first, largely by growing tobacco for export. This New World leaf, long used by Amerindians for recreation and medicine, was finding a new market among seventeenth-century Europeans. Despite the opposition of individuals like King James I of England, who condemned tobacco smoke as "dangerous to the eye, hateful to the nose, harmful to the brain, and dangerous to the lungs," the habit spread. By 1614 tobacco was reportedly being sold in seven thousand shops in and around London, and some English businessmen were dreaming of a tobacco trade as valuable as Spain's silver fleets.

Turning such pipe dreams into reality was not easy. Diseases, hurricanes, and attacks by the Caribs and the Spanish scourged the early French and English West Indian colonists. They also suffered from shortages of supplies from Europe and of labor sufficient to clear and plant virgin land with tobacco. Two changes improved the colonies' prospects. One was the formation of chartered companies. To promote national claims without government expense, France and England gave groups of private investors monopolies over trade to their West Indian colonies in exchange for the payment of an annual fee. The other change was that the companies began to provide passage to the colonies for poor Europeans, who paid off their debt by working three or four years for the established colonists. They were called *indentured servants* or *bondservants*.

Under this system the French and English population on several tobacco islands grew rapidly in the 1630s and 1640s. By the middle of the century, however, the Caribbean colonies were in crisis because of stiff competition from milder Virginia-grown tobacco, also cultivated by indentured servants. The cultivation of sugar cane, introduced by Dutch investors expelled from Brazil, provided the Caribbean colonies a way out of this crisis but in the process transformed their labor force from European to African.

The Portuguese had introduced sugar cultivation into Brazil from islands along the African coast after 1550 and had soon introduced enslaved African labor as well (see Chapter 19). By 1600 Brazil was the Atlantic world's greatest sugar producer. Some Dutch merchants invested in Brazilian sugar plantations so that they might profit from transporting the sugar across the Atlantic and distributing it in Europe. However, in the first half of the seventeenth century the Netherlands were fighting for their independence from the Spanish crown, which then ruled Portugal and Brazil (see Chapter 18). As part of that struggle, the Netherlands government chartered the Dutch West India Company in 1621 to carry the conflict to Spain's overseas possessions.

Not just a disguised form of the Dutch navy, the Dutch West India Company was a private trading company. People who invested in it expected it to cover its expenses and pay its investors dividends. The capture of a Spanish treasure fleet in 1628 enabled the company to pay its stockholders a dividend of 50 percent and to finance an assault on Brazil's valuable sugar-producing areas. By 1635 the Dutch company controlled 1,000 miles (1,600 kilometers) of northeastern Brazil's coast. Over the next fifteen years the new Dutch owners improved the efficiency of the Brazilian sugar industry, and the company prospered by supplying the plantations with African slaves and European goods and carrying the sugar back to Europe.

Like its assault on Brazil, the Dutch West India Company's entry into the African slave trade combined economic and political motives. It seized the important West African trading station of Elmina from the Portuguese in 1638 and took their port of Luanda on the Angolan coast in 1641. From these coasts the Dutch shipped slaves to Brazil and the West Indies. Although the Portuguese were able to drive the Dutch out of Angola after a few years, Elmina remained the Dutch West India Company's headquarters in West Africa.

Once free of Spanish rule in 1640, the Portuguese crown turned its attention to reconquering Brazil. By 1654 Portuguese armies had driven the last of the Dutch sugar planters from Brazil. Some of the expelled planters transplanted their capital and knowledge of sugar production to small colonies, which the Dutch had founded earlier as trading bases with Spanish colonies; others introduced the Brazilian system into English and French Caribbean islands. This was a momentous turning point in the history of the Atlantic economy.

Sugar and Slaves

The Dutch infusion of expertise and money revived the French colonies of Guadeloupe and Martinique, but the English colony of Barbados best illustrates the dramatic transformation that sugar brought to the seventeenth-century Caribbean. In 1640 Barbados's economy depended largely on tobacco, mostly grown by European settlers, both free and indentured. By the 1680s sugar had become the colony's principal crop, and enslaved Africans were three times as numerous as Europeans. Exporting up to 15,000 tons of sugar a year, Barbados had become the wealthiest and most populous of England's American colonies. By 1700, the West Indies had surpassed Brazil as the world's principal source of sugar.

The expansion of sugar plantations in the West Indies was made possible by a jump in the volume of the slave trade from Africa (see Figure 20.1). During the first half of the seventeenth century about 10,000 slaves a year had been brought from Africa. Most were destined for Brazil and the mainland Spanish colonies. In the second half of the century the trade averaged 25,000 slaves a year. More than half were intended for the English, French, and Dutch West Indies and most of

Figure 20.1   Transatlantic Slave Trade, 1551–1850 (in millions)

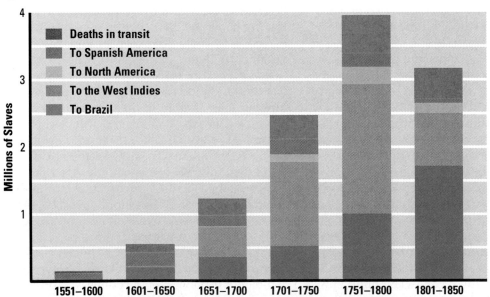

Legend:
- Deaths in transit
- To Spanish America
- To North America
- To the West Indies
- To Brazil

Y-axis: Millions of Slaves

X-axis categories: 1551–1600, 1601–1650, 1651–1700, 1701–1750, 1751–1800, 1801–1850

Source: Philip D. Curtin, *The Atlantic Slave Trade: A Census* (Madison: University of Wisconsin Press, 1969), tables 33, 34, 65; Paul E. Lovejoy, "The Volume of the Atlantic Slave Trade: A Synthesis," *Journal of African History* 23 (1982): 473–501; David Eltis, *Economic Growth and the Ending of the Transatlantic Slave Trade* (New York: Oxford University Press, 1987), table A.8.

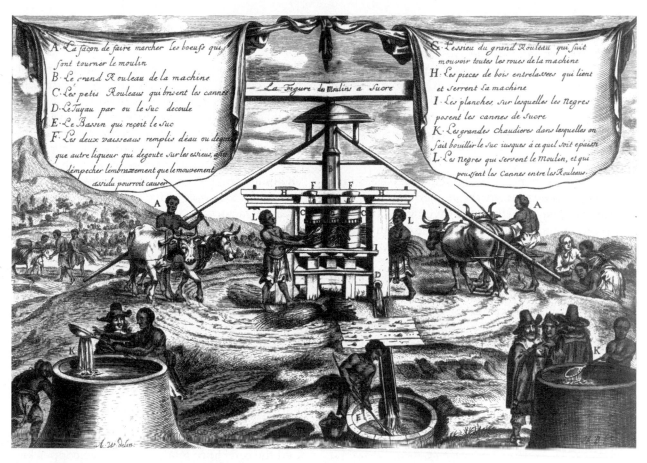

Sugar mill Even this fairly small sugar mill in the French West Indies illustrates the complexity of the crushing process. Two slaves (A) drive oxen attached to poles that turn the rollers (C) that crush the canes (L) The cane juice runs down the trough to a basin (E), from which it is ladled into cauldrons (K) and boiled down. (Library of Congress)

the rest for Brazil. A century later the volume of the Atlantic slave trade was three times larger.

The shift in favor of African slaves was a product of many factors. Recent scholarship has cast doubt on the once-common assertion that Africans were more suited than Europeans to field labor, since newly arrived Africans and Europeans both died in large numbers in the American tropics. Africans' slightly higher survival rate was not decisive because mortality was about the same among later generations of blacks and whites born in the West Indies and acclimated to its diseases.

The West Indian historian Eric Williams also refuted the idea that the rise of African slave labor was primarily motivated by prejudice. Citing the West Indian colonies' prior use of enslaved Amerindians and indentured Europeans, along with European convicts and prisoners of war, he argued, "Slavery was not born of racism: rather, racism was the consequence of slavery."[1] Williams suggested the shift was due to the lower cost of African labor.

Yet slaves were far from cheap. Cash-short tobacco planters in the seventeenth century preferred indentured Europeans because they cost half as much as African slaves. Poor European men and women were willing to work for little in order to get to the Americas, where they could acquire their own land cheaply at the end of their term of service. However, as the cultivation of sugar spread after 1750, rich speculators drove the price of land in the West Indies up so high that end-of-term indentured servants could not afford to buy it. As a result, poor Europeans chose to indenture themselves in the mainland North American colonies, where cheap land was still available. Rather than raise wages to attract European laborers, Caribbean sugar planters switched to slaves.

Rising sugar prices helped the West Indian sugar planters afford the higher cost of African slaves. The fact that the average slave lived seven years, while the typical indentured labor contract was for only three or four years, also made slaves a better investment. The planters could rely on the Dutch and other traders to supply them with enough new slaves to meet the demands of the expanding plantations. Rising demand for slaves (see Figure 20.1) drove their sale price up steadily during the eighteenth century. These high labor costs were one more factor favoring large plantations over smaller operations.

PLANTATION LIFE IN THE EIGHTEENTH CENTURY

To find more land for sugar plantations, France and England founded new Caribbean colonies. By 1660 the English had wrested the island of Jamaica from the Spanish (see Map 19.1). The French seized the western half of the large Spanish island of Hispaniola in the 1670s. During the eighteenth century this new French colony of Saint Domingue (present-day Haiti) became the greatest producer of sugar in the Atlantic world, while Jamaica surpassed Barbados as England's most important sugar colony. The technological, environmental, and social transformation of these island colonies illustrates the power of the new Atlantic system.

Technology and Environment

The cultivation of sugar cane was fairly straightforward. From fourteen to eighteen months after planting, the canes were ready to be cut. The roots continued to produce new shoots that could be harvested about every nine months. Only simple tools were needed: spades for planting, hoes to control the weeds, and sharp machetes to cut the canes. What made the sugar plantation a complex investment was that it had to be a factory as well as a farm. Freshly cut canes needed to be crushed within a few hours to extract the sugary sap. Thus, for maximum efficiency, each plantation needed its own expensive crushing and processing equipment.

At the heart of the sugar works was the mill where canes were crushed between sets of heavy rollers. Small mills could be turned by animal or human power, but larger, more efficient mills needed more sophisticated sources of power. Eighteenth-century Barbados went in heavily for windmills, and the French sugar islands and Jamaica used costly water-powered mills often fed by elaborate aqueducts.

From the mill, lead-lined wooden troughs carried the cane juice to a series of large copper kettles in the boiling shed, where the excess water boiled off, leaving a thick syrup. Workers poured the syrup into conical molds in the drying shed. The sugar crystals that formed in the molds were packed in wooden barrels for shipment to Europe. The dark molasses that drained off was made into rum in yet another building, or it was barreled for export.

To make their operation more efficient and profitable, investors gradually increased the size of the typical West Indian plantation from around 100 acres (40 hectares) in the seventeenth century to at least twice that size in the eighteenth century. Some plantations were even larger. In 1774 Jamaica's 680 sugar plantations averaged 441 acres (178 hectares) each; some spread over 2,000 acres (800 hectares). Jamaica so specialized in sugar production that the island had to import most of its food. Saint Domingue had a comparable number of plantations of smaller average size but generally higher productivity. The French colony was also more diverse in its economy. Although sugar production was paramount, some planters raised provisions for local consumption or crops such as coffee and cacao for export.

In some ways the mature sugar plantation was environmentally responsible. The crushing mill was powered by water, wind, or animal power, not fossil fuels. The boilers were largely fueled by burning the crushed canes, and the fields were fertilized by manure of the cattle. In two respects, however, the plantation was very damaging to the environment: soil exhaustion and deforestation.

The repeated cultivation of a single crop removed from the soil more nutrients than animal fertilizer and fallow periods could restore. Instead of rotating sugar with other crops in order to restore the nutrients naturally, planters found it more profitable to clear new lands when yields declined too much in the old fields. When land close to the sea on the early sugar islands was exhausted, planters moved on to new islands. Many of the English who first settled Jamaica were from Barbados, and the pioneer planters on Saint Domingue came from older French sugar colonies. In the second half of the eighteenth century Jamaican sugar production began to fall behind that of Saint Domingue, which still had access to virgin land. Thus the plantations of this period were not a stable form of agriculture but one that gradually laid waste to the landscape.

Deforestation, the second form of environmental damage, continued a trend begun in the sixteenth century. The Spanish had cut down some forests in the Caribbean to make pastures for the cattle they introduced. Sugar cultivation rapidly accelerated land clearing. Forests near the coast were the first to disappear, and by the end of the eighteenth century only land in the interior of the islands retained dense forests.

Other changes, combined with soil exhaustion and deforestation, profoundly altered the ecology balance of the West Indies. By the eighteenth century virtually all of the domesticated animals and cultivated plants in the Caribbean were ones that Europeans had introduced. The Spanish had brought cattle, pigs, and horses, all of which multiplied so rapidly that no new imports had been necessary after 1503. They had also introduced new plants. Of these, bananas and plantain from the Canary Islands were a valuable

Plantation scene, Antigua, British West Indies Even in this romanticized painting the slaves' simple earthen huts contrast sharply with the planter's elegant great house on the rising ground on the left. Note the large church in the center background and the women performing domestic tasks. (West India Committee)

Table 20.1   Slave Occupations on a Jamaican Sugar Plantation, 1788

Occupations and Conditions	Men	Women	Boys and Girls	Total
Field laborers	62	78		140
Tradesmen	29			29
Field drivers	4			4
Field cooks		4		4
Mule-, cattle-, and stablemen	12			12
Watchmen	18			18
Nurse		1		1
Midwife		1		1
Domestics and gardeners		5	3	8
Grass-gang			20	20
Total employed	*125*	*89*	*23*	*237*
Infants			23	23
Invalids (18 with yaws)				32
Absent on roads				5
Superannuated [elderly]				7
Overall total				*304*

Source: Adapted from Edward Long to William Pitt, in Michael Craton, James Walvin, and David Wright, eds., *Slavery, Abolition, and Emancipation* (London: Longman, 1976), 103. Published and reprinted by permission of Addison Wesley Longman, Ltd.

omy spread, the Caribs surviving on the smaller islands were also pushed to the point of extinction. Far earlier and more completely than in any mainland colony, the West Indies were repeopled from across the Atlantic—first from Europe and then from Africa.

Slaves' Lives

During the eighteenth century, West Indian plantation colonies had the world's most polarized societies. On most islands 90 percent or more of the inhabitants were slaves. Power resided in the hands of the *plantocracy*, a small number of very rich men who owned most of the slaves and most of the land as well. Between the slaves and the masters might be found only a few others—a few estate managers and government officials and, in the French islands, some small farmers, both white and black. Thus it is only a slight simplification to describe eighteenth-century Caribbean society as being made up of a large, abject class of slaves and a small, powerful class of masters.

The profitability of a Caribbean plantation depended on extracting as much work as possible from the slaves. Their long workday might stretch to eighteen hours or more when the cane harvest and milling were in full swing. Sugar plantations achieved exceptional productivity through the use of force and the threat of force. As Table 20.1 shows, on a typical Jamaican plantation about 80 percent of the slaves actively engaged in productive tasks; the only exceptions were infants, the seriously ill, and the very old. Everyone on the plantation, except those disabled by age or infirmity, had an assigned task.

Table 20.1 also illustrates how slave labor was organized by age, sex, and ability. As in other Caribbean colonies, only 2 or 3 percent of the slaves served as house servants. About 70 percent of the able-bodied slaves worked in the fields, generally in one of three labor gangs. A "great gang," made up of the strongest slaves in the prime of life, did the heaviest work, such as breaking up the soil at the beginning of the planting season. A second gang of youths, elders, and less fit slaves did somewhat lighter work. A

addition to the food supply, and sugar and rice formed the basis of plantation agriculture, along with native tobacco. Other food crops arrived with the slaves from Africa, including okra, black-eyed peas, yams, grains such as millet and sorghum, and mangoes. Many of these new animals and plants were useful additions to the islands, but they crowded out indigenous species.

The most tragic and dramatic transformation in the West Indies occurred in the human population. Chapter 17 detailed how the indigenous Arawak peoples of the large islands were wiped out by disease and abuse within fifty years of Columbus's first voyage. As the plantation econ-

"grass gang," composed of children under the supervision of an elderly slave, was responsible for weeding and other simple work, such as collecting grass for the animals. Women formed the majority of the field laborers, even in the great gang. Nursing mothers took their babies with them to the fields. Slaves too old for field labor tended the toddlers.

Because slave ships brought twice as many males as females from Africa, men outnumbered women on Caribbean plantations. As Table 20.1 shows, a little over half of the adult males were employed in nongang work. Some tended the livestock, including the mules and oxen that did the heavy carrying work; others were skilled tradesmen, such as blacksmiths and carpenters. The most important artisan slave was the head boiler, who oversaw the delicate process of reducing the cane sap to crystallized sugar and molasses.

Skilled slaves received rewards of food and clothing or time off for good work, but the most common reason for working hard was to escape punishment. The slave gangs were headed by privileged male slaves, appropriately called "drivers," whose job was to ensure that the gangs completed their work. Since production quotas were high, slaves toiled in the fields from sunup to sunset, except for meal breaks. Those who fell behind due to fatigue or illness soon felt the sting of the whip. Openly rebellious slaves, who refused to work, disobeyed orders, or tried to escape, were punished with flogging, confinement in irons, or mutilation. On a Virginia plantation Equiano was shocked to see a woman slave being punished with an "iron muzzle" that "locked her mouth so fast that she could scarcely speak, and could not eat nor drink."

Even though slaves did not work in the fields on Sunday, it was no day of rest, for they had to farm their own provisioning grounds, maintain their dwellings, and do other chores, such as washing and mending their rough clothes. Sunday markets, where slaves sold small amounts of produce or animals they had raised to get a little spending money, were common in the British West Indies.

Except for occasional holidays—including the Christmas-week revels in the British West In-

Punishment for slaves In addition to whipping and other cruel punishments, slave owners devised other ways to shame and intimidate slaves into obedience. This metal face mask prevented the wearer from eating or drinking. (By permission of the Syndics of Cambridge University Library)

dies—there was little time for recreation and relaxation. Slaves might sing in the fields, but singing was simply a way to distract themselves from their fatigue and the monotony of the work. There was certainly no time for schooling, and no willingness to educate slaves, beyond skills useful to the plantation.

Time for family life was also inadequate. Although the large proportion of young adults in plantation colonies ought to have led to a high rate of natural increase, the opposite occurred. Poor nutrition and overwork lowered fertility. A woman who did become pregnant found it difficult to carry a child to term while continuing heavy fieldwork or to ensure her infant's survival. As a result of these conditions, along with disease and accidents from dangerous mill equipment, deaths heavily outnumbered births on West Indian plantations (see Table 20.2). Life expectancy for slaves in nineteenth-century Brazil was only 23 years of age for males and 25.5 years for females. The figures were probably

Table 20.2   Birth and Death on a Jamaican Sugar Plantation, 1779–1785

Year	Born Males	Born Females	Purchased	Died Males	Died Females	Proportion of Deaths
1779	5	2	6	7	5	1 in 26
1780	4	3	—	3	2	1 in 62
1781	2	3	—	4	2	1 in 52
1782	1	3	9	4	5	1 in 35
1783	3	3	—	8	10	1 in 17
1784	2	1	12	9	10	1 in 17
1785	2	3	—	0	3	1 in 99
Total	19	18	27	35	37	
	Born 37			Died 72		

Source: Edward Long to William Pitt, in Michael Craton, James Walvin, and David Wright, eds., *Slavery, Abolition, and Emancipation* (London: Longman, 1976), 105. Published and reprinted by permission of Addison Wesley Longman, Ltd.

similar for the eighteenth-century Caribbean. A callous opinion, common among slave owners in the Caribbean and in parts of Brazil, held that it was cheaper to import a youthful new slave from Africa than to raise one to the same age on a plantation.

The harsh conditions of plantation life played a major role in shortening slaves' lives, but the greatest killer was disease. The very young were carried off by dysentery caused by contaminated food and water. Slaves newly arrived from Africa went through a period of "seasoning," during which one-third on average died of unfamiliar diseases. Slaves also suffered from diseases brought with them, including malaria. On the plantation profiled in Table 20.1, for example, more than half of the slaves incapacitated by illness had yaws, a painful and debilitating skin disease common in Africa. As Figure 20.2 suggests, only slave populations in the healthier temperate zones of North America experienced natural increase; those in tropical Brazil and the Caribbean had a negative rate of growth.

Such high mortality greatly added to the volume of the Atlantic slave trade, since plantations had to purchase new slaves every year or two just to replace those that died (see Table 20.2). The additional imports of slaves to permit the expansion of the sugar plantations meant that the majority of slaves were African-born on most West Indian plantations. As a result, African religious beliefs, patterns of speech, styles of dress and adornment, and music were prominent parts of West Indian life.

Given the harsh conditions of their lives, it is not surprising that slaves in the West Indies often sought to regain the freedom into which most had been born. Individual slaves often ran away, hoping to elude the men and dogs who would track them. Sometimes large groups of plantation slaves rose in rebellion against their bondage and abuse. For example, a large rebellion in Jamaica in 1760 was led by a slave named Tacky, who had been a chief on the Gold Coast of Africa. One night his followers broke into a fort and armed themselves. Joined by slaves from other nearby plantations, they stormed several plantations, setting them on fire and killing the planter families. Tacky died in the fighting that followed, and three other rebel leaders stoically endured cruel deaths by torture that were meant to deter others from rebellion.

Figure 20.2 Slave Imports and Black Populations in the Americas, 1500–1825

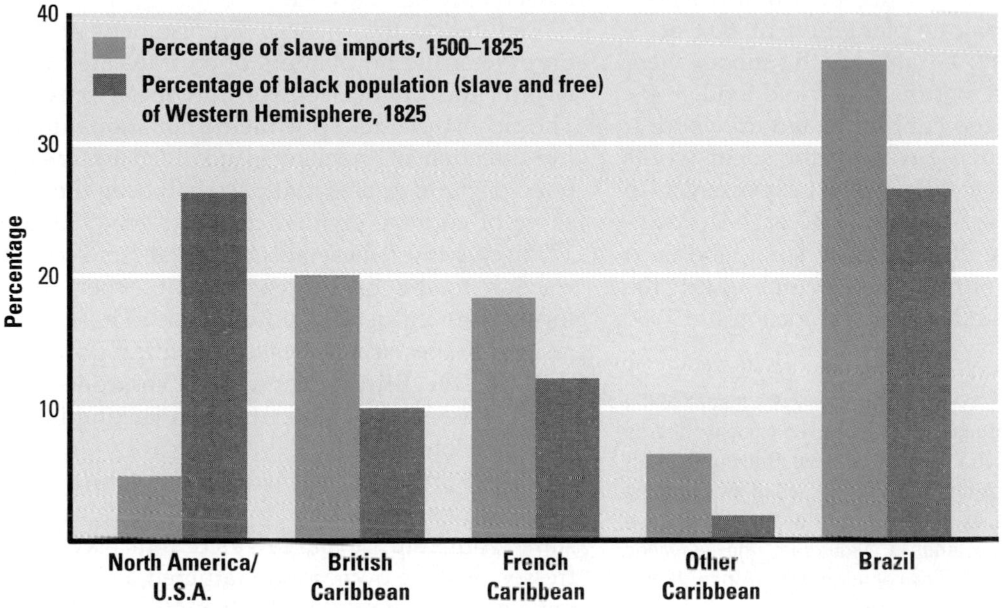

Source: From Robert William Fogel and Stanley L. Engerman, *Time on the Cross: The Economics of American Negro Slavery*. Copyright © 1974 by Robert William Fogel and Stanley L. Engerman. Reprinted by permission of W. W. Norton & Company, Inc.

Because they believed rebellions were usually led by slaves with the strongest African heritage, European planters tried to curtail African cultural traditions. They required slaves to learn the colonial language and discouraged the use of African languages by deliberately mixing slaves from different parts of Africa. In French and Portuguese colonies, slaves were encouraged to adopt Catholic religious practices, though African deities and beliefs also survived. In the British West Indies, where only Quaker slave owners encouraged Christianity among their slaves before 1800, African herbal medicine remained strong, as did African beliefs concerning nature spirits and witchcraft.

Free Whites and Free Blacks

The lives of the small minority of free people were very different from the lives of slaves. In the French colony of Saint Domingue, which had nearly half of the slaves in the Caribbean in the eighteenth century, free people fell into three distinct groups. First, at the top of free society were the wealthy owners of large sugar plantations (the *grands blancs,* or "great whites"), who dominated the economy and society of the island. Second came less-well-off Europeans (*petits blancs,* or "little whites"), most of whom raised provisions for local consumption and crops such as coffee, indigo, and cotton for export, relying on their own and slave labor. Third came the free blacks. Though nearly as numerous as the free whites and engaged in similar occupations, they ranked below whites socially. A few free blacks became wealthy enough to own their own slaves.

The dominance of the plantocracy was even greater in British colonies. Whereas sugar constituted about half of Saint Domingue's exports, in Jamaica the figure was over 80 percent. Such concentration on sugar cane left much less room for small cultivators, white or black, and confined most landholding to a few larger owners. Three-quarters of the farmland in Jamaica at mid century belonged to individuals who owned 1,000 acres (400 hectares) or more.

One source estimated that a planter had to invest nearly £20,000 sterling to acquire even a medium-size Jamaican plantation of 600 acres (240 hectares) in 1774. A third of this money went for land on which to grow sugar and food crops, pasture animals, and cut timber and firewood. A quarter of the expense was for the sugar works and other equipment. The largest expense was to purchase 200 slaves at about £40 each. In comparison, the wage of an English rural laborer at this time was about £10 a year (one-fourth the price of a slave), and the annual incomes in 1760

Jamaican Maroon Leonard Parkinson was a leader of the Trelawney Town Maroons, the largest community of free blacks in Jamaica, who rebelled against British mistreatment in 1795. Although the Maroons agreed to a peace, the British treacherously exiled five hundred of them to frigid Nova Scotia in 1796, and in 1800 sent the surviving Trelawney Maroons to Sierra Leone in West Africa. (Courtesy of National Library of Jamaica)

of the ten wealthiest noble families in Britain averaged only £20,000 each.

Reputedly the richest Englishmen of this time, West Indian planters often translated their wealth into political power and social prestige. The richest planters put their plantations under the direction of managers and lived in Britain, often on rural estates that once had been the preserve of country gentlemen. Between 1730 and 1775 seventy of these absentee planters secured election to the British Parliament, where they formed an influential voting bloc. Those who resided in the West Indies had political power as well, for the British plantocracy controlled the colonial assemblies, an institution lacking in the French colonies.

Most Europeans in plantation colonies were single males, many of whom took advantage of slave women for sexual favors or took slave mistresses. A slave owner who fathered a child by a female slave often gave both mother and child their freedom. In some colonies such *manumissions* (legal grants of freedom to individual slaves) produced a significant free black population. By the late eighteenth century, free blacks were more numerous than slaves in most of the Spanish colonies. They were almost 30 percent of the black population of Brazil, and they existed in significant numbers in the French colonies. Free blacks were far less common in the British colonies and the United States, where manumission was rare.

As in Brazil (see Chapter 19), escaped slaves constituted another part of the free black population. In the Caribbean runaways were known as *maroons*. Maroon communities were especially numerous in the mountainous interiors of Jamaica and Hispaniola as well as in the inland parts of the Guianas (see Voices and Visions: A Maroon Village in French Guiana). The Jamaican Maroons, after withstanding several attacks by the colony's militia, signed a treaty in 1739 that recognized their independence in return for their cooperation in stopping new runaways and suppressing slave revolts. Similar treaties with the large maroon population in the Dutch colony of Surinam (Dutch Guiana) recognized their possession of large inland regions.

A Maroon Village in French Guiana, 1748

Runaway slaves, called maroons, *were common in plantation colonies. Colonial officials regularly tried to recapture them and destroy their villages. In 1748 a captured maroon youth named Louis gave the following testimony to officials in French Guiana in South America.*

He declared and admitted that he has been a maroon for about eighteen moons [lunar months] with Rémy, his father, and other Negroes belonging to [M. Gourgues]; that Rémy having displeased the said M. Gourgues and having been whipped by him, had planned this maronnage, having first gotten together a supply of . . . cassava and bananas for the trip . . . ; that after an unknown number of weeks, a certain André [guided them] to the maroon village . . . ; that in the said village there are twenty-seven houses and three open sheds . . . ; that the said houses belong to and are inhabited by twenty-nine strong male Negroes . . . , twenty-two female Negroes . . . , nine Negro boys, and twelve Negro girls, making in all seventy-two slaves. . . .

[Louis further declared that the captain of the village,] Bernard, nicknamed Couacou, . . . takes care of wounds [with herbal medicines,] baptizes with holy water and recites daily prayer. . . . That no member of the troop has died during the past two years.

That the captain's orders are obeyed perfectly; it is in his yard that prayers are recited in the morning and evening, as they are on well-run plantations; those who are sick recite their prayers in their houses.

That André either whips or has whipped those who deserve punishment. . . . That André and some of his trusted followers make sorties from time to time to recruit new members in the area. . . . That no whites ever entered the village, nor any Negroes other than the ones who are recruited . . . and who promise never to betray them nor to run away, under penalty of being hunted down and killed. . . .

That whenever land has to be cleared, everyone works together, and that once a large area has been burned, everyone is allotted a plot according to the needs of the family to plant and maintain. That the wild pigs that they kill frequently are divided among them, as is other large game, even fish that they dry when there are large numbers of them. . . .

That . . . they maintain and repair their arms themselves, keeping them in good condition at all times, but that when having hunted a great deal they are without powder and shot, . . . they use tiny stones, which . . . are found in abundance in the area . . . .

That the women spin cotton when the weather is bad and work in the fields in good weather. That [men] weave cotton cloth, which serves to make skirts for the women and loincloths for the men; that this cotton material is woven piece by piece and then assembled and decorated with Siamese cotton thread. . . .

That they get salt from the ashes of the Maracoupy palm. That they make a beverage out of sweet potatoes, yams, bananas, and various grains, in addition to their [cassava beer].

That they store all their belongings in [baskets, and they all] are equipped with axes and machetes and that there are spares . . . and that they have no tools other than a few files, gimlets, and hammers; that they have no saws or adzes [wood-working axes]. That they had at the said Negro village two Negro drums, which they played on certain holidays.

What is the significance of the maroons employing African forms of communal ownership, herbal medicine, brewing, cloth making, and musical instruments? How much did they rely on tools, weapons, beliefs, and practices that they acquired from the French?

Source: Richard Price, ed., *Maroon Societies: Rebel Slave Communities in the Americas,* 2d ed. (Baltimore: Johns Hopkins University Press, 1979), 313–318. Reprinted by permission of the Johns Hopkins University Press.

CREATING THE ATLANTIC ECONOMY

At once archaic in their cruel system of slavery and oddly modern in their specialization in a single product, the West Indian plantation colonies were the bittersweet fruits of a new Atlantic trading system. The rise of the new system is illustrated by the transformation of the type and number of ships crossing the Atlantic since the first European conquests of the Americas. The symbol of the Atlantic trade of the sixteenth century was the Treasure Fleet, an annual convoy of from twenty to sixty ships laden with silver and gold bullion from Spanish America. Two different vessels typify the far more numerous Atlantic voyages of the late seventeenth and eighteenth centuries. One was the sugar ship, returning to Europe from the West Indies or Brazil crammed with barrels of brown sugar destined for further refinement. At the end of the seventeenth century an average of 266 sugar ships sailed just from the small island of Barbados every year. The second type of vessel was the slave ship. At the trade's peak between 1760 and 1800, some 300 ships, crammed with an average of 250 African captives each, made this passage every year.

Many separate pieces went into the creation of the new Atlantic economy. Besides the plantation system itself, the development of three other elements merits further investigation: new economic institutions, new partnerships between private investors and governments in Europe, and new working relationships between European and African merchants. The new trading system is a prime example of how European capitalist relationships were reshaping the world.

Capitalism and Mercantilism

The Spanish and Portuguese voyages of exploration in the fifteenth and sixteenth centuries were government ventures, and both countries tried to keep their overseas trade and colonies royal monopolies (see Chapters 17 and 18). Monopoly control, however, proved both expensive and inefficient. The success of the Atlantic economy in the seventeenth and eighteenth centuries owed much to private participation, which made trading ventures more efficient and profitable. European private investors were attracted by the profits they could make from an established and growing trading and colonial system, but their successful participation in the Atlantic economy depended on new institutions and a significant measure of government protection that reduced the likelihood of catastrophic loss.

Two European innovations enabled private investors to fund the rapid growth of the Atlantic economy. One was the ability to manage large financial resources through mechanisms that modern historians have labeled *capitalism*. The essence of early modern capitalism was a system of large financial institutions—banks, stock exchanges, and chartered trading companies—that enabled wealthy investors to reduce risks and increase profits. Originally developed for business dealings within Europe, the capitalist system expanded overseas in the seventeenth century, when slow economic growth in Europe led many investors to seek greater profits abroad. The capitalism of these centuries was buttressed by *mercantilism*, policies adopted by European states to promote their citizens' overseas trade and defend their interests, including by armed force when necessary.

Banks were a central capitalist institution. By the early seventeenth century, Dutch banks had developed such a reputation for security that individuals and governments from all over western Europe entrusted them with large sums of money. To make a profit, the banks invested these funds in real estate, local industries, loans to governments, and overseas trade.

Individuals seeking returns higher than the low rate of interest paid by banks could purchase shares in *joint-stock companies,* sixteenth-century forerunners of modern corporations. Shares were bought and sold in specialized financial markets called *stock exchanges*. The Amsterdam Exchange, founded in 1530, became the greatest stock market in the seventeenth and eighteenth centuries.

To reduce the risks of overseas trading, merchants and trading companies insured their ships and cargoes with specialized companies that agreed to cover losses.

Chartered companies were one of the first examples of mercantilist capitalism. A charter issued by the government of the Netherlands in 1602 gave the Dutch East India Company a legal monopoly over all Dutch trade in the Indian Ocean. This privilege encouraged private investors to buy shares in the company. They were amply rewarded when Dutch East India Company captured control of the long-distance trade routes in the Indian Ocean from the Portuguese (see Chapter 21). As we have seen, a sister firm, the Dutch West India Company, was chartered in 1621 to engage in the Atlantic trade and to seize sugar-producing areas in Brazil and African slaving ports from the Portuguese.

Such successes inspired other governments to set up their own chartered companies. By 1672, all English trade with West Africa was in the hands of the Royal African Company, which established its headquarters at Cape Coast Castle, just east of Elmina on the Gold Coast. The French government also played an active role in chartering companies and promoting overseas trade and colonization. Jean Baptiste Colbert, King Louis XIV's minister of finance from 1661 to 1683, chartered French East India and French West India Companies to reduce French colonies' dependence on Dutch and English traders.

French and English governments also used military force in pursuit of commercial dominance, especially to break the trading advantage of the Dutch in the Americas. Restrictions on Dutch access to French and English colonies provoked a series of wars with the Netherlands between 1652 and 1678 (see Chapter 18), during which the larger English and French navies defeated the Dutch and drove the Dutch West India Company into bankruptcy.

With Dutch competition in the Atlantic reduced, the French and English governments moved to revoke the monopoly privileges of their chartered companies. England opened trade in Africa to any English subject in 1698 on the grounds that ending monopolies would be "highly beneficial and advantageous to this kingdom." It was hoped that such competition would also cut the cost of slaves to West Indian planters, though the demand for slaves soon drove the prices up again.

Such new mercantilist polices fostered competition among a nation's own citizens, while using high tariffs and restrictions to exclude foreigners. In the 1660s England had passed a series of Navigation Acts that confined trade with its colonies to English ships and cargoes. The French called their mercantilist legislation, first codified in 1698, the *Exclusif*, highlighting its exclusionary intentions. Other mercantilist laws defended manufacturing and processing interests in Europe against competition from colonies, imposing prohibitively high taxes on any manufactured goods and refined sugar imported from the colonies.

As a result of such mercantilist measures, the Atlantic became Britain, France, and Portugal's most important overseas trading area in the eighteenth century. Britain's imports from its West Indian colonies in this period accounted for over one-fifth of the value of total British imports. The French West Indian colonies played an even larger role in France's overseas trade. Only the Dutch, closed out of much of the American trade, found Asian trade of greater importance (see Chapter 21). Profits from the Atlantic economy, in turn, helped promote further economic expansion and increase the revenues of European governments.

The Great Circuit and the Middle Passage

At the heart of the Atlantic system was a great clockwise network of trade routes known as the "Great Circuit" (see Map 20.1). It began in Europe, ran south to Africa, turned west across the Atlantic Ocean to the Americas, and then swept back to Europe. Like Asian sailors in the Indian Ocean, Atlantic mariners depended on the prevailing winds and currents to propel their ships. What drove the ships as much as the winds and currents was the desire for the profits that each leg of the circuit was expected to produce.

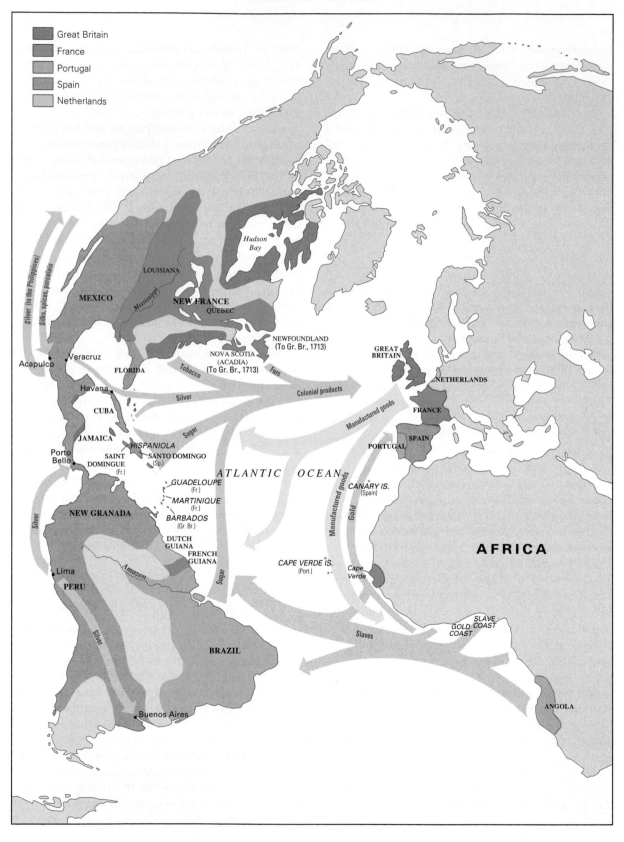

Great Britain
France
Portugal
Spain
Netherlands

Silver (to the Philippines)
Silks, spices, porcelain

Hudson Bay

LOUISIANA

MEXICO

NEW FRANCE
QUÉBEC

NEWFOUNDLAND
(To Gr. Br., 1713)

NOVA SCOTIA
(ACADIA)
(To Gr. Br., 1713)

GREAT
BRITAIN

NETHERLANDS

Acapulco
Veracruz

FLORIDA

Tobacco

Furs

FRANCE

Silver

Colonial products

PORTUGAL

Havana

SPAIN

CUBA

Sugar

JAMAICA

Manufactured goods

Porto
Bello

SAINT
DOMINGUE
(Fr.)

HISPANIOLA
SANTO DOMINGO
(Sp.)

ATLANTIC OCEAN

CANARY IS.
(Spain)

GUADELOUPE
(Fr.)

MARTINIQUE
(Fr.)

NEW GRANADA

BARBADOS
(Gr. Br.)

Manufactured goods

Gold

AFRICA

DUTCH
GUIANA
FRENCH
GUIANA

CAPE VERDE IS.
(Port.)

Cape
Verde

Silver

Lima

Amazon

PERU

Sugar

SLAVE
COAST

GOLD
COAST

Silver

Slaves

BRAZIL

ANGOLA

Buenos Aires

The first leg, from Europe to Africa, carried European manufactures—notably metal bars, hardware, and guns—as well as great quantities of cotton textiles brought from India. Some of these goods were traded for West African gold, timber, and other products, which were taken back to Europe. More goods went to purchase slaves, who were transported across the Atlantic to the plantation colonies in the part of the Great Circuit known as the "Middle Passage." On the third leg, plantation goods from the colonies returned to Europe. Each leg of the circuit carried goods from where they were abundant and relatively cheap to where they were scarce and therefore more valuable. Thus, in theory, each leg of the Great Circuit could earn much more than its costs, and a ship that completed all three legs could return a handsome profit to its owners. In practice, the risks of these ventures could turn profit into loss.

The three-sided Great Circuit is only the simplest model of Atlantic trade. Many other trading voyages supplemented the basic circuit. Cargo ships made long voyages from Europe to the Indian Ocean, passed southward through the Atlantic with quantities of African gold and American silver, and returned with the cotton textiles necessary to the African trade. Other sea routes brought to the West Indies manufactured goods from Europe or foodstuffs and lumber from New England. In addition, some Rhode Island and Massachusetts merchants participated in a "Triangular Trade" that carried rum to West Africa, slaves to the West Indies, and molasses and rum back to New England. There was also a considerable two-way trade between Brazil and Angola, which exchanged Brazilian liquor and other goods for slaves. On another route, Brazil and Portugal exchanged sugar and gold for European imports.

European interests dominated the Atlantic system. The manufacturers who supplied the

Map 20.1 The Atlantic Economy By 1700 the volume of maritime exchanges among the Atlantic continents had begun to rival the trade of the Indian Ocean Basin. Note the trade in consumer products, slave labor, precious metals, and other goods. A silver trade to East Asia lay the basis for a Pacific Ocean economy.

trade goods and the investors who provided the capital were all based in Europe, but so too were the principal consumers of the plantation products. Before the seventeenth century, sugar had been rare and fairly expensive in western Europe. By 1700 annual consumption of sugar in England had risen to about 4 pounds (nearly 2 kilograms) per person. Rising western European prosperity and declining sugar prices promoted additional consumption, starting with the upper classes and working its way down the social ladder. People spooned sugar into popular new beverages imported from overseas—tea, coffee, and chocolate—to overcome the beverages' natural bitterness. By 1750 annual sugar consumption in Britain had doubled, and it doubled again to about 18 pounds (8 kilograms) per person by the early nineteenth century (well below the American average of about 100 pounds [45 kilograms] a year in 1960).

The flow of sugar to Europe depended on another key component of the Atlantic trading system: the flow of slaves from Africa (see Map 20.2). The rising volume of the Middle Passage also measures the Atlantic system's expansion. During the first 150 years after the European discovery of the Americas, some 800,000 Africans had begun the journey across the Atlantic. During the boom in sugar production between 1650 and 1800, the slave trade rose to nearly 7,500,000. Of the survivors, over half landed in the West Indies and nearly one third in Brazil. Plantations in North America imported another 5 percent, and the rest went to other parts of Spanish America (see Figure 20.1).

The transportation of slaves from Africa became a highly specialized trade, although it regularly attracted some amateur traders hoping to make a quick profit. Most slaves were carried in ships that had been specially built or modified for the slave trade by the construction between the ships' decks of additional platforms on which the human cargoes were packed as tightly as possible.

Seventeenth-century mercantilist policies placed much of the Atlantic slave trade in the hands of chartered companies. During their existence the Dutch West India Company and the English Royal Africa Company each carried

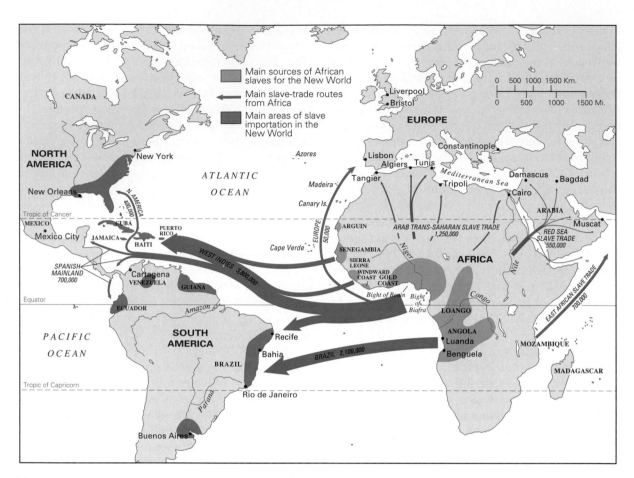

Map 20.2 The African Slave Trade, 1500-1800 After 1500 a vast new trade in slaves from sub-Saharan Africa to the Americas joined the on-going slave trade to the Islamic states of North Africa, the Middle East, and India. The West Indies were the major destination of the Atlantic slave trade, followed by Brazil.

about 100,000 slaves across the Atlantic. In the eighteenth century, private English traders from Liverpool and Bristol controlled about 40 percent of the slave trade. The French, operating out of Nantes and Bordeaux, handled about half as much, but the Dutch hung on to only 6 percent. The Portuguese supplying Brazil and other places had nearly 30 percent of the Atlantic slave trade, in contrast to the 3 percent carried in North American ships.

To make a profit, European slave traders had to buy slaves in Africa for less than the cost of the goods they traded in return. Then they had to

deliver as many healthy slaves as possible across the Atlantic for resale in the plantation colonies. The treacherous voyage to the Americas lasted from six to ten weeks. Some ships completed it with all of their slaves alive, but large, even catastrophic, losses of life were common. On average between 1650 and 1800, about one slave in every six perished during the Middle Passage (see Figure 20.1).

Some deaths resulted from the efforts of the captives to escape. On his voyage Equiano witnessed two of his Igbo countrymen, who were chained together, jump into the sea, "preferring death to such a life of misery." To inhibit such attempts, most male slaves were confined below deck during most of the voyage, and special netting was installed around the outside of the ship. Some slaves fell into deep psychological depression, known to contemporaries as "fixed melancholy," from which many perished. Others, including Equiano, refused to eat, so forced feeding was used to keep slaves alive. When opportunities presented themselves (nearness to land, illness among the crew), some cargoes of enslaved Africans tried to overpower their captors. Such "mutinies" were rarely successful and were put down with brutality that occasioned further losses of life.

Other deaths during the Middle Passage were due to the ill treatment slaves received. Although it was in the interests of the captain and crew to deliver their slave cargoes in good condition, whippings, beatings, and even executions were used to maintain order and force the captives to take nourishment. Moreover, the dangers and brutalities of the slave trade were so notorious that many ordinary seamen shunned such work. As a consequence, many of the officers and crews on slave ships were cruel and brutal characters.

Although examples of unspeakable cruelties abound in the records, most deaths in the Middle Passage were the result of disease rather than abuse, just as on the plantations. Dysentery spread by contaminated food and water caused many deaths. Others died of contagious diseases such as smallpox carried by persons whose infections were not detected during the medical examinations of slaves prior to boarding. Such maladies spread quickly in the crowded and unsanitary confines of the ships, claiming the lives of many slaves already physically weakened and mentally traumatized by their ordeals.

The crew who were in close contact with the slaves were equally exposed to the epidemics and regularly suffered heavy losses. Moreover, sailors often fell victim to tropical diseases, such as malaria, to which Africans had acquired resistance. It is a measure of the callousness of the age, as well as the cheapness of European labor, that over the course of a Great Circuit voyage the proportion of crew deaths could be as high as the slave deaths on the Middle Passage.

Selling Africans This 1785 newspaper advertisement caters to the interests of British West Indian slave buyers. The short passage time from Africa should ensure the slaves' good health; the "naturally industrious" Africans from the Gambia river already know how to cultivate rice; credit or a discount for cash are available to buyers. (Courtesy, Wilberforce House, Hull)

AFRICA, THE ATLANTIC, AND ISLAM

The Atlantic system took a terrible toll in African lives both during the Middle Passage and under the harsh conditions of plantation slavery. Many others died while being marched to the African coastal ports for sale overseas. The overall effects on Africa of these losses and of other aspects of the slave trade have been the subject of considerable historical debate. It is clear that the trade's impact depended on the intensity and terms of different African regions' involvement.

Any assessment of the Atlantic system's effects in Africa must also take into consideration the fact that some Africans profited from the trade by capturing and selling slaves. They chained the slaves together or bound them to forked sticks for the march to the coast, then bartered them to the European slavers for trade goods. The effects on the enslaver were different from the effects on the enslaved. Finally, a broader understanding of the Atlantic system's effects in sub-Saharan Africa comes from comparisons with the effects of Islamic contacts.

The Gold Coast and the Slave Coast

As Chapter 17 showed, early European visitors to Africa's Atlantic coast were interested more in trading than in colonizing or controlling the continent. As the Atlantic trade mushroomed after 1650, this pattern continued. African kings and merchants sold slaves and other goods at many new coastal sites, but the growing slave trade did not lead to any substantial European colonization.

The transition to slave trading was not sudden. Even as slaves were becoming Atlantic Africa's most valuable export, nonslave goods such as gold, ivory, and timber remained a significant part of the total trade. For example, during its eight decades of operation from 1672 to 1752, the English Royal African Company made 40 percent of its profits from dealings in gold, ivory, and forest products. In some parts of West Africa, such nonslave exports remained predominant even at the peak of the trade.

African merchants were very discriminating about what merchandise they received in return for slaves or other goods. A European ship that arrived with goods of low quality or not suited to local tastes found it hard to purchase a cargo at a profitable price. European guidebooks to the African trade carefully noted the color and shape of beads, the pattern of textiles, the type of guns, and the sort of metals that each section of the coast preferred. In the early eighteenth century, for example, the people of Sierra Leone had a strong preference for large iron kettles, whereas brass pans were preferred on the Gold Coast, and iron and copper bars were in demand in the

Niger Delta, where smiths turned them into useful objects (see Map 20.3).

Although preferences for merchandise varied, Africans' greatest demands were for textiles, hardware, and guns. Of the goods the Royal African Company traded in West Africa in the 1680s, over 60 percent were Indian and European textiles, 30 percent hardware and weaponry. Beads and other jewelry formed 3 percent. The rest consisted of cowrie shells that were used as money. In the eighteenth century, tobacco and rum from the Americas also were among the imports.

Both Europeans and Africans naturally attempted to drive the best bargain for themselves and sometimes engaged in deceitful practices. The strength of the African bargaining position, however, may be inferred from the fact that as the demand for slaves rose, so too did their price in Africa. In the course of the eighteenth century the goods needed to purchase a slave on the Gold Coast doubled and in some places tripled or quadrupled.

West Africans' trading strengths were reinforced by African governments on the Gold and Slave Coasts that forced Europeans to observe African trading customs and prevented them from taking control of African territory. Indeed, some African states grew stronger as a result of their participation in the trade. Rivalry among the several European nations, each of which established its own trading "castles" along the Gold Coast, also reduced Europeans' bargaining strength. In 1700 the head of the Dutch East India Company in West Africa, Willem Bosman, bemoaned the fact that, to stay competitive against the other European traders, his company had to include large quantities of muskets and gunpowder in the goods it exchanged, thereby adding to Africans' military power. Bosman also related that before being allowed to buy slaves at Whydah on the Slave Coast his agents first had to pay the king a substantial customs duty and buy at a premium price whatever slaves the king had to sell. By African standards, Whydah was a rather small kingdom controlling only that port and its immediate hinterland. In 1727 it was annexed by the larger kingdom of Dahomey, which maintained a strong trading posi-

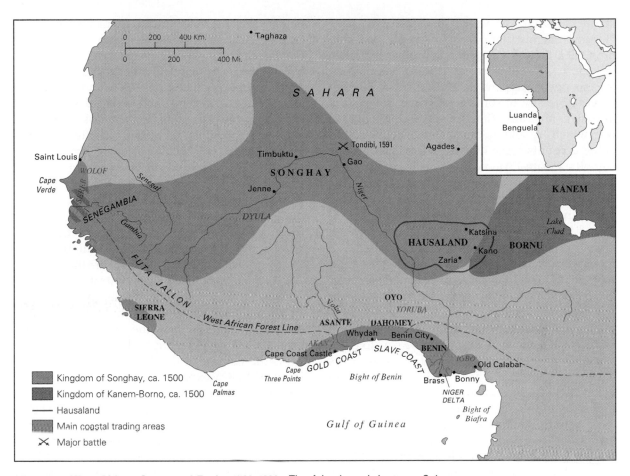

Map 20.3 West African States and Trade, 1500-1800 The Atlantic and the trans-Saharan trade brought West Africans new goods and promoted the rise of powerful states and trading communities. The Moroccan invasion of Songhai and Portuguese colonization of the Angolan ports of Luanda and Benguela showed the political dangers of such relations. (Jean-Loup Charmet)

tion with Europeans at the coast. Dahomey's rise depended heavily on the firearms that the slave trade supplied for its well-trained armies of men and women.

In the cases of two of Dahomey's neighbors, the connections between state growth and the Atlantic trade were more complex. One was the inland Oyo kingdom to the northeast. Oyo cavalry overran Dahomey in 1730 and forced it to pay an annual tribute to keep its independence. The other was the newer kingdom of Asante, west of Dahomey along the Gold Coast, which expanded rapidly after 1680. While both Oyo and Asante

participated in the Atlantic trade, neither kingdom was so dependent on it as Dahomey. Overseas trade formed a relatively modest part of the economies of these large and populous states and was balanced by their extensive overland trade with their northern neighbors and with states across the Sahara. Like the great medieval empires of the western Sudan, Oyo and Asante were stimulated by external trade, but they were not controlled by it.

How did African kings and merchants obtain slaves for sale? Bosman dismissed misconceptions prevailing in Europe in his day. "Not a few in our country," he wrote to a friend in 1700, "fondly imagine that parents here sell their children, men their wives, and one brother the other. But those who think so, do deceive themselves; for this never happens on any other account but that of necessity, or some great crime; but most of the slaves that are offered to us are prisoners of war, which are sold by the victors as their booty."[2] Other accounts agree that prisoners taken in war were the greatest source of slaves for the Atlantic trade, but it is difficult to say how often capturing slaves for export was the main cause of warfare. "Here and there," conclude two respected historians of Africa, "there are indications that captives taken in the later and more peripheral stages of these wars were exported overseas, but it would seem that the main impetus of conquest was only incidentally concerned with the slave-trade in any external direction."[3]

An early-nineteenth-century king of Asante had a similar view: "I cannot make war to catch slaves in the bush, like a thief. My ancestors never did so. But if I fight a king, and kill him when he is insolent, then certainly I must have his gold, and his slaves, and his people are mine too. Do not the white kings act like this?"[4] English rulers had indeed sentenced seventeenth-century Scottish and Irish prisoners to forced labor in the West Indies. One may imagine that the African and the European prisoners did not share their kings' view that such actions were legitimate.

The Bight of Biafra and Angola

In the eighteenth century the slave trade expanded eastward to the Bight (bay) of Biafra. In contrast to the Gold and Slave Coasts, where strong kingdoms predominated, the densely populated interior of the Bight of Biafra contained no large states. Even so, the powerful merchant princes of the coastal ports still made European traders give them rich presents. Because of the absence of sizable states, there were no large-scale wars and consequently few prisoners of war. Instead, kidnapping was the major source of slaves, as Equiano's autobiography indicates. In about 1756, while their parents were away working in the

fields, the eleven-year-old Equiano and his younger sister were snatched from their yard by two men and a woman. After passing through many hands, Equiano finally reached a coastal port, where, he relates, he was astonished at the sight of the slave ship and alarmed at his first sight of "white men with horrible looks, red faces, and loose hair." By then he had become separated from his sister, whose fate he never learned.

As Equiano learned on his way to the coast, some inland African merchants were experienced in procuring debtors, victims of kidnapping, and convicted criminals and shepherding them through a network of markets to the coast. The largest of the inland trading communities of the Bight of Biafra was that of the Aro of Arochukwu, who used their control of a famous religious oracle to enhance their prestige. The Aro cemented their business links with powerful inland families and the coastal merchants through gifts and marriage alliances.

As the volume of the Atlantic trade along the Bight of Biafra expanded in the late eighteenth century, some inland markets evolved into giant fairs with different sections specializing in slaves and imported goods. An English ship's doctor reported that in the 1780s slaves were "bought by the black traders at fairs, which are held for that purpose, at a distance of upwards of two hundred miles from the sea coast." He reported seeing from twelve hundred to fifteen hundred enslaved men and women arriving at the coast from a single fair.[5]

The local context of the Atlantic trade was different south of the Congo estuary at Angola, the greatest source of slaves for the Atlantic trade (see Map 20.2). This was also the one place along the Atlantic coast where a single European nation, Portugal, controlled a significant amount of territory. Except when overrun by the Dutch for a time in the seventeenth century, Portuguese residents of the main coastal ports of Luanda and Benguela served as middlemen between the caravans that arrived from the far interior and the ships that crossed from Brazil. From the coastal cities Afro-Portuguese traders guided large caravans of trade goods inland to exchange for slaves at special markets. Some markets met in the shadow of Portuguese frontier forts; powerful African kings controlled others.

Many of the slaves sold at these markets were prisoners of war captured by expanding African states. By the late eighteenth century, slaves sold from Angolan ports were prisoners of wars fought from as far as 600 to 800 miles (1,000 to 1,300 kilometers) inland. Many were victims of wars of expansion fought by the giant federation of Lunda kingdoms. As elsewhere in Africa, such prisoners usually seem to have been a byproduct of African wars rather than the purpose for which the wars were fought.

Recent research has linked other enslavement with environmental crises in the hinterland of Angola.[6] During the eighteenth century these southern grasslands periodically suffered severe droughts, which drove famished refugees to better-watered areas. Powerful African leaders gained control of such refugees in return for supplying them with food and water. These leaders built up their followings by assimilating refugee children, along with adult women, who were valued as food producers and for reproduction. However, they often sold into the Atlantic trade the adult male refugees, who were more likely than the women and children to escape or challenge the ruler's authority. Rising Angolan leaders parceled out the Indian textiles, weapons, and alcohol they received in return for such slaves as gifts to attract new followers and to cement the loyalty of their established allies.

The most successful of these inland Angolan leaders became heads of powerful new states that stabilized areas devastated by war and drought and repopulated them with the refugees and prisoners they retained. The slave frontier then moved farther inland. This cruel system

Queen Nzinga of Angola, 1622 This formidable African woman went to great lengths to maintain her royal dignity when negotiating a treaty for her brother with the Portuguese governor of Luanda. To avoid having to stand in his presence, she had one of her women bend herself into a human seat. Nzinga later ruled in her own name and revolted against the Portuguese with the aid of Dutch and African allies. (Jean-Loup Charmet)

worked to the benefit of a few African rulers and merchants at the expense of the many thousands of Africans who were sent to death or perpetual bondage in the Americas.

Although the organization of the Atlantic trade in Africa varied, it was based on a partnership between European and African elites. To obtain foreign textiles, metals, and weapons, African rulers and merchants sold slaves and many other products. Most of the exported slaves were prisoners taken in wars associated with African state growth. But strong African states also helped offset the Europeans' economic advantage and hindered them from taking control of African territory. Even in the absence of strong states, powerful African merchant communities everywhere dominated the movement of goods and people. The Africans who gained from these exchanges were the rich and powerful few. Many more Africans were losers in these exchanges.

As Angola illustrates, the Atlantic system also touched the lives of those affected by famine. During droughts in the northern grasslands south of the Sahara, refugees were also being assimilated by African warlords or sold away as slaves. To understand this context, it is necessary to adopt a broader view of sub-Saharan Africa's external relations.

Comparing European and Islamic Contacts

While Atlantic Africa was being drawn into closer relations with the Europeans between 1500 and 1800, the Islamic world continued to be the most significant external influence along the southern border of the Sahara and in eastern Africa, as it had been for centuries before 1500. There are both similarities and differences in the impact of these two external influences on sub-Saharan Africa.

Despite all their commercial expansion in the centuries before 1800, Europeans had acquired control of little African territory. Their trading posts along the Gold and Slave Coasts were largely dependent on the goodwill of local African rulers. Only on islands and in Angola did the Atlantic trade lead to significant European colonies. Ironically, the largest European colony in Africa in 1800, the Dutch East India Company's Cape Colony at the southern tip of the continent, was tied to the Indian Ocean trade, not to the Atlantic trade. The Cape Colony did not export slaves; rather the 25,750 slaves in its population were mostly derived from persons *imported* from Madagascar, South Asia, and the East Indies.

Muslim territorial dominance was more extensive. Arab conquests in the seventh century permanently brought North Africa into the Muslim world. Muslim practices and traders spread south of the Sahara, but Arab and North African Muslims had little success in extending their territorial dominance southward before 1500. During the sixteenth century, all of North Africa except Morocco was annexed to the new Ottoman Islamic empire, while Ethiopia lost extensive territory to other Muslim conquerors (see Chapter 17).

In the 1580s, Morocco began a southward expansion aimed at gaining control of the Saharan trade. To that end it sent a military expedition of 4,000 men and 10,000 camels from Marrakesh to attack the indigenously ruled Muslim empire of Songhai in the western Sudan. Half of the men perished on their way across the desert. The remainder, armed with 2,500 muskets, succeeded in besting Songhai's army of 40,000 cavalry and foot soldiers in 1591, reducing the empire to a shadow of its former self. Although Morocco was never able to annex the western Sudan, for the next two centuries the occupying troops extracted a massive tribute of slaves and goods from the local population and collected tolls from passing merchants.

Morocco's destruction of Songhai weakened the trans-Saharan trade in the western Sudan. Caravans continued to cross the desert bringing textiles, hardware, and weapons, but much of the trade shifted eastward to the central Sudan. Except for the absence of tobacco and alcohol (both of which were prohibited to Muslims), these goods were similar to those in the Atlantic trade. There was also a continuation of the salt trade southward from Saharan mines. Communities of Dyula traders in the western Sudan and Hausa traders in the central Sudan distributed these imports and local goods throughout West Africa. They also collected goods for shipment northward, including gold, caffeine-rich kola nuts from Asante and other parts of the forest (a stimulant allowed by Muslim law), African textiles and leather goods, as well as slaves.

Fewer slaves crossed the Sahara than crossed the Atlantic, but their numbers were substantial. It is estimated that between 1600 and 1800 about 850,000 slaves trudged across the desert's various routes (see Map 20.2). A nearly equal number of slaves from sub-Saharan Africa entered the Islamic Middle East and India by way of the Red Sea and the Indian Ocean.

The tasks that African slaves performed in the Islamic world were very different from their tasks in the Americas. In the late seventeenth and eighteenth centuries, Morocco's rulers employed an army of 150,000 slaves obtained from the south to keep them in power. Other slaves worked for Moroccans on sugar plantations, as servants, and as artisans. In contrast to the make-up of the Atlantic slave trade, the majority of the slaves crossing the desert were women, intended to serve wealthy households as concubines and servants. The trans-Saharan slave trade also included a much higher proportion of children than did the Atlantic trade, including eunuchs meant for eventual service as harem guards. It is estimated that only one in ten of these boys survived the surgical removal of their genitals.

The central Sudanese kingdom of Bornu illustrates some aspects of trans-Saharan contacts. This ancient Muslim state had grown and expanded in the sixteenth century as the result of guns imported from the Ottoman Empire. Bornu retained many captives from its wars, or sold them as slaves to the north in return for the firearms and horses that underpinned the kingdom's military power. Bornu's king, Mai Ali, conspicuously displayed his kingdom's new power and wealth while on four pilgrimages to Mecca between 1642 and 1667. On the last, an enormous entourage of slaves—said to number fifteen thousand—accompanied him.

Ayuba Suleiman Diallo (1701–??) Known as Job ben Solomon to the Maryland planter who owned him as a slave from 1731 to 1735, this Muslim from the West African state of Bondu, was able to regain his freedom and return to Africa. Note the booklet of Quranic verses around his neck. (British Library)

Like Christians, Muslims of this period saw no moral impediment to owning and trading in slaves. Indeed, Islam recognized the *jihad* (holy war) as a means by which their religion could be spread and considered enslaving "pagans" to be a meritorious act because it brought them into the faith. Although Islam forbade the enslavement of Muslims, some Muslim states south of the Sahara did not strictly observe that law. Ahmad Baba, a Muslim scholar of Timbuktu, in a 1614 treatise on slavery lamented that the enslavement of free Muslims was much practiced, notably by Muslim Hausa rulers.

A West African named Ayuba Suleiman Diallo is a revealing example of an enslaved Muslim. In 1730 his father, a prominent Muslim scholar, sent Ayuba to sell two slaves to an English ship on the Gambia River so as to buy paper and other necessities. On his way home a few days later, other Africans kidnapped Ayuba, shaved his head to make him appear to have been a war captive, and sold him to the same English ship. A planter from Maryland purchased Ayuba. Soon after, an English scholar, impressed by Ayuba's knowledge of Arabic and his elevated social origins, bought his freedom and arranged for him to return home.[6]

Because of sub-Saharan Africa's long and deep exposure to Islam, Muslim cultural influences were much greater than European ones before 1800. The Arabic language, long dominant in North Africa, continued to expand as a means of communication among scholars and merchants south of the Sahara. The Islamic religion also increased the number of its adherents south of the desert, reaching well beyond the urban centers that had been its medieval strength.

In contrast, African conversion to Christianity was limited to coastal Angola and the immediate vicinity of small European trading posts. The use of European languages was also largely confined to the trading coasts. Still it is notable that some African merchants sent their sons to Europe to learn European ways. One of these young men, Philip Quaque, was educated and ordained as an Anglican priest in England and became the official chaplain of the Cape Coast Castle from 1766 until his death in 1816. Not only men of Quaque's stature but many African merchants learned to write a European language. A leading trader of Old Calabar on the Bight of Biafra kept a diary in pidgin English in the late eighteenth century.

The interesting details of the lives of elite and culturally sophisticated individuals such as Ayuba Suleiman and Philip Quaque must not distract us from the grim, sordid details of this era of slave trading. It is easy to rejoice in Ayuba's return to Africa while forgetting the unrecorded fates of the two persons whom he sold into slavery. In admiring Quaque's achievement of a position second only to the British governor on the Gold Coast, we should not overlook that his principal duties were to tend the spiritual needs of the slave traders, not the slaves. Unfortunately, surviving records tell us much less about the large number of Africans who suffered than about the small number who prospered from the European and Muslim trades.

Despite uncertainty over many details, it is still possible to assess some of the effects of the Atlantic and Islamic trades on sub-Saharan Africa. One key issue is how the European and Islamic slave trades affected Africa's population. Most scholars who have looked deeply into the question agree on two points: (1) the effect of slave exports could not have been large when measured against the population of the entire continent, but (2) losses in regions that contributed heavily to the slave trade were severe. The lands behind the Slave Coast are thought to have been acutely affected. The large slave trade may also have caused serious depopulation in Angola. To some extent, however, losses from famine in this region may have been reduced by the increasing cultivation of high-yielding food plants from the Americas (see Environment and Technology: Amerindian Foods in Africa).

Although both foreign Muslims and Europeans obtained slaves from sub-Saharan Africa, there was a significant difference in the numbers they obtained and thus in the overall effects of the two slave trades. Between 1550 and 1800 some 8 million Africans were exported into the Atlantic trade, four times as many as were taken from sub-Saharan Africa to North Africa and the Middle East. The families of all those sent abroad suffered from their individual loss, but the ability of the population to replenish its numbers through natural increase depended on the proportion of women lost to these slave trades. The much higher proportion of women in the Muslim slave trade would have multiplied its lasting effects on sub-Saharan African populations.

It is impossible to assess with precision the complex effects of the goods received in sub-Saharan Africa from these trades. Africans were very particular about what they received, so it is unlikely that they could have been consistently cheated. Some researchers have suggested that imports of textiles and metals undermined African weavers and metalworkers, but most economic historians calculate that on a per capita basis the volume of these imports was too small to have idled many African artisans. Imports

Amerindian Foods in Africa

The migration of European plants and animals across the Atlantic to the New World was one side of the Columbian exchange (see Chapter 19). The Andean potato, for example, became a staple crop of the poor in Europe, and cassava (a Brazilian plant cultivated for its edible roots) and maize (the Amerindian grain) moved across the Atlantic to Africa.

Maize was a high-yielding grain that could produce much more food per acre than many grains indigenous to Africa. The varieties of maize that spread to Africa were not modern high-bred "sweet corn" but starchier types found in white and yellow corn meal. Cassava—not well known to modern North Americans except perhaps in the form of tapioca—became the most important New World food in Africa. Truly a marvel, cassava had the highest yield of calories per acre of any staple food and thrived even in poor soils and during droughts. Both the leaves and the root could be eaten. Ground into meal, the root could be made into a bread that would keep for up to six months, or it could be fermented into a beverage.

Cassava and maize were probably introduced accidentally into Africa by Portuguese ships from Brazil that discarded leftover supplies after reaching Angola. It did not take long for local Africans to recognize the food value of these new crops, especially in drought-prone areas. As the principal farmers in Central Africa, women must have played an important role in learning how to cultivate, harvest, and prepare these foods. By the eighteenth century, Lunda rulers hundreds of miles from the Angolan coast were actively promoting the cultivation of maize and cassava on their royal estates in order to provide a more secure food supply.

Some historians of Africa believe that in the inland areas these Amerindian food crops provided the nutritional base for a population increase that partially offset losses due to the Atlantic slave trade. By supplementing the range of food crops available and by enabling populations to increase in once lightly settled or famine-prone areas, cassava and maize, along with peanuts and other New World legumes, permanently altered Africans' environmental prospects.

Cultivation of cassava, 1554 drawing   (Engraving from the book by Hans Staden, 1554)

supplemented rather than replaced local production. Although it is true, as some have pointed out, that the goods received in sub-Saharan Africa were intended for consumption and thus did not serve to develop the economy, neither did the sugar, tea, or chocolate that the Atlantic economy directed to European consumers promote economic development in Europe.

Historians disagree in their assessment of how deeply European capitalism dominated Africa before 1800, but it is clear that European political and economic power was far less in Africa than in the West Indies or in other parts of the Americas. However, it is significant that Western capitalism was expanding rapidly in the eighteenth century, while the Ottoman Empire, the dominant state of the Middle East, was entering a period of economic and political decline (see Chapter 27). The tide of influence in Africa was thus running in the Europeans' direction.

CONCLUSION

The new Atlantic trading system had great importance and momentous implications for world history. In the first phase of their expansion Europeans had conquered and colonized the Americas and captured major Indian Ocean trade routes. The development of the Atlantic system showed Europeans' ability to move beyond the conquest and capture of existing systems to create a major new trading system that could transform a region almost beyond recognition.

The West Indies felt the transforming power of capitalism more profoundly than did any other place outside Europe in this period. The establishment of sugar plantation societies was not just a matter of replacing native vegetation with alien plants and native peoples with Europeans and Africans. More fundamentally it made these once isolated islands part of a dynamic trading system controlled from Europe. To be sure, the West Indies was not the only place affected. Parts of northern Brazil were touched as deeply by the sugar revolution, and other parts of the Americas were yielding to the power of European colonization and capitalism.

Africa played an essential role in the Atlantic system, importing trade goods and exporting slaves to the Americas. Africa, however, was less dominated by the Atlantic system than were Europe's American colonies. Africans remained in control of their continent and interacted culturally and politically with the Islamic world more than with the Atlantic.

Historians have seen the Atlantic system as a model of the kind of highly interactive economy that became global in later centuries. For that reason the Atlantic system was a milestone in a much larger historical process, but not a monument to be admired. Its transformations were destructive as well as creative, producing victims as well as victors. Yet one cannot ignore that the system's awesome power came from its ability to create wealth. As the next chapter describes, southern Asia and the Indian Ocean basin were also beginning to feel the effects of Europeans' rising power.

SUGGESTED READING

The larger structures and dynamics of early modern capitalism and the Atlantic economy have been examined by Immanuel Wallerstein, *The Modern World-System*, 3 vols. (1974–1989), and by Fernand Braudel, *Civilization and Capitalism, 15th–18th Century*, 3 vols. (1982–1984); both works cover much more than the Atlantic system. James D. Tracy has edited two volumes of similarly wide-ranging scholarly papers: *The Rise of Merchant Empires* (1990) and *The Political Economy of Merchant Empires* (1991). Especially relevant are the chapters in *The Rise of Merchant Empires* by Herbert S. Klein, summarizing scholarship on the Middle Passage, and by Ralph A. Austen, on the trans-Saharan caravan trade between 1500 and 1800. Alan K. Smith, *Creating a World Economy: Merchant Capital, Capitalism, and World Trade, 1400–1825* (1991), provides a useful overview.

The best introduction to the Atlantic slave trade and New World slavery is Philip D. Curtin, *The Rise and Fall of the Plantation Complex* (1990), which Curtin has summarized in an American Historical Association pamphlet, *The Tropical Atlantic in the Age of the Slave Trade* (1991). Recent scholarly articles on subjects considered in this chapter are available in *The Atlantic Slave Trade: Effects on Economies, Societies, and Peoples in Africa, the Americas and Europe*, ed. Joseph E. Inikori and Stanley L. Engerman (1992); in *Slavery and the Rise of the Atlantic System*, ed. Barbara L. Solow (1991); and in *Africans in Bondage: Studies in Slavery and the Slave Trade*, ed. Paul Lovejoy (1986). Sidney Mintz, *Sweetness and Power: The Place of Sugar in Modern History* (1985), considers the rise of sugar plantations in a broad historical context.

The cultural connections among African communities on both sides of the Atlantic are explored by John Thornton, *Africa and Africans in the Making of the Atlantic World, 1400–1680* (1992), and Margaret E. Crahan and Franklin W. Knight, eds., *Africa and the Caribbean: The Legacies of a Link* (1979). See also the collection edited by Richard Price, *Maroon Societies: Rebel Slave Communities in the Americas*, 2d ed. (1979).

Edward Reynolds, *Stand the Storm: A History of the Atlantic Slave Trade* (1985), provides an up-to-date overview of research on that subject. A useful collection of primary and secondary sources is David Northrup, ed., *The Atlantic Slave Trade* (1994). James A. Rawley's *The Trans-Atlantic Slave Trade* (1981) and Basil Davidson's *The African Slave Trade*, rev. ed. (1980), are other useful historical narratives.

Herbert S. Klein's *African Slavery in Latin America and the Caribbean* (1986) is an exceptionally fine synthesis of recent research on New World slavery, including North American slave systems. The larger context of Caribbean history is skillfully surveyed by Eric Williams, *From Columbus to Castro: the History of the Caribbean* (1984), and more simply surveyed by William Claypole and John Robottom, *Caribbean Story*, vol. 1, *Foundations*, 2d ed. (1990). Michael Craton, James Walvin, and David Wright, eds., *Slavery, Abolition, and Emancipation* (1976) is a valuable collection of primary sources about slavery in the British West Indies.

Roland Oliver and Anthony Atmore, *The African Middle Ages, 1400–1800* (1981) summarize African history in this period. Students can pursue specific topics in more detail in Richard Gray, ed., *The Cambridge History of Africa*, vol. 4 (1975), and B. A. Ogot, ed., *UNESCO General History of Africa*, vol. 5 (1992). For recent research on slavery and the African, Atlantic, and Muslim slave trades within Africa see Paul Lovejoy, *Transformations in Slavery: A History of Slavery in Africa* (1983); Claire C. Robertson and Martin A. Klein, eds., *Women and Slavery in Africa* (1983); and Patrick Manning, *Slavery and African Life: Occidental, Oriental, and African Slave Trades* (1990). Case studies are found in J. E. Inikori, ed., *Forced Migration: The Impact of the Export Slave Trade on African Societies* (1982). *The Interesting Narrative of the Life of Olaudah Equiano* (1789) exists in several old and modern editions,

and a critical edition of the portion relevant to the slave trade is reprinted in Philip D. Curtin, ed., *Africa Remembered: Narratives by West Africans from the Era of the Slave Trade* (1968), along with other African voices.

Students interested in Islam's cultural and commercial contacts with sub-Saharan Africa will find useful information in Allan G. B. Fisher and Humphrey J. Fisher, *Slavery and Muslim Society in Africa* (1971), and J. Spencer Trimingham, *The Influence of Islam upon Africa* (1968).

NOTES

1. Eric Williams, *Capitalism and Slavery* (Charlotte: University of North Carolina Press, 1944), 7.

2. Willem Bosman, *A New and Accurate Description of Guinea, etc.* (London, 1705), quoted in David Northrup, ed., *The Atlantic Slave Trade* (Lexington, MA: D. C. Heath, 1994), 72.

3. Roland Oliver and Anthony Atmore, *The African Middle Ages, 1400–1800* (Cambridge, England: Cambridge University Press, 1981), 100.

4. King Osei Bonsu, quoted in Northrup, ed., *The Atlantic Slave Trade*, 93.

5. Alexander Falconbridge, *Account of the Slave Trade on the Coast of Africa* (London: J. Phillips, 1788), 12.

6. Joseph C. Miller, "The Significance of Drought, Disease, and Famine in the Agriculturally Marginal Zones of West-Central Africa," *Journal of African History* 23.1 (1982), 17–61.

7. In Philip D. Curtin, ed., *Africa Remembered: Narratives by West Africans from the Era of the Slave Trade* (Madison: University of Wisconsin Press, 1968).

CHAPTER TWENTY-ONE

Southwest Asia and the Indian Ocean, 1500–1750

The Ottoman Empire · The Safavid Empire · The Mughal Empire

Trade Empires in the Indian Ocean

In 1637, John Greaves, a professor of geometry and astronomy at Oxford, set forth on a scientific journey to the East. When he returned from Istanbul and Cairo two years later, he had acquired five copies of the Samarkand Tables, an exhaustive and precise record of astronomical observations made under the sponsorship of the Central Asian astronomer-king Ulugh Beg (r. 1447–1449). At the time of their compilation, in an observatory whose primary observing instrument had a phenomenally large radius of over 120 feet (36 meters), they were the most accurate astronomical readings ever made; and two centuries later, they were still an impressive achievement.

Although only a handful of scientists in England knew of Ulugh Beg, his grandfather had become a figure of sensation in London in 1587 as the title character in Christopher Marlowe's play *Tamburlaine the Great*. The Tamburlaine, or Tamerlane, of Marlowe's imagination—"I that am termed the scourge and wrath of God,/the only fear and terror of the world"— fit well the European image of Central Asian conquerors established long before by the Mongol leader Genghis Khan (ca. 1162–1227).

His real name was Timur. Although he claimed descent from the great Mongol conqueror Genghis Khan, he actually was the son of a Turkish nomad chieftain. Being lamed in youth, he was called Timur Lenk, "Timur the Lame," from which we get the usual English rendering: Tamerlane. Between 1369 and his death in 1405, he brilliantly and brutally conquered an empire that stretched from Ankara and Damascus in the west to Delhi in the east. He died on the way to a projected conquest of China.

The sensational stories of Tamerlane's bloody conquests overshadowed the flowering of arts and sciences that he and his descendants fostered. Samarkand to this day is spectacularly adorned with brilliantly tiled Timurid mosques, schools, and tombs. Timurid painters perfected the art of miniature painting in which they depicted scenes of court life. And the colossal observatory on a hill outside the city, continuing a tradition of serious astronomical observation and theorizing strongly supported earlier by the Mongols, became a model for later observatories built by Muslim rulers in Istanbul and Delhi.

Timur and Ulugh Beg, grandfather and grandson, embody the two sides of Muslim imperial greatness in the post-Mongol centuries: one was a conqueror with a lust for territory to support his giant army and luxurious capital city; the other was a patron of the arts and scientific investigator cultivating the most refined expressions of civilized life.

The great land empires of the post-Mongol era—the Ottoman, Safavid, and Mughal Empires—would be superseded by the globe-spanning maritime empires of Europe (see Chapters 26, 28, and 29), partly because of the problems they encountered in adopting their new military technologies that made payment of part-time soldiers by land grants obsolete. But their ultimate failure does not diminish their innovations and achievements in social and religious organization and manufacturing and trade, as well as in the arts and sciences.

THE OTTOMAN EMPIRE

The most long-lived of the post-Mongol Muslim empires was that of the Ottoman sultans. By extending Islamic conquests into eastern Europe, starting in the late fourteenth century, and by absorbing the Arab lands of Syria and Egypt, previously ruled by the Mamluk sultans, the Ottomans seemed to recreate the might of the original Islamic caliphate, the empire established by the Muslim Arab conquests in the seventh century. However, they were very much an empire of their time, not greatly dissimilar to the

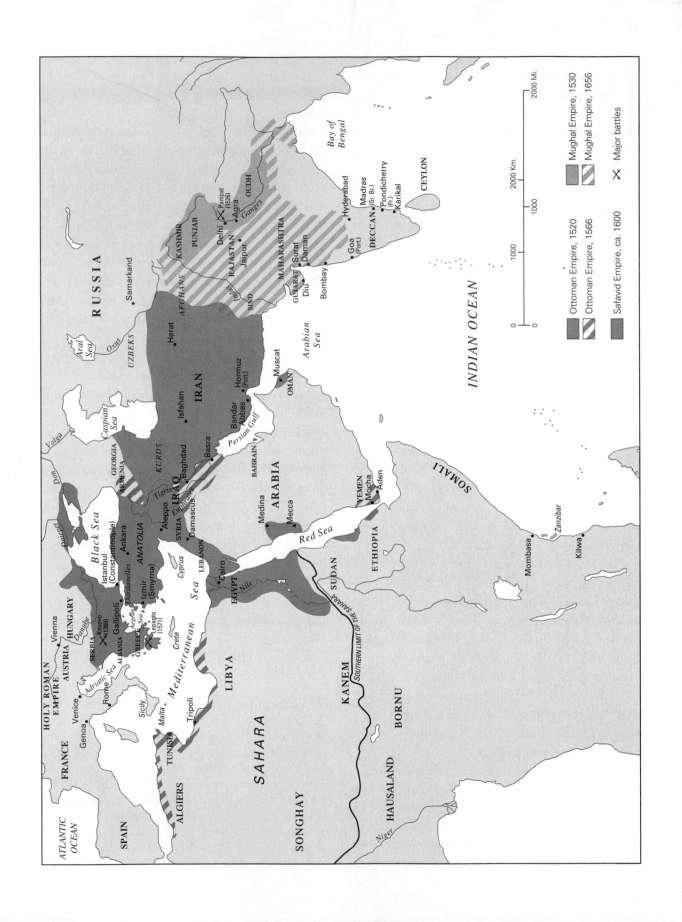

RUSSIA

Samarkand

Bay of
Bengal

CEYLON

Madras
(Gr. Br.)
Pondicherry
(Fr.)
Karikal

Hyderabad

DECCAN

Goa
(Port.)

Surat
Daman

GUJARAT
Diu
Bombay

MAHARASHTRA

RAJASTAN
Jaipur

SIND

INDIAN OCEAN

KASHMIR
PUNJAB

Delhi
Panipat
(1526)
Agra
Ganges

OUDH

AFGHANS

Herat

IRAN

Isfahan

Bandar
Abbas
Hormuz
(Port.)

Muscat

OMAN

Arabian
Sea

Aral
Sea

Oxus

Caspian
Sea

Volga

KURDS

Baghdad
Basra

Persian Gulf

BAHRAIN

ARABIA

Mecca
Medina

YEMEN
Mocha
Aden

SOMALI

Zanzibar

Mombasa

Kilwa

GEORGIA
ARMENIA

Tigris

IRAQ

Euphrates

Aleppo
Damascus
SYRIA

LEBANON

Red Sea

ETHIOPIA

Don

Black Sea

Dnieper

Istanbul
(Constantinople)
Ankara

ANATOLIA

Izmir
(Smyrna)

Cyprus

Cairo
EGYPT
Nile

SUDAN

SOUTHERN LIMIT OF THE SAHARA

HOLY ROMAN
EMPIRE

Vienna

AUSTRIA
HUNGARY

SERBIA

Kosovo
(1389)

ALBANIA
GREECE

Gallipoli

Dardanelles

Aegean
Sea

Lepanto
(1571)

Crete

Mediterranean
Sea

LIBYA

SAHARA

KANEM

BORNU

FRANCE

Venice
Genoa
Rome

Adriatic Sea

Sicily

Malta

Tripoli

TUNISIA

ALGIERS

SPAIN

ATLANTIC
OCEAN

SONGHAY

Niger

HAUSALAND

Ottoman Empire, 1520
Ottoman Empire, 1566

Safavid Empire, ca. 1600

Mughal Empire, 1530
Mughal Empire, 1656

✕ Major battles

2000 Mi.

2000 Km.

1000

1000

0

new centralized monarchies of France and Spain taking shape at the same time elsewhere in Europe (see Chapter 18).

Enduring more than five centuries, until World War I, the Ottoman Empire survived several periods of wrenching change, some caused by internal problems, others by the growing power of European adversaries. These periods of change reveal the problems that huge, land-based empires in various parts of the world faced.

Expansion and Frontiers

The Ottoman Empire grew primarily by land conquest (see Map 21.1). It began around 1300 as a tiny state built on the strength of an army of Turkish nomad warriors and a few Christian converts to Islam in northwestern Anatolia. The expansion of this state into an empire, first in the Balkans and then at the expense of other small Turkish principalities in Anatolia, was due to three factors: (1) the shrewdness of its founder Osman (from which the name "Ottoman" comes) and his descendants, (2) control of a strategic link between Europe and Asia at Gallipoli on the Dardanelles strait, and (3) the creation of an army that combined the traditional skills of the Turkish cavalryman with the new military possibilities opened up by the use of gunpowder.

At first, Ottoman armies concentrated on Christian enemies in Greece and the Balkans, in 1389 conquering a strong Serbian kingdom at the Battle of Kosovo (in present-day Yugoslavia). Much of southeastern Europe and Anatolia had come under the control of the sultans by 1402, when Bayazid I, "the Thunderbolt," returned to Anatolia to face Timur's challenge from Central Asia. After Timur defeated and captured Bayazid at the Battle of Ankara (1402), a generation of civil war followed, until Mehmed I reunified the sultanate.

During a century and a half of fighting for territory both east and west of Constantinople, the sultans repeatedly had been tempted by the heavily fortified capital of the slowly dying

Map 21.1 Muslim empires in the sixteenth to seventeenth centuries

Byzantine Empire. In 1453, Sultan Mehmed II, "the Conqueror," laid siege to Constantinople. His forces used enormous cannon to bash in the city's walls, dragged warships over a high hill from the Bosporus strait to the city's inner harbor to get around its sea defenses, and finally penetrated the city's land defenses through a series of direct infantry assaults. The fall of Constantinople—henceforth commonly known as Istanbul—brought to an end over eleven hundred years of Byzantine rule and made the Ottomans seem once again invincible.

When Selim I, "the Inexorable," conquered the Mamluk Sultanate of Egypt and Syria in 1516 and 1517, the Red Sea became the Ottomans' southern frontier. Selim also quelled a potential threat on his eastern frontier from the new and expansive realm of the Safavid shah in Iran. Although further wars were to be fought with Iran, the general border between the Ottomans and their eastern neighbors was essentially established at this time, leaving Iraq a contested and repeatedly ravaged frontier province. As for the Ottomans' western frontier, the rulers of the major port cities of Algeria and Tunisia, some of them Greek or Italian converts to Islam, voluntarily joined the empire in the early sixteenth century, thereby greatly strengthening its naval forces.

While Ottoman armies pressed deeper and deeper into eastern Europe, the sultans also fought to become the dominant power in the Mediterranean. Between 1453 and 1502, the Ottomans fought the opening engagements of a two-century war with Venice, the most powerful of Italy's commercial city-states. From the Fourth Crusade of 1204 onward, Venice had assembled a profitable maritime empire that included major islands such as Crete and Cyprus along with strategic coastal strongpoints in Greece. Venice thereby became more than just a trading nation. Its island sugar plantations, making use of cheap slave labor, competed favorably with the Egyptian sugar industry in the international trade of the fifteenth century. With their rivals, the Genoese, trading by way of the strategic island of Chios, the Venetians stifled Ottoman maritime activities in the Aegean Sea.

The first round of fighting left Venice in control of its lucrative islands for another century.

But the fighting also left Venice a reduced military power compelled to pay tribute to the Ottomans in return for trading rights. The Ottomans, like the Chinese, were willing to let other nations carry trade to and from their ports—they preferred trade of this sort—as long as those other nations acknowledged Ottoman authority. It never occurred to them that a sea empire held together by flimsy ships could truly rival a great land empire capable of fielding an army of a hundred thousand fighting men.

On their southern frontier, the Ottomans inherited the Mamluks' involvement with the Muslims of the Red Sea and Indian Ocean region, who were accustomed to trading by way of Egypt and Syria. In the early sixteenth century, Muslim merchants from southern India and Sumatra sent emissaries to Istanbul to request naval support against the Portuguese. The Ottomans were vigorous in responding to Portuguese threats close to their territories, such as at Aden at the southern entrance to the Red Sea, but their efforts farther afield were insufficient to derail the growing Portuguese domination.

Eastern luxury products were still flowing abundantly to Ottoman markets. And Portuguese power was territorially limited to a few fortified coastal points, such as Hormuz at the entrance to the Persian Gulf, Goa in western India, and Malacca in Malaya (see Chapter 17). Why commit major resources to subduing an enemy whose main threat was a demand that merchant vessels, mostly belonging to non-Ottoman Muslims, buy protection from Portuguese attack? The Ottomans did send a naval force all the way to Indonesia, but they never formulated a consistent or aggressive policy with regard to political and economic developments on their southern maritime frontier.

Central Institutions

Like other Turkish principalities inheriting the military traditions of Central Asia, the Ottoman army originally consisted of lightly armored mounted warriors who were adept at shooting a short bow that was greatly strengthened by compressed layers of bone, wood, and leather. The conquest of Christian territories in the Balkans in the late fourteenth century, however, gave the Ottomans access to a unique military resource: Christian prisoners of war forced to serve as military slaves.

The use of slaves as soldiers had a long history in Islamic lands, and the contemporary Mamluk Sultanate in Egypt and Syria was built on that practice. The Mamluks, however, acquired their new blood from slave markets in Central Asia. Enslaving Christian prisoners of war, an action of questionable legality in Islamic law, was an Ottoman innovation. Induced to convert to Islam, these "new troops," called in Turkish *yeni cheri*, and in English "Janissary," gave the Ottomans unusual military flexibility. Being Christian by upbringing, the Janissaries had no misgivings about fighting against Turks and Muslims when the sultans wished to expand their territories in Anatolia. Moreover, since horseback riding and bowmanship were not engrained elements of their cultural backgrounds, they readily accepted the idea of fighting on foot and learning to use guns, which at that time were still too heavy and awkward for a horseman to load and fire.

The Janissaries lived in barracks and trained all year round. Up to the middle of the sixteenth century, they were barred both from holding jobs and from marrying. They adhered to the Bektashi Sufi brotherhood, named after the semilegendary fourteenth-century figure Hajji Bektash. The Bektashis, who maintained a chaplain in every Janissary unit, believed in an eclectic form of Islam that had a number of traits of seemingly Christian origin, such as a ritual meal of bread and wine. This connection may have encouraged the attachment of Janissaries who remembered their Christian upbringing prior to being selected for Janissary training.

The process of selection had changed early in the fifteenth century. Recruitment from Christian prisoners of war was unreliable and raised questions of allegiance. A new system was devised called the *devshirme* (literally "selection"), a regular levy of male children imposed on Christian villages in the Balkans and occasionally elsewhere. Devshirme children first were placed with Turkish families to learn their language and then were sent to the sultan's palace in Istanbul for an education that included instruction in

Islam, military training, and, for the most talented, what we might call liberal arts. This training regime, remarkably sophisticated for its time, produced not only the Janissary soldiery but also, for the chosen few who went on to special training in the inner service of the palace, senior military commanders and heads of government departments up to the rank of grand vizier.

Thus the Ottoman Empire was cosmopolitan in character. The sophisticated court language, Osmanli (the Turkish form of "Ottoman"), shared basic grammar and vocabulary with the Turkish spoken by Anatolia's nomads and villagers, but the addition of Arabic and Persian ingredients made it as distinct from that language as the Latin of educated Europeans was from the various Latin-derived Romance languages. Everyone who served in the military or the bureaucracy and conversed in Osmanli was considered to belong to the *askeri*, or "military," class. Members of this class were exempt from taxes and owed their entire well-being to the sultan. The mass of the population, whether Muslims, Christians, or Jews—the latter of whom flooded into Ottoman territory after their expulsion from Spain in 1492 (see Chapter 17)—constituted the *raya*, literally "flock of sheep."

By 1520, the beginning of the reign of Sultan Suleiman, known to Europeans as "the Magnificent" and to his subjects as "the Lawgiver," the Ottoman Empire was clearly the most powerful and best-organized state in either Europe or the Islamic world. Its military was balanced between mounted archers and Janissaries trained in the most advanced weaponry. The former were primarily Turks and were supported by grants of land in return for their military service. The latter were Turkified Albanians, Serbs, and Macedonians and were paid from the central treasury. The galley-equipped navy was manned by Greek, Turkish, Algerian, and Tunisian sailors, usually under the command of an admiral from one of the North African ports.

The balance of the Ottoman land forces brought success to Ottoman arms in recurrent wars with the Safavids, who were much slower to adopt firearms, and in the inexorable conquest of the Balkans. Ottoman forces reached the gates of Vienna in unsuccessful sieges in 1529 and 1683. Expansion by sea was less dramatic.

Sultan Ahmet mosque in Istanbul   Located opposite the old Byzantine hippodrome (chariot race track) and near the sultan's palace and the Aya Sofya Mosque—the old Byzantine Hagia Sophia cathedral—the Mosque of Sultan Ahmet I (r. 1603-1617) is also called the Blue Mosque because of the tile work inside. The Bosporus strait is in the background. (JHC Wilson/Robert Harding Picture Library)

Rhodes (1523), Cyprus (1571), and Crete (1669) fell to the Ottomans, but a major expedition against Malta that would have given them a foothold in the western Mediterranean failed in 1565. Combined Christian forces also achieved a massive naval victory at the Battle of Lepanto, off Greece, in 1571. But Ottoman resources were so extensive that in a year's time they had replaced all of the galleys sunk in that battle.

The government mustered its resources in different ways. Under the land-grant system, resident cavalrymen administered most rural areas in Anatolia and the Balkans. They dispensed justice, collected taxes, and reported for each summer's campaign with their horses, retainers, and

Top Kapi palace   The Ottoman sultans' palace, on the site of an earlier Byzantine palace, was both governing center and royal residence. The outer courtyard, shown here, was used for occasions of state. Note different headdresses indicating rank or military unit. The palace is now a museum. (Topkapi Saray Museum)

normally succeed his father, the grant holders did have an interest in productivity.

According to the Ottoman conception of the world, the sultan provided justice for his "flock of sheep" *(raya)*, and the military protected them; in return, the raya paid the taxes that supported both sultan and soldiery. In reality, the sultan's government, like most large territorial governments in premodern times, remained comparatively isolated from the lives of most of his subjects. Most Arab, Turkish, and Balkan townsfolk depended on local notables and religious leaders to represent them before the Ottoman provincial governor and his staff. Islam was the ruling religion and gradually became the majority religion in Balkan regions like Albania and Bosnia that had large numbers of converts. Thus the law of Islam (the Shari'a), as interpreted by local *ulama* (religious scholars), overshadowed urban institutions and social life. But local customs prevailed among non-Muslims and in many rural areas; and non-Muslims looked to their own religious leaders for guidance in family and spiritual matters.

Crisis of the Military State

As military technology evolved, cannon and lighter-weight firearms played an ever-larger role on the battlefield, both for the Ottomans and for their European opponents: Venice, Hungary, Russia, and the Holy Roman Empire (this was less true in conflicts with Iran, which only slowly adopted gunpowder). Accordingly, the size of the Janissary corps grew steadily and with it increased the cost of government. By contrast, the role of the Turkish cavalry, which continued to disdain firearms even as they became lighter and easier to use, diminished.

To fill state coffers and pay the Janissaries, in the mid-sixteenth century the sultan started reducing the number of landholding cavalrymen. The revenues they previously had spent for their own living expenses and military equipment now went directly to the imperial treasury. Offsetting these new imperial revenues, however, was the expense of providing tax collectors and local administrators to take over the functions of the deposed landholders. As for the displaced

supplies, all paid for from the taxes they collected. When not campaigning, they stayed at home. Some historians maintain that these cavalrymen, who did not own their land, had little interest in encouraging production or introducing new technologies, but since a militarily able son could

cavalrymen themselves, they constituted an armed and unhappy group concentrated in rural Anatolia.

At about the same time, in the late sixteenth century, a flood of cheap silver from the New World engulfed the economies of the Islamic world. Substantial inflation had already occurred in Europe (see Chapter 18), as the uncontrolled minting of silver coins gave rise to a superabundance of money available to pay for a less rapidly expanding supply of goods and services. With few silver sources of its own, the Ottoman mint could not match European production of coins. A bolt of cloth priced at three pieces of silver might be expensive by Ottoman standards, representing, perhaps, a month's pay. By European standards, however, three pieces of silver was comparatively cheap. This difference in value led to European merchants sending whole boatloads of coin to Ottoman port cities and bidding up the price of commodities and manufactured goods. Reacting to the weakness of its currency, the Ottoman government increased the minting of coins and lowered their silver content. This measure simply worsened the inflation by throwing yet more currency on the market without increasing the supply of goods, which flowed relentlessly westward to Europe.

As in most periods of inflation, people who depended on fixed sums of money suffered. Many of the remaining landholders—restricted by law to collecting a fixed amount of taxes—saw their purchasing power decline so much that they were unable to report for military service. Because this delinquency played into the hands of the sultan's government, which wanted to reduce the cavalry and increase the Janissary corps, no reforms were made to allow landholders to keep their land grants. The land returned to the state, and the cavalrymen joined the ranks of dispossessed troopers. Students and professors in religious colleges (*madrasas*) similarly found it impossible to live on fixed stipends from the madrasa endowments.

Constrained by religious law from fundamentally changing the tax system, the government levied emergency surtaxes to collect enough funds to pay the Janissaries and bureaucrats. For additional military strength, particularly in the

wars with Iran, the government reinforced the Janissary ranks with partially trained, salaried soldiers hired for the duration of a campaign. Once the summer campaign season was over, however, these soldiers found themselves out of work and short on cash.

This complicated situation resulted in massive revolts that devastated Anatolia between 1596 and 1658. Former landholding cavalrymen, temporary soldiers released at the end of the campaign season, peasants overburdened by emergency taxes, and even impoverished students of religion formed bands of marauders. Anatolia experienced the worst of the rebellions and suffered greatly from emigration and the loss of agricultural production. But an increase in banditry, made worse by the government's inability to stem the spread of muskets among the general public, beset other parts of the empire as well.

In the meantime, the Janissaries used their growing influence to gain relief from the prohibitions on their marrying and engaging in business. Janissaries who involved themselves in commerce lessened the burden on the state budget, and married Janissaries who enrolled sons or relatives in the corps made it possible in the seventeenth century for the government to save state funds by abolishing the devshirme system with its traveling selection officers. These savings, however, were more than offset by the increase in the total number of Janissaries and in their steady deterioration as a military force, which entailed hiring more and more supplemental troops.

Economic Change and Growing Weakness

A very different Ottoman Empire emerged from this period of crisis. The sultans once had led armies. Now they were likely to reside in their palace and have little experience of the real world. This manner of living was the product of the gradually developed policy of keeping the sultan's male relatives confined to the palace to prevent them from plotting coups or meddling in politics. The sultan's mother and the chief eunuch overseeing the private quarters of the palace thus became important arbiters of royal favor, and even of succession to the sultanate, and the affairs of government were overseen more and more by the chief administrators, the grand viziers. (Ottoman historians draw special attention to the negative influence of women in the palace after the time of Suleiman, but to some degree they are reflecting traditional male, and Muslim, fears about women in politics.)

The devshirme had been discontinued, and the Janissaries had taken advantage of their increased power and privileges to make membership in their corps hereditary. Together with several other newly prominent infantry regiments, they added to their roles in the army extensive involvement in crafts and trading, both in Istanbul and in provincial capitals like Cairo, Aleppo, and Baghdad. This took a toll on their military skills, but they continued to be a powerful faction in urban politics that the sultans could neither ignore nor reform. Moreover, since the Janissaries and members of the special regiments were responsible solely to their own officers, workshops under their control were free to ignore the rules established by the craft guilds. Since the guilds were quite conservative and preferred constant and equitable distribution of work for all members to economic growth or innovation, this military involvement in commerce disturbed the pattern of economic life.

Land grants in return for military service also disappeared. Tax farmers arose in their place. They paid specific taxes, such as customs duties, in advance in return for the privilege of collecting a greater amount from the actual taxpayers. Between 1604 and 1607, for example, two Jews named David the son of Abraham and Abraham the son of David advanced the government 18 million akches (small silver coins) for the customs duties of Izmir, collecting a total of 19,169,203 akches, a profit of 6.5 percent.

Rural administration, already disrupted by the rebellions, suffered from the transition to tax farms. The former landholders had been military men who readily kept order on their lands in order to maintain their incomes. Tax farmers were less likely to live on the land, and their tax collection rights could vary from year to year. The imperial government, therefore, faced greater administrative burdens and came to rely heavily on powerful provincial governors or on wealthy men who purchased lifelong tax collection rights that prompted them to behave more or less like private landowners.

Rural disorder and decline in administrative control opened the way, in some cases, for new economic opportunities. The Aegean port of Izmir, known to Europeans by the ancient name "Smyrna," had a population of around 2,000 in 1580. By 1650 the population had increased almost twentyfold to between 30,000 and 40,000. Along with refugees from the uprisings and from European pirate attacks along the coast came European merchants and large colonies of Armenians, Greeks, and Jews. A French traveler in 1621 wrote: "At present, Izmir has a great traffic in wool, beeswax, cotton, and silk, which the Armenians bring there instead of going to Aleppo . . . because they do not pay as many dues."[1]

Izmir's transformation between 1580 and 1650 from a small Muslim Turkish town to a multiethnic, multireligious, multilinguistic entrepôt was affected by the Ottoman government's inability to control trade—and by the slowly growing dominance of European traders in the Indian Ocean. Spices from the East, though still traded in Aleppo and other long-established centers, were not to be found in Izmir. Aside from Iranian silk brought in by caravan, European traders purchased local agricultural products—dried fruits, sesame seeds, nuts, and olive oil. As a consequence, farmers who had previously grown grain for subsistence shifted their plantings more and more to cotton and other cash crops, including, after its introduction in the 1590s, tobacco, which quickly became very popular in the Ottoman Empire despite government prohibitions. In this way the agricultural economy of western Anatolia, the Balkans, and the Mediterranean coast—the Ottoman lands most accessible to Europe—became enmeshed in the seventeenth century in a growing European commercial network.

At the same time, Ottoman military power slowly ebbed. The ill-trained Janissaries sometimes resorted to hiring substitutes to go on campaign, and the sultans relied on partially trained seasonal recruits and on armies raised by the governors of frontier provinces. By the middle of the eighteenth century, it was obvious to the Ottomans' Austrian and Russian opponents that the empire was in decline. On the eastern front, however, Ottoman exhaustion after many wars was matched by the demise in 1722 of their perennial adversary, the Safavid state of Iran.

The Ottoman Empire lacked both the wealth and the inclination to match European economic advances. Overland trade from the east dwindled as political disorder cut deeply into Iranian silk production. Coffee, an Arabian product that rose from obscurity in the fifteenth century to become the rage first in the Ottoman empire and then in Europe, was grown in the highlands of Yemen and exported by way of Egypt. By 1770, however, Muslim merchants trading in the Yemeni port of Mocha (literally "the coffee place") were charged 15 percent in duties and fees, while English traders, benefiting, like certain other European powers, from trade agreements with the Ottoman Empire going back to the mid-fifteenth century—the time of Mehmed the Conqueror—paid little more than 3 percent.

Such trade agreements led to European domination of Ottoman import and export trade by sea. Nevertheless, the Europeans did not control strategic ports in the Mediterranean comparable to Malacca in the Indian Ocean and Hormuz on the Persian Gulf, so their economic power stopped short of colonial settlement and direct political administration in Ottoman territories.

A few astute Ottoman statesmen observed the growing disarray of the empire and advised the sultans to reestablish the land-grant and devshirme system of Suleiman's reign. They failed to understand that the disarray had begun with technological changes in the conduct of war—changes necessitating reliance on a standing army outfitted with firearms. This could not be ignored; and despite its enormous territory, the Ottoman government did not find an effective way to muster the military resources it needed.

To most people, the downward course of imperial power was far from evident, much less the reasons behind it. Ottoman historians named the period between 1718 and 1730 "the Tulip Period" because of the craze for high-priced tulip bulbs that swept Ottoman ruling circles. The craze replicated a Dutch tulip mania that had begun in the mid-sixteenth century, when the flower was introduced into Holland from Istanbul, and peaked in 1636 with particularly rare bulbs going

for 2,500 florins apiece—the value of twenty-two oxen. Far from seeing Europe as the enemy that eventually would dismantle the weakening Ottoman Empire, the Istanbul elite experimented with European clothing and furniture styles and purchased printed books from the empire's first (and short-lived) press.

In 1730, however, the gala soirees, at which guests watched turtles with candles on their backs wander in the dark through massive tulip beds, gave way to a conservative Janissary revolt with strong religious overtones. Sultan Ahmed III abdicated, and the leader of the revolt, Patrona Halil, an Albanian former seaman and stoker of the public baths, swaggered around the capital for several months dictating government policies before being seized and executed.

The Patrona Halil rebellion confirmed the perceptions of a few that the Ottoman Empire was facing severe difficulties. But decay at the center spelled benefit elsewhere. In the provinces, ambitious and competent governors, wealthy landholders, urban notables, and nomad chieftains were well placed to take advantage of the central government's weakness. By the middle of the eighteenth century, groups of Mamluks had regained a dominant position in Egypt, Janissary commanders had become virtually independent rulers in Baghdad, and Muhammad ibn Abd al-Wahhab's conservative Sunni movement had begun its remarkable rise beyond the reach of Ottoman power in central Arabia. Although no region declared full independence, the sultan's power was slipping away to the advantage of a broad array of lower officials and upstart chieftains in all parts of the empire, and the Ottoman economy was reorienting itself toward Europe.

THE SAFAVID EMPIRE

The Safavid state of Iran, the Ottomans' longtime foe, had many of the characteristics of a large, land-based empire: It initially relied militarily on cavalry paid through land grants, its population spoke several different languages, and it was oriented inward away from the sea. It

Textile Production

Different regions specialized in different textiles. Safavid Iran exported silk and knotted carpets. Mughal India was noted for its cottons (calico is named for Calicut, an Indian port on the Bay of Bengal). And the Malay world of Southeast Asia pro-duced cotton prints called *batik*. The technology of textile production varied greatly, but everywhere much of the labor was performed by women. To make a rug, an Iranian girl, left, knots colored yarn around a vertically strong warp. To make cotton cloth for Batik printing, right, an Indonesian woman works on a loom.

Textile production in Iran (left) and Southeast Asia (right)   (Photo Researchers, Inc. (l.) and Mattiebelle Gittinger, The Textile Museum, Washington D. C. (r.))

also had distinct qualities that to this day continue to set Iran off from its neighbors: It derived part of its legitimacy from the pre-Islamic dynasties of ancient Iran, and it adopted the Shi'ite form of Islam. Although Timur had been a great conqueror, his children and grandchildren contented themselves with modest realms in Afghanistan and Central Asia, while a number of would-be rulers vied for control elsewhere. In Iran itself, the ultimate victor in a complicated struggle for power among Turkish chieftains was Ismail, a boy of Kurdish, Iranian, and Greek ancestry, the hereditary leader of a militant Sufi brotherhood named "Safaviya" for his ancestor Safi al-Din. In 1502, at the age of sixteen, Ismail proclaimed himself shah of Iran. At around the

same time, he declared that from that time forward his realm would be devoted to Shi'ite Islam, and he called on all of his subjects to abandon their Sunni beliefs.

Most of the members of the Safavi brotherhood were Turkish-speakers from nomadic groups known as *qizilbash*, or "redheads," because of their distinctive turbans. They believed that Ismail was virtually a god incarnate and fought ferociously on his behalf. If Ismail wished his state to be Shi'ite, his word was law to the qizilbash. The Iranian subject population, however, was not so easily persuaded. Neighboring lands received Sunni refugees from Safavid rule. Their preaching and intriguing helped stoke the fires that kept Ismail (d. 1524) and his son Tahmasp (d. 1576) engaged in war after war. Almost a century passed and a series of brutal persecutions occurred before Iran became an overwhelmingly Shi'ite land. The transformation also required the importation of Arab Shi'ite scholars from Lebanon and Bahrain to institute a high level of Shi'ite religious education.

Although Ismail's reasons for compelling Iran's conversion to Shi'ism are unknown, the effect of this radical act was to create a deep chasm between Iran and its eastern and western neighbors, all of which were Sunni. Iran became a truly separate country for the first time since its incorporation into the Islamic empire in the seventh century.

Society and Religion

Although the imposition of Shi'ite belief made permanent the split between Iran and its neighbors, differences between them had long been in the making. Persian, written in the Arabic script from the tenth century onward, had emerged as the second language of Islam. By 1500, an immense library of legal and theological writings; epic, lyric, and mystic poetry; histories; and drama and fiction had come into being. Iranian scholars and writers normally read Arabic as well as Persian and amply sprinkled their writings with Arabic phrases, but their Arab counterparts were much less inclined to learn Persian. This divergence between the two language areas had intensified after the Mongols destroyed Baghdad, the capital of the Islamic caliphate, in 1258 and diminished the importance of Arabic-speaking Iraq. Syria and Egypt had become the heartland of the Arab world while Iran developed largely on its own, having more extensive contacts with India—where Muslim rulers favored the Persian language—than with the Arabs.

In the heyday of the Islamic caliphate in the seventh through ninth centuries, cultural styles had radiated in all directions from Baghdad. In the post-Mongol period—a time of immense artistic creativity and innovation in Iran, Afghanistan, and Central Asia—styles in the East went their own way. Painted and molded tiles and tile mosaics, often in vivid turquoise blue, became the standard exterior decoration of mosques in Iran but never were used in Syria and Egypt. Persian poets like Saadi (d. 1291) and Hafiz (d. 1389) raised morally instructive and mystical-allegorical verse to peaks of perfection that had no reflection in Arabic poetry, generally considered to be in a state of decline.

The Turks, who steadily came to dominate the political scene from Bengal to Algeria, generally preferred Persian as a vehicle for literary or religious expression. The Mamluks in Egypt and Syria showed greatest respect for Arabic. The Turkish language, which had a vigorous tradition of folk poetry, developed only slowly, primarily in the Ottoman Empire, as a language of literature and administration. Ironically, Ismail Safavi was a noted religious poet in the Turkish language of his qizilbash followers, and his mortal adversary, the Ottoman Selim II, was known for the elegance of his Persian poetry.

To be sure, Islam provided a shared tradition across ethnic and linguistic borders. Mosque architecture differed, but Iranians, Arabs, and Turks, as well as Muslims in India, all had mosques. They also had madrasas that trained the ulama to sustain and interpret the Shari'a as the all-encompassing law of Islam. Yet they differed substantially in local understandings of their common tradition.

Notable Sufi orders included the Bektashi and Mevlevi in Ottoman Anatolia, the Chishti and Naqshbandi in India, and the Qadiri and Suhrawardi in the central Arab lands. All had distinctive rituals and concepts of mystical union with God. These orders also were present in pre-Safavid Iran, but Iran stood out as the land where Sufism most often fused with militant political objectives. The Safavi order was not the first to deploy armies and use the point of a sword to promote love of God. The Safavid shahs were unique, however, in eventually banning, somewhat ineffectively, all Sufi orders from their domain.

Even prior to Shah Ismail's imposition of Shi'ism, therefore, Iran had become a distinctive society. Nevertheless, the impact of Shi'ism was significant. Shi'ite doctrine dictated that all temporal rulers, regardless of title, were only temporary stand-ins for the "Hidden Imam." The "Hidden Imam" was the twelfth descendant of Ali, the prophet Muhammad's cousin and son-in-law. Shi'ites believe that leadership of the Muslim community belongs solely to divinely appointed Imams from Ali's family, but the twelfth Imam disappeared as a child in the ninth century. Until he returns, the Shi'ite community lacks a proper religious authority. Some Shi'ite scholars concluded that the faithful should calmly accept the world as it was and wait quietly for the Imam's return. Others maintained that they themselves should play a stronger role in political affairs because they were best qualified to know the wishes of the Hidden Imam. These two positions, which still play a role in Iranian Shi'sm, tended to enhance the self-image of the ulama as independent of imperial authority and stood in

the way of ulama members becoming government functionaries, as happened with many Ottoman ulama.

Shi'ism also affected the psychological life of the people. Commemoration of the martyrdom of Imam Husain (d. 680), Ali's son who was the third Imam, during the first two weeks of every lunar year regularized an emotional outpouring that had no parallel in Sunni lands. Day after day (as they do today) preachers recited the woeful tale to crowds of weeping believers, and elaborate street processions, often organized by the guilds, paraded chanting and self-flagellating men past crowds of reverent onlookers. Passion plays in which Husain and his family are mercilessly killed by the agents of the Umayyad caliph Yazid became a unique form of Iranian public theater.

Of course, Shi'ites elsewhere observed some of the same rites of mourning for Imam Husain, particularly in the Shi'ite pilgrimage cities of Karbala and Najaf in Ottoman Iraq. But the impact of these rites on society as a whole was far greater in Iran, where 90 percent of the population was Shi'ite. Over time, the subjects of the Safavid shahs came to feel more than ever a people apart, despite the fact that many of them had been Shi'ite for only two or three generations.

A Tale of Two Cities: Istanbul and Isfahan

Outwardly, Istanbul and Isfahan, which became Iran's capital in 1598 by decree of Shah Abbas I (r. 1587–1628), looked quite different. Built on seven hills on the south side of the narrow Golden Horn inlet, Istanbul's skyline was punctuated by the gray stone domes and thin, pointed minarets of the great imperial mosques. Their design, brought to perfection by the architect Sinan (d. ca. 1578) in some eighty mosque designs, was inspired by Hagia Sophia, the Byzantine cathedral converted to a mosque and renamed Aya Sofya after 1453. The mosques surrounding the royal plaza in Isfahan, in contrast, had unobtrusive minarets and brightly tiled domes that rose to gentle peaks. The sultan's palace in Istanbul was surrounded by high walls. Shah Abbas fo-

The Masjid-i Shah (Royal Mosque) in Isfahan   The dome is covered with glazed tile mosaic—a floral arabesque pattern above two tiers of religious calligraphy. Domes were used in both grand and humble Iranian buildings. The minarets contrast strikingly with the lofty spires of Ottoman mosques (see photo on p. 603). (Robert Harding Picture Library)

cused his capital on the giant royal plaza, which was large enough for his army to play polo, and he used a palace overlooking the plaza to receive dignitaries and review his troops. This public imagery contributed to Shah Abbas's being "the Great."

As the primary Ottoman seaport, Istanbul's harbor teemed with sailing ships and smaller craft, many of them belonging to a colony of European merchants perched on a hilltop on the north side of the Golden Horn. Isfahan, far from the sea, was only occasionally visited by Europeans. Its trade was largely in the hands of Jews, Hindus, and especially a colony of Armenian Christians brought in by Shah Abbas.

Beneath these superficial differences, the two capitals had much in common. Wheeled vehicles were scarce in hilly Istanbul and nonexistent in Isfahan, which was within the broad zone where camels supplanted wheeled transport after the rise of the Arab caravan cities in the pre-Islamic centuries. In size and layout both cities were built for walking and lacked, aside from the royal plaza in Isfahan, the open spaces characteristic of contemporary European cities. Away from the major mosque complexes, streets were narrow and irregular. Houses crowded against each other in dead-end lanes. Open areas were interior courtyards where residents could enjoy their privacy. Artisans and merchants organized themselves into guilds that had strong social and religious as well as economic bonds. The shops of each guild adjoined each other in the markets.

Women were seldom seen in public, even in Istanbul's mazelike covered market or in Isfahan's long, serpentine bazaar. At home, the women's quarters—called *anderun,* or "interior," in Iran and *harem,* or "forbidden area," in Istanbul—were separate from the public rooms where the men of the family received visitors. In both areas, low cushions, braziers for warmth, carpets, and small tables constituted most of the furnishings. In Iran and the Arab provinces, shelves and niches for books could be cut into the thick, mud-brick walls. Residences in Istanbul were usually built of wood. Glazed tile in geometric or floral patterns covered the walls of wealthy men's reception areas.

The private side of family life has left few traces, but it is apparent that women's society—

consisting of wives, children, female servants, and possibly one or more eunuchs—was not entirely cut off from the outside world. Ottoman court records reveal that women, using male agents, were very active in the urban real estate market. Often they were selling inherited shares of their father's estate, but some both bought and sold real estate on a regular basis and even established religious endowments for pious purposes. The fact that Islamic law, unlike some European codes, permitted a wife to retain her property after marriage gave some women a stake in the general economy and a degree of independence from their spouses. Women also appeared in other types of court cases, where they often testified for themselves, for Islamic courts did not recognize the role of attorney. Although comparable Safavid court records do not survive, historians assume that a parallel situation prevailed in Iran.

European travelers commented on the veiling of women outside the home, but miniature paintings indicate that ordinary female garb consisted of a long, ample dress with a scarf or long shawl pulled tight over the forehead to conceal

Istanbul family on its way to the bath house   Public baths, an important feature of Islamic cities, set different hours for men and women. Young boys, such as the lad in the turban shown here, went with their mothers and sisters. Note how the children wear the same costumes as adults. (Osterreichische Nationalbibliothek)

the hair. Lightweight trousers, either close-fitting or baggy, were often worn under the dress. This mode of dress was not far different from that of men. Poor men wore light trousers, a long shirt, a jacket, and a hat or turban. Wealthier men wore over their trousers ankle-length caftans, often closely fitted around the chest. The norm for both sexes was complete coverage of arms, legs, and hair.

Public life was almost entirely the domain of men. Poetry and art, both somewhat more elegantly developed in Isfahan than in Istanbul, were as likely to extol the charms of beardless boys as pretty women. Despite religious disapproval of homosexuality, attachments to adolescent boys were neither unusual nor hidden. Women who appeared in public—aside from non-Muslims, the aged, and the very poor—were likely to be slaves. Miniature paintings frequently depict female dancers, musicians, and even acrobats in attitudes and costumes that range from decorous to decidedly erotic.

Despite social similarities, the overall flavors of Isfahan and Istanbul were not the same. Isfahan had a prosperous Armenian quarter across the river from the city's center, but it was not a truly cosmopolitan capital, just as the peoples of the Safavid realm were not remarkably diverse. Like other rulers of extensive land empires, Shah Abbas located his capital toward the center of his domain within comparatively easy reach of any threatened frontier. Istanbul, in contrast, was a great seaport and crossroads located on the straits separating the sultan's European and Asian possessions. People of all sorts lived or spent time in Istanbul—Venetians, Genoese, Arabs, Turks, Greeks, Armenians, Albanians, Serbs, Jews, Bulgarians, Circassians, and more. In this respect Istanbul conveyed the cosmopolitan character of other major seaports from London to Canton (Guangzhou) and belied the fact that its prosperity rested on the vast reach of the sultan's territories rather than on the voyages of its merchants.

Economic Crisis and Political Collapse

The silk of northern Iran, monopolized by the shahs, was the mainstay of the country's foreign trade. However, most of the shah's subjects, whether Iranians, Turks, Kurds, or Arabs, lived by subsistence farming or herding. Neither area of activity recorded significant technological advances during the Safavid period. Large sections of the country were granted to the qizilbash nomads in return for their furnishing mounted warriors for the army. These lands were held by the groups in common, however, and were not subdivided into individual landholdings as in the Ottoman Empire. Thus many people in rural areas lived according to the will of a nomad chieftain who had little interest in building the agricultural economy.

The crisis of finding the money to pay troops armed with firearms that struck the Ottomans also affected Iran, though somewhat later because of Iran's comparative distance from Europe. By the end of the sixteenth century, it was evident that a more systematic adoption of cannon and firearms in the Safavid Empire would be needed to hold off the Ottomans and the Uzbeks (Turkish rulers who had succeeded the Timurids on Iran's Central Asian frontier, see Map 21.1). Like the Ottoman cavalry a century earlier, however, the warriors furnished by the nomad leaders were not inclined to trade in their bows for firearms. Shah Abbas responded by establishing a slave corps of year-round soldiers and arming them with guns. These converts to Islam who initially provided the manpower for the new corps were mostly captives taken in raids on Georgia in the Caucasus. Some became powerful members of the court. They formed a counterweight to the nomad chiefs just as the Janissaries had earlier challenged the landholding Turkish cavalry in the Ottoman Empire. Under the strong hand of Shah Abbas, the inevitable rivalries and intrigues between the factions were kept under control. His successors were less fortunate.

In the late seventeenth century, the inflation caused by cheap silver spread into Iran, and overland trade through Safavid territory declined because of mismanagement of the silk monopoly after Shah Abbas's death. As a result, the country faced the unsolvable problem of finding money to pay the army and bureaucracy. Trying to unseat the nomads from their lands to regain control of taxes was more difficult and more disruptive militarily than the piecemeal dismantlement of the land-grant system in the Ottoman Empire. The nomads were a still cohesive military force, and pressure from the center simply caused them to withdraw to their mountain pastures until the pressure subsided. By 1722, the government had become so weak and commanded so little support from the nomadic groups that an army of marauding Afghans was able to capture Isfahan and effectively end Safavid rule.

Despite Iran's long coastline, the Safavids never possessed a navy. The Portuguese seized the strategic Persian Gulf island of Hormuz in 1517 and were expelled only in 1622, when the English ferried Iranian soldiers to the attack. Typical of land-oriented rulers, the shahs relied on the English and Dutch for naval support and never considered competing with them at sea. Nader Shah, a general who emerged from the confusion of the Safavids' fall to reunify Iran briefly between 1736 and 1747, purchased some naval vessels from the English and used them in the Persian Gulf. But his navy decayed after his death, and Iran did not again have a navy until the twentieth century.

New Year celebration at court of Shah Jahan (r. 1628–1658) The pre-Islamic Iranian tradition of celebrating New Year (Persian No Ruz, "New Day") on March 21, the vernal equinox, spread with Islamic rule. The dancing girls are a characteristically Indian aspect of the celebration. (The Royal Collection © Her Majesty Queen Elizabeth II)

THE MUGHAL EMPIRE

What distinguished the Indian empire of the Mughal sultans from the empires of the Ottomans and Safavids was the fact that India was preeminently a land of Hindus ruled by a Muslim minority. To be sure, the Ottoman provinces in the Balkans, except for Albania and Bosnia, remained mostly Christian, but the remainder of the Ottoman Empire was overwhelmingly Muslim with small Christian and Jewish minorities. The Ottoman sultans made much of their control of Mecca and Medina and resulting supervision of the annual pilgrimage caravans just as the Safavids fostered pilgrimages to a shrine in Mashhad in northeastern Iran for their overwhelmingly Shi'ite subjects.

India, in contrast, was far from the Islamic homelands. Muslim dominion in India was the result of repeated military campaigns from the early eleventh century onward, and the Mughals had to contend with the Hindus' long-standing resentment of the destruction of their culture by Muslims. Unlike the Balkan peoples, who had struggled to maintain their identities in relation to the Byzantines, the Crusaders, and one another before the arrival of the Turks, the peoples of the Indian subcontinent had used centuries of freedom from foreign intrusion to forge a distinctive Hindu civilization that could not easily accommodate the world-view of Islam. Thus the challenge facing the Mughals was not just conquering and organizing a large territorial state but also searching for a formula for Hindu-Muslim coexistence.

Political Foundations

The founder of the Mughal Empire, Babur (1483–1530), was a Muslim descendant of both Genghis Khan and Timur (*Mughal* is Persian for "Mongol"). Invading from Central Asia, he defeated the last Muslim sultan of Delhi at the Battle of Panipat in 1526. Babur's grandson Akbar (r. 1556–1605), a brilliant but mercurial man whose lifelong illiteracy betrayed his upbringing in the wilds of Afghanistan, established the central administration of the expanding state. Under him and his three successors—the last of whom, Aurangzeb, died in 1707—all but the southern tip of India fell under Mughal rule, administered first from Agra and then from Delhi.

Akbar granted land revenues to military officers and government officials in return for their service. Ranks, called *mansabs,* some high and some low, entitled holders of each rank to revenue assignments. As in the other Islamic empires, revenue grants were not considered hereditary, and the central government kept careful track of their issuance.

With a population of 100 million, a thriving trading economy based on cotton cloth, and a generally efficient administration, India under Akbar was probably the most prosperous empire of the sixteenth century. He and his successors faced few external threats and experienced generally peaceful conditions in their northern Indian heartland. Nevertheless, they were capable of squandering immense amounts of blood and treasure to subdue Hindu kings and rebels in the Deccan region or Afghans on their western frontier (see Map 21.1).

Foreign trade boomed at the port of Surat in the northwest, which also served as embarkation point for pilgrims to Mecca. Like the Safavids, the Mughals had no navy or merchant ships. The government saw the Europeans—now primarily Dutch and English, the Portuguese having lost most of their Indian ports—less as enemies than as shipmasters whose naval support could be procured as needed in return for trading privileges. It never questioned the wisdom of selling Indian cottons for European coin—no one understood how cheap silver had become in Europe—and shipping them off to European customers in English and Dutch vessels.

Hindus and Muslims

India had not been dominated by a single ruler since the time of Harsha (606–647). Though horrified by Muslims' destruction of Hindu cultural monuments, the expansion of Muslim territory, and the practice, until Akbar's time, of enslaving prisoners of war and compelling them to convert to Islam, Hindu efforts to oppose Muslim rule were piecemeal rather than concerted. The Mughal state, in contrast, inherited traditions of unified imperial rule both from the Islamic caliphate and the more recent examples of Genghis Khan and Timur. Those Mongol-based traditions, however, did not necessarily mean religious intolerance. Seventy percent of the *mansabdars* (officials holding land revenues) appointed under Akbar were Muslim soldiers born outside India, but 15 percent were Hindus. Most of the Hindu appointees were warriors from the north called Rajputs, one of whom rose to be a powerful revenue minister. Their status as mansabdars was a manifestation of the policy of religious accommodation adopted by Akbar and more or less maintained by his successors—until the reign of his militantly Muslim great-grandson Aurangzeb (r. 1658–1707).

Akbar (1542–1605), the most illustrious ruler of his dynasty, differed from his Ottoman and Safavid counterparts—Suleiman the Magnificent and Shah Abbas the Great—in his striving for social harmony and not just for more territory and revenue. Though he succeeded to the throne at the age of thirteen, his actions were dominated first by a regent and then by his strong-minded childhood nurse. At the age of twenty, he took command of the government; married a Rajput princess, whose name is not recorded; and welcomed her father and brother to the court in Agra. Other rulers might have used such a marriage as a means of humiliating a subject group. But Akbar signaled by this marriage his desire for reconciliation and even intermarriage between Muslims and Hindus. A year later he rescinded the *jizya*, the head tax that Muslim rulers traditionally levied on tolerated non-Muslims. This measure was more symbolic than real because the tax had not been regularly collected, but the gesture helped cement the allegiance of the Rajputs.

Akbar longed for an heir. Much to his relief, his Rajput wife gave birth to a son in 1569, ensuring that future rulers would have both Muslim and Hindu ancestry.

Akbar ruled that in legal disputes between two Hindus, decisions would be made according to village custom or Hindu law as interpreted by local Hindu scholars. Shari'a law was in force for Muslims. Akbar made himself the legal court of last resort in a 1579 declaration that he was God's infallible earthly representative. Thus appeals could be made to Akbar personally, a possibility not usually present in Islamic jurisprudence.

Akbar tried to make himself the center of a new "Divine Faith" incorporating Muslim, Hindu, Zoroastrian, Sikh, and Christian beliefs. He was strongly attracted by Sufi ideas, which permeated the religious rituals he instituted at his court. To promote serious consideration of his religious principles, he oversaw, from a catwalk high above the audience, debates among scholars of all religions assembled in his octagonal private audience chamber. When courtiers uttered the Muslim exclamation "Allahu Akbar"— "God is great"—they also understood it in its second grammatical meaning: "God is Akbar."

Akbar's religious views did not survive him, but the court culture he fostered, reflecting a mixture of Muslim and Hindu traditions, flourished until Aurangzeb reinstituted many restrictions on Hindus. Though inspired by Timurid and Safavid miniatures, Mughal and Rajput paintings reveled in precise portraits of political figures and depictions of scantily clad women, even though they brought frowns to the faces of pious Muslims, who deplored the representation of human beings in art. Most of the leading painters were Hindus. In poetry, in addition to the florid style of Persian verse favored at court, a new taste developed for poetry and prose in the popular language of the Delhi region. The Turkish word *ordu*, meaning "army," led to the modern descendant of this language being called *Urdu* in Pakistan (in India it is called *Hindi*).

Akbar's policy of toleration does not explain the pattern of conversion to Islam in Mughal India. Some scholars maintain that most converts came from members of the lowest Hindu social groups, or castes, who hoped to better their social lot, but there is little data to confirm this theory. Others argue that Sufi brotherhoods, which developed strongly in India, led the way in converting people to Islam, but this proposition has not been proved. The most heavily Muslim regions were in the valley of the Indus River and east Bengal. The Indus center dates from the establishment of Muslim rule there as early as the eighth century.

A careful study of local records and traditions from east Bengal indicates that the eastward movement of the delta of the Ganges River and the spread of rice cultivation into forest clearings played the primary role in conversions to Islam there. Mansabdars (mostly Muslims) with land grants in east Bengal contracted with local entrepreneurs to collect a labor force, cut down the forest, and establish rice paddies. Some of the entrepreneurs were Hindus, but most were non-Sufi Muslim religious figures. Like the Hindus, those Muslims used religion, represented by the construction of mosques and shrines, as a cement to maintain their farming communities. Since most natives of the region were accustomed to worshiping local forest deities rather than the main Hindu gods, the shift to Islam represented a move to a more sophisticated, literate culture appropriate to their new status as farmers producing for the commercial rice market. Gradual religious change of this kind, which has parallels in other parts of India, often produced Muslim communities that in social customs, such as the strict seclusion of women, differed little from neighboring Hindu communities. In east Bengal, common Muslim social institutions, such as madrasas, the ulama, and law courts, were little in evidence.

Another change in Indian religious life in the Mughal period was the appearance of the Sikh religion in the Punjab region of northwest India. Nanak (1469–1539), the movement's first *guru* (spiritual teacher), stressed meditation as a means of seeking enlightenment and drew upon both Muslim and Hindu imagery in his teachings. His followers formed a single community without differences of caste. However, after Aurangzeb ordered the ninth guru beheaded in 1675 for refusing to convert to Islam, the tenth and final guru dedicated himself to avenging his father's death and reorganized his followers into "the army of the pure," a religious order dedicated to defending Sikh beliefs. These devotees signaled their faith by leaving their hair uncut; carrying a comb, a steel bracelet, and a sword or dagger; and wearing military-style breeches. By the eighteenth century, the Mughals were encountering fierce opposition from the Sikhs as well as from Hindu guerrilla forces in the rugged and ravine-scarred province of Maharashtra on India's west coast.

Central Decay and Regional Challenges

Mughal power did not long survive Aurangzeb's death in 1707. Some historians consider the land-grant system a central element in the rapid decline of imperial authority, but other factors were at play as well. Aurangzeb's additions to Mughal territory in southern India were not all well integrated into the imperial structure, and a number of strong regional powers arose to challenge Mughal military supremacy. The Marathas proved a formidable enemy as they carved out a swath of territory across India's middle, and Sikhs, Hindu Rajputs, and Muslim Afghans exerted intense pressure from the northwest. A climax came in 1739 when Nader Shah, the warlord who had seized power in Iran after the fall of the Safavids, invaded the subcontinent and sacked Delhi, which Akbar's grandson Shah Jahan had rebuilt and beautified as the Mughal capital some decades before. The "peacock throne," the priceless, jewel-encrusted symbol of Mughal grandeur, was carried off to Iran as part of the booty. Another throne was found for the later Mughals to sit on; but the empire, which survived in name to 1857, was finished.

In 1723, Nizam al-Mulk, the powerful vizier of the Mughal sultan, gave up on the central government and established his own virtually independent state at Hyderabad in the eastern Deccan. Other officials bearing the title *nawab*, Anglicized as "nabob," became similarly independent in Bengal and Oudh in the northeast, as did the Marathas. In the northwest, simultaneous Iranian and Mughal weakness allowed the Afghans to establish an independent kingdom as well.

Some of these regional powers, and the smaller princely states that arose on former Mughal territory, were prosperous and benefited from the removal of the sultan's heavy hand. Linguistic and religious communities, freed from the religious intolerance instituted during the reign of Aurangzeb, similarly enjoyed greater opportunity for political expression. However, this disintegration of central power favored the intrusion of European powers.

Joseph François Dupleix took over the presidency of the French stronghold of Pondicherry in 1741 and began a new phase of European involvement in India. He captured the English trading center of Madras and used his small contingent of European and European-trained Indian troops to become a power broker in southern India. Though offered the title *nawab*, Dupleix preferred to operate behind the scenes, using Indian princes as puppets. His career ended in 1754 when he was called home. Deeply involved in wars in Europe, the French government was unwilling to pursue further adventures in India. Dupleix's departure opened the way for the British, whose ventures in India are described in Chapter 26.

TRADE EMPIRES IN THE INDIAN OCEAN

I t is no coincidence that the Mughal, Safavid, and Ottoman Empires declined simultaneously in the seventeenth and eighteenth centuries. Complex changes in military technology and in the world economy, along with the increasing difficulty of basing an extensive land empire on military forces paid through land grants, affected them all adversely. The opposite was true for seafaring countries intent on turning trade networks into maritime empires. Improvements in ship design, navigation accuracy, and the use of cannon gave an ever-increasing edge to European powers competing with local seafaring peoples. Moreover, the development of joint-stock companies in which many merchants pooled their capital provided a flexible and efficient financial instrument for exploiting new possibilities.

Neither the Ottomans, nor the Safavids, nor the Mughals seriously contested the growth of Portuguese and then Dutch, English, and French maritime power. Yet the majority of non-European shipbuilders, captains, sailors, and traders were Muslim. There were also active groups of Armenian, Jewish, and Hindu traders, but they remained almost as aloof from the Europeans as the Muslims did. The presence in every port of fellow Muslims following the same legal traditions and practicing their faith in similar ways cemented the Muslims' trading network. Islam, from its very outset in the life and preachings of Muhammad (570–632), had been congenial toward trade and traders. Unlike Hinduism, it was a proselytizing religion, a factor that encouraged the growth of coastal Muslim communities as local non-Muslims were drawn into Muslim commercial activities, converted, and intermarried with Muslims from abroad.

Although European missionaries, particularly the Jesuits, tried to extend Christianity into Asia and Africa (see Chapters 17 and 22), most Europeans, the Portuguese excepted, were less inclined than the Muslims to treat local converts or the offspring of mixed marriages as full members of their communities. As a consequence, Islam spread extensively into East Africa and Southeast Asia during precisely the time of rapid European commercial expansion. Even without the support of the Muslim land empires, Islam became a source of resistance to growing European domination.

Muslims in the East Indies

Historians disagree about the chronology and manner of Islam's spread in Southeast Asia. Arab traders were well known in southern China as early as the eighth century, so Muslims probably reached the East Indies at a similarly early date. Nevertheless, Indian cultural influences dominated in the area for several centuries thereafter, indicating that early Muslim visitors had little impact on local beliefs. Clearer indications of

Scene from Indonesia in Mughal manuscript   Wonders of foreign lands were a common theme in Islamic literature. Though India and Indonesia had been in trading contact for over a thousand years, fancy still played a major role in such works as is evident in the little men perched in trees. (Reproduced by kind permission of the Trustees of the Chester Beatty Library, Dublin)

conversion and the formation of Muslim communities date from roughly the fourteenth century. The strongest overseas linkage is to the port of Cambay in India rather than to the Arab world. Islam took root first in port cities and in some royal courts and spread inland slowly, possibly transmitted by itinerant Sufis.

Although appeals to the Ottoman sultan for support against the Europeans ultimately

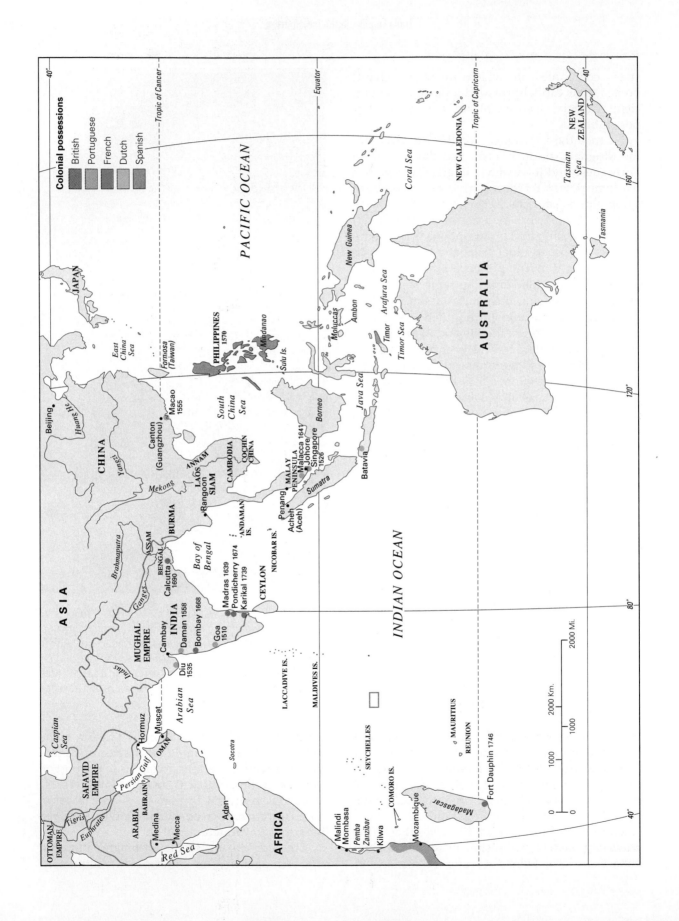

Colonial possessions
- British
- Portuguese
- French
- Dutch
- Spanish

40°

Tropic of Cancer

Equator

Tropic of Capricorn

160°

40°

PACIFIC OCEAN

NEW CALEDONIA

NEW ZEALAND

Coral Sea

Tasman Sea

Tasmania

AUSTRALIA

Arafura Sea

Timor Sea

Timor

Ambon

Moluccas

New Guinea

Java Sea

Borneo

120°

JAPAN

East China Sea

Formosa (Taiwan)

PHILIPPINES 1570

Mindanao

Sulu Is.

South China Sea

Macao 1555

Canton (Guangzhou)

Beijing

CHINA

Huang He

Yangzi

Mekong

ANNAM

LAOS

CAMBODIA

COCHIN CHINA

SIAM

Rangoon

BURMA

ASIA

Brahmaputra

ASSAM

BENGAL

Calcutta 1690

Penang

MALAY PENINSULA

Malacca 1641

Johore

Singapore 1526

Acheh (Aceh)

Sumatra

Batavia

ANDAMAN IS.

NICOBAR IS.

CEYLON

Bay of Bengal

Madras 1639

Pondicherry 1674

Karikal 1739

MUGHAL EMPIRE

INDIA

Cambay

Daman 1558

Bombay 1668

Goa 1510

Diu 1535

Ganges

Indus

LACCADIVE IS.

MALDIVES IS.

Arabian Sea

Socotra

INDIAN OCEAN

80°

Muscat

Hormuz

OMAN

Persian Gulf

BAHRAIN

SAFAVID EMPIRE

Caspian Sea

OTTOMAN EMPIRE

Tigris

Euphrates

ARABIA

Medina

Mecca

Aden

Red Sea

AFRICA

Malindi

Mombasa

Pemba

Zanzibar

Kilwa

Mozambique

COMORO IS.

SEYCHELLES

MAURITIUS

REUNION

Madagascar

Fort Dauphin 1746

0   1000   2000 Km.

0   1000   2000 Mi.

40°

Indian Merchants in Russia

Despite the growth and eventual importance for the history of imperialism of European trade in the Indian Ocean, overland commerce through central Asia continued throughout this period. Few traders from eastern lands reached western Europe, but trading missions from India visited Russia and a small but important colony of Indian merchants developed in Astrakhan, at the mouth of the Volga River, where they dealt primarily in cotton and silk cloth. In 1675, Indian merchants in Moscow informed Russian officials that:

I n the Indian state the highest demand for Russian goods is for high-priced sables—10, 20, 30 roubles a pair, good, red broad cloth and green broad cloth, red leather, walrus teeth, coral, large middle sized and small mirrors, gold and silver velvet and Turkish velvet. . . . And the Indian rulers love Borzoi dogs. (p. 91)

One Indian merchant of Astrakhan, Marwar Bara, wrote in 1735:

Previously there were favorable conditions for trade from India to Russia and merchants comfortably went [abroad]. Each year about two hundred exported . . .

goods, and then when disturbances occurred in Persia and passage became difficult because of robbers the number of merchants declined year by year. Now exceedingly few came, less than eighty. (p. 128)

Nevertheless, in 1777 the Russian governor of Astrakhan complained:

It is not a secret that they, the Indians, having trade with Russian subjects, attempt, in exchange for Russian money and for goods, to receive Russian silver money, and especially heavy silver of the best kind with the portrait of Peter the Great. . . . Silver is in short supply in Russia and is aggravated by these non-citizens, the Indians. (p. 111)

How do the circumstances of Indian traders in Russia compare with those of Europeans in India? How do the goods exchanged between India and Russia compare with goods exchanged across the Indian Ocean?

Source: Stephen Frederic Dale, *Indian Merchants and Eurasian Trade, 1600–1750*, Cambridge: Cambridge University Press, 1994.

proved of little use, Islam as a political ideology strengthened resistance to Portuguese, Spanish, and Dutch intruders. When the Spaniards conquered the Philippines during the decades following the establishment of their first fort in 1565 (see Chapter 17), they encountered Muslims on the southern island of Mindanao and the nearby Sulu archipelago. They called them "Moros," the Spanish term for their old enemies, the Muslims of North Africa. In the ensuing Moro wars, the Spaniards portrayed the Moros as greedy pirates who raided non-Muslim territories for slaves. In fact, they were political, religious, and commercial competitors whose perseverance enabled them to establish the Sulu Empire based in the

Map 21.2 European colonization in the Indian Ocean to 1750

southern Philippines, one of the strongest states in Southeast Asia from 1768 to 1848.

Other local kingdoms that looked on Islam as a force to counter the aggressive Christianity of the Europeans included the actively proselytizing Brunei Sultanate in northern Borneo and the Acheh Sultanate in northern Sumatra. At its peak in the early seventeenth century, Acheh succeeded Malacca as the main center of Islamic expansion in Southeast Asia. It prospered from trade in pepper and cotton cloth from Gujarat in India. Acheh declined after the Dutch seized Malacca from Portugal in 1641.

How well Islam was understood in these Muslim kingdoms is open to question. In Acheh, for example, a series of women ruled between 1641 and 1699. This practice came to an end when local Muslim scholars obtained a ruling from scholars in Mecca and Medina that Islam did not approve of female rulers. This ruling became a turning point after which scholarly understandings of Islam gained greater prominence in the East Indies.

Historians have theorized that the first propagators of Islam in Southeast Asia were merchants, Sufi preachers, or both. The scholarly vision of Islam, however, took root in the sixteenth century by way of pilgrims returning from years of study in Mecca and Medina. Islam was the primary force in the dissemination of writing in the region. Some of the returning pilgrims wrote in Arabic, others in Malay or Javanese. As Islam continued to spread, *adat*, a form of Islam rooted in pre-Muslim religious and social practices, retained its preeminence in rural areas over practices centered on the Shari'a, the religious law. But the royal courts in the port cities began to heed the views of the pilgrim teachers, as in the case of their condemnation of female rulers. Though different in many ways, both varieties of Islam provided believers with a firm basis of identification in the face of the growing European presence. Christian missionaries gained most of their converts in regions that had not yet converted to Islam, like the northern Philippines.

Muslims in East Africa

The East African ports the Portuguese began to visit in the fifteenth century were governed by Muslim rulers but were not linked politically (see Map 21.2). People living in the slave-cultivated millet and rice lands of the Swahili coast—from the Arabic *sawahil* meaning "coasts"—had little contact with those in the dry hinterlands. Throughout this period, the East African lakes region and the highlands of Kenya witnessed unprecedented migration and relocation of peoples because of drought conditions that persisted from the late sixteenth through most of the seventeenth century. The expansion of what was to be the powerful kingdom of Buganda in Uganda did not begin until 1674 and the reign of King Mawanda (d. 1704).

Cooperation among trading ports like Kilwa, Mombasa, and Malindi was hindered by the thick bush country that separated the cultivated tracts of coastal land and by the fact that the ports competed with one another in the export of ivory; ambergris (a whale by-product used as a fixative in perfumes), and forest products like beeswax, copal tree resin, and wood (Kilwa also exported gold). In the eighteenth century, slave trading, primarily to Arabian ports but also to India, increased in importance. Because Europeans—the only peoples who kept consistent records of slave-trading activities—never played a major role in this slave trade, few records have survived to indicate its extent. Perhaps the best estimate is 2.1 million slaves exported between 1500 and 1890, a little over 12.5 percent of the total traffic in African slaves during that period (see Chapter 20).

The Portuguese conquered all of the coastal ports from Mozambique northward except Malindi, with whose ruler Portugal cooperated. A Portuguese description of the ruler indicates some of the cloth and metal goods that Malindi imported, as well as some local manufactures:

> The King wore a robe of damask trimmed with green satin and a rich [cap]. He was seated on two cushioned chairs of bronze, beneath a rough sunshade of crimson satin attached to a pole. An old man, who attended him as a page, carried a short sword in a silver sheath. There were many players on [horns], and two trumpets of ivory richly carved and of the size of a man, which were blown through a hole in the side, and made sweet harmony with the [horns].[2]

Although the Portuguese favored the port of Malindi throughout the sixteenth century, towns like Kilwa, Lamu, and Mombasa declined. They pillaged Mombasa in 1505, 1528, and 1589. Portuguese influence in East Africa began to wane when the Arabs of Oman captured the Portuguese stronghold of Musqat on the southeast Arabian coast in 1650. After a siege lasting from 1696 to 1698, the Omanis captured Mombasa, which by then had become the local Portuguese capital. Portugal strove to regain its position and in 1727 succeeded in retaking and holding Mombasa for two years, but it was a last gasp. Omani domination of the Swahili Coast soon reasserted itself, gradually shifting its center of operations to the island of Zanzibar. The Portuguese had to content themselves with Mozambique and a few remaining ports in India (Goa) and farther east (Macao and Timor).

Omani success derived in part from the fact that no other European power wished to take the place of the Portuguese. Compared with India and the East Indies, East Africa was less appealing as a source of trade goods. More important than trade goods to the Arabs of Oman, however, was the bringing of the port cities under one ruler and the extension and consolidation of Islam as a unifying force on the Swahili Coast. The mixture of Arabic and Bantu spoken in the coastal cities developed into a distinctive Swahili language, further distancing the peoples of coastal East Africa from those of the interior and bringing them more into the orbit of Islam. Arabs and other Muslims who settled in the region intermarried with local families, giving rise to a mixed population that played an important role in the towns.

Islam also spread in the southern regions of the Sudan in this period, particularly in the dry regions away from the Nile River. But no significant contact occurred between the emerging Muslim Swahili culture and that of the Muslims in the Sudan, farther to the north.

The Coming of the Dutch

The Dutch played a major role in driving the Portuguese from their possessions in the East Indies. They were better organized than the Portuguese through the institution of the joint-stock company, the prime example being the Dutch East India Company established in 1602 (see Chapter 20). Just as the Portuguese had tried to dominate the trade in spices, so the Dutch concentrated at first on the spice-producing islands of Southeast Asia. The Portuguese had seized Malacca, a strategic town on the narrow strait at the end of the Malay Peninsula, from a local Malay ruler in 1511 (see Chapter 17). The Dutch took it away from them in 1641, leaving Portugal little foothold in the East Indies except the islands of Ambon and Timor (see Map 21.2).

Although the seven provinces of the United Netherlands constituted one of the least autocratic countries of Europe, the governors-general appointed by the Dutch East Asia Company deployed almost unlimited powers in their efforts to maintain their trade monopoly. They could even order the execution of their own employees for "smuggling"—that is, trading on their own. Under strong governors-general, the Dutch fought a series of wars against Acheh and other local kingdoms on Sumatra and Java. In 1628 and 1629, their new capital at Batavia, now the city of Jakarta on Java, was besieged by a fleet of fifty ships belonging to Sultan Agung of Mataram, a Javanese kingdom. The Dutch held out with difficulty and eventually prevailed when Agung was unable to get effective help from the English.

Suppressing local rulers, however, was not enough to control the spice trade once other European countries adopted Dutch methods, became more knowledgeable about where goods might be acquired, and started to send more ships to Southeast Asia. In the course of the eighteenth century, therefore, the Dutch gradually turned from being a middleman for Southeast Asian producers and European buyers to being a producer of crops in areas they controlled, notably in Java. Javanese teak forests yielded high-quality lumber, and coffee, transplanted from Yemen, grew well in the hilly regions of western Java. In this new phase of colonial export production, Batavia developed from being the headquarters town of a far-flung enterprise to being the administrative capital of a conquered land. To dilute the impact of being the only foreigners in Java, the Dutch encouraged Chinese immigrants to establish service and business enterprises in Batavia.

Beyond the East Indies, the Dutch utilized their discovery of a powerful band of eastward-blowing winds (the "Roaring Forties," named for being 40–50° south of the equator) to reach Australia at the beginning of the seventeenth century. In 1642 and 1643 Abel Tasman became the first European to set foot on Tasmania and New Zealand and to sail around Australia, foreshadowing the European involvement in that region (see Chapter 26).

CONCLUSION

That a major shift in world economic and political alignments was well under way by the late seventeenth century was scarcely perceivable in the parts of Asia and Africa ruled by the Ottoman and Mughal sultans and the Safavid shahs. To be sure, more and more trade was being carried in European vessels, and Europeans had enclaves in a handful of port cities and islands. But the age-old tradition of Asia was that imperial wealth came from the control of broad expanses of agricultural land. Except in the case of state monopolies, such as Iranian silk, governments did not greatly concern themselves with what farmers planted. To fill the government coffers, they relied mostly on land taxes, usually indirectly collected through holders of land grants or tax farmers, rather than on customs duties or control of markets.

With ever-increasing military expenditures, these taxes fell short of the rulers' needs. Few people, however, realized that this revenue shortfall was a problem basic to the entire economic system rather than a temporary inconvenience. Imperial courtiers pursued their luxurious ways, poetry and the arts continued to flourish, and the quality of manufacturing and craft production remained generally high. Eighteenth-century European observers marveled no less at the riches and industry of these Eastern lands than at the fundamental weakness of their political and military systems, thoughts they would also entertain in confronting societies to the north and east, as will be discussed in the next chapter.

SUGGESTED READING

The best comprehensive and comparative account of the post-Mongol Islamic land empires, with an emphasis on social history, is Ira Lapidus, *A History of Islamic Societies* (1988). For a work of similar scope concentrating on intellectual history see Marshall G. S. Hodgson,

The Ventury of Islam. Volume 3. The Gunpowder Empires and Modern Times (1974).

On the Ottoman Empire, the standard political history is Stanford J. Shaw, *History of the Ottoman Empire and Modern Turkey. Volume I, Empire of the Ghazis: The Rise and Decline of the Ottoman Empire, 1280–1808* (1976). For a collection of articles on non-political matters, see Halil Inalcik and Donald Quataert, eds., *An Economic and Social History of the Ottoman Empire, 1300–1914* (1994).

The world's foremost Ottoman historian, Halil Inalcik, analyzes the history and structure of the empire in *The Ottoman Empire: The Classical Age, 1300–1600* (1989). There is no equivalent analysis for the period 1600 to 1750, but suggestive studies have been written by Rifa'at Ali Abou-El-Haj, *Formation of the Modern State: The Ottoman Empire Sixteenth to Eighteenth Centuries* (1991) and Haim Gerber, *The Social Origins of the Modern Middle East* (1987).

Among the specialized studies of cities and regions that give a good sense of some of the major changes in Ottoman society and economy after the sixteenth century are Daniel Goffman, *Izmir and the Levantine World, 1550–1650* (1990); Abraham Marcus, *The Middle East on the Eve of Modernity: Aleppo in the Eighteenth Century* (1989); and Bruce McGowan, *Economic Life in the Ottoman Empire: Taxation, Trade, and the Struggle for Land, 1600–1800* (1981).

Questions relating to religious minorities in the Ottoman Empire are best covered by the articles in Benjamin Braude and Bernard Lewis, eds., *Christians and Jews in the Ottoman Empire: The Functioning of a Plural Society* (1982). The role of women in the governance of the empire is skillfully treated by Leslie Pierce, *The Imperial Harem: Women and Sovereignty in the Ottoman Empire* (1993). Ralph S. Hattox, *Coffee and Coffeehouses: The Origins of a Social Beverage in the Medieval Near East* (1988) is an excellent contribution to Ottoman social history.

The most comprehensive treatment of the history of Safavid Iran is in the articles in Peter Jackson and Laurence Lockhart, eds., *The Cambridge History of Iran. Volume 6. The Timurid and Safavid Periods* (1986). The articles by Hans Roemer in this volume provide the best political narratives of the pre-Safavid and Safavid period. Roger Savory's important article on the structure of the Safavid state is available in a more extensive form in his *Iran Under the Safavids* (1980).

For the artistic side of Safavid history, abundantly illustrated, see Anthony Welch, *Shah 'Abbas and the Arts of Isfahan* (1973). Said Amir Arjomand, *The Shadow of God and the Hidden Imam: Religion, Political Order, and Societal Change in Shiite Iran from the Beginning to 1890* (1984) contains the best analysis of the complicated relationship between Shi'ism and monarchy. Safavid economic history is not well developed, but useful studies have been published by Ann K. S. Lambton, *Landlord and Peasant in Persia: A Study of Land Tenure and Land Revenue Administration*, rev. ed. (1991) and Mehdi Keyvani, *Artisans and Guild Life in the Later Safavid Period: Contribution to the Social-Economic History of Persia* (1982).

A highly readable work that situates the Mughal Empire within the overall history of the subcontinent is Stanley Wolpert, *A New History of India*, 4th ed. (1993). For a broad treatment of the entire development of Islamic society in India with emphasis on the Mughal period see S. M. Ikram, *History of Muslim Civilization in India and Pakistan* (1989). Douglas E. Streusand, *The Formation of the Mughal Empire* (1989) provides a more detailed and analytical account of the early period of the Mughal Empire. For the history of the Sikhs see W. H. McLeod *The Sikhs: History, Religion, and Society* (1989). Two specialized works on the economic and trading history of India are Ashin Das Gupta and M. N. Pearson, eds., *India and the Indian Ocean, 1500–1800* (1987) and Stephen Frederic Dale, *Indian Merchants and Eurasian Trade, 1600–1750* (1994).

The history of East Africa in this period is not well documented, but B. A. Ogot, ed., *UNESCO General History of Africa*, Vol. 5, *Africa from the Sixteenth to the Eighteenth Century* (1992) provides an excellent collection of articles reflecting the current state of knowledge. John Middleton, *The World of the Swahili: An African Mercantile Civilization* (1993) is balanced and up to date.

For a brief, general introduction to the relations between the Muslim land empires and the development of Indian Ocean trade see Patricia Risso, *Merchants and Faith: Muslim Commerce and Culture in the Indian Ocean* (1995). Esmond Bradley Martin and Chryssee Perry Martin have written a popular and well illustrated work on the western Indian Ocean entitled *Cargoes of the East: The Ports, Trade and Culture of the Arabian Seas and Western Indian Ocean* (1978). C. R. Boxer, *The Dutch Seaborne Empire, 1600–1800* (1973) is a classic account of all aspects of Dutch maritime expansion.

NOTES

1. Daniel Goffman, *Izmir and the Levantine World, 1550–1650* (Seattle, 1990), p. 52.

2. Esmond Bradley Martin and Chrysee Perry Martin, *Cargoes of the East* (London, 1978), p. 17.

CHAPTER TWENTY-TWO

Central and Eastern Asia,

1500–1800

The Ming to Qing Transition • The Qing Empire at Its Height

Decentralization and Innovation: Tokugawa Japan

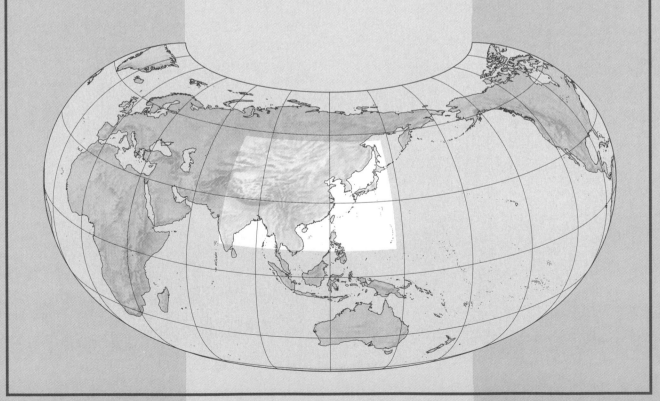

The pull of Asian power, wealth, and resources inspired one of the great events of European exploration and colonization—the expedition of the Portuguese navigator Vasco da Gama in 1499 that opened the sea route to Asia by way of the African Cape of Good Hope (see Chapter 17). The Portuguese rulers hoped to dominate the spice trade of India—Melaka (Malacca) and beyond—and take away profits from Muslim merchants based in areas ranging from Mogadishu in East Africa to Jakarta in the East Indies. To enhance his credibility with the Asians he expected to encounter, Da Gama carried a letter from the Portuguese king to Prester John, the mythical Christian monarch of Central Asia. Europeans since before the time of Genghis Khan had been hoping that Prester John would destroy Muslim power in the Middle East. As reports of the power and opulence of Genghis Khan's court had inspired travel, trade, diplomacy, and cultural exchange by land routes between western Europe and eastern Asia, so the legend of Prester John and the lure of Indian spice helped motivate European societies to seek riches through exploitation of sea travel.

It was primarily by sea trade that Europe and the Middle East were connected to East Asia after decline of the caravan trade in the 1400s. This maritime trade helped to develop the coastal cities of India and Southeast Asia, which became important stopping places on the routes. Because there was no longer continuous contact across the Eurasian continent Europeans, particularly, came to think of their world as special and remote from Asia and Africa.

Like the Romanovs of Russia (see Map 22.1), the Ottomans based in Anatolia (modern Turkey), and the Mughals of India, the Qing of China (1636–1912) ruled a great land-based empire that attempted in the early modern period to protect the privileges of agriculture over commerce, to maintain centralized imperial rule, and to sustain military control over lands that were strategically important even if economically unprofitable. In the long run, all of these empires were at a disadvantage in the struggle against the sea-based empires of Europe, which primarily concentrated on the colonization of profitable areas, linked the development of commerce to the enrichment of the central government, and enlisted the aid of semiprivate organizations to find, develop, and govern territories brought under their rule.

At the same time, few Europeans were aware of another remarkable society in East Asia, one that had lived for centuries in the shadow of China: Japan. Unlike continental Asia, Japan had not been dominated by empires in the medieval and early modern periods, nor had it developed an empire that dominated others. Thus Japan was often isolated from the cultural and economic developments of continental Asia. Yet independently Japan developed a vigorous economic and technological life—sometimes profitably connected to the developments of mainland Asia, sometimes securely insulated. By the end of the 1700s, as China was experiencing economic deterioration and social stagnation, Japan was poised for centralization and industrialization.

THE MING TO QING TRANSITION

Historians have long debated the reasons for the decline of the Ming Empire (1368–1644) in China in the 1500s and early 1600s. During that time, China was not only unified but also dominated most of East and Central Asia. Through *the tribute system*—the practice of political, economic, and military of countries not actually conquered by the Ming subordination—many Asian and a few European countries expressed their ritual acceptance of the material and moral superiority of China.

The Ming "Golden Age"

In many ways, the cultural achievements of Ming China in the 1500s were brilliant. Literature reached new heights with the publication of massive novels. Some, like Wu Cheng'en's *Journey to the West*, were based on well-known historical incidents or on folktales and shared the spirit of novel writing of the 1400s. Others were completely original. For example, Wu Jingzi's *The Scholars*—a satirical excursion into the complex relationships of men competing for success in the examination system by which officials were selected—focuses exclusively on the dramas of elite life but is distinguished above all for its structure, narrative style, and many layers of meaning.

By far the most notorious of the original novels was *The Golden Lotus*, possibly written by Xu Wei. It has been praised as among the earliest true novels and possibly the best, but its subject matter is so cynical and some passages are so explicitly sexual that in the modern period publishers have rarely printed all of it. In the 1500s, however, *The Golden Lotus* was an instant success. In the city of Suzhou, where the story is set, copies of the book were everywhere, and soon it was available in all the major cities. The work was praised as the necessary reading of drunkards and libertines who wanted to show some intellectual chic. After the fall of the Ming, the Qing Empire sternly suppressed the novel. In the great literary inquisition of the 1700s it was ordered that those who printed, sold, or read the novel were to be subjected to severe corporal punishment. Nevertheless, *The Golden Lotus* remained an underground classic and was even translated into Manchu, the Qing imperial language, so that princes, aristocrats, and soldiers could secretly enjoy it.

Later Ming achievements in the design and export of porcelain products were also astonishing. By the 1500s Europe had learned of the high-grade blue-on-white porcelain that was common among the elites of China. Portuguese merchants had begun not only exporting the products to Europe but requesting special designs that imitated European pitchers and bowls that otherwise would have been made of metal or wood.

In many cases, these commissioned items had distinctive gold fittings and designs that were copied from European paintings. By 1600 the Dutch were also heavily involved in this trade, and Europeans were becoming accustomed to the fine new porcelain, "china" (see Chapter 21).

This apparent golden age, however, was beset by serious problems that by the year 1600 left the Ming Empire economically exhausted, in political deterioration, and technologically behind its East Asian neighbors and Europe. Some of these problems were the result of natural disasters associated with climate, soils, and disease. Others were political and military stresses, particularly from Central Asia—which was still largely under Mongol control—and from Manchuria. There Manchus had joined together with Chinese settlers to create an economically strong and militarily assertive state, the Qing. Still other pressures on the Ming resulted from domestic unrest, as rebellions spread among the poor farmers, renters, and soldiers, whose misery deepened during the early 1600s.

The "Seventeenth-Century Crisis"

Recently historians have seen the fall of the Ming Empire and the conquest of China by the Qing in the middle 1600s as being connected to trends in global development and not merely as an event particular to Chinese history. This interpretation is partly derived from evidence of climatic change in the seventeenth century. Annual temperatures dropped and finally reached their low point about 1645, remaining low until the early 1700s. The effects on the Ming took many forms. Development of a centralized political and military system among the Manchus in Northeast Asia was at least partly stimulated by declines in agricultural production and in the size of livestock herds, which intensified competition in the region. Later, the Manchus invaded Ming territory in search of greater agricultural resources and cattle. The Mongols on the north and west of the Ming domain were affected by greater difficulties in pasturing their livestock, and peaceful migrations into Ming territory, as well as aggressive violations of the borders, were common in the early 1600s. Clearly, the Mongols and Manchus who applied increasing pressure on the Ming in the seventeenth century were themselves pressured by changes in the climate and in the environment.

It is also possible to see the effects of the climatic changes inside China. During the last decades of the Ming, there is evidence of agricultural distress, the migration of peoples away from less productive areas, and the spread of epidemic diseases. The two large peasant uprisings that hastened the end of the Ming Empire were fueled by the dissatisfactions of tenant farmers and day workers who were being squeezed by high rents, low wages, and low land yields. An increase in banditry deepened the unhappiness of the rural population and led to greater disorders as farmers and farm worker rebellions in Shaanxi province—once the capital of China from about 1100 B.C.E. to about 900 C.E., but by the late Ming a rustic backwater—and Sichuan province, the heart of China's agricultural production. The devastation caused by the two great rebellions resulted in deep declines in the local populations and grinding distress for those who were left.

Another component of the global "seventeenth-century crisis" also affected China. As Europeans colonized Mexico and Central America, they exploited the new sources of silver and flooded the global trade networks with silver coins (see Chapter 19). As China became more involved in this trade in the 1500s and early 1600s, silver flowed into China in exchange for goods sold to Europe. Silver dollars from the Spanish Empire were fully accepted in the Chinese economy, and the Chinese government began to mint its own silver and to remint foreign silver in imitation of the Spanish design.

As the amount of silver in circulation rose, its relative value fell. But the Ming government maintained a strict ratio in price between silver and copper coins. Taxes and prices were tied to silver values. Most transactions, however, required the conversion of copper coinage to silver, and because silver had declined in value, much more copper was needed to meet the rises in prices and in taxation. In a time of worsening economic and population conditions, the decline in the value of silver and consequent inflation in prices and taxes worsened the hardships of the rural population. The Ming government found it

more and more difficult to maintain order and eventually was overwhelmed by the rebellion of the peasant leader Li Zicheng. He declared himself emperor and occupied Beijing briefly in 1644 before being driven out by the Manchus, who proceeded to establish their own capital at Beijing and begin the conquest of China.

Environmental and economic stress by themselves do not destroy societies. Indeed, both the Mongols in eastern Asia and the Manchus centralized their political systems and increased the territories under their control in the 1600s, all at the expense of the Ming Empire. We need to consider the importance of global factors in the demise of the Ming in the context of the special factors operating on China.

Because of a deterioration in roads, bridges, canals, dams, and dikes, the Ming were not in a position to sustain the productivity of their lands or the reliability of their transportation systems. Corruption and inefficiency in government prevented the court from making and enforcing policies that would have minimized the spread of disorder and disease. And because of poor policy for the management of their borders, the Ming could not maintain competent communications and trade relations with their immediate neighbors or with the new arrivals from Europe. The magnitude of the environmental changes and the novelty of the economic changes of the middle 1600s challenged the Ming, but the critical issue is that the empire could not respond effectively to those challenges.

Economic and Technological Stagnation

The hardship of rural life in China of the 1600s was a contrast to the cities, which were culturally and commercially vibrant. Many absentee landlords lived in the cities, as well as officials, artists, and rich merchants who had purchased ranks or prepared their sons for the examinations. The elites had created a brilliant culture in which novels, operas, poetry, porcelain, and painting were all closely interwoven. This meant that for small businessmen—such as printers, restaurant owners, tailors, artisans, and shop keepers specializing in paper, ink, inkstones, and writing brushes—there was money to be made.

The imperial government catered to the tastes of the urban elites by operating its own factories for the production of ceramics and silks. Enormous government complexes at Jingdezhen and at Dehua, where the distinctive white and blue porcelain of the Ming period was produced, invented assembly-line techniques and produced large quantities of high-quality ceramics for sale in China and abroad.

But by the end of the Ming period the factories were plagued by disorder and inefficiency. The situation became so bad that workers held strikes with increasing frequency during the late sixteenth and seventeenth centuries. During such a work action at Jingdezhen in 1601, workers threw themselves into the kilns to protest working conditions.

Urban and industrial sectors of later Ming society fared much better than the rural, agricultural part. After an initial recovery from the depression in population and economic growth of the thirteenth century, the rural Ming economy failed to sustain growth. This was partly due to the fact that technological improvements in methods of harvesting and processing grains, and in the production of cotton and silk, were not adapted and exploited in China as they were in Korea and Japan. After the beginning of the sixteenth century, China had knowledge, from European traders, of new crops from Africa and

Ceramics manufacture   The porcelain factories at Jingdezhen and Dehua were already famous for their elegant blue-on-white pattern when Europeans began importing them in the 1500s. As shown here, the processes were based on assembly-line techniques that assured regularity of quality, efficient use of worker's expertise, and high output. By early Qing period, many of the inland factories were making porcelain to the designs of European importers, who picked up the finished products at Canton and took them west. (From *Tiangong Kaiwu*)

America, but these crops were introduced slowly and did not have a real impact until after the Ming period. Neither regions growing rice in southern China nor those growing wheat in northern China experienced a meaningful increase in productivity during the second half of the Ming period.

At the same time, population growth stabilized. In the early Ming period, the population—recovering from the wars that had led to the overthrow of the Mongols and establishment of the Ming in the fourteenth century—grew rapidly and once again surpassed a hundred million. This rapid growth was enough to shock some sectors of the economy, but it was not sustained. After 1500, economic depression in the countryside, combined with recurring epidemics in central and southern China, kept population growth in check. Large and devastating peasant revolts hastened the political disintegration of the Ming empire and shrank the population of many of the most critical agricultural areas. As a result, the Ming population at its height probably did not much surpass that of four hundred years earlier.

External Pressure on the Ming

By the year 1500, the Ming empire had reached the farthest extent of its military power. It controlled all of China and some of Manchuria and Mongolia. Its tributary states included Annam (the modern state of Vietnam) Korea, Japan, many of the khanates of Central Asia, kingdoms of Southeast Asia, and some states of the Middle East. However, the Ming were under constant pressure from the powerful Mongol federations of Central Asia. In the late 1500s a large portion of the Mongols were unified again. This time, a Mongol khan used Tibetan religion to centralize his power. To legitimate his authority, the khan designated for the first time a *Dalai Lama*, meaning "universal priest," of Tibetan Buddhism, who in turn recognized the khan as the universal Buddhist king. Since that time, the Dalai Lamas (each of whom is believed to be an incarnation of previous lamas) have continued to play important political roles in Mongolia, China, and Tibet.

This unification of the Mongols in the 1500s was a significant step in the reemergence of Mongolia as a regional military power around 1600. In its last decades the Ming Empire was squeezed by Mongol forces on the west and north, and by Manchu forces on the north and east, until it was finally conquered by the Qing in 1644.

In the final years of the 1500s, as Ming resources critically declined, Japanese leaders mounted a series of invasions of Korea. The campaigns threw East Asia into crisis. Korea was a tributary state of the Ming, so the Ming were required to send a major defense force. The Manchus, who controlled the region north of Korea, contributed troops to the international force under Ming leadership. For their part, the Koreans had to employ all the technological and military skill for which the Yi period was renowned. General Yi Son-sin devised and used the covered warships, or "turtle boats," that intercepted a portion of the Japanese fleet.

The effects of the invasion on the continent of Asia were lasting. The impoverished Ming had to pay a high price to bring northeastern peoples like the Manchus into the struggle against the Japanese. In addition, the Ming decline in military strength was hastened by the strain of repelling the invaders, while leaders of the Manchus, in particular, were strengthened. In Korea, factionalism that had afflicted the Yi court before the Japanese invasions was worsened by the devastation of the land and the struggle for leadership after the invaders were turned back. Korea was so weakened that the rising Manchu power soon brought the country under its sway.

For the entire later Ming period, conditions at the boundaries of the empire were critical to its health. The Mongols remained strong in the north and west and disrupted Ming overland contact with Central and West Asia. The Manchus grew stronger in the north and east and severed the traditional relationship between China and Korea, at the same time preventing Ming development of the agricultural regions of Manchuria. In the southwest, there were repeated uprisings among native peoples who were being crowded by the immigration of Chinese farmers.

The Ming could not look to the seas for relief. Pirates, often of Japanese or partial Japanese ancestry, based in Okinawa and in Taiwan, roamed

Korean turtle boats   After Japanese forces attacked Korea in 1592, Yi Son-sin mobilized his "turtle boats." Plates of iron were erected over the boats' wooden frame to defend against on-slaughts of long-distance fire-arrows and percussive shells, which had been used in East Asia for four centuries. With this new ship design Yi was able to control the sea between Korea and Japan, so that the landed invasion forces were isolated and eventually crushed by combined forces of Ming troops, Korean infantry, and Korean civilians. (Courtesy, Yushin Yoo)

the entire southeastern coast of China, frequently landing at and looting trading towns. Ming military resources, concentrated against the Mongols and the Manchus in the north, could not be deployed to make the coasts hospitable to Chinese traders. Many southern Chinese, frustrated by conditions and despairing of ever making a living at home, migrated in unprecedented numbers to all areas of Southeast Asia, where they began to profit from the sea-trading networks of the Indian Ocean.

New Global Influences: The Society of Jesus and the East India Companies

The Ming situation was further complicated by the arrival of Europeans in the 1500s. Ignatius of Loyola had founded the Society of Jesus in 1534 in order to join the Catholic Reformation—the effort to undermine Protestantism (see Chapter

18). Part of the Jesuits' campaign was to concentrate on the conversion to Catholicism of peoples in Asia, the Americas, and North Africa. One of the original Jesuits, Francis Xavier, went to India in the middle sixteenth century looking for converts and later traveled throughout Southeast and East Asia. He spent two years in Japan and died in 1552 in China. Following Xavier, other Jesuits had a significant influence in China and also presented to Europeans an intriguing picture of Asian life.

China derived some material benefits from contact with the Jesuits. Chinese converts to Catholicism, foremost among them Xu Guangqi, were important in introducing European techniques of agronomy, hydraulics, and engineering. Matteo Ricci, the outstanding Jesuit of late Ming China, became expert in Chinese and an accomplished scholar of the Confucian classics. Although he gained some high-ranking converts to Catholicism, including members of the imperial family, Ricci himself was deeply affected by Chinese elite culture, and in later times the influence of Confucian philosophy over the Jesuits would become a matter of controversy in Rome. Unfortunately for the Ming, some of the skills the Jesuits introduced—particularly mapmaking and the casting of cannon—were used by the Manchus in the conquest of China between 1644 and 1685. On November 4, 1650, as Manchus finally drove the Ming imperial family into the highlands of Southeast Asia, Grand Dowager Empress Wang sent a delegation of Jesuits to Rome requesting the pope to "take pity on us sinners in God's presence and, when we die, to bestow a special absolution." Wang further noted that all members of the imperial family had been converted and that if the papacy could help repel the Manchus, "ambassadors will be dispatched to perform proper ceremonies at the altars of Saints Peter and Paul."

Michel Boym, the Jesuit priest acting as Wang's envoy, did not reach Rome until 1652 and could gain no papal audience until 1656. Then, with an encouraging letter from Pope Alexander VI, Boym returned to a China that had been virtually conquered by the Manchus, who refused to let him travel inland from Canton (Guangzhou). Wang and her family were dead by that time. Boym himself died attempting to contact them and was buried in the highlands between China and Annam in 1659.[1]

By the time the Jesuits first arrived in East Asia, European merchants already were present. The earliest arrivals were the Portuguese, who (as we saw in Chapter 17) after 1500 dominated

From the Jesuits library at Beijing Jesuits such as Matteo Ricci and Michel Boym were willing to share their published works on technology and science with Chinese scholars, but without practical knowledge it was impossible for Chinese writers to accurately convey the basic ideas behind the mechanisms. It was not usual for Chinese scholars to have real contact with mechanical things, and though their own libraries often contained illustrations of working people and their tools, the drawings were not really intended to convey precise knowledge to the reader. Information from Europe conveyed by means of drawing alone was, as in this instance, likely to be garbled beyond recognition in the Chinese version. (Left, from Zonca, *Tromba Da Rota per Cavar Aqua*, 1607. Right, "The eighth diagram," from *Chhi Thushuo*, 1627. Both courtesy of Joseph Needham, *Science and Civilization In China*, Vol. 4)

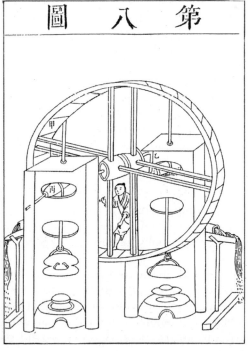

the spice trade of Malacca and Java as well as the trade routes around India. The Spanish were also interested in the trade and established a small base on Taiwan, an island off the coast of southeast China. Soon after 1600, however, the Portuguese and Spanish were dislodged from Taiwan by the Dutch, whose East India Company (EIC) was chartered by the monarchy of the Netherlands to manage all commerce in the Indian and Pacific Oceans. To secure their influence in East Asia and to discredit their rivals, the Dutch East India Company willingly complied with both Chinese and Japanese demands in the style of communications with their rulers. They performed the ritual kowtow to the Ming and Qing emperors in China and managed to retain exclusive permission to live on the Japanese island of Deshima, off Nagasaki, after Japan had been formally closed to all foreign contact in the early 1600s.

Outside Japan, however, the Dutch East India Company had a strong rival in the British East India Company (BEIC), chartered by Queen Elizabeth I in 1600. The British company had hoped to take the spice trade away from the Dutch but gave up that idea after the murders of English merchants in Java. Instead the BEIC concentrated on India. Gradually the company was given powers to coin money in India and to make and enforce laws as if it were a government. The British crown gave the BEIC the right to control Bombay (previously a Portuguese colony), and slowly the BEIC began to expand its base of political as well as economic control. By dominating the trade in goods from India—including cotton, silk, and the minerals needed for gunpowder—the BEIC made enormous profits for its British investors, particularly between 1660 and 1700. The company became so powerful that the Mughal rulers of northern India (see Chapter 21) granted BEIC the right to control Bengal and Bihar provinces in the mid-eighteenth century, and the company rapidly evolved into a quasi-government, waging wars, police actions, diplomacy, and its own powerful lobbying efforts in Britain as well as in India.

In China, also, the British East India Company became a force. As part of its plan to regulate BEIC activities, the British government attempted to open its own direct diplomatic relations with China. Like many Europeans, the directors of the BEIC believed that China's technological achievements and its gigantic potential markets made it the key to limitless profit. China had tea, rhubarb, porcelain, and silk to offer, and Dutch merchants had been energetic in their transport of Chinese goods to Europe.

By the early 1700s the BEIC dominated the community of European "factories"—the combined residences and offices of the European merchants residing in Canton—and families such as the Barings, Jardines, and Mathesons had established themselves as quasi-political powers. By the end of the 1700s, the British government was suspicious of the influence of the BEIC, sought still more privileges by interfering in British politics.

The European trading companies and the Society of Jesus are two examples of global organizations that brought new opportunities for enrichment by supplying goods to the growing markets of the West, and European technologies to the diverse societies of East Asia. They were also conduits of knowledge between Asia and Europe, and this two-way communication sparked enormous changes in the ways that eastern and western Eurasia related to each other. But as the British government eventually became wary of the power and independence of the BEIC, so the Roman Catholic Church eventually became wary of the worldwide power of the Jesuits. In 1773 (the same year in which a series of new laws passed by the British Parliament restrained the independence of the BEIC), Pope Clement XIV suppressed the Society of Jesus. It was later revived but never again was a great independent influence in Asia.

THE QING EMPIRE AT ITS HEIGHT

The forces led by the Manchus conquered north China quickly after 1644 but required nearly a century to secure their control over the peripheries that the Ming never had managed effectively. Before the year 1700 the Qing had gained south China, and for the first time the island of Taiwan was incorporated into an empire based in China. By the same year, the Qing Empire was also in the process of conquering Mongolia and Central Asia. The seventeenth and eighteenth centuries in China—and particularly the reigns of the Kangxi (1662–1722) and Qianlong (1736–1796) emperors—were the period of greatest economic, military, and cultural achievement under the Qing.

Thanks to the tribute system and to regional patterns of trade, Chinese influence was strong throughout eastern Asia. Korean ambassadors and students were numerous in Beijing and readily absorbed the tastes of the Qing elite. Vietnam, Burma, and Nepal sent regular embassies to the Qing tribute court and carried the latest Chinese fashions back home. Standing screens in lacquer and precious stones, cloisonné ceramics from the imperial factories, delicate silks, fine porcelain tableware and vases, and ornately carved and lacquered furniture were among the Chinese products popular in East Asia that increased in quantity and, for a time, in quality.

Consolidation of the Qing Empire

The early Qing emperors wished to create an economic and demographic recovery in China. They repaired the roads and waterworks, lowered transit taxes (a fee for transporting items on roads and canals) on goods, mandated comparatively low rents and interest rates, and established economic incentives for people to move into areas that had been devastated in the peasant rebellions of the late Ming period. After the end of the 1600s the eastern Mongols, who had been such a threat to the Ming, were neutralized as a military and political challenge. By the middle 1700s western Mongolia, Central Asia, and Tibet were all under Qing control. With the reestablishment of unity in eastern Eurasia, the overland routes of communication from Samarkand to Korea were revived, though the economic and cultural influence of those routes was a shadow of what it had been under the Mongols in the 1200s. Nevertheless, through its conquests in Central Asia the Qing Empire gained access to the superior horses of Afghanistan, to new sources of coal, iron, gold, and silver and, most important, was eventually

able to eliminate the military danger posed by the Mongols.

In the course of its conquest of Mongolia and Northeast Asia, the Qing came into increasing conflict with the Romanov empire in Russia (see Map 22.1). In the 1500s Russia had already begun to dominate Siberia, which became important for its furs, timber products, and rich mineral deposits. But a century later the Romanovs and the Qing came into direct competition for the Amur River, which flows through Manchuria to the Pacific Ocean. Rising military tensions were resolved by treaties in the late 1600s and the early 1700s, and domination of the northeastern peoples was split between the Romanovs and the Qing. The treaties permitted Russia to peacefully maintain its access to the Pacific. From there Russia launched in the early 1700s the explorations of North America that made the peoples of Alaska subjects of the Russian tsar, as well as nominal adherents of the Russian Orthodox Church.

The effectiveness of Qing expansion before 1800 was due in part to the ability of the growing empire to incorporate ideas and technologies from vastly different regions. Before invading China, the Qing had already begun to use the Mongol system of political organization. They also adapted a program of religious legitimation of the emperor's power that was Tibetan in origin but had been used by Mongol emperors in the past. Many of the agricultural policies of the early Qing state were influenced by the practices of the Korean and Chinese governments.

As the Qing conquest was consolidated in north China, south China, Northeast Asia, and Central Asia, maps in the European style—thanks to the century of Jesuit influence at the Ming court—were created both as practical guides to the newly conquered regions and also as symbols of Qing dominance. In the early years of the conquest of China the Qing also considered introducing the European calendar. Protests were so strong, however, that an anti-Jesuit backlash developed among the Confucian elites, and the plan was dropped. The emperors personally remained friendly with the Jesuits and frequently discussed scientific and philosophical issues with them. When the Kangxi emperor fell ill with malaria in the 1690s, he relied on Jesuit medical

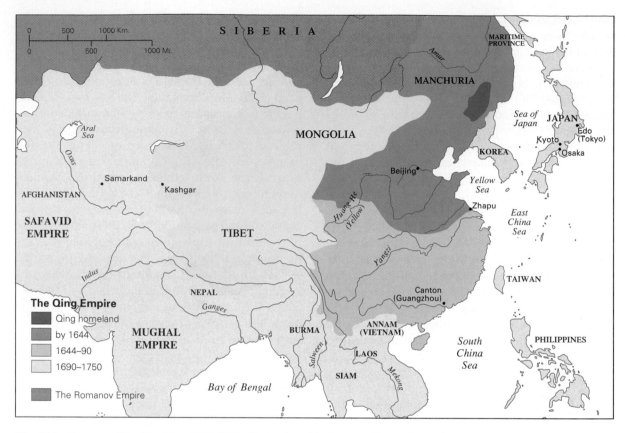

Map 22.1   Romanov-Qing Rivalries, 1650–1750   During its critical years of formation and expansion, the Qing empire struggled against the Romanov empire of Russia for control of Siberia, the Amur River and Mongolia. The conflict was stabilized by the equal treaties of Nerchinsk (1687) and Kiakhta (1727), which established borders and tariffs between the two great powers.

expertise (in this case, the administration of quinine) for his recovery and ordered the creation of illustrated books in the Manchu language detailing European anatomical and pharmaceutical knowledge. The Jesuits influenced the early Qing emperors in their knowledge of and attitudes toward mathematics, astronomy, medicine, and European civilization generally.

To gain converts among the Chinese elite, the Jesuits learned classical Chinese, memorized the Confucian classics, adopted the traditional dress of Chinese scholar-officials, and made important compromises in their religious teaching in order not to offend Chinese feelings. One compromise was Jesuit acceptance of Confucian ancestor worship as a practice compatible with the teachings of Christianity. The matter caused great con-

troversy between the Jesuits and their Catholic rivals, the Franciscans and Dominicans, in China, and also between the Jesuits and the popes. In 1690 the disagreement reached a high pitch. The Kangxi emperor wrote to Rome in support of the Jesuit position, but the matter was dropped, inconclusively, in the early 1700s.

By that time, the influx of Jesuits to China had slowed, and for the remainder of the 1700s a small population of Jesuits remained at the Qing court, though their cultural and religious influence did not rival that of their predecessors in the 1600s. An example of this change in the late 1700s was the Jesuit painter Giuseppe Castiglione, a court portrait artist and landscape painter who profoundly influenced Chinese artists' ways of representing light, depth, and dimension. Castiglione introduced new ways in which Qing emperors presented themselves and their environment to their contemporaries and to later generations, but he was not, as the Jesuits had been in the 1600s, an important adviser to the emperor.

Though Jesuit influence declined and eventually disappeared in the Qing empire in the 1700s, the influence of Jesuit reports in Europe about the Qing increased. The exchange of information between the Qing and the Europeans had never been one way. The Jesuits informed the Qing court on matters of anatomy, for instance, and the Qing demonstrated to the Jesuits an early form of inoculation—variolation—that they had used to stem the spread of smallpox after the Qing conquest of Beijing. The technique was the inspiration for the vaccines later developed by Europeans. Similarly, the enormous imperial factories that produced porcelain inspired the industrial management practices of Josiah Wedgwood in England (see Chapter 23).

The success of porcelain in England was in some ways symptomatic of the tremendous popularity of "chinoiserie" throughout Europe. Things Chinese—or things that looked to Europeans as if they could be Chinese—became items desired by the wealthy and the aspiring middle classes. Not only silk, porcelain, and tea, but also cloisonné jewelry, tableware, and decorative items, lacquered and jeweled room dividers, painted fans, carved jade, and ivory (which originated in Africa and was finished in China) were sought. Perhaps most striking in its effect on the interior of European homes was wallpaper, an adaptation of the Chinese practice of covering walls with enormous loose-hanging watercolors or calligraphy scrolls. By the middle 1700s, special workshops throughout China were producing wallpaper and other consumer items according to the specifications of European merchants. The items were shipped to Canton for export to Europe.

In political philosophy, too, the Europeans felt they had something to learn from the early Qing emperors. In the late 1770s, poems supposedly written by the Qianlong emperor were translated into French and disseminated through the intellectual circles of western Europe. These works depicted the Qing emperors as benevolent

Transferring European designs, Canton By 1800, the economy and the mercantile culture of Canton were grounded in the trade between China and Europe. Chinese entrepreneurs specialized in the reproduction of European motifs on Chinese porcelain or lacquerware for export to Europe. Cantonese merchants even made the culture founded on this international trade a commercialized object in itself. This painting shows a Chinese artisan transferring European painted scenes to glass, from which they can be transferred again to Chinese items for export. The painting itself was specially made for the export trade. (Victoria & Albert Museum)

despots who campaigned against superstition and ignorance, curbed the excesses of the aristocracy, and patronized science and the arts. Among European intellectuals who were questioning the political systems of their own societies, this image of a practical, secular, compassionate ruler was intriguing (see Chapter 24). Voltaire proclaimed the Qing emperors model philosopher-kings and advocated such rulership as a protection against the growth of aristocratic privilege. Although the Jesuits' interest in China was in decline by this time, the works the Jesuits bequeathed stimulated Europeans' interest in the languages and civilizations of East Asia and intensified their efforts to establish direct communications with the Qing court.

Tea and Diplomacy

The early trade relationship between Europe and China developed considerably until the 1700s. In addition to silk and porcelain, tea became an enormously popular Chinese product in western Europe. It had earlier been a prized import to Russia, Central Asia, and the Middle East, all of which knew it as *cha*, its northern Chinese name, and all of which originally acquired it by the overland Eurasian routes of medieval and early modern times. All of western Europe, however, knew the product from sea routes first exploited by the Portuguese and Dutch and thus from its name in Fujian province of coastal China and Taiwan, *te*. From the time of its introduction to England in the middle 1600s, tea displaced chocolate and coffee as the favored drink.

Like all the contemporary governments of East Asia, the Qing empire attempted to regulate commercial activity closely. Qing rulers did this in part because they wanted agriculture to remain the most important and best-protected source of wealth. Such regulation was also consistent with the government's Confucian philosophy that merchants should always be on the lowest rungs of the social and political ladders.

Those ideas, combined with increasing concern about banditry and piracy, led the Qing Empire to strictly limit the access of foreign merchants to the commercial cities of China in the 1700s (a policy that, for similar reasons, had been followed in the earliest years of the Ming empire). This was true whether the merchants were caravan traders on camels attempting to sell dried dates at Kashgar in Central Asia (see Map 22.1), or Japanese merchants trying to sell lacquer ware at Zhapu on the eastern coast of China. It was also true for European merchants at Canton. Restrictions on Europeans at Canton began in 1729, and by 1784 the practices known

as the "Canton system" were fixed: European merchants were permitted to trade only at Canton; they were to be insured, protected, and vouchsafed by Chinese merchants in the city; and all tax revenues from the Canton trade were to be directly rendered to the imperial family through its resident commissioner, known to the Europeans as the "hoppo."

To the Europeans, who imagined this system was uniquely directly against them and whose sea-based empires were built on entirely different principles, the Canton system seemed irrational. Great fortunes had been made in the tea trade, but the search for a suitable product to sell to China had not been successful. British and some American merchants believed that China was a vast unexploited market, with hundreds of millions of potential consumers of lamp oil made from whale blubber, cotton grown in India or the American south, or guns manufactured in London or Connecticut. Britain particularly after the loss of its North American colonies (see Chapter 24), feared that its markets would diminish. Only the Canton system seemed to be standing in the way of opening new paths for commerce.

Because few products from Europe found a market in China, European silver went to China to pay for the exported products. The Qing government, whose revenues were declining in the later 1700s while its expenses rose, needed the silver. In Britain, the imbalance of payments created anxiety and anger over the Qing empire's alleged unfair restrictions on the import of foreign goods.

To make matters worse, the British East India Company had managed its worldwide holdings badly, and as it teetered on bankruptcy, its attempts to manipulate the Parliament became more intrusive. In 1773 the British Parliament passed a series of laws designed to curb the political activities of the BEIC and dismantle some of its monopolies. At the same time, to allow the BEIC to recoup some of its income, Parliament granted it a market monopoly for the American colonies, where it began to sell inferior tea at high prices. British Americans resented being forced to purchase the BEIC product. Protests— "tea parties"—later broke out in Boston, New York, Philadelphia, and elsewhere, and the members of the Sons of Liberty—an association of merchants, tradesmen, and lawyers—warned fellow American colonials that the BEIC represented the greatest threat to their freedoms. Hoping to quiet British America and destroy the influence of the BEIC in domestic politics, the British government decided to undercut the company's ability to control access to Asian tea. For that to happen, the trade in China needed to be restructured. In 1792, George Macartney was dispatched to China to open diplomatic relations with the Qing Empire (see Voices and Visions: The Macartney Mission).

Although historians usually consider the Macartney mission to be an intriguing failure, it had a strong influence over later developments in both Europe and China. Both the British and the Qing insisted on certain rituals, and it may appear that their inflexibility doomed the Macartney mission. But beyond ritual, the Qing rulers wanted to keep the Canton system intact because it was working very well for them. It brought the imperial family money; it created lucrative monopolies for certain merchant families in Canton (who in turn were careful to enrich the officials who allowed them their privileges); and it simplified some problems related to the control of contraband. Moreover, although the Qing court was fascinated by some of the goods that Macartney brought as gifts (really as advertisements)—especially ornamental and amusing timepieces and landscape paintings—neither Europe nor America had a product that really appealed to the Qing in 1793. Realizing that the export of tea, furs, silk, rhubarb, and porcelain was a major advantage, the Qing government did not feel a need to exert itself to improve the relative trade position of Britain.

Dutch, French, and Russian embassies soon attempted to achieve what Macartney had failed to. When they failed also, European frustration with China mounted. To the British government, the imbalance in trade between Britain and China was more worrisome after the Macartney mission, because the likelihood of a political solution to the problem appeared to be diminishing. The British realized, however, that they needed greater familiarity with the Qing Empire and its cultures. Macartney's group had included only one English member who knew Chinese—a child, Thomas Staunton, who learned it on the sea voyage. In Britain and elsewhere in Europe,

scholarship on Chinese and Manchu languages increased, and greater efforts to understand the history and political philosophy of China were made. For their part, the officials of the Qing Empire realized that although they had rejected Macartney, the presence of Europeans in East Asia would only grow. And so they began to investigate the geography, cultures, economies, and armaments of Europe.

Literature and Gender

In the 1700s censorship of all forms of literature became more intense. Nevertheless, the Qianlong emperor considered himself a champion of the printing of imperial encyclopedias, approved collections of poetry and history, and selected works on technology. Imperial libraries were

Education of elite women   Since ancient times, the limited education of women had been advocated by male elites because as mothers women would encourage their sons to study and advance up the social and political ladders. In the Ming period, however, there was widespread interest in the education of women. The development of merchant networks widened the opportunities for women to write letters to each other, to encourage other women to continue their studies, and to share their impressions of literature. (Reproduced courtesy of the Harvard-Yenching Library)

The Macartney Mission

One of the stumbling blocks of Britain's Macartney mission in their attempts to establish diplomatic relations with the Qing empire in 1793 was their inability or unwillingness to use the customary rituals by which countries acknowledged the moral superiority of the emperor of China. Some of these problems were worked out early, thanks to the efforts of eleven-year-old Thomas Staunton, who had come along with his father on the journey. Thomas was the only member of the British party who learned to speak and write Chinese. Curiously, his diary of the trip still mystifies historians over the question of whether the British party did or did not perform the elaborate and, in British eyes, humiliating ritual of the kowtow. In that ceremony, Qing officials and foreign visitors would kneel to the ground three times, after each kneeling performing three prostrations, with the body flat upon the ground, face down.

Chinese records state that the Macartney party was instructed in the ritual and performed it when they encountered the emperor at his summer palace at Rehe. But most historians have accepted the reports that the British party knelt on one knee to the emperor, as they would have to British king. Thomas's diary, however, states that the British joined a crowd of dignitaries (primarily Bannermen and ambassadors from Mongolia, Burma, and Central Asia):

"We were told that the Emperor was coming. We then stood by the side of the road which the Emperor was to pass. He came in a gilt chair supported by 16 men. As he passed we went upon one knee and bowed out heads down to the Ground."

Thus, Thomas agreed with Macartney that the British movements began upon one knee, but his insistence that they had bent their heads to the ground describes almost exactly the prostrating of the body in the kowtow. Somebody—perhaps Thomas himself, but more likely his father who read his words later—realized the seriousness of the implication, and the words "to the Ground" are crossed out in his original diary. Actually, Thomas' account is very similar to that of another Briton in the group, who wrote that: "As [the emperor] passed . . . we paid our respect in the usual form of the country, by kneeling nine times to the

ground," an even more precise description of the kowtow. And to make the waters even murkier, Thomas says that when the party stopped at Canton on their way out of China,

"We went through the tent and entered a handsome furnished room with a throne at the end. There we met . . . great [officials] who were preparing to make nine bows and three genuflections to the throne at the end of the room, as thanking the Emperor for our safe and pleasant arrival here. We followed their example."

So Thomas describes the British as kowtowing yet again, this time before an empty throne.

Why does Thomas' disagreement with his father and with Lord Macartney matter so much? Macartney had been instructed by the British government that he was not to humiliate Britain by prostrating himself before the Qing emperor. And there is ample evidence that Macartney made clear that if presented alone or with his small party to the emperor, he would never kowtow. Thomas's evidence, however, suggests that when the British party were reduced to insignificant presences in large crowds (their normal situation while in China), they tended to go along with the movements of the crowd, not making themselves stick out or disrupting the proceedings. Under those circumstances, the Britons with Macartney may in fact have kowtowed numerous times during their stay. Nevertheless, they staunchly insisted after their return to Britain that no kowtow had ever been performed, meaning that Britain had never acknowledged the superiority of the Qing emperor. This oversimplification of the issue became a serious international matter when a second British embassy, the Amherst mission, arrived in China in 1816 and was told that because Macartney had kowtowed, all British ambassadors would have to do the same. The Amherst talks broke down immediately, the British government branded the Qing as liars, and the two countries remained at stalemate until the outbreak of the Opium War (Chapter 27).

How does the kowtow relate to the "tributary system" in China (Chapter 11)? Why is it so different from the "diplomatic relations" that were familiar to Europeans in the 1700s?

built in locations throughout central China to give the elite access to the new publications. Private literature—including contemporary poetry, fiction, and travel writing—was also important. The novels of the Ming period were reproduced in movable-print editions and could be purchased at low prices. But not until the later eighteenth century was perhaps the greatest Chinese novel, and one of the finest works in any language written. *Dream of the Red Chamber* (*Honglou meng* in Chinese), by Cao Xueqin, has endured as one of the most absorbing of all stories; it is also rich with reflections of Chinese elite culture at the height of the Qing Empire.

Baoyu, the hero of the novel, is a boy growing up in the portion of his family's mansion (the "red chamber") that is reserved for women and girls. Time, the pressure of society, and family expectations all demand that Baoyu grow up and assume the stereotypically male responsibilities of marriage and the examination system, but he resists. Part of the background of this story is the fact that in comparison to the Ming before it, Qing society did indeed demand more rigid behavior in terms of both ethnic identity and gender. During the Qing period, for instance, there was a tendency to criminalize male dress and sexual behaviors that the Ming had tolerated. *Dream of the Red Chamber* is full of nostalgia for the effectiveness, achievement, and dynamism of the Kangxi period, but it also protests the demands of the Qianlong period for strict adherence to norms of dress, behavior, and legal obligations. Baoyu's predicament reflects the elite's discomfort with the transition from military to civil society, from a protected environment to increasing uncertainties, from prosperity to decline.

Baoyu's opposite in the novel is Daiyu, an educated girl of the household. In late Ming and in Qing times, the education of women became a topic of debate among the elite. In the novel, Daiyu suffers the fate of most educated heroines in fiction: she dies an early death. A conservative group of Confucian scholars predicted this outcome as the usual result of female education, because the worldly concerns, ambitions, and complexities of intellectual life would cause the delicate female psyche to collapse.

The argument on the other side was that educated women would make the best mothers for the male elites of the future. Educated women would value education, guide their infant sons through their early lessons, and require continuing discipline in the preparations for the examinations. To a large extent, however, elite women valued education for its own sake, for what it brought to their lives. Many encouraged or oversaw the education of their daughters without the permission or the help of the men of the household. To the end of the Qing period, the education of women remained a frequently debated subject among men, while a minority of women created educational and literary traditions that were passed from generation to generation.

This written communication and exchange of literature among elite women was made possible by the development of mercantile activity between 1500 and 1800. The women in merchant families often were the real managers of the household and had a relatively independent existence despite their bound feet and the complete absence of property rights. Merchant families had the resources to extend education to girls, and the movement of goods and communications on the merchant network allowed the exchange of letters, poems, and essays among wealthy women. Literary pursuits by elite women were tolerated because they were a product of leisure and thus a symbol of status. In some ways they were the counterpart of the social symbolism of footbinding, which also demonstrated the fact that elite women did not work, since their feet were systematically destroyed by the binding process.

For women of the laboring classes, neither education nor footbinding was a consideration. Like their husbands and fathers, these women were workers and largely illiterate. From their points of view, the elite women poets and household managers might as well have been in another universe.

Population Growth and Decline of the Infrastructure

When Macartney's entourage visited China in 1793, they were carefully guided through the most prosperous cities and the most productive farmland. They did not see the evidence of economic and environmental decline that was beginning to affect China in the last decades of the 1700s. The population explosion had led to intense demand for greater cultivation of rice and wheat, for new lands to be opened for the planting of crops imported from Africa and the Americas, and for more thorough exploitation of land already in use. Eventually land and water management failed, and both economic and environmental decline contributed to increasing social disorder.

The narratives of Marco Polo's adventures in the 1200s had fixed the image of packed Chinese cities in Europeans minds. But between the time of Marco Polo and the time of Macartney the Chinese population had tripled. This growth was partly the result of the peace that the Qing enforced after the conquest. Instead of the wars, rebellions, epidemics, and agricultural disasters that afflicted the late Ming, the Qing enjoyed peace and prosperity, and as a result the population increased (see Map 22.2).

Map 22.2 Population Growth in China, 1700–1800   During the first half of the Qing period, conditions of peace, land reclamation, and better transportation contributed to an explosion of population. By 1800 it is probable that the population had reached well over 300 million, double what it was at the beginning of the Qing. At first new crops helped sustain the population, but soon deforestation and soil exhaustion led to increased flooding, massive internal migration and steep declines in living standards in many areas.

In addition, foreign crops known in the late Ming but not widely exploited were commonly used in the Qing period to supplement or replace traditional crops. For instance, in regions of northern China, years of planting wheat and barley had exhausted nutrients from the top most layer of soil. In these areas, the introduction of corn from America temporarily revived agricultural productivity, because the roots of corn grow much further and can find more nutrients at lower levels of the soil. In central and southern China, the use of crops from the Americas such as sweet potatoes made possible the opening of agricultural land that had not been suitable for the cultivation of rice or wheat. As Macartney observed when he was in China, field crops were sown in neat rows by a mechanical seeder. Most of Europe still used the broadcast method, which wasted much of the seed. Because of the efficiency of Chinese planting, the fact that population growth had made the amount of land that could be planted per person three times less than what it had been a century before had not yet created general poverty. With these stimulants, and in the absence of major inhibiting factors such as war or disease, the early Qing population exploded, reaching between 350 million and 400 million by the end of the 1700s.

Woodlands present in China at the beginning of the 1700s had greatly diminished by the end of the century. Houses could thereafter be built of brick, but deforestation joined soil exhaustion as a cause of more and more erosion. As erosion advanced, flooding became a danger. But, because of government corruption and general inefficiency, there was less ability to prevent flooding or to recover from its effects. Waterworks—dams, dikes, and the dredging of silted-up river channels—were not maintained. Local gentry could sometimes make up the deficit but soon were unable to carry the burden. By the end of the eighteenth century even the Grand Canal, which linked the Yellow and Yangzi Rivers, was virtually unusable, its towns starved for commerce.

The result was misery in many parts of interior China by the year 1800. Environmental deterioration and the decline of agriculture prompted many people to move. They sought seasonal work in the better agricultural areas, or they worked as barge pullers, charcoal burners,

nightsoil carriers or in other low-status trades. Many drifted to the cities to make their way by begging, prostitution, or theft. In central China and the southwest, where indigenous peoples had been driven off their lands and farmers had been impoverished by serious flooding from the Xiang and other rivers, rebellions became endemic. By 1796 a series of persistent rural revolts had been linked by the White Lotus sect of millennarian Buddhism, which wished to restore stability and prosperity in China by driving out the Manchu conquerors. The rebellions were still raging when the Qianlong emperor died in 1799.

Because the population growth of the early Qing was one facet of the general economic growth of the empire, it is a sign of the way in which the size and complexity of Qing society outgrew the ability of the state to control it. The Qing government employed about the same number of officials as had the Ming even though the Qing empire was twice as large as the Ming geographically and had more than three times as many people. For local control the Qing depended on a working alliance with local elites, including gentry and aspiring official families. But this dependence often undercut the ability of the government to enforce tax regulations or to control the standards for admission to government service. The resulting semiprivatization of governance in the late 1700s promoted a situation in which corruption was widespread, military policies were inconsistent and ineffective, and banditry was growing, while government revenues were shrinking.

DECENTRALIZATION AND INNOVATION: TOKUGAWA JAPAN

Like continental East Asia under the Qing Empire, Japan under the Tokugawa shoguns had to deal with the transition from the intense militarization of the early 1600s to the comparative peace and secularization of the 1700s. At the same time, Japanese leaders confronted problems of decreasing state revenues, and mounting foreign pressure for trade. In virtually every as-

Women and Tokugawa Technology

In the early-modern period the balance between available resources and demand was better in Japan than in China. In Qing China, population rapidly outstripped farmers' ability to increase agricultural output. In addition, the population of China was unevenly distributed, and when the population far exceeded the demand for labor, not everyone who needed work could find it. In such circumstances, many working women were forced to relinquish skilled, specialized jobs to men and to consider themselves lucky if they were able to find lower-paying, unskilled work.

In Tokugawa Japan, in contrast, women's labor remained valuable through the 1700s and became increasingly specialized. In the countryside and in the industries of the towns, women were regularly employed. In Japan as in China, they were indispensable in agricultural labor. But in Japan, because of the social coherence and comparative uniformity of the work in all regions, women's roles were well integrated with those of men, and women maintained a role in the political as well as economic life of the village. As mechanization was introduced, the value of women's work did not decline. Indeed, women's skills actually became more specialized, and mechanization became a normal part of their work.

The silk industry traditionally had been dominated by women working at home, where they oversaw the breeding and feeding of silkworms and the production of raw silk. In the Tokugawa period, these skills were mechanized—sometimes on so large a scale that the making of silk could no longer be considered a cottage industry. Nevertheless, the demand for labor remained so high that women were able to maintain their role in silk weaving.

Women also were active in mining. They were believed to be highly skilled at separating desired metals from the surrounding stone. This was a lowly trade that was expected to attract humble workers. But as the Tokugawa economy grew, the demand for iron, copper, silver, and gold increased, and these workers, despite their low social standing, were critical to advancement of the society.

Watercolors and drawings of the period commonly depict the integration of women into the Tokugawa economic scene. There was, however, a firm ceiling beyond which Tokugawa women could not rise. Although they enjoyed more economic leverage than their equally hard-working counterparts in China and Korea, they had no property rights. Moreover, despite the fact that Tokugawa women maintained their position in mechanized trades, they generally were not instructed in the most advanced techniques until after they had married, because if a girl were instructed at a very young age before marriage, her skills would benefit not her own birth family but the family of her future husband. Thus, in the 1800s, when increasing complexity demanded earlier and more prolonged training in some trades, women were denied this training. In the last decades of the Tokugawa shogunates, they became more and more restricted to unskilled, small-scale, less-well-paid, and less-visible work.

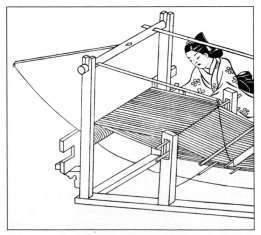 

(From Hishikawa Moronobu *Wakoku hyakujo* (1695). Reproduced courtesy of the Harvard-Yenching Library)

pect the Japanese reaction strongly contrasted to the continental Asian response, with lasting consequences for the region.

Shogunate and Economy

Around 1600 a new military leader, or shogun—Tokugawa Ieyasu—reunified Japan. Under his successors the country would remain at domestic peace until the middle nineteenth century. Although Japan was brought under a single military government, the structure of the shogunate had a very important influence on the development of the Japanese economy in the early modern period. Tokugawa Ieyasu ended decades of civil war by defeating his enemies at the battle of Sekigahara in 1600. The regional lords who fought for Tokugawa at Sekigahara were understood to have an especially close relationship to the shoguns. The Shogunate's original intention was to reward those who had supported the Tokugawa with well-developed rice lands in central Japan—relatively close to the shogunal capital— and to punish those who had not supported the Tokugawa by granting them only remote, undeveloped lands at the northern and southern extremes of the Japanese islands.

The emperors of Japan had no political power; they remained at Kyoto, the medieval capital. The shoguns built a new capital for themselves at Edo (present-day Tokyo). Kyoto and Edo were connected by a network of well-maintained and frequently traveled roads. Not only trade but trading centers developed along this route.

Each regional lord supported a castle town, a small bureaucracy, a population of warriors (*samurai*) and military support personnel, and often an academy. The shogun paid the lords in rice, and the lords paid their followers in rice. To meet their personal expenses, recipients of rice had to convert a large portion of it into cash. This transaction stimulated the development of huge rice exchanges at Edo and at Osaka, where merchants speculated in rice prices. The Tokugawa shoguns required the lords to visit Edo frequently. This requirement led to the extension of good roads, traffic, and commerce to three of the four main islands of Japan.

The result of this controlled decentralization in Tokugawa Japan was the establishment of well-spaced urban centers between which there was frequent traffic. Transport and credit were important businesses in the early 1600s, and traditional small industries enlarged their geographical scope. Because of the domestic peace of the Tokugawa era, the warrior class—the samurai—was required to adapt itself to the growing bureaucratic needs of the state. As the samurai became more educated, more attuned to the tastes of the civil elite, and more involved in conspicuous consumption, merchants dealing in silks, *sake* (rice wine), fans, porcelain, lacquer ware, books, and loans were well positioned to exploit the new opportunities (see Environment and Technology: Women and Tokugawa Technology). The state attempted—unsuccessfully—to curb the independence of the merchants when the interests of the samurai were in danger, particularly when rice prices went too low or interest rates went too high.

The 1600s and 1700s were a period of high achievement in artisanship and commerce. Japanese skills in steelmaking, in pottery, and in lacquer ware were joined by excellence in the production and decoration of porcelain, thanks to Korean experts brought to Japan by the forces that invaded Korea in the late 1500s. Manufacturers and merchants won enormous family fortunes in the early 1600s. The origins of the industrial and financial combines that in the twentieth century would be known as the *zaibatsu* are to be found in this era. Several of the most important—such as the Mitsui companies—had their origins in *sake* or beer breweries. They branched out into early banks, restaurants, lacquer and other table ware, and transport.

These industrial families usually cultivated alliances with their regional lords and, if possible, with the shogun. In this way they sometimes could weaken the strict control on merchant activity that was an official part of Tokugawa policy. By the end of the 1700s, the industrial families of Tokugawa Japan were the key to modernization and the development of heavy industry, particularly in the prosperous provinces. Their political influence was critical to the later transformation of Japan into an industrialized society.

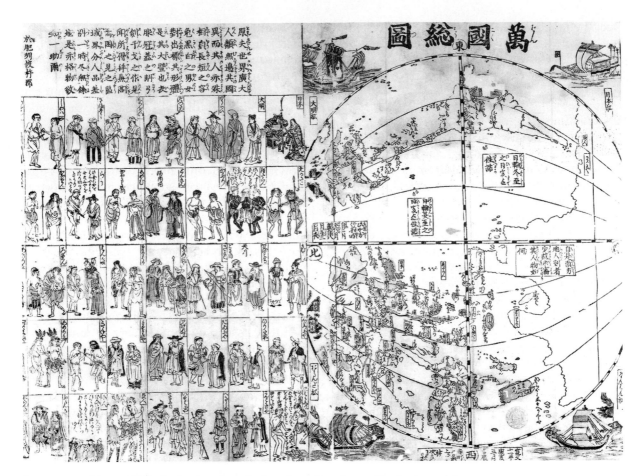

Japanese world map, 1671   Technology transfer in early modern Japan: The Japanese inter-mediaries between the Dutch merchants on the island of Deshima learned the Dutch lan-guage and were as interested in European political ideas as they were in the specifics of science or engineering. From maps such as this, for instance, they learned the geographical extent of the emerging European mercantile systems, and were able to absorb some of the history and economic management behind European exploration and conquest. (British Mu-seum/Fotomas Index)

The "Closing" of Japan

Like China, Japan at the end of the 1500s was a target of missionary activity by the Jesuits. But whereas the Chinese elite was comparatively open to the Jesuits as long as they accommodated Confucian values and became acquainted with Chinese culture, converts to Catholic Christianity among the Japanese elite were comparatively few. Missionaries could selectively gain the favor of regional lords while bypassing the shogunal court in Edo, which was consistently hostile to Christianity. This was the case with Date Masamuni, the fierce and independent warlord

of northern Honshu, who sent his own embassy to the Vatican in 1613 by way of the Philippines (where there were significant communities of Japanese merchants and pirates) and Mexico City.

Generally, Christianity was more successful among farmers in the countryside. Jesuits had their greatest success in the southern and eastern regions of Japan. But in the late 1630s these same regions were the scenes of massive uprisings by farmers who had been impoverished by local rents and taxes. The rebellions, which were ruth-lessly suppressed, were blamed on Christian in-fluence. Hundreds of Japanese Christians were crucified as a warning to others. Belief in Christianity was banned by law. Then in 1649 the shogunate imposed the "closing" of the country, making it illegal and punishable by death for foreigners to come in or for Japanese to go out. The objective was to prevent the spread of foreign influence in Japan, not necessarily to exclude from Japan all knowledge of foreign cultures.

A few Europeans, primarily Netherlanders, were permitted to reside on the small island of Deshima near Nagasaki, and a few Japanese were licensed to supply their needs. These intermediaries concentrated first on learning Dutch, so the body of knowledge that eventually spread from Nagasaki came to be known as "Dutch studies." Familiarity with European weapons technology, shipbuilding, mathematics and astronomy, anatomy and medicine, and geography was common among the "Dutch studies" school. In the 1700s some Japanese theorists advocated that Japan abandon its decentralized, agriculturally oriented system in favor of the centralized, mercantilistic systems of the European empires. This criticism of the government system would later combine with other influences to destroy the Tokugawa shogunate in the nineteenth century.

The closing of Japan was not honored by some of the regional lords whose fortunes depended on the overseas trade with Korea, Okinawa, Taiwan, China, and Southeast Asia. The lords at the northern and southern extremes of Japan tended to be relatively free from control by the shogun. Many of them not only pursued the overseas trade but also claimed personal dominion over islands lying between Japan and Korea to the west and between Japan and Taiwan to the south, including present-day Okinawa.

Qing authorities attempted to limit Japan's access to China's trading ports by issuing a limited number of passes to Japanese merchants (a version of the Canton system so resented by European merchants). Without these passes, Japanese merchants could not enter the port. A black market in the passes soon developed. Pirates of mixed Japanese, Taiwanese, and Chinese descent began to waylay legitimate vessels in order to seize the passes; and the lords of southern Japan soon learned to counterfeit them. Through these means and others, the southern Japanese lords became wealthy and powerful by controlling sea trade. Their violation of Tokugawa law helped make

some of them so powerful that the shogunate could no longer control them, a factor that also undermined the Tokugawa regime.

Elite Decline and Social Crisis

By the year 1700, the relative fortunes of the "inner" and the "outer" lords were reversing. The productivity of the well-developed lands of central Japan was not increasing, and population growth was putting a great strain on them. In the remoter provinces, the lords had sponsored programs to settle and develop new agricultural lands, so the rate of economic growth there far outstripped the rate in the centrally located domains. This economic situation, in combination with the shogun's relatively loose control over the remoter areas, presented a distinct threat to the Tokugawa government.

Also destabilizing to the Tokugawa government in the 1700s was the inability to control the price of rice and the economic decline of the samurai class. To finance their living, the samurai had to convert their rice to cash in the market. The transactions sustained an industry of agents, speculators, and short-term moneylenders, particularly in the rice-market towns of Edo and Osaka. The Tokugawa government realized that these merchants and financiers might easily enrich themselves at the expense of the samurai if the price of rice, and the rate of interest, were not strictly controlled. Laws designed to regulate these two factors were passed early in the Tokugawa period, and more laws requiring moneylenders to forgive samurai debts were added later. But these laws were not always enforced, partly in accord with the wishes of the lords and samurai, who by the early 1700s were already dependent on the willingness of merchants to provide them credit.

The Tokugawa government strongly resisted the forces that were tending to weaken the traditional elite and to strengthen the merchant class. One reason for this resistance was that the Tokugawa regime was primarily a military government. It depended for its legitimacy on its ability to reward and to protect the interests of those who had supported the Tokugawa conquest. The samurai remained important to the ability of the

Woodblock print of the Forty-Seven Ronin story The saga of the Forty-Seven Ronin and their search to avenge their fallen leader has fascinated the Japanese public since it occurred in 1702. As pure embodiment of samurai virtue, the Ronin were deserving of respect and sympathy. But in being willing to resort to military action in order to carry out the private obligation to their leader, they were an intolerable menace to social stability.

Tokugawa to defend, police, and govern Japan. Another reason for Tokugawa support for the traditional elite was that the Tokugawa government, like the governments of the Qing Empire, Korea, and Annam, believed in the Confucian philosophy of keeping agriculture the basis of state wealth and of keeping merchants in lowly positions because of their reputed lack of moral character. This Confucian view was advantageous to agricultural interests and to traditional elite interests. Governments throughout East Asia used this policy to attempt to limit the growing influence and power of merchants.

The Tokugawa government, however, was at a special disadvantage. Its decentralized system of rule by lords of domains limited its ability to regulate merchant activities, but it stimulated the development of commercial activities associated with travel, transport, finance, luxury goods, and many aspects of urban life. In the first two centuries of the Tokugawa shogunate—from 1600 to 1800—the economy grew faster than the population. Household amenities and cultural resources that in China normally would have been found only in the cities were common in the Japanese countryside, and the overall literacy rate was as high as 35 percent.

Despite official disapproval, merchants and others involved in the growing economy enjoyed relative freedom and influence in eighteenth-century Japan. They produced a vivid culture of their own, which fostered the development of kabuki theater, colorful woodblock prints and silkscreened fabrics, and restaurants. They also began to amass the capital resources that eventually would make the centralization and industrialization of Japan possible. Not surprisingly, Japan was able at a much earlier date than any other East Asian nation to accord merchants, financiers, and industrialists the status and influence that made possible its emergence as an international power.

The ideological and social crisis of Tokugawa Japan's transformation from a military to a civil society is captured in the "Forty-seven Ronin" incident of 1702. A senior minister provoked a young regional lord into drawing his sword at the shogun's court. For this action the young lord was sentenced to commit *seppuku*, the ritual suicide of the samurai. His own followers were then *ronin*, or "masterless samurai," and the traditional code of the warrior obliged them to avenge their master. This ethic had been promoted by the Tokugawa shogunate, which had authorized a modified "Confucian" code of conduct designed to assure the samurai's loyalty to their overlords, up to the shogun and the emperor. The ronin broke into the house of the senior minister who had provoked their own lord, and they killed him as well as others in his household. They then withdrew to a Buddhist temple in Edo, where they were beyond the reach of the law. They petitioned the shogun to acknowledge their duty to be loyal to their lord and to avenge his death.

A legal debate began in the shogun's government. To deny the righteousness of the ronin would deny the ideological foundation of the shogunal form of government, which was based on samurai values. But to approve the actions of the ronin would create chaos in society, make it impossible to have laws against murder, and deny the shogunal government itself the right to try cases of samurai violence. As a compromise, the shogun determined that the ronin had to die, but could die honorably by committing *seppuku*.

The compromise exposed a fatal flaw in the structure of shogunal government. To maintain a state based on military values, the state would have to place the military itself outside the law. Centralization, standardization of laws, and the ability of the state to enforce laws for protection of the public would be impossible. The ronin's purity of purpose is still celebrated in Japan today, but from the time of the case in 1702 it was recognized that the self-sacrifice of the *ronin* for the sake of upholding civil law was necessary.

Despite all the advantages that decentralization offered Tokugawa society, it was fatal to the shogunal form of government, which ended in 1868. The Tokugawa shogunate put into place a political and economic system that fostered great innovation, but the government itself could not exploit it. Thus the Tokugawa period is one in which the government remained quite traditional while other segments of society developed new methods of productivity and management. The beneficiaries of this period were not the shoguns but the regional elites, who eventually destroyed the shogunate and created a centralized, industrially based state in the late 1800s.

CONCLUSION

By the 1700s, the technological gap between Europe and China was the reverse of what it had been two centuries before. China had previously been in advance of Europe in military, agricultural, and industrial technologies. After the spread of technological knowledge under the Mongol empires and its specialized adaptation in Europe, the Europeans possessed more powerful military technologies than the Chinese, and

Korea and Japan were advancing in many traditional industries. Despite remaining artistic brilliance and a new market for both raw and manufactured goods in Europe, the Qing Empire did not succeed in increasing state revenues or revitalizing public works.

This was a sharp and instructive contrast with Tokugawa Japan. Whether in terms of economic development, political structure, public values, or popular culture, Japan was a society rapidly bursting the shell of shogunal rule. The controlled decentralization of shogunal government from 1185 to 1868 encouraged economic and technological competition among the regional domains, and by the late 1700s new skills in agricultural mechanization, light industries, finance, and transport had created a vigorous and culturally independent merchant class, as well as generations of young men impatient with the rigid social system of the Tokugawa period. By the middle 1800s Japanese society had the resources to respond quickly and effectively to the threat of Western domination.

The Qing, in contrast, was left with no resources, whether of capital or of skills. While the population of China exploded and by the year 1800 was far outpacing economic growth, in Japan both the population and the economy grew fast, with the economy perhaps even a bit ahead. While the Qing Empire managed through the 1700s to contain mercantile activity and the political influence of economic cliques, in Japan artisans, industrialists, bankers, speculators, and commercial artists and writers wrested a certain social and cultural autonomy of their own. And while the Qing expended its resources on increasingly futile attempts to maintain military dominance over Central Asia, Japan abandoned expansionism after 1600 and concentrated on the creation of wealth, which eventually would propel it into competition with the West.

The 1700s contributed a final element to the cataclysmic encounters to come between Europe and East Asia. The technological strength of Europe combined with political developments to produce the beginnings of European commercial colonization in Asia. The decline of Mughal India, the Ottoman empire, and the Qing empire fostered the idea of a world divided between "East" and "West." By the end of the 1700s, the

"East" of this concept would be seen in the "West" as a world without law or industry, whose people lived in fear and poverty. It was believed to be a passive world that could only respond to the energy and the guidance of the "West." Colonization of that "East" was seen as not only profitable but justifiable in the name of "civilization." When Europe shortly gained the resources and technology to pursue its campaigns against the "East," China and Japan met the onslaught in very different ways.

SUGGESTED READING

On problems relating to the development of global systems and the coherence of the empires, see William W. Fitzhugh and Aron Crowell, eds., *Crossroads of Continents* (1988), and Paul M. Kennedy, *The Rise and Fall of the Great Powers: Economic Change and Military Conflict from 1500 to 2000* (1987).

There is a great deal of literature focused on the history of the Jesuits in various countries. See these general histories: Christopher Hollis, *The Jesuits: A History* (1968), and Georg Schurhammer, *Francis Xavier: His Life, His Times,* trans. M. Joseph Costelloe (1973–1982). For China see David E. Mungello, *Curious Land: Jesuit Accommodation and the Origins of Sinology* (1985); and Jonathan D. Spence, *The Memory Palace of Matteo Ricci* (1984). For Japan see C. R. Boxer, *The Christian Century in Japan, 1549–1650* (1951).

On the East India companies see John E. Wills, *Pepper, Guns, and Parleys: The Dutch East India Company and China, 1662–1681* (1974); Dianne Lewis, *Jan Compagnie in the Straits of Malacca, 1641–1795* (1995); John Keay, *The Honourable Company: A History of the English East India Company* (1991); and Brian Gardner, *The East India Company* (1971).

On China see previously cited textbooks, and these more specialized works: On the transition from the Ming to Qing periods see James W. Tong, *Disorder Under Heaven: Collective Violence in the Ming Dynasty* (1991); Frederic Wakeman, *The Great Enterprise* (1985); Lynn Struve, *Voices from the Ming-Qing Cataclysm: In Tiger's Jaws* (1993).

There are early abridged translations of popular fiction, such as Arthur Waley's of *The Monkey* (*Journey to the West*) or *Chin P'ing Mei* (*The Golden Lotus*). For more recent translations see Anthony C. Yu, ed. and trans., *The Journey to the West,* 4 vols. (1977–1983); Clement Egerton, *The Golden Lotus: A Translation, from the Chinese Original, of the Novel Chin Ping Mei* (1972); and Wu Ching-Tzu, *The Scholars,* trans. Yang Hsien-yi and Gladys Yang (1957).

On Chinese society generally in this period see two classic (though slightly dated) works by Ping-ti Ho: *The Ladder of Success in Imperial China: Aspects of Social Mobility, 1368–1911* (1962) and *Studies in the Population of China, 1368–1953* (1959); see also the general study by Susan Naquin and Evelyn S. Rawski, *Chinese Society in the Eighteenth Century* (1987). On the two greatest of the Qing emperors and their times see Jonathan D. Spence, *Emperor of China: Self Portrait of K'ang Hsi, 1654–1722* (1974).

On the Qing trade systems see John E. Wills, *Embassies and Illusions: Dutch and Portuguese Envoys to K'ang-hsi, 1666–1687* (1984), and Craig Clunas, *Chinese Export Art and Design* (1987).

A great deal has been published on the Macartney mission, much of it originating in the diaries and memoirs of participants. See the exhaustively detailed Alain Peyrefitte, *The Immobile Empire,* trans. Jon Rothschild (1992), and for a more theoretical discussion see James L. Hevia, *Cherishing Men from Afar: Qing Guest Ritual and the Macartney Embassy of 1793* (1995).

On Japan in this period see Chie Nakane and Shinzaburô Ôishi, *Tokugawa Japan: The Social and Economic Antecedents of Modern Japan,* trans. Conrad Totman (1990), and Tessa Morris-Suzuki, *The Technological Transformation of Japan from the Seventeenth to the Twenty-first Century* (1994). Mary Elizabeth Berry, *Hideyoshi* (1982) is an account of the reunification of Japan at the end of the sixteenth century and the invasion of Korea. On technological advancement, capital formation, and competition in the Tokugawa period see the classic by Thomas C. Smith, *Agrarian Origins of Modern Japan* (1959); and the first chapter of Albert Craig, *Chôshû in the Meiji Restoration* (1961).

NOTE

1. See Lynn Struve, *Voices from the Ming-Qing Cataclysm: In Tiger's Jaws* (New Haven, CT: Yale University Press, 1993), 235–237.

PART SIX

Revolutions Reshape the World,

1750–1870

Between 1750 and 1870, Europe and its American colonies experienced dramatic economic, political, and social change. The beginnings of industrialization, the American and French Revolutions, and the breakdown of traditional social controls posed powerful challenges to the established order. Revolution, war, labor violence, and social dislocations convulsed Africa, Asia, the Americas, and the Middle East as well as many European nations. Though transformed by these forces, Europe and the United States established unprecedented global domination within a century.

The introduction of new technologies, often called the "Industrial Revolution," quickly spread from Great Britain to western Europe and the United States, rapidly increasing the productivity and efficiency of Western economies. Economic competition within the industrializing nations accelerated the development and diffusion of new technologies.

Industrialization also changed the nature of work. Factories replaced artisan workshops and home production. The combined effects of mechanization and the factory system improved the quality and lowered the costs of goods. The mechanization of agriculture had a similar impact on rural life, increasing the scale and productivity of farms.

Industrial societies were wealthier, more socially fluid, and more physically mobile than traditional societies. But not all groups benefited: as artisans, small farmers, and agricultural laborers, among others, were threatened by mechanization. At the same time, Europe's rapid population growth stiffened competition for jobs and housing. As a result, millions of Europeans decided to emigrate to the open landscapes of the United States, Canada, Argentina, and Australia.

In similar ways, the American Revolution (1776–1783) and the French Revolution (1789–1799) transformed Western political culture. After the American Revolution, nearly all of the European colonies in the Americas gained their independence. In Europe, constitutional republicanism made slower progress. Monarchies survived but were generally weakened by constitutions. The revolutionary era also unleashed powerful forces of nationalism (the association of a shared culture and language with a specific territory) that enabled Western governments to harness more effectively the energies and resources of their citizens.

In the wake of these revolutionary events, both traditional monarchists and modern charismatic political leaders challenged the partisans of constitutional democracy. Monarchs who secured their positions usually did so by embracing nationalist objectives and by permitting some electoral participation. But in the difficult transition from monarchy or colonialism to democracy, many nations discovered that nationalism and mass politics sometimes led to dictatorship in times of crisis. Popular forms of authoritarian rule appeared first in France with Napoleon Bonaparte. Although the United States successfully established a constitutional order, military leaders or popular politicians who represented regional or class interests often overthrew constitutional governments in Latin America.

Other revolutionary changes were also taking place. Western abolitionist movements and revolts by slaves in Haiti and other parts of the Americas brought an end to the slave trade and slavery in the Western Hemisphere. Political revolutions created reformist Muslim states in West Africa and powerful kingdoms in southeastern Africa. In China and Japan as well, established political orders were challenged.

Even while Europe's colonial empires in Latin America were being dismantled, machine-made textiles and iron tools from Europe and later from the United States were completing a new conquest, overwhelming the competition of small local producers. Simultaneously, the products of the industrializing nations were entering Africa and Asia. When this economic penetration was resisted, as it was in East Asia, the industrial nations of the West—equipped with modern rifles, cannon, and iron ships—commonly used military force to open markets. Elsewhere, Western economic expansion was more peaceful. To

obtain European manufactures, Africans created a new "legitimate trade" in palm oil, gold, and ivory to replace the declining Atlantic slave trade. Some Africans used firearms obtained in trade with the West to create new empires or expand and strengthen existing states.

New colonization for economic reasons or for settlement was another form of Western expansion. France conquered Algeria. Britain added the Cape Colony at the southern tip of Africa as a link to its Indian Ocean empire. Britain also annexed and sent settlers to the distant lands of Australia and New Zealand, with consequences for the indigenous populations that paralleled those suffered by Amerindians in the wake of sixteenth-century European expansion. But nowhere was British expansion more momentous than in India. When the British government assumed direct political control after the Indian Rebellion of 1875–1858, it took possession of a colony with a larger population and greater commercial potential than that of all the colonies lost by Europe in the Americas.

The Ottoman Empire, China, and Japan were deeply influenced by the economic and military expansion of Europe and the United States, but

Technology

1750–1800—Steam engine, mechanization of textile production, iron foundries, industrial potteries

1800–1870—Cotton gin, spread of railroads and steamships, telegraph, repeating firearms, iron ships

Environment

After 1840—Rapid settlement of North American West

Increased urbanization in Europe, United States, and Ottoman Empire

Expansion of coal mining to support steam power

Growing industrial pollution

Settlement of Australia and New Zealand

1800–1860—Repeated flooding of Yellow River; erosion and soil exhaustion in China

Boom in cotton cultivation in U.S. south (after 1810) and Egypt (after 1860)

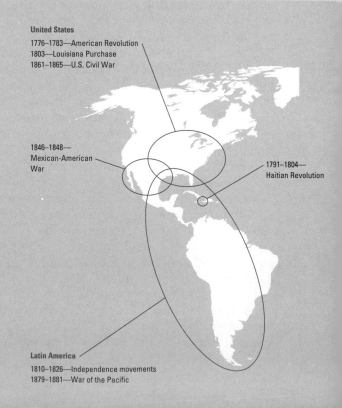

United States
1776–1783—American Revolution
1803—Louisiana Purchase
1861–1865—U.S. Civil War

1846–1848—Mexican-American War

1791–1804—Haitian Revolution

Latin America
1810–1826—Independence movements
1879–1881—War of the Pacific

they remained politically independent. In each case, local rulers met the Western challenge by adopting elements of Western technology and culture. The Ottoman Empire was forced to react early to developments in Europe. By the end of the 1820s, military rebellions and European support for Greek independence led the Ottoman court to introduce Western-style reforms in education, the military, and law. But despite these reforms, the Ottoman state found it difficult to resist Europe's economic penetration.

As Western power grew, China, like the Ottoman empire, was weakened by regionalism, political corruption, and the lack of economic integration. Although China survived the period of European expansion as an independent nation, a series of military defeats seriously compromised Chinese sovereignty. The result was humiliating treaties that gave citizens of Great Britain, France, and the United States living in China freedom to ignore Chinese law. Efforts by the Chinese government to strengthen its position by modernizing the military and promoting industrialization were largely failures.

Japan proved more successful than China and the Ottoman empire in modernizing its political institutions and economy and in resisting European and American domination. Japan's relative geographic isolation and smaller economy limited European interest. The narrow nature of the forced opening of Japanese markets by the United States at the end of the 1850s combined with long-standing social tensions in Japan to force a clean break with the former political system.

The economic, political, and social revolutions that began in the mid-eighteenth century both shook the foundations of European culture and led to Western global dominance. Yet by 1870 the full consequences of this revolutionary period were not yet apparent. Throughout Asia, Africa, and Latin America, societies attempted to meet the challenges posed by the growing power of the industrializing nations of Europe. Some sought to resist these new currents by using local culture and experience to guide change. But to protect the integrity and autonomy of their own cultural traditions, many others adopted Western commercial policies, industrial technologies, and government institutions.

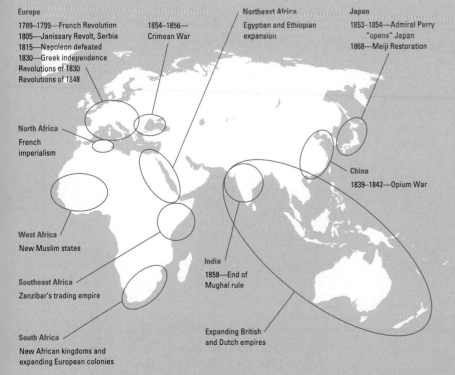

Europe
1789–1799—French Revolution
1805—Janissary Revolt, Serbia
1815—Napoleon defeated
1830—Greek independence
Revolutions of 1830
Revolutions of 1848

1854–1856—Crimean War

Northeast Africa
Egyptian and Ethiopian expansion

Japan
1853–1854—Admiral Perry "opens" Japan
1868—Meiji Restoration

North Africa
French imperialism

China
1839–1842—Opium War

West Africa
New Muslim states

India
1858—End of Mughal rule

Southeast Africa
Zanzibar's trading empire

South Africa
New African kingdoms and expanding European colonies

Expanding British and Dutch empires

Society
Beginning of industrial labor movement in West
1808–1850—End of Atlantic slave trade
1810–1840—Growing use of child labor in industry
1830–1870—Secularization movement in Ottoman Empire
1840s—Women's rights movement begins in West
1840–1870—Increased emigration from Europe and Asia to Americas
1850–1888—Abolition of slavery in Americas
After 1850—Expansion of legitimate trade in West Africa

Culture
Islam expands in East and West Africa
Christian missionary activity in Africa and Asia
Expansion of public schools in West
1800–1850—Modernization movements in Egypt, Ethiopia, and Ottoman Empire
1850s—Rise of Indian nationalism

The Industrial Revolution, 1760–1870

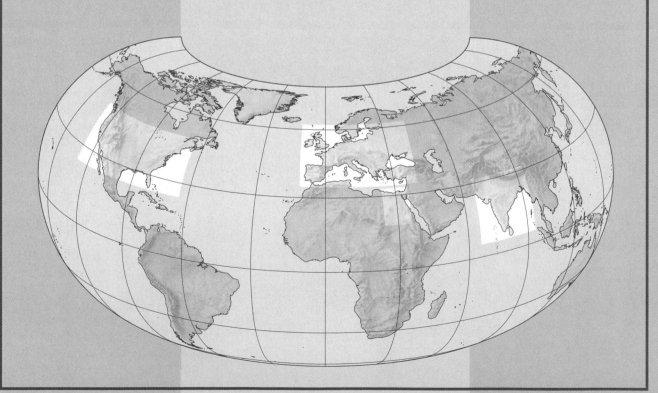

In the early nineteenth century, new textile machines put many craftsmen in the English Midlands out of work. In late 1811 and early 1812, bands of unemployed workers calling themselves "Luddites" came out at night to attack factories and workshops and smash the hated machines that had cost them their livelihood. As one poor English weaver testified to Parliament: "I have five children and a wife, the children all under 8 years of age. . . . I work sixteen hours a day. . . . My family live on potatoes chiefly and we have one pint of milk per day." The poet Lord Byron spoke out in the Luddites' defense: "However we may rejoice in any improvement in the arts which may be beneficial to mankind, we must not allow mankind to be sacrificed to improvements in Mechanism."

Although the British army crushed the Luddites, in the long run it was not military force that doomed them and their counterparts in other countries but the greater productivity of the machines and the profits they brought to their owners. Neither uprisings by displaced workers nor protests by sympathetic intellectuals could slow the coming of industrial machines. Historians often refer to this great transformation as the "Industrial Revolution."

The late eighteenth and early nineteenth centuries witnessed dramatic innovations in manufacturing, mining, transportation, and communications and equally rapid changes in society and commerce. The people who controlled these innovations achieved unprecedented power over nature and access to energy and natural resources. But this power and wealth was unevenly distributed. In the industrializing countries, some people benefited tremendously, while others suffered. At the time, the political upheavals—the American and French Revolutions and the Napoleonic Wars—attracted more attention (see Chapter 24). In the long run, however, industrialization had a more profound impact on the economy, society, environment, and culture of the countries where it took root.

The Industrial Revolution affected the entire world, but very unevenly. The first countries to be transformed—Britain, then western Europe and the United States—became wealthy and powerful. In Russia and eastern Europe, mechanization came slowly, and it is not until the end of the nineteenth century that historians can speak of an industrial revolution there. Industrialization also began, tentatively, in a few countries outside the West such as Egypt and India, but the economic and military power of the European countries soon stifled these beginnings. The disparity between the industrial and the nonindustrial worlds, which prevails today, dates from the early nineteenth century.

BRITAIN: A SOCIETY OPEN TO INNOVATION

The Industrial Revolution began in Great Britain (see Map 23.1), a country with many technologically creative people, though no more than in France at the time or in China a few centuries before. Until the mid-eighteenth century, the British were better known for their cheap imitations of foreign goods than for their innovativeness or the quality of their products. But they put inventions into practice more quickly than other people, as the engineer John Farey told a parliamentary committee in 1829: "The prevailing talent of English and Scotch people is to apply new ideas to use and to bring such applications to perfection, but they do not imagine as much as foreigners."

Britain had many advantages. It was the world's leading exporter of tools, guns, hardware, and other craft goods. Its mining and metal industries employed engineers willing to experiment with new ideas. Its craftsmen

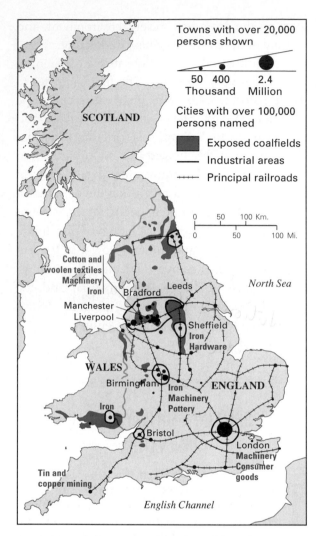

Towns with over 20,000
persons shown

50   400   2.4
Thousand   Million

Cities with over 100,000
persons named

■ Exposed coalfields

— Industrial areas

┼┼┼┼ Principal railroads

0   50   100 Km.
0   50   100 Mi.

SCOTLAND

Cotton and
woolen textiles
Machinery
Iron
Bradford   Leeds   *North Sea*

Manchester
Liverpool
Sheffield
Iron
Hardware

WALES
Birmingham
Iron
Machinery
Pottery   ENGLAND

Iron

Bristol

London
Machinery
Consumer
goods

Tin and
copper mining

English Channel

Map 23.1 The Industrial Revolution in Britain, ca. 1850
The first industries arose in northern and western England
regions that had abundant coal and iron-ore deposits for the
iron industry and a moist climate and fast-flowing rivers,
factors that were important for the cotton industry.

European continent, and the government employed fewer bureaucrats and officials. Members
of the gentry, and even some aristocrats, married
into merchant families. Farther down the social
scale, intermarriage among the families of small
merchants, yeoman farmers, and town craftsmen
was quite common. Ancestry remained important, but wealth also commanded respect. With
enough money, a businessman could buy a country estate, a seat in Parliament, and the social status that accompanied them. Standards of living
were the highest in Europe, perhaps the world.

At a time when transportation by land was
very costly, Great Britain had the best water
transportation system in Europe, thanks to its indented coastline, navigable rivers, and growing
network of canals. It had a unified market, with
none of the duties and tolls that goods had to
pay every few miles in France. This encouraged
specialization and trade.

Britain was highly commercial: more of its
people were involved in production for export
and in trade and finance than in any other major
country. It had financial and insurance institutions able to support growing business enterprises and a patent system that offered inventors
the hope of rich rewards. The example of men
who became wealthy and respected for their inventions, like Richard Arkwright the cotton mag-
nate and James Watt the steam engine designer,
stimulated others. In this respect, Britain contrasted with China and most of the European
continent, where aristocrats, politicians, and intellectuals competed for the limelight, craftsmen
were looked down upon, and inventors were seldom rewarded.

supplied ships with clocks and navigation instruments. Many of its skilled workers were foreigners who had fled persecution and found
refuge in Britain, bringing their talents with
them.

British society was more fluid than others at
the time. Compared with France or Austria, the
English royal court was less ostentatious, the
aristocracy was less powerful, and the lines separating the social classes were less sharply drawn.
Political power was not as centralized as on the

THE TECHNOLOGICAL REVOLUTION

Industrialization involved four revolutionary
innovations: (1) mass production through the
division of labor, (2) new machines and mechanization, (3) a great increase in the supply of
iron, and, most important of all, (4) the steam engine and the changes it permitted.

The New Manufactures

The pottery industry is a good example of the new mass production methods. East Asian potters had long known how to make fine glazed porcelain, or "china." In Europe before the mid-eighteenth century only the wealthy could afford fine porcelain imported from Asia; middle-class people used pewter tableware, and the poor ate out of wooden or earthenware bowls. Several royal manufactures—Meissen in Saxony, Delft in Holland, and Sèvres in France—were founded to produce exquisite handmade products for the courts and aristocracy, but their products were much too expensive for mass consumption. Meanwhile, more and more Europeans acquired a taste for tea, cocoa, and coffee, and with it a demand for porcelain that would not spoil the flavor of hot beverages (see Chapter 20). This created opportunities for inventive entrepreneurs.

Britain, like other countries, had many small potters' workshops where craftsmen made a few plates and cups at a time. Much of this activity was located in a part of the Midlands called the Potteries, which possessed good clay, coal for firing, and lead for glazing. There Josiah Wedgwood (1730–1795) opened a business in 1759. Today, the name Wedgwood is associated with expensive, highly decorated china. But Wedgwood's most important contribution lay in producing ordinary porcelain cheaply.

To do so, he applied mass production methods long used at the Chinese porcelain works at Jingdezhen and Dehua. He subdivided the work into highly specialized and repetitive tasks, such as unloading the clay, mixing it, pressing flat pieces, dipping the pieces in glaze, putting handles on cups, packing kilns, and carrying things from one part of his plant to another. He substituted the use of molds for the potter's wheel wherever possible, a process that not only saved labor but made identical plates and bowls that could be stacked. Wedgwood was also interested in new technologies. He invested in toll roads and canals so that clay could be shipped economically from Cornwall to his factories. In 1782, to mix clay and grind flint, he purchased one of the first steam engines to be used in industry.

Wedgwood's potteries In Staffordshire, England, Josiah Wedgwood established a factory to mass produce beautiful and inexpensive china. The bottle-shape buildings are kilns in which thousands of pieces of china could be fired at one time. In Etruria and other pottery towns, kilns, factories, and housing were all mixed together, and smoke from burning coal filled the air. (Mary Evans Picture Library)

These were radical departures from the age-old methods of craftsmanship that prevailed until then. By the minute division of labor, new machinery, and strict discipline, Wedgwood lowered the cost of his products while improving their quality. As a result, he could offer his wares at lower prices. His factory grew far larger than any other and employed several hundred workers. He had his own traveling salesmen touting his goods throughout England.

Wedgwood's interest in applying technology to manufacturing was connected with his membership in the Birmingham Lunar Society, so named because members met when the moon was full so they could see their way home after dark. This club included such luminaries as the chemist Joseph Priestley, the inventor James Watt, the manufacturer Matthew Boulton, and the naturalist Erasmus Darwin, grandfather of the biologist Charles Darwin (see Chapter 28). This critical mass of creative thinkers living in close proximity and willing to exchange ideas and discoveries encouraged the atmosphere of experimentation and innovation that characterized late-eighteenth-century England. Similar societies throughout Britain were creating a vogue for science and giving the word *progress* a new meaning: "change for the better."

The cotton industry was the largest industry in this period and illustrates the role of mechanization. Cotton had long been the most common fabric in China, India, and the Middle East, where it was spun and woven by hand. The plant did not grow in Europe, but the fabric was so much cooler, softer, and cleaner than wool that wealthy Europeans developed a taste for this costly import. When the powerful English woolen industry persuaded Parliament to forbid the import of cotton cloth into England, it stimulated attempts to import the fiber and make the cloth locally. Here was an inviting opportunity for enterprising inventors to reduce costs through labor-saving machinery.

Beginning in the 1760s, a series of inventions revolutionized the spinning of cotton thread. The first was the spinning jenny, invented by James Hargreaves in 1764. The jenny drew out the cotton fibers and twisted them into thread. It was simple and cheap to build and easy for one person to operate. Early models spun six or seven threads at once, later ones up to eighty. The thread, however, was soft and irregular and could only be used in combination with linen.

In 1769 Richard Arkwright invented another spinning device, the water frame, which produced thread strong enough to be used without linen. Arkwright was both a gifted inventor and a successful businessman. His machine was larger and more complex than the jenny and required a source of power such as a water wheel, hence the name "water frame." To obtain the necessary energy, he installed many machines in one building, next to a fast-flowing river. The resemblance to a flour mill gave such enterprises the name "cotton mill."

In 1785 another inventor, Samuel Crompton, patented a machine that combined the best features of the jenny and the frame. This device, called a mule, produced a thread that was both strong and fine enough to be used in the finer qualities of cotton called muslins. In fact, the mule could make a finer, more even thread than any human, and at a lower cost. Now British industry could undersell high-quality handmade Indian cloth. As a result, British cotton output increased tenfold between 1770 and 1790.

The boom in thread production and the soaring demand for cloth created bottlenecks in weaving. Inventors were not far behind. The first power loom was introduced by Edmund Cartwright in 1784 but was not perfected until after 1815. Other inventions of that period included carding machines, chlorine bleach, and cylindrical printing presses. By the 1830s, the cotton industry consisted of large mills powered by steam engines that turned raw cotton into printed cloth. It was a far cry from the home spinning and weaving of the previous century (see Chapter 18).

Mechanization offered two advantages: (1) productivity for the manufacturer and (2) price for the consumer. Whereas in India it took 500 hours to spin a pound of cotton, the mule of 1790 could do so in 3 person-hours, and the self-acting mule—an improved version introduced in 1830—required only 1 hour and 20 minutes. Cotton mills needed few skilled workers, and managers often hired children to tend the spinning machines. The same was true of power looms, which gradually replaced handloom weaving: the number of power looms rose from 2,400 in 1813 to 500,000 by 1850. Meanwhile, the price of cloth fell by 90 percent from 1782 to 1812 and kept dropping after that.

Iron making was also transformed during the Industrial Revolution. Iron had been used for thousands of years throughout Eurasia and Africa. In eleventh-century Song China, forges had produced cast iron in large quantities. Although production declined after the Song period, iron continued to be common and inexpensive in China. Wherever iron was produced, however, deforestation eventually drove up the cost of charcoal and restricted output. Further-

Crystal Palace interior The Crystal Palace, built for the Universal Exposition of 1851, was the largest structure in England. It was entirely prefabricated of iron and glass, a forerunner of great railroad stations of the late nineteenth century and the skyscrapers of the twentieth century. (Houghton Library)

more, iron had to be repeatedly heated and hammered to drive out the impurities, a difficult and costly process. Because of limited wood supplies and the high cost of skilled labor, iron was a rare and valuable metal outside China before the eighteenth century and was used only for weapons, cutlery, and hardware.

A major breakthrough occurred in 1709 when Abraham Darby discovered that coke (coal from which the impurities have been cooked out) could be used in place of charcoal. The resulting metal was of lower quality but much cheaper than charcoal-iron. Then in 1784 Henry Cort found a way to remove some of the impurities in the iron by stirring the molten iron with long rods. Already by 1790 four-fifths of Britain's iron was made with coke, while other countries still used charcoal. Coke-iron not only was cheaper and less destructive of forests but allowed a great expansion in the size of individual blast furnaces, substantially reducing the cost of iron. There seemed almost no limit to the quantity of iron that could be produced with coke instead of charcoal. Britain's iron production began rising fast, from 17,000 tons in 1740 to 3 million tons in 1844, as much as the rest of the world put together.

In turn, there seemed no limit to the amount of iron that an industrializing society would purchase or to the novel applications for this cheap and useful material. In 1779 the iron manufacturer Abraham Darby built a bridge of iron across the Severn River. In 1851 Londoners marveled at the Crystal Palace, a huge greenhouse made entirely of iron and glass and large enough to enclose the tallest trees. Six years later they witnessed the launching of the *Great Eastern*, the largest ship built before the twentieth century, made entirely of iron.

The Energy Revolution

Although the mechanization of manufacturing was very important, the most revolutionary invention of the Industrial Revolution was surely the steam engine. By the late seventeenth century many activities had run into serious bottlenecks because of a lack of energy. In particular, deep mines filled with water faster than horses could pump it out. Between 1702 and 1712 Thomas Newcomen developed the first steam engine, a crude and inefficient device (see the picture on page 000). Its voracious appetite for fuel mattered little in coal mines where fuel was cheap, but it was too costly for other uses. When James Watt, an instrument maker at Glasgow University, was asked to repair a model of a Newcomen engine, he realized that it wasted fuel because the cylinder had to be alternately heated and cooled. He therefore developed a separate condenser, a vessel into which the steam was allowed to escape after it had done its work, leaving the cylinder always hot and the condenser always cold. Watt patented his idea in 1769. Seven years later, he and the manufacturer Matthew Boulton began selling steam engines to manufacturers of iron, pottery, and cotton.

Watt's steam engine was the most celebrated invention of the eighteenth century. It was more than an ingenious invention or a substitute for other forms of energy. It differed from previous devices in two ways: first, there seemed almost no limit to the amount of coal in the ground, and therefore of available energy; and second, it could be used where animal, wind, and water power

were lacking. Without the steam engine, industrialization would have been a limited phenomenon.

The new manufactures and engines that appeared in the late eighteenth century mark the beginning of the Industrial Revolution, but their impact on the British economy was not immediate. Some inventions, like the power looms and steam engines, needed further refinements before they could be widely used. Meanwhile, the frequent wars with France between 1792 and 1815 hampered trade and drove up interest rates, slowing economic growth (see Chapter 24). By the 1820s and 1830s, however, the British economy was growing fast, thanks to its new cotton, iron, machine, and hardware industries and the export of their products.

Transportation and Communications

Inspired by the success of Watt's engine, inventors thought of using it for transportation. They first put steam engines on boats in France in 1783, in America in 1787, and in England in 1788. The first commercially successful steamboat was Robert Fulton's *Clermont*, which steamed on the Hudson River between New York City and Albany in 1807. Soon thereafter, steamboats were launched on other American rivers, especially the Ohio and the Mississippi, gateways to the midwestern United States.

Oceangoing steamships were much more difficult to build than riverboats, for steam engines used so much fuel that no ship could carry more than a few days' worth. The *Savannah*, which crossed the Atlantic in 1819, was a sailing ship with an auxiliary steam engine that was used for only 90 hours of its 29-day trip. But engineers were developing more efficient engines, and in 1838 two steamers, the *Great Western* and the *Sirius*, crossed the Atlantic on steam alone. Elsewhere, sailing ships held their own until late in the century, for world trade was growing so fast that there was enough business for every kind of ship.

On land as on water, the problem was not imagining uses for steam-powered vehicles but building ones that worked. The Frenchman Nicolas Cugnot built a three-wheeled steam carriage in 1769 as a curiosity. At the time, steam engines were too heavy and weak to pull any weight. After Watt's patent expired in 1800, inventors experimented with lighter, more powerful high-pressure engines—an idea Watt had rejected as too dangerous. In 1804, the engineer Richard Trevithick built an engine that consumed only 2½ pounds (1.1 kilograms) of coal per horsepower per hour, twelve times less coal than Newcomen's and three times less than Watt's. With it, he built several steam-powered vehicles able to travel on roads or rails.

Horses could pull heavier wagons on wooden or iron rails than on cobblestone roads. By the 1820s England had many such horse-powered

Newcomen's atmospheric engine, 1712   Newcomen's was the first practical fossil-fuel engine. It used a cylinder that was first filled with steam, then sprayed with cold water to make the steam condense. The resulting vacuum allowed the pressure of the atmosphere to push down the piston, hence the name "atmospheric." A beam then transmitted the power to a pump underground that pumped water out of a mine. Not until the end of the eighteenth century did better engines, made by Boulton and Watt, replace Newcomen's awkward but effective machine. (Science & Society Picture Library)

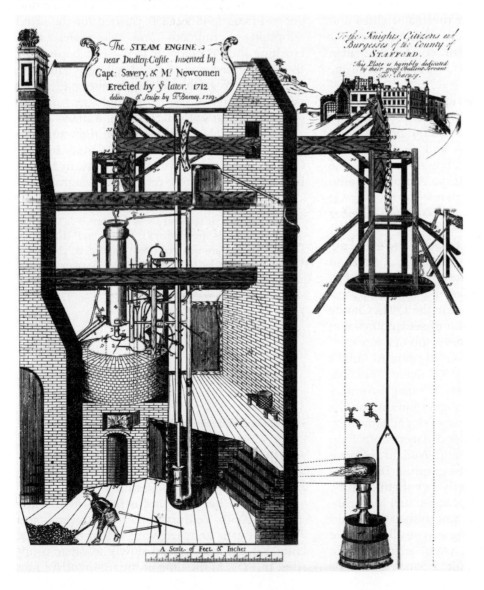

railways. On one of them, the Stockton and Darlington Railway, the chief engineer, George Stephenson, began using steam locomotives in 1825. Four years later, the owners of the Liverpool and Manchester Railway organized a contest between locomotives, stationary engines, and horse-drawn wagons. Stephenson and his son Robert easily won the contest with their locomotive *Rocket*, which pulled a 20-ton train at up to 30 miles (48 kilometers) per hour. After the triumph of the *Rocket*, Britain was swept by a railroad-building mania that lasted for twenty years. The first lines linked towns and mines with the nearest harbor or waterway. In the late 1830s, passenger traffic soared, and entrepreneurs built lines between the major cities and then to small towns as well. Railroads were far cheaper, faster, and more comfortable than stagecoaches, and millions of people got in the habit of traveling.

The railway boom soon spread to other countries. Over the next fifty years, Britain built 13,000 miles (20,930 kilometers) of railroads, Germany 13,000, (20,930) and France almost 10,000 (16,100). No people, however, took to the railroad as enthusiastically as Americans, who lived in a huge country with few roads or canals; by 1870 their rail network stretched 53,000 miles (85,330 kilometers).

The advent of railroads coincided with the development of the electric telegraph. Already in the eighteenth century, many people recognized a need to communicate faster than a ship or a horse could travel. In France in the 1790s, Claude Chappe developed a system of semaphores that transmitted messages from the top of a tower by waving wooden arms. After Alessandro Volta's invention of the battery in 1800 made it possible to produce an electric current, many inventors tried to apply electricity to communication. The first practical systems were developed almost simultaneously in England and America. In England, Charles Wheatstone and William F. Cooke introduced a five-needle telegraph in 1837; it remained in use until the early twentieth century. That same year, the American Samuel Morse introduced his code of dots and dashes that could be transmitted with a single wire. By the late 1840s, telegraph wires were being strung throughout the eastern United States and western Europe. The first successful long-distance telegraph cable, laid between Britain and America in 1866, was quickly followed by cables to India, China, Australia, and Africa. The world was rapidly shrinking, to the applause of Europeans and Americans for whom speed was a clear measure of progress (see Environment and Technology: "The Annihilation of Time and Space").

In other parts of the world, people had mixed reactions to railroads and telegraphs. In the Middle East and Latin America, governments quickly perceived their value and borrowed money to obtain these new technologies. In India, Lord Dalhousie, the British governor-general from 1848 to 1856, pushed for the rapid adoption of railroads and telegraphs. After crushing the Rebellion of 1857 (see Chapter 26), the British hastened to build railroads and telegraph lines to safeguard their power and to develop commerce. Both technologies quickly proved popular with all classes of Indians.

Europeans also demanded the right to build railroads and telegraph lines in China, but the Chinese government resisted strongly. In 1868, it responded to a Western request for telegraphs:

> All countries have cast their greedy eyes on the construction of telegraphs in China. . . . [Their request] sounds quite proper. Yet the evil intentions they harbor are not voiced. It should be clear that this is to pander to all foreign ambassadors' desire to take an opportunity to get in, and one successful case will lead to demands for more.[1]

When foreigners built railroads and telegraphs without official authorization, officially sponsored "mobs" ripped them up. As a result, China was very late in obtaining these alien artifacts.

THE INDUSTRIAL REVOLUTION SPREADS

As Britain began to industrialize in the late eighteenth century, other Europeans and Americans watched with astonishment and envy. Yet industry spread slowly to other countries. In 1851, at the time of the first world's fair,

"The Annihilation of Time and Space"

In the 1780s, it took from five to eight months to sail from England to India, and a European writing a letter to someone in India usually had to wait two years for an answer. Fifty years later, when the first steamships and telegraph lines appeared, telegraph pioneer William O'Shaughnessy, serving with the British army in India, wrote:

> The progress of science is hourly adding to the catalogue of triumphs effected by the sagacity of man over the seeming impossibilities of nature . . . . A conquest still greater than all which I have quoted would be the annihilation of time and space in the accomplishment of correspondence.

By 1870, the voyage to India by ship had been shortened to three weeks, and correspondents could expect answers to their letters in less than two months. It was the beginning of what O'Shaughnessy called "the annihilation of time and space."

The telegraph had an even more astonishing impact on global communications. Beginning in the 1860s, cables laid on the ocean floor allowed telegrams to be sent across oceans as readily as on land. When the first cable to India was completed in June 1870, the chairman of the Eastern Telegraph Company, John Pender, sent a telegram to Bombay and received an answer 4 minutes and 22 seconds later. The *Daily Telegraph* of London reported this astonishing news:

> Aladdin . . . must have dropped his wonderful lamp in sheer amazement and neglect, and sold his magic ring for old gold. Time itself is telegraphed out of existence. Today communicates on one hand with Yesterday, on the other, with tomorrow.

Today, many of us take for granted that we can communicate easily, almost instantaneously, with any country in the world. This astonishing ability to leap over distances began in the mid-nineteenth century. Since that time, communications technologies have made the world a much smaller and more intimate place—for those who can afford them.

Sources: Sir William Brooke O'Shaughnessy, "Memoranda relative to experiments on the communication of Telegraphic Signals by induced electricity," *Journal of the Asiatic Society of Bengal* (September 1839): 720–21. Quoted in G. R. M. Garratt, *One Hundred Years of Submarine Cables* (London: HMSO, 1950), p. 29.

Transatlantic travel   In 1938, two ships equipped with both sails and steam engines, the Sirius and the Great Western, sailed from England to New York. Although the Sirius left a few days earlier, the Great Western—shown here arriving in New York harbor—almost caught up with it, arriving just four hours after the Sirius. This race inaugurated regular transatlantic steamship service. (Courtesy of the Mariner's Museum, Newport News, VA)

the Great Exhibition in London, Britain still produced half of the world's iron and cotton cloth and two-thirds of the world's coal. Why the delay?

Western Europe

In the eighteenth century, the economies of western Europe were hampered by high transportation costs, misguided government regulations, rigid social structures, and a general antipathy toward innovations, business competition, and financial success. The ruling monarchies made feeble attempts to import British techniques and organize factory production, but those attempts all floundered for lack of markets or management skills. Then, from 1789 to 1815, revolutions and wars convulsed Europe (see Chapter 24). Although war created opportunities for suppliers of weapons and uniforms, the insecurity of the times and the interruption of trade with Britain weakened the incentive to invest in new technologies. Neither the arms trade nor efforts by local manufacturers to replace imports sufficed to stimulate an industrial revolution. The only advantage of these upheavals for the continental economies was to sweep away the restrictions of the old regimes.

Only after conditions of peace were reestablished in the 1820s were the economies of the European continent ready to begin industrializing (see Map 23.2). Industrialization first spread to Belgium and northern France, as businessmen there visited Britain to observe the changes and to spy out industrial secrets. In spite of British laws forbidding the emigration of skilled workers and the export of textile machinery, many workers and technical diagrams slipped through. By the 1820s, several thousand Britons were at work on the European continent setting up machines, training workers in the new methods, and even starting their own businesses.

European governments were acutely aware of Britain's lead and of the need to stimulate their own industrialization. They created technical schools. They eliminated internal tariff barriers, tolls, and other hindrances to trade. They encouraged the formation of joint-stock companies and

of banks like the French Crédit Mobilier to channel private savings into industrial investments. In continental Europe as in Britain, cotton was the first industry. The mills of France, Belgium, and Germany served local markets but could not compete abroad with the more advanced British industry. By 1830, the political climate in western Europe was as favorable to business as Britain's had been a half-century earlier.

It was railways that triggered the industrialization of Europe. Belgium, independent since 1830, quickly copied the British. In France and Prussia, the state planned and supervised railroad construction from the start in order to avoid the technical and financial problems that had plagued the early British railroads. This precaution delayed construction until the mid-1840s. When it began, however, it had a greater impact than in Britain, for it not only satisfied the long-standing need for transportation but also stimulated the iron, machinery, and construction industries.

Abundant deposits of coal and iron ore determined the concentration of industries in a swath of territories running from northern France through Belgium and the Ruhr district of western Germany to Silesia in Prussia (now part of Poland). In the 1850s and 1860s, the states of Germany experienced an industrial boom, as did France and Belgium. Countries farther from Britain—Spain, Italy, Austria, Sweden, and Russia—were just beginning to build cotton mills and railroads by 1870.

The United States

The only other part of the world that underwent an industrial revolution before 1870 was the United States. Thanks to immigration, the American population rose from 9.6 million in 1820 to 31.5 million in 1860, faster than in any other part of the world at the time. More and more Americans lived in towns and cities. In the 1840s alone, the urban population almost doubled. New York City, already 100,000 strong in 1815, reached 600,000 (including Brooklyn) in 1850. By then, the American standard of living was, on average, the highest in the world despite the poverty of immigrant slum dwellers and southern black

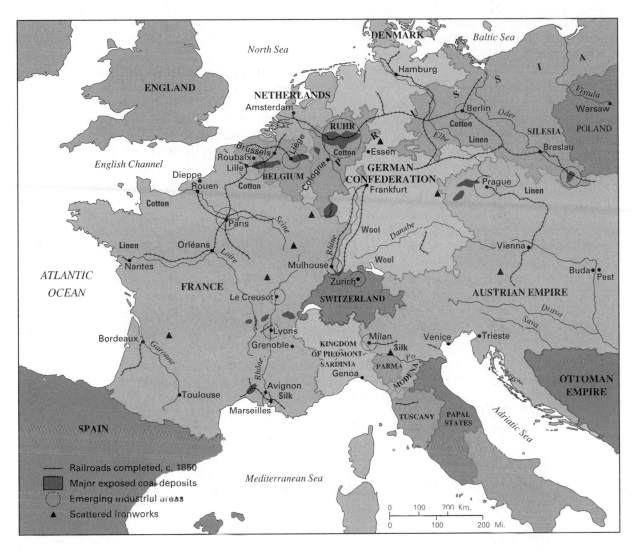

Map 23.2 Industrialization in Europe, ca. 1850 By 1850, industrialization was only beginning on the European continent. The first industrial regions were those located closest to England and possessing rich coal deposits: Belgium and the Ruhr region of Germany. Politics determined the location of railroads; notice the star-shaped French network emanating from Paris and the lines linking the different parts of the German Confederation.

slaves. The combination of population increase and relatively high income created a growing demand for the products of industry.

American industrialization differed substantially from its British predecessor. The United States was a land of enormous distances separating eastern cities, southern cotton plantations, and Midwestern farms. The need to overcome these great distances explains the success of Robert Fulton's steamboat and Samuel Morse's telegraph. In the 1820s, the Erie Canal linked the Atlantic seaboard with the Great Lakes and opened up Ohio, Indiana, and Illinois to European settlement. Steamboats proliferated west of the Appalachian Mountains; by 1830 some three hundred plied the Mississippi and its tributaries. To counter the competition from New York State, Pennsylvania built 1,000 miles (1,600 kilometers) of canals by 1840. The United States was fast becoming a nation that moved by water.

Then came the railroads, and Americans discovered a new love affair. Entrepreneurs built railroads as fast and cheaply as possible with an eye to quick profits, not long-term durability. By the 1840s, 6,000 miles (9,660 kilometers) of track radiated westward from Boston, New York, Philadelphia, and Baltimore and connected these cities to one another. The boom of the 1840s was dwarfed by the mania of the 1850s, when 21,000 miles (33,800 kilometers) of new track were laid, many of them westward across the Appalachians to Memphis, St. Louis, and Chicago. After 1856, the trip from New York to Chicago, which once took three weeks by boat and on horseback, could be made in 48 hours. More than anything else, it was the railroads that opened up the American Midwest, turning the vast prairie into wheat fields and pasture for cattle to feed the industrial cities of the east.

Cotton became America's most valuable crop. In the 1790s, most of Britain's cotton came from India, as the United States produced a mere 750 tons, mostly long-fiber cotton from South Carolina. In 1793, the American Eli Whitney patented his cotton gin, a simple device that separated the cotton seeds from the fiber and made it economical to grow short-staple cotton. This permitted the spread of cotton farming into Georgia, then into Alabama, Mississippi, and Louisiana, and finally as far west as Texas. By 1861, when the Civil War began, the southern states were producing over a million tons of cotton a year, five-sixths of the world's total.

While the South became an economic colony of the cotton mills of England, the northern states were heading in the opposite direction.

The De Witt Clinton locomotive, 1835–1840 The De Witt Clinton was the first steam locomotive built in the United States. Notice the high smokestack, designed to let the hot cinders cool off so they would not set fire to nearby trees, an important consideration at a time when eastern North America was still covered with forests. Also, the three passenger cars are clearly horse-carriages fitted with railroad wheels. (The Bettman Archive)

With the help of British craftsmen who introduced jennies, mules, and power looms, Americans developed a cotton industry in the 1820s. By 1840, the United States had twelve hundred cotton mills, two-thirds of them in New England, powered by water rather than steam. The 1830s and 1840s were a period of tremendous technological creativity or, as Americans liked to call it, "Yankee ingenuity." In 1843, Samuel Morse erected a telegraph line from Washington to Baltimore. In 1834, Cyrus McCormick patented his reaper, a godsend for midwestern farmers who had too much land and not enough labor. The sewing machine, perfected by Isaac Singer in the 1850s, became the first popular domestic appliance and the basis for the ready-to-wear clothing industry. In the western territories, people quickly adopted Samuel Colt's revolver for self-defense and personal adornment.

At the Great Exhibition of 1851, Europeans admired what was called the "American system of manufactures." Although the idea of interchangeable parts had originated in Europe in the eighteenth century, it was gradually adopted in the mid-nineteenth century in the manufacture of firearms, farm equipment, and sewing machines. In the next hundred years, the use of machinery to mass-produce consumer items was to become the hallmark of American industry.

ENVIRONMENTAL IMPACT OF THE INDUSTRIAL REVOLUTION

Long before the Industrial Revolution began, practically no wilderness areas remained in Britain, as almost every piece of land was covered with cultivated fields, forests, pastures, or towns. Yet humans continued to use up the environment. The most serious problem was deforestation, as people cut timber to build ships and houses, to heat homes, and to manufacture bricks, iron, glass, beer, bread, and many other items. As the cost of wood rose, Britons substituted coal for firewood and suffered the conse-

quences; Londoners in particular breathed dense and noxious coal smoke. Although humans tolerated the burning of coal, it was too polluting for smelting iron or baking bread.

In many ways, industrialization relieved the pressures on the environment. Raw materials once grown on British soil, such as wood, hay, or wool, were replaced by those found underground like iron ore and coal or overseas like cotton. While forested countries like Russia, Sweden, and the United States continued to smelt iron with charcoal, the British substituted coke made from coal. As the British population increased and land grew scarcer, the cost of growing feed for horses rose, creating incentives to find new, less land-hungry means of transportation. Likewise, as iron became cheaper and wood more expensive, many objects formerly made of wood, such as ships, came to be made of iron.

The Urban Environment

The Industrial Revolution involved far more than substitution. It accelerated change, introduced new activities, and unleashed new forces, many of which impacted on the environment. The most dramatic changes occurred in the towns.

Never before had towns grown so fast. London, already the largest city in Europe in 1700 with its 500,000 inhabitants, grew to 1,117,000 by 1801, 2,239,000 by 1841, and 4,770,000 by 1881; it was then the largest city the world had ever known. Smaller towns grew even faster. Manchester, a small town of 20,000 in 1758, reached 399,000 in 1861, a twenty-fold increase. Liverpool grew sixfold in sixty years, from 82,000 in 1801 to 472,000 in 1861. These were not isolated instances. In some areas, towns merged together to form megalopolises, like Greater London, the English Midlands, central Belgium, and the Ruhr district of Germany.

Industrialization made some people very prosperous. A great deal of this new wealth went to building fine homes, churches, museums, and theaters in wealthy neighborhoods in London, Berlin, and New York. Much of the beauty of

Overcrowded London   The French artist Gustave Dore depicted the tenements of industrial London where workers and their families lived in crowded and unsanitary conditions. This famous image shows row houses, each one room wide, with tiny back yards, while trains pass on viaducts overhead. (Prints Division, New York Public Library, Astor, Lenox, and Tilden Foundations)

London dates from the time of the Industrial Revolution.

Yet, by all accounts, the industrial cities grew much too fast. Air pollution from burning coal got steadily worse. Factories and workers' housing were mixed together. As poor migrants poured in from the countryside, developers built cheap, shoddy row houses to rent out to them. These tenements were dangerously overcrowded, with several families packed into one small room. New town dwellers, recently arrived from the country, brought country ways with them. People threw their sewage and trash out the windows to be washed down the gutters. The poor kept pigs and chickens, the rich kept horses, and pedestrians stepped into the street at their own risk. People drank water drawn from wells and rivers contaminated by sewage and industrial effluents. The River Irwell, which ran through Manchester, was, in the words of one visitor, "considerably less a river than a flood of liquid manure." "Every day that I live," wrote an American visitor to Manchester, "I thank Heaven that I am not a poor man with a family in England." The poet William Blake (1757–1827) expressed the revulsion of sensitive people at the spoliation of England's "mountains green" and "pleasant pastures" when he wrote:

> And did the Countenance Divine
> Shine forth upon our clouded hills?
> And was Jerusalem builded here
> Among these dark Satanic Mills?[2]

Under these conditions, diseases proliferated. To the long list of preindustrial urban diseases like smallpox, dysentery, and tuberculosis, industrialization added new ailments. Rickets, a bone disease caused by a lack of sunshine, became endemic in the dark and smoky industrial cities. Steamships brought cholera from India, causing great epidemics that struck the poor neighborhoods especially hard. In the 1850s, when the average life expectancy in England was 40 years, it was only 24 years in Manchester, and around 17 years in Manchester's poorest neighborhoods, because of the high infant mortality. Although cities had historically been associated with diseases, observers of nineteenth-century industrial cities documented the horrors of slum life in vivid detail. Their shocking reports led to municipal reforms, such as garbage removal, water and sewage systems, and parks and schools. These measures began to alleviate the ills of urban life after the midcentury.

Rural Environments in Britain and Western Europe

The Industrial Revolution also transformed the countryside. Some of the transformation was destructive, filling the air with smoke and leaving huge mounds of tailings around mine shafts. Many contemporaries, however, called such changes "improvements." Rich landowners petitioned Parliament to force out the small farmers and sell the "waste"—that is, the woods and pasture used in common by villagers. This process, though socially unjust and offensive to those who waxed nostalgic about "merry olde England," improved the efficiency and productivity of agriculture, for it permitted new methods that small farmers could not afford: drainage, soil improvements, mechanization, crop rotations, and the breeding of better animal stock. In many ways, the agricultural revolution paralleled the industrial one.

In eastern Europe, as in Britain, large estates predominated and aristocratic landowners used "improvements" to increase their incomes at the expense of the peasants. Only in western Europe was enclosure hampered by the fact that land was scattered among many smallholders.

To contemporaries, the most obvious changes in rural life were those brought about by the new transportation systems. In the eighteenth century, only France had a national network of quality roads, later extended into Italy and Germany in the nineteenth century. In Britain, local governments neglected the roads that served long-distance traffic. In response to the growing demand, private enterprises—"Turnpike Trusts" —built numerous toll roads.

For heavy goods, horse-drawn wagons were too costly, even on good roads. The growing volume of heavy freight triggered canal-building booms in Britain, France, and the Low Countries in the late eighteenth century. Some canals, like the duke of Bridgewater's canal in England, connected coal mines to towns or navigable rivers. Others were built to link up the various navigable rivers and create national transportation networks.

In their day, canals were marvels of construction, with deep cuttings, tunnels, and even aqueducts carrying barges over rivers. They were also a school where engineers learned the skills they were to apply to the next great transportation system: the railroads. They laid straight tracks across rolling country by cutting deeply through hills and throwing daringly long bridges of stone and iron across valleys. Lesser lines snaked their way to small towns hidden in remote valleys. Soon, long-isolated districts were invaded by clanking trains pulled by puffing, smoke-belching locomotives.

Railroads also invaded the towns. The railroad companies built their stations—gigantic imitations of Gothic cathedrals or Roman temples made of stone, iron, and glass—as close to the heart of cities as they could. On the outskirts of cities, railroad yards, sidings, and repair shops covered acres of land, surrounded by miles of warehouses and workers' housing. Farther out, far from the dangerous and polluted cities where their factories were located, newly rich industrialists created an environment halfway between country homes and townhouses: the first suburbs.

Thus, in the century after industrialization began, the landscape of industrial countries was transformed more rapidly than ever before. Yet ecological changes, like the technological and economic changes that caused them, were only beginning.

Environmental Changes in the United States

In the United States as in Europe, cities mushroomed, rivers were channeled to drive machinery, and canals and railroads sliced through the landscape and covered vast amounts of land. But Americans transformed their environment even faster than Europeans, for land was not precious but practically free, and, east of the Appalachian Mountains, forests were not a valuable resource but a hindrance to development. In their haste to "conquer the wilderness" and "open up the West," pioneer settlers felled trees and burned them, built houses and abandoned them, and moved on. Cotton was especially harmful, as planters cut down forests, grew cotton for a few years until it depleted the soil, then moved west, abandoning the land to scrub pines. This was slash-and-burn agriculture on an industrial scale.

At the time, America seemed immune to human depredations. In the process of "taming the wilderness," Americans thought of nature as an obstacle to be overcome and dominated. This mindset persisted long after the entire continent was occupied and the environment truly was endangered.

THE SOCIAL TRANSFORMATION

Although inventions were the most visible aspect of the Industrial Revolution, many other changes in society, politics, and the economy also took place, interacting with one another. As the population rose rapidly, people flocked to crowded, unsanitary cities. Working conditions were harsh and dangerous, especially for the children, who formed a large part of the work force. The growing economy created a prosperous middle class but did not improve the lives of the poor until several decades later.

Population

We know that the European population was rising in the eighteenth century, slowly at first, faster after 1780, and fastest of all in the early nineteenth century. The population of England and Wales rose from 5.5 million in 1688 to 9 million in 1801 and to 18 million by 1851. Such increases had never before been experienced in world history.

Historians are not sure what caused this boom. Perhaps it was a more reliable food supply or more widespread resistance to disease. We know that industrialization was not the cause, for the populations of China and eastern and southern Europe were also growing; nor did the population boom cause industrialization. But when industrialization and population growth occurred simultaneously, they reinforced each other. More regular food supplies and job opportunities led people to marry at an earlier age and have more children. A high birthrate meant a high proportion of children: in the early nineteenth century some 40 percent of the population of Britain was under fifteen years of age. This high proportion of youths explains both the vitality of the British people in that period and the widespread use of child labor. People also migrated at an unprecedented rate, from the land into the cities, from Ireland to the industrial areas of England, and, more generally, from Europe to the United States, Canada, and Latin America.

Working Conditions

Industrialization offered new opportunities to the enterprising. Carpenters, metalworkers, and machinists were in great demand. Since industrial machines were fairly simple, some workers became engineers or went into business for themselves. The boldest moved to the continent of Europe, the Americas, or India, taking their skills with them to establish new industries.

The successful, however, were a minority. Most industrial jobs were unskilled, monotonous, and boring. Factory work did not vary with the seasons or the time of day but began and ended by the clock. Hours were long, there were few breaks, and foremen watched constantly. Workers who performed one simple task over and over got little sense of achievement or connection to the final product. Industrial accidents were frequent and could ruin a family. Unlike even the poorest preindustrial farmer or craftsman, factory workers had no control over their tools, their jobs, or their working hours.

Industrial work, by definition, was physically removed from the home. This had a major impact on women and on family life. Women workers were concentrated in textile mills, partly because of ancient traditions, partly because textile work required less strength than metalworking, construction, or hauling. They earned, on average, from one-third to one-half as much as men. Young unmarried women worked to support themselves or to save for marriage. Married women took factory jobs when their husbands were unable to support the family. Mothers of infants faced a hard choice: either to leave their babies with wet nurses (women who nursed other people's babies) at great expense and danger or to bring them to the factory and keep them drugged with opiates so that they stayed quiet. Rather than working together as family units, husbands and wives increasingly saw their work fall into "separate spheres."

Even where factory work was available, it was never the main occupation of working women in the early years of industrialization. Most young women became domestic servants in spite of the low pay, the constant drudgery, and the risk of sexual abuse by male employers. Women with small children tried hard to find work they could do at home, such as laundry, sewing, embroidery, making or decorating hats, or taking in lodgers.

Even with both parents working, poor families found it hard to make ends meet. As in preindustrial societies, parents thought children should contribute to their upkeep as soon as they were able to. The first generation of workers brought their children with them to the factories and mines as early as age five or six; they had little choice, since there were no public schools or day-care centers. Employers encouraged the practice and even hired orphans. They preferred children because they were cheaper and more docile than adults and were better able to tie broken threads or crawl under machines to sweep the dust. In Arkwright's cotton mills, two-thirds of the workers were children. In Samuel Greg's mill, 17 percent were under ten years of age and 53 percent were between ten and seventeen; they worked from 14 to 16 hours a day and were beaten if they made a mistake or fell asleep. Mine operators used children to pull coal carts along the low passageways from the coal face to the mine shaft. In the mid-nineteenth century, when the British government began restricting child labor, mill owners increasingly recruited Irish immigrants.

American industry began on a somewhat different note than the British. In the early nineteenth century, Americans still remembered their revolutionary ideals (see Chapter 24). When Francis Cabot Lowell built a cotton mill in Massachusetts, he deliberately hired the unmarried daughters of New England farmers, promising them decent wages and housing in dormitories under careful moral supervision. Other manufacturers eager to combine profits with morality followed his example. But soon the profit motive won out, and manufacturers imposed longer hours, harsher working conditions, and lower wages. The young women protested: "As our fathers resisted with blood the lordly avarice of the British ministry, so we, their daughters, never will wear the yoke which has been prepared for us." When they went on strike, the factory owners replaced them with Irish immigrant women who were willing to accept lower pay and worse conditions.

Child labor This photo, taken in a cotton mill in Georgia, U.S.A., illustrates a common phenomenon of early industrialization. Not only are children working in factories but there is no protection against industrial accidents; the boys are barefoot and work close to an unshielded drive-belt. (The Bettman Archive)

While the cotton boom enriched planters, merchants, and manufacturers, African-Americans paid for it with their freedom. In the 1790s, 700,000 slaves of African descent lived in the United States, but their numbers were diminishing and the founders of the Republic did not consider slavery a serious problem. Cotton, however, could be grown profitably only with slave labor, and as the planting of cotton expanded, so did the number of slaves. By 1850 the United States had 3,200,000 slaves, 60 percent of whom grew cotton. Similarly, surging demand for tea and coffee in Europe and North America prolonged, and even expanded, slavery in the sugar plantations of Brazil and the West Indies (see Chapter 20). Slavery was not, as southerners maintained, a "peculiar institution," a consequence of biological differences, biblical injunctions, or African traditions. Slavery was part and parcel of the Industrial Revolution, just as much as child labor

in Britain, the clothes that people wore, and the beverages they drank.

Changes in Society

Industrialization caused profound social changes, benefiting some people and harming others. In Britain, the worst-off were those who clung to an obsolete skill or craft. The cotton-spinning boom of the 1790s briefly brought prosperity to weavers. Their high wages and low productivity, however, induced inventors to develop power looms. As a result, the wages of handloom weavers had fallen a third by 1811 and two-thirds by 1832. Even working ever longer hours they could not escape destitution.

The wages and standard of living of factory workers did not decline steadily like those of handloom weavers; they fluctuated wildly through the boom-and-bust cycles of an unrestrained capitalist economy. During the war years—from 1792 to 1815—the price of food, on which the poor spent most of their income, rose faster than wages, causing widespread hardship. As urban populations swelled, the poor were forced into overcrowded, unsanitary slums.

In the 1820s real wages and public health began to improve. Industrial production grew at over 3 percent a year, pulling the rest of the economy along. Prices fell and wages rose. Even the poor could now afford comfortable, washable cotton clothes and underwear.

Improvement was not steady, however. Business cycles caused booms and depressions and periodic unemployment. Bad times returned in the "hungry forties," when refugees from the Irish famine flooded England and America. The benefits of industrialization—cheaper food, clothing, and utensils—did not improve the workers' standard of living until the 1850s.

The real beneficiaries of the Industrial Revolution were the middle class. In Britain, landowning gentry and the merchants had long shared wealth and influence. In the late eighteenth century, a new group arose—entrepreneurs whose money came from manufacturing. Most, like Arkwright and Wedgwood, were the sons of middling shopkeepers, craftsmen, or farmers.

Their enterprises were usually self-financed, for little capital was needed to enter the cotton-spinning or machine-building business. Many tried and some succeeded, largely by plowing their profits back into the business. A generation later, in the nineteenth century, some newly rich industrialists bought their way into high society.

Before the Industrial Revolution, wives of merchants had often participated in the family business; occasionally, widows managed sizable businesses on their own. With industrialization came a "cult of domesticity" to justify removing middle-class women from contact with the business world. Instead, they were responsible for the home, the servants, the education of children, and the family's social life. As we will see in Chapter 28, by the late nineteenth century, the idea of separate spheres for men and women influenced the elaborate culture of the Victorian Age.

Middle-class people who attributed their success, often correctly, to their own efforts and virtues believed in an ethic of individual responsibility: if some people could succeed through hard work, thrift, and temperance, then those who did not succeed bore the blame for their own failure. Many of the workers, newcomers from rural districts, earned too little to provide for the long stretches of unemployment they suffered. The squalor and misery of life in factory towns led to a noticeable increase in drunkenness on paydays. While the life of the poor remained brutal, the well-to-do espoused a morality of sobriety, thrift, work, and responsibility. It may sound hypocritical to us, but at the time it demonstrated the sincere concern of middle-class moralists, combined with a feeling of helplessness in the face of terrible social problems.

IDEOLOGICAL AND POLITICAL RESPONSES TO INDUSTRIALIZATION

C hanges as profound as the Industrial Revolution could not occur without political ferment and conflicts of ideologies. So many other momentous events took place during those years—the American and French Revolutions, the Napoleonic Wars, the reactions and revolts that periodically swept over Europe after 1815 (see Chapter 24)—that we cannot neatly separate out the consequences of industrialization from the rest. Nevertheless, it is clear that the Industrial Revolution stimulated *laissez-faire*, economic policies, socialism, and workers' protests.

Laissez Faire and Its Critics

The most celebrated exponent of *laissez faire* ("let them do") was the Scottish economist Adam Smith (1723–1790). In *The Wealth of Nations* (1776) he argued that if individuals were allowed to seek their personal gain, the effect, as though guided by an "invisible hand," would be to increase the general welfare. Other than protecting private property, the government should refrain from interfering in business; it should even allow duty-free trade with foreign countries.

Although it was true that governments at the time were incompetent at managing national economies, it was also becoming obvious that industrialization was not improving the general welfare but causing great misery. Two other thinkers, Thomas Malthus (1766–1834) and David Ricardo (1772–1832), attempted to explain the poverty they saw without changing the basic premises of laissez faire. The cause of the workers' plight, Malthaus and Ricardo said, was a population boom that outstripped the food supply and led to falling wages. The workers' poverty was as much a result of "natural law" as the wealth of successful businessmen was, and the only way the working class could avoid mass famine was to delay marriage and practice self-restraint and sexual abstinence.

Business people in Britain eagerly adopted a philosophy that justified their activities and kept the government at bay, but not everyone accepted the grim conclusions of the "dismal science," as economics was then known. Jeremy Bentham (1748–1832) believed that it was possible to maximize "the greatest happiness of the greatest number" if a Parliament of enlightened reformers studied the social problems of the day and passed appropriate legislation. Bentham's philosophy became known as *utilitarianism*.

The German economist Friedrich List (1789–1846) rejected laissez faire and free trade as a British trick "to make the rest of the world, like the Hindus, its serfs in all industrial and commercial relations." To protect their "infant" industries from British competition, he argued, countries like Germany had to erect high tariff barriers. On the European continent, List's ideas were as influential as those of Smith and Ricardo and led to the formation of a German customs union, or *Zollverein*, in 1834.

Positivists and Utopian Socialists

Bentham's optimistic philosophy advocated gradual improvements. Not so some French social thinkers, who, moved by a sincere humanitarian concern for the poor, offered a radically new vision of a just civilization. Espousing a philosophy called *positivism*, the count of Saint-Simon (1760–1825) argued that the scientific method could solve social as well as technical problems. According to him, the poor, guided by scientists and artists, should form workers' communities under the protection of benevolent business leaders. Although his ideas found no following among workers, they attracted the enthusiastic support of bankers and entrepreneurs, inspired by visions of railroads, canals, and other symbols of progress.

Meanwhile, the socialist Charles Fourier (1722–1837), who loathed capitalists, imagined an ideal society in which groups of sixteen hundred workers would live in communal dormitories and work together on the land and in workshops where the hardships of labor would be softened by music, wine, and pastries. For this, his critics called him "utopian," a dreamer.

The person who came closest to creating a Utopian community was the Englishman Robert Owen (1771–1858). A successful cotton manufacturer, Owen believed that industry could provide prosperity for all. Conscience-stricken by the appalling plight of the workers, he rebuilt the mill town of New Lanark, improved the housing, and added schools, a church, and other amenities. He also testified before Parliament against child labor and for government inspection of working conditions, thereby angering his fellow industrialists.

The ideas of the Utopians were unrealistic (hence their name), yet they had a great influence on Karl Marx and the socialists of the late nineteenth century, as we shall see in Chapter 28.

Protests and Reforms

Workers benefited little from the ideas of those middle-class philosophers. Instead, they resisted the harsh working conditions in their own way. They changed jobs often; they were often absent, especially on Mondays; and when they were not closely watched, the quality of their work was often poor.

Periodically, workers rioted or went on strike. In England between 1810 and 1820, Luddites broke into factories and destroyed the machines that threatened their livelihood. Such acts of resistance, however, did nothing to change the nature of industrial work. Not until workers learned to act together could they hope to have much influence.

Gradually they formed benevolent societies and organizations to demand universal male suffrage and shorter work days. In the 1830s, Robert Owen tried but failed to organize a "General Union." The Chartist movement had more success, gathering petitions by the thousands to present to Parliament. Although Chartism collapsed in 1848, it left a legacy of labor organizing.

Mass movements persuaded political leaders to look into the abuses of industrial life. This action was a long time coming because it conflicted with the prevailing laissez-faire philosophy. In the 1820s and 1830s, the British Parliament began investigating conditions in the factories and mines. The Factory Act of 1833 prohibited the employment of children under the age of nine in textile mills; limited the working hours of children between nine and thirteen years of age to 8 hours a day, and limited the working hours of those between fourteen and eighteen to 12 hours a day (see Voices and Visions: Child Labor in the Early Cotton Mills). The Mines Act of 1842 prohibited the employment of all women and of

Child Labor in the Early Cotton Mills

In agrarian societies everywhere in the world, children were expected to work and contribute to the family economy. Thus, when industrialization began, both parents and employers thought child labor was perfectly normal. But working conditions in factories were very different from working conditions on farms and in home workshops. Child labor became a contentious issue in Britain in the 1830s. Parliamentary committees investigated the problem, and writers published books and pamphlets debating the issue. In The Philosophy of Manufactures *(1835) the English economist Andrew Ure wrote in defense of the cotton industry:*

I have visited many factories, both in Manchester and in the surrounding districts, during a period of several months, entering the spinning rooms, unexpectedly, and often alone, at different times of the day, and I never saw a single instance of corporal chastisement inflicted on a child, nor indeed did I ever see children in ill-humour. They seemed to be always cheerful and alert, taking pleasure in the light play of their muscles,—enjoying the mobility natural to their age. The scene of industry, so far from exciting sad emotions in my mind, was always exhilarating. It was delightful to observe the nimbleness with which they pieced the broken ends, as the mule-carriage began to recede from the fixed roller beam, and to see them at leisure, after a few seconds' exercise of their tiny fingers, to amuse themselves in any attitude they chose, till the stretch and winding-on were once more completed. The work of these lively elves seemed to resemble a sport, in which habit gave them a pleasing dexterity. Conscious of their skill, they were delighted to show it off to any stranger. As to exhaustion by the day's work, they evinced no trace of it on emerging from the mill in the evening; for they immediately began to skip about any neighborhood play-ground, and to commence their little amusements with the same alacrity as boys issuing from a school.

In contrast, the German socialist Friedrich Engels reported in The Condition of the Working Class in England in 1844 *(1892):*

The great mortality among children of the working-class, and especially among those of the factory operatives, is proof enough of the unwholesome conditions under which they pass their first year. . . . The result in the most favourable case is a tendency to disease, or some check in development, and consequent less than normal vigour of the constitution. A nine year old child of a factory operative that has grown up in want, privation, and changing conditions, in cold and damp; with insufficient clothing and unwholesome dwellings, is far from having the working force of a child brought up under healthier conditions. At nine years of age it is sent into the mill to work 6½ hours (formerly 8, earlier still, 12 to 14, even 16 hours) daily, until the thirteenth year; then twelve hours until the eighteenth year. . . . In no case can its presence in the damp, heavy air of the factory, often at once warm and wet, contribute to good health; and, in any case, it is unpardonable to sacrifice to the greed of an unfeeling bourgeoisie the time of children which should be devoted solely to their physical and mental development, withdraw them from school and the fresh air, in order to wear them out for the benefit of the manufacturers.

Compare these two statements. How could the same situation lead to such contradictory evaluations? What alternative occupation for children were these two authors thinking of when they described factory work. In the long run, which of the two views prevailed?

Sources: **1.** Andrew Ure, *The Philosophy of Manufactures,* 2nd ed. (London: C. Knight, 1835), p. 301. **2.** Friedrich Engels, *The Condition of the Working Class in England in 1844* (1892, reprinted London: George Allen & Unwin, 1952), pp. 150–151.

boys under age ten underground. In 1846 Parliament repealed the Corn Laws (duties on imported grain), lowering the cost of food. Even then, several decades went by before there were enough inspectors to enforce the new laws.

Thus the British learned to seek reform through accommodation. On the European continent, in contrast, the revolutions of 1848 (see Chapter 24) revealed widespread discontent with the repressive governments of the time but in the end failed to soften the hardships of industrialization.

INDUSTRIALIZATION AND THE NONINDUSTRIAL WORLD BEFORE 1870

Long before 1870, the industrialization of the West began to affect the rest of the world, often for the worse. In most places, trade with the West meant exporting raw materials instead of locally made handicraft products. The few countries that attempted to build industries of their own had little success, for the competition with established industries, backed by the might of Britain, was too great. Let us consider three cases where industrialization was not successful: Russia, whose society and institutions delayed industrialization by a century, and Egypt and India, where industrialization was stifled at the outset. In these three cases, we can discern the outlines of the Western domination that has characterized the history of the world since the late nineteenth century (as we shall see in Part Seven).

Russia

Russia had been in close contact with western Europe since the seventeenth century. Its aristocrats spoke French, its army was modeled on those of western Europe, and it participated in European wars and diplomacy. Yet Russia differed from western Europe in one important aspect: it had almost no middle class. Thus its

industrialization arose not from the initiative of local entrepreneurs but by government decree and through the work of foreign engineers.

To overcome Russia's enormous distances, Tsar Alexander I (r. 1801–1825) introduced steamboat service on the Volga River in 1820. His successor Nicholas I (r. 1825–1855) built the first railroad from St. Petersburg, the capital, to his summer palace in 1837; a few years later, he insisted that the trunk line from St. Petersburg to Moscow run in a perfectly straight line. American engineers built locomotive workshops, and British engineers set up textile mills. These projects, though well publicized, were isolated islands in a society that was still largely medieval, where most of the population were serfs tied to the estates of powerful noble landowners and towns were few and far apart.

Until the late nineteenth century, the government's interest in industry was limited and hesitant. An industrial revolution, to be successful, required large numbers of educated and independent-minded artisans and entrepreneurs. The Russian government, suspicious of Western ideas—especially anything smacking of liberalism, socialism, or revolution—feared the spread of literacy and of modern education beyond the minimum needed to train the officer corps and the bureaucracy. Rather than run the risk of allowing a bourgeoisie and a working class to arise that might challenge its control, the ultraconservative regime kept the peasants in serfdom and preferred to import most industrial goods and pay for them with exports of grain and timber. As a result, it fell further behind western Europe, economically and technologically, than it had been a half-century before. When France and Britain went to war against Russia in 1854 (see Chapter 27), they faced a Russian army that was equipped with obsolete weapons and bogged down for lack of transportation.

Egypt

Like Russia, Egypt also began to industrialize in the early nineteenth century. The driving force was its ruler, Muhammad Ali (1769–1849), a man who was to play a major role not only in the history of Egypt but in the Middle East and East

Africa as well (see Chapter 26). He wanted to build up the Egyptian economy and military in order to become less dependent on the Ottoman sultan, his nominal overlord. To do so, he imported advisers and technicians from Europe and founded cotton mills, foundries, shipyards, weapons factories, and other industrial enterprises. To pay for all this, he made the peasants grow wheat and cotton, which the government bought at a low price and exported at a profit. He also imposed high tariffs on imported goods. In effect, Egypt set up a system of state capitalism to force the pace of industrialization.

Mohammad Ali's efforts, however, fell afoul of the British, who did not want a powerful country interrupting the flow of travelers and mail crossing Egypt, the shortest route between Europe and India. When Egypt went to war against the Ottoman Empire in 1839, Britain intervened and forced Muhammed Ali to eliminate all import duties in the name of free trade. Unprotected, Egypt's fledgling industries could not compete with the flood of cheap British products. Thereafter, Egypt exported raw cotton and imported manufactured goods and became, in effect, an economic dependency of Britain.

Mohammed Ali's successors, Abbas (r. 1848–1854) and Said (r. 1854–1863), opened up Egypt to foreign investment. Foreign banks funded projects that benefited foreign trade, such as railways, telegraphs, harbors, and irrigation schemes. Most important of all these projects was the Suez Canal, built between 1859 and 1869 (see Chapter 29). Only a few Egyptians gained from these projects, which compromised and eventually doomed Egypt's independence.

India

Until the late eighteenth century, India had been the world's largest producer and exporter of cotton textiles, handmade by skilled spinners and weavers. The British East India Company took over large parts of India just as Britain was embarking on its Industrial Revolution (see Chapter 22). Thus cheap British factory-made textiles

A steam tractor in India   Power machinery was introduced slowly into India because of the abundance of skilled low-cost labor. In this scene, a steam-tractor fords a shallow stream, to the delight of onlookers. The construction in the background is probably a pier for a railroad bridge. (Billie Love Historical Collection)

began flooding India duty-free, putting first spinners and then handloom weavers out of work. Unlike Britain, however, India had no factories to which displaced handicraft workers could turn for work. Most of them became landless peasants, eking out a precarious living.

Like other tropical regions, India became an exporter of raw materials and an importer of British industrial goods. To hasten the process, British entrepreneurs and colonial officials introduced railroads into the subcontinent. The construction of India's railroad network began in the mid-1850s, along with coal mining to fuel the locomotives and telegraph lines connecting the cities.

Some Indian entrepreneurs saw opportunities in the atmosphere of change that the British had created. In 1854 the Bombay merchant Cowasjee Nanabhoy Davar imported an engineer, four skilled workers, and several textile machines from Britain and started India's first textile mill. This was the beginning of India's cotton industry. Although India had many gifted entrepreneurs, its industrialization proceeded at a snail's pace, for the government was in British hands, and the British did nothing to encourage Indian industry.

The spread of the Industrial Revolution to western Europe and North America in the early nineteenth century delayed the industrialization of the rest of the world. Even in countries whose governments were tempted to imitate the West, cheap Western imports, backed by the power of Great Britain, thwarted the spread of industry for a century or more.

CONCLUSION

In the period from 1760 to 1870 the new technologies of the Industrial Revolution gave humans greatly increased power over nature. Goods could be manufactured in vast quantities at low cost. People and messages could travel at unprecedented speeds. In addition to utilizing the energy produced by muscles, wind, and water, humans now had access to the energy stored in coal. Faster than ever before, they turned forests into farmlands, dug canals and laid track, bridged rivers and cut through mountains, and covered the countryside with towns and cities.

This newfound power over nature, far from benefiting all people, increased the disparities among individuals and between societies. Industrialization brought forth entrepreneurs—whether in the mills of England or the plantations of the American south—with enormous power over their workers or slaves, a power that they found easy and profitable to abuse. Some people acquired great wealth while others lived in poverty and squalor. Middle-class women were restricted to the care of their home and children, while many working-class women had to leave home to earn an income in factories or as domestic servants. These changes in work and family life provoked intense debates among intellectuals, some defending the disparities in the name of laissez faire, others criticizing the injustices that industrialization brought. These abuses were only gradually brought under control. After a lag of a generation or more, reform legislation reduced child labor, increased the suffrage, and provided education to increasing numbers of children. By the mid-nineteenth century, workers and their families were better clothed, fed, and housed than earlier generations.

By 1870, the Industrial Revolution had spread from Britain to western Europe and the United States, but its impact was already being felt around the world. To make a product that was sold on every continent, the British cotton industry used African slaves, American land, British machines, and Irish workers. Iron ships and steam engines shifted the historic balance between Europe and China. After 1870—as we shall see in Chapter 29—no part of the world would remain unscathed by the power of industry.

SUGGESTED READING

General works on the history of technology give pride of place to industrialization. For an optimistic overview see Joel Mokyr, *The Lever of Riches: Technolog-*

ical Creativity and Economic Progress (1990). The most complete encyclopedic work is *The Industrial Revolution, c. 1750–c. 1850* (1958), volume 4 in the five-volume *History of Technology*, ed. Charles Singer, E. J. Holmyard, A. R. Hall, and Trevor I. Williams.

There is a rich literature on the British Industrial Revolution. The best short introduction is T. S. Ashton's often reprinted *Industrial Revolution, 1760–1830* (1948). See also the essays in Carlo Cipolla, ed., *Industrial Revolution, 1700–1914* (1973). More detailed works include Phyllis Deane, *The First Industrial Revolution* (1969); Peter Mathias, *The First Industrial Nation: An Economic History of Britain 1700–1914* (1969); and Eric Hobsbawm, *Industry and Empire* (1969). The best new economic history is Joel Mokyr, ed., *The Economics of the Industrial Revolution* (1985).

The social impact of industrialization is the theme of E. P. Thompson, *The Making of the English Working Class* (1968), but see also E. R. Pike, ed., *"Hard Times": Human Documents of the Industrial Revolution* (1966), and Peter Stearns and Herrick Chapman, *European Society in Upheaval*, 3rd ed. (1991). Important aspects of the social transformations are treated in François Crouzet, *The First Industrialists* (1985), and Peter Stearns, *Paths to Authority: The Middle Class and the Industrial Labor Force in France, 1820–1848* (1978).

The role of women is most ably revealed in Lynn Y. Weiner, *From Working Girl to Working Mother: The Female Labor Force in the United States, 1820–1980* (1985), and in Louise Tilly and Joan Scott, *Women, Work, and Family* (1978). The classic account of urbanization is Asa Briggs's *Victorian Cities* (1965).

European industrialization outside Britain is dealt with in J. Goodman and K. Honeyman, *Gainful Pursuits: The Making of Industrial Europe: 1600–1914* (1988), and David Landes, *The Unbound Prometheus: Technological Change and Industrial Development in Western Europe from 1750 to the Present* (1972). On American industrialization, see H. J. Habakkuk, *American and British Technology in the Nineteenth Century* (1962), and Jonathan Prude, *The Coming of Industrial Order: Town and Factory Life in Rural Massachusetts, 1810–1860* (1983).

The first book to treat industrialization as a global phenomenon is Peter Stearns, *The Industrial Revolution in World History* (1993); see also Louise Tilly's important article "Connections" in *American Historical Review* 99 (1994): 1–20. On Russia, see William Blackwell, *The Beginnings of Russian Industrialization* (1970). On Egypt, see Charles Issawi, ed., *The Middle East in the World Economy, 1800–1914* (1987). The beginnings of Indian industrialization are described in S. D. Mehta, *The Cotton Mills of India, 1854 to 1954* (1954).

On the environmental impact of industrialization, see Richard Wilkinson, *Poverty and Progress: An Ecological Perspective on Economic Development* (1973), and Richard Tucker and John Richards, *Global Deforestation in the Nineteenth-Century World Economy* (1983).

NOTE

1. Zhong Zhang, "The Transfer of Networks Technology to China, 1860–1898" (Ph.D. Dissertation, University of Pennsylvania, 1989) p. 14.

CHAPTER TWENTY-FOUR

Revolutionary Changes to the Old Order, 1750–1850

Prelude to Revolution: The Eighteenth-Century Crisis • The American Revolution

The French Revolution • Revolution Spreads, Conservatives Respond

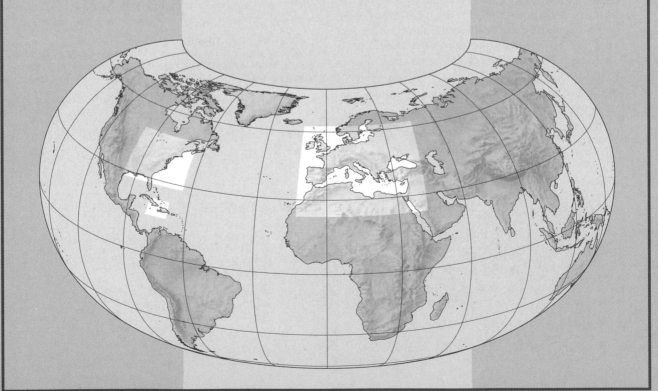

On the evening of August 14, 1791, more than two hundred slaves and black freedmen met in secret in the plantation district of northern Saint Domingue (present-day Haiti) to set the date for an insurrection against the local slave owners. Although the delegates agreed to put off the uprising for a week, violence began almost immediately. During the following decade, Haiti's rebels would end slavery, defeat the military forces of Britain and France, and gain independence.

News and rumors about revolutionary events in France had spread throughout the island and prompted the slaves to organize themselves politically. The same news and rumors had divided the island's white population between royalists (supporters of French King Louis XVI) and republicans (supporters of democracy) and led to the revolt of the free mixed-race population, *gens de couleur,* who had sought to gain the rights of citizens.

Among those planning the insurrection was a black freedman named Toussaint L'Ouverture. He would prove to be one of the most remarkable representatives of the revolutionary era. Toussaint organized military forces, negotiated locally with royalist and republican factions and internationally with Britain and France, and wrote his nation's first constitution. Although commonly portrayed as a fiend by slave owners throughout the Western Hemisphere, he became for slaves a towering symbol of resistance to oppression.

The Haitian slave rebellion was an important episode in the long and painful political and cultural transformation of the modern Western world. Economic expansion and the growth of trade were creating unprecedented wealth. The first stage of the Industrial Revolution (described in Chapter 23) was multiplying human productivity, bringing new patterns of consumerism, and altering long-established social structures.

At the same time, intellectuals were questioning the traditional place of monarchy and religion in society. The rising economic power of merchants, industrialists, and professionals coincided with the stirring of new intellectual currents that supported the transformation of political culture.

This revolutionary era turned the Western world "upside down." The *ancien régime,* the French term for Europe's old order, rested on medieval principles: politics dominated by powerful monarchs, intellectual and cultural life dominated by religion, and economics dominated by a hereditary agricultural elite. In the West's new order, politics was opened to vastly greater participation, science and secular inquiry took the place of religion in intellectual life, and economies were increasingly opened to competition.

This radical transformation did not take place without false starts and temporary setbacks. Imperial powers resisted the loss of colonies, monarchs and nobles struggled to retain their ancient privileges, and the church fought against the claims of science. As a result, revolutionary steps forward were often matched by reactionary steps backward. The liberal and nationalist ideals of the eighteenth-century revolutionary movements were only imperfectly realized in Europe and the Americas. National self-determination, universal suffrage, and the remediation of social injustices—these goals would continue to animate reformers into the twentieth century.

PRELUDE TO REVOLUTION: THE EIGHTEENTH-CENTURY CRISIS

The revolutionary cycle that began in 1775 with the American Revolution was precipitated in large measure by the cost of wars fought among Europe's major powers for colonies and trade. Britain, France, and Spain were the central actors in these global struggles, but other imperial powers were affected as well. In an intellectual environment transformed by the increasing popularity of John Locke's idea that governments derived their authority from the consent of the governed (see Chapter 18), efforts to impose new taxes or to more efficiently collect traditional revenues necessarily raised questions about the rights of individuals and authority of institutions.

Colonial Wars and Fiscal Crises

The rivalry among European powers intensified early in the seventeenth century when the newly independent Netherlands began an assault on the American and Asian colonies of Spain and Portugal (see Chapter 20). The Dutch attacked Spanish treasure fleets in the Caribbean and Pacific and seized parts of Portugal's colonial empire in Brazil and Angola. Europe's other emerging sea power, Great Britain, also attacked Spanish fleets and seaports in the Americas. British sea power then checked Dutch commercial and colonial ambitions in three wars between 1652 and 1674.

As Dutch power ebbed, Britain and France began a long struggle for political preeminence in western Europe and for territory and trade outlets in the Americas and Asia (see Chapter 18). Both the geographic scale and the expense of this conflict expanded during the eighteenth century. Nearly all of Europe's great powers were engaged in the War of Spanish Succession (1701–1714). War between Britain and Spain, begun in 1739 over smuggling in the Americas, quickly broadened into a generalized European conflict, the War of Austrian Succession (1740–1748). Then England and France initiated yet another in a series of wars, this time for control of North America. When Britain won the Seven Years War, known as the French and Indian War (1756–1763) in America, it not only gained undisputed control of North America east of the Mississippi River but also forced France to surrender most of its holdings in India.

The enormous costs of those conflicts distinguished them from earlier wars. Traditional taxes collected in traditional ways no longer covered the obligations of governments. For example, at the end of the Seven Years War in 1763, Britain's war debt had reached £137 million. Although Britain's total budget before the war had averaged only £8 million, annual interest on the war debt alone came to exceed £5 million. Even as European economies expanded because of increased trade and the early stages of the Industrial Revolution, fiscal crises overtook one European government after another. In an intellectual environment transformed by the Enlightenment, the need for new revenues provoked debate and confrontation within a vastly expanded and more critical public.

The Cultural Crisis of the Old Order

As Chapter 18 demonstrated, the Enlightenment drew on the scientific revolution of the seventeenth century. Dazzled by Copernicus's ability to explain the structure of the solar system and Newton's representation of the law of gravity, European intellectuals began to apply the logical tools of scientific inquiry to other questions. Some labored to systematize knowledge or organize reference materials. For example, Carolus Linnaeus (a Swedish botanist known by the Latin form of his name) sought to categorize all living organisms, and Samuel Johnson published a comprehensive English dictionary with over forty thousand definitions. In France Denis Diderot worked with other Enlightenment thinkers to create a compendium of human knowledge, the thirty-five-volume *Encyclopédie*.

Other thinkers pursued lines of inquiry which challenged long-established religious and political institutions. Some argued that if scientists could understand the laws of nature then surely similar forms of disciplined investigation might reveal laws of human nature. Others wondered whether society and government might be better regulated and more productive if guided by science rather than by hereditary rulers and the church. These new perspectives and the intellectual optimism that fed them would help guide the revolutionary movements of the late eighteenth century.

All Enlightenment thinkers were not radicals. There was never a uniform program for political and social reform, and the era's intellectuals often disagreed about principles and objectives.

Even though the Enlightenment is commonly associated with hostility toward religion and monarchy, very few European intellectuals openly expressed republican or atheist sentiments. The church was most commonly attacked when it attempted to censor ideas or ban books. Critics of monarchial authority were as likely to point

Beer Street, 1751 engraving by Hogarth This engraving shows an idealized London street scene where beer drinking is associated with manly strength, good humor, and prosperity. The self-satisfied corpulent figure in the left foreground has been reading a copy of the king's speech to Parliament. We can imagine him offering a running commentary to his drinking companions as he read the speech. (E. T. Archive)

out violations of ancient custom as to suggest democratic alternatives. Even Voltaire, one of the Enlightenment's most critical intellects and one of the era's great celebrities, believed that Europe's monarchs were likely agents of political and economic reform and wrote favorably of China's Qing emperors (discussed in Chapter 22).

Indeed, sympathetic members of the nobility and reforming European monarchs such as Charles III of Spain (1759–1788), Catherine the Great of Russia (1762–1796), and Frederick the Great of Prussia (1740–1786) actively sponsored and promoted the dissemination of new ideas and provided patronage for many of the era's best-known intellectuals. They recognized that elements of the Enlightenment critique of the ancien régime buttressed their efforts to expand royal authority at the expense of religious institutions, the nobility, and regional autonomy. Such goals as the development of national bureaucracies staffed by civil servants selected on merit, the creation of national legal systems, and the modernization of tax systems were objectives that united many of Europe's monarchs and intellectuals.

Though willing to embrace reform proposals when they served royal interests, Europe's monarchs moved quickly to suppress or ban radical ideas that promoted republicanism or directly attacked religion. However, too many channels of communication were open to permit a thoroughgoing suppression of these ideas. In fact, censorship tended to enhance intellectual reputations, and persecuted intellectuals generally found patronage in the courts of foreign rivals.

Many of the major intellectuals of the Enlightenment maintained an extensive correspondence with each other as well as with political leaders. This led to numerous firsthand contacts among the intellectuals of different nations. French philosopher Jean Jacques Rousseau, for example, briefly sought refuge in Britain, where he befriended the English philosopher David Hume. Voltaire lived in Prussia and England for extended periods.

The intellectual ferment of the era deeply influenced the expanding middle class of Europe and the Western Hemisphere. Members of this class were eager consumers of books and the inexpensive newspapers and journals that were widely available in the eighteenth century. It was this broadening of the intellectual audience that overwhelmed traditional institutions of censorship. Scientific discoveries, new technologies, and controversial work on human nature and politics were also discussed in the thousands of coffeehouses and teashops opening in major cities and market towns.

Many European intellectuals were interested in the Americas. Although some Europeans continued to dismiss the New World as barbaric and inferior, others used idealized accounts of the New World to support their critiques of European society. These thinkers looked to Britain's North American colonies for confirmation of their belief that human nature unconstrained by the corrupted practices of Europe's old order would quickly produce material abundance and social justice. More than any other American, Benjamin Franklin came to symbolize both the natural genius and the vast potential of America.

Born in 1706 in Boston, the young Franklin was apprenticed to his older brother, a printer. At seventeen he ran away to Philadelphia, where he succeeded as a printer and publisher, best known for his *Poor Richard's Almanac*. By age forty-two he was a wealthy man. He retired from active business to pursue writing, science, and public affairs. In Philadelphia, Franklin was instrumental in the creation of what would later become the Philadelphia Free Library, the American Philosophical Society, and the University of Pennsylvania.

His contributions were both practical and theoretical. He was the inventor of bifocal glasses, the lightning rod, and an efficient wood stove. In 1751 he published a scientific work on electricity, *Experiments and Observations on Electricity*, that established his intellectual reputation in Europe. Intellectuals heralded the book as proof that the simple and unsophisticated world of America was a particularly hospitable environment for genius.

Franklin was also an important political figure. He served Pennsylvania as a delegate to the Albany (New York) Congress in 1754, which sought to coordinate colonial defense against at-

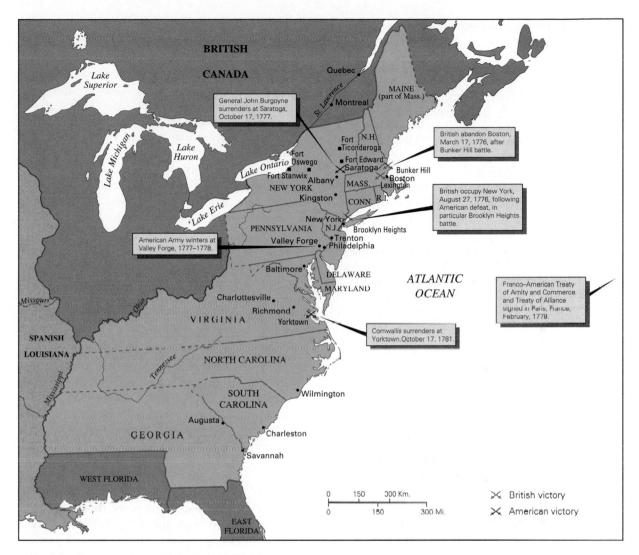

Map 24.1 The American Revolutionary War Although the British army won most of the major battles of the war and British troops held most of the major cities, the American revolutionaries eventually won a comprehensive military and political victory.

ple who were pro-British—and to enforce the boycott of British goods.

By the time the Second Continental Congress met in Philadelphia in 1775, military confrontation had occurred. Patriot militia units had fought British troops at Lexington and Concord, Massachusetts (see Map 24.1). As events propelled the colonies toward revolution, Congress created its own currency and organized an army with George Washington (1732–1799), a Virgin-

ian who served in the French and Indian War, as commander.

Popular support for independence was given a hard edge by the angry rhetoric of thousands of street-corner speakers and the inflammatory pamphlet *Common Sense*, written by Thomas Paine, a recent immigrant from England. Paine's pamphlet alone sold 120,000 copies. On July 4, 1776, Congress approved the Declaration of Independence, a document that would prove to be the most enduring statement of the revolutionary era's ideology:

> We hold these truths to be self evident: That all men are created equal; that they are endowed by their creator with certain unalienable rights; that among these are life, liberty and the pursuit of happiness; that, to secure these rights, governments are instituted among men, deriving their just powers from the consent of the governed.

This affirmation of popular sovereignty and individual rights would influence the language of revolution and popular protest all around the world.

Hoping to end the downward spiral of British authority, Great Britain sent a huge expeditionary force, 32,000 soldiers and an armada of more than 400 ships, to pacify the colonies. By 1778, British land forces had grown to 50,000 supported by 30,000 German mercenaries. But this military commitment proved futile. The American Revolution would prove to be the first war of national liberation. Although British forces won most of the battles, the small, poorly armed, and sometimes badly led Continental army could depend on a sympathetic civilian population to provide supplies and recruits.

Two decisive battles determined the war's outcome. In late 1777, British General "Gentleman Johnny" Burgoyne was defeated by General Horatio Gates at Saratoga, New York. This victory gave heart to patriot forces who had recently suffered a string of defeats. More important, the victory brought France into the conflict as an ally of the Americans. French military help proved important at many points in the war and decisive in the final great battle, fought at Yorktown, Virginia (see Map 24.1). Here a British army led by General Charles Cornwallis was besieged by American and French forces. With escape cut off by a French fleet, Cornwallis surrendered to Washington as the British military band played "The World Turned Upside-Down."

Even before American success on the battlefield, Britain had lost the more important political struggle. The British government was never able to discover a compromise solution that would satisfy colonial grievances. Half-hearted efforts to resolve the bitter conflict over taxes failed. An offer after the loss at Saratoga to roll back the clock and reestablish the administrative arrangements of 1763 made little headway after the Declaration of Independence. By delaying attempts at compromise until blood was spilled and revolutionary organizations were in place, the British government lost the opportunity to mobilize and give direction to the considerable loyalist minority in the colonies.

Although instructed by the Continental Congress to work in tandem with the French, America's peace delegation signed a separate agreement with British negotiators in late 1782. The delegates recognized that both France and Spain, ostensibly allies, were more concerned with containing British power than with furthering the development of a strong and unified America. The final treaty of peace (1783) granted unconditional independence and established generous boundaries for the former colonies. The United States, in return, promised to repay prewar debts due to British merchants and to allow loyalists to recover property confiscated by patriot forces.

The Construction of Republican Institutions

Even before the Declaration of Independence, most of the states—as the former colonies were called—had created new governments. Ignoring the British example of an unwritten constitution, state leaders summoned constitutional conventions to draft formal charters and submitted the results to voters for ratification. Europeans were fascinated by the new idea of written constitutions and by the formal ratification of those constitutions by the people. Thus many of those documents were quickly translated and published in Europe. Remembering conflicts between royal governors and colonial legislatures, the authors of state constitutions placed severe limits on executive authority. Legislatures, in contrast, were granted greater powers than in colonial times. Many states also inserted in their constitutions a bill of rights to provide further protection against government tyranny.

An effective constitution for the new national government was developed slowly and hesitantly. The Second Continental Congress sent the Articles of Confederation—the first constitution of the United States—to the states for approval in 1777, but it was not accepted by all the states until 1781. A one-house legislature in which each state was granted a single vote dominated this government. A simple majority of the thirteen states was sufficient to pass minor legislation, but nine votes were necessary for declaring war, imposing taxes, and coining or borrowing money. Executive power was exercised by committees. Given the intended weakness of this government, it is remarkable that it successfully organized the human and material resources to defeat Great Britain.

With the coming of peace, many of the most powerful political figures in the United States began an effort to fashion a new constitution. The Confederation government had proved unable to enforce unpopular requirements of the peace treaty such as the recognition of loyalist property claims, the payment of prewar debts, and even the payment of military salaries and pensions. In September 1786 Virginia invited the other states to discuss the government's failure to deal with trade issues. This led to a call for a new convention to meet in Philadelphia nine months later. A rebellion led by Revolutionary War veterans in western Massachusetts gave the assembling delegates a sense of urgency.

The Constitutional Convention, which began meeting in May 1787, achieved a nonviolent second American Revolution. The delegates pushed aside the announced purpose of the convention—"to render the constitution of the federal government adequate to the exigencies of the

The signing of the United States Constitution The signing of the Constitution inspired many artists. In this version, Washington is shown at the center of the ceremony, sitting elevated above the delegates. His authority and stature, in effect, giving meaning to the document. (The Bettman Archive)

union"—and in secret undertook to write a new constitution. George Washington was elected presiding officer; his reputation and popularity providing the solid foundation on which the delegates could contemplate an alternative political model. The real leader of the convention was James Madison of Virginia.

Debate focused on several issues: representation, electoral procedures, executive powers, and the relationship between the federal government and the states. The compromise solutions included distribution of political power among the executive, legislative, and judicial branches and the division of authority between the federal government and the states. The final compromise provided for a two-house legislature: the lower house to be elected directly by voters and the upper house to be elected by the state legislatures. The president would be elected indirectly by "electors" selected by ballot in the states (each state had a number of electors equal to the number of representatives and senators).

Although the Constitution created the most democratic government of the era, only a minority of the adult population was given full rights. In some northern states where large numbers of free blacks had fought in patriot forces, there was hostility to the continuation of slavery, but southern leaders were able to protect the institution. Slaves were denied participation in the political process, although they were counted as three-fifths of a person for purposes of representation. Southern delegates also gained a twenty-year continuation of the slave trade to 1808.

Women had been powerfully affected by their participation in revolutionary politics and by the changes in the economy brought on by the break with Britain. Many had led prewar boycotts, and during the war women had organized relief and charitable organizations. Nevertheless, they were denied political rights in the new republic. New Jersey briefly stood as an exception. Without specifically excluding women, the framers of that state's constitution had granted the right to vote to free residents who met modest property-holding requirements. As a result, women and African-Americans who met property requirements were able to vote in New Jersey until 1807, when lawmakers eliminated this right.

THE FRENCH REVOLUTION

B ecause of French support for American independence, a fiscal crisis in France deepened, overwhelming the government's resources and precipitating revolution.

The French Revolution accelerated Europe's momentum toward republican government and secular culture. It did not create an enduring form of representative democracy, as the American Revolution had done. But the colonial revolution produced no symbolic drama comparable to the public beheading of the French king Louis XVI in early 1793. The French Revolution expanded mass participation in political life and radicalized the democratic tradition inherited from English and American experience. But the passions unleashed by revolutionary events could not be sustained. In the end, democratic reform would be undermined by popular demagogues and the establishment of the dictatorship of Napoleon.

French Society and Fiscal Crisis

French society was divided into three estates. The clergy, the First Estate, numbered about 130,000 in a nation of 28 million. The Catholic Church owned about 10 percent of the nation's land and extracted substantial amounts of wealth from the economy in the form of tithes and ecclesiastical fees. Despite its substantial wealth, the church was exempted from nearly all taxes. The clergy was organized hierarchically, and members of the high nobility held almost all the upper positions in the church.

The 300,000 members of the nobility, the Second Estate, controlled about 30 percent of the land and retained feudal rights on much of the rest. Nobles held the vast majority of high administrative, judicial, military, and church positions. Though traditionally barred from some types of commercial activity, nobles were actually important participants in wholesale trade, banking, manufacturing, and mining. Like the

The Pencil

From early times, Europeans had used sharp points, lead, and other implements to sketch, make marks, and write brief notes. At the end of the seventeenth century, a source of high-quality graphite was discovered at Borrowdale in the northwest of England. Borrowdale graphite gained acceptance among artists, artisans, and merchants. At first, pure graphite was simply wrapped in string. By the eighteenth century, pieces of graphite were being encased in wooden sheaths and resembled modern pencils. Widespread use of this useful tool was retarded by the limited supply of high-quality graphite from the English mines.

The English crown periodically closed the Borrowdale mines or restricted production to keep prices high and maintain adequate supplies for future needs. As a result, artisans in other European nations developed alternatives that used lower-quality graphite or, most commonly, graphite mixed with sulfur and glues.

The major breakthrough occurred in 1793 in France when war with England ruptured trade links. The government of revolutionary France responded to the shortage of graphite by assigning a thirty-nine-year-old scientist, Nicolas-Jacques Conté, to find an alternative. Conté had earlier promoted the military use of balloons and conducted experiments with hydrogen. He also had had experience using graphite alloys in the development of crucibles for melting metal.

Within a short period, Conté had produced a graphite that is the basis for most lead pencils today. He succeeded by mixing finely ground graphite with potter's clay and water. The resulting paste was dried in a long mold, sealed in a ceramic box, and fired in an oven. The graphite strips were then placed in a wooden case. Although some believed the Conté pencils were inferior to the pencils made from Borrowdale graphite, Conté had produced a very serviceable pencil that could be produced in uniform quality and unlimited amounts.

Henry Petroski, summarizing the achievement of Conté in his *The Pencil*, wrote: "The laboratory is really the modern workshop. And modern engineering results when the scientific method is united with experience with the tools and products of craftsmen. . . . Modern engineering, in spirit if not in name, would come to play a more and more active role in turning the craft tradition into modern technology, with its base of research and development."

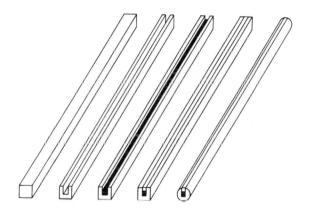

Source: This discussion depends on Henry Petroski, *The Pencil: A History of Design and Circumstance* (New York: Knopf, 1990); the quotation is on pp. 50–78. Drawing by Fred Avent for Henry Petroski. Reproduced by permission.

---

clergy, this estate was hierarchical: important differences in wealth, power, and outlook separated the higher from the lower nobility. The nobility was also a highly permeable class: the Second Estate in the eighteenth century saw an enormous infusion of wealthy commoners who purchased administrative and judicial offices that conferred noble status.

The Third Estate included everyone else. The bourgeoisie, or middle class, grew rapidly in the eighteenth century: there were three times as many members of this class in 1774, when Louis XVI took the throne, as there had been in 1715, at the end of Louis XIV's reign. Commerce, finance, and manufacturing accounted for much of the wealth of the Third Estate. Wealthy commoners also owned nearly a third of the nation's land. This literate and socially ambitious class supported an expanding publishing industry, subsidized the fine arts, and purchased many of the extravagant new homes being built in Paris and other cities.

Artisans and other skilled workers, small shopkeepers and peddlers, and small landowners made up the largest sector of society. They owned some property and lived decently when crops were good and prices stable. By 1780 poor harvests and weak consumer demand were threatening these groups.

The poor were a large, growing, and troublesome sector. The poverty and vulnerability of peasant families forced younger children to seek seasonal work away from home and led many to crime and beggary. Poor people who stayed on the land were threatened by large groups of roving vagabonds who raided isolated farms. In Paris and other French cities, the vile living conditions and unhealthy diet of the working poor were startling to visitors from other European nations. Urban streets swarmed with beggars and prostitutes. The wretchedness of the French poor is perhaps best indicated by the growing problem of child abandonment. By 1780 at least forty thousand children a year were given up by their parents.

Unable to afford decent housing, obtain steady employment, or protect their children, the poor periodically erupted in violent protest and rage. In the countryside violence was often the reaction when the nobility or clergy increased dues and fees. In towns and cities an increase in the price of bread often provided the spark, for bread prices largely determined the quality of life of the poor. These explosive episodes, however, were not revolutionary in character. The remedies sought were conventional and immediate rather than structural and long-term. That was to change when the Crown tried to solve its fiscal crisis.

The expenses of the War of Austrian Succession began the crisis. An effort by Louis XV (r. 1715–1774) to impose taxes on the nobility and on other groups that in the past had enjoyed exemptions led to widespread protest and the refusal of the Parlement of Paris, a court of appeal that heard appeals from local courts throughout France, to register the new tax. Crisis reappeared when debts from the Seven Years War compelled the king to impose emergency fiscal measures. Again, the king met resistance from the Parlement of Paris. In 1768 Crown authorities exiled the members of that Parlement and pushed through a series of unpopular fiscal measures. When the twenty-two-year-old Louis XVI assumed the throne in 1774, he attempted to gain popular support by recalling the exiled members of the Parlement of Paris. He soon learned, however, that provincial parlements had also come to see themselves as having a constitutional power to check any growth in monarchial authority.

In 1774 Louis's chief financial adviser warned that the government could barely afford to operate; as he put it, "the first gunshot [act of war] will drive the state to bankruptcy." Despite this warning, the French took on the heavy burden of supporting the American Revolution, delaying collapse by borrowing enormous sums and disguising the growing debt in misleading fiscal accounts. By the end of the war with Britain, more than half of France's national budget was required to service the debt alone. It soon became clear that fiscal reforms and new taxes, not new loans, were necessary.

In 1787 the desperate king called an Assembly of Notables to approve a radical and comprehensive reform of the economy and fiscal policy. Members of this assembly were selected by the king's advisers from the high nobility, the judiciary, and the clergy. The Notables proved unwilling to act as a rubber stamp for the proposed reform, however. They began to raise issues of representation and legitimacy. The fiscal crisis was becoming a political crisis.

Protest Turns to Revolution

In frustration, the king dismissed the Notables and attempted to implement some reforms on his own, but this effort was met by an increasingly hostile judiciary and by popular demonstrations. Because the king was unable to extract needed tax concessions from the French elite, he was forced to call the Estates General, the French national legislature, which had not met since 1614. The narrow self-interest and greed of the rich—who would not tolerate an increase in their taxes—rather than the grinding poverty of the common people had created conditions favorable for revolution.

In late 1788 and early 1789 members of the three estates came together throughout the nation to discuss grievances and elect representatives who would meet at Versailles. Although wealthy men dominated the Third Estate, it was committed to radical reform. Both the First and the Second Estates were deeply divided over procedural and policy issues and many nobles and members of the clergy sympathized with the reform agenda of the Third Estate. Traditionally the three estates met separately, and a positive vote by two of the three was required for action. Tradition, however, was quickly overturned when the Third Estate refused to conduct business until the king ordered the other two estates to sit with it in a single body.

After six weeks of stalemate, many parish priests from the First Estate began to meet with the commoners. When this expanded Third Estate declared itself the National Assembly, the king and his advisers recognized that the reformers intended to force them to accept a constitutional monarchy. Louis's vain hope for fiscal reform was being overwhelmed by the central ideas of the era: the people were sovereign, and the legitimacy of political institutions and individual rulers ultimately depended on their carrying out the people's will. Louis prepared for a confrontation with the National Assembly by moving military forces to Versailles. But before he could act, the people of Paris intervened.

A succession of bad harvests beginning in 1785 had propelled bread prices upward throughout France and provoked an economic depression as demand for nonessential goods collapsed. By the time that the Estates General met, nearly a third of the Parisian work force was unemployed. Hunger and anger marched hand in hand through working-class neighborhoods.

When the people of Paris heard that the king was massing troops in Versailles to arrest the representatives, crowds of common people began to seize arms and mobilize. On July 14 a crowd searching for military supplies attacked the Bastille, a medieval fortress used as a prison. The futile defense of the Bastille cost ninety-eight lives before its garrison surrendered. Enraged, the attackers hacked the commander to death and then paraded through the city with his head and that of the mayor of Paris stuck on pikes.

These events coincided with uprisings by peasants in the country. Peasants sacked manor houses and destroyed documents that recorded their feudal obligations. They refused to pay taxes and dues to landowners and seized common lands. Forced to recognize the fury raging through rural areas, the National Assembly voted to end feudal obligations and to reform the tax system. Having forced acceptance of their narrow agenda, the peasants ceased their revolt.

These popular uprisings strengthened the hand of the National Assembly in its dealings with the king. One manifestation of this altered relationship was passage of the Declaration of the Rights of Man. There were clear similarities between this declaration and the U.S. Declaration of Independence. Indeed, Thomas Jefferson, who had written the American document, was U.S. ambassador to Paris and offered his opinion to those involved in the drafting of the French statement. The French declaration, however, was more sweeping in its language than the American one. Among the enumerated natural rights were "liberty, property, security, and resistance to oppression." The Declaration of the Rights of Man also guaranteed free expression of ideas, equality before the law, and representative government.

While delegates debated political issues in Versailles, the economic crisis worsened in Paris. Women employed in the garment industry and in small retailing were particularly hard hit. Because the working women of Paris faced high food prices every day as they struggled to feed their families, their anger had a hard edge. Public markets became political arenas where the urban poor met daily in angry assembly. Here the revolutionary link between the material deprivation of the French poor and the political aspirations of the French bourgeoisie was forged.

On October 5, market women organized a

crowd of thousands to march the 12 miles (19 kilometers) to Versailles. Once there, they forced their way into the National Assembly to demand action from the frightened representatives: "the point is that we want bread." The crowd then entered the royal apartments, killed some of the king's bodyguards, and searched for Queen Marie Antoinette, whom they loathed as a symbol of extravagance. Eventually, the crowd demanded that the royal family relocate to Paris. Preceded by the heads of two aristocrats carried on pikes and hauling away the palace's supply of flour, the triumphant crowd escorted the royal family to Paris.

With the king's ability to resist democratic change overcome by the Paris crowd, the National Assembly achieved a radically restructured French society in the next two years. It passed a new constitution that dramatically limited monarchial power and abolished the nobility as a hereditary class. Economic reforms swept away monopolies and trade barriers within France. The Legislative Assembly (the new constitution's new name for the National Assembly) seized church lands to use as collateral for a new paper currency, and priests—who were to be elected—were put on the state payroll. When the government tried to force priests to take a loyalty oath, many Catholics joined a growing counterrevolutionary movement.

At first, many European monarchs had welcomed the weakening of the French king, but by 1791 Austria and Prussia threatened to intervene in support of the monarchy. The Legislative Assembly responded by declaring war. Although the war went badly at first for French forces, people across France responded patriotically to foreign invasions, forming huge new volunteer armies and mobilizing national resources to meet the challenge. By the end of 1792 French armies had gained the upper hand everywhere.

The Terror

In this period of national crisis and foreign threat, the French Revolution entered its most radical phase. A failed effort by the king and queen to escape from Paris and find foreign allies cost the king any remaining popular support. As

Parisian women march on Versailles   When the market women of Paris marched on Versailles and forced the royal family to return with them, they altered the course of the French Revolution. In this drawing the women are armed with pikes and swords and drag a cannon. Only the woman on the far left is clearly middle class and she is pictured hesitating or turning away from the resolute actions of the poor women around her. (Bibliotheque nationale de France)

foreign armies crossed into France, his behavior was increasingly viewed as treasonous. On August 10, 1792, a crowd similar to the one that had marched on Versailles invaded his palace in Paris and forced the king to seek protection in the Legislative Assembly. The Assembly suspended the king, ordered his imprisonment, and called for the formation of a new National Convention to be elected by the vote of all men.

Rumors of counterrevolutionary plots kept working-class neighborhoods in an uproar. In September mobs surged through the city's prisons, killing nearly half of the prisoners. Swept along by popular passion, the newly elected National Convention convicted Louis XVI of treason, sentenced him to death, and proclaimed France a republic. (In January 1793 the king was beheaded by the guillotine, the machine that would become the bloody symbol of the era.)

The National Convention—the new legislature of the new First Republic of France—convened in September. Almost all of its members were from the middle class and nearly all were "Jacobins"—the most uncompromising democrats. Deep political differences, however, separated moderate Jacobins—called "Girondists," after a region in southern France—and radicals known as "the Mountain," a faction led by Maximilien Robespierre and Georges Jacques Danton. Members of the Mountain—so named because their seats were on the highest level in the assembly hall—were more sympathetic than the Girondists to the demands of the Parisian working class and more impatient with parliamentary procedure and constitutional constraints on government action.

With the French economy still in crisis and Paris suffering from inflation, high unemployment, and scarcity, Robespierre used the popular press and political clubs to forge an alliance with the volatile Parisian working class. His growing strength in the streets allowed him to purge the National Convention of his enemies and to restructure the government. Executive power was placed in the hands of the newly formed Committee of Public Safety, which created special courts to seek out and punish domestic enemies.

Among the groups that lost ground were the active feminists of the Parisian middle class and the working-class women who had sought the right to bear arms in defense of the Revolution (see Voices and Visions: Revolutionary Women in Paris). These women had provided decisive leadership at crucial times, helping propel the Revolution toward a widened suffrage and a more democratic structure. Armed women had actively participated in every confrontation with conservative forces. It is ironic that the National Convention—the revolutionary era's most radical legislative body, one elected by universal male suffrage—would repress the militant feminist forces that had prepared the ground for its creation.

Faced with rebellion in the provinces and foreign invasion, Robespierre and his allies unleashed a period of repression called the Reign of Terror (1793–1794). During the Terror approximately 40,000 people were executed and another 300,000 thrown into prison. New actions against the clergy were also approved, including in some places the forced marriage of priests. Even time was subject to revolutionary change. A new republican calendar created twelve thirty-day months divided into ten-day weeks. Sunday, with its Christian meanings, disappeared from the calendar. By the spring of 1794 the Revolution was secure from foreign and domestic enemies, but repression continued.

Among the victims were some who had been Robespierre's closest political collaborators, including Danton. The execution of these people prepared the way for Robespierre's own fall by undermining the sense of invulnerability that had secured the loyalty of his remaining allies in the National Convention. After French victories eliminated the immediate foreign threat, conservatives in the Convention felt secure enough to vote for the arrest of Robespierre on July 27, 1794. Over the next two days, Robespierre and nearly a hundred of his remaining allies were executed by guillotine.

Reaction and Dictatorship

Purged of Robespierre's collaborators, the Convention began to undo the radical reforms. It removed many of the emergency economic controls that had held down prices and protected

Revolutionary Women in Paris

In 1791, Pauline Léon and three hundred other women petitioned the National Assembly for the right to bear arms. Léon would later serve as the president of a radical club, the Society of Revolutionary Republican Women. This petition demonstrates that the radical republican ideology of the Revolution had stirred a strong feminist current.

Legislators: Patriotic women come before you to claim the right which any individual has to defend his life and liberty.

Everyone predicts that a violent shock is coming; our fathers, husbands, and brothers may be the victims of the fury of our enemies. Could we be denied the joy of avenging them or of dying at their sides? We are *citoyennes* [citizens], and we cannot be indifferent to the fate of the fatherland.

Your predecessors deposited the Constitution as much in our hands as in yours. Oh, how to save it, if we have no arms to defend it from the attacks of its enemies?

Yes, Gentlemen, we need arms, and we come to ask your permission to procure them. May our weakness be no obstacle; courage and intrepidity will supplant it, and the love of the fatherland and hatred of tyrants will allow us to brave all dangers with ease. Do not believe, however, that our plan is to abandon the care of our families and home, always dear to our hearts, to run to meet the enemy.

No, Gentlemen. We wish only to defend ourselves the same as you; you cannot refuse us, and society cannot deny the right nature gives us, unless you pretend the Declaration of Rights does not apply to women, and that they should let their throats be cut like lambs, without the right to defend themselves. . . . But, you say, men are armed for your defense. Of course, but we reply, why deprive us of the right to join that defense, and of the pleasure of saving their days by using ours? . . . Is our life dearer than theirs? Are our children not orphaned by the loss of their fathers as much as their mothers? Why then not terrorize aristocracy and tyranny with all the resources of civic effort [*civisme*] and the purest zeal, zeal which cold men can well call fanaticism and exaggeration, but which is only the natural result of a heart burning with love for the public weal?

Without doubt, Gentlemen, the most joyous success will crown the justice of our cause. Well then, we shall have the pleasure of having contributed to the victory. But if, by the wiles of our enemies or the treachery of some on our side, the evil ones win victory, then is it not cruel to condemn us to await in our homes a shameful death and all the horrors which will precede it? Or—an even worse misfortune—to survive the loss of what we hold most dear, our families and our liberty?

No, Gentlemen, do not imagine it. If, for reasons we cannot guess, you refuse our just demands, these women you have raised to the ranks of *citoyennes* by granting that title to their husbands, these women who have sampled the promises of liberty, who have conceived the hope of placing free men in the world, and who have sworn to live free or die—such women, I say, will never consent to concede the day to slaves; they will die first. . . .

But, Gentlemen, let us cast our eyes away from these cruel extremes. Whatever the rages and plots of aristocrats, they will not succeed in vanquishing a whole people of united brothers armed to defend their rights. We also demand only the honor of sharing their exhaustion and glorious labors and of making tyrants see that women also have blood to shed for the service of the fatherland in danger.

Gentlemen, here is what we hope to obtain from your justice and equity:

1. Permission to procure pikes, pistols, and sabres (even muskets for those who are strong enough to use them), within police regulations.

2. Permission to assemble on festival days and Sundays on the Champ de la Fédération, or in some other suitable places, to practice maneuvers with these arms.

3. Permission to name the former French Guards to command us, always in conformity with the rules which the mayor's wisdom prescribes for good order and public calm.

Were the petitioners asking for equality with men? Was the demand to bear arms and defend the revolution more radical than a demand to vote? How had the revolution altered the political understandings of these French women?

Source: From *Women in Revolutionary Paris, 1789–1795* by Darline Gay Levy, Harriat Branson Appelwaite, and Mary Durham Johnson, 72–74. Copyright © 1979 by the Board of Trustees of the University of Illinois. Used with permission of the University of Illinois Press.

The execution of Louis XVI   There was no more potent symbol of the overturning of the old order than the beheading of the French king. In this illustration, the executioner stands in front of the guillotine holding aloft the head of the king. (Bibliotheque nationale de France)

the working class. When the Paris working class revolted in 1795, the Convention approved the use of overwhelming military force. The Catholic Church was allowed to regain much of its former influence, but confiscated wealth was not returned. A more conservative constitution was also ratified. It protected property, established a voting process that reduced the power of the masses, and created a new executive authority, the Directory. Once installed in power, however, the Directory proved unable to end the foreign wars or solve domestic economic problems.

Having lost the election of 1797, the Directory suspended the results. The republican phase of the Revolution was clearly dead. Legitimacy was now based on coercive power, rather than on elections. Two years later, Napoleon Bonaparte (1769–1821), a brilliant young general in the French army, seized power. Just as the American and French Revolutions had been the start of the modern democratic tradition, the military intervention that brought Napoleon to power in 1799

marked the advent of another modern form of government: popular authoritarianism.

The American and French Revolutions had resulted in part from conflicts over representation. If the people were sovereign, what institutions best expressed popular will? In the United States, the answer was to expand the electorate and institute representative government. The French Revolution had taken a different direction with the Terror. Interventions on the floor of the National Convention by market women and soldiers, the presence of common people at revolutionary tribunals and at public executions, and expanded military service were all forms of political communication that satisfied, temporarily, people's desire to influence their government. Napoleon tamed these forms of political expression to organize Europe's first popular dictatorship. He succeeded because his military reputation promised order to a society exhausted by a decade of crisis and turmoil.

In contrast to the National Convention,

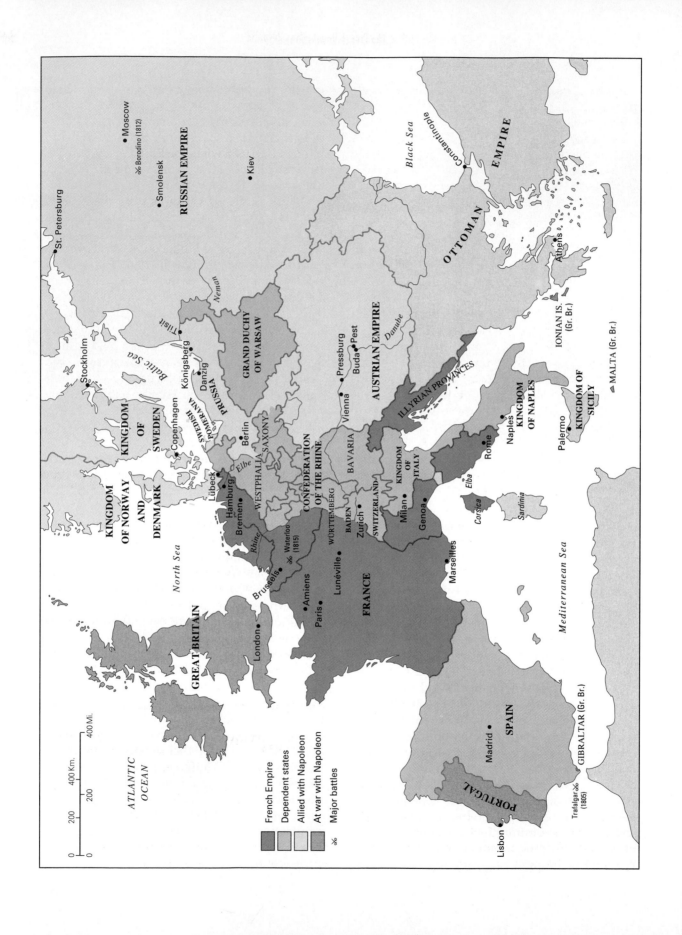

Moscow •
✕ Borodino (1812)
Smolensk •

RUSSIAN EMPIRE

Kiev •

St. Petersburg •

Black Sea

Constantinople •

OTTOMAN EMPIRE

Athens •

IONIAN IS.
(Gr. Br.)

MALTA (Gr. Br.)

Stockholm •
Baltic Sea
Neman
Tilsit
Königsberg •
Danzig •

KINGDOM
OF
SWEDEN

GRAND DUCHY
OF WARSAW

Pressburg •
Buda • Pest

AUSTRIAN EMPIRE

Danube

ILLYRIAN PROVINCES

KINGDOM OF NAPLES

KINGDOM OF SICILY

Copenhagen •

PRUSSIA

SWEDISH POMERANIA

Berlin •

Vienna •

KINGDOM
OF
NORWAY
AND
DENMARK

Lübeck •
Hamburg •
Bremen •

Elbe

WESTPHALIA
SAXONY

CONFEDERATION OF THE RHINE

BAVARIA

KINGDOM
OF
ITALY

Milan •
Genoa •

Naples •
Rome •

Palermo •

Elba
Corsica
Sardinia

North Sea

Rhine

Waterloo (1815) ✕
Brussels •

WÜRTTEMBERG
BADEN
Zürich •
SWITZERLAND

Amiens •
Lunéville •

FRANCE

Marseilles •

Mediterranean Sea

GREAT BRITAIN

London •

Paris •

ATLANTIC
OCEAN

400 Mi.
400 Km.
200
200
0
0

French Empire
Dependent states
Allied with Napoleon
At war with Napoleon
Major battles ✕

SPAIN

Madrid •

GIBRALTAR (Gr. Br.)

Trafalgar ✕ (1805)

PORTUGAL

Lisbon •

Napoleon proved capable of realizing France's dream of dominating Europe and providing effective protection for persons and property at home. Negotiations with the Catholic Church led to the Concordat of 1801. This agreement gave French Catholics the right to freely practice their religion and recognized the French government's authority to nominate bishops and retain priests on the state payroll. In his comprehensive rewriting of French law, the Civil Code of 1804, Napoleon won the support of the peasantry and of the middle class by asserting two basic principles inherited from the moderate first stage of the French Revolution: equality in law and protection of property. Even some members of the nobility became supporters after Napoleon declared himself emperor and France an empire in 1804. However, the discrimination against women that had begun during the Terror was extended by the Napoleonic Code. Women were denied basic political rights and were able to participate in the economy only with the guidance and supervision of their fathers and husbands.

While providing personal security, the Napoleonic system denied or restricted many individual rights. Free speech and free expression were limited. Criticism of the government, viewed as subversive, was proscribed, and most opposition newspapers disappeared. Spies and informers directed by the minister of police enforced these limits to political freedom. Thousands of the regime's enemies and critics were questioned or detained in the name of domestic tranquillity.

Ultimately, the Napoleonic system depended on the success of French arms and French diplomacy (see Map 24.2). From Napoleon's assumption of power until his fall, no single European state could defeat the French military. Even powerful alliances like that of Austria and Prussia were brushed aside with humiliating defeats and forced to become allies of France. By 1802 Napoleon dominated continental Europe. But his effort to mobilize forces for an invasion of Britain failed in late 1805 when the British navy defeated the French and allied Spanish fleets at Cape Trafalgar, off the coast of Spain.

Following their invasion of the Iberian Peninsula, French armies became tied down by 1809 in a costly conflict with Spanish and Portuguese patriots who had forged alliances with the British. Frustrated by events in the Iberian Peninsula and faced with a faltering economy, Napoleon made the fateful decision to invade Russia. In June 1812 Napoleon began his campaign with the largest army ever assembled in Europe, approximately 600,000 men. After fighting an inconclusive battle at Borodino, Napoleon pressed on to Moscow. Five weeks after occupying Moscow, he was beset by fires set by Russian patriots and by oncoming armies. He ordered a retreat, but the brutal Russian winter and attacks by Russian forces destroyed his army. A broken and battered fragment of 30,000 men returned home to France.

After the debacle in Russia, Austria and Prussia deserted Napoleon and entered an alliance with England and Russia. Unable to defend Paris, Napoleon was forced to abdicate the French throne in April 1814. The allies exiled Napoleon to the island of Elba off the coast of Italy and restored the French monarchy. The next year Napoleon escaped from Elba and returned to France. But his moment had passed. He was defeated by an allied army at Waterloo, in Belgium, after only one hundred days in power. His final exile was on the distant island of St. Helena in the South Atlantic, where he died in 1821.

REVOLUTION SPREADS, CONSERVATIVES RESPOND

Even as the dictatorship of Napoleon was undermining the achievements of the French Revolution, revolutionary ideology was spreading and taking hold in Europe and the

Map 24.2 Napoleon's Europe, 1810 By 1810, Great Britain was the only remaining European power at war with Napoleon. Because of the loss of the French fleet at Trafalgar in 1805, Napoleon was unable to threaten Britain with invasion. Britain was therefore able to actively assist the resistance movements in Spain and Portugal that helped to weaken French power.

Americas. In Europe, the French Revolution promoted nationalism and republicanism. In the Americas the legacies of the American and French Revolutions led to a new round of struggles for independence. News of revolutionary events in France destabilized the colonial regime in Saint Domingue, a small French colony on the western half of the island of Hispaniola, and resulted in the first successful slave rebellion. In Europe, however, the spread of revolutionary fervor was checked by reaction as monarchs formed an alliance to protect themselves from further revolutionary outbreaks.

Toussaint L'Ouverture negotiating with the British The former slave Toussaint L'Ouverture led the successful slave rebellion in Saint Domingue (Haiti). He then defended the revolution against British and French military interventions. Notice that in this print Toussaint seems to command the scene, directing the attention of the British officers to the document he holds in his hand. (Bibliotheque nationale de France)

The Haitian Revolution

In 1789 the French colony of Saint Domingue was among the richest European colonies in the Americas. Its plantations produced sugar, cotton, indigo, and coffee. In fact, the colony produced two-thirds of France's tropical imports and generated nearly a third of all French foreign trade. The island's wealth rested on a brutal slave regime. Saint Domingue's harsh punishments and poor living conditions were notorious in the Caribbean. Because of high mortality rates and expanding demand for labor, the majority of the colony's 500,000 slaves were African-born.

In 1789, when news of the calling of France's Estates General arrived on the island, the wealthy planters sent to Paris a delegation charged with seeking more home rule and greater economic freedom for Saint Domingue. The gens de couleur also sent representatives. Mostly small planters or urban merchants who owned slaves, these free mixed-race delegates sought an end to race discrimination and a measure of political equality with whites. They did not seek freedom for slaves because many of them were slave owners themselves. As the French Revolution became more radical, the gens de couleur forged an alliance with sympathetic French radicals, who identified the wealthy planters on the island as royalists.

Colonial administration weakened as a result of turmoil in France, permitting rich whites, poor whites, and the gens de couleur to pursue their narrow interests in an increasingly bitter struggle. Given the island's brutal slave regime, there was no way to control the violence once it was under way. When Vincent Ogé, the leader of the gens de couleur mission in France, returned to organize a military force, he was captured, tortured, and executed by planter forces. This cruelty was soon repaid in kind.

By 1791 the island's whites, who were led by the planters, and the gens de couleur were engaged in open warfare. This division among the two groups of slave owners gave the slaves an opening. A slave rebellion began in the north and spread throughout the colony (see Map 24.3). Plantations were destroyed, masters and over-

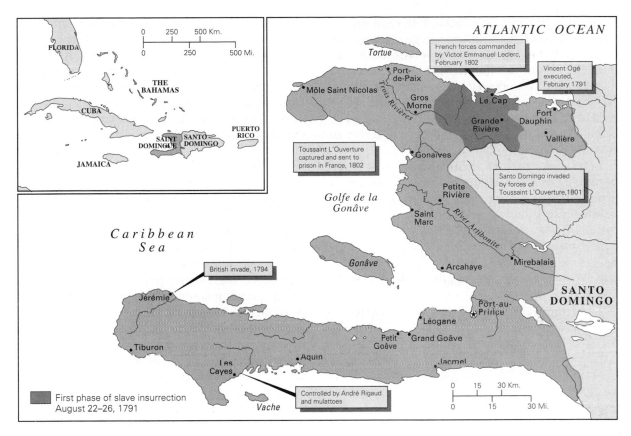

Map 24.3 The Haitian Revolution On their way to achieving an end to slavery and gaining national independence the Haitian revolutionaries were forced to defeat British and French military interventions as well as the local authority of the slave masters.

seers killed, and crops burned. An emerging rebel leadership that combined elements of African political culture with revolutionary ideology from France mobilized and directed the rebelling slaves.

The rebellious slaves eventually gained the upper hand under the leadership of François Dominique Toussaint L'Ouverture, a former domestic slave. He was politically strengthened when the radical National Convention in France abolished slavery in 1793. He overcame his rivals in Saint Domingue, defeated a British expeditionary force in 1798, and then invaded neighboring Santo Domingo, freeing the slaves there. Although Toussaint continued to assert his loyalty to France, he gave the French government no effective role in local affairs.

As reaction overtook revolution in France, both slave emancipation and Toussaint's political position were threatened. When the Directory contemplated the reestablishment of slavery, Toussaint protested,

> Do they think that men who have been able to enjoy the blessing of liberty will calmly see it snatched away? They supported their chains only so long as they did not know any condition of life more happy than slavery. But today when they have left it, if they had a thousand lives they would sacrifice them all rather than be forced into slavery again.[1]

In 1802 Napoleon sent a large military force to Saint Domingue to reestablish French authority and slavery (see Map 24.3). Few women had taken up arms during the first stages of the

Revolution in Saint Domingue, but, with the arrival of these French troops, large numbers of women actively supported the resistance. In less than two years the French lost forty thousand men to wounds and yellow fever. Toussaint was captured and sent to France, where he died. Nevertheless, Napoleon's ambitions were defeated. Saint Domingue became the free republic of Haiti.

Independence and emancipation had been purchased at a terrible price. Tens of thousands had died, the economy was destroyed, and public administration was corrupted by more than a decade of violence. Dictatorship, not democracy, would take hold and civil war and military uprisings would trouble Haiti throughout the nineteenth century (see Chapter 28).

The Congress of Vienna and Conservative Retrenchment

In March 1814, Britain, Russia, Austria, and Prussia agreed to work together to restrain French expansionism once Napoleon was defeated. The ideology of the French Revolution and Napoleon's imperial ambitions had threatened the very survival of the European old order. Ancient monarchies had been overturned and dynasties had been replaced with interlopers. Long-established political institutions had been tossed aside, and long-recognized international borders had been ignored. The very existence of the nobility and church had been put at risk. Under the leadership of the Austrian foreign minister Prince Klemens von Metternich (1773–1859), the allies worked to create a comprehensive peace settlement that would ensure the survival of the conservative order.

The central objective of the allies meeting in Vienna was to roll back the clock in France. Because a strong and stable France was understood to be the best guarantee of future peace, the French monarchy was reestablished and France's 1792 borders were recognized. Most of the continental European powers received some territorial gains, for Metternich sought to offset French power with a balance of power. In addition, Austria, Russia, and Prussia formed a separate

alliance to confront more actively the revolutionary and nationalist energies that the French Revolution had unleashed. This "Holy Alliance" acted decisively in 1820 to defeat liberal revolutions in Spain and Italy. By repressing republican and nationalist ideas in universities and the press, the Holy Alliance also attempted to meet the potential challenge posed by subversive ideas.

Nationalism, Reform, and Revolution

Despite the power of these conservative monarchs, popular support for national self-determination and democratic reform grew throughout Europe. In 1821, Greek patriots, their homeland under Ottoman control since the fifteenth century, launched an independence movement. Metternich and other conservatives opposed Greek independence, but many European artists and writers used the cultural legacy of ancient Greece to rally political support for intervention. After years of struggle, Russia, France, and Great Britain forced Ottoman recognition of Greek independence in 1830.

Placed on the throne of France by the victorious allies in 1814, Louis XVIII ruled as a constitutional monarch until his death in 1824. His brother, Charles X, sought to rule in the pre-revolutionary style of his ancestors. When Charles repudiated the constitution in 1830, a popular revolution in Paris soon forced him to abdicate. His successor, his cousin Louis Philippe (r. 1830–1848), accepted the constitution and expanded voting privileges.

Democratic reform movements appeared contemporaneously in the United States and Great Britain. In the United States, new western states entered the Union after 1790 with constitutions that provided for broad voting rights among free males. Following the War of 1812, the right to vote was expanded in older states as well. This broadening of the franchise led in 1828 to the election of the populist president Andrew Jackson (see Chapter 25).

Britain was the most democratic society in Europe prior to the French Revolution. However, the violence of the Revolution in France made the British aristocracy and the conservative Tory

The Revolution of 1830 in Belgium Following the 1830 uprising that overturned the restored monarchy in France, the Belgians rose up to declare their independence from Holland. In Poland and Italy , similar uprisings, combining nationalism and a desire for self governance, failed. This painting by Gustave Wappers romantically illustrates the popular nature of the Belgian uprising by bringing to the barricades men, women, and children drawn from both the middle and working classes. (Musees royaux des Beaux-Arts de Belgique, Bruxelles)

Party fearful of any mass movement. When the British government limited the importation of foreign grain in 1815, thus increasing food prices, poor consumers protested. The government responded by outlawing most public meetings and, in Manchester, by using troops against protesters.

Reacting against these policies, reformers gained the passage of laws that increased the power of the House of Commons, redistributed votes from agricultural to industrial districts, and expanded voting rights. Although the more radical demands of reformers called Chartists were defeated in the 1830s, new labor and economic reforms addressing the grievances of workers were passed (see Chapter 23).

Despite the achievement of Greek independence and limited political reform in France and Great Britain, conservatives continued to hold the upper hand in Europe. The desire for democratic reform and for national self-determination and the frustrations of urban workers led finally to a vast upheaval in 1848. In Paris, members of the middle class united with workers to overthrow the regime of Louis Philippe and create the Second French Republic. All adult males were given voting rights, slavery was abolished in French colonies, the death penalty was ended, and a ten-hour workday was legislated for Paris. However, Parisian workers' demand for programs to reduce unemployment and lower prices provoked conflicts with the middle class, which wanted to protect property rights. When workers rose up against the government, French troops were called out to crush them. Desiring the reestablishment of order, the French elected Louis Napoleon, nephew of the former emperor, president in December 1848. Three years later, he overturned the constitution, ruling briefly as dictator and then as Emperor Napoleon III until 1871.

Nationalism and the desire for political liberty also challenged the Austrian Empire and Prussia. Reformers in Hungary, Italy, Bohemia, and elsewhere pressed for greater national self-determination. When the Austrian monarchy hesitated to meet these demands, students and workers in Vienna took to the streets to force political reforms similar to those sought in Paris. With revolution spreading throughout the empire, Metternich, the symbol of reaction, fled Vienna in disguise. Little lasting change occurred, however, because the new Austrian emperor, Franz Joseph (r. 1848–1916), was able to use Russian military assistance and loyal Austrian troops to reestablish central authority.

Simultaneously, middle-class reformers and workers in Berlin joined forces to compel the Prussian king to accept a liberal constitution and seek unification of the German states. But the Constituent Assembly called to write a constitution and arrange for national integration became entangled in diplomatic conflicts with Austria and Denmark. As a result, Frederick William IV (r. 1840–1861) was able to reassert his authority, thwarting both constitutional reform and unification.

Despite their heroism on the barricades of Paris, Vienna, and Berlin, the revolutionaries of 1848 failed to gain either their nationalist or their republican objectives. Throughout these crises, monarchs retained the support not only of aristocrats but of professional militaries, largely recruited from peasants who had little sympathy for urban workers. Revolutionary coalitions, in contrast, were fragile and lacked clear objectives. Workers' demands for higher wages, lower prices, and labor reform often drove their middle-class allies into the arms of the reactionaries.

CONCLUSION

Although Metternich's program of conservative retrenchment succeeded in the short term, the interaction of liberalism and nationalism reemerged in the revolutions of 1830 and 1848 to threaten the old order. In Europe, monarchy, multinational empires, and the established church retained the loyalty of millions and could call on large fiscal resources. Yet, within a century, the nation-state and the Enlightenment's legacy of rational inquiry, broadened political participation, and a secular intellectual culture would prevail. In the Americas, the desire for independence would lead to the overthrow of the Portuguese and Spanish Empires.

This outcome was determined in large measure by the old order's inability to satisfy the new social classes that appeared with the emerging industrial economy. The material transformation produced by industrial capitalism could not be contained in the narrow confines of a hereditary social system, nor could the rapid expansion of scientific learning be contained within the doctrines of traditional religion. The revolutions of the late eighteenth century began the transformation of Western society but did not complete it. Only a minority gained full political rights. Women would achieve full political rights only in the twentieth century. Democratic institutions, as in revolutionary France, often failed. Moreover, as Chapter 25 will discuss, slavery endured in the Americas past midcentury, despite the revolutionary era's enthusiasm for individual liberty.

SUGGESTED READING

The American Revolutions has received a great amount of attention from scholars. Colin Bonwick, *The American Revolution* (1991), and Edward Countryman, *The American Revolution* (1985), provide excellent introductions. Edmund S. Morgan, *The Challenge of the American Revolution* (1976), remains a major work of interpretation. Gordon S. Wood, *The Radicalism of the American Revolution* (1992), is a brilliant examination of the ideological and cultural meanings of the Revolution.

For the role of women in the American Revolution see Linda K. Kerber, *Women of the Republic: Intellect and Ideology in Revolutionary America* (1980), and Mary Beth Norton, *Liberty's Daughters: The Revolutionary Experience of American Women, 1750–1800* (1980). Among the many works that deal with African-Americans and Amerindians during the era, see Sylvia Frey, *Water from Rock: Black Resistance in a Revolutionary Age* (1991), and Barbara Graymont, *The Iroquois in the American Revolution* (1972).

For the French Revolution, François Furet, *Interpreting the French Revolution* (1981), breaks with interpretations that emphasized class and ideological interpretations. Georges Lefebve, *The Coming of the French Revolution*, trans. R. R. Palmer (1947), presents the classic class-based analysis. George Rudé, *The Crowd in History: Popular Disturbances in France and England* (1981), remains the best introduction to the role of mass protest in the period. Lynn Hunt, *The Family Romance of the French Revolution* (1992), examines the gender content of revolutionary politics. Joan Landes, *Women and the Public Sphere in the Age of the French Revolution* (1988), also examines gender-related issues of the period. Felix Markham, *Napoleon* (1963), and Robert B. Holtman, *The Napoleonic Revolution* (1967), provide reliable summaries of the period.

The Haitian Revolution has received less extensive coverage than the revolutions in America and France. C. L. R. James, *The Black Jacobins*, 2d ed. (1963), is the classic study. Anna J. Cooper, *Slavery and the French Revolutionists, 1788–1805* (1988), also provides an overview of this important topic. Carolyn E. Fick, *The Making of Haiti: The Saint Domingue Revolution from Below* (1990), is the best recent synthesis of the Revolution. David P. Geggus, *Slavery, War, and Revolution* (1982), examines the British role in the revolutionary period.

For the revolutions of 1830 and 1848 see Arthur J. May, *The Age of Metternich, 1814–48*, rev. ed. (1963), for a brief survey. Henry Kissinger's *A World Restored* (1957) remains among the most interesting discussions of the Congress of Vienna. Eric Hobsbawm's *The Age of Revolution* (1962) provides a clear analysis of the class issues that appeared during this era. Paul Robertson's *Revolutions of 1848: A Social History* (1960) remains a valuable introduction to the period's social history. See also Peter Stearns and Herrick Chapman, *European Society in Upheaval* (1991). For the development of European social reform movements see Albert Lindemann, *History of European Socialism* (1983).

For national events see István Deák's examination of Hungary, *The Lawful Revolution: Louis Kossuth and the Hungarians, 1848–49* (1979). See Theodore S. Hamerow, *Restoration, Revolution, and Reaction, 1815–1871* (1966), for Germany, and Roger Price, *A Social History of Nineteenth-Century France* (1987), for French events. Barbara Taylor, *Eve and the New Jerusalem: Socialism and Feminism in the Nineteenth Century* (1983), analyzes connections between workers' and women's rights issues in England.

NOTE

1. Quoted in C. L. R. James, *The Black Jacobins*, 2nd ed., revised (Vintage Books: New York, 1963), 196.

Nation Building and Economic Transformation in the Americas, 1800–1890

Independence in Latin America · The Problem of Order

The Challenge of Economic and Social Change

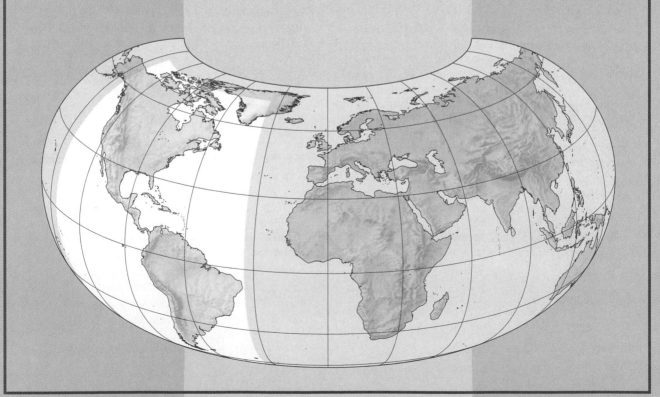

On the morning of June 19, 1867, Maximilian of Hapsburg, brother of Emperor Franz Joseph of Austria and, since 1864, emperor of Mexico, was executed by firing squad in Querétaro in central Mexico. His young wife Charlotte, daughter of Leopold, king of Belgium, had already returned to Europe in the hope that Napoleon III, emperor of France, or the pope would intervene to save her husband. News of her husband's death swept her into insanity. She died in her native Belgium in 1927.

With Mexico divided by violent factional conflicts and the United States convulsed by the Civil War, Napoleon III had seized the opportunity to send a large military force to Mexico. The invasion was supported by Mexican conservatives who resented their government's efforts to introduce democratic reforms and limit the power of the Catholic Church.

After driving the liberal president, Benito Juárez, from Mexico City, Napoleon III and a group of Mexican conservatives had convinced Archduke Maximilian to accept the throne of Mexico. Despite embracing patriotic symbols and accepting some of Juárez's reforms, Maximilian failed to win the affection of the Mexicans. The armed resistance of Mexican liberals and diplomatic pressure by the United States led to a French pullout. The defeat and execution of Maximilian signaled the triumph of Mexican republicanism.

As the successful struggle for independence by Britain's thirteen North American colonies revealed, a radical transformation had begun in the New World in the last quarter of the eighteenth century. In a new environment, European colonists had become a new people, perceiving themselves as different and eager to protect their own interests. Spurred by this sense of distinct identity and buttressed both by Enlightenment ideology, which exalted political freedom (see Chapter 18), and by the example of the United States (see Chapter 24), most of the Spanish and Portuguese colonies of the New World declared their independence in the early decades of the nineteenth century. As the French intervention in Mexico illustrates, however, the sovereignty of many American nations would be challenged.

During the remainder of the nineteenth century, all the new nations of the Americas wrestled with the difficult questions that independence raised. If colonies could reject submission to imperial powers, could not regions with distinct cultures, social structures, and economies refuse to accept the political authority of the newly formed nation-states? How could nations born in revolution accept the political strictures of written constitutions—even those they had written themselves? How could the ideals of liberty and freedom expressed in those constitutions be reconciled with the denial of rights to Amerindians, slaves, recent immigrants, and women?

While trying to resolve these political questions, the new nations also attempted to promote economic growth. Just as the legacy of class and racial division thwarted the realization of political ideals, colonial economic development, with its emphasis on agricultural and mining exports, inhibited efforts to promote diversification and industrialization.

INDEPENDENCE IN LATIN AMERICA

As the eighteenth century drew to a close, Spain and Portugal still held vast colonial possessions in the Western Hemisphere, although their power had declined relative to that of their British and French rivals. Both empires had reformed colonial administration and strengthened their military forces in the eighteenth century. Despite these efforts, the same economic and political forces that had undermined British rule in the thirteen colonies were present in Spanish America and Brazil.

Roots of Revolution

Wealthy colonial residents of Latin America were frustrated by the political and economic power of colonial officials and angered by high taxes and monopolies. By 1800, the examples of the American and French Revolutions had stirred enthusiasm for self-government (see Chapter 24). The great works of the Enlightenment as well as revolutionary documents like the Declaration of Independence and the Declaration of

Simón Bolívar Simón Bolívar was the greatest of Latin America's independence era leaders. There are many portraits of Bolívar, each suggesting distinct elements of his political legacy. This portrait shows him in uniform and cape mounted on a white horse. His gaze is focused on the horizon, suggesting his unique ability to foresee the future's challenges. (Organization of American States)

the Rights of Man circulated widely in Latin America. Ironically, though, it was Napoleon's decision to invade Portugal (1807) and Spain (1808), not revolutionary ideas, that ignited Latin America's struggle for independence.

As the French invaded Portugal, the royal family fled to Brazil, where King John VI would maintain his court for over a decade. In Spain, in contrast, Napoleon forced King Ferdinand VII to abdicate and then placed his brother Joseph Bonaparte on the throne. Spanish patriots fighting against the French created a new political body, the *Junta Central*, to administer the areas they controlled. With King Ferdinand imprisoned, the Junta claimed the right to exercise the Spanish king's powers over the colonies.

These events provoked a crisis of legitimacy in the Spanish colonies. Large numbers of colonists, perhaps a majority, favored obedience to the Spanish Junta. But a vocal minority, which included many wealthy and powerful individuals, wondered why the Junta in Spain, rather than local elites, should rule them. In late 1808 and 1809, Spanish officials in Venezuela, Mexico, and Bolivia were overthrown by popular movements led by local elites who then created Juntas. In each case, Spanish officials quickly reasserted control and punished those responsible. The harsh repression that followed these early uprisings further polarized public opinion and gave rise to a greater sense of a separate American nationality. By 1810 Spanish colonial authorities were facing a new round of revolutions more clearly focused on the achievement of independence.

Spanish South America

In Caracas (the capital city of modern Venezuela), a revolutionary coalition led by creoles (colonial-born whites) declared independence in 1811. Although this Junta espoused popular sovereignty and representative democracy, its leaders were large landowners who defended slavery and opposed full citizenship for the black and mixed-race majority. Their aim was to maintain their own privileges by eliminating Spaniards from the upper levels of government and from the church. This narrow, selfish agenda permitted Spanish loyalists in the colonial administration and church hierarchy to rally thousands of free blacks and slaves to defend the empire. Faced with determined resistance, the revolutionary movement placed overwhelming political authority in the hands of its military leader Simón Bolívar (1783–1830), who became the preeminent leader of the independence movement in Spanish South America.

The son of wealthy Venezuelan planters, Bolívar had studied both the classics and the works of the Enlightenment. He used the force of his personality to mobilize political support and to hold the loyalty of his troops. Defeated on many occasions, Bolívar successfully adapted his objectives and policies to attract new allies and build coalitions. Although initially opposed to the abolition of slavery, for example, he agreed to support emancipation in order to draw slaves and freemen to his cause and to gain supplies from Haiti. Bolívar was also capable of using harsh methods to ensure victory. Attempting to force resident Spaniards to join the rebellion in 1813, he proclaimed: "Any Spaniard who does not . . . work against tyranny in behalf of this just cause will be considered an enemy and punished; as a traitor to the nation, he will inevitably be shot by a firing squad."[1]

Between 1813 and 1817 military advantage shifted back and forth between the patriots and loyalists. Bolívar's ultimate success was ensured by his decision to enlist demobilized English veterans of the Napoleonic Wars and by a military revolt in Spain in 1820. The English veterans, hardened by combat, helped improve the battlefield performance of Bolívar's army. The revolt in Spain forced Ferdinand VII to accept a constitution that limited the powers of the monarch and the church. Colonial loyalists who for a decade had fought to maintain the authority of monarch and church viewed those reforms as unacceptably liberal.

With the king's supporters divided, momentum swung irreversibly to the patriots. After liberating present-day Venezuela, Colombia, and Ecuador, Bolívar's army occupied the area that is now Peru and Bolivia. Finally defeating the last Spanish armies in 1824, Bolívar and his closest supporters attempted to draw the former Spanish colonies into a formal confederation. The first step

was to unify Venezuela, Colombia, and Ecuador into a single nation: Gran Colombia. With Bolívar's encouragement, Peru and Bolivia also experimented with unification. Despite his prestige, however, all of these initiatives had failed by 1830.

Buenos Aires (the capital city of modern Argentina) was the second important center of revolutionary activity in Spanish South America. When news of Ferdinand VII's abdication, forced by Napoleon in 1808, reached Buenos Aires, a coalition of militia commanders, merchants, and ranchers forced the local viceroy to step down and created a Junta. To ward off the potential opposition of loyalists and Spanish officials, the Junta claimed loyalty to the imprisoned Ferdinand VII. Once Ferdinand regained the Spanish throne after the defeat of Napoleon, however, Junta leaders dropped this pretense. In 1816 they declared independence as the United Provinces of the Río de la Plata.

Patriot leaders in Buenos Aires at first sought to retain control over the territory of the Viceroyalty of Río de la Plata, which had been created in 1776 and included modern Argentina, Uruguay, Paraguay, and Bolivia. But Spanish loyalists in Uruguay and Bolivia and a separatist movement in Paraguay defeated these ambitions. Even within the territory of Argentina, the government in Buenos Aires was unable to control regional rivalries and political differences. As a result, the region rapidly descended into political chaos.

A weak succession of Juntas, collective presidencies, and dictators soon lost control over much of the interior of the future Argentina. In 1817, the government in Buenos Aires did manage to support a mixed force of Chileans and Argentines led by José de San Martín (1778–1850), who planned to attack Spanish military forces across the Andes Mountains in Chile and Peru. During this long campaign, San Martín's most effective troops were former slaves who had gained freedom by enlisting in the army, and *gauchos*, the cowboys of the Argentine *pampas* (prairies). After gaining victory in Chile, San Martín pushed on to Peru in 1820 but failed to gain a clear victory there. The violent and destructive uprising of Tupac Amaru II in 1780 (see Chapter 19) had traumatized the colony and left property owners fearful that support for

Nation Building in the Americas

1789	U.S. Constitution ratified
1810–1825	Spanish American wars of independence
1822	Brazilian independence
1836	Texas secedes from Mexico
1846–1848	Mexican-American War
1847–1870	Caste War of Yucatán
1850–1888	Abolition of slavery in the Americas
1862–1867	French intervention in Mexico
1865–1870	Paraguayan War (Paraguay versus Argentina, Brazil, and Uruguay)
1870s	Governments of Argentina and Chile wage war against indigenous peoples
1876	Sioux and allies defeat U.S. Seventh Cavalry at Little Big Horn
1879–1881	War of the Pacific (Chile versus Peru and Bolivia)

independence might unleash another Amerindian uprising. Unable to make progress, San Martín surrendered command of patriot forces in Peru to Simón Bolívar, who overcame final Spanish resistance in 1824.

Mexico

In 1810, Mexico was Spain's richest and most populous colony. Its silver mines were the richest in the world; the colony's capital, Mexico City, was larger than any city in Spain. Mexico also had the largest population of Spanish immigrants among the colonies. They dominated the government, the church, and the economy. When news of Napoleon's invasion of Spain reached the colony, conservative Spaniards in Mexico City overthrew the local viceroy, who they thought was too sympathetic to the creoles. By doing so, however, these Spanish loyalists undermined the legitimacy of colonial institutions.

The first stage of the revolution occurred in the Bajío region of north-central Mexico, where many Amerindian communities had lost lands to growing mining and commercial agricultural enterprises. Resulting tensions had been worsened by a cycle of crop failures and epidemics that began in 1780. When news of Napoleon's invasion of Spain reached Mexico, the Bajío region was already afflicted with high grain prices, unemployment, and privation.

On September 16, 1810, Father Miguel Hidalgo y Costilla, the parish priest of the small town of Dolores, rang the church bells, attracting a crowd of thousands. In a fiery speech he urged the crowd to rise up against the oppression of Spanish officials. The rural and urban poor who joined his movement in the tens of thousands lacked military discipline and adequate weapons but knew who their oppressors were. They attacked the ranches and mines that had exploited them. Many Spaniards and colonial-born whites were murdered or assaulted. Wealthy Mexicans at first were sympathetic to Hidalgo's objectives, but they soon recognized the threat that the angry masses who followed Hidalgo posed to their interests, and they offered their support to Spanish authorities. The military tide soon turned against Hidalgo. He was captured, tried, and executed in 1811.

The revolution did not die, however, but continued under the leadership of the priest José María Morelos, a former student of Hidalgo. A more adept military and political leader than his mentor, Morelos created a formidable fighting force and, in 1813, convened a congress that declared independence and drafted a constitution. Despite these achievements, loyalist forces proved too strong for Morelos. He was defeated and executed in 1815.

Although small numbers of insurgents continued to wage war against Spanish forces, colonial rule seemed secure in 1820. However, news of the military revolt in Spain unsettled the conservative groups and church officials who had defended Spanish rule against Hidalgo and Morelos. In 1821, Colonel Agustín Iturbide and other loyalist commanders forged an alliance with remaining insurgents and declared Mexico's independence. The conservative origins of Mexico's transition to independence were revealed by the creation of a monarchial form of government with Iturbide as emperor. In early

1823, however, Iturbide was overthrown, and Mexico became a republic.

Brazil

The arrival of the Portuguese royal family in Brazil in 1808 helped to maintain the loyalty of the colonial elite and to stimulate the local economy. The defeat of French forces in Portugal led to calls for King John VI to return. In 1820 a liberal revolt in Portugal similar to the military uprising in neighboring Spain forced John VI to return to Europe. He left his son Pedro in Brazil as regent.

Many Brazilians had grown tired of economic dependence and of the arrogance of Portuguese soldiers and bureaucrats. Portuguese demands that Pedro also return to Lisbon and growing fears that troops would be sent to discipline Brazil increased support for independence. In 1822, Pedro declared Brazilian independence. Unlike its neighbors, which all became constitutional republics, Brazil established a constitutional monarchy with Pedro I as emperor. The monarchy would survive until his son Pedro II was overthrown in 1889 by republicans.

THE PROBLEM OF ORDER

A ll the newly independent nations of the Western Hemisphere had difficulties establishing stable political institutions. The idea of popular sovereignty found broad support across the hemisphere. As a result, written constitutions and elected assemblies were put in place, often before the actual achievement of independence. Even in the hemisphere's two monarchies, Mexico and Brazil, the emperors sought to legitimate their authority by agreeing to the creation of representative assemblies. Nevertheless, widespread support for constitutional order and for representative government failed to prevent bitter factional conflict, regionalism, the appearance of personalist leaders, and in some cases military uprisings.

Constitutional Experiments

In reaction to the arbitrary and tyrannical authority of colonial rulers, revolutionary leaders in both the United States and Latin America espoused constitutionalism. They believed that the careful description of political powers in written constitutions offered the best protection for individual rights and liberties. In practice, however, many new constitutions proved unworkable. In the United States, George Washington, James Madison, and other leaders abandoned the Articles of Confederation to write a new constitution, which was put into effect in 1789. In Latin America, few constitutions survived the rough-and-tumble of national politics. Between 1811 and 1833 Venezuela and Chile alone ratified and then rejected a combined total of nine constitutions.

Important differences in colonial political experience influenced later developments in the Americas. The ratification of a new constitution in the United States was the culmination of a long historical process that had begun with the development of English constitutional law and continued under colonial charters. Colonial government in British North America was more democratic and more tolerant of parties and factions than were the colonial governments in Portuguese and Spanish America. Even though women and the poor were denied the vote, many more residents of the British colonies voted and held political office than in Latin America. One important result of these differences was that viceroys and royal judges in the Portuguese and Spanish Empires were much more powerful than the highest-ranking British colonial officials in North America.

Democratic passions and the desire for effective self-rule in the Americas led to significant political reform even in the region's remaining colonies. Through the 1830s Canada was without strong central government. Political life was dominated by a colonial governor and by appointed advisory councils drawn from the local elites. Elected assemblies existed within each of the major administrative subdivisions, but they exercised limited power. Agitation to end oligarchic rule and make government responsive to the will of the assemblies led, in 1837 and 1838, to armed rebellions. Britain's response to these conflicts was to accept a broad political reform that expanded self-rule and recognized Canada's "national" character by creating a Confederation with a strengthened central government in 1867.

The path to effective constitutional government was rockier to the south. Because neither Spain nor Portugal had permitted anything like colonial North America's elected legislatures and municipal governments, the drafters of Latin American constitutions were less constrained by practical political experience. As a result, many of the new Latin American nations experimented with untested political institutions. For example, Simón Bolívar, who authored the first constitutions of five South American republics, included in Bolivia's constitution a fourth branch of government that had "jurisdiction over the youth, the hearts of men, public spirit, good customs, and republican ethics."

Most Latin American nations found it difficult to define the proper political role for the Catholic Church after independence. In the colonial period the Catholic Church held a religious monopoly, controlled all levels of education, and dominated intellectual life. Many early constitutions aimed to reduce this power by making education secular and by permitting the practice of other religions. The church responded by organizing its allies and financing conservative political movements. In Mexico, Colombia, Chile, and Argentina conflicts between liberals who sought the separation of church and state and supporters of the church's traditional powers dominated political life until late in the nineteenth century.

Limiting the military's power proved to be a constitutional stumbling block in Latin America. The wars for independence had elevated the prestige of military leaders. Once the wars were over, Bolívar and other former military commanders seldom proved willing to subordinate themselves to civilian authorities. At the same time, frustrated by the often chaotic workings of constitutional democracy, few citizens were willing to support civilian politicians in any contest with the military. As a result, many Latin American militaries successfully resisted civilian control. Brazil, ruled by Emperor Pedro I, was the principal exception to this pattern.

Personalist Leaders

Successful patriot leaders in both the United States and Latin America gained mass followings during the wars for independence. They recruited and mobilized popular support by using patriotic symbols and by carefully associating their actions with national objectives. After independence, many patriot military leaders were able to use their personal followings to gain national political leadership. George Washington's ability to dominate the political scene in the early republican United States anticipated the later political ascendancy of revolutionary heroes like Iturbide in Mexico and Bolívar in Gran Colombia. In each case, military reputation provided the foundation for personal political power.

In Latin America, personalist leaders who gained and held political power without constitutional sanction were commonly called *caudillos*. This region's slow development of stable political institutions made personalist politics more influential than was the case in the United States. Nevertheless, charismatic politicians in the United States such as Andrew Jackson did sometimes challenge constitutional limits to their authority as did the caudillos of Latin America. Unlike Latin America, however, the United States would not experience an armed rebellion provoked by an unfavorable electoral result.

Throughout the Western Hemisphere, charismatic military men played a key role in attracting mass support for independence movements that were commonly dominated by colonial elites. Although this popular support was often decisive in the struggle for independence, the first constitutions of nearly all the American republics excluded large numbers of poor citizens from full political participation. But nearly everywhere in the Americas marginalized groups found populist leaders to articulate their concerns and challenge these limits on political participation. Using informal means, these leaders sought to influence the selection of officeholders and to place their concerns in the public arena. Despite their success in overturning the deference-based politics of the colonial past, this populist political style at times threatened constitutional order and led to dictatorship.

Andrew Jackson of the United States and José Antonio Páez of Venezuela were political leaders whose powerful personal followings allowed them to challenge constitutional limits to their authority. During the independence wars in Venezuela and Colombia, Páez (1790–1873) organized and led Bolívar's most successful cavalry force. Like most of his followers, Páez was uneducated and poor, but his physical strength, courage, and guile made him a natural guerrilla leader and helped him build a powerful political base in Venezuela. Páez described his authority in the following manner: "[the soldiers] resolved to confer on me the supreme command and blindly to obey my will, confident . . . that I was the only one who could save them."[2]

After independence, Bolívar pursued his dream of forging a permanent union of former Spanish colonies modeled on the federal constitution of the United States. But he failed to appreciate the nationalist sentiments unleashed during the independence wars. Having overturned colonialism, Páez and other Venezuelan leaders resisted the surrender of their hard-won power to Bolívar's government in distant Bogotá (the capital city of modern Colombia). Finding Bolívar's authority challenged by political opponents in 1829, Páez declared Venezuela's independence. Merciless to his enemies and indulgent with his followers, Páez ruled the country as president or dictator for the next eighteen years. Despite implementing an economic program favorable to the elite, Páez remained popular with the masses by skillfully manipulating popular political symbols. Even as his personal wealth grew through land acquisitions and commerce, Páez took care to present himself as a common man.

Andrew Jackson (1767–1845) was the first president of the United States born in humble circumstances. A self-made man who eventually acquired substantial property and owned over a hundred slaves, Jackson was extremely popular among frontier residents, urban workers, and small farmers. Although he was notorious for his untidy personal life as well as for dueling, his courage, individualism, and willingness to challenge authority helped him lead a successful political career as judge, general, congressman, senator, and president.

During his military career, Jackson sometimes ignored the instructions of civilian authorities, but his defeat of British forces at the Battle of New Orleans in 1815, his seizure of Florida from the Spanish in 1818, and his later victories over the Creek and Seminole peoples elevated him to the pinnacle of American politics. In 1824, he received a plurality of the popular vote for the presidency, but, because he failed to get a majority of electoral votes, he was denied the presidency when the House of Representatives chose John Quincy Adams.

Jackson's landslide election in 1828 and reelection in 1832 were welcomed by his followers as the triumph of democracy over entrenched aristocracy. During his presidency, Jackson substantially increased presidential power at the expense of Congress and the courts. Like Páez, Jackson was able to dominate national politics by blending a populist political style that celebrated the virtues and cultural enthusiasms of common people without threatening the economic interests of the most powerful propertied groups.

Personalist leaders were common in both Latin America and the United States, but Latin America's weaker constitutional tradition, more limited protection of property rights, lower literacy levels, and less developed communications systems provided fewer checks on the ambitions of popular politicians. The Constitution of the United States was never suspended, and no national election result in the United States was ever successfully overturned by violence. Latin America's personalist leaders, however, often ignored constitutional restraints on their authority, and election results seldom determined access to presidential power. As a result, by 1900, every Latin American nation had experienced dictatorship.

The Threat of Regionalism

After independence, new national governments were generally weaker than the colonial governments they replaced. In debates over tariffs, tax and monetary policies, and, in many nations, slavery and the slave trade, regional elites often were willing to lead secessionist movements or to provoke civil war rather than accept laws that threatened their interests. Some of the hemisphere's newly independent nations would not survive these struggles; others would lose territories to aggressive neighbors.

In Spanish America, all of the postindependence efforts to forge large multistate federations failed. For example, Central America and Mexico maintained their colonial-era administrative association following independence in 1821. After the overthrow of Iturbide's imperial rule in Mexico in 1823, regional politicians created an independent Republic of Central America. Regional rivalries and civil wars during the 1820s and 1830s forced the breakup of that entity as well, leading to the creation of five separate nations. After independence, Bolívar attempted to maintain the colonial unity of Venezuela, Colombia, and Ecuador by creating the nation of Gran Colombia with its capital in Bogotá. Even before his death in 1830, Venezuela and Ecuador had achieved independence from Colombia. Argentina, Uruguay, Paraguay, and Bolivia had also been united in colonial times, but, with the defeat of Spain, political leaders in Paraguay, Uruguay, and Bolivia all elected to declare independence.

The powerful centrifugal forces that led to the creation of these independent nations almost resulted in the breakup of Argentina itself. After independence, Argentine liberals had attempted to create a strong central government to promote secular education, free trade, and European immigration. Conservative elites of the interior provinces organized to support the Catholic Church's traditional control of education as well as to protect local textile and winemaking industries from European imports. When, in 1819, political leaders in Buenos Aires imposed a national constitution that ignored these concerns, the interior provinces rose in rebellion.

For more than four decades Argentina was dominated by powerful local caudillos like Juan Manuel de Rosas, who between 1829 and 1852 ran the province of Buenos Aires as if it were his private domain. The economy expanded under Rosas, but his use of intimidation, mob violence, and assassination created many enemies. Finally in 1852, an alliance of foreign and domestic enemies overthrew the dictator. However, a new cycle of provincial rivalry and civil wars prevented the creation of a strong central government until 1861.

In the United States the defense of both state and regional interests played an important role in the framing of the Constitution. Many important constitutional provisions represented compromises forged among competing state or regional leaders. The creation of a Senate with equal representation was an attempt to calm small states, which feared domination by larger states. Similarly, slave states were able to force free states to accept a compromise that counted three-fifths of the slave population for purposes of representation in the House of Representatives. Yet, despite these constitutional compromises, the nation was still threatened by regional rivalries.

Slavery divided the republic into two separate and increasingly competitive societies. A rising tide of immigration to the northern states in the 1830s and 1840s began to move the center of power in the House of Representatives away from the South. Although southern leaders had supported the Louisiana Purchase (1803 purchase from France of a vast territory extending from the Gulf of Mexico to Minnesota), the admission of Texas to the Union, and a war with Mexico (discussed later in the chapter) territorial expansion posed a direct threat since it placed the issue of slavery at the center of national debate. Would slavery be allowed to expand into new territories? Could slavery be protected if new states admitted to the Union were overwhelmingly free?

In 1860 Abraham Lincoln (1809–1865), who was committed to checking the spread of slavery, was elected president of the United States. In response, the southern planter elite chose the dangerous course of secession. Lincoln was able to preserve the Union, but his victory was purchased at an enormous cost. The U.S. Civil War was the most destructive and bloody conflict in the history of the Western Hemisphere. More

Map 25.1 Latin America in 1830 By 1830, patriot forces had overturned the Spanish and Portuguese empires of the Western Hemisphere. Regional conflicts, local wars, and foreign interventions challenged the survival of many of these new nations following independence.

OREGON
COUNTRY
(Joint U.S.-British
occupation)

BRITISH NORTH AMERICA
(Gr. Br.)

Mississippi

UNITED STATES

Colorado

Rio Grande

MEXICO
1821

San
Antonio

*ATLANTIC
OCEAN*

Gulf of Mexico

Havana

BAHAMA IS.
(Gr. Br.)

Mexico City • Veracruz

CUBA
(Spain)

HAITI 1804

PUERTO RICO (Spain)

BRITISH
HONDURAS (Gr. Br.)

GUATEMALA
Guatemala

JAMAICA (Gr. Br.)

*Caribbean
Sea*

UNITED PROVINCES OF
CENTRAL AMERICA
1823–1839

Panama

Caracas

TRINIDAD (Gr. Br.)

VENEZUELA

BR. GUIANA (Gr. Br.)

DUTCH GUIANA (Neth.)

FRENCH GUIANA (France)

Magdalena

Bogotá

GRAN COLOMBIA
1819–1830

*Galápagos
Islands*

Quito

ECUADOR

Amazon

EMPIRE OF BRAZIL
1822

PERU
1821

Lima

*PACIFIC
OCEAN*

Bahia

BOLIVIA
1825

Sucre

Paraná

PARAGUAY
1811

São Paulo

Rio de Janeiro

CHILE
1817

Santiago

UNITED
PROVINCES OF
LA PLATA
1816

ARGENTINA

Buenos Aires

URUGUAY
1828

Montevideo

PATAGONIA
(Disputed between
Argentina and Chile)

| 0 | 500 | 1000 Km. |

| 0 | 500 | 1000 Mi. |

*Islas Malvinas
(Falkland Islands)*
(La Plata)

than 500,000 lives were lost before the South surrendered in 1865. Victory not only permitted the abolition of slavery but transferred national political power to a northern elite committed to industrial expansion and federal support for railroads and other internal improvements.

The South's failed secession shared essential characteristics with the secessionist movements that had led to the breakup of Gran Colombia and the other Spanish American federations. In fact, the South was better prepared politically and economically for independence than were those successful separatist movements. It failed in part because of poor timing. The new nations of the Western Hemisphere were most vulnerable during the early years of their existence; indeed, all the successful secessions occurred within the first decades following independence. In the case of the United States, secession was defeated by an experienced national government that had been legitimated and strengthened by more than seventy-five years of stability and reinforced by economic and population growth.

Foreign Interventions and Regional Wars

With the exception of the U.S. Civil War, the scale of military conflict in the Western Hemisphere in the nineteenth century was far smaller than in Europe. Nevertheless, wars often determined national borders, access to natural resources, and control of markets in the hemisphere. Even after independence, some Western Hemisphere nations had to defend themselves against Europe's great powers. Contested national borders and regional rivalries also led to wars between Western Hemisphere nations. By the end of the nineteenth century, the United States, Brazil, Argentina, and Chile had successfully waged wars against their neighbors and established themselves as regional powers.

Within thirty years of independence, the United States fought a second war with England— the War of 1812. The weakness of the new republic was symbolized by the burning of the White House and Capitol by British troops in 1814. This humiliation was soon overcome, how-

ever, and by the end of the nineteenth century the United States was the hemisphere's greatest military power. Its war against Spain in 1898 created an American empire that reached from the Philippines and Hawaii in the Pacific Ocean to Puerto Rico in the Caribbean Sea.

Latin American nations were also challenged by Europe. Mexico defeated a weak Spanish invasion in 1829 and a French assault on Veracruz in 1838. In 1863, a large French army invaded Mexico and installed the Austrian Archduke Maximilian as emperor. President Benito Juárez finally drove out the French army in 1867 and executed Maximilian. Argentina faced British and French naval blockades during the Rosas years, and in the 1850s British naval forces violated Brazil's territorial waters to stop the importation of slaves.

Wars between Western Hemisphere nations commonly produced more enduring results. The United States greatly expanded its land area through military conflicts. In the 1820s Mexico had encouraged Americans to immigrate to Texas, which at that time was Mexican territory. By the early 1830s Americans outnumbered Mexican nationals in Texas by four to one and were aggressively challenging Mexican laws such as the prohibition of slavery. In 1835, political turmoil in Mexico led to a rebellion in Texas by an alliance of Mexican liberals and American settlers. Mexico was defeated in a brief war, and Texas became an independent nation. The U.S. decision to make Texas a state in 1845 provoked war with Mexico a year later. Although Mexican forces fought well, U.S. forces captured Mexico City, and the United States imposed a punitive peace treaty. Mexico lost 50 percent of its territory, including present-day New Mexico, Arizona, and California. In return it received $15 million. When gold was discovered in California in 1848, the magnitude of Mexico's loss became clear.

Other groups of American citizens, acting without formal government support, attempted to imitate the Texans but had less success. Two invasions of Cuba in the early 1850s failed as did William Walker's invasion of Nicaragua in 1855. Walker declared himself president but was soon deposed and executed.

In two wars with neighbors, Chile established itself as the leading military and economic

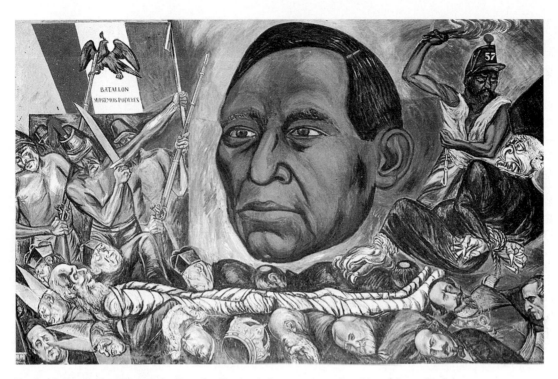

Benito Juárez's triumph over the French   Benito Juárez overcame humble origins to lead the overthrow of Emperor Maximilian and the defeat of French imperialism. He has remained a powerful symbol of secularism and republican virtue in Mexico. In this 1948 mural by José Clemente Orozco, Juárez's face dominates a scene of struggle that pits Mexican patriots against the allied forces of the Catholic Church, Mexican conservatives, and foreign invaders. (Museo Nacional de Historia/CENDIAP-INBA)

power on the west coast of South America. Chile defeated the Confederation of Peru and Bolivia between 1836 and 1839. A second war with Peru and Bolivia occurred over disputed control of rich mining territories. Chilean and British investors in nitrate mines provoked the war in 1879. The modern Chilean army and navy won a crushing victory, forcing Bolivia to cede its outlet to the sea and Peru to yield the mining districts.

Argentina and Brazil fought each other over control of Uruguay in the 1820s, but a military stalemate eventually forced them to recognize Uruguayan independence. In 1865 Argentina and Uruguay joined Brazil to wage war against Paraguay. After five years of warfare, the Paraguayan dictator Francisco Solano López and more than 20 percent of the national population were dead. Paraguay lost territory to the victors, was forced to open its markets to foreign trade, and suffered military occupation.

Native Peoples and the Nation-State

Relations between the Western Hemisphere's new nation-states and indigenous peoples were negotiated by both diplomacy and military action. During late colonial times, to avoid armed conflict and to limit the costs of frontier defense, Spanish, Portuguese, and British imperial governments attempted to limit the expansion of settlements into territories already occupied by Amerindians. The colonial powers' role as mediator and protector of native peoples ended with independence.

The military potential of still-independent Amerindian peoples posed a significant challenge to many Western Hemisphere republics, however. Weakened by civil wars and constitutional crises, many new nations were less able to maintain frontier peace than earlier colonial

Navajo leaders travel to Washington to negotiate   As settlers, ranchers, and miners pushed west in the nineteenth century, leaders of Amerindian peoples were forced to negotiate territorial concessions with representatives of the United States government. In order to impress Amerindian peoples with the wealth and power of the United States, many leaders were invited to Washington, D.C. In this 1874 photo, Navajo leaders are shown together with their Anglo translators in Washington, D.C. (#5851 Frank McNill Collection, State Records Center & Archives, Sante Fe, NM)

governments had been. After independence, Amerindian peoples succeeded in pushing back some frontier settlements in Argentina, the United States, Chile, and Mexico. Despite these early victories, native military resistance was finally overcome by the end of the 1880s in both North and South America.

After the end of the American Revolution, rapidly expanding agricultural settlements threatened native peoples. Between 1790 and 1810 tens of thousands of settlers entered territories guaranteed to Amerindians by treaty. In Ohio alone more than 200,000 white settlers were present by 1810. Native leaders responded by seeking the support of British officials in Canada and by forging broad intertribal alliances. American forces decisively defeated one such Amerindian alliance in 1794 at the Battle of Fallen

Timbers in Ohio. After 1800 two Shawnee leaders, the brothers Tecumseh and The Prophet (Tenskwatawa), created a larger and better organized alliance among southern and western Indian peoples. Although Tecumseh forged a military alliance with Great Britain, the American military defeated his forces in 1813. By 1840 the once numerous and powerful Amerindian cultures located east of the Mississippi River had been defeated and, in many cases forced to relocate farther west.

White settlers then pushed across the Mississippi into Arkansas and Missouri, forcing native peoples to cede those lands. The 1828 presidential election of Andrew Jackson, a veteran of wars against native peoples, brought matters to a head. In 1830 Congress passed the Indian Removal Act, forcing the removal of Cherokees and remnants of other eastern peoples to lands west of the Mississippi. When the removal was carried out in 1837 and 1838, nearly half of the forced migrants died on this "Trail of Tears."

The Amerindians of the Great Plains offered formidable resistance to further expansion. By the 1850s, when buffalo hunters, cattlemen, and settlers reached the American West in substantial numbers, indigenous peoples had adopted the horse and firearms. These new technologies had transformed the cultures of Plains peoples such as the Sioux, Comanche, Pawnee, and Kiowa. Among the Pawnee, for example, the improved efficiency of the buffalo hunt reduced earlier dependence on agriculture. As a result, women, who had primary responsibility for crops, lost prestige and social power to male hunters. Living arrangements were also affected as the single-family tepees of migratory buffalo hunters replaced the multigenerational lodges associated with the earlier farming economy.

After the U.S. Civil War, these Plains cultures were menaced by a growing population of settlers. Buffalo herds were hunted to near extinction for their hides, and traditional lands were lost to farmers and cattlemen. Over a period of nearly four decades of armed conflict with the United States Army, many Amerindian peoples were forced to give up their land and their traditional ways. The Comanche, who had dominated the southern plains during the period of Spanish and Mexican rule, were forced by the U.S. government to cede most of their land in Texas in 1865. The Sioux and their allies resisted for more than another decade. Although in 1876 they overwhelmed General George Armstrong Custer and the Seventh Cavalry in the Battle of Little Bighorn (in the southern part of the present-day state of Montana), the Sioux finally were forced to accept reservation life. A series of military campaigns then broke the resistance of the Apache in the 1870s and 1880s.

A similar pattern of adaptation, resistance, and defeat developed in Argentina and Chile. The proliferation of herds of wild cattle provided indigenous peoples with a limitless food supply, and the acquisition of the horse and metal weapons increased their military capacities. The native peoples of Argentina and Chile effectively checked the southern expansion of agriculture and ranching until the 1850s. In fact, Amerindian raiders operated within 100 miles (160 kilometers) of Buenos Aires into the 1860s. Unable to defeat these resourceful enemies, the governments of both nations relied on an elaborate system of gift giving and prisoner exchanges to maintain peace on the frontier.

By the 1860s, population increase, political stability, and military modernization allowed Argentina and Chile to take the offensive. In 1870 General Julio Roca organized an overwhelming military force to crush all native resistance in Argentina. Thousands of Amerindians were killed and the survivors driven onto marginal lands.

The story in Chile was the same. When civil war and an economic depression weakened the Chilean government at the end of the 1850s, the Araucanian people attempted to push back frontier settlements. Despite early successes, the Araucanians were eventually defeated in the 1870s by Chilean forces armed with modern weaponry. In Chile, as in the United States and Argentina, in an attempt to justify upcoming military campaigns against native peoples, Amerindians were demonized as brutal and cruel obstacles to progress. In April 1859, a Chilean newspaper commented:

> The necessity, not only to punish the Araucanian race, but also to make it impotent to harm us, is well recognized . . . as the only way to rid the country of a million evils. It is well understood that they are odious and prejudicial guests in Chile . . . conciliatory measures have accomplished nothing with this stupid race—the infamy and disgrace of the Chilean nation.[3]

Political divisions and civil wars within new nations sometimes provided an opportunity for long-pacified native peoples to rebel as well. In the Yucatán region of Mexico, owners of henequen (the agave plant that produces fiber used in twine) and sugar plantations had forced many Maya communities off traditional lands and compelled thousands of other Amerindians to become peons. In the late 1840s, when Mexico was convulsed by civil war and an invasion by the United States, the Maya rose in rebellion. After the war with the United States ended, Mexico forced Maya rebels to retreat to unoccupied territories. There they created an independent state, which they called the "Empire of the Cross." Organized around a mix of traditional beliefs and Christian symbols, this indigenous state resisted Mexican forces through the 1860s. The last of the Maya strongholds would hold out until 1901.

THE CHALLENGE OF ECONOMIC AND SOCIAL CHANGE

During the nineteenth century, the newly independent nations of the Western Hemisphere struggled to realize the Enlightenment ideals of freedom and individual liberty. The achievement of these objectives was slowed by the persistence of oppressive colonial era institutions like slavery. The cultural and racial diversity of the hemisphere presented many obstacles to reformers. Nevertheless, by century's end reform movements in many of the hemisphere's nations had succeeded in ending the slave trade, abolishing slavery, expanding voting rights, and integrating new waves of immigrants from Asia and Europe.

The consequences of increased industrialization and greater integration in the evolving world economy also challenged the region's political stability and social arrangements. Although a small number of nations embraced industrialization, most Western Hemisphere economies became increasingly dependent on the export of agricultural goods and minerals during the nineteenth century. While the industrializing nations of the hemisphere became richer than the nations that remained exporters of raw materials, all the region's economies became more vulnerable and volatile as a result of greater integration in international markets. Efforts to assert national economic control, as with contemporary movements for social reform, produced powerful new political forces in the American nations.

Abolition

Throughout the hemisphere, strong antislavery sentiments were expressed during the struggles for independence. In nearly every new nation, revolutionary leaders asserted universal ideals of freedom and citizenship that contrasted harshly with slavery. Nevertheless, slavery survived throughout most of the hemisphere until the 1850s. In regions where the export of plantation products was most important—such as the United States, Brazil, and Cuba—abolition was achieved with great difficulty (the character of Cuban slavery is the topic of the Voices and Visions feature).

With independence, slavery in the United States was weakened by abolition in some northern states and by the termination of the African slave trade in 1808. This tentative progress toward the abolition of slavery was stalled by the profitable expansion of cotton agriculture following the War of 1812. In Spanish America, tens of thousands of slaves gained freedom by joining revolutionary armies during the wars for independence. After independence, most Spanish American republics prohibited the slave trade. Counteracting that trend, the growing international demand for sugar and coffee in the nineteenth century led to an increase in slave importations to Brazil and Cuba (the island was a Spanish colony until 1899), despite Great Britain's efforts to end the slave trade.

During the long struggle to end slavery, U.S. abolitionists argued that slavery offended both morality and the universal rights asserted in the Declaration of Independence. Abolitionist Theodore Weld articulated the religious objection to slavery in 1834:

No condition of birth, no shade of color, no mere misfortune of circumstance, can annul the birthright charter, which God has bequeathed to every being upon whom he has stamped his own image, by making him a free *moral agent* [emphasis in original], and that he who robs his fellow man of this tramples upon right, subverts justice, outrages humanity . . . and sacrilegiously assumes the prerogative of God.[4]

Two groups that were denied full rights of citizenship, women and free African-Americans, played important roles in the abolitionist cause. Women served on the executive committee of the American Anti-Slavery Society and produced some of the most effective propaganda against slavery. Angelina and Sarah Grimké of South Carolina moved to the north to pursue abolition. Their ally, Maria Child, became an editor of the American Anti-Slavery Society's periodical. Thousands of other women joined abolitionist groups, where they provided leadership and were effective speakers and propagandists. When social conservatives attacked this highly visible public role, many women abolitionists responded by becoming public advocates of female suffrage as well.

Frederick Douglass, a former slave, became one of the most effective abolitionist speakers and writers. Other more radical black leaders pushed the abolitionist movement to accept the inevitability of violence—either civil war or slave insurrection—in ending slavery. Charles Lenox Redmond, for example, declared that slaves should "RISE AT ONCE, en masse, and THROW OFF THEIR FETTERS" (capitalization in original).

In the 1850s the growing electoral strength of the newly formed Republican Party forced a confrontation between slave and free states. After the election of Abraham Lincoln in 1860, thirteen southern states seceded from the Union. During the war, pressure for emancipation mounted as tens of thousands of black freemen and escaped slaves joined the Union Army. Hundreds of thousands of other slaves fled their masters' plantations and farms for the protection of advancing northern armies. Finally in 1863, in the midst of the Civil War and two years after the abolition of serfdom in Russia (see Chapter 27), President Lincoln began the abolition of slavery by issuing the Emancipation Proclamation, which ended slavery in rebel states. Final abolition was accomplished after the war by the Thirteenth Amendment to the Constitution.

Slavery survived in Brazil for more than two decades after it was abolished in the United States. Not only was progress slower but it also depended in large measure on foreign pressure. Once Great Britain ended the slave trade to its Carribean colonies, it began to pressure other slave societies to end slave importations. In 1830, Brazil signed a treaty with the British ending the slave trade. Despite this agreement, Brazil illegally imported over a half-million more African slaves before the British navy finally forced compliance in the 1850s. The Emperor Pedro II and many Brazilian liberals worked to abolish slavery in the 1850s and 1860s, but their desire to find a form of gradual emancipation acceptable to slave owners slowed progress.

During the Paraguayan War (1865–1870), large numbers of slaves joined the Brazilian army in exchange for freedom. Their loyalty and heroism undermined the military's support for slavery, and by the 1880s army leaders were resisting demands that they capture and return runaway slaves. Educated Brazilians increasingly viewed slavery as an obstacle to economic development and as an impediment to democratic

A former Brazilian slave returns from military service   The heroic participation of black freemen and slaves in the Paraguayan War (1865–1870) led many Brazilians to advocate the abolition of slavery. The caption for this cartoon reads: "On his return from the war in Paraguay: Full of glory, covered with laurels, after having spilled his blood in defense of the fatherland and to free a people from slavery, the volunteer sees his own mother bound and whipped! Awful reality!" (Courtesy, Fundacao Biblioteca Nacional)

reforms. As abolitionist sentiment grew, reformers forced the passage of a series of laws that provided for the gradual emancipation of slaves in the 1870s. With political support for slaves weakening in the 1880s, growing numbers of slaves forced the issue by fleeing from bondage. Legislation abolishing slavery finally was passed by the Brazilian parliament and accepted by Emperor Pedro II in 1888.

The plantations of the Caribbean region received just under 50 percent of all African slaves shipped to the New World. As a result, tiny white minorities lived surrounded by slave and free colored majorities throughout the region. At the end of the eighteenth century, the slave rebellion in Saint Domingue (see Chapter 24) spread terror across the Caribbean. Because of fear that any effort to overthrow colonial rule might unleash new slave rebellions, there was little enthusiasm among free settlers in Caribbean colonies for independence. Nor did local support for abolition appear among white settlers or free colored populations. Thus abolition in most Caribbean colonies commonly resulted from political decisions made in Europe by colonial powers.

Nevertheless, slaves in these colonies also helped propel the movement toward abolition by rebelling, running away, and resisting in more subtle ways as they had done in Brazil, the United States, and in Spanish America. Although initially unsuccessful, the rebellions that threatened France's other Caribbean colonies following the Haitian Revolution weakened metropolitan support for slavery. Jamaica and other British colonies also experienced rebellions and the creation of communities of runaways. In Spanish Cuba as well, slave resistance forced an increase in police expenditure in the nineteenth century.

After 1800, the sugar plantations of the British West Indian colonies became less profitable, and a coalition of organized labor groups, Protestant dissenters, and free traders in Britain pushed for the abolition of slavery. Britain, the major participant in the eighteenth century expansion of slavery in the Americas, ended its participation in the slave trade in 1808. It then negotiated a series of treaties with Spain, Brazil, and other slave powers to eliminate the slave trade to America. Once these treaties were in place, British naval forces actively sought to enforce compliance. In

1834, slavery in British colonies was abolished, although former slaves were compelled to remain with former masters as "apprentices." Abuses by planters and resistance to apprenticeship by former slaves led to complete abolition in 1838. Slavery in the French Caribbean was abolished a decade later after upheavals in France led to the overthrow of the government of Louis Philippe (see Chapter 24).

Slavery persisted in Spain's remaining Caribbean colonies until the 1880s. It was weakened first by Britain's use of diplomatic pressure and naval force to limit the arrival of African slaves after 1820. More important, however, was the development of support for abolition in the colonies. Both Cuba and Puerto Rico had larger white and free colored populations than the Caribbean colonies of Britain and France. As a result, there was less fear in Cuba and Puerto Rico that abolition would lead to the political ascendancy of former slaves, as had occurred in Haiti. In Puerto Rico, where slaves numbered approximately thirty thousand, local reformers sought and gained the abolition of slavery in 1873. In the midst of a decade-long war to defeat forces seeking the independence of Cuba, the Spanish government moved gradually toward abolition. Initially, slave children born after September 18, 1868 were freed but obligated to work for their former masters for eighteen years. This requirement was followed in 1880 by a law that freed all other slaves on the condition that they serve their masters for eight additional years (see Voices & Visions: Opportunities for Freedom Within the Cuban Slave System). Finally, in 1886, these conditions were eliminated and slavery was abolished. With slavery abolished, Cuban patriots forged a multiracial alliance that would initiate a new war for independence in 1895.

Immigration

During the colonial period, free Europeans were a minority among immigrants to the Western Hemisphere. Between 1500 and 1760, African slaves entering the Western Hemisphere outnumbered European immigrants by nearly two to one. Another 4 million or so African slaves were imported before the effective end of the

Opportunities for Freedom Within the Cuban Slave System

During the nineteenth century, visitors from the United States to Cuba sometimes commented on differences in the systems of slavery that had developed in the two nations. Nearly all of these observers remarked on the greater opportunities for freedom provided for in Spanish law. Slave states in the United States had severely limited manumission in the decades that preceded abolition, but Cuban slaves continued to escape bondage in large numbers in slavery's final years. Here are the observations of one American visitor in his 1885 book:

There are said to be three hundred thousand free negroes on the island [and] about one hundred and forty thousand male and about sixty thousand female slaves. To carry on the great industry of the island as systematized by the planters, this number of hands is entirely inadequate. It is sometimes asked how there came to be so many free negroes in the island. It should be clearly understood that the laws which govern Cuba are made by the home government, not by the planters or natives of Cuba, and that indirectly these laws have long favored emancipation of the blacks. For many years any slave has enjoyed the right to go to a magistrate and have himself appraised, and upon paying the price thus set upon himself he can receive his free papers. The valuation is made by three persons, of whom the master appoints one, and the magistrate two. The slave may pay by installments of fifty dollars at a time but he owes his full service to his master until the last and entire payment is made. If the valuation be twelve hundred dollars, after the slave has paid one hundred he owns one twelfth of himself, and the master eleven twelfths, and so on. Until all is paid, however, the master's dominion over the slave is complete. There has also long been another peculiar law in operation. A slave may on the same valuation compel his master to transfer him to any person who will pay the money in full, and this has often been done where slave and master disagree. This law, as will be seen, must have operated as it was designed to do, as a check upon masters, and as an inducement for them to remove special causes of complaint and dissatisfaction. It has also enabled slaveholders of the better class, in the case of ill-usage of blacks, to relieve them by paying down their appraised value and appropriating their services to themselves. All this relates to the past rather than the present, since, as we have explained, the relationship of slave and master is now so nearly at an end as to render such arrangements inoperative.

Why would the Spanish colonial government of Cuba pass laws that limited the power of slave owners? Does this commentator seem to approve of Spanish laws permitting emancipation? How did slavery in Cuba differ from slavery in the United States? How would this system affect relations between slaves and masters?

Source: Abridged from Louis A. Perez, ed., *Slaves, Sugar, and Colonial Society: Travel Accounts of Cuba, 1801–1899* (Wilmington, DE: Scholarly Resources, 1992), 243–244.

---

slave trade at the end of the 1850s. As the African slave trade came to an end, the arrival of millions of immigrants from Europe and Asia in the nineteenth century contributed to the further transformation of the Western Hemisphere. This new wave of immigration fostered rapid economic growth and the occupation of frontier regions in the United States, Canada, Argentina, Chile, and Brazil. It also promoted urbanization. By century's end, nearly all of the hemisphere's fastest-growing cities (Buenos Aires, Chicago, New York, and São Paulo, for example) had large immigrant populations.

During the nineteenth century Europe provided the majority of immigrants to the Western Hemisphere. For much of the century, these immigrants came primarily from western Europe, but after 1870, the majority came from southern and eastern Europe. The scale of immigration increased dramatically in the second half of the century. The United States received approximately 600,000 European immigrants in the 1830s, 1.5 million in the 1840s, and then 2.5 million *per decade* until 1880. In the 1890s, an astonishing total of 5.2 million immigrants arrived. European immigration to Latin America also increased dramatically after 1880. Combined immigration to Argentina and Brazil rose from just under 130,000 in the 1860s to 1.7 million in the 1890s. By 1910, 30 percent of the Argentine population was foreign-born, more than twice the proportion of the U.S. population. Argentina was an extremely attractive destination for European immigrants, receiving more than twice as many immigrants as Canada between 1870 and 1930. Even so, immigration to Canada increased tenfold during this same period.

Asian immigration to the Western Hemisphere increased after 1850. Approximately 100,000 Chinese immigrants arrived in Peru between 1849 and 1875; more than 120,000 Chinese entered Cuba between 1847 and 1873; and about 50,000 Chinese immigrated to Canada by 1900. The United States, however, was the primary North American destination for Chinese immigrants, receiving 300,000 between 1854 and 1882. India also contributed to the social transformation of the Western Hemisphere, sending more than a half million immigrants to the Caribbean region. British Guiana alone received 238,000 immigrants from the subcontinent.

Despite the obvious economic benefits stemming from this inflow of people, hostility to immigration mounted in many nations. Nativist political movements argued that large numbers of new immigrants could not be successfully integrated into national political cultures. By the end of the century these fears and prejudices led many governments in the Western Hemisphere to limit immigration or to distinguish between "desirable" and "undesirable" immigrants, commonly favoring Europeans over Asians.

Asians faced more obstacles to immigration than did Europeans and were more often victims of violence and extreme forms of discrimination in the New World. In the 1870s and 1880s, anti-Chinese riots erupted in many western cities in the United States. Congress responded to this wave of racism by passing the Chinese Exclusion Act in 1882, which eliminated most Chinese immigration. In 1886, fears that Canada was being threatened by "inferior races" led to the imposition of a head tax that made immigration to

Canada more difficult for Chinese families. During this same period, strong anti-Chinese prejudice surfaced in Peru, Mexico, and Cuba. Similar prejudice faced Japanese immigrants in Brazil and East Indians in the English-speaking Caribbean.

Immigrants from Europe also faced prejudice and discrimination. In the United States, Italians were commonly portrayed as criminals or anarchists. In Argentina, social scientists attempted to prove that Italian immigrants were more violent and less honest than the native-born population. Immigrants from Spain were popularly stereotyped in Argentina as miserly and dishonest. Eastern European Jews seeking to escape pogroms and discrimination at home found themselves barred from many educational institutions and professional careers in both the United States and Latin America. Negative stereotypes were invented for German, Swedish, Polish, and Middle Eastern immigrants as well. The perceived grievances used to justify these common prejudices were remarkably similar from Canada to Argentina. Immigrants, it was argued, threatened the well-being of native-born workers by accepting low wages, and they threatened national culture by resisting assimilation.

Many intellectuals and political leaders wondered if the evolving mix of culturally diverse populations could sustain a common citizenship. As a result, efforts were directed toward compelling immigrants to assimilate. Schools became cultural battlegrounds where language, cultural values, and patriotic feelings were transmitted to the children of immigrants. From Argentina to Canada, school curricula were reformed to promote national culture. Ignoring Canada's large French-speaking population, an English-speaking Canadian reformer commented on recent immigration by stating, "[I]f Canada is to become in a real sense a nation, if our people are to become one people, we must have one language."[5] These fears and prejudices led to the proliferation of patriotic songs, the veneration of national flags and other symbols, and the development of national histories that emphasized patriotism and civic virtue. Nearly everywhere in the Americas schools worked to create more homogeneous national cultures.

Immigrants to Argentina await processing Argentina was one of the most important destinations for European immigrants in the nineteenth century. In this photo, thousands of recent arrivals are packed into an assembly hall to await processing. (Library of Congress)

American Cultures

Despite discrimination, immigrants continued to flood into the Western Hemisphere, introducing new languages, living arrangements, technologies, and work customs. Immigrants also altered the politics of many of the hemisphere's nations as they sought to influence government policies. Where immigrants arrived in the greatest numbers, they put enormous pressure on housing, schools, and social welfare services. To compensate for their isolation from home, language, and culture, immigrants often created ethnically based mutual aid societies, sports and leisure clubs, and neighborhoods. These ethnic patterns provided valuable social and economic support for recent arrivals while sometimes worsening the fears of the native-born that immigration was a threat to national culture.

While immigrants were being changed by programs of forced acculturation and by their experiences in their adopted nations, they and their children in turn were altering the cultures of these nations. Immigrants learned the language of their adopted countries as fast as possible in order to improve their earning capacity. At the same time, words and phrases from their native languages entered the language of host nations. Languages as diverse as Yiddish and Italian strongly influenced American English, Argentine Spanish, and Brazilian Portuguese. The cuisine of nearly every American nation was altered by dietary practices introduced from Europe and Asia. In turn, immigrants commonly added native foods to their diets, especially the hemisphere's abundant and relatively cheap meats.

American popular music changed as well. For example, the Argentine tango, based on African-Argentine rhythms, was transformed by new instrumentation and orchestral arrangements brought by Italian immigrants. Mexican ballads blended with English folk music in the U.S. southwest, and Italian operas played to packed houses in Buenos Aires. Sports, games of chance, and fashion also experienced this process of borrowing and exchange.

Union movements and electoral politics in the hemisphere also felt the influence of new arrivals who aggressively sought to influence government and gain improved working conditions. The labor movements of Mexico, Argentina, and the United States, in particular, were influenced by the anarchist and socialist beliefs of European immigrants. Mutual benevolent societies and less formal ethnic associations pooled resources to help immigrants open businesses, aid the immigration of their relatives, or bury their family members. They also established links with political movements, sometimes exchanging votes for favors.

The Children's Aid Society of Toronto Throughout the Western Hemisphere, women led the effort to develop social welfare institutions. Their leadership was most clearly evident in providing protection for poor and abandoned children. This photo shows a social worker and children sitting on the front step of the Children's Aid Society of Toronto in 1895. (City of Toronto Archives, #SC1-3)

Women's Rights and the Struggle for Social Justice

The abolition of slavery in the Western Hemisphere did not end racial discrimination or provide full political rights for every citizen. Not only did blacks suffer the effects of political and economic discrimination, but women, new immigrants, and native peoples also experienced similar obstacles in nearly every Western Hemisphere nation. During the second half of the nineteenth century, reformers struggled to remove these limits on citizenship while also addressing the welfare needs of workers and the poor.

As early as 1848, a group of activists meeting as The Women's Rights Convention issued a statement that said in part, "We hold these truths to be self-evident: that all men and women are equal." While moderates sought greater economic independence and full legal rights, increasing numbers of women demanded the right to vote. Other women lobbied to provide better conditions for women working outside the home, especially in textile factories. Sarah Grimké responded to criticism of women's activism:

> "This has been the language of man since he laid aside the whip as a means to keep woman in subjection. He spares her body, but the war he has waged against her mind, her heart, and her soul, has been no less to her a moral being. How monstrous is the doctrine that woman is to be dependent on man!"[6]

Progress toward equality between men and women was equally slow in Canada and Latin America. Canada's first women doctors were forced to train in the United States, since no woman was able to receive a medical degree in Canada until 1895. Full enfranchisement occurred in the twentieth century, but Canadian women did gain the right to vote in some provincial and municipal elections before 1900. Like women in the United States, Canadian women provided leadership in temperance, child welfare, and labor reform movements. Argentina and Uruguay were among the first Latin American nations to provide public education for women. Both nations introduced coeducation in the 1870s. Chilean women gained access to some professional careers in the 1870s. In Argentina, the first woman doctor would graduate in 1899. In Brazil, where many women had been active in the abolitionist movement, four women had graduated in medicine by 1882. More rapid progress was achieved in lower status careers that less directly threatened male economic power. By the end of the century women dominated elementary school teaching throughout the Western Hemisphere.

From Canada to Argentina and Chile, the majority of working-class women had no direct involvement in these reform movements, but in their daily lives they succeeded in transforming gender relations. By the end of the nineteenth century, the majority of these women worked outside the home on farms, in markets, and, increasingly, in factories. Many bore full responsibility for providing for their children. Whether men thought women should remain in the home or not, by the end of the century women were unambiguously present in the economy (see also Chapter 28).

Throughout the hemisphere there was little progress toward eliminating racial discrimination. Blacks were denied the vote throughout the south in the United States. They were also subjected to the indignity of segregation—allocated to separate schools, hotels, restaurants, seats in public transportation, and even separate water fountains. Racial discrimination against blacks was also common in Latin America, though seldom spelled out in legal codes. After abolition, black men and women organized to force an end to these oppressive systems. Often forging links with sympathetic white reformers, they commonly demanded the right to vote and greater economic opportunity. In Brazil, Argentina, and Cuba as well as in the United States, blacks came together to launch political and literary magazines and to promote reform and celebrate black cultural achievements.

Development and Underdevelopment

Although the Atlantic economy experienced three periods of economic contraction during the nineteenth century, nearly all the nations of the Western Hemisphere were richer in 1900 than in 1800. The Industrial Revolution, worldwide population growth, and an increasingly integrated world market stimulated economic expansion (see Environment & Technology: The McCormick Reaper). Wheat, corn, wool, meats, and nonprecious minerals were added to the region's earlier exports of silver, sugar, dyes, coffee, and cotton. The United States was the only Western Hemisphere nation to industrialize in the nineteenth century. To service distant markets, governments throughout the hemisphere invested in improved roads, railroads, canals, and telegraphs. They also sought to use tariff and monetary policies to sponsor economic diversification and growth. Yet only three Western Hemisphere nations—the United States, Canada, and Argentina—had achieved levels of prosperity similar to those of western Europe by 1900.

New demands for copper, zinc, lead, coal, and tin unleashed by the Industrial Revolution led to mining booms in the west of the United States and in Mexico and Chile. Unlike the small-scale and often short-term gold- and silver-mining operations of the colonial era, the mining companies of the late nineteenth century were heavily capitalized international corporations that could bully governments and buy political favors. During this period, European or North American Corporations owned most new mining enterprises in Latin America. Petroleum development, which occurred at the end of the century, followed this pattern as well.

New technology accelerated economic integration, but the high cost of this technology often increased dependence on foreign capital. Many of the hemisphere's governments promoted railroads by granting tax benefits, free land, and monopoly rights to both domestic and foreign investors. By 1890 vast areas of the Great Plains in the United States and Canada, the Argentine pampas, and the northern part of Mexico were producing grains and livestock for foreign markets opened by the development of railroads. Steamships also lowered the cost of transportation to distant markets, and the telegraph stimulated expansion by speeding up the spread of information about the demand for and availability of products.

The McCormick Reaper

The McCormick reaper was one of the great industrial success stories of the nineteenth century. McCormick reapers and other agricultural implements dominated the industry and gained export markets throughout the Western Hemisphere and Europe. By leading the mechanization of agriculture, the McCormick Havesting Machine Company reduced labor costs and promoted the development of large-scale commercial farming in the Midwestern United States and Canada. Aided by mechanization, wheat production grew by 70 percent in the 1850s alone.

Cyrus McCormick and his family began building reapers in their blacksmith shop in Rockbridge County, Virginia, in 1840. In the early years, slaves owned by the family helped hand-craft the reapers from raw materials found locally. Although McCormick faced competition from other manufacturers, the business grew quickly, in part because McCormick was a great promoter who effectively used advertising to develop his business. As demand rose, he increased production by adding new skilled workers and by licensing other manufacturers to produce the company's reapers.

These licensing agreements caused problems of quality control that led McCormick to move all the company's production to a custom-built factory in Chicago in 1848. Production in the new factory quickly reached 1,500 units per year, far outstripping the 200 units per year produced in the Virginia operation. Nearly all this increase came from adding more skilled workers and from the closer supervision of subcontractors who supplied blades and other parts. By 1876, 14,000 reapers were produced.

At the end of the 1870s, Cyrus broke with his brother, Leander, and brought in a factory manager who had worked at Colt firearms and the Wilson Sewing Machine Company. Under this new leadership, the company introduced a new industrial process that emphasized standardization and special-purpose machine tools for fabrication. Production reached 48,000 units in 1885 and then soared to 100,000 in 1889. These changes in technology and production methods, however, changed the work force from skilled to unskilled labor and contributed to increased numbers of strikes and stoppages.

Source: This discussion follows the analysis in David A. Hounshell, *From the American System to Mass Production, 1800–1932: The Development of Manufacturing Technology in the United States* (Baltimore: Johns Hopkins University Press, 1984), 153–189.

The McCormick Reaper (Navistar (International Harvester Archives))

The acquisition of bundles of new technologies at the same time often multiplied the cumulative effects of individual technologies. In Argentina, for example, the railroad, telegraph, barbed wire, and refrigeration all appeared in a single generation in the 1870s and 1880s. Although Argentina had abundant livestock herds from the colonial period, the great distance separating Argentina from Europe's markets meant that Argentine cattle raisers could not efficiently export either fresh meat or live animals. This situation changed when the combination of railroads and the telegraph lowered freight costs and improved information about markets, steamships reduced the length of time needed for crossing the Atlantic, and refrigeration made it possible to ship to Europe cattle that had been fattened and slaughtered in Argentina. As land values rose and livestock breeding improved, new investments were protected by barbed wire, the first inexpensive fencing available on the nearly treeless plains.

Despite these shared experiences, growing interdependence and increased competition had produced deep structural differences among Western Hemisphere economies by 1900. Two distinct economic tracks were clearly visible. One led to industrialization and prosperity, what is now called *development*. The other continued colonial dependence on the export of raw materials and low wage industries, now commonly called *underdevelopment*. By the end of the nineteenth century, material prosperity was greater and economic development was more diversified in English-speaking North America than in the nations of Latin America. Argentina was the only Latin American nation to achieve levels of per capita wealth similar to those in the United States and Canada by 1900. Argentina's economy would then lose ground after 1914.

Cyclical swings in international markets influenced these important differences in regional economic development. The world capitalist economy was in the first years of a four-decade period of rapid growth when the United States gained independence in 1783. With a large merchant fleet, a diversified economy that included some manufacturing, and adequate banking and insurance services, the United States benefited from an expanding world economy. Rapid population growth due in large measure to immigration, high levels of per capita wealth, widespread landownership, and relatively high literacy rates also fostered rapid economic development in the United States.

Canada's struggle for greater political autonomy, which culminated with the Confederation in 1867, coincided with a second period of global economic expansion. Canada also benefited from its special trading relationship with the preeminent industrial power, Britain, and from a rising tide of immigrants after 1850. Nevertheless, some regions within both of these prosperous nations—the southern part of the United States and Canada's maritime provinces, for example—demonstrated the patterns of underdevelopment found in Latin America.

Latin American nations, in contrast, gained independence in the 1820s, when the global economy was experiencing contraction due to the end of the Napoleonic Wars and market saturation provoked by the early stages of European industrialization. During the colonial period the region's economic resources had been concentrated on the production of agricultural and mining exports that faced increased competition once independence was achieved. Although these sectors experienced some periods of great prosperity in the nineteenth century, their markets experienced sharp moves not only up but down. The history of these specialized economies, subject to periodic problems of oversupply and low prices, was one of boom and bust. The efforts of Latin American governments to gain competitive market advantages by defeating union activity, holding down wages, and opening markets to foreign manufactures further complicated the movement toward industrialization.

Weak governments, political instability, and, in some cases, civil war also slowed Latin American economic development. Because of the region's dependence on both capital and technology obtained from abroad, Great Britain and, by the end of the century, the United States often were able to impose unfavorable trade conditions on Latin American governments and to protect British and American investments in Latin

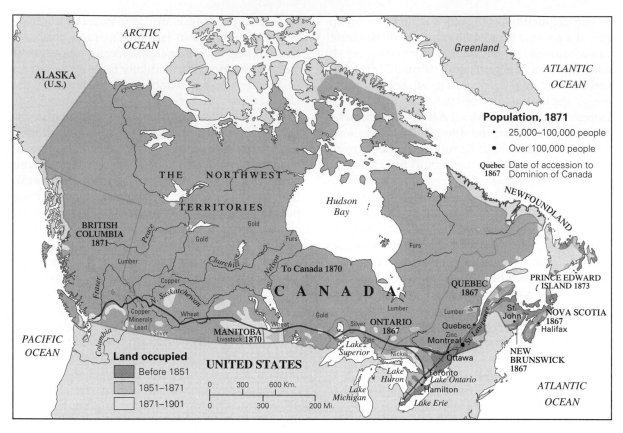

Map 25.2 Canada, 1871 Although independence was not yet achieved and settlement remained concentrated along the United States border, Canada had established effective political and economic control over its western territories by 1871.

America from taxation and regulation by those governments. The combined impact of these domestic and international impediments to development became clear when Mexico, Chile, and Argentina failed to achieve high levels of domestic investment in manufacturing late in the nineteenth century, despite a rapid accumulation of wealth induced by a rising tide of income derived from traditional exports.

Altered Environments

Population growth, economic expansion, new technologies, and the introduction of plants and animals to new regions dramatically altered the Western Hemisphere's environment. Many of Cuba's forests were cut in the early nineteenth century to expand sugar production. The expansion of livestock raising put heavy pressure on often fragile environments in Argentina, Uruguay, southern Brazil, and the southwest of the United States. Other forms of commercial agriculture also threatened the environment. For example, in South Carolina and Georgia, farmers gained a short-term increase in cotton production by abandoning crop rotation after 1870, but this practice quickly led to soil exhaustion and erosion. On the North American prairies and the Argentine pampas, the use of plows eliminated many native grasses and increased the threat of soil erosion. In Brazil, coffee planters exhausted soil fertility with a destructive cycle of overplanting followed by expansion onto forest reserves cleared by cutting and burning.

Rapid urbanization also put heavy pressure on the environment. New York, Chicago, Rio de

Janeiro, Buenos Aires, and Mexico City were among the world's fastest-growing cities in the nineteenth century. Governments strained to keep up with the need for sewers, clean water, and garbage disposal. A rising demand for building materials led to the rapid expansion of the timber industry in many countries. By 1900 more than 3.5 million acres (1.4 million hectares) of public land in the United States had been claimed at low cost under the Timber and Stone Act of 1878. Similar transfers of land from public to private ownership occurred in Argentina and Brazil as well.

As the mining frontier advanced into Nevada, Montana, and California after 1860, erosion and pollution resulted. Similar results occurred in other mining areas. The expansion of nitrate mining and, later, open-pit copper mining in Chile scarred and polluted the environment. The state of Minas Gerais in Brazil experienced a series of mining booms that began with gold in the late seventeenth century and continued with iron ore in the nineteenth. By the end of the century, its red soil was ripped open, forests were depleted, and erosion was left uncontrolled. Similar devastation afflicted parts of Bolivia and Mexico.

Efforts to meet increasing domestic demands for food and housing and to satisfy foreign demands for exports led to environmental degradation, but they also contributed significantly to the growth of the world economy and to regional prosperity. By the end of the nineteenth century, small-scale conservation efforts were under way in many nations. The first national parks and nature reserves had also been created. But when confronted by a choice between economic growth and the protection of the environment, all of the hemisphere's nations embraced growth.

The Cananea copper mine in Sonora, Mexico In the late nineteenth century, American and European investments transformed the scale of mining in Latin America. Larger, more mechanized mines with thousands of workers dramatically affected the environment in once isolated regions. The Cananea mine, developed by Col. William Greene of the United States, was also the site of ongoing labor conflict. (Arizona State Historical Society/Tucson)

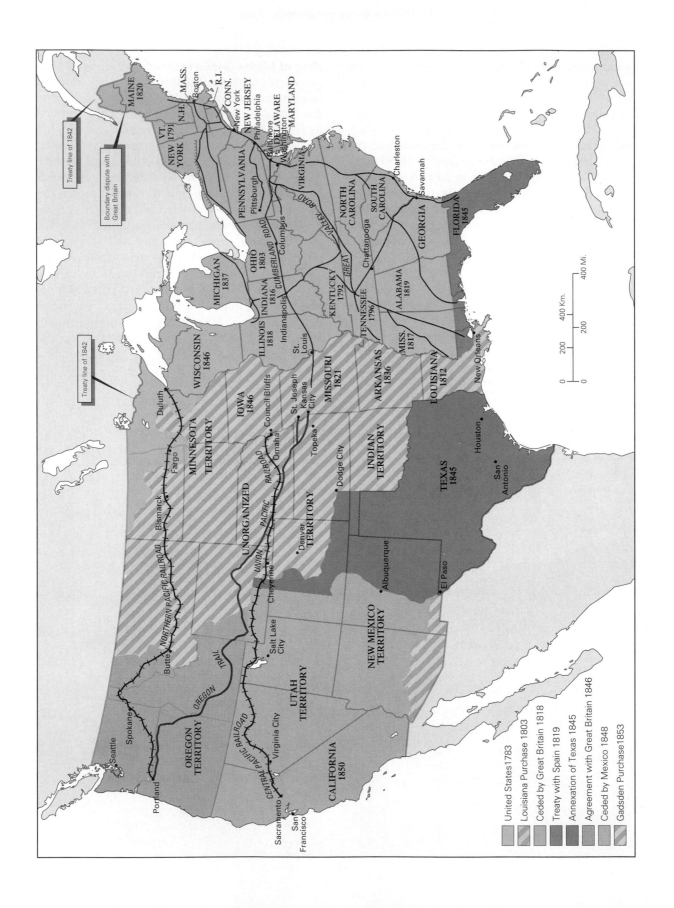

Treaty line of 1842

Boundary dispute with Great Britain

Treaty line of 1842

MAINE 1820

MASS.
R.I.
Boston
CONN.
New York
NEW JERSEY
DELAWARE
MARYLAND
N.H.
VT.
NEW YORK 1791
PENNSYLVANIA
Pittsburgh
Philadelphia
Baltimore
Washington
VIRGINIA

OHIO 1803
Columbus
INDIANA 1816
Indianapolis
ILLINOIS 1818
MICHIGAN 1837
St. Louis
CUMBERLAND ROAD
GREAT VALLEY ROAD
KENTUCKY 1792
TENNESSEE 1796
NORTH CAROLINA
SOUTH CAROLINA
Chattanooga
Charleston
Savannah
GEORGIA
ALABAMA 1819
MISS. 1817
FLORIDA 1845

WISCONSIN 1846
IOWA 1846
Council Bluffs
MINNESOTA TERRITORY
Duluth
Fargo
Bismarck
Butte
Spokane
Seattle
Portland
NORTHERN PACIFIC RAILROAD
OREGON TERRITORY
OREGON TRAIL
CENTRAL PACIFIC RAILROAD
Virginia City
Sacramento
San Francisco
CALIFORNIA 1850
UTAH TERRITORY
Salt Lake City
Cheyenne
UNION PACIFIC RAILROAD
Omaha
St. Joseph
Kansas City
Topeka
MISSOURI 1821
ARKANSAS 1836
LOUISIANA 1812
New Orleans
UNORGANIZED TERRITORY
Denver
Dodge City
INDIAN TERRITORY
NEW MEXICO TERRITORY
Albuquerque
El Paso
TEXAS 1845
San Antonio
Houston

400 Mi.
400 Km.
200
0
200
0

United States 1783
Louisiana Purchase 1803
Ceded by Great Britain 1818
Treaty with Spain 1819
Annexation of Texas 1845
Agreement with Great Britain 1846
Ceded by Mexico 1848
Gadsden Purchase 1853

CONCLUSION

The nineteenth century witnessed enormous changes in the Western Hemisphere. With the exception of Canada and many Caribbean islands, colonial rule had been overturned. Throughout the hemisphere, republican forms of government had triumphed. By 1900, national governments were much stronger than they had been at independence. Although Latin America lagged behind the United States and Canada in institutionalizing democratic political reforms, Latin American nations were stronger and more open in 1900 than in 1850. All of the hemisphere's nations were better able to meet the threats of foreign intervention and regionalism as well. The increased strength of national governments had made possible the abolition of slavery and the expansion of political rights.

Serious challenges remained. Amerindian peoples were relegated to reservations, excluded from national political life, and, in some countries, still burdened with special tribute and tax obligations. Women had begun to enter occupations previously reserved to men but would not receive full citizenship rights until the twentieth century. The baneful legacy of slavery and colonial racial stratification remained a barrier to many men and women. The benefits of economic growth were not equitably distributed among the nations of the Western Hemisphere or within the individual nations. In 1900, nearly every American nation was wealthier, better educated, more democratic, and more populous than at independence. They were also generally more vulnerable to distant economic forces, more profoundly split into haves and have-nots, and more clearly divided into a rich North and a poorer South.

Map 25.3 Territorial Growth of the United States, 1783–1853 The rapid western expansion of the United States resulted from aggressive diplomacy and warfare against Mexico and Amerindian peoples. Railroad development helped integrate the trans Mississippi west and promote economic expansion.

SUGGESTED READING

For the independence era in Latin America see John Lynch, *The Spanish American Revolutions, 1808–1826*, 2d ed. (1986); Jay Kinsbruner, *Independence in Spanish America* (1994); and A. J. R. Russell-Wood, ed., *From Colony to Nation: Essays on the Independence of Brazil* (1976).

The postindependence political and economic struggles in Latin America can be traced in David Bushnell and Neil Macaulay, *The Emergence of Latin America in the Nineteenth Century* (1988). Tulio Halperin-Donghi, *The Contemporary History of Latin America* (1993), and E. Bradford Burns, *The Poverty of Progress: Latin America in the Nineteenth Century* (1980), argue in different ways that Latin America's economic and social problems originated in unfavorable trade relationships with more-developed nations. See also an excellent collection of essays, Leslie Bethell, ed., *The Cambridge History of Latin America*, vol. 3, *From Independence to c. 1870* (1985).

There is an enormous literature on politics and nation building in the United States and Canada. Among the many worthy studies of the United States are William J. Cooper, *The South and the Politics of Slavery, 1828–1856* (1978); Kenneth M. Stampp, *America in 1857* (1991); and Lawrence Frederick Kohl, *The Politics of Individualism: Parties and the American Character in the Jacksonian Era* (1989). For Canada see J. M. S. Careless, *The Union of the Canadas: The Growth of Canadian Institutions, 1841–1857* (1967); Ged Martin, ed., *The Causes of Canadian Confederation* (1990); and Arthur I. Silver, *The French-Canadian Idea of Confederation, 1864–1900* (1982).

The social and cultural issues raised in this chapter are also the subject of a vast literature. For an excellent summary of immigration see also Walter Nugent, *Crossing: The Great Transatlantic Migrations, 1870–1914* (1992). See also Gunther Barth, *Bitter Strength: A History of Chinese in the United States, 1850–1870* (1964), and Nicolás Sánchez-Albornoz, *The Population of Latin America: A History* (1974).

On the issue of slavery see David Brion Davis, *Slavery and Human Progress* (1984); George M. Frederickson, *The Black Image in the White Mind: The Debate on Afro-American Character and Destiny, 1817–1914* (1971); and Benjamin Quarles, *Black Abolitionists* (1969). For the women's rights movement see Ellen C. Du Bois, *Feminism and Suffrage: The Emergence of an Independent Woman's Movement in the Nineteenth Century* (1984);

Lori D. Ginzberg, *Women and the Work of Benevolence: Morality, Politics, and Class in the Nineteenth-Century United States* (1990). Among numerous excellent studies of Indian policies see Robert M. Utley, *The Indian Frontier of the American West, 1846–1890* (1984). On those topics for Canada see J. R. Miller, *Skyscrapers Hide the Heavens: A History of Indian White Relations in Canada* (1989); Olive Patricia Dickason, *Canada's First Nations* (1993); and Alison Prentice, *Canadian Women: A History* (1988).

For abolition in Latin America and the Caribbean see Rebecca Scott, *Slave Emancipation in Cuba: The Transition to Free Labor, 1860–1899* (1985); Robert Conrad, *The Destruction of Brazilian Slavery, 1850–1888* (1973); and William A. Green, *British Slave Emancipation: The Sugar Colonies and the Great Experiment, 1830–1865.* An introduction to the place of women in Latin American society is found in Francesca Miller, *Latin American Women and the Search for Social Justice* (1991); and Jane Jaquette, ed., *The Women's Movement in Latin America* (1989).

An introduction to environmental consequence of North American development is provided by William Cronon, *Nature's Metropolis: Chicago and the Great West* (1991); Joseph M. Petulla, *American Environmental History* (1973); and Donald Worster, *Rivers of Empire: Water, Aridity, and the Growth of the American West* (1985). For Brazil see Warren Dean, *With Broadax and Firebrand: The Destruction of the Brazilian Atlantic Forest* (1995); and for Argentina, Uruguay, and Chile, Alfred

Crosby, *Ecological Imperialism: The Biological Expansion of Europe, 900–1900* (1986).

NOTES

1. Quoted in Lyman L. Johnson, "Spanish American Independence and Its Consequences," in *Problems in Modern Latin American History, A Reader*, eds., John Charles Chasteen and Joseph S. Tulchin (Scholarly Resources: Wilmington, Delaware: 1994), 21.

2. José Antonio Páez, *Autobiografía del General José Antonio Páez*, 2 vols (Caracas, Venzuela, 1973), I, 83.

3. Quoted in Brian Loveman, *Chile, The Legacy of Hispanic Capitalism* (New York: Oxford University Press, 1979), 170.

4. Quoted in Bernard Bailyn, David Brion Davis, David Herbert Donald, John L. Thomas, Robert H. Wiebe, and Gordon S. Wood, *The Great Republic: A History of the American People* (Lexington, MA: D. C. Heath, 1981), 398.

5. J. S. Woodsworth in 1909, quoted in R. Douglas Francis, Richard Jones, and Donald B. Smith, *Destinies: Canadian History Since Confederation*, 2d ed. (Toronto: Holt, Rinehart and Winston, 1992), 141.

6. Sarah Grimké, "Reply to the Massachusetts Clergy," in Nancy Woloch, ed., *Early American Women. A Documentary History, 1600–1900* (Wadsworth Publishing Company: Belmont, California, 1992), 343.

CHAPTER TWENTY-SIX

Africa, India, and the New British Empire, 1750–1870

Changes and Exchanges in Africa · India under Company Rule

Britain's Eastern Empire

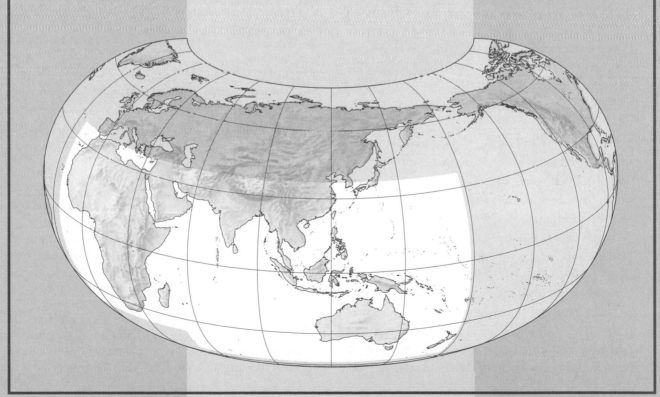

In 1782 Tipu Sahib inherited the throne of the state of Mysore, which his father had made the most powerful state in South India. The ambitious and talented new ruler also inherited a healthy distrust of the British East India Company's territorial ambitions. Before the company could invade Mysore, Tipu Sahib launched his own attack in 1785. He then sent an embassy to France in 1788 seeking an alliance against Britain. Neither of these ventures was immediately successful.

A decade later, the French chose to enter into a loose alliance with Tipu Sahib as part of a scheme to challenge Britain's colonial and commercial supremacy in the Indian Ocean. General Napoleon Bonaparte invaded Egypt in 1798 to threaten British trade routes to India and hoped to use the alliance with Tipu Sahib to drive the British out of India. The French invasion of Egypt went well enough at first, but a British naval blockade and the ravages of disease crippled the French force. When the French withdrew, another military adventurer, Muhammad Ali, the commander of the Ottoman army in Egypt, took advantage of the situation to revitalize Egypt and expand its rule. Sahib's struggle with the British East India Company was going badly. A military defeat in 1792 forced him to surrender most of his coastal lands. Despite a loose alliance with France, he was unable to stop further British advances. Tipu lost his life in 1799 while defending his capital against a British assault. Mysore was divided between the British and their Indian allies.

These events illustrate that both talented local leaders and European intruders were vying to build powerful states in South Asia and Africa between 1750 and 1870. Midway through that period, it was by no means clear that the Europeans would gain the upper hand. Britain and France were as likely to fight each other as they were to fight any Asian or African state. In 1800,

the two nations were engaged in their third major war for overseas supremacy since 1750.

By 1870, however, superior naval and industrial strength had gained Britain a decisive advantage over France. A new British empire in the East included the giant subcontinent of India, settler colonies in Australia and New Zealand, and a growing network of trading outposts. By then Britain had completed the campaign to replace the overseas slave trade from Africa with "legitimate" trade and had spearheaded new Asian and South Pacific labor migrations into a rejuvenated string of tropical colonies.

Like Portugal and the Netherlands in earlier times, Britain was able to enlarge its empire not only because of its military and economic strength but also because it did not face united opposition. By 1750 the Mughal Empire, which had ruled India since the end of the fifteenth century, was crumbling. Indigenous peoples elsewhere were split into many distinct units. Each state or society decided individually whether its interests were best served by resistance, cooperation, or even by alliance with the European intruders.

CHANGES AND EXCHANGES IN AFRICA

During the century before 1870, Africa underwent dynamic political changes and a great expansion of foreign trade. Indigenous African leaders as well as Middle Eastern and European imperialists built powerful new states or expanded old ones. As the continent's external slave trades to the Americas and to Islamic lands died slowly under British pressure, trade in goods such as palm oil, ivory, timber, and gold expanded sharply. In return Africans imported large quantities of machine-made textiles and firearms. These complex changes are best understood by looking at African regions separately.

New States in Southern and Inland West Africa

Most state growth in Africa between 1750 and 1870 was due to internal changes and leaders. The Zulu and other new kingdoms in southern Africa were the product of forces quite different from those giving rise to the Sokoto Caliphate and other reformist Islamic states in inland West Africa (see Map 26.1).

In the fertile coastlands of southeastern Africa (in modern South Africa), the Nguni peoples for many centuries had pursued a life based on cattle and agriculture. Small independent chiefdoms suited their political needs until a serious drought hit the region at the beginning of the nineteenth century. Out of the conflict for grazing and farming lands arose the Zulu kingdom. Its founder, an upstart military genius named Shaka (r. 1818–1828), developed strict military drill and close-combat warfare featuring oxhide shields and lethal stabbing spears. The Zulu became the most powerful and most feared fighters in southern Africa.

Shaka expanded his kingdom by raiding his African neighbors, seizing their cattle, and incorporating their women and children. Breakaway military bands spread this system of warfare and state building inland to the high plateau country, across the Limpopo River (in modern Zimbabwe), and as far north as Lake Victoria. As the power and population of these new kingdoms increased, so too did the number of displaced and demoralized refugees around them. To protect themselves from the Zulu, some neighboring Africans created their own states. The Swazi kingdom consolidated north of the Zulu and the kingdom of Lesotho grew by attracting refugees to strongholds in southern Africa's highest

Zulu regimental camp Under King Shaka's leadership young men from across the kingdom were gathered together in camps, where they learned the arts of war and military discipline. In the center of the camp youths are performing a dance. Note the neat rows of "beehive" sleeping huts, the cattle enclosure in the upper right of the center, and the horses at the lower left—probably owned by European visitors. (National Archives, Zimbabwe)

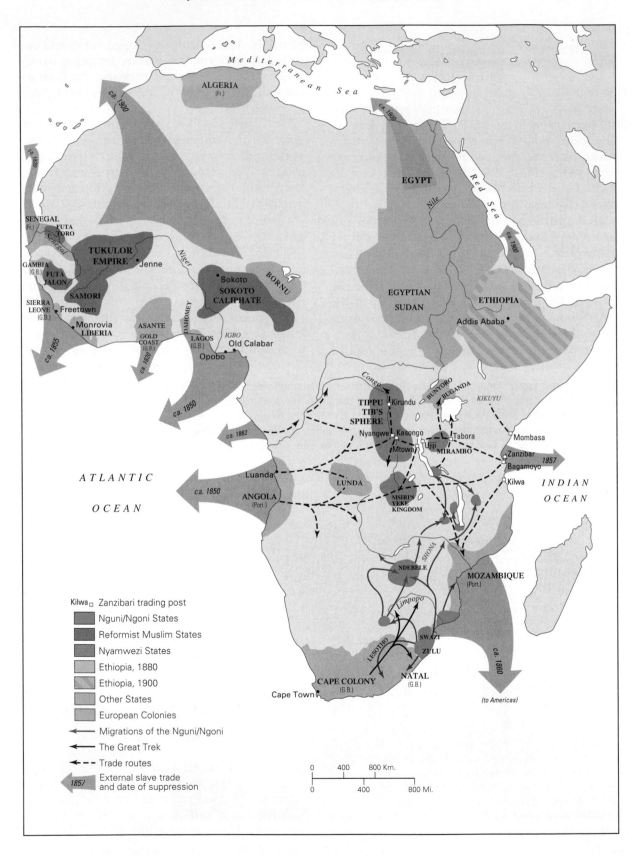

Kilwa □ Zanzibari trading post

Nguni/Ngoni States

Reformist Muslim States

Nyamwezi States

Ethiopia, 1880

Ethiopia, 1900

Other States

European Colonies

→ Migrations of the Nguni/Ngoni

→ The Great Trek

--→ Trade routes

→ External slave trade
   and date of suppression

ALGERIA (Fr.)

Mediterranean Sea

EGYPT

Nile

Red Sea

SENEGAL (Fr.)

FUTA
TORO

Senegal

**TUKULOR
EMPIRE** • Jenne

Niger

GAMBIA (G.B.)

FUTA
JALON

SAMORI

SIERRA
LEONE (G.B.) • Freetown

Monrovia
LIBERIA

ASANTE
GOLD
COAST (G.B.)

DAHOMEY

LAGOS (G.B.)

IGBO

Old Calabar

Opobo

• Sokoto

**SOKOTO
CALIPHATE**

BORNU

**EGYPTIAN
SUDAN**

ETHIOPIA

Addis Ababa •

Congo

**TIPPU
TIB'S
SPHERE**
Nyangwe • Kasongo

Kirundu

BUNYORO
BUGANDA

KIKUYU

□ Mombasa

• Mtowa

Ujiji

Tabora

MIRAMBO

□ Zanzibar

Bagamoyo

□ Kilwa

1857

ATLANTIC

OCEAN

Luanda

LUNDA

ANGOLA (Port.)

**MSIRI'S
YEKE
KINGDOM**

*INDIAN
OCEAN*

SHONA

NDEBELE

MOZAMBIQUE (Port.)

Limpopo

SWAZI

ZULU

LESOTHO

CAPE COLONY (G.B.)

NATAL (G.B.)

Cape Town •

(to Americas)

ca. 1900

ca. 1820

ca. 1885

ca. 1850

ca. 1862

ca. 1850

ca. 1890

ca. 1900

ca. 1860

| 0 | 400 | 800 Km. |
| 0 | 400 | 800 Mi. |

mountains. Both Lesotho and Swaziland survive as independent states to this day.

Although Shaka ruled for little more than a decade, he succeeded in creating a new national identity as well as a new kingdom. He grouped all the young people in his domains by age into regiments. Regiment members lived together and immersed themselves in learning Zulu lore and customs, including fighting methods for the males. A British trader named Henry Francis Fynn expressed his "astonishment at the order and discipline" he found everywhere in the Zulu kingdom. He witnessed public festivals of loyalty to Shaka at which regiments of young men and women numbering in the tens of thousands danced around the king for hours. Parades showed off the king's enormous herds of cattle, a symbol of Zulu wealth.

Meanwhile, Islamic reform movements in West Africa were creating another cluster of powerful states in the savannas south of the Sahara. Islam had been a force in the politics and cities of this region for centuries (see Chapter 20), but it had made only slow progress among most rural people. As a consequence, most Muslim rulers had found it prudent to tolerate the older religious practices of their rural subjects. In the 1770s, local Muslim scholars began preaching the need for a vigorous reform of Islamic practices. They condemned the accommodations Muslim rulers had made with older traditions and called for a forcible conquest of rural "pagans." The reformers followed a classic Muslim pattern: a *jihad* (holy war) added new lands, where governments enforced Islamic laws and promoted the religion's spread among conquered people.

The largest of the new Muslim reform movements occurred in the Hausa states (in what is now northern Nigeria) under the leadership of Usuman dan Fodio (1745–1817), a Muslim cleric of the Fulani people. He charged that the Hausa kings, despite their official profession of Islam,

Map 26.1 Africa in the Nineteenth Century Africans created important new states as the result of Islamic reform movements in the west, new trade in the east, the Zulu revolution in the southeast, and Ethiopian and Egyptian expansion in the northeast. Aside from some coastal enclaves on the Atlantic coast, European colonization by 1870 was confined to Algeria and southern Africa.

were "undoubtedly unbelievers . . . because they practice polytheistic rituals and turn people away from the path of God." Distressed by the lapses of a former pupil, the king of Gobir, Usuman issued a call in 1804 for a jihad to overthrow him. Muslims unhappy with their social or religious position spread the movement to other Hausa states. The successful armies united the conquered Hausa states and neighboring areas under a caliph (sultan) who ruled from the city of Sokoto. The Sokoto Caliphate (1809–1906) was the largest state in West Africa since the fall of Songhai in the sixteenth century (see Chapter 20).

The new Muslim states were centers of Islamic learning and reform. Schools for training boys in Quranic subjects spread rapidly, and the great library at Sokoto attracted many scholars. Although officials permitted non-Muslims within the empire to follow their religions in exchange for paying a special tax, they suppressed public performances of dances and ceremonies associated with traditional religions. Many who resisted the expansion of Muslim rule were killed, enslaved, or forced to convert by the continuing jihads.

Sokoto's leaders sold some captives into the Atlantic slave trade and many more into the trans-Saharan slave trade, which carried ten thousand slaves a year, mostly women and children, across the desert to North Africa and the Middle East. Slavery also increased greatly within the Sokoto Caliphate and other new Muslim states. It is estimated that by 1865 there were more slaves in the Sokoto Caliphate than in any remaining slaveholding state in the Americas.[1] Most of the enslaved persons raised food, making possible the seclusion of free women in their homes in accordance with reformed Muslim practice.

Modernization and Expansion in Egypt and Ethiopia

To the northeast, the ancient African states of Egypt and Ethiopia were undergoing a period of growth and modernization. Napoleon's invading army had withdrawn from Egypt by 1801, but the shock of this display of European strength and Egyptian weakness was long lasting. The successor to Napoleon's rule was Muhammad Ali (1769–1849), who eliminated his rivals and ruled Egypt from 1805 to 1848. He began the political, social, and economic reforms that created modern Egypt.

Muhammad Ali's central aim was to give Egypt sufficient military strength to prevent another European conquest, but he was pragmatic enough to make use of European experts and techniques to achieve that goal. His reforms transformed Egyptian landholding, increased agricultural production, and created a modern administration and army. To train candidates for the army and administration Muhammad Ali set up a European-style state school system and opened a military college at Aswan. He paid for these ventures and for the European experts and equipment that he imported by encouraging Egyptian peasants to cultivate cotton and other crops for export.

In the 1830s Muhammad Ali headed the strongest state in the Islamic world and the first to employ Western methods and technology for modernization. The process was far from a blind imitation of the West. Rather, the technical expertise of the West was combined with Islamic religious and cultural traditions. For example, the Egyptian printing industry, begun to provide Arabic translations of technical manuals, also turned out critical editions of Islamic classics and promoted a revival of Arabic writing and literature later in the century.

By the end of Muhammad Ali's reign in 1848, the modernization of Egypt was well under way. The population had nearly doubled, trade with Europe had expanded by almost 600 percent, and a new class of educated Egyptians had begun to replace the old ruling aristocracy. Egyptians were replacing many of the foreign experts, and the fledgling program of industrialization was providing the country with its own textiles, paper, weapons, and military uniforms. The demands on peasant families for labor and military service, however, were acutely disruptive.

Ali's grandson Ismail (r. 1863–1879) placed even more emphasis on westernizing Egypt. "My country is no longer in Africa," Ismail declared, "it is in Europe."[2] His efforts increased the number of European advisers in Egypt—and

Egypt's debts to French and British banks. In the first decade of his reign, revenues increased thirty-fold and exports doubled (largely because of a huge increase in cotton exports during the American Civil War). By 1870 there was a network of new irrigation canals, 800 miles (1,300 kilometers) of railroads, a modern postal service, and the dazzlingly new capital city of Cairo. When the market for Egyptian cotton collapsed after the American Civil War, however, Egypt's debts to British and French investors led to the country's partial occupation (see Chapter 29).

From the middle of the century, another process of state building and reform was under way in the ancient kingdom of Ethiopia, whose rulers had been Christian for fifteen hundred years. Weakened by internal divisions and the pressures of its Muslim neighbors, Ethiopia was a shadow of what it had been in the sixteenth century (see Chapter 17), but under Emperor Téwodros II (r. 1833–1868) and his successor Yohannes IV (r. 1872–1889) most highland regions were brought back under imperial rule. The only large part of ancient Ethiopia that remained outside Emperor Yohannes's rule was the Shoa kingdom, ruled by King Menelik from 1865. When Menelik succeeded Yohannes as emperor in 1889, the merger of their separate realms created the modern boundaries of Ethiopia.

Beginning in the 1840s, Ethiopian rulers purchased modern weapons from European sources and created strong armies loyal to the ruler. Emperor Téwodros also encouraged the manufacture of weapons locally. With the aid of Protestant missionaries his craftsmen even constructed a giant cannon capable of firing a half-ton shell. However, his efforts to coerce more technical aid by holding some British officials captive backfired when the British invaded instead. As the British forces advanced, Téwodros committed suicide to avoid being taken prisoner. Satisfied that their honor was avenged, the British withdrew. Later Ethiopian emperors kept up the program of reform and modernization.

European Invaders and Explorers

More lasting than Britain's punitive invasion of Ethiopia was France's conquest of Algeria, a

Téwodros's mighty cannon Like other "modernizers" of the nineteenth century, Emperor Téwodros of Ethiopia sought to reform his military forces. In 1861 he forced resident European missionaries and craftsmen to build guns and cannons, including this seven-ton behemoth, which was named "Sebastapol" after the Black Sea port that had been the center of the Crimean War. It took five hundred men to haul the cannon across Ethiopia's hilly terrain. (From Hormuzd Rassam, *Narrative of the British Mission to Theodore, King of Abyssinia, II,* London 1869, John Murray)

move that anticipated the general European "Scramble for Africa" after 1870 (see Chapter 29). Equally pregnant with future meaning was the Europeans' exploration of the inland parts of Africa in the middle decades of the century.

Long an exporter of grain and olive oil to France, the North African state of Algeria had even supplied Napoleon with grain for his 1798 invasion of Egypt. The failure of French governments to repay this debt led to many disputes between Algeria and France and eventually to a severing of diplomatic relations in 1827, after the ruler of Algeria allegedly struck the French ambassador in annoyance with his fly whisk. Three years later an unpopular French government, hoping to stir French nationalism with an easy overseas victory, attacked Algeria on the pretext of avenging this insult.

The invasion of 1830 proved a costly mistake. The French government was soon overthrown, but the war in Algeria dragged on for eighteen years. The attack by an alien Christian power united the Algerians behind 'Abd al-Qadir, a gifted and resourceful Muslim holy man. To achieve victory, the French built up an army of over 100,000 that broke Algerian resistance by destroying farm animals and crops and massacring villagers by the tens of thousands. After 'Abd al-Qadir was captured and exiled in 1847, the resistance movement fragmented, but the French occupiers faced resistance in the mountains for another thirty years. By 1871 poor European settlers, who rushed in to take possession of Algeria's rich coastlands, numbered 130,000.

Meanwhile, a more peaceful European intrusion was penetrating Africa's geographical secrets. Small expeditions of adventurous explorers, using their own funds or financed by private geographical societies, were seeking to uncover the mysteries of inner Africa that had eluded Europeans for four centuries. Besides discovering more about the course of Africa's mighty rivers, these explorers wished to assess the continent's mineral wealth or convert the African millions to Christianity.

Many of the explorers were concerned with tracing the course of Africa's great rivers. Explorers learned in 1795 that the Niger River in West Africa flowed from west to east (not the other way as had often been supposed) and in 1830 that the great morass of small streams entering the Gulf of Guinea was in fact the Niger Delta.

The north-flowing Nile, whose annual floods made Egypt bloom, similarly attracted explorers bent on finding the headwaters of the world's longest river. In 1770 Lake Tana in Ethiopia was established as a major source, and in 1861–1862 Lake Victoria (named for the British sovereign) was found to be the other main source.

In contrast to the heavily financed expeditions with hundreds of African porters that searched the Nile, the Scottish missionary David Livingstone (1813–1873) organized quite modest treks through southern and central Africa. The missionary doctor's primary goal was to scout out locations for Christian missions, but he was also highly influential in tracing the course of the Zambezi River, between 1853 and 1856. He named its greatest waterfall for the British monarch Queen Victoria. Livingstone also traced the course of the upper Congo River, where in 1871 he was met by the Welsh-American journalist Henry Morton Stanley (1841–1904) on a publicity-motivated search for the "lost" missionary doctor. On an expedition from 1874 to 1877, Stanley descended the Congo River to its mouth.

One of the most remarkable features of the explorers' experiences in Africa was their ability to move unmolested from place to place. The strangers were seldom harmed without provocation. Stanley preferred large expeditions that fought their way across the continent, but Livingstone's modest expeditions, which posed no threat to anyone, regularly received warm hospitality.

Abolition and Legitimate Trade in Coastal West Africa

No sooner was the mouth of the Niger River discovered than eager entrepreneurs began to send expeditions up the river to scout out its potential for trade. Along much of coastal Africa, commercial relations with Europeans remained dominant between 1750 and 1870. The value of trade between Africa and the other Atlantic continents more than doubled between the 1730s and the 1780s, then doubled again by 1870.[3] Before about 1825 the slave trade accounted for most of that increase, but thereafter African exports of vegetable oils, gold, ivory, and other goods drove overseas trade to new heights.

Europeans played a critical role in this transformation and expansion of Africa's overseas trade. The Atlantic slave trade had arisen to serve the needs of the first European empires, and its end—along with the rise of the new "legitimate" trade—was linked to the ideas and industrial needs of Britain's new economy and empire.

One step in the Atlantic slave trade's extinction had been the successful slave revolt in Saint Domingue in the 1790s (see Chapter 24). It ended slavery in the largest plantation colony in the West Indies, and elsewhere in the Americas it inspired slave revolts that were brutally repressed. As news of the slave revolts and their repression spread, humanitarians and religious reformers called for an end to the slave trade. Since it was widely believed that African-born slaves were more likely to rebel than were persons born into slavery, support for abolition of the slave trade was found even among Americans wanting to preserve slavery. In 1808 both Great Britain and the United States made carrying and importing slaves from Africa illegal for their citizens. Most other Western countries followed suit by 1850, but few enforced their abolition with the vigor of the British.

Once the world's greatest slave traders, the British became the most aggressive abolitionists. Britain sent a naval patrol to enforce the ban along the African coast and negotiated treaties allowing the patrol to search other nations' vessels suspected of carrying slaves. During the half-century after 1815, Britain spent some $60 million (£12 million) in its efforts to end the slave trade, ironically a sum equal to the profits British slave traders had made in the fifty years before 1808.

Although the British patrols captured 1,635 slave ships and liberated over 160,000 enslaved Africans, the trade proved difficult to stop, for Cuba and Brazil continued to import huge numbers of slaves. Such demand drove slave prices up and persuaded some African rulers and merchants to continue to sell slaves and to help foreign slavers evade the British patrols. After British patrols quashed the slave trade along the Gold Coast, the powerful king of Asante even tried to persuade a British official in 1820 that reopening the trade would be to their mutual profit. Because the slave trade moved to other parts of Africa, the slave trade to the Americas did not end until 1867.

The demand for slaves in the Americas claimed the lives and endangered the safety of untold numbers of Africans, but it also satisfied other Africans' desires for the cloth, metals, and other goods that European traders brought in return. To continue their access to those trade goods, Africans revived old trades or developed new exports as the Atlantic slave trade was shut down. On the Gold Coast, for example, annual exports of gold climbed to nearly 25,000 ounces (750 kilograms) in the 1840s and 1850s, compared to 10,000 ounces (300 kilograms) in the 1790s.

The most successful of the new exports from West Africa was palm oil, a vegetable oil used by British manufacturers for soap, candles, and lubricants. While still a major source of slaves until the mid-1830s, the trading states of the Niger Delta simultaneously emerged as the premier exporters of palm oil. In inland forests men climbed tall oil palms and cut down large palm-nut clusters, which women pounded to extract the thick oil. Coastal African traders bought the palm oil at inland markets and brought it to European ships at the coast.

The dramatic increase in palm-oil exports—from a few hundred tons at the beginning of the century to tens of thousands of tons by midcentury—did not require any new technology, but it did alter the social structure of the coastal trad-

ing communities. Coastal traders grew rich and used their wealth to buy large numbers of male slaves to paddle the giant dugout canoes that transported palm oil from inland markets along the narrow delta creeks to the trading ports. Niger Delta slavery could be as harsh and brutal as that on New World plantations (see Chapters 19 and 20), but it offered some male and female slaves a chance to gain wealth and power. Some female slaves who married big traders exercised great authority over junior members of trading households. Male slaves who supervised canoe fleets were well compensated, and a few even became wealthy enough to take over the leadership of the coastal "canoe houses" (companies). The most famous, known as "Jaja" (ca. 1821–1891), rose from being a canoe slave to the head of a major canoe house. To escape discrimination by free-born Africans, he founded the new port of Opobo, which he ruled as king. In the 1870s Jaja of Opobo was the greatest palm-oil trader in the Niger Delta.

Another effect of the suppression of the slave trade was the spread of Western cultural influences in West Africa. To serve as a base for their antislave-trade naval squadron, in 1808 the British had taken over the small colony of Sierra Leone. Over the next several years, 130,000 men, women, and children taken from "captured" vessels were liberated in Sierra Leone. Christian missionaries helped settle these impoverished and dispirited "recaptives" in and around Freetown, the capital. In time the mission churches and schools made many willing converts among such men and women.

Sierra Leone's schools also produced a number of distinguished graduates. For example, Samuel Adjai Crowther (1808–1891), freed as a youth from a slave ship in 1821 by the British squadron, became the first Anglican bishop in West Africa in 1864, administering a pioneering diocese along the lower Niger River. James Africanus Horton (1835–1882), the son of a slave liberated in Sierra Leone, became a doctor and the author of many studies of West Africa.

Other Western cultural influences came from people of African birth or descent returning to their ancestral homeland in this era. Free black Americans began a settlement to the south of Sierra Leone in 1821 that grew into the republic

King Jaja of Opobo   This talented man rose from slavery in the Niger Delta port of Bonny to head one of the town's major palm-oil trading firms, the Anna Pepple House, in 1863. Six years later, Jaja founded and ruled his own trading port of Opobo. (Reproduced from *West Africa: An Introduction to Its History,* Michael Crowder, by courtesy of the publishers, Addison Wesley Longman)

dence and run a school for his children. Edward Wilmot Blyden (1832–1912), born in the Danish West Indies and proud of his West African parentage, emigrated to Liberia in 1851 and became a professor of Greek and Latin (and later Arabic) at the fledgling Liberia College. Other free blacks from Brazil and Cuba chartered ships to return to their West African homelands, bringing with them Roman Catholicism, architectural motifs, and clothing fashions from the New World. Although the number of Africans exposed to Western culture in 1870 was still small, this influence grew rapidly in later decades.

Slaves and Secondary Empires in Eastern Africa

As British patrols hampered the slave trade in West Africa, slavers moved southward and then around the tip of southern Africa to eastern Africa. There the Atlantic slave trade joined an existing trade in slaves to the Islamic world that was also expanding in this period. Two-thirds of the 1.2 million slaves exported from eastern Africa in the nineteenth century went to markets in North Africa and the Middle East; the other third went to plantations in the Americas and to European-controlled Indian Ocean islands.

Slavery also became more prominent within eastern Africa itself. Between 1800 and 1873, Arab and Swahili owners of clove plantations along the coast purchased some 700,000 slaves from inland eastern Africa to do the labor-intensive work of harvesting this spice. The plantations were on Zanzibar Island and in neighboring territories belonging to the Sultanate of Oman, an Arabian kingdom on the Persian Gulf that had been expanding its control over the East African coast since 1698 (see Chapter 21). The sultan had even moved his court to Zanzibar in 1828 to take better advantage of the burgeoning trade in cloves. Zanzibar was also an important center of slaves and ivory. Most of the ivory was shipped to India, where much of it was carved into decorative objects for European markets.

The ivory caravans came to the coast from hundreds of miles inland under the direction of African and Arab merchants. Some of these mer-

of Liberia, a place of liberty at a time when slavery was still legal and flourishing in the United States. After their emancipation in 1865 other African-Americans followed. Emma White, a literate black woman from Kentucky, moved from Liberia to Opobo in 1875, where King Jaja employed her to write his commercial correspon-

chants brought large personal empires under their control by using capital they had borrowed from Indian bankers and modern firearms they had bought from Europeans and Americans. Some trading empires were created by inland Nyamwezi traders, who worked closely with the indigenous Swahili and Arabs in Zanzibar to develop the long-distance caravan routes.

The largest of these personal empires, along the upper Congo River, was created by Tippu Tip (ca. 1830–1905), a trader from Zanzibar, who was Swahili and Nyamwezi on his father's side and Omani Arab on his mother's. Livingstone, Stanley, and other explorers who received Tippu Tip's gracious hospitality in the remote center of the continent praised their host's intelligence and refinement. On an 1876 visit, for example, Stanley recorded in his journal that Tippu Tip was "a remarkable man," a "picture of energy and strength" with "a fine intelligent face: almost courtier-like in his manner."

Tippu Tip also composed a detailed memoir of his adventures in the heart of Africa, written in the Swahili language of the coast. In it he mocked innocent African villagers for believing that his gunshots were thunder. As the memoir and other sources make clear, these modern rifles not only felled countless elephants for their ivory tusks but also inflicted widespread devastation and misery on the people of this isolated area.

One can blame Tippu Tip and other Zanzibari traders for the pillage and havoc in the once-peaceful center of Africa, along with their master, the sultan of Oman. However, the circle of responsibility was still broader. Europeans supplied the weapons used by the invaders and were major consumers of ivory and cloves. For this reason historians have referred to the states carved out of eastern Africa by the sultans of Oman, Tippu Tip, and others as "secondary empires," in contrast to the empire that Britain was establishing directly. At the same time, Britain was working to bring the Indian Ocean slave trade to an end in eastern Africa. British officials pressured the sultan of Oman into halting the Indian Ocean slave trade from Zanzibar in 1857 and ending the import of slaves into Zanzibar in 1873.

Egypt's expansion southward during the nineteenth century can also be considered a sec-ondary empire. Muhammad Ali had pioneered the conquest of the upper Nile, establishing at Khartoum a major base that became the capital of the Egyptian Sudan. A major reason for his invasion of the Sudan was to secure slaves for his army so that more Egyptian peasants could be left free to grow cotton for export. From the 1840s unscrupulous traders of many origins, leading forces armed with European weapons, pushed south to the modern frontiers of Uganda and Zaire in search of cattle, ivory, and slaves. They set one African community against another and reaped profit from the devastation they sowed.

Africa in the Nineteenth Century

1798	Napoleon invades Egypt
1806	Britain takes permanent control of the Cape Colony
1808	Britain and U.S. outlaw Atlantic slave trade
1808	Britain takes control of Sierra Leone
1809	Usuman dan Fodio founds Sokoto Caliphate
1811	Muhammad Ali starts Egypt's modernization
1818	Shaka founds the Zulu kingdom
1821	African-Americans found Republic of Liberia
1821	Egypt establishes control of the Sudan
1828	Sultan of Oman moves capital to Zanzibar
1831–1847	Abd al-Qadir leads resistance to the French in Algeria
1834	Britain ends slavery in the Cape Colony
1836–1839	Afrikaners' Great Trek
1845	Britain annexes Natal
1864	Samuel Adjai Crowther consecrated as Anglican bishop
1866–1867	Last slave ship crosses the Atlantic
1869	Jaja founds Opobo
1871	Stanley "finds" Livingstone
1873	Zanzibar stops importing slaves from the African mainland
1875	Tippu Tip begins empire-building in central Africa
1889	Menelik unites modern Ethiopia

INDIA UNDER COMPANY RULE

The people of South Asia felt the impact of European commercial, cultural, and colonial expansion more immediately and profoundly than did the people of Africa. While Europeans were laying claim to only small parts of Africa between 1750 and 1870, virtually all of India (with three times the population of all of Africa) came under Britain's direct or indirect rule. After founding the British East India Company in 1600, it took British interests over 250 years to commandeer the colonies and trade of the Dutch East India Company, fight off rival French interests, and pick up the pieces of the decaying Mughal Empire (see Chapter 21). By 1763 the French were stymied, in 1795 the Dutch company was dissolved, and in 1858 the last Mughal emperor was dethroned, leaving the vast subcontinent in British hands.

Company Men

When Mughal power weakened in the early eighteenth century, Europeans were not the first outsiders to intrude. In 1739, Iranian armies defeated the Mughal forces, sacked Delhi, and returned home with a vast booty. Indian states also took advantage of Mughal weakness to assert their independence. By midcentury, the Maratha Confederation, a coalition of states on the Deccan

British Mem-sahib, ca. 1782 This charming painting by a Bengali artist shows Lady Impey, the wife of the British East India Company's Chief Justice of Bengal, surrounded by her Indian servants in a room that mixes Indian and European decor. The Hindi word *sahib* was an honorific title; *mem-sahib* was the Anglo-Indian feminine form reserved for European women, whose status was first determined by race and then by gender. (E. T. Archives)

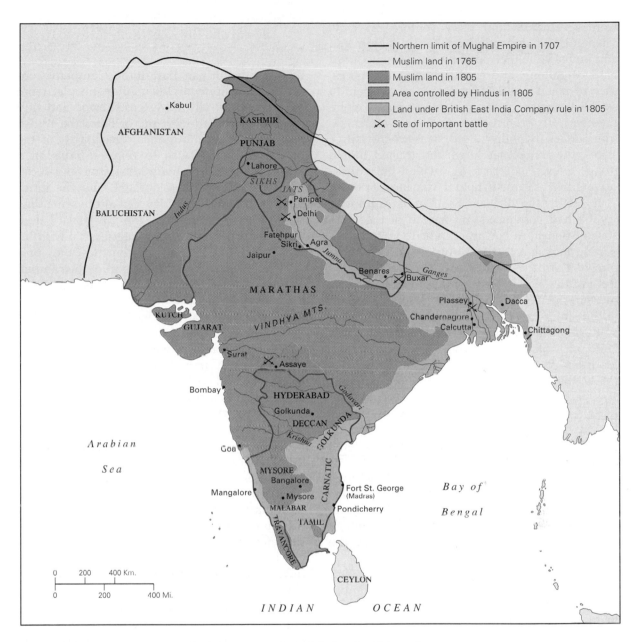

Map 26.2 India, 1707–1805 As Mughal power weakened during the eighteenth century, other Indian states and the British East Indian Company expanded their territories.

Plateau in central India, controlled more land than the Mughals did (see Map 26.2). Also ruling their own powerful states were the *nawabs* (the term used for Muslim princes who were deputies of the Mughal emperor, though in name only): the nawab of Bengal in the northeast; the nawab of Arcot in the southeast, Haidar Ali

(1722–1782)—the father of Tipu Sahib and ruler of the southwestern state of Mysore; and many others.

The British, Dutch, and French East India Companies were also eager to expand their profitable trade into India in the eighteenth century. Such far-flung European trading companies were speculative and risky ventures in 1750. Their success depended on hard-drinking and ambitious young "Company Men," who used hard bargaining, and hard fighting when necessary, to persuade Indian rulers to allow them to establish trading posts at strategic points along the coast. To protect their fortified warehouses from attack by other Europeans or by native states, the companies hired and trained Indian troops known as *sepoys*. In divided India these private armies came to hold the balance of power.

In 1691, the British East India Company (BEIC) had convinced the nawab of the large state of Bengal in northeast India to let the company establish a fortified outpost at the fishing port of Calcutta. A new nawab, pressing claims for additional tribute from the prospering port, overran the fort in 1756 and imprisoned a group of BEIC men in a cell so small that many died of suffocation. To avenge their deaths in this "Black Hole of Calcutta," a large BEIC force from Madras, led by the young Robert Clive, overthrew the nawab. The weak Mughal emperor was persuaded to acknowledge the British East India Company's right to rule Bengal in 1765. Fed by the tax revenues of Bengal as well as by profits from trade, Calcutta grew into a city of 250,000 by 1788.

In southern India, Clive had used BEIC forces from Madras to secure victory for the British Indian candidate for nawab of Arcot during the Seven Years War, thereby gaining an advantage over French traders who had supported the loser. The defeat of Tipu Sahib of Mysore at the end of the century (described at the start of the chapter) secured South India for the company and prevented a French resurgence.

Along with Calcutta and Madras, the third major center of British power in India was Bombay, on the western coast. There, after a long series of contests with the Maratha Confederation rulers, the British East India Company gained a decisive advantage in 1818, annexing large territories to form the core of what was called the "Bombay Presidency." Some states were taken over completely, as Bengal had been, but very many others remained in the hands of local princes who accepted the political control of the company.

The Raj and the Rebellion, 1818-1857

By 1818 the British East India Company controlled an empire of 130 million people, more people than in all of western Europe and fifty times the population of the colonies the British had lost in North America. One thrust of the British *raj* (reign) was to remake India on a British model through administrative and social reform, economic development, and the introduction of new technology. But at the same time the company men—like the Mughals before them—had to temper their interference with Indian social and religious customs lest they provoke rebellion or lose the support of their Indian princely allies. For this reason and because of the complexity of the task of ruling such a vast empire, there were many inconsistencies in Britain's policy toward India.

The central reform was to create a powerful and efficient system of government. British rule before 1850 relied heavily on military power—170 sepoy regiments and 16 European regiments. Another reform very much in the interests of India's new rulers was to disarm approximately 2 million warriors who had served India's many states and turn them to civilian tasks, mostly cultivation. A third reform was to give freer rein to Christian missionaries eager to convert and uplift India's masses. Few converts were made, but the missionaries kept up steady pressure for social reforms.

Another key state reform was to substitute private property for India's complex and overlapping patterns of landholding. In Bengal this worked to the advantage of large landowners, but in Mysore the peasantry gained. Private ownership made it easier for the state to collect the taxes that were necessary to pay for the costs of administration, the army, and economic reform.

Such policies of "westernization, Anglicization, and modernization," as they have been called, were only one side of British rule. The other side was the bolstering of "traditions"—both real and newly invented. In the name of tradition the Indian princes who ruled nearly half of British India were frequently endowed by their British overlords with greater power and splendor and longer tenure than their predecessors had ever had. Hindu and Muslim holy men were able to expand their "traditional" power over property and people far beyond what had ever been the case in earlier times. Princes, holy men, and other Indians frequently used claims of tradition to resist British rule as well as to turn it to their advantage. The British rulers themselves invented many "traditions"—including elaborate parades and displays—half borrowed from European royal pomp, half freely improvised from Mughal ceremonies (see Voices and Visions: Ceremonials of Imperial Domination).

While the British and Indian elites danced sometimes in close partnership, sometimes in apparent opposition, it was the ordinary people of India who suffered. Women of every status, members of subordinate Hindu castes, the "untouchables" and "tribals" outside the caste system, and the poor generally found little benefit in the British reforms and much new oppression in the taxes and "traditions" that exalted their superiors' status.

The transformation of British India's economy was also double-edged. On the one hand, the British raj created many new jobs as a result of the growth of internal and external trade and the expansion of agricultural production, such as in opium in Bengal—largely for export to China (see Chapter 27)—coffee in Ceylon (an island off the tip of India), and tea in Assam (a state in northeastern India). On the other hand, competition from cheap cotton goods produced in Britain's industrial mills drove many Indians out of the handicraft textile industry. In the eighteenth century India had been the world's greatest exporter of cotton textiles; in the nineteenth century India increasingly shipped raw cotton fiber to Britain.

Even the beneficial economic changes introduced under British rule were disruptive, and there were no safety nets for the needy. Officials were constantly wary of rebellion by displaced ruling elites, disgruntled religious traditionalists, and the economically dispossessed. Indeed, localized revolts were almost constant during the first half of the nineteenth century. The greatest concern was over the continuing loyalty of Indi-

an sepoys in the British East India Company's army. Their numbers had increased to 200,000 in 1857, along with 38,000 British officers. Armed with the latest rifles and disciplined in fighting methods, the sepoys had a potential for successful rebellion that other groups lacked.

In fact, discontent was growing among Indian soldiers. In the early decades of BEIC rule, most sepoys came from Bengal, one of the first states the company had annexed. The Bengali sepoys resented the active recruitment of other ethnic groups into the army after 1848, such as Sikhs from Punjab and Gurkhas from Nepal. Many Hindus objected to a new law in 1856 requiring new recruits to be available for service overseas in the growing Indian Ocean empire, for their religion prohibited ocean travel. The replacement of the standard military musket by the far more accurate Enfield rifle in 1857 also caused problems. Soldiers were ordered to use their teeth to tear open the ammunition cartridges, which were greased with animal fat. Hindus were offended by this order if the fat came from cattle, which they considered sacred. Muslims were offended if the fat came from pigs, which they considered unclean.

Although the cartridge-opening procedure was quickly changed, the cartridges transformed discontent into rebellion by Hindu sepoys in May 1857, and British troubles mushroomed when Muslim sepoys, peasants, and discontented elites joined in. The rebels asserted old traditions to challenge British authority: sepoy officers in Delhi proclaimed their loyalty to the Mughal emperor; others rallied behind the Maratha leader Nana Sahib. The rebellion was put down by March 1858, but it shook this piecemeal empire to its core.

Historians have attached different names and meanings to the events of 1857 and 1858. Concentrating on the technical fact that the uprising was an unlawful action by soldiers, nineteenth-century British historians labeled it the "Sepoy Rebellion" or the "Mutiny," and these names are still commonly used. Seeing in these events the beginnings of the later movement for independence, some modern Indian historians have termed it the "Revolution of 1857." In reality, it was much more than a simple mutiny, because

Ceremonials of Imperial Domination

These excerpts from a letter written to Queen Victoria by the Viceroy of India, Lord Lytton, describe the elaborate ceremonies the colony staged in 1876 in anticipation of her being named "Empress of India" and the effects they had on the Indian princes who governed many parts of India. Although British India's power still rested on the threat of military force, its leaders grew increasingly skilled at using symbolic displays of authority and material rewards to win the support of Indian allies.

The day before yesterday (December 23), I arrived, with Lady Lytton and all my staff at Delhi. . . . I was received at the [railroad] station by all the native chiefs and princes, and, . . . after shaking hands . . . , I immediately mounted my elephant, accompanied by Lady Lytton, our two little girls following us on another elephant. The procession through Delhi to the camp . . . lasted upwards of three hours. . . . The streets were lined for many miles with troops; those of the native princes being brigaded with those of your Majesty. The crowd along the way, behind the troops, was dense, and apparently enthusiastic; the windows, walls, and housetops being thronged with natives, who salaamed, and Europeans, who cheered as we passed along. . . .

My reception by the native princes at the station was most cordial. The Maharaja of Jeypore (who has lighted the Viceroy's camp with gas of his own manufacture) informed Sir John Strachey that India had never seen such a gathering as this, in which not only all the great native princes (many of whom have never met before), but also chiefs and envoys from Khelat, Burmah, Siam, and the remotest parts of the East, are assembled to do homage to your Majesty. . . .

On Tuesday (December 26) from 10 A.M. till past 7 P.M., I was, without a moment's intermission, occupied in receiving visits from native chiefs, and bestowing on those entitled to them the banners, medals, and other honours given by your Majesty. The durbar, which lasted all day and long after dark, was most successful. . . . Your Majesty's portrait, which was placed over the Viceregal throne in the great durbar tent, was thought by all to be an excellent likeness of your Majesty. The native chiefs examined it with special interest.

On Wednesday, the 27th, I received visits from native chiefs, as before, from 10 A.M.. til 1 P.M., and from 1:30 P.M. to 7:30 P.M., was passed in returning visits. I forgot to mention that on Tuesday and Wednesday evenings I gave great State dinners to the Governors of Bombay and Madras. Every subsequent evening of my stay at Delhi was similarly occupied by State banquets and receptions [for officials, foreign dignitaries, and] many distinguished natives. After dinner on Thursday, I held a levee [reception], which lasted till one o'clock at night, and is said to have been attended by 2,500 persons—the largest, I believe, ever held by any Viceroy or Governor-General in India.

. . . your Majesty will, perhaps, allow me to mention, in connection with [the ruler of Kashmir], one little circumstance which appears to me very illustrative of the effect which the assemblage has had on him and others. In the first interviews which took place months ago between myself and Kashmir, . . . I noticed that, though perfectly courteous, he was extremely mistrustful of the British Government and myself. . . . On the day following the Imperial assemblage, I had another private interview with Kashmir for the settlement of some further details. His whole manner and language on this last occasion were strikingly different. [He said:] "I am now convinced that you mean nothing that is not for the good of me and mine. Our interests are identical with those of the empire. Give me your orders and they shall be obeyed."

What is significant about the fact that Lord Lytton and his family arrived in Delhi by train and then chose to move through the city on elephants? What impression did the viceroy intend to create in the minds of the Indian dignitaries by assembling so many of them together and bestowing banners, medals, and honors on them? What might account for the Indian ruler of Kashmir's remarkable change of attitude toward the viceroy and the empire? How differently might a member of the Indian middle class or an unemployed weaver have reacted?

Source: Lady Betty Balfour, *The History of Lord Lytton's Indian Administration, 1876 to 1880* (London: Longmans, Green, and Co., 1899), 116–121, 132.

it involved more than soldiers, but it was not yet a nationalist revolution, for the rebels' sense of a common Indian national identity was weak.

Political Reform and Industrial Impact, 1858-1900

Whatever it is called, the rebellion of 1857–1858 was a turning point in the history of modern India. Some say it marks the beginning of modern India. In its wake Indians gained a new centralized government, entered a period of rapid economic growth, and began to develop a new national consciousness.

The changes in government were immediate. In 1858 Britain eliminated the last traces of Mughal and Company rule. In their place, a new secretary of state for India in London now oversaw Indian policy, and a new governor-general in Delhi acted as the British monarch's viceroy on the spot. A proclamation by Queen Victoria in November 1858 guaranteed all Indians equal protection of the law and the freedom to practice their religions and social customs; it also assured Indian princes that so long as they were loyal to the queen British India would respect their control of territories and "their rights, dignity and honour."[4]

British rule continued to emphasize both tradition and reform after 1857. At the top, the British viceroys lived in enormous palaces amid hundreds of servants and gaudy displays of luxury meant to convince Indians that the British viceroys were legitimate successors to the Mughal emperors. They treated the quasi-independent Indian princes with elaborate ceremonial courtesy and maintained them in splendor. When Queen Victoria was proclaimed "Empress of India" in 1877 and periodically thereafter, the viceroys put on great pageants known as *durbars*. The most elaborate of all was the durbar at Delhi in 1902 to celebrate the coronation of King Edward VII, at which Viceroy Lord Curzon honored himself with a 101-gun salute and a parade of 34,000 troops in front of 50 princes and 173,000 lesser visitors.

Behind the pomp and glitter, a powerful and efficient bureaucracy controlled the Indian masses. Members of the elite Indian Civil Service (ICS), mostly graduates of Oxford and Cambridge Universities, held the senior administrative and judicial posts. Only a thousand men at the end of the nineteenth century, they visited the villages in their districts, heard lawsuits and complaints, and passed judgments. Beneath them were a far greater number of Indian officials and employees. Recruitment into the ICS was by open examinations. In theory any British subject could take these exams. But they were given in England, so in practice the system worked to exclude Indians. In 1870 there was only one Indian among the 916 members of the ICS. Subsequent reforms by Viceroy Lord Lytton led to fifty-seven Indian appointments by 1887, but there the process stalled.

The key reason blocking qualified Indians' entry into the upper administration of their country was the racist contempt most British officials felt for the people they ruled. When he became commander-in-chief of the Indian Army in 1892, Lord Kitchener declared:

> It is this consciousness of the inherent superiority of the European which had won for us India. However well educated and clever a native may be, and however brave he may have proved himself, I believe that no rank we can bestow on him would cause him to be considered an equal of the British officer.

A second transformation of India after 1857 resulted from involvement with industrial Britain. The government invested millions of pounds sterling in harbors, cities, irrigation canals, and other public works. British interests felled forests to make way for tea plantations, persuaded Indian farmers to grow cotton and jute for export, and created great irrigation systems to alleviate the famines that periodically had decimated whole provinces. As a result, India's trade expanded rapidly.

Most of the exports were agricultural commodities for processing elsewhere: cotton fiber, opium, tea, silk, and sugar. In return India imported manufactured goods from Britain, including the flood of machine-made cotton textiles that severely undercut Indian hand-loom weavers. The effects on individual Indians varied enormously. Some women found new jobs, though at very low pay, on plantations or in the growing cities, where prostitution flourished. Others struggled to hold families together or ran away from abusive husbands. Everywhere in India poverty remained the norm.

The Indian government also promoted the introduction of new technologies into India not long after their appearance in Britain. Earlier in the century there had been steamboats on the rivers and a massive program of canal building for irrigation. Beginning in the 1840s, a railroad boom (paid for out of government revenues) gave India its first national transportation network, followed shortly by telegraph lines. Indeed, in 1870 India had the greatest rail network in Asia and the fifth largest in the world. Originally designed to serve British commerce, the railroads were owned by British companies, constructed with British rails and equipment, and paid dividends to British investors. Ninety-nine percent of the railroad employees were Indians, but Europeans occupied all the top positions— "like a thin film of oil on top of a glass of water, resting upon but hardly mixing with [those] below," as one official report put it.

Although some Indians opposed the railroads at first because the trains mixed people of different castes, faiths, and sexes, the Indian people took to rail travel with great enthusiasm. The trains carried Indians on business, on pilgrimage, and in search of work. In 1870 over 18 million passengers traveled along the network's 4,775 miles (7,685 kilometers) of track, and more than a half-million messages were sent up and down the 14,000 miles (22,500 kilometers) of telegraph wire. By 1900 India's trains were carrying 188 million passengers a year.

But the freer movement of Indian pilgrims and the flood of poor Indians in the cities also promoted the spread of cholera, a disease transmitted through water contaminated by human feces. Cholera deaths rose rapidly during the nineteenth century and eventually spread to Europe (see Chapter 23). In many Indian minds *kala mari* ("the black death") was a divine punishment for failing to prevent the British takeover. This chastisement also fell heavily on British residents, who died in large numbers. In 1867 officials demonstrated the close connection between cholera and pilgrims who bathed in and drank from sacred pools and rivers. The installation of a new sewerage system (1865) and a filtered water supply (1869) in Calcutta dramatically reduced cholera deaths there. Similar measures in Bombay and Madras also led to great reductions, but most Indians lived in small villages where famine and lack of sanitation kept cholera deaths high. In 1900 an extraordinary four out of every thousand residents of British India died of cholera. Sanitary improvements lowered the rate later in the twentieth century.

Rising Indian Nationalism, 1828–1900

Ironically, both the successes and the failures of British India stimulated the development of Indian nationalism. Stung by the inability of the rebellion of 1857 to overthrow British rule, some thoughtful Indians began to argue that the only way for Indians to regain control of their destiny was to reduce their country's social and ethnic divisions and promote Pan-Indian nationalism.

Individuals such as Rammohun Roy (1772–1833) had promoted development along these lines a generation earlier. A Western-educated Bengali from a Brahmin family, Roy was a successful administrator for the British East India Company and a thoughtful student of comparative religion. His Brahmo Samaj (Divine Society), founded in 1828, attracted Indians who sought to reconcile the values they found in the West with the ancient religious traditions of India. They supported efforts to reform some Hindu customs, including the restrictions on widows and the practice of child marriage. They advocated reforming the caste system, encouraged a monotheistic form of Hinduism, and urged a return to the founding principles found in the Upanishads, ancient sacred writings of Hinduism.

Roy and his supporters had backed earlier British efforts to reform or ban some practices they found repugnant. Widow burning (*sati*) was outlawed in 1829 and slavery in 1843. Reformers sought to correct other abuses of women: prohibitions against widows remarrying were revoked in 1856, and female infanticide was made a crime in 1870.

Although Brahmo Samaj remained an influential movement after the rebellion of 1857, many Indian intellectuals turned to Western secular values and nationalism as the way to reclaim India for its people. In this process the spread of Western education played an important role. Roy had studied both Indian and Western subjects, mastering ten languages in the process, and helped found the Hindu College in Calcutta in 1816. Other Western-curriculum schools quickly followed, including Bethune College in Calcutta, the first secular school for Indian women, in 1849. European and American missionaries played a prominent role in the spread of Western education. In 1870 there were 790,000 Indians in over 24,000 elementary and secondary schools, and India's three universities (established in 1857) awarded 345 degrees. The graduates of these schools articulated a new Pan-Indian nationalism that transcended regional and religious differences.

Many of the new nationalists came from the Indian middle class, which had prospered from the increase of trade and manufacturing. Such educated and ambitious people were angered by the obstacles that British rules and prejudices put in the way of their advancement. Hoping to increase their influence and improve their employment opportunities in the Indian government, they convened the first Indian National Congress in 1885. The members sought a larger role for Indians in the Civil Service. They also called for reductions in military expenditures, which consumed 40 percent of the government's budget, so that more could be spent on alleviating the poverty of the Indian masses. The Indian National Congress promoted unity among the country's many religions and social groups, but most early members were upper-caste Western-educated Hindus and Parsis (members of a Zoroastrian religious sect descended from Persians). The Congress effectively voiced the opinions of elite Indians, but until it attracted the support of the masses, it could not hope to challenge British rule (see Chapter 32).

BRITAIN'S EASTERN EMPIRE

In 1750 Britain's empire had been centered on slave-based plantation and settler colonies in the Americas. A century later its main focus was on commercial networks and colonies in the East. In 1750 the French and Dutch were also serious contenders for global dominion. A century later they had been eclipsed by the British colossus straddling the world. Several distinct changes facilitated this expansion and transformation of Britain's overseas empire: a string of military victories pushed aside other rivals for overseas trade and colonies; new policies favored free trade over mercantilism; and changes in shipbuilding techniques increased the speed and volume of maritime commerce. Linked to these changes were new European settlements in southern Africa, Australia, and New Zealand and the growth of a new long-distance labor trade.

Colonial Rivalries and Trading Networks

As the story of Tipu Sahib told at the beginning of this chapter illustrates, France was still a serious rival to Britain for dominion in the Indian Ocean at the end of the eighteenth century. However, France's defeats in the wars of the French Revolution (see Chapter 24) ended Napoleon's dream of restoring French dominance overseas. The wars also dismantled much of the Netherlands' Indian Ocean empire. When French armies occupied the Netherlands, the Dutch ruler, who had fled to Britain in January 1795, authorized the British to take over Dutch possessions overseas so they could be kept out of French hands. During 1795 and 1796 British forces quickly occupied the Cape Colony at the tip of southern Africa, the strategic Dutch port of Malacca on the strait between the Indian Ocean and the South China Sea, and the island of Ceylon (see Map 26.3).

Then the British occupied Dutch Guiana and Trinidad in the southern Caribbean. In 1811 they

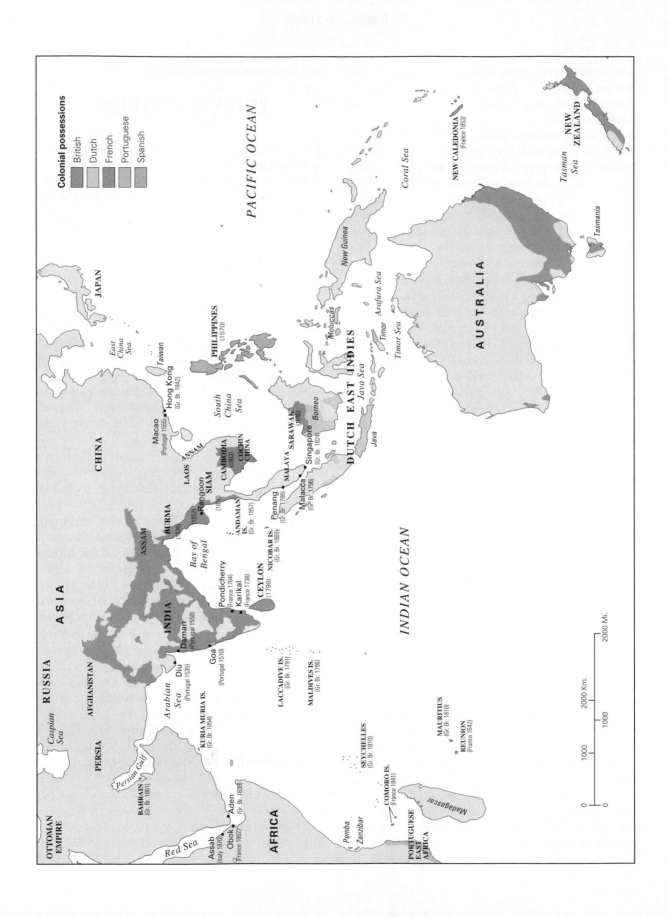

Colonial possessions

British
Dutch
French
Portuguese
Spanish

PACIFIC OCEAN

NEW CALEDONIA
(France 1853)

NEW ZEALAND

Tasman Sea

Tasmania

AUSTRALIA

New Guinea

Moluccas

Timor
Timor Sea
Arafura Sea

Coral Sea

Java Sea

Java

Borneo

DUTCH EAST INDIES

PHILIPPINES
(1570)

East China Sea

Taiwan

JAPAN

CHINA

South China Sea

Hong Kong
(Gr. Br. 1842)

Macao
(Portugal 1555)

ANNAM

LAOS

COCHIN CHINA

CAMBODIA
(1863)

SIAM
(1826)

Rangoon

BURMA
(1852)

ASSAM

SARAWAK
(1846)

MALAYA

Singapore
(Gr. Br. 1824)

Malacca
(Gr. Br. 1796)

Penang
(Gr. Br. 1786)

ANDAMAN IS.
(Gr. Br. 1857)

NICOBAR IS.
(Gr. Br. 1869)

Bay of Bengal

CEYLON
(1798)

Pondicherry
(France 1764)

Karikal
(France 1738)

INDIA

Damar
(Portugal 1558)

Diu
(Portugal 1535)

Goa
(Portugal 1510)

Arabian Sea

ASIA

RUSSIA

Caspian Sea

AFGHANISTAN

PERSIA

Persian Gulf

BAHRAIN
(Gr. Br. 1861)

KURIA MURIA IS.
(Gr. Br. 1854)

OTTOMAN EMPIRE

Red Sea

Assab
(Italy 1870)

Obok
(France 1862)

Aden
(Gr. Br. 1839)

AFRICA

Pemba
Zanzibar

COMORO IS.
(France 1841)

Madagascar

PORTUGUESE EAST AFRICA

SEYCHELLES
(Gr. Br. 1810)

LACCADIVE IS.
(Gr. Br. 1791)

MALDIVES IS.
(Gr. Br. 1796)

MAURITIUS
(Gr. Br. 1810)

RÉUNION
(France 1642)

INDIAN OCEAN

0   1000   2000 Mi.

0   1000   2000 Km.

even seized the island of Java, the center of the Netherlands' East Indian empire. British forces had also attacked French possessions, gaining control of the islands of Mauritius and Réunion in the southwestern Indian Ocean. At the end of the Napoleonic Wars in 1814, Britain returned Java to the Dutch and Réunion to the French but kept the Cape Colony, British Guiana (once part of Dutch Guiana), Trinidad, Ceylon, Malacca, and Mauritius.

The Cape Colony was valuable because of Cape Town's strategic importance as a supply station for ships making the long voyages between Britain and India. With the port city came some twenty thousand descendants of earlier Dutch and French settlers who occupied far-flung farms and ranches in its hinterland. Despite their European origins, these people thought of themselves as permanent residents of Africa and were beginning to refer to themselves as *Afrikaners,* "Africans" in their dialect of Dutch. British governors prohibited any expansion of the white settler frontier because such expansion invariably led to wars with indigenous Africans on the other side. This decision, along with the imposition of laws protecting African rights within Cape Colony (including the emancipation of slaves in 1834), alienated many Afrikaners.

In the late 1830s parties of Afrikaners embarked on a "Great Trek," leaving the British-ruled Cape Colony for the fertile high *veld* (plateau) to the north that two decades of Zulu wars had depopulated. The Great Trek led to the foundation of three new settler colonies in southern Africa by 1850: the Afrikaners' Orange Free State and Transvaal on the high veld and the British colony of Natal on the Indian Ocean coast. Although firearms enabled the settlers to win some important battles against the Zulu and other Africans, they were still a tiny minority surrounded by the populous and powerful independent African kingdoms that had grown up at the beginning of the century. A few thousand British settlers came to Natal and the Cape Colony by midcentury, but only Cape Colony had any strategic importance to Britain, because of its role as a stopover for ships between Britain and British India.

Meanwhile, another strategic British outpost was being established in Southeast Asia. One prong of the advance was led by Thomas Stamford Raffles, who had governed Java during the period of British occupation from 1811 to 1814. After Java's return to the Dutch, Raffles helped the British East India Company establish a new free port at Singapore in 1824, on the site of a small Malay fishing village with a superb harbor. By attracting British merchants and Chinese businessmen and laborers, Singapore soon became the center of trade and shipping between the Indian Ocean and China. Along with Malacca and other possessions on the strait, Singapore formed the "Straits Settlements," which British India administered until 1867.

Further British expansion in Malaya (now Malaysia) did not occur until after 1874, but in neighboring Burma it came more quickly. Burma had emerged as a powerful kingdom by 1750, with plans for expansion. In 1785 Burma tried to annex neighboring territories of Siam (now Thailand) to the east, but a coalition of Thai leaders thwarted Burmese advances by 1802. Burma next attacked Assam to the west, but this action led to war with British India, which was concerned for the security of its own frontier with Assam. After a two-year war, India annexed Assam in 1826 and occupied two coastal provinces of northern Burma. As rice and timber trade from these provinces grew important, the occupation became permanent, and in 1852 British India annexed the port of Rangoon and the rest of coastal Burma.

Map 26.3 European Possessions in the Indian Ocean and South Pacific, 1870. After 1750 French and British competition for new territories greatly expanded the European presence established earlier by the Portuguese, Spanish, and Dutch. By 1870 the British controlled much of India, were settling Australia and New Zealand, and possessed important trading enclaves throughout the region.

Imperial Policies and Shipping

Through such piecemeal acquisitions, by 1870 Britain had added several dozen colonies to the twenty-six colonies it had in 1792, after the loss of the thirteen in North America (see Chapter 24). Nevertheless, historians usually portray

Singapore, ca. 1840 The tall-masted ships in the harbor signal the rise of this sleepy Malayan fishing village to Southeast Asia's most important port city after its takeover by the British in 1824. (Hulton Getty Picture Collection Ltd.)

Britain in this period as a reluctant empire builder, its leaders unwilling to acquire new outposts that could prove difficult and expensive to administer. This apparent contradiction is resolved when one recognizes that the underlying goal of most British imperial expansion during these decades was trade rather than territory. Most of the new colonies were meant to serve as ports in the growing network of shipping that encircled the globe or as centers of production and distribution for those networks.

This new commercial expansion was closely tied to the needs of Britain's growing industrial economy and reflected a new philosophy of overseas trade. Rather than rebuilding the closed network of trade with its colonies known as *mercantilism* (whose rise is charted in Chapter 20), Britain sought to trade freely with all parts of the world. Free trade was also a wise policy in light of the independence of so many former colonies in the Americas (see Chapter 25).

Whether colonized or not, more and more African, Asian, and Pacific lands were being drawn into the commercial networks created by British expansion and industrialization. As was pointed out earlier, uncolonized parts of West Africa became major exporters to Britain of vegetable oils for industrial and domestic use and forest products for dyes and construction, while areas of eastern Africa free of European control exported ivory that ended up as piano keys and decorations for the elegant homes of the industrial middle class. From the far corners of the world came coffee, cocoa, and tea for the tables of the new industrial classes in Britain and other parts of Europe (along with sugar to sweeten these beverages), and indigo dyes and cotton fibers for their expanding textile factories.

In return, the factories of the industrialized nations supplied manufactured goods at very attractive prices. By the mid-nineteenth century a major part of their textile production was destined for overseas markets. Sales of cotton cloth to Africa increased 950 percent from the 1820s to the 1860s. British trade to India grew 350 percent between 1841 and 1870 while India's exports increased 400 percent. Trade with other regions also expanded rapidly. In most cases such trade benefited both sides, but there is no question that the industrial nations were the dominant partners.

A second impetus to global commercial expansion was the technological revolution in the construction of oceangoing ships under way in nineteenth century. The middle decades of the century were the golden age of the sailing ship. New techniques, using iron to fasten timbers together, permitted shipbuilders to construct much larger vessels. Merchant ships in the eighteenth century rarely exceeded 300 tons, but after 1850 swift American-built "clipper" ships of 2,000 tons were commonplace in the British merchant fleet. Huge canvas sails hung from tall masts also made the streamlined clippers faster than earlier vessels. Ships from the East Indies or India had taken six months to reach Europe in the seventeenth century; after 1850 the new ships could complete the voyage in half that time.

This increase in size and speed resulted in much lower shipping costs, which further stimulated maritime trade. The growth in size and numbers of ships increased the tonnage of British merchant shipping by 400 percent between 1778 and 1860. To extend the life of such ships in tropical lands, clippers intended for Eastern service generally were built of teak and other tropical hardwoods from new British colonies in South and Southeast Asia. Although tropical forests began to be cleared for rice and sugar plantations as well as for timbers, the effects on the environment and people of Southeast Asia came primarily after 1870 (see Chapter 29).

Colonization of Australia and New Zealand

The development of new ships and shipping contributed to a third form of British rule in the once-remote South Pacific. In contrast to the rule over an indigenous population in India or the commercial empire overseen from Singapore and Cape Town, in the new British colonies of Australia and New Zealand British settlers displaced indigenous populations, just as had happened earlier in North America (see Chapter 19).

Portuguese mariners had sighted the continent of Australia in the early seventeenth century, but its remoteness made the land of little interest to Europeans. However, after the English adventurer Captain James Cook made the first systematic European exploration of New Zealand and the fertile eastern coast of Australia between 1769 and 1778, expanding shipping networks brought in growing numbers of visitors and settlers.

At the time of Cook's visits Australia was the home of about 650,000 hunting and gathering people, whose Melanesian ancestors had settled there some 40,000 years earlier. The two islands of New Zealand, lying 1,000 miles (1,600 kilometers) southeast of Australia, were inhabited by about 250,000 Maoris, who practiced hunting, fishing, and simple forms of agriculture, which their Polynesian ancestors had introduced around 1200 C.E. (see Chapter 17). Because of their long isolation from the rest of humanity, the populations of Australia and New Zealand were as vulnerable as the Amerindians had been to unfamiliar diseases introduced by new overseas contacts. By the late nineteenth century only 93,000 aboriginal Australians and 42,000 Maoris survived. By then they were outnumbered and dominated by British settler populations.

The first permanent British settlers in Australia were 736 convicts, of whom 188 were women, sent into exile from British prisons in 1788. For the next few decades Australian penal colonies grew slowly and had only slight contact with the indigenous population, whom they called "Aborigines." However, the discovery of gold in 1851 brought a flood of free European settlers (and some Chinese) and hastened the end of the penal colonies. After 1850 tens of thousands of British settlers received government-subsidized passages "down under" on the improved sailing ships of that era, although the voyage still took more than three months. By 1860 the settler population had reached 1 million, and it doubled in the next fifteen years.

British settlers were drawn more slowly to New Zealand. Some of the first were temporary

Whaling

The rapid expansion of hunting for whales aptly illustrates the growing power of technology over nature in this period. Many contemporaries, like many people today, were sickened by the killing of the planet's largest living mammals. American novelist Herman Melville captured the conflicting sentiments in his epic whaling story, *Moby Dick* (1851). One of his characters enthusiastically explains why such a grisly and dangerous business existed:

"But, though the world scorns us as whale hunters, yet does it unwittingly pay us the profoundest homage; yea, an all abounding adoration! for almost all the tapers, lamps, and candles that burn around the globe, burn, as before so many shrines, to our glory!"

Melville's character overstates the degree to which whale oil dominated illumination and does not mention its many other industrial uses. Neither does he describe the commercial importance of whalebone (baleen). For a time its use in corsets allowed fashionable women to achieve the hourglass shape that they desired. Whalebones use for umbrella stays, carriage springs, fishing rods, suitcase frames, combs, brushes, and many other items made it the plastic of its day.

New manufacturing technologies went hand in hand with new hunting technologies. The revolution in ship design enabled whalers from Europe and North America to extend their hunts into the southern oceans, including extensive hunting off New Zealand. By the nineteenth century whaling ships were armed with guns that propelled a steel harpoon armed with vicious barbs deep into the whale. In the 1840s explosive charges on harpoon heads ensured the whale's immediate death. Yet, as this 1838 engraving of an expedition off the north cape of New Zealand shows, flinging small harpoons from rowboats in the open sea continued to be part of the dangerous work.

Another century of extensive hunting would devastate many whale species before international agreements finally curtailed the killing of these giant sea creatures.

Whaling expedition, 1838 engraving (Courtesy, National Library of New Zealand)

residents along the coast who slaughtered seals and exported seal pelts to Western countries to be made into men's felt hats. A single ship in 1806 took away sixty thousand sealskins. By the early 1820s overhunting had virtually exterminated the seal population. Sperm whales were also hunted extensively near New Zealand for their oil, used for lubrication, soap, and lamps; ambergris, an ingredient in perfume; and bone, used in women's corsets (see Environment and Technology: Whaling). Military action that overcame Maori resistance, a brief gold rush, and the availability of faster ships and subsidized passages attracted more British immigrants after 1860. The colony especially courted women immigrants to offset the preponderance of single men. By the early 1880s, fertile agricultural lands of this farthest frontier of the British Empire had a settler population of 500,000.

The model that in 1867 had formed the giant Dominion of Canada out of the very diverse and thinly settled colonies of British North America was applied to the newer colonies in Australia and New Zealand. In 1901 Australia emerged from the federation of the separate colonies of New South Wales, Tasmania, South Australia, Victoria, Queensland, and Western Australia. Originally administered as part of New South Wales, New Zealand became a separate colony in 1840 and a self-governing dominion in 1907.

Britain's policies toward its settler colonies in Canada and the South Pacific were shaped by a desire to avoid the conflicts that had led to the American Revolution in the eighteenth century. By gradually turning over governing power to the colonies' inhabitants, Britain accomplished three things. It satisfied the settlers' desire for greater control over their own territories, it muted demands for independence, and it made the colonial governments responsible for most of their own expenses. Indigenous peoples were outvoted by the settlers or even excluded from voting. An 1897 Australian law segregated the remaining Aborigines onto reservations, where they lacked the rights of Australian citizenship. The requirement that voters had to be able to read and write English kept Maori from voting in early New Zealand elections, but four seats in the lower house of the legislature were reserved for Maori from 1867.

British proclamation to the Australian aborigines, ca. 1830 Affixed to trees in rural areas of Tasmania, this poster was intended to convey the message that the indigenous population could expect the European settlers to be their friends and that the settler government would punish murderers with equal severity, regardless of their race. The poster failed to produce mutual trust. (Tasmanian Museum & Art Gallery)

In other ways the new settler colonies were more progressive. Australia developed very powerful trade unions, which improved the welfare of skilled and semiskilled urban white male workers, promoted democratic values, and exercised considerable political clout. In New Zealand, where sheep raising was the main occupation, populist and progressive sentiments promoted the availability of land for the common person. Australia and New Zealand were also among the first states in the world to grant women the right to vote, beginning in 1894.

New Labor Migrations

Europeans were not the only people to transplant themselves overseas in the mid-nineteenth century. Between 1834 and 1870 large numbers of Indians, Chinese, and Africans were recruited to overseas locations, especially to work on sugar plantations. In the half-century after 1870 tens of thousands of Asians and Pacific Islanders made similar voyages. The scale of such population movements and fact that many of these migrants traveled halfway around the world show the capacities of the new sailing ships. The power and interdependence of the British Empire are revealed in the fact that British India was the greatest source of such laborers and other British colonies were their principal destinations.

After Britain's emancipation of slaves in 1834, the freed Africans were no longer willing to work such long hours as they had been forced to do as slaves. When given full freedom of movement in 1838, many men and most women left the plantations entirely. British colonies had to find other laborers if they were to compete successfully with sugar plantations in Cuba, Brazil,

Asian laborers in British Guiana   The manager of the sugar estate reposes on the near end of the gallery of his house with the proprietor's attorney. At the other end of the galley European overseers review the plantation's record books, while a servant brings them a cup. In the yard other cups of lifeblood are being drained from bound Chinese and Indian laborers. This allegorical drawing by a Chinese laborer represents the exploitation of Asian laborers by Europeans. (Boston Athenaeum)

and the French Caribbean that were still using slave labor.

India's teeming masses seemed one obvious alternative. After planters on Mauritius successfully introduced Indian laborers, the Indian labor trade was extended to the British Caribbean in 1838. Free Africans were another possibility. In 1841, the British government allowed Caribbean planters to recruit Africans whom British patrols had rescued from slave ships and brought to liberation depots in Sierra Leone and elsewhere. By 1870, over a half-million Indians had left their homes for Mauritius or the British Caribbean along with nearly 40,000 Africans and over 18,000 Chinese for the British Caribbean colonies. After the French abolished slavery in 1848, their colonies also recruited 19,000 laborers from Africa and nearly 80,000 from India. Also ending slavery in 1848, Dutch Guiana recruited 57,000 new Asian workers for its plantations.

Although African slave labor was not abolished in Cuba until 1886, the rising cost of slaves led the burgeoning sugar plantations to recruit 138,000 new laborers from China between 1847 and 1873. Such labor recruitment also became the mainstay of new sugar plantations in places that had never known slave labor: after 1850 American planters in Hawaii recruited labor from China and Japan; British planters in Natal recruited from India; and those in Queensland (in northeastern Australia) relied on laborers from neighboring South Pacific islands.

Larger, faster ships made transporting laborers halfway around the world affordable, though voyages from Asia to the Caribbean still took an average of three months. Despite close regulation and supervision of shipboard conditions, the crowded accommodations on the long voyages encouraged the spread of cholera and other contagious diseases that took many migrants' lives.

All of these laborers served under contracts of indenture, which bound them to work for a specified period (usually from five to seven years) in return for free passage to their overseas destination. They were also paid a small salary and were provided with housing, clothing, and medical care. Indian indentured laborers also received the right to a free passage home if they worked a second five-year contract. British Caribbean colonies required that forty women be recruited for every hundred men as a way to promote family life. So many Indians chose to stay on in Mauritius, Trinidad, British Guiana, and Fiji that they constituted a third or more of the total population of these colonies by the early twentieth century.

Although many early recruits from China and the Pacific Islands were kidnapped or otherwise coerced into leaving their homes, in most cases the new indentured migrants had much in common with contemporary emigrants from Europe (described in Chapter 23). Both groups chose to leave their homelands in hopes of improving their economic and social conditions. Both earned modest salaries. Many saved to bring money back with them when they returned home, or they used their earnings to buy land or to start a business in their new countries, where large numbers chose to remain. One major difference was that people recruited as indentured laborers were generally so much poorer than emigrants from Europe that they had to accept lower-paying jobs in less desirable areas because they could not pay their own way. However, it is also true that many European immigrants into distant places like Australia and New Zealand had their passages subsidized but did not have to sign a contract of indenture. It is clear that racial and cultural preferences, not just economics, shaped the flow of labor into European colonies.

A person's decision to accept an indentured labor contract could also be shaped by political circumstances. In India, disruption brought by British colonial policies and the suppression of the 1857 rebellion contributed significantly to people's desire to emigrate. Poverty, famine, and warfare had not been strangers in precolonial India. Nor, as Chapter 27 relates, were these causes of emigration absent in China and Japan.

Not simply the creation of Western imperialism, the indentured labor trade was a model of the repulsions and attractions presented to Asians and Africans by the commercial and industrial expansion of the West. Growing Western power created an unequal relationship but not an entirely one-sided one. Most men and women who signed indentured contracts were trying to improve their lives by emigrating, and many succeeded in manipulating the system to their own advantage. Whether for good or ill, more and more of the world's peoples saw their lives being influenced by the existence of Western colonies, Western ships, and Western markets.

CONCLUSION

What is the global significance of these complex political and economic changes in southern Asia, Africa, and the South Pacific? One perspective stresses the continuing exploitation of the weak by the strong, of African, Asian, and Pacific peoples by aggressive Europeans. In this view, the emergence of Britain as a dominant power in the Indian Ocean basin and South Pacific continues the European expansion that the Portuguese and the Spanish pioneered and the Dutch continued. Likewise, Britain's control over the densely populated lands of South and Southeast Asia and over the less populated lands of Australia and New Zealand was a continuation of the conquest and colonization of the Americas.

From another perspective what was most important about this period was not the political and military strength of the Europeans but their growing dominance of the world's commerce, especially through long-distance ocean shipping. In this view, like other Europeans, the British were drawn to Africa and southern Asia by a desire to obtain new materials, but Britain's commercial expansion in the nineteenth century was increasingly the product of Easterners' demand for industrial manufactures. The growing exchanges could be mutually beneficial. African and Asian consumers found industrially produced goods far cheaper and sometimes better than the handicrafts they replaced or supplemented. Industrialization also created new markets for African and Asian goods, as in the case of the vegetable-oil trade in West Africa or cotton in Egypt and India. But there was a negative impact, too, in the case of the weavers of India and the damage to species of seals and whales.

The emphasis on Europeans' military and commercial strength did not mean that African,

Asian, and Pacific peoples were reduced to appendages of Europe. The balance of power was shifting in the Europeans' favor between 1750 and 1870, but local cultures were still vibrant and local initiatives often dominant. Islamic reform movements and the rise of the Zulu nation had greater significance for their respective regions of Africa than did Western forces. Despite some ominous concessions to European power, Southeast Asians were still largely in control of their own destinies. Even in India, most people's lives and beliefs showed more continuity with the past than change due to British rule.

Finally, it must not be imagined that Asians and Africans were powerless in dealing with European expansion. The Indian princes who extracted concessions from the British raj in return for their cooperation and the Indians who rebelled against the raj both forced the system to accommodate their needs. Moreover, some Asians and Africans were beginning to use European education, technology, and methods to transform their own societies. Leaders in Egypt, India, and other lands, like those in Russia, the Ottoman Empire, China, and Japan—the subject of Chapter 27—were learning to challenge the power of the West on its own terms. In 1870 no one could say how long and how difficult that learning process would be, but Africans and Asians would continue to shape their own futures.

SUGGESTED READING

Until the publication of *The Oxford History of the British Empire*, ed. William Roger Louis, vol. 3, *The Nineteenth Century*, ed. A. R. Porter (forthcoming), the broadest global survey of this period remains *The Cambridge History of the British Empire*, vol. 2, *The Growth of the New Empire, 1783–1870* (1940), ed. J. Holland Rose, A. P. Newton, and E. A. Benians. Less Anglocentric in their interpretations of the era are Immanuel Wallerstein's *The Modern World-System III: The Second Era of Great Expansion of the Capitalist World-Economy, 1730–1840s* (1989) and William Wodruff's *Impact of Western Man: A Study of Europe's Role in the World Economy, 1750–1960* (1982). Atlantic relations are well handled by David Eltis, *Economic Growth and the Ending of the Transatlantic Slave Trade* (1987). For the Indian Ocean basin see Sugata Bose, ed., *South Asia and World Capitalism* (1990).

Roland Oliver and Anthony Atmore provide a brief introduction to Africa in *Africa Since 1800*, 4th ed. (1994). More advanced works are J. F. Ade Ajayi, ed., *UNESCO General History of Africa*, vol. 6, *Africa in the Nineteenth Century until the 1880s* (1989), and John E. Flint, ed., *The Cambridge History of Africa*, vol. 5, *From c. 1790 to c. 1870* (1976). Although specialized literature has refined some of their interpretations, the following are excellent introductions to their subjects: J. D. Omer-Cooper, *The Zulu Aftermath* (1966); Murray Last, *The Sokoto Caliphate* (1967); A. G. Hopkins, *An Economic History of West Africa* (1973); Robert W. July, *The Origins of Modern African Thought* (1967); and Robert I. Rotberg, ed., *Africa and Its Explorers: Motives, Methods, and Impact* (1970). For eastern and northeastern Africa see Norman R. Bennett, *Arab Versus European: War and Diplomacy in Nineteenth Century East Central Africa* (1985); P. J. Vatikiotis, *The History of Modern Egypt: From Muhammad Ali to Mubarak*, 4th ed. (1991); and, for the negative social impact of Egyptian modernization, Judith Tucker, "Decline of the Family Economy in Mid-Nineteenth-Century Egypt," *Arab Studies Quarterly* 1 (1979): 245–271.

Very readable introductions to India in this period are Percival Spear, *India: A Modern History* (1961), chapters 16–26, and Stanley Wolpert, *A New History of India*, 4th ed. (1993), chapters 12–16. More advanced treatments in the "New Cambridge History of India" series are P. J. Marshall, *Bengal: The British Bridgehead: Eastern India, 1740–1828* (1988); C. A. Bayly, *Indian Society and the Making of the British Empire* (1988); Sugata Bose, *Peasant Labour and Colonial Capital: Rural Bengal Since 1700* (1993); and Kenneth W. Jones, *Socio-Religious Reform Movements in British India* (1989). Environmental and technological perspectives on India are offered in the appropriate parts of Daniel Headrick, *The Tentacles of Progress: Technology Transfer in the Age of Imperialism, 1850–1940* (1988); Mashav Gadgil and Ramachandra Guha, *This Fissured Land: An Ecological History of India* (1992); and David Arnold, *Colonizing the Body: State Medicine and Epidemic Disease in Nineteenth-Century India* (1993).

A good introduction to the complexities of Southeast Asian history is D. R. SarDesai, *Southeast Asia: Past and Present*, 2d ed. (1989). More detail can be found in the appropriate chapters of Nicholas Tarling, ed., *The Cambridge History of South East Asia*, 2 vols. (1992). The second and third volumes of *The Oxford History of Australia*, ed. Geoffrey Bolton (1992, 1988), deal with the period covered by this chapter. A very readable multicultural and gendered perspective is provided by *Images of Australia*, ed. Gillian Whitlock and David Carter (1992). *The Oxford Illustrated History of New Zealand*, ed. Keith Sinclair (1990), provides a wide-ranging introduction to that nation.

For summaries of recent scholarship on the indentured labor trade see David Northrup, *Indentured Labor in the Age of Imperialism, 1834–1922* (1995), and Robin Cohen, ed., *The Cambridge Survey of World Migration*, part 3, "Asian Indentured and Colonial Migration" (1995).

An outstanding analysis of British whaling is Gordon Jackson's *The British Whaling Trade* (1978). Edouard A. Stackpole's *Whales & Destiny: The Rivalry Between America, France, and Britain for Control of the Southern Whale Fishery, 1785–1825* (1972) is more anecdotal.

NOTES

1. Paul E. Lovejoy and Jan S. Hogendorn, *Slow Death for Slavery: the Course of Abolition in Northern Nigeria, 1897–1936* (New York: Cambridge University Press, 1993).

2. Cited in P. J. Vatikiotis, *The History of Modern Egypt: From Muhammad Ali to Mubarak*, 4th ed. (Baltimore: Johns Hopkins University Press, 1991), 74.

3. David Eltis, "Precolonial Western Africa and the Atlantic Economy," in *Slavery and the Rise of the Atlantic Economy*, ed. Barbara Solow (New York: Cambridge University Press, 1991), table 1.

4. Quoted by Bernard S. Cohn, "Representing Authority in Victorian India," in *The Invention of Tradition*, ed. Eric Hobsbawm and Terence Ranger (Cambridge, England: Cambridge University Press, 1983), 165.

CHAPTER TWENTY-SEVEN

The Ottoman Empire and East Asia, 1800–1870

The Ottoman Empire and the European Model

The Qing Empire and Foreign Coercion

Japan, from Shogunate to Empire

When the Qianlong emperor of the Qing died in 1799, the court received a shock. It was known for decades that the emperor had indulged his handsome young court favorite, Heshen, allowing him extraordinary privileges and power. Senior bureaucrats had come to hate Heshen, suspecting him of overseeing a widespread network of corruption. Part of his scheme, they believed, had been to prolong the inconclusive wars against the native Miao peoples of southwest China in the late 1700s. While glowing reports of successes against the rebels poured into the capital, enormous sums of government money flowed to the battlefields. But there was no evidence that the war was actually progressing, and no adequate accounting for the funds.

After the emperor's death, Heshen's enemies ordered his arrest. When they searched his mansion, they discovered magnificent hoards of silk, furs, priceless porcelain, furniture, and gold and silver. His cash alone exceeded what remained in the imperial treasury. The new emperor ordered Heshen to commit suicide with a rope of golden silk. But the damage Heshen exemplified could not be undone. Even with the recovery of his fortune, the expenses of the Qing government were so great that it was permanently bankrupt. The declining agricultural base could not replenish the state coffers, and the pressures for internal police and military action rose after 1800. Repeated investigations of the bureaucracy revealed growing corruption. In the 1800s, then, the Qing Empire faced a period of increasing challenge from the sea-based powers of western Europe with an empty treasury, a stagnant economy, and a troubled society.

The problems of the Qing were not unique. They were shared by all of the land-based empires of Eurasia: the Ottoman in the Middle East, the Mughal in India, and the Romanov in Russia. During the early 1800s, much of Eurasia was affected by rapidly increasing population and by a slowing of the agricultural growth that had been so important in the 1700s. Meanwhile, military expansion had overstretched the resources of their treasuries. In the 1800s these traditional regimes reached a crisis point in their economies and societies, and simultaneously they were confronted with aggressive demands for economic concessions from western Europe. The result was the general indebtedness—either through direct loans or failure to pay indemnities after losing military conflicts—of the Eurasian empires to western Europe.

Westernizers argued for the adoption of the technological and managerial techniques that appeared to underlie the strength and aggressiveness of the European powers. But many sectors of these Eurasian societies—often including the Westernizers themselves—were anxious to protect the traditional cultural values that legitimated the status of their elites and offered some symbols for national definition. Thus the challenge of importing certain European goods, knowledge, and advisers while trying to limit their influence was complex and ultimately created political instabilities. Perhaps more important, that challenge inspired these empires to pursue programs of military and financial reform, rather than undertaking a more thoroughgoing restructuring of their economies and of their political life. In many cases there was indeed improvement, but it occurred in too small a degree and too slowly to rebalance the power between the great land-based empires of Eurasia and the increasingly expansive sea-based regimes of Europe and America.

Although the situation of the Eurasian empires with respect to the economic and military challenges of western Europe were similar, there are distinct and important differences in the ways those empires managed their internal and foreign problems. The central Ottoman territories fared best. Ottoman reforms began early, and despite frequent tensions with Europe in the

1800s, the empire managed to work out a cooperative relationship with western Europe. The Qing Empire, in contrast, experienced the arrival of European military forces and cultural influences as a shock. That empire began reforms far too late to permit even its central territories to unite themselves during the 1800s.

Because Russia shared boundaries with Europe, the Ottoman Empire, and the Qing Empire, it played a special role in their fates. The enormous size of the Russian Empire as well as its position between the networks of Europe and those of Asia constantly frustrated reform attempts in the 1800s, and the history of Russia since 1917—the end of the Romanov empire—has been a troubled and unstable one. Geographically, Russia and the Ottomans were located in such a way that both of them were in continuous communication with European courts and commercial centers. The Qing, in contrast, knew the empire of the Romanovs primarily through Russia's eastward campaigns of expansion, which had begun in the 1600s (see Map 22.1 in Chapter 22). In the 1800s the Qing continued to see the Russian problem along their northern borders as unconnected to the Western incursions that plagued the southern coasts.

This chapter concentrates on the experience of two of these land-based Eurasian empires: the Ottoman and the Qing. But to understand the significance of the similarities between them, we need to examine a dramatic contrasting case: Japan. Like the Ottoman and Qing Empires, Japan in the 1800s was in the late decades of a long-lived political system: the Tokugawa shogunate. Also like the Ottoman and Qing Empires, the Tokugawa government experienced steeply declining revenues, a stagnating agricultural base, and corruption in the central government. Moreover, Japan like all East Asian countries experienced the shock of military and economic confrontation with the West in the middle 1800s.

Because of the uniquely decentralized system of rule under the Tokugawa, however, Japan could not attempt the top-down reforms that the Ottoman and Qing Empires tried. Instead, Japan's first direct contact with a foreign sea power led to the destruction of the traditional Japanese state. It was replaced by a centralized and relatively efficient order whose leaders were determined not to be victims of European expansion but to be participants in the evolving colonial order in Asia. The effects of the transformation of Japan—felt first in Korea, then in China, then in Central and Southeast Asia, and now throughout the world—have been profound.

THE OTTOMAN EMPIRE AND THE EUROPEAN MODEL

Although the Ottoman Empire experienced the problems and challenges sketched above, its position close to Europe gave it a relatively early exposure to European ambitions and capabilities (see Map 27.1). Consequently, the Ottoman rulers were earlier than those of other empires to experiment with financial and military modernization (see Chapter 21). Not until the mid-nineteenth century, however, did the Ottoman government overcome entrenched opposition to change and put into place a series of reforms designed to remove the influence of religious elites from many areas of the state and

Map 27.1 The Expansion of Russia to 1800 Much of the background of the Crimean War can be understood through the European reaction to the expansion of Russian territory and influence under the Romanov Empire. Though the westward growth toward Europe had stopped by the end of the eighteenth century, Russian acquisition of territory in the Caucasus (Georgia) and Central Asia showed the inability of the Ottomans to contain further enlargement of the Russian empire. This prompted France and Britain to join the Ottomans in attempting to retake control of the Black Sea.

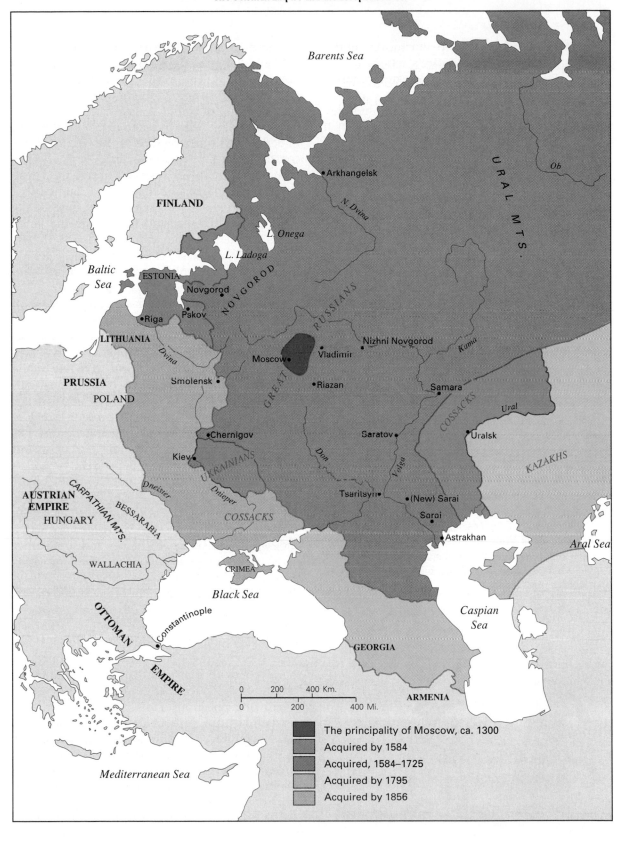

Barents Sea

• Arkhangelsk

FINLAND

URAL MTS.

Ob

N. Dvina

L. Onega

L. Ladoga

Baltic
Sea

ESTONIA

Novgorod •

NOVGOROD

GREAT   RUSSIANS

• Riga   • Pskov

• Nizhni Novgorod

Kama

LITHUANIA

Moscow •   • Vladimir

PRUSSIA

• Smolensk

• Samara

POLAND

• Riazan

COSSACKS

Dvina

Ural

• Uralsk

• Chernigov

Saratov •

KAZAKHS

Kiev •

UKRAINIANS

Don

Volga

AUSTRIAN
EMPIRE

CARPATHIAN MTS.

BESSARABIA

Dneister

Dnieper

COSSACKS

Tsaritsyn •

• (New) Sarai

HUNGARY

Sarai •

WALLACHIA

CRIMEA

Astrakhan •

Aral Sea

Black Sea

Caspian
Sea

OTTOMAN

• Constantinople

GEORGIA

EMPIRE

0   200   400 Km.

0   200   400 Mi.

ARMENIA

Mediterranean Sea

	The principality of Moscow, ca. 1300
	Acquired by 1584
	Acquired, 1584–1725
	Acquired by 1795
	Acquired by 1856

economy. The reforms could not move rapidly enough to preserve the empire's independence from western Europe, but they created momentum for centralization and helped promote nationalism in the late nineteenth century, and they created a practical base for the founding of a Turkish republic in the twentieth century (see Chapter 30).

Early Struggles for Reform

Because of its geographical proximity to Europe (where the Ottomans established diplomatic embassies), and because of the predisposition of some of its late-eighteenth-century rulers, the Ottoman Empire experienced some reforms in the early 1800s. Their purpose was to make the military more effective, bring provincial governors more under the control of the central government, and standardize taxation and land tenure. The cost of these reforms was to be covered by taxes, primarily on tobacco and coffee.

Army dress Changes in the Ottoman armies were gradual, beginning with the introduction of European guns and artillery. The Janissaries were required to modify their dress and their beards in order to use the new weapons efficiently and safely. Beards were trimmed and elaborate headgear was reserved for ritual occasions. Traditional military units attempted to retain distinctive dress whenever possible, and one compromise was the brimless cap, the fez, adapted from the high hats that some Janissaries had traditionally worn. (Osterreichisches Nationalbibliotek)

Those reforms made by the ruler Selim III (r. 1789–1807) failed for political more than economic reasons. The most violent and persistent opposition arose among the traditional, specially trained corps of military slaves, the Janissaries, who had become an independent political force in Serbia and other regions of the empire. Their control in Serbia, where they acted as local governors, was intensely resented by the local residents, particularly Christians, who claimed that the Janissaries abused them. In response to the charges, Selim threatened to reassign the Janissaries to the Ottoman capital at Istanbul. The Janissaries suspected that this threat signaled their steady removal from political power—and possibly from existence.

In 1805 the Janissaries rose in a bloody revolt against Selim's reforms in Serbia, and massacres of Christians in Serbia followed. Selim was unable to reestablish central Ottoman rule over Serbia. Instead, the Ottoman court had to rely on the governor of Bosnia, who joined his troops with the peasants of Serbia to suppress the Janissary uprising. Afterwards the ever-present threat of intervention from Russia frustrated the Ottomans' attempts to disarm the Serbians, and Serbia became effectively independent.

The Janissaries were the most dramatic opponents of the imperial reforms of the early 1800s, but they were not alone. Other portions of the military, including reserves, engaged in active and passive resistance. In Turkey and some other parts of the empire, revolts of the Janissaries were encouraged by noblemen who had been early supporters of reform but now feared the effects of revised taxation procedures and resented Selim's adoration of France (he had acknowledged Napoleon as emperor). Also in opposition were the congregations of Muslim councilors, the *ulama*, who distrusted the secularization of law and taxation that Selim proposed. In the face of growing rejection of his reforms, Selim suspended his program in 1806. Nevertheless, a massive military uprising at Istanbul resulted in his overthrow and imprisonment. Reform forces rallied and recaptured the capital but were too late to rescue Selim. He had been executed at the order of his successor.

The reforms that began in the time of Selim and continued—though not always with perfect consistency—into the later 1800s were partly a response to the inability of the Ottoman Empire to maintain control over the enormous expanse of territory that it had subjugated in the previous two centuries (see Chapter 21). The most stunning loss of the early 1800s, and the issue that most threatened relations with Europe, was the achievement of Greek independence in 1827.

Europeans considered the war for Greek independence from the Ottomans a campaign to recapture the classical roots of their civilization from Muslim influence, and many—including the "mad, bad and dangerous to know" poet Lord Byron, who lost his life in the war—volunteered to fight for the cause. The Ottomans depended on Ibrahim Pasha of Egypt—son of Muhammad Ali (see Chapter 26)—to preserve their rule in Greece, but he was handily defeated by the French fleet. Not only was Ottoman control of Greece ended, but the tenuous Ottoman rule in Egypt was further damaged.

The Tanzimat Reforms

In 1826 Mahmud II (r. 1808–1839) revived the reform movement. Traumatic episodes such as the Janissary revolt in Serbia and the execution of Selim III taught the Ottoman court that reform, if it was to be pursued, had to be more systematic and ruthless than had been the case earlier. Mahmud II targeted the Janissaries for dissolution and by 1826, after many bloody incidents, achieved this goal. He also reduced the political power of the religious elite. This action necessitated a restructuring of the bureaucracy, because education and law would now be under the authority of the civil government. Property laws were amended to make the charitable trusts (*auqaf*) by which religious communities and families managed their wealth subject to civil review and regulation. Even the public judgments of the ulama were to be regulated by Ottoman bureaucratics.

In most of his attempts to secularize the state, Mahmud II relied on laws to establish a uniform civil code of government, and he cultivated for himself the image of a progressive legal reformer. Many of his ideas were given their widest expression in the Tanzimat Reforms, announced by his

sixteen-year-old son and successor, Abdul Mejid, soon after Mahmud's death in 1839.

A striking feature of the Tanzimat proclamations (*tanzimat* means "restructuring") was a set of guaranteed political rights, which have been compared to Magna Carta, the charter of limited political and civil liberties that the king of England issued in 1215. Among other provisions, the Tanzimat called for public trials and for equal protection for all under the law, regardless of religious affiliation. It also guaranteed some rights of privacy, equalized the eligibility of men for conscription into the army, and provided for a new, formalized method of tax collecting that legally ended tax farming in the empire.

No Islamic country had ever produced anything so nearly approaching a constitution, and

European exposure Increasing exposure to French and British influence stimulated the programs on the part of the Ottoman rulers to completely modernize their armies. By the time of the Crimean War, the Janissaries had been replaced by a professional military, trained in special schools, adept in the use of modern artillery, and dressed in the fashion of the European infantry and cavalry. (Hulton-Getty Picture Collection)

the Ottoman Empire enjoyed a renewed reputation as a progressive influence in the Middle East. The successors to Mahmud II and Abdul Mejid were less zealous in their legal ideologies and later created a mixed court system that permitted religious judges (*qadi*) to decide certain matters. Nevertheless, the distinction between religious and secular law continued to be observed, and in the middle 1800s the commercial code was remodeled along the lines of the French system. Trade and finance, in this instance, were affirmed by the rulers to be outside the jurisdiction of religious law.

Army and Society in the Tanzimat

In the military and in education, Mahmud II also revived reforms that Selim III had begun. A conscript army was mandated, and with it came the educational reforms that attempted to promote the appeal of secular, international, urban cultural attitudes. Military cadets were sent to France and to the German states for training, and military uniforms were modeled on those of France. In the 1830s an Ottoman imperial school of military sciences was established at Istanbul. Most of its instructors and advisers were imported from Europe to teach chemistry, engineering, mathematics, and physics in addition to military history. Reforms in military education became the model for general educational reforms. The first medical school in the Ottoman Empire, for instance, was established for army doctors and surgeons in 1834. In 1838 a national system of preparatory schools was created.

Since the subjects that students studied and many of the teachers themselves were foreign in origin, the issue of whether Turkish would be a language of instruction in the new schools was a serious one. The easiest course of action was to import and use foreign teaching texts. French was the preferred language of instruction in all advanced professional and scientific training. Translating the works into Turkish was a long and complex task that had not been completed by the end of the 1800s.

The importance of educational institutions in these early reforms accelerated the growth in wealth and influence of the urban elites, particularly at Istanbul. There, a cosmopolitan milieu embracing European languages and culture, as well as military professionalism and an interest in progressive political reform, thrived. Newspapers, printed mostly in French, were published at Istanbul, and travel to Europe—particularly to England and France—by wealthy Turks became more common. Among self-consciously progressive men, European dress was the fashion in the Ottoman cities of the later 1800s. Traditional dress was retained as a symbol of the religious, the rural, and the parochial.

Although the reforming rulers from Mahmud II on were conscious of the immediate importance of military change, they quickly appreciated that limited technical improvements could not be isolated from more general issues of society and culture. Within the military alone, technical reforms were quickly politicized. Under Mahmud II, the introduction of modern weaponry and drill organization required a change in the traditional military dress. Beards were now regarded as unhygienic and, among the artillery units, a fire hazard. They were restricted, along with the wearing of loose trousers and turbans.

Headgear became a controversial issue. European military caps, which had leather bills on the front to protect against the glare of the sun, were not acceptable, because soldiers wearing them would be unable to touch their foreheads to the ground while bowing to Mecca in daily prayer. The compromise was the brimless cap now called the *fez*, which the military and then Ottoman civil officials adopted in the early years of Mahmud II's reign. Military castes had been an important part of traditional Ottoman society, and the alteration in military dress—so soon after the vanquishing of the Janissaries—was universally recognized as symbolizing change in the social meaning of military service.

Secularization of the legal code had profound implications for the non-Muslim subjects of the Ottomans. Neither Christianity nor Judaism was forbidden in the Islamic state. Non-Muslims, however, were frequently under special tax obligations and were excluded from certain professions, including the military, unless they converted to Islam. In addition, the role of Islamic judges in the legal process often limited the extent to which non-Muslims could seek redress or protection.

Secularization of the law gave all male subjects, regardless of their religion, access to the courts. It also resulted in equalization of taxation. Thus, in the 1860s and 1870s, as a constitution was debated and the possibility of a male franchise was discussed, the prospect of the Muslim loss of all political privilege arose. The Muslim majority not only was disturbed by the apparent loss of a consensus that the Ottoman Empire was a Muslim society but was also suspicious of the motives of Christians, many of whom were not of Turkish descent. Muslims remembered the championing of Christian causes by Russia and France, and could rationalize hostilities against the Christians of Ottoman territories in Europe, Armenia, and the Middle East on the grounds of Turkish patriotism.

The Tanzimat Reforms were explicitly limited to the public rights of, and political participation by, men. Private life—including everything connected to marriage and divorce—was left within the sphere of religious law, and at no time was there a question of political participation by, or reformed education for, women. But it is not enough to say that women were by omission denied the new rights and privileges that the reforms guaranteed to all men. Paradoxically, the reforms actually decreased women's influence.

First of all, like China in the Ming and Qing periods, the Ottoman territories had been affected by the growth in European commerce in the 1600s and the inflow of silver from the Americas (see Chapters 18 and 19). The increase in silver may have intensified the use of money instead of barter in some parts of the Ottoman economy—as it did in some parts of Europe. Money in turn led to price fluctuations for both goods and labor, bringing new value to the work done by men in new industries, and hiding the value of work done by women, particularly in the home-based industries such as weaving and embroidery (see Environment and Technology in Chapter 22). Economically, women became more isolated from public life in the 1700s, and Muslim prescriptions for female behavior reinforced these social trends.

Nevertheless, before the Tanzimat reforms women in Ottoman society had retained considerable influence, particularly in the management and disposal of their property. After marriage, women were often pressured to convert their landholdings to cash, the better to transfer their wealth to the family of their husbands, with whom they would reside. But many women had retained influence over the distribution of property through the creation of charitable trusts for their sons. Because these trusts were negotiated through the religious courts, they could conform to the wishes of family members, and women of wealthy families could exercise significant indirect control over property.

The secularizing reforms of Mahmud II in the 1820s and 1830s, however, specifically removed the charitable trusts from the jurisdiction of the religious courts and brought trusts under the regulation of the state. The general effect was to destroy women's control over their own and their families' property and to lower the status of women in the nineteenth-century Ottoman Empire. Meanwhile, reforms in the military, in higher education, in the professions, and in commerce all bypassed women. By the late 1800s, the isolation of women was a highly valued symbol of Turkish nativism and Muslim traditionalism.

The Crimean War

Russian rulers since Peter the Great (r. 1682–1725) had decried Ottoman occupation of the former Byzantine capital at Constantinople (now Istanbul). But their protests were often empty political rhetoric. By the end of the 1700s the Romanov empire of Russia had taken control of Hungary, Transylvania, and the eastern shores of the Caspian Sea away from the Ottomans (see Map 27.2). The threat of Russian intervention had forced the Ottomans to leave Serbia effectively independent after the 1805 uprising of the Janissaries, and in 1829 the two empires were squabbling over the Georgian region of the Caucasus, which Russia seized and kept. In contrast, when the forces of the industrializing leader Muhammad Ali of Egypt had threatened to

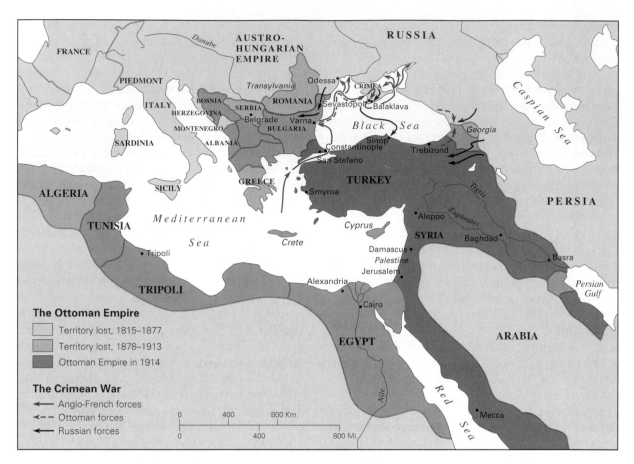

Map 27.2   The Ottoman Empire and the Crimean War   At its height the Ottoman Empire had controlled most of the perimeter of the Mediterranean Sea. But in the 1800s the Ottoman territories shrank, as many countries gained their independence—frequently with the aid of France or Russia. The Black Sea, which left the Turkish coast vulnerable to assault by the Russian navy, was a great weak spot that was intensely contested in the Crimean dispute.

depose the Ottoman rulers, Russia had announced itself in support of the Ottomans (see Chapter 26). Nevertheless, Russia seemed poised to exploit Ottoman weakness and seize key territories in the Balkans and in Central Asia.

Cracks in Ottoman control had also appeared in the Middle East. Although Egypt remained formally under Ottoman rule, the real power there was held by the local governor. In the Arab lands, the leaders of nomadic federations constantly challenged Ottoman domination. During the last years of the 1700s, France itself—then in its expansionary imperial phase under Napoleon—began to battle the Ottomans for

control of Egypt. In 1798 French troops landed at Cairo, and open warfare between France and the Ottoman Empire was declared. But three years later French forces left Egypt, and the Ottomans resumed close cooperation with France in their mutual struggle against Russia, which had assumed an assertive political role in Europe after the end of the Napoleonic Wars.

Those developments contributed to the outbreak of war in Crimea (see Map 27.2). Britain and France were resentful and distrustful of Russia because successive tsars had played a reactionary role in Europe after the Congress of Vienna (1815). Russian forcefulness had also squeezed the Ottoman Empire in the early 1800s, not just as military but also as ideological pressure. The tsars demanded to be acknowledged as the spiritual and political patrons of Orthodox Christians living in the Ottoman territories. Not to be outdone, France insisted that Catholics in the Ottoman territories of Palestine—where French influence had been growing since the late eighteenth century—should have status equal or superior to the status of Orthodox believers. Bolstered by the promised support of Britain and France, the Ottomans rejected the demands of the Romanov tsar Nicholas I (r. 1825–1855) and mobilized to drive the Russian forces out of what is now Romania. The Ottomans held their own in the land engagements, but the Russians swiftly won the naval battles on the Black Sea.

Britain and France entered the war on the side of the Ottoman Empire in 1854, and these countries decided to conquer the Russian territory of Crimea—which until 1783 had been ruled by descendants of Genghis Khan. Later the Italian kingdom of Sardinia-Piedmont joined the fray on the Ottoman side, and the Austro-Hungarian Empire—previously Russia's long-standing ally—threatened to support the Ottomans.

The Crimean War was one of the critical confrontations of the mid-1800s. It not only employed recently developed military technology but stimulated the development of communications, transportation, and battlefield medicine. The carnage caused by rapid-fire weapons, long-range rifles, mines, infection, and disease reached unprecedented levels and was reported with unprecedented speed to the populations of the fighting states (see Environment and Technology: The New Web of War). In 1856 the isolated Russians were forced to negotiate the Treaty of Paris, ending the war.

The treaty guaranteed the territorial integrity of the Ottoman Empire. The formal alliance of Britain and France with the Ottoman rulers blocked Romanov expansion into eastern Europe and into the Middle East. The terms of the treaty also gave Britain and France a means of checking each other's colonial ambitions in the Middle East: neither, according to the Paris terms, was entitled to take Ottoman territory for its exclusive use.

European Patronage and Economic Decline

The declining state revenues and the increasing integration with the European commercial networks created hazardous economic conditions in the Ottoman Empire by the middle 1800s. Mahmud II's successors continued to secularize financial and commercial institutions and to model them closely on European counterparts. The Ottoman imperial bank was founded in 1840, and a few years later a currency reform linked the value of Ottoman gold coins to the British pound. Sweeping changes in the 1850s expedited the creation throughout the empire of banks, insurance companies, and legal firms. These and other reforms fostering trade contributed to a strong demographic shift in the Ottoman Empire between about 1850 and 1880. Within this period many of the major cities of the empire doubled—in some cases, tripled—in size. A strong urban professional class emerged, as well as a considerable class of wage laborers.

Although the Ottoman reforms influenced the growth of international commerce and the urbanization of the empire in the later 1800s, they were ineffective in correcting the insolvency of the imperial government. Ottoman finances were damaged by declining revenues from agricultural yields and by widespread corruption, some of which received spectacular exposure in the early 1840s. From the conclusion of the Crimean War in 1856 on, the imperial government of the Ottomans became heavily dependent on foreign loans for reform and for survival. Commercial and financial life was rapidly restructured to fit European practices. Trade tariffs were altered to favor European imports, and European banks were established in the Ottoman cities. The Ottoman currency was changed to allow more systematic conversion with European currency. Urban residence laws were revised to allow Europeans to live in Istanbul and other commercial centers in their own enclaves, under their own laws (a practice called *extraterritoriality*).

Because of the stimulation that the inflow of European trade, money, and culture provided,

The New Web of War

The Crimean War and the Taiping Rebellion were part of a set of very large and extremely bloody wars of the middle 1800s which saw the application of far more lethal technologies, the invention of new generations of killing machines, and the resulting slaughter of soldiers and civilians at a rate that had never before witnessed. These technologies, once used on battlefields in the U. S.., Russia, India, or China were rapidly transmitted to the next theater of conflict. This was partly because of a new international network of soldiers moving around the globe, bringing with them expertise in the new techniques.

Some of these soldiers, such as General Charles Gordon, moved from battlefield to battlefield according to the contours of imperial interest. Gordon, for instance, was commissioned in the British army in 1852, then served in the Crimean War after Britain entered on the side of the Ottomans. Three years after the end of that conflict, in 1860, he was dispatched to China, serving the British forces during the Arrow War and taking part in the sack of Beijing. He stayed in China, seconded to the Qing imperial government, until the suppression of the Taipings in 1864, earning himself the nickname of "Chinese" Gordon. In later years Gordon served as governor of territory along the Nile for the rulers of Egypt, and was killed there in 1885 attempting to lead his Egyptian troops in defense of the city of Khartoum against the uprising of the local religious leader, the Mahdi.

Journalism was an important part of the developing web of telegraph communications that speeded orders to and from the battlefields. Readers in London could learn in detail of the dramas in the Crimea or in China a week—or in some cases, days—after they had occurred. Print and, later, photographic journalism also created new "stars" from these war experiences. Charles Gordon was one himself, but of equal stature was Florence Nightingale.

In these great wars of the 1800s, the vast majority of deaths resulted from infections or unnecessary bleeding to death rather than the wounds themselves. Nightingale had, since her youth, distinguished herself for her interest in hospital management and nursing. She had gone to Prussia and to France to study advanced techniques, and was credited with leading a marked improvement in British health care before the outbreak of the Crimean War. As the public reacted to reports of the suffering, Nightingale was sent to the Crimea by the British government. Within a year of her arrival the fatality rate in the military hospitals had dropped from 45 percent to under 5 percent. Her techniques for preventing septicemia, dysentery, and for promoting healing therapies were quickly adopted by those working under and alongside her. On her return to London, Nightingale established institutes for nursing that were quickly recognized as leaders in the world, and she herself was lionized by the British public, receiving the Order of Merit in 1907, three years before her death. The new efficiency of the killing machines of the 1800s made her work necessary, and the new efficiency of the era's communications made her an international celebrity.

One of many variations on the depictions that appeared in British newspapers of Florence Nightingale administering to the wounded in the Crimean War. (Mary Evans Picture Library)

the cities became attractive to laborers, and the movement of people from the countryside to the cities continued to be massive. For the wage-dependent workers of the bloated cities, the economic situation worsened. The growing foreign trade brought large numbers of imports to the empire, but few exports went abroad, apart from the Turkish opium that American traders took to China to compete against the Indian opium of the British. Together with the growing national debt, these factors in the middle 1800s aggravated inflationary trends that left the urban populations in a precarious position.

This vicious circle was frustrating to the ruling elite, but it had a much sharper impact on the generations of young men who, in the mid-1800s, aspired to wealth and influence. These groups, who were primarily urban based, were educated but did not wield political power. In their view, the Ottoman rulers would be forced to—or indeed would be willing to—allow the continued domination of the empire's political, economic, and cultural life by Europeans. Inspired, ironically, by the European nationalist movements of 1848 (see Chapter 24), they began to band together in the 1860s, as the "Young Turks." To these men, freedom from European domination required the destruction of the Ottoman Empire from within. They proposed that the empire should be replaced by a national republic structure—a Turkish national state, their "Fatherland." Nationalism continued to be fostered by the leaders of the Young Turks—who exploited the new institutions of newspapers and private schools to spread their message—but the Ottoman empire continued its weakened existence under the sponsorship of Western powers until 1922.

THE QING EMPIRE AND FOREIGN COERCION

Around the year 1800 the Qing Empire was facing many of the same crises as the Ottomans, but no early reform movement of the kind that Selim III initiated emerged in China. The reasons are not difficult to understand. The primary European influences in China before 1800 were not writers of the Enlightenment or nationalist leaders like Napoleon. They were instead the Jesuits, who centuries before had sought out China and other societies in Asia to find converts to Catholicism as the church's influence in Europe declined (see Chapter 22). The Qing felt no threat from western Europe and had successfully negotiated both military and diplomatic coexistence with the Russian Empire (see Map 27.3). Complaints from European merchants at Canton (Guangzhou) who chafed against the restrictions of the Canton system (see Chapter 22) were brushed off as the dissatisfactions of wealthy and privileged men who simply desired more wealth and privilege.

Disorder was primarily domestic and was regarded as familiar: rebellions among displaced indigenous peoples, among the poor in areas experiencing economic or environmental distress, among those protesting injustices of the local magistrates. These troubles, thought the Qing rulers, could be dealt with in the usual way: by suppressing rebels and dismissing incompetent or untrustworthy officials. The Qing rulers of 1800 had no compelling reason to think that revolutionary challenges were headed their way.

In 1842, however, the Qing Empire lost the first Opium War (1839–1842) to Britain and was forced to agree to the first of a series of economic and political measures grossly favoring European and American merchants. Only then did Chinese elites begin to press the government to advance its military technology and strategic practices. But European and American assaults came in such rapid waves that there was no time for any sort of recovery or reform until the period of "cooperation" with the West that followed suppression of the Taiping Rebellion in 1864 (see Voices and Visions: Lin Zexu).

Economic and Social Disorder

The successes of the early Qing Empire created much of the domestic and political chaos of the later period. The Qing conquest had brought stability to central China, which previously had

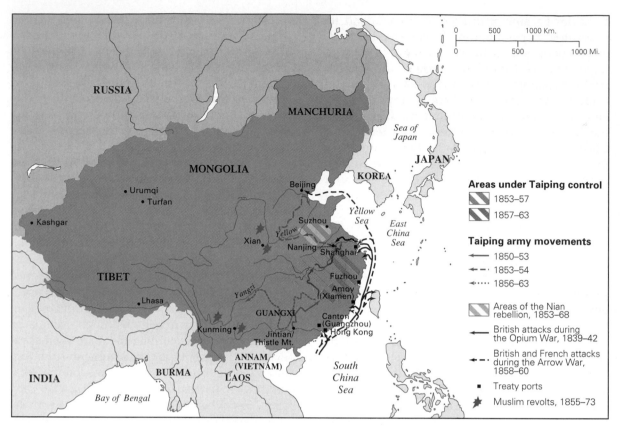

Map 27.3 Sites of Conflict in the Qing Empire of the 1800s   In both the opium wars of 1839–1842 and 1856–1860, the sea coasts saw most of the action. Since the Qing had no imperial navy, the well-armed British ships encountered little resistance as they shelled the southern coasts. But inland conflicts such as the prolonged Taiping Rebellion found Qing combatants—whether rebels or imperial troops—on ground much more favorable to them. Armies were massive, slow-moving, and battles were often prolonged attempts to starve out the other side before making a major assault.

been subjected to decades of rebellion and agricultural shortages. The Qing encouraged the recovery of farmland, the opening of previously uncultivated areas, and the restoration and expansion of the road and canal system. The result was dramatic expansion of the agricultural base together with a gigantic leap in population (see Chapter 22). Enormous numbers of farmers, merchants, and day laborers migrated across China in search of less crowded conditions, and a permanent "floating population" of the unemployed and homeless emerged. By the end of the 1700s, population strain on the land had resulted

in serious environmental damage in some parts of central and western China: Deforestation, erosion, and soil exhaustion left swollen populations stranded on land that was deteriorating rapidly.

The dissatisfactions of this population were joined by those of other groups: minority peoples in central and southwestern China who had been driven off their lands during the boom of the 1700s; Mongols who resented the appropriation of their grazing lands and the displacement of their traditional elites; village vigilante organizations that had grown used to policing and virtually governing regions that the Qing had become too weak to manage; and growing numbers of people who mistrusted the government, suspecting that all officials were corrupt. In the 1800s, the increasing presence and privileges of foreign merchants and missionaries in the treaty ports aggravated these endemic social problems. Both to the poor and to the Confucian gentry, the missionaries were a visible reminder of the inability or unwillingness of the Qing court to protect the country from foreign intrusion. In some parts of China the Qing were hated because they themselves were a foreign conquest regime and were suspected of having sympathies with the newly arrived foreigners from Europe.

As the nineteenth century opened, the White Lotus Rebellion—partly inspired by a mystical ideology that predicted the restoration of the Chinese Ming dynasty and the coming of the Buddha—was raging across central China and could not be suppressed until 1804. The White Lotus was the first large rebellion in a series of internal conflicts that continued through the 1800s. Ignited by deepening social instabilities, these movements were sometimes intensified by local ethnic conflicts and sometimes by the unorthodox religion. They clearly were dependent on regional populations' increasingly sophisticated use of village organization for self-defense, traditional weapons, and the management of long-range communications. Southern coastal populations attempting to fend off British invasion during the first Opium War effectively used some of these techniques.

The Opium War

Unlike the Ottomans, the Qing until the mid-1800s believed that the Europeans were remote and only casually interested in trade. They knew little of the enormous fortunes that European and American merchants in this period were reaping from smuggling opium into China. They did not know that silver gained in the illegal opium trade was financing part of the industrial transformation of locations such as Birmingham,

England, and Providence, Rhode Island. But, as Qing officials slowly learned, Britain was not far away. In India it had colonies where opium was grown. At Singapore, it had a major naval base through which it could transport opium to China and other parts of eastern Asia. Moreover, it was determined to right the trade imbalance that had occurred with China as a result of the tea trade, and opium seemed the key.

For more than a century, British officials had been dissatisfied with the enormous trade deficit between Britain and China. The deficit had resulted from the British demand for tea and the Qing failure to facilitate the importation to China of any British product (see Chapter 22). In the early 1700s, a few European merchants and their Chinese partners were importing small quantities of opium, and in 1729 the first Qing law making the importing of opium illegal was promulgated.

Historians have estimated that at the time as few as 200 chests of opium were being imported to China, and neither Britain nor the Qing considered opium a major issue. By 1800, however, smuggling had increased the quantity to as many as 4,000 chests a year. British merchants had discovered an extremely profitable trade, and a large Chinese commerce had arisen around the distribution of the drugs that foreigners brought to shore. Most devastating to Chinese society, however, was the dramatic increase in the early 1800s of the use of, and addiction to, the drug. British importers by then were competing with Americans, and a price war in the early 1820s raised demand sharply. By the 1830s as many as 30,000 chests were being imported, and addiction had spread to all levels of Chinese society. Many very high-ranking officials were affected.

For a time the Qing court debated whether to legalize opium and tax it or to enforce the existing ban on the drug more strictly. The decision was to root out the use and importation of opium, and in 1839 Lin Zexu was sent to Canton to deal with the matter.

The Qing insistence on banning the opium trade appeared to Britain an intolerable restraint on trade, a direct threat to Britain's economic

Lin Zexu

In early 1839, Lin Zexu resigned his post as a provincial governor in order to act as a special imperial commissioner at Canton. The court felt that local officials were so partial to the interests of the Canton merchants that enforcement of the new anti-opium policy would be impossible without an agent as determined and as honest as Lin Zexu. In the short term, the combined Chinese and European merchants were no match for Lin: they surrendered their opium and a majority signed bonds swearing they would import no more.

Shortly afterward Lin wrote to Queen Victoria, hoping to persuade her to prevent British merchants from continuing the opium trade.

We find that your country is [very far] from China. Yet there are barbarian ships that strive to come here for trade for the purpose of making a great profit. . . . That is to say, the great profit made by barbarians is all taken from the rightful share of China. By what right do they in return use the poisonous drug to injure the Chinese people? Even though the barbarians may not necessarily intend to do us harm, yet in coveting profit to an extreme, they have no regard for injuring others. Let us ask, where is your conscience? I have heard that the smoking of opium is very strictly forbidden by your country; that is because the harm caused by opium is clearly understood. Since it is not permitted to do harm to your own country, then even less should you let it be passed on to the harm of other countries—how much less to China! Of all that China exports to foreign countries, there is not a single thing which is not beneficial to people: they are of benefit when eaten, or of benefit when used, or of benefit when resold: all are beneficial. Is there a single article from China that has done harm to other countries?"

When open warfare broke out between the Qing and British empires, Lin was blamed by the governments of both coun- tries for the conflict. The Qing court banished him to the remote Xinjiang province. In a letter to a friend he reflected upon the consequences of the empire's technology gap with Britain.*

"When I was in office in [Canton] I had made plans regarding the problems of ships and cannon and a water force. Afraid that there was not enough time to build ships, I at first rented them. Afraid that there was not enough time to cast cannon and that it would not be done according to the regulations, I at first bought foreign ones. The most painful thing was that when the [harbor] was broken into, a large number of good cannon fell into the hands of the rebellious barbarians. I recall that after I had been punished two years ago, I still took the risk of calling the Emperor's attention to two things: ships and guns."

Lin's appreciation of the dangers of losing advanced weapons to the enemy foreshadowed many of the dangers of the later period of the Taiping conflict. Though his analysis of the predicament the empire had found itself in because of its neglect of technology was penetrating, it was also very late, and by the time Lin came to this conclusion the Qing was already in the process of coming under the constant pressure from European powers and the United States that made systematic, centralized reforms very difficult to accomplish.

How do the attitudes in these two passages from Lin's writings contrast to each other?

How do they compare to the attitudes of Ottoman elites in the 1830s and 1840s?

Source: Adapted from Teng and Fairbank, *China's Response to the West:* 24–29.

health, and indirectly a cause for war. The British declared war when their naval and marine forces arrived off the coast of China in late 1839. The significance of naval power, which the Ottomans had appreciated but had not mastered in the Mediterranean and Black Seas, was understood by the Qing slowly. Indeed, the difference between a naval invasion and piracy was not clear to Qing strategists until the first Opium War was nearly over.

The Opium War that lasted from 1839 to 1842 exposed the fact that the traditional, hereditary soldiers of the Qing Empire—the Bannermen—were, like the Janissaries of the Ottoman Empire, hopelessly obsolete. The war had been fought mostly from the sea. British ships landed troops who pillaged coastal cities and then returned to their ships and sailed to new destinations. The Qing had no national navy at all, and until they were able to engage the British in prolonged fighting on land, they were unable to defend themselves against the attacks. Even in the land engagements, Qing resources proved spectacularly inadequate. The British could quickly move their forces by ship along the coast and land them at strategic sites. Qing troops moved primarily by walking. The movement of Qing reinforcements from central China to eastern China took more than three months.

Once the Qing defense forces arrived, they were not only exhausted but basically without weapons. Against the British invaders the Bannermen used the few muskets the empire had imported during the 1700s. These weapons were unreliable and unsafe. They were matchlocks, requiring the soldiers to ignite the load of gunpowder in the gun barrel by hand. Firing the weapons was dangerous, and the canisters of gunpowder that each musketeer carried on his belt were likely to explode if a fire broke out on the battlefield—a frequent occurrence in encounters with the artillery of the British. Most of the Bannermen, however, were without guns and were forced to fight, if they got the chance, with swords, knives, spears, and clubs.

The soldiers under British command—many of whom were Indians from South Asia—carried rifles fired by percussion caps, far quicker, safer, and more accurate than the Qing soldiers' antique matchlocks. The long-distance artillery of the British was flexible and deadly in the cities and villages of eastern China.

The Qing commanders believed that the British gunboats would be too large and heavy to sail upriver and that evacuating people from the coasts would protect China from the British threat. They were mistaken. New gunboats like the *Nemesis* could proceed in shallow water and sailed without difficulty up the Yangzi River.

When the invaders approached Nanjing, the revered former Ming capital, the Qing decided to negotiate an end to the war. In 1842 the terms of the Treaty of Nanking were concluded. The treaty guaranteed "most-favored nation" status to Britain, meaning that any privileges granted to future signatories of treaties with China would also accrue to Britain. This system would in effect prevent the colonization of Chinese territory, because giving land to one Western country would necessitate giving it to all. The British established their rights of residence in five Chinese "treaty ports," a very low tariff on imports, and a long-standing debt of the Qing Empire to Britain in the form of an indemnity, or penalty for having started the war. Soon after, an American treaty established extraterritoriality and legalized the right of foreigners to import opium to China. French treaties later established the rights of foreign missionaries to travel extensively in the Chinese countryside and preach their religion.

European Pressures and Privilege

The treaty system in China resulted in the colonization of very small pockets of Qing territory, where foreign merchants, missionaries, and their military guards lived but Qing law did not apply. This was the same extraterritorial system that existed in the Ottoman Empire and elsewhere in Asia. As in the Ottoman Empire, the greatest territorial losses for the Qing rulers resulted from the actual or nominal independence of the regions they had dominated. In the early 1800s, both Britain and Russia were actively trying to erase the last vestiges of Qing sovereignty from Central Asia. In the late 1800s France would force the court of Vietnam to end its vassalage to the Qing, while Britain encouraged Tibetan independence. But it was Japan that snapped the critical Qing hold over Korea.

There were small but violent conflicts between Japanese and Chinese forces in Korea in the 1870s and 1880s, and in the 1890s Japan sponsored a movement for Korean national independence from China. By the end of the century Japan had by force or the threat of force taken from the Qing the Liuqiu Islands (including Okinawa) and Taiwan and had established military domination over Korea.

An important result of the treaty system was the creation of small urban pockets and some rural channels where there was intense exposure to Western people, culture, and economic power. In Canton, Shanghai, and some other coastal cities, Westerners were seen entertaining themselves in exclusive restaurants and bars, maintaining offices and factories where all but a few of the Chinese people present were engaged in menial labor, or building comfortable housing in zones where they refused to allow the Chinese to live. Around the foreign establishments, gambling and prostitution offered employment to some of the urban "floating population."

Often, Chinese regarded the work of Christian missionaries both in the cities and in the countryside as benevolent, as when the congregations sponsored hospitals, shelters, and soup kitchens or gave out stipends to Chinese men and women who attended church on Sundays. But just as often the missionaries themselves were regarded by local people as an additional evil. At every turn they seemed to subvert Confucian beliefs, whether by condemning ancestor worship, pressuring poor families to put their children into orphanages, or denouncing footbinding. The growing numbers of Westerners, and their growing privileges, quickly became a target of resentment for a deeply dissatisfied, daily more impoverished, and increasingly militarized society.

The Taiping Rebellion

The most startling demonstration of the inflammatory mixture of social unhappiness and foreign intrusion was the Taiping Rebellion (see Map 27.2). The region of Guangxi where the Taiping movement originated was an example of the entrenched social problems that had been generating disorders throughout the empire for a half-century. Agriculture in the region was unstable, and many people made their living from arduous and despised trades such as carrying human waste, producing charcoal, and mining.

Economic distress was complicated by ethnic divisions. A minority group, the Hakkas, were frequently to be found in the lowliest trades, and tensions between them and the majority were rising.

All these factors were significant in the experience of Hong Xiuquan (1813–1864), the founder of the Taiping movement. He came from a humble Hakka background, and after years of study competed in the provincial Confucian examinations, hoping for a post in government. He failed the examinations repeatedly, and in his late thirties he seems to have suffered a nervous breakdown. Afterward he spent some time in Canton and there met both Chinese and American missionaries of Protestant Christianity, who inspired him with their teachings. Hong, however, had his own interpretation of the Christian message. He saw himself as the younger brother of Jesus, commissioned by God to found a new kingdom on earth and drive the Manchu conquerors, the Qing, out of China. The result would be universal peace, and Hong called his new religious movement the "Heavenly Kingdom of Great Peace" (*Taiping tianguo*).

Beginning with a circle of friends and relatives, Hong quickly amassed a community of believers, primarily Hakkas, around him at Thistle Mountain in Guangxi. Their ideas and their practices alarmed the local people. The Taipings believed in the prophecy of dreams, and they claimed they could walk on air. Hong and his rivals for leadership in the movement went in and out of ecstatic trances. They denounced the Manchus as creatures of Satan. News of the heresy reached the government, and Qing troops were dispatched to arrest the Taiping leaders. But the imperial troops were soundly repelled. Local loyalty to the Taipings spread quickly, their numbers multiplied, and they began to enlarge their domain.

At first it appears that the Taipings relied on Hakka sympathies and the charismatic appeal of their religious doctrine to attract followers. But as their numbers and power grew, they altered their methods of preaching and governing. They stopped enlisting Hakkas against the majority and began to enlist the majority against the Manchus. They forced the populations of cap-

Advance of the Taipings Units of the Taiping army were strictly divided between men and women, but women were fully included in the work of the Taiping communities. They were also mobilized on the field of battle, as shown here. The minority Hakka group had never practiced footbinding, and as other peoples—including the majority Han Chinese—were pressed into the Taiping units, the ban on footbinding was extended to them. (Culver Pictures)

tured villages to join their movement, and once people were absorbed, their activities were strictly monitored. Men and women were segregated and organized into work and military teams. Women were forbidden to bind their feet (foot binding had never been a practice of the Hakkas) and participated fully in farming and laboring. Brigades of women soldiers took to the field against the Qing forces.

As the Taiping movement grew, it edged toward eastern and northern China. Panic preceded them. Villagers feared being forced into the Taiping units, and the Confucian elites recoiled in horror from the bizarre ideology of foreign gods, of totalitarian rule, and of walking, working, warring women. Local officials and gentry led the self-defense works, first repairing and strengthening village and town walls, then provisioning the communities within them, then arming and drilling the male residents. In the early 1850s these attempts at local defense were overwhelmed by the huge numbers the Taipings

were able to muster in their campaigns in the central provinces of China. But soon the local communities began to achieve greater success with their defenses. When, in 1853, the Taiping armies crossed the Yangzi River and made their way to Nanjing, their momentum was slowing, and they were looking for a permanent base.

Qing military commanders were already gaining some ground in their attempts to stem the spread of the Taipings. The empire's successes were mainly due to the flexibility of the commanders of the imperial forces in the face of this unprecedented challenge. The military commanders were also powerfully backed by a group of civilian provincial governors who had studied the techniques that local militia forces used for self defense. In essence, certain of the provincial governors, foremost Zeng Guofan, combined their knowledge of civilian self defense and local terrain with more efficient organization and the use of modern weaponry. The result was the formation of new military units in which many of the Bannermen voluntarily served under civilian governors. The Qing court agreed to special taxes to fund the new armies and acknowledged the new combined leadership of the civilian and professional force. When the Taipings settled into Nanjing, these new armies quickly surrounded that city, hoping to starve out the rebels.

This was not easily done. The Taipings had provisioned and fortified themselves well. Also, they had the advantage of several brilliant young military commanders who at intervals mobilized enormous campaigns that moved through nearby parts of eastern China, scavenging supplies and attempting to break the encirclement of Nanjing. For more than a decade the Taiping leadership remained ensconced at Nanjing, and their "Heavenly Kingdom" endured. The Qing forces had contained the rebellion, but there was no certainty that they could eradicate it.

By 1856, Britain and France were concerned about the situation in China and freed from their preoccupation with the Crimean War. European and American missionaries had visited Nanjing,

Nanjing encircled   For a decade the Taipings held the city of Nanjing as their capital. For years imperial and international troops attempted to break the Taiping hold. By summer of 1864 the imperial forces had built tunnels leading to the foundations of the Nanjing city walls and planted explosives in them. The detonation of the explosives signalled the final Qing assault upon the rebel capital. As shown here, the common people of the city, along with their starving livestock, were caught in the cross-fire first. Many of the Taiping leaders escaped the debacle at Nanjing, through nearly all were hunted down and executed. (Roger-Viollet)

Bannermen at rest The Qing emperors were never successful in completely replacing the traditional military, the Bannermen, with a modern army. Since Bannerman status was hereditary, the number of Bannermen soon outgrew the ability of the imperial government to support them. Law and custom nevertheless pressured a large number of Bannermen to continue to live in their distinct communities, though a majority were unemployed and very poor. They were easy targets in time of civil strife. During the Taiping Rebellion, tens of thousands of Bannermen and their families were slaughtered. (Royal Asiatic Society, London)

curious to see what their fellow Christians were up to. The reports they sent home were surprising and, for the faithful, discouraging. Hong Xiuquan and the other leaders appeared to lead lives of indulgence and abandon, and more than one missionary accused them of homosexual practices. Now having no fear of being accused of quashing an appealing Christian movement, the British and French considered the situation.

Although the Taipings were not going to topple the Qing, the outbreak of a new rebellion in northern China, the Nian Rebellion, in the 1850s was ominous, for a series of simultaneous large

insurrections might indeed destroy the empire. Perhaps more important, Britain and France were now considering making war on the Qing themselves, again. The Qing had not observed the provisions of the treaties signed after the first Opium War, and European patience was exhausted. How would the Qing survive both multiple domestic wars and another foreign assault?

The decision was to make a swift, brutal series of coastal attacks which began in 1856 and culminated in a British and French invasion of Beijing in 1860, followed by a new round of treaties punishing the Qing for not enacting the provisions of the treaties that followed the Opium War of 1839 to 1842. When the new wars were concluded, British and French forces joined the Qing in the campaign against the Taipings. Attempts to coordinate the international forces were sometimes riotous and sometimes tragic, but the injection of European weaponry and money aided in the quelling of both the Taiping and the Nian Rebellions during the 1860s.

The Taiping Rebellion ranks as the world's bloodiest civil war and greatest armed conflict before the twentieth century (see Map 27.2). Estimates of deaths in the years of fighting between 1850 and 1864 range between 20 million and 30 million. The loss of life was due primarily to starvation and disease, since most engagements consisted of surrounding the enemy in walled fortifications and waiting until they died, surrendered, or were so weakened that they could be vanquished easily. Many sieges continued for a year or more, and the populations of some cities found that after starving for a year under the occupation of the rebels, they would be starved for another year under occupation of the imperial forces. Reports of the eating of grass, leather, hemp, and human flesh were widespread. The dead were rarely buried properly, and epidemic disease was common in the war zone.

The area of early Taiping fighting was close to the regions of southwest China where bubonic plague had been lingering for centuries. When the rebellion was suppressed, many Taiping adherents sought safety in the highlands of Laos and Annam (Vietnam). These areas soon showed infestation by plague, and within a few years the disease had reached Hongkong. From there it spread to Singapore, San Francisco, Calcutta, and London. So the late 1800s saw not only a brief revival of bubonic plague but intense fear over the possibility of a worldwide outbreak. In Europe and America, Chinese immigrants were suspected as likely carriers.

Internal and External Restructuring

The agricultural centers of China were devastated in the Taiping Rebellion. Many of the most intensely and successfully cultivated regions of central and eastern China were depopulated and laid barren after years of fighting. By the late 1800s some were still uninhabited, and provincial population figures suggest that major portions of the country did not recover until the twentieth century.

Cities, too, were hit very hard. Shanghai, which was primarily known as a foreign treaty port and had been modest in size before the Taiping Rebellion, saw its population multiply many times with the arrival of refugees from the war-blasted neighboring provinces. The city itself had been under attack by the Taipings and with its bloated population endured months without food supplies. Major cultural centers in eastern China lost masterpieces of art and architecture, imperial libraries were burned or their collections were exposed to the weather, and not only books but the printing blocks used to make the books were destroyed.

The Qing government emerged from this civil war with no hope of achieving solvency again. Even before the uprising at Thistle Mountain in 1850, the Qing treasury had been bankrupted by the corruption of the 1700s, by the attempts of the very early 1800s to restore waterworks and roads, by declining yields from land taxes, and by the geometrically increasing burden of indemnities demanded by Europeans in treaties that followed the Opium War. By about 1850, the Qing government was already spending about ten times what it took in. The Taiping Rebellion worsened this situation profoundly. Vast stretches of what had once been productive rice land were devastated. The population was dispersed. Immediate relief for refugees was demanded. The array of imperial, volunteer, foreign, and mercenary troops that had suppressed the Taipings was demanding that their unpaid wages, provisions, and weapons costs be made good.

With the Qing government so profoundly in their debt, Britain and France became active participants in the period of recovery in China that followed conclusion of the Taiping Rebellion. This period of political quiescence and remedial economic development is sometimes called the "Tongzhi Restoration," since it occurred during the reign of the Tongzhi emperor (1862–1875). To ensure that the Qing government began repaying at least a portion of its debt to Britain, Robert

Hart was installed as inspector-general of a newly created Imperial Maritime Customs Service. The revenues he collected were split between Britain and the Qing. Britons and Americans put themselves in the employ of the Qing government as advisers and ambassadors, attempting to smooth communications between the Qing, Europe, and the United States while the Chinese imperial government started up the diplomatic machinery demanded by Europe in its latest treaties.

The real work of the recovery, however, was managed by the civilian provincial governors who had come to the forefront in the struggle against the Taipings. To prosecute the war, they had gained from the Qing court permission to levy their own taxes, raise their own troops, and run their own bureaucracies. These special powers were not entirely canceled when the war ended. Chief among these governors was Zeng Guofan, who in the 1860s oversaw not only programs to restore agriculture, communications, education, and publishing, but also attempts to start programs for reform and industrialization that would be necessary to regain some measure of independence for China.

Like many provincial governors, Zeng preferred to look to the United States—rather than

Cixi's allies Though in the 1860s and 1870s Cixi was a supporter of reformers, in her later years she was widely regarded as corrupt, self-centered, and the primary obstacle to reform. Her greatest allies were the court eunuchs. First introduced to palace life as managers of the imperial harems, the eunuchs became powerful political parties at court in early China. At first the Qing emperors refused to allow the eunuchs any political influence, but by Cixi's time the eunuchs were once again a political factor. (Freer Gallery, Smithsonian Institution)

to Britain—for models and aid. He hired American advisers to run his arsenals for the manufacture of modern weapons, his shipyards, and his military academies. He sponsored a daring program in which promising Chinese boys were sent not to traditional Confucian academies but to Hartford, Connecticut, to be educated in English, science, mathematics, engineering, and history. They returned to China to assume some of the positions that foreign advisers had previously held in Zeng's industries and schools. Although Zeng was never an advocate of participation by women in public life, he was a firm adherent of the Confucian elite view that educated mothers were a necessity, perhaps now more than ever—and he not only encouraged but partly oversaw the advanced classical education of his own daughters. Among the provincial governors, Zeng was esteemed as the most capable, loyal, incorruptible, and flexible. His death in 1872 deprived the empire of a major force for vigorous reform.

The period of recovery marked a fundamental structural change in the Qing Empire. After the Taiping Rebellion, the emperors were ineffective rulers, but a coalition of members of the aristocracy supported the reform and recovery programs. If they had been unwilling to legitimate the new powers of governors such as Zeng Guofan, the empire might have evaporated within a generation. A crucial member of this alliance was Cixi (1835–1908), after the 1880s known as the "Empress Dowager." Though later observers, both Chinese and foreign, reviled her as a monster of corruption and arrogance, in the 1860s and 1870s Cixi was a supporter of the provincial governors, some of whom became so powerful that they were managing Qing foreign policy as well as domestic affairs.

Instead of a conquest regime dominated by a Manchu military caste and its Chinese civilian appointees, the empire was now controlled by a group of reformist aristocrats and military men, independently powerful civilian governors, and a small number of foreign advisers. But in the complex international situation, the Qing now lacked strong, central, unified leadership. Moreover, the powers of taxation, legislation, and military command could not be recovered once they had been granted to the provincial governors. From the 1860s forward, the Qing Empire fragmented into a set of large power zones in which leadership was handed by governors to their protégés.

JAPAN, FROM SHOGUNATE TO EMPIRE

In the early 1800s, the Tokugawa shogunate in Japan also responded to the threat of foreign invasion by attempting to strengthen its finances and its military forces exclusively. But unlike the Qing and Ottoman empires, the Tokugawa government was fundamentally decentralized by design, and decentralization prevented the state from forming and carrying out a single policy that would have resisted European and American encroachment. Instead, some of the regional governments of Japan, which did not trust the Tokugawa shogunate to have the ability or the will to protect the islands, developed their own reformed armies, arsenals, and shipyards.

The arrival of a small American fleet in 1853 with demands for an opening of Japan to trade with the United States started a process that in 1868 ended with the destruction of the Tokugawa shogunate by leaders of the most powerful provinces. They banded together to create a profound political, economic, and technological transformation of Japan. Within an astoundingly short period of time, Japan joined several of the European sea empires and the United States at the pinnacle of international power and prestige (see Map 27.4).

Collapse of the Shogunate

By the 1800s, several of the regional provinces were much wealthier and more ambitious than others. This was particularly true of Satsuma and

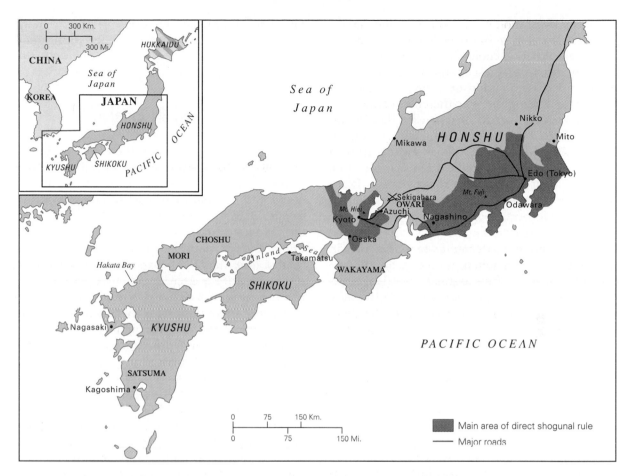

Map 27.4 Japan in the 1800s The Tokugawa shogunate was the last of the decentralized governments of Japan that had put primary power into the hands of a military leader and protector of the emperor since medieval times. In the Tokugawa case, provincial leaders at the western extreme of Honshu island—regarded as undesirable sites in the early Tokugawa period—experienced higher rates of economic growth and managerial innovation than did the central provinces. In eastern Honshu, the provincial leaders were exploiting the northern island of Hokkaido, which in the 1800s was only beginning to reveal its potential for development in the industries of fishing, mining, and animal husbandry.

Choshu, two large provinces in southern Japan. Because the ancestors of their ruling houses had not been supporters of the Tokugawa lineage (see Chapter 22), they were chastised by being given sparsely settled lands far from the shogunal court at Edo (present-day Tokyo). Over time, this relatively remote location proved to be a distinct advantage. The ability of these regions to rapidly expand their agricultural base when centrally located regions had reached their limit allowed them to enjoy high rates of growth in revenue and population during the early 1800s. The remoteness and the economic vigor of these provinces also fostered local self-reliance. When, in the late 1700s, Choshu was alarmed by the arrival of Russian and British ships, the local lords began to prepare to defend themselves against a possible invasion—with or without the aid of the shogunate.

The economic and political weakness of the shogunate prompted some leaders in the Tokugawa government to attempt a restrengthening, primarily by placing new burdens on the hereditary provincial governors. Some academies for aspiring soldiers, scholars, and bureaucrats in the provinces became centers for the development and dissemination of a new ideology of loyalty to the shoguns, who depended on the politically weak emperors of Japan for their legitimacy. But the arrival of the American Commodore Matthew C. Perry and his fleet in 1853 shattered the shoguns' attempts to restore their influence across the provinces. Perry promised to return in 1854, and demanded that Japan open its ports to American ships for refueling and for trade.

The commodore's demand sparked a crisis in the shogunate. Consultation among the provincial governors and the shogunal officials was extensive. Finally, the shogunal advisers advocated capitulation to Perry. They pointed to the demonstration of foreign power to which China had been subjected, and they expressed doubt that the treaty powers in China would be discouraged from seeking other ports in East Asia. Those arguing for rejecting Perry's demands pointed out that the British and the Americans were not the same people, and that the Americans could not both protect their merchants in China and also initiate an invasion of Japan.

When Perry's fleet returned in 1854, representatives of the Tokugawa shogun indicated their willingness to sign the Treaty of Kanagawa—modeled on the unequal treaties between the West and China. The signing occurred in 1858. Some provincial governors, angry and disappointed, began to encourage an underground movement calling for the destruction of the Tokugawa regime and expulsion of foreigners from Japan.

Tensions between the shogunate and some provinces increased in the early 1860s. At first the ambitious provincial leaders were struggling against each other, hoping to gain an individual advantage in the coming struggle to depose the Tokugawa shoguns. But samurai strategists in Satsuma, Choshu, and other large provinces concluded that the rebellious provinces would do better to join forces, and in 1867 these allied provinces declared war on the Tokugawa. The fighting was intense but brief. In 1868, a new government was founded, and the young emperor Mutsuhito (r. 1868–1912) was declared "restored."

The "Meiji Restoration"

It was one thing to destroy the old state, but it was another to assemble a new state that had the resources and the experience to deal with economic and military problems. Although Japan is smaller than the landmass of either the Qing or the Ottoman Empires, its many islands are far-flung, and its natural resources are extremely limited (see Map 27.3). So the size of Japan was not necessarily a decisive advantage in the apparent ease with which it was reformed.

Perhaps more important was the fact that, unlike the Qing and Ottoman Empires, Japan was of no great strategic importance to Europe or to the United States. American merchants theorized that Japan, like China, would be a rich market for their goods, and American naval planners wished to have a reprovisioning station in Japan to facilitate their movements along the China coast. But neither of these considerations would have propelled the United States to have begun a war with Japan in the 1850s, and the European powers showed only a casual interest in Japan. Thus there was no foreign effort to sustain the Tokugawa shogunate economically or strategically. When it was destroyed, the strategists were unimpeded in their plans for a centralized, industrialized national state.

The new state was known by Mutsuhito's reign name, *Meiji*, meaning "brilliant rule." The ideology of the state was one source of its power. The new leaders claimed that by "restoring" the emperor they had ended centuries of imperial seclusion and disempowerment by the shoguns. Taking advantage of the mystique of the emperor, nationalism, and anxiety over the foreign threat, for a decade the leaders focused efforts to transform Japan from a decentralized, traditional military government to a centralized, civil, industrializing state. The distinctively nationalistic ideology of the "Restoration" coexisted in the early

Meiji period with an intense interest in European practices in government, education, industry, and dress, and sometimes in popular culture.

The achievements of the Meiji Restoration were remarkable. A group of extraordinarily talented and farsighted men—often referred to as the "Meiji oligarchs"—oversaw the military and political reforms. They overcame regional resistance to political and social reform, and gradually but systematically they brought about the downfall of the traditional provincial governors and of their own samurai class. Although the Tokugawa government had been impoverished, in some of the provinces there was wealth, and throughout the country the literacy rate may have been as high as 35 percent. This was the highest literacy rate in Asia at the time, and the oligarchs shrewdly exploited it in their introduction of new educational systems, a conscript army, and new communications. Judicious deficit financing without extensive foreign debt paid for heavy industry, thanks to the decades of experimentation with industrial development and financing in the provinces in the earlier 1800s.

With a conscript army and a revamped educational system the oligarchs attempted to create a citizenry that was literate, competent, and loyal. When nationalistic passions ran high and threatened to disrupt the political process, they permitted a small incursion into Korean territory in 1874. It resulted in Japan forcing on Korea a treaty modeled on the treaty that Commodore Perry had forced on Japan.

European music, dance, literature, dress, architecture, theater, and political systems were all popular in Japan after the Restoration. Then as tensions with the European powers in East Asia mounted in the later 1800s, a nativist movement appeared. As Japan approached the end of the century, the unwillingness of the oligarchs to permit the development of institutions for popular participation in policymaking took its toll. A constitution issued in 1890 was a design for an authoritarian system that legislated imperial charisma, institutionalized military prestige, and strictly limited the role of political leaders. As Japan's military security and economic influence

Yamagata Aritomo The young provincial leaders who banded together to overthrow the Tokugawa shogunate in 1867–1868 overcame regional rivalries and many personal conflicts to form a new government. Though the Meiji leaders were brilliant in guiding Japan out of the dangers of subjugation to the powers of Europe and the United States, in initiating the industrialization of the country and modernizing its military, they distrusted emerging political parties, which they regarded as short-sighted and corruptible. Yamagata Aritomo, who designed the modern army and its educational policies, remained a formidable force in Japanese policymaking until his death in 1922. (Asahi Shimbun Photo)

increased in the late 1800s, the new empire was accepted into the international power elite that held the fate of the Qing Empire and of Korea, Okinawa, Annam (Vietnam), and the Philippines in its hands. At the same time, however, the Japanese political system remained undeveloped, heavily dependent on personal authority, and unable to adapt either to the passing of the oligarchs or to domestic crises.

CONCLUSION

The response of Japan to the challenge of the industrializing nations was a striking contrast to outcomes in the Ottoman and Qing Empires. An important point of comparison is the relationship between financial resources and top-down reform. In the Ottoman and Qing (as well as the Romanov) Empires, the courts attempted to mandate reforms in the military. To meet the cost, these revenue-starved empires debased their currencies and thereby stimulated inflation. To continue the reforms, they became dependent on loans from the Western powers, which ultimately gained control of their finances, their commercial strategies, and in some cases their revenue-producing organs. Japan, in contrast, experienced comparatively few top-down major reforms under the Tokugawa shoguns. Instead, the decentralized provinces provided their own means of experimenting with local military improvement, new educational programs, and deficit financing before the Meiji Restoration of 1868. Afterward, they could compare their experiences and apply what they had learned.

Japan's exposure to the military and economic pressure of the Western sea powers was also much more limited than that of the Ottoman and Qing Empires. One reason for this difference was that Japan was not an empire in the same sense that the Ottoman and Qing were empires. Japan did not control extensive trade networks and urban centers to which Britain and France wished to gain privileged access. Nor was its position, on the far side of the Eurasian continent, regarded as strategically significant by the Western powers. The American treaty that Commodore Perry forced on Japan was virtually Japan's only experience with "unequal treaties." In contrast, the terms demanded by the British in the Treaty of Nanking of 1842 were harsh, and it ushered in the period of "unequal treaties" that resulted in the installation of a vast system of foreign privilege in China. European and American pressure on the Qing Empire became so intense in this period that the Chinese could neither learn to finance the industries necessary for a strong military nor find a period of peace in which to develop the educational institutions that would have produced a new generation of leaders.

The oligarchs of Japan hoped that its relatively remote location and relatively insignificant political status would protect Japan from Western domination. The Qing and the Ottoman rulers could only hope that mutual distrust among the European powers would limit the ambitions of any individual European state. In China, this strategy was referred to as "using the barbarians against the barbarians." But it meant that the Qing Empire was continually embroiled in short, rather localized wars—or threatened wars—with aspiring signatories in the "unequal treaty" system. With each round of treaties came a new round of privileges to be distributed among the European and American participants. With each round of treaties, the number of treaty ports grew, too, so that by the end of the 1800s they numbered more than ninety.

In the Ottoman Empire, as in the Qing territories, it was not necessary for Europeans or Americans to establish colonies in order to enjoy privileged status. They had pockets of wealth—primarily in the cities—that could be exploited, and exploitation was best done through strategic alliances or diplomatic instruments, not by the expensive and risky methods of colonization. It is not a coincidence that both of the empires whose territorial integrity the European powers—and, in the case of China, the United States—swore themselves to defend were ultimately derided as "sick men" of Eurasia, unable to defend themselves against their "defenders," and kept in a state of low-grade survival to provide markets, raw materials, and strategic advantages to smaller, more dynamic nations.

In Japan, as in China, long-standing social tensions combined with foreign provocation to spark a civil war. But in Japan the war was short, featured little foreign involvement, and ended in a clean break with the former political system. In China, the civil war was long and monstrously destructive of life, economy, and culture, and it gradually incorporated massive involvement of foreign weapons and advisers. In this sense the

Taiping Rebellion shared with the Crimean War the distinction of being part of a set of very large and extremely bloody wars of the middle 1800s—including the American Civil War (see Chapter 25) and the Indian "Mutiny," or "Sepoy Rebellion" (see Chapter 26). These conflicts saw the application of far more lethal technologies, the invention of new generations of killing machines, and the resulting slaughter of soldiers and civilians at a rate never before witnessed.

The Crimean War and the Taiping Rebellion were watershed points in the loss of centralization and autonomy for the Ottoman and Qing Empires, respectively. The processes bear some striking similarities, not least of which was that in each conflict the empire in question emerged as nominally victorious. Both land-based Eurasian empires were overextended. They suffered from declining revenues and social dislocation, to which the state had made a limited reformist response. Ironically, there remained in these empires enclaves of merchants and artisans who were enriched by the trade with Europe and America, but the empires never found a way of taxing these new incomes.

Much domestic wealth flowed from the Ottoman and Qing Empires to the West in payment for legal as well as illegal commodities, although these states could not find resources for arms and education. Increasing pressure from Britain and France deepened the financial woes and political tensions of the two empires and heightened elite Ottoman and Qing awareness of the necessity for military reform. During the wars themselves, the financial obligations of the empires and the strategic advantages of their existence led to the formation of alliances with Britain and France. And in the aftermath of the conflicts, the empires experienced serious problems with decentralization, a loss of control over their borders, permanent indebtedness and inflation, a progressive loss of international and domestic credibility, and dependence on foreign protection.

The differences between the Ottoman and Qing are also illuminating. Before the end of the 1700s, the Ottomans made an attempt to modernize their military and make their government more efficient. Their proximity to Europe gave them direct experience with the Napoleonic era and the rising nationalism of the 1800s. The intense struggle between France and Russia gave the Ottomans a strategic position that made it distinctly to the advantage of France to side with the Ottomans in their territorial struggles. For their part, the Ottomans were comparatively swift in their adaptation of aspects of French culture, military practices, and commercial institutions. This adaptability sustained Ottoman political credibility in Europe through the critical period of the war for Greek independence, and it later allowed design and implementation of the reform program under Mahmud II that through the middle of the 1800s recentralized the Ottoman state. On the strength of that recentralization, the secular programs that defined a civil sphere and a Turkish identity gave strength to the very nationalist movement that eventually helped destroy the Ottoman Empire.

Unlike the Ottomans, the Qing were not able to achieve even a modest degree of recentralization and reform before or after the Taiping Rebellion. Suppression of the rebellion required the systematic dissolution of the traditional military structures, regionalization of command and support, and the use of foreign commanders, soldiers, and weapons to end the civil war. The alliance formed by Britain and France at this time would become more active in the very late 1800s, as the European powers and the United States attempted repeatedly to prevent colonization of Qing territory by Japan. This was a local chapter in the growing global struggle to balance new emerging economic and military powers.

SUGGESTED READING

For the Ottoman Empire, there is a large and interesting literature, much based on original documents, some in translation, relating to Ottoman administration throughout Europe and the Middle East. Two widely available general histories are Stanford Shaw,

History of the Ottoman Empire and Modern Turkey (1976–1977), and J.P.D.B. Kinross, *The Ottoman Centuries: The Rise and Fall of the Turkish Empire* (1977).

On the economy and society of the nineteenth-century empire see Huri Islamoglu-Inan, ed., *The Ottoman Empire and the World-Economy* (1987); Sevket Pamuk, *The Ottoman Empire and European Capitalism, 1820–1913: Trade, Investment, and Production* (1987); Kemal H. Karpat, *Ottoman Population, 1830–1914: Demographic and Social Characteristics* (1985); and Carter V. Findley, *Bureaucratic Reform in the Ottoman Empire: The Sublime Porte, 1789–1922* (1980).

On the Qing Empire of the nineteenth century see Pamela Kyle Crossley, *Orphan Warriors: Three Manchu Generations and the End of the Qing World* (1990). For a more detailed political history see Mary C. Wright, *The Last Stand of Chinese Conservatism: The T'ung-chih Restoration, 1862–1874* (1971). There is a very large literature on both the Opium War and the Taiping Rebellion, including reprinted editions by contemporary observers. For general histories of the Opium War see Peter Ward Fay, *The Opium War, 1840–1842: Barbarians in the Celestial Empire in the Early Part of the Nineteenth Century and the War by Which They Forced Her Gates Ajar* (1975); Christopher Hibbert, *The Dragon Wakes: China and the West, 1793–1911* (1970); and the classic study by Chang Hsin-pao, *Commissioner Lin and the Opium War* 1964. For a recent, more scholarly treatment see James M. Polachek, *The Inner Opium War* (1992). Enduring sources on the Taiping Rebellion are S. Y. Têng, *The Taiping Rebellion and the Western Powers: A Comprehensive Survey* (1971), and C. A. Curwen, *Taiping Rebel: The Deposition of Li Hsiu-ch'eng* (1976). See also Caleb Carr, *The Devil Soldier: The Story of Frederick Townsend Ward* (1992). The most recent study is Jonathan D. Spence, *God's Chinese Son: The Taiping Heavenly Kingdom of Hong Xiuquan* (1996).

The classic work on the period leading to the Meiji Restoration in Japan is Albert M. Craig, *Choshu in the Meiji Restoration* (1961). See also Conrad Totman, *The Collapse of the Tokugawa Bakufu, 1862–1868* (1980); Bob Tadashi Wakabayashi, *Anti-Foreignism and Western Learning in Early-Modern Japan: The New Theses of 1825* (1986); Peter Booth Wiley with Korogi Ichiro, *Yankees in the Land of the Gods: Commodore Perry and the Opening of Japan* (1990); and George M. Wilson, *Patriots and Redeemers in Japan: Motives in the Meiji Restoration* (1992).

Global Dominance and Diversity,
1850–1945

The era of Western global hegemony includes two distinct periods: from 1850 to the outbreak of World War I in 1914, a period of increasing Western—and, to a lesser degree, Japanese—ascendancy over the nonindustrialized parts of the world; and the period of world wars from 1914 to 1945, a struggle among the industrialized countries for global dominance, in which the energies of millions of people were channeled into mass destruction.

From the mid-nineteenth to the mid-twentieth centuries, one cultural area dominated the rest of the world in a way that had never happened before. In a phenomenon that historians call the *New Imperialism*, the major nations of Europe extended their commercial and political influence over Africa and most of Asia, while the United States did the same in Latin America. One non-European country, Japan, escaped subordination to the West. By the end of the nineteenth century it had joined the Western powers in their imperialist expansion.

The preeminence of Europe, the United States, and Japan had many causes, but two, introduced in Part Six, were crucial. One was nationalism, a bond uniting the people of a state or territory who have a common culture or a shared history. The expanded participation of ordinary citizens in politics and the emergence of politicians who appealed to the general public were among the major consequences of the revolutions in England, America, and France (see Chapter 24). In those three nations, public participation eventu-

ally resulted in such democratic institutions as a free press, universal suffrage, and strong parliamentary institutions, and in the lessening or elimination of monarchial privileges. Elsewhere, mass participation and democratization did not always go hand in hand. In Germany and Russia, autocratic monarchies and conservative politicians learned to use nationalist feelings to mobilize mass support. Similarly, the leaders of Japan harnessed public opinion behind a program of rapid industrialization. Despite their differences, all those nations—whether democratic or authoritarian—competed for global influence and resources, first by building colonial empires and later by fighting one another.

The other cause of Western and Japanese power in this period was industrialization. As we saw in Chapter 23, the Industrial Revolution began in England in the mid-eighteenth century and spread to Europe and North America in the nineteenth. The period from 1850 to 1945 saw the introduction or the spread of automobiles, aircraft, electricity, steel, radio, motion pictures, home appliances, and other important innovations. Most of these technologies operated in large-scale networks that fostered the growth of powerful organizations such as corporations, labor unions, and state enterprises.

The array of new technologies and economic arrangements transformed the lives of people of all classes and professions—not always for the better. Industrialization increased the power and wealth of entrepreneurs, managers, and engineers but did little to help those whose income was derived from the land. Work increasingly took place in factories and offices, separating employment from home life, husbands from wives, children from parents. A growing proportion of married women became housewives, while compulsory education systems took over the care of children. The United States and Canada experienced the first wave of mass consumption in this period.

Intensifying industrial activities transformed the natural environment. Pollution from manufacturing, long a local problem, began to affect whole regions, such as the German Ruhr and the English Midlands. Cities like New York and London expanded into giant metropolitan areas. The industrial world's commercial and strategic dependence on raw materials from distant sources raised fears of depletion and sped the search for synthetic substitutes.

Warfare also was transformed by industrialization, as military forces adopted increasingly destructive weapons. These changes gave the first industrializing countries the means to conquer traditional societies. They also stimulated further the demand for foreign markets, resources, and military bases.

The same factors that had given Europe, the United States, and Japan such an advantage over the rest of the world were also the causes of their own worst troubles. Modern life, a product of industrialization, threatened older values and customs. Cycles of economic boom and bust worsened tensions between nations and social classes. Nationalism, which originally emphasized the bonds between the inhabitants of a particular state or territory, developed in the twentieth century into feelings of contempt for foreigners and ethnic minorities, especially in wartime.

Until 1914, Britain, France, and the United States dominated, in one way or another, over half of the area and peoples of the world. Others were less successful. Germany and Japan, latecomers to mass politics and industrialization, entered the competition for overseas colonial empires when few unconquered territories remained. Germany's desire to become a global power was a major cause of the First World War (1914–1918). Its defeat by France, Britain, and the United States did not restore the prewar equilibrium, as the victorious Allied nations had hoped. A major consequence of the war was a revolution in Russia that threatened to destabilize the rest of the world.

Technology

Industrial expansion

Mass production of consumer goods in the United States and
    western Europe

Railroad networks in Europe, North America, India, and Russia

Telegraphs (intercontinental from 1866) and telephones (from 1880s)

Construction of Suez (1869) and Panama (1914) Canals

From early twentieth century—automobiles, highways, airplanes in
    the United States and western Europe

New weapons and military technologies inspired by the world wars

Environment

Rise of mega-cities and industrial regions

Pollution from cities and factories

New lands opened in North and South America

Irrigation projects in India, Egypt, the United States, and Australia

Wartime environmental destruction

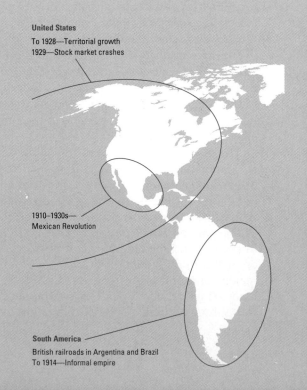

United States
To 1928—Territorial growth
1929—Stock market crashes

1910–1930s—
Mexican Revolution

South America
British railroads in Argentina and Brazil
To 1914—Informal empire

Shaky in the 1920s, the world economy collapsed in the Great Depression of the 1930s. The resulting social disruption allowed extremist politicians in Germany and Japan to take power. Once in office, they sought redress for the economic problems and perceived national humiliations by seizing the territories of their neighbors through intimidation or force.

Nationalism assumed its most hideous form in the Second World War (1937–1945). This conflict resulted from the social dislocations of the Depression and the territorial ambitions of the Japanese military and of Adolf Hitler, the dictator of Germany. By 1941, it was pitting Japan and Germany against Great Britain, the Soviet Union, and the United States, and the fighting had spread over half of the world. In addition to the enormous damage to cities and civilian populations caused by mechanized military forces, the war also encouraged racial hatreds and the deliberate massacre of millions of innocent people.

Nationalism and rivalries among the industrialized nations affected other areas of the world in radical ways. In Asia, Africa, and Latin America, domination by the great powers weakened traditional cultures and political structures, while population growth kept living standards low and put stress on the natural environment. The ideas that had made the West and Japan powerful inspired leaders of a new generation in Asia, Africa, and Latin America to attempt to rescue their people through revolutions of national liberation. Many of those new leaders had been educated in the West; others were influenced by the West; still others were motivated by their fear of growing Western interference. Their political aspirations gave voice to the distress of the poor—especially the peasants—brought on by population growth, economic ups and downs, and the dislocations of war. As the great powers fought each other for mastery of the world, non-Western societies prepared to overcome their long subjection. Mexico and China succeeded only after years of warfare and social upheaval. In contrast, India erupted in violent ethnic conflicts at the moment of independence.

The year 1945 marks the end of western European dominance. After the defeat of Germany and Japan in World War II, only the United States and the Soviet Union remained to compete for global influence. Meanwhile, nationalism was rapidly spreading to the rest of the world, bringing with it the urge to acquire the benefits and power of industrial technology.

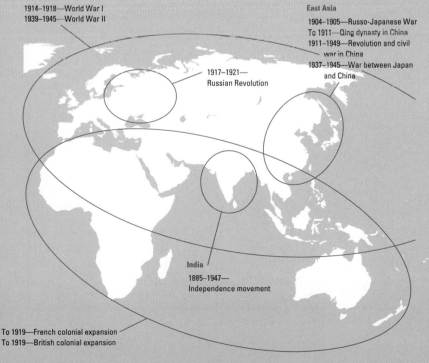

1914–1918—World War I
1939–1945—World War II

1917–1921—
Russian Revolution

East Asia
1904–1905—Russo-Japanese War
To 1911—Qing dynasty in China
1911–1949—Revolution and civil
   war in China
1937–1945—War between Japan
   and China

India
1885–1947—
Independence movement

To 1919—French colonial expansion
To 1919—British colonial expansion

Society

Expansion of nationalism and mass politics
Increased racial and ethnic tensions; maximum
   violence in Nazi Germany (1933–1945)
Escalation of mass migrations
To World War I—"Victorian" morality and gender
   relations (Europe and North America)
Independence movements in India (from 1885)
   and Middle East (from World War I)
Social revolutions and peasant uprisings in
   Mexico (from 1910), China (from 1911),
   and Russia (1917–1921)
1929–1940—Great Depression

Culture

Spread of Islam and Christianity in Africa
Revolution in physics
Spread of Marxism in Europe
New social sciences
From 1920s—mass media (North America
   and Europe)

CHAPTER TWENTY-EIGHT

The New Power Balance,

1850–1914

New Technologies and the World Economy · Social Transformations

Women and Gender Relations in the Victorian Age

Nationalism and the Unification of Germany

The Great Powers of Europe in the Late Nineteenth Century · Great Powers Overseas

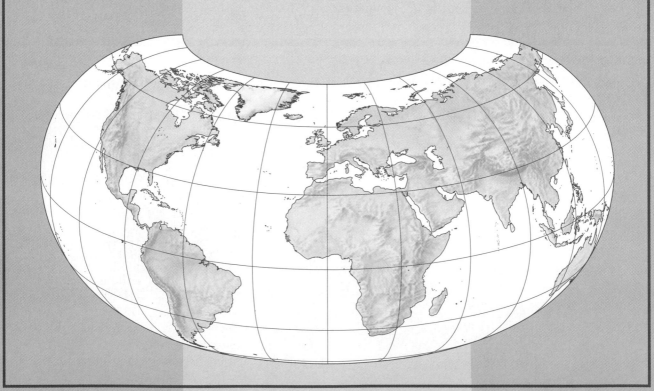

On January 18, 1871, in the great Hall of Mirrors of the palace of Versailles, King Wilhelm I of Prussia was proclaimed emperor of Germany before a crowd of officers and other German rulers. This ceremony marked the unification of many small German states into one nation. Off to one side stood Otto von Bismarck, the man responsible for the creation of a united Germany. A few years earlier, he had declared: "The great issues of the day will be decided not by speeches and votes of the majority—that was the great mistake of 1848 and 1849—but by iron and blood." Indeed it was "blood,"—that is, victories on the battlefield—rather than popular participation that had led to the unification of Germany; among the dignitaries in the Hall of Mirrors that day, only two or three were civilians. As for "iron," it meant not only weapons but, more important, the industries required to produce such weapons. Thus, after 1871, nationalism, once a dream of revolutionaries and romantics, became ever more closely associated with military forces and with industry.

In this chapter we will see how industry and nationalism transformed the economies and environments, the societies, and the politics of the great powers—Germany, France, Britain, Russia, the United States, and Japan—from 1850 to the start of World War I in 1914. This was an age when Western culture exalted the powerful over the weak, men over women, rich over poor, Europeans over other races. In the next chapter, which deals with the era of the "New Imperialism" (1870–1914), we will see how these nations used their power to conquer colonial empires in Asia and Africa and to control Latin America. Together, Chapters 28 and 29 describe an era in which a handful of wealthy industrialized nations—all but one of them of European culture—imposed on the other peoples of the world a domination more powerful than any experienced before or since.

NEW TECHNOLOGIES AND THE WORLD ECONOMY

After the mid-nineteenth century, industrialization took off in new directions. It spread to new countries, especially Germany and the United States, which soon surpassed Great Britain as the world's leading industrial powers. Small companies, like those that had flourished in Britain in the late eighteenth century, were overshadowed by large corporations, some owned by wealthy capitalists, others (especially in Russia and Japan) by governments.

New technologies, based on advances in physics and chemistry, revolutionized everyday life and transformed the world economy. Some of the inventions of this period—the automobile, airplane, and radio in particular—aroused tremendous excitement, but did not make an impact on people's lives until after World War I (see Chapter 30). Others advances, such as the steel and chemical industries, electricity, and the spreading networks of steamships, telegraphs, and railroads, were already important before 1914.

The Steel and Chemical Industries

Steel is a special form of iron, both hard and elastic. Until the eighteenth century, it could be made only by skilled blacksmiths in very small quantities at a very high cost and thus was reserved for swords, knives, axes, and watch springs. The invention of the crucible (a container in which molten iron was stirred until it turned to steel) in the 1740s made steel cheap enough for tools, weapons, and machines. By 1850 Britain was producing some 60,000 tons a year.

Then came a series of inventions that made steel the cheapest and most versatile metal ever known. In the 1850s, William Kelly, a Kentucky iron master, discovered that air forced through molten pig iron turned it into steel without additional fuel. In the 1860s the Englishman Henry

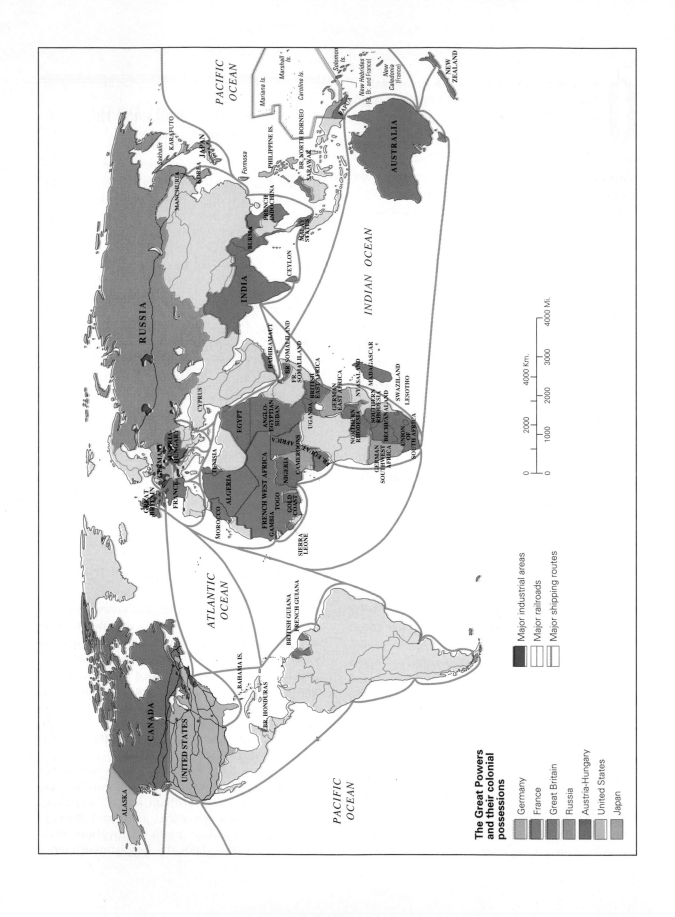

The Great Powers
and their colonial
possessions

Germany
France
Great Britain
Russia
Austria-Hungary
United States
Japan

Major industrial areas
Major railroads
Major shipping routes

PACIFIC OCEAN

ATLANTIC OCEAN

PACIFIC OCEAN

INDIAN OCEAN

ALASKA

CANADA

UNITED STATES

BR. HONDURAS

BAHAMA IS.

BRITISH GUIANA
FRENCH GUIANA

GREAT BRITAIN

FRANCE
GERMANY
AUSTRIA-HUNGARY

MOROCCO
ALGERIA
TUNISIA
GAMBIA
TOGO
GOLD COAST
SIERRA LEONE
FRENCH WEST AFRICA
NIGERIA
CAMEROONS
FR. EQUATORIAL AFRICA
GERMAN SOUTHWEST AFRICA
UNION OF SOUTH AFRICA
BECHUANALAND
SOUTHERN RHODESIA
NORTHERN RHODESIA
GERMAN EAST AFRICA
UGANDA
ANGLO-EGYPTIAN SUDAN
EGYPT
BR. SOMALILAND
FR. SOMALILAND
HADHRAMAUT
BRITISH EAST AFRICA
NYASALAND
MADAGASCAR
SWAZILAND
LESOTHO

CYPRUS

RUSSIA

INDIA
CEYLON
BURMA
FRENCH INDOCHINA
MALAY STATES

MANCHURIA
KOREA
JAPAN
KARAFUTO
Sakhalin
Formosa

PHILIPPINE IS.
BR. NORTH BORNEO
SARAWAK

Mariana Is.
Marshall Is.
Caroline Is.
Solomon Is.
New Hebrides (Gt. Br. and France)
New Caledonia (France)

AUSTRALIA

NEW ZEALAND

0   2000   4000 Km.
0   1000   2000   3000   4000 Mi.

Bessemer improved Kelly's method. Bessemer's converters produced steel at one-tenth the cost of the crucible method. Other new processes permitted steel to be made from scrap iron, an increasingly important raw material, and from the phosphoric iron ores common in western Europe. As a result, world steel production rose from a half-million tons in 1870 to 28 million in 1900, of which the United States produced 10 million, Germany 8, and Britain 4.9. Steel became cheap and abundant enough to make rails, bridges, ships, and even "tin" cans meant to be used once and thrown away.

The new steel mills were hungry consumers of coal, iron ore, limestone, and other raw materials. They took up as much space as whole towns, belched smoke and particles of rust night and day, and left behind huge hills of slag and other waste products. Environmental degradation, long familiar in certain communities, now covered entire regions such as the English Midlands, the German Ruhr, and parts of Pennsylvania (Map 28.1).

The chemical industry followed a similar pattern. Until the late eighteenth century, chemicals were produced by trial and error in small workshops. In 1787, the Frenchman Nicolas Leblanc invented a way to make sodium carbonate, or soda, from salt. By the early nineteenth century, soda, sulfuric acid, and chlorine bleach (used in the cotton industry) were manufactured on a large scale, especially in Britain. In 1856 the Englishman William Perkin created the first synthetic dye, aniline purple; the next few years were known in Europe as the "mauve decade" from the color of fashionable women's clothes. Industry began mass-producing other organic chemicals—compounds containing carbon atoms. Toward the end of the century, German chemists synthesized red, violet, blue, brown, and black

Map 28.1 The Great Powers and Their Colonial Possessions in 1913 By 1913, a small handful of countries claimed sovereignty over more than half the land area of the earth. Global power was closely connected with industries and a merchant marine, rather than with a large territory. This explains why Great Britain, the smallest of the great powers, possessed the largest empire.

dyes as well. These bright, long-lasting colors delighted consumers but damaged the natural-dye exports of many tropical countries, especially hurting the plantations of India that produced indigo, a blue vegetable dye.

Another area where chemistry made important advances was in the manufacture of explosives. The first of these were nitrocellulose and nitroglycerin, a liquid so dangerous that it explodes when jarred. In 1866, the Swedish scientist Alfred Nobel found a way to turn nitroglycerin into a stable solid—dynamite. This and other new explosives enabled the armies and navies of the great powers to replace their weapons with far more accurate and powerful rifles and cannon.

The increasing complexity of industrial chemistry made it one of the first fields where science and technology interacted on a daily basis. This development gave a great advantage to Germany, which had the most advanced engineering schools and scientific institutes of its time. While the British government paid little attention to science and engineering, the German government funded research and encouraged cooperation between universities and industries. By the end of the nineteenth century Germany was the world's leading producer of dyes, drugs, synthetic fertilizers, ammonia, and nitrates used in making explosives.

Electricity

The third innovation that transformed the world of the late nineteenth century was electricity. At first, producing electric current was so costly that it was used only for electroplating and telegraphy. In 1831 the Englishman Michael Faraday showed that the motion of a copper wire through a magnetic field induced an electric current in the wire. Based on his discovery, inventors in the 1870s devised increasingly efficient generators that turned mechanical energy into electric current and opened the way to a host of new applications.

Arc lamps lit up public squares, theaters, and stores; homes relied on gas lamps, which produced a softer light. Between 1878 and 1881, Joseph Swan in England and Thomas Edison in the United States developed incandescent lamps

Paris lit up by electricity, 1900   The electric light bulb was invented in the United States and Britain, but Paris made such extensive use of the new technology that it was nicknamed "city of lights." To mark the Paris Exposition of 1900, the Eiffel Tower and all the surrounding buildings were illuminated with strings of lightbulbs while powerful spotlights swept the sky. (Civica Raccolta delle Stempe Achille Bertarelli, Castella Sforzesco, Milan. Photographer: Roberto Alberti)

well suited to lighting small rooms. In 1882, Edison created the first electrical distribution network, in New York. By the turn of the century, electric lighting was rapidly replacing the dim and smelly gas lamps in the cities of Europe and America.

Other uses of electricity appeared in quick succession. Beginning in the 1880s, electric streetcars and, later, subways helped alleviate the horrendous traffic jams that clogged the large cities of Europe and America. In industry, electric motors replaced steam engines and power belts, increasing productivity and improving workers'

safety. As the demand for electricity grew, engineers learned to extract energy from falling water. The hydroelectric plant at Niagara Falls on the St. Lawrence River, bordering Ontario, Canada and New York State, opened in 1895 and produced an incredible 11,000 horsepower.

Electricity helped alleviate some of the environmental problems caused by its predecessors. Electric motors and lamps did not pollute the air. Power plants were built at a distance from cities. When electric trains and streetcars replaced horse-drawn trolleys and steam locomotives, cities became noticeably cleaner and healthier. At the same time, electricity created a huge demand for copper, bringing Chile, Montana, and southern Africa into the world economy as never before.

Shipping and Telegraph Cables

The late nineteenth century saw a tremendous expansion of railroads and shipping, linked to growth in world trade and to technological innovations. Steam-powered ships dated back to the 1830s but were too costly at first for anything but first-class passenger traffic. Then, in the midcentury, a series of developments radically transformed ocean shipping. First iron, next steel, replaced the wood that had been used for hulls since shipbuilding began. Propellers replaced paddle wheels. Engineers built more powerful and fuel-efficient engines. By the turn of the century a marine engine could convert the heat produced by burning a sheet of paper into the power to move one ton over half a mile. The average size of freighters increased from 200 tons in 1850 to 7,500 tons in 1900. Coaling stations and ports able to handle large ships were built around the world. Most of all, the Suez Canal constructed in 1869 shortened the distance between Europe and Asia and triggered a massive switch from sail to steam (see Chapter 29).

The steamers of the turn of the century were so costly they had to be used as efficiently as possible. As the world's fleet of merchant ships grew from 9 million to 35 million tons between 1850 and 1910, new organizations developed to make the best use of ships. One such organization was the shipping line, a company that offered fast, punctual, and reliable service on a fixed schedule. Passengers, mail, and perishable freight traveled on scheduled liners. Most ships, however, were tramp freighters that voyaged from one port to another under orders from their company headquarters in Europe or America.

To control their ships around the globe, shipping companies used a new medium of communications: cables laid along the ocean floor linking the continents. Submarine cables were laid across the Atlantic in 1866, to India in 1870, to China, Japan, and Australia in 1871 and 1872, to Latin America in 1872 and 1873, to East and South Africa in 1879, and to West Africa in 1886. By the turn of the century, cables connected every country and almost every inhabited island. As the public and the press extolled the "annihilation of time and space" (see the Environment and Technology feature in Chapter 23), cables became the indispensable tools of modern shipping and business.

Railroads

After a rapid spurt of building new lines, British railroad mileage leveled off at around 20,000 miles (32,220 kilometers) in the 1870s. France and Germany built networks longer than Britain's, as did Canada and Russia. The largest of all, by far, was the rail network of the United States. At the end of its Civil War in 1865, the United States already had 35,000 miles (56,350 kilometers) of track, three times as much as Britain. By 1915, the American network reached 390,000 miles (627,900 kilometers), more than the next seven longest networks combined.

Railroads were not confined to the industrialized nations that built them; they could be constructed almost anywhere they promised to be of value to business or government. That included regions with abundant raw materials or agricultural products, like South Africa, Mexico, or Argentina, and densely populated countries like Egypt. The British built the fourth longest rail network in the world in India in order to reinforce their presence and develop their trade with their largest colony (see Chapter 26).

Everywhere they were built, railroads consumed huge amounts of land. Many old cities doubled in size to accommodate railroad stations, sidings, tracks, warehouses, and repair shops. In the countryside, railroads required bridges, tunnels, and embankments. They consumed vast quantities of timber for ties to hold the rails, for bridges, and for fuel, often using up whole forests for miles on either side of the tracks. Throughout the world, they opened new lands to agriculture, mining, and other human exploitation of the natural resources, whether for the benefit of the local inhabitants, as in Europe and North America, or for a distant power, as in the colonial empires.

World Trade and Finance

Between 1850 and 1913 world trade expanded tenfold. Because steamships were much more efficient than sailing ships, the cost of freight dropped between 50 and 95 percent, making it worthwhile to ship even cheap and heavy products halfway around the world. For instance, Europe imported wheat from the United States and India, wool from Australia, and beef from Argentina, and exported coal, railroad equipment, textiles, and machinery.

The growth of world trade transformed the economies of different parts of the world in different ways. The economies of western Europe and North America, the first to industrialize, grew more prosperous and diversified. Their capitalist economies, however, were prey to sudden swings in the business cycles—booms followed by deep depressions in which workers lost their jobs and investors their fortunes. For example, because of the close connections among the industrial economies, the collapse of a bank in Austria in 1873 triggered a depression that spread to the United States, causing mass unemployment. Worldwide recessions occurred in the mid-1880s and mid-1890s as well.

In the late 1870s and early 1880s, Germany, the United States, and other late-industrializing Western nations raised tariffs to protect their industries from foreign competition. Yet trade barriers could not insulate countries from the business cycles, for money continued to flow almost unhindered around the world. One of the main causes of the growing interdependence of the global economy was the financial power of Great Britain. Long after German and American in-dustries surpassed the British, Britain continued to dominate the world's flows of trade, finance, and information. By 1900, two-thirds of the world's submarine cables were British or passed through Britain. Over half of the world's shipping was British-owned. Britain invested

one-fourth of its national wealth overseas, much of it in the United States and Argentina. British money financed many of the railroads, harbors, mines, and other big projects outside Europe. While other currencies fluctuated, the pound sterling was as good as gold, and nine-tenths of international transactions used sterling.

The nonindustrial parts of the world were also tied to the world economy as never before. They were more vulnerable than the industrialized ones, for many of them produced raw materials that could be replaced by synthetic substitutes or alternative sources of supply. Even products in constant demand, like Cuban sugar or Bolivian tin, were subject to prices that fluctuated wildly on the world market. Nevertheless, until World War I, the value of exports from the tropical countries generally remained high, and their populations were still moderate.

SOCIAL TRANSFORMATIONS

Profound social changes in the industrial nations accompanied the technological and economic changes of the late nineteenth century. A fast-growing population swelled cities to unprecedented size, while millions of Europeans emigrated to the Americas. Relations between industrial employers and their workers were often strained, leading to labor movements and new forms of radical politics.

Population and Migrations

The population of Europe grew faster from 1850 to 1914 than ever before or since, almost doubling from 265 million to 468 million. In other countries of predominantly white population— the United States, Canada, Australia, New Zealand, and Argentina—the increase was even greater, because of the inflow of Europeans. There were many reasons for the mass migrations of this period: the Irish famine; the persecution of Jews in Russia; poverty and population growth in Italy, Spain, Poland, and Scandinavia; and the cultural ties between Great Britain and English-speaking countries overseas (see Voices and Visions: The English Language). Equally important was the availability of cheap and rapid steamships and railroads serving travelers at both ends (see Environment and Technology: Railroads and Immigration). Between 1850 and 1900 an average of 400,000 Europeans migrated overseas every year, and between 1900 and 1914 the flood rose to over 1 million each year. From 1850 to 1914, the population of North America rose from 7 million to 82 million, nearly a twelve-fold increase. The proportion of Caucasians in the world's population rose from one-fifth to one-third.

Why did the number of Europeans and their descendants overseas jump so dramatically? Largely, the increase came from a drop in the death rate, as epidemics and starvation became less common. The Irish famine of 1847 and 1848 was the last peacetime famine in European history. As farmers plowed up the midwestern plains of North America and planted wheat, much of which was shipped to Europe, the food supply rose faster than the population. Fertilizers increased the yields of all crops. Canning and refrigeration made food abundant year-round. The diet of Europeans and North Americans improved as meat, fruit, vegetables, and oils became part of the daily fare of city dwellers, in winter as well as in summer.

Many of the European migrants were peasants who hoped to become farmers in their new homelands. In the process of "opening up" the midwest regions of the United States and Canada, the pampas of Argentina, and large areas of Australia, New Zealand, and South Africa, these settlers evicted the original inhabitants and transformed the landscape. They used mechanical devices produced by the new industries, especially steel plows and farm implements and steam-powered sawmills. Forests were clear-cut for lumber, open grasslands were fenced in and plowed under or turned into cattle ranches, and railroads cut across the landscape. Everywhere, houses were built and towns sprang up.

Urbanization and Social Structures

In 1851, Britain became the first nation in history to have a majority of its population living in towns and cities. By 1914, 80 percent of its population was urban, as were 60 percent of German and 45 percent of the French populations. As a result, cities grew to unprecedented size. London, already the world's largest city in 1800 with 900,000 inhabitants, grew to 2.7 million in 1850 and to 6.6 million in 1900, a sevenfold increase in a century. New York, a small town of 64,000 people in 1800, reached 3.4 million by 1900, a fifty-fold increase. Population growth and the building of railroads and industries allowed cities to invade the countryside, swallowing up nearby towns and villages. In 1800, New York covered only the southernmost quarter of Manhattan Island, some 3 square miles (7.8 square kilometers); by 1900 it covered 150 square miles (390 square kilometers). London in 1800 measured about 4 square miles (10.4 square kilometers); by 1900 it covered twenty times more area. In the English Midlands and the German Ruhr, towns fused into one another, filling in the fields and woods that had once separated them.

As cities grew, they changed in character. Newly built railroads not only brought goods into the cities on a predictable schedule, but they also allowed people to live farther apart. At first only the well-to-do could afford to commute by train; by the end of the century, electric streetcars and subways allowed working-class people to live miles from their workplaces.

In preindustrial and early industrial cities, the poor crowded together several in a room, sanitation was bad, water was often contaminated with sewage, and darkness made life dangerous. New urban technologies transformed city life. The most important change was the installation of pipes to bring clean water into the cities and to get rid of sewage. First gas and then electric lighting made cities safer and more pleasant at night. By the turn of the century, municipal governments provided police and fire departments, sanitation and garbage removal, building and health inspection,

Railroads and Immigration

Why did so many Europeans immigrate to North America in the late nineteenth and early twentieth centuries? The quick answer is they needed to. Millions of people felt a strong urge to escape the poverty or tyranny of their home countries and make a new life for themselves in a new land of freedom and opportunity.

Yet motivation alone does not explain migrations. After all, poverty and tyranny existed long before the late nineteenth century. Two other reasons helped determine when and where people migrated: were they allowed to migrate, and were they able to?

In the nineteenth century, Asians were recruited to build railroads and work on farms. But from the 1890s on, the United States and Canada began closing their doors to non-Europeans. Emigrants from Europe were still legally admitted and socially tolerated until after the First World War.

The ability to travel was a result of transportation. Until the 1890s, most immigrants came from Ireland, England, or Germany—countries that had good rail transportation to their own harbors and low steamship fares to North America. As railroad lines were extended into the poorer regions of eastern and southern Europe, more and more immigrants came from Italy, Austria-Hungary, and Russia.

The same was true at the other end. Until the 1870s, most immigrants to North America settled on the east coast. After that, as railroads pushed west across the continent, a growing proportion settled on farms in the central and western parts of the continent. The power of steam moved people as much as their desires did.

Emigrant waiting room   (Library of Congress)

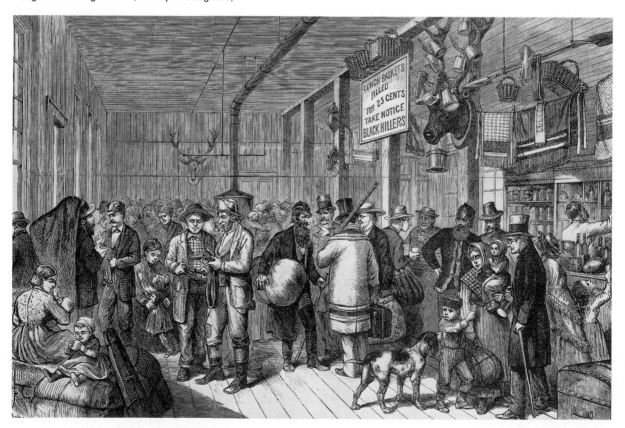

Urban growth: Vienna in 1873 During the nineteenth century, European cities grew at an unprecedented speed. This bird's-eye view of the Austro-Hungarian capital shows the transformation. The densely populated inner city surrounded the cathedral. In 1857 the high walls, which had once protected the old city from attack, were torn down. This made room for the Ringstrasse, a broad, tree-shaded boulevard lined with public buildings, museums, churches, and a university. Beyond the Ring, the newly wealthy bourgeoisie built new neighborhoods of large houses and apartment buildings. (Museen der Stadt, Vienna)

schools, parks, and other amenities unheard of a century earlier.

As sanitary conditions improved, epidemics became rare. For the first time in history, urban death rates fell below birthrates. The decline in infant mortality was especially significant. Confident that their children would survive infancy, couples began to limit the number of children they had, and ancient scourges like infanticide and child abandonment became less frequent. By the beginning of the twentieth century, middle- and even working-class couples began using contraceptives.

To accommodate the growing population, builders created new neighborhoods, from the crowded tenements of the poor to the opulent mansions of the newly rich. In America, planners laid out new cities like Chicago on a rectangular grid, and middle-class families moved to the new developments on the edges of cities. In Paris, older downtown neighborhoods with their narrow crooked streets and rickety tenements were replaced with broad boulevards and modern apartment buildings. Brilliantly lit by gas and electricity, Paris became the "city of lights," a model for city planners from New Delhi to Buenos Aires. The rich continued to live in inner cities that contained the monuments, churches, and palaces of preindustrial times, while workers moved to the outskirts.

Lower population densities and better transportation divided cities into industrial, commercial, and residential neighborhoods for different social classes. Improvements such as water and sewerage, electricity, and streetcars always benefited the wealthy first, then the middle class, and the working class last of all. In the complex of urban life, businesses of all kinds arose, and the professions—engineering, accounting, research, journalism, the law, among others—took on an increased importance. The new middle class exhibited its wealth in fine houses, many servants, and elegant entertainment.

In fast-growing cities like London, New York, or Chicago, newcomers arrived so quickly that housing construction and municipal services could not keep up. Immigrants who saved their money to help reunite their families could not afford costly municipal services. As a result, poorer neighborhoods retained the overcrowded, unhealthy, and dangerous conditions that had marked the early decades of industrialization.

While urban environments improved in many ways, air quality worsened during this period. Coal, burned to power steam engines and heat buildings, polluted the air, creating unpleasant and sometimes dangerous "pea-soup" fog and coating everything with a film of grimy dust. And the thousands of horses that pulled the carts and carriages covered the streets with their wastes, causing a terrible stench.

Labor Movements and Socialist Politics

Industrialization combined with the revolutionary ideas of the late eighteenth century to produce two kinds of movements—socialism and labor movements—calling for further changes. Socialism was an ideology developed by radical thinkers who questioned the sanctity of private property and argued in defense of industrial workers against their employers. Labor unions were organizations formed by industrial workers to defend their interests. The socialist and labor movements were never identical. Most of the time they were allies; occasionally they were rivals.

Since the beginning of the nineteenth century, workers had united to create "friendly societies" for mutual assistance in times of illness, unemployment, or disability. Anticombination laws, however, forbade them to strike. These laws were abolished in Britain in the 1850s and in the rest of Europe in subsequent decades. Labor unions sought not only better wages but also improved working conditions and insurance against illness, accidents, disability, and old age. They grew slowly because they required a permanent staff and a great deal of money to sustain their members during strikes. By the end of the century, British labor unions counted 2 million members, and German and American unions had one million members each.

Socialism began as an intellectual movement. By far the best-known socialist was Karl Marx (1818–1883), a German who lived most of his life in England. He combined German philosophy, French revolutionary ideas, and knowledge of British industrial conditions. He expressed his ideas succinctly in the *Communist Manifesto* (1848) and in great detail in *Das Kapital* (1867). He argued that the capitalist system allowed the bourgeoisie (the owners of businesses and factories) to extract the "surplus value" of workers' labor—that is, the difference between workers' wages and the value of the goods they manufactured. He saw business enterprises becoming larger and more monopolistic and workers growing more numerous and impoverished with every downturn in the business cycle.

Marx gave an intellectual structure to the growing dissatisfaction with raw industrial capitalism. In the late nineteenth century, business tycoons and playboys spent money lavishly on mansions, yachts, private railroad cars, and other ostentatious displays of wealth that contrasted sharply with the poverty of the workers. Even though industrial workers were not becoming poorer as Marx believed, the class struggle between workers and employers was brutally real. What Marx did was to offer a persuasive explanation of the causes of this contrast and the antagonisms it bred.

Marx was not just a philosopher; he also made a direct impact on politics. In 1864, he helped found the International Working Man's Association (later known as the First International), a movement he hoped would bring about the radical overthrow of the bourgeoisie. However, it attracted more intellectuals than workers. Despite Marx's predictions, workers did not flock to the revolutionary banner, not because they "lacked consciousness" but because they found other means of redressing their grievances, such as the vote and labor unions.

Just as labor unions strove to enable workers to share in the benefits of a capitalist economy, so did electoral politics persuade workers to become part of the existing political system instead of seeking to overthrow it. The nineteenth century saw a gradual extension of the right to vote throughout Europe and North America. Universal male suffrage became law in the United States in 1870, in France and Germany in 1871, in Britain in 1885, and in the rest of Europe soon thereafter. With universal male suffrage, socialist politicians could expect to capture many seats in their national parliaments, since the newly enfranchised working class was so numerous. Their goal was to use their voting power to gain concessions from government and eventually even to win elections.

The classic case of socialist electoral politics is the Social Democratic Party of Germany. Founded in 1875 with a revolutionary socialist program, within two years it won a half-million votes and several seats in the *Reichstag* (the lower house of the German parliament). Through superb organizing efforts and important concessions wrung from the government, the party grew fast, by 1912 garnering 4.2 million votes and winning more seats in the Reichstag than any other party. In pursuit of electoral success, the Social Democrats became more reformist and less radical. By joining the electoral process, they abandoned the idea of violent revolution.

Working-class women, burdened with both job and family responsibilities, found little time for politics and were not welcome in the male-dominated trade unions or radical political parties. Female suffrage did not come about until well into the twentieth century. A few radical women, such as the anarchist Emma Goldman in the United States and the German socialist Rosa Luxemburg, became famous but never had a large following. It was never easy to reconcile the demands of workers and those of women. In 1889 the German socialist Clara Zetkin wrote: "Just as the male worker is subjected by the capitalist, so is the woman by the man, and she will always remain in subjugation until she is eco-nomically independent. Work is the indispensable condition for economic independence." Six years later, she added: "The proletarian woman cannot attain her highest ideal through a movement for the equality of the female sex, she attains salvation only through the fight for the emancipation of labor."[1]

WOMEN AND GENDER RELATIONS IN THE VICTORIAN AGE

In English-speaking countries, the period from 1850 to 1914 is known as the "Victorian Age." The expression refers not only to the reign of Queen Victoria of England but to rules of behavior and to an ideology surrounding the family and the relations between men and women. The Victorians emphasized the differences between people more than their common humanity: white- versus dark-skinned, rich versus poor, men versus women. They stressed the romantic aspects of love and marriage and both partners' duty to family and religious values. They contrasted the masculine ideals of strength and courage with the feminine virtues of beauty and kindness, and they idealized the home as a peaceful and loving refuge from the dog-eat-dog world of competitive capitalism. Although Victorian ideas contained elements of racism, sexism, and class discrimination, they were widely and sincerely felt at the time and have had an enormous impact on Western gender relations ever since.

Upper- and Middle-Class Women

Victorian morality claimed to be universal, yet it best fit the European upper- and middle-class family. Men and women were thought to belong in "separate spheres." Successful businessmen spent their time at work or relaxing in men's clubs. They put their wives in charge of rearing the children, running the household, and spending the family money to enhance the family's social status.

The word *lady*, once the feminine equivalent of *lord*, came to mean the wife of a *gentleman*, a member of the genteel bourgeoisie. As the Englishwoman Margaretta Greg explained in 1853: "A lady, to be such, must be a mere lady. She must not work for profit, or engage in any occupation that money can command, lest she invade the rights of the working classes, who live by their labour."

Before electric appliances, however, a middle-class home demanded enormous amounts of work. Not only were families larger, but middle-class couples entertained often and lavishly. To carry out all these tasks required servants. A family's status and the activities and lifestyle of the "mistress of the house" depended on the availability of servants to help her with the household tasks. Only families that employed at least one full-time servant were considered middle class.

Toward the turn of the century, modern technology began to transform middle-class homes. Plumbing eliminated the pump and the outhouse. Central heating replaced fireplaces, stoves, trips to the basement for coal, and endless dusting. Gas and electricity lit houses and cooked food without soot, smoke, and ashes. By the early twentieth century, a few wealthy families acquired the first vacuum cleaners and washing machines. Did these technological advances mean less housework for women? Not right away. As families acquired new household technologies, they raised their standards of cleanliness, thus demanding just as much labor as before from homemakers and their servants.

In spite of servants and household technologies, middle-class women found themselves ever busier with a variety of socially acceptable duties, the most important of which was rearing children. Before contraception became common at the turn of the century, young brides usually got pregnant soon after marriage. Unlike the rich of previous eras, who handed their children over to wet nurses and tutors, Victorian mothers nursed their own babies and showered their children with love and attention. Even those who could afford nannies and governesses remained personally involved in their children's education. However, girls received an education very different from that of boys. While boys were being prepared for the business world or the professions, girls were taught such skills as embroidery, drawing, and music, which offered no monetary reward or professional preparation but enhanced their social graces and marriage prospects.

Victorian morality glorified the home life of women, but it frowned on their career ambitions and other outside interests. Governments enforced the legal discrimination against women. Until the end of the century, most European countries considered women minors for life—that is, subject to their fathers before marriage and to their husbands after. Even Britain, among the most progressive countries, did not give women the right to control their own property until 1882.

Young middle-class women were allowed to work temporarily until they got married, but only in genteel occupations like retail and office work where a young woman could display her fine manners. When the typewriter and telephone were first introduced into the business world in the 1880s, only men could use these "high-technology" devices. Soon, however, businessmen found they could get better work at lower wages from educated young women, and operating these machines was typecast as women's work.

Jobs that required higher education, especially those in the professions, were long closed to women. Until late in the century, few universities granted degrees to women. In America, women's higher education was restricted to elite colleges like Smith, Wellesley, and Radcliffe in the east and to teachers' colleges in the midwest. European women had fewer opportunities. Before 1914, very few women became doctors, lawyers, or professional musicians and artists.

The first profession open to women was teaching, as more and more countries passed laws calling for universal compulsory education. By 1911, for instance, 73 percent of all teachers in England were women. They were considered especially suited to teaching young children and girls—an extension of the duties of Victorian mothers. However, teaching was considered suitable only for single women, for married women were expected to get pregnant right away and stay home taking care of their own children rather than the children of other people. In 1901, Mary Murphy, a teacher with ten years' experience, was charged with misconduct and fired from her teaching job in a Brooklyn school when she got married. After a three-year legal battle, a judge ruled that marriage was not misconduct, and she was reinstated with back pay.

A home life, no matter how busy, did not satisfy all middle-class women. Some became volunteer nurses or social workers, at little or no pay. Others organized to fight prostitution, alcohol, and child labor. By the turn of the century, a few challenged male domination of politics and the law. Women suffragists, led in Britain by Emmeline Pankhurst and in America by Elizabeth Cady Stanton and Susan B. Anthony, demanded the right to vote. The more radical used violent tactics such as breaking windows, setting fire to houses, or throwing themselves under horses' hoofs. By 1914, women had won the right to vote

in twelve states of the United States, but British women did not vote until 1918.

Working-Class Women

The life of middle-class women in the Victorian Age was a mixture of luxuries and discrimination, but working-class women led a life of toil and pain, considerably harder than that of their menfolks. Although the worst abuses of child labor had been banned in most European countries by the midcentury, parents expected girls as young as ten to contribute to the household budget and to their own upkeep. Many became servants in the homes of the well-to-do, where they commonly worked sixteen or more hours a day, six and a half days a week, for little more than room and board. Their living quarters, usually in the attic or basement, contrasted with the luxurious quarters of their masters. Without appliances, much of their work was physically hard:

Women's work in the Victorian Age As industrialization spread, increasing numbers of young women found employment in factories but always in specifically designated "female" jobs requiring manual dexterity rather than physical strength. In this picture, women workers are packing matches into boxes in a London match factory. (Courtesy, Bryant & May)

hauling coal and water up stairs, washing laundry by hand.

Female servants were vulnerable to sexual abuse by their masters or their masters' sons. A well-known case is that of Helene Demuth, who worked for Karl and Jenny Marx all her life. At age thirty-one she bore a son by Karl Marx and put him with foster parents rather than leave the family. She was more fortunate than most, for most families fired a servant who got pregnant, rather than embarrass the master of the house.

When young women could find work in a factory, they often preferred it to domestic service. Here, too, Victorian society practiced a strict sexual division of labor. Men worked in construction, iron and steel, heavy machinery, or on railroads; women worked in textiles and the clothing trades, two extensions of traditional women's household work. Appalled by the abuses of women and children in the early phase of industrialization, most industrial countries passed protective legislation limiting the hours or forbidding the employment of women in the hardest and most dangerous occupations, such as mining and foundry work. Such legislation, while limiting abuses, also reinforced gender divisions in industry, keeping women in low-paid subordinate positions. Denied access to the better-paid jobs of foremen or machine repairmen, female factory workers earned, on average, between one-third and two-thirds of men's wages.

Married women with children were expected to stay home, even when their husbands did not make enough to support them. Thus most married women of the working class had double responsibilities within the home: not only the work of child rearing and housework but also that of contributing to their family's income. Families who had room to spare, even a bed or a corner of the kitchen, took in boarders. Many women did piecework such as sewing dresses, making lace, hats, or gloves, or weaving baskets. The hardest and worst-paid work was washing other people's clothes. Often women worked at home ten to twelve hours a day and enlisted the help of their small children, perpetuating practices long outlawed in factories. Since electric lighting and indoor plumbing cost more than most working-class families could afford, even ordinary household duties like cooking and washing remained heavy burdens.

The poorest of the poor were orphans and single women with children. Unable to find jobs or support themselves at home, many turned to prostitution. The wealth of middle-class men made it easy for them to take advantage of the poverty of working-class women.

NATIONALISM AND THE UNIFICATION OF GERMANY

The most influential idea of the nineteenth century was nationalism. According to the French revolutionary ideology described in Chapter 24, with its stress on *fraternité* (brotherhood) and *patrie* (fatherland), people were not the subjects of a sovereign but citizens of a *nation*—a concept identified with a territory, the state that ruled it, and the culture of its people. Since the most widely spoken language in nineteenth-century Europe was German, the unification of most German-speaking people into a single state in 1871 had momentous consequences for the world.

Language and National Identity Before 1871

Language was often the crucial element in creating a feeling of national unity. It was important both as a way to unite the people of a nation and as the means of persuasion by which political leaders could inspire their followers (see Voices and Visions: The English Language). Language was the tool of the new generation of political activists, most of them lawyers, teachers, students, and journalists. Yet language and nationality seldom coincided.

The fit between France and the French language was exceptional. The Italian- and German-speaking peoples were divided among

The English Language

Two hundred years ago, English was hardly spoken outside Britain and the eastern seaboard of North America. A century later, not only was it the language of the United States, Canada, Britain, Australia, and New Zealand, but it had spread to the intellectual and business elites of other continents as well. Today it is the language of business, science and technology, and international politics throughout the world. In 1835, the English historian Thomas Babington Macaulay attributed its success to the works written in it:

[English] stands pre-eminent even among the languages of the West. It abounds with works of imagination not inferior to the noblest which Greece has bequeathed to us; with models of every species of eloquence; with historical compositions, which, considered merely as narratives, have seldom been surpassed, and which, considered as vehicles of ethical and political instruction, have never been equalled; . . . with the most profound speculations on metaphysics, morals, government, jurisprudence, and trade; with full and correct information respecting every experimental science. . . . Whoever knows that language has ready access to all the intellectual wealth which all the wisest nations of the earth have created and hoarded in the course of ninety generations. . . . the literature now extant in that language is of far greater value than all the literature which three hundred years ago was extant in all the languages of the world together. Nor is this all. In India, English is the language spoken by the ruling class. It is spoken by the higher class of natives at the seats of government. It is likely to become the language of commerce throughout the seas of the East.

Not everyone agreed with Macaulay that English was the best language and that its spread was beneficial. Here are the words of the Indian nationalist Bipin Chandra Pal, writing a century after Macaulay:

. . . the India-born Civilian [i.e., government official] practically cut himself off from his parent society, and lived and moved and had his being in the atmosphere so beloved of his British colleagues. In mind and manners he was as much an Englishman as any Englishman. It was no small sacrifice for him, because in this way he completely estranged himself from the society of his own people and became socially and morally a pariah among them. . . . He was as much a stranger in his own native land as the European residents in the country.

The success of the English language had much to do with the spread of the British Empire. Today, we live in a world of independent nations, yet the use of English is far more widespread than it ever was. Why is that? Is it the quality of works written in English, as Macaulay believed? Is it the political power of the English-speaking nations? Or is there another cause? And can we, the English-speaking writers and readers of this book, ever judge the issue impartially?

Source: G. O. Trevelyan, Life and Letters of Lord Macaulay, vol. 1 (New York: Harper & Brothers, 1877), 353–355; and Bipin Chandra Pal, Memories of My Life and Times, 2nd ed. (Calcutta: Bipin Chandra Pal Institute, 1973), 331–332.

---

many small states. The Austrian Empire included peoples who spoke German, Czech, Slovak, Hungarian, Polish, and other languages. Even where people spoke a common language, they could be divided by religion or institutions. For example, the Irish, though English-speaking, were Catholics, whereas the English were Protestants; and in the United States, the issue of slavery divided the South from the North, creating a southern identity.

The idea of realigning the boundaries of states to fit linguistic, religious, or cultural divisions was revolutionary. In Italy and Germany, it would lead to the forging of large new states out of many small ones. In Central and eastern Europe, nationalism was divisive and threatened to break up large states into smaller ones.

Until the 1860s, nationalism was also associated with liberalism, the revolutionary middle-class ideology that asserted the sovereignty of

Wilhelm I proclaimed emperor of Germany   On January 18, 1871, Prussia and the smaller states of Germany united to form the German Reich (empire). King Wilhelm I of Prussia was proclaimed kaiser (emperor) as his chancellor, Otto von Bismarck (in a white jacket), and dozens of generals and lesser princes cheered. The ceremony took place in the Great Hall of Mirrors in the palace of Versailles, near Paris, to mark Prussia's stunning victory over France. (Bismarck Museum, Friedrichsruh)

the people and demanded constitutional government, a national parliament, and freedom of expression. The most famous nationalist of the early nineteenth century was the Italian liberal Giuseppe Mazzini (1805–1872), who not only sought to unify the Italian peninsula into one nation but associated with like-minded revolutionaries elsewhere to bring nationhood and liberty to all peoples oppressed by tyrants and foreigners. Although such revolutionaries aroused sympathy in liberal England, the governments of Russia, Prussia, and Austria persecuted them. But the new ideas could not be quashed. To staff

their bureaucracies and police forces to maintain law and order, even conservative regimes required educated personnel, and education meant universities, the breeding ground of new ideas transmitted by a national language.

The revolutions of 1848 were a major turning point in this process (see Chapter 24). Although they failed, the strength of the revolutionary movements convinced conservatives that governments could not forever keep their citizens out of politics, and that mass politics, if properly managed, could strengthen rather than weaken the state. A new generation of conservative political leaders learned how to preserve the social status quo through public education, universal military service, and colonial conquests, all of which built a sense of national unity.

The Unification of Germany

Until the 1860s, the region of Central Europe where people spoke German (the former Holy Roman Empire) consisted of Prussia, the German-speaking parts of the Austrian Empire, and numerous smaller states. Nationalists were divided into those who wanted to unite all Germans under the Austrian throne and those who sought to exclude Austria with its many non-Germanic peoples and unite all other German-speaking areas under Prussia. The divisions were also religious: Austria and southwestern Germany were Catholic; Prussia and the northeast were Lutheran. And the divisions were economic: the western sections were more urban and industrial than the eastern. The Prussian state had two advantages: (1) the newly developed industries of the Rhineland and (2) the first European army to make use of railroads, telegraphs, breechloading rifles, steel artillery, and other products of modern industry.

The king of Prussia, Wilhelm I (r. 1861–1888), had entrusted the running of his government to his chancellor, the brilliant and authoritarian aristocrat Otto von Bismarck (1815–1898). Bismarck was determined to use Prussian industry and German nationalism to advance the interests of the Prussian state. In 1864, after a quick victory against Denmark, he set his sights higher.

In 1866, Prussia defeated Austria. To everyone's surprise, Prussia took no Austrian territory. Instead, Prussia and some smaller states formed the North German Confederation, the nucleus of a future Germany. Then in 1871, confident that Austria would not hinder him, Bismarck provoked with France the war known as the "Franco-Prussian War." The Prussian armies, joined by troops from southern as well as northern Germany, used their superior firepower and tactics to achieve a quick victory.

The spoils of victory included a large indemnity and two provinces of France bordering on Germany: Alsace and Lorraine. The French paid the indemnity easily enough but resented the loss of their provinces. To the Germans, this region was German because a majority of its inhabitants spoke a dialect of German. To the French, it was French because it had been so when the nation of France was forged in the Revolution and because most of its inhabitants considered themselves French. These two conflicting definitions of *nationalism* guaranteed permanent enmity between France and Germany. It was to be the first of a long series of such disagreements, as nationalism turned out to be more often divisive than unifying.

Nationalism After 1871

The Franco-Prussian War of 1871 changed the political climate of Europe. France and Britain became wholeheartedly liberal. Germany, Austria-Hungary (the Austrian Empire had renamed itself in 1867 to please its Hungarian people), and Russia remained conservative and used nationalism to maintain the status quo.

All politicians tried to use popular feelings to bolster their governments. They were greatly aided by the press, especially cheap daily newspapers that sought to increase their circulation by publishing sensational articles about overseas conquests and foreign threats. As governments increasingly came to recognize the advantages of an educated population in the competition between states, they opened public schools in every town, opening public service jobs to women for the first time. The spread of literacy allowed politicians and journalists to appeal to the emotions of the poor, diverting their anger from their employers to foreigners and their votes from socialist to nationalist parties.

In many countries, the dominant group used nationalism as a reason to impose its language, religion, or customs on its minorities. The Russian Empire attempted to "Russify" its diverse ethnic populations. The Spanish government made the Spanish language compulsory in the

The Doss house   Late nineteenth century cities showed more physical than social improvements. This painting by Makovsky of a street in St. Petersburg contrasts the broad avenue and impressive new buildings with the poverty of the crowd. (The State Russian Museum/Smithsonian Institution Traveling Exhibit)

schools, newspapers, and courts of its Basque- and Catalan-speaking provinces. Immigrants to the United States were expected to learn English, in the name of national unity.

Nationalism soon spread to other continents (see Chapters 26, 27, and 32). By the 1880s signs of national consciousness appeared in Egypt, Japan, India, and other non-Western countries, inspiring anti-Western and anticolonial movements.

Western culture in the late nineteenth century exalted the powerful over the weak, men over women, rich over poor, Europeans over other races, and humans over nature. Some people even sought to enlist science in support of political dominance. One of the most influential scientists of the century, and the one whose ideas were most

widely cited and misinterpreted, was the English biologist Charles Darwin (1809–1882).

As a young man, Darwin spent several years traveling through South America and the South Pacific studying the plant and animal life. On his return to England, he found an explanation for the great variety of natural life forms he had seen, which he published in 1859 as *On the Origin of the Species by the Means of Natural Selection*. In it, he showed that the earth was extremely old and that living beings over hundreds of thousands of years had either evolved in the struggle for survival or become extinct.

The philosopher Herbert Spencer (1820–1903) and others took up Darwin's ideas of "natural selection" and "survival of the fittest" and applied them to human society. Extreme social Darwinists developed elaborate pseudo scientific theories of racial differences, claiming that they were the result not of history but of biology. If Europeans had conquered empires in Asia and Africa, if men had more political power than women, if workers earned less than the well-to-do, they argued, these differences must have "natural" causes. These ideas were not at all what Darwin had meant, nor were they based on any research. Nevertheless, they became very popular at the turn of the century, for they gave a scientific-sounding justification for the power of the privileged.

THE GREAT POWERS OF EUROPE IN THE LATE NINETEENTH CENTURY

After 1871, politicians and journalists discovered how easily they could whip up popular frenzy against neighboring countries. Military officers, impressed by the awesome power of the weapons that industry provided, began to think these weapons were invincible. Rivalries over colonial territories, ideological differences between liberal and conservative governments, and even minor border incidents or trade disagreements contributed to a growing atmosphere of international tension.

Germany at the Center of Europe

International relations revolved around a united Germany, both because it was located in the center of Europe and because it had the most powerful army on the European continent. After creating a unified German Empire in 1871, Bismarck declared his country "satiated" and put his effort into maintaining the peace in Europe. To isolate France, the only country with a grudge against Germany, he forged a loose coalition with Austria-Hungary and Russia, the other two conservative powers. Despite the rival ambitions

of Austria and Russia in the Balkans, he was able to keep this coalition alive for twenty years.

At home, Bismarck proved adept at manipulating mass politics. To weaken the influence of middle-class liberals, he extended the vote to all adult males. By imposing high tariffs on manufactured goods and wheat, he gained the support of both the wealthy industrialists of the Rhineland and the great landowners of eastern Germany, traditional rivals for power. He stole the thunder of the socialists by introducing social legislation—medical, unemployment, and disability insurance and old-age pensions—long before other industrial countries. Under his leadership, the German people developed a tremendous sense of national unity and pride in their industrial and military power.

In 1888 Wilhelm I was succeeded by his grandson Wilhelm II (r. 1888–1918), a vulgar, insecure, and arrogant man who tried to gain respect by using bullying tactics. Within two years he had dismissed Chancellor Bismarck and surrounded himself with yes men and flatterers. Whereas Bismarck had shown little interest in acquiring colonies overseas, Wilhelm II talked about his "global policy" and demanded a colonial empire. Ruler of the nation with the mightiest army and the largest industrial economy in Europe, he felt that Germany deserved "a place in the sun."

The Liberal Powers: France and Great Britain

The French, once the dominant nation in Europe, had difficulty reconciling themselves to being in second place. Though a prosperous country with a flourishing agriculture and a large colonial empire, France had some serious weaknesses. Its population was almost stagnant; in 1911 it had only 39 million people compared to Germany's 64 million. In an age when the power of nations was roughly proportional to the size of their army, France could field an army only two-thirds the size of Germany's. Another weakness was the slow growth of French industry compared to

Germany's, due to the loss of the iron and coal mines of Lorraine.

The French people were deeply divided over the very nature of the state: some were monarchists and Catholic; a growing number held republican and anticlerical views. These divisions came to a head at the turn of the century over the case of Captain Alfred Dreyfus, a Jewish officer falsely convicted of spying for the Germans in 1894. French society, even families, split between those who felt that reopening the case would only dishonor the army and those who believed that letting injustice go unchallenged dishonored the nation. The case reawakened a dormant anti-Semitism in French society. Not until 1906, after twelve painful years, was Dreyfus exonerated. Yet if French political life seemed fragile and frequently in crisis, a long tradition of popular participation in politics and a strong sense of nationhood, reinforced by a fine system of universal public education, had given the French people a deeper cohesion than appeared on the surface.

Great Britain was the only other country in Europe with something approaching a democratic tradition. The British government alternated smoothly between the Liberal and Conservative Parties, and the income gap between the rich and the poor gradually narrowed. Nevertheless, Britain had problems that grew more apparent as time went on.

One was the resentment of the Irish against English rule. Nationalism had strengthened the allegiance of the English, Scots, and Welsh to the Crown and the state. But it had left out the Irish, who felt excluded because they were Catholic and predominantly poor.

Another problem was the British economy. Once the workshop of the world, Great Britain fell behind the United States and Germany in such important industries as iron and steel, chemicals, electricity, and textiles. Even in shipbuilding and shipping, Britain's traditional specialties, Germany was catching up.

Britain was also preoccupied with its enormous and fast-growing empire. The empire was a source of wealth for investors and the envy of other imperialist nations, but it was also a constant worry and a drain on Britain's finances.

The revolt of 1857 against British rule in India (see Chapter 26) was crushed with difficulty and kept British politicians worried thereafter. The empire required Britain to maintain several costly fleets of warships stationed throughout the world.

For most of the nineteenth century, Britain turned its back on Europe and pursued a policy of "splendid isolation." Only once, in 1854, did it intervene militarily in Europe, joining France in the Crimean War of 1854–1856 against Russia (see Chapter 27). Britain's preoccupation with India and the shipping routes through the Mediterranean led British statesmen to exaggerate the Russian threat to the Ottoman Empire and to the Central Asian approaches to India. Periodic "Russian scares" and Britain's age-old rivalry with France for overseas colonies diverted the attention of British politicians away from the rise of a large, powerful, united Germany.

The Conservative Powers: Russia and Austria-Hungary

Two of the great powers of Europe, Russia and Austria-Hungary, were weakened rather than strengthened by the forces of nationalism. The reason for this effect was that their populations were far more divided, socially and ethnically, than were the German, French, or British peoples.

Russia was the most misunderstood country in Europe. Its enormous size and population led many Europeans to exaggerate its military potential. Yet it was easily defeated by France and Britain in the brief Crimean War.

In 1861, the moderate conservative Tsar Alexander II (r. 1855–1881) emancipated the peasants from serfdom. That half-hearted measure, however, did not create a modern society on the western European model. It only turned serfs into tenant farmers indebted to their former owners. Though technically "emancipated," the great majority of Russians had little education, few legal rights, and no say in their government. After Alexander's assassination in 1881, his successors Alexander III (r. 1881–1894) and Nicholas II (r. 1894–1917) opposed all forms of social change. Although the Russian government employed many bureaucrats and policemen, its commercial middle class was small and had little influence. Wealthy landowning aristocrats continued to dominate the Russian court and administration and succeeded in blocking most reforms.

The weaknesses in Russia's society and government became glaringly obvious during a war with Japan in 1904 and 1905. The fighting took place in Manchuria, a Chinese province far from European Russia. The Russian army, which received all its supplies by means of the inefficient Trans-Siberian Railway, was soon defeated by the better trained and equipped Japanese. The Russian navy, after a long journey around Europe, Africa, and Asia, was met and sunk by the Japanese fleet at the Battle of Tsushima Strait in 1905.

The shock of defeat caused a popular uprising, the Revolution of 1905, that forced Tsar Nicholas II to grant a constitution and an elected *Duma* (parliament). But as soon as he was able to rebuild the army and the police, he reverted to the traditional despotism of his forefathers. Small groups of radical intellectuals, angered by the contrast between the wealth of the elite and the poverty of the common people, plotted the violent overthrow of the tsarist autocracy.

The ethnic diversity of imperial Russia also contributed to its instability. The Polish people, never reconciled to being annexed by Russia in the eighteenth century, rebelled in 1830 and 1863–1864. The tsarist empire also included Finland, Estonia, Latvia, Lithuania, and Ukraine, the very mixed peoples of the Caucasus, and the Muslim population of Central Asia conquered between 1865 and 1881. Furthermore, Russia had the largest Jewish population in Europe, and the harshness of its anti-Semitic laws and periodic *pogroms* (massacres) forced many Jews to flee to America. All in all, only 45 percent of the peoples of the tsarist empire spoke Russian. This meant that Russian nationalism and the state's attempts to impose the Russian language on its subjects were a divisive instead of a unifying force in the empire.

Nationalism was also divisive in south-central Europe, where many different language groups lived in close proximity. In 1867, when the Austrian Empire renamed itself the Austro-Hungarian Empire, it pleased its Hungarian population but alienated its Czechs, Slovaks, Poles, and other Slavic minorities. The Austro-Hungarian Empire still thought of itself as a great power. Instead of seeking conquests in Asia or Africa, however, it attempted to dominate the nearby Balkans. This strategy irritated Russia, which thought of itself as the protector of Slavic peoples everywhere. The Austrian annexation of the former Turkish province of Bosnia-Herzegovina in 1908 worsened relations between the two empires. Festering quarrels over the Balkans—the "tinderbox of Europe"—would eventually lead Europe to war (see Chapter 30).

GREAT POWERS OVERSEAS

Since the sixteenth century, Europeans had come to regard their continent as the center of the universe and their states as the only great powers in the world. The rest of the world was either ignored or used as bargaining chips in the game of power politics. The late nineteenth century marked the high point of European power and arrogance, as the nations of Europe, in a frenzy known as the "New Imperialism," rushed to gobble up the last remaining unclaimed pieces of the world (see Chapter 29).

Yet at that very moment two nations outside Europe were becoming great powers. One of them, the United States, was mainly inhabited by people of European origin, and its rise to great-power status had been predicted early in the nineteenth century by astute observers like the French statesman Alexis de Tocqueville. The other one, Japan, seemed so distant and exotic in 1850 that no Europeans guessed it would soon join the ranks of the great powers.

The United States

After the Civil War ended in 1865, the United States entered a period of vigorous growth (see Chapter 25). Hundreds of thousands of immigrants arrived every year, mainly from Russia,

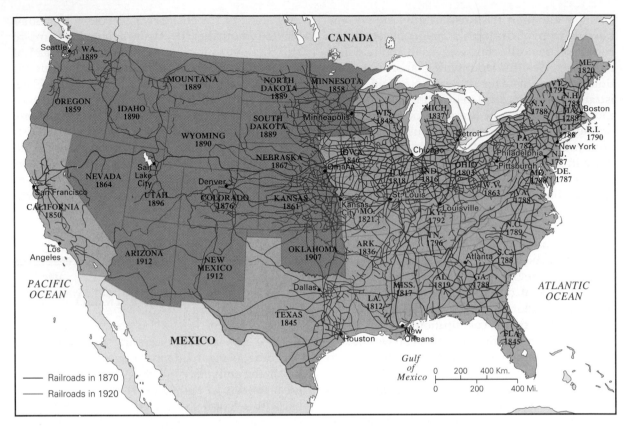

Map 28.2   The United States, 1850–1920   This map shows the expansion of the United States from the coasts into the interior of the continent. In the western half of the continent, only California and Texas were states in 1850; territories located further from the coasts became states later. The economic development, shown by the railroad lines, followed much the same pattern, radiating west and south from the northeastern states and—to a lesser extent—eastward from California.

Italy, and Central Europe, raising the population from 39 million in 1871 to 63 million in 1891, an increase of 62 percent. Although many settled on the newly opened lands west of the Mississippi (see Map 28.2), most of the migrants moved to the towns, which mushroomed into cities in a few years. Chicago, for example, grew fourfold, from 444,000 in 1870 to 1,700,000 in 1900. In the process, the nation became an industrial giant. The rail network, already the world's longest in 1865, multiplied eleven-fold by 1915, creating the largest single integrated market in the world. To make the rails, locomotives, bridges, and other material, industry produced 20 million tons of

steel annually in 1900. By then the United States had overtaken Britain and Germany as the world's leading industrial power.

This explosive growth was accomplished with few government restrictions. In fact, in the last years of the nineteenth century, the federal, state, and local governments seemed to be influenced by (if not in the pay of) the business sector, on which they lavished free land, tariffs, and other benefits. Giant monopolies, like John D. Rockefeller's Standard Oil Company, and steel and railroad trusts dominated American life. In this atmosphere of unfettered free enterprise, the nation got rich fast, as did its upper and middle classes.

The sudden expansion created many victims, however. First among them were the American Indians. When the railroads penetrated the west after the Civil War, they brought white colonists eager to start farming, ranching, or mining. The indigenous Indians, whose lands they invaded fought back with great courage but were outnumbered and outgunned. In Canada, the government tried to protect the Indians from the whites. The United States Army, however, always sided with the settlers. The U.S. government had signed numerous treaties with the Indians, but tore them up when settlers demanded more land. After decades of wars, massacres, and starvation, the government confined the remaining Indians to reservations on the poorest lands.

The U.S. government also abandoned African-Americans after the Civil War, especially in the defeated South. Though freed from slavery in 1865, most of them became sharecroppers who were at the mercy of their landowners. In the 1890s, the southern states instituted "Jim Crow" laws segregating blacks in public transportation, jobs, and schools. Not only did southern judges apply harsh laws in a biased manner, but black Americans were also subject to the lawless violence of mobs, which lynched an average of fifty blacks a year until well into the twentieth century.

Racism also affected Asian immigrants, many of whom had come to the United States to build railroads in the western states. In 1882 the U.S. government barred the Chinese from immigrating by enacting the first of many racial exclusion laws.

Working-class whites benefited little from the booming economy. The depressions of 1873 and 1893 caused more distress in the United States than in Europe, because the United States had few labor laws and little unemployment compensation to soften the hardships. Police or the army repressed strikes and unions. The courts

Deforestation As European settlers moved into the forested regions of North America, they cut the trees, both as a source of timber and to clear the land for farming. In the process, much of Michigan, Wisconsin, and Ontario were deforested. This picture shows a farmer contemplating his newly cleared land. (State Historical Society of Wisconsin)

consistently supported employers against their employees, capital against labor, and business against government.

Working-class women bore the brunt of repressive labor practices, because they earned less than men, had more responsibilities, and seldom were members of labor unions. As in Britain, middle-class women activists organized to demand female suffrage and to fight against alcohol, prostitution, and other social evils.

The booming economy and the waves of immigrants radically transformed the environment. Timber companies clear-cut large areas of Michigan, Wisconsin, and the Appalachian Mountains to provide lumber for railroad ties and frame houses, pulp for paper, and fuel for locomotives and iron foundries. Farmers cleared the forests and plowed up the prairies. Buffalo, the dominant animals of the western territories, were massacred by the hundreds of thousands to starve out the Indians and clear the land for cattle. In the west, the government began massive irrigation projects. In the industrial northeast, iron foundries, steel mills, and steam engines caused severe, local air pollution problems.

In spite of all the assaults, the North American continent was so huge that large parts of it remained unspoiled. A few especially beautiful areas were declared national parks, beginning with Yellowstone in Wyoming in 1872, thereby marking a new stage in Americans' attitude toward nature. Thanks to the efforts of the naturalist John Muir, the forestry expert Gifford Pinchot, and President Theodore Roosevelt, large parts of the western states were set aside as national forests.

Most citizens showed little interest in foreign affairs. Patriots tended to celebrate American freedom and democracy, the conquest of a huge continent, and the country's remarkable technological achievements. In this period, the inventor Thomas Edison was probably the most admired man in America.

The expansionism of the United States and its businesses did not stop at the borders but exerted a strong influence on Mexico and the Caribbean. Naval officers, bankers, and politicians urged active intervention in the Western Hemisphere. In 1898 the United States defeated Spain, annexed Hawaii, Puerto Rico, and the Philippines and turned Cuba into an American protectorate (see Chapter 29). Long recognized as the leading power in the Americas, the United States now found itself involved in Asian affairs as well. Nevertheless, although their country was fast becoming a global power, most Americans still preferred George Washington's policy of "no European entanglements."

China and Japan

In the late nineteenth century, the power of Europe and the United States reached around the world. Its impact on the two most influential countries of East Asia, China and Japan, was completely opposite. While China resisted the Western influence and became weaker, Japan transformed itself into a major industrial and military power on a par with the West.

In the 1860s, China had not yet recovered from the Taiping Rebellion (see Chapter 27), and the French and British took advantage of its troubles to demand treaty ports where they could trade at will. The British took over China's customs and allowed the free import of opium until 1917. Foreign influence penetrated inland as well. By 1894, some two thousand Christian missionaries (many of them Americans) were founding churches, hospitals, and schools throughout the country, taking over the traditional role of the Chinese gentry. Although Christians had little success in gaining converts, the gentry resented their special privileges.

A Chinese "self-strengthening movement" tried in vain to bring about significant reforms by reducing government expenditures and eliminating corruption. Empress Dowager Cixi became hostile to all reforms and viewed the telegraph, railways, mines, and other foreign technologies as a wedge to carry foreign influences into the interior, threatening the political status quo. Government officials, who did not dare resist the Westerners outright, secretly encouraged crowds to attack and destroy the intru-

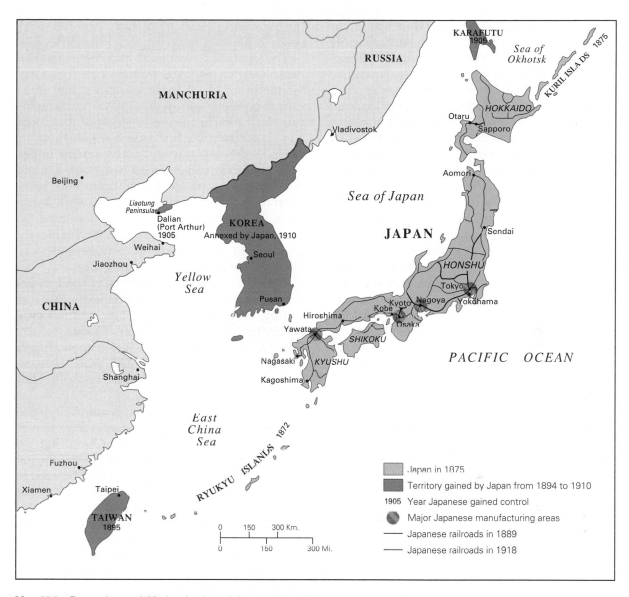

Map 28.3 Expansion and Modernization of Japan, 1868–1914 As Japan acquired modern industry, it followed the example of the European powers in seeking overseas colonies. Its colonial empire grew at the expense of its neighbors: Taiwan was taken from China in 1895, Karafutu (now Sakhalin) from Russia in 1905, and all of Korea became a colony in 1910.

sive devices. They were able to slow down the foreign intrusion, but in doing so, they denied themselves the best means of defense against foreign pressure.

Unlike China, Japan had little contact with the outside world until the 1850s. As we saw in Chapter 27, the arrival in Tokyo Bay in 1853 and 1854 of American warships commanded by Commodore Matthew Perry came as a shock to Japanese society. In 1867 and 1868, after thirteen years of violence and uncertainty, provincial rebels overthrew the Tokugawa shogunate and proclaimed the Meiji era. Unlike the Chinese, the Japanese were under no illusions that they could fend off the powerful Westerners without changing their institutions or their society. Japan had a long history of adopting technologies from China and Korea. In the same spirit, the Japanese eagerly sought to learn the technological secrets of Western strength. From 1868 until the early twentieth century, the "Meiji oligarchs" kept Japan free of Western imperialism by encouraging Japan's transformation into a world-class industrial and military power, under an authoritarian system of government.

In the Charter Oath issued in 1868, the young Emperor Mutsuhito included the prophetic phrase: "Knowledge shall be sought throughout the world and thus shall be strengthened the foundation of the imperial polity." This was to be the motto of a new Japan that embraced all foreign ideas, institutions, and techniques useful to strengthen the nation. Throughout the 1870s and 1880s, the new Japanese government sent hundreds of students to Britain, Germany, and the United States. It hired foreign experts to teach Japanese how to build railroads, organize a modern army and navy, and operate a bureaucracy. It opened vocational, technical, and agricultural schools and founded four imperial universities. It brought in an Englishman, William Ayrton, to the newly created Imperial College of Engineering as the first professor of electrical engineering anywhere in the world. His students later went on to found major corporations and government research institutes.

The Meiji leaders created a government structure similar to that of imperial Germany. They modeled the Japanese navy on the British navy and the Japanese army on the Prussian army, and they introduced Western-style postal and telegraph systems, railroads and harbors, banking, clocks, and calendars. Though imposed by aristocrats, the Meiji Restoration marked as profound a change in political and social life as the French Revolution. All this was done in the name of the emperor, who was worshiped as the embodiment of the nation in a cult known as *Shinto*. By the end of the century, Japan was sufficiently Westernized that the Western powers rescinded the unequal treaties they had imposed forty years earlier.

The Japanese government also encouraged industrialization. It taxed farmers heavily to pay for the purchase of ships, machines, and other capital goods. It set up enterprises to manufacture cloth and cheap consumer goods that could be sold abroad. The first Japanese industries exploited workers ruthlessly, just as the first industries in Europe and America had done. Peasant families, squeezed by rising taxes and rents, often had to send their daughters to work in textile mills in a form of indentured servitude. As soon as these enterprises became profitable, the government sold them to private investors, mainly large *zaibatsu*, or conglomerates.

The classic pattern of industrialization brought not only mass production and the exploitation of factory labor to Japan but also technological creativity. Thus the carpenter Toyoda Sakichi founded the Toyoda Loom Works (now Toyota Motor Company) in 1906. Ten years later, he patented the world's most advanced automatic loom.

The motive for the transformation of Japan was to prevent the Western powers from undermining the nation as they had China. But the methods that strengthened Japan against the imperial ambitions of others could also be used to carry out its own conquests (see Map 28.3). Once involved with the outside world, Japan quickly moved from defensive to offensive action. In 1876, having purchased some modern warships from Britain, it sent them to Korea to extort the same privileges that Westerners had obtained in Japan. This action provoked the intervention of China, which had long claimed suzerainty over Korea. But China was growing weaker as Japan grew stronger. In 1894, the two nations went to war. In less than six months, the Japanese defeated China, forcing it to evacuate Korea, to cede Taiwan and the Liaodong Peninsula, and to pay a heavy indemnity.

France, Germany, Britain, Russia, and the United States, upset at seeing a newcomer join the ranks of the imperialists, made Japan give up Liaodong in the name of the "territorial integrity" of China. In exchange for their "protec-

A silk factory in Japan in the 1870s Silk manufacture had long been one of Japan's best known industries. In 1872, the Japanese government built a modern silk factory using the latest silk-reeling equipment and technology imported from Europe. This inspired private entrepreneurs to do likewise. Notice that all the workers in this factory in Tokyo were women, as was true in most textile mills of that period. (The Metropolitan Museum of Art, Gift of Lincoln Kirstein, 1959. (JP 3346))

tion," the Western powers then made China grant them territorial and trade concessions, including ninety treaty ports where foreigners enjoyed the privilege of extraterritoriality.

Hopes for reform in China modeled on the Meiji Restoration were crushed in 1898, when the Empress Dowager Cixi imprisoned the young Guangxu emperor and ended the "Hundred Days Reform." In 1900, the conservatives who took over encouraged the "Boxer Uprising," a series of antiforeign riots that gave the European powers, Japan, and the United States an excuse to occupy Beijing.

These events underlined how helpless China had become. During those years of humiliation and partial occupation, thousands of young Chinese went abroad—at one point fifteen thousand were studying in Japan—hoping to learn how to modernize their country and make it strong. These young foreign-educated Chinese were to lead a revolution that would overthrow the Manchu rulers in 1911 (see Chapter 32).

In contrast, Japan's participation in the suppression of the Boxer Uprising showed how quickly it had become a military power in East Asia. In the Russo-Japanese War of 1905, Japan surprised the world by defeating the Russian Empire. In spite of Western attempts to restrict it to the role of junior partner, Japan continued to increase its military and economic influence. It gained control of southern Manchuria, one of China's richest provinces, with its industries and railroads. In 1910, it annexed Korea, thereby joining the ranks of the world's colonial powers.

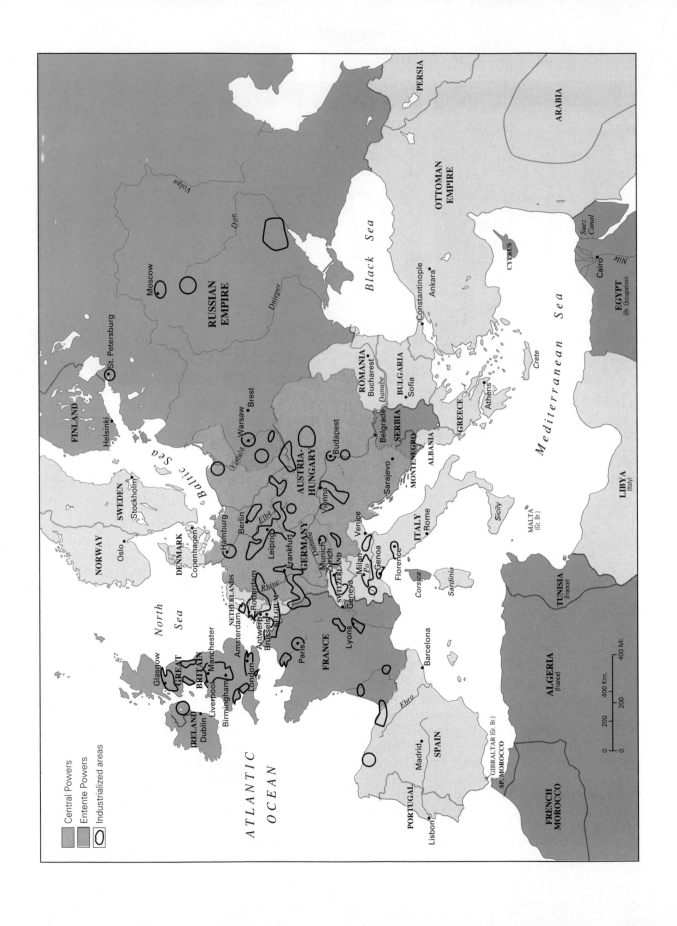

Central Powers
Entente Powers
Industrialized areas

PERSIA

ARABIA

OTTOMAN
EMPIRE

Suez
Canal

Nile

Cairo

EGYPT
(Br. Occupation)

Black Sea

Volga

Don

Moscow

RUSSIAN
EMPIRE

Dnieper

St. Petersburg

Helsinki

FINLAND

Warsaw

Brest

Vistula

Budapest

ROMANIA

Bucharest

Danube

BULGARIA

Sofia

Belgrade

SERBIA

Sarajevo

MONTENEGRO

ALBANIA

GREECE

Athens

Constantinople

Ankara

CYPRUS

Crete

Mediterranean Sea

Stockholm

SWEDEN

NORWAY

Oslo

Copenhagen

DENMARK

Baltic Sea

Berlin

Hamburg

Elbe

Leipzig

Frankfurt

GERMANY

Munich

Zurich

SWITZERLAND

Geneva

Danube

Vienna

AUSTRIA-
HUNGARY

Venice

Milan

Po

Genoa

Florence

ITALY

Rome

Sicily

MALTA
(Gr. Br.)

LIBYA
(Italy)

Corsica

Sardinia

TUNISIA
(France)

Rhine

NETHERLANDS

Amsterdam

Rotterdam

Antwerp

Brussels

BELGIUM

Paris

FRANCE

Lyons

*North
Sea*

Glasgow

GREAT
BRITAIN

Manchester

Liverpool

Birmingham

London

IRELAND

Dublin

*ATLANTIC
OCEAN*

Barcelona

Ebro

SPAIN

Madrid

PORTUGAL

Lisbon

GIBRALTAR (Gr. Br.)

SP. MOROCCO

ALGERIA
(France)

FRENCH
MOROCCO

400 Mi.

400 Km.

200

200

0

0

CONCLUSION

After World War I broke out in 1914, many people, especially in Europe, looked back on the period from 1850 to 1914 as a golden age. For some, and in certain ways, it was. Industrialization was now a powerful torrent changing Europe, North America, and East Asia. The great scourges—famines, wars, and epidemics—receded in people's memories. Clean water, electric lights, and railways began to improve the lives of city dwellers, even the poor. Goods from distant lands, even travel to other continents, fell within the reach of millions.

European and American society seemed to be heading toward better organization and greater security for its members. Municipal services made city life less dangerous and chaotic. Through labor unions, workers achieved some measure of recognition and security. By the turn of the century, liberal political reforms had taken hold in western Europe and the United States and seemed about to triumph in Russia as well. Morality and legislation aimed at providing security for women and families, though equality between the sexes was still beyond reach.

The framework for all these changes was the nation-state. The world economy, international politics, even cultural and social issues revolved around a handful of countries—the great powers—that believed themselves in control of the destiny of the world. Seldom in history had there been such a concentration of wealth, of power, and of self-confidence.

The success of the great powers rested on their ability to extract resources from nature and from other societies, especially in Asia, Africa, and Latin America. In a global context, the counterpart of the rise of the great powers is the story of imperialism and colonialism. To complete our understanding of the period before 1914, let us turn now to the relations between the great powers and the rest of the world.

Map 28.4 Europe in 1913 On the eve of World War I, Europe was divided between two great alliance systems: the Central Powers (Germany, Austria-Hungary, and Italy) and the Entente (France, Great Britain, and Russia), and their respective colonial empires. These alliances were not stable, however; when war broke out, the Central Powers lost Italy but gained the Ottoman Empire (see Chapter 30).

SUGGESTED READING

More has been written on the great powers in the late nineteenth century than on any previous period in their histories. The following are some interesting recent works and a few classics.

Industrialization is the subject of David Landes, *The Unbound Prometheus: Technological Change and Industrial Development in Western Europe from 1750 to the Present* (1969), and Peter Stearns, *The Industrial Revolution in World History* (1993). Two interesting works on nationalism are E. J. Hobsbawm, *Nations and Nationalism Since 1780* (1990), and Hans Kohn, *The Age of Nationalism* (1976).

Barrington Moore, *The Social Origins of Dictatorship and Democracy* (1966), is a classic essay on European society. On European women see Renate Bridenthal, Claudia Koonz, and Susan Stuard, eds., *Becoming Visible: Women in European History* (1987); Patricia Branca, *Silent Sisterhood: Middle-Class Women in the Victorian Home* (1975); Louise Tilly and Joan Scott, *Women, Work, and Family* (1987); and Theresa McBride, *The Domestic Revolution: The Modernization of Household Service in England and France 1820–1920* (1976). The history of family life is told in Beatrice Gottlieb, *The Family in the Western World from the Black Death to the Industrial Age* (1993). Albert Lindemann, *A History of European Socialism* (1983), covers the labor movements as well.

There are many excellent histories of individual countries. Germany in the late nineteenth century is well treated in Erich Eyck, *Bismarck and the German Empire* (1964). On Britain see Donald Read, *The Age of Urban Democracy: England, 1868–1914* (1994), and David Thomson, *England in the Nineteenth Century, 1815–1914* (1978). On France, Eugen Weber, *Peasants into Frenchmen* (1976), and Roger Price, *A Social History of Nineteenth-Century France* (1987), are especially recommended. A good introduction to Russian history is Hans Rogger, *Russia in the Age of Modernization and Revolution, 1881–1917* (1983). Carl Schorske, *Fin de Siècle Vienna*

(1980), is a most interesting book on the politics and culture of Austria-Hungary.

Three very different aspects of American life are described in Carl Degler's *Out of Our Past: The Forces That Shaped Modern America* (1970), David Nye's *Electrifying America: Social Meaning of a New Technology* (1992), and Emily Rosenberg's *Spreading the American Dream: American Economic and Cultural Expansion, 1890–1945* (1982).

There are several interesting books on Japan, in particular Richard Storry, *A History of Modern Japan* (1982), and Tessa Morris-Suzuki, *The Technological Transformation of Japan* (1994). Two fine books cover the history of modern China: John King Fairbank, *The Great Chinese Revolution, 1800–1985* (1987), and Jonathan D. Spence, *The Search for Modern China* (1990).

NOTE

1. Quoted in Bonnie S. Anderson and Judith P. Zinsser, *A History of Their Own: Women in Europe from Prehistory to the Present* (New York: Harper & Row, 1988), vol. 2, pp. 372 and 387.

The New Imperialism, 1869–1914

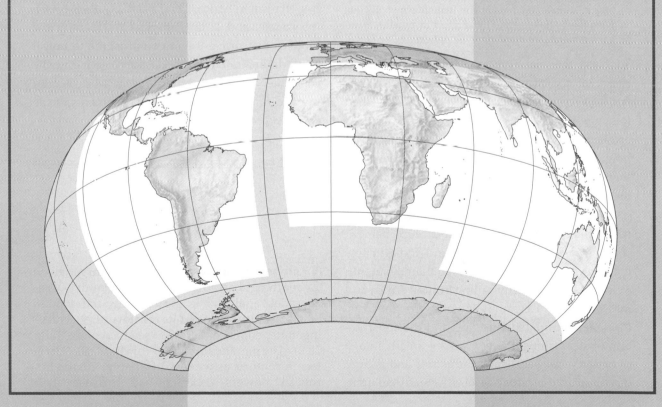

In November 1869, Empress Eugénie of France, Emperor Francis Joseph of Austria-Hungary, and sixteen hundred other dignitaries from the Middle East and Europe assembled at Port Said in Egypt to celebrate the inauguration of the greatest construction project of the century: the Suez Canal. In his invitations, Ismail, the khedive of Egypt, had included all the Christian princes of Europe and all the Muslim princes of Asia and Africa, except the Ottoman sultan, his nominal overlord. He wanted to show that Egypt was not only independent but an equal of the great powers.

Ismail also used this occasion to emphasize the harmony and cooperation between the peoples of Africa, Asia, and Europe. A French journalist wrote:

> This multitude, coming from all parts of the world, presented the most varied and singular spectacle. All races were represented. . . . We saw, coming to attend this festival of civilization, men of the Orient wearing clothes of dazzling colors, chiefs of African tribes wrapped in their great coats, Circassians in war costumes, officers of the British army of India with their shakos [hats] wrapped in muslin, Hungarian magnates wearing their national costumes.[1]

To bless the inauguration, Ismail had invited clergy of the Muslim, Orthodox, and Catholic faiths. A reported note: "The Khedive . . . wished to symbolize thereby the unity of men and their brotherhood before God, without distinction of religion; it was the first time that the Orient had seen such a meeting of faiths to celebrate and bless together a great event and a great work."[2]

The canal was a great success, but not in the way Ismail had intended it to be. Ships using it could travel between Europe and India in less than two weeks—much less time than the month or longer consumed by sailing around Africa and into the Indian Ocean. By lowering freight costs, the canal stimulated shipping and the construction of steamships, thereby giving an advantage to nations that had heavy industries and a large maritime trade. Great Britain, which had long opposed the construction of the canal for fear that it might fall into enemy hands, benefited more than any other nation. France, which had provided half of the capital and most of the engineers, came in a distant second, for it had less trade with Asia than Britain did. Egypt, which had contributed the other half of the money and most of the labor, was the loser in this affair. Instead of making Egypt powerful and independent, the Suez Canal provided the excuse for a British invasion and occupation of Egypt. Far from inaugurating an era of harmony among the peoples of three continents and three faiths, the canal triggered a wave of European domination over Africa and Asia.

Between 1869 and 1914 Germany, France, Britain, Russia, and the United States (great powers discussed in Chapter 28) used industrial technology to impose their will on the nonindustrial parts of the world. Historians use the expression *New Imperialism* to describe this exercise of power. In this chapter, we study the workings of the New Imperialism in Africa, Central and Southeast Asia, the Pacific, and Latin America. We identify the motives that drove the imperialists; the technical and administrative methods they used, and the consequences of their actions for the world economy and for the peoples and environments of the colonized countries.

THE NEW IMPERIALISM: MOTIVES AND METHODS

Europe had a long tradition of imperialism reaching back to the twelfth-century Crusades against the Arabs, and the United States greatly expanded its territory after achieving independence in 1783 (see Maps 25.3 and 28.2). During the first two-thirds of the nineteenth century, as we saw in Chapter 26, the European powers continued to increase their influence overseas. The New Imperialism was characterized by an explosion of territorial conquests. Between 1869 and 1914, in a land grab of unprecedented speed, Europeans took territories in Africa and Central Asia, and both Europeans and Americans took territories in Southeast Asia and the Pacific. Approximately 10 million square miles (26 million square kilometers) and 150 million people fell under the rule of Europe and the United States in this period.

The New Imperialism, however, was more than a gigantic land grab. It also involved the use of economic and technological means to reorganize dependent regions and bring them into the world economy as suppliers of foodstuffs and raw materials and as consumers of industrial products. In Africa and other parts of the world, this was done by conquest and colonial administration. In the Latin American republics, the same result was achieved indirectly. Those republics became economic dependencies of the United States and Europe even though they remained politically independent.

What inspired Europeans and Americans to venture overseas and impose their will on other societies? There is no simple answer to this question. Economic, cultural, and political motives were involved in each case.

Political Motives

The great powers of the late nineteenth century, as well as less powerful countries like Italy, Portugal, and Belgium, were competitive and hypersensitive about their status. French leaders, humiliated by their defeat at the hands of Prussia in 1871 (see Chapter 28), sought to reestablish their nation's prestige through territorial acquisitions overseas. Great Britain, already in possession of the largest and richest empire in the world, felt the need to protect India, its "jewel in the crown," by acquiring colonies in East Africa and Southeast Asia. Although German chancellor Otto von Bismarck had little interest in acquiring colonies, many Germans believed that a country as important as theirs required an equally impressive empire overseas.

Political motives were not limited to statesmen in the capital cities. Colonial governors, even officers posted to the farthest outposts of colonies, practiced their own diplomacy. They often decided on their own to claim a piece of land before some rival got it. Armies involved in frontier wars found it easier to defeat their neighbors than to make peace with them. In response to border skirmishes with neighboring states, the colonial agents were likely to send in troops, take over their neighbors' territories, and then inform their home governments. Governments felt obligated to back up their men-on-the-spot in order not to lose face. Much of West Africa, Southeast Asia, and the Pacific islands were acquired in this manner.

Cultural Motives

The late nineteenth century saw a Christian revival in Europe and North America, as both Catholics and Protestants founded new missionary societies.

Religion and Imperialism The European penetration into Africa was accompanied by enthusiastic efforts to convert the Africans to Christianity. European missionaries built schools and clinics as well as churches. Here African schoolchildren are shown a picture of the Virgin Mary holding the baby Jesus, an image clearly designed to replace traditional African religious objects. Mary and Jesus are represented as Europeans. (Ikon/USGP)

Their purpose was not only religious—to convert nonbelievers, whom they regarded as "heathen"—but also cultural in a broader sense. They sought to export their own norms of "civilized" behavior: they were determined to abolish slavery in Africa and bring Western education, medicine, hygiene, and monogamous marriages to all the world's peoples.

Among those attracted by religious work overseas were many women, who joined missionary societies to become teachers and nurses, positions of greater authority than they could hope to find at home. Although they did not challenge colonialism directly, their influence often helped soften the harshness of colonial rule—for example, by calling attention to issues of maternity and women's health. Mary Slessor, a British missionary who lived for forty years among the people of southeastern Nigeria, campaigned against slavery, human sacrifice, and the killing of twins and, generally, for women's rights. In India, missionaries denounced the customs of child marriages and *sati* (the burning of widows on their husbands' funeral pyres). Such views often clashed with the customs of the people among whom they settled.

The sense of moral duty and cultural superiority was not limited to missionaries. Many Europeans and Americans, equating technological innovations with "progress" and "change for the better" believed that the power of Western technology proved the superiority of Western ideas, customs, and culture. This attitude, though self-congratulatory, at least included the idea that non-Western peoples could achieve, through education, the same cultural level as Europeans and Americans. More harmful were the racist ideas prevailing at the time, which relegated non-Europeans to a status of permanent inferiority. Social Darwinists (see Chapter 28) assigned different stages of biological development to peoples of different races and cultures. They divided humankind into several races based on physical appearance and ranked these races in a hierarchy that ranged from "civilized" at the highest level down through "semibarbarous," "barbarian," and finally, at the bottom, "savage." Caucasians—whites—were always at the top of this ranking. Such ideas were often presented as excuses for the permanent rule over Africans and Asians.

Imperialism first interested small groups of academics, clergy, and businessmen but soon attracted people from other walks of life. Young men, finding few opportunities for adventure and glory at home in an era of peace, sought them overseas as the Spanish *conquistadores* of Europe's "Age of Discovery" had done over three centuries earlier. At first, the European public and parliaments were indifferent or hostile to overseas adventures, but a few easy victories in the 1880s helped to overcome their reluctance. The United States was fully preoccupied with its westward expansion until the 1880s, but in the 1890s popular attention shifted to lands outside U.S. borders. Newspapers, which achieved a wide readership in the second half of the nineteenth century, discovered they could boost circulation with reports of wars and conquests. By the 1890s, imperialism had become a popular cause; it was the overseas extension of the nationalism that characterized the power politics of the time.

Economic Motives

The industrialization of Europe and North America stimulated the demand for minerals such as copper for electrical wiring, tin for canning, chrome and manganese for the steel industry, coal for steam engines, and, most of all, gold and diamonds. The demand for such industrial crops as cotton and rubber and for stimulants like sugar, coffee, tea, and tobacco also grew. These products were found in the tropics, but never in sufficient quantities. An economic depression lasting from the mid-1870s to the mid-1890s caused European merchants, manufacturers, and shippers to seek protection against foreign competition (see below). They argued that their respective countries needed secure sources of tropical raw materials and foodstuffs and protected markets for their industries. Declining business opportunities at home prompted entrepreneurs and investors to look for profits from mines, plantations, and railroads in Asia, Africa, and Latin America. Investment in countries so different from their own, however, was extremely risky. Businessmen and bankers therefore eagerly sought the political backing of their government, preferably with soldiers.

These reasons explain why Europeans and Americans wished to expand their influence over other societies in the late nineteenth and early twentieth centuries. Yet motives alone are not enough to explain the events of that time. What made the motives effective, what made it seem desirable and even relatively simple to conquer a piece of Africa, to convert the "heathen," or to start a plantation, was the sudden increase in the power at the disposal of industrial peoples over nonindustrial peoples and over the forces of nature. Technological advances explain both the surge of motives and the outcome of the New Imperialism.

The Tools of the Imperialists

To succeed, empire builders needed the means to achieve their objectives at a reasonable cost. These means were a consequence of the Industrial Revolution (see Chapter 23). Since the early part of the nineteenth century, technological innovations had begun to tip the balance of power in favor of Europe. Europeans had dominated the oceans since the end of the fifteenth century, and their naval power increased still more with the introduction of steamships. The first steamer reached India in 1825 and was soon followed by regular mail service in the 1830s. The long voyage around Africa was at first too costly for cargo steamers, for coal had to be shipped from England. The building of the Suez Canal and the development of increasingly efficient engines solved this problem and led to a boom in shipping to the Indian Ocean and East Asia. Whenever fighting broke out, passenger liners were requisitioned as troopships, giving European forces greater mobility than Asians and Africans. Their advantage was enhanced even more by the development of a global network of submarine telegraph cables connecting Europe with North America in the 1860s, with Latin America and Asia in the 1870s, with Africa in the 1880s, and finally across the Pacific in 1904 (see Environment and Technolo-

gy: The Annihilation of Time and Space, in Chapter 23.)

Until the middle of the nineteenth century, Europeans were much weaker on land than at sea. Thereafter, Europeans used gunboats with considerable success in China, Burma, Indochina, and the Congo Basin. Although gunboats opened up the major river basins to European penetration, the invaders often found themselves hampered by other natural obstacles. *Falciparum* malaria, found only in Africa, was so deadly to Europeans that few explorers survived before the 1850s. In 1854 a British doctor discovered that the drug quinine, taken regularly during one's stay in Africa, could prevent the disease. These and a few sanitary precautions reduced the annual death rate among whites in West Africa from between 250 and 750 per thousand in the early nineteenth century to between 50 and 100 per thousand after the midcentury. This reduction was sufficient to open the continent to merchants, officials, and missionaries.

Muzzleloading smoothbore muskets had been used in Europe, Asia, and the Americas since the late seventeenth century, and by the early nineteenth century they were also common in much of Africa. The development of new and much deadlier firearms in the 1860s and 1870s shifted the balance of power on land between Westerners and other peoples. One of these was the breechloader, which could be fired accurately ten times as fast as, and five or six times farther than, a musket. By the 1870s armies in Europe and the United States had all switched to these new rifles. Two more innovations appeared in the 1880s: smokeless powder, which did not foul the gun or reveal the soldier's position, and repeating rifles, which could shoot fifteen rounds in fifteen seconds. In the 1890s, European and American armies began using machine guns, which could fire eleven bullets per second.

In the course of the century, Asians and Africans also acquired better firearms, mostly old weapons that European armies had discarded. As European firearms improved, the firepower gap widened, making colonial conquests easier than ever before. By the 1880s and 1890s, European-led forces of a few hundred could defeat non-European armies of thousands. Against

The Battle of Omdurman   In the late nineteenth century, battles between European (or European-led) troops and African forces were largely one-sided because of the disparity of firearms and tactics between the two sides. The Battle of Omdurman in the Sudan in 1898 is a dramatic example. The forces of the Mahdi, some on horseback, were armed with spears and single-shot muskets. The British troops and their Egyptian allies, in the foreground, used repeating rifles and machine guns with a much longer range than the Sudanese weapons. As a result, there were many Sudanese casualties but very few British or Egyptian. (E. T. Archive)

the latest weapons, African and Asian soldiers armed with muskets or, in some cases, with spears did not stand a chance, no matter how numerous and courageous they were.

A classic example is the Battle of Omdurman in the Sudan. On September 2, 1898, 40,000 Sudanese attacked an Anglo-Egyptian expedition that had come up the Nile on six steamers and four other boats. General Horatio Kitchener's troops had twenty machine guns and four artillery pieces; the Sudanese were equipped with muskets and spears. Within a few hours, 11,000 Sudanese and 48 British lay dead. Winston Churchill, the future British prime minister, witnessed the battle and called it

the most signal triumph ever gained by the arms of science over barbarians. Within the space of five hours the strongest and best-armed savage army yet arrayed against a modern European Power had been destroyed and dispersed, with hardly any difficulty, comparatively small risk, and insignificant loss to the victors.[3]

Colonial Agents and Administration

Once colonial agents had taken over a territory, their home government expected them to cover their own costs and, if possible, bring some profit to their home country. In some cases, such as along the West African coast or in Indochina, there was already a considerable trade that could be taxed. In many other places, however, the profits of colonialism could come only from investments and from a thorough reorganization of the indigenous societies. In applying modern scientific and industrial methods to the exploitation of their colonies, colonialists started the transformation of Asian and African societies and landscapes that has continued to our day.

Legal experts and academics placed a great emphasis on the differences between various systems of colonial government and debated whether colonies eventually should be assimilated into the ruling nation, associated in a federation, or allowed to rule themselves. Colonies that were *protectorates* retained their traditional governments, even their monarchs, but had a European "resident" or "consul general" to "advise" them. Other colonies were directly administered by a European governor. In fact, the impact of colonial rule depended much more on economic and social conditions than on narrow legal distinctions.

One important factor was the presence or absence of European settlers. In Canada, Australia, and New Zealand, whites were already in the majority by 1869, and their colonial "mother-country," Britain, encouraged them to elect parliaments and rule themselves. Where European settlers were numerous but nonetheless a minority of the population, as in Algeria and South Africa, colonialism involved a struggle between the settlers and the home country for control over the indigenous population. In colonies with few white settlers, the European governors ruled autocratically.

In the early years, colonial administrations consisted of a governor and his staff, a few troops to keep order, and a small number of tax collectors and magistrates. Nowhere could colonialism operate without the cooperation of an indigenous elite, because no colony was wealthy enough to pay the salaries of more than a handful of European officials. In most cases, the colonial governors exercised power through traditional rulers willing to cooperate. In addition, colonial governments also educated a few local youths for "modern" jobs as clerks, nurses, policemen, customs inspectors, and the like. Thus colonialism relied on two rival indigenous elites.

European and American women seldom took part in the early stages of colonial expansion. As conquest gave way to peaceful colonialism, however, and as steamships and railroads made travel less difficult, colonial officials and settlers began bringing their wives to the colonies. By the 1880s, the British Women's Emigration Association was recruiting single women to go out to the colonies to marry British settlers. As one of its founders, Ellen Joyce, explained, "The possibility of the settler marrying his own countrywoman is of imperial as well as family importance."

The arrival of white women in Asia and Africa coincided with increasing racial segregation. As Sylvia Leith-Ross, wife of a colonial officer in Nigeria, explained, "When you are alone, among thousands of unknown, unpredictable people, dazed by unaccustomed sights and sounds, bemused by strange ways of life and thought, you need to remember who you are, where you come from, what your standards are." Many colonial wives found themselves in command of numerous servants and expected to follow the complex etiquette of colonial entertainment in support of their husbands' official positions. Only occasionally did these women find opportunities to exercise personal initiatives, usually charitable work involving indigenous women and children. However well meaning, their efforts were always subordinated to the work of men.

THE SCRAMBLE FOR AFRICA

Until the 1870s, African history was largely shaped by internal forces and local initiatives (see Chapter 26). Outside Algeria and southern Africa, only a handful of Europeans had ever visited the interior of Africa, and European countries possessed only small enclaves on the coasts. As late as 1879, Africans ruled more than 90 percent of the continent. Then in a decade Africa was invaded and divided among

The Scramble for Africa

1868	Diamonds discovered at Kimberly (South Africa)
1869	Opening of the Suez Canal
1873–74, 1893–94, 1895–96	Anglo-Asante Wars (Gold Coast)
1877–78	Anglo-Xhosa and Anglo-Zulu Wars (South Africa)
1882	British forces occupy Egypt
1883–88	French conquer upper Niger region (West Africa)
1885	Berlin Conference; Leopold obtains Congo Free State
1896–98	British conquer Sudan
1896	Ethiopians defeat Italian army at Adowa (Ethiopia)
1899	Nigeria becomes British protectorate
1899–1902	South African or Anglo-Boer War
1908	Congo annexed by Belgium
1912	Morocco becomes French protectorate

the European powers in a movement often referred to as the "Scramble for Africa" (see Map 29.1). This invasion affected all regions of the continent. Let us look at the most significant cases, beginning with Egypt, the wealthiest and most populated part of the continent.

Egypt

Ironically, European involvement in Egypt resulted from an Egyptian attempt to free itself from Ottoman Turkish influence. Throughout the mid-nineteenth century, the khedives of Egypt had tried to modernize their armed forces; build canals, harbors, railroads, and other public works; and reorient Egyptian agriculture toward export crops, especially cotton (see Chapters 23 and 26). Their interest in the Suez Canal was also part of this policy. Khedive Ismail even tried to make Egypt the center of an empire reaching south into the Sudan and Ethiopia.

These ambitions cost vast sums of money, which the khedives borrowed from various European creditors at high interest rates. By 1876, Egypt's foreign debt had risen to £100 million sterling, and the interest payments alone consumed one-third of its foreign export earnings. To avoid bankruptcy, the Egyptian government had to sell its shares in the Suez Canal to Great Britain and accept four foreign "commissioners of the debt" to oversee its finances. French and British bankers, still not satisfied, lobbied their governments to secure the loans by stronger measures. In 1878 the two governments obliged Ismail to appoint a Frenchman as minister of public works and a Briton as minister of finance. When high taxes caused hardship and popular discontent, the French and British had Ismail deposed by the Ottoman sultan. This provoked a military uprising under Egyptian army colonel Arabi Pasha, which threatened the Suez Canal.

Fearing for their investments, the British sent an army into Egypt in 1882. Originally they intended to occupy Egypt for only a year or two, but so important was the Suez Canal to their maritime supremacy that they stayed for seventy years. During those years the British ruled Egypt "indirectly"—that is, they maintained the Egyptian government and the fiction of Egyptian sovereignty but retained the real power in their own hands.

Sir Evelyn Baring, British consul-general from 1883 to 1907, was eager to develop Egyptian agriculture, especially cotton production. He brought in engineers and contractors to build the first dam across the Nile at Aswan in upper Egypt. When it was completed in 1902, it was one of the largest dams in the world. It captured the annual Nile flood and released its waters throughout the year, allowing farmers to grow two, sometimes three, crops a year. This doubled the effective acreage compared with the basin system of irrigation practiced since the time of the pharaohs, in which the annual floodwaters of the Nile were retained by low dikes around the fields.

The economic development of the country enriched a small elite of landowners and merchants, many of them foreigners. Egyptian peasants got little relief from the heavy taxes collected to pay for their country's crushing for-

The opening of the Suez Canal The inauguration of the Suez Canal in 1869 was the scene of tremendous celebrations. Not only did hundreds of princes and high officials attend the official ceremonies, but tens of thousands of ordinary Egyptians and foreign tourists lined the banks of the new canal to watch the long procession of ships making their way from the Mediterranean to the Red Sea. (Staatsbibliothek, Berlin)

eign debt and the expenses of the British army of occupation. Western ways that conflicted with the teachings of Islam offended Muslim religious leaders. By the 1890s, most Egyptian politicians and intellectuals were demanding that the British leave, but to no avail.

Western and Equatorial Africa

While the British were taking over Egypt, the French were planning to extend their empire into the interior of West Africa. Starting from the coast of Senegal, which had been in French hands for centuries, they hoped to build a railroad from the upper Senegal River to the upper Niger, thereby opening up the trade of the interior to French merchants.

Meanwhile, it was the actions of three individuals, rather than a government, that brought about the occupation of the Congo Basin, an enormous forested region in the heart of equatorial Africa (see Map 29.1). In 1879, the American journalist Henry Morton Stanley, who had explored the area, persuaded Leopold II, king of Belgium, to invest his personal fortune in "opening up" equatorial Africa. With Leopold's money, Stanley returned to Africa from 1879 to 1884 to establish trading posts along the left bank of the Congo River. At the same time, the Italian explorer Savorgnan de Brazza obtained from Makoko, an African ruler living on the opposite bank, a treaty that placed the area under the "protection" of France.

These events sparked a flurry of diplomatic activity. German chancellor Bismarck called the Berlin Conference of 1884 and 1885. There the major powers agreed that henceforth "effective occupation" would replace the former trading relations between Africans and Europeans. This meant that every country with colonial ambitions had to send troops into Africa and participate in the division of the spoils. As a reward for

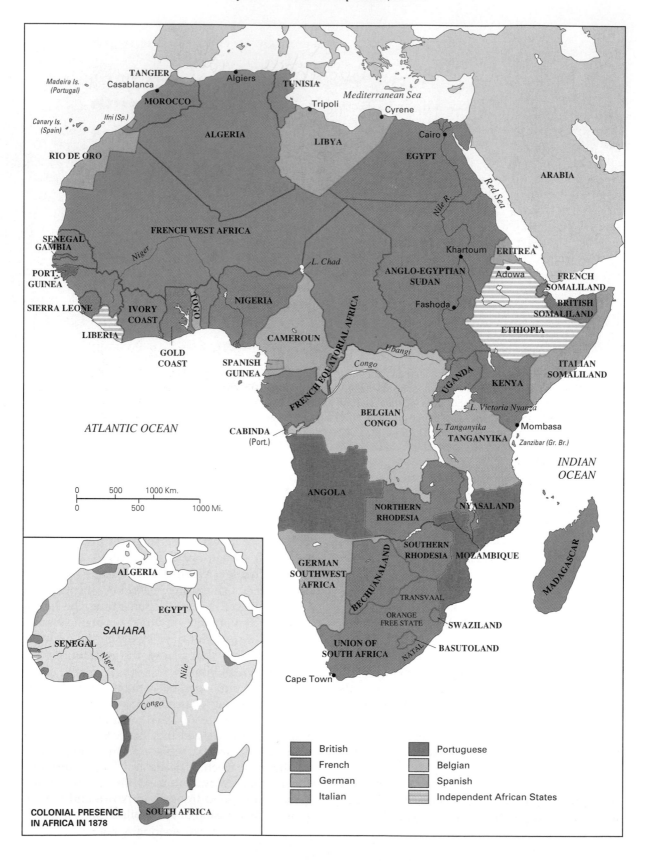

Madeira Is.
(Portugal)

Canary Is.
(Spain)

Ifni (Sp.)

TANGIER
Casablanca

Algiers

TUNISIA

Mediterranean Sea

Tripoli

Cyrene

MOROCCO

RIO DE ORO

ALGERIA

LIBYA

EGYPT

Cairo

Nile R.

Red Sea

ARABIA

FRENCH WEST AFRICA

Niger

L. Chad

Khartoum

ANGLO-EGYPTIAN
SUDAN

ERITREA

Adowa

FRENCH
SOMALILAND

SENEGAL
GAMBIA

PORT.
GUINEA

SIERRA LEONE

IVORY
COAST

TOGO

NIGERIA

CAMEROUN

FRENCH EQUATORIAL AFRICA

Fashoda

Ubangi

BRITISH
SOMALILAND

ETHIOPIA

LIBERIA

GOLD
COAST

SPANISH
GUINEA

Congo

ITALIAN
SOMALILAND

ATLANTIC OCEAN

CABINDA
(Port.)

BELGIAN
CONGO

UGANDA

L. Victoria Nyanza

L. Tanganyika

KENYA

Mombasa

Zanzibar (Gr. Br.)

TANGANYIKA

INDIAN
OCEAN

0   500   1000 Km.

0   500   1000 Mi.

ANGOLA

NORTHERN
RHODESIA

NYASALAND

GERMAN
SOUTHWEST
AFRICA

BECHUANALAND

SOUTHERN
RHODESIA

MOZAMBIQUE

MADAGASCAR

TRANSVAAL

ORANGE
FREE STATE

SWAZILAND

UNION OF
SOUTH AFRICA

NATAL

BASUTOLAND

Cape Town

ALGERIA

EGYPT

SAHARA

SENEGAL

Niger

Nile

Congo

SOUTH AFRICA

**COLONIAL PRESENCE
IN AFRICA IN 1878**

British

French

German

Italian

Portuguese

Belgian

Spanish

Independent African States

A steamboat for the Congo River   Soon after Henry Morton Stanley and Savorgnan de Brazza opened the Congo Basin to European conquest, the new colonial rulers realized they needed better transportation. Since access from the sea was blocked by rapids on the lower Congo River, steamboats had to be brought in sections, hauled from the coast by thousands of Congolese over very difficult terrain. This picture shows the pieces arriving at Stanley Pool, ready to be reassembled. (From H. M. Stanley, *The Congo*, vol. II, London, 1885)

triggering the Scramble for Africa, Leopold II acquired a personal domain under the name "Congo Free State" (now Zaire), while France and Portugal took most of the rest of equatorial Africa. In this manner, the European powers and King Leopold managed to divide Africa among them, at least on paper.

"Effective occupation" required many years of effort. In the interior of West Africa, French troops encountered the determined opposition of Mus-

Map 29.1 Africa in 1878 and 1914   These two maps show the expansion of the European colonial empires into Africa at the end of the nineteenth century. In 1878, the European colonial presence was limited to a few coastal enclaves, plus portions of Algeria and South Africa. By 1914, all of Africa, except Ethiopia and Liberia, had been taken over by Europeans.

lim rulers who resisted the invasion for up to thirty years. The French advance encouraged the Germans to stake claims to parts of the region and the British to move north from their coastal enclaves, until the entire region was occupied by Britain, France, and Germany.

Because West Africa had long had a flourishing trade, the new rulers took advantage of existing trade networks, taxing merchants and farmers, investing the profits in railroads and harbors, and paying dividends to European stockholders. In the Gold Coast (now Ghana), British trading companies bought at low prices the cocoa grown by African farmers and resold it for large profits. The interior of French West Africa lagged behind. Although the region could produce cotton, peanuts, and other crops, the difficulties of transportation limited its development before 1914.

Compared to West Africa, equatorial Africa had few inhabitants and little trade. Rather than try to govern these vast territories directly, the Congo Free State, the French Congo, and the Portuguese colonies of Angola and Mozambique farmed out huge pieces of land to private concession companies, offering them a monopoly on the natural resources and trade of their territories and the right to employ soldiers and to tax the inhabitants. The inhabitants, however, had no cash crops they could sell to raise the money they needed to pay their taxes.

Freed from outside supervision, the companies forced the African inhabitants at gunpoint to produce cash crops and carry them, on their heads or backs, to the nearest railroad or navigable river. The worst abuses took place in the Congo Free State, where a rubber boom lasting from 1895 to 1905 made it profitable for private companies to coerce Africans to collect latex from vines that grew in the forests. After 1906 the British press began publicizing the horrors. The public outcry that followed, coinciding with the end of the rubber boom, convinced the Belgian government to take over Leopold's private empire in 1908.

Southern Africa

The history of southern Africa between 1869 and 1914 differs from that of the rest of the continent in several important respects. One was that the land had long attracted settlers. African pastoralists and farmers had inhabited the region for centuries. Afrikaners, descendants of Dutch settlers on the Cape of Good Hope, moved inland throughout the nineteenth century; British prospectors and settlers arrived later in the century; and, finally, Indians were brought over by the British and stayed.

The reason southern Africa attracted European settlers was its good pastures and farmland and its phenomenal deposits of diamonds, gold, and copper, as well as coal and iron ore. This was the new El Dorado that imperialists had dreamed of since the heyday of the Spanish Empire in Peru and Mexico (see Chapter 17).

The discovery of diamonds at Kimberley in 1868 immediately lured numerous European prospectors as well as Africans looking for work. It also attracted the interest of Great Britain, colonial ruler of the Cape Colony, which annexed the diamond area in 1871, thereby angering the Afrikaners. Once in the interior, the British got involved in a war with the Xhosa people in 1877 and 1878. Then in 1879 they confronted the Zulu, militarily the most powerful of the African peoples in the region.

The Zulu, led by their king Cetshwayo, resented their encirclement by Afrikaners and British. A growing sense of nationalism and their proud military tradition led them into a war with the British in 1879. At first they held their own, defeating the British at Isandhlwana, but a few months later they were in turn defeated. Cetshwayo was captured and sent into exile, and the Zulu's lands were given to white ranchers. Yet throughout those bitter times, their sense of nationhood remained strong.

Relations between the British and the Afrikaners, already tense as a result of British encroachments, took a turn for the worse when gold was discovered in the Afrikaner republic of Transvaal in 1886. In the gold rush that ensued, the Afrikaners were soon outnumbered by the British.

Britain's invasion of southern Africa was driven in part by the ambition of Cecil Rhodes (1853–1902), who once declared that he would "annex the stars" if he could. Rhodes made his fortune in the Kimberley diamond fields, founding De Beers Consolidated, a company that has dominated the world's diamond trade ever since. He then turned to politics. He led a concession company, the British South Africa Company, to push north into Central Africa, where he named two new colonies after himself: Southern Rhodesia (now Zimbabwe) and Northern Rhodesia (now Zambia). The Ndebele and Shona peoples, who inhabited the region, resisted this invasion, but the machine guns of the British finally defeated them.

British attempts to annex the two Afrikaner republics, Transvaal and Orange Free State, and the inflow of English-speaking whites into the gold and diamond mining areas led to the South African War, which lasted from 1899 to 1902. At first the Afrikaners had the upper hand, for they were highly motivated, possessed modern rifles, and knew the land. In 1901, however, Great Britain brought in 450,000 troops and crushed the Afrikaner armies. Ironically, the Afrikaners' defeat in 1902 led to their ultimate victory. The British government, wary of costly commitments overseas, expected European settlers to manage their own affairs, as they were doing in Canada, Australia, and New Zealand. Thus the European settlers created the Union of South Africa in 1910, in which the Afrikaners eventually emerged as the ruling element.

Unlike Canada, Australia, and New Zealand, South Africa had a majority of indigenous inhabitants and substantial numbers of Indians and "Cape Coloureds" (people of mixed ancestry). Yet the Europeans were both numerous enough to demand self-rule and powerful enough to

deny the vote and other civil rights to the majority. In 1913 the South African parliament passed the Natives Land Act, assigning Africans to reservations and forbidding them to own land elsewhere. This and other racial policies turned South Africa into a land of segregation, oppression, and bitter antagonism.

Political and Social Consequences

Africa at the time of the European invasion contained a wide variety of societies. Some parts of the continent had long-established kingdoms with aristocracies or commercial towns dominated by a merchant class. In other places, agricultural peoples lived in villages without any

An Ethiopian victory   Among the states of Africa, Ethiopia alone was able to defend itself against European imperialism. In the 1880s, Ethiopia, hemmed in by Italian advances to its east and north and British advances to its south and west, purchased modern weapons and trained its army to use them. Thus prepared, the Ethiopians defeated an Italian invasion in 1896. Here we see Ethiopian army officers, dressed in their most elaborate finery, posing for a photograph after their victory. (National Archives)

outside government. Still elsewhere, pastoral nomads were organized along military lines. In some remote areas, people lived from hunting and gathering. It is not surprising, then, that these societies responded in very different ways to the European invasion.

Some peoples adapted readily to the European invasion, welcoming the invaders as allies against local enemies. Under colonial rule, they sought a Western education and work in government service or in European firms. In exchange, they were often the first to receive benefits such as schools and roads.

Others, especially peoples with a pastoral or a warrior tradition, fought tenaciously. Examples abound, from the Zulu and Ndebele peoples of southern Africa to the followers of charismatic leaders such as the Mahdi in the eastern Sudan or Samori in the western Sudan (now Mali). In Southwest Africa (now Namibia), the pastoral Herero people rose up against German invaders in 1904; in repressing the uprising, the Germans exterminated two-thirds of them.

Some commercial states with a long history of contact with Europeans also fought back. The kingdom of Asante in Gold Coast rose up three times (in 1874, 1896, and 1900) before it was finally overwhelmed. In the Niger Delta, the ancient city of Benin, rich with artistic treasures, resisted colonial control until 1897, when a British "punitive expedition" set it on fire and carted its works of art off to Europe.

One resistance movement succeeded, to the astonishment of Europeans and Africans alike. When Menelik became emperor of Ethiopia in 1889, his country was threatened by Sudanese Muslims to the west and by France and Italy, which controlled the Red Sea coast to the east. By the Treaty of Wichelle (1889), Italy had agreed to sell modern weapons to Ethiopia. Six years later, when Italians attempted to establish a protectorate over Ethiopia, they found the Ethiopians armed with thousands of rifles and even a few machine guns and artillery pieces. Although Italy sent twenty thousand troops to attack Ethiopia, they were defeated at Adowa in 1896 by a larger and better-trained Ethiopian army.

Most Africans neither joined nor fought the European invaders but tried to continue living as they had been. They found this increasingly difficult, however, for colonial rule disrupted every traditional society. The presence of colonial officials meant that rights to land, commercial transactions, and legal disputes were handled very differently from the way they had been before, and that traditional rulers lost all authority, except where Europeans used them as local administrators.

Changes in landholding were especially disruptive, for most Africans were farmers or herders for whom access to land was a necessity of life. In places with a high population density, such as Egypt and West Africa, the colonial rulers left peasants in place but encouraged them to grow cash crops and then collected taxes on the product of their labor. Elsewhere, the new rulers declared any land that was not farmed to be "waste" or "vacant" and gave it to private concession companies or to European planters and ranchers. Thus Africans found themselves squatters, sharecroppers, or ranch hands on land where they had grown crops or raised animals for generations. In the worst cases, as in South Africa, many were forced off their lands and onto "reserves," like the Indians of the United States (see Chapter 25).

While the colonial rulers harbored designs on the land, they were even more interested in African labor. Yet they did not want to pay wages high enough to attract workers voluntarily. Instead, they imposed various taxes, such as the hut tax or the head tax, which Africans had to pay regardless of their income. To find the money, Africans had little choice but to accept whatever work the Europeans offered, no matter how poorly paid. In this way, Africans were recruited to work on plantations, railroads, and other modern enterprises. In the South African mines, African miners were paid, on average, one-tenth as much as European miners.

Despite the low wages, Africans came to the cities and mining camps seeking a better life than they had on the land. Many migrated great distances and stayed away for years at a time. Most migrant workers were men who left their wives and children behind in villages and on reserves. In some cases, the authorities did not allow them to bring their families and settle permanently in the towns. This caused great hardship for African women, who had to grow food for their families during the men's absences.

Some African women welcomed colonial rule, for it brought an end to fighting and slave raiding (see Voices and Visions: A Nigerian Woman Remembers Her Childhood). On the whole, however, African women benefited less than men from the economic changes that colonialism introduced. In areas where the colonial rulers replaced communal property (traditional in most of Africa) with private property, property rights were assigned to the head of the household—that is, to the man. Almost all the jobs open to Africans, even those considered "women's work" in Europe such as nursing or domestic service, were reserved for men.

Cultural Responses

More Africans probably came into contact with missionaries than with any other Europeans. Missionaries, both men and women, opened schools to teach reading, writing, and arithmetic to village children. Boys were taught crafts such as carpentry and blacksmithing, while girls learned domestic skills such as cooking, laundry, and child care.

Education opened the doors to more than jobs. Along with basic skills, the first generation of Africans educated in mission schools also acquired Western ideas of justice and progress. Samuel Ajayi Crowther, a Yoruba rescued from slavery as a boy and educated in mission schools in Sierra Leone, went on to become an ordained minister and, in 1864, the first African bishop. Crowther thought that Africa needed European assistance in achieving both spiritual and economic development:

> Africa has neither knowledge nor skill . . . to bring out her vast resources for her own improvement. . . . Therefore to claim Africa for the Africans alone, is to claim for her the right of a continued ignorance. . . . For it is certain, unless help [comes] from without, a nation can never rise above its present state.[4]

After the first generation, many of the teachers in mission schools were Africans, themselves the products of a mission education. They discovered that Christian ideals clashed with the reality of colonial exploitation. As a convert named Charles Domingo wrote in 1911:

> There is too much failure among all Europeans in Nyasaland. The three combined bodies—Missionaries, Government and Companies or gainers of money—do form the same rule to look upon the native with mockery eyes. . . . If we had enough power to communicate ourselves to Europe, we would advise them not to call themselves Christendom, but Europeandom. Therefore the life of the three combined bodies is altogether too cheaty, too thefty, too mockery. Instead of "Give," they say "Take away from." There is too much breakage of God's pure law.[5]

Christian missionaries from Europe and America were not the only ones to bring religious change to Africa. In southern and Central Africa, indigenous preachers adapted Christianity to African values and customs and founded new denominations known as "Ethiopian" churches.

Christianity proved successful in converting followers of traditional religions but made no inroads among Muslims. Instead, Islam, long predominant in northern and eastern Africa, spread southward as Muslim teachers established Koranic schools in the villages and founded Muslim brotherhoods. European colonialism may have unwittingly helped the diffusion of Islam by building cities and increasing trade, which not only permitted Muslims to travel and settle in new areas but made Islam—a universal religion without the taint of colonialism—increasingly relevant to Africans. As a result, the number of Muslims in sub-Saharan Africa probably doubled between 1869 and 1914.

ASIA AND WESTERN DOMINANCE

During the period from 1869 to 1914, the pressure of the industrial powers was felt throughout Asia, the East Indies, and the Pacific islands. As trade between these regions and

A Nigerian Woman Remembers Her Childhood

First-person accounts of the period from 1869 to 1914 by African women are extremely rare, for few African women knew how to write and almost none wrote their memoirs. One exception is Baba of Karo, a woman from Zarewa in the Sokoto caliphate (now northern Nigeria), who told her life story to a visiting American anthropologist. This is her recollection of the arrival of the British who conquered Sokoto between 1901 and 1903, when she was a young girl.

When I was a maiden the Europeans first arrived. Ever since we were quite small the *malams* [Koranic scholars] had been saying that the Europeans would come with a thing called a train, they would come with a thing called a motor-car, in them you would go and come back in a trice. They would stop wars, they would repair the world, they would stop oppression and lawlessness, we should live at peace with them. We used to go and sit quietly and listen to the prophecies. They would come, fine handsome people, they would not kill anyone, they would not oppress anyone, they would bring all their strange things. We were young girls when a European came with his attendants—"See, there's a white man, what has brought him?" He was asking the way to some town, we ran away and shut the door and he passed by and went on his way. . . .

I remember when a European came to Karo on a horse, and some of his foot soldiers went into the town. Everyone came out to look at them, but in Zarewa they didn't see the European. Everyone at Karo ran away—"There's a European! There's a European!" He came from Zaria with a few black men, two on horses and four on foot. We were inside the town. Later on we heard that they were there in Zaria in crowds, clearing spaces and building houses. One of my younger "sisters" was at Karo, she was pregnant, and when she saw the European she ran away and shut the door.

At that time Yusufu was the king of Karo. He did not like the Europeans, he did not wish them, he would not sign their treaty. When he saw that perforce he would have to agree, so he did. We Habe [Hausa] wanted them to come, it was the Fulani [ruling class of Sokoto] who did not like it. When the Europeans came the Habe saw that if you worked for them they paid you for it, they didn't say, like the Fulani, "Commoner, give me this! Commoner, bring me that!" Yes, the Habe wanted them; they saw no harm in them. From Zaria they came to Rogo, they were building their big road to Karo City. They called out the people and said they were to come and make the road, if there were trees in the way they cut them down. The Europeans paid them with goods, they collected the villagers together and each man brought his large hoe. Money was not much use to them, so the Europeans paid them with food and other things.

The Europeans said that there were to be no more slaves; if someone said "Slave!" you could complain to the *alkali* [judge] who would punish the master who said it, the judge said "That is what the Europeans have decreed." The first order said that any slave, if he was younger than you, was your younger brother, if he was older than you he was your elder bother—they were all brothers of their master's family. No one used the word "slave" any more. When slavery was stopped, nothing much happened at our *rinji* [slave quarters] except that some slaves whom we had bought in the market ran away. Our own father went to his farm and worked, he and his son took up their large hoes; they loaned out their spare farms. Tsoho our father and Kadiri my brother with whom I live now and Balambo worked, they farmed guineacorn and millet and groundnuts and everything; before this they had supervised the slaves' work—now they did their own. . . .

In the old days if the chief liked the look of your daughter he would take her and put her in his house; you could do nothing about it. Now they don't do that.

This account raises a number of important questions. How did the people in this part of Africa anticipate the arrival of the Europeans? Who favored their coming, and who did not? Why? What impact did the Europeans have on slavery and on labor in this area? Overall, did Baba of Karo approve or disapprove of their coming? Why?

Source: From M. F. Smith, ed., *Baba of Karo: A Woman of the Muslim Hausa* (New York: Philosophical Library, 1955), 66–68. Reprinted by permission of Philosophical Library, New York.

the industrial countries grew in the late nineteenth century, so did their attractiveness to imperialists eager for economic benefits and national prestige.

Europeans had traded along the coasts of Asia and the East Indies since the early sixteenth century (see Chapter 17). By 1869, Britain already controlled most of India and Burma, Spain occupied the Philippines, the Netherlands held large parts of the East Indies (now Indonesia), and France had established a foothold in Indochina (now Vietnam, Kampuchea, and Laos). Here, the opening of the Suez Canal did not trigger a new era of imperialism; rather, it was the existence of these Asian colonial possessions that had inspired the building of the canal.

We have already seen the special cases of British imperialism in India (Chapter 26) and of Japanese imperialism in China and Korea (Chapter 28). Here let us look at the impact of the New Imperialism on Central and Southeast Asia, Indonesia, the Philippines, and Hawaii (see Map 29.2).

Central Asia

For over seven centuries, Russians had been at the mercy of the nomads of the Eurasian steppe that extended from the Black Sea to Manchuria. When the nomadic tribesmen were united, as they were under the Mongol ruler Genghis Khan (r. 1206–1227), they could defeat the Russians; when they were not, the Russians advanced into the steppe. This age-old ebb and flow ended when Russia acquired modern rifles and artillery.

Nomads like the Kazakhs, who lived east of the Caspian Sea, fought bravely but in vain against such weapons. The fertile agricultural land of Kazakhstan attracted 200,000 Russian settlers. Although the governments of Tsar Alexander II (r. 1855–1881) and Tsar Alexander III (r. 1881–1894) claimed not to interfere in indigenous customs, they declared communally owned grazing lands "waste" or "vacant" and turned them over to farmers from Russia. By the end of the nineteenth century, the nomads had been fenced out and reduced to starvation. Echoing the beliefs of other European imperialists, the eminent Russian jurist Fyodor Martens declared: "In-

Asia and Western Dominance

1862–95	French conquer Indochina piecemeal
1865–76	Russian forces advance into Central Asia
1867–1914	British take over Malayan Peninsula piecemeal
1869	Opening of Suez Canal; increase in shipping between Europe and Asia
1870	U.S. obtains Pago Pago harbor (Samoa)
1884	U.S. obtains Pearl Harbor (Hawaii)
1884–87	Russia completes conquest of Central Asia to borders of Afghanistan
1885	Britain completes conquest of Burma
1891–1903	Russia builds Trans-Siberian Railway, penetrates Manchuria and Korea
1894–95	Sino-Japanese War; China defeated
1898	Filipinos rebel against Spain
1898	U.S. annexes Hawaii, purchases Philippines from Spain
1899–1902	U.S. forces conquer and occupy Philippines
1904–05	Russo-Japanese War; Russia defeated
1905	British partition Bengal (India); mass demonstrations

ternational rights cannot be taken into account when dealing with semibarbarous peoples."

South of the Kazakh steppe land were deserts dotted with oases where the fabled cities of Tashkent, Bokhara, and Samarkand served the caravan trade between China and the Middle East. For centuries the peoples of the region—Uzbeks, Tajiks, and Turks—had lived under the protection of the Mongols and later the Qing Empire. But by the 1860s and 1870s, the Qing Empire was losing control over Central Asia (see Chapter 27), so it was fairly easy for Russian expeditions to conquer the indigenous peoples. Russia thereby acquired land suitable for cotton, along with a large and growing Muslim population.

Southeast Asia and Indonesia

The peoples of the Southeast Asian peninsula and the Indonesian archipelago had been in contact with outsiders—Chinese, Indians, Arabs, Europeans—for centuries. Java and the

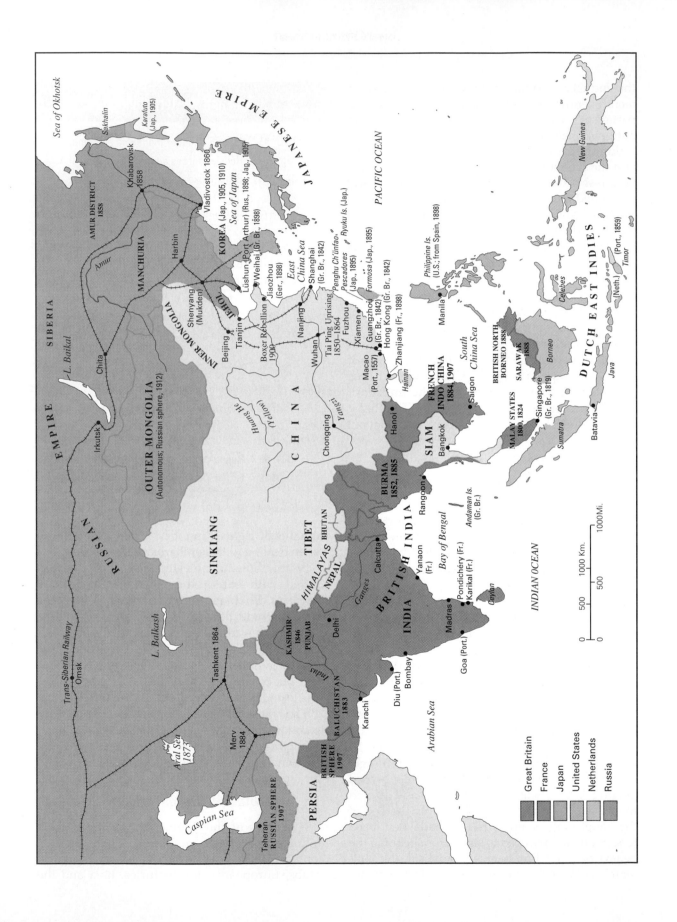

Sea of Okhotsk

JAPANESE EMPIRE

Karafuto (Jap., 1905)

Sakhalin

Khabarovsk 1858

PACIFIC OCEAN

Vladivostok 1860

MANCHURIA

Harbin

Sea of Japan

KOREA (Jap., 1905, 1910)

Lüshun (Port Arthur) (Rus., 1898; Jap., 1905)

Weihai (Gr. Br., 1898)

Ryuku Is. (Jap.)

New Guinea

DUTCH EAST INDIES

Shenyang (Mukden)

JEHOL

Beijing

Jiaozhou (Ger., 1898)

Tianjin

East China Sea

Shanghai (Gr. Br., 1842)

Penghu Chünfao, Pescadores (Jap., 1895)

Formosa (Jap., 1895)

Philippine Is. (U.S.; from Spain, 1898)

Manila

Celebes

Timor (Port., 1859)

SIBERIA

AMUR DISTRICT 1858

Amur

INNER MONGOLIA

Boxer Rebellion 1900

Nanjing

Wuhan

Tai Ping Uprising 1850-1864

Xiamen

Fuzhou (Gr. Br., 1842)

Guangzhou (Gr. Br., 1842)

Hong Kong (Gr. Br., 1842)

Zhanjiang (Fr., 1898)

Java

Batavia (Neth.)

RUSSIAN EMPIRE

L. Baikal

Chita

Huang He (Yellow)

C H I N A

Chongqing

Yangzi

Macao (Port., 1557)

Hainan

South China Sea

BRITISH NORTH BORNEO 1888

SARAWAK 1888

Borneo

Sumatra

Irkutsk

OUTER MONGOLIA (Autonomous; Russian sphere, 1912)

SINKIANG

TIBET

BHUTAN

HIMALAYAS

NEPAL

FRENCH INDO CHINA 1884, 1907

Hanoi

SIAM

Bangkok

Saigon

MALAY STATES 1800, 1824

Singapore (Gr. Br., 1819)

RUSSIAN EMPIRE

Trans-Siberian Railway

Omsk

L. Balkash

Tashkent 1864

BURMA 1852, 1885

Rangoon

Andaman Is. (Gr. Br.)

1000 Mi.

1000 Km.

INDIAN OCEAN

KASHMIR 1846

PUNJAB

Delhi

BRITISH INDIA

Calcutta

Yanaon (Fr.)

Bay of Bengal

Ganges

Pondichéry (Fr.)

Karikal (Fr.)

Ceylon

500

500

Aral Sea 187

Merv 1884

Indus

BALUCHISTAN 1883

I N D I A

Madras

Goa (Port.)

0

0

PERSIA

BRITISH SPHERE 1907

Diu (Port.)

Bombay

Karachi

Arabian Sea

Teheran

RUSSIAN SPHERE 1907

Caspian Sea

Great Britain

France

Japan

United States

Netherlands

Russia

smaller islands—the fabled Spice Islands (the Moluccas)—had long been subject to Portuguese and later to Dutch domination. Until the mid-nineteenth century, however, most of the region was made up of independent kingdoms.

As in Africa, there is considerable variation in the history of different parts of the region, yet they all came under intense imperialist pressure during the nineteenth century. Burma, nearest India, was gradually taken over by the British in the course of the century, until the last piece was annexed in 1885. Indochina fell piece by piece under French control until it was finally subdued in 1895. Similarly, Malaya (now Malaysia) came under British rule in stages during the 1870s and 1880s. By the early 1900s the Dutch had subdued northern Sumatra, the last part of the Dutch East Indies to be conquered. Only Siam (now Thailand) remained independent, although it had lost several border provinces.

Despite their varied political histories, all these regions had three features in common. First was their economic potential. They all had fertile soil, constant warmth, and heavy rains. Second, the peoples of the region had a long tradition of intensive gardening, irrigation, and terracing. In those parts of the region where the population was not very dense, the Europeans found it easy to import landless laborers from China and India seeking better opportunities overseas. The third reason for the region's wealth was the transfer of commercially valuable plants from other parts of the world: tobacco, cinchona (an anti-malarial drug), manioc (an edible root crop), maize (corn), and natural rubber from the Americas; sugar from India; tea from China; and coffee and oil palms from Africa. By 1914, much of the world's supply of these valuable products—in the case of rubber, almost all—came from Southeast Asia and Indonesia (see Environment and Technology: Imperialism and Tropical Ecology).

Map 29.2 Asia in 1914 By 1914, much of Asia was claimed by the colonial powers: the southern rim, from the Persian Gulf to the Pacific, was occupied by Great Britain and, to a lesser extent, by France, the Netherlands, and the United States. Siberia, in the north, had been incorporated into the Russian Empire. Japan, now industrialized, had joined the Western imperialist powers in expanding its territory and influence at the expense of China.

The wealth of the region certainly attracted the European imperialists, even when, as in the case of the French in Indochina, their original motivation was political. Most of this wealth was exported to Europe and North America. In exchange, the inhabitants of the region received two benefits from colonial rule: peace and a reliable food supply. As a result, their numbers increased at an unprecedented rate. For instance, the population of Java (an island the size of Pennsylvania) doubled from 16 million in 1870 to over 30 million in 1914.

Colonialism and the growth of population brought many social changes to this region. The more numerous agricultural and commercial peoples gradually moved into mountainous and forest areas, displacing the earlier inhabitants who practiced hunting and gathering or shifting agriculture. The migrations of the Javanese to Borneo and Sumatra are but one example. Similarly, immigrants from China and India (see Chapter 26) changed the ethnic composition and culture of every country in the region. Thus the population of the Malay Peninsula became one-third Malay, one-third Chinese, and one-third Indian.

As in Africa, European missionaries attempted to spread Christianity under the colonial umbrella. Islam, however, was much more successful in gaining converts, for it had been established in the region for centuries and people did not consider it a religion imposed on them by foreigners.

Education and European ideas had an impact on the political perceptions of the peoples of Southeast Asia and Indonesia. Just as important, however, was their awareness of events in neighboring Asian countries: India, where a nationalist movement arose in the 1880s (see Chapter 26); China, where modernizers were undermining the authority of the Qing (Chapter 27); and especially Japan, whose rapid industrialization culminated in its brilliant victory over Russia in 1905 (Chapter 28). The spirit of a rising generation was expressed by a young Vietnamese writing soon after the Russo-Japanese War:

> I, . . . an obscure student, having had occasion to study new books and new doctrines, have discovered in a recent history of Japan how they have been able to conquer the impotent Europeans. This is the reason why we have formed an organization.

. . . We have selected from young Annamites [Vietnamese] the most energetic, with great capacities for courage, and are sending them to Japan for study. . . . Several years have passed without the French being aware of the movement. . . . Our only aim is to prepare the population for the future.[6]

Hawaii and the Philippines

By the 1890s, the United States had a fast-growing population and industries that produced more manufactured goods than they could sell. Merchants and bankers began to look to export markets. The political mood was also expansionist, and many echoed the feelings of the naval historian Alfred T. Mahan: "Whether they will it or no, Americans must now begin to look outward."

Some Americans had been looking outward for quite some time, especially across the Pacific to China and Japan. In 1870 the United States obtained the harbor of Pago Pago in Samoa, and in 1884 it acquired Pearl Harbor in Hawaii. Nine years later, American settlers in Hawaii deposed Queen Liliuokalani (1838–1917) and offered the islands to the United States. At the time, Congress was reluctant to acquire so many dark-skinned subjects all at once, and the settlers had to content themselves with an informal protectorate. By 1898, however, the United States had become openly imperialistic. During a war with Spain, it annexed Hawaii for strategic reasons as a steppingstone to Asia. As the United States became ever more involved in Asian affairs, Hawaii's strategic location brought an inflow of U.S. military personnel, and its fertile land

Emilio Aguinaldo   In 1896, a revolt led by Emilio Aguinaldo attempted to expel Spaniards from the Philippines. When the United States purchased the Philippines from Spain two years later, the Filipino people were not consulted. Aguinaldo continued his campaign, this time against the American occupation forces, until his capture in 1901. In this picture, he is shown on horseback, surrounded by some of his troops. (UPI-Corbis-Bettmann)

caused planters to import farm laborers from Japan, China, and the Philippines. These immigrants soon outnumbered the native Hawaiians.

While large parts of Asia were falling under colonial domination, the people of the Philippines were chafing under their Spanish rulers. The movement for independence began among young Filipinos studying in Europe. José Rizal, a young doctor working in Spain, was arrested and executed in 1896 for writing patriotic and anticlerical novels. Thereafter, the center of resistance shifted to the Philippines, where Emilio Aguinaldo, leader of a secret society, rose in revolt and proclaimed a republic in 1898. The revolutionaries had a good chance of winning independence, for Spain had its hands full with a revolution in Cuba (see below).

Unfortunately for Aguinaldo and his followers, the United States went to war against Spain in April 1898 and quickly overcame the Spanish forces in the Philippines and in Cuba. President William McKinley (1897–1901) had not originally intended to acquire the Philippines. But after the Spanish defeat, he soon changed his mind and bought them from Spain for $20 million rather than let them fall into the hands of Germany or Japan, which, operating from the Philippines, could have threatened American business interests in China.

The Filipinos were not eager to trade one master for another. In January 1899, Aguinaldo rose up again and proclaimed the independence of his country. In spite of protests by anti-imperialists in the United States, the U.S. government decided that its global interests outweighed those of the Filipino people. In rebel areas, the American occupation army tortured prisoners, burned villages and crops, and forced the inhabitants into "reconcentration camps." Many American soldiers tended to look on Filipinos with the same racial contempt with which Europeans viewed their colonial subjects. By the end of the insurrection in 1902, the war had cost the lives of 5,000 Americans and 200,000 Filipinos.

After the end of the insurrection, the United States attempted to soften its rule with public works and economic development projects. New buildings went up in the city of Manila, roads, harbors, and railroads were built, and the Philippine economy was tied ever more closely to that of the United States. In 1907 Filipinos were allowed to elect representatives to a legislative assembly; however, ultimate authority remained in the hands of a governor appointed by the president of the United States. In 1916, the Philippines were the first colony to be promised eventual independence, a promise that was fulfilled thirty years later.

IMPERIALISM IN LATIN AMERICA

Nations in the Americas followed two divergent paths (see Chapter 25). In Canada and the United States there arose manufacturing industries, powerful corporations, and wealthy financial institutions. Latin America and the Caribbean exported raw materials and foodstuffs and imported manufactured goods. The poverty of their people, the preferences of their elites, and the pressures of the world economy made them increasingly dependent on the industrialized countries. Their political systems and the American Monroe Doctrine (1823) saved them from outright annexation by the colonial empires. But their natural resources made them attractive targets for manipulation by the industrial powers, including the United States, in a form of economic dependence called *free trade imperialism.*

In the Western Hemisphere, therefore, the New Imperialism manifested itself not by a scramble for territories but in two other ways. In the larger republics of South America, the pressure was mostly financial and economic. In Central America and the Caribbean, it also included military intervention by the United States.

Railroads and the Imperialism of Free Trade

As both inhabitants and outsiders realized, Latin America's potential for economic growth was huge, for the region could produce many agricultural and mineral products in demand in the

Imperialism in Latin America

1880–1910	Railroad building boom: British companies in Argentina and Brazil; U.S. companies in Mexico
1881–91	French company tries but fails to build a canal across the Isthmus of Panama
1895–98	Cubans revolt against Spanish rule
1898	Spanish-American War; U.S. wins, annexes Puerto Rico, occupies Cuba to 1902
1901	U.S. imposes Platt Amendment on Cuba, permitting U.S. troops to occupy island in1906–09, 1912, and 1917–22
1903	U.S. backs secession of Panama from Colombia
1904–1907, 1916	U.S. troops occupy Dominican Republic
1906–1914	U.S. builds Panama Canal
1912	U.S. troops occupy Nicaragua and Honduras
1914	U.S. troops occupy Veracruz (Mexico)
1915	U.S. troops occupy Haiti
1916–1917	U.S. forces invade northern Mexico

industrial countries. What was most urgently needed was a means of opening up the interior to development. For this, railroads seemed the perfect answer.

Foreign merchants and bankers as well as Latin American landowners and politicians embraced the new technology. Starting in the 1870s, almost every country in Latin America acquired railroads, usually connecting mines or agricultural regions with the nearest port rather than linking up the different parts of the interior. Since Latin America did not have any steel or mechanical industries, all the equipment and materiel came from Britain or the United States. So did the money to build the networks, the engineers who designed and maintained them, and the managers who ran them.

Argentina, a land of rich soil that produced wheat, beef, and hides, obtained the longest and best-developed rail network south of the United

States. By 1914, 86 percent of the railroads in Argentina were owned by British firms, 40 percent of the employees were British, and the official language of the railroads was not Spanish but English. The same was true of mining and industrial enterprises and public utilities throughout Latin America.

In many ways, the situation resembled that of India or Ireland, which also obtained a rail network in exchange for raw materials and agricultural products. The Argentine nationalist Juan Justo saw the parallel:

> English capital has done what English armies could not do. Today our country is tributary to England . . . the gold that the English capitalists take out of Argentina or carry off in the form of products does us no more good than the Irish get from the revenues that the English lords take out of Ireland.[7]

The difference was that Indians and Irish had little say in the matter, since they were under British rule. But in Latin America the political elites, most of whom considered themselves culturally European, encouraged foreign companies with generous concessions as the most rapid way to modernize their countries and enrich their property owners.

American Expansionism and the Spanish-American War

After 1865, the European powers used their financial power to penetrate Latin America. But they avoided territorial acquisitions, for four reasons: (1) they were already overextended in Africa and Asia; (2) there was no need, because the Latin American governments provided the political backing for the economic arrangements; (3) the Latin Americans had shown themselves capable of resisting invasions, most recently when Mexico fought off the French in the 1860s (see Chapter 25); and (4) the United States, itself a former colony, claimed to defend the entire Western Hemisphere against all outside intervention. This claim, made in the Monroe Doctrine, did not prevent the United States itself from intervening in Latin American affairs.

The United States had long had interests in Cuba, the closest and richest of the Caribbean islands. American businesses had invested great sums of money in Cuba's sugar and tobacco industries, and tens of thousands of Cubans had migrated to the United States. In 1895, when the Cuban nationalists José Martí and Máximo Gómez started a revolution against Spanish rule, American newspapers thrilled readers with lurid stories of Spanish atrocities, businessmen worried about their investments, and politicians demanded that the U.S. government help liberate Cuba.

Then on February 15, 1898, the U.S. battleship *Maine* accidentally blew up in Havana harbor, killing 266 Americans. The U.S. government immediately blamed Spain and issued an ultimatum that the Spanish evacuate Cuba. Spain caved in before the ultimatum, but the American press and Congress were so eager for war that President McKinley could not restrain them.

The Spanish-American War was over quickly. On May 1, 1898, American warships destroyed the Spanish fleet at Manila in the Philippines. Two months later, the United States Navy sank the Spanish Atlantic fleet off Santiago, Cuba. By mid-August, Spain was suing for peace. U.S. Secretary of State John Hay called it "a splendid little war." As war booty, the United States purchased the Philippines from Spain and took over Puerto Rico and Guam, which remain American possessions to this day.

Railroads penetrate South America The late nineteenth century saw the construction of several railroad networks in South America, often through rugged and dangerous terrain. This photograph shows the inauguration of a bridge on the Transandine Railroad in Peru. Flags were raised in honor of American construction and British ownership of the railroad. (Tony Morrison/South American Pictures)

American Intervention in the Caribbean and Central America

The nations of the Caribbean and Central America were all small and poor, and their governments were corrupt, unstable, and often bankrupt. They seemed to offer an open invitation to foreign interference. The excuse was often the same one that led to the British takeover of Egypt. A government would borrow money to pay for railroads, harbors, electric power, and other symbols of modernity. When it could not pay back the loan, the banks in Europe or the United States asked for assistance from their home governments, which sometimes threatened to intervene. To preempt any European intervention, the United States sent in the Marines.

Presidents Theodore Roosevelt (1901–1909), William Taft (1909–1913), and Woodrow Wilson (1913–1921) differed sharply on the proper policy the United States should follow toward the small nations to the south. But all three felt impelled to intervene in the region. Having "liberated" Cuba from Spain, the United States forced the Cuban government to accept the Platt Amendment, which gave the United States the "right to intervene" to maintain order on the island. The United States used this excuse to occupy Cuba militarily from 1906 to 1909, in 1912, and again from 1917 to 1922. In all but name, Cuba became an American protectorate. American troops also occupied the Dominican Republic from 1904 to 1907 and again in 1916, Nicaragua and Honduras in 1912, and Haiti in 1915. They brought sanitation and material progress but no political improvements.

The United States was especially forceful in Panama. Here the issue was not corruption or debts but a more vital interest: a canal across the isthmus of Panama that would benefit shipping between the east and west coasts of the United States. In 1878 the Frenchman Ferdinand de Lesseps, builder of the Suez Canal, had obtained a concession from Colombia to construct a canal across the isthmus, which lay in Colombian territory. Financial scandals and yellow fever, however, doomed his project.

When the United States acquired Hawaii and the Philippines in 1898, it recognized the strategic value of a canal that would allow warships to move quickly between the Atlantic and Pacific Oceans. The main obstacle was Colombia, whose Senate refused to give away a piece of its territory. In 1903, the U.S. government supported a Panamanian rebellion against Colombia and quickly recognized the independence of Panama. In exchange, it obtained the right to build a canal and to occupy a zone 5 miles (8 kilometers) wide on either side of it. Work began in 1904, and the Panama Canal opened on August 15, 1914.

THE WORLD ECONOMY AND TROPICAL ENVIRONMENTS

The New Imperialists were not traditional conquerors or empire builders like the Spanish conquistadores. Their aim was not only to extend their power over new territories and peoples but to control both the natural world and indigenous societies and put them to work more efficiently than had ever been done before. Both their goals and their methods were industrial. A railroad, for example, was an act of faith as well as a means of transportation. They expressed their belief in progress and their good intentions in the clichés of the time: "the conquest of nature," "the annihilation of time and space," "the taming of the wilderness," and "our civilizing mission."

Expansion of the World Economy

For centuries, exotic or tropical products like spices, sugar, and silk had found a ready market in Europe. The Industrial Revolution vastly expanded this demand. Imports of foods and of stimulants like tea, coffee, and cocoa increased substantially during the nineteenth century. The trade in industrial raw materials grew even faster. Some were the products of agriculture, such as cotton, jute for bags, and palm oil for soap and lubricants. Others were minerals like diamonds, gold, and copper. There also were wild forest products that only later came to be cultivated: timber for buildings and railroad ties, cinchona bark, rubber for rainwear and tires, and gutta-percha to insulate electric cables.

The growing needs of the industrial world could not be met by the traditional methods of production and transportation of the nonindustrial world. For instance, when the U.S. Civil War interrupted the export of cotton to England in the 1860s, the British turned to India but found that Indian cotton was ruined by exposure to rain and dust during the long trip on bullock carts from the interior of the country to the harbors. To prevent the expansion of their industry from being stifled by the technological backwardness of their newly conquered territories, the imperialists made every effort to bring those territories into the mainstream of the world market.

The first great change was transportation. The Suez Canal cut travel time and lowered freight costs dramatically. The ever-increasing size of steamships required deeper harbors. The Europeans built railroads throughout the world; India alone had 37,000 miles (nearly 60,000 kilometers) of railroad track by 1915, almost as much as Germany or Russia. Railroads reached into the interior of Latin America, Canada, China, and Australia. In 1903 the Russians completed the Trans-Siberian Railway from Moscow to Vladivostok on the Pacific. Visionaries even made plans for railroads from Europe to India and from Egypt to South Africa.

Transformation of Tropical Environments

The economic changes brought by Europeans and Americans also changed environments around the world. The British, whose craving for tea could not be satisfied with the limited exports available from China, introduced tea into the warm, rainy hill country of Ceylon and northeastern India. In those areas and in Java, thousands of square miles of tropical rain forests were felled to make way for tea plantations.

Economic botany and agricultural science were applied to every promising plant species. Rubber was used after the mid-nineteenth century for waterproof rainwear, industrial belts, and bicycle tires. For two decades the latex used to make rubber came only from *Hevea* trees that grew wild in Brazil. Then in the 1870s British agents smuggled seedlings from Brazil to Malaya, forming the basis of an enormous plantation economy. Cinchona, tobacco, sugar, and other crops were also introduced, improved, and vastly expanded in the colonies of Southeast Asia and Indonesia (see Environment and Technology: Imperialism and Tropical Ecology). Cocoa and coffee growing spread over large areas of Brazil and Africa; oil-palm plantations were established in Nigeria and the Congo Basin. Throughout the tropics, lands once covered with forests or devoted to shifting slash-and-burn agriculture were transformed into permanent farms and plantations.

Even in areas not devoted to export crops, growing populations put pressure on the land. In Java and India, farmers felled trees to provide arable land and firewood. They terraced hillsides, drained swamps, and dug wells.

Irrigation and water control transformed the dry parts of the tropics as well. In the 1830s, British engineers in India had restored ancient canals that had fallen into disrepair. Their success led them to build new irrigation canals, turning thousands of previously barren acres into well-watered, densely populated farmland. The migration of European experts spread the new science of irrigation engineering around the world. By the turn of the century, irrigation projects proliferated wherever rivers flowed through dry lands. In Egypt, Central Asia, California, and Australia, irrigation brought more acres under cultivation in one forty-year span than in all previous history.

Railroads had voracious appetites for land and resources. They cut into mountains, spanned rivers and canyons with trestles, and covered as much land with their freight yards as whole cities had needed in previous centuries. They also used up vast quantities of iron, timber for ties, and coal or wood for fuel. Most important of all, railroads brought people and their cities,

Imperialism and Tropical Ecology

Like all conquerors before them, the European imperialists of the nineteenth century exacted taxes and rents from the peoples they conquered. But they also sent botanists and agricultural experts to their tropical colonies to increase the production of commercial crops. In doing so, they radically changed the landscapes of their tropical dependencies.

The most dramatic effects were brought about by the deliberate introduction of new crops—an acceleration of the Columbian Exchange that had begun in the fifteenth century (see Chapter 19). In the early nineteenth century, tea was transferred from China to India and Ceylon. In the 1850s, British and Dutch botanists smuggled seeds of the cinchona tree from the

Tea pickers in Ceylon, ca. 1900 As the world's consumption of tea soared in the nineteenth century, entrepreneurs sought out new areas in which the tea bushes could be grown profitably. This picture shows a hillside in Ceylon (now Sri Lanka), a former rain forest turned into a tea plantation. Harvesting the tea leaves is very labor intensive, requiring the work of hundreds of Ceylonese women. (Archive Photos/Popperfoto)

Andes in South America to India and Java. They had to operate in secret, because the South American republics, knowing the value of these crops, prohibited the export of seeds. With the seeds, the British and Dutch established cinchona plantations in Ceylon and Java, respectively, to produce quinine, which was essential as an antimalarial drug and a flavoring for tonic water. Similarly, in the 1870s, British agents stole seeds of the rubber tree from the Amazon rain forest and transferred them to Malaya and Sumatra.

Before these transfers, vast forests covered the highlands of India, Southeast Asia, and Indonesia, precisely the lands where the new plants grew best. And so European planters had the forests cut down and replaced with thousands of acres of commercially profitable trees and bushes, all lined up in perfect rows and tended by thousands of native laborers to satisfy the demands of customers in faraway lands. The crops that poured forth from the transformed environments brought great wealth to the European planters and the imperial powers. In 1909, the British botanist John Willis justified the transformation in these terms:

> Whether planting in the tropics will always continue to be under European management is another question, but the northern powers will not permit that the rich and as yet comparatively undeveloped countries of the tropics should be entirely wasted by being devoted merely to the supply of the food and clothing wants of their own people, when they can also supply the wants of the colder zones in so many indispensable products.

This quotation raises important questions about trade versus self-sufficiency. If a region's economy supplies the food and clothing wants of its own people, is its output "entirely wasted"? What is the advantage of trading the products of one region (such as the tropics) for those of another (such as the colder zones)? Is this trade an obligation? Should one part of the world (such as "the northern powers") let another refuse to develop and sell its "indispensable products"? Can you think of a case where a powerful country forced a weaker one to trade?

Source: John Christopher Willis, *Agriculture in the Tropics: An Elementary Treatise* (Cambridge: Cambridge University Press, 1909), pp. 38–39.

farms, and industries to areas that previously had held small, scattered populations.

Prospectors looking for valuable minerals opened the earth to reveal its riches: gold in South Africa, Australia, and Alaska; tin in Nigeria, Malaya, and Bolivia; copper in Chile and Central Africa; iron ore in northern India; and much else. Where mines were dug deep inside the earth, the dirt and rocks brought up with the ores formed huge mounds near the mine opening. For ores found closer to the surface, open mines turned the earth into a landscape of lunar craters, and runoff from the minerals poisoned the water for miles around. The refineries that treated the ores also fouled the environment with slag heaps and toxic effluents.

The transformation of the land by human beings, a constant throughout history, accelerated sharply. Only the changes that have taken place since 1914 can compare with the transformation of the global environment between 1869 and 1914.

CONCLUSION

The industrialization of the late nineteenth century increased the power of Europeans and North Americans over nature and over the peoples of other continents. They used their new-found power to conquer empires.

The opening of the Suez Canal in 1869 symbolized the beginning of the New Imperialism. It demonstrated the power of modern industry to subdue nature by carving the land. It stimulated shipping and trade between the industrial countries and the tropics. It deepened the involvement of Europeans in the affairs of the Middle East, Africa, and Asia. From that year until 1914, not only the great powers but smaller countries too—even, in some cases, individual Europeans or Americans—could decide the fate of whole countries. Their motivation to conquer or control other lands surely helps explain the New Imperialism of the time. But the means at the disposal of the imperialists—that is, the gap that opened between their technologies and forms of organi-

zation and those available to Asians, Africans, and Latin Americans—is equally important.

The opening of the Panama Canal in August 1914 confirmed the new powers of the industrializing nations—but with a twist, for it was the United States, a latecomer to the game of imperialism, that created the canal. In that same month, the other imperialist nations turned their weapons against one another and began a life-or-death struggle for supremacy in Europe. That conflict is the subject of our next chapter.

SUGGESTED READING

D. K. Fieldhouse, *Colonialism, 1870–1945* (1981), is a good introduction to the topic of imperialism. The debate on the theories of imperialism is presented in Roger Owen and Robert Sutcliffe, *Studies in the Theory of Imperialism* (1972), and in Winfried Baumgart, *Imperialism* (1982). The British Empire is the subject of Bernard Porter, *The Lion's Share: A Short History of British Imperialism, 1850–1970* (1976).

On Africa in this period see Roland Oliver and Anthony Atmore, *Africa Since 1800*, new ed. (1994); Roland Oliver and G. N. Sanderson, eds., *From 1870 to 1905* (1985), and A. D. Roberts, ed., *From 1905 to 1940* (1986), in *The Cambridge History of Africa;* and A. Adu Boahen, ed., *Africa Under Colonial Domination, 1880–1935* (1985), in *UNESCO General History of Africa*. The European conquest of Africa is recounted in Thomas Pakenham, *The Scramble for Africa* (1991), and Ronald Robinson and John Gallagher, *Africa and the Victorians: The Climax of Imperialism* (1961). The classic novel about the impact of colonial rule on African society is Chinua Achebe's *Things Fall Apart* (1958).

Imperial rivalries in Asia are the subject of David Gillard, *The Struggle for Asia, 1828–1914: A Study in British and Russian Imperialism* (1977), and Peter Hopkirk, *The Great Game: The Struggle for Empire in Central Asia* (1994). On other aspects of imperialism in Asia see Clifford Geertz, *Agricultural Involution: The Process of Ecological Change in Indonesia* (1963), especially chapters 4 and 5, and Stanley Karnow, *In Our Image: America's Empire in the Philippines* (1989).

On Latin America in this period see David Bushnell and Neill Macauley, *The Emergence of Latin America in the Nineteenth Century* (1994). Free-trade imperialism is the subject of D. C. M. Platt, *Latin America and British Trade, 1806–1914* (1973). On American expansionism see David Healy, *Drive to Hegemony: The United States in the Caribbean, 1898–1917* (1989), and Walter LaFeber, *The Panama Canal,* rev. ed. (1990).

On race relations in the colonial world see Noel Mostert, *Frontiers: The Epic of South Africa's Creation and the Tragedy of the Xhosa People* (1992), and Robert Huttenback, *Racism and Empire: White Settlers and Colored Immigrants in the British Self-Governing Colonies, 1830–1910* (1976). Gender relations are the subject of Caroline Oliver, *Western Women in Colonial Africa* (1982), and Cheryl Walker, ed., *Women and Gender in Southern Africa to 1945* (1990). David Northrup's *Indentured Labor in the Age of Imperialism, 1834–1922* (1995), discusses migrations and labor. The point of view of the colonized is examined in Frantz Fanon, *The Wretched of the Earth* (1966), and Albert Memmi, *The Colonizer and the Colonized* (1967). The impact of technology on the New Imperialism is the subject of Daniel R. Headrick's *The Tools of Empire: Technology and European Imperialism in the Nineteenth Century* (1981) and *The Tentacles of Progress: Technology Transfer in the Age of Imperialism, 1850–1940* (1988).

On the economic and demographic transformation of Africa and Asia see Eric Wolf, *Europe and the People Without History* (1982), especially chapters 11 and 12, and L. S. Stavrianos, *Global Rift: The Third World Comes of Age* (1981). The impact on the environment is the subject of R. P. Tucker and J. F. Richards, *Deforestation and the Nineteenth-Century World Economy* (1983).

NOTES

1. *Journal officiel* (November 29, 1869), quoted in Georges Douin, *Histoire du règne du khédive Ismaïl* (Rome: Reale Societá di geografia d'Egitto, 1933), 453.

2. E. Desplaces in *Journal de l'Union des Deux Mers* (December 15, 1869), quoted in Douin, op. cit., p. 453.

3. Winston Churchill, *The River War: An Account of the Reconquest of the Soudan* (New York: Charles Scribner's Sons, 1933), p. 300.

4. Robert W. July, *A History of the Africa People,* 3rd ed. (New York: Charles Scribner's Sons, 1980), p. 323.

5. George Shepperson and Thomas Price, *Independent African* (Edinburgh: University Press, 1958), pp. 163–64, quoted in Roland Oliver and Anthony Atmore, *Africa Since 1800,* 4th ed. (Cambridge: Cambridge University Press, 1994), p. 150.

6. Thomas Edson Ennis, *French Policy and Developments in Indochina* (Chicago: University of Chicago Press, 1936), p. 178, quoted in K. M. Panikkar, *Asia and Western Dominance* (New York: Collier, 1969), p. 167.

7. Quoted in Stanley J. Stein and Barbara H. Stein, *The Colonial Heritage of Latin America* (New York: Oxford University Press, 1970), p. 151.

CHAPTER THIRTY

The First World War and Its Aftermath, 1914–1929

Causes of the "Great War" · War in the West · War and Revolution in Russia

War in the Middle East and Africa · Europe and America in the Twenties

Aftermath of War in the Middle East

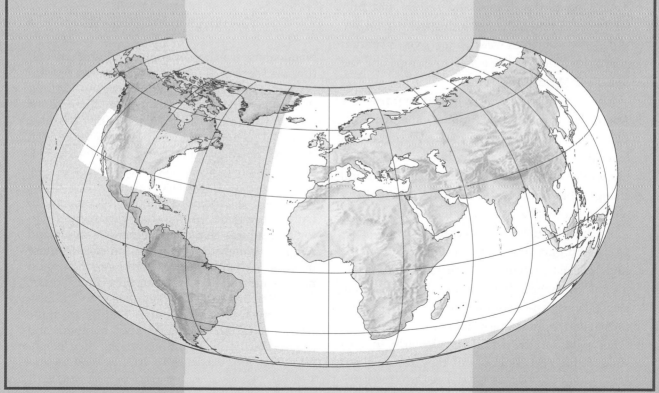

O
n June 28, 1914, Archduke Franz Ferdinand, heir to the throne of Austria-Hungary, was riding in an open carriage through Sarajevo, capital of the province of Bosnia-Herzegovina, which Austria had annexed six years before. When the carriage stopped momentarily, Gavrilo Princip, member of a pro-Serbian conspiracy, fired his pistol twice, killing the archduke and his wife.

Those shots ignited a war that spread throughout Europe. It soon turned into a global war, for the Ottoman Empire fought against Britain in the Middle East and Japan attacked German positions in China. France and Britain involved their empires in the war and brought Africans, Indians, Australians, and Canadians to Europe to fight and labor on the front lines. Finally, in 1917, the United States entered the fray.

The war involved weapons and tactics never seen before, and it demanded unprecedented efforts from civilian populations. It caused greater environmental changes than any previous war, destroying towns, farms, and forests and provoking an unprecedented industrial expansion. When it ended four years later, over 8 million people had died, and the map of Europe and the Middle East was transformed.

The war replaced three great empires—the Austro-Hungarian, the Ottoman, and the Russian—with over a dozen new states. It triggered a revolution in Russia that sent tremors throughout the world. And it provoked social and cultural changes that undermined Europe's two-century-old hegemony over the rest of the world.

In this chapter, we concentrate on three regions—Europe, the Russian Empire, and the Middle East—where the crucial battles were fought and where postwar developments were direct consequences of the war. Equally momentous events were taking place at the same time in other parts of the world, particularly in East Asia, India, and Mexico, but they resulted primarily from local causes and were less directly influenced by the war. We therefore turn to them in Chapter 32.

CAUSES OF THE "GREAT WAR"

T
he war that started in July 1914 was known as the "great war" until the 1940s, when a far greater one overshadowed it (see Chapter 31). Although the assassination of the archduke ignited it, its underlying causes had been simmering for many years. One of them was the ideas and feelings we call *nationalism*, which bound citizens to their country and led them to obey their government and, when called upon, to willingly kill the citizens of other countries. Another was the system of alliances and military plans that governments devised to protect themselves from their rivals. A third was the German leaders' desire to dominate Europe.

The Spread of Nationalism

Nationalism was deeply rooted in European culture. As we saw in Chapter 28, it united the citizens of France, Britain, and Germany behind their governments and gave them tremendous cohesion and strength of purpose. Only the most powerful feelings could inspire millions of men to march obediently into battle and sustain civilian populations through years of hardship.

Nationalism could also be a dividing rather than a unifying force. The large but fragile multinational Russian, Austro-Hungarian, and Ottoman Empires contained numerous ethnic and religious minorities. Having repressed those peoples for centuries, the governments could never count on their full support. The Greeks, Serbs, Romanians, and Bulgarians who had broken away from the Ottoman Empire over the previous century fought one another and aroused territorial ambitions among their neighbors. The very existence of an independent Serbia threatened Austria-Hungary by stirring up the hopes and resentments of its Slavic populations.

Because of the spread of nationalism, most people viewed war as a crusade for liberty and victory or a long-overdue revenge for past injustices. In the course of the nineteenth century, as memories of the misery and carnage caused by the Napoleonic Wars (see Chapter 24) faded, revulsion against warfare gradually weakened. The few wars fought in Europe after 1815, such as the Crimean War of 1854 (see Chapter 27) and the Franco-Prussian War of 1871 (Chapter 28), had been short and caused few casualties or long-term consequences. And in the wars of the New Imperialism (see Chapter 29), Europeans almost always had been victorious at a small cost in money and manpower. The well-to-do had forgotten their fears that war would trigger dangerous social revolution; on the contrary, many believed that only war could heal the divisions in their societies and make workers unite behind their "natural" leaders.

Throughout Europe, the outbreak of war was greeted with parades and flags and hopes for a quick and easy victory. German troops marched off to the front shouting "To Paris!" In France, spectators encouraged marching troops with shouts of "Send me the Kaiser's moustache!" The British poet Rupert Brooke began a poem with the line "Now God be thanked Who has matched us with His hour." The German sociologist Max Weber wrote: "This war, with all its ghastliness, is nevertheless grand and wonderful. It is worth experiencing." When the war began, very few imagined that their side might not win. And no one foresaw that in the war to come, everyone would lose.

Alliances and Military Plans

What turned an incident in a small town in the Balkans into a conflict involving all the great powers was the system of alliances that had grown up over the previous decades (see Chapter 28). Germany and Austria-Hungary formed the Central Powers. In response, France allied itself with Russia. In 1904 Britain joined France in an Entente ("understanding"), and in 1907 it buried its differences with its old rival, Russia. Europe was thus divided into two blocs of roughly equal power: Germany and Austria-Hungary on one side; France, Russia, and Britain on the other.

What made the alliance system unstable, however, was inflexible military planning. In 1914 western and Central Europe had highly developed railroad networks but very few motor vehicles. The armies on the European continent had grown to include millions of soldiers and more millions of reservists. To mobilize these masses and transport them to battle was an enormous project requiring thousands of trains running on precise schedules. As a result, once under way, no country's mobilization could be canceled or postponed without creating chaos.

The French and German general staffs had worked out elaborate railroad timetables to mobilize their armies in a few days, but other countries were less well prepared. Russia, a large country with an underdeveloped rail system, needed several weeks to mobilize its forces. Britain had only a tiny volunteer army and no mobilization plans, which made the German leaders believe that the British would stay out of a war on the continent. To avoid having to fight both France and Russia at the same time, the German generals planned to defeat the smaller French army in a few days, then transport their entire army by train east across Germany to the Russian border before Russia could fully mobilize, and quickly defeat Russia. Unlike the other great powers, the political and military leaders of Germany looked forward to a war they expected to win in a hurry.

Meanwhile, the Austro-Hungarian government wanted to punish Serbia for stirring up anti-Austrian feelings. On July 23 it demanded that Serbia prosecute its nationalists. Serbia quickly agreed to do so. Nevertheless, Austria-Hungary, eager to crush Serbian nationalism once and for all and emboldened by the backing of Germany, declared war on Serbia on July 28.

Diplomats and statesmen, even the monarchs of Europe, sent one another frantic telegrams, but they had lost control of events, for the Austro-Hungarian declaration of war had triggered

The Road to World War One

1882	Triple Alliance among Germany, Austria-Hungary, Italy
1891–1905	German Schlieffen Plan
1894	Franco-Russian alliance
1898	Germany begins to build a High Seas Fleet, triggering Anglo-German naval armaments race
1902	Anglo-Japanese alliance
1904	Anglo-French Entente
1906	British launch *Dreadnought*, first all-big-gun battleship
1907	Anglo-Russian Entente
1911	Moroccan Crisis; tension between Germany and France over Morocco
1914:	
June 28	Serbian nationalist assassinates Austrian Archduke Franz Ferdinand
July 23	Austro-Hungarian ultimatum to Serbia
July 28	Austria-Hungary declares war on Serbia
July 30	Russia declares general mobilization of its army
August 1	Germany declares war on Russia
August 3	Germany declares war on France, invades Belgium
August 4	Britain declares war on Germany

all the mobilization plans. On July 29 the Russian government, feeling duty-bound to protect Serbia, ordered a general mobilization in order to force Austria to back down. On August 1, France honored its treaty obligation to Russia and ordered general mobilization. Minutes later Germany did likewise. Because of the rigid railroad timetables, war not only was inevitable but was automatic. Three hours after issuing its mobilization order, Germany declared war on Russia.

There remained an enigma: what would Britain do? The German plan was to avoid the French defenses along the Franco-German border and instead wheel around through neutral Belgium and into northwestern France. The German general staff did not expect Britain to go to war over Belgium, for in the past Britain had al-

ways hesitated before getting involved in European wars. In any case, the Germans expected France to capitulate before the British could get involved. On August 3, when German troops entered Belgium, Britain demanded their withdrawal, but Germany refused. At midnight Britain declared war on Germany.

WAR IN THE WEST

Warfare, when it came, was a complete surprise to all the belligerents, from the generals on down. Every officer had studied military tactics: from the classic battles of Alexander the Great in the fourth century B.C.E. to those of Napoleon in the nineteenth, the advantage had gone to the fastest-moving army led by the boldest general. Few had paid any attention to the American Civil War (see Chapter 25) or the Russo-Japanese War (Chapter 28), the first major conflicts fought with industrial weapons. They assumed that in the coming war, victory would depend on speed, courage, and firepower. Instead, the evolution of military technology imposed a stalemate that lasted four years.

Stalemate, 1914–1918

The plans that the generals had so carefully drawn up went awry almost from the start. The French generals, led by Joseph Joffre, believed that a spirited attack would always prevail. They hurled their troops, dressed in bright blue-and-red uniforms, against the well-defended German border and suffered a crushing defeat. The Germans had expected to cross Belgium unopposed, but Belgian resistance held them up for several days. Nevertheless, large German armies defeated the French and the British in battle after battle. By early September they held Belgium and northern France and were fast approaching Paris.

German victory seemed assured. But their troops, who had marched and fought for a month, were weary and their generals wavered. Then Russia attacked eastern Germany, and German troops needed for the final push into France

The Experience of Battle

Battles have often been described, but almost always from the point of view of the generals. What is it like to be a soldier on a battlefield? And how can this experience be conveyed to readers who have never been to war?

Here is how the German writer Erich-Maria Remarque, a veteran of World War I, describes a soldier's experience in his classic war novel All Quiet on the Western Front *(1928):*

Night again. We are deadened by the strain—a deadly tension that scrapes along one's spine like a gapped knife. Our legs refuse to move, our hands tremble, our bodies are a thin skin stretched painfully over repressed madness, over an almost irresistible, bursting roar. We have neither flesh nor muscles any longer, we dare not look at one another for fear of some incalculable thing. So we shut our teeth—it will end—it will end—perhaps we will come through.

Suddenly the nearer explosions cease. The shelling continues but it has lifted and falls behind us, our trench is free. We seize the hand-grenades, pitch them out in front of the dug-out and jump after them. The bombardment has stopped and a heavy barrage now falls behind us. The attack has come.

No one would believe that in this howling waste there could still be men; but steel helmets now appear on all sides of the trench, and fifty yards from us a machine-gun is already in position and barking.

The wire entanglements are torn to pieces. Yet they offer some obstacle. We see the storm-troops coming. Our artillery opens fire. Machine-guns rattle, rifles crack. The charge works its way across. Haie and Kropp begin with the hand-grenades. They throw as fast as they can, others pass them the handles with the strings already pulled. . . .

We recognize the smooth distorted faces, the helmets: they are French. They have already suffered heavily when they reach the remnants of the barbed wire entanglements. A whole line has gone down before our machine-guns; then we have a lot of stoppages and they come nearer.

I see one of them, his face upturned, fall into a wire cradle. His body collapses, his hands remain suspended as though he were praying. Then his body drops clean away and only his hands with the stumps of his arms, shot off, now hang in the wire.

During the war and for years thereafter, many people asked: What makes men put their lives at risk, even in nearly hopeless situations like the one Remarque describes? Is it hatred of the enemy? Is it the slender hope of winning? Or are they simply trained, from early childhood, to obey their superiors? Is battle a primitive urge or the result of centuries of culture and civilization?

Source: Erich Maria Remarque, All Quiet on the Western Front, *trans. A. W. Wheen (Boston: Little, Brown, 1958), 98–99.*

---

were shifted to the Russian front. When a gap opened between two German armies along the Marne River, Joffre requisitioned the taxis of Paris and moved the army of Paris, France's last reserves, into the gap. At the Battle of the Marne (September 5–12, 1914), the Germans were thrown back several miles, then came to a stop, their plans in tatters.

During the next month, both sides spread out until they formed an unbroken line over 300 miles (483 kilometers) long from the North Sea to the border of Switzerland. All along this line, the troops prepared their defenses. Their most potent weapon was the machine gun, an almost im-penetrable defense against advancing infantry but useless for the offensive, for it was too heavy for one man to carry and took time to set up. To escape the deadly stream of bullets, soldiers quickly dug foxholes in the ground. Soon, they connected the holes to form a shallow trench, then dug communications trenches to the rear. Within weeks, the battlefields were chopped up with lines of trenches several feet deep, their tops protected by sandbags and their floors covered with planks. Despite all the work they put into them, the soldiers spent much of the year soaked and covered with mud (see Voices and Visions: The Experience of Battle).

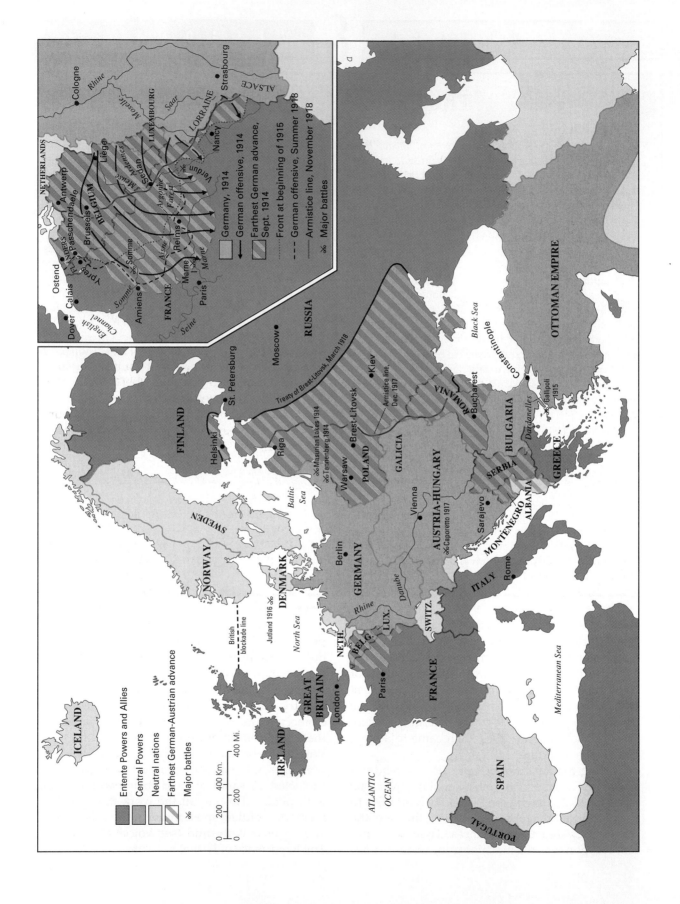

ICELAND

Entente Powers and Allies
Central Powers
Neutral nations
Farthest German-Austrian advance
⚔ Major battles

0   200   400 Km.
0   200   400 Mi.

British blockade line

Jutland 1916 ⚔

NORWAY

SWEDEN

FINLAND

Helsinki

St. Petersburg

Moscow

RUSSIA

Riga

Baltic Sea

DENMARK

North Sea

GREAT BRITAIN

London

IRELAND

ATLANTIC OCEAN

NETH.

BELG.

LUX.

Paris

FRANCE

Berlin

GERMANY

Rhine

Danube

SWITZ.

ITALY

Rome

Vienna

AUSTRIA-HUNGARY

⚔ Caporetto 1917

Warsaw

POLAND

GALICIA

⚔ Tannenberg 1914
⚔ Masurian Lakes 1914

Brest-Litovsk

Kiev

Treaty of Brest-Litovsk, March 1918

Armistice line, Dec. 1917

ROMANIA

Bucharest

Black Sea

Constantinople

OTTOMAN EMPIRE

Gallipoli 1915

Dardanelles

BULGARIA

SERBIA

Sarajevo

MONTENEGRO

ALBANIA

GREECE

Mediterranean Sea

SPAIN

PORTUGAL

Germany, 1914
German offensive, 1914
Farthest German advance, Sept. 1914
Front at beginning of 1915
German offensive, Summer 1918
Armistice line, November 1918
⚔ Major battles

Rhine

Cologne

Strasbourg

ALSACE

LORRAINE

LUXEMBOURG

Saar

Moselle

Nancy

Verdun

Meuse

Argonne Forest

Aisne

Marne

Reims

Somme

Sedan

Ardennes

Liège

NETHERLANDS

Antwerp

Brussels

BELGIUM

FLANDERS

Passchendaele

Ypres

Ostend

Calais

Dover

English Channel

Amiens

Somme

Seine

PARIS

FRANCE

Marne

Trenches were nothing new. What was extraordinary about the First World War was that the trenches along the entire western front were all connected, leaving no gaps through which armies could advance (see Map 30.1). How, then, could either side ever hope to win?

In May 1915, Italy joined the war on the side of the Entente, henceforth known as the Allied Powers. Battles between the Italian and Austro-Hungarian armies proved as inconclusive as those on the western front. During the next four years, from 1914 to 1918, generals on both sides again and again ordered their troops to attack. In one great battle after another, thousands of men climbed out of their trenches, raced across the open fields, and were mowed down by enemy fire. Sometimes, attacking troops released poison gas to kill or blind the defenders, only to find that the gas immobilized the attackers as well. In the end, poison gas gave no military advantage but only added to the horror of battle and suffering of the soldiers.

The year 1916 saw the bloodiest and most futile battles of the war. The Germans attacked the French forts at Verdun, losing 281,000 men and causing 315,000 French casualties. In retaliation, the British attacked the Germans at the Somme River and suffered 420,000 casualties—60,000 on the first day alone—while the Germans lost 450,000 and the French 200,000.

This was not warfare as it had ever been practiced before; instead, it was mass slaughter in a moonscape of mud, steel, and flesh where no human could long survive. Everyone attacked, but no one could win, for the most powerful armies in the world were paralyzed by trenches and machine guns. In four years of the bloodiest fighting the world had ever seen, the western front never moved more than a few miles one way or another. War was beyond the control of soldiers and generals alike.

The reason for the stalemate was that the defensive was mechanized but the offensive was not. Railroad trains could operate only behind the lines; near the front, soldiers had to walk. Machine guns could kill anyone who approached, and attacking soldiers, once out of their trenches, faced an almost certain death. Hoping to destroy the machine-gun nests, the attacking force saturated the enemy lines with artillery barrages. This action only alerted the defenders that an attack was coming and allowed them to rush in reinforcements, to set up new machine guns, and to stop the attack.

The generals refused to admit that a few men with machine guns were more powerful than hundreds of soldiers rushing toward them with bayonets, for that admission would have meant that they could never win. Obstinately, they promised victory, prepared ever bigger offensives, and ordered a whole generation of young men to their deaths. They knew the casualties were enormous, but they expected the enemy to run out of young men before their side did, a gruesome calculation called the "war of attrition."

At sea, the war was just as inconclusive as on land. Before 1914, Germany had tried to intimidate Britain by building up its navy, but that attempt only provoked the British to build an even larger fleet. As soon as the war broke out, the British cut the German telegraph cables overseas, blockaded the German and Austrian coasts, and set out to capture or sink all enemy ships still at sea. For a few months, German warships in the Pacific and Indian Oceans caused considerable damage. The German High Seas Fleet, however, seldom ventured out for a quick raid. Only once, on May 31, 1916, did it emerge in force to confront the British Grand Fleet. At the Battle of Jutland, off the coast of Denmark, the two fleets lost roughly equal numbers of ships, and the Germans escaped back to their harbors.

Britain still ruled the waves—but not the water under them. In early 1915, in retaliation for the British blockade, Germany declared a blockade of Britain by submarines. Unlike surface ships, submarines could not rescue the passen-

Map 30.1 The First World War in Europe During World War I, most of the fighting took place on two fronts. After an initial surge through Belgium into northern France, the German offensive bogged down for four years along the Western Front. To the east, the German armies conquered a large part of Russia during 1917 and early 1918. Despite Germany's spectacular victories in the east, it lost the war because its armies collapsed along the strategically important Western Front.

Trench warfare in World War I   As they faced each other across the Western Front, the German and Allied soldiers dug elaborate networks of trenches. Attacking meant jumping out of one's trenches and racing across a no-man's land of mud and barbed wire. Here we see Princess Patricia's Canadian Light Infantry repelling a German attack near Ypres, in northern France, in March 1915, using machine guns, rifles, and hand grenades. (Courtesy, The Princess Patricia's Canadian Light Infantry, Regimental Museum and Archives)

gers of a sinking ship or even distinguish a neutral ship from an enemy. German submarines therefore sank everything they could, including the British ocean liner *Lusitania*, on which 1,198 people died, 139 of them Americans. When the United States protested, Germany ceased its submarine campaign, hoping to keep America neutral.

The Home Front and the War Economy

The optimism that greeted the outbreak of war did not last long. Within a few months, shortages appeared. As the armies demanded ever more weapons, ammunition, and food, civilians had to work harder, eat less, and pay higher taxes. Textiles, coal, meat, fats, and imported products like tea and sugar were strictly rationed. To coordinate vital war supplies, governments gradually imposed stringent controls over all aspects of their economies. Socialists and labor unions participated actively in the war effort, for they found government regulation more to their liking than unfettered free enterprise.

The war economy transformed civilian life. Because food rations were allocated according to need, not wealth, nutrition actually improved among the poor in France and Britain. Unemployment vanished in all countries at war. Thousands of Africans, Indians, and Chinese were recruited for heavy labor in Europe. To fill the positions in steel mills, mines, and munitions plants vacated by soldiers, employers hired women. Although many men found women's new roles hard to accept at first, women became streetcar drivers, mail carriers, and police, and some found work in the suddenly burgeoning bureaucracies. Many women joined the auxiliary military services as doctors, nurses, mechanics, or ambulance drivers. After 1917, as the war took its toll of young men, the British government established women's auxiliary units for the army, navy, and air force. Though clearly intended "for the duration only," these positions gave thousands of women a sense of participation in the war effort and a taste of personal and financial independence.

German civilians paid an especially high price for the war, for the British blockade severed the Central Powers' overseas trade. The German chemical industry was able to develop synthetic explosives and fuel, but synthetic food was harder to swallow. Wheat flour disappeared, replaced first by rye, then by potatoes and turnips, then by acorns and chestnuts, and finally by sawdust. After the failure of the potato crop in 1916 came the "turnip winter," when people had to survive on 1,000 calories per day, half the normal nutrition of an active adult. Women, children, and the elderly were especially hard hit, but even soldiers on the front went hungry and raided enemy lines just to scavenge food.

By 1916, Russians were also faced with shortages and widespread hunger. The reason was less a lack of food than confusion and bureaucratic incompetence. With so many men in the army, Russian railroads broke down for lack of fuel and parts, and crops rotted in the fields. Rationing never worked efficiently, and during the bitterly cold winter of 1916–1917, Russian factory workers and housewives had to line up long before dawn in front of grocery stores in order to get something to eat.

One country grew rich during the war: the United States. For two and a half years, the United States stayed technically neutral—that is, it did not fight but did a roaring business supplying France and Britain. When it entered the war in 1917, the government set up boards to coordinate business and government. As a result, busi-

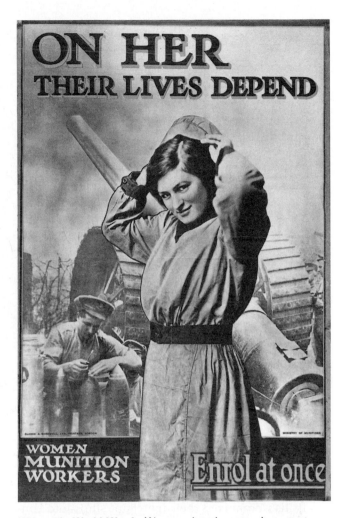

Women in World War I Women played a more important role in World War I than in previous wars. As the armies drafted millions of men, employers hired women for essential war work. This poster extolling the importance of women workers in supplying munitions was probably designed to recruit women for factory jobs. (Trustees of the Imperial War Museum)

nesses involved in war production made spectacular profits. Civilians were exhorted to help the war effort by investing their savings in war bonds and growing food in backyard "victory gardens." Employers hired women to replace men in offices and factories. As they still faced a labor shortage, they recruited African-Americans. The war thus played a major role in the migration of black Americans from the rural south to the cities of the north.

The Last Years of the War, 1917-1918

When 1917 began, the two sides were so evenly matched that it seemed the war would not end until one side or the other ran out of young men. Losing hope of winning, soldiers began to mutiny. In May 1917, 54 of the 100 French divisions along the western front refused to attack. During the summer, Russian and Italian troops also mutinied, panicked, or deserted. In the fall, just as the situation seemed deadlocked forever, the Russian army collapsed.

Meanwhile, the United States was drawn into the war. Like many Americans, President Woodrow Wilson had wanted to stay out of the European conflict. He tried to keep the United States neutral and persuade the belligerents to compromise. In late 1916, the German leaders decided the only way they could win was to starve the British people by sinking the ships that brought Britain's food supply. They knew that unrestricted submarine warfare was likely to bring the United States into the war on the side of France and Britain, but they expected France and Britain to collapse before the United States could send over enough troops to help them. The submarine campaign resumed on February 1, 1917, but did not prove as effective as the German High Command had hoped, for the British organized their merchant ships into convoys protected by destroyers. On April 6, Wilson declared war on Germany. The German gamble had failed.

By early 1918, Erich von Ludendorff, since 1917 the leading German general, realized Germany's only hope of victory was to defeat the French and British before American troops arrived in sufficient numbers to tip the balance. Between March and August he launched a series of surprise attacks that broke through the front at several places and pushed to within 40 miles (64 kilometers) of Paris. But his troops were tired, and victory eluded him. Meanwhile, every month brought another 250,000 American troops to the front. In August, the Allies counterattacked, and the Germans began a retreat that could not be halted, for the German soldiers, like the French the year before, had lost the will to

fight. Ludendorff resigned, the German fleet mutinied, and Kaiser Wilhelm II, having lost all support, fled to Holland. A new government signed an armistice. On November 11 at 11 A.M., the guns went silent, and the war was over.

The war left behind more dead and wounded and more physical destruction than any previous conflict. It is estimated that between 8 million and 10 million died, almost all of them young men. Among them were about 2 million Germans, 1.75 million Russians, 1.5 million Frenchmen; the Austro-Hungarian Empire lost over 1 million, Britain 750,000, Italy nearly 500,000, and the United States approximately 100,000. Perhaps twice that many men returned home wounded, gassed, or shell-shocked, many of them for life.

Peace Treaties

Delegates of the victorious Allies—France, Britain, the United States, Italy, Japan, and a host of other nations—met in Paris in early 1919. Russia, in the throes of civil war, was not invited, and the defeated powers were kept out until the treaties were ready for their signatures.

From the start, three men dominated the conference: President Wilson, British Prime Minister David Lloyd George, and French Premier Georges Clemenceau. They paid scant attention to the Italians, even less to the delegates of smaller European nations, and none at all to non-European nationalities. They rejected the Japanese proposal that all races be treated equally. They ignored the Pan-African Congress organized by the African-American W. E. B. Du Bois to call attention to the concerns of African peoples around the world. They also ignored the ten thousand other delegates of various nationalities that did not represent sovereign states—including the Arab leader Faisal, the Zionist Chaim Weizmann, and forty-two Armenian delegations—who came to Paris to lobby for their cause. They were, in the words of British Foreign Secretary Sir Arthur Balfour, "three all-powerful, all-ignorant men, sitting there and carving up continents" (see Map 30.2).

Map 30.2 Territorial Changes in Europe After World War I Although the heaviest fighting took place in western Europe, the territorial changes were relatively minor; two provinces taken by Germany in 1871, Alsace and Lorraine, were returned to France. In eastern Europe, in contrast, the changes were enormous. The disintegration of the Austro-Hungarian Empire and the defeat of Russia allowed a belt of new countries to arise, stretching from Finland in the north to Yugoslavia in the south.

Each one had his own agenda. Wilson, a high-minded idealist, wanted to apply the principle of *self-determination* to European affairs, by which he meant creating nations that reflected ethnic or linguistic divisions. He also proposed a League of Nations, a world organization that would con-

demn aggression, safeguard the peace, and foster international cooperation. His idealism clashed with the more hardheaded and self-serving nationalism of the Europeans. To satisfy his constituents, Lloyd George insisted that Germany pay a heavy indemnity. Clemenceau wanted Germany to give Alsace-Lorraine (a part of France before 1871) and the industrial Saar region to France, and he demanded that the Rhineland be detached from Germany to form a buffer state.

The result was a series of compromises that satisfied no one. The European powers formed a League of Nations, but the U.S. Congress, reflecting the isolationist feelings of the American people, refused to let the United States join it. France recovered Alsace and Lorraine but was unable to weaken Germany by detaching the Rhineland and had to content itself with vague promises of British and American protection in the event Germany rebuilt its army. Although Britain gained land in Africa from Germany and in the Middle East from Turkey, it was greatly weakened by human losses and the disruption of its trade.

On June 28, 1919, the Allied Powers made Germany sign the Treaty of Versailles. Germany was forbidden to have an air force or more than a token army and navy. It lost little land in the west but had to give up large parts of its eastern territory to a newly reconstituted Poland. The Allies made Germany promise vast sums as "reparations," without setting either a figure or a period of time for payment. In the infamous "guilt clause" that was to rankle the Germans for years to come, the Allies made Germany accept "responsibility for causing all the loss and damage" of the war. The Treaty of Versailles left Germany humiliated but essentially intact and potentially the most powerful nation in Europe. A peace neither of punishment nor of reconciliation, Versailles was one of the greatest failures in history.

When the war ended, the old Austro-Hungarian Empire fell apart. By the Treaties of St. Germain and Trianon, Austria and Hungary each lost three-quarters of their territory. Several new countries appeared in the lands lost by Russia, Germany, and Austria-Hungary: Poland, resurrected after over a century; Czechoslovakia, created from the northern third of Austria-Hungary; and Yugoslavia, combining Serbia and the former South Slav provinces of Austria. The new boundaries coincided with the major linguistic groups of eastern Europe, but the new countries all contained disaffected minorities. These smaller nations were safe only as long as Germany

and Russia lay defeated and prostrate. In the Middle East, a similar breakup of the Ottoman Empire caused such instability that it left the victorious Allies weaker than they had been before the war.

WAR AND REVOLUTION IN RUSSIA

Although the war caused great suffering in western Europe, its effect on Russia was far more devastating, for it destroyed the old society, opened the door to revolution and civil war, and introduced a radically new political system. By clearing away the old, however, the years of upheaval prepared Russia to industrialize at breakneck speed under the leadership of professional revolutionaries.

Russia at War

By 1914, Russia had made impressive strides toward modernity: railroads and heavy industries, an elaborate bureaucracy, and an education system designed to train government officials. Yet in many ways, Russia remained an eighteenth-century society with a majority of peasants, a small middle class, a wealthy aristocracy, and an autocratic government. Peasants hated their landlords, and industrial workers lived in wretched conditions. The intellectuals, among the most creative in modern history, loved their country but blamed the government for its backwardness compared to western Europe.

At the beginning of World War I, Russia had the largest army in the world, but its generals were incompetent, supplies were lacking, and soldiers were poorly trained and equipped. In August 1914, two Russian armies attacked East Prussia, the easternmost province of Germany. Though greatly outnumbered, the Germans achieved a stunning victory at Tannnenberg. Yet at the time they had neither the troops nor the desire to advance into Russia.

Though outclassed by Germany, Russia did have an enemy that was its equal. The Austro-

Hungarian army was also poorly trained and equipped and could not trust its Slavic troops. Several times the Russians defeated the Austro-Hungarians, only to be defeated in turn by the Germans. In the end, the outcome was decided not on the battlefield but within Russia and Austria-Hungary—societies that crumbled under the stress of a prolonged war.

In 1916, after a string of defeats, the Russian army scored several victories against the Austrians, only to be pushed back again by the Germans with a loss of a million soldiers killed, wounded, or taken prisoner. At that point the Russians ran out of ammunition and other essential supplies. Russian troops were ordered into battle unarmed and told to pick up the rifle of a fallen comrade. Disorganization spread from the front to the interior, as railroad equipment wore out, industries deprived of labor and raw materials slowed down, and agricultural production declined. The court of Tsar Nicholas II, meanwhile, remained as wasteful and corrupt as ever.

Double Revolution

In the cities food and fuel became scarce. In early March 1917 (February by the old Russian calendar), food ran out in Petrograd, the capital. Housewives and female factory workers staged mass demonstrations that quickly were followed

Lenin the orator   Lenin, the leader of the Bolshevik revolutionaries, was a spellbinding orator. Here he is seen addressing Red Army soldiers in Sverdlov Square, Moscow, in 1920. At the time, the Bolsheviks were mopping up the last of the "White" (anti-Bolshevik) forces, but were fully engaged in a war with Poland. The fate of the revolution depended on the fighting spirit of the Red Army soldiers and on their loyalty to Lenin. (David King Collection)

by widespread strikes and a mutiny of the garrison. Male workers and soldiers formed *soviets* (councils) to take over factories and barracks. A few days later, the tsar abdicated, and leaders of the parliamentary parties, led by Alexander Kerensky, formed a Provisional Government. Thus began what Russians called the "February Revolution."

Meanwhile, revolutionary groups, formerly hunted by the police, came out of hiding. The most numerous were the Social Revolutionaries, who advocated the redistribution of property among the peasants. The Social Democrats, a Marxist party, were divided into two factions. The Mensheviks, who advocated electoral politics and reform in the tradition of European Socialists, had a large following among intellectuals and factory workers. Their rivals, the Bolsheviks, were a small but tightly disciplined group of radicals obedient to the will of their leader, Vladimir Lenin (1870–1924).

Lenin, the son of a government official, became a revolutionary in his teens when his older brother was executed for plotting to kill the tsar. He spent years in exile, first in Siberia and later in Switzerland. There, with a will of iron, he devoted his full attention to organizing his followers. Although he professed Marx's ideas concerning class conflict (see Chapter 28), he never visited a factory or a farm. His goal was to create a party that would lead the revolution rather than wait for it. As he explained: "Classes are led by parties and parties are led by individuals. . . . The will of a class is sometimes fulfilled by a dictator."

In early April 1917, the German government, hoping to destabilize Russia, allowed Lenin to cross Germany from Switzerland to Russia in a sealed railway car. As soon as he arrived in Petrograd on April 16, he announced his program: immediate peace, all power to the soviets, and the distribution of land to the peasants and of factories to the workers. This plan proved immensely popular among the soldiers and workers, exhausted by the war.

The next few months witnessed a tug-of-war between the Provisional Government and the various revolutionary factions in Petrograd. Kerensky ordered yet another offensive, but this time the soldiers began to desert by the hundreds of thousands, throwing away their rifles and walking back to their villages. As the Germans began advancing, Russian resistance melted, and the government lost what little support it had.

The Bolshevik Party, meanwhile, was gaining support among the workers of Petrograd and the soldiers and sailors of the garrison. On November 6, 1917 (October 24 in the Russian calendar), they rose up and took over the city, calling this action the "October Revolution." Their sudden move surprised the other revolutionaries, who believed that a "socialist" revolution could happen only after many years of "bourgeois" rule. But Lenin was more interested in power than in the finer points of Marxist doctrine. He overthrew the Provisional Government and arrested Mensheviks, Social Revolutionaries, and other rivals.

Seizing Petrograd was only the beginning, for the rest of the country was in chaos. The Bolsheviks nationalized all private land and ordered the peasants to hand over their crops without compensation. The peasants, having already seized their landlords' estates, resisted the Bolsheviks. In the cities, the Bolsheviks took over the factories and drafted the workers into compulsory labor brigades. To enforce his rule, Lenin created the Cheka, a secret police with powers to arrest and execute all enemies of the Bolsheviks.

Meanwhile, the Germans were still advancing, and the Bolsheviks had no choice but to sue for peace. By the Treaty of Brest-Litovsk, signed on March 3, 1918, Russia lost Poland, Finland, the Baltic states, the Ukraine, and the Caucasus, along with a third of its population and wealth.

Civil War and Communist Victory

The October Revolution soon attracted foreign intervention. French troops occupied Odessa in the south, the British and Americans landed in Archangel and Murmansk in the north, and the Japanese occupied Vladivostok in the far east. Liberated Czech prisoners of war briefly seized the Trans-Siberian Railway.

In December 1918, a civil war began that damaged Russia more than the world war. Although the Communists—as the Bolsheviks were called after March 1918—held central Russia, all the surrounding provinces rose up against them. Counterrevolutionary armies, led by former tsarist officers, obtained weapons and supplies from the Allies. For three years the Communists and their enemies burned farms and confiscated crops, causing a famine that claimed 3 million victims, more than had died in Russia in seven years of fighting. In 1920 the Communists fought an inconclusive war with Poland. By 1921, they had defeated most of their enemies one after another, for the anti-Bolshevik forces were never united and the peasants were afraid of a tsarist victory and the return of their landlords. The Communists' victory was also due to their central position, the superior discipline of their Red Army, and the military genius of its commander, Leon Trotsky.

Finland, the Baltic states, and Poland remained independent, but other parts of the tsar's empire were reconquered one by one. In December 1920 the Communists first recognized the independence of a Soviet Ukraine, then annexed it to Russia to form the Union of Soviet Socialist Republics (USSR).

The provinces of the tsarist empire in the Caucasus and Central Asia had also declared their independence in 1918. While the Bolsheviks staunchly supported anticolonialist movements in Africa and Asia, they also opposed what they called "feudalism" in the former Russian colonies. Between 1918 and 1921, the Red Army reconquered these states one by one, replacing the indigenous leaders with Russians and annexing them to the USSR. Thus did the Bolsheviks rid Russia of the taint of tsarist colonialism while still retaining control over the lands and peoples that once had belonged to the Russian Empire.

Lenin and the New Economic Policy

By 1921 economic production of the USSR had declined to only one-sixth of Russia's prewar level. Factories and railroads had shut down for lack of fuel, raw materials, and parts. Farms were devastated and their livestock killed, leaving the urban population hungry. Lenin and his followers found themselves masters of a country in ruins and were not sure how to organize a productive economy.

At that point, Lenin decided to release the economy from party and government control. The New Economic Policy (NEP) that he announced in March 1921 allowed peasants to own land and sell their crops, private merchants to trade, and private workshops to produce goods and sell them on the free market. Only the biggest businesses, such as banks, railroads, and large enterprises, remained under government ownership.

The relaxation of controls had an immediate effect. Production began to climb, and food and other goods became available. Yet the NEP reflected no change in the ultimate goals of the Communist Party. It was merely a breathing space, what Lenin called "two steps back to advance one step forward," for the Communists had every intention of creating a modern industrial economy without private property, under party guidance. This goal meant investing in heavy industry and electrification and moving rural people to the cities to work in the new industries. It also meant providing food for the urban workers without spending scarce resources to purchase it from the peasants. In other words, it meant making the peasants, the great majority of the Soviet people, pay for the industrialization of Russia. This strategy turned the peasants and the Communists into bitter enemies and made a clash inevitable.

When Lenin died in January 1924 without naming a successor, his associates jockeyed for power. The leading contenders were Leon Trotsky, commander of the Red Army, and Party Secretary Joseph Stalin. Trotsky had the support of many "Old Bolsheviks" who had joined the party before the Revolution. He had spent years in exile and saw the Revolution in Marxist terms, as the spark that would ignite a world revolution of the working class against the rich. Stalin, the only leading Communist who had never lived abroad, took a less internationalist view, insisting that socialism could survive "in one country."

To gain power, Stalin filled the party with bureaucrats loyal to himself. During 1926 and 1927 he outmaneuvered Trotsky and had him expelled from the Party for what Stalin called "deviation from the party line." Finally, in January 1929, he forced Trotsky to flee the country. Now absolute master of the party, Stalin prepared to industrialize the Soviet Union at breakneck speed.

WAR IN THE MIDDLE EAST AND AFRICA

The First World War had a profound impact on many other parts of the world besides Russia. Within days of its outbreak in Europe in 1914, it spread to other continents and oceans. One reason was the existence of German colonies and naval bases in Africa, East Asia, and the Pacific. Overseas extensions of European wars were nothing new: between 1650 and 1815 ships and soldiers from England, France, and Spain had frequently fought far from Europe. What was new was the involvement of two non-European powers, the Ottoman Empire and Japan, which transformed a quarrel between Europeans into a true world war. Japan seized German enclaves in China but was less interested in defeating Germany than in gaining a foothold in China; for that reason, we turn to it in Chapter 32. The involvement of the Ottoman Empire, however, directly affected the outcome of the war and transformed the entire Middle East.

The Middle East in 1914

At the turn of the century, most of the Middle East was still nominally under Ottoman Turkish rule. The Ottoman Empire was slowly declining, though it had not collapsed completely (see Chapter 27). It survived partly because many Muslims regarded the sultan as the true leader of Islam, partly because the Ottomans left provincial affairs to local notables, and partly because Great Britain rescued it several times to keep Russia from gaining access to the Mediterranean Sea.

The European powers took advantage of the Ottoman Empire's weakness to meddle in its internal affairs. Russia and France posed as defenders of the empire's Christian minorities. Britain occupied Egypt in 1882 to guarantee its access to the vital Suez Canal. After 1900, the imperial decline accelerated, as Italy took Libya (1911) and the Ottomans lost most of their Balkan provinces (1912–1913). The Europeans seemed about to partition the Ottoman Empire as they had sub-Saharan Africa (see Chapter 29).

As in China and Japan, the European influence caused a tug-of-war in the Ottoman Empire between reformers and conservatives. Modernization of the army and administration promised to bring economic development, military power, and eventual freedom from foreign interference. But any serious reform required foreign technicians and advisers, loans from European banks, and concessions to foreign governments and businesses. This would open the country even more to foreign interference, at least for a while. Halfhearted attempts to reform the administration made little difference.

In the early years of the century, a conspiracy of professionals and army officers calling themselves the Committee of Union and Progress, or "Young Turks," began plotting to take over the government. In 1909 they deposed Sultan Abd el-Hamid, and in 1913 they installed a dictatorship. They were eager to reform the army and the administration but were suspicious of Britain and Russia. To achieve their aims, they relied increasingly on German advice and assistance.

The Ottoman Empire at War

When the war broke out, the Turks hesitated, then sided with the Central Powers. In November 1914, they joined the fighting, hoping to gain land at Russia's expense, but the fighting in the Caucasus proved disastrous for both armies and for the civilian populations as well. The Turks deported the Armenians, whom they suspected of being pro-Russian, from their homelands in eastern Anatolia to Syria and other parts of the empire. During the forced march across the mountains in the winter, hundreds of thousands of Armenians were murdered or died of hunger and exposure. It was a precedent for even ghastlier tragedies still to come.

The Turks also closed the Dardanelles, the straits between the Mediterranean and Black Seas (see Map 30.3). In the spring of 1915 British officials, seeing little hope of victory on the western front, proposed to force open the Dardanelles by landing troops on the nearby Gallipoli Peninsula. The campaign, mismanaged from the start, gave the defenders ample warning. Turkish troops, led by the German general Liman von Sanders, mounted a strong resistance and pushed the invaders into the sea.

Having failed at the Dardanelles, the British tried to subvert the Ottoman Empire from within by promising the emir (prince) of Mecca, Hussein ibn Ali, a kingdom of his own if he would lead an Arab revolt against the Turks. In 1916, Hussein rose up and was proclaimed king of Hijaz (western Arabia). Thereafter his son Faisal led an Arab army in support of the British advance from Egypt into Palestine and Syria. Although the Arab Revolt of 1916 did not affect the struggle in Europe, it contributed to the defeat of the Ottoman Empire and the subsequent Anglo-French occupation of the Levant.

British intrigues in the Middle East involved Jews as well as Arabs. For centuries, minorities of Jews had lived in eastern and central Europe, where they developed a thriving culture despite frequent persecutions. By the early twentieth century a movement called Zionism, led by Theodore Herzl, arose among Jews who wanted to return to their ancestral homeland in Palestine. The concept of a Jewish nationality with a homeland of its own appealed to many Europeans, Jews and gentiles alike, as a humanitarian solution to the problem of anti-Semitism.

By 1917, Chaim Weizmann, leader of the British Zionists, had persuaded several British politicians that a Jewish homeland in Palestine should be carved out of the Ottoman Empire and placed under British protection, thereby strengthening the Allied cause. In November, as British armies were advancing on Jerusalem, Foreign Secretary Balfour wrote to Weizmann that "His Majesty's Government view with favor the establishment in Palestine of a national home for the Jewish people and will use their best endeavours to facilitate the achievement of that object, it being clearly understood that nothing shall be done which may prejudice the civil and religious rights of existing non-Jewish communities in Palestine." At the time, the British did not foresee that this statement, known as the Balfour Declaration, would lead to conflicts between Palestinians and Jewish settlers.

Britain also sent troops to southern Mesopotamia to secure the oil pipeline from Iran. Having done so, they slowly moved north, taking Baghdad in early 1917. Although the officers for the Mesopotamian campaign were British, most of the troops and equipment came from India. Most Indians, like other colonial subjects of Britain, supported the war effort despite the hardships it caused. Their involvement in the war contributed to the movement for Indian independence (see Chapter 32).

Africa and the War

The war in the Middle East was, in part, a conflict between two peoples of the region: Turks and Arabs. The fighting in Africa, in contrast, reflected the quarrels of Europeans, not of Africans. When the war began, the British and French quickly overran German Togo, on the West African coast. The much larger colonies of Southwest Africa and German Cameroon (in equatorial Africa) were not fully conquered until 1915. In Tanganyika, their East African colony, the Germans remained undefeated until the end of the war (see Map 29.1).

From the Africans' point of view, the changeover from one European ruler to another was less significant than the hardships the war brought. The Europeans requisitioned foodstuffs, imposed heavy taxes, and forced Africans to grow export crops such as cotton, cocoa, and palm oil, and sell them at low prices. Many of the Europeans stationed in Africa left to join the war, leaving large areas with little or no European presence. The combination of increased demands on Africans and fewer European officials led to uprisings in Nigeria, Libya, Nyasaland (now Malawi), and other colonies. The Europeans needed several years to repress some of them.

Over a million Africans served at one time in the various armies, and perhaps three times that number were drafted as porters to carry the armies' equipment. France, faced with a shortage

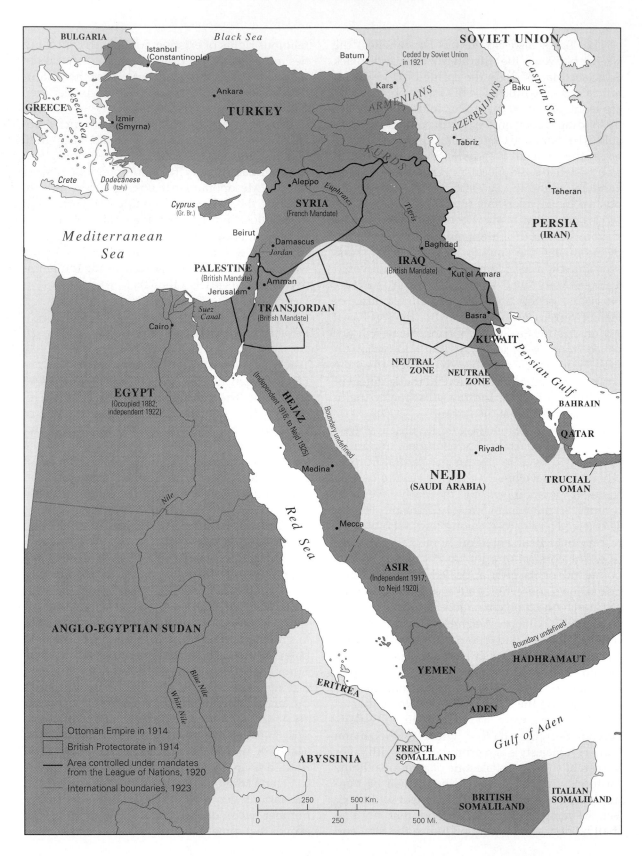

BULGARIA

Black Sea

SOVIET UNION

Istanbul
(Constantinople)

Batum

Ceded by Soviet Union
in 1921

Kars

Caspian Sea

Baku

GREECE

Aegean Sea

Ankara

TURKEY

ARMENIANS

AZERBAIJANIS

Izmir
(Smyrna)

Tabriz

KURDS

Crete

Dodecanese
(Italy)

Cyprus
(Gr. Br.)

Aleppo

Euphrates

Teheran

Tigris

SYRIA
(French Mandate)

PERSIA
(IRAN)

*Mediterranean
Sea*

Beirut

Damascus

Baghdad

Jordan

IRAQ
(British Mandate)

PALESTINE
(British Mandate)

Amman

Kut el Amara

Jerusalem

TRANSJORDAN
(British Mandate)

Basra

*Suez
Canal*

Cairo

KUWAIT

NEUTRAL
ZONE

NEUTRAL
ZONE

Persian Gulf

EGYPT
(Occupied 1882;
independent 1922)

HEJAZ
(Independent 1916; to Nejd 1925)

Boundary undefined

BAHRAIN

Riyadh

QATAR

Medina

Nile

Red Sea

NEJD
(SAUDI ARABIA)

**TRUCIAL
OMAN**

Mecca

ANGLO-EGYPTIAN SUDAN

ASIR
(Independent 1917;
to Nejd 1920)

Boundary undefined

HADHRAMAUT

Blue Nile

White Nile

YEMEN

ERITREA

ADEN

Gulf of Aden

☐ Ottoman Empire in 1914

☐ British Protectorate in 1914

▬ Area controlled under mandates
from the League of Nations, 1920

— International boundaries, 1923

ABYSSINIA

**FRENCH
SOMALILAND**

**BRITISH
SOMALILAND**

**ITALIAN
SOMALILAND**

0   250   500 Km.

0   250   500 Mi.

The Twenties flappers After the traumatic experience of World War I, the young and well-to-do celebrated the return to peace with flamboyance. The decorative paint job of this open convertible, shown at a Paris exposition, matches the coat of the elegant flapper standing next to it. (UPI/Corbis-Bettmann)

of young Frenchmen, drafted Africans into its army, where many fought side by side with Europeans. The Senegalese Blaise Diagne, the first African elected to France's Chamber of Deputies in 1914, campaigned for African support of the war effort. Put in charge of recruiting African soldiers, he insisted on equal rights for African and European soldiers and an extension of the franchise to educated Africans, demands that were only partially successful.

Map 30.3 Territorial Changes in the Middle East after World War I World War I transformed the Middle East. The collapse of the Ottoman Empire encouraged Arab nationalists to strive for independence; one Arab state, Saudi Arabia, did constitute itself in the 1920s. Elsewhere, however, Arab nationalism was thwarted by the intervention of France and Britain, which took over the Arab provinces of the Ottoman Empire as mandates of the League of Nations.

EUROPE AND AMERICA IN THE TWENTIES

The 1920s was a decade of apparent progress hiding irreconcilable tensions. On the one side were the victors, especially British and French conservatives who longed for a return to the stable order of the prewar era, with its hierarchy of social classes, its prosperous world trade, and its European dominance over the rest of the world. On the other were people all over the world whose hopes had first been raised by the rhetoric of the war, then dashed by its outcome. Among them were Germans who felt cheated out of a victory that had been almost within their grasp; Italians disappointed that their sacrifices had not been rewarded with large territorial gains; Indians and Arabs who longed for independence; Chinese who looked for a lessening of foreign intrusion; Japanese who hoped to expand their influence in China; Bolsheviks eager to consolidate their power within Russia and export their revolution to the rest of the world; and many others. The war that had sparked hopes for change also produced unresolved conflicts and faith in violent action. Thus the peace of 1919 proved to be short-lived.

An Ephemeral Peace, 1919–1929

The decade after the end of the war can be divided into two distinct periods: five years of painful recovery and readjustment (1919–1923), followed by six years of growing peace and prosperity (1924–1929).

To force the Germans to pay the unspecified reparations promised in the Versailles Treaty, the French army took over the Ruhr, Germany's primary industrial area, in 1923. In retaliation, the German government began printing money recklessly, causing the most severe inflation the world has ever seen. Soon German money was worth less than the paper it was printed on, and a wheelbarrow full of paper money was needed to buy a loaf of bread. As the country teetered on the brink of civil war, radical nationalists called for revenge and tried to overthrow the government. Finally in November the German government issued a new currency at a rate of 1 trillion old marks to 1 new one. Germany promised to resume reparations, and the French agreed to end the occupation.

Beginning in 1924, the world enjoyed a few years of calm and prosperity. After the end of the German crisis of 1923, the western European nations became less confrontational, and Germany joined the League of Nations. The vexed issue of reparations also seemed to vanish, as Germany borrowed money from New York banks to meet its payments—money that France and Britain then used to pay back their wartime loans from the United States. This triangular flow of money, based on credit, stimulated a rapid recovery of the European economies. France began rebuilding its war-torn northern zone. Germany recov-

ered from its hyperinflation. In the United States a boom began that was to last over five years.

While their economies flourished, governments grew more cautious and businesslike. Even the Communists, after Lenin's death, seemed to give up their attempts to spread revolution abroad. Yet problems remained. Germany and the Soviet Union did not accept their borders with the small nations that had arisen between them. In 1922, they signed a secret pact at Rapallo, Italy, allowing the German army to conduct secret maneuvers in Russia in violation of the Versailles Treaty in exchange for German help in building up Russian industry and military potential.

The League of Nations proved adept at resolving numerous international issues of a technical nature such as health, postal and telegraph communications, and labor relations. However, in its main function—preserving the peace—it was successful only when the great powers were in agreement. Without American participation, sanctions against transgressors had little meaning.

Social Changes

Besides costing over 8 million lives, the war dislocated whole populations, creating millions of refugees. War and revolution forced almost 2 million Russians, 750,000 Germans, and 400,000 Hungarians to flee their homes. At the same time, bitter Greco-Turkish war led to the expulsion of hundreds of thousands of Greeks from Anatolia and Turks from Greece (see below).

Many refugees found shelter in France, which welcomed 1.5 million to bolster its declining population. The preferred destination, however, was the United States, the most prosperous country in the world. Eight hundred thousand immigrants succeeded in reaching it before the U.S. Immigration Acts of 1921 and 1924 closed the door to eastern and southern Europeans. Canada, Australia, and New Zealand adopted similar restrictions on immigration. The Latin American republics still welcomed European refugees, but their economies were hard hit by the drop in the prices of their main exports (sugar, coffee, copper, and tin) after the war, and their poverty and unemployment discouraged potential immigrants.

In Western countries, class distinctions were becoming less sharply defined. The United States and Canada led the way. North America had never had so rigidly defined a class structure as European societies nor so elaborate a set of traditions and manners. During the war, ostentatious displays of wealth and privilege were deemed unpatriotic and remained so after the war. Many European aristocrats had died on the battlefields, and with them went their long-standing ascendancy in the army, the diplomatic corps, banking, and other sections of elite society. In both North America and Europe, the twenties saw engineers, businessmen, lawyers, and other professionals rising to prominence, increasing the relative importance of the middle class.

The activities of governments, which had expanded during the war, continued to grow as municipal, provincial, and national administrations increasingly provided housing, highways, schools, public health facilities, broadcasting, and other services. This growth required thousands more bureaucrats than there had been before the war. Department stores, banks, insurance companies, and other businesses also increased their white-collar work force.

The middle class expanded during the twenties, but the working class did not. In industry, the introduction of new machines and methods such as Henry Ford's auto assembly line raised the productivity of workers so that a greater output did not require an expanded labor force. In North America and western Europe, the proportion of blue-collar workers shrank while that of white-collar employees grew.

Women's lives changed more rapidly in the twenties than in any previous decade. Although the end of the war marked a retreat from wartime job opportunities, some women remained in the work force as wage earners and as salaried professionals. The young and wealthy enjoyed more personal freedoms than their mothers had before the war. They drove cars, played sports, traveled alone, and smoked in public. Emancipated from the corsets and long dresses of prewar fashions, they wore their skirts and their hair short and danced to jazz instead of waltzes, to the consternation of their elders. Many others, however, found that the upheavals of war and revolution brought more suffering than liberation. Millions of women had lost their fathers, brothers, sons, husbands, and fiancés in the war. After the war, the shortage of young men caused many single women to lead lives of loneliness and destitution.

European and American women's rights advocates—labeled "suffragettes" by their critics—had been demanding the vote since the 1890s. Women first obtained it under the Russian Provisional Government of 1917, a right later confirmed by the Bolsheviks. Germany followed in 1919. Britain gave women over age thirty the suffrage in 1918 and later extended it to younger women. The United States followed in 1920 with the Nineteenth Amendment to the Constitution. In Turkey (which replaced the Ottoman Empire in 1921), women began voting in 1934. Most other countries, however, did not allow women to vote until after 1945. In dictatorships, voting rights for women made no difference, and in democratic countries, women tended to vote like their male relatives. In the British elections of 1918 the first to include women—they overwhelmingly voted for the Conservative Party. Their influence on politics was less radical than feminists had hoped and conservatives had feared. Even when it did not alter the political situation, however, the right to vote was a potent symbol.

Technology and Mass Consumption

People had long been aware that scientific discoveries could lead to remarkable new products and services, such as electricity, the telephone, and aircraft. Only in the 1920s, however, did such innovations change the lives of millions of people.

In 1903, two young American mechanics, Wilbur and Orville Wright, built the first aircraft that was heavier than air and that could maneuver in flight. From that moment on, airplanes fascinated people wherever they appeared. During

The archetypal automobile city   As Los Angeles grew from a modest town into a sprawling metropolis, it built broad avenues, parking lots, and garages to accommodate automobiles. By 1929, most families had a car, and streetcar lines closed down for lack of passengers. This photograph shows a street in the downtown business district. (Ralph Morris Archives/Los Angeles Public Library)

the war, the exploits of air aces relieved the tedium of news from the front.

In the twenties, aviation became a sport and a form of entertainment, and daredevil pilots achieved fame by pushing their planes to the very limit, and often beyond it. Among the most celebrated were three American pilots: Amelia Earhart, winner of numerous air races; Richard Byrd, who flew over the North Pole in 1926; and the most adulated of all, Charles Lindbergh, the first to fly solo across the Atlantic in 1927. The heroic age of flight lasted until the late 1930s, when aviation became a means of transportation, a business, and a male preserve.

The twenties also marked the advent of mass consumption in North America and western Eu-

rope. Even office and factory workers could afford the products of industry. The cause was a technological revolution similar in scope to the Industrial Revolution (see Chapter 23) or to the late-nineteenth-century wave of innovations (Chapter 28). Henry Ford's assembly line and Frederick Taylor's scientific management techniques made it possible to mass-produce vehicles and appliances in ever-greater volume and at falling prices.

Buses and trucks connected remote villages to cities and railroad lines, ending generations of rural isolation. By 1929, the United States had one car for every five people, five-sixths of the world's automobiles. As middle- and working-class families bought cars, cities were surrounded by rings of automobile suburbs. In western Europe, business and professional people owned cars, but for workers, cars remained luxuries until the 1950s.

With the introduction of electricity into urban homes (see Chapter 28), middle-class homemakers bought not only electric lights but also irons and washing machines. Electricity was more than a consumer utility, however; it was the basis for whole new systems, like electric railways and the aluminum industry. So important was electricity that Lenin once defined Bolshevism as "electrification and soviets."

Science and Culture

The traumatic experience of the war and the new technologies combined to transform both popular and elite cultures. Before the war the radio had been used primarily as a "wireless telegraph" for ships; in the 1920s, it became a means of broadcasting music, news, entertainment, and advertisements. The United States allowed broadcasting to become a private industry, but most nations imposed government ownership in order to use the new medium for educational, cultural, and propaganda purposes.

Other mass media flourished in a more creative atmosphere; here too, America took the lead, quickly followed by western Europe. As literacy spread, the press found increasing audiences for tabloids with huge headlines and sensational photographs. Advertisements, using techniques learned in wartime propaganda campaigns, enticed consumers to buy the latest products. Inexpensive phonograph records allowed even families of modest means to enjoy music in their homes, once the privilege of the well-to-do. The cinema brought entertainment to large numbers of people at once. Jazz, cartoons, and gangster movies were easily transported to every continent, forming the beginning of an emerging global popular culture (see Chapter 35).

While popular culture was changing under the influence of technology, elite culture was being transformed by discoveries in the natural and social sciences in the aftermath of war. Among the many theories and discoveries that appeared in the first decades of the century, some had global repercussions.

In the natural sciences, a revolution in physics undermined all the old certainties about nature. At the very end of the nineteenth century, physicists had discovered that the atoms that made up matter were not solid but consisted of far smaller particles. In 1900 the German physicist Max Planck (1858–1947) found that light and energy did not form a continuous stream but traveled in small units called quanta.

Those findings seemed strange enough, but what really called Newtonian physics into question was Albert Einstein's (1879–1955) general theory of relativity (1916). Not only was matter made of insubstantial particles, but—according to Einstein's theory—time, space, and mass were not fixed but were all relative to one another. Other physicists found that light consists either of waves or of particles, depending on the vantage point of observer, and that an experiment could determine either the speed or the position of a particle, but never both.

To nonscientists it seemed as though theories expressed in incomprehensible mathematics had replaced truth and common sense. Far from being mere speculation, however, the new physics promised to unlock the secrets of matter and provide humans with plentiful—and potentially dangerous—new sources of energy.

The new social sciences were even more unsettling than the new physics, for they challenged Victorian morality, bourgeois values, and the very idea of Western superiority. Sigmund Freud (1856–1939), a Viennese physician, developed the techniques of psychoanalysis to probe the mind of his patients. He found not only rationality but also hidden layers of emotion and desire repressed by social restraints. He wrote: "the primitive, savage and evil impulses have not vanished from any individual, but continue their existence, although in a repressed state." Meanwhile, sociologists and anthropologists had begun the empirical study of societies, both Western and non-Western. Already before the war, the French sociologist Émile Durkheim (1858–1917) had come to the then-shocking conclusion that "there are no religions that are false. All are true in their own fashion."

Although these ideas had been expressed before 1914, it was the experience of the First World War that made these ideas relevant by calling into question the Europeans' faith in reason and progress. If the words *primitive* and *savage* applied to Europeans as well as to other peoples, and if religions were all equally "true," then what remained of the superiority of Western civilization? *Cultural relativism*, as the new approach to human societies was called, was the analogue of *relativity* in the physical world. While some accepted the new ideas with enthusiasm, others condemned and rejected them. The confident sense of order and progress that had characterized European and American culture before World War I was shattered.

The Environment Transformed

No place on earth had ever been so completely devastated as the western front, a 300-mile-long (483-kilometer-long) scar across France and Belgium. The fighting ravaged and burned forests and demolished towns. The earth was gouged by trenches, pitted with craters, and filled with ammunition, broken weapons, chunks of concrete, and the bones of countless soldiers. After the war, it took a decade to clear the debris, rebuild the towns, and create dozens of military cemeteries with neat rows of crosses stretching for miles. To this day, farmers plow up fragments of old weapons and ammunition; every so often, a long-buried shell suddenly explodes. Elsewhere, the war hastened the buildup of industry, with its mines, factories, and railroad tracks.

The return of peace accelerated environmental changes. In India, Australia, and the western United States, where little virgin rain-watered land was left to be plowed under, engineers built many dams and canals to irrigate dry lands. In their calculations, the immediate benefits of irrigation—land, food, and electricity—far outweighed distant consequences such as salt deposits on irrigated lands and harm to wildlife.

More than any other technology, however, the automobile transformed the landscape of North America and western Europe. Roads were paved and highways built at an unprecedented pace. By the late 1920s, networks of paved roads rivaled rail networks both in length and in the surface they occupied, especially near cities. Far from being blamed for their exhaust emissions, automobiles were praised as the solution to urban pollution. As they replaced carts and carriages, horses disappeared from city streets, as did the tons of manure they formerly had left behind.

The most important environmental effect of automobiles was suburban sprawl, for middle-class families could now live in single-family homes too spread apart to be served by public transportation. Los Angeles, the first true automobile city, consisted of suburbs spread over hundreds of square miles and linked together by broad avenues. In those sections of the city where streetcar lines went out of business, the automobile, once a plaything for the wealthy, became a necessity for commuters. Many Americans saw Los Angeles as the portent of a glorious future when everyone would have a car. Only a few foresaw the congestion and pollution that would ensue.

AFTERMATH OF WAR IN THE MIDDLE EAST

The peoples of the Middle East had been directly involved in the fighting and thus hoped to have a say at the peace conference. But the victorious French and British expected to treat the Middle East like a non-Western territory open to colonial rule. The result was a legacy of instability that has persisted to this day.

Recasting Colonialism: The Mandate System

At the Paris Peace Conference of 1919, France, Britain, Italy, and Japan wanted to divide up the former German colonies and the territories of the Ottoman Empire as spoils of war. Their ambitions clashed with President Wilson's ideal of national self-determination. Although Wilson intended self-determination to apply only to Europeans, it changed the political atmosphere of the time. Eventually, the victors arrived at a compromise: the mandate system. It was a form of colonialism tempered by the novel idea that the colonial rulers were accountable for what the peace treaties called "the material and moral well-being and the social progress of the inhabitants."

Class C Mandates—the colonies with the smallest populations—were simply annexed by their conquerors. Thus South Africa acquired Southwest Africa (now Namibia), while Britain, Australia, New Zealand, and Japan took the German islands in the Pacific. Class B Mandates were larger but still underdeveloped. In theory they were to be ruled for the benefit of their inhabitants under League of Nations supervision, with a view to eventual autonomy at some unspecified time in the future. Most of Germany's African colonies fit into this category.

Class A Mandates included the Arab-speaking territories of the old Ottoman Empire. The League of Nations declared that they had "reached a state of development where their existence as independent nations can be provisionally recognized subject to the rendering of administrative advice and assistance by a Mandatory, until such time as they are able to stand alone." Arabs interpreted this ambiguous wording as a promise of independence. Britain and France, however, sent troops into the region "for the benefit of its inhabitants." Palestine (now Israel), Transjordan (now Jordan), and Iraq (formerly Mesopotamia) became British mandates, while France claimed Syria and Lebanon (see Map 30.3).

The Rise of Modern Turkey

As the Ottoman Empire teetered on the brink of collapse, France, Britain, and Italy saw an opportunity to expand their empires. Greece wanted all lands inhabited by Greeks, perhaps even a resurrection of the Byzantine Empire that had existed from the fifth to the mid-fifteenth century. In 1919 French, British, Italian, and Greek forces occupied Constantinople and parts of Anatolia.

Mustafa Kemal Atatürk   Mustafa Kemal, leader of Turkey after World War I, was determined to modernize his country on the Western model as rapidly as possible. Among the many changes he introduced were the Roman alphabet to replace the Arabic one, and European-style clothing. Here he is shown wearing a suit and teaching the Roman alphabet. (Stock Montage)

By the Treaty of Sèvres, the Allies made the sultan give up most of his lands, including much of Anatolia, but were foiled by the sudden reemergence of Turkish nationalism.

In 1919, when the sultan's government gave in to Allied pressures, Mustafa Kemal, a hero of the Gallipoli campaign, rose in revolt. Backed by fellow army officers, he formed a national government in central Anatolia. After a short but fierce war against the invading Greeks, his armies reconquered Anatolia and the area around Constantinople in 1922. Turks and Greeks agreed to an exchange of populations. As a result, hundreds of thousands of Greeks had to leave their ancestral homes in Anatolia, and all Muslims were expelled from Greece. This practically ended the ethnic diversity that had prevailed in the region for centuries.

As a war hero and the proclaimed savior of his country, Kemal was able to impose wrenching changes on his people faster than any other reformer would have dared. He was an outspoken modernizer eager to bring Turkey closer to Europe as quickly as possible. In the 1920s he abolished the sultanate, declared Turkey a secular republic, and introduced European laws. In a radical break with Islamic tradition, he suppressed the Muslim courts, schools, and religious orders and replaced the Arabic with the Latin alphabet.

Kemal also attempted to bring the traditional Turkish family closer to the European model. Women received civil equality, including the right to vote and be elected to the national assembly. Kemal forbade polygamy and instituted civil marriage and divorce. He even changed people's clothing, strongly discouraging women from veiling their faces and replacing the fez, until then the traditional Turkish men's hat, with the European brimmed hat. He ordered everyone to take a family name, choosing the name Atatürk ("father of the Turks") for himself. His reforms spread quickly in the cities but were long resisted in rural areas, where traditional Islamic customs remained strong.

Arab Lands and the Question of Palestine

Among the Arab people, the thinly disguised colonialism of the mandate system set off protests and rebellions, not only in the mandated territories but even as far away as Morocco. Arabs viewed the European presence not as "liberation" from Ottoman "oppression" but as a foreign occupation.

The British attempted to control the Middle East with a mixture of bribery and intimidation. They helped Faisal, leader of the Arab Revolt, become king of Syria; then, when the French ousted him, they made him king of Iraq. They used bombers to quell rural insurrections. In 1931 they reached an agreement with King Faisal's govern-

ment: official independence in exchange for the right to keep two air bases, a military alliance, and an assured flow of petroleum. France, meanwhile, sent thousands of troops to Syria and Lebanon to crush nationalist uprisings.

In Egypt as in Iraq, the British substituted phony independence for official colonialism. Having made Egypt a protectorate in 1914, they declared it independent in 1922 but reserved the right to station troops along the Suez Canal to secure their communications with India in the event of war. Most galling to the Egyptian Wafd (Nationalist) Party was the British attempt to remove Egyptian troops from the Sudan, a land many Egyptians considered a colony of Egypt. Britain was successful in keeping Egypt in limbo—neither independent nor a colony—thanks to an alliance with King Farouk and conservative Egyptian politicians who feared both secular and Islamic radicalism.

As soon as Palestine became a British mandate in 1920, Jewish immigrants arrived, encouraged by the Balfour Declaration of 1917. While most settled in the cities, others purchased land to establish *kibbutzim* (communal farms). Their goals were to become self-sufficient pioneers and reestablish their ties to the land of their ancestors. The purchases of land by Jewish agencies angered the indigenous Palestinians, especially tenant farmers evicted from their lands to make room for settlers. In 1920 and 1921, riots erupted between Jews and Arabs. When far more Jewish immigrants arrived than they had anticipated, the British tried to limit immigration, thereby alienating the Jews without mollifying the Arabs. Increasingly, Jews arrived without papers, smuggled in by audacious militant organizations. In the 1930s, the country was torn by strikes and guerrilla warfare that the British could not control. In the process, Britain earned the hatred of both sides and of much of the Arab world as well.

Social Change in the Middle East

After World War I, Middle Eastern society underwent dramatic changes. Nomads disappeared from the deserts as trucks replaced the camel caravans. The rural population grew fast,

Cities Old and New

Cities do not just grow larger; they change, sometimes radically, in response to culture and technology.

The impact of cultural dominance and technological innovations on urban design is evident in these photographs of Cairo.

The European colonial presence was felt more strongly in cities than in the countryside. Cairo, the largest city in the Arab world before the British conquest, grew much larger after 1882. The construction of modern quarters for Europeans and wealthy Egyptians had little impact on the older quarters where most Cairenes lived, however. In the picture of the old quarter of Cairo in 1900 with its narrow streets and open stalls, men wear the burnoose and women cover their faces with a veil. The later picture, taken in 1904, shows Shepheard's Hotel, one of the most luxurious in the world, built on a broad avenue in the city's modern quarter.

The picture at right reflects the traditional architecture of hot desert countries: narrow streets, thick whitewashed walls, small windows, and heavy doors, all designed to keep out the heat of the day and protect privacy.

The picture below shows the ideas Europeans brought with them about how a city should look. The wide streets and high airy buildings with windows and balconies mimic the urban design of late-nineteenth-century Paris, London, or Rome.

Cairo, traditional and modern   (Billie Love Historical Collection)

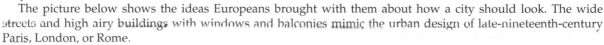

and many landless peasants migrated to the swelling cities. All together, the population of the region is estimated to have increased by half between 1914 and 1939, while that of the largest cities—such as Constantinople, Baghdad, and Cairo—doubled (see Environment and Technology: Cities Old and New).

Encouraged by the transformation of Turkey, the urban and mercantile middle class adopted Western ideas, customs, and styles of housing and clothing. Some families sent their sons to European secular or mission schools, then to Western colleges in Cairo and Beirut or to universities abroad, to prepare for jobs in government and business. Among the educated elite were a few women who became schoolteachers or nurses. There were great variations, ranging at one extreme from Lebanon, with its strong French influence, to Arabia or Iran, which retained a great diversity of cultural traditions.

The region in closest contact with Europe was the Maghrib—that is, Algeria, Tunisia, and Morocco—which the French army considered its private domain. Alongside the older native quarters, the French built modern neighborhoods inhabited mainly by Europeans. France had occupied Algeria since 1830 and had encouraged European immigration. The settlers owned the best lands and monopolized government jobs and businesses; Arabs and Berbers remained poor and suffered intense discrimination. Nationalism was only beginning to appear before the Second World War, and the settlers quickly blocked any attempt at reform.

CONCLUSION

Briefly in the late 1920s it seemed as though the victors of World War I could somehow reestablish the prewar prosperity and European dominance of the globe. But the spirit of the twenties was an illusion—not real peace but the eye of a hurricane. World War I left many problems unresolved and worsened others.

One such problem was Germany, which had tried to become a world power and almost succeeded. Defeat and the Treaty of Versailles humiliated Germany but did not reduce its military or industrial potential. Russia seemed to have collapsed into chaos and civil war, from which the victorious powers sought to isolate themselves; not until the 1930s would it recover, as we shall see in Chapter 31. Similarly, at the end of the war the Middle East seemed ripe for a new wave of European imperialism. Here too, however, the war unleashed forces that severely limited European influence. Far from emerging stronger from the war, the European victors found themselves challenged on many fronts: from within by revolutionary movements and throughout the world by nationalist movements and the growing power of nations overseas. Only in sub-Saharan Africa was European power still on the rise.

Modern technology and industrial organization had long been praised in the name of "progress" for their ability to reduce toil and disease and improve living standards. The war showed that they possessed an equally awesome potential to massacre and destroy. As we shall see in the next chapter, most survivors wanted no more of such a nightmare. But a small minority worshiped violence and saw in the new weaponry a means to dominate those who feared conflict and death.

SUGGESTED READING

Bernadotte Schmitt and Harold C. Bedeler, *The World in the Crucible, 1914–1918* (1984), is an engaging overview of the First World War. Imanuel Geiss, *July 1914: The Outbreak of the First World War* (1967), presents the documentary evidence of Germany's role in causing the conflict. Barbara Tuchman's *The Guns of August* (1962) and Alexander Solzhenitsyn's *August 1914* (1972) recount the first month of the war in minute detail. John Keegan's *The Face of Battle* (1976) vividly describes the Battle of the Somme from the soldiers' perspective. On the technology of warfare see William H. McNeill, *The Pursuit of Power: Technology, Armed Force, and Society* (1982), and John Ellis, *The Social History of the Machine Gun* (1975). The role of women and the home front is the subject of essays in Margaret Randolph Higonnet, Jane Jenson, Sonya Michel, and Margaret Collins Weitz, eds., *Behind the Lines: Gender and the Two World Wars* (1987), and sections of Lynn Weiner, *From Working Girl to Working Mother* (1985). Two famous novels about the war are Erich Maria Remarque's *All Quiet on the Western Front* (1928) and Robert Graves's *Goodbye to All That* (1929). The war in English literature is the subject of Paul Fussell, *The Great War and Modern Memory* (1975).

On the background to the Russian Revolution read Theodore von Laue's *Why Lenin? Why Stalin?* 2d ed. (1971). The classic eyewitness account of the Revolution is John Reed's *Ten Days That Shook the World* (1919), but see also Richard Pipes, *The Russian Revolution* (1990). The best-known novel about the Russian Revolution and civil war is Boris Pasternak's *Doctor Zhivago* (1958).

John Maynard Keynes's *The Economic Consequences of the Peace* (1920) is a classic critique of the Paris Peace Conference. Arno Mayer's *Political Origins of the New Diplomacy, 1917–1918* (1959), analyzes the tensions and

failures of great-power politics. The 1920s are discussed in Raymond Sontag's *A Broken World, 1919–1939* (1971).

On war and its aftermath in the Middle East see David Fromkin, *A Peace to End All Peace* (1989), and M. E. Yapp, *The Near East Since the First World War* (1991). Bernard Lewis, *The Emergence of Modern Turkey* (1968), is a good introduction to modern Turkey. On Africa in this period see A. Adu Boahen, ed., *Africa Under Colonial Domination, 1880–1935* (1985), vol. 7 of *UNESCO General History of Africa*, and A. D. Roberts, ed., *From 1905 to 1940* (1986), vol. 7 of *The Cambridge History of Africa*.

The cultural transformation is captured in H. Stuart Hughes, *Consciousness and Society: The Reorientation of European Social Thought, 1890–1930* (1958). The towering intellectuals of that era are the subject of Peter Gay, *Freud: A Life for Our Time* (1988), and Abraham Pais, *Subtle Is the Lord: The Science and Life of Albert Einstein* (1982). Two books capture the enthusiastic popular response to technological innovations: David E. Nye, *Electrifying America: Social Meanings of a New Technology* (1990), and Peter Fritzsche, *A Nation of Fliers: German Aviation and the Popular Imagination* (1992).

CHAPTER THIRTY-ONE

The Depression and the Second World War, 1929–1945

The Depression · The Stalin Revolution · Japan Goes to War

Fascism in Europe · The Second World War · The Character of Warfare

For six years, from 1924 to 1929, the world seemed to return to what U.S. president Warren G. Harding called "normalcy": prosperity in the West, no major wars, European domination of Asia and Africa, and U.S. domination of Latin America. Conservative politicians and wealthy investors looked to the future with optimism. In June 1929 the American financier Bernard Baruch declared: "The economic condition of the world is on the verge of a great forward movement."

Four months later, the American economy imploded. On October 24—"Black Thursday"—stockholders, afraid that the value of their stocks might fall, sold 16 million shares, causing the very price drop they were afraid of. Stock prices fell by half in three weeks and continued to drop. A share of General Electric, worth $403 at its peak in 1929, dropped to a low of $8.50 in 1932, while the price of a share of RCA stock fell from $114.75 to $2.50.

Millions of investors lost their savings, as did the banks and brokers that had lent them money. People who had savings accounts rushed to withdraw their money, causing thousands of banks to collapse. Very soon, the economic crisis spread around the world, as businesses went bankrupt, prices fell, factories closed, and workers were laid off. Even wholly agricultural nations and colonies suffered as the markets for their exports shriveled.

The international system forged at Versailles proved too fragile to preserve the peace in such desperate times. In the Soviet Union, Joseph Stalin pushed his people to industrialize their country at breakneck speed. In Germany and Japan, the Depression awakened resentments against the victors of the Great War; those who harbored grievances against the old order or who feared communism increasingly called for violent methods to revive their societies and to dominate others.

The result was another war. The Second World War engulfed more lands and peoples than any previous conflict and caused far more deaths and destruction. At the end of it, much of Europe and East Asia had been reduced to ruins, and millions of destitute refugees sought safety in other lands. The European colonial powers were either defeated or so weakened that they could no longer hold onto their empires. As the long era of European dominance came to an end, Asian and African peoples asserted their independence.

THE DEPRESSION

What began as a stock market crash soon turned into the deepest and most widespread economic depression in history. Because the United States had the largest economy in the world, its collapse was felt around the world, especially in those nations and colonies that relied on trade and exports. The collapse of the global economy in turn had profound and dangerous political consequences. Let us consider these effects.

Economic Crisis

The first reaction of traditional politicians to the stock market crash was to issue cheerful exhortations and to hope that business would recover on its own. In January 1930 U.S. president Herbert Hoover announced: "Business and industry have turned the corner"; then in May: "We have now passed the worst."

Despite such brave words, fear and pessimism quickly spread from finance to industry. As American consumers reduced their purchases, businesses cut production. For example, General Motors, which had built 5,500,000 cars in 1929, made only 2,500,000 in 1931. In the process, businesses laid off workers, throwing thousands out of work and rendering them dependent on charity. Businesses and government agencies that employed women replaced them with men, arguing that men had to support their families whereas women worked only for "pin money." As farm prices fell, small farmers went bankrupt and lost their land.

By mid-1932, the American gross national product (GNP) had fallen by half, and unemployment had risen to an unprecedented 25 percent of the work force. As unemployment rose, many jobless men deserted their families. Government spending on welfare and public works projects alleviated misery but was insufficient to restore prosperity. Many observers thought the free-enterprise system was collapsing, to be replaced by bread lines, soup kitchens, men selling apples on street corners, and hoboes riding freight trains.

Frightened by the stock market collapse, the New York banks called in their loans to Germany and Austria. In May 1931 the Austrian bank Creditanstalt suspended payments, triggering panic throughout Central Europe. Without American money, Germany and Austria stopped paying reparations to France and Britain, which could no longer pay back their war loans to America. Governments canceled both reparations and war loans but did so too late to save the world economy.

In 1930 the U.S. government, hoping to protect domestic industries from foreign competition, imposed the Smoot-Hawley tariff, the highest import duty in American history. In retaliation, other countries raised their tariffs in a wave of "beggar thy neighbor" protectionism. The result was to cripple export industries and shrink world trade. While global industrial production declined by 36 percent between 1929 and 1932, world trade dropped by a breathtaking 62 percent.

Depression in Industrial Nations

Every capitalist nation saw its economy shrivel. France and Britain escaped the worst of it by making their colonial empires purchase their products rather than those of other countries. Nations that relied on exports to pay for import-

ed food and fuel—in particular Japan and Germany—suffered much more. In Germany, unemployment reached 6 million by 1932, affecting twice as many people as in Britain. Half of the German population was plunged into poverty. Thousands of schoolteachers and engineers were laid off, and those who kept their jobs saw their salaries cut and their living standards fall. In Japan, the burden of the Depression was shifted to the farmers and fishermen, who saw their incomes drop sharply; some, in desperation, revived the ancient practice of selling their daughters.

Such a massive economic upheaval had profound political repercussions. Many people in capitalist countries began losing faith in laissez-faire economic policies (see Chapter 23) and calling for government intervention in the economy. In America, Franklin D. Roosevelt defeated Hoover and was elected president in 1932 on a "New Deal" platform promising government programs to stimulate and revitalize the economy. Although the American, British, and French governments took on more responsibilities, they remained democratic. In Germany and Japan, as economic grievances worsened long-festering political resentments, radical politicians took over the economy and turned their nations into machines to make war.

Even government control of a national economy could be jeopardized by the swings of the world market. Thus nationalists everywhere yearned for *autarchy*, independence from the world economy. Only two industrial nations—the United States and the Soviet Union—even came close to self-sufficiency. Two others, Britain and France, could have survived by trading with their colonial empires. For Germany, Italy, and Japan, however, the yearning for autarchy meant acquiring, by war if necessary, an empire large enough to support a self-sufficient economy.

Depression in Nonindustrial Regions

The Depression soon spread to Asia, Africa, and Latin America, but very unevenly. India, a large and mainly agricultural country, by 1930 had erected a wall of import duties to protect its infant industries from foreign competition. As a result,

The depression in Japan Japan depended on world trade for its imports of fuel and raw materials. The depression caused unemployment and hardships, which led in turn to political agitation. This picture shows a speaker addressing a crowd before a May Day parade in 1931, the annual celebration of workers and labor unions. (UPI/Corbis-Bettmann)

living standards in India stagnated but did not drop. China, except in its coastal regions, was little affected by trade with other countries; as we shall see, its problems were political, not economic.

Countries that depended on the export of a few products were hard hit by the Depression. Malaya and the Dutch East Indies produced most of the world's natural rubber. When U.S. and European automobile production dropped by half, so did imports of rubber, devastating the Malayan and East Indian economies. Cuba had become a tourist haven during the 1920s, a playground for rich Americans who basked in the sun and quaffed liquor forbidden at home by Prohibition. When the Depression hit, the tourists vanished, and with them went Cuba's prosperity.

Sugar from the Caribbean, coffee from Brazil and Colombia, wheat and beef from Argentina, tea from Ceylon and Java, tin from Malaya and Bolivia, and many other products felt the heavy hand of the Depression. Argentina and Brazil, which had started on the road to industrialization, were set back a decade or more. Throughout Latin America, unemployment and homelessness increased markedly. In response to the Depression, military officers seized power in several Latin American countries. Consciously imitating Fascist dictatorships in Europe, they imposed authoritarian control over their economies, hoping to stimulate local industries and curb imports.

Outside the USSR, only southern Africa boomed during the 1930s. As most prices dropped, gold became relatively more valuable, enriching the white South African mine owners. Copper deposits, found in Northern Rhodesia (now Zambia) and the Belgian Congo (now Zaire), proved to be cheaper to mine than Chilean copper. But this mining boom benefited only a small minority of Europeans. For Africans it was at best a mixed blessing, for mining offered jobs and cash wages to men while women stayed behind in the villages, farming, herding, and raising children without their husbands' help.

THE STALIN REVOLUTION

The Soviet Union was as conspicuously absent from the Depression as it had been from the "normalcy" of the 1920s. Ostracized by most other countries, it underwent two revolutions in quick succession: first the Bolshevik Revolution described in Chapter 30; then, from 1928 to 1940, an economic and social transformation that turned it into a great industrial and military power and intensified both admiration for and fear of communism throughout the world.

Five-Year Plans

Joseph Stalin (1879–1953) was born Joseph Vissarionovich Dzhugashvili into the family of a poor shoemaker. Before becoming a revolutionary, he studied for the priesthood. He played only a small part in the Revolution of 1917, but he was a hard-working and skillful administrator who rose within the party bureaucracy and filled its upper ranks with men loyal to himself. By 1925, he had ousted Leon Trotsky, the best-known revolutionary after Lenin, from the party. He then proceeded to squeeze all other rivals out of positions of power, make himself absolute dictator, and transform Soviet society.

Stalin's ambition was to turn the USSR into an industrial nation. Industrialization, however, would serve a different purpose in the USSR

than in other countries. It was not expected to produce consumer goods for a mass market, as in Britain or the United States, or to enrich individuals. Instead, its aim was to increase the power of the Communist Party and the power of the Soviet Union in relation to other countries.

Stalin was determined to prevent a repeat of the kind of humiliating defeat that Russia had suffered at the hands of Germany in 1917. So he stressed heavy industries, especially steel. It was no coincidence that he had chosen for himself the revolutionary name "Stalin" (meaning "man of steel"). His goal was to quintuple the output of electricity and double that of heavy industries—iron, steel, coal, and machinery—in five years. To do so, he devised the First Five-Year Plan, a system of centralized control copied from the German experience of World War I. In every way except actual fighting, Stalin's Russia resembled a nation at war.

Beginning in October 1928, the Communist Party and government created whole industries and cities from scratch, recruiting millions of peasants and training them to work in the new factories, mines, and offices. Rapid industrialization hastened environmental changes. Hydroelectric dams turned rivers into strings of reservoirs. Roads, canals, and railroad tracks cut the landscape. Forests and grasslands were turned into farmland. From an environmental perspective, the outcome of the Five-Year Plans resembled the outcome of economic expansion and new technologies in the United States and Canada a few decades earlier (see Chapter 25).

Since the Soviet Union was still a predominantly agrarian country, the only way to pay for these massive investments, provide the labor, and feed the millions of new industrial workers was to squeeze the peasantry. Stalin therefore proceeded with the most radical social experiment ever conceived up to that time: the collectivization of agriculture.

Collectivization of Agriculture

Collectivization meant consolidating small private farms into vast collective farms and making farmers work together in commonly owned fields. As economic units, collectives were to become outdoor "factories" where food was manufactured through the techniques of mass production and the application of machinery. Each collective was expected to supply the government with a fixed amount of food and distribute what was left among its members. Machine tractor stations leased agricultural machinery to several farms and in exchange collected the portion of the crop owed to the government. Collectivization was an attempt to impose an urban-industrial way of life—the only lifestyle Communists accepted—on the peasants to replace what Lenin had called their "petty bourgeois" attitudes. It was expected to bring them once and for all under government control so they never again could withhold food supplies as they had done when Lenin was trying to carry out the New Economic Policy (see Chapter 30).

When collectivization was announced, the government mounted a massive propaganda campaign. Party members fanned out across the countryside to enlist the farmers' support. At first all seemed to go well, but soon the *kulaks* (fists), the better-off peasants, began to resist giving up all their property. When soldiers came to force them into collectives at gunpoint, the farmers burned their crops, smashed their equipment,

The collectivization of agriculture   During the 1930s, agricultural land in Russia was organized into huge collective farms, several of which depended on a machine tractor station for their equipment and supplies. This way, the Communist Party could keep the peasants under tight control. This picture shows a row of tractors at the Lenin collective farm in 1933. (Endeavor Group UK. Photo: G. Petrusov)

and slaughtered their livestock. Within a few months, they destroyed half of the country's horses and cattle and two-thirds of its sheep and goats. In retaliation, Stalin ruthlessly ordered the "liquidation of kulaks as a class" and incited the poorest peasants to attack their wealthier neighbors. Over 8 million kulaks were arrested. Many were executed, and the rest were sent to slave labor camps in Siberia or northern Russia, where most starved to death.

The peasants who were left had been the least successful before collectivization and proved to be least competent after. Many were sent to work in factories. The rest were not allowed to leave their farms. With half of their draft animals gone, they could not plant or harvest enough to meet the swelling demands of the cities. Yet the government took what it could find, leaving little or nothing for the farmers. After bad harvests in 1933 and 1934, a famine swept through the country, killing some 5 million people, about one in every twenty farmers.

Stalin's Second Five-Year Plan, designed to run from 1933 to 1937, was originally intended to increase the output of consumer goods. But when the Nazis took over Germany in 1933 (see below), Stalin changed the plan to emphasize heavy industries that could produce armaments. Between 1927 and 1937 the Soviet output of metals and machines increased fourteen-fold while consumer goods became scarce and food was rationed. After a decade of Stalinism, the Soviet people were more poorly clothed, fed, and housed than they had been under the New Economic Policy.

Terror and Opportunities

The 1930s brought both terror and new opportunities to the Soviet people. The forced pace of industrialization, the collectivization of agriculture, and the uprooting of millions of people could be accomplished only under duress. To prevent resistance or rebellion, Stalin created a climate of suspicion and fear enforced by the NKVD, or secret police. In large measure, the terror that pervaded the country was a reflection of his own paranoia, for he distrusted everyone and feared for his life.

As early as 1930, he had hundreds of engineers and technicians arrested on trumped-up charges of counterrevolutionary ideas and sabotage. Three years later, he expelled a million members of the Communist Party—one-third of the membership—on similar charges. He then turned on his most trusted associates. In December 1934 he secretly ordered the assassination of Sergei Kirov, the party boss of Leningrad, then made a public display of mourning Kirov while blaming others for his death.

The years 1934 to 1938 were marked by a series of spectacular purge trials, in which Stalin accused most of Lenin's associates of "anti-party activities," the worst form of treason. In 1937 he had the eight top generals and many lesser officers accused of treason and executed, leaving the Red Army dangerously weakened. He even executed the head of the NKVD, which was enforcing the terror. Under torture or psychological pressure, almost all confessed to the "crimes" they were charged with.

While Old Bolsheviks and high officials were being put on trial, terror spread steadily downward. The government regularly made demands on people that they could not meet, making everyone guilty of breaking some regulation or other. People from all walks of life were arrested, sometimes on a mere suspicion or a false accusation by a jealous coworker or neighbor, sometimes for expressing a doubt or working too hard or too little, sometimes for being related to someone previously arrested, and sometimes for no reason at all. Such people were convicted and sentenced without trial. At the height of the terror, some 8 million were sent to *gulags* (labor camps), where perhaps a million died each year of exposure or malnutrition. To its victims, the terror seemed capricious and random. Yet it served to turn a sullen and resentful people into docile, hard-working subjects.

In spite of the fear and hardships, Stalin's regime received the support of many, if not most, Soviet citizens. Suddenly, with so many people gone and new industries and cities being built everywhere, there were new opportunities for those who remained, especially the poor and the young. Women entered careers and jobs previously closed to them, becoming steelworkers, physicians, and office managers; but they retained their household and child-rearing duties, receiving little help from men. People who moved to the cities, worked enthusiastically, and asked no questions could hope to rise into the upper ranks of the Communist Party, the military, the government, or the professions—where the privileges and rewards were many.

In the process they helped the Soviet Union industrialize faster than any country had ever done before. By the late 1930s, the USSR had become the world's third largest industrial power, after the United States and Germany. To foreign observers it seemed to be booming with construction projects, production increases, and labor shortages. Even anti-Communist observers admitted that only a planned economy subject to strict government control could avoid the Depression. To millions of Soviet citizens who took pride in the new strength of their country, and to many foreigners who contrasted it with the unemployment and despair in the West, Stalin's achievement seemed worth any price.

JAPAN GOES TO WAR

B y the 1920s Japan was a respected member of the international community, the only non-European nation among the major powers. The pride of its armed forces and the collapse of its foreign trade in the Depression, however, led Japan to wager its very existence on the creation of a great empire.

Japan from 1914 to 1931

The Japanese had been quick to join World War I, which they saw as a golden opportunity to advance their national interests while the Europeans were occupied elsewhere. In short order, they conquered the German colonies in the northern Pacific and on the coast of China, then turned their attention to the rest of China.

At the time, as we shall see in Chapter 32, China was in the grip of a revolution and seemed about to break apart. In January 1915, Japan presented China with a list of Twenty-One Demands that would have turned it into a virtual protectorate. Britain and the United States persuaded Japan to soften its demands but could not prevent it from keeping the German enclaves and extracting railroad and mining concessions in Manchuria and Mongolia at China's expense. The Chinese people greeted these concessions with riots and boycotts of Japanese goods. The relationship between the two countries became one of aggressor and victim, the beginning of a bitter struggle that was to last for thirty years.

As had happened after Japan's victory over Russia in 1905, the United States stood in the way of Japan's ambitions. At the Versailles peace conference in 1919, Woodrow Wilson and the Europeans had rejected Japan's statement on racial equality. Three years later, the United States demanded that Japan limit its navy to three-fifths the size of the American or British navies, a blow to Japanese pride. Under its long-standing Open Door policy, the United States also claimed to defend China's independence and territorial integrity and keep China open to all foreign business interests. The Japanese people felt insulted by each of these measures and the immigration law of 1924, which excluded Japanese from the United States.

Japan had limited farmland and few natural resources. Yet its population, which reached 60 million in 1925, was increasing by a million a year. To break out of underdevelopment, as we saw in Chapter 28, Japan had industrialized at breathtaking speed, especially during the First World War, when it exported textiles, consumer goods, and munitions. Its economy grew by over 4 percent a year, four times as fast as western Europe's, eight times faster than China's. Its industrial work force increased from 700,000 in 1921 to 5 million in 1930.

Economic growth worsened social tensions. The main beneficiaries of prosperity were *zaibatsu*, giant corporations—such as Mitsubishi, Sumitomo, Yasuda, and Mitsui—that controlled most

The Japanese invasion of China   When the Japanese Army invaded northern and eastern China in December 1937, Chinese infantry soldiers were quickly overwhelmed by Japanese tanks and aircraft. In this picture of the Japanese attack on the Chinese city of Nanjing, a tank is making its way across a half-destroyed railroad bridge, opening a path for the infantry to follow. (Ullstein Bilderdienst, Berlin)

of Japan's industry and commerce. In the big cities, *mobos* (modern boys) and *mogas* (modern girls) shocked traditionalists with their foreign ways: dancing together, wearing tight pants and short skirts, behaving like Americans. Farmers, who constituted half of the population, remained poor; some, in desperation, sold their daughters to textile mills, where young women formed the bulk of the labor force. Labor unions were weak, and only a few workers enjoyed lifetime employment with big companies.

Japanese prosperity depended to a large extent on foreign trade and imperialism in Asia. The country imported almost all its fuel, raw materials, and machine tools and exported silk and light manufactures. As long as business was

good, Japan cooperated with the League of Nations. But Japan was vulnerable to swings in the world economy and to great-power politics in East Asia.

When the Depression hit, China and the United States erected barriers against Japanese imports. The collapse of demand for silk and rice ruined thousands of Japanese farmers; many sold their daughters into prostitution while their sons flocked to the military. Japanese nationalists turned once again to imperialism, believing that if Japan had a colonial empire, it would not be beholden to the rest of the world. But the Europeans and Americans had already taken most potential colonies in Asia, leaving Japan with Korea, Taiwan, and a railroad in Manchuria. The conquest of China, with its vast population and resources, seemed like the solution to Japan's problems.

The Manchurian Incident of 1931

Junior army officers, most of them from peasant backgrounds, determined to take action. Their first move took place in Manchuria, a Chinese province rich in coal and iron ore and dominated by the Japanese-owned South Manchurian Railway. In September 1931, an explosion on a railroad track gave officers of the Japanese force guarding the railway an excuse to conquer the entire province. In the Japanese government, weak civilian ministers were intimidated by the military; informed after the fact, they acquiesced to the attack in order to avoid losing face. Chinese politicians were too weakened by years of revolution and internal division to resist. When Chinese students, workers, and housewives boycotted Japanese goods, Japanese troops briefly took over Shanghai, China's major industrial city, and the area around Beijing. Japan thereupon recognized the "independence" of Manchuria under the name "Manchukuo."

The response of the great powers was swift but ineffective. The U.S. State Department issued a statement condemning the Japanese conquest. The League of Nations refused to recognize Manchukuo and urged the Japanese to remove their troops from China. Persuaded that the Western powers would not fight, Japan resigned from the League of Nations.

During the next few years, the Japanese built railways and heavy industries in Manchuria and northeastern China and sped up their rearmament. At home, life became harsher and more repressive as more and more production was diverted to the military, especially to building warships. The government grew more authoritarian, jailing thousands of dissidents. On several occasions super-patriotic junior officers mutinied or assassinated leading political figures. Although the mutineers were punished, generals and admirals sympathetic to their views replaced more moderate civilian politicians.

War with China

Japanese economists argued that freeing Japan from its dependence on world trade would require several years of peace. Some Japanese army officers advocated a quick conquest of China; others anticipated a war with the Soviet Union. While their superiors hesitated, junior Japanese officers, the only faction with a clear plan, took actions that had momentous consequences.

European and American historians date the beginning of the Second World War from the German invasion of Poland in September 1939 (see below). In fact, fighting between the major powers erupted two years earlier, on July 7, 1937, when Japanese troops attacked Chinese forces at the Marco Polo Bridge near Beijing. Junior officers ordered the attack, and, as in 1931, they quickly obtained the support of their commanders and then, reluctantly, of the government.

Within weeks, Japanese troops had seized Beijing, Tianjin, Shanghai, and other coastal cities, and the Japanese navy had blockaded the entire coast of China. Although the Chinese armies were large and fought bravely, they were poorly led and armed and lost every battle. Japanese planes bombed Nanjing, Hankou, and Canton, and Japanese soldiers on the ground broke dikes and burned villages, killing thousands of civilians. Within a year, Japan controlled the coastal provinces of China and the lower Yangzi and Yellow river valleys. The Chinese government, led by General Chiang Kaishek, escaped to mountainous Sichuan province in the center of the country.

Once again, the United States and the League of Nations denounced the Japanese atrocities. But the Western powers were too preoccupied with events in Europe and with their own economic problems to risk a military confrontation in Asia. Even after the Japanese sank an American gunboat and shelled a British ship on the Yangzi River, their only responses were pious resolutions and righteous indignation.

In spite of Japanese organizational and fighting skills, Japan's attack on China was only partially successful. Although China had lost its richest and most populated regions, the Chinese people continued to fight, either in the army or, increasingly, with Communist guerrilla forces. Japan's attempts to win the war by conquering one more piece of China only pushed Japan deeper into the quagmire. Its conquests turned out to be a drain on the Japanese economy and manpower rather than a source of wealth and strength.

At home, life became harsher for the Japanese people. Taxes rose. Food, fuel, and other necessities became scarce. More and more young men were drafted. Worst of all in the eyes of Japanese leaders was the painful realization that the war with China was not making their country self-sufficient. On the contrary, the Japanese war machine was becoming increasingly dependent on the United States for steel and machine tools and for nine-tenths of its oil.

Japanese leaders continued to keep a watchful eye on the international situation. With the outbreak of war in Europe in 1939, they thought they saw a chance to seize the French and Dutch colonies in Southeast Asia without a fight. In July 1941, when the French government allowed Japanese forces to occupy Indochina, the United States and Britain, instead of merely complaining, stopped supplying steel, scrap iron, oil, and other products that Japan desperately needed. This action left Japan with a hard choice: either to abandon China and Manchuria, as the Americans insisted, or to fight the United States and Britain. The Japanese government chose war.

FASCISM IN EUROPE

The Russian Revolution and its Stalinist aftermath frightened property owners in Europe and America. Although governments everywhere repressed Communist movements, their response to the threat of social revolution varied. In the democracies of western Europe and North America, there was little fear of Communist uprisings or electoral victories, and middle- and upper-income voters took refuge in traditional conservative politics and in police action to pre-

vent subversion. The societies of southern and Central Europe, in contrast, lacked stable political systems.

Italy and Germany had been unified in the 1860s and 1870s. Most Balkan states had become independent in the nineteenth century; the states of eastern Europe had been independent only since World War I. The political institutions of states in southern and central Europe were frail imitations of those in the West and lacked popular legitimacy. The war had turned their inflated hopes of victory to bitter disappointment. Many people felt bewildered by modernity—with its cities, factories, and department stores—which they blamed on ethnic minorities, especially Jews. In their yearning for a mythical past of family farms and small shops, increasing numbers lost faith in representative political parties and sought more dramatic solutions.

Radical politicians quickly learned to use wartime propaganda techniques to appeal to a confused citizenry, especially young men and the unemployed. They promised to use any means necessary to bring back prosperity, prevent the spread of communism, and achieve the territorial conquests that the First World War had denied them. They borrowed their tactics from the Bolsheviks and their goals from the war.

Mussolini's Italy

The first country to seek radical answers was Italy. World War I, which had never been popular, left behind thousands of veterans who found neither pride in their victory nor jobs in the postwar economy. Unemployed veterans and violent youths banded together into *fasci di combattimento* (fighting units) to intimidate politicians and demand action. When workers threatened to strike, factory and property owners hired gangs of these *fascisti* to defend them.

Benito Mussolini (1883–1945) had once been a member of the Socialist Party but was expelled for supporting Italy's entry into the war. A veteran and a spellbinding orator, he quickly became the leader of the Fascist Party, which glorified warfare and the Italian nation. By 1921 it had 300,000 members, many of whom used violent methods to repress strikes, intimidate voters, and seize municipal governments. A year later, Mussolini threatened to march on Rome if he was not appointed prime minister. The government, composed of timid parliamentarians, gave in.

No sooner was Mussolini in office than he proceeded to install Fascist Party members in all government jobs, crush all opposition parties, and jail anyone who dared criticize him. The party took over the press, public education, and youth activities and gave employers control over their workers. The Fascists tried to make Italy self-sufficient in foodstuffs, lowering living standards. However, they reduced unemployment and provided social security and public services. On the whole, they proved to be neither ruthless radicals nor competent administrators.

What Mussolini and the Fascist movement really excelled at was publicity: bombastic speeches, spectacular parades, news bulletins full of praise and adulation for *Il Duce* (the Leader), signs everywhere proclaiming "Il Duce is always right!" Billboards, movie footage, radio news bulletins, and other modern public relations techniques were new to politics and galvanized the masses of citizens in ways never before seen in peacetime. Mussolini's genius was to apply the psychology of war to peacetime life. Although his rhetoric was filled with words like *war*, *violence*, and *struggle*, until the mid-1930s his foreign policy was cautious and friendly toward France and Britain. But his methods of whipping up patriotism and public enthusiasm were not lost on other radicals with more sinister ambitions.

Hitler's Germany

Postwar Germany suffered far deeper traumas than Italy. It had lost the First World War after coming very close to winning. The inflation of 1923 wiped out the savings of middle-class families. Less than ten years later, the Depression caused more unemployment and misery in Germany than in any other country. Millions of Germans lost faith in democracy and blamed Socialists, Jews, and foreigners for their troubles.

Hitler haranguing an audience   Adolf Hitler was a masterful public speaker who often used his oratorical gift to captivate mass audiences at Nazi Party rallies. (Roger Viollet)

What few realized—even those who hoped for a radical change—was that they were about to get not just an authoritarian dictatorship but one dedicated to war and mass murder.

Adolf Hitler (1889–1945) was born in Austria, the son of a minor government official. He tried to become an artist but failed and spent his youth in dire poverty. At the start of World War I, he joined the German army and was wounded at the front. He later looked back fondly on the clearly defined lines of authority and the camaraderie he had experienced in battle. After the war, using his gifts as an orator, he quickly rose in a political splinter group, the National Socialist German Workers' Party—Nazis for short. In 1924, while Germany was in political chaos and reeling from hyperinflation, Hitler led a small and unsuccessful uprising in Munich. While serving a brief jail sentence, he wrote *Mein Kampf* (*My Struggle*), a book in which he outlined his goals and beliefs.

Hitler went far beyond ordinary nationalism. Shocked by the demise of the Austro-Hungarian Empire, he believed that Germany should incorporate all German-speaking people, even those who lived in neighboring countries. He took the racist ideas commonly held by whites toward people of color and applied them to Europeans. He distinguished among a "master race" of Aryans (he meant Germans, Scandinavians, and Britons), a degenerate "Alpine" race of French and Italians, and an inferior race of Russian and eastern European Slavs, who he believed were fit only to be slaves of the master race. His most intense hatred was reserved for Jews, whom he blamed for every disaster that had befallen Germany, especially the defeat of 1918. He glorified violence, interpreting the Darwinian idea of "survival of the fittest" (see Chapter 28) to mean that in a future war the "master race" would defeat and subjugate all others.

His first goal was to repeal the humiliation and military restrictions of the Versailles Treaty. Then he planned to annex all German-speaking territories to a greater Germany, by war if necessary, and later to conquer *Lebensraum* (room to live) in the east at the expense of Poland, Russia, and Ukraine. Finally, he planned to eliminate all Jews from Europe. When it was first published in 1925, *Mein Kampf* attracted little notice. Its ideas seemed so insane that almost no one took it, or its author, seriously.

The years from 1924 to 1930 were a time of prosperity for Germany (see Chapter 30). Hitler's followers remained a tiny minority, for most found his ideas too extreme. But when the Depression hit, the Nazis gained supporters among the unemployed who believed Nazi promises of jobs for all and among property owners frightened by the growing popularity of Communists. In March 1933, as leader of the largest party in Germany, Hitler became chancellor.

Once in office, he quickly assumed dictatorial power. From the *Reichstag* (parliament) he obtained the power to govern by decree, legally ending democracy in Germany. A policy of "coordination" put Nazis in charge of all government agencies, education, and professional organizations. All other political parties were abolished and their leaders thrown into concentration camps. The Nazis deprived Jews of their citizenship and civil rights, prohibited them from marrying "Aryans," ousted them from the professions, and confiscated their property. In August 1934, when President Paul von Hindenburg died, Hitler proclaimed himself *Führer*, or leader, and called Germany the "Third Reich" (empire)—the third after the Holy Roman Empire of medieval times and the German Empire of 1871 to 1918.

The Nazis' economic and social policies were spectacularly effective. They replaced labor unions with a National Labor Front that controlled both labor and employers. The government undertook massive public works projects. Businesses hired workers to manufacture weapons for the armed forces. Women, who had entered the work force during and after World War I, were urged to return to *Kinder, Kirche, Küche* (children, church, kitchen), releasing jobs for men. By 1936 business was booming, unemployment dropped to its lowest level since the 1920s, and living standards were rising. Hitler's popularity soared, because most Germans believed their economic well-being outweighed the loss of liberty.

The Road to War, 1933–1939

To Hitler, being a dictator was only the means to an end, for his goal was not prosperity or popularity but conquest. As soon as he came to office, he began to build up the armed forces. Meanwhile, he tested the reactions of the other powers through a series of surprise moves followed by protestations of peace.

In 1933, he withdrew Germany from the League of Nations. France and Britain disapproved but hesitated to retaliate by blockading or invading Germany. Two years later he announced that Germany was going to introduce conscription, build up its army, and create an air force in violation of the Versailles Treaty. Instead of protesting, Britain signed a naval agreement with Germany. The message was clear: neither Britain nor France was willing to risk war by standing up to Germany. The United States, absorbed in its domestic economic problems, reverted to isolationism and refused to accept responsibility for the condition of Europe, which it had helped create in 1919.

In 1935, emboldened by the weakness of the democracies toward Japan and Germany, Mussolini invaded Ethiopia, the last independent state in Africa and a member of the League of Nations. The League and the democracies protested feebly but refused to stop the Italian campaign by closing the Suez Canal to Italian ships and imposing an oil embargo. The following year, Hitler sent troops into the Rhineland on the borders of France and Belgium; the other powers merely protested.

In July 1936, the Spanish army rose up against the government of the Republic of Spain, which it considered too leftist and anti-Catholic. In the civil war that followed, Italy and Germany aided the Nationalists (as the rebels called themselves), and the USSR supported the Republic. In 1936 Hitler and Mussolini, seeing that the democracies refused to help the Spanish government, concluded that aggression paid off and formed an alliance called the Axis, aimed at furthering their territorial ambitions.

By 1938 Hitler decided his rearmament plans were far enough advanced that he could afford to escalate his demands. In March, Germany invaded Austria. Most of its citizens were German-speakers and accepted the annexation of their country to Hitler's Reich without protest. Then came the turn of Czechoslovakia, where a German-speaking minority lived along the German border. Hitler first demanded their autonomy from Czech rule, then their annexation to Germany. Throughout the summer he threatened to go to war. Finally in September 1938 at the Munich Conference he met with the leaders of France, Britain, and Italy, who gave him everything he wanted without consulting Czechoslovakia. Once again, the fascist powers learned that aggression paid off and that the democracies would always give in.

The weakness of the democracies—now called "appeasement"—is hard to explain, for it ran counter to the traditional European balance of power. It had three causes. The first was the deep-seated fear of war among all people who had lived through World War I. Unlike the dictators, politicians in the democracies could not ignore their peoples' yearnings for peace. Politicians and people alike hoped that if they wished for peace fervently enough, the threat of war might go away.

The second reason was the fear of communism among the conservative politicians who ruled France and Britain. Until very late in the day, they were more afraid of Stalin than of Hitler, for Hitler, at least, claimed to respect Christianity and private property. Distrust of the Soviet Union was a psychological block to recreating the only viable counterweight to Germany: the pre–World War I alliance of Britain, France, and Russia.

The third reason was the very novelty of fascist tactics. For generations, politicians had learned that countries negotiated their differences and resorted to war only when their differences could not be reconciled. Neville Chamberlain, prime minister of Britain at the Munich Conference, believed that political leaders (except the Bolsheviks) were basically honorable men and that an agreement was as valid as a business contract. Thus, when Hitler promised that he wanted to incorporate only German-speaking people into Germany and had "no further territorial demands," Chamberlain believed him.

After Munich it was too late to stop Hitler, short of war. In March 1939, Germany invaded what was left of Czechoslovakia. Belatedly realizing that Hitler was not to be trusted, France and Britain sought Soviet help. Stalin, however, distrusted the "capitalists" as much as they distrusted him, and Hitler beat the French and British at their own game. He offered to divide

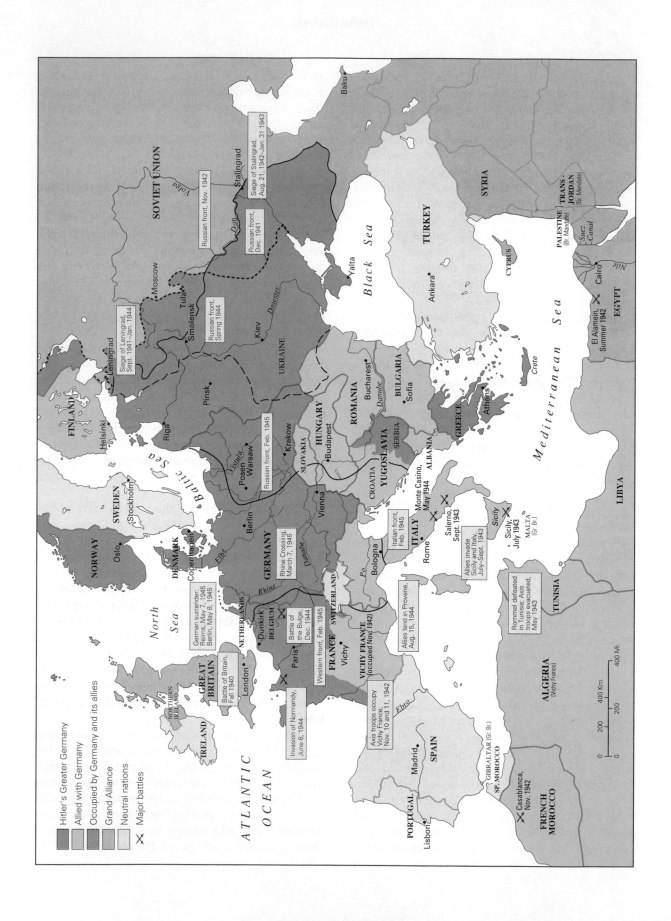

Poland and the rest of eastern Europe between Germany and the Soviet Union. On August 23, Stalin accepted. The Nazi-Soviet Pact freed Hitler from the fear of a two-front war and gave Stalin two more years of peace to build up his armies. One week later, on September 1, 1939, German forces swept into Poland. The war was on.

THE SECOND WORLD WAR

Many people feared the Second World War would be a repetition of the First. Instead, it was much bigger in every way. It was fought around the world—from Norway to New Guinea, from Hawaii to Egypt—and on every ocean. It killed far more people than World War I. It was a total war involving all productive forces and all civilians, and it showed how effectively industry, science, and nationalism could be channeled into mass destruction.

The War of Movement

World War II marked a return to a classic type of warfare. The defense had dominated in World War I; in this war, motorized weapons gave the advantage back to the offense. Opposing forces moved fast, their victories hinging as much on the aggressive spirit of their commanders and the military intelligence they obtained as it did on numbers of troops or firepower.

The *Wehrmacht* (German armed forces) was the first to learn this lesson. It not only had

Map 31.1 The Second World War in Europe and North Africa In World War II, the German conquests were much more extensive than in World War I. By late 1942, Germany and its allies had conquered most of western and central Europe, much of north Africa, and half of European Russia. These conquests were not enough to ensure victory, however, for the Soviet Union was rebuilding its armies, Great Britain remained undefeated, and the United States was becoming more powerful with every passing week.

tanks, trucks, and fighter planes but also perfected their combined use in a tactic called *Blitzkrieg* (lightning war), in which fighter planes scattered enemy troops and disrupted communications, tanks punctured the enemy's defenses, and then, with the help of the infantry, encircled and captured the enemy troops. At sea, both the Japanese and the U.S. navies had developed aircraft carriers that could launch planes against targets hundreds of miles away.

The very size and mobility of the opposing forces made the fighting far different from any the world had ever seen. Instead of fighting localized battles, armies ranged over vast theaters of operation. Countries were conquered in a matter of days or weeks. The belligerents mobilized the economies of entire continents, squeezing them for every possible resource. They tried not only to defeat their enemies' armed forces but to damage the economies that supported those armed forces by means of blockades, submarine attacks on shipping, and bombing raids on industrial areas. They no longer thought of civilians as innocent bystanders but as legitimate targets and later as vermin to be exterminated.

War in Europe and North Africa

The Wehrmacht needed less than a month to conquer Poland. Britain and France declared war on Germany but took no military action. Meanwhile, the Soviet Union invaded eastern Poland and the Baltic republics of Lithuania, Latvia, and Estonia. Although the Poles fought bravely, their infantry and cavalry were no match for German or Russian tanks. During the winter of 1939–1940, Germany and the Western democracies faced each other in what soldiers called a "phony war" and watched as the USSR attacked Finland, which resisted for many months.

In March 1940, Hitler went on the offensive again, conquering Denmark, Norway, the Netherlands, and Belgium in less than two months. In May, he attacked France. The French army had as many soldiers, tanks, and aircraft as the Wehrmacht, but its morale was low, and it quickly collapsed. By the end of June, Hitler was master of all of Europe between Russia and Spain (see Map 31.1).

Germany still had one enemy left: Great Britain. Although Britain had no army to speak of, it had other assets: the English Channel, the Royal Navy and Royal Air Force, and a tough new prime minister, Winston Churchill. Knowing they could invade Britain only by gaining control of the airspace over the Channel, the Germans launched a massive air attack lasting from June through September. They failed, however, because the Royal Air Force had better fighters and used radar and code breaking to detect approaching flights.

Frustrated in the west, Hitler turned his attention eastward. So far he had gotten the utmost cooperation from Stalin, who was supplying Germany with grain, oil, and strategic raw materials. Yet he had always wanted to conquer Lebensraum in the east and enslave the Slavic peoples who lived there, and he feared that if he waited, Stalin would build up a dangerously strong army. So in June 1941 Hitler launched the largest attack in history, with 3 million soldiers and thousands of planes and tanks.

Within five months the Wehrmacht had conquered the Baltic states, Ukraine, and half of European Russia, captured a million prisoners of war, and stood at the very gates of Moscow and Leningrad (now St. Petersburg). The USSR seemed on the verge of collapse when suddenly the weather turned cold, machinery froze, and the fighting came to a halt. Like Napoleon, Hitler had ignored the environment of Russia to his peril.

The next spring the Wehrmacht renewed its offensive. It surrounded Leningrad in a siege that was to cost a million lives. Leaving Moscow aside, it turned toward the Caucasus and its oil wells. In August 1942 the Germans attacked Stalingrad (now Volgagrad), the key to the Volga River and the supply of oil. For months, German and Soviet soldiers fought over every street and every house. When winter came, the Red Army counterattacked and encircled the city. In February 1943 the remnants of the German army in Stalingrad surrendered. Hitler had lost his greatest gamble.

From Europe, the war spread to Africa (see Map 31.1). When France fell in 1940, Mussolini began imagining himself a latter-day Roman emperor and decided the time had come to realize his imperial ambitions. Italian forces quickly overran British Somaliland, then invaded Egypt. Their victories were short-lived, however, for when the British counterattacked, Italian resistance crumbled. During 1941, British forces ousted the Italians from Ethiopia and invaded Libya as well. The Italian rout in North Africa brought the Germans to their rescue. During 1942 the German and British Commonwealth armies seesawed back and forth across the deserts of Libya and Egypt. At El Alamein in northern Egypt the British prevailed because they had more weapons and supplies. Thanks to their success at breaking German codes, they were also better informed about their enemies' plans. The Germans were finally expelled from Africa in May 1943. The Mediterranean was now in Allied hands, and the way to an invasion of Italy lay open.

War in Asia and the Pacific

The fall of France and the involvement of Britain and the USSR against Germany presented Japan with the opportunity it had been looking for. Suddenly the European colonies in Southeast Asia, with their abundant oil, rubber, and other strategic materials, seemed ripe for the taking. The only obstacle was the United States, which controlled the Philippines and proclaimed a paternalistic concern for China.

The Japanese generals, frustrated by the stalemate in China, demanded a rapid conquest of Southeast Asia, but the admirals hesitated. They knew Japan did not yet have sufficient industrial resources, nor was the navy prepared to fight a war with the United States and Britain. Admiral Isoroku Yamamoto, commander of the Japanese fleet, told Prime Minister Fumimaro Konoye: "If I am told to fight regardless of the consequences, I shall run wild for the first six months or a year, but I have utterly no confidence for the second or third year. . . . I hope that you will endeavor to avoid a Japanese-American war." Finally they agreed on a plan for a surprise attack on the United States Navy, followed by an invasion of Southeast Asia. They knew they could not hope to defeat the United States, but they calculated that the shock would be so great that isolationist Americans would accept the Japanese conquest

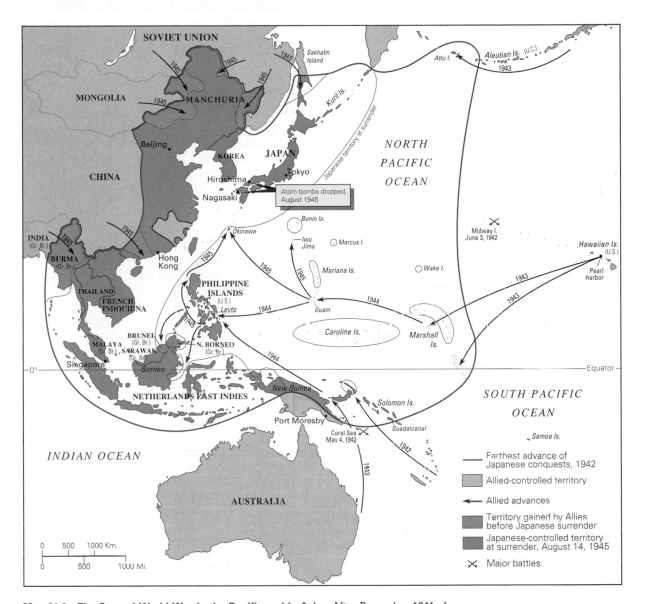

Map 31.2 The Second World War in the Pacific and in Asia After December 1941, Japan found itself simultaneously fighting two very different wars. In China, its armies were bogged down in a war of attrition. In the Pacific, its navy was spectacularly successful, extending its power over the western half of the Pacific Ocean and Southeast Asia. Victory at sea, however, is not measured in square miles of ocean or in the number of islands taken but in the relative strength of navies. When the United States sank four Japanese aircraft carriers at the battle of Midway in June 1942, the Japanese navy never recovered.

of Southeast Asia as readily as they had acquiesced to Hitler's conquests in Europe.

On December 7, 1941, Japanese planes bombed the U.S. naval base at Pearl Harbor on the island of Oahu in the Hawaiian Islands, sinking or damaging scores of warships but missing the aircraft carriers, which were at sea. Soon thereafter, the Japanese bombed Hong Kong and Singapore and invaded Thailand, the Philippines, and Malaya. Within a few months they occupied all of Southeast Asia and the Dutch East Indies (see Map 31.2). Japan's dream of an East

Japan's Mission in Asia

In the summer of 1941, to justify the sacrifices the Japanese people were asked to make, the Japanese Ministry of Education published "The Way of the Subjects," a pamphlet aimed at high school and university students. Among its major themes was Japan's "mission" to rescue Asia from British and American domination. Here are some excerpts.

The orientation of world history has made the collapse of the old order a certainty. Japan has hereby initiated the construction of a new world order based on moral principles.

Japan's position was raised suddenly to the world's forefront as a result of the Russo-Japanese War of 1904–05. . . . Japan's victory attracted the attention of the entire world, and this caused a reawakening of Asiatic countries, which had been forced to lie prostrate under British and American influence, with the result that an independence movement was started.

Hopes to be free of the shackles and bondage of Europe and America were ablaze among the nations of India, Turkey, Arabia, Thailand, Vietnam, and others. This also inspired a new national movement in China. Amid this stormy atmosphere of Asia's reawakening, Japan has come to be keenly conscious of the fact that the stabilization of East Asia is her mission, and that the emancipation of East Asian nations rests solely on her efforts. . . .

Viewed from the standpoint of world history, the China Affair [Japan's invasion of China] is a step toward the construction of a world of moral principles by Japan. . . . Until the evils of European and American influences in East Asia that had led China astray are eliminated, until Japan's cooperation with New China as one of the links in the chain of the Greater East Asian Coprosperity Sphere yields satisfactory results, and East Asia and the rest of the world are united as one on the basis of moral principles, Japan's indefatigable efforts are sorely needed. . . .

Japan has a political mission to help various regions in the Greater East Asian Coprosperity Sphere, which are reduced to a state of quasi-colony by Europe and America, and rescue them from their control. Economically, this country will have to eradicate the evils of their exploitation and then set up an economic structure for coexistence and coprosperity. Culturally, Japan must strive to fashion East Asian nations to abandon their following of European and American culture and to develop Eastern culture for the purpose of contributing to the creation of a just world. The East has been left to destruction for the past several hundred years. Its rehabilitation is not an easy task. It is natural that unusual difficulties attend the establishment of a new order and the creation of a new culture. Overcoming these difficulties will do much to help in establishing a world dominated by morality, in which all nations can co-operate and all people can secure their proper positions.

This document tells us how the Japanese government justified the war to its own people—as a moral crusade undertaken for the sake of other Asian peoples. This rationale raises both historical and ethical issues. Historically, was the "reawakening of Asiatic countries" the result of the Japanese victory over Russia in 1905, or did it predate that victory? How does this document portray Europe and America? How does it describe the other Asian nations, especially China? Ethically, why did the Japanese government feel responsible for emancipating East Asia? Why did it see that emancipation as resting "solely" on "Japan's indefatigable efforts"? How does the document describe the future of East Asia after Japan has rescued it from Europe and America? How would you compare this description with what you know of East Asia today?

Source: Alfred J. Andrea and James H. Overfield, eds., The Human Record: Sources of Global History, vol. 2 (Boston: Houghton Mifflin, 1994), 405–409.

Asian empire seemed within reach, for its victories surpassed even Hitler's in Europe (see Voices and Visions: Japan's Mission in Asia).

Yet Yamamoto's fears were justified. While Japanese forces were overrunning land and sea, the United States, far from being cowed into submission, suddenly began preparing for war. In April 1942, American planes bombed Tokyo. In May the United States Navy defeated a Japanese fleet in the Coral Sea, ending Japanese plans to conquer Australia. A month later, at the Battle of Midway, Japan lost four of its six largest aircraft carriers. Japan did not have enough industry to replace them, for its war production was only one-tenth that of the United States. In the vastness of the Pacific Ocean, aircraft carriers held the key to victory, and without them Japan faced a long and hopeless war.

The End of the War and Its Human Cost

After Stalingrad, the advantage on the eastern front shifted to the Soviet Union. By 1943 the Red Army was receiving a growing stream of supplies from factories in Russia and the United States. Slowly at first and then with increasing vigor, it pushed the Wehrmacht back toward Germany.

The Western powers, meanwhile, staged two invasions of Europe. Beginning in July 1943, they captured Sicily and invaded Italy. Mussolini resigned and Italy signed an armistice, but German troops held off the Allied advance for two years. Then on June 6, 1944, 156,000 British, American, and Canadian troops landed on the coast of Normandy in western France—the largest shipborne assault ever staged. Within a week, the Allies had more troops in France than Germany did, and by September Germany faced an Allied army of over 2 million men with half a million vehicles of all sorts.

Although the Red Army was on the eastern border of Germany, ready for the final push, Hitler transferred part of the Wehrmacht westward. Despite overwhelming odds, Germany was able to hold on for almost a year because of the fighting qualities of its soldiers and the terror inspired by the Nazi regime, which commanded obedience to the end. On May 7, 1945, a week after Hitler committed suicide, the German military leaders surrendered.

Japan fought on a while longer, in large part because the United States had been aiming most of its war effort at Germany. In the Pacific, U.S. forces leap-frogged over some heavily fortified Japanese island bases in order to capture others closer to Japan. By June 1944, U.S. bombers were able to reach Japan itself. Meanwhile, U.S. submarines sank ever larger numbers of Japanese merchant ships, cutting Japan off from its sources of oil and other raw materials. After May 1945, with the Japanese air force grounded for lack of fuel, U.S. planes began destroying Japanese ship-

Key Events of World War II	
1937 July 7	Japanese troops invade China
1939 Sept 1	German forces invade Poland
1940 Mar–Apr	German forces conquer Denmark, Norway, the Netherlands, and Belgium
May–June	German forces conquer France
June–Sept	Battle of Britain: German Luftwaffe fails to defeat Royal Air Force
1941 June 21	German forces invade USSR
Dec 7	Japanese aircraft bomb Pearl Harbor (Hawaii)
1942 Jan–Mar	Japanese conquer Philippines, Malaya, Indonesia
1942 April	U.S. planes bomb Tokyo
June	U.S. Navy defeats Japanese at Battle of Midway
1942–1943	British and Germans battle for control of North Africa; Soviet victory in Battle of Stalingrad
1943–1944	Red Army slowly pushes Wehrmacht back to Germany
1944 June 6	U.S., British, Canadian troops land in Normandy
1945 May 7	Germany surrenders
August 6	U.S. drops atomic bomb on Hiroshima, Japan
August 14	Japan surrenders

ping, industries, and cities practically at will.

Even as their homeland was being pounded, the Japanese still held strong positions in Asia. At first Asian nationalists like the Indonesian Achmed Sukarno were glad to get rid of the white colonialists and welcomed the Japanese. The Japanese occupation, however, was harsh and brutal despite its name: "Greater East Asian Coprosperity Sphere." By 1945 Asians were ready to see the Japanese leave but not to welcome back the Europeans; instead, they looked forward to independence (see Chapters 32 and 33).

On August 6, 1945, the United States dropped an atomic bomb on the Japanese city of Hiroshima. Over eighty thousand people were killed in

Hiroshima after the atomic bomb   On August 6, 1945, an atomic bomb destroyed the city of Hiroshima, killing over 50,000 people. This photo, taken from the air, shows the devastation of the city center, in which only a few concrete buildings remained standing. (UPI-Bettmann Newsphotos)

a flash, and thousands more died an agonizing death from burns and radiation. Three days later, another atomic bomb destroyed another city: Nagasaki.

Was the use of these atomic weapons necessary? At the time, Americans believed that the conquest of the Japanese homeland would take more than a year and cost the lives of hundreds of thousands of American soldiers. Although some Japanese were determined to fight to the bitter end, others were willing to surrender if they could retain their emperor. Had the Allies agreed sooner to keep the monarchy, Japan might have surrendered without the nuclear devastation. On August 14, Japan offered to surrender and Emperor Hirohito himself gave the order to lay down arms. Two weeks later, Japanese leaders signed the terms of surrender. The war was officially over.

The war left an enormous death toll. Recent estimates place the figure at close to 60 million deaths, six to eight times more than in World War I. Over half of the dead were civilian victims of massacres, famines, or bombs. The Soviet Union lost between 20 million and 25 million people, more than any other country. China suffered 15 million deaths, Poland some 6 million, of whom half were Jewish; in addition, the Jewish people lost 3 million outside Poland. Over 4 million Germans and over 2 million Japanese died. In much of the world, almost every family mourned one or more of its members. In contrast, Great Britain lost 400,000 people, the United States 300,000.

Many parts of the world were flooded with refugees. Some 90 million Chinese fled the Japanese advance. In Europe millions fled from the Nazis or the Red Army or were herded back and forth on government orders. Many refugees never returned to their homes, creating new ethnic mixtures more reminiscent of the New World than of the Old.

THE CHARACTER OF WARFARE

One reason for the terrible toll in human lives and suffering was a change in moral values, as belligerents targeted not just soldiers but entire peoples as enemies. Some belligerents even labeled their own ethnic minorities as enemies. Another reason for the devastation was the appearance of new technologies that carried destruction deep into enemy territory, far beyond the traditional battlefields. Let us consider the new technologies of warfare, the changes in morality, and their lethal combination.

The War of Science

As fighting spread around the world, the features that had characterized the early years of the war—the mobilization of manpower and economies and the mobility of the armed forces—grew increasingly powerful. Meanwhile, new aspects of war took on a growing importance. One of these was the impact of science on the technology of warfare (see Environment and Technology: Birth of the Computer). Chemists found ways to make synthetic rubber from coal or oil. Physicists perfected radar, which warned of approaching enemy aircraft and submarines. Cryptanalysts broke enemy codes, allowing them to penetrate secret military communications.

Aircraft development was especially striking. As war approached, German, British, and Japanese aircraft manufacturers developed fast, maneuverable fighter planes. U.S. industry produced aircraft of every sort but was especially noted for its heavy bombers designed to fly in huge formations and drop tons of bombs on enemy cities. Germany, unable to produce heavy planes in large numbers, responded with radically new designs, including the first jet fighters, low-flying buzz bombs, and, finally, V-2 missiles, against which there was no warning or defense.

Leaders of the military no longer dismissed the creations of civilian inventors, as they had before World War I. Instead, they expected scientists to furnish secret weapons that could doom the enemy. In October 1939, President Franklin Roosevelt received a letter from physicist Albert Einstein, a Jewish refugee from Nazism, warning of the dangers of nuclear power: "There is no doubt that subatomic energy is available all around us, and that one day man will release and control its almost infinite power. We cannot prevent him from doing so and can only hope that he will not use it exclusively in blowing up his next door neighbor." Fearing that Germany might develop a nuclear bomb first, Roosevelt placed the vast resources of the U.S. government at the disposal of physicists and engineers, both Americans and refugees from Europe. By 1945 they had built two atomic bombs, each one powerful enough to annihilate an entire city.

Bombing Raids

German bombers had damaged Warsaw in 1939 and Rotterdam and London in 1940. Yet Germany lacked a strategic bomber force capable of destroying whole cities. In this area, the British and Americans excelled. Since it was very hard to pinpoint individual buildings, especially at night, the British Air Staff under British Air Chief Marshal Arthur "Bomber" Harris decided that "operations should now be focused on the morale of the enemy civilian population and in particular the industrial workers."

In May 1942 a thousand British planes dropped incendiary bombs on Cologne, setting fire to most of the old city. Between July 24 and August 2, 1943, thirty-three hundred British and American bombers set fire to Hamburg, killing 50,000 people, mostly women and children. Later raids destroyed Berlin, Dresden, and other German cities. All in all, the bombing raids against Germany killed 600,000 people—more than half of them women and children—and injured 800,000. But if the air strategists had hoped to

Birth of the Computer

Nowadays, computers are found in almost every office and home. One day they may be on every wrist and in every pocket. When the first computers were built, however, people thought of them only as big, fast calculators and could not imagine any use beyond mathematical computation.

World War II stimulated the invention of computers, for the many complex weapons systems that the war brought forth required enormous numbers of mathematical calculations. In the early 1940s, the German engineer Konrad Zuse built a large calculator to solve aircraft design problems. At the same time, the Harvard mathematician Howard Aiken built a similar machine, the Mark I, to perform quickly the tedious calculations needed in physics experiments. Aiken's device could multiply two 10-digit numbers in three seconds. These machines, which used electromagnetic relays of the kind then used in central telephone offices, were reliable but large, noisy, and slow.

The most important advance in computing involved replacing mechanical control switches with vacuum tubes of the kind then used in radios (vacuum tubes had no moving parts). The first purely electronic computer, the Electronic Numerical Integrator and Computer, or ENIAC, was built by J. Presper Eckert and John Mauchley of the University of Pennsylvania. When completed in 1946, the ENIAC filled a room 40 feet (12 meters) long by 20 feet (6 meters) wide and weighed 30 tons; its 18,000 vacuum tubes used as much electricity as a sizable town. For each problem, it had to be set up (or "programmed") by plugging wires into sockets, like an old telephone switchboard. Once set up, however, ENIAC could solve mathematical problems—for example, calculating the trajectories of artillery shells—a thousand times faster than Aiken's Mark I. To do the same number of calculations in the same amount of time would have required seventy-five thousand skilled mathmeticians!

These early machines revolutionized computation in the same way that the telegraph had "annihilated" time in long-distance communications a hundred years before (see Chapter 23). The physicists, mathematicians, and engineers who worked with the first computers figured that three or four—ten at the very most—would suffice for all conceivable computing needs in the United States for years to come.

As it turned out, that was only the beginning. Soon after World War II ended, the mathematician John von Neumann devised a way to integrate the program and the data. Meanwhile, engineers developed magnetic memory devices to store data, programs, and output quickly and economically. These and other improvements made it possible for computers to perform any number of tricks, such as word processing, filing and sorting data, handling images, and communicating. Whether they will ever be able to "think" is another question.

The first computer   The ENIAC (Electronic Numerical Integrator and Computer) was unveiled in February 1946. It occupied a large room and its 18,000 vacuum tubes used as much electricity as a small town. Its purpose was to calculate the trajectories of artillery shells, a tedious series of calculations done before by several hundred women mathematics majors, called "computers." (Bettmann Archive)

break the morale of the German people, they failed. German armament production continued to increase until late 1944, and the population remained obedient and hard working. The only effective bombing raids were those directed against oil depots and synthetic fuel plants; by early 1945, they had almost brought the German war effort to a standstill.

Japanese cities also were targets of American bombing raids. As early as April 1942, sixteen planes launched from an aircraft carrier bombed Tokyo. Later, as American forces captured islands close to Japan, the raids intensified. Their effect was even more devastating than the raids on Germany, for Japanese cities were made of wood and exploded in firestorms. In March 1945 Tokyo was set ablaze; 80,000 people were killed and a million were made homeless. That attack was a portent of worse destruction to come.

The Holocaust

In World War II, for the first time, more civilians than soldiers were deliberately put to death. The champions in the killing of defenseless civilians were the Nazis. Their murders were not the accidental byproducts of some military goal but a

Germans confront the Holocaust   When the Allies entered Germany in 1945, they found Nazi extermination camps filled with corpses and with emaciated prisoners condemned to death. Here, American soldiers have brought German townspeople to a camp to see a cartload of corpses and to personally witness the horrors of the Holocaust. (UPI-Bettmann Newsphotos)

calculated policy of exterminating whole races of people.

Their first targets were Jews. Soon after Hitler came to power, he deprived German Jews of their citizenship and legal rights. When eastern Europe fell under Nazi rule, its large Jewish population was herded into ghettos in the major cities, where many died of starvation and disease. Then, in early 1942, the Nazis decided to carry out what Hitler called his "final solution to the Jewish problem" by applying modern industrial methods to the slaughter of human beings. German companies built huge extermination camps in eastern Europe. Every day trainloads of cattle cars arrived at the camps, disgorging thousands of captives and the corpses of those who had died of starvation or asphyxiation along the way. The strongest survivors were put to work and fed almost nothing until they died. Women, children, the elderly, and the sick were shoved into gas chambers and asphyxiated with poison gas. The biggest camp, Auschwitz, in southern Poland, was designed to kill up to twelve thousand people a day. Most horrifying of all were the tortures inflicted on prisoners selected by Nazi doctors for "medical experiments." This mass extermination, now called the Holocaust ("burning"), claimed some 6 million Jewish lives.

Besides the Jews, the Nazis also killed 3 million Polish Catholics, especially professionals, army officers, and the educated, in an effort to reduce the Polish people to slavery. They also exterminated homosexuals, Jehovah's Witnesses, Gypsies, the disabled, and the mentally ill, all in the interests of "racial purity." Whenever a German was killed in an occupied country, the Nazis retaliated by burning a village and all its inhabitants. After the invasion of Russia, the Wehrmacht was given orders to execute all captured communists, government employees, and officers. The German military also worked millions of prisoners of war to death or let them die of starvation.

The Home Front in Europe and Asia

In the First World War, there had been a clear distinction between the "front" and the "home front." Not so in World War II. Rapid military movements and air power carried the war into people's homes. For the civilian populations of China, Japan, Southeast Asia, and Europe, the war was far more terrifying than their worst nightmares. Armies swept through the land, confiscating food, fuel, and anything else of value. Bombers and heavy artillery pounded cities into rubble, leaving only the skeletons of buildings, while survivors hid in cellars and scurried around like rats. Even when a city was not targeted, air-raid sirens awakened people throughout the night. In countries occupied by the Germans, the police arrested civilians, deporting many to die in concentration camps or to work as slave labor in armaments factories. Millions fled their homes in terror, losing their friends and families. Even in Britain, which was never invaded, children and the elderly were taken from their families and sent for safety to live in the countryside.

The war demanded an enormous and sustained effort from all civilians, but more so in some countries than in others. In 1941, even as the Wehrmacht was routing the Red Army, the Soviets dismantled over fifteen hundred factories and rebuilt them in the Ural Mountains and in Siberia, where they soon turned out more tanks and artillery than the Axis. The Red Army eventually mobilized 22 million men, while Soviet women took over half of all industrial and three-quarters of all agricultural jobs. In the other belligerent countries, women also played a major role in the war effort, replacing men in the fields, factories, and offices. In Germany, in contrast, the Nazis believed that women should stay home and bear children. The Nazis therefore imported 7 million "guest workers," a euphemism for war prisoners and captured foreigners.

Half the ships afloat in 1939 were sunk during the war. American shipyards more than made up for the Allied losses, but Axis shipping was reduced to nothing by 1945. The production of aircraft, trucks, tanks, and other military supplies showed a similar imbalance. Although the Axis powers made strenuous efforts to increase their production, they could not compete with the vast outpouring of Soviet tanks and American materiel.

The Home Front in the United States

Unlike the other belligerents, the United States did not suffer during the war. Indeed, it flourished. Safe behind their oceans, American civilians felt no bombs, saw no enemy soldiers, and suffered few military casualties and almost no civilian ones. The economy, still depressed in 1939, went into a prolonged boom after 1940. By 1944 the United States alone was producing twice as much as all the Axis powers combined. Thanks to huge military orders, jobs were plentiful and opportunities beckoned. Bread lines disappeared, and nutrition and health improved. While consumer goods ranging from automobiles to nylon stockings were in short supply, most Americans saved part of their paychecks. Their savings would be the basis for the phenomenal post-World War II consumer boom (see Chapters 34 and 35). Many Americans later looked back on that time as "the good war."

War always exalts supposedly masculine attributes such as physical courage, violence, and domination. The Axis powers glorified these qualities, but they existed in America as well. Yet World War II also did much to weaken the hold of traditional ideas. On a much larger scale than in World War I, employers recruited women and members of racial minorities to work in jobs once reserved for white men. For example, 6 million women entered the labor force during the war, 2.5 million of them in manufacturing jobs previously considered "man's work." In a book entitled *Shipyard Diary of a Woman Welder* (1944), Augusta Clawson recounts her experiences in a shipyard in Oregon:

> The job confirmed my strong conviction—I have stated it before—what exhausts the woman welder is not the work, not the heat, nor the demands upon physical strength. It is the apprehension that arises from inadequate skill and consequent lack of confidence; and this *can* be overcome by the right kind of training. . . . I know I can do it if my machine is correctly set, and I have learned enough of the vagaries of machines to be able to set them. And so, in spite of the discomforts of climbing, heavy equipment, and heat, I enjoyed the work today because *I could do it.*[1]

The expansion of job opportunities did not take place without friction. At the beginning, many men resisted the idea that women, especially mothers of young children, should take jobs that would take them away from their families. As the labor shortage got worse, however, employers and politicians grudgingly admitted that the government ought to help provide day care for the children of working mothers. The entry of women into the labor force proved to be one of the most significant consequences of the war. As one woman put it: "War jobs have uncovered unsuspected abilities in American women. Why lose all these abilities because of a belief that 'a woman's place is in the home'? For some it is, for others not."

The war loosened racial bonds as well, bringing hardships for some and benefits for others. Seeking jobs in war industries, 1.2 million African-Americans migrated to the north and west. In the southwest, Mexican immigrants took jobs in agriculture and war industries. But no new housing was built to accommodate the inflow of migrants to the industrial cities, and as a result many suffered from overcrowding and discrimination. Much worse was the fate of 112,000 Japanese-Americans living on the west coast of the United States: they were rounded up and herded into internment camps in the desert until the war was over, ostensibly for fear of spying and sabotage but actually because of their race.

War and the Environment

During the Depression, construction and industry had slowed to a crawl, reducing environmental stress. The war reversed this trend, sharply accelerating pressures on the environment.

One cause was the fighting itself. Battles scarred the landscape, leaving spent ammunition and damaged equipment. Retreating armies flooded large parts of China and the Netherlands. The bombing of cities left ruins that survived for a generation or more. Much of the damage was repaired after the war, although the rusted hulks of ships still litter the lagoons of once-pristine coral islands in the Pacific.

Positive effects of war   Although World War II caused terrible destruction, it also had some positive consequences. Among the most important were the revival of the American economy after the Depression and the opportunities that opened up for American women in jobs previously held by men. This picture shows three women welders at the Bethlehem Steel Shipyard. They have lifted their welding masks in order to hold a conversation. (Corbin-Bettman)

The main cause of environmental stress, however, was not the fighting but the economic development that sustained it. The war's half-million aircraft required thousands of air bases, many of them in the Pacific, in China, in Africa, and in other parts of the world that seldom had seen an airplane before. Similarly, barracks, shipyards, docks, warehouses, and other military constructions sprouted on every continent.

As war industries boomed—the United States increased its industrial production fourfold during the war—so did their demand for raw materials. Mining companies opened new mines and towns in Central Africa to supply strategic minerals. The large Latin American countries, especially Argentina and Brazil, deprived of manufactured imports, began building their own steel mills, factories, and shipyards. In India, China, and Europe, timber felling accelerated far beyond the reproduction rate of trees, replacing forests with denuded land. In a few instances, ironically, the war was good for the environment. Submarine warfare, for example, made fishing and whaling very dangerous and allowed fish and whale populations to increase.

Yet we must keep the environmental effects of the war in perspective. Except for the destruction of cities, much of the impact was simply the result of industrial development, only temporarily slowed by the Depression. During the war, the damage caused by military demand was tempered by the restraints placed on civilian consumption. The environmental impact of the war seems quite modest compared to the damage inflicted on the earth by the long consumer boom that followed it.

CONCLUSION

Despite its name, World War II was the *first* truly global conflict, covering oceans and continents and involving over half of the world's people. Not surprisingly, it left a powerful legacy.

Into the power vacuum left by the collapse of the Axis powers stepped the two "superpowers," the United States and the USSR. When the war ended, American soldiers were stationed in Australia, Japan, and western Europe, and the Soviet army occupied all of eastern Europe and parts of northern China. Within months of their victory, these one-time allies become first rivals and then ideological enemies hovering on the brink of war.

The war had been so widespread and destructive because a rapidly advancing technology could readily be converted from civilian to military production. Machines that had made cars could also manufacture bombers or tanks. Engineers could design factories to kill people with maximum efficiency. The accelerating technology of missiles and nuclear bombs made the entire planet vulnerable, for the first time in history, to destruction by human beings.

But the reverse was also true. Nuclear power, jet aircraft, chemicals, electronics, and other wartime technologies could be used to improve living standards. After the war western Europe, Japan, and the United States became more prosperous than ever. The organization and technology that had allowed them to fight produced amazing results when applied to peaceful pursuits.

In the first half of the twentieth century, two world wars overturned the global relations inherited from the nineteenth century. World War I brought revolution to Russia, undermined the global economy, and led to the rise of totalitarian regimes. Then came World War II, which weakened the old colonial powers of Europe.

While the great powers were engaged in their struggles for world domination, the ideas of nationalism and social justice awakened mass political movements around the world. We have already seen the impact of such revolutionary and nationalist movements in Russia and the Middle East. In the next chapter, we will study three other influential upheavals that took place during the age of world wars. They are the Mexican revolution, the Chinese wars and revolutions, and the Indian independence movement.

SUGGESTED READING

The literature on the period from 1929 to 1945 is enormous and growing fast. The following list is a very brief introduction.

On the Depression, Charles Kindelberger, *The World in Depression, 1929–39* (1973), provides a sophisticated economic analysis, and A. J. H. Latham, *The Depression and the Developing World, 1914–1939* (1981), gives a global perspective.

The best recent book on Japan in the twentieth century is Daikichi Irokawa, *The Age of Hirohito: In Search of Modern Japan* (1995). On Japanese expansion see W. G. Beasley, *Japanese Imperialism, 1894–1945* (1987). The race to war is covered in Akira Iriye, *The Origins of the Second World War in Asia and the Pacific* (1987). Michael Barnhart's *Japan Prepares for Total War* (1987) is short and well written.

The classic biography of Stalin is Isaac Deutscher's *Stalin*, 2d ed. (1966). On the transformation of the USSR see Roy Medvedev's *Let History Judge: The Origins and Consequences of Stalinism* (1989). Stalin's collectivization of agriculture is vividly portrayed in Robert Conquest's *Harvest of Sorrow* (1986); Conquest's *The Great Terror: A Reassessment* (1990) describes the purges of the 1930s. Alexander Solzhenitsyn, a veteran of Stalin's prisons, explores them in a detailed history, *The Gulag Archipelago, 1918–1956,* 3 vols. (1974–1978), and in a short but brilliant novel, *One Day in the Life of Ivan Denisovich* (1978).

Alexander De Grand provides an excellent interpretation of fascism in *Italian Fascism: Its Origins and Development*, 2d ed. (1989). William Shirer's *The Rise and Fall of the Third Reich* (1960) is a long but dramatic eyewitness description of Nazi Germany by a journalist. The dictators are the subject of two fine biographies: Denis Mack Smith's *Mussolini* (1982) and Alan Bullock's *Hitler: A Study in Tyranny* (1965). See also A. J. P. Taylor's controversial classic *The Origins of the Second World War* (1966).

Two recent and detailed books on World War II are John Keegan, *The Second World War* (1990), and Gerhard Weinberg, *A World at Arms: A Global History of World War II* (1994). Particular aspects of the war in Europe are covered in Alexander Werth, *Russia at War, 1941–1945* (1965), and Conrad Crane, *Bombs, Cities, and Civilians* (1993). The most readable account of the war in Asia and the Pacific is Ronald Spector's *Eagle Against the Sun* (1988); but see also Akira Iriye, *Power and Culture: The Japanese-American War, 1941–1945* (1981), and James Hsiung and Steven Levine, eds., *China's Bitter Victory: The War with Japan, 1937–1945* (1992).

The terror of life under Nazi rule is the subject of two powerful memoirs: Anne Frank's *The Diary of a Young Girl* (1952) and Eli Wiesel's *Night* (1960). On the Holo-

caust see Lucy Dawidowicz, *The War Against the Jews, 1933–1945*, 2d ed. (1986), and Leni Yahil, *The Holocaust: The Fate of European Jewry* (1990).

Among the many books that capture the scientific side of warfare, two are especially recommended: Richard Rhodes's long but fascinating *The Making of the Atomic Bomb* (1986) and F. H. Hinsley and Alan Stripp, eds., *Code Breakers* (1993).

Among the many books on the home front in the United States, the most vivid is Studs Terkel, *"The Good War": An Oral History of World War Two* (1984). Margaret Randolph Higonnet, Jane Jenson, Sonya Michel, and Margaret Collins Weitz, eds., *Behind the Lines: Gender and the Two World Wars* (1987), discusses the role of women in the war.

NOTE

1. Augusta Clawson, *Shipyard Diary of a Woman Welder* (New York: Penguin, 1944), quoted in Rosalyn Baxandall, Linda Gordon, and Susan Reverby, eds., *America's Working Women: A Documentary History—1600 to the Present* (New York: Random House, 1976), p. 290.

CHAPTER THIRTY-TWO

Revolutions and National Independence,

1900–1950

Zenith and Sunset of the New Imperialism · The Chinese Revolution

The Indian Independence Movement · The Mexican Revolution

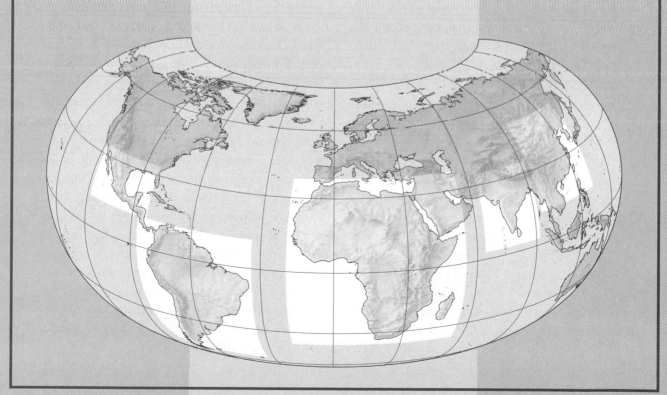

In April 1947, as Chinese Communist forces surrounded Nanjing, the British frigate *Amethyst* sailed up the Yangzi River to evacuate British civilians. Dozens of times since the Opium War of 1839 to 1842, foreign powers had dispatched warships up the rivers of China to rescue their citizens, enforce their treaty rights, or intimidate the Chinese. Foreign warships deep in the heart of China were the very symbols of its weakness. This time, however, the Chinese Communist artillery damaged the *Amethyst* and beat back other British warships sent to its rescue. No nation has invaded China since that year.

As we saw in Chapters 30 and 31, between 1914 and 1945 the industrialized powers of the world fought one another in two world wars, and Russia underwent a revolution. Yet the nonindustrial regions of the world were by no means passive spectators during this period. Momentous revolutions and nationalist movements were taking place in Asia and Latin America and soon thereafter in Africa. The age of gunboat imperialism, so dramatically inaugurated by the *Nemesis* a century before (see Chapter 27), came to an end after World War II.

What sparked these revolutions and nationalist movements? The reasons varied from one place to another, but overall we can identify three causes of revolution.

One was increasing poverty among the peasants and a widening gap between their incomes and those of the rich. In poor countries such as those described in this chapter, the population consisted mainly of peasants who had little land and kept little of their harvest. Population growth that outstripped both the opening of new land and improvements in productivity worsened the plight of these peoples. Such societies, which have existed since the first civilizations, often experienced peasant revolts but seldom

went through revolutions. For that, they had to await the impact of modern politics.

The second cause was the appearance of a new generation of city people, many of them educated in Western ideas of equality and national independence, who were inspired by the rise of Japan and the Russian Revolution. This new generation channeled the despair of their followers into movements against both foreign domination and the older traditional elites.

The third cause of revolution was a growing alliance between this new generation and the dissatisfied peasantry. Together they created the politics of mass participation by calling for social justice, national unity, and independence. Although mass politics first appeared in the West, it found tremendous resonance throughout the nonindustrial world and helped end the long era of Western dominance.

Modern mass politics came to different societies at different times, depending on local circumstances. As we saw in Chapter 30, in the Middle East the transformation was hastened by the experience of World War I. Africa south of the Sahara had to wait until World War II to challenge European colonialism. In China, India, and Mexico, the transformation was long and sometimes violent.

In this chapter we look in detail at the three most crucial non-Western revolutionary and nationalist movements of the first half of the twentieth century: the Chinese and Mexican Revolutions and the independence of India. They are important because they involved almost half of the world's population and because they were the forerunners of many other movements in Asia, Africa, and Latin America after 1950. Before we turn to these revolutionary upheavals, let us consider the last stages of colonialism, which were formal in Africa and informal in Latin America and China.

ZENITH AND SUNSET OF THE NEW IMPERIALISM

The new imperialism was a product of the tremendous disparities of wealth and power between the industrializing countries and the non-Western world (see Chapter 29). It continued well into the twentieth century, in both formal and informal guises.

At the end of World War I, the victorious Allies took over the colonies of their enemies. Britain, France, Belgium, and South Africa divided up Germany's African colonies between them. On several occasions in the 1920s, U.S. troops invaded the nations of the Caribbean and Central America. When the Ottoman Empire collapsed, France and Britain occupied Iraq, Syria, Lebanon, and Palestine. In the 1920s, the Soviet Union reconquered its Central Asian and Caucasian territories, which briefly had asserted their independence. In the 1930s, Italy invaded Ethiopia. The colonial empires reached their peak just before World War II.

At the same time, the industrialized countries took advantage of the continuing weakness of China and Latin America for their own economic gain.

Colonial Africa: Economic and Social Changes

Of all the continents, Africa had been the last to come under European rule (see Map 29.1 in Chapter 29). The first half of the twentieth century, when nationalist movements threatened European rule in Asia, was the period of classic colonialism in Africa. Except in Algeria, Kenya, and South Africa, few Europeans lived in Africa. In 1930, Nigeria, with a population of 20 million, was ruled by 386 British officials and by 8,000 policemen and military, of whom 150 were European. Yet even such a small presence stimulated deep social and economic changes.

The years between the world wars witnessed an economic boom from which Africans benefited little. The colonial powers invested great sums in railroads, harbors, mines, and other infrastructures intended to produce raw materials for the industrial world. Governments took lands that Africans owned communally and sold or leased them to European companies or, in eastern and southern Africa, to white settlers. Large European companies dominated wholesale commerce, while immigrants from various countries—Indians in East Africa, Greeks and Syrians in West Africa—handled much of the retail trade.

Where land was divided into small farms, some Africans benefited from the boom. Farmers in the Gold Coast (now Ghana) profited from the high prices of cocoa, as did palm-oil producers in Nigeria and coffee growers in East Africa. In most of Africa, women played a major role in the retail trades, selling pots and pans and other hardware, toys, cloth, and food in the markets, and maintaining households and finances separate from those of their husbands.

For many Africans, economic development meant working in European-owned mines and plantations, often under compulsion. In many colonies, African men were required to work up to one month a year for the government without pay. Paid "contract" labor was often worse, for it could last for months. In the 1920s, when the government of French Equatorial Africa decided to build a railroad from Brazzaville to the Atlantic coast, a distance of 312 miles (502 kilometers), it drafted 127,000 men to carve a roadbed across mountains and through rain forests. For lack of food, clothing, and medical care, 20,000 of them died, an average of 64 deaths per mile of track.

Europeans prided themselves on bringing modern health care to Africa; yet before the 1930s, there was too little of it to help the majority of Africans, and other aspects of colonialism were worsening public health. As people migrated to cities, mines, and plantations, and as soldiers moved from post to post, they spread syphilis, gonorrhea, tuberculosis, and malaria. Epidemics of sleeping sickness and smallpox

Diamond mining in South Africa   The discovery of diamonds in the Transvaal in 1867 attracted prospectors to the area around Kimberley. The first wave consisted of individual "diggers,"
including a few Africans. By the late 1870s, the surface deposits had been exhausted and further mining required complex and costly machinery. After 1889, one company, De Beers Consolidated, owned all the diamond mines. This photograph shows the entrance to a mine shaft,
with mine workers surrounded by heavy equipment. (Royal Commonwealth Society)

raged throughout Central Africa. Labor conscription and food requisitions caused malnutrition,
making people more vulnerable to diseases.
Only in the 1930s do statistics begin to show improvements in health and a growing population.

In 1900 the only city in sub-Saharan Africa
with more than 100,000 inhabitants was Ibadan
in Nigeria. Fifty years later, dozens of cities had
reached that size, including Nairobi in Kenya, Jo-
hannesburg in South Africa, Lagos in Nigeria,
Accra in Gold Coast, and Dakar in Senegal.
Africans migrated to cities because they offered
hope of jobs and excitement and, for a few, the
chance to become wealthy.

Migrations damaged the family life of those
involved, for almost all the migrants were men.
Women stayed in the countryside to farm and
raise children. Cities built during the colonial period reflected the attitudes of the colonialists in
their racially segregated housing, clubs, restaurants, hospitals, and other institutions. Patterns
of racial discrimination were most rigid in the
white-settler colonies of eastern and southern
Africa.

In much of Africa, traditional beliefs could not
meet the spiritual needs of those whose lives had
been dislocated by foreign rule, migrations, and
economic changes. Under these circumstances,

many Africans converted to Christianity or to Islam. A major attraction of the Christian denominations was their mission schools, which taught both craft skills and basic literacy, providing access to employment as minor functionaries, teachers, clergy, or shopkeepers. These schools educated a new elite, especially in West Africa. Islam was spread by example among African traders, rather than by foreign missionaries. It also emphasized literacy—in Arabic rather than in a European language—but was less disruptive of traditional African customs such as polygamy.

Beginnings of African Nationalism

The contrast between the ideas imparted by education and the realities of racial discrimination under colonial rule contributed to the rise of African nationalism. As we saw in Chapter 30, the Senegalese Blaise Diagne agitated for African participation in politics and fair treatment in the French army. In British West Africa, J. E. Casely Hayford began organizing a nationalist movement for greater autonomy. Organizations like the Young Kikuyu in Kenya and the African National Congress in South Africa were founded to defend the interests of Africans. These nationalist movements drew inspiration from the ideas of Pan-Africanists from America like W. E. B. Du Bois and Marcus Garvey, as well as from European ideas of liberty and nationhood. Until World War II, however, they were small and had little influence.

The Second World War had a profound effect on the peoples of Africa, even those far removed from the theaters of war. The war brought hardships—forced labor, inflation, requisitions of raw materials—but it also brought hope. During the campaign to oust the Italians from Ethiopia in 1941, Emperor Haile Selassie (r. 1930–1974) led his own troops into his capital Addis Ababa and reclaimed his title. A million Africans served as soldiers and carriers in Burma, North Africa, and Europe, where many became aware of Africa's role in helping the Allied war effort. They listened to Allied propaganda in favor of European liberation movements and against Nazi racism,

and they returned to their countries with new and radical ideas.

Informal Empire in Latin America and China

Territorial annexations were not the only form of imperialism. More complex were the various informal ways in which the leading industrial powers dominated other countries economically and politically while maintaining the fiction of independence.

From the late nineteenth century until the 1930s, Great Britain and the United States controlled the economies of many Latin American countries through investments in railroads, mines, and plantations (see Chapter 29). The equipment for these enterprises came from Britain and America, as did the capital to purchase it. Foreign engineers and managers supervised the construction and operation of the enterprises, and foreign ships carried their imports and exports. The Latin American nations contributed cheap labor and low-cost agricultural and mineral resources.

The best-known example is the American-owned United Fruit Company, which operated vast banana plantations in Guatemala and Nicaragua, along with its own harbors, railroads, shipping lines, and radio stations. Equally important was the Standard Oil Company of New Jersey, which controlled the oil industry of Venezuela.

Not all Latin American countries were so easily manipulated by foreign interests. The large republics of South America, especially Argentina and Brazil, gradually became more nationalistic and more able to free themselves from foreign interference. During the First World War, they had no alternative but to produce for themselves many manufactured goods that formerly they had imported. Thereafter, they deliberately distanced themselves, both politically and economically, from Britain and the United States.

Informal imperialism existed in China until the 1930s. For a century, the British, followed by other Western powers, had taken advantage of

China's internal weaknesses to exact special concessions, such as naval bases and control over China's customs revenues. They also obtained special neighborhoods in Shanghai and Beijing for their citizens and the right of extraterritoriality (see Chapter 27), which meant that their citizens could not be tried in Chinese courts. In China, as in Latin America, foreign firms controlled public utilities and much of the country's import and export business. Whenever the Chinese government balked at these exactions or Chinese people revolted against them, European, American, and Japanese forces went in to reestablish order and enforce compliance with the treaties that had imposed such inequities. Not until the 1920s was China able to revise these unequal treaties.

This informal imperialism did not appear on maps and was not mentioned in the pronouncements of government officials, but it was just as significant in its effects as the formal, official variety. Industrial countries obtained the economic advantages of colonialism without incurring the political costs of maintaining an army or providing education, health, and other social services. Foreign powers took no responsibility for the maintenance of order, except when their citizens or properties were threatened. They often sold arms to rebels and governments alike, profiting from civil disturbances as well as from peaceful trade. From the turn of the century to the 1930s, China and Latin America suffered far more from civil unrest than did Africa, India, and other areas of formal colonialism.

THE CHINESE REVOLUTION

At the beginning of the twentieth century, China stood poised at the brink of two upheavals: (1) a revolt by the peasants against their landlords and against the Qing government, which did little to protect them from natural disasters; (2) a revolt of intellectuals and city dwellers against national humiliation and the government that tolerated it. When these two movements joined together, they sparked one of the most profound social upheavals in modern history.

The People and the Land

China's population was the largest of any country in the world and growing: from about 350 million in 1850 to a half-billion by 1950 and over a billion by 1980. China had little new land to put under the plow and few industries to absorb these people. By the early twentieth century, peasant plots averaged between 1 and 4 acres (0.4 and 1.6 hectares) apiece, roughly half as large as they had been two generations earlier. Farming methods, though ingenious, had not changed in centuries. As the land available per farmer diminished with each generation, more people became landless farm laborers. Rents and taxes took over half of the harvest. Most Chinese worked incessantly, survived on a diet of grain and vegetables, and spent their lives in fear of floods, bandits, and tax collectors.

The most populated parts of China were the rich alluvial plains of the Yangzi and Yellow Rivers. The Yellow River carried silt, which it deposited on its eastern stretches, gradually raising its bed above the floodplains. Constant labor was needed to prevent the river from overflowing its dikes and flooding the low-lying fields and villages on either side. In times of war and civil disorder, these precautions were neglected and disasters ensued.

Between 1853 and 1855 the Yellow River, which flowed into the Yellow Sea south of the Shandong Peninsula, broke out of its channel and carved a new bed hundreds of miles to the north. In 1931 the Yangzi flooded an area the size of New York State, causing 14 million people to flee their homes. Between 1913 and 1938 the Yellow River burst its dikes seventeen times. The flood of 1933 killed 18,000 people and forced 3.4 million to flee. Throughout their history, the Chinese emphasized the connections between politics and the environment. Floods were the result of official neglect and corruption and thus a sign that the ruling dynasty was losing the Mandate of Heaven.

Not only were most Chinese poor and vulnerable to vagaries of war and nature, they also suffered from deeply rooted social injustices. This was especially true of women who were subjected to the ancient custom of footbinding. Parents broke their young daughters' arches and bound their feet tightly with strips of cloth, causing excruciating pain; girls grew up with tiny feet, ostensibly to make them sexually attractive to men, who would never, many believed, marry a girl with big feet. Footbinding made women virtually incapable of getting about on their own, physically tying them to their homes and families.

This painful custom was not imposed from above but persisted despite centuries of official disapproval. The Manchus, a foreign people who ruled China until 1911, never bound their own daughters' feet. Government officials, revolutionaries, and Christian missionaries alike inveighed against footbinding. Yet the practice continued among conservative families in some parts of China as late as the 1930s. In perpetuating the domination of men over women, footbinding also impoverished their families by reducing the productivity of women in a land that relied almost entirely on human labor for agricultural tasks.

Above the peasantry, Chinese society was divided into many groups and strata. Landowners, big and small, associated with local officials to form the gentry. High officials, chosen through an elaborate examination system, enriched themselves through their control of the courts, the taxation system, and the government monopolies on salt, iron, and other products. In the treaty ports, wealthy merchants handled China's growing import-export trade in collaboration with foreign companies. In the late nineteenth and early twentieth centuries, Shanghai, China's financial and commercial center, became famous for its "concessions"—neighborhoods reserved for wealthy foreigners—its opium addicts and prostitutes, and its criminal gangs.

Although foreign trade represented only a small part of China's economy, contact with the outside world had a tremendous impact on Chinese politics. In the treaty ports of the turn of the century, there arose a generation that saw no hope for advancement in the old system of examinations and official positions. Some learned foreign ideas in Christian mission schools or in Japan and the United States. These Westernized intellectuals grew up smarting from the humiliations of foreign imperialism yet also eager to emulate the foreign thinking that they saw as the key to national power and self-respect.

The Fall of the Qing Dynasty

In June 1898 the young Emperor Guangxu issued a series of decrees reforming the Qing bureaucracy, the examination system, and the army in order to make the government more efficient and the country better able to defend itself against foreign pressures. These reforms, however, threatened the position and privileges of senior officials grouped around Guangxu's aunt, the Empress Dowager Cixi (last mentioned in Chapter 27). In September she suddenly returned to the palace, announced that Guangxu had asked her to rule in his place, and had him imprisoned. His associates either fled into exile or were captured and executed. Thus ended the last attempt under Qing rule to reform China from above.

Two years later, in 1900, Cixi encouraged a secret society, the Righteous Fists, or Boxers, to rise up and expel all foreigners and their influences from China. In retaliation, the Western powers and Japan captured Beijing, forced a huge indemnity on China, and seemed about to carve China up into colonies. Although the foreign powers could not agree to divide China, their influence grew rapidly. Thousands of Chinese students went to Japan and the United States, where many became convinced that China needed a revolution to get rid of the Qing and make their country strong and modern. In Shanghai, a city dominated by the British, Chinese dissidents published works that never would have been allowed elsewhere in China. The contrast between the squalor in which most of the city's residents lived and the blatant luxury of the foreigners' concession areas sharpened the resentment of Chinese intellectuals.

Cixi died in 1908, leaving the country without leadership. Two groups, however, had been preparing to take over. One was the Revolutionary

Alliance led by Sun Yatsen (1867–1925). Educated in Hawaii and Hong Kong, Sun had spent much of his life in exile in Japan, England, and the United States plotting the overthrow of the Qing dynasty. His ideas were a mixture of nationalism, socialism, and Confucian philosophy. In 1896, when Sun was living in London, Chinese diplomats tried to kidnap him. The attempt failed but made him famous. The sincerity of his patriotism, his powerful ambition, and his tenacious spirit attracted a large following. The most famous of his followers was Qiu Jin, who fled an unhappy marriage to become a schoolteacher and radical activist. In 1907, she tried to organize an uprising against the government but was arrested and executed.

The other group that had been preparing to take over China consisted of army officers, especially the generals commanding the regional armies. After China's defeat in the war with Japan in 1895 (see Chapter 28), the government belatedly had agreed to train officers and equip the army with modern rifles and machine guns. The combination of traditional regional autonomy with modern tactics and equipment led to the creation of local armies beholden to their generals rather than to the central government. Militarism in China, unlike militarism in Japan or Germany, was not aimed at the outside world; its purpose was to conquer and hold China itself.

In October 1911, when a regional army mutinied against the central government, the most powerful of the generals, Yuan Shikai, refused to uphold the authority of the Qing. A revolutionary assembly elected Sun president of China in December 1911. But Sun had no military forces at his command, and to avoid a clash with the army, he resigned a few weeks later. A new national assembly then elected Yuan president. The first round of the struggle to create a new China had gone to the military.

Although Yuan Shikai was an able military man, he had no political program. While Sun reorganized his followers into a political party called Guomindang (National People's Party), Yuan quashed all attempts to create a Western-style government and harassed Sun's followers. In 1915, when Yuan announced his intention of becoming emperor, he lost all his supporters and died soon after.

Warlords and the Guomindang

From then until well into the 1920s, China was ruled by regional generals known as "warlords." They supported their armies through plunder and arbitrary taxation and fought one another or formed fleeting alliances. They protected the opium trade and the gangsters who ran it. They neglected the dikes and canals on which the livelihood of Chinese farmers depended. They frightened off trade and investments in railroads, industries, and agricultural improvement. Although the treaty ports prospered, the rest of China grew poorer during the warlord era. China had never seemed so weak and vulnerable.

Had the great powers acted together, as they had done in 1900, China might have fared much worse. But from 1914 to 1918 the Western powers were occupied fighting one another. Japan, an ally of Britain, took advantage of the situation to seize a German enclave on the Chinese coast. And at the Paris Peace Conference in 1919 the great powers awarded Germany's enclaves to Japan instead of returning them to China. To many educated Chinese, this was a cruel insult. On May 4, 1919, students demonstrated in front of the Forbidden City of Beijing, the seat of government. Despite a government crackdown, this May Fourth movement spread to other parts of China. A new generation was growing up to challenge the old officials, the warlords, and the foreigners.

Sun Yatsen tried to make a comeback in Canton (Guangzhou) in the early 1920s. Though not a Communist, he was impressed with the efficiency of Lenin's revolutionary tactics and let a Soviet adviser reorganize the Guomindang along Leninist lines. He also welcomed members of the newly created Chinese Communist Party into the Guomindang. When he died in 1925, the leadership of his party passed to Chiang Kaishek (1887–1975).

An officer and director of the military academy, Chiang trained several hundred young officers who remained loyal to him thereafter. In 1927, he determined to crush the regional warlords. As his army moved north from its base in Canton, he briefly formed an alliance with the Communists. Once his troops had occupied

Shanghai, however, he allied himself with local gangsters to crush the labor unions and decimate his former allies, the Communists, whom he considered a threat to his regime. Then he defeated or co-opted most of the other warlords and established a dictatorship.

As peace returned, China seemed poised to become independent and perhaps even prosperous. In the conciliatory mood of the 1920s (see Chapter 30), Japan, the United States, and Great Britain expected to do business without resorting to military threats; they even gave up most of the privileges they had exacted from China in the heyday of imperialism. Many foreign observers hailed Chiang's success as a "Nationalist Revolution."

Chiang's government issued ambitious plans to build railroads, develop agriculture and industries, and modernize China from the top down. However, his followers were neither competent administrators like the Japanese officials of the Meiji Restoration nor ruthless modernizers like the Russian Bolsheviks (see Chapters 28 and 31). Instead, they attracted thousands of opportunists whose goal was to "become an official and get rich" by taxing and plundering businesses. In the countryside, tax collectors and landowners squeezed the peasants ever harder, even at times of natural disaster. What little money reached the government's coffers went to the military.

Mao on the Long March   In 1934–1935, Mao Zedong led his rag-tag army of guerrillas on a year-long march across the rugged mountains of southern and western China. In this romanticized painting, young Mao is speaking to a group of soldiers in spotless uniforms who look up at him with worshipful expressions. (Library of Congress)

Mao Zedong, the Chinese Communists, and the Long March

The main challenge to Chiang's government came from the Communists. The Chinese Communist Party had been founded in 1921 by a handful of intellectuals. For several years it lived in the shadow of the Guomindang, kept there by orders of Joseph Stalin, who expected it to subvert the government from within. In 1927 its efforts to manipulate the Guomindang and to recruit members among industrial workers came to nought when Chiang Kaishek arrested and executed all the Communists and labor leaders he could catch.

The few Communists who escaped the mass arrests in Shanghai tried to establish bases in the remote mountainous parts of Jiangxi, in southeastern China. Among them was Mao Zedong (1893–1976), a farmer's son who had left home to study philosophy. He was not a contemplative thinker but a man of action whose first impulse was to call for violent effort: "To be able to leap on horseback and to shoot at the same time; to go from battle to battle; to shake the mountains by one's cries, and the colors of the sky by one's roars of anger." In the early 1920s, he had discovered the works of Karl Marx, joined the Communist Party, and soon became one of its leaders.

In Jiangxi, Mao began studying conditions among the peasants, in whom Communists previously had shown no interest. He planned to redistribute the properties of landowners to the poorest peasants, thus gaining adherents for the coming struggle with the Guomindang army. In this, he was following the example of innumerable leaders of peasant rebellions over the centuries. His goal, however, was not just a nationalist revolution against the traditional government and foreign intervention but a complete social revolution from the bottom up. Mao's reliance on the peasantry was a radical departure from Marxist-Leninist ideology, which stressed the backwardness of the peasants and pinned its hopes on the industrial workers. He therefore had to be careful to cloak his pragmatic tactics in Communist rhetoric, to allay the suspicions of Stalin and his agents.

Mao was also a radical advocate of women's equality. Even before becoming a Communist, he had written several tracts on women's rights, an issue among Chinese thinkers since the nineteenth century. Radical ideas such as those of Margaret Sanger, the American leader of the birth-control movement, and the feminist play *A Doll's House* by the Norwegian dramatist Henrik Ibsen had inspired veterans of the May Fourth Movement and young women attending universities and medical or nursing schools. Before 1927 the Communists had organized the women who worked in Shanghai's textile mills, the most exploited of all Chinese workers. Later in their mountain stronghold in Jiangxi, they allowed divorce, banned arranged marriages, and organized women farmers. They worked to end footbinding, which survived in remote rural areas. However, they did not admit women to leadership positions, for the party was still run by men whose primary task was warfare.

The government pursued the Communists into the mountains. The army made forays up the valleys and built forts throughout the countryside. Rather than risk direct confrontations, Mao responded with guerrilla warfare. He harassed the army at its weak points with hit-and-run tactics, relying on the terrain and the support of the peasantry. Government troops often mistreated civilians, but Mao insisted that his soldiers help the peasants, pay a fair price for food and supplies, and treat women with respect.

In spite of their good relations with the peasants of Jiangxi, the Communists gradually found themselves encircled by government forces. In 1934, Mao and his followers decided to break out of the southern mountains and trek to Shaanxi, an even more remote province in northwestern China (see Map 32.1). This "Long March" took them 6,000 miles (9,660 kilometers) in one year, 17 miles (27 kilometers) a day over desolate mountains and through swamps and deserts, pursued by the army and bombed by Chiang's aircraft. Of the 100,000 Communists who left Jiangxi in October 1934, only 4,000 reached Shaanxi a year later. The government thought it was finally rid of the Communists.

War with Japan

Meanwhile, Chiang Kaishek had a much more urgent problem on his hands: the revival of Japanese imperialism described in Chapter 31. In late 1931 Japanese forces seized Manchuria and a few months later briefly occupied Shanghai. The Chinese government, deprived of some of its richest provinces, faced the prospect of further Japanese advances. From 1937 to 1941, the Guomindang and the Communists formed a united front against the Japanese. This did not mean real cooperation but only a lessening of the conflicts between the two sides.

Beginning in July 1937, Japanese forces quickly seized China's richest agricultural lands and industrial cities (see Map 32.1). Warfare between Chinese and Japanese was often incredibly violent. In the winter of 1937–1938, Japanese troops took Nanjing, raped 20,000 women, killed 200,000 prisoners and civilians, and looted and burned the city. To slow them down, Chiang ordered the Yellow River dikes blasted open, caus-

Map 32.1 The Chinese Communist Movement and the War with Japan In 1934–1935, the Nationalists, in control of most of China, forced the Communists out of the mountains of Kiangsi and pursued them across southern and western China but could not defeat them. Then in 1937, Japanese armies invaded northern and eastern China, but could not pursue the Nationalists into their stronghold of Sichuan in central China. Thus, China remained divided into three hostile camps until the Japanese defeat in 1945.

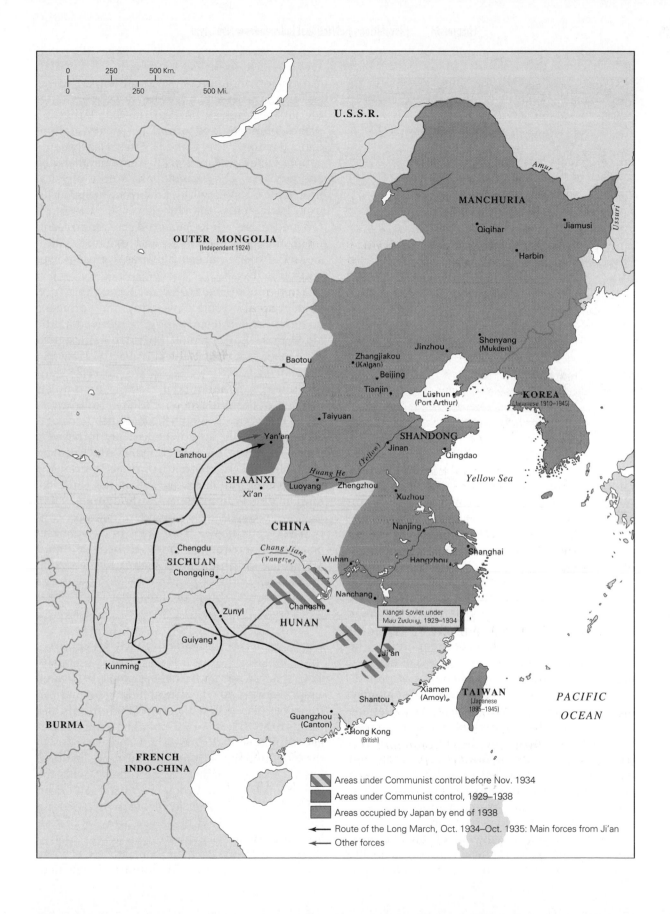

Areas under Communist control before Nov. 1934

Areas under Communist control, 1929–1938

Areas occupied by Japan by end of 1938

Route of the Long March, Oct. 1934–Oct. 1935: Main forces from Ji'an

Other forces

The Chinese Revolution

1911	Qing Dynasty overthrown
1915	Japan presents Twenty-one Demands to China
1919	May Fourth Movement; student demonstrations
1921	Chinese Communist Party founded
1925	Chiang Kaishek becomes head of Guomindang
1927	Guomindang forces occupy Shanghai; Mao Zedong and Communists flee
1931	Japanese forces occupy Manchuria
1934–35	Mao leads Communists on Long March
1937	Japanese attack China, conquer coastal provinces; Guomindang flees to Sichuan
1941–45	Guomindang receive U.S. aid to fight Japanese
1945 Aug	Japanese forces surrender
1945–49	Civil War
1949 Oct	Communists defeat Guomindang; Mao proclaims People's Republic

ing a flood that destroyed 4,000 villages, killed 890,000 people, and made 12.5 million people homeless. Two years later, when the Communists ordered a massive offensive against the Japanese, the latter retaliated with a "kill all, burn all, loot all" campaign, destroying hundreds of villages down to the last person, building, and farm animal.

The Guomindang fled to the interior province of Sichuan, isolated from the rest of China by rugged mountains. There Chiang built up a huge army, not so much to fight Japan as to prepare for a future confrontation with the Communists. The army drafted over 3 million men, even though it had only 1 million rifles and could not provide food or clothing for all its soldiers. The Guomindang raised taxes on farmers, even when famine forced them to eat the bark of trees. Such taxes, however, were not enough to support both a large army and the thousands of officials and hangers-on who had fled to Sichuan. To avoid alienating its wealthy supporters by raising their taxes, the government printed money, causing inflation, hoarding, and corruption.

The United States, angered by Japan's invasion of China, got unofficially involved in the war as early as 1940. Claire Chennault, an Ameri-

can aviator, organized a private air force, the Flying Tigers, with U.S. government support. After the Japanese attack on Pearl Harbor, American planes bombed Japan from bases in Guomindang territory. The United States also tried to supply Chiang's forces with weapons, materiel, and advisers. The Guomindang's only physical link to the outside world, however, was by airlift from India across the Himalayas. As a result, it received more advice than aid, creating resentment among the Chinese and dangerous illusions in America about China as a great power and a friendly ally.

From Yan'an, his capital in Shaanxi province, Mao gradually rebuilt his army and formed a government. Until early 1941, he received a little aid from the Soviet Union. But after Stalin signed the Soviet-Japanese Neutrality Pact (1941), that aid ended.

Unlike the Guomindang, the Communists listened to the grievances of the peasants, especially the poor, to whom they distributed land confiscated from landowners. They imposed a rigid discipline on their officials and soldiers and tolerated no dissent or criticism from the intellectuals who had fled the Japanese and lost faith in the Guomindang. Although they had few weapons, the Communists obtained support and intelligence from farmers in Japanese-occupied territory. They turned military reversals into propaganda victories, presenting themselves as the only group in China that was serious about fighting the Japanese.

Civil War and Communist Victory

The Japanese surrender in September 1945 came as a surprise to the Guomindang. American transport planes flew Guomindang officials and troops to all the cities of China. The United States gave millions of dollars of aid and weapons to the Guomindang, all the while urging "national unity" and a "coalition government" with the Communists. Chiang, however, used American aid and all other means available to prepare for a civil war. By late 1945 he had an army of 2.7 million, more than twice the size of Mao's army.

From 1945 to 1949 the contest between the Guomindang and the Communists intensified.

Guomindang forces started with many advantages: more troops and weapons, U.S. backing, and control of the cities. But their behavior eroded whatever popular support they had. As they moved into formerly Japanese-held territory, they acted like an occupation force. They taxed the people they "liberated" more heavily than the Japanese had. They looted businesses, confiscated supplies, and enriched themselves at the expense of the population. To pay its bills, the government printed money so fast that it soon lost all its value, ruining merchants and causing hoarding and shortages. In the countryside, the Guomindang's brutality alienated the peasants.

Meanwhile, the Communists obtained immense amounts of Japanese equipment seized by the Soviets in the last weeks of the war and American weapons surrendered by deserting Guomindang soldiers. In Manchuria, where they were strongest, the Communists pushed through a radical land reform program, distributing the properties of landowners among the poorest peasants. In battles against government forces, the higher morale and popular support that the Communists enjoyed proved to be more valuable than the heavy equipment of the Guomindang, whose soldiers began deserting by the thousands. By 1949 Guomindang armies were collapsing everywhere, defeated more by their own greed and ineptness than by the Communists. As the Communists advanced, high-ranking members of the Guomindang fled to Taiwan, an island protected from the mainland by the United States Navy. On October 1, 1949, Mao Zedong proclaimed the founding of the People's Republic of China.

China in revolution   In 1948, with the Guomindang government of China on the verge of defeat, people became desperate. In this photograph by French photojournalist Henri Cartier-Bresson, citizens of Shanghai line up before a bank to exchange their near-worthless currency for gold and silver. In the ensuing panic, several were crushed to death. (Cartier-Bresson/Magnum Photos, Inc.)

THE INDIAN INDEPENDENCE MOVEMENT

India and China are similar in size and population, yet their modern histories differ significantly. China retained its formal independence, but India was a colony of Great Britain until 1947. China experienced a series of violent upheavals that lasted for two generations, but the violent conflict that struck the Indian people came only after they had achieved independence.

The Land and the People

Much of India is fertile land, but it is very vulnerable to the vagaries of nature, especially the droughts caused by the periodic failure of the monsoons. When the rains failed from 1896 to 1900, 2 million people died of starvation. Unlike the Chinese, who expected their government to maintain the dikes that protected the lowlands from floods, the Indian people did not blame natural disasters on government policies, for no government in India had ever claimed the Mandate of Heaven.

Despite periodic famines, the Indian population grew from 250 million in 1900 to 319 million in 1921 and 389 million in 1941. This growth created pressure in many areas. Landless young men converged on the cities, far exceeding the number of jobs available in the slowly expanding industries. To produce timber for construction, shipbuilding, and railroad ties, and to clear land for tea and rubber plantations, government foresters cut down most of the tropical hardwood forests that had covered the subcontinent in the nineteenth century. In spite of deforestation and extensive irrigation, the amount of land available to peasant families shrank with each successive generation. Economic development—what the British called the "moral and material progress of India"—hardly benefited the average Indian.

Indians were divided into many classes. Peasants—always the great majority—paid rents to the landowner, interest to the village moneylender, and taxes to the government, and had little money left to improve their land or raise their standard of living. The government protected property owners, from the village moneylender all the way up to the princes and maharajahs who owned huge tracts of land. The cities were crowded with craftsmen, traders, and workers of all sorts, mostly very poor. Although the British had banned *sati* (the burning of widows on their husbands' funeral pyres), in all other respects women's lives had changed very little.

So many different languages were spoken in the subcontinent that English became—like Latin in medieval Europe—the common medium of communication among the educated. This helped create a new class of English-speaking, Western-educated government officials, professionals, and merchants, who would play a prominent role in the independence movement.

The majority of Indians practiced Hinduism and were subdivided into hundreds of castes, each affiliated with a particular occupation. Their religion discouraged intermarriage and other social interactions among castes and with people who were not Hindus. Muslims constituted one-quarter of the people of India but formed a majority in the northwest, especially in the Sind and Punjab regions, and in eastern Bengal. Over a millennium, many poor people had converted to Islam to escape the caste system. Muslims had dominated northern and central India until the eighteenth century but had fared poorly under the British. More reluctant than Hindus to learn English, they felt discriminated against by both British and Hindus.

British Rule and Indian Nationalism

Colonial India was ruled by a viceroy appointed by the British government; the country was administered by a few thousand members of the Indian Civil Service (see Chapter 26). Imbued with a sense of duty toward their subjects, members of the Civil Service formed one of the least corrupt bureaucracies of all time. Drawn mostly from the English gentry, they liked to think of India as a land of lords and peasants that it was their duty to protect from the dangers of industrialization and radical politics.

As Europeans, the Civil Service members admired modern technology but tried to control its introduction into India so as to maximize the benefits to Britain and to themselves. For example, they encouraged railroads, harbors, telegraphs, and other communications technologies, as well as irrigation and plantations. But at the same time, to minimize the disruptive impact of industrialization on Indian society, they discouraged the cotton and steel industries and limited the training of Indian engineers.

At the turn of the century, the majority of Indians—especially the peasants, the landowners, and the princes—accepted British rule. But the Europeans' condescending attitude toward darker-skinned peoples increasingly offended Indians who had learned English and absorbed English ideas of freedom and representative government and then discovered that thinly disguised racial quotas excluded them from the Indian Civil Service, the officer corps, and the most prestigious country clubs.

In 1885 a small group of English-speaking Indian professionals founded a political organization called the Indian National Congress. For twenty years, members respectfully petitioned the government for access to higher administrative positions and a voice in official decisions but had little influence outside intellectual circles. Then, in 1905, Viceroy Lord Curzon divided the province of Bengal in two, to improve the efficiency of its administration (see Map 32.2). This decision, made without consulting anyone, angered not only educated Indians, who saw it as a step taken to lessen their influence, but also millions of uneducated Hindu Bengalis, who suddenly found themselves outnumbered by Muslims in both East and West Bengal.

News of Japan's victory in the Russo-Japanese War in 1905 (see Chapter 28) encouraged nationalist sentiment in India. It proved that Europeans were not invincible. Soon Bengal was the scene of demonstrations, boycotts of British goods, and even incidents of violence against the British.

In 1906, while the Hindus of Bengal were protesting the partition of their province, Muslims, fearful of Hindu dominance, founded the All-India Muslim League. Caught in an awkward situation, the government responded by granting Indians a limited franchise based on wealth. Muslims, however, were, on average, poorer than Hindus, so the British instituted separate representation and different qualifications for Hindus and Muslims. In 1911 the British transferred the national capital from Calcutta to Delhi, the old capital of the Mughal emperors. These changes disturbed Indians of all classes and religions and raised their political consciousness. Politics, once the concern of Westernized intellectuals, turned into two mass movements: one by Hindus and one by Muslims.

During World War I, Indians supported Britain enthusiastically; 1.2 million men volunteered for the army, and millions more Indians gave money to the government. Many expected that the British would reward such loyalty with political concessions; others organized to demand such concessions. In 1916 two leading nationalists formed the Home Rule League to demand the right of Indians to control the internal affairs of India. One of them was Bal Tilak, head of the Indian National Congress, a forceful and provocative Hindu traditionalist who had once been jailed for inciting a riot. The other was an Englishwoman, Annie Besant, who had moved to India and become a labor organizer; she then founded the Hindu University of Benares (now Varanasi) and became active in the Indian National Congress, to which she was later elected president.

In 1917, in response to the agitation, the British government announced "the gradual development of self-governing institutions with a view to the progressive realization of responsible government in India as an integral part of the British Empire." This announcement sounded like a promise of self-government, but the timetable was left so vague that nationalists denounced it as a devious maneuver to postpone India's independence.

Soon after the end of World War I, a violent epidemic of influenza spread to every country on earth. India was especially hard hit; of the 20 million people who died worldwide, one out of four was Indian. This dreadful toll increased the mounting political tensions. Congress leaders

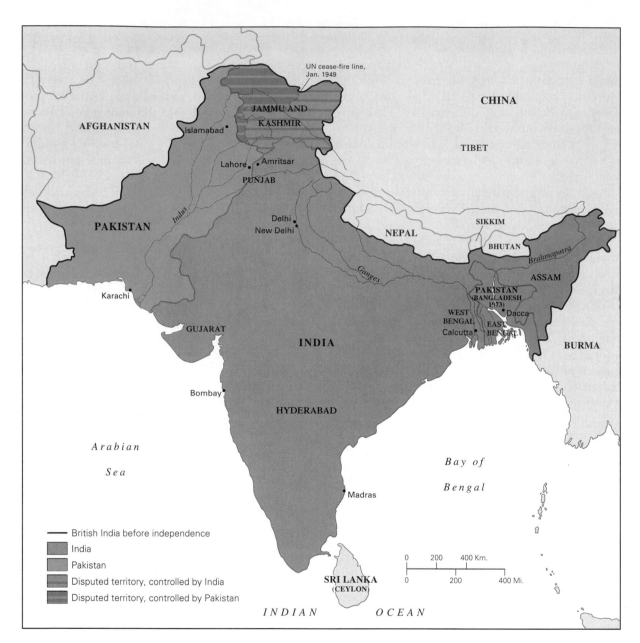

Map 32.2 The Partition of India, 1947 Before the British, India had been divided among many states, ethnic groups, and religions. When the British left in 1947, the sub-continent split along religious lines. The predominantly Muslim regions of Sind and Punjab in the northwest and East Bengal in the east formed the new nation of Pakistan, while the predominantly Hindu center became the Republic of India. Disputed territories of Jammu and Kashmir remained, however, to poison the relations between the two new countries for the years to come.

declared that the British reform proposals were too little too late. Muslims were angry at the Allies' harsh treatment of Turkey (a Muslim country) after World War I (see Chapter 30). On April 13, 1919, in the city of Amritsar in Punjab, General Reginald Dyer ordered his troops to fire into a peaceful crowd of some 10,000 demonstrators, killing at least 379 and wounding 1,200. As waves of angry demonstrations swept over India, the time of gradual accommodation came to a close.

Mahatma Gandhi and Militant Nonviolence

For the next twenty years, India teetered on the edge of violent uprisings and harsh repression, possibly even war. The fact that it did not succumb was due to Mohandas K. Gandhi (1869–1948), a man known to his followers as Mahatma, "the great soul."

Gandhi began life with every advantage. His family was wealthy enough to send him to England for his education. After his studies, he lived in South Africa, where he practiced law for the small Indian community living there. During World War I he returned to India and was one of many Western-educated intellectuals who joined the Indian National Congress.

Gandhi had some unusual political ideas. Unlike Bal Tilak, Benito Mussolini, Mao Zedong, and other radical political thinkers of his time, he denounced the popular ideals of power and struggle and combat. Instead, inspired by both Hindu and Christian concepts, he preached the saintly virtues of *ahimsa* (nonviolence) and *satyagraha* (the search for truth). He refused to countenance violence among his followers, and several times he called off demonstrations when they turned violent.

Gandhi had an affinity for the poor that was unusual even among socialist politicians. In 1921 he gave up the Western-style suits worn by lawyers and the fine raiment of wealthy Indians and henceforth wore nothing but simple peasant garb: a length of homespun cloth below his waist and a shawl to cover his torso (see Environment and Technology: Gandhi and Technology). Though married, he practiced total chastity. He spoke for the farmers and the outcasts, whom he named *harijan*, "the children of God." He attracted ever-larger numbers of followers among the poor and the illiterate, who soon began worshiping him as a saint, and he transformed the cause of Indian independence from an elite movement of the educated into a mass movement with a quasi-religious aura.

Gandhi was a brilliant political tactician and a master of public relations gestures. In 1929, for instance, he led a few followers on an 80-mile (129-kilometer) walk, camped on a beach, and gathered salt from the sea, in a blatant and well-publicized act of civil disobedience to the government's salt monopoly. But he discovered that unleashing the power of popular participation was one thing and controlling its direction was quite another. Within days of his "Walk to the Sea," popular demonstrations of support broke out all over India, in which the police killed 100 demonstrators and arrested over 60,000.

Many times, Gandhi threatened to fast "unto death," and several times he did come close to death, to protest the violence of both the police and his followers. He was repeatedly arrested and spent a total of six years in jail, yet every arrest made him more popular. He became a cult figure, not only in his own country but also in the West. He never won a battle or an election; instead, in the words of historian Percival Spear, he made the British "uncomfortable in their cherished field of moral rectitude," and he gave Indians the feeling that theirs was the ethically superior cause.

India Moves Toward Independence

In the 1920s, slowly and reluctantly, the British began to give in to the pressure of the Indian National Congress and the Muslim League. While reserving "imperial" questions of law and order, defense, and finance for themselves, they handed control over "national" areas like education, the economy, and public works to Indians. They also gradually admitted more Indians into the Civil Service and the officer corps.

Gandhi and Technology

In the twentieth century, all political leaders but one have embraced modern industrial technology. That one exception is Gandhi.

After deciding to wear only handmade cloth, Gandhi made a bonfire of imported factory-made cloth and began spending half an hour every day spinning yarn on a simple spinning wheel, a task he called a "sacrament." The spinning wheel became the symbol of his movement. Any Indian who wished to come before him had to dress in handwoven cloth.

Gandhi had several reasons for reviving this ancient craft. One was revulsion against the materialism of the West, which he contrasted with the poverty of his own people:

> The incessant search for material comforts and their multiplication is such an evil, and I make bold to say that the Europeans themselves will have to remodel their outlook if they are not to perish under the weight of the comforts to which they are becoming slaves.

Gandhi believed that foreign cotton mills had impoverished his people:

> A hundred and fifty years ago, we manufactured all our cloth. Our women spun fine yarns in their own cottages, and supplemented the earnings of their husbands. . . . India grows all the cotton she needs. She exports several million bales of cotton to Japan and Lancashire and receives much of it back in manufactured calico, though she is capable of producing all the cloth and all the yarn necessary for supplying her wants by hand-weaving and hand-spinning. . . . The spinning wheel was presented to the nation for giving occupation to the millions who had, at least four months of the year, nothing to do.

But most of all, to Gandhi, the spinning wheel was a political symbol of "national consciousness and a contribution by every individual to a definite constructive national work":

> If three hundred million people did the same thing every day . . . because they were inspired by the same ideal, we would have enough unity of purpose to achieve independence.

Nevertheless, Gandhi was a shrewd politician who understood the usefulness of modern devices for mobilizing the masses and organizing his followers. He wore a watch and used the telephone and the printing press to keep in touch with his followers. When he traveled by train, he rode third class—but in a third-class railroad car of his own. His goal was the independence of his country, and he pursued it with every nonviolent means he could find.

Gandhi's ideas challenge us to rethink the purpose of technology. Was he opposed on principle to all modern devices? Was he an opportunist who used those devices that served his political ends and rejected those that did not? Or did he have a higher principle that accounts for his willingless to use the telephone and the railroad but not factory-made cloth?

Source: Louis Fischer, *Gandhi: His Life and Message for the World* (New York: New American Library, 1954), 82–83.

Gandhi at the spinning wheel Mahatma Gandhi chose the spinning wheel as his symbol because it represented the traditional activity of millions of rural Indians whose livelihood was threatened by industrialization. Margaret Bourke-White took this photograph of Gandhi and his spinning wheel for *Life* magazine. (Margaret Bourke-White, *LIFE Magazine* @ Time Warner Inc.)

In the years between the First and Second World Wars India took its first steps toward industrialization. Protected by high tariff barriers against imports—even from Britain—Indian entrepreneurs built plants to manufacture iron and steel, cement, paper, cotton and jute textiles, sugar, and other products. This early industrialization provided jobs, but not enough to improve the lives of the Indian peasants or urban poor.

These manufactures, however, helped create a class of wealthy Indian businessmen, especially in Bombay, the city with the largest trade and the most contact with the West. Far from being satisfied with the government's policies, they supported the Indian National Congress and its demands for independence. Though paying homage to Gandhi, they preferred his designated heir, Jawaharlal Nehru (1889–1964). A highly educated nationalist and subtle thinker, Nehru, in contrast to Gandhi, looked forward to creating a modern industrial India.

Congress politicians won regional elections but continued to be excluded from the viceroy's cabinet, the true center of power. When World War II began in September 1939, Viceroy Lord Linlithgow declared war without consulting a single Indian. The Congress-dominated provincial governments resigned in protest and found that boycotting government office increased their popular support. When the British offered to give India its independence once the war ended, Gandhi called the offer a "postdated cheque on a failing bank" and demanded full independence immediately. He started a "Quit India" campaign that aroused popular demonstrations against the British and provoked a wave of arrests, including his own.

As in World War I, Indians contributed heavily to the Allied war effort, supplying 2 million soldiers and enormous amounts of materiel. Once again, India was called on to contribute its resources, particularly timber, needed for emergency construction.

Indian soldiers felt they were fighting to defend their country rather than to support the British Empire. For many of Gandhi's followers, nonviolence was not a creed but a tactic. As Nehru explained: "I would fight Japan sword in hand, but I can only do so as a free man." A small number of Indians, however, were so anti-British

The Indian Independence Movement

1857–1947	India under British Rule
1885	Indian National Congress founded
1905	Viceroy Curzon splits Bengal province; mass demonstrations
1906	Muslims found All-India Muslim League
1911	British transfer capital from Calcutta to Delhi
1916	Amritsar Massacre
1921	Gandhi leads Indian National Congress
1929	Gandhi leads March to the Sea
1930s	Gandhi calls for independence, is repeatedly arrested
1939	British bring India into World War II
1940	Muhammad Ali Jinnah demands a separate nation for Muslims
1947 Aug 15	Partition and independence of India and Pakistan

that they joined the Japanese side under the leadership of Subhas Chandra Bose, a former follower of Gandhi. Although the British considered Bose a traitor, many Indians thought that he and his followers deserved as much respect as those who fought on the British side.

India's subordination to foreign interests was vividly demonstrated in the famine of 1943 in Bengal. Unlike previous famines, this one was caused not by drought but by the Japanese conquest of Burma, which cut off supplies of Burmese rice. Food was available elsewhere in India, but the railroads were occupied with the transport needs of the military, then frantically preparing to face an imminent Japanese invasion. As a result, supplies ran short in Bengal and surrounding areas, speculators hoarded what little food there was, and some 2 million people starved before the army was ordered to supply food.

Partition and Independence

When the war ended, Britain's new Labour government prepared for Indian independence, but the deep suspicions between Hindus and Mus-

The partition of India As India approached independence from British colonial rule, the country erupted into a bloody civil war between Muslims and Hindus, forcing millions to flee their homes. This photograph by *Life* magazine photographer Margaret Bourke-White shows Muslims heading for safety in Pakistan, the predominantly Muslim part of the subcontinent. Along the way they pass the remains of victims of earlier attacks on refugees. (Margaret Bourke-White, *LIFE Magazine* @ Time Warner Inc.)

on deaf ears. Unable to control the tiger of Hindu-Muslim hatred, the leaders of the Congress and of the League chose to ride it to power. In despair, Gandhi retreated to his home near Ahmadabad. The British made frantic proposals to keep India united, but their authority was waning fast.

By early 1947 the Congress had accepted the idea of a partition of India into two states, one secular, the other Muslim. In June, Lord Mountbatten, the last viceroy, decided that independence must come immediately. On August 15, amid jubilation and a genuine outpouring of friendliness toward the departing British, British India gave way to a new India and Pakistan.

The rejoicing over independence, however, was marred by violent outbreaks of ethnic strife. In protest over the mounting chaos, Gandhi refused to attend the independence-day celebration. Throughout the land, Muslim and Hindu neighbors turned against each other, and armed gangs of people of one religion hunted down people of the other faith. For centuries Hindus and Muslims had intermingled throughout most of India. Leaving all their possessions behind, Hindus now fled from predominantly Muslim areas, and Muslims fled from Hindu areas. Trainloads of desperate refugees of one faith were attacked and massacred or left stranded in the middle of deserts by members of the other. Within a few months, some 12 million people had abandoned their ancestral homes, and half a million lay dead. In January 1948, Gandhi died too, gunned down by an angry Hindu refugee.

lims complicated the process. The break between the two communities had started in 1937, when the Congress won the provincial elections and refused to share power with the Muslim League. In 1940, the leader of the League, Muhammad Ali Jinnah (1876–1948), demanded what many Muslims had been dreaming of for years: a country of their own, to be called Pakistan.

As independence approached, talks between Jinnah and Nehru broke down, and battle lines were drawn. Violent rioting broke out in Bengal and Bihar, states with mixed populations. Gandhi's appeals for tolerance and cooperation fell

THE MEXICAN REVOLUTION

In the nineteenth century, Latin America successfully achieved independence from Spain and Portugal but did not industrialize. Throughout much of the century most Latin American republics suffered from ideological divisions, unstable governments, and violent upheavals (see Chapter 25). By trading their raw materials and agricultural products for foreign

Map 32.3 The Mexican Revolution The Mexican Revolution originated in two distinct regions of the country. One was the mountainous and densely populated area south of Mexico City, particularly Morelos, the homeland of Emiliano Zapata. The other was the dry and thinly populated ranch country of the north, such as Chihuahua, the home of Pancho Villa. The fighting that ensued, however, crisscrossed the country along the main railroad lines marked on the map.

manufactures, they became economically dependent on the wealthier countries to the north, especially the United States and Great Britain. Their societies, far from fulfilling the promises of their independence, remained deeply split between wealthy landowners and desperately poor peasants.

Nowhere was this more true than in Mexico, a country of ancient civilization and, in all Latin America, the country most influenced by the Spanish during three centuries of colonial rule. Few countries in Latin America suffered as many foreign invasions and interventions. A Mexican saying observed wryly: "Poor Mexico: so far from God, so close to the United States" (see

Map 32.3). In Mexico the chasm between rich and poor was so deep and the hold of tradition so strong that only a revolution could move the country toward prosperity and democracy.

Mexico in 1910

Despite the upheavals of the nineteenth century (see Chapter 25), at the beginning of the twentieth the society of Mexico was still divided between rich and poor and between persons of Spanish, Indian, and mixed ancestry. A few very wealthy families of Spanish origin, less than 1 percent of the population, owned 85 percent of the land, mostly in huge *haciendas* (estates). Closely tied to this elite were the American and British companies that controlled most of Mexico's railroads, silver mines, plantations, and other productive enterprises. At the other end of the social scale were Indians and *mestizos* (people of mixed Indian and European ancestry). Most of them were peasants who worked on the haciendas or farmed small communal plots near their ancestral villages.

The urban middle class was small and had little political influence. There were few professional and government positions for them to fill, and foreigners owned most of the businesses. Industrial workers also were few in number; the only significant groups were textile workers in the port of Veracruz on the Gulf of Mexico and railroad workers spread throughout the country.

During the colonial period (see Chapter 19), the Spanish government had made halfhearted efforts to defend the Indians from the land-grabbing tactics of the haciendas. After independence, wealthy Mexican families and American companies used bribery and force to acquire millions of acres of good agricultural land from the villages. The peasants lost not only their fields but also their access to firewood and pasture for their animals. As sugar, cotton, and other commercial crops replaced the cultivation of corn and beans, the peasants had little choice but to work on haciendas. To survive, they had to buy food and other necessities on credit from the landowner's store until they fell into perpetual debt.

Sometimes whole communities were forced to relocate. In the 1880s, American investors purchased from the government dubious claims to more than 2.5 million acres (1 million hectares) traditionally held by the Yaqui people of Sonora. When the Yaqui resisted the expropriation of their lands, they were brutally repressed by the Mexican army.

Extremes of wealth and poverty were common in agricultural civilizations. In Mexico, however, the peasants knew that their situation had gotten dramatically worse in recent memory.

Northern Mexicans had no peasant tradition of communal ownership, for the northern half of the country was too dry for farming, unlike the tropical and densely populated south. The north was a region of silver mines and cattle ranches, some of them enormous. It was sparsely populated by cowboys, miners, and bandits. The brutality of their lives and the vast inequities of income made northern Mexicans as resentful as the people of the south.

In 1910 the government seemed all-powerful, and no one expected a revolution to break out. For thirty years, General Porfirio Díaz (1830–1915) had ruled Mexico under the motto "Liberty, order, progress." To Díaz, "liberty" meant freedom for rich hacienda owners and foreign investors to acquire more land. The government imposed order through rigged elections and a policy of *pan o palo* (bread or the stick)—that is, bribes for Díaz's supporters and summary justice for those who opposed him. And "progress" meant mainly the importing of foreign capital, machinery, and technicians to take advantage of Mexico's labor, soil, and natural resources.

During the Díaz years, Mexico City—with its paved streets, streetcar lines, electric street lighting, and public parks—became a showplace, and throughout Mexico new telegraph and railroad lines connected cities and towns. Of all these improvements, railroads had the most dramatic effect on the nation. By 1910, more than 15,000 miles (24,150 kilometers) of track had been laid. Eighty percent of the capital for the expansion of the railroads, however, came not from Mexico but from the United States. Material progress of that sort benefited only a handful of well-connected businessmen. The great boom in railroads, agriculture, and mining at the turn of the century actually caused a decline in the average Mexican's standard of living.

Though a mestizo himself, Díaz favored whites over the nonwhite majority of Mexicans. He and his supporters tried to eradicate what they saw as Mexico's embarrassingly rustic traditions. On many middle- and upper-class tables, French cuisine replaced traditional Mexican dishes. The wealthy replaced sombreros and ponchos with European garments and preferred horse racing and soccer to the traditional bullfighting and cockfighting. To the educated middle class—the only group with a strong sense of nationhood—this devaluation of Mexican culture became a symbol of the Díaz regime's failure to defend national interests.

Mexican Society in Upheaval, 1911–1920

Unlike the Chinese Revolution or the Indian independence movement, the Mexican Revolution was not the work of one man or one party with a well-defined ideology. Instead, it developed haphazardly, led by a series of ambitious but limited leaders, each representing a different segment of Mexican society.

The first was Francisco Madero (1873–1913), the son of a wealthy landowning and mining family, educated in the United States. Appalled by the corruption and nepotism of the Díaz regime, he ran for president under the slogan "Effective suffrage and no reelection." When he was defeated, he called on the Mexican people to rebel. In early 1911, minor uprisings broke out here and there, the local authorities wavered, the government collapsed, and Díaz fled into exile. After two years as president, Madero was overthrown and murdered by one of his supporters, General Victoriano Huerta. Woodrow Wilson, the president of the United States, showed his displeasure with Huerta by sending the United States Marines to occupy Veracruz.

These events—military coups, assassinations, U.S. intervention—could have taken place anywhere in the Caribbean or Central America and at any time in the nineteenth and early twentieth centuries. But as the revolt spread throughout Mexico and more and more people became involved, the story departed from the traditional scenario.

Mexico's urban middle class and industrial workers were angered by the inequities of Mexican society and by foreign intervention in the affairs of their country. They found leaders in Venustiano Carranza, a landowner, and in Alvaro Obregón, a former schoolteacher. Calling themselves Constitutionalists, Carranza and Obregón organized private armies and in 1914 succeeded in overthrowing Huerta.

By then the revolution had spread to the countryside. As early as 1911, the Indian farmer Emiliano Zapata (1879–1919) had led a revolt against the haciendas in the mountains of Morelos, south of Mexico City (see Map 32.3). His soldiers were peasants, some of them women, mounted on horseback and armed with pistols and rifles. For several years, they periodically came down from the mountains, burning hacienda buildings and returning land to the Indian villages to which it had once belonged.

Another leader appeared in Chihuahua, a northern state where seventeen persons owned two-fifths of the land and 95 percent of the people had no land at all. Starting in 1913, Pancho

Emiliano Zapata and Pancho Villa Zapata and Villa were the two most famous guerrilla leaders in the Mexican revolution. In this photograph, they are shown riding together during one of their rare encounters. Zapata, center, wears the broad *sombrero* of rural Mexico; Villa, on the right, has donned a military uniform.

Villa (1877–1923), a former ranch hand, mule driver, and bandit, organized an army of three thousand men, most of them cowboys. They too seized land from the large haciendas, not to rebuild traditional communities as in southern Mexico, but to create family ranches.

Zapata and Villa were part agrarian rebels, part social revolutionaries. They enjoyed tremendous popular support but could never transcend their regional and peasant origins and lead a national revolution. They constantly clashed with the forces led by Carranza and Obregón. Although the Constitutionalists had fewer soldiers than Zapata and Villa, they held the major cities and controlled the country's exports of oil, and they used the proceeds to buy modern weapons. In 1915 Obregón's machine gunners decimated Villa's rifle-toting cavalry, sending Villa back north.

To rebuild his popularity within Mexico, Villa tried to provoke foreign intervention by raiding towns across the U.S. border. Once again, President Wilson ordered American troops into Mexico to pursue the "bandits." Inciting U.S. intervention did Villa little good, however, for he did not have the forces to capture Mexico City. Fighting continued for years, but gradually the Constitutionalists took over most of Mexico. In 1919 they defeated and killed Zapata; Villa was assassinated four years later. An estimated 2 million people lost their lives in the civil war, and much of Mexico lay in ruin.

During their struggle to win support against Zapata and Villa, the Constitutionalists had adopted many of their agrarian reforms, such as the restitution of communal lands to the Indians of Morelos. The Constitutionalists also proposed a number of social programs designed to appeal to workers and to the middle class. The Constitution of 1917 promised universal suffrage and no reelection of a president; state-run education to free the poor from the hold of the Catholic Church; the end of debt peonage; restrictions on foreign ownership of property; and laws to protect laborers, specifying minimum wages and maximum hours.

These reforms were too costly to implement right away. Nevertheless, they had important symbolic significance, for they enshrined the dignity of Mexicans and the equality of Indians,

Diego Rivera, "The Agitator"   Diego Rivera was both politically committed to the Mexican Revolution and widely admired as an artist. This mural, painted at the National Agricultural School at Chapingo near Mexico City, shows a political agitator addressing a crowd of peasants and workers. With one hand, the speakers points to miners in a silver mine and, with the other, to a hammer and sickle. (Universidad Autonoma de Chapingo/CENDIAP-INBA)

mestizos, and whites, as well as of peasants and city people.

The Revolution Institutionalized, 1920–1940

In the early 1920s, after a decade of violence that had exhausted all classes, the Mexican Revolution lost momentum. The government was reluctant to implement the reforms promised by the Constitution of 1917. Only in Morelos did peasants receive land. All important decisions were made by President Obregón and his closest associates, mostly surviving revolutionary generals. Nevertheless, the Revolution had changed the social makeup of the governing class in important ways. For the first time in Mexican history representatives of rural communities, unionized workers, and public employees were admitted to the inner circle.

In the arts, the Mexican Revolution produced a surge of creativity, best represented by the political murals of José Clemente Orozco and Diego Rivera (see Voices and Visions: Revolutionary Art) and the paintings of Frida Kahlo. Much of their work focused on social themes, showing peasants, workers, and soldiers in scenes from the Revolution.

In 1928, after Obregón was assassinated, his successor, Plutarco Elías Calles, founded the National Revolutionary Party, or PNR (the abbreviation of its name in Spanish), as a means of ensuring political continuity. Calles's aim was to put his protégés into the presidency (they could legally serve only one term) while he kept control of the country as party boss. By doing so, he departed from the tradition of military coups and assassinations that had so long plagued Mexico. Unlike the totalitarian fascist and communist parties of Europe, the PNR was a forum where all the pressure groups and vested interests—labor, peasants, businessmen, landowners, military, and others—worked out compromises. The establishment of the PRN gave the Mexican Revolution a second wind.

Lázaro Cárdenas, chosen by Calles to be president in 1933, was a man with a mind of his own.

The Mexican Revolution

1876–1910	Porfirio Díaz, dictator of Mexico
1910	Francisco Madero calls for revolution
1911	Revolution breaks out; Madero is assassinated by Gen. Victoriano Huerta; U.S. troops occupy Veracruz
1914	Huerta overthrown; Venustiano Carranza becomes president
1911–20	Regional leaders: Emiliano Zapata in south, Pancho Villa in north
1916–17	U.S. troops pursue Villa in northern Mexico
1917	New Constitution proclaimed
1920	Carranza killed; Obregón becomes president; violence subsides
1928	National Revolutionary Party founded
1933	Lázaro Cárdenas elected president
1938	Cárdenas nationalizes oil industry

He came from a poor Indian family and always felt close to the common people. He constantly traveled to remote areas, spending time with farmers, workers, and other ordinary citizens and building up popular support. He brought peasants' and workers' organizations into the party, renamed it the Mexican Revolutionary Party (PRM), and removed the generals. Then he set to work implementing the reforms promised in the Constitution of 1917.

In short order, Cárdenas redistributed 44 million acres (17.6 million hectares) to peasant communes, twice as much land as had been distributed since the Revolution began. He closed church-run schools, replacing them with government teachers. He nationalized the railroads and numerous other businesses. Although his policies offended landowners and the Catholic Church, they made him the most popular president in twentieth-century Mexico.

Cárdenas's most dramatic move was the expropriation of foreign-owned oil companies. In the early 1920s, Mexico had been the world's leading producer of oil, but a handful of American and British companies exported almost all of it. The Mexican people received little benefit from their plentiful supplies of this natural re-

Revolutionary Art

Art is often somewhat political because it must appeal to the members of the elite who commission or purchase it. But in revolutionary times, political leaders see art as a means of serving the cause of revolution.

Sometimes the heavy hand of politics stifles creativity, resulting in clumsy propaganda pieces such as the works of socialist realism produced during the regimes of Stalin and Mao.

In other cases, a revolution inspires artists to produce works of great power and beauty that appeal to people who have no particular interest in the revolution itself. Diego Rivera's The Agitator *(1926) on p. 936 is such a work. It has aroused the admiration of critics and art lovers even in distant countries and long after the events that inspired it.*

Is the image in Rivera's painting about Mexicans? Is it about workers and farmers? Or is it about agitation and the spread of political ideas? What interest does this painting have other than as a historical document?

Which of these two works of art is aesthetically more appealing? Which one conveys a more powerful political message?

Social realism   This painting by Sergei Gerasimov is an example of the social realist style prevalent in the USSR under Stalin. It shows Lenin addressing a group of soldiers, sailors, and peasants at the Second Congress of Soviets. (Russian Museum, Lenigrad/Sovfoto)

source. In 1938, Cárdenas seized the foreign-owned oil industry, more as a matter of national pride than of economics. The oil companies expected the governments of the United States and Britain to come to their rescue, perhaps with military force, and they tried to punish Mexico by refusing to ship any Mexican oil overseas.

In an earlier day, such action by Mexico could easily have led to a punitive expedition from the United States. But U.S. president Franklin D. Roosevelt had replaced the traditional send-in-the-marines response with a Good Neighbor pol-

icy that emphasized respect for Latin American sovereignty. In the end, Mexico and the United States resolved the issue through negotiation.

When Cárdenas's term ended in 1940, Mexico, like India and China, was still a land of poor farmers with a small industrial base. The Revolution had brought great changes, however. The political system was free of both chaos and dictatorships. Land and other resources were no longer monopolized by a small group of wealthy people. The military was tamed, and the Catholic Church no longer controlled education. And the nationalization of oil had demonstrated Mexico's independence from foreign corporations and military intervention.

Nevertheless, the democratic promise of Francisco Madero's campaign remained unfulfilled. With the return of stability Mexico would prosper again, but this fragile prosperity would be threatened by growing population and an increasingly corrupt public administration.

CONCLUSION

The first half of the twentieth century witnessed many revolutionary upheavals around the world. Russia underwent a revolution in 1917. After World War II, revolutions and national independence movements occurred in Indochina, Cuba, and many parts of Africa. Events in China, India, and Mexico, however, were especially important, for two reasons. First, they involved half of the world's population. Second, by joining the rebellion of the poor with the ideas and methods of modern mass politics, they were the forerunners of revolutions elsewhere.

Mass participation in politics was often provoked by Western-educated leaders like Sun Yat-sen, Mahatma Gandhi, and Francisco Madero. But charismatic leaders with little formal education like Mao Zedong and Emiliano Zapata also moved people to act. The leaders who were most successful were the ones who appealed not only to the masses of peasants but also to urban workers, soldiers, and educated people. Mao, Gandhi, and Cárdenas were successful because what they had to say made sense to the poor and to the educated. The basis of their appeal was a nationalistic promise: if the people united to free themselves from foreign domination, then not only would the whole nation benefit politically, but all classes of people would gain economically as well.

This promise could not be fulfilled without a struggle. In India, revolution meant liberation from colonialism. The process could have been bloody, but because of Gandhi's philosophy of nonviolence and Britain's policy of gradual withdrawal, independence was achieved by mutual consent. By then, however, nationalism had stirred religious differences into a bloody ethnic conflict.

Mexico and China, unlike India, were formally independent in the twentieth century. In those two nations revolution and civil war went hand in hand, not because the old elites clung to power but because rival groups representing different social classes fought to fill the power vacuum that those elites left. All the rivals for power claimed to represent the nation against foreigners. The winners were the ones who most clearly stood up to foreign interests, whether the Japanese in China or the American oil companies in Mexico.

Through revolution, all three regions achieved their political aims: mass participation, less foreign interference, and the replacement of traditional or foreign rulers by nationalistic and modernizing elites. These political and social changes were perhaps necessary to improve the lives of ordinary people, but they certainly were not sufficient. In the end, China, India, and Mexico remained underdeveloped and poor because of the destruction of war and the growth of population. For them, the economic revolution, the advent of prosperity, lay in the future.

SUGGESTED READING

An important book on popular revolutions in developing countries is Eric Wolf, *Peasant Wars of the Twentieth Century* (1969). The emergence of nationalism is the subject of Benedict Anderson, *Imagined Communities: Reflection on the Origin and Spread of Nationalism*, rev. ed. (1981).

The classic overview of Africa under colonial rule is Melville Herskovits, *The Human Factor in Changing Africa* (1958). Two excellent general introductions are Roland Oliver and Anthony Atmore, *Africa Since 1800*, 4th ed. (1994), and A. E. Afigbo, E. A. Ayandele, R. J. Gavin, J. D. Omer-Cooper, and R. Palmer, *The Making of Modern Africa*, vol. 2, *The Twentieth Century* (1986).

More detailed and challenging are *UNESCO General History of Africa*, vol. 7, *Africa under Colonial Domination 1880–1935*, ed. A. Adu Boahen (1985), and vol. 8, *Africa since 1935*, ed. Ali Mazrui and C. Wondji (1993); *The Cambridge History of Africa*, vol. 7, *From 1905 to 1940*, ed. A. D. Roberts (1986), and vol. 8, *From c. 1940 to c. 1975*, ed. Michael Crowder (1984); and A. Adu Boahen, *African Perspectives on Colonialism* (1987). Outstanding novels about Africa in the colonial era include Chinua Achebe, *Arrow of God* (1964); Buchi Emecheta, *The Joys of Motherhood* (1980); and Peter Abraham, *Mine Boy* (1946).

In the large and fast-growing literature on twentieth-century China, two general introductions are especially useful: John K. Fairbank, *The Great Chinese Revolution, 1800–1985* (1986), and Jonathan Spence, *The Search for Modern China* (1990). On the warlord and Guomindang periods see Lucien Bianco, *Origins of the Chinese Revolution, 1915–1949* (1971). The Japanese invasion of China is the subject of James Hsiung and Steven Levine, eds., *China's Bitter Victory: The War with Japan, 1937–1945* (1992). Jung Chang, *Wild Swans: Three Daughters of China* (1991), is a fascinating account of women's experiences during the Chinese Revolution and the Mao era by the daughter of two Communist officials.

For a general introduction to Indian history see Sumit Sarkar, *Modern India, 1885–1947* (1983), and Percival

Spear, *India: A Modern History*, rev. ed. (1972). The Indian independence movement has received a great deal of attention. Judith M. Brown has written many books on Gandhi; her most recent is *Gandhi: Prisoner of Hope* (1989). *Gandhi's Truth: On the Origin of Militant Nonviolence* (1969) by noted psychoanalyst Erik Erikson is also recommended. Two collections of memoirs of the last decades of British rule are worth looking at: Charles Allen, ed. *Plain Tales of the Raj: Image of British India in the Twentieth Century* (1975), and Zareer Masani, ed., *Indian Tales of the Raj* (1988). The environment is discussed in M. Gadgil and R. Guha, *This Fissured Land: An Ecological History of India* (1993).

A fine general overview of modern Mexican history is Jan S. Bazant, *A Concise History of Mexico from Hidalgo to Cárdenas, 1805–1940* (1977). On the Mexican Revolution, two recent books are essential: Alan Knight, *The Mexican Revolution*, 2 vols. (1986), and John M. Hart, *Revolutionary Mexico: The Coming and Process of the Mexican Revolution* (1987). But see also two old classics by sympathetic Americans: Frank Tannenbaum, *Peace by Revolution: Mexico After 1910* (1933), and Robert E. Quirk, *The Mexican Revolution, 1914–1915* (1960). Mexico's most celebrated revolutionary is the subject of Manuel Machado, *Centaur of the North: Francisco Villa, the Mexican Revolution, and Northern Mexico* (1988). Mariano Azuela, *The Underdogs* (1988), is an interesting fictional account of this period.

PART EIGHT

The Perils and Promises of a Global Community, 1945 to the Present

For thirty years or more after World War II, historians, journalists, and many others, routinely used the term "postwar era" when referring to the times they were living in. The two world wars and the intervening global economic depression had firmly established the idea that in the twentieth century the world's societies were more closely interrelated than they ever had been before. Yet the notion of a "postwar era" in which all the peoples of the world could rejoice in the defeat of totalitarianism became increasingly hollow as the Cold War set in between the United States and the Soviet Union and more and more peoples became engrossed in national struggles for independence. With the end of the Cold War in 1991 the last of Europe's colonies gained their freedom, but by then much uncertainty had arisen about how the second

Technology

1952—First hydrogen bomb
1953—Structure of DNA identified
1956—First videotape recorder
1957—Sputnik space satellite
1959—First dry copier (xerography)
1967—First heart transplant
1969—U.S. astronaut Neil Armstrong first person on moon
1976—First personal computer

Environment

1962—Rachel Carson, *Silent Spring*
1974—OPEC oil-price increases begin
1980s–1990s—Burning of Amazon rain forest
1985, 1994—International whaling conventions
1986—Chernobyl nuclear disaster spreads contamination
1992—International treaty to limit chemicals causing ozone depletion
1996—Mexico City the world's largest city

United States
1945–1991—Cold War between United States and USSR
1962—Cuban missile crisis
1963—John F. Kennedy assassinated; Lyndon B. Johnson assumes the presidency, launches the "Great Society"
1970—United States expands Vietnam War by invading Cambodia
1974—Richard M. Nixon resigns presidency in wake of Watergate scandal
1981–1989—Presidency of Ronald Reagan

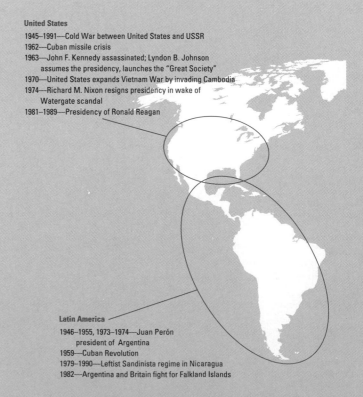

Latin America
1946–1955, 1973–1974—Juan Perón president of Argentina
1959—Cuban Revolution
1979–1990—Leftist Sandinista regime in Nicaragua
1982—Argentina and Britain fight for Falkland Islands

half of the twentieth century should be seen and what the world would be like in the next century.

In much of the world, freedom from European imperial domination challenged formerly colonized peoples to develop new political, social, and economic institutions. Each of these new nations saw the postwar period in terms of its own needs and aspirations. By contrast, western Europe, North America, and the bloc of states dominated by the USSR saw the entire world as a rivalry between two superpowers, the United States and the Soviet Union.

The domestic or regional concerns of the emerging nations and the global concerns of Cold War strategists in Washington and Moscow converged or conflicted in often bewildering ways. Throughout the entire period from 1945 to 1991, local struggles between communist and noncommunist forces repeatedly involved the two superpowers. Sometimes the superpowers were arms suppliers or political allies, as in eastern Europe and Iran at the end of World War II, or El Salvador and Nicaragua in the 1980s. Sometimes they were combatants. The Korean War (1950–1953) and the Vietnam War (1954–1975) engaged American troops and arms; the Soviet Union intervened

massively in Afghanistan in 1979. European powers waged other wars in hopes of averting the collapse of their empires. Newly independent states seeking to resolve problems with their neighbors, as in the case of Israel and the Arab states also waged war. In other instances, newly independent countries, that saw themselves as nonaligned states, sought economic or political benefits from both superpowers by leaning first toward one, then toward the other.

The collapse of the Soviet Union in 1991 triggered the last phase of decolonization. American and Soviet development of ever-more-destructive and expensive nuclear weapons and delivery systems taxed the American economy but drove the Soviet Union into bankruptcy. Distressed by economic disruption and declining standards of living, Soviet citizens vented their anger and frustration by rejecting their government. The non-Russian peoples of the Soviet republics of Lithuania, Estonia, and Latvia seceded from the USSR, followed by a dozen other constituent republics. These events marked the end of an era that, in retrospect, seems to be most accurately characterized not as the "postwar era" but as a time of Cold War and decolonization.

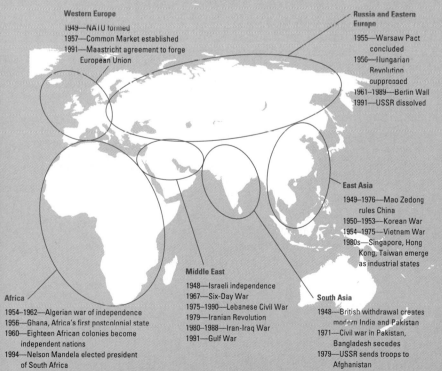

Western Europe

1949—NATO formed
1957—Common Market established
1991—Maastricht agreement to forge European Union

Russia and Eastern Europe

1955—Warsaw Pact concluded
1956—Hungarian Revolution suppressed
1961–1989—Berlin Wall
1991—USSR dissolved

East Asia

1949–1976—Mao Zedong rules China
1950–1953—Korean War
1954–1975—Vietnam War
1980s—Singapore, Hong Kong, Taiwan emerge as industrial states

Middle East

1948—Israeli independence
1967—Six-Day War
1975–1990—Lebanese Civil War
1979—Iranian Revolution
1980–1988—Iran-Iraq War
1991—Gulf War

South Asia

1948—British withdrawal creates modern India and Pakistan
1971—Civil war in Pakistan, Bangladesh secedes
1979—USSR sends troops to Afghanistan

Africa

1954–1962—Algerian war of independence
1956—Ghana, Africa's first postcolonial state
1960—Eighteen African colonies become independent nations
1994—Nelson Mandela elected president of South Africa

Society

1945—United Nations charter signed
1948—Universal Declaration of Human Rights
From 1959—Cuban Revolution inspires Latin American liberation movements
1960s—Resurgence of feminist movement in United States; Japan becomes industrial power
1964, 1965, 1968—U.S. civil rights legislation
1966–1969—Cultural Revolution in China
1968–1975—U.S. antiwar movement
1979—Islamic revolution in Iran
1991—Fall of USSR and eastern European communist regimes; end of apartheid in South Africa

Culture

1956—Elvis Presley becomes a star
1962—Vatican II council
From ca. 1975—Postmodernism in architecture
1981—MTV (Music Television)
1993—World Wide Web popularizes the Internet

Changes in technology and economic relations accompanied the political changes of the twentieth century. In the second half of the century, the limitations of time and space, the historic barriers to human interconnection, were almost entirely overcome. Supersonic speed remained the preserve of the military, but instantaneous communication became commonplace. New technologies eased international financial and business transactions and fostered the growth of transnational corporations.

In the relatively nonindustrialized parts of the world, population grew rapidly in all postwar decades, partly because public health improved and epidemic diseases were contained, and partly, perhaps, in response to the hope for a better future that new-found independence seemed to promise. Consequently, Latin America, Africa, South Asia, China, and parts of the Middle East faced serious problems in providing their people with food, housing, and work opportunities as millions left agricultural life and sought their livelihoods in rapidly growing cities. Technological advances in agriculture and control of reproduction helped countries cope with these problems. Some countries exported large numbers of workers to richer countries as well. But strains on society continued to grow in many regions, both domestically because of unemployment and poverty and internationally because of resentment against low-paid foreign workers, and the social customs they often brought with them.

In addition, various nonpolitical factors seemed increasingly to shape social and cultural life. According to some critics, international business interests, rooted in the United States and other industrialized nations, seemed to be coercing all the world's peoples into accepting a single cultural model. To substantiate their theory of Western cultural imperialism, they cited the rise and worldwide spread of Western popular culture through the media of motion pictures, recordings, broadcasting, and advertising. Other people—particularly in Islamic, Hindu, and Buddhist societies—rededicated themselves to renewing and energizing cultural and religious traditions that were not of Western origin.

Running parallel to this late-twentieth-century contest between Western cultural domination and the reassertion of other identities were forces that tended to draw the world together. Foremost among them was the United Nations. Though often inefficient in action the United Nations provided a forum for all the peoples of the world to voice their concerns. Human rights, gender equality, and the quest for peace were not exclusive United Nations concerns, but they found expression in United Nations activities and those of other international organizations.

But even while the world was edging closer to common standards in the areas of human rights and gender equality, the quest for peace among nations was proving to be frustrating. Most governments were unwilling to surrender sovereignty to international bodies, and new currents of unrest flowing from religious and ethnic identity were coursing around the world. At the same time, sophisticated news reporting through the electronic media was giving new impetus to the old political tool of terrorism, and the Cold War arms race was replaced by fears of smaller-scale nuclear threats, either from countries developing the means to build nuclear weapons or from states or terrorist organizations acquiring those weapons by theft or purchase.

How far will the earth's peoples go in accepting common values, cultural outlooks, and economic preferences? The centuries-long trend toward greater global interaction and interdependence accelerated during the twentieth century even as the number of independent nations multiplied several-fold through decolonization. But throughout history different peoples have repeatedly asserted their separate identities even when subjected to centuries of imperial control. Will human diversity finally succumb to the domination of economic forces? Or are the new assertions of difference in religious movements, struggles for ethnic autonomy, and distinctive adaptations of modern industrial life to local values and traditions better indicators of how the world will develop in the twenty-first century?

CHAPTER THIRTY-THREE

Decolonization and the Cold War, 1945–1991

Decolonization and Nation Building · The Cold War

Limits to Superpower Influence · The End of the Bipolar World

In 1946, in a speech at Fulton, Missouri, Great Britain's wartime leader Winston Churchill said: "From Stettin in the Baltic to Trieste in the Adriatic, an iron curtain has descended across the Continent. . . . I am convinced there is nothing they [the communists] so much admire as strength, and there is nothing for which they have less respect than weakness, especially military weakness."

Though less elegant in formulation than some of the speeches Churchill made in the darkest hours of World War II, the phrase "iron curtain" became a watchword for the Cold War between the United States and its allies—"running dogs of capitalism" in Soviet parlance—and the Soviet Union and its allies—"satellites" in American parlance. This psychological curtain of understanding and communication between the two sides took palpable form in 1961 when the communist government of the German Democratic Republic erected a wall in Berlin—as much to prevent its citizens from fleeing to the noncommunist western part of the city as to keep westerners from entering its territory.

Fittingly, the demolition of the Berlin Wall in 1989 and the subsequent reuniting of Germany symbolized the collapse of communism and the end of the Cold War. With the dissolution of the Union of Soviet Socialist Republics in 1991, the process was complete, and the world entered a new and uncertain era unexpectedly relieved of the constant fear of nuclear destruction and the suffocating burden of east-west rivalry.

The intensity of that rivalry sometimes obscured another postwar phenomenon, a development that changed the lives of millions of people. The western domination of Asia, Africa, and Latin America was largely ended, and the colonial empires of the New Imperialism (see Chapter 29) dismantled. The new generation of world leaders to head these states sometimes skillfully played Cold War antagonism to their own advantage. These moves simply formed the background to the real business, however: nation building. Many of these leaders sought unique ways to achieve their national goals without embracing either the communist or capitalist camp.

DECOLONIZATION AND NATION BUILDING

Whereas the losing countries in World War I—Germany, Austria-Hungary, and the Ottoman Empire—were stripped of colonies and torn apart to be reborn as new nations in the Balkans and the Middle East (see Chapter 30), it was primarily the winning side in World War II—Great Britain, France, the Netherlands, and Belgium—that ended up losing its colonies (see Map 33.1). However, this did not come about through a series of war-ending treaties or through the mechanism of a League of Nations.

Instead, each colony raised its demand for freedom and recognition, sometimes making that demand at the point of a bayonet. While each country's road to independence was separate, they shared a feeling of excitement and rebirth. Circumstances differed profoundly. In some Asian instances, where colonial rule was of long standing, the newly independent states found themselves in possession of viable industries, communications networks, and educational systems. In others, notably in Africa, decolonization gave birth to nations facing dire economic problems and internal sources of disunity based on language or ethnicity. And in Latin America, where political independence had been achieved long before, the quest was for freedom from foreign economic domination, particularly from the United States. Despite these differences, a kinship arose among the new and old nations of Latin America, Africa, and Asia. As the North Americans, Europeans, and Chinese settled into the exhausting deadlock of the Cold War, visions of independence and national growth captivated the rest of the world.

New Nations in South and Southeast Asia

Britain's partition of India in 1947 into the independent states of India and Pakistan has been described in Chapter 32. The two states were strikingly dissimilar. Muslim Pakistan—half centered on the valley of the Indus River in the west and half in Bengal in the east—defined itself according to religion and quickly fell under the control of military leaders. India, a secular republic led by Prime Minister Jawaharlal Nehru, was much larger and inherited most of the considerable industrial and educational resources the British had developed, along with the larger share of trained civil servants and military officers. Ninety percent of its population was Hindu and most of the rest Muslim.

Adding to the tensions of independence (see Chapter 32) was the decision of the Hindu ruler of the northwestern state of Jammu and Kashmir to join India without consulting his overwhelmingly Muslim subjects. War between India and Pakistan over Kashmir broke out in 1947 and ended with an uneasy truce, only to resume briefly in 1965. Though Kashmir remained a flashpoint of patriotic feeling, the two countries managed to avoid open warfare even as India developed a nuclear weapons capacity in 1974 and Pakistan followed suit in the 1990s.

Despite recurrent predictions that multilingual India might break up into a number of linguistically homogeneous states, most Indians recognized that unity benefited everyone; and the country pursued a generally democratic and socialist line of development. Pakistan, on the other hand, did break up when its Bengali-speaking eastern section seceded to become the independent country of Bangladesh in 1971. Their shared political heritage notwithstanding, these South Asian countries grew steadily apart after independence following markedly different

From Colonies to Independent Nations

1945	United Nations Charter signed
1946–1954	French fight to hold Indochina
1948	British withdrawal creates modern India and Pakistan; Israeli independence, first Israeli-Arab war
1954–1962	Algerian war of independence
1956	Suez War, Nasser at peak of power
From 1959	Cuban Revolution inspires Latin American liberation movements
1991	End of apartheid in South Africa; constituent republics of USSR gain independence
1994	Nelson Mandela elected president of South Africa

paths, economically, politically, religiously, and socially.

As the Japanese had supported anti-British Indian nationalists, so they encouraged the dreams of some anticolonialists in the countries they occupied in Southeast Asia. Other nationalists, particularly those belonging to communist groups, saw the Japanese as an imperialist enemy; and the harsh character of Japanese occupation eventually alienated the mass of the population. Nevertheless, the defeats the Japanese inflicted on British, French, and Dutch colonial armies at the beginning of World War II (see Chapter 31) set a stirring example throughout the region of an Asian people standing up to European colonizers.

In the Dutch East Indies, a man named simply Sukarno cooperated with the Japanese in hopes that the Dutch, who had dominated the region economically since the seventeenth century, would never return. Though they had suffered badly from wartime Nazi occupation and enjoyed little international support, the Dutch after the war fought Sukarno's independence movement. Dutch withdrawal was finally negotiated in 1949, and Sukarno went on to become the dictator of his poor, populous, sprawling island nation. He ruled until 1965 when a military coup

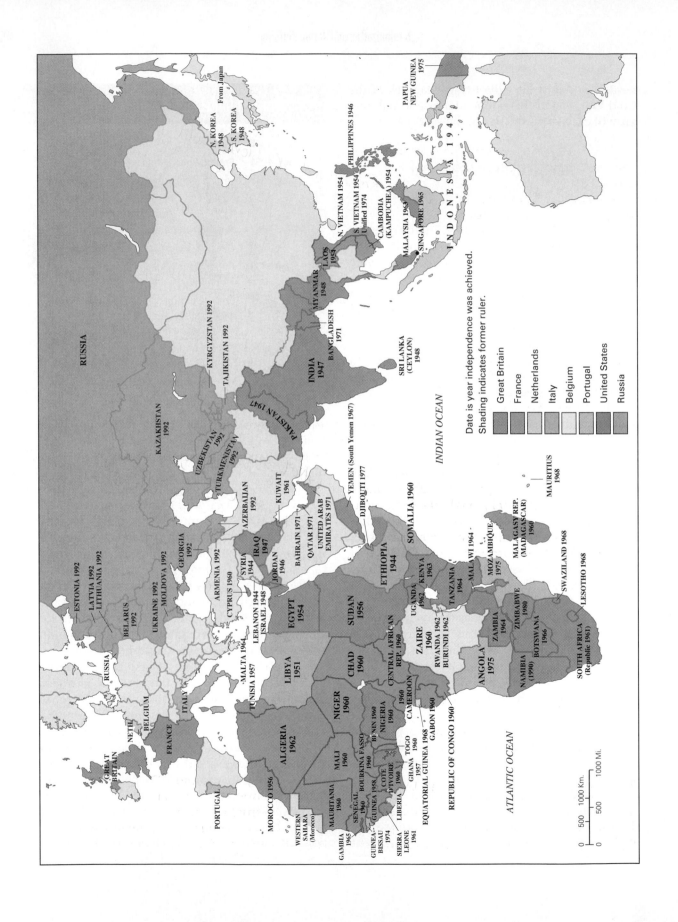

ousted him and brutally eliminated Indonesia's powerful communist party.

Elsewhere in the region, nationalist movements won independence as well. Britain granted independence to Burma (now Myanmar) in 1948 and established the Malay Federation that same year. (Singapore, once a member of the federation, became an independent city-state itself in 1950.) The United States met its public commitment to grant independence to the Philippines after the war as well.

In all these cases, communist insurgents plagued the departing colonial powers and the newly formed governments. But the most important postwar communist movement arose in the part of Southeast Asia known as French Indochina. There Ho Chi Minh, who had spent several years in France during World War I, played the pivotal role. In France, Ho had joined the communist party. After training in Moscow, he returned to Vietnam to found the Indochina Communist Party in 1930. He and his supporters took refuge in China during World War II.

At war's end, the new French government was determined to retain its prewar colonial possessions. Ho Chi Minh's nationalist coalition, now called the Viet Minh, fought the French with help from the People's Republic of China (see Chapter 32). After a brutal struggle, the French stronghold of Dienbienphu fell in 1954, marking the doom of France's colonial enterprise. Ho's Viet Minh government took over in the north while a noncommunist nationalist government ruled the south. Fighting between the two sections eventually became a major conflict in the Cold War, as we shall see.

French soldiers on patrol in Algeria The Algerian war was one of the most savage struggles for independence in the era of decolonization. The French held out a more secular, Western-style view of life but did not hesitate to intrude into homes and populated residential areas in search of their enemies. At independence in 1961, most Algerian leaders spoke French more readily than Arabic. (Marc Riboud/Magnum Photos, Inc.)

The Struggle for Independence in Africa

The postwar French government was as determined to hold Algeria as it was Vietnam. Since

Map 33.1 Decolonization Numerous countries that gained independence after World War II in the Caribbean, in South and Central America, and in the Pacific are not shown. Note that independence came a decade or so earlier in South and Southeast Asia than in Africa, and that disintegration of the Soviet empire into independent states occurred some three decades later.

invading the country in 1830, France had followed policies very different from those of the British in India. French settlement had been strongly encouraged and Algeria had eventually been declared an actual part of France rather than a colony. By the mid-1950s, 10 percent of the Algerian population was French, and the country's economy had become strongly oriented toward France. Though Islam, the religion of the other 90 percent, prohibited drinking alcohol, Algerian vineyards produced immense quantities of wine for French tables. Algerian oil and gas fields had become the mainstay of the French petroleum industry.

A revolt that broke out in 1954 was pursued with great brutality by both sides. The Algerian revolutionary organization, the Front de Libération National (FLN), was supported by Egypt and other Arab countries on the principle that all Arab peoples should be able to choose their own governments. However, French colonists considered the country rightfully theirs and swore to fight to the bitter end. When Algeria finally won independence in 1962, a flood of angry colonists returned to France, causing severe political unrest. Their departure also undermined the Algerian economy since very few Arabs had received technical training or acquired management experience. Despite the bitter feelings left by the war, Algeria retained close, and seemingly indissoluble, economic ties to France, and Algerians increasingly fled unemployment at home by emigrating to France and taking low-level jobs.

None of the several wars for independence in sub-Saharan Africa matched the Algerian struggle in scale. But even without war, most of the new states suffered from many problems. Boundaries established in the nineteenth century by competition among imperial powers did not coincide with natural geographic or ethnic divisions. Neglect of education under colonial rule left too few educated Africans to run government ministries and staff newly established schools without European assistance. In some places, overdependence on export crops like cacao or peanuts made economies hostage to international price fluctuations. Transportation facilities designed by colonial overlords to bring export crops or minerals to seaports rather than to create national road and railroad networks made for poor communications within and between countries. And population increases, resulting in part from colonial improvements in medical care and public health, foreshadowed worsening poverty and unemployment in the absence of the massive investment needed for education, industrialization, and agricultural expansion.

In the 1950s and 1960s, enthusiasm for liberation overcame worries about these material problems. Some of the politicians who led the nationalist movements had devoted their lives to ridding their homelands of foreign occupation. Their skills as government administrators frequently proved unequal to the problems that faced them, however. An example is Kwame Nkrumah, who in 1957 became prime minister of Ghana (formerly the Gold Coast), the first British colony in Africa to achieve independence. Only a few hundred Ghanaian children of his generation graduated each year from the seven-year elementary schools, and he was one of only a handful who made it through teacher training college. After graduation he spent a decade reading philosophy and theology in the United States, learning the notions of black pride and independence then being propounded by W. E. B. Du Bois and Marcus Garvey.

After a brief stay in Britain—where he joined Kenyan nationalist Jomo Kenyatta to found an organization devoted to African freedom—Nkrumah returned in 1947 to the Gold Coast to work for independence. The time was propitious. Great Britain was exhausted by war and unwilling to squander money and blood to hold restive colonies that were not particularly valuable in terms of resources. Independent Ghana thus came into being without war or protracted bloodshed. After becoming president in 1960, however, Nkrumah made a grander impression internationally than he did at home; and in 1966 a group of army officers overthrew him in a coup.

Kenyatta faced a more difficult road in Kenya, where the presence of a substantial number of European coffee planters enhanced Britain's desire to retain control. A movement known as the Mau Mau, formed mostly of the Kikuyu people, began its activities in 1952. When violence between settlers and Mau Mau fighters escalated, British troops hunted down the Mau Mau leaders and resettled the Kikuyu. The British charged Kenyatta with being a Mau Mau leader and held him in prison, and then in internal exile, during a declared state of emergency. In 1961, however, they released him. Negotiations with the British to write a constitution for an independent Kenya followed, and in 1964 he was elected the first president of the Kenyan republic. He proved to be an effective, if autocratic, ruler, and Kenya benefited from greater stability and prosperity than Ghana.

In contrast with the African nationalists in the British colonies and their counterparts in Algeria, the African leadership of the sub-Saharan French colonies were reluctant to call for independence. They visualized change in terms of the promises made by the Free French movement of General Charles de Gaulle at a conference in Brazzaville, French Equatorial Africa, in 1944. Acknowledging the value of his African territorial base, his many African troops, and the food supplied by African farmers, de Gaulle promised the colonial leaders who attended the conference—none of them African—more democratic government and broader suffrage, though not representation in the French National Assembly. He also promised to abolish forced labor and the *indigénat*, which permitted French administrators to imprison any African subject without charge for two weeks; to expand education, in French only, down to the village level; to improve health services; and to open more administrative positions, though not the top ones, to Africans.

Though the word independence was never mentioned, the politics of postwar colonial self-government led in that direction. Most of the new group of African politicians seeking election in the colonies of French West Africa were trained as civil servants. They had typically served in a number of different colonies according to the French policy of rotation of jobs and thus had a broad outlook. They realized that while some colonies had good economic prospects—such as Ivory Coast with coffee and cacao exports, fishing, and hardwood forests—others, such as land-locked, desert Niger, did not. Furthermore, they recognized the importance of French public investment in the region—a billion dollars between 1947 and 1956—and their own dependence on civil service salaries, which in places totaled 60 percent of government expenditures.

As the Malagasy politician Philibert Tsirinana said in a press conference in 1958: "When I let my heart talk, I am a partisan of total and immediate independence [for Madagascar]; when I make my reason speak, I realize that it is impossible." Charles de Gaulle, returned to power in France in 1958, at the height of the Algerian war, spoke to the issue of rationality when he said: "One cannot conceive of both an independent territory and a France which continues to aid it."

Ultimately, however, the heart prevailed everywhere. Guinea, under the dynamic leadership of Sékou Touré, led the way in 1958. Some leaders, like Senegal's Léopold Senghor, advocated a West African federation. Others, like Félix Houphouet-Boigny of the Ivory Coast, favored each country going its own way. The latter view predominated, and by the time Nigeria, the most populous West African state, achieved independence from Great Britain in 1960, the leaders of the former French colonies of Ivory Coast (now Cote d'Ivoire), Niger, Dahomey (now Benin), Senegal, and Upper Volta (now Burkina Faso) could attend the celebrations as independent heads of state.

Though decolonization in Africa presented innumerable scenes of people of European descent struggling with indigenous Africans to retain personal privileges, control of resources, and political power, race conflict became particularly severe in the temperate southern part of the continent. In 1970, European settlers in the British colony of Southern Rhodesia proclaimed independence for themselves and fought tenaciously against indigenous African guerrilla forces and an international economic boycott. Ten years later they conceded the hopelessness of their position and acceded to majority African rule. The new government changed the country's name, which had honored the memory of the British imperialist Cecil Rhodes, to Zimbabwe, the name of a great stone city built by indigenous Africans long before the arrival of European settlers.

In the meantime, African guerrillas struggled against Portuguese rule in Angola and Mozambique, prompting the Portuguese army to revolt against the home government in 1974. The new Portuguese government granted independence to its African colonies the following year. This left only South Africa and neighboring Southwest Africa, which it had governed since World War I, in the hands of ruling European minorities. The change had been swift; Africa had entered the postwar period almost entirely under European control.

After World War II, a succession of South African governments had constructed a state and society based on a policy of racial separation, or *apartheid*. Indians and people of mixed parentage, approximately 12 percent of the population, were classified as "nonwhite" along with the 74 percent of the population who were indigenous Africans. These groups were subjected to strict limitations on place of residence, right to travel, and access to jobs and public facilities. "Homelands" somewhat similar to Amerindian reservations in the United States were created in comparatively undesirable parts of the country. The largest and most productive tracts of land were held by the 14 percent of the population descended from Dutch and English settlers.

Rising in opposition was the African National Congress (ANC), formed in 1912. After police fired on demonstrators in the African town of Sharpeville in 1960, a lawyer named Nelson Mandela organized ANC guerrilla resistance to the government. Mandela was sentenced to life in prison in 1964, but he was released in 1990. Recently elected president F. W. de Klerk had decided, under pressure from international boycotts and isolation as well as worsening internal disorder, to dismantle the *apartheid* system. Negotiations with the de Klerk government outlined a new political process that resulted, in 1994, in Mandela being elected president with 63 percent of the vote in South Africa's first multiracial election. This was the final step in the process of indigenous Africans regaining control of their countries. (Southwest Africa, under United Nations guidance, made the transition to majority rule in 1990, as the country of Namibia.)

South African leaders F. W. de Klerk and Nelson Mandela De Klerk became president in 1989 when his predecessor P. W. Botha resigned. Botha had relaxed some apartheid restrictions but maintained a policy of suppressing African political activism. De Klerk freed Nelson Mandela from prison and opened negotiations with Mandela's African National Congress. Under a new constitution, Mandela became president in 1994, fifty years after joining the ANC. (S. Silva/Sygma)

The Quest for Economic Freedom in Latin America

In Latin America, independence from European rule had been achieved long before, but American and European economic domination had only increased (see Chapter 29). Chile's copper, Cuba's sugar, Colombia's coffee, and Guatemala's bananas were all controlled from abroad, just as the largest resort hotel in Havana was owned by the American organized crime figure Meyer Lansky and the communications networks of several countries were in the hands of ITT (International Telephone and Telegraph Company).

An army colonel turned politician, Argentina's Juan Perón set a dramatic, though ultimately unsuccessful, example by declaring economic independence. His initial support came from conservative forces in the army and the Catholic Church; but with the help of his popular and dynamic second wife Eva Duarte Perón, he built support among trade unionists that carried him to the presidency by a huge majority in 1946. He called his program the "third position" between communism and capitalism. It combined populism, nationalization of some foreign enterprises, a welfare program for the working class, and authoritarian controls on society, thus leading some critics to call him a fascist and others a socialist. His popularity waned with the fall of international prices for wheat and beef, Argentina's main exports, in the early 1950s. The weakened economy gave conservative forces a chance, and his slide was hastened both by the death of his wife in 1952 and his excommunication from the church in 1955 for his anticlerical policies. Later that year, a military coup forced him into exile, but Peronism remained an electoral force for decades to come.

Perón was an example of the personalist, authoritarian ruler, strong of speech and decisive of action, that had been known in Latin America for a century or more (see Chapter 25). Typically, in a speech on May 1, 1944, he declared: "I believe that programs, as revolutions, should not be announced, but simply carried out." But few of these personalist leaders came close to Perón's popularity or skill in building a working class party and thus freeing himself from wealthy and foreign interests. More frequently, these conservative forces prevailed after a period of personalist rule.

The fate of Jacobo Arbenz Guzmán of Guatemala was more typical of Latin American leaders who tried to confront the power of foreign economic interests. Elected in 1951, Arbenz continued the policies of agrarian and labor reform pursued since 1944 by his predecessor, Juan José Arévalo. His expropriation of large estates angered large landowners, the United Fruit Company in particular. This U.S. corporation not only dominated the banana exports but also held vast tracts of land in reserve for possible future use. Reacting to reports that Arbenz was becoming friendly toward communism, the U.S. Central Intelligence Agency (CIA), in one of its first major overseas operations, prompted a takeover by the Guatemalan military in 1954. The action did more than remove Arbenz from the scene; it also condemned Guatemala to decades of governmental instability and growing violence between leftist and rightist elements in society.

The rise of Fidel Castro's revolutionary regime in Cuba wedded personalist traditions with Cold War politics. American domination of the Cuban economy prior to 1960 was overwhelming. U.S. companies owned 40 percent of raw sugar production, 23 percent of nonsugar industry, 90 percent of telephone and electrical services, and 50 percent of public service railways. Moreover, many American-owned industries depended on factories in the United States for essential supplies. The needs of the U.S. economy largely determined Cuban foreign trade. A 1934 treaty granted Cuban sugar preferential treatment in the American market in return for U.S. manufacturers gaining access to the Cuban market. As a consequence, by 1956 sugar accounted for 80 percent of exports and 25 percent of national income. But U.S. demand dictated that only 39 percent of the land owned by the sugar companies was under production. Similarly, immense deposits of nickel went untapped because the U.S. government, which owned them, considered them only a reserve.

Fidel Castro entering Havana in 1959   A charismatic orator, Castro was initially extremely popular with most Cubans and even with many Americans. His acceptance of Soviet aid and adoption of communist economic planning led to U.S. naval blockade and economic sanctions and eventually produced a severe decline in the Cuban economy. Nevertheless, the Cuban example inspired many other revolutionaries in Central and South America. (Burt Glinn/Magnum Photos, Inc.)

Profits went north to the United States or to a small class of wealthy Cubans, many of whom, like the owners of the Bacardi rum company, were of foreign origin. The economic growth rate between 1951 and 1958 was 1.4 percent per year, less than the rate of population increase; and a quarter of the working population was unemployed for the better part of every year. Cuba's ruler during that period was Fulgencio Batista, who had originally come to power in 1933 and asserted dictatorial control in 1952. Batista became a symbol of corruption, repression, and foreign economic domination.

The forces that compelled Batista to flee the country in 1959 never numbered more than about 2,000 armed rebels. His fall resulted more from the growing public belief in denunciations of his regime broadcast by clandestine radio and a lack of firm support from any strong popular institutions than it did from military pressure. His 30,000-man army was intact at the time of his flight.

Fidel Castro, a lawyer; his brother Raul; and the main theorist of communist revolution in Latin America, Ernesto "Che" Guevara, provided the new regime with charismatic leadership for a time. Even in the United States, where Castro gave a number of speeches in the wake of his victory, large crowds cheered him as a heroic champion against dictatorship and American economic imperialism. Within a year, his government redistributed land, lowered urban rents, and raised wages, effectively transferring 15 percent of the national income from rich to poor. Within twenty-two months it had seized almost all U.S. property in Cuba and most Cuban corporations. This resulted in a blockade by the United States, a flight of bourgeois and technically trained Cubans, a drop in investment, and the beginning of chronic food shortages.

Though communists had been part of the anti-Batista coalition from the start, little evidence supports the view that Castro undertook his rebellion on the basis of communist theories or to install a communist government. However, international politics of the time were increasingly influenced by the east-west rivalry of the Cold War. Soon Castro turned to the Soviet Union for economic aid. In doing so, he was essentially committing his nation to economic stagnation and dependence on a foreign power as damaging as the previous relationship with the United States.

In April 1961, some 1,500 Cuban exiles, whom the CIA had trained for a year in Guatemala, landed at the Bay of Pigs in an effort to overthrow Castro. The Cuban army defeated the attempted invasion in a matter of days, partly because the new American president, John F. Kennedy, decided not to supply all the air support called for in the plan, which had originated in the Eisenhower administration. The Bay of Pigs fiasco not only tarnished the reputation of the United States and the CIA but also prompted Castro to declare that he and his revolution were and always had been Marxist-Leninist.

Though the dream of a thriving, egalitarian communist state subsequently attracted downtrodden people in many parts of Latin America, Castro seemed unable to make the dream come true for his own people. Cuba encouraged revolutionaries in El Salvador, Nicaragua, and elsewhere, but conservative forces backed by the United States fought them to a stalemate, often at a dreadful cost in innocent human life.

Challenges of Nation Building

Decolonization occurred on a vast scale. Fifty-one nations signed the Charter of the United Nations (to be discussed in Chapter 35) when the victorious allies created that organization in the closing months of 1945. During its first decade, twenty-five new members joined, a third of them upon gaining independence. During the next decade, forty-six new members were admitted, virtually all of them former colonial territories, as were most of the sixty-some nations that joined after 1976.

Each of these hundred-plus nations had to organize and institute a form of government. Comparatively few were able to do so without experiencing coups, rewritten constitutions, or regional rebellions. This recapitulated the experience of European peoples that freed themselves of monarchical rule (such as France, Germany, and Italy; see Chapter 28) and of the Western Hemisphere colonies (such as the United States, Mexico, Venezuela, and Argentina) that gained independence in the eighteenth and nineteenth centuries (see Chapter 25; also see Voices and Visions: The Falklands War). Leaders do not always agree on the form that independence should take. In the absence of an established constitutional tradition, they frequently try to assert their own vision by force.

Most of these new nations, while trying to establish political stability, also faced severe economic challenges. These included foreign ownership and operation of key resources, the need to build an effective infrastructure, and the twin desires to reduce dependence on capricious world commodity markets and to conserve domestic wealth by reducing imports of manufactured goods.

Since achievement of political and economic goals depended on educated and skilled personnel, education was the third common concern of the newly emerging nations. Addressing that concern was not merely a matter of building and staffing schools. In some countries, leaders had to decide which language to teach and how to inculcate a sense of national unity in students

The Falkland War

The imperialist countries of Europe adjusted with difficulty to being second-class powers after losing their colonies. Despite much-reduced military forces, they still prided themselves, somewhat unrealistically, on their importance in the global east-west struggle. In 1982, Argentina invaded the cold, lightly populated Falkland Islands (which they called the Malvinas) in the south Atlantic. They claimed sovereignty, but Great Britain had long considered the islands a British colony. Britain dispatched an invasion force and retook the islands within six weeks. Compared with the many colonial wars Britain fought in the nineteenth century, this was a minor conflict. But the effort of projecting power so far from home taxed British military resources, once supreme on the seas, to the utmost.

Margaret Thatcher, Britain's Conservative Party prime minister at the time, saw the successful expedition not just as a defense of British rights, but as an assertion of Britain's continuing importance in global military affairs.

The significance of the Falklands War was enormous, both for Britain's self-confidence and for our standing in the world. Since the Suez fiasco in 1956, British foreign policy had been one long retreat. The tacit assumption made by British and foreign governments alike was that our world role was doomed steadily to diminish. We had come to be seen by both friends and enemies as a nation which lacked the will and the capability to defend its interests in peace, let alone in war. Victory in the Falklands changed that. Everywhere I went after the war, Britain's name meant something more than it had. The war also had real importance in relations between East and West: years later I was told by a Russian general that the Soviets had been firmly convinced that we would not fight for the Falklands, and that if we did fight we would lose. We proved them wrong on both counts, and they did not forget the fact.

How might one of the superpowers have handled the crisis if they claimed sovereignty over the Falklands and found their claim contested by a minor power such as Argentina?

How might the crisis have been affected if the Falklands had been in a crucial strategic location, for example, off the southern coast of China, instead of the south Atlantic?

Source: Margaret Thatcher, *The Downing Street Years* (New York: HarperCollins, 1993), pp. 173–174.

from different—sometimes historically antagonistic—ethnic, religious, and linguistic groups. Another problem was how to provide satisfying jobs for new graduates. These graduates often had very high expectations by virtue of their education.

Only rarely were the new nations able to surmount these three hurdles. Even the most successful economically and educationally—such as Singapore, South Korea, and Taiwan (see Chapter 34)—suffered from tendencies toward authoritarian rule. Similarly, Costa Rica, with a remarkably stable parliamentary regime from 1949 onward and a literacy rate of 90 percent, remained heavily dependent on world prices for agricultural commodities and on the importation of manufactured goods.

THE COLD WAR

The wartime alliance between the United States, Great Britain, and the USSR had been an uneasy one (see Chapter 31). Fear of the working class, which had fueled the rise of Nazism, was not confined to Germany. Political and economic leaders committed to democratic choice, free markets, and untrammeled capital investment had loathed socialism in its several forms for more than a century. When unionists fought to organize, anarchists contrived political disruption through bombings and assassinations, and the Bolsheviks established a revolutionary state in Russia, conservatives in Europe and America felt threatened. After World War II, communist insurgencies in China and elsewhere seemed to confirm the threat of worldwide worker revolution.

In the postwar years the west perceived the Soviet Union not only as a nerve center of world revolution but also as a military power capable of launching a war as destructive and terrible as the one recently ended. Soviet leaders, particularly after the United States and the countries of western Europe established a military alliance in 1949, felt themselves surrounded by hostile forces. Having lost 20 million people in the war with Germany and, in their view, been denied credit for the leading role they took in defeating the Nazis, the Soviets felt cheated of the dominant role in world affairs they had earned at great cost. As events unfolded, both sides saw their worst fears confirmed. It is far from clear, however, whether the Cold War evolved as the product of those fears or whether a different and more trusting cast of minds among the principal nations' leaders could have averted a world-threatening arms race and a generation of destructive competition worldwide (see Environment and Technology: Rocketry and Space Exploration).

The Onset of the Cold War

For Germany, Austria, and Japan, relief from the rain of Allied bombs was accompanied by foreign military occupation and the installation of new governments subordinate to the occupiers' wishes. For the Soviet Union, war's end offered opportunities to resume the Bolsheviks' self-defined mission to assist proletarian movements struggling for power. The USSR had particular success in eastern Europe, where military occupation facilitated communist victories. Western leaders saw the rapid emergence of communist regimes in Poland, Czechoslovakia, Hungary, Bulgaria, Romania, Yugoslavia, and Albania as Stalin taking advantage of agreements reached at Yalta (February 1945) and Potsdam (July–August 1945) on the postwar political order.

Both winners and losers concentrated first on reconstruction. What money and resources re-

The Major Events of the Cold War	
1948–1949	Berlin airlift
1949	NATO formed
1950–1953	Korean War
1952	First hydrogen bomb
1953	Stalin dies
1954–1975	Vietnam War
1955	Warsaw Pact concluded
1956	Hungarian revolution suppressed
1961	Berlin Wall built
1962	Cuban Missile crisis
1976	Mao Zedong dies
1979	USSR sends troops to Afghanistan
1989	Berlin Wall destroyed
1991	USSR dissolved

mained were mustered to clear rubble, repair infrastructure, rebuild factories, and rehouse the homeless. Western Europe and Japan slowly entered into a period of economic renewal that eventually rebuilt their economies, changed their landscapes, and enabled them to compete with the United States in world markets. The Soviet Union—and the new governments in eastern Europe that followed Soviet bidding—pressed industrial reconstruction and production to the maximum to compete with the United States. In the process, they denied most consumer goods to their citizens and prolonged housing shortages caused by the war.

For the United States, the fateful transition from viewing the Soviet Union as an ally against Germany to seeing it as a worldwide enemy took two years to accomplish. In the waning days of World War II, the United States had seemed quite amenable to the Soviet desire to gain free access to the Bosphorus and Dardanelles straits that, under Turkish control, restricted Soviet naval movement from the Black Sea to the Mediterranean. Two years later, in July 1947, the Truman Doctrine offered military aid to both Turkey and Greece to help them resist Soviet military pressure and subversion. This initiative quickly grew into a full-scale American effort to

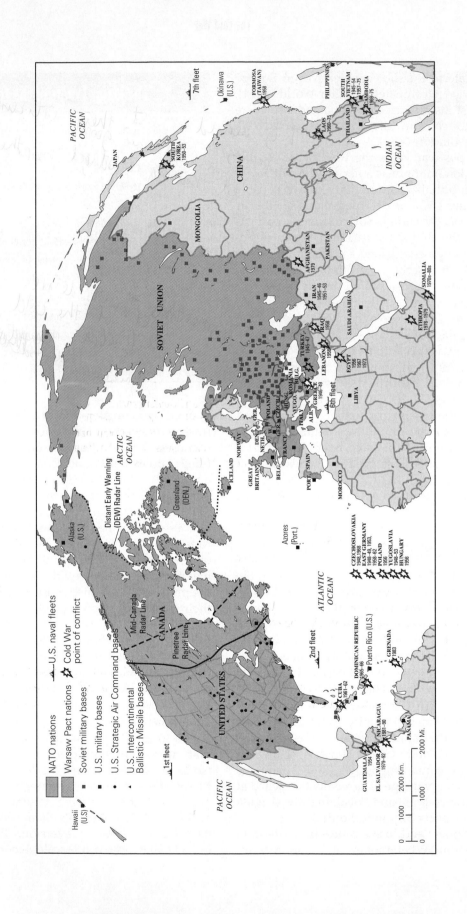

Cold War confrontation in 1959 Vice-president Richard M. Nixon and Soviet premier Nikita Khrushchev had a heated exchange of views during Nixon's visit to a Moscow trade fair. Two years before, the Soviet Union had launched the world's first space satellite. Nixon had achieved political prominence as a ferocious opponent of communism, and Khrushchev had chilled American hearts with his prediction, "We will bury you!" (Seymour Raskin/Magnum Photos, Inc.)

spur European recovery. The Marshall Plan, named after U.S. Secretary of State George C. Marshall, dispersed over $12.5 billion to friendly European countries between 1948 and 1951. In 1949, the formation of the North Atlantic Treaty Organization (NATO) committed the United States, Canada, and several countries of western Europe to joint preparations for a war against the USSR. In 1951, Greece and Turkey were admitted to NATO. The Soviet counterpart of NATO, the Warsaw Pact, did not come into being until 1955 as a response to the decision of the western powers to allow West Germany to rearm within the context of NATO (see Map 33.2).

Map 33.2 Cold War Confrontation A polar projection is shown on this map because Soviet and America strategists planned to attack one another by missile in the polar region, hence the Canadian-American radar lines. Military installations along the southern border of the Soviet Union were directed primarily at China.

The much-feared and long-prepared-for third great war in Europe never occurred. The Soviet Union tested western resolve in 1948–1949 by blockading the areas of Berlin occupied by British, French, and American forces, which were surrounded by Soviet-controlled East Germany. An airlift of food and fuel defeated the blockade. In 1961 the East German government accentuated the country's political division by building the Berlin Wall. The west tested the east, in turn, by encouraging a rift between Stalin and Yugoslavia, led by the wartime communist resistance leader Josip Broz Tito. Western aid and encouragement resulted in Yugoslavia signing a defensive treaty with Greece and Turkey (but not with NATO) and not joining the Warsaw Pact alliance. Stalin, in the meantime, died in 1953. Three years later, after a period of political infighting in Moscow, he was denounced for fostering a cult of personality by Nikita Khrushchev, the new leader of the USSR.

Rocketry and Space Exploration

A dvances in military technology arising from the Cold War arms race had significant impact in civilian life. Rocketry provides an excellent example. Robert Goddard (1882–1945), an American physicist, was the foremost rocket pioneer in the interwar period, building the first liquid-fueled rocket, developing automatic steering devices, and proving that rockets could work efficiently in the near vacuum of the upper atmosphere.

Practical application of his ideas did not come until the waning months of World War II when Nazi Germany launched V2 rocket bombs against England. These weapons were ballistic missiles, that is, they were powered on take-off and then, once their fuel was exhausted, glided along a parabolic arc to the target. The V2 was not very accurate, but American and Soviet strategists realized by war's end that it was the weapon of the future, particularly if it could be designed to carry an atomic bomb, which had enough power to compensate for inaccuracy.

The contest to build larger and more accurate ballistic missiles with ever more sophisticated nuclear warheads lasted throughout the Cold War. The United States benefited from the skills of German V2 designers whom they recruited to the American side. Soviet rocket designs tended to be less sophisticated in controls but were often equipped with more powerful engines.

Using rockets designed for the military, the Soviet Union placed a small satellite into orbit around the earth in October 1957; the United States responded with its own satellite three months later. The space race was on, a contest in which accomplishments in space exploration were understood to imply equivalent achievements in military missile technology. The Saturn V rocket that carried Americans Neil A. Armstrong and Edwin E. "Buzz" Aldrin, Jr. to the first human landing on the moon on July 20, 1969, was 363 feet (110.6 meters) tall, more than 7 times the size of the V2.

Saturn V rocket on launch pad This three-stage rocket was the main vehicle in American missions to the moon. Three sets of engines and fuel tanks stacked on top of one another and fired consecutively account for most of the Saturn's size, which roughly equals that of the Statue of Liberty with a World War II V-2 rocket perched on its torch. (National Aeronautics and Space Administration)

It was apparent that the communist parties that vied for elections in western Europe would never be allowed to take power. Similarly, Soviet power set clear limits on how far any eastern European country might stray from Soviet domination. In 1956, an anti-Soviet revolt in Hungary was crushed by Soviet troops; some 190,000 refugees fled to the west. That same year, Poland saw student and worker riots and mass demonstrations. No troops entered the country, however, as the government stayed within the Soviet orbit. Czechoslovakia repeated Hungary's fate in 1968. The west was a passive onlooker in all these instances. It had no recourse but to acknowledge that the USSR had the right to intervene in the domestic affairs of any Soviet bloc nation whenever it wished.

A more explosive crisis erupted in Korea. At war's end, a division of responsibility based on expedience left Soviet troops in control north of the 38° latitude line and American troops in control in the south. When no agreement could be reached on holding elections throughout the country, communist North Korea and noncommunist South Korea became independent states in 1948. Two years later, the former invaded the latter. The United Nations Security Council, acting in the absence of the Soviet delegation, voted to condemn the invasion and called on UN members to come to the defense of South Korea. The ensuing war lasted until 1953. The United States was the primary ally of South Korea. The People's Republic of China (see Chapter 32) supported North Korea.

The conflict in Korea was the first major war of the Cold War era. It remained limited to the Korean peninsula because the United States feared that launching attacks into China might prompt China's ally, the USSR, to retaliate and bring about the dreaded World War III. Americans and South Koreans advanced from a small toehold in the south all the way to the North Korean–Chinese border. Then, after China sent troops across the border, the North Koreans and Chinese pushed them back, and the fighting settled into a static war in the mountains along the 38° parallel. The two sides eventually agreed to a truce along that line, but the ceasefire lines remained fortified, no peace treaty was concluded, and the possibility of renewed warfare between the two Koreas continued well past the end of the Cold War.

The Race for Nuclear Supremacy

Just as fear of nuclear warfare affected strategic decisions in the Korean War, so the existence of these massively destructive weapons underlay all aspects of Cold War confrontation. The American devastation of Hiroshima and Nagasaki with atomic weapons (see Chapter 31) had ushered in a new era in the history of war. Nuclear weapons fed into a logic of total war that was already reaching a peak in Nazi genocide and terror bombing and in massive allied air raids on large cities. After the Soviet Union exploded its first nuclear device in 1949, fears of a world holocaust grew rampant, becoming even more dire when the United States exploded a far more powerful weapon, the hydrogen bomb, in 1952, and the Soviet Union followed suit less than a year later. Fear of theft of nuclear secrets by Soviet spies, both real and suspected, contributed to a sense of paranoia in the United States. The conviction that the nuclear superpowers would be willing to use their terrible weapons if their vital interests were threatened spread despair around the world.

In 1954, President Dwight D. Eisenhower warned the Soviet leaders against attacking western Europe. The U.S. response, he said, would reduce the USSR to "a smoking, radiating ruin at the end of two hours." A few years later, the new Soviet leader Nikita Khrushchev offered an equally stark promise: "We will bury you." Rhetoric aside, both men—and their successors—had the capacity to deliver upon these threats, and everyone in the world knew that all-out war with nuclear weapons would produce the greatest global devastation in human history.

Worst fears seemed about to be realized in 1962 when the Soviet Union deployed nuclear missiles to Cuba as a response to the American installation of similar missiles in Turkey. The world held its breath. Confronted by unyielding diplomatic pressure and military threats from President John F. Kennedy, Khrushchev backed off and pulled the missiles from Cuba. Subsequently the Americans removed their missiles from Turkey. As frightening as the crisis was, the fact that leaders actually accepted tactical defeat rather than launching an attack gave reason to hope that nuclear weapons might be contained.

The following thirty years saw rapid increases in the number, means of delivery, and destructive force of nuclear weapons. The bomb dropped on Hiroshima, equal in strength to 12,500 tons of TNT, had destroyed an entire city. By the 1960s, explosive yields were measured in megatons (millions of tons of TNT), and it became possible to load a single missile with several weapons of this scale, each of which could be targeted to different sites. By placing these missiles on submarines, a major component of American nuclear forces, the weapon seemingly could not be defended against. By 1990 the arsenals of eight nuclear powers held more than 23,000 nuclear warheads.

Paradoxically, the same period saw progress in arms limitation. In 1963, Great Britain, the United States, and the USSR agreed to ban the testing of nuclear weapons in the atmosphere, in space, and under water, thus reducing the environmental danger of radioactive fallout. In 1968, the United States and the USSR jointly proposed a world treaty against further proliferation of nuclear weapons. It was signed by 137 countries, but a few refused to do so. Not until 1972, however, did the two superpowers recognize the futility of squandering their wealth on ever-larger missile forces. That year they began the arduous and extremely slow process of negotiating weapons limits. As the Cold War ebbed and the Soviet Union faced financial exhaustion, they even agreed to reduce nuclear arms.

Despite bouts of rhetorical saber-rattling between Soviet and American leaders, the threat of nuclear war that haunted the world for the forty-five years of the Cold War also forced a measure of restraint on the superpowers. Since fighting each other directly risked escalation to the level of nuclear exchange, they carefully avoided crises that might provoke such confrontations. Even when arming third parties to do their fighting by proxy, they set limits on how far such fighting could go. Some of these proxy combatants, however, understood the limitations of the superpowers well enough to manipulate them for their own purposes.

LIMITS TO SUPERPOWER INFLUENCE

Though no one doubted the dominating role of the superpower rivalry in world affairs, the newly independent states had concerns that were primarily domestic and regional. Their challenge was to find a way to pursue their ends within the framework of the bi-polar structure of the Cold War—and possibly to make profitable use of that rivalry. Where nationalist forces sought to assert political or economic independence, Cold War antagonists provided arms and political support, even when the nationalist goals were quite different from those of the superpowers. For other nations, the ruinously expensive superpower arms race opened opportunities to expand their industries and export capabilities.

In short, the superpowers dominated the world, but did not control it. And as time progressed, they even dominated it less and less. Yet the worldwide scope of their rivalry impeded the emergence of any other global political structure so that the end of the Cold War left the world in a state of confusion.

Exploiting Superpower Rivalries

As one of the most successful leaders of the decolonization movement, Indonesia's President Sukarno was an appropriate figure to host a meeting in 1955 of twenty-nine African and Asian countries. The conferees proclaimed solidarity among all peoples fighting against colonial rule. The conference marked the beginning of an effort by the many new, poor, mostly non-European nations emerging from colonialism to gain more weight in world affairs by banding together. The terms *nonaligned nations* and *Third World*, which became commonplace in the following years, signaled the determination of these countries to define their collective position within the context of, but uninvolved with, the Cold War. If the west, led by the United States, and the eastern bloc, led by the Soviet Union, represented two worlds locked in mortal struggle, the Third World consisted of everyone else.

Leaders of the so-called Third World countries preferred the label *nonaligned*, which signified freedom from membership on either side. However, many leaders in the west noted that the Soviet Union supported national liberation movements and that the group included communist countries such as China and Yugoslavia. As a result, they decided not to take the term nonaligned seriously. In a polarized world, they saw Sukarno, Tito, Nehru, Nkrumah, and Egypt's Gamal Abd al-Nasir as stalking horses for a communist takeover of the world. This may also have been the view of some Soviet leaders since the Soviet Union was quick to offer some of these countries military and financial aid.

From the point of view of the movement's leaders, nonalignment was primarily a device to extract money and support from one or both superpowers. Flirting with the Soviets or the communist Chinese could gain a country cheap or free weapons and training and barter agreements that offered an alternative to selling agricultural or mineral products in western-dominated world markets. The same flirtation might also prompt the United States and its allies to proffer grants and loans, cheap or free grain from America's agricultural surplus, and investment in industry and infrastructure.

When played skillfully, this balancing game allowed countries to teeter one way and then the other and gain from both sides in the process. For example, Egypt under Nasir, who led a military coup against the monarchy in 1952, and his successor Anwar al-Sadat gained substantial benefits in this fashion. The United States offered to build a dam at Aswan, on the Nile River, to increase Egypt's electrical generating and irrigation capacity. When Egypt turned to the Soviets for arms, the United States reneged on the dam project, but the Soviet Union picked it up and brought it to conclusion. In the meantime, Israel, Great Britain, and France conspired to invade Egypt in 1956. Their objective was to overthrow Nasir, regain the Suez Canal, which he had recently nationalized, and secure Israel from any Egyptian threat. Though the invasion succeeded militarily, the United States and the Soviet Union both put pressure on the invaders to withdraw, thus saving Nasir's government. Then, in 1972, Sadat evicted his Soviet military advisors but used his Soviet weapons a year later to attack Israel. In the aftermath of defeat in that war, he announced his utmost faith in the power of the United States to solve Egypt's political and economic problems, a strategy that earned Egypt about $3 billion per year in U.S. aid after it made peace with Israel in 1979.

Numerous other countries adopted similar balancing strategies. If one sympathized with the Soviet view of the world, as India often seemed to do under Nehru, a regional rival, such as Pakistan, could be expected to court the United States. In Ethiopia, a leftist military coup in 1974 led to a switch of allegiances from the United States to the Soviet Union. As a result, neighboring Somalia, until then the recipient of Soviet aid, turned to the United States for support. Sometimes the two superpowers backed rival factions within the same country. Such was the case in the former Belgian Congo (after 1971 the country of Zaïre), wracked by factional and ethnic fighting for years after formal independence was granted in 1960. In all of these cases, the underlying dilemma of local leaders was how to develop their economies and assert or preserve their national interests. Manipulating the superpowers was simply a means toward those ends, implying very little about true ideological orientations.

U.S. Defeat in Vietnam

President Eisenhower and his foreign policy advisors had debated long and hard in 1954 whether to send aid to the French in their failing effort to sustain colonial rule in Vietnam. They decided against it, correctly perceiving that the days of the European colonial empires were numbered. After winning independence, however, communist North Vietnam supported a communist guerrilla movement—the Viet Cong—against the noncommunist government of South Vietnam. At issue was the ideological and economic orientation of an independent Vietnam.

When John F. Kennedy succeeded to the presidency seven years later, he and his advisors decided to support the South Vietnamese government of President Ngo Dinh Diem. Though they realized that this government was corrupt and unpopular, they feared that a communist victory would encourage similar movements throughout Southeast Asia and alter the balance of power in the Cold War. Kennedy steadily increased the number of American military advisors from 685 to almost 16,000 while se-

cretly encouraging the overthrow and execution of Diem in hopes of a more popular and honest government coming to power.

Lyndon Johnson, who became president after Kennedy's assassination in 1963, gained support from Congress for an unlimited expansion of American military deployment after an apparent North Vietnamese attack on two U.S. destroyers in the Gulf of Tonkin. By the end of 1966, 365,000 American troops were engaged in the Vietnam War. Nothing the Americans tried, however, succeeded in stopping the Viet Cong guerrillas and their North Vietnamese allies. Diem's successors turned out to be just as corrupt and unpopular, and the heroic nationalist image of North Vietnam's Ho Chi Minh evoked strong sympathies among many South Vietnamese.

Scene of destruction in Vietnam   Images like this, resulting from American bombing raids, helped galvanize popular opposition to the war in the United States and around the world. The Viet Cong and North Vietnamese countered American air superiority by effective guerrilla tactics, popular support by many South Vietnamese, and routing supplies through neighboring Laos and Cambodia. American attacks on these neighbors further intensified the anti-war movement. (J. A. Paulvony/Sygma)

In 1973, a treaty between North Vietnam and the United States ended American involvement in the war and promised future elections. Two years later, in violation of the treaty, Viet Cong and North Vietnamese troops overran the South Vietnamese army and captured the southern capital of Saigon, renaming it Ho Chi Minh City. The two halves of Vietnam were reunited in a single state ruled from the north.

The war was bloody and traumatic. The Vietnamese were hit by over a million casualties. The 58,000 deaths suffered by the United States seared the national consciousness ensuring that the U.S. would not easily be drawn into another shooting war. The war effort had given rise to serious economic problems at home because President Johnson refused to curtail his ambitious program of welfare measures. Moreover, the conflict had excited a domestic antiwar movement that was instrumental in convincing the government that the people did not support the war. At the same time, many in the military and their civilian supporters were angry about restrictions placed on the conduct of operations. These restrictions were designed to prevent China from entering the war and possibly touching off a nuclear confrontation, but many people saw them as depriving the armed forces of a chance to win the war.

The searing experience of the Vietnam War prompted the United States to look to proxy combatants subsequently. The Soviet Union had already adopted this practice since revolutionary communist movements in dozens of countries only asked for money and arms. In the 1970s and 1980s, Cubans fought for the newly independent and Soviet-supported government of Angola against a rival nationalist movement backed by South Africa and the United States. In El Salvador, American-equipped government forces fought a prolonged Soviet-backed rebellion, while next door in Nicaragua the situation was reversed—the Soviets supported the leftist Sandinista government and the United States armed right-wing guerrillas known as Contras.

In these and other cases, the animosities and political ambitions that led to war were largely local or regional in nature, quite removed from the primary struggle between the United States and the Soviet Union. But the wars were fought within the overarching geopolitical framework of the two superpowers' jockeying for position. What was at stake for the superpowers might be basing rights for air forces, navies, and missiles; governmental participation or exclusion of a local communist party; or access to oil or other mineral resources. What was at stake for the actual participants, on the other hand, was more often national survival or control over the national government.

Japan and China

No one took better advantage of the opportunities presented by the superpowers' preoccupation than did Japan and China. By the end of the Cold War, the Soviet Union had fallen to pieces and the United States was weary and uncertain of its role in the world. Japan and China, however, were poised to become major world forces in the post Cold War era.

Japan, which signed a peace treaty with most of its former enemies in 1951, regained independence from American occupation the following year. Renouncing militarism and its imperialist past (see Chapter 28), Japan remained on the sidelines, concerned only with domestic and economic affairs, throughout the Korean War. Its new constitution, written under American supervision in 1946, prohibited any military beyond a limited self-defense force and banned the deployment of Japanese troops abroad.

Firmly committed to peace, the Japanese turned their talents and energies to rebuilding industries and engaging in world commerce. Peace treaties with countries in Southeast Asia included reparations payable in the form of goods and services, thus reintroducing Japan to that region as a force for economic development rather than as a military occupier. Nevertheless, bitterness over the oppression of the wartime occupying forces remained strong, and Japan had to move slowly in developing new regional markets for its manufactured goods.

The emergence of Japan as a worldwide economic power will be discussed in Chapter 34. The point to be made here is that the Cold War, by isolating Japan and excluding it from most world political issues, provided an exceptionally favorable environment for it to develop its economic strength.

By contrast, China was deeply involved in, though not controlled by, Cold War politics. When the communist party won its war with the nationalists in 1949 and established the People's Republic of China (PRC) (see Chapter 32), its main ally and source of arms was unquestionably the Soviet Union. By 1956, however, the PRC and the USSR were beginning to diverge politically, partly in reaction to the Soviet rejection of Stalinism and partly because of China's reluctance to be cast forever in the role of student. Mao Zedong had his own notions of communism focusing strongly on the peasantry, who were ignored by the Soviets in favor of the industrial proletariat.

In 1958 Mao inaugurated the Great Leap Forward, a policy designed to vault China into the ranks of world industrial powers by maximizing utilization of labor in small-scale, village-level industries. The policy failed because the diversion of labor reduced food production and the small industries overproduced inferior goods. This failure was compounded by the withdrawal of Soviet aid and technical advisors in 1960. Furthermore, the conversion of rural cooperatives into communes disrupted traditional patterns of family life. Nevertheless, the Great Leap Forward demonstrated the willingness of the Chinese government to carry out massive economic and social projects of its own devising.

At the age of seventy-three, in 1966, Mao Zedong instituted another radical nationwide program, the Cultural Revolution. He ordered a mass mobilization of Chinese youth into Red Guard units. His goal was to kindle revolutionary fervor in a new generation that had never known the hardship and self-sacrifice of the party's founding fathers. He also wished to ward off the stagnation and bureaucratization he saw in the Soviet Union. Red Guard units criticized and purged teachers, party officials, and intellectuals for "bourgeois values" but suffered themselves from factionalism. As social upheaval increased and industrial production fell, Mao called on the army to control the Red Guards, but also to adopt their revolutionary goals.

Internal party conflict continued until 1971 when Mao admitted that some aspects of the Cultural Revolution had gotten out of hand. Meanwhile, the continuing policy of small-scale industrialization finally resulted in records being set for both agriculture and industry. The last years of the Cultural Revolution were dominated by radicals led by Mao's wife Jiang Qing, who focused on restrictions on artistic and intellectual activity. This repressive phase lasted until Mao's death in 1976, after which the radicals were imprisoned and a more pragmatic Chinese leadership emerged.

In the meantime, the rift between the PRC and the USSR had opened so wide that President Richard Nixon, by reputation a staunch anticommunist, put out secret diplomatic feelers to revive relations. In 1971, the United States dropped objections to the PRC joining the United Nations and taking up China's permanent seat on that body's Security Council. This necessitated the expulsion from the UN of the Chinese nationalist government based on the island of Taiwan, which had persistently claimed to be the only legal Chinese authority. The following year, Nixon visited Beijing and in later years American-Chinese relations continued to improve steadily. The violent military suppression of prodemocracy student demonstrators in Beijing's Tiananmen Square in 1989, followed by other incidents of human rights abuses, gave rise to strong pressures in the United States to cool relations with China. But the opening up of the world's largest country, with well over a billion people, to foreign trade and economic development offered such phenomenal prospects for American business that no permanent rupture took place in Chinese-American relations.

Arab-Israeli Conflict and the Politics of Oil

One arena of seemingly unending regional conflict illustrates the inability of the superpowers to control dangerous international disputes. Independence had come gradually to the Arab countries of the Middle East. Britain granted Syria and Lebanon independence after World War II. Other Arab countries—Iraq, Egypt, Jordan—enjoyed nominal independence but were actually under indirect British control until the 1950s. Military coups overthrew King Faruq of Egypt in 1952 and King Faysal II of Iraq in 1958. King Husain of Jordan dismissed his British military commander in 1956 in response to the Suez crisis, but his poor desert country long remained dependent on British, and later American, financial aid.

Overshadowing all Arab politics, however, was the struggle with Israel. British policy on Palestine between the wars oscillated between sentiment favoring Zionist Jews—who emigrated to Palestine, encouraged by the Balfour Declaration (see Chapter 30)—and sentiment for the indigenous Palestinian Arabs—who felt themselves being pushed aside and suspected that the Zionists were aiming at an independent state. These pressures increased after the Nazis came to power in 1933. As more and more Jews sought a safe haven from persecution, Arabs felt more and more threatened by mass immigration. Arabs unleashed a guerrilla uprising against the British in 1936, and Jewish groups turned to militant tactics a few years later as well. Occasionally, Arabs and Jews bloodily confronted each other in riots or killings, making it clear that peaceful coexistence in Palestine would be difficult or impossible to achieve.

After the war, under intense pressure to resettle European Jewish refugees, Britain conceded that it saw no way of resolving the dilemma and turned the problem over to the United Nations. In November 1947, the UN General Assembly voted in favor of partitioning Palestine into two states, one Jewish and one Arab. The Jewish community made plans for declaring independence; the Palestinians, having lost most of their leadership during the earlier guerrilla war, reacted in horror and took up arms. When Israel declared its independence in May 1948, neighboring Arab countries sent armies to help the Palestinians crush the newborn state.

Israel prevailed on all fronts. Some 700,000 Palestinians became refugees either by fleeing the battle zones or being forced out by the Israeli army. They found shelter in United Nations refugee camps in Jordan, Syria, Lebanon, and the Gaza Strip, a bit of coastal land on the Egyptian-Israeli border. The right of these refugees to return home became a focal point in Arab politics. In 1967, Israel responded to threatening military moves by Egypt's Nasir by preemptively attacking Egyptian and Syrian airbases. In six days, Israel won a smashing victory. When Jordan entered the war, Israel won complete control of Jerusalem, which it had previously split with Jordan, and the West Bank, the part of Palestine west of the Jordan River. Acquiring all of Jerusalem satisfied a deep Jewish longing to return to their holiest city, but Palestinians still regarded it as their destined capital, and Muslims in many countries protested Israeli control of the Dome of the Rock, a revered Islamic shrine located there. Israel also occupied the Gaza Strip, the strategic Golan Heights in southern Syria, and the entire Sinai peninsula (see Map 33.3). These acquisitions resulted in a new wave of Palestinian refugees.

The rival claims to Palestine continued to plague Middle Eastern politics. Palestinian resistance groups joined together in the Palestine Liberation Organization (PLO), headed by Yasir Arafat. The PLO waged guerrilla war against Israel, frequently engaging in acts of terrorism. The militarized Israelis were able to blunt or absorb these attacks and launch counterstrikes that also involved assassinations and bombings. This standoff lasted until 1993 when Israel and the PLO reached an agreement in principle that granted the Palestinians on the West Bank and in the Gaza Strip relief from military occupation and a measure of autonomy.

Though the United States proved a firm friend of Israel, and the Soviet Union armed the Arab states throughout much of this period, neither superpower saw the struggle between Zionism and Palestinian nationalism as a vital concern. The involvement of oil changed their view of conflict in that region.

The phenomenal concentration of oil wealth in the Persian Gulf states—Iran, Iraq, Kuwait, Saudi Arabia, Qatar, Bahrain, and the United Arab Emirates—was not fully realized until after World War II. Demand for oil rose sharply after the war, particularly in the United States where automobile ownership became almost universal and trucks hauled an ever-increasing amount of

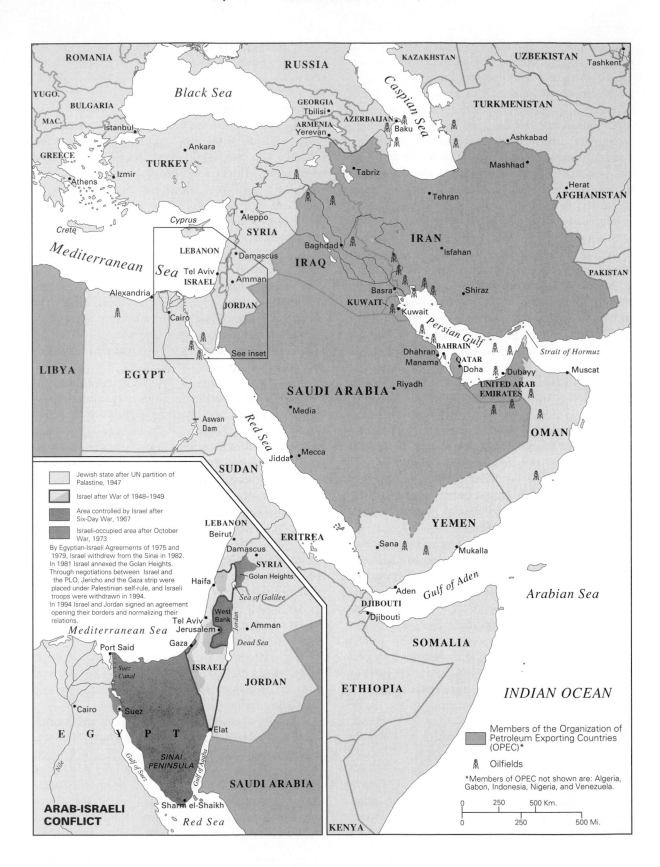

ROMANIA

YUGO.

BULGARIA

MAC.

GREECE

Black Sea

RUSSIA

KAZAKHSTAN

UZBEKISTAN

Tashkent

Istanbul

Ankara

TURKEY

Izmir

Athens

Crete

Cyprus

Mediterranean

Sea

Aleppo

SYRIA

LEBANON

Damascus

Tel Aviv

ISRAEL

Amman

JORDAN

Alexandria

Cairo

See inset

GEORGIA

Tbilisi

AZERBAIJAN

ARMENIA

Yerevan

Baku

Caspian Sea

TURKMENISTAN

Ashkabad

Mashhad

Herat

AFGHANISTAN

Tabriz

Tehran

IRAN

Isfahan

Baghdad

IRAQ

Basra

KUWAIT

Kuwait

Shiraz

PAKISTAN

Persian Gulf

Strait of Hormuz

Dhahran

BAHRAIN

Manama

QATAR

Doha

Dubayy

Muscat

LIBYA

EGYPT

Aswan Dam

Red Sea

SUDAN

Media

Jidda

Mecca

SAUDI ARABIA

Riyadh

UNITED ARAB EMIRATES

OMAN

YEMEN

Sana

Mukalla

Aden

Gulf of Aden

Arabian Sea

DJIBOUTI

Djibouti

SOMALIA

ETHIOPIA

INDIAN OCEAN

KENYA

Inset (ARAB-ISRAELI CONFLICT):

Jewish state after UN partition of
Palestine, 1947

Israel after War of 1948–1949

Area controlled by Israel after
Six-Day War, 1967

Israeli-occupied area after October
War, 1973

By Egyptian-Israeli Agreements of 1975 and
1979, Israel withdrew from the Sinai in 1982.
In 1981 Israel annexed the Golan Heights.
Through negotiations between Israel and
the PLO, Jericho and the Gaza strip were
placed under Palestinian self-rule, and Israeli
troops were withdrawn in 1994.
In 1994 Israel and Jordan signed an agreement
opening their borders and normalizing their
relations.

LEBANON

Beirut

Damascus

SYRIA

Golan Heights

Haifa

Sea of Galilee

ERITREA

Mediterranean Sea

Tel Aviv

Jerusalem

West Bank

Amman

Dead Sea

Jordan

Gaza

Port Said

Suez Canal

Cairo

Suez

ISRAEL

JORDAN

E   G   Y   P   T

Nile

Gulf of Suez

Gulf of Aqaba

Elat

SINAI PENINSULA

SAUDI ARABIA

Sharm el-Shaikh

Red Sea

**ARAB-ISRAELI
CONFLICT**

Members of the Organization of
Petroleum Exporting Countries
(OPEC)*

Oilfields

*Members of OPEC not shown are: Algeria,
Gabon, Indonesia, Nigeria, and Venezuela.

0   250   500 Km.

0   250   500 Mi.

freight. The recovery of European and Japanese industry added to the demand for oil.

As a world oversupply of oil diminished in the face of rising demand, the oil-producing states used political pressure and threats of nationalization during the 1960s to gain greater shares of ownership and profits from the foreign oil companies that developed their oil fields. In 1960 they formed the Organization of Petroleum Exporting Countries (OPEC), including some members from outside the Middle East, to express their collective interest in higher revenues.

Oil politics and the Arab-Israeli conflict intersected in October 1973. A surprise Egyptian attack across the Suez Canal breached the Israeli defenses in the occupied Sinai and threw the Israelis into temporary disarray. Within days the war turned in Israel's favor and an Egyptian army was trapped at the canal's southern end. The United States then arranged a ceasefire and disengagement of forces. But before that could happen, the Arab oil-producing countries voted to embargo oil shipments to the United States and the Netherlands as punishment for their support of Israel.

This use of oil as an economic weapon had little immediate impact, but its implications profoundly disturbed the worldwide oil industry. Prices rose—along with feelings of insecurity. In 1974 OPEC responded to the turmoil in the oil market by quadrupling prices. Prices continued to rise for a decade, during which time hundreds of billions of dollars flowed into the treasuries of the oil-producing countries (see Chapter 34). The political outcome of the decade-long crisis was deeper and deeper American commitment to the stability of the oil-producing states and increasing anxiety about the Soviet Union somehow gaining access to the region. The United States thus pursued an inconsistent policy of political and military support for Arab oil producers

Map 33.3 Middle East Oil and the Arab-Israeli Conflict Oil resources were controlled by private European and American companies until the 1960s when most countries, guided by OPEC, negotiated agreements for sharing control, leading eventually to national ownership. This set the stage for the use of oil as a weapon in the Arab-Israeli war of 1973 and for the succeeding oil price increases.

along with a commitment to guarantee the survival of Israel, the Arabs' enemy.

Iran and Afghanistan

While the Arab-Israel conflict and the oil crisis concerned and perplexed the superpowers, the prospect of direct military involvement or confrontation remained remote. When unexpected crises developed in Iran and Afghanistan, however, significant strategic issues were more directly involved because these countries adjoined Soviet territory, thus making military intervention more likely. With post–Vietnam War caution, the United States reacted to the crises with restraint. The Soviet Union took a bolder but ultimately disastrous course.

The Iranian Revolution of 1979 proved enormously frustrating to the United States. Mohammad Reza Pahlavi had succeeded his father as Shah of Iran at the outbreak of World War II. In 1953, covert intervention by the American CIA had helped him retain his throne in the face of a movement to usurp royal power and nationalize the Anglo-Iranian Oil Company. Thereafter, the shah enjoyed special favor in American eyes even when he finally nationalized oil. The United States encouraged him to spend the wealth he gained from the OPEC price increases on equipping the Iranian army with the most advanced American weaponry.

Resentment against the Pahlavi family's autocracy, particularly in some Shi'ite Muslim circles, dated from the 1925 seizure of power by the shah's father. The shah's dependence on the United States stimulated further opposition. In the 1970s, the ballooning wealth of the elite families around the throne and inefficiency, malfeasance, and corruption in efforts to improve the lot of the masses swelled resentment into mass opposition.

Ayatollah Ruhollah Khomeini, a Shi'ite philosopher-cleric who had spent most of his eighty-plus years in religious and academic pursuits, became the voice and symbolic center of the opposition. Massive street demonstrations and crippling strikes forced the shah to flee the country the following year. Under the Islamic

Ayatollah Khomeini returns to Iran   Khomeini's return from Paris, where he had inspired a revolution from exile, quickly followed Mohammed Reza Shah's flight in 1979. Immensely popular, the octogenarian religious philosopher tried to weld various revolutionary factions into an effective government. When President Jimmy Carter allowed the Shah to come to the U.S. for medical treatment, Khomeini and most Iranians became convinced that the United States was opposed to their revolution. (Dejean/Sygma)

Republic of Iran that replaced the monarchy, Ayatollah Khomeini was supreme arbiter of disputes and guarantor of religious legitimacy, overseeing a parliamentary regime based on European models but embodying religious control of legislation and public morals. Elections were held, but the process was not open to all; monarchists, communists, and other groups opposed to the idea of an Islamic Republic were barred from running. Clerics with little training for government emerged in many of the highest posts, and stringent measures were taken to combat Western styles and culture. Universities were temporarily closed and their faculties purged of secularists and monarchists. Women were compelled to wear modest Islamic garments outside the house, and semi-official vigilante committees policed public morals and cast a pall over entertainment and social life.

Though the United States under President Jimmy Carter had criticized the shah's repres-

sion, the rise of this Islamic Republic was a blow to American power and prestige. Not only was the new regime religiously doctrinaire, anti-Israeli, and anti-American—Khomeini saw the United States as a "Great Satan" opposed to Islam—but in its early years it fostered similar Islamic revolutionary movements in other countries. Moreover, when radicals seized the U.S. embassy in Tehran and held 52 diplomats hostage for 444 days, Americans felt humiliated at their inability to do anything, particularly after the failure of a military rescue attempt.

In the fall of 1980, shortly after negotiations for the release of the hostages began, Saddam Husain, the ruler of neighboring Iraq, invaded Iran to topple the Islamic Republic. His own dictatorial rule rested on a secular, Arab nationalist philosophy and long-standing friendship with the Soviet Union. He feared that Iran's revolutionary fervor would infect his country's Shi'ite majority. The war pitted American weapons in the hands of the Iranians against Soviet weapons in the hands of the Iraqis, but the superpowers avoided overt involvement during eight years of bloodshed. Covertly, however, the United States sent arms to Iran, hoping to gain the release of other American hostages held by radical Islamic groups in Lebanon. When this came to light in 1986, the resulting political scandal intensified American hostility toward Iran. Now openly tilting toward Iraq, the Americans sent their navy to the Persian Gulf ostensibly to protect nonbelligerent shipping. The move forced Iran to accept a ceasefire in 1989.

While the United States faced anguish and frustration in Iran, the Soviet Union got involved in problems of a more serious nature in neighboring Afghanistan. Since World War II, the Soviet Union had succeeded in staying out of shooting wars by using proxies. But in 1978, the Soviet Union sent its army to Afghanistan to support a fledgling communist regime against a hodgepodge of local, religiously inspired guerrilla bands that had taken control of much of the countryside.

With the United States, Saudi Arabia, and Pakistan paying, equipping, and training the Afghan rebels, the Soviet Union found itself in the same kind of unwinnable war the United States had stumbled into in Vietnam. Unable to justify the continuing drain on manpower, morale, and economic resources and facing widespread domestic discontent over the war, Soviet leaders finally withdrew the troops in 1989. The Afghan communists managed to hold on for another three years, but eventually the rebel groups took control of the entire country—only to fight among themselves over who should rule.

THE END OF THE BIPOLAR WORLD

Under President Ronald Reagan, elected in 1978, and the Soviet Union's General Secretary Leonid Brezhnev, the rhetoric of the Cold War remained intense. Massive U.S. investment in armaments, including a space-based missile protection system that never became operational, marked a new and extremely expensive stage in the arms race that had been going on continuously since 1945. Ultimately, the challenge to the inefficient Soviet economy proved too much. Obsolete industrial plants and techniques and a system of centralized planning that stifled initiative and responsiveness to market demand added up to a declining standard of living. Government functionaries and communist party favorites received special privileges, including permission to shop in stores that stocked western goods, but the average citizen faced long lines for meager food supplies and scarce consumer goods. Soviet citizens compared their lot with the free and prosperous life of the west—depicted in the increasingly accessible western media. Western tourists became accustomed to people offering to buy their clothes.

Despite the increasing unpopularity of the prolonged war in Afghanistan and growing discontent, Brezhnev refused to modify his rigid and unsuccessful policies. But he was unable to contain an underground current of protest. Novelist Alexander Solzhenitzyn castigated the Soviet system, and particularly the Stalinist prison camps, in a series of novels. He won a Nobel Prize in literature but was charged with treason and expelled from the country in 1974. Physicist Andrei Sakharov and his wife Yelena Bonner protested the nuclear arms race and human rights violations and were condemned to banishment within the country. Numerous Jewish dissidents spoke out against anti-Semitism. Self-published underground writings circulated widely despite government efforts to suppress them.

By the time Mikhail Gorbachev took up the reins of government in 1985 after two short-lived successors to Brezhnev, war weariness, economic decay, and vocal protest had reached critical levels. Casting aside Brezhnev's hard line, Gorbachev imaginatively inaugurated major reforms in an attempt to stave off total collapse. He instituted a policy of openness (*glasnost*) that permitted opinions critical of the government and the party to be aired. At the same time, he struggled to address long-suppressed economic problems by moving away from central state planning toward a free enterprise economic system, a process he called *perestroika* ("restructuring"). In 1989, he abandoned the war in Afghanistan.

Events in eastern Europe played an important role in forcing change upon the Soviet Union. Protests by Polish shipyard workers in the city of Gdansk led to the formation of a labor union called Solidarity that soon enrolled 9 million members. The Polish Catholic church, strengthened by the elevation of a Pole, Karol Wojtyla, to

the papacy as John Paul II in 1978, gave strong moral support to the protest movement.

The reluctance of the Soviet Union to send troops to Poland, as they had done in Hungary and Czechoslovakia in earlier decades, emboldened critics and reformers throughout eastern Europe (see Map 33.4). Beleaguered governments vacillated between relaxation of control and militant suppression of dissent. At the same time, many of them sought solutions to their own severe economic problems, resulting from

Map 33.4 The End of Soviet Domination in Eastern Europe   The creation of new countries out of Yugoslavia and Czechoslovakia, and the reintegration of Germany into a single country marked the most complicated changes of national borders and state identities since World War I. As always in such matters, this process affected majority-minority relationships and led, in some cases, to bitterness and bloodshed, particularly in the states that formerly constituted Yugoslavia: Serbia (still called Yugoslavia), Slovenia, Croatia, Macedonia, and Bosnia and Herzegovina.

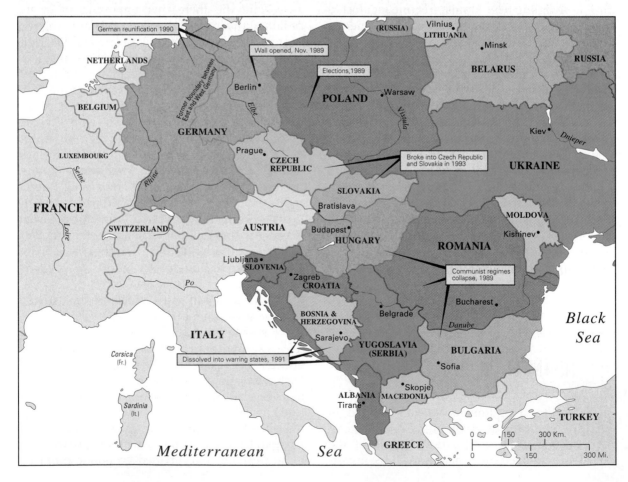

Demonstration by Polish Solidarity labor union   Founded in 1980 by Lech Walesa, Solidarity sponsored strikes and public protests and quickly gained nine million members. Communist leader General Wojciech Jaruzelski, with Soviet backing, suppressed Solidarity in 1982. It remained active underground, however, with the support of the Catholic Church. Taking to the streets in the late 1980s, it achieved government recognition in 1989. A year later, Walesa was elected president of Poland. (Michel Philippot/Sygma)

Soviet-style industrial policies, by turning to the west for trade and financial assistance. The flow of travelers, ideas, styles, and money from western countries accelerated the demand for change.

By the end of 1989, the communist governments of eastern Europe had fallen, a transformation vividly symbolized by the dismantling of the Berlin Wall. In some places the government collapsed and resigned. Rebellion occurred in others, notably in Romania where dictator Nicolae Ceausescu and his wife Elena were arrested and executed. The changeover was demonstrated in 1990, when Solidarity leader Lech Walesa was elected president of Poland and dissident playwright Vaclav Havel was elected president of Czechoslovakia.

Looking on with dismay at the collapse of communism in five allied Warsaw Pact countries, the Soviet leadership could see that a crisis was at hand. The year 1990 brought declarations of independence by Lithuania, Estonia, and Latvia, three small states on the Baltic Sea that the Soviet Union had annexed in 1939. Soon, the other constituent republics of the USSR demanded independence as well. Gorbachev, with sympathy from the United States—dismayed by the rapidity of communism's collapse because it was uncertain as to what might come next—tried to accommodate the rising pressures for change. But the tide was running too fast.

The end came in 1991. After communist hardliners botched a poorly conceived coup against

Gorbachev in August, disgust with communism boiled over. Boris Yeltsin, the president of the Russian republic, led popular resistance to the coup in Moscow and emerged as the most powerful authority in the country. Russia, the largest republic in the Soviet Union, was effectively taking the place of the USSR. With the central government of the Soviet Union scarcely functioning, the elected assemblies of the various republics proclaimed independence. In September, the Congress of People's Deputies—the central legislature of the USSR and long subservient to the communist party—voted to dissolve the union, and Mikhail Gorbachev went into retirement.

standing the history of the last half of the twentieth century. Environmental issues, population concerns, world economic competition, and the transformation of culture under the influence of electronic media would have evolved regardless of Cold War or the decolonization movements. The final chapters of this book therefore examine the historical backgrounds and manifestations of these other areas of current world concern: the transformation of the natural and economic environment in which we live and developments in the area of global unification, cultural diversity, and changing patterns of interaction between societies.

CONCLUSION

When a historian cites as an important turning point a date from long ago, such as Columbus' voyage to the New World in 1492, few readers wonder whether or not the historian is right. Dividing history by time period, region, and theme is part of the historian's job. Yet people are likely to disagree strongly when similar historical turning points are suggested for their own times. Time divisions based on events during the Cold War may make sense to most Americans and Russians but be irrelevant to Arabs and Israelis, who may measure history by the sequence of Arab-Israeli wars.

From almost any political viewpoint, however, 1991 marked an historical watershed. The Cold War ended; communism collapsed almost everywhere; fear of global nuclear holocaust disappeared; and the last great colonial empire, that of the Soviet Union, dissolved into fledgling independent states. Above and beyond these momentous developments, however, three centuries of world history shaped overwhelmingly by the ambitions and rivalries of European and American powers came to an end, leaving the world uncertain as to what would come next.

Nevertheless, war and politics should not be allowed to overshadow other ways of under-

SUGGESTED READING

The period since 1945 has been particularly rich in memoirs by government leaders. Some that are particularly relevant to the Cold War and decolonization are Dean Acheson (U.S. Secretary of State under Truman), *Present at the Creation* (1969); Nikita Khrushchev, *Khrushchev Remembers* (1970); Margaret Thatcher, *The Downing Street Years* (1993); and Anthony Eden (British Prime Minister), *Full Circle* (1960).

Geoffrey Barraclough, *An Introduction to Contemporary History* (1964), is a remarkable early effort at understanding the broad sweep of history during this period.

Scholarship on the origins of the Cold War is extensive and includes Akira Iriye, *The Cold War in Asia: A Historical Introduction* (1974); Bruce Kuniholm, *The Origins of the Cold War in the Near East* (1980); Madelaine Kalb, *The Congo Cables: The Cold War in Africa—From Eisenhower to Kennedy* (1982); and Daniel Yergin, *Shattered Peace: The Origins of the Cold War and the National Security State* (1977). For good general histories of the Cold War, see Martin Walker, *The Cold War: A History* (1993); and Walter Lafeber, *America, Russia, and the Cold War, 1945–1992* (1993). The latter puts an emphasis on how the Cold War eroded American democratic values. For a look at the Cold War from the Soviet perspective see William Taubman, *Stalin's America Policy* (1981); for the American perspective see John Lewis Gaddis, *Strategies of Containment: A Critical Appraisal of Postwar American National Security Policy* (1982). The Cuban missile crisis is well covered in Michael Beschloss, *The Crisis Years: Kennedy and Khrushchev, 1960–1963* (1991). On Europe during and after the Cold War see David Calleo, *Beyond American Hegemony* (1987) and Tina Rosenberg, *The Haunted Land: Facing Europe's Ghosts After Communism* (1995).

The nuclear arms race and the associated Soviet-American competition in space are well covered by McGeorge Bundy, *Danger and Survival: Choices About the Bomb in the First Fifty Years* (1988) and Walter McDougall, *The Heavens and the Earth: A Political History of the Space Age* (1985). An example of an American strategist's thinking at the height of the arms race is Herman Kahn, *Thinking About the Unthinkable in the 1980s* (1984). Among the many novels illustrating the alarming impact of the arms race on the general public are Philip Wylie, *Tomorrow!* (1954) and Nevil Shute, *On the Beach* (1970).

The end of the European empires is broadly treated by D. K. Fieldhouse, *The Colonial Empires* (1982); the British Empire in particular by Brian Lapping, *End of Empire* (1985). For a critical view of American policies toward the decolonized world see Gabriel Kolko, *Confronting the Third World: United States Foreign Policy, 1945–1980* (1988).

For books on some of the specific episodes of decolonization treated in this chapter see, on Algeria, Alistaire Horne, *A Savage War of Peace: Algeria, 1954–1962* (1987); on Cuba, Hugh Thomas, *Cuba: The Pursuit of Freedom* (1971); on the Suez crisis of 1956, Keith Kyle, *Suez 1956* (1991); on Britain's role in the Middle East over the period of the birth of Israel, William Roger Louis, *The British Empire in the Middle East, 1945–1951* (1984); on Vietnam, George Herring, *America's Longest War: The United States and Vietnam, 1950–1975* (1986); on Latin America, Eric Wolf, *The Human Condition in Latin America* (1972).

The special cases of Japan and China in this period are covered by Edwin O. Reischauer, *The Japanese* (1981); Marius B. Jansen, *Japan and China: From War to Peace, 1894–1972* (1975); and Maurice Meisner, *Mao's China and After: A History of the People's Republic* (1986). John Merrill, *Korea: The Peninsular Origins of the War* (1989) presents the Korean war as a civil and revolutionary conflict as well as an episode of the Cold War. The story of the Iranian Revolution and the early days of the Islamic Republic of Iran is well told by Shaul Bakhash, *The Reign of the Ayatollahs: Iran and the Iranian Revolution* (1990). Barnet Rubin, *The Fragmentation of Afghanistan* (1995), provides excellent coverage of the struggle between Soviet forces and the Muslim resistance in that country. Among hundreds of books on the Arab-Israeli conflict Charles D. Smith, *Palestine and the Arab-Israeli Conflict* (1992), stands out as one of the most thoughtful and well written.

CHAPTER THIRTY-FOUR

The Global Contest for Resources,

1945–1991

Competition and Integration in a Global Economy • The Challenge of Population Growth

The Movement of People • The Challenge of Technological and Environmental Change

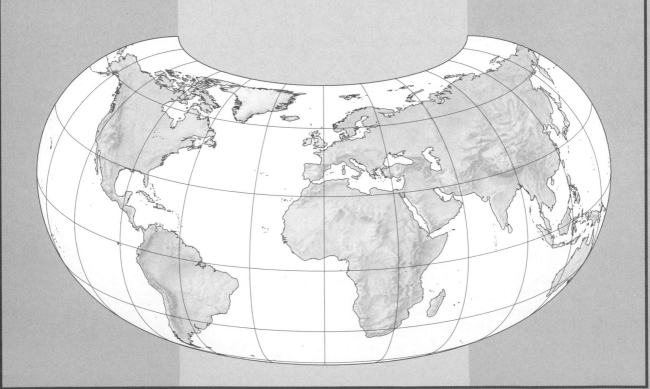

On Thursday July 22, 1993, police officers attempting to arrest a young boy for sniffing glue were assaulted by a group of stone-throwing homeless children who live on the streets of Rio de Janeiro's banking district. One police officer was injured. Late the following night, two cars of hooded vigilantes fired hundreds of shots at a group of about 45 of these children sleeping on the steps of a nearby church. The attackers killed five children there and two more in a nearby park. The murderers were later identified as off-duty police officers.

In 1993, death squads and drug dealers killed more than four hundred of Rio's street children. Few people sympathize with the victims. One person living near the scene of the July shooting said, "Those street kids are bandits, and bandits have to die. They are a rotten branch that has to be pruned."

The victims came from Rio's streets and parks where more than 350,000 abandoned children survive by begging, selling drugs, stealing, and prostitution. The brutality of their lives is an increasingly common feature of life in the developing world where rapid population growth is outstripping economic resources.[1]

Similar problems of violence, poverty, and social breakdown can be found today in many developing nations. In industrialized nations as well, politicians and social reformers worry about increasing levels of unemployment, family breakdown, and homelessness. As was true during the eighteenth-century Industrial Revolution (see Chapter 23), the dramatic economic growth and rapid technological progress of the post–World War II era has coincided with growing social dislocation and inequality.

The world economy is now more integrated than at any time in the past. Trade agreements have opened markets at the same time that new technologies have transformed the workplace.

Today, industrial and agricultural corporations produce and market goods and services globally. The benefits of expansion and integration have been enjoyed disproportionally by the advanced industrial nations. This period has also witnessed a dramatic increase in world population. The most rapid increases have occurred in the poorest nations.

The combination of population growth and increasing levels of industrialization, in turn, have had a dramatic impact on global environment. On every continent, the depletion of forests, loss of farmland, destructive effects of mining, and pollution have been felt. Wealthy nations with slow rates of population growth have found it easier to respond to these environmental challenges than have poor nations experiencing rapid population growth. These then are the challenges facing the late twentieth century: the unequal distribution of wealth, growing population pressures, and threats to the environment.

COMPETITION AND INTEGRATION IN A GLOBAL ECONOMY

Since 1945 global economic productivity has expanded more rapidly than at any time in the past. Faster, cheaper communications and transportation have combined with improvements in industrial and agricultural technologies to create levels of material abundance that would have amazed those who experienced the First Industrial Revolution (see Chapter 23). Despite this remarkable economic expansion and growing market integration, a majority of the world's population remain in poverty. In fact, the industrialized nations of the Northern Hemisphere nations now enjoy a larger share of the world's wealth than was true a century ago.

The Confrontation Between Capitalism and Socialism

The Cold War was more than a military and political rivalry (see Chapter 33): it was also a confrontation between two economic systems. For nearly 40 years following the end of World War II, many critics of capitalism, especially in the Third World, viewed the Soviet Union's socialist economy as an alternative to capitalism. In this competition of east and west, success or failure was measured in terms of economic growth, changes in per-capita income, and productivity gains rather than in terms of military divisions or atomic weapons.

During World War II, the American economy had finally escaped the lingering effects of the Depression and grown stronger (see Chapter 31). High military spending and the draft led to full employment and high wages. The wartime conversion of factories from the production of consumer goods created pent-up demand for those goods. With peace, the United States enjoyed prosperity. From a position of economic strength, the United States supported recovery in western Europe and Japan. The Marshall Plan was the primary instrument of American economic assistance to Europe. Between 1948 and 1952, the United States provided $12.5 billion in Marshall Plan assistance. By 1961 more than $20 billion in economic aid had been received.

Although at the end of the Cold War the U.S. economy remained the world's largest and Americans were still well off, enormous defense costs, competition from the revitalized European and Japanese economies, and the oil price shocks of the 1970s combined to diminish U.S. economic preeminence. Average income adjusted for inflation has stagnated in the last twenty years. Industries that had been centers of strength for the American economy in 1950 had become uncompetitive by 1980. Shipbuilding nearly disappeared, and the nation's largest steel companies declined. Makers of automobiles and consumer electronics also struggled for nearly two decades to meet the challenges of quality and price posed by Japan and other rapidly developing nations

of the Pacific Rim. These problems were highlighted by U.S. President Richard Nixon's decision in 1971 to end the postwar monetary agreements that had made the U.S. dollar the international financial standard. Freed to float against other currencies, the once-stable dollar declined relative to the currencies of Germany and Japan through the 1970s and 1980s.

Nevertheless, it was the U.S. economy that led the developed nations' slow escape from the recession that characterized the 1970s and 1980s. Faced with increased competition from Europe and Asia, U.S. industry undertook a massive restructuring that included reducing and reorganizing the workforce as well as corporate mergers. New technologies (including computers, fiber optics, and industrial robots) also increased efficiency and improved competitiveness. American business leaders—and politicians—also actively promoted international trade agreements meant to reduce tariffs and open access to international markets. U.S. negotiators consistently pushed free trade principles in international talks aimed at writing a General Agreement on Trade and Tariffs (GATT), and the United States joined Canada and Mexico in creating a free trade zone in the Western Hemisphere with the North American Free Trade Agreement (NAFTA) signed in 1992. Although the debate continues, American industry and agriculture are now integrated in a global marketplace, and American workers now compete directly with workers in Mexico and South Korea as well as those in Germany or Japan.

The western European economy was heavily damaged during World War II. The bombing of industrial zones, the death or displacement of millions of skilled and experienced workers, the loss of capital, and the destruction of transportation networks created enormous obstacles to economic recovery. Not surprisingly, then, the early postwar years were bleak in many European nations. Nevertheless, the efforts of European governments combined with American aid to promote rapid recovery. By 1963, a resurgent European economy had doubled 1940 output.

Western European governments generally increased their role in economic management during this period. In Great Britain, the Labour Party government of the 1950s nationalized coal, steel, railroads, and health care. The French government nationalized public utilities, the auto, banking, and insurance industries, and parts of the mining industry. The Italian and West German governments intervened as well, though more modestly. Initially, these steps contributed significantly to the economic recovery by providing the large infusions of capital needed for rebuilding and for acquiring new technologies.

European governments also began a process of economic cooperation and integration, launched in 1948 with the creation of the Organization of European Economic Cooperation. After successful experiences with cooperative policies in the coal and steel industries, some countries were ready to begin lowering tariffs and encouraging the movement of goods and capital. In 1957 France, West Germany, Italy, the Netherlands, Belgium, and Luxembourg signed a treaty creating the European Economic Community, also called the Common Market. Although integration was slowed by French President Charles De Gaulle's fears of a resurgent German economy and by Britain's decision to stay outside the community, by the 1970s the Common Market nations had nearly overtaken the United States in industrial production. Now called the European Community (EC), the economic alliance expanded after 1970, eventually adding Great Britain, Denmark, Greece, Ireland, Spain, Portugal, Finland, Sweden, and Austria.

Prosperity dramatically changed European society. Average wages increased, unemployment fell, and social welfare benefits were expanded. Governments spent more than before the war on health care, unemployment benefits, old age benefits, public housing, and grants to poor families with children. By the 1980s, European workers had the most generous paid vacations in the world. The combination of economic growth and income redistribution raised living standards and fueled demand for consumer goods. Automobile ownership, for example, grew approximately ninefold between 1950 and 1970. Millions of Europeans bought dishwashers, televisions, and, more recently, computers, and

videocassette recorders (VCRs). Tourism was another sign of increased leisure time and growing affluence, as large numbers of European wage workers vacationed abroad. However, there remain significant differences in income levels among EC nations, with the German average income nearly four times that of the poorest members, Greece and Portugal.

Following the oil price shocks of the 1970s (see Chapter 33) and the resulting worldwide recession, western European economies slowed and unemployment levels rose. High wages and costly welfare benefits made European goods expensive relative to competing products from North America and the Pacific Rim. In addition, the costs of funding reunification (see Chapter 33) slowed growth in Germany, Europe's strongest economy. In response, major corporations, like Mercedes Benz and BMW, have located new factories in the United States to lower labor costs and European politicians have begun to discuss benefits cuts. With increased international economic competition, Europe's ability to maintain traditional high wage levels and generous social welfare benefits will remain a question.

The rapid development of a powerful Soviet state after 1917 challenged traditional Western assumptions about economic development and social policy as well as posing a strategic threat. From the 1920s, the Soviet state relied on bureaucratic agencies and political processes, rather than market forces, to determine the production, distribution, and price of goods. Housing, medical services, retail shops, factories, the land—even intellectual properties like music and literature—were viewed as collective property and, therefore, were regulated and administered by the state. The state decided what would be produced, how it would be distributed, and what it would cost.

At the end of the war, the economies of the Soviet Union and its eastern European allies were just as devastated as those of western Europe. The Soviet command economy had enormous natural resources, a large population, and abundant energy at its disposal. Moreover, Soviet planners had made large investments in technical and scientific education. As a result, initial recovery was rapid. The Soviet economy grew at an estimated annual rate of approximately 5 percent per year from war's end to the end of the 1960s.

The ability of the Soviet state to allocate labor, capital, and raw materials succeeded in developing heavy industry in the 1930s and war years. However, bureaucratic control of the economy proved inefficient in the postwar years, when industrial might was increasingly measured by the production of televisions and automobiles rather than tons of coal and steel. In communications, transportation, and consumer goods, the gap with the west widened in the 1970s and gaped in the 1980s when the Soviet economy failed to meet domestic demand for clothing, housing, food, automobiles, and consumer electronics. Socialist agriculture also proved inefficient and unproductive, forcing the Soviet Union to rely on food imports.

The socialist nations of eastern Europe were compelled to follow the Soviet economic model, but some national differences appeared. For example, Poland and Hungary implemented agricultural collectivization more slowly than did Czechoslovakia. Despite these differences, however, economic planners throughout the region concentrated resources to accelerate industrialization. Although significant growth occurred among these socialist economics, the same inefficiencies and failures that plagued the Soviet economy appeared here as well.

The Pacific Rim

At the end of World War II, Japan was occupied by American military forces, and General Douglas MacArthur, the American commander, held

Worker unrest in Eastern Europe   After the collapse of the Soviet Union, workers began to more forcefully demand improvement in working conditions. This photo shows a group of angry women factory workers in Minsk, capital of Belarus, surrounding plant managers and demanding action on their grievances. (Yuri Ivanon/Time, Inc.)

nearly unconditional power (see Chapter 33). After removing Japan's wartime leaders and imposing a new democratic constitution, the occupation government set out to help rebuild the economy. Unions were given greater freedom, land reform was undertaken, and some of the large industrial firms associated with the war effort were broken up. However, with the triumph of the Communists in China, the United States moderated its reform agenda, allowing the reappearance of powerful industrial conglomerates that had been banned by the anti-trust policies of the U.S. occupation authorities. In 1952, the U.S. finally ended the occupation.

Although Japan's economic recovery was at first slow, the Korean War provided a dramatic boost by pumping American money into the economy. The Japanese economy then grew at about 10 percent a year for the next two decades. Average income also increased rapidly, overtaking the United States in 1986.

Japanese success had its origins in prewar industrialization as well as in postwar reforms. Japan had developed heavy industry, a disciplined industrial workforce, and modern transportation and communication networks before the war (see Chapter 31). Although many of these assets were destroyed in air raids, the nation retained the knowledge and political will necessary to recreate them. With U.S. aid, a government committed to rebuilding the industrial base, relatively inexpensive labor, and a global demand for consumer goods, Japanese corporations quickly achieved competitiveness. By 1960, Japanese factories were among the most modern and efficient in the world.

As in western Europe, the Japanese government played a leading role in directing recovery and expansion. Government bureaucracies worked with corporate leaders to organize resources, provide capital, and develop technologies. While the American government sometimes used the courts to prevent the creation of monopolies and cartels, Japanese policy continued to favor the creation of huge corporations, called *zaibatsu* before the war, and promoted cooperation among competitors. Moreover, businesses developed corporate cultures that emphasized loyalty, commitment, and responsibility. Workers were given job security and a role in decision making; in return, they were expected to dedicate themselves to the corporation's success.

The Japanese miracle began with the production of inexpensive, low technology products for the mass markets of America and Europe. Japanese industry quickly progressed to the production of high value, technologically sophisticated products. In the 1950s, western consumers commonly dismissed Japanese goods as cheap and inferior. Today, Japanese products, from automobiles to computers and consumer electronics, set global standards for quality. This revolution was accomplished at enormous expense. During the period of most rapid growth, the Japanese held down wages and domestic consumption levels to promote savings (the basis of investment in new technology) and to maintain the nation's competitive advantage in international markets.

By the 1970s and 1980s, Japanese success at exporting goods produced huge trade surpluses with other nations, prompting the United States and the European Community to try, through tough negotiating, to force an opening of the Japanese market. Today, Japan is also faced with competition from new lower-cost producers elsewhere in Asia. As a result, Japanese industries are currently struggling to retain their technological advantages and their traditional commitment to lifetime employment while increasing their competitiveness.

The Japanese model was successfully imitated by a small number of Asian states, the most important of which is South Korea. As in Japan, the government there entered into an informal partnership with industry to promote growth. With inexpensive labor, strong technical education, and substantial domestic capital reserves, South Korea overcame the devastation of the Korean War (see Chapter 33) in little more than a decade. Despite heavy defense expenditures, South Korea developed both heavy industries such as steel and shipbuilding as well as consumer industries such as automobiles and consumer electronics. Led by four giant corporations, which account for nearly half the gross domestic product and produce a broad mix of goods, the Korean economy matched Japanese economic growth rates by the 1980s. Hyundai, one of these four

Pacific Rim industrialization   Since the late 1950s, Korea has experienced rapid economic growth. The world's largest dry docks owned by Hyundai Corporation symbolize the Korean economic achievement. (Paul Chesley/Tony Stone Worldwide)

corporations, manufactures products as diverse as supertankers, cars, electronics, and housing.

Taiwan, Hong Kong, and Singapore developed modern industrial and commercial economies as well. Taiwan has suffered a number of political reverses recently, including the loss of its United Nations seat and the withdrawal of recognition by the United States (see Chapter 33). Nevertheless, it has achieved remarkable economic progress. Unlike South Korea, Taiwan's development has been led by smaller, more specialized companies. In recent years, Taiwan has gained a foothold in the economy of the People's Republic of China while maintaining its traditional markets in the United States and South Asia.

Hong Kong and Singapore are small societies with fewer resources that nevertheless have also enjoyed rapid economic development. Singapore's initial economic takeoff was based on its busy port and on banking and commercial services. As capital accumulated in these profitable sectors, this society of around 3 million people diversified by building textile and electronics industries. Like Singapore, Hong Kong's economic prosperity is tied to its port and to the development of banking and commercial services, which are increasingly linked to the growing economy of China. It has also developed a highly competitive industrial sector dominated by textile and consumer electronics production.

All of these Newly Industrialized Economies (NIEs) share many characteristics that help explain their rapid achievement of industrialization. All have disciplined and hardworking workforces. All have invested heavily in education. As early as 1980 Korea, for example, had as many engineering graduates as Germany,

Britain, and Sweden combined. All have high rates of personal saving, which allow them to fund investment in new technology. In 1987, the saving rates for Taiwan and South Korea were 38.8 percent and 37 percent respectively while that for the United States was 12.7 percent. And, like Japan, all these dynamic Pacific Rim economies have benefited from government sponsorship and protection.

Following the Communist victory in 1949, Mao Zedong and the new Chinese leadership put in place an economic plan that followed the Soviet model and emphasized heavy industry. During the 1950s, progressive political pressure was brought upon professionals and specialists, and upon centers of industrialization. This pressure became a flood in 1957 and led to the radicalization of agriculture and industry in 1958–1961, the so-called "Great Leap Forward," intended to decentralize and bring all economic activity under the control of the Chinese Communist party. By the time this disastrous policy was abandoned, agricultural and industrial production had fallen and millions had lost their lives. When relations with the USSR were broken, an important source of aid was lost and the economy further damaged. Following Mao's death in 1976, China's leaders introduced a comprehensive economic reform that allowed more individual initiative and permitted individuals to accumulate wealth. This process has created rapid growth, but per-capita measures of wealth indicate that China remains a poor nation.

The "Third World"

Decolonization (see Chapter 33) produced scores of new nations which were immediately confronted with the need to chart their own economic course. Most faced their new future with a set of problems inherited from their colonial past—low levels of industrialization, an underdeveloped infrastructure, and dependence on mineral or agricultural exports. The question of which course to follow was often colored by the passions and ideology of the independence movements. During the 1950s and 1960s, foreign investment and capitalist development strategies came under broad attack for their association with the colonial past. The leaders of these emerging nations asked if political independence could be fully enjoyed without meaningful economic autonomy. Although few of these nations completely embraced socialism, many created state enterprises to foster basic industries and expand infrastructure as well as limiting foreign investments.

Resentment toward former colonial masters—or, in the case of Latin America, toward earlier U.S. interventions—led in many cases to the nationalization of foreign-owned businesses. In these contests, developing nations commonly faced the possibility of military intervention or economic retaliation. The U.S. government justified military intervention in Guatemala in 1954 and in Cuba in 1961, in part, as the defense of American corporations (see Chapter 33). Economic nationalism also led to foreign intervention elsewhere. Following the independence of Zaïre (the former Belgian Congo), for example, European-owned copper companies promoted secessionist movements that launched a long, bloody, destructive civil war.

More common than the nationalization of foreign-owned industries was the use of tariffs, import restrictions, and domestic content laws to protect manufacturers in developing nations from the competition of producers in the industrialized nations. These import-substitution policies produced some successes in Asia and Latin America. Both Brazil and Mexico created competitive and efficient auto industries, and South Korea and Taiwan developed formidable consumer electronics industries, for example. More commonly, however, import substitution created inefficient and expensive new industries that forced domestic consumers to purchase inferior locally produced goods at high prices.

The rapid economic recovery of Europe and Japan and the continued economic growth of the U.S. throughout the 1960s provided steady demand for the products of many "Third World" nations. This demand helped to disguise the relative inefficiency and low productivity associated with Third World policies of high public sector employment and subsidized industrialization. Many developing nations also gained substantial

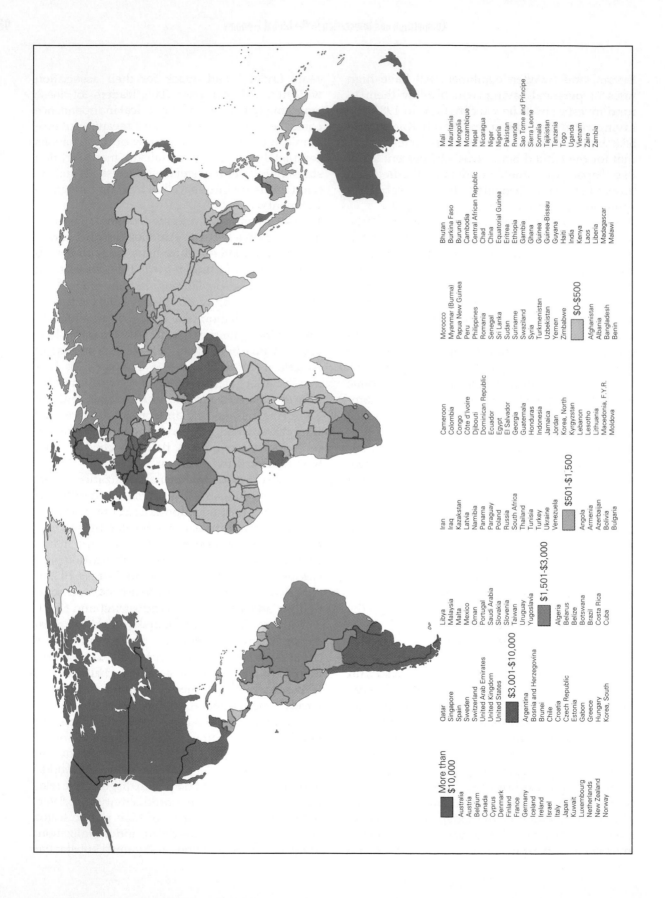

foreign aid from the rival super powers, both of which provided assistance for high profile projects such as hydroelectric plants and highways. These relatively good economic times ended in the 1970s.

Beginning in 1973, OPEC (the Organization of Petroleum Exporting Countries) forced two dramatic increases in oil prices (see Chapter 33). While the industrialized western nations suffered a recession, the oil-importing nations of the developing world were devastated. Many developing nations attempted to ride out the crisis by borrowing from international lenders, but debt payments drained off scarce resources. In Latin America, Argentina, Brazil, and Chile alone owed nearly $200 billion to foreign lenders by 1990. African nations' foreign debt also increased, rising from $14 billion in 1973 to well over $125 billion in 1990.

Ironically, many oil-exporting nations also accumulated new debt. Twenty years after the first price shocks, it was clear that only those oil producers with both small populations and large oil reserves—Saudi Arabia, Kuwait, and the United Arab Emirates in particular—would become rich. Oil producing nations with large populations like Mexico, Iran, and Nigeria benefited only marginally. When oil prices fell due to lessened demand caused by conservation and worldwide recession, many oil-exporting nations were saddled with huge foreign debts.

Hit hard by the oil price shocks, the worldwide recession, and growing indebtedness, the "Third World" suffered another blow when the end of the Cold War led to dramatic reductions in foreign aid. In the early 1990s, many developing nations began to reexamine the free market policies they had rejected during the Cold War era. Although responses to this crisis differed from region to region and nation to nation, laws restricting foreign investment were amended to attract investment capital throughout the "Third

Map 34.1 Estimated GNP Per Capita Income in the Early 1990s Since World War II, wealth has increasingly been concentrated in a small number of industrialized nations located in the Northern Hemisphere. The cost of developing and acquiring new technologies has widened the gap between rich and poor nations.

World." Many developing nations began to sell off public utilities and even some industries nationalized during the 1950s and 1960s.

The Problem of Growing Inequality

Clearly the benefits of postwar material progress have been unevenly distributed. Since 1945, remarkable changes in technology, productivity, and commercial relations have coincided with growing levels of wealth inequality both among nations and among regions and individuals within nations. The thousands of homeless street children who live among the gleaming glass and steel towers of Rio's banking district might be viewed as a metaphor for the social consequences of postwar economic development.

Internationally, the gap between rich and poor nations has grown much wider since 1945. In 1993, Switzerland and Japan had the highest GNP per capita with $35,760 and $31,490 respectively; that of the United States was $24,740. The poorest nation in the Common Market, Greece, had an estimated GNP per capita of $7,220, equal to Argentina's. The nations of the former Soviet Union and eastern Europe have per-capita GNPs similar to those found in the better-off nations of the Third World. Russia's per-capita GNP in 1993 was $2,340, similar to Brazil's $2,930 though substantially less than Mexico's $3,610. Among other developing economies, Algeria and Thailand had per-capita GNPs of approximately $2,000 while Nigeria, India, and China were below $500 (see Map 34.1). Today one billion of the world's people, approximately 20 percent, live on less than $500 a year. Overwhelmingly, this poverty is concentrated in the developing nations of Africa, Latin America, and Asia though pockets of grinding poverty can be found in every developed nation as well.

The gulf that separates rich and poor nations continues to expand even as worldwide economic output grows. Only a few Asian nations have been able to compete successfully with the traditional industrial powers of western Europe and North America since 1945. Otherwise, little progress has been made. In fact, most of the na-

A garbage dump in Manila, Philippines   Garbage pickers are a common feature of Third World urban development. Bottles, aluminum cans, plastic, and newspapers are sorted and sold to provide the household income for thousands of poor families in nearly every Third World city. (Geoff Tompkinson/Aspect Picture Library Ltd.)

tions of the Third World are relatively worse off now than they were in 1945.

Wealth inequality has grown within nations as well. Those regions tied to new technologies that provide competitive advantages have become wealthier while other regions have lost ground. In the United States, for example, the South and Southwest grew richer in the last three decades relative to the older industrial regions of the Midwest and East. In addition, per-capita income in the suburbs has grown relative to that in urban areas. A similar pattern has appeared in Britain, where older industrial regions like Wales and the Midlands have declined relative to the booming area south of London. Regional inequalities have also appeared in developing na-

tions. Generally, capitals like Buenos Aires, Argentina, or Lagos, Nigeria, attract large numbers of migrants from rural areas because they offer more opportunities, even if those opportunities cannot compare to those available in developed nations.

Even in the industrialized world, people are divided into haves and have nots. During the presidency of Ronald Reagan, wealth inequality in the United States reached its highest level since the 1929 stock market crash. Some scholars estimate that the wealthiest 1 percent of households in the United States control more than 30 percent of the nation's total wealth. In 1992, households collecting Aid to Families with Dependent Children (AFDC) received an average of

$4,680 while the 1,059 partners in New York's largest law firms averaged $957,000 in income and the head of General Electric earned $15 million.[2] Although wealth is less concentrated in the mature industrial economies of Europe, where tax and inheritance laws redistribute wealth, unemployment, homelessness, and substandard housing are now increasingly common.

THE CHALLENGE OF POPULATION GROWTH

From 1850 to 1914, European population more than doubled, putting enormous pressure on rural land resources and urban housing, and overwhelming fragile institutions of public assistance (see Chapter 28). This dramatic surge in population forced a large wave of immigration across the Atlantic, helping to develop North and South America and invigorating the Atlantic economy. Population growth also contributed to Europe's industrial revolution by lowering labor costs and increasing consumer demand.

Educated Europeans of the nineteenth century had ambivalent feelings about this rapid increase in human population. Some saw population growth as a blessing that would promote economic well-being. Pessimists, on the other hand, claimed that the seemingly relentless increase in human population would bring eventual disaster. Best known of these pessimists was the English cleric Thomas Malthus, who in 1798 argued convincingly that unchecked population growth would outstrip food production. Looking at Europe's future, he saw a replication of what he took to be China's desperate present, where a visitor "will not be surprised that mothers destroy or expose many of their children; that parents sell their daughters for a trifle; . . . and that there should be such a number of robbers. The

Chinese family planning campaign The Chinese government has used billboards and other forms of mass advertising to promote compliance with family-planning directives. The objective has been to limit parents to a single child. (Picard/Sipa Press)

surprise is that nothing still more dreadful should happen."[3]

The generation that came of age in the years immediately following World War II inherited a world in which Malthus and the other pessimists were casually dismissed. Increased industrial and agricultural productivity had multiplied supplies of food and other necessities. And, cultural changes associated with expanded female employment, older age at marriage, and more effective family planning had combined to retard the rate of population increase. By the late 1960s, Europe and other industrial societies had made what was called the "demographic transition"— they now enjoyed lowered fertility rates and reduced mortality. Birthrates, as a result, were just adequate for the maintenance of existing population levels.

Many experts argued, therefore, that the population growth then being seen in developing nations was a short-term phenomenon that would be ended by the same combination of economic and social changes that had altered European patterns. Since it was assumed that industrialization and urbanization would occur more rapidly in the twentieth century than earlier, many believed that the demographic transition would appear earlier in the developing nations.

By the 1970s, the demographic transition had not appeared in the Third World and the issues had become politicized. The leaders of some developing nations actively sponsored pronatalist policies, arguing that population was power. For example, Luís Echeverría, president of Mexico in the 1970s, encouraged high fertility and was rewarded by population growth of more than 3 percent per year. At that rate, the population of Mexico would double in less than twenty-five years. Pronatalist rhetoric was a minor, if persistent, component of an increasingly angry debate between the developed nations and developing nations. As industrialized, mostly white, nations raised concerns about rapid population growth in Asia, Africa, and Latin America, populist political leaders in those regions asked if this concern was not at its root racist.

The question exposed the continued influence of racism in the population debate and temporarily disarmed western advocates of birth control. However, once the economic shocks of the 1970s and 1980s exposed the vulnerability of developing economies, governments in the developing world jettisoned pronatalist policy. Mexico began to promote birth control and succeeded in pushing its annual growth rate down to 2.3 percent.

As can be seen in Table 34.1, world population exploded in the twentieth century. At current rates of growth, world population increases by a number equal to the total population of the United States every three years. Unlike the population growth in the eighteenth and nineteenth centuries when much of the world's population increase occurred in the era's wealthiest nations, population growth today is overwhelmingly in the poorest nations. Although fertility rates have dropped in most developing nations, they remain much higher than in the industrialized nations. Moreover, mortality rates have been reduced by improvements in hygiene and medical treatments. The result has been rapid population growth.

The Industrialized Nations

In the developed industrial nations of western Europe and Japan and in the former socialist republics of eastern Europe, low fertility and increased life expectancy present challenges for the future very different from that foreseen by Malthus. In Russia and other former socialist nations, current birthrates are now actually lower than death rates. That is, births are inadequate to maintain existing population levels. Birthrates— already low before the collapse of the socialist system—have contracted further with recent economic problems. The United States falls between the low birth levels of Europe and Japan and the higher levels of developing countries.

The low birthrates of the mature industrial nations are commonly associated with higher levels of female employment outside the home, the material values of consumer culture, improvements in contraception, and greater access to abortion. Armed with modern contraceptive technology, adults in the industrial nations commonly adapt family planning to fit altered economic circumstances. When the planned economies of eastern Europe stagnated, birthrates plunged. In the former German Democratic Republic, for example, births fell below deaths by 1974, and only an ambitious pronatalist government program turned the decline around. In socialist Romania, Yugoslavia, and Bulgaria, in the early 1980s, abortions were as common as births—in some years more common.

The Developing Nations

Even if the industrialized nations were to pursue pronatalist policies, they would continue to decline relative to the developing nations as a proportion of world population. In fact, 95 percent of all future population growth will be in developing nations (see Map 34.2). A comparison between Europe and Africa illustrates the recent transformation in world demography. In 1950, Europe had twice the population of Africa. By 1985, Africa had drawn even. According to projections, by 2025 Africa's population will be three times larger than Europe's. Given the performance of African economies, future generations seem likely to face increased levels of famine, epidemics, and social breakdown.

Other developing regions have rapid population growth as well. While all other developing nations have an average birthrate of 33.6 per thousand (33.6 births per 1000 inhabitants), Muslim countries have a rate of 42.1. This rate is more than 300 percent higher than that for industrial nations (13.1). Fertility rates present a similar pattern. Muslim nations average 6 children per female with other developing nations averaging 4.5 and industrial nations 1.7. Since World War II, the rate of population growth in these nations has been influenced by relatively lower life expectancy and higher crude death rates as well. While the crude death rate (deaths per 1,000 population) in the developed nations is 9.4 per 1,000, it is nearly 14 in the Muslim nations.

The populations of Latin America and Asia are expanding dramatically also, but at rates

Table 34.1   Growth of World Population

Year	Population
1825	1.0 billion
1925	2.0 billion
1976	4.0 billion
1990	5.3 billion
2025 (projected)	8.5 billion

Source: Paul Kennedy, *Preparing for the Twenty-first Century* (New York, 1993), pp. 22–23.

slower than sub-Saharan Africa or the Muslim nations. Latin America's population increased from 165 million in 1950 to 405 million in 1985 and is projected to reach 778 million in 2025, despite declining birthrates. These aggregate figures mask a broad range of distinct national experiences. Since the early 1960s, Argentina, Uruguay, and Chile have had crude birthrates similar to those of poorer European nations like Ireland, Greece, and Spain and only slightly higher than those of the United States, Germany, and France. Mexico, Brazil, and Peru have birthrates more than 70 percent higher. The nations of Central America have birthrates similar to those of the fast-growing Muslim nations.

Latin America and other developing regions face continuing population increases even though fertility is declining. The number of births per woman in Brazil fell from 5.8 in 1965 to 4.0 in 1980, a decline of 30 percent, yet the birthrate has fallen only 19 percent and the actual number of births per year has actually increased. This is because the number of women of child-bearing age was dramatically increased by earlier rounds of population growth following the end of World War II. National population continues to climb due to the momentum of high birth rates in the 1970s and 1980s.

In Asia, the populations of India and China continue to grow despite sometimes ruthless government efforts to reduce family size (see Voices & Visions: China's Family Planning

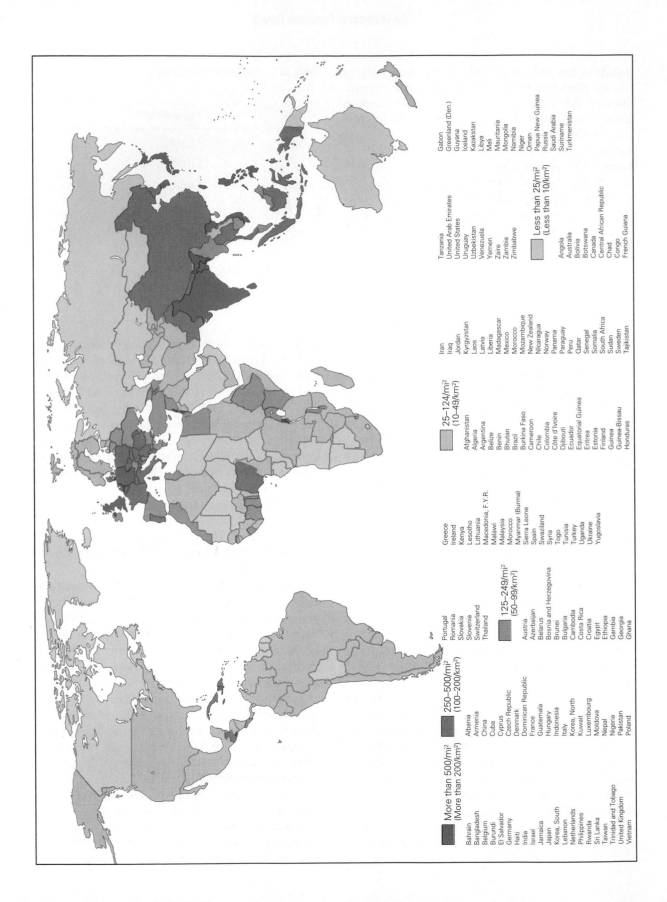

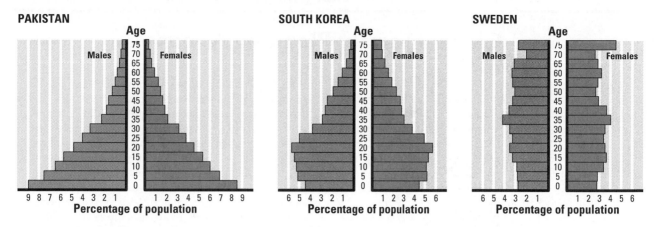

Figure 34.1 Age Structure Comparison: Islamic Nation (Pakistan), Non-Islamic Developing Nation (South Korea), and Developed Nation (Sweden), 1985
Source: World Bank

Needs). In the case of China, efforts to enforce a one-child-per-family law led to large-scale female infanticide as peasant families sought to guarantee male heirs. India's policies of forced sterilization created widespread outrage and led to the electoral defeat of the ruling Congress Party. Yet both countries achieved some successes. Between 1960 and 1982, India's birthrate fell from 48 to 34 per 1000. China's rate declined even more sharply, from 39 to 19, in the same period. Still, by 2025 China, which today has 1.13 billion and India today with 853 million, will both reach 1.5 billion.

Bangladesh, Sri Lanka, Pakistan, and Afghanistan all have high levels of fertility and declining mortality. Pakistan and Bangladesh remain among the most rapidly growing populations in South Asia despite receiving the highest levels of population assistance from the U.S. government. Pakistan's birthrate has dropped slightly since 1960, but Bangladesh has experienced no improvement and Afghanistan has actually increased its crude birthrate from 50 to 54.

It is unclear, therefore, whether the nations of Asia, Africa, and Latin America will imitate the "demographic transition" experienced in the

Map 34.2 World Population Density World population has grown rapidly in the twentieth century. The most rapid growth has occurred in the developing nations of Asia, Africa, and Latin America.

West during the Industrial Revolution. It appears that education levels, particularly those of women, are closely tied to fertility rates. Where women in the developing world have uninhibited access to education and work outside the home in large numbers, Argentina for example, fertility rates are similar to those of the developed nations. But obstacles to the education and employment of women remain strong in much of the world.

"Old" and "Young" Populations

The profound transformation in human reproductive patterns and life expectancy in the fifty years since World War II is clearly illustrated by the population pyramids generated by demographers. Figure 34.1 shows the age distributions of Pakistan, South Korea, and Sweden in 1985, nations at three distinct points in terms of economic development. Sweden is a mature industrial nation. South Korea is a rapidly industrializing nation that has already overtaken many European nations in both industrial output and per-capita wealth. Pakistan is a poor, traditional Muslim nation with rudimentary industrialization, low educational levels, and little effective family planning.

As can be seen, Pakistan has nearly 50 percent of its population under age 16. The resulting pressures on the economy are extraordinary.

China's Family Planning Needs

China has the world's largest population, with over one billion people. Although China enjoyed rapid economic growth in the closing years of the century, population pressures continue to present the government with severe problems. In 1993, the Chinese economy became the world's tenth largest. Nevertheless, its per-capita GDP (Gross Domestic Product) of $370 remained at Third World levels.

The Chinese government's family planning policies have been harshly criticized. Families are under heavy pressure to have only one child, resulting in the killing of female infants and the abandonment of children with disabilities. In the following quote, Peng Yu, vice-minister of the State Family Planning Commission, explains the need for efforts at population control:

China is a developing country with a huge population but limited cultivated land, inadequate per-capita resources and a weak economic foundation. . . . Despite continuous efforts in family planning, the huge base has created an annual net increase of around 14 million in recent years, equal to the total population of a medium-sized country. At present, per-capita cultivated land in China has declined to less than 0.1 hectare, equivalent to only one-fourth the world average as are per-capita freshwater resources. . . . Although national income has been climbing by 25 percent annually, the increase has been eaten up by new population growth, resulting in reduced fund accumulation and also holding up the speed of economic construction. A fast-growing population has also created great difficulties in employment, education, housing, transportation, and health care. Confronted by such grim realities, to guarantee basic living conditions and constantly improve standards of living, China cannot follow the Western mode under which natural falling birth rates coincide with gradual economic growth.

Why has the Chinese government sought to control population growth? What effect does population growth have on the environment and economic development? Are there more and ethical questions raised by the effort of any government to limit population growth?

Every year 150,000 men reach age 65—and another 1.2 million turn 16. Pakistan, therefore, must create more than 1 million new jobs per year or face a steadily growing problem of unemployment and declining wages. Sweden, on the other hand, confronts a different problem. With an aging population, a growing demand for social welfare benefits, and declining labor pool, Sweden's industries could become less competitive and its citizens could be forced to confront declining living standards. South Korea had an age-sex structure similar to Pakistan until recently but a decline in fertility has dramatically altered the ratio of children to adults. It now faces neither Pakistan's pressure to create jobs or Sweden's growing demands for welfare benefits for the aged.

Nevertheless, the demographic challenges faced by Sweden and other developed nations are less daunting than those confronting the developing nations. Poor nations must overcome problems such as the shortage of investment capital, poor quality transportation and communication networks, and low educational levels at the same time they struggle to produce jobs. Wealthy, well-educated, and politically stable nations can invest in robots and other new technologies to reduce labor needs and increase industrial and agricultural efficiency as their populations age. Among industrialized nations, both the demographic problem and the potential technological fix are most clearly visible in Japan.

Unless current demographic patterns are reversed, Japan will have the oldest population among industrial nations by 2025. More so than the United States and western Europe, Japan has resisted immigration, instead investing heavily in technological solutions to the problems created by an aging labor force. As of 1994, Japan had 75 percent of the world's industrial robots. Although Japanese industries are now able to produce more goods with fewer workers, Japan will face long-term increases in social welfare payments. In most other industrialized nations, such as Canada and Germany for example, young immigrants from poorer nations are entering the workforce in large numbers.

THE MOVEMENT OF PEOPLE

Two characteristics of the postwar world should now be clear. First, despite decades of experimentation with state-directed economic development, most nations that were poor in 1960 are as poor or poorer now. The only exceptions to this general rule are a few rapidly developing Asian industrial nations and an equally small number of oil-exporting nations. Second, world population is increasing to startlingly high levels. More importantly, most of this increase in population is in the poorest nations.

These two characteristics of the modern era come together in a surge of international immigration. Few issues in the recent past have created more controversy and even moderate voices sometimes frame the discussion of immigration as a competition among peoples. One recent commentator summarized his analysis this way: "As the better-off families of the northern hemisphere individually decide that having only one or at the most two children is sufficient, they may not recognize that they are in a small way vacating future space (that is, jobs, parts of inner cities, shares of population, shares of market preferences) to faster-growing ethnic groups both inside and outside their boundaries. But that, in fact, is what they are doing."[4] This competitive model may be rejected, but the general patterns are clear. All the developed industrial

Illegal immigration Despite increased efforts by developed nations to restrict immigration, the growing populations and limited economic opportunities of poorer nations have led to increased levels of population movement. In this photo, a border patrol vehicle keeps hundreds of hopeful immigrants from entering the United States near Tijuana, Mexico. (Don Barletti)

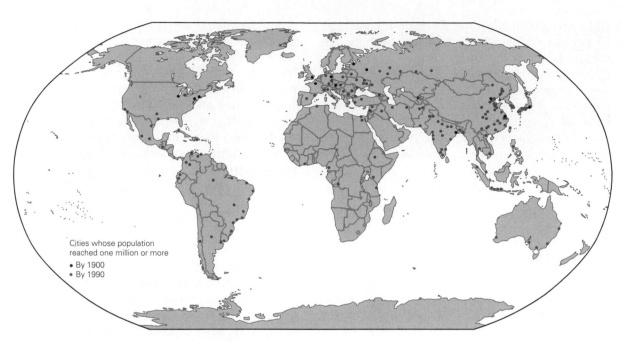

Map 34.3 Cities with a Million or More Inhabitants   The number of cities with a million or more inhabitants has increased dramatically due to a tidal wave of rural to urban migration in the twentieth century. In developing nations with scarce resources, squatter settlements and shanty towns have proliferated to meet the housing needs of recent migrants.

nations except Japan are receiving large numbers of legal and illegal immigrants from poor nations with growing populations.

Large-scale migrations within developing countries are a related phenomenon. The movement of impoverished rural residents helps feed the rapid growth of urban populations in Asia, Africa, and Latin America (see Map 34.3 and Table 34.2). In fact, this internal migration is often the first step toward migration abroad.

Internal Migration: The Growth of Cities

Migration to urban centers in developing nations increased threefold from 1925 to 1950. Since then, the pace has accelerated. The sprawling shanty towns that have grown up around major cities in developing nations are commonly seen as symptomatic of wholesale social breakdown and economic failure. The residents of these makeshift

neighborhoods do indeed live in conditions far inferior to those experienced by the most impoverished residents of rich nations. Nevertheless, life in the urban centers is better than life in the countryside.

Migration to a city brings enhanced opportunities and access to better services. A World Bank study estimated that three out of four migrants to cities make gains. Residents of cities in sub-Saharan Africa are six times more likely than rural residents to have safe water, for example. An unskilled migrant from the depressed northeast of Brazil can triple his or her income by moving to Rio de Janeiro. Despite higher housing and food costs in São Paulo, the wages of manual laborers there are five times higher than in the nation's poorest agricultural zones.

As the scale of rural to urban migration has grown, these benefits have proved more elusive, however. In many West African cities, basic services are crumbling under the pressure of rapid population growth. Hygiene, public order, and transportation have declined. In the world's largest city, Mexico City, more than thirty thousand people live in the garbage dumps and scavenge for food and clothing. Worsening conditions and the threat of crime and political instability have led many governments to try to slow the migration to cities and, in some cases, to return people to the countryside. Indonesia, for example, has relocated more than half a million urban residents since 1969. Despite some successes with slowing the rate of internal migration, nearly every poor nation will face the challenges posed by rapidly growing cities in the next century.

Table 34.2   Urban Residents as Percentage of Total Population

Nation	1960	1985
Nigeria	18%	31%
Tanzania	4%	24%
Morocco	29%	45%
Tunisia	40%	53%
India	18%	26%
Brazil	46%	73%
Mexico	51%	69%

Source: World Tables 1976 (Baltimore, 1976); and The Economist Book of Vital World Statistics (London, 1990).

International Immigration

Each year hundreds of thousands of men and women leave the agricultural regions and the cities of the developing world to emigrate to the industrialized nations. As this movement increased in scale after 1960, ethnic and racial tensions in the host nations grew worse. Political refugees and immigrants have faced murderous violence in Germany; growing anti-immigrant sentiment led to a new right-wing political movement in France; and an expanded Border Patrol recently attempted to more effectively seal the U.S. border with Mexico. Current levels of immigration pose daunting social and cultural challenges for both host nations and immigrants.

Immigrants from the developing nations offer many of the same benefits to host nations provided by the great migration of Europeans to the Americas in the nineteenth century (see Chapter 25). In fact, many European nations actively promoted guest worker programs and other inducements to immigration in the 1960s when an expanding European economy first confronted labor shortages. However, attitudes toward immigrants changed as the size of the immigrant population grew and as European economies slowed in the 1980s. Facing higher levels of unemployment, native-born workers saw immigrants as competitors willing to work for lower wages and less likely to support unions.

Although the economic slowdown of the 1970s and 1980s explains the timing of efforts to lower official immigration quotas and end illegal immigration, worsening relations between immigrants and the native-born were inevitable given that cultural characteristics form the basis of national identity in many European countries (see Chapter 28). Put simply, many Germans are unable to think of the German-born son or daughter of Turkish immigrants as a German. Throughout Europe, the legal definition of citizenship tends to reflect this narrow, culturally and ethnically derived, sense of nationality.

Because immigrants are generally young adults and because they commonly retain the positive attitudes toward early marriage and large families dominant in their native cultures, immigrant communities in Europe and the United States tend to have higher fertility rates than host populations. In Germany in 1975, for example, immigrants made up only about 7 percent of the population but accounted for nearly 15 percent of all births.

Recent studies demonstrate that immigrant fertility declines with prolonged residence in industrialized societies. The family size of second-generation immigrants living in developed nations is almost always smaller than that of their parents, but remains larger than that of the host population. Therefore, even without additional immigration, these groups grow faster than the longer-established population. Although the fertility of the Hispanic population in the United States is lower than that for Mexico and other sources of Latin American immigrants, for example, Hispanic groups will contribute well over 20 percent of all population growth during the next 25 years.

In every developed nation, immigration is now portrayed as both economically useful and culturally threatening. These economic and cultural issues are, of course, understood differently by different social groups. In the United States, large-scale agricultural companies, dependent on immigrants for labor, oppose efforts to substantially lower the current rate of immigration or effectively enforce immigration law. Unions and other groups that represent workers see immigrants as a threat to wage levels and job security. States that are the primary entry points for legal and illegal immigrants—Florida, Texas, and California—are also the primary arenas for cultural conflict while these issues receive little interest in states with few immigrants.

As the Muslim population in Europe and the Asian and Latin American populations in the United States expand in the next century, cultural conflicts will test definitions of citizenship and nationality. The United States has some advantages in meeting these challenges by its long experience with immigration and relatively open access to citizenship. Yet, the United States is already moving slowly in the direction of European efforts to restrict immigration and defend a culturally conservative definition of nationality.

THE CHALLENGE OF TECHNOLOGICAL AND ENVIRONMENTAL CHANGE

The economic expansion that began with the end of World War II was led by technological innovation. New technologies increased productivity and disseminated human creativity. They also altered the way we live, work, and play. Because the economic benefits of these changes have been largely concentrated in the advanced industrialized nations, technology has increased their power relative to the developing world. Even within developed nations, postwar technological innovations have not benefited all classes, industries, and regions equally. There have been losers as well as winners.

Population growth and increased levels of migration and urbanization have led to the expansion of agricultural and industrial production globally. This multiplication of farms and factories has intensified environmental threats. Loss of rain forest, soil erosion, global warming, pollution of air and water, and extinction of species represent threats to our quality of life and to the survival of our societies. Here again, differences between industrialized and developing nations have appeared. Environmental protection, like the acquistion of new technology, has progressed furthest in those societies with the greatest economic resources.

New Technologies and the World Economy

The war effort provided the initial impetus for the proliferation and dissemination of new technologies (see Chapter 31). Nuclear energy, jet engines, radar, and tape recording were among the many wartime developments that later had an impact on consumers' lives. When applied to industry, new technology increased productivity, reduced labor requirements, and improved the flow of information. Pent-up demand for consumer goods also contributed to research and development of new technologies. As the western economies recovered from the war and incomes rose, consumers sought new products that reduced their work or entertained them. The consumer electronics industry responded by rapidly developing new products.

Improvements in existing technologies accounted for much of the developed world's productivity increases during the 1950s and 1960s. Larger and faster trucks, trains, and airplanes cut transportation costs. Both capitalist and socialist governments played central roles in making these changes possible by building highway systems, improving railroad track, and constructing airports. These governments also provided essential funding and guidance in meeting expanding energy needs by bearing much of the cost for developing and constructing nuclear power plants.

No technology better symbolizes the innovations of the last fifty years than the computer. The first computers were expensive, large, and slow. Only large corporations, governments, and universities could afford them. IBM and other industry leaders recognized the potential market and worked to lower costs while, reducing the size, and increasing the speed of computers. Progress was rapid. By the mid-1980s, desktop computers had replaced typewriters in most of the developed world's offices. Technological advances have continued. Each new generation of computers is smaller, faster, and more powerful than the previous.

Linked via modems (which connect computers over phone lines) and satellites, computers have had a revolutionary effect on how work is organized and conducted. Along with cellular phones and fiber optics, modern computers make possible the nearly instantaneous transmission of large amounts of information. Commodity and stock markets across the globe are now linked electronically. Financial markets have also been integrated such that national currencies are continuously traded in response to a constant flow of political and economic information (see Environment & Technology: The Computer Revolution).

Computers have also altered manufacturing. Small dedicated computers now form a part of most production machinery. In the developed world, companies forced by increased competition to seek improvements in efficiency and product quality have introduced robots on the shop floor. Europe has followed Japan's initiative in this field, especially in automobile production and mining. With lower labor costs than Japan

An interconnected world In a remote part of Kenya, a member of the Samburu people makes a call using a cellular phone. (Sally Wiener Grotta/The Stock Market)

and Europe, the United States has introduced robots more slowly. Nevertheless, a quick comparison of photos of U.S. automobile assembly lines from 1935 and from 1995 should demonstrate the revolutionary nature of technological change.

The Computer Revolution

Not only have computers, the Internet, and cellular phones transformed the world of work, they have also transformed protest and revolution as well. On January 1, 1994, the Zapatista National Liberation Army took over the the state capital of the Mexican state of Chiapas. A movement of mostly Amerindian peasants lightly armed with World War II–era guns, the Zapatistas proved adept at keeping the world informed about events in remote Chiapas. Two days after the seizure, the leaders of the revolution were on the Internet spreading their version of events. The chief of the rebellion, Subcomandante Marcos, carried a laptop in his backpack as he traveled through rebel territory, and a raid on a Zapatista safe house in Mexico City produced more diskettes and computers than guns and bullets. Dissidents and rebels in other parts of the world are embracing this new technology as well, finding an effective way of countering the traditional control of the media enjoyed by governments.

A subcomandante carries a backpack laptop as well as more traditional arms   (Jeremy Bigwood)

The multinational corporation has been a primary agent of these changes. From the eighteenth century, powerful commercial companies have conducted business across national borders. By this century, the growing economic power of corporations in the industrialized nations has allowed them to invest directly in the mines, plantations, and public utilities of less developed regions. In the postwar years, many of these companies have become truly multinational (multinational ownership and management).

This process has been furthered by international trade agreements and open markets. Ford not only produces and sells cars internationally, but its shareholders, workers, and managers also have an international character. The Japanese automaker Honda imports into Japan cars it manufactures in Ohio. Similarly, German Volkswagen makes cars in Mexico for sale in the United States.

As multinational manufacturers, agricultural conglomerates, and financial giants become wealthier and more powerful, they increasingly can escape the controls imposed by national governments. If labor costs are too high in Japan, antipollution measures too intrusive in the United States, or taxes too high in Great Britain, multinational companies can relocate—or threaten to do so. Multinationals often have overwhelming power relative to governments in the developing world. It is usually in these settings that the worst abuses of labor or of the environment occur.

Technology and the Way We Work

The revolution in communication has permitted people today to modify the nature of work in fundamental ways. It is no longer necessary for a company's employees to arrive together at a shared workplace. Computers, cellular phones, and satellite links make it possible to conduct business from nearly any location. Editors, software designers, engineers, architects, and members of many other professions now work efficiently from their homes. Indeed, thousands of information specialists now commute via modem to work in Los Angeles from their homes in Idaho or Colorado. Today, a European researcher or manager flying over the Atlantic can compose a report on a laptop computer and send it simultaneously to associates in Japan and the United States. Even in developing nations, engineers, software writers, and other specialists are now linked via modems and satellites to corporate headquarters or manufacturing plants in more advanced industrialized nations.

These technologically induced changes have costs as well as benefits. Corporate managers, engineers, and information specialists of various kinds have been liberated from the traditional workplace at the cost of greater isolation. Will faxes, cellular conversations, and e-mail provide the same social and intellectual stimuli previously enjoyed through human contact in the lab, shop, and studio? Will these changes in work accentuate divisions of class, race, and culture? In the developed nations, those groups participat-

ing most fully in these technological changes are benefiting disproportionately from the economic growth of the last decades. The current concentration of technology in developed nations also suggests that future efforts to improve the economies of developing societies will confront many difficulties. Can nations leapfrog into the modern industrial age without having first developed basic industries and infrastructure?

Conserving and Sharing Resources

Since the 1960s, a growing number of environmental activists and concerned political leaders have warned of the devastating environmental consequences of population growth, industrialization, and the expansion of agriculture onto marginal lands. Assaults on the rain forest and redwoods, the disappearance of species, and the poisoning of streams and rivers have raised public consciousness. These signs of environmental damage are found in both advanced industrial economies and in the poorest of the developing nations. Perhaps the worst environmental record was achieved in the former Soviet Union, where industrial and even nuclear waste was often dumped with little concern for environmental consequences. The accumulated effect of scientific studies and public debate has led to both national and international efforts to slow, if not turn back, damage to the environment.

The larger global population discussed above requires more food, housing, energy, and other resources. In the developed world, industrial activity has increased much more rapidly than population growth. As a result, consumption of energy (coal, electricity, and petroleum) has risen proportionally. Indeed, the nature of the consumer-driven economic expansion of the postwar years may itself be an obstacle to addressing environmental problems. Modern economies depend for their well-being on the profligate consumption of goods and, therefore, resources. Stock markets closely follow measures of consumer confidence—the willingness of people to buy. When consumption slows, industrial

Brazilian gold rush   Mining booms have the potential of rapidly altering previously pristine natural environments. This dramatic photo illustrates the environmental impact that the arrival of thousands of gold miners have had on one region of the Brazilian state of Pará. (Sebastiao Salgado)

nations enter a recession. How could the United States, Germany, or Japan change consumption patterns to protect the environment without endangering corporate profits, wages, and employment levels?

In the developing countries, where population growth has been most dramatic since 1945, environmental pressures are often more extreme. In Brazil, India, and China, for example, the need to expand food production has led to rapid deforestation and the extension of farming and grazing onto marginal lands with the predictable results of erosion and water pollution. Population growth in Indonesia has led the government to sanction cutting nearly 20 percent of total forest area. These nations and many other poor nations are also attempting to force industrialization, fearing that their rapidly growing populations cannot be provided for unless the transition from agriculture to manufacturing is completed. Indeed, the argument for this policy is compelling. Why should Indians or Brazilians remain poor while Americans, Europeans, and Japanese remain rich?

Responding to Environmental Threats

Despite the grave nature of the environmental threats we face, there have been many successes in the effort to preserve and protect the environment. The early 1970s witnessed the passage of the Clean Air Act, the Clean Water Act, and the Endangered Species Act in the United States. These laws were part of a larger environmental effort that included the nations of the European Community and Japan. Environmental awareness has spread via changes in school curricula, the media, and grassroots political movements such as the various "green" parties active in European politics. Most nations in the developed world enforce strict antipollution laws and sponsor massive recycling efforts. Many also encourage resource conservation by rewarding energy-efficient factories and cars and by promoting alternative energy sources such as solar power.

These efforts have produced significant progress in the developed world. In western Europe and the United States, air quality has improved dramatically. In the United States, smog levels are down nearly a third in the last thirty years even though the number of automobiles has increased more than 80 percent. Emissions of lead and sulfur dioxide are down as well. The Great Lakes, Long Island Sound, and Chesapeake Bay are all much cleaner than they had been in 1970. The rivers of North America and Europe have also improved due to the introduction of new sewage treatment facilities and the implementation of stiff laws against industrial dumping.

Underlying many of these improvements is the introduction of new technologies. Adding pollution controls to automobiles, planes, and factory smokestacks lowered emissions of harmful chemicals into the environment. In 1996, a new car emits 80 percent less pollution than a similar vehicle of 1970. Similar progress has been made in the chemical industry. During the last decade scientists have identified chlorofluorocarbons or CFCs as a contributor to the loss of the ozone layer. As these chemicals are used widely in air conditioning and refrigeration, there has been strong resistance to phasing them out. Nevertheless, the transition is now nearly complete in new appliances and cars. Whether this technological change will lead to the reversal of ozone loss is not clear.

What is clear, however, is that the desire to preserve our natural environment is growing around the world. In the developed nations, continued political organization and enhanced awareness of environmental issues should lead to an incremental improvement in environmental policy. In the developing world and most of the former Soviet bloc, however, population pressures and weak governments will probably hinder effective environmental policies. It is likely, therefore, that global improvements will have to be funded by the industrialized nations—and the cost is likely to be high. Achieving this global redistribution of wealth and political power will be the most difficult task facing the environmental movement in the coming years.

CONCLUSION

In the five decades since the end of World War II, the world has been altered by economic growth and integration, by population growth and movement, and by technological and environmental change. Led by the postwar recovery of the industrial powers and the remarkable economic expansion of Japan, the world economy has grown dramatically. The development and application of new technology has contributed significantly to this process. International markets are more open and integrated than at any time in the past.

The new wealth and exciting technologies of the postwar era have not been shared equally, however. The capitalist west and a small number of Pacific Rim nations have grown richer and more powerful while most of the world's nations remain poor. Population growth in the developing world is one of the reasons for this divided experience. Unable to find adequate employment or, in many cases, bare subsistence, people in these nations migrate across borders looking to improve their lives. These movements often provide valuable labor in the factories and farms of the developed world, but also provoke cultural, racial, and ethnic tension. Meeting the problems of inequality, population growth, and international migration will challenge the global community in the coming decades.

Technology offers one of the best hopes for meeting these challenges. Engineers, stockbrokers, professors, and other professionals now have an international character thanks to the communications revolution. Ambitious and talented people in the developing world can now fully participate in global intellectual and economic life. However, the vast majority of people in these countries remain disconnected from this liberating technology by poverty. Technology is also tied in intimate ways to our efforts to protect the environment. It has provided the means to clean auto and factory emissions—even while it helped produce much of the world's pollution. Technology and human culture have been intertwined since the beginning. Our ability to control and direct this most human of assets will determine the future.

SUGGESTED READING

There is an enormous literature devoted to postwar economic performance. Among the works that should be consulted are W. L. M. Adriaasen and J. G. Waardensburg, eds. *A Dual World Economy: Forty Years of Development Experience* (1989); G. Ambrosius and W. Hibbard, *A Social and Economic History of Twentieth-Century Europe* (1989); P. Krugman, *The Age of Diminished Expectations: U.S. Economic Policy in the 1990s* (1990); B. J. McCormick, *The World Economy: Patterns of Growth and Change* (1988); and H. van der Wee, *Prosperity and Upheaval: The World Economy, 1945–1980* (1986).

There are many fine studies of nations and regions. See, for example, Volker Berghahn, *Modern Germany: Society, Economy and Politics in the 20th Century* (1983); and C. Kindleberger, *Europe's Postwar Growth* (1976). For the Soviet bloc see K. Dawisha, *Eastern Europe, Gorbachev and Reform: The Great Challenge* (1988); Barbara Engel and Christine Worobec, eds., *Russia's Women: Accommodation, Resistance, Transformation* (1990); and David Remnick, *Lenin's Tomb, The Last Days of the Soviet Empire* (1993). For the Pacific Rim, see Jonathan Spence, *The Search for Modern China* (1990); Edwin O. Reischauer, *The Japanese* (1988); H. Patrick and H. Rosovsky, *Asia's New Giant: How the Japanese Economy Works* (1976); Staffan B. Linder, *Pacific Century: Economic and Political Consequences of Asian-Pacific Dynamism* (1986). For the Third World, see R. N. Gwynne, *New Horizons? Third World Industrialization in an International Framework* (1990); G. Hancock, *Lords of Poverty: The Power, Prestige, and Corruption of the International Aid Business* (1990); E. Hermassi, *The Third World Reassessed* (1980).

There are a number of studies that examine the special problems faced by women in the postwar period. See, for example, Elisabeth Croll, *Feminism and Socialism in China* (1978); J. Ginat, *Women in Muslim Rural Society: Status and Role in Family and Community* (1982); June Hahner, *Women in Latin America* (1976); P. Hudson, *Third World Women Speak Out* (1979); A. de Souza, *Women in Contemporary India and South Asia* (1980); and M. Wolf, *Revolution Postponed: Women in Contemporary China* (1985).

For general discussions of economic, demographic, and environmental problems facing the world, see W. Alonso, ed., *Population in an Interacting World* (1987); P. R. Ehrlich and A. E. Ehrlich, *The Population Explosion* (1990); James Fallows, *More Like Us: Making America Great Again* (1989); Paul M. Kennedy, *Preparing for the Twenty-first Century* (1993); J. L. Simon, *Population Matters: People, Resources, Environment and Immigration* (1990).

For issues associated with technological and environmental change, see M. Feshbach and A. Friendly, *Ecocide in the U.S.S.R.* (1992); John Bellamy Foster, *Economic History of the Environment* (1994); S. Hecht and A. Cockburn, *The Fate of the Forest: Developers, Destroyers, and Defenders of the Amazon* (1989); K. Marton, *Multinationals, Technology, and Industrialization: Implications and Impact in Third World Countries* (1986); S. P. Huntington, *The Third Wave: Demoralization in the Late Twentieth Century* (1993); L. Solomon, *Multinational Corporations and the Emerging World Order* (1978); B. L. Turner II et al., eds., *The Earth as Transformed by Human Action: Global and Regional Changes in the Biosphere over the Past 300 Years* (1990).

NOTES

1. *New York Times,* vol. 142 (July 24, 1993), 1.

2. Andrew Hacker, "Unjust Desserts?," *The New York Review of Books,* vol. 41, no. 5 (March 3, 1994), p. 20.

3. Quoted in Antony Flew, "Introduction," to Thomas Robert Malthus, *An Essay on the Principle of Population and A Summary View of the Principle of Population* (New York, 1970), p. 30.

4. Paul Kennedy, *Preparing for the Twenty-first Century* (New York, 1993), p. 45.

CHAPTER THIRTY-FIVE

The World at the End of the Twentieth Century: A Global Culture?

Toward a Global Culture?   •   Toward a Global Government?

Toward a Fragmented World?   •   The Endurance of Cultural Diversity

At the height of World War II, German radio listeners were treated to round-the-clock political speeches and late-night performances of the Berlin Philharmonic Orchestra. United States Army Signal Corps specialists, impressed by the quality of the sound but doubting the stamina of the orators and musicians, deduced that German engineers had devised a recording system that sounded as good as a live broadcast. It was the first tape recorder, called the Magnetophon. After the Allied invasion of France (see Chapter 31), the Signal Corps searched for the mysterious device, but every Magnetophon they found had been smashed to protect the secrets of its design. When the war was nearly over, they finally discovered one intact.

Meanwhile, back in the United States, the country's most popular singer and movie star, Bing Crosby, was battling the radio networks for permission to prerecord his broadcasts. In 1946, all radio shows were live. The networks refused to allow prerecording for fear that the sound quality would be too poor. This meant that performers like Crosby had to be present at the studio at broadcast time almost every week of the year.

ABC Radio, the weakest network, hoped to benefit from Crosby's popularity and finally granted his wish. In October 1946, he began to prerecord his show on wax disks. Since this permitted him to edit the show and broadcast only the best parts, it was a success—but only a partial one. Listeners complained that the sound was tinny and fuzzy. Looking around for a better recording technique, Crosby's production company found former Signal Corps officer Jack Mullin, who had shipped home two German Magnetophons after the war. A year later, Crosby broadcast his first tape-recorded show on a machine built to Mullin's design. Its superior sound quality, essentially indistinguishable from a live broadcast, transformed radio broadcasting

overnight, with Bing Crosby Enterprises serving as the distributor for the new technology.

Tape-recording technology progressed rapidly, and within a decade engineers had developed the first practical videotape recorder. Tape recording made it increasingly convenient for ordinary people to preserve the high points of their own lives and to accumulate their own libraries of music, television broadcasts, and motion pictures. Other new technology followed, including photocopying, first offered commercially in 1959; the Internet, which originated in the 1960s; and fax machines, an old idea that became practical and cheap in the 1980s. These advances transferred to the general population the power to reproduce and distribute words, sounds, and images. Hitherto, because of the cost and technical complication of printing and recording, governments and wealthy corporations had virtually monopolized these activities.

The unanticipated consequences of this power soon became apparent. The leader of the Iranian Revolution of 1979, Ayatollah Ruhollah Khomeini (see Chapter 33), roused Iranians against the monarchy by smuggling audiotapes of sermons into the country. Scores of would-be revolutionaries around the world followed his example. Hand reproduction and distribution of underground protest literature played an important role in stirring up discontent against the failing Soviet Union. And terrorist and revolutionary groups increasingly conveyed their demands and pronouncements by way of fax transmissions or the Internet (see the Environment & Technology feature in Chapter 34). Power resided even in recordings made for private use. Tape recordings of office conversations by U.S. President Richard M. Nixon revealed wrongdoing and led to his resignation.

The availability of recording technology not only threatened the dominance of government, but it also facilitated the preservation of local cultural traditions and the development of new ones. Minivan drivers in Istanbul played audiocassettes of Arabesk music (Arab-style Turkish singing), pleasing their customers but offending polite Turkish society. Peruvian Amerindian bands played in New York City subway stations to sell their audiocassettes to passers-by. And archivists, scholars, and enthusiasts taped myriad cultural performances and rituals on the verge of extinction around the world.

TOWARD A GLOBAL CULTURE?

The process of decolonization, more or less completed with the collapse of the Soviet Union, made political imperialism an increasingly distant memory (see Chapter 33). At the same time, concerns grew in many quarters about cultural imperialism, a form of domination attributed to Western business. To these critics, entertainment conglomerates flooded the world's movie theaters and television screens with Western tastes and styles, and Western manufacturers flooded world markets with Western goods—both relying on sophisticated advertising techniques vigorously promoting this worldwide consumption. In this view, global marketing represented an insidious effort not only to overwhelm the world with a single cultural outlook formed by capitalist ideology, but also to suppress or devalue traditional cultures and alternative ideologies. The primary culprit in this conceptualization of cultural imperialism was the United States.

In truth, technology more than ideology played the central role in making Western culture available to the entire world. And a closer

First videotape recorder   Broadcast use of the Ampex VRX-1000 began on November 30, 1956. Forty years later, with a profile smaller than one of the first model's control panels, it was an essential appliance in millions of homes. Videotapes changed entertainment and posed a threat to culturally and politically repressive regimes. (Ampex Corporation)

analysis of cultural trends reveals a diversity of voices that the case for cultural imperialism overlooks.

The Medium and the Message

The position that the West engaged in cultural imperialism rested in part on the fact that American invention and industry pioneered so many of the technological means by which culture formed and spread in the twentieth century. Though the content conveyed by these new technologies was not always American, American tastes and preoccupations were highly influential, as developments in the motion picture and television industries demonstrate.

Motion pictures began in France in 1895 and flourished there and elsewhere in Europe, where the dominant concern was to reproduce stage plays. In fact, famous actors delivered every line of their speeches even though these first films were silent. In the United States, filmmaking started at almost the same time; but American filmmakers considered it their business to entertain audiences rather than to preserve outstanding theatrical performances. In competition for those audiences, they looked to cinematic innovation, broad humor, and exciting spectacles. In the process, they developed a style of filmmaking that was quite different from traditional theater and immensely popular with the general public.

After World War I, filmmaking took root and flourished in Japan, India, Turkey, Egypt, and elsewhere. American and European studios exported films successfully—partly because a silent film presented no language problems—but diversity became a hallmark of the world's film industry. In 1929, the year talking films were introduced, out of an estimated 2,100 films produced worldwide, 510 were made in the United States and 750 in Japan.

After World War II, which left much of the European and Japanese industry in ruins, the United States became the world's paramount exporter of films. Hollywood productions exported an image of the United States as a land of gangsters and cowboys, pratfalls and musical romance. By the 1960s, depictions of American life broadened. Still, emphasis on crime, luxurious living, and—from the 1970s on—explicit sexuality presented to the world a distorted but influential and consistent image of America.

European and Japanese cinema recovered slowly from the war. Filmmakers earned high marks for artistic accomplishment, but their work generally appealed to much smaller international markets. Hollywood's main international competition in the field of popular cinema came from Bombay, whose joyous musicals had wide appeal; Egypt, famed for musicals and comedies; and Hong Kong, which specialized in martial arts films. Films of high artistic merit made in the USSR, Brazil, China, India, and, after the 1979 revolution, Iran, won international prizes but did not attract mass international audiences.

Hollywood's preponderant role in the world movie industry was not replicated in television, partly because videotape technology and satellite broadcasting did not develop until after decolonization had sensitized newly independent governments to the use of broadcasting as a tool of nation building. American Vladimir Zworykin's invention of an electron scanning gun in 1928 made television possible, but it became widely available to consumers only after World War II and did not spread to most non-Western countries until the 1960s. Commercial competition in the American market spurred a steady stream of innovations, most notably color broadcasting in 1953, videotaping in 1956, and transoceanic satellite transmission in 1962.

Moviemaking tended to be privately organized or inspired even in countries that imposed government censorship. Television outside the United States, on the other hand, usually became a government monopoly, following the pattern of telegraph and postal service and radio broadcasting. Government control of news reports and approval of entertainment programs guaranteed a unified national television viewpoint and limited American cultural influence. Nevertheless, the new medium's insatiable demand for shows to broadcast eventually caused many state broadcasters to turn to American sources. It was

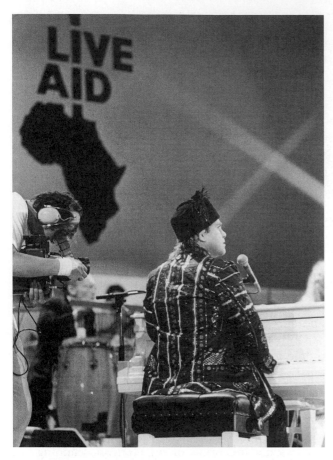

Rock concert for African famine relief Rock singer and pianist Elton John was one of many performers who donated their efforts to the Live Aid benefit concert. The concert in Britain was carried throughout the world via television and paved the way for later concerts of a similar nature. Popular music had been used for centuries to mobilize public concern and engage the feelings of young people, but radio, television, and inexpensive recordings multiplied its impact in the second half of the century. (J. Langevin/Sygma)

cheaper to broadcast American soap operas, adventure series, and situation comedies than to produce so many shows domestically. Still, the United States was not the only source of programming. Many nations purchased shows from Brazil, Mexico, and Great Britain.

At the same time, American producers saw satellite transmission as an opening to an international market. Music Television (MTV), specializing in rock music videos aimed at a youth

audience, became an international enterprise with special editions for different parts of the world. The music videos broadcast to Uzbekistan were often of Russian groups; those sent to Singapore were of Chinese groups. None of these bands were known to the average young American viewer. The Cable News Network (CNN) also developed its international potential after proving itself as the most viewed and informative news source during the 1991 Gulf War, when a U.S.–led coalition attacked Iraq for its invasion of Kuwait. With news around the clock, CNN began to supplant both other commercial and government news programming as the best source for news about rapidly developing crises. Still, since CNN embodied a fundamentally American view of the news, even in its international editions, governments in other countries often limited its reception.

Zworykin's electron scanning gun also made possible the computer screen. The computer industry, which mushroomed for defense and business purposes in the postwar decades, initially had little connection with television or movies. At base, the three technologies differed. Movies recorded light and shadow on film, and television used electromagnetic waves. Computers were based on a digital system in which every bit of information was a 0 or a 1, with millions of bits required for even a simple screen display. In principle, however, given adequate electronic storage capacity and enough speed in recovering stored information, every point on a photographic image or electron wave could be expressed digitally and transmitted to the computer screen as a moving picture. Japan introduced the first digital television broadcasting in the 1990s, about the same time that disks containing digitized movies and computer programs with movielike action became increasingly available. (See Environment and Technology: Compact Disc Technology.) More widespread, however, was communication through the Internet, a linkage of academic, government, and business computer networks. Developed originally for U.S. defense research purposes in the 1960s, the Internet expanded to become a major cultural phenomenon with the proliferation of personal computers in the 1980s.

Compact Disc Technology

When the spinning disc replaced Thomas Edison's original revolving cylinder as the preferred means of recording sound, a fragile, single-sided wax disc could play some three to ten minutes of music, depending upon whether it was 10 or 12 inches in diameter. Pressing both sides of the disc doubled the information that could be stored in its grooves. By making the grooves narrower, packing them closer, and slowing the speed of rotation from 78 revolutions per minute to 33 1/3 rpm, a whole symphony could be recorded on the two sides of a single 12-inch disc. These long-playing, or LP, records, made of durable vinyl became standard for the recording industry in the 1960s.

The compact disc, introduced by Sony and Philips Electronics in the 1980s, used a recording technique in which a laser burned tiny pits, representing the zeros and ones of digitized sound, into a five-inch plastic disc. Between 1982 and 1996, 400 million CD players and 6 billion discs were sold. The 12-inch LP became obsolete since both of its sides could be recorded on a single-sided CD with more precise sound, less noise, and greater durability.

In 1997, several electronics companies began to market digital versatile discs (DVD). With smaller pits and a narrower data track, the DVD has a data spiral twice as long as the same-sized CD and can store 14 times the amount of information. Future plans visualize a quadrupling of DVD capacity through recording on two layers.

Each major change in recording capacity has expanded the range of materials—music, movies, computer programs—that can efficiently be reproduced and lowered the cost of reproduction. Thus the information age ushered in by Thomas Edison's phonograph seems likely to evolve dramatically in the twenty-first century.

Compact disc (IBM Corporation, Research Division, Almaden Research Center)

As had happened so often throughout history, technological developments led the world in unanticipated directions. The new telecommunications and entertainment technologies did indeed derive disproportionately from American invention, industry, and cultural creativity (with Japan becoming a powerful secondary factor on the industrial side in the 1970s). To that degree, then, these changes could be seen as foreboding Western, especially American, cultural domination. In fact, however, the American input was rather uneven. The more widespread the new technologies became, the greater the opportunities afforded to people around the world to adapt them to their own purposes.

The Spread of Popular Culture

Just as new technologies affected international currents of cultural influence, so they changed perceptions of culture. At the beginning of the twentieth century, sophisticated Europeans and Americans, like elite groups from imperial Rome to Ming China, valued most what they considered "high culture" and thought of "popular culture" as localized entertainment for villagers and common folk—vigorous, picturesque, and quaint, but essentially vulgar. Influenced by the tastes of the European imperialist powers, modernizing elite groups around the world had

Japanese adult male comic book Comic magazines emerged after World War II as a major form of publication in Japan and a distinctive product of Japanese culture. Different series are directed to different age and gender groups. Issued weekly and running to some 300 pages in black and white, the most popular magazines sell as many copies as major newsmagazines do in the United States.

turned their backs on their own artistic traditions in the nineteenth century. Instead, they built opera houses, established symphony orchestras, and experimented with European literary forms as extensions of their fascination with everything Western. Thus a Europe-dominated concept of "high culture," with a canon of masterworks created exclusively by composers, artists, and

thinkers of European descent, took root in many parts of the world. Non-Western cultural forms lost prestige in their own homes.

While European tastes were thus becoming influential internationally, popular culture was becoming more and more visible. Illustrious European composers and choreographers had been turning to folk tunes and dances for inspiration since the eighteenth century. But the search for fresh sounds and images intensified with the advent of modernism in Europe in the mid-nineteenth century. Modern writers, composers, and artists valued novelty and individuality of expression over classical structures and traditional formal narratives. These artists explored the workings of the subconscious rather than attempting to portray an objective reality. Since patrons of the arts were often outraged and offended by experimental or unconventional modernist works, sensationalism became a hallmark of modernism. Artists and composers strove to explore ever broader frontiers of feeling and experience. Some were captivated by the sounds and images of Europe's new industrial society; others drew their ideas from popular culture. Spanish artist Pablo Picasso, one of the most consistent modernist innovators, borrowed the imagery of African masks in some paintings, circuses and carnivals in others, and newspaper typography in still others.

This mining of popular cultures for ideas did little to inspire a wide interest in those cultures, however. Thomas Edison's phonograph was the key invention that opened popular culture to global audiences. Through inexpensive recordings, American popular music spread around the world. Jazz and blues had originated in the black culture of the American South after the Civil War and moved north in the twentieth century when black musicians migrated northward. The newborn recording industry made their creations available to a nation that was rapidly exchanging the parlor piano for a phonograph. Musicians like Jelly Roll Morton set a high standard of achievement.

Though blues remained primarily a black American taste, jazz recordings and jazz musicians became popular in Europe in the 1920s. The driving force behind jazz remained the creative skill of black musicians like Duke Ellington, Louis Armstrong, Bessie Smith, and Billie Holiday. Serious orchestral composers like the Russian Igor Stravinsky and the Frenchman Maurice Ravel utilized jazz rhythms and themes just as Picasso borrowed ideas from African masks. However, jazz remained the music of nightclubs and dance parties instead of concert halls. By World War II, black jazz musicians had become so much a part of the international image of the United States that Nazi propaganda frequently incorporated vile racial caricatures of them. Ironically, while jazz was widely perceived abroad as quintessential American popular culture, it remained largely the preserve of the African-American minority at home. Millions of white Americans preferred the tunes published by New York's commercial music houses, which employed some of the musical language of jazz but seldom displayed the black sensibility.

The popularity of jazz derived from the appeal of its rhythms and naturalness, not from imitation of a colonial ruling class, as with the nineteenth-century vogue for grand opera. The same was true of rock'n'roll, a dynamic, sensual, and audacious popular music that arose in the 1950s and became even more widespread than jazz. Rock grew out of black rhythm-and-blues and derived initially from black American performers like Chuck Berry. The rise to international stardom in the early 1960s of Britain's Beatles helped make rock'n'roll a worldwide phenomenon. The core of rock remained American and British, but popular musicians from all over the world recorded in rock-influenced styles. Some achieved broad acclaim, as did Jamaica's Bob Marley with his Caribbean reggae style. Others gained strong local followings by blending rock with traditional forms, as happened with Malagasy music in Madagascar and Rai music in Algeria.

The rhythms and feelings of former black slaves in the American South could never have evolved into a core element of global culture without the recording industry. The preponderant role of the United States in the postwar world also played a role. The equally African-inspired rhythms of the Brazilian samba and Cuban rumba, for example, never gained a significant international following.

Mass production and advertising, the latter developed largely in the United States, opened a second avenue to the worldwide spread of popular culture. Prior to World War II, each industrialized country followed its own path in terms of consumer goods. In the postwar era, however, in part because of the destruction of so much industry in Europe and Japan, American consumer products began to find international markets. In time, European, Japanese, and multinational companies became equally aggressive in international marketing, making it harder and harder for homegrown industries in smaller or poorer countries to hold their own without government protection. In marketplaces around the world, domestically produced consumer goods, from children's toys to copper cooking pots, were displaced by imports.

In the 1970s and 1980s, the U.S. economy suffered from inflation fueled by soaring oil prices and intense competition from Japanese manufacturers (see Chapter 34). Ironically, critics around the world chose this time to identify the United States as the chief propagator of a worldwide consumer culture. This analysis seemed to be confirmed by the international cachet of American brand names like Levi, Coca-Cola, Marlboro, Gillette, McDonald's, and Kentucky Fried Chicken. But the names blazoned in neon atop the skyscrapers of Tokyo—Hitachi, Sony, Sanyo, and Mitsubishi—commanded instant recognition as well, as did such European names as Nestlé, Mercedes, Pirelli, and Lacoste. The concept of a globe-girdling American consumer culture had, in fact, been overtaken by internationalization.

A sidewalk stand in Amman, Jordan, in 1986 symbolized the fact. It featured inexpensive yellow sweatshirts bearing the legend "Oklahoma" with a large number beneath it. The shirts were made in Hong Kong; the buyers were Arabs; and the reference was to American football, then rarely played outside North America. At the same time, sidewalk stands in New York's Greenwich Village were stocked with checked Arab *kaffiyas,* or headscarves. The internationalization of styles, as of music, had become a two-way street. Yet, on balance, the overall direction of change in popular culture and consumer taste during the decades following World War II was indeed toward the United States. Two years after the breakup of the Soviet Union, a shopper in Bishkek, the capital of Kyrgyzstan in the heart of Central Asia, could buy women's underpants stenciled with a picture of a Marlboro cigarette pack and a diner in Moscow could go to Pizza Hut for an exotic, if fairly expensive, treat.

Marxist theorists argued that the tendency of capitalist economies to produce too many goods compelled industrialized nations to seek ever-larger markets, thereby exploiting the entire world for the benefit of corporate shareholders.

By their interpretation, the spread of American products, or of the enticing image of American products, was simply another form of imperialism, insidiously but inevitably destroying local crafts, styles, and cultural traditions. Yet most young Turks, Nigerians, and Taiwanese who liked to wear Levis, drink Coke, smoke Camels, and listen to Michael Jackson had little sense of being under the thumb of the imperialists. Though their economies may, indeed, have been in thrall to multinational business concerns, they themselves generally felt free to condemn American foreign policy and considered their personal style preferences simply an aspect of living within an increasingly global culture. The issue of cultural imperialism remained far more ambigu-

Pyramid entrance to the Louvre   I. M. Pei, a Chinese-American architect born in 1917, designed elegant office buildings such as Boston's John Hancock Tower in the international style. His 1987–1989 plan for refurbishing Paris' Louvre museum with a glass pyramid in its courtyard initially outraged critics who said that its stark geometric modernism ignored the city's architectural traditions. Since opening, it has proven popular as well as functionally effective. (Bill Wassman/The Stock Market)

ous than European imperialism had been in the days of colonial viceroys and gunboat diplomacy (see Chapter 29).

Global Connections and Elite Culture

While the real or apparent globalization of popular culture became a subject of concern, the implications of cultural links across national and ethnic boundaries at a more elite level were less controversial. The end of the Cold War (see Chapter 33) reopened intellectual and cultural contacts between the former adversaries, making possible such things as Russian–American collaboration on space missions and extensive business contacts among former rivals. European and American scientific laboratories benefited as well from the intellectual gifts of an increasing number of graduate students and researchers from China, India, Pakistan, Turkey, and elsewhere. Given the scarcity of high-level research laboratories outside of Europe, America, and Japan, many of these students chose to remain in their countries of training after graduation, contributing to a "brain drain" that primarily benefited the West.

In this way, technical training helped contribute to the rising importance of English as a global second language. British imperialism had planted English on every continent by the beginning of the twentieth century (see Chapters 26 and 29). Spurred by American economic and political eminence in the second half of the century, as well as by American movies and television, the language spread even as the British Empire faded away. English became the most commonly taught second language in the world, and a number of technology-intensive industries, including air transportation and computers, used it extensively. In newly independent countries, universities that took pride in teaching in the national language often had science faculties that operated in English. The emergence of this potential global language made travel for business and pleasure increasingly easy and greatly facilitated the operations of multinational corporations. Still, the future of the trend and its long-run implications could not be foreseen.

Architectural design and engineering afford an instructive example of globalization at the higher cultural level. In the 1920s, the Swiss architect Charles Édouard Jeanneret, known as Le Corbusier, outlined a new approach to architecture that featured simplicity of form, absence of surface ornamentation, easy manufacture, and inexpensive materials. Among his influential designs were the main buildings of Chandigarh, the new capital of the Indian state of Punjab.

Postmodern Japanese architecture Kiyoshi Sey Takeyama, born in 1954, designed the D-Hotel in Osaka in 1985. "Relations can often be clarified by interrupting things.... I built massive, incomplete walls, simultaneously expressing desire for and renunciation of communication with others. This ambivalence sums up our life in the contemporary city." Takeyama and other young Japanese architects pursue an architecture that reponds more to modern Japanese culture than to the earlier modernism of the international style. (Courtesy, AMORPHE Takeyama and Associates)

Other architects—including the Finn Eero Saarinen, the Germans Ludwig Mies van der Rohe and Walter Gropius, and the American Frank Lloyd Wright—advanced his lines of thought and added their own to create what was known as the International Style after World War II.

Glass and steel skyscrapers in the International Style began to sprout in world capitals in the 1960s. At the same time, people were traveling to those capitals along highways that followed limited access designs pioneered by the German autobahns. The causeway linking the island nation of Bahrain with mainland Saudi Arabia, for example, was indistinguishable in design from an American superhighway. The designs of new underground rail systems in Cairo and Mexico City similarly reflected the internationalization of engineering and design. It became commonplace for a project in one country to be designed by an architectural firm in another and built by a construction firm from a third.

The International Style came to be criticized, however, for neglecting local architectural traditions. Critics either blasted the designs for indulging the creative fancies of the architects or complained that architects turned out boringly similar designs that imparted an unattractive uniformity to previously distinctive cities. In the United States, this criticism formed the foundation of a movement called postmodernism. Postmodernist theoreticians called for abandoning the rigid rules of architectural modernism and showing greater sensitivity to history and local context. There was a call for allowing more diverse voices, such as those of minorities, to be heard in determining aesthetic criteria and for making the arts more accessible to ordinary people.

Some architects, including a growing number from non-Western countries, reacted to the postmodern critique. They retained modernism's advances in technology and materials while experimenting with a broader array of forms, surface decoration, and references to earlier architectural traditions. Though conventional glass and steel skyscrapers continued to be built, liberation from Le Corbusier's confining vision permitted architects in different countries to follow their own inclinations. Designs by such young Japanese postmodernists as Kiyoshi Takeyama and Norihiko Dan differed markedly from those of their Western counterparts Philip Johnson of the United States and James Stirling of Great Britain. Yet they were by no means a return to traditional Japanese forms.

Situated at the juncture of artistic vision and new building technologies, architecture stood out as the counterpart of rock music in fostering local diversity within the context of overall global change. But it was not unique. The ten winners of the Nobel Prize for Literature between 1982 and 1991 included writers from Colombia, Nigeria, Egypt, Mexico, and the West Indies. By contrast, the previous decade's winners had included only one non-European. Seeming to heed the call of the postmodernists for opening the door to voices from beyond the European perimeter, the prize committee helped the world recognize the growing strength of its cultural diversity.

Only time will tell how correct is the apprehension that cultural globalization will ultimately lead to the triumph of stultifying homogeneity, mediocrity, and vulgarity. The West, for good or ill, dominated the immediate postimperialist era. However, the web of international contact based on advanced technologies had not yet reached its full extent or become accessible to the bulk of the world's peoples. By the end of the century, according to one estimate, half the world's people had never spoken on a telephone. The cultural changes spurred by technology seemed only to be in mid-course. Technology could still become a means of releasing profound creative energies in unexpected locales.

TOWARD A GLOBAL GOVERNMENT?

Economic and technological forces had the side effect of fostering a global culture. Globalization of political and social behavior, on the other hand, resulted from deliberate institution building. Many such institutions grew from initial agreements among a small group of nations. The Universal Postal Union, facilitating international mail deliveries, began in 1875 following agreement among a handful of European countries and the United States. It is now a U.N. agency. The International Committee of the Red Cross included fewer than 20 countries at its outset in 1880. Now it has over 100 national members in all parts of the world. Some derived from the need for standards for new technologies. For example, the ASCII (American Standard Code for Information Interchange) code was originally designed to standardize the transmission of letter characters to teletype machines. IBM expanded its use in 1981 to become the most common system for representing keyboard characters on personal computers.

The most ambitious attempt to create an international institution was undoubtedly the United Nations, the postwar successor to the League of Nations (see Chapter 30). Few political leaders anywhere fully embraced the notion of world governance. Most remained reluctant to surrender national sovereignty or permit outsiders to intervene in national affairs. But the widespread desire to avert future wars, address international problems collectively, and allow voices from all over the world to be heard induced most countries to participate actively in the United Nations.

The United Nations

U.S. President Franklin Delano Roosevelt first used the term "United Nations" in 1941 to describe those countries allied in the war against Germany and Italy. In 1942, twenty-six governments agreed not to make peace separately. Two years later, representatives from the United States, Great Britain, the USSR, and China, met at Dumbarton Oaks, New York. There they drafted specific charter proposals that finally bore fruit in the treaty called the United Nations Charter signed in San Francisco in the spring of 1945 and ratified by fifty-one original member nations on October 24, United Nations Day.

Like its predecessor, the League of Nations (see Chapter 30), the United Nations had two houses. The assembly of all member states was called the General Assembly; the inner council was named the Security Council. A full-time bureaucracy headed by a secretary general carried out the day-to-day business of both groups, and numerous agencies concerned themselves with specialized international problems. These include UNICEF (United Nations Children's Fund), the FAO (Food and Agriculture Organization), and UNESCO (United Nations Educational, Scientific, and Cultural Organization). Unlike the League, which required unanimous agreement in both its deliberative bodies, the United Nations operated by majority rule, except that five permanent members of the Security Council—China, France, Great Britain, the United States, and the USSR—had veto power in that chamber. (Until 1971, the China seat on the Security Council was held by the government of Taiwan. That year, the United States agreed to oust Taiwan from the U.N. and establish the People's Republic of China in its place [see Chapter 33].)

The decolonization of Africa and Asia (see Chapter 33) greatly swelled the size of the General Assembly while the Security Council remained at a fixed number of members. Many of these new nations looked to the United Nations, with its internationalist and egalitarian philosophy, for assistance and access to a wider political world. While the vetoes of the Security Council's permanent members often stymied action touching even indirectly on Cold War concerns, the General Assembly became the arena for expressing opinions on many issues involving decolonization. In the organization's early years, General Assembly resolutions carried great weight. An example is the 1947 order that divided Palestine into sovereign Jewish and Arab states (see Chapter 33). Gradually, though, the flood of new members produced a voting majority more concerned with poverty and racial discrimination than with the Cold War. As a result, the superpowers and their allies increasingly disregarded the General Assembly, effectively allowing the new nations of the world to speak, but not to act collectively.

All signatories to the United Nations Charter renounced war and territorial conquest. Nevertheless, peacekeeping, the sole preserve of the Security Council, became a particularly vexing problem. An ill-advised Soviet boycott of Council proceedings in 1950 resulted in a vote to send troops to resist the North Korean invasion of South Korea. Having learned its lesson, the Soviet Union subsequently exercised its veto to prevent further United Nations interference against allies or Soviet-supported revolutionary movements. The other permanent members acted in the same way to protect their own friends and interests. Throughout the Cold War, then, the United Nations was seldom able to deploy forces to forestall or quell international conflicts, though it did from time to time send observers to monitor truces or agreements otherwise arrived at. This failure to act ended dramatically in 1990 when the organization authorized creation of a multinational military coalition to oppose the Iraqi annexation of Kuwait. Iraqi troops were expelled in the Gulf War of 1991. Afterwards, a serious debate arose as to whether this was a fluke occurrence or the harbinger of new forcefulness by the United Nations.

Human Rights

The United Nations was not just concerned with relations between states; it also aimed to protect the individual. The human rights movement was anchored in a United Nations General Assembly resolution of December 10, 1948 called the Universal Declaration of Human Rights. The declaration contained thirty articles, which it proclaimed to be "a common standard of achievement for all peoples and nations."[1] It condemned slavery; torture; cruel and inhuman punishment; and arbitrary arrest, detention, or exile. It called for freedom of movement, assembly, and thought. It asserted rights to life, liberty, and security of person; to impartial public trials; and to education, employment, and leisure. Throughout, the declaration ringingly asserted the principle of equality, most fully set forth in article 2:

> Everyone is entitled to all the rights and freedoms set forth in this Declaration, without distinction of any kind, such as race, color, sex, language, religion, or political or other opinion, national or social origin, property, birth or other status.[2]

The roots of the declaration lay mostly in European and American history. Religious tolerance emerged from Europe's bloody religious wars between Catholics and Protestants (see Chapter 18). The U.S. Constitution and Bill of Rights and the French Declaration of the Rights of Man contributed Enlightenment ideas of inalienable rights (see Chapter 25). The struggle against slavery and the women's suffrage movement in the nineteenth and twentieth centuries extended the concept of tolerance to all races and both sexes (see Chapters 25 and 28). The concept of social justice steadily advanced with the recognition of labor unions, the spread of universal education, and the establishment of government programs to care for the needy and ensure an adequate standard of living for all citizens.

Not all the countries that initially voted for the declaration shared this European heritage. However, its principles dovetailed with humanitarian outlooks in a variety of cultures and nations. Most countries joining the United Nations later willingly signed the declaration since it implicitly condemned the persistence of discriminatory European colonial regimes. Despite this apparent agreement, some people had philosophical reservations about the declaration's formulation of human rights. They asked whether such a set of principles could be called universal when so many of the world's religious and cultural traditions had not been consulted in its drafting.

Did the declaration's assertion of total equality, for example, mean that the traditional social distinctions represented by the Hindu castes were unacceptable? Was the declaration breached by nations that used religion, language, skin color, or membership in a particular ethnic group to distinguish more privileged from less privileged citizens—a group that included Israel, the United States, South Africa, and Saudi Arabia, among many others? Did the article declaring that "everyone has a right to a nationality" implicitly condemn the suppression of ethnic minorities—as Turkey, Iraq, and Iran did with their Kurdish populations; China did with Tibetans; and France did with immigrant Muslims from North Africa?

In practice, human rights activists ignored these more troubling issues. Instead, they focused on easily agreed upon violations of human decency, such as torture, imprisonment without trial, summary execution by government death squads, and famine and refugee relief. International organizations devoted to relieving hunger and oppression and bringing human rights abuses to world attention proliferated in the 1970s. Amnesty International, founded in 1961 and numbering 1.2 million members by 1993, concentrated on gaining freedom for people illegally imprisoned. The Conference on Security and Cooperation in Europe, founded in 1972, became an effective human rights monitoring group after the Soviet Union reaffirmed its commitment to human rights at a convention in Helsinki in 1975. Famine relief gave rise to heavily publicized rock concerts that inspired an international outpouring of sympathy and money.

Such efforts raised the prominence of human rights as a global concern and put pressure on governments to consider the issue when making foreign policy decisions. But increasing concern did not answer the questions of people who felt that the rights referred to in the declaration were solely of Western derivation and therefore insensitive to other cultural and religious traditions. Skeptics observed that when a Western country prodded a non-Western country to improve its human rights performance—for example, by barring the government from cutting off a thief's hand as stipulated by Islamic law—reverse criticism of the Western country—for example, condemnation of persistent racial discrimination in America—often fell on deaf ears. Thus the human rights movement was sometimes seen not as an effort to make the world as a whole more humane, but as a form of Western cultural imperialism, a club with which to beat former colonial societies into submission.

Women's Rights

No issue exemplified this dichotomy of views so clearly as women's rights. The feminist movement that peaked in the early twentieth century had concentrated on acquiring voting rights, expecting that any further gains in equality could be achieved through the ballot (see Chapters 28

Beijing women's conference in 1995 This gathering of women, under United Nations auspices, from every part of the world illustrated the challenges posed by women's search for equality. The Chinese government, consistent with its policies of suppressing dissent and closely regulating social life, tried to limit press access to the conference. As in many other instances, these efforts to silence or control women's voices on issues like abortion and family planning proved ineffective. (Alexandra Boulat/Sipa Press)

and 30). Feminist activism revived in the United States in the 1960s inspired by parallel efforts to combat racial discrimination and end the war in Vietnam. Spread subsequently to Europe and then around the world, feminism focused on equal access to education and jobs as well as on quality of life matters such as eradicating anti-female language and behavior, ending sexual exploitation, and abandoning confining clothing styles. Ironically, the decades that saw the feminist movement (followed by movements for gay and lesbian rights in the United States and Europe) become a major force also saw sexuality become a more explicit and prominent aspect of commercial, artistic, and social life.

Feminists in the West decried the oppression of women in other parts of the world. At the same time, some non-Western women complained about the deterioration of morality and family life in the West and a misplaced feminist concern with matters such as clothing. As with human rights, non-Western peoples disputed the West's definition of priorities. Though Western women and secularized Muslim women called Islamic dress codes discriminatory, many outspoken Muslim women chose to cover their hair and conceal their bodies, whether as an expression of personal belief, a statement of resistance to secular dictatorship, or a defense against coarse male behavior. Some African women saw their real problems as deteriorating economic conditions, AIDS (see Voices and Visions: AIDS and Society), and customary genital mutilation.

Efforts to coordinate the struggle for women's rights internationally began with the formation in 1946 of the United Nations Commission on the Status of Women. After lagging for several decades, these efforts gained momentum in the 1970s with a series of highly publicized international conferences. The search for a universally accepted women's rights agenda proved elusive, given these local concerns and strong disagreement on issues like abortion. Still, a rising global tide of women's education, access to employment, political participation, and control of fertility augured well for the eventual achievement of gender equality.

Nevertheless, culturally shaped disagreement on this and other philosophical and social issues persisted at century's end. The greatest likelihood was that the diverse peoples of the world would seldom be able to do more than agree to disagree. And with world developmental patterns pointing to worsening social and economic problems in Africa and growing economic power in Asia (see Chapter 34), the continuing appeal of standards too closely identified with European and American values seemed to be in doubt.

TOWARD A FRAGMENTED WORLD?

Running counter to the various trends toward globalization, political and social division along religious, ethnic, and racial lines increased during the final decades of the century. While the world economy became more integrated (see Chapter 34), diversity came increasingly to be valued. Indeed, in a significant number of countries, the call for diversity evolved into militant movements for separation or secession.

From the onset of European imperialism down to the peace settlement at the close of World War I (see Chapter 30), the European powers had readily—often arbitrarily—drawn and redrawn lines on maps. Ironically, these arbitrary boundaries became accepted borders for new nations in the era of decolonization. Superpower fear of regional instability during the Cold War combined with desire in the newly independent states to legitimize and institutionalize their national identities to produce a broad unwillingness to redraw national boundaries. Regional groups like the Organization of African Unity affirmed the unchangeable status of colonial borders despite their lack of relationship to ethnic and linguistic realities. Secession efforts—whether by the Ibos of southern Nigeria (1967–1970) or Canada's Quebecois (from the 1970s to the 1990s)—aroused little support in other countries, who favored the status quo. This generally conservative attitude toward change was reinforced by a number of violent episodes that aroused fears of the world order somehow dissolving.

Challenges to the Nation-State

A frequently invoked image of the latter part of the twentieth century was that some place or other might become "like Lebanon" or "like Beirut." The reference was to the prolonged period of civil war and anarchy that Lebanon experienced between 1975 and 1991. A closer look at this conflict illustrates the complexity and diver-

AIDS and Society

Acquired Immune Deficiency Syndrome (AIDS) was identified in 1981 as a fatal disease caused by human immunodeficiency virus, or HIV. It has spread worldwide, affecting a large proportion of the population in parts of sub-Saharan Africa. Since transmission of the virus occurs only through exchange of bodily fluids—mainly blood or semen—AIDS is most closely associated with sexual activities or reuse of hypodermic needles. Some cases have arisen from blood transfusions or accidental contact with infected blood. Though homosexual or bisexual men and drug users who share needles thus far account for the preponderance of AIDS victims, heterosexual relations are an important vector for the spread of the disease in Africa. There women and newborn babies make up a significant proportion of those infected. Because the disease has a multi-year latency period during which the infected person is unaware of his or her condition, efforts to curb the epidemic have focused not only on finding a cure but on instilling safe-sex practices, such as using condoms and refraining from promiscuous behavior.

AIDS normally strikes people in the prime of life, and it has claimed some of the world's most artistic and talented people as well as its most deprived. Arthur Ashe, a black American tennis player who was an outspoken advocate of racial equality as well as Wimbledon champion in 1975, acquired his HIV infection through a heart operation in 1983. He died ten years later. In his memoirs he writes:

Sometimes, gloomily, I wonder about a connection between AIDS and where we in the United States are headed as a people and a nation as this century moves to a close. Too many people seem determined to forget that although we are of different colors and beliefs, we are all members of the same human race, united by much more than the factors and forces that separate us. Sometimes I wonder what is becoming of our vaunted American society, or even Western civilization, as an unmistakable darkness seems to settle over our lives and our history, blocking out the sun. Our national destiny, which at times seems as bright as in the past, sometimes also appears tragically foreshortened, even doomed, as the fabric of our society is threatened by endless waves of crime, by the weakening of our family structures, by the deterioration of our schools, and by the decline of religion and spiritual values. AIDS then takes on a specially ominous cast, as if in its savagery and mystery it mirrors our fate.

Surely we need to resist surrendering to such a fatalistic analogy. Some people profess to see little purpose to the struggle for life. And yet that is precisely the task to which, in my fight against the ravages of AIDS, I devote myself every day: the struggle for life, aided by science in my fight with this disease. . . .

I know that I must govern that part of my imagination that endows AIDS with properties it does not intrinsically possess. I must be as resolute and poised as I can be in the face of its threat. I tell myself that I must never surrender to its power to terrify, even under its constant threat of death."

Why do cultural heroes—athletes, movie stars, popular musicians—play such an important role in contemporary life? According to Ashe, does an ongoing tragedy such as AIDS serve more to bring society together, or to divide it? Why?

Source: Arthur Ashe and Arnold Rampersad, *Days of Grace* (New York: Alfred A. Knopf, 1993), p. 221.

sity of forces that could come into play in an ostensibly local conflict. It also shows how fragile were the new states born during the period of decolonization.

Lebanon became independent of France after World War II. A small country of 3 million people divided among various Christian and Muslim sects, its unwritten national pact stipulated that the president would be a Maronite Christian, the prime minister a Sunni Muslim, and the speaker for its religiously proportioned parliament a Shi'ite Muslim. This formula worked for thirty years. Lebanon became a dynamic, prosperous country with a well-educated and enterprising population even while giving refuge (but not citizenship) to thousands of Palestinians who fled Israel after the 1948 war in the Middle East (see Chapter 33). Many of these Palestinian refugees looked to the Palestine Liberation Organization (PLO) for political leadership.

When a Lebanese civil war broke out in 1975, the issue of whether the PLO should remain free to organize militarily against Israel became intermixed with long simmering tensions between the religious groups. Since each religious group had one or more private militias ready to defend territory and privileges, the situation turned bloody. Neighboring Syria intervened to balance the political scales, first on behalf of the Palestinians and then in support of the Maronites. Finally it settled into a quasi-occupation of uncertain intent. Israel, meanwhile, took up the Maronite cause in hopes of gaining a friendly and avowedly Christian neighbor. The Islamic Republic of Iran supported the Shi'ites, the poorest Lebanese community but a large one. Beirut became a battlefield, and the national government more or less ceased to function.

In 1982, a highly destructive Israeli invasion expelled the PLO from Lebanon but failed to secure a Maronite-dominated government. Other countries sent troops to facilitate a PLO withdrawal, but they became subject to terrorist attack. Chaos resulted, and the civil war resumed. Finally, in 1991, the Syrian army suppressed the last Maronite efforts to prolong their dominance, and an uneasy peace fell over the exhausted nation. By 1996, new construction in Beirut indicated that the civil war was over—but trouble lurked beneath the surface. Syria still occupied eastern Lebanon, and Israel still patrolled the largely Shi'ite south, where violence sometimes flared between Israel and Shi'ite militants.

Sometimes the Lebanese conflict seemed to hinge on old religious and economic rivalries; at other times, the country seemed to be an arena for indirect warfare between Israel, the PLO, and Syria. It is not altogether clear why the status quo broke down in 1975. Once the guns stopped firing, a new Lebanese government still divided the top posts religiously just as before even though many Christians had emigrated and the Shi'ites were generally considered to have become the majority population.

Other countries experienced conflicts similar to the Lebanese disaster. The Tamil-speaking Hindu population in Sri Lanka fought a prolonged and merciless guerrilla struggle against the dominant Singhalese-speaking Buddhists. Yugoslavia's postcommunist dissolution in 1991 and 1992 into five independent states led to a bewildering and intractable war among Eastern Orthodox Serbians, Muslim Bosnians, and Roman Catholic Croatians, all of whom shared the same ethnic and linguistic identity. Basque separatists in northern Spain pursued their political goals through terrorist bombings. Eritrea fought successfully for independence from religiously and linguistically different Ethiopia. And ethnic hatreds wracked Rwanda and Burundi repeatedly.

In other instances, large-scale violence was avoided. The linguistically dissimilar Czechs and Slovaks agreed to divide postcommunist Czechoslovakia into a Czech Republic and a Slovak Republic. A brief uprising among the Maya population of southern Mexico drew needed government attention and aid to that part of the country. And Malay-Chinese animosities in Malaysia were largely submerged in economic prosperity.

Compared with nineteenth-century nationalist movements, a hallmark of these and other instances of ethnic, linguistic, or religious autonomy was the comparative unimportance of ideology. Some leaders did eloquently proclaim their people's right to national identity and statehood. More often, though, leaders inveighed against the intolerance, insolence, or oppressive acts of some other group. The primary stress was on social differentiation rather than a group's destiny or god's will. As a consequence, there was a good deal of bewilderment worldwide as to where such desires to cling together and resist assimilation might lead in the future.

Religion in the Contemporary World

While the role of religious feeling in the conflicts in Lebanon and Bosnia was uncertain, no one could doubt the enhanced global role of religion in the closing decades of the twentieth century

Scene from Lebanese civil war In the city of Beirut, where a dozen or more militias fought to protect their neighborhoods or extend their control, many fighters were masked gunmen rather than uniformed troops. Many prosperous citizens fled abroad leaving room for villagers to occupy abandoned and damaged buildings. Beirut's reputation as the Arab city with the most European way of life did not survive the war. By the mid-1990s, when rebuilding got underway, the city was much more heavily Muslim and Shi'ite than it had been, and Lebanese political life was dominated by Syria. In southern Lebanon, Israel exerted authority in a security zone several miles deep. (F. Demulder/Frank Spooner Pictures/Liaison International)

(see Map 35.1). Heightened religiosity did not necessarily lead to conflict, however. Essentially peaceful missionary and revival movements made great headway in many areas. Examples include evangelical Protestantism in the United States, Central and South America, and the former Soviet Union; Mormonism in American Samoa and Chile; and the completely nonpolitical Jam'at-i Tabligh movement throughout the Islamic world.

Appeals for a return to family-based moral uprightness found enthusiastic audiences whether made to African-Americans by the Nation of Islam or to secular Jews by the Lubavitcher sect. Pope John Paul II traveled tirelessly to visit Roman Catholics in every part of the world and spoke forcefully on behalf of the moral teachings of the church. He counseled peace, social justice, and the setting aside of historical animosities by the world's religions. Polish by origin, he also played an important role in encouraging Catholics in Eastern Europe to confront and bring down their atheistic communist regimes. Yet he also met disagreement when he reiterated the Church's opposition to birth control, abortion, and the ordination of women priests.

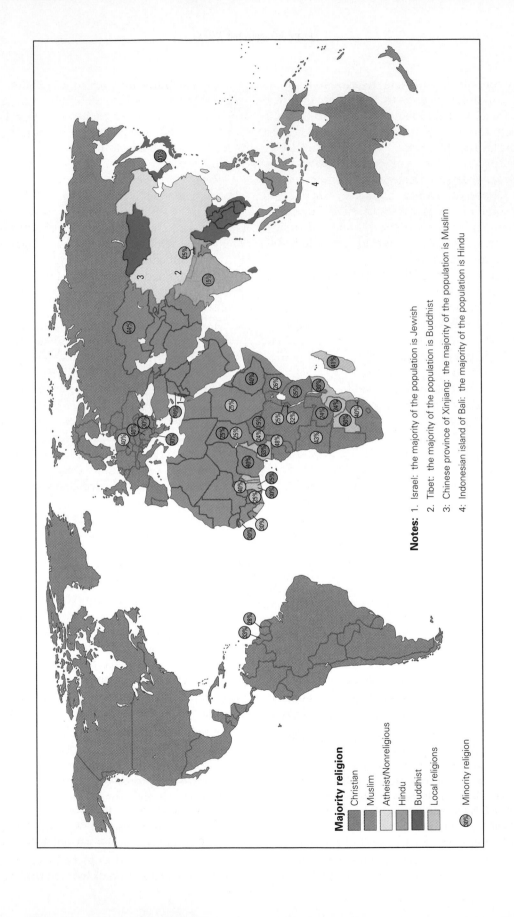

Majority religion

- Christian
- Muslim
- Atheist/Nonreligious
- Hindu
- Buddhist
- Local religions

⬤ Minority religion

Notes: 1. Israel: the majority of the population is Jewish
2. Tibet: the majority of the population is Buddhist
3. Chinese province of Xinjiang: the majority of the population is Muslim
4. Indonesian island of Bali: the majority of the population is Hindu

Many people in the late twentieth century looked to religion as a basis for moral life in a world where political ideologies seemed to have failed. Others, brought up in secular societies and maintaining few ties to organized religion, looked upon this heightened religiosity with foreboding. They saw religious revival groups as a force whose ultimate goal was to impose on everyone their own moral standards, educational curricula, lifestyles, artistic vision, and political systems. The Islamic world provided the most dramatic examples.

The first Kingdom of Saudi Arabia had arisen in the eighteenth century as an alliance between a nomad chieftain named Ibn Saud and a puritanical reformer named Muhammad ibn Abd al-Wahhab. Basing their policies on Wahhabi legal views, the Saudi government eliminated forms of ritual observance it considered heretical, applied severe corporal punishments, drastically restricted the movement of women and their entry into the labor force, and banned non-Muslim religious activities. In the late twentieth century, the kingdom's conservatism, stability, and, most important, huge petroleum reserves (the world's largest), made it a close ally of the United States. This alliance existed despite the fact that many Americans deplored the kingdom's religious rigidity. In Saudi Arabia, Islam was seen as a socially conservative and coercive force, but not a political threat.

Iran, on the other hand, embodied the threatening aspect of religion in government. The 1979 revolution (see Chapter 33) terminated the rapid growth of secularism in Iran. Ironically, women in the Islamic Republic of Iran suffered fewer restrictions than did those in Saudi Arabia and Iranians could vote for a parliament and openly criticize their government, as Saudis could not. Nevertheless, Iran became an international sym-

Map 35.1 World Religions Believers in Islam, Christianity, and Buddhism make up large percentages of the population in many countries. Differing forms of these religions seldom coincide with national boundaries. As religion revives as a focus of social identity, political assertion, or mass mobilization, the possibility of religious activism spreading across broad geographic regions becomes greater, as does the likelihood of domestic discord in multi-religious states.

bol of instability and terrorist activity. In 1991, the Algerian army suspended that country's first free elections in order to forestall the certain victory of the Islamic Salvation Front (FIS). France and the United States tacitly approved its banning of the FIS and bloody crackdown on Islamic militants in order to prevent "another Iran." Basic differences—the fact that the Shah's fall had been caused by largely uncoordinated mass demonstrations and strikes in an entirely Shi'ite country whereas the FIS was a legal, entirely Sunni, political party seeking a mandate to govern—seemed less important than the fact that both movements were rooted in the Islamic religion.

Some people in the West contended that Islam was taking the place of communism as the great enemy of the West. This newly defined East-West conflict appealed to people looking for a simple international structure in the post–Cold War world. In fact, Islamic movements, like Christian, Buddhist, and other religious movements, differed so much from place to place and depended so much on local circumstances that religion seemed more a source of increasing difference in the world than the basis for a new world order.

Threats to Order

Ethnic and religious tensions combined with technology to create instability by giving extremist groups and nations powerful tools of destruction. One technique was to launch violent terrorist attacks. Terrorism rests on the belief that horrendous acts of violence can provoke harsh reprisals—or, if repeated frequently, demonstrate such government incompetence that existing regimes will lose legitimacy and the people will look to the terrorists as a strong, organized, determined replacement. By no means a new force in world affairs, terrorism thrived in the late twentieth century. Ironically, its influence derived largely from the same technological developments that in other guises brought the world closer together: television. Global dissemination of news gave terrorist acts greater publicity, thus generating greater fear in the government and the general public and increasing the likelihood of the government losing control.

Palestinian groups dedicated to destroying Israel set the tone for modern media-centered terrorism with airplane hijackings in 1968 and the capture and eventual murder of eleven Israeli athletes during the Munich Olympic Games of 1972. Each of these outrages became a media event that galvanized sympathy for Israel, but also led fearful television viewers to believe that the Palestinian groups were much stronger than they actually were. Following the Palestinian lead, political groups around the world staged innumerable terrorist acts, from countless bombings in the British Isles by the Irish Republican Army to the assassinations in India of prime ministers Indira Gandhi and Rajiv Gandhi to the release of nerve gas in the Tokyo subway system by an apocalyptic Buddhist sect in 1995.

Terrorism occasionally contributed to political success. Israeli prime ministers Menahem Begin and Yitzhak Shamir had led Jewish terrorist organizations before the creation of the state of Israel, and Yasir Arafat became leader of an incipient Palestinian state in 1996 partly due to the worldwide publicity gained by PLO terrorism. Nevertheless, it was much more often a source of tragedy and needless loss of innocent life. Part of the tragedy, unfortunately, was the growing reality that terrorism could strike anywhere—including New York's World Trade Center and Oklahoma City's federal office building—and the corresponding fear that even after the end of the Cold War, the world was still an unsafe and threatening place.

While individuals feared terrorism, the fear of nuclear proliferation, a far more plausible threat to world peace, was concentrated in government circles. Throughout the Cold War, the world had lived with a sense of impending nuclear doom. This sense quickly evaporated after communism collapsed in Europe in 1991. Yet thousands of nuclear weapons remained. Despite safeguards to keep them from being sold or stolen, the possibility of a nuclear weapon falling into the hands of terrorists or states interested in blackmailing their neighbors could not be discounted, particularly given the economic and political disorder of post–Soviet Russia. Nor was there adequate assurance that radioactive materials could be disposed of safely without environmental contamination.

In addition, a number of countries undertook to construct their own nuclear devices, usually in secret. Oddly, the balance of nuclear forces between the United States and the Soviet Union throughout the Cold War came increasingly to be seen as an element of stability. As neither side could have started a nuclear war without facing total annihilation, both sides were bound never to use their ghastly arsenals. Without the threat of mutual destruction, however, the possibility of just one or two nuclear weapons being used in a restricted regional context gave rise to a new form of nuclear anxiety. The problem for the world community was how to prevent a country like North Korea or Iraq, whose nuclear ambitions have been well proven, from deploying nuclear weapons. Economic sanctions and international agreements against nuclear proliferation were tried but were found not to be effective. Yet no country wished to go to war to forestall nuclear weapons acquisition.

THE ENDURANCE OF CULTURAL DIVERSITY

The persistence of diverse cultural traditions remained evident at the twentieth century's end despite the globalization of industrial society and the integration of economic markets. Japan demonstrated that a country with a non-Western culture could perform at a high economic level. The Western concern for the individual is less valued in Japan than the ability of each individual to fit into a group, whether as a corporation employee, a member of an athletic team, or a student in a class. Moreover, it is considered unmannerly to directly contradict, correct, or refuse the request of another person.

From a Western point of view, these Japanese customs seem to discourage individual initiative and personality development and to preserve traditional hierarchies. Japanese women, for example, even though they often work outside the home, are responding only slowly to the American and European feminist yearning for equality in economic and social relations.

The Japanese approach to social relations is well suited to an industrial economy. The efficiency, pride in workmanship, and group solidarity of Japanese workers, accompanied by government and corporate policies, played a major role in catapulting Japan from a defeated nation with a largely demolished industrial base in 1945 to an economic power by the 1980s (see Chapter 34).

Japan's success in the modern industrial world calls into question an assumption common in the immediate postwar era. Since industrialization was pioneered by Europeans and Americans, many Westerners thought that the spread of industrialization to different parts of the world would require the adoption of Western culture in nonscientific areas as well. As an awareness of the economic impact of Japanese culture and society began to spread in the 1980s, however, it became apparent that Taiwan and South Korea, along with Singapore and Hong Kong, were developing dynamic industrial economies of their own. In the 1990s, Muslim Malaysia and Buddhist Thailand appeared to be following the same pattern. Had Japan been unique, or would cultural variety prove fully compatible with industrial growth and prosperity?

Clearly, the long-standing Western assumption of European and American exceptionalism—the belief that all of world history culminated in the exceptional convergence of political freedom, secularism, and industrialism of the west—needed to be abandoned. So, too, did the corollary that the twenty-first century would be as thoroughly dominated by Western culture and economic and political power as had the previous two centuries.

Also coming into question, however, was whether industrialization was the only viable route to prosperity. As computer technology continued to change almost all aspects of life, the idea of a country living primarily from its control of information and telecommunications seemed a possibility in the coming century.

The lesson to be drawn from Japan and the other rising economic powers of Asia was not that Western technology had provided a potential source of universal well-being, but rather that human ingenuity and adaptability are endlessly fertile and creative. Human cultural achievement has historically followed unpredictable paths, reaching one sort of climax in one time and place and another in another. In the same spirit, the future locus of spiritual and cultural achievement remained essentially unpredictable at the start of a new millennium.

CONCLUSION

Throughout history, the human species has been marked by cultural diversity. Languages, foods, costumes, customs, social organization, artistic expression, and spiritual beliefs have developed locally—both shaped by and shaping available technologies and local environmental constraints. Over the millennia, political entities have grown greatly in scale, as has the size of the human population. Consequently isolation has diminished. Increasing contact between groups has produced cultural and technological cross-fertilization. Unfortunately, it also led from time to time to conflict and the total disappearance of peoples, languages, and cultural traditions.

Yet a rich diversity of human experience has always persisted beneath the changing patterns of domination. People have repeatedly shown strong yearnings to be distinctly themselves, either as individuals or as part of social groups. Even within today's highly integrated and media-saturated societies, many groups take justifiable pride in their ancestry, language, religion, and culture. The world of today is, as it has always been, multicultural and pluralistic.

But today's world is also home to a growing sense of global culture. A Coke, a Big Mac, and a pair of Levi's provide basic—perhaps simplistic—artifacts of an almost universal culture. The question is whether these artifacts, which economic integration seems destined to make worldwide, will gradually push out manifestations of indigenous culture that have survived for centuries, such as Malaysian kite flying, Persian carpet making, African dancing, or Mexican cooking. Or, as a more hopeful outcome, will our ability to interact ever more closely within a common global culture foster a greater respect for the earth and its peoples?

SUGGESTED READING

The interrelationships between high culture and popular culture during the twentieth century are treated from very different perspectives by Greil Marcus, *Lipstick Traces: A Secret History of the Twentieth Century* (1989), and Kurt Varnedoe, *High and Low: Modern Art and Popular Culture* (1991). The former concentrates on the avant garde from Dada to Punk Rock, the latter on images from popular culture used in art. Two very readable books by James B. Twitchell, *Carnival Culture: The Trashing of Taste in America* (1992) and *Adcult USA: The Triumph of Advertising in American Culture* (1996), detail the rise of popular culture in the United States and present various reactions to this phenomenon.

Many interpretations of and approaches to postmodernism are sampled in Thomas Docherty, ed., *Postmodernism: A Reader* (1993). These may be compared with a classic early statement of modernism, Amédée Ozenfant, *Foundations of Modern Art* (1931).

Thomas P. Hughes, *American Genesis: A Century of Invention and Technological Enthusiasm, 1870–1970* (1989) offers a far-ranging account of the American role in twentieth-century technological change by an outstanding historian of technology. For a comprehensive, highly detailed treatment of telephone, telegraph, radio, and television in particular, see George P. Oslin, *The Story of Telecommunications* (1992).

Books on films and the film industry around the world are legion. A good place to start is George Mast, *A Short History of the Movies* (1986). A similar survey of jazz music is available from Marshall W. Stearns, *The Story of Jazz* (1970). For the rock video phenomenon see E. Ann Kaplan, *Rocking Around the Clock: Music Television, Postmodernism, and Consumer Culture* (1987).

A good, if optimistic, starting point for studying the United Nations is Leland M. Goodrich, *The United Nations in a Changing World* (1974). The broader range of transnational forces affecting international relations is covered by Werner J. Feld, *Nongovernmental Forces and World Politics: A Study of Business, Labor, and Political Groups* (1972). Harold K. Jacobson, *Networks of Interdependence: International Organizations and the Global Political System* (1984) offers a wide-ranging discussion that touches on security, economics, welfare, and human rights.

A seminal book in the awakening of the feminist movement in the 1970s is Betty Friedan, *The Feminine Mystique* (1974). For the revival of feminism in Europe see Gisela Kaplan, *Contemporary Western European Feminism* (1992). For non-Western perspectives see Phyllis Andors, *The Unfinished Liberation of Chinese Women, 1949–1980* (1983); Nermin Abadan-Unat, Deniz Kandiyoti, and Mübeccel R. Kiray, eds., *Women in Turkish Society* (1981); and Chandra Talpade Mohanty, Ann Russo, and Lourdes Torres, eds., *Third World Women and the Politics of Feminism* (1991).

Gilles Kepel, *The Revenge of God: The Resurgence of Islam, Christianity, and Judaism in the Modern World* (1994) deals with recent religio-political movements. On sectarian conflict and the Lebanese civil war see Itamar Rabinovitch, *The War for Lebanon, 1970–1985* (1985); Elizabeth Picard, *Lebanon: A Shattered Country* (1996) and Augustus Richard Norton, *Amal and the Shi'a: Struggle for the Soul of Lebanon* (1987).

Some noteworthy novels that have attempted to visualize the near future on the basis of current perceptions of technological change, environmental deterioration, and growth of transnational corporations are David Brin, *Earth* (1990) and Bruce Sterling, *Islands in the Net* (1988). See too William Gibson's "Sprawl" trilogy *Neuromancer* (1984), *Count Zero* (1987), and *Mona Lisa Overdrive* (1988).

NOTES

1. "Universal Declaration of Human Rights," in *Twenty-five Human Rights Documents,* New York: Center for the Study of Human Rights, Columbia University, 1994, p. 6.

2. Ibid.

This guide provides pronunciation information for words in *The Earth and Its Peoples* that may be unfamiliar to you. Using this guide to pronounce proper names and other terms in the text should both aid your understanding of the material and build your confidence in speaking (and listening) in class.

To make the guide easy to read, the pronunciation for each word is spelled by syllable, with pronunciation symbols used for vowel sounds, as shown in the key below. The primary stress syllable in each word is capitalized, this shows which syllable should be emphasized in pronunciation.

Pronunciation Key:

a	h*a*t	ā	d*a*te	âr	d*are*	ah	f*a*ther
e	p*e*t	ē	f*ee*d	îr	p*ier*	ou	h*ou*se
i	s*i*t	ī	f*i*ne	ô	s*aw*	uh	*a*lone, h*er*
o	n*o*t	ō	s*o*	ûr	b*ur*n	œ	as in French, p*eu*
u	b*u*t	oo	n*oo*n	ŏŏ	f*oo*t		

The following references were used in compiling the pronunciations:

American Heritage Dictionary of the English Language, Third Edition (Boston: Houghton Mifflin Company, 1992)
Concise Cambridge Italian Dictionary (London: Cambridge University Press, 1975)
Ehrlich, Eugene H. and Hand, Raymond, Jr., *NBC Handbook of Pronunciation,* 4th ed. (New York: HarperPerennial, 1991)
The International Geographic Encyclopedia and Atlas (Boston: Houghton Mifflin Company, 1979)

The New Cassell's French Dictionary (New York: Funk & Wagnalls Co., 1962)
The New Century Cyclopedia of Names (New York: Appleton-Century-Crofts, 1954)
Papinot, E., *Historical and Geographical Dictionary of Japan* (Ann Arbor, MI: Overbeck Co., 1948)
Pronouncing Dictionary of Proper Names (Detroit, MI: Omnigraphics, Inc., 1993)
Spanish and English Dictionary (New York: Holt, Rinehart & Winston, 1955)
Webster's New Geographical Dictionary (Springfield, MA: Merriam-Webster, Inc., 1988)

A'isha AH-ē-shah
Abbasa ah-BAS-uh
Abbasid ah-BA-sid
'Abd al-Qadir AHB-d al—KAH-dėr
Abd al-Rahman AHB-d al—ruh-MAHN
Abd al-Wahhab ABD uhl—wuh-HAHB
Abu Bakr a-BOO BAK-uhr
Achaean uh-KĒ-uhn
Achaemenid a-KĒ-muh-nid
Aceh ah-CHE
Achilles uh-KIL-ēz
adat AH-daht
Adena ah-DAY-nah
Adowa AH-dŏŏ-wah
Aegean i-JĒ-uhn
Afrikaner af-ri-KAH-nuhr
Agamemnon ag-uh-MEM-non
Agincourt AJ-in-kort
Aguinaldo ah-gē-NAHL-dō
Agung of Mataram AH-gŏŏng ŭv mah-tah-RAHM
Ahaggar uh-HAG-uhr
Ahasuerus uh-HAZ-yoo-ēr-uhs
Ahhijawa uh-kē-YÔ-wuh
ahimsa uh-HIM-sah
Ahl al-Sunra wa'l-Jama'a AHL as—SUUN-uh wel—jah-MAH-uh
Ahmadabad AH-muhd-ah-bahd
Ahmose AH-mōs
Ahuramazda ah-HŎŎR-uh-MAZ-duh
Ain Jalut YYN jah-LOOL
Akkad AH-kahd
Akkadian uh-KĀ-dē-uhn
Aksum AHK-soom
al-Andalus al—AN-duh-lus
al-Ghaba al—GAH-buh
Ala-ud-din Khaliji uh-LAH—uh-DĒN KAL-jee
Alalakh UH-luh-luhk
Aleutian uh-LOO-shuhn
Algonquin al-GONG-kwin
Alighieri, Dante ah-lē-GYE-rē, DAHN-tā
alkali AL-kuh-lī
Allah AH-luh
alluvial uh-LOO-vē-uhl
Almoravid al-muh-RAH-vid
Alsace-Lorraine al-SAHS—lô-REN
Altai AL-tī
Amarna uh-MAHR-nuh
Amaterasu ah-mah-te-RAH-sŏŏ
ambergris AM-buhr-grēs
Ambon AHM-bôn
Amenhotep ah-muhn-HŌ-tep
Amitabha u-mi-TAH-buh
Amon AH-muhn

Amorite AM-uh-rīt
Anasazi ah-nuh-SAH-zē
Andalusian an-duh-LOO-zhuhn
anderun ahn-duh-ROON
Angra Mainyu ANG-ruh MĪN-yoo
Anjou AN-joo
Ankara ANG-kuhr-uh
Annam uh-NAHM
anthropomorphic an-thruh-puh-MÔR-fik
Antigonid an-TIG-uh-nid
Antioch AN-tē-ok
Anyang AHN YAHNG
Apache uh-PACH-ē
apartheid uh-PAHRT-hāt
apiru uh-PĒ-roo
Aquinas, Thomas a-KWĪ-nuhs, tō-MAHS
Aquitaine AK-wi-tān
Arafat AR-uh-fat
Aramaic ar-uh-MĀ-ik
Araucanian ahr-ô-KĀ-nē-uhn
Arawak AR-uh-wahk
Archangel AHRK-ān-juhl
Archilochus ahr-KIL-uh-kuhs
archipelago ahr-kuh-PEL-uh-gō
Ardashir ahr-dah-SHĒR
Argentina ahr-juhn-TĒ-nuh
Arianism ÂR-ē-uh-niz-uhm
Aristophanes ar-uh-STOF-uh-nēz
Arjuna AHR-joo-nuh
armillary AR-muh-ler-ē
Aro AH-rō
Arochukwu AH-rō-CHOO-kwoo
Asante uh-SHAHN-tē
Ashdod ASH-dod
Ashikaga ah-shē-KAH-gah
Ashurbanipal ah-shŏŏr-BAH-nuh-pahl
askeri AS-kuh-rē
Assiniboine uh-SIN-uh-boin
Astarte uh-STAHR-tē
Astrakhan AS-truh-kan
astrolabe AS-truh-lāb
Aswan AS-wahn
Atacama at-uh-KAM-uh
Atahualpa ah-tuh-WAHL-puh
Aten AHT-n
Athanasius ath-uh-NĀ-shuhs
atlatl aht-LAHT-l
auqaf OU-kahf
Aurangzeb OR-uhng-zeb
australopithecine ô-strä-lō-PITH-uh-sēn
Australopithecus africanus ô-strä-lō-PITH-uh-kuhs af-ri-KAH-nuhs
Avar AH-vahr
Averroës uh-VER-ō-ēz

Avicenna av-uh-SEN-uh
Avignon ah-vē-NYŌN
Awdaghost OU-duh-gust
awilum uh-WĒ-loom
Axum AHK-soom
ayatollah ī-uh-TŌ-luh
ayllu ī-LYOO
Azambuja, Diogo da ah-zahm-BOO-yah
Azcapotzalco ahs-kah-pô-TSAHL-kô
Azerbaijan ah-zuhr-bī-JAHN
Azores Ā-zorz

Babur BAH-buhr
Bactria BAK-tre-uh
Bahia buh-HĒ-uh
Bahrain bah-RĀN
Bajio bah-Ē-oh
Bal Tilak BAHL tē-LAHK
balam BAH-lam
Balboa, Vasco Núñez de bal-BŌ-uh
Balkh BAHLK
Baluchistan buh-loo-chi-STAN
Bani Hilal BAH-nē hē-LAHL
Baoyu BOU-yoo
Barbados bahr-BĀ-dōz
Barmakids BAHR-muh-kidz
bas-relief bah—ri-LĒF
Basque BASK
Bastille ba-STĒL
Batavia buh-TĀ-vē-uh
batik buh-TĒK
Batista, Fulgencio bah-TĒS-tah, fool-HEN-syō
Bayazid BAH-yah-zēd
Bayeux bah-YOO
Beauvais bō-VĀ
Begin, Menachem BĀ-gin, muh-NAH-kem
Behistun bā-hi-STOON
Beijing bā-JING
Bektashi bek-TAH-shē
Beltaine BEL-tān
Benguela ben-GĀ-luh
Berytus buh-RĪ-tus
biblion bi-BLE-ahn
Bight of Biafra BĪT of bē-AH-fruh
bilad al-Sudan bi-LAD uhs—soo-DAN
Bis im Pharrhof BĒS ēm FAHR-hôf
Blaise Diagne BLĀZ dē-AHN-yuh
blitzkrieg BLITS-krēg
Boccaccio, Giovanni bō-KAH-chē-ō, jē-uh-VAH-nē
bodhisattva bō-di-SUT-vuh
Bohai BŌ-HĪ
Bolívar, Simón bō-LĒ-vahr
Bologna buh-LŌN-yuh

Boniface BON-uh-fās
Bordeaux bor-DŌ
Bosch, Hieronymus BOSH, hī-RON-uh-muhs
Bosnia-Herzegovina BOZ-nē-uh—her-tsuh-gō-VĒ-nuh
Bosporus BOS-puhr-uhs
bourgeoisie bŏŏr-zhwah-ZĒ
Brahe, Tycho BRAH-hē, TĒ-kō
Brazza, Savorgnan de brah-ZAH, sa-vor-NYAHN
Brescia BRE-shah
Bruges BROOZH
Brunei broo-NĪ
Buenos Aires BWE-nôs Ī-res
Bukhara boo-KAHR-uh
burgess BÛR-jis
burgh BÛRG
Burgoyne, "Gentleman Johnny" buhr-GOIN
Burma BÛR-muh
Buyid BOO-yid
Byblos BIB-los
Byrsa BÛR-suh
Byzantine BIZ-uhn-tēn

Cabral, Pedro Alvares KA-brahl
cacao kuh-KĀ-ō
Caesar SĒ-zuhr
caesaropapism sē-zuh-rō-PĀ-piz-uhm
Caffa KAH-fah
Cahokia kuh-HŌ-kē-uh
Cakchiquel kahk-chē-KEL
caliphal KAL-uh-fuhl
Calixtus kuh-LIK-stuhs
Cambyses kam-BĪ-sēz
Camões, Luís de kuh-MOINSH
Cao Cao TSOU TSOU
Cao Xueqin TSOU SHOO-EH-CHIN
Caramansa kah-rah-MAHN-sah
caravel KAR-uh-vel
Cárdenas, Lázaro KAHR-dn-ahs, LAH-sah-rō
Carnelian kahr-NĒL-yuhn
Carolingian kar-uh-LIN-juhn
Carranza, Venustiano kah-RAHN-sah
Carthaginian kahr-thuh-JIN-ē-uhn
Cartier, Jacques KAHR-tē-ā
Casas, Bartolomé de las KAH-sahs
cassia KASH-uh
castas KAH-stahs
Castiglione, Giuseppe kah-stē-LYÔ-nē
Castillo kahs-TĒ-lyō
Çatal Huyuk cha-TAHL hoo-YOOK
Catalan KAT-l-an

Caucasian kô-KĀ-zhuhn
Caucasus KÔ-kuh-suhs
caudillo kô-DĒL-yō
Ceausescu, Nicolae chou-SHES-koo, nē-kô-LĪ
celadon SEL-uh-don
Celt KELT
Cernunnos KÛRN-yoo-nuhs
Cervantes, Miguel de suhr-VAN-tes
Cetshwayo ke-CHWĪ-ō
Ceuta sā-OO-tuh
Champagne shahm-PAHN-yuh
Champlain, Samuel de shahm-PLĀN
Chan CHAHN
Chandigarh CHUN-dē-guhr
Chang'an CHAHNG AHN
Charlemagne SHAHR-luh-mān
Cheka CHĀ-kuh
cheque CHEK
Chiang Kai-shek CHANG KĪ-SHEK
Chiapas chē-AH-pahs
Chihuahua chuh-WAH-wah
Chile CHĒ-le
chinoiserie shēn-wah-zuh-RĒ
Chishti CHISH-tē
Choctaw CHOK-tô
cinchona sing-KŌ-nuh
Circassian suhr-KASH-ē-uhn
Clairvaux klär-VŌ
Clemenceau, Georges klem-uhn-SŌ
cloisonné kloi-zuh-NĀ
Cluny KLOO-nē
Cnossus KNOS-uhs
Coeur, Jacques KÛR
Colbert, Jean Baptiste kôl-BÂR
Comanche kuh-MAN-chē
Comnenus, Alexius kom-NĒ-nuhs, uh-LEK-sē-uhs
Condorcanqui kon-dor-KAHN-kē
conquistadore kon-KĒ-stuh-dor
Constantinople kon-stan-tuh-NŌ-puhl
Le Corbusier luh kor-boo-ZYĀ
Cortés, Hernán kor-TEZ, âr-NAHN
costaria coh-STAH-rē-uh
Costilla, Hidalgo y Ē kōs-TĒ-yah
Coucacou koo-KAH-koo
courtiers KOR-tē-uhr
Creditanstalt crā-DĒT-ahn-shtahlt
creole KRĒ-ōl
Crimea krī-MĒ-uh
Crimean krī-MĒ-uhn
cruzado kroo-ZAH-dō
Cugnot coo-NYŌ
cuneiform kyoo-NĒ-uh-form
curia KYŎŎR-ē-uh
Cuzco KOOS-kō
Cyclopes sī-KLŌ-pēz

Cyrillic si-RIL-ik
Czech CHEK

Daedalus DED-l-uhs
Dahomey duh-HŌ-mē
Daiyu DĪ-yoo
Dalai lama DAH-lī LAH-muh
Daoist DOU-ist
Dardanelles dahr-dn-ELZ
Darius duh-RĪ-uhs
Date Masamuni DAH-tā mah-sah-MOO-nē
Daulatabad dou-LAT-ah-bahd
Davar dah-VAHR
Deccan DEK-uhn
Dehua DUH-HWAH
Deir el-Bahri DYYR uhl—BAH-rē
Delft DELFT
Delhi DEL-ē
Deshima DE-shē-mah
Deuteronomic doo-tuhr-uh-NOM-ik
devshirme dev-shēr-MEE
dhikr DIK-uhr
dhow DOU
Dhuoda doo-WOH-duh
Diderot, Denis DE-duh-rō, duh-NĒ
Dido DĪ-dō
Dienbienphu dyen-byen-FOO
dinar di-NAHR
Diodorus dī-ō-DOR-uhs
Dionysia dī-uh-NIZH-ē-uh
diorite DĪ-uh-rīt
dirham di-RAM
Djoser JŌ-sûr
Donatism DON-uh-tiz-uhm
Dravidian druh-VID-ē-uhn
dromedary DROM-i-der-ē
Druids DROO-ids
Du Bois, Eugene doo-BWAH
Du Bois, W. E. B. doo-BOIS
ducat DUK-uht
duchy DUCH-e
Dur DOOR
Durkheim, Émile DÛRK-hīm, ā-MĒL
Dyula DYŎŎ-la

Ebla Ē-bluh
Eblaite Ē-bluh-īt
ecclesiastical i-klē-zē-AS-ti-kuhl
Ecuador EK-wuh-dor
Edessa i-DES-uh
Ekwesh EK-wesh
Elamites Ē-luh-mīt
emir i-MÎR
encomenderos en-kō-MĒN-der-ōs
encomienda en-kō-mē-EN-duh
Enkidu EN-kē-doo

ensete en-SE-tā
entente on-TONT
entrepôt ON-truh-pō
épée ā-PĀ
Epistle i-PIS-uhl
epoch EP-uhk
Epona e-PŌ-nuh
Equiano, Olaudah ā-kwē-AH-noo,
    ō-LOU-duh
Erasmus i-RAZ-muhs
Eritrea er-i-TRĒ-uh
Erythraean er-i-THRĒ-uhn
Eugenie œ-zhā-NĒ
eunuch YOO-nuhk
Euphrates yoo-FRĀ-tēz
Exchequer EKS-chek-uhr
Ezana ē-ZAH-nah

Faisal FĪ-suhl
Faiyum fī-YOOM
Falasha fuh-LAH-shuh
Faruq fuh-ROOK
fascisti fah-SHĒ-stē
Fatimid FAT-uh-mid
Ferghana fuhr-GAH-nuh
feudum FYOO-duhm
Fibonacci fē-bō-NAH-chē
fief FĒF
frater FRĀ-tuhr
Frumentius froo-MEN-shuhs
Fuggers FOOG-uhrz
Führer FYŎOR-uhr
Fujiwara foo-jē-WAHR-uh
Fustat fus-TAHT

Gabriel, José gah-BRĒ-el
Gabriol GĀ-brē-uhl
Galilei, Galileo gal-uh-LĀ,
    gal-uh-LĒ-ō
Gallipoli guh-LIP-uh-lē
Gamal Abd al-Nasir gah-MAHL
    abd—uhn-NAH-suhr
Gandhi, Indira or Rajiv GAHN-dē
Ganges GAN-jēz
Gansu GAHN-SOO
Gath GATH
gaucho GOU-chō
Gaugemela GÔ-guh-mē-luh
Gdansk guh-DAHNSK
Ge Hong GUH HOONG
Gebel Barkal JEB-uhl BAHR-kahl
Genghis Khan JEN-gis KAHN
genista juh-NIS-tuh
Genoese JEN-ō-ēz
Gezer GE-zuhr
Ghana GAH-nuh
Ghat GAHT
Ghazan gah-ZAHN

Ghent GENT
Ghiyas al-Din GĒ-YAHS ad-DĒN
Ghurkhas GUHR-kuhz
Gila River HĒ-luh
Giotto JOT-ō
Girondist juh-RON-dist
Giza GĒ-zuh
glasnost GLAHS-nôst
Go-Daigo GŌ—DĪ-gō
Goa GO-uh
Gobi Desert GŌ-bē
Gomorrah guh-MOR-uh
Graeci GRĪ-kē
Gran, Ahmed GRAHN, AH-muhd
Guadeloupe GWOD-l-oop
Guangxu GWAHNG-JOO
Guangzhou GWAHNG-JŌ
Guangzi GWAHNG-SHĒ
Guatemala gwah-tuh-MAH-luh
guerrilla guh-RIL-uh
Guevara, Che guh-VAHR-uh, CHĀ
Guiana gē-AH-nuh
Guillaume gē-YŌM
guillotine GĒ-uh-tēn
Gujarat goo-juh-RAHT
gulag GOO-lahg
Guo Shijie GWŌ SHÛR-jē-yeh
Guomindang GWŌ-MIN-DAHNG
Guyuk GUH-YOOK

hadith hah-DĒTH
Hafiz HAH-fiz
Hagia Sophia HĀ-jē-uh SŌ-fē-uh
Hainan HĪ-NAHN
Hajj Bektash HAH-jee bek-TAHSH
Hakkas HAHK-kahz
Hakra River HAK-ruh
halal hah-LAHL
Halevi, Judah hah-LĀ-vē
Halicarnassus hal-i-kahr-NAS-uhs
Hamadan ham-uh-DAN
Hammurabi HAM-uh-rah-bē
Hangzhou HAHNG JŌ
Hanoverian han-ō-VÎR-ē-uhn
Hanseatic han-sē-AT-ik
harem HÂR-uhm
harijan HAH-rē-jahn
Harkhuf HAHR-koof
Harun al-Rashid hah-ROON al—
    rah-SHĒD
Hatshepsut hat-SHEP-sŏŏt
Hattusha haht-tŏŏ-SHAH
hauberk HÔ-bûrk
Hausa HOU-suh
Havel, Vaclav hah-VEL
hectare HEK-târ
Heike HĀ-KEH
heknu HEK-noo

Heliopolis hē-lē-OP-uh-lis
Hellenes HE-lēnz
helot HEL-uht
Henan HŒ-NAHN
henequen HEN-i-kwin
Herat he-RAHT
Herero huh-RÂR-ō
heretical huh-RET-i-kuhl
Herodotus he-ROD-uh-tuhs
Heshen huh-SHUN
Heyerdhal, Thor HĀ-uhr-dahl
hieroglyphics hī-ruh-GLIF-iks
hijra HIJ-ruh
Himalaya HIM-uh-lā-uh
Himyar HIM-yuhr
Hippalus HIP-uh-luhs
Hittite HIT-īt
Ho Chi Minh HŌ CHĒ MIN
Hohenstaufen hō-uhn-SHTOU-fuhn
Hokulea hō-koo-LĀ-ah
hominid HOM-uh-nid
Homo erectus HŌ-mō I-REK-tuhs
Homo habilis HŌ-mō HAB-uh-luhs
Homo sapiens HŌ-mō SĀ-pē-enz
Hong Xiuquan HOONG SHĒ-Ō-
    choo-wan
Honglou Meng HOONG-lō MUNG
Houphouet-Boigny, Félix oo-FWĀ—
    bwah-NYĒ, fā-LĒKS
Huang Chao HWANG CHOU
Huang Da Po HWAHNG DAH PŌ
Huang He HWANG HUH
Huantar, Chavin de HWAHN-tahr,
    CHAH-vēn dā
Huaqing HWA-CHING
Huari HWAHR-ē
Huguenot HYOO-guh-not
Huitzilopochtli wē-tsē-lō-POCH-tlē
Hulegu HOO-luh-goo
Huna Capac WĪ-nah kah-PAHK
Husayn, Saddam hoo-SAYN, Sah-
    DAHM
Hwangnyang-sa HWAHNG-
    NYUHNG SAH
Hyksos HIK-sōs
Hystaspes his-TAS-pēz

Ibadan ē-BAH-dahn
Ibn al-Arabi IB-uhn ahl-AH-rah-bē
Ibn Battuta IB-uhn ba-TOOT-tuh
ibn Ezra, Abraham IB-uhn ĒZ-ruh
Ibn Khaldun IB-uhn khahl-DOON
Ibn Rushd IB-uhn RUSHD
Ibn Saud IB-uhn sah-OOD
Ibn Sina IB-uhn SĒ-nah
Ibn Tufayl IB-uhn too-FAYL
Ibn Tumart IB-uhn TOO-mahrt
Ibo Ē-bō

Il Duce il DOO-chā
Il-khan ĒL-KAHN
Iliad IL-ē-ad
indigénat in-di-jay-NOT
ingenio in-HĒN-yoh
Iolcus YOL-kuhs
Iona ī-Ō-nuh
iqta ik-TUH
Iranian i-RAH-nē-uhn
Iroquois IR-uh-kwoi
Isandhlwana ē-sahn-LWAHN-nuh
Isfahan is-fuh-HAHN
Ismail is-MAH-ēl
Iturbide, Augustín ē-tŏŏr-BĒ-dā
Ituri ē-TOO-rē
Izmir IZ-mēr

Ja'far JAH-far
Jacobin JAK-uh-bin
Jacquerie zhahk-uh-RĒ
Jagadai JAH-gah-dī
Jam'at-i Tabligh jam-AHT-uh tab-LĒG
Janissary JAN-i-ser-ē
Jeanneret, Charles Édouard Zhe-nuh-RAY
Jericho JER-i-kō
Jiang Qing JYAHN CHING
Jiménez hē-ME-nes
Jin JIN
Jingdezhen JING-DUH-JŒN
Jinnah jē-NAH
jizya JIZ-yuh
Juárez, Benito HWAH-res
Junta HŎŎN-tuh
Jurchen JUHR-CHEN
Juvaini JOO-VĪ-NĒ

Ka'ba KΛH-buh
Kabul KAH-buhl
kaffiya kah-FĒ-uh
Kahlo, Frida KAHI-lō, FRĒ-duh
Kaifeng kī-FUNG
Kaiser KĪ-zuhr
Kalahari kah-luh-HAHR-ē
Kalhu KAL-oo
Kamakura kah-mah-KOO-rah
Kanagawa kah-nah-GAH-wah
Kanem kah-NEHM
Kanem-Bornu KAH-nuhm—BOR-noo
Kangxi KAHNG-SHĒ
Kanishka ka-NISH-kuh
Kara-Khitai KARA—Kē-TĪ
Karakorum kahr-uh-KOR-uhm
Kashgar KASH-gahr
Kassite KAS-īt
Kathiawar kah-tē-uh-WAHR
Kazakh KAH-zahk
Kazakhstan KAH-zahk-stahn

Kepler, Johannes KEP-luhr, YO-hahn
Keraits KEH-RĪTS
Khadija ka-DĒ-juh
Khalifa kah-LĒ-fuh
Khan-balikh KAHN—BAH-lik
Khanate KAH-nāt
Kharijite KAHR-uh-jīt
Khartoum kahr-TOOM
Khayyam, Omar kī-YAM
Khedive kuh-DĒV
Khefren KEF ren
Khelat kuh-LAHT
Khitai kē-TĪ
Kho KŌ
Khoisan KOI-sahn
Khomeini, Ruhollah khoh-MAY-nee, ROO-hoh-luh
Khrushchev, Nikita KRUUSH-chyof
Khubilai KOO-buh-lī
Khufu KOO-foo
Khurasan kor-uh-SAHN
khuriltai KOO-ril-tī
Khwarasm KWAH-RAZ-um
Kiet Siel KΛYT SEL
Kiev KĒ-ef
Kikuyu ki-KOO-yoo
Kitans KĒ-TANS
Kivas KĒ-vuhs
Kojiki KŌ-JĒ-kē
Kongjo KONG-JŌ
Koryo KOR-yō
Kosovo KÔ-sô-vô
Krac des Chevalliers KRAHK day shuh-vahl-YAY
Krishna KRISH-nuh
kulak KOO-lak
Kyrgyzstan KÎR-gē-stahn

Lab'ayu luh-BAH-yoo
labyrinth LAB-uh-rinth
Lahore luh-HOR
laissez-faire LES-ā FÂR
Lamaism LAH-muh-iz-uhm
Lambeyeque lam-bay-YAY-kay
Languedoc lahng-DÔK
Laos LOUS
lapis lazuli LAP-is LAZ-uh-lē
Lascaux la-SKŌ
Lebensraum LĀ-buhns-roum
legume LEG-yoom
Leiden LĪD-n
Leptis Magna LEP-tis MAG-nuh
Lesotho luh-SŌ-tō
Levant luh-VANT
Li Qingzhao LĒ CHING-JOU
Li Shizhen LĒ shûr-JEN
Liao LYOU
Liaodong LYOU-DONG

Liège lē-EZH
Liliuokalani lē-lē-oo-ō-kah-LAH-nē
Lima LĒ-muh
Lin Zexu LĒN zuh-SHOO
lineage LIN-ē-ij
Liuqiu lē-Ō-chē-ō
loess LES
Lucca LOOK-kah
Luddite LUD-īt
lugal LOO-guhl
Luo Guanzhong LÔ GWAHNG-JOONG
Luoyang LWŌ-yahng
Lusiads loo-SĒ-uds
Lusitania loo-si-TĀ-nē-uh
Lysistrata lis-uh-STRAH-tuh

ma'at muh-AHT
Ma Huan MAH HWAHN
Macao muh-KOU
Madeira muh-DĒR-uh
madrasa MA-dras-uh
Maharaja mah-huh-RAH-juh
Maharashtra mah-huh-RAHSH-truh
Mahayana mah-huh-YAH-nuh
Mainz MĪNTS
maize MĀZ
Malagasy mal-uh-GAS-ē
malam MAH-lahm
Malawi muh-LAH-wē
Malay muh-LĀ
Malinke muh-LING-kā
Mallia mahl-YAH
Manchukuo MAN-CHOO-KWŌ
manganese MANG-guh-nēs
Manichaean man-i-KĒ-uhn
Manichee MAN-i-kē
manikongo mah-NĒ-KÔNG-gō
manioc MAN-ē-ok
Mansa Kankan Musa MAHN-suh KΛHN-kahn MOO-suh
mansab MAN-suhb
mansabdar man-suhb-DAHR
Mantua MAN-choo-uh
Manzikert MANZ-i-kuhrt
Mao Zedong MOU DZUH-DONG
Maori MAH-ô-rē
Maraga mah-rah-GAH
Maratha muh-RAH-tuh
mare librum MAH-rā LĒ-brum
mare nostrum MAH-rā NO-struhm
Mari MAH-rē
Marne MAHRN
Maronnage mah-ruh-NAHZH
Marquesas mahr-KĀ-suhs
Marquis mahr-KĒ
Marrakesh mar-uh-KESH
Martinique mahr-ti-NĒK

martyr MAHR-tuhr
Maruz muh-ROOZ
Mashhad mahsh-HAHD
matriarchy MĀ-trē-ahr-kē
matrilineal mat-ruh-LIN-ē-uhl
Maule MÔL
Mauritius mô-RISH-uhs
Maurya MORYA
Maya MAH-yuh
Mazzini, Giuseppe maht-SĒ-nē,
    joo-ZEP-pe
Mbuti uhm-BOO-tē
Mede MĒD
Medici MED-i-chē
Medoi MĀ-doy
Megara MEG-uh-ruh
Mehmed ME-met
Meiji MĀ-jē
Mein Kampf MĪN KAHMPF
Mejid, Abdul me-JĒD
Melanesia mel-uh-NĒ-zhuh
Melgart MEL-kahrt
Menes MĒ-nēz
Meroë MER-ō-ē
Merovingian mer-uh-VIN-juhn
mestizo mes-TĒ-zō
Metternich MET-uhr-nik
Mevlevi MEV-le-vē
Mexica MEK-si-kah
Michaelangelo mī-kuhl-AN-juh-lō
Michoacán MĒ-chô-ah-kahn
Minas Gerais MĒN-ahs JAYR-yys
Mindanao min-duh-NAH-ō
Minoan mi-NŌ-uhn
Minotaur MIN-uh-tor
Mitanni mi-TAH-nē
Mitsui mē-TSOO-yē
mitt'a MIT-uh
Moche MOK
Mochica mō-CHĒ-kuh
Moctezuma môk-ti-ZOO-muh
Mohenjo-Daro mō-hen-jō—
    DAHR-ō
monasticism muh-NAS-tuh-siz-uhm
Mongke MUHNG-KUH
monophysite muh-NOF-uh-sīt
Montpellier mōn-pel-YĀ
Mosul MOH-suhl
Mozambique mō-zam-BĒK
Mu'awiya moo-AH-wē-yuh
muezzin moo-EZ-in
Mughal MOO-guhl
muhtasib muh-TAH-sib
mulatto mŏŏ-LAH-tō
Muscovite MUS-kuh-vīt
Musqat MUS-kat
Mutsuhito moo-tsoo-HĒ-tō
Myanmar myahn-MAH

Mycenae mī-SĒ-nē
Mycenaean mī-suh-NĒ-uhn
myrrh MÛR
Mysore mī-SOR

Nabataean nab-uh-TĒ-uhn
Nabopolassar NAB-ō-pō-las-uhr
Najaf NA-jaf
Nanking NAN-king
Nantes NAHNT
Nanzhao nahn-JOU
Napata na-PĀ-tuh
naphtha NAF-thuh
Naqshbandi naksh-BAN-dē
Nasir al-Din NAH-zuhr ad—DĒN
nawab nuh-WOB
Nazi NAHT-sē
nazir NA-zir
Ndebele nn-duh-BĀ-lā
Neanderthal nē-AN-duhr-thôl
Nebuchadnezzar NAB-oo-kuhd-nez-
    uhr
Nefertiti nef-uhr-TĒ-tē
Nehru, Jawaharlal NĀ-roo
New Guinea new GIN-ē
Ngo Dinh Diem NGŌ DĒN DYEM
Nguni nn-GOO-nē
Nian NYAHN
Nicaea nī-SĒ-uh
Nineveh NIN-uh-vuh
Nishapur ni-shah-PŎŎR
Nizam al-Mulk nee-ZAHM ulh—
    MOOLK
Nkrumah, Kwame nn-KROO-muh,
    KWAH-mee
Novgorod NOV-guh-rod
Nuer NOO-uhr
Nyamwezi nn-nyahm-WĀ-zē
Nyasaland NYAH-sah-land
Nyssa NĪ-suh

oba Ō-buh
ochre Ō-kuhr
Oduduwa o-DOO-doo-wah
Ogodei UH-GUH-DĀ
Olduvai ol-DOO-vī
oligarchy OL-i-gahr-kē
Omani ō-MAH-nē
Ophir ō-FĒR
ordu OR-doo
Orinoco or-uh-NŌ-kō
orthopraxy or-thuh-PRAK-sē
Osiris ō-SĪ-ris
Oudh OUD

Páez, José Antonio PAH-es
pagani pah-GAH-nē

Pahlavi, Mohammad Reza PAH-luh-
    vē
Palenque pah-LENG-ke
Palmares PAL-muh-ruhs
Palmyra pal-MĪ-ruh
Palmyrene pal-MĪ-rēn
Pamir pah-MĒR
Pampas PAM-puhz
Panathenaea pan-ath-uh-NĒ-uh
papacy PĀ-puh-sē
papyrus puh-PĪ-ruhs
Paraguay PAR-uh-gwī
Pasha, Ibrahim PAH-shuh, ib-rah-
    HĒM
patriarchate PĀ-trē-ahr-kit
patrie PAH-trē
patrilineal pat-ruh-LIN-ē-uhl
Peng Yu PUHNG YOO
perestroika per-i-STROI-kuh
Pericles PER-i-klēz
Pernambuco PÛR-nuhm-byoo-kō
Petrarch, Francesco PĒ-trahrk,
    fran-CHES-kō
Phaistos FĪ-stuhs
phalanx FĀ-langks
Phnom Penh puh-NOM PEN
Phoenician fi-NĒ-shuhn
Phoinikes FOY-nē-kes
Phosphoric fos-FOR-ik
Piccolomini PĒ-kuh-lō-MĒ-nē
piety PĪ-i-tē
Piraeus pi-RĀ-uhs
Pisistratus pī-SIS-truh-tuhs
Pizarro pi-ZAHR-ō
Plateau pla-TŌ
Pleistocene PLĪ-stuh-sēn
Po Zhuyi BŌ JOO-YĒ
pogrom PŌ-gruhm
polis PŌ-lis
Pondicherry pon-di-CHER-ē
pontifex maximus PON-tuh-feks
    MAK-suh-muhs
Prometheus pruh-MĒ-thē-uhs
Provençal prō-vuhn-SAHL
Ptah ptah
Ptolemy TOL-uh-mē
Pueblo Bonito PWEB-lō buh-NĒ-tō
Punt pŏŏnt
Pygmy PIG-mē
Pylos PĒ-lōs
pyre PĪR
Pyrenees PIR-uh-nēz
Pythagoras pi-THAG-uhr-uhs
Pythia PITH-ē-uh

Qadiri KAH-duh-rē
Qairawan kyyr-ah-WAHN
qanat Kah-NAHT

Qatabah KA-tuh-buh
Qatar KAH-tar
Qianlong CHĒ-EN-LONG
Qiantang CHĒ-EN-TAHNG
Qin CHIN
Qing CHING
Qinghai CHING-HĪ
qizilbash ki-zil-BAHSH
Québec kā-BEK
Québecois kā-be-KWAH
Querétaro ke-RE-tah-rō
Quetzalcoatl ket-sahl-kō-AHT-l
quilombos kē-LŌM-bōs
quinoa KĒN-wah
quipu KĒ-poo
Quixote ē-HŌ-tē
Quran kŏŏ-RAHN
Quraysh kuu-RYYSH

Rabban Sauma RAH-BAHN
   SOU-mah
Rabelais, François RAB-uh-lā
rah RAH
Rai RYY
Rajput RAHJ-poot
Ramesses ram-i-SĒZ
Rashid al-Din rah-SHĒD ad—DĒN
Ravenna ruh-VEN-uh
raya RAH-yuh
Rayy RĀ
Re RĀ
Reichstag RĪKS-tahg
Remarque ri-MAHRK
Ricci, Matteo RĒ-chē, mah-TĀ-ō
Richelieu rē-shuh-LYŎŎ
rinji RIN-jē
Rio de Janeiro RĒ-ō dā zhuh-
   NĀR-ō
Rio de la Plata RĒ-ō dā lah
   PLAH-tah
Robespierre, Maximilien ROBZ-pē-âr
Roca, Julio RŌ-kuh
Romanesque rō-muh-NESK
ronin RŌ-nin
Rosas, Huan Manuel de duh RŌ-sahs
rouble ROO-buhl
Ruhr RŎŎR
Rwanda roo-AHN-duh

Saadi SAH-dē
Saarinen, Eero SAHR-uh-nuhn
Safavid SAH-fah-vid
Sahel SAH-hil
Said sah-ĒD
Sake SAH-kē
Salamis SAH-lah-mēs
Samaj, Brahmo suh-MAHJ, BRAH-mō
Samarkand SAM-uhr-kand

samorin SAH-muh-rin
samurai SAM-ŏŏ-rī
São Tomé SOU tō-MĀ
saqiya suh-KĒ-yuh
Saqqara suh-KAHR-uh
Saracen SAR-uh-suhn
Sarepta suh-REP-tuh
Sargon SAHR-gon
Sasanid suh-SAH-nid
sati su-TĒ
satrap SĀ-trap
satyagraha suh-TYAH-gruh-huh
sawahil suh-WAH-hil
Shechem SHĒ-kuhm
schism SKIZ-uhm
Schliemann SHLĒ-mahn
Scythian SITH-ē-uhn
Seine SEN
Sekigahara se-kē-GA-HAH-ra
Seleucid si-LOO-sid
Selim se-LEEM
Seljuk sel-JOOK
Semitic suh MIT ik
Senegalese sen-uh-gah-LĒZ
sepoy SĒ-poi
seppuku SE-poo-kŏŏ
Sesshu ses-SHOO
Seville suh-VIL
Sèvres SEV-ruh
Shaanxi SHAHN-SHĒ
Shahansha SHAH-han-SHAH
shahid sha-HĒD
shaitan shī-TAHN
Shalmaneser shal-muh-NĒ-zuhr
Shamir, Yitzhak shah-MĒR
Shang SHAHNG
Shari´a shah-RĒ-ah
Sharrukin SHAH-roo-kēn
shawabti shuh-WAB-tē
Shechem shuh-KEM
Shephelah she-FE-luh
Shi´a SHĒ-uh
Shi´ism SHĒ-iz-uhm
Shi´ite SHĒ-īt
Shiraz shē-RAHZ
Shuwardata shoo-wuhr-DUH-tuh
sian SĒ-ahn
Sichuan SECH-WAHN
Sidon SĪD-n
Siena sē-EN-uh
Sierra Leone sē-ER-uh lē-ŌN
Sijilmasa si-jil-MA-suh
Sikh SĒK
Sind SIND
Singhalese sing-guh-LĒZ
Sinhalese sin-huh-LĒZ
Sioux SOO
Socotra suh-KŌ-truh

Sodom SOD-uhm
Sogdian SOG-dē-uhn
Sogdiana sog-dē-AN-uh
Solzhenitzyn, Alexander sōl-zhuh-
   NĒT-sin
Son SUN
sorghum SOR-guhm
Sousse SOOS
Sri Lanka SRĒ LAHNG-kuh
Srivijaya srē-VI-juh-yuh
Sry Darya SHRĒ DAHR-yah
Steppe STEP
Strabo STRĀ-bō
Strachey, John STRA-chē
styrax STĪ-raks
Subudei SUH-BUH-DĀ
suffetes SOO-fētz
Suhrawardi suh-ruh-WAHR-dē
Sui SWĒ
Suleiman SOO-lā-mahn
Sumanguru soo-muhn-GOO-roo
Summa Theologica SŎŎM-uh thē-uh-
   LOJ-i-kuh
Sundiata soon-JAH-tuh
Surat SŎŎR-uht
suzerainty SOO-zuh-rin-tē
Suzhou SOO-JŌ
Swahili swah-HĒ-lē
Swidden SWID-n
Sylvius, Aeneas SIL-vē-uhs,
   in-Ē-uhs

Tabriz tah-BRĒZ
Tahert TAH-huhrt
Tahmasp tah-MAHSP
Tahyast TAH-yast
Ta sety TUH-SE-tē
Taika TĪ-kah
Taiping TĪ ping
Tajik tah-JIK
Takla Makan TAH-kluh muh-KAHN
Talmud TAHL-mŏŏd
Tamburlaine TAM-buhr-lān
Tamerlane TAM-uhr-lān
Tang TAHNG
Tanganyika tahn-guh-NYĒ-kuh
Tangguts TAHNG-GOOTS
Tangier tan-JĪR
Tanit TAH-nit
Tarim TAH-rēm
Tashkent tahsh-KENT
Tassili ta-SEE-lee
Tawantinsuyu tah-wahn-teen-SOO-
   yoo
te TĀ
Techuacán te-choo-uh-KAHN
Tecumseh ti-KUM-suh
Temeh TĒM

Temüjin TEM-oo-chin
La Tene lah TEN
tenno TEN-NŌ
Tenochtitlán te-NŌCH-tē-tlahn
Tenskwatawa ten-SKWAHT-uh-wah
Teotihuacán tā-uh-tē-wah-KAHN
terik te-RĒK
Teutonic too-TON-ik
Téwodros tā-WŌ-druhs
Thar Desert TAHR
Theodosius thē-uh-DŌ-shuhs
Thermopylae thuhr-MOP-uh-lē
Theseus THĒ-sē-uhs
Thesmophoria thes-mō-FŌ-rē-uh
Thucydides thoo-SID-i-dēz
Tiahuanaco tē-uh-wuh-NAH-kō
Tiamat TYAH-maht
Tian TĒ-EN
Tibesti tē-BES-tē
Tien Shan TYEN SHAHN
Tiglathpileser TIG-lath-pi-LĒ-zuhr
Tigris TĪ-gris
Tikal tē-KAHL
Timur Lenk ti-MŎOR LENK
Timur-i lang tē-MOOR—yē LAHNG
Timurid ti-MŎOR-id
Tiryns TĪR-inz
Tito TĒ-tō
Tlaloc tlah-LŌK
Tlateloca tlah-tay-LOH-koh
Tlemcen tlem-SEN
Tocqueville, Alexis de TŌK-vil
Todaiji tō-DĪ-jē
Toghoril TŌ-guh-rul
Tokugawa Ieyasu tō-kō-GA-wa
    Ē-yeh-YAH-suh
Tongzhi toong-JŪR
tophets TŌ-fet
Topiltzin toh-PĒLT-seen
Tordesillas tor-duh-SĒ-yuhs
Toulouse too-LOOZ
Touré, Sékou too-RĀ, SĀ-koo
Transoxiana trans-ox-ē-AHN-ah
Trianon trē-ah-NŌ
Tripitaka tri-PIT-uh-kuh
Tripoli TRIP-uh-lē
trireme TRĪ-rēm
Trujillo troo-HĒ-ō
tsar ZAHR
Tsirinana, Philibert tsē-RAH-nah-nah
Tsushima TSOO-shē-mah
Tuareg TWAH-reg
Tughril TUUG-ruhl

Tunisia too-NĒ-zhuh
Tupac Amaru TOO-pahk ah-MAH-roo
Turkic TÛR-kik
Tuscany TUS-kuh-nē
Tutankhamun toot-ahng-KAH-muhn
Tuthmosis tuth-MŌ-sis
Tyre TĪR
Tyrolian Alps ti-RŌ-lē-uhn

Uaxactún wahsh-ahk-TOON
Ugarit OO-guh-rēt
Uigur WĒ-gŏŏr
ulamai OO-luh-mā
Umayyad oo-MĪ-ad
umma UM-uh
Upanishads oo-PAHN-i-shahds
Urartu ŏŏ-RAHR-too
Urdu ŌOR-doo
Urugu YŎOR-uh-gwī
Uruk OO-rŏŏk
Usuman dan Fodio OO-soo-mahn
    duhn FŌD-yō
Uthman uuth-MAHN
Uzbekistan ŏŏz-BEK-i-stan

Vairocana VĪ-rō-chah-nah
Vallon-Pont-d'Arc vah-LON—
    pon—DAHRK
van Eyck, Jan vahn ĪK, YAHN
Verde VÛRD
Versailles vuhr-SĪ
Vijayanagar vē-juh-yah-NAH-gahr
Vizier vi-ZĪR
Vladivostok vlad-uh-VOS-tok

Wafd WAHFT
Walesa, Lech wah-LEN-suh, LEK
Walpurga val-POOR-gah
Wang Jinghong WAHNG JING-hong
Wazir wuh-ZĒR
Wehrmacht VĀR-mahkt
Wei WĀ
Weizmann, Chaim WĪTS-muhn,
    KHĪ-im
Whorl HWORL
Whydah HWĪ-duh
Wojtyla, Karol voy-TĒ-luh
Wu Cheng'en WOO CHUNG-UHN
Wu Jingzi WOO JING-zuh
Wu Zhao WOO JOU

Xanadu ZAN-uh-doo
Xavier, Francis ZĀ-vē-uhr

Xenophon ZĒN-uh-fuhn
Xhosa KŌ-suh
Xi'an SHĒ-AN
Xia SHYAH
Xiang SHYAHNG
Xinjiang SHIN-JYAHNG
Xiongnu SHĒ-OONG-noo
Xu Guangqi SOO GWAHNG-CHĒ
Xu Wei SOO WĀ
Xuan de SHOO-WEN-DEH
Xuanzang SHOO-WEN-ZAHNG

Yahweh YAH-wā
Yang Guifei YAHNG GWĀ-FĀ
Yangdi YAHNG-DĒ
Yangzi YANG-ZUH
Yaqui YAH-kē
Yazdigird YAZ-duh-guhrd
Yazid ya-ZĒD
Yelu Chucai YEH-LŌ CHOO-tsī
yeni cheri YEN-i CHE-rē
yerba YÂR-buh
Yi Son-sin YĒ SUN-shin
Yongle YOONG-LÔ
Ypres Ē-pruh
Yuan Shihkai yoo-AHN shē-KĪ
Yucatán yoo-kuh-TAN

Za-ar ZAH—ahr
Zagros ZAG-ruhs
Zaibatsu ZĪ-bah-tsoo
Zaire zah-ĒR
Zarathushtra zar-uh-THOO-struh
zealots ZEL-uht
Zeng Guofan TSUNG GWŌ-FAN
Zhang Qian JAHNG CHĒ-EN
Zhapu JAH-poo
Zheng He JUNG HUH
Zhou JŌ
Zhu Shijie JOO SHŪR-jē-yeh
Zhu Yuanzhang JOO YOO-WEN-
    JAHNG
ziggurat ZIG-uh-rat
Zimbabwe zim-BAHB-wā
Zin CHIN
Zollverein TSOL-fer-īn
Zoroastrianism zor-ō-AS-trē-uh-niz-
    uhm
Zumárraga zoo-MAH-rah-gah
Zworykin, Vladimir ZWOR-i-kin,
    VLAD-uh-mír

Index

and central Europe, 123; trade routes and, 221–223; compared with trade, 224, along Silk Road, 227; of Bantu-speaking peoples, 241–242; by Turkic peoples, 316; Tang Empire and, 319; in southern China, 333; from Asia to Americas, 340; in tropical regions, 428; agricultural distress as cause of, 626–627; to industrial cities and towns, 668; of Cherokee, 718–719; of labor, 760–762; industrialization, population, and, 802–803; by African laborers, 840–841; of African-Americans, 863, 909; in colonial Africa, 916; of peoples, 993–996; internal, 994–995. *See also* Colonies and colonization; Germanic peoples; Immigration

Milinda, *see* Menander

Militarism: of Germanic peoples, 250; of Islamic empire, 290; in Huari, 363. *See also* Wars and warfare

Military: in Mesopotamia, 45; in Assyrian Empire, 103; under Philip II (Macedon), 152; Roman, 167, 168, 174; in China, 179; Chinese weapons and, 185; conscription and, 187; Germanic, 254; in feudal Europe, 254–255; in Japan, 327; Song Chinese innovations and, 335; East Asian resources and, 336; in Teotihuacán, 345; Mayan, 346–347; Toltec, 350; Aztec, 353; Mongol, 381–382, 392; Egypt and, 395; Korean, 418; slaves and, 447–448; weaponry and, 474–476; European, 493; revolution in, 522–523; Ottoman, 602–605; decline of Ottoman, 606–607; in Safavid Empire, 612; of Ming China, 629; Japanese samurai as, 643; Tokugawa regime and, 645–646; Napoleon Bonaparte and, 697, 699; charismatic leaders from, 712; limiting power in Latin America, 712; in Ethiopia, 741 (illus.); *sepoys* as, 748; discontent in India and, 749–751; Ottoman, 768 and *illus.*, 770–771; in Crimean War, 773, 774; in Qing Empire, 775; Taiping Rebellion and, 781–782; in Japan, 789, 822; weaponry of, 794; explosives and, 799; imperialism and, 831; intervention, in Latin America, 850; planning, for World War I, 857–858; in Russia, 866; in Japan, 891–894; in Germany, 897; mobility of, in World War II, 899; in China, 920. *See also* Armed forces; Janissaries; Military technology; Navy; Wars and warfare

Military technology, 45, 103, 152, 523, 647; of Assyrians, 122–123; in Crimean War, 773; in World War I, 858; in World War II, 905. *See also* Armaments; Wars and warfare; Weapons and weaponry

Militia, of American patriots, 687

Mills: in western Europe, 457–458; cotton industry and, 656. *See also* Textiles and textile industry

Milvian Bridge, Battle at, 176

Minaret, architecture of, 447 (illus.). *See also* Architecture

Mind Emie, Japan and, 629

Minerals: in Mesopotamian trade, 38; in ancient China, 68; in Iran, 128; in Mesoamerica, 341; in tropical regions, 429–431; in Americas, 727; in southern Africa, 838; worldwide need for, 851; environment and, 853. *See also* Coinage; Mining

Mines Act (England), 672–674

Ming Empire (China), 399, 400 (map), 405–409; Mongols and, 402; seafaring and exploration under, 406–408; trade with Middle East, 408; technology in, 409–413; observatory of, 410 (illus.); population growth of, 411; fear of technology transfer in, 411–413; fine arts and, 413; conquest of Annam, 421; Mongol collapse and, 486; trade contacts of, 486–487; Golden Age in, 625; worldwide trends and fall of, 626–627; economic and technological stagnation in, 627–629; military power of, 629; external pressures on, 629–630; Jesuit missionaries in, 630–631. *See also* China; Porcelain

Ming "ware," *see* Porcelain

Mining: in Gupta Empire, 205; in Song China, 335; in Ming China, 409–410; in western Europe, 458; in Latin America, 551, 553; in Americas, 727; erosion and, 731; in Latin America, 731 (illus.); environmental impact of, 853; in South Africa, 916 (illus.). *See also* Metals; Minerals

Minoan civilization, 82, 83–84 and *map*; commerce, settlement, and aggression of, 86–87

Minority peoples, 794; in Qing China, 776–777. *See also* Ethnic groups; groups by name

Minos (Greece), 83; legend of, 85

Minotaur, legend of, 85

Minyak people, 320, 323

Missions and missionaries, 257; from India, 211; spread of Buddhism and, 243; Carpini as, 401; in Africa, 482; in Americas, 483; in West Africa, 500; in Kongo, 501; European male dominance and, 507; in French Canada, 562; Christian vs. Islamic attitudes, 617; in British India, 748;

in Qing China, 779; New Imperialism and, 829–830, 829 (illus.); in colonial Africa, 841, 917; in Southeast Asia and Indonesia, 845. *See also* Christianity; Conversion; Evangelization; Latin America

Mississippian culture, 358

Mita (labor obligations), in Andean civilizations, 359, 551

Mitanni (city-state), 73

Mobile, Alabama, 558

Mobilization: in France, 693; for World War I, 857–858. *See also* Wars and warfare

Moby Dick (Melville), whaling and, 758

Mocha, Yemeni port of, 607

Moche civilization, in Andean region, 361–362

Mochica people, 360. *See also* Moche civilization

Moctezuma II (Aztec), 352, 505–506 and *illus.*

Modems, 997

Modernization, in China, 921. *See also* Industrialization

Modern period, use of term, 509

Mogadishu, 425, 440

Mohenjo-Daro, 56

Moisture, *see* Rainfall

Moksha, 196

Molucca Islands, as Spice Islands, 499

Mombasa, 620

Mona Lisa (Leonardo da Vinci), 469

Monarchs and monarchies: as Sumerian rulers, 37–38; Sargon as, 38; in ancient Egypt, 48–49, 52; in River Valley civilizations, 60; Hatshepsut, 64; in Shang China, 68; in New Kingdom Egypt, 74–77; in Assyrian Empire, 101–103; in Assyrian art, 102–103; Israelite, 110–112; in Persian Empire, 130–133; Persian women and, 131–132; Chinese Emperor and, 184; in Mauryan Empire, 201; Buddhism and, 202; of Gupta Empire, 205; in Srivijayan Empire, 212–213; in kingdom of Ghana, 238; in sub-Saharan Africa, 240; in England, 275; Magna Carta and, 275; Mayan, 346; in Andean civilizations, 359; of Incas, 364; Russian tsars and, 391; in Korea, 416; in western Europe, 471–478; advisers to, 519–520; Enlightenment challenge to, 540; criticisms of, 681–682; sympathy with Enlightenment and, 682; consolidation of power by, 683; restoration in France, 699; in Mexico and Brazil, 711. *See also* Caliphs and caliphates; Divination; Government; Pharaoh; Royal power; monarchs by name

C.T.